William Smith

A Smaller Dictionary of Greek and Roman Antiquities

Ninth Edition

William Smith

A Smaller Dictionary of Greek and Roman Antiquities
Ninth Edition

ISBN/EAN: 9783337021948

Printed in Europe, USA, Canada, Australia, Japan

Cover: Foto ©ninafisch / pixelio.de

More available books at **www.hansebooks.com**

SMALLER DICTIONARY

OF

Greek and Roman Antiquities.

By WILLIAM SMITH, D.C.L., LL.D.,

ABRIDGED FROM THE LARGER DICTIONARY.

NINTH EDITION.

ILLUSTRATED WITH TWO HUNDRED WOODCUTS.

LONDON:
JOHN MURRAY, ALBEMARLE STREET.
1874.

DR. WM. SMITH'S DICTIONARIES.

A DICTIONARY OF THE BIBLE; Its ANTIQUITIES, BIOGRAPHY, GEOGRAPHY, AND NATURAL HISTORY. With Illustrations. 3 vols. Medium 8vo. 5l. 5s.

A CONCISE BIBLE DICTIONARY. Condensed from the above. With Maps and 300 Illustrations. Medium 8vo. 21s.

A SMALLER BIBLE DICTIONARY. Abridged from the above. With Maps and 40 Illustrations. Crown 8vo. 7s. 6d.

A DICTIONARY OF GREEK AND ROMAN ANTIQUITIES. Including the Laws, Institutions, Domestic Usages, Painting, Sculpture, Music, the Drama, &c. With 500 Illustrations. Medium 8vo. 28s.

A DICTIONARY OF GREEK AND ROMAN BIOGRAPHY AND MYTHOLOGY. Containing a History of the Ancient World, civil, literary, and ecclesiastical. With 564 Illustrations. 3 vols. Medium 8vo. 84s.

A DICTIONARY OF GREEK AND ROMAN GEOGRAPHY. Including the political history of both countries and cities, as well as their geography. With 530 Illustrations. 2 vols. Medium 8vo. 56s.

A CLASSICAL DICTIONARY OF MYTHOLOGY, BIOGRAPHY, AND GEOGRAPHY. With 750 Woodcuts. 8vo. 18s.

A SMALLER CLASSICAL DICTIONARY. Abridged from the above. With 200 Woodcuts. Crown 8vo. 7s. 6d.

A SMALLER DICTIONARY OF GREEK AND ROMAN ANTIQUITIES. Abridged from the larger Work. With 200 Woodcuts. Crown 8vo. 7s. 6d.

A LATIN-ENGLISH DICTIONARY, Based on the Works of FORCELLINI and FREUND. With Tables of the Roman Calendar, Measures, Weights, and Monies. Medium 8vo. 21s.

A SMALLER LATIN-ENGLISH DICTIONARY: with Dictionary of Proper Names and Tables of Roman Calendar, etc. Abridged from the above. Square 12mo. 7s. 6d.

A COPIOUS AND CRITICAL ENGLISH-LATIN DICTIONARY. Medium 8vo. 21s.

A SMALLER ENGLISH-LATIN DICTIONARY. Abridged from the above. Square 12mo. 7s. 6d.

A SMALLER DICTIONARY OF GREEK AND ROMAN ANTIQUITIES.

ABACUS.

ABACUS (ἄβαξ), denoted primarily a square tablet of any description, and was hence employed in the following significations:— (1) A table, or side-board, chiefly used for the display of gold and silver cups, and other kinds of valuable and ornamental utensils. The use of abaci was first introduced at Rome from Asia Minor after the victories of Cn. Manlius Vulso, B.C. 187, and their introduction was regarded as one of the marks of the growing luxury of the age.—(2) A draught-board or chess-board.—(3) A board used by mathematicians for drawing diagrams, and by arithmeticians for the purposes of calculation.—(4) A painted panel, coffer, or square compartment in the wall or ceiling of a chamber.—(5) In architecture, the flat square stone which constituted the highest member of a column, being placed immediately under the architrave.

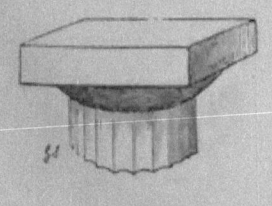

Abacus.

ABOLLA, a cloak chiefly worn by soldiers, and thus opposed to the toga, the [garb] of peace. [TOGA.] The abolla was [worn] by the lower classes at Rome, and consequently by the philosophers who affected [severi]ty of manners and life. Hence the ex[pr]ession of Juvenal, *facinus majoris abollae*,

ACCENSUS.

—"a crime committed by a very deep philosopher."

Abolla. (Bellori, Arc. Triumph., pl. 11, 12.)

ABROGATIO. [LEX.]
ABSOLUTIO. [JUDEX.]
ACAENA (ἀκαίνη, ἄκαινα, or in later Greek ἄκενα, in one place ἄκαινον), a measuring rod of the length of ten Greek feet. It was used in measuring land, and thus resembles the Roman *decempeda*.

ACATIUM (ἀκάτιον, a diminutive of ἄκατος), a small vessel or boat used by the Greeks, which appears to have been the same as the Roman *scapha*. The *Acatia* were also sails adapted for fast sailing.

ACCENSUS. (1) A public officer, who attended on several of the Roman magistrates. The Accensi summoned the people to the assemblies, and those who had lawsuits to court; they preserved order in the courts, and proclaimed the time of the day when it was the third hour, the sixth hour, and the ninth hour. An accensus anciently preceded the consul who had not the fasces, which custom, after being long disused, was restored by Julius Cæsar in his first consulship. Accensi also attended on the governors of provinces.—(2) The accensi were also a class of soldiers in the Roman army, who were enlisted after the full number of the legion had been completed, in order to supply any vacancies that might occur in the legion. They were taken, according to the census of Servius Tullius, from the fifth class of citizens, and were placed in battle in the rear of the army, behind the triarii.

ACCLAMĀTIO, was the public expression of approbation or disapprobation, pleasure or displeasure, by loud acclamations. On many occasions, there appear to have been certain forms of acclamations always used by the Romans; as, for instance, at marriages, *Io Hymen, Hymenaee,* or *Talassio;* at triumphs, *Io Triumphe;* at the conclusion of plays, the last actor called out *Plaudite* to the spectators; orators were usually praised by such expressions as *Bene et praeclare, Belle et festive, Non potest melius,* &c. Under the empire the name of *acclamationes* was given to the praises and flatteries bestowed by the senate upon the reigning emperor and his family.

ACCUBĀTIO, the act of reclining at meals. The Greeks and Romans were accustomed, in later times, to recline at their meals; but this practice could not have been of great antiquity in Greece, since Homer always describes persons as sitting at their meals; and Isidore of Seville, an ancient grammarian, also attributes the same custom to the ancient Romans. Even in the time of the early Roman emperors, children in families of the highest rank used to sit together, while their fathers and elders reclined on couches at the upper part of the room. Roman ladies continued the practice of sitting at table, even after the recumbent position had become common with the other sex. It appears to have been considered more decent, and more agreeable to the severity and purity of ancient manners, for women to sit, more especially if many persons were present. But, on the other hand, we find cases of women reclining, where there was conceived to be nothing bold or indelicate in their posture. Such is the case in the preceding woodcut, which seems intended to represent a scene of matrimonial felicity. For an account of the disposition of the couches, and of the place which each guest occupied in a Greek and Roman entertainment, see SYMPOSIUM and TRICLINIUM.

ACCŪSĀTOR, ACCŪSĀTIO. [JUDEX.]

ACERRA (θυμιατήριον, λιβανωτρίς), the incense-box or censer used in sacrifices. The acerra was also a small moveable altar placed before the dead, on which perfumes were burnt. The use of acerrae at funerals was forbidden by a law of the Twelve Tables as an unnecessary expense.

Acerra. (From a Frieze in the Museum Capitolinum.)

ACĒTABŪLUM (ὀξίς, ὀξύβαφον, ὀξυβάφιον). (1) A vinegar-cup, wide and open above, as we see in the annexed cut. The name was

Acetabulum. (Dennis, Etruria, p. xcvi.)

also given to all cups resembling it in size and form, to whatever use they might be applied. —(2) A Roman measure of capacity, fluid and dry. It was one-fourth of the hemina, and therefore one-eighth of the sextarius.

Accubatio Act of Reclining. (Montfaucon, Ant. Exp., Suppl., in. 60.)

ĀCHĀĪCUM FOEDUS. The Achaean league is divided into two periods. 1. *The earlier period.*—When the Heracleidae took possession of Peloponnesus, which had until then been chiefly inhabited by Achaeans, a portion of the latter, under Tisamenus, turned northwards and occupied the north coast of Peloponnesus. The country thus occupied derived from them its name of Achaia, and contained twelve confederate towns, which were governed by the descendants of Tisamenus, till at length they abolished the kingly rule after the death of Ogyges, and established a democracy. In the time of Herodotus the twelve towns of which the league consisted were: Pellene, Aegeira, Aegae, Bura, Helice, Aegium, Rhypes (Rhypae), Patreis (ae), Phareis (ae), Olenus, Dyme, and Tritaeeis (Tritaea). After the time of Herodotus, Rhypes and Aegae disappeared from the number, and Ceryncia and Leontium stepped into their place. The bond which united the towns of the league was not so much a political as a religious one, as is shown by the common sacrifice offered at Helice to Poseidon, and after the destruction of that town, at Aegium to Zeus, surnamed Homagyrius, and to Demeter Panachaea. The confederation exercised no great influence in the affairs of Greece down to the time when it was broken up by the Macedonians. 2. *The later period.*—When Antigonus in B.C. 281 made the unsuccessful attempt to deprive Ptolemaeus Ceraunus of the Macedonian throne, the Achaeans availed themselves of the opportunity of shaking off the Macedonian yoke, and renewing their ancient confederation. The grand object however now was no longer a common worship, but a real political union among the confederates. The fundamental laws were, that henceforth the confederacy should form one inseparable state, that each town, which should join it, should have equal rights with the others, and that all members, in regard to foreign countries, should be considered as dependent, and bound to obey in every respect the federal government, and those officers who were entrusted with the executive. Aegium was the seat of the government, and it was there that the citizens of the various towns met at regular and stated times, to deliberate upon the common affairs of the league, and if it was thought necessary, upon those of separate towns, and even of individuals, and to elect the officers of the league. The league acquired its great strength in B.C. 251, when Aratus united Sicyon, his native place, with it, and some years later gained Corinth also for it. Megara, Troezene, and Epidaurus soon followed their example. Afterwards Aratus persuaded all the more important towns of Peloponnesus to join the confederacy, and thus Megalopolis, Argos, Hermione, Phlius, and others were added to it. In a short period the league reached the height of its power, for it embraced Athens, Megara, Aegina, Salamis, and the whole of Peloponnesus, with the exception of Sparta, Elis, Tegea, Orchomenos, and Mantineia. The common affairs of the confederate towns were regulated at general meetings attended by the citizens of all the towns, and held regularly twice every year, in the spring and in the autumn. These meetings, which lasted three days, were held in a grove of Zeus Homagyrius in the neighbourhood of Aegium, and near a sanctuary of Demeter Panachaea. Every citizen, both rich and poor, who had attained the age of thirty, might attend the assemblies, to which they were invited by a public herald, and might speak and propose any measure. The subjects which were to be brought before the assembly were prepared by a council (βουλή), which seems to have been permanent. The principal officers of the confederacy were: 1. At first two strategi (στρατηγοί), but after the year B.C. 255 there was only one, who in conjunction with an hipparchus (ἵππαρχος) or commander of the cavalry and an under-strategus (ὑποστρατηγός) commanded the army furnished by the confederacy, and was entrusted with the whole conduct of war; 2. A public secretary (γραμματεύς); and, 3. Ten demiurgi (δημιουργοί). All the officers of the league were elected in the assembly held in the spring, at the rising of the Pleiades, and legally they were invested with their several offices only for one year, though it frequently happened that men of great merit and distinction were re-elected for several successive years. If one of the officers died during the period of his office, his place was filled by his predecessor, until the time for the new elections arrived. The perpetual discord of the members of the league, the hostility of Sparta, the intrigues of the Romans, and the folly and rashness of the later strategi, brought about not only the destruction and dissolution of the confederacy, but of the freedom of all Greece, which after the fall of Corinth, in B.C. 146, became a Roman province under the name of Achaia.

ĀCIES. [EXERCITUS.]

ĀCĬNĂCĒS (ἀκινάκης), a Persian sword, whence Horace speaks of the *Medus acinaces.* The acinaces was a short and straight weapon, and thus differed from the Roman *sica* which was curved. It was worn on the right side of the body, whereas the Greeks and Romans usually had their swords suspended on the left side. The form of the acinaces, with the mode of wearing it, is illustrated by the following Persepolitan figures.

Acinaces, Persian Sword. (From bas-reliefs at Persepolis.)

ACISCŬLUS. [Ascia.]

ĀCLIS, a kind of dart with a leathern thong attached to it. [Amentum.]

ACROĀMA (ἀκούαμα), which properly means any thing heard, was the name given to a concert of players on different musical instruments, and also to an interlude performed during the exhibition of the public games. The word is also applied to the actors and musicians who were employed to amuse guests during an entertainment, and is sometimes used to designate the anagnostae. [Anagnostes.]

ACRŎLĪTHI (ἀκρόλιθοι), statues, of which the extremities only were of marble, and the remaining part of the body of wood either gilt or covered with drapery.

ACRŎPŎLIS (ἀκρόπολις). In almost all Greek states, which were usually built upon a hill, rock, or some natural elevation, there was a castle or a citadel, erected upon the highest part of the rock or hill, to which the name of *Acropolis*, higher or upper city, was given. Thus we read of an acropolis at Athens, Corinth, Argos, Messene, and many other places. The Capitolium at Rome answered the same purpose as the Acropolis in the Greek cities; and of the same kind were the tower of Agathocles at Utica, and that of Antonia at Jerusalem.

ACROSTŎLĬUM. [Navis.]

ACRŌTĒRĬUM (ἀκρωτήριον), signifies the extremity of any thing, and was applied by the Greeks to the extremities of the prow of a vessel (ἀκροστόλιον), which were usually taken from a conquered vessel as a mark of victory: the act of doing so was called ἀκρωτηριάζειν. In architecture it signifies, 1. The sloping roof of a building. 2. The pediment. 3. The pedestals for statues placed on the summit of a pediment. In sculpture it signifies the extremities of a statue, as wings, feet, hands, &c.

ACTA. (1) The public acts and orders of a Roman magistrate, which after the expiration of his office were submitted to the senate for approval or rejection. Under the empire, all the magistrates when entering upon their office on the 1st of January swore approval of the acts of the reigning emperor.—(2) Acta Forensia were of two kinds: first, those relating to the government, as leges, plebiscita, edicta, the names of all the magistrates, &c., which formed part of the *tabulae publicae;* and secondly, those connected with the courts of law.—(3) Acta Militaria, contained an account of the duties, numbers, and expenses of each legion, and were probably preserved in the military treasury founded by Augustus.—(4) Acta Senatus, called also Commentarii Senatus and Acta Patrum, contained an account of the various matters brought before the senate, the opinions of the chief speakers, and the decision of the house. By command of Julius Caesar they were published regularly every day as part of the government gazette. Augustus forbade the publication of the proceedings of the senate, but they still continued to be preserved, and one of the most distinguished senators was chosen by the emperor to compile the account.—(5) Acta Diurna, a gazette published daily at Rome by the authority of the government, during the later times of the republic and under the empire, corresponding in some measure to our newspapers. They were also called *Acta Publica, Acta Urbana, Acta Rerum Urbanarum, Acta Populi,* and sometimes simply *Acta* or *Diurna.* They contained, 1. A list of births and deaths in the city, an account of the money paid into the treasury from the provinces, and every thing relating to the supply of corn. 2. Extracts from the Acta Forensia. 3. Extracts from the Acta Senatus. 4. A court circular, containing an account of the births, deaths, festivals, and movements of the imperial family. 5. An account of such public affairs and foreign wars as the government thought proper to publish. 6. Curious and interesting occurrences, such as prodigies and miracles, the erection of new edifices, the conflagration of buildings, funerals, sacrifices, a list of the various games, and especially curious tales and adventures, with the names of the parties.

ACTIA (ἄκτια), a festival celebrated every four years at Actium in Epirus, with wrestling, horse-racing, and sea-fights, in honour of Apollo. There was a celebrated temple of Apollo at Actium. After the defeat of Antony off Actium, Augustus enlarged the temple, and instituted games to be celebrated every five years in commemoration of his victory.

ACTIO, is defined by a Roman jurist to be the right of pursuing by judicial means what is a man's due. The old actions of the Roman law were called *legis actiones* or *legitimae*, either because they were expressly provided for by the laws of the Twelve Tables, or because they were strictly adapted to the words of the laws, and therefore could not be varied. But these forms of action gradually fell into disuse, in consequence of the excessive nicety required, and the failure consequent on the slightest error in the pleadings, and they were eventually abolished by the Lex Aebutia, and two Leges Juliae, except in a few cases. In the old Roman constitution, the knowledge of the law was most closely connected with the institutes and ceremonial of religion, and was accordingly in the hands of the patricians alone, whose aid their clients were obliged to ask in all their legal disputes. App. Claudius Caecus, perhaps one of the earliest writers on law, drew up the various forms of actions, probably for his own use and that of his friends: the manuscript was stolen or copied by his scribe Cn. Flavius, who made it public; and thus, according to the story, the plebeians became acquainted with those legal forms which hitherto had been the exclusive property of the patricians. After the abolition of the old legal actions, a suit was prosecuted in the following manner:—An action was commenced by the plaintiff summoning the defendant to appear before the praetor or other magistrate who had *jurisdictio;* this process was called *in jus vocatio;* and, according to the laws of the Twelve Tables, was in effect a dragging of the defendant before the praetor, if he refused to go quietly; and although this rude proceeding was somewhat modified in later times, we find in the time of Horace that if the defendant would not go quietly, the plaintiff called on any bystander to witness, and dragged the defendant into court. The parties might settle their dispute on their way to the court, or the defendant might be bailed by a vindex. The vindex must not be confounded with the vades. This settlement of disputes on the way was called *transactio in via,* and serves to explain a passage in St. Matthew, v. 25. When before the praetor, the parties were said *jure agere.*

The plaintiff then prayed for an action, and if the praetor allowed it *(dabat actionem),* he then declared what action he intended to bring against the defendant, which he called *edere actionem.* This might be done in writing, or orally, or by the plaintiff taking the defendant to the *album* [ALBUM], and showing him which action he intended to rely on. As the *formulae* on the album comprehended, or were supposed to comprehend, every possible form of action that could be required by a plaintiff, it was presumed that he could find among all the formulae some one which was adapted to his case; and he was, accordingly, supposed to be without excuse if he did not take pains to select the proper formula. If he took the wrong one, or if he claimed more than his due, he lost his cause *(causa cadebat);* but the praetor sometimes gave him leave to amend his claim or *intentio.* It will be observed, that as the formulae were so numerous and comprehensive, the plaintiff had only to select the formula which he supposed to be suitable to his case, and it would require no further variation than the insertion of the names of the parties and of the thing claimed, or the subject-matter of the suit, with the amount of damages, &c., as the case might be. When the praetor had granted an action, the plaintiff required the defendant to give security for his appearance before the praetor *(in jure)* on a day named, commonly the day but one after the *in jus vocatio,* unless the matter in dispute was settled at once. The defendant, on finding a surety, was said *vades dare, vadimonium promittere,* or *facere;* the surety, *vas,* was said *spondere;* the plaintiff, when satisfied with the surety, was said *vadari reum,* to let him go on his sureties, or to have sureties from him. When the defendant promised to appear *in jure* on the day named, without giving any surety, this was called *vadimonium purum.* In some cases, *recuperatores* [JUDEX] were named, who, in case of the defendant making default, condemned him in the sum of money named in the *vadimonium.* If the defendant appeared on the day appointed, he was said *vadimonium sistere;* if he did not appear, he was said *vadimonium deseruisse;* and the praetor gave to the plaintiff the *bonorum possessio.* Both parties, on the day appointed, were summoned by a crier *(praeco),* when the plaintiff made his claim or demand, which was very briefly expressed, and may be considered as corresponding to our declaration at law. The defendant might either deny the plaintiff's claim, or he might reply to it by a plea, *exceptio.* If he simply denied the plaintiff's claim, the cause was at issue, and a judex might be demanded. The forms of the *exceptio*, also, were contained in the praetor's edict, or, upon hearing the facts, the praetor adapted the plea to the case. The plaintiff might reply to the defendant's *exceptio*. The plaintiff's answer was called *replicatio*. If the defendant answered the *replicatio*, his answer was called *duplicatio*; and the parties might go on to the *triplicatio* and *quadruplicatio*, and even further, if the matters in question were such that they could not otherwise be brought to an issue. A person might maintain or defend an action by his *cognitor* or *procurator*, or, as we should say, by his attorney. The plaintiff and defendant used a certain form of words in appointing a cognitor, and it would appear that the appointment was made in the presence of both parties. The cognitor needed not to be present, and his appointment was complete when by his acts he had signified his assent. When the cause was brought to an issue, a judex or judices might be demanded of the praetor, who named or appointed a judex, and delivered to him the formula, which contained his instructions. The judices were said *dari* or *addici*. So far the proceedings were said to be *in jure:* the prosecution of the actio before the judex requires a separate discussion. [JUDEX.]

ACTOR, signified generally a plaintiff. In a civil or private action, the plaintiff was often called *petitor*; in a public action (*causa publica*), he was called *accusator*. The defendant was called *reus*, both in private and public causes: this term, however, according to Cicero, might signify either party, as indeed we might conclude from the word itself. In a private action the defendant was often called *adversarius*, but either party might be called *adversarius* with respect to the other. Wards brought their actions by their guardian or tutor. *Peregrini*, or aliens, originally brought their action through their patronus; but afterwards in their own name, by a fiction of law, that they were Roman citizens. A Roman citizen might also generally bring his action by means of a cognitor or procurator. [ACTIO.] Actor has also the sense of an agent or manager of another's business generally. The *actor publicus* was an officer who had the superintendence or care of slaves and property belonging to the state.

ACTUARIAE NAVES, transport-vessels, seem to have been built in a lighter style than the ordinary ships of burden, from which they also differed in being always furnished with oars, whereas the others were chiefly propelled by sails.

ACTUARII, short-hand writers, who took down the speeches in the senate and the public assemblies. In the debate in the Roman senate upon the punishment of those who had been concerned in the conspiracy of Catiline, we find the first mention of short-hand writers, who were employed by Cicero to take down the speech of Cato.

ACTUS, a Roman measure of length, also called *actus quadratus*, was equal to half a jugerum, or 14,400 square Roman feet. The *actus minimus*, or *simplex*, was 120 feet long, and four broad, and therefore equal to 480 square Roman feet. Actus was also used to signify a bridle-way.

ACUS (βελόνη, βελονίς, ῥαφίς), a needle, a pin. Pins were made not only of metal, but also of wood, bone, and ivory. They were used for the same purposes as with us, and also in dressing the hair. The mode of platting the hair, and then fastening it with a pin or needle, is shown in the annexed figure of a female head. This fashion has been continued to our own times by the females of Italy.

Acus. (Montfaucon, Ant. Exp., Suppl., iii. 3.)

ADDICTI. [NEXI.]
ADFINES. [AFFINES.]
ADLECTI, or ALLECTI, those persons under the empire who were admitted to the privileges and honours of the praetorship, quaestorship, aedileship, and other public offices, without having any duties to perform. The senators called *adlecti* seem to have been the same as the conscripti.

ADLOCUTIO. [ALLOCUTIO.]
ADMISSIONALES, chamberlains at the imperial court, who introduced persons into the presence of the emperor. They were divided into four classes; the chief officer of each class was called *proximus admissionum;* and the *proximi* were under the *magister admissionum*. Their duty was called *officium admissionis*. They were usually freedmen.

ADOLESCENS, was applied in the Roman law to a person from the end of his twelfth or fourteenth to the end of his twenty-fifth year, during which period a person was also called *adultus*. The word adolescens, however, is frequently used in a less strict sense in the Latin writers in referring to a person much older than the above-mentioned age.

ADONIA (ἀδώνια), a festival celebrated in honour of Aphrodite and Adonis in most of the Grecian cities. It lasted two days, and was celebrated by women exclusively. On the first day they brought into the streets statues of Adonis, which were laid out as corpses; and they observed all the rites customary at funerals, beating themselves and uttering lamentations. The second day was spent in merriment and feasting; because Adonis was allowed to return to life, and spend half the year with Aphrodite.

ADOPTIO, adoption. (1) GREEK.—Adoption was called by the Athenians εἰσποίησις, or sometimes simply ποίησις, or θέσις. The adoptive father was said ποιεῖσθαι, εἰσποιεῖσθαι, or sometimes ποιεῖν: and the father or mother (for a mother after the death of her husband could consent to her son being adopted) was said ἐκποιεῖν: the son was said ἐκποιεῖσθαι with reference to the family which he left; and εἰσποιεῖσθαι with reference to the family into which he was received. The son, when adopted, was called ποιητός, εἰσποιητός, or θετός, in opposition to the legitimate son born of the body of the father, who was called γνήσιος. A man might adopt a son either in his lifetime or by his testament, provided he had no male offspring, and was of sound mind. He might also, by testament, name a person to take his property, in case his son or sons should die under age. Only Athenian citizens could be adopted; but females could be adopted (by testament at least) as well as males. The adopted child was transferred from his own family and demus into those of the adoptive father; he inherited his property, and maintained the sacra of his adoptive father. It was not necessary for him to take his new father's name, but he was registered as his son in the register of his phratria (φρατρικὸν γραμματεῖον). Subsequently to this, it was necessary to enter him in the register of the adoptive father's demus (ληξιαρχικὸν γραμματεῖον), without which registration it appears that he did not possess the full rights of citizenship as a member of his new demus.—(2) ROMAN.— The Roman relation of parent and child arose either from a lawful marriage or from adoption. Adoptio was the general name which comprehended the two species, adoptio and adrogatio; and as the adopted person passed from his own familia into that of the person adopting, adoptio caused a capitis diminutio, and the lowest of the three kinds. [CAPUT.] Adoption, in its specific sense, was the ceremony by which a person who was in the power of his parent (in potestate parentum),

whether child or grandchild, male or female, was transferred to the power of the person adopting him. It was effected under the authority of a magistrate (magistratus), the praetor, for instance, at Rome, or a governor (praeses) in the provinces. The person to be adopted was emancipated [MANCIPATIO] by his natural father before the competent authority, and surrendered to the adoptive father by the legal form called in jure cessio. When a person was not in the power of his parent (sui juris), the ceremony of adoption was called adrogatio. Originally, it could only be effected at Rome, and only by a vote of the populus (populi auctoritate) in the comitia curiata (lege curiata); the reason of this being that the caput or status of a Roman citizen could not, according to the laws of the Twelve Tables, be effected except by a vote of the populus in the comitia curiata. Clodius, the enemy of Cicero, was adrogated into a plebeian family, in order to qualify himself to be elected a tribune of the plebs. Females could not be adopted by adrogatio. Under the emperors it became the practice to effect the adrogatio by an imperial rescript. The effect of adoption was to create the legal relation of father and son, just as if the adopted son were born of the blood of the adoptive father in lawful marriage. The adopted child was intitled to the name and sacra privata of the adopting parent. A person, on passing from one gens into another, and taking the name of his new familia, generally retained the name of his old gens also, with the addition to it of the termination anus. Thus Aemilius, the son of L. Aemilius Paullus, upon being adopted by P. Cornelius Scipio, assumed the name of P. Cornelius Scipio Aemilianus, and C. Octavius, afterwards the emperor Augustus, upon being adopted by the testament of his great-uncle the dictator, assumed the name of C. Julius Caesar Octavianus.

ADORATIO (προσκύνησις), adoration, was paid to the gods in the following manner:— The individual stretched out his right hand to the statue of the god whom he wished to honour, then kissed his hand, and waved it to the statue. The adoration differed from the oratio or prayers, which were offered with the hands folded together and stretched out to the gods. The adoration paid to the Roman emperors was borrowed from the Eastern mode, and consisted in prostration on the ground, and kissing the feet and knees of the emperor.

ADROGATIO. [ADOPTIO, (ROMAN).]

ADULTERIUM, adultery. (1) GREEK.— Among the Athenians, if a man caught another man in the act of criminal intercourse (μοιχεία) with his wife, he might kill him with impunity; and the law was also the same with respect to a concubine (παλλακή). He might also inflict other punishment on the offender. It appears that there was no adultery, unless a married woman was concerned. The husband might, if he pleased, take a sum of money from the adulterer, by way of compensation, and detain him till he found sureties for the payment. The husband might also prosecute the adulterer in the action called μοιχείας γραφή. If the act of adultery was proved, the husband could no longer cohabit with his wife, under pain of losing his privileges of a citizen (ἀτιμία). The adulteress was excluded even from those temples which foreign women and slaves were allowed to enter; and if she was seen there, any one might treat her as he pleased, provided he did not kill her or mutilate her.—(2) ROMAN.— The word adulterium properly signifies, in the Roman law, the offence committed by a man's having sexual intercourse with another man's wife. *Stuprum* (called by the Greeks ϕθορά) signifies the like offence with a widow or virgin. In the time of Augustus a law was enacted (probably about B. C. 17), entitled *Lex Julia de adulteriis coercendis*, which seems to have contained special penal provisions against adultery; and it is also not improbable that, by the old law or custom, if the adulterer was caught in the fact, he was at the mercy of the injured husband, and that the husband might punish with death his adulterous wife. By the Julian law, a woman convicted of adultery was mulcted in half of her dowry (*dos*) and the third part of her property (*bona*), and banished (*relegata*) to some miserable island, such as Scriphos, for instance. The adulterer was mulcted in half his property, and banished in like manner. This law did not inflict the punishment of death on either party; and in those instances under the emperors in which death was inflicted, it must be considered as an extraordinary punishment, and beyond the provisions of the Julian law. The Julian law permitted the father (both adoptive and natural) to kill the adulterer and adulteress in certain cases, as to which there were several nice distinctions established by the law. If the wife was divorced for adultery, the husband was entitled to retain part of the dowry. By a constitution of the Emperor Constantine, the offence in the adulterer was made capital.

ADVERSĀRIA, a note-book, memorandum-book, posting-book, in which the Romans entered memoranda of any importance, especially of money received and expended, which were afterwards transcribed, usually every month, into a kind of ledger. (*Tabulae justae, codex accepti et expensi.*)

ADVERSĀRIUS. [ACTOR.]
ĂDŬNĀTI (ἀδύνατοι), were persons supported by the Athenian state, who, on account of infirmity or bodily defects, were unable to obtain a livelihood. The sum which they received from the state appears to have varied at different times. In the time of Lysias and Aristotle, one obolus a day was given; but it appears to have been afterwards increased to two oboli. The bounty was restricted to persons whose property was under three minae; and the examination of those who were entitled to it belonged to the senate of the Five Hundred. Peisistratus is said to have been the first to introduce a law for the maintenance of those persons who had been mutilated in war.

ADVOCATUS, seems originally to have signified any person who gave another his aid in any affair or business, as a witness for instance; or for the purpose of aiding and protecting him in taking possession of a piece of property. It was also used to express a person who in any way gave his advice and aid to another in the management of a cause; but, in the time of Cicero, the word did not signify the orator or patronus who made the speech. Under the emperors it signified a person who in any way assisted in the conduct of a cause, and was sometimes equivalent to orator. The advocate's fee was then called *Honorarium*.

ĀDȲTUM. [TEMPLUM.]
AEDES. [DOMUS; TEMPLUM.]
AEDĪLES (ἀγορανόμοι). The name of these functionaries is said to be derived from their having the care of the temple (*aedes*) of Ceres. The aediles were originally two in number: they were elected from the plebs, and the institution of the office dates from the same time as that of the tribunes of the plebs, B. C. 494. Their duties at first seem to have been merely ministerial; they were the assistants of the tribunes in such matters as the tribunes entrusted to them, among which are enumerated the hearing of causes of smaller importance. At an early period after their institution (B. C. 446), we find them appointed the keepers of the senatus-consulta, which the consuls had hitherto arbitrarily suppressed or altered. They were also the keepers of the plebiscita. Other functions were gradually entrusted to them, and it is not always easy to distinguish their duties from some of those which belong to the censors. They had the general superintendence of buildings, both sacred and private; under this power they provided for the support and repair of temples, curiae, &c., and took care that private buildings which were in a ruinous state were repaired

by the owners or pulled down. The care of the supply and distribution of water, of the streets and pavements, with the cleansing and draining of the city, belonged to the aediles; and, of course, the care of the cloacae. They had the office of distributing corn among the plebs, but this distribution of corn at Rome must not be confounded with the duty of purchasing or procuring it from foreign parts, which was performed by the consuls, quaestors, and praetors, and sometimes by an extraordinary magistrate, as the praefectus annonae. The aediles had to see that the public lands were not improperly used, and that the pasture grounds of the state were not trespassed on; and they had power to punish by fine any unlawful act in this respect. They had a general superintendence over buying and selling, and, as a consequence, the supervision of the markets, of things exposed to sale, such as slaves, and of weights and measures; from this part of their duty is derived the name under which the aediles are mentioned by the Greek writers (ἀγορανόμοι). It was their business to see that no new deities or religious rites were introduced into the city, to look after the observance of religious ceremonies, and the celebrations of the ancient feasts and festivals. The general superintendence of police comprehended the duty of preserving order, regard to decency, and the inspection of the baths and houses of entertainment. The aediles had various officers under them, as praecones, scribae, and viatores. The AEDILES CURULES, who were also two in number, were originally chosen only from the patricians, afterwards alternately from the patricians and the plebs, and at last indifferently from both. The office of curule aediles was instituted B. C. 365, and, according to Livy, on the occasion of the plebeian aediles refusing to consent to celebrate the Ludi Maximi for the space of four days instead of three; upon which a senatus-consultum was passed, by which two aediles were to be chosen from the patricians. From this time four aediles, two plebeian and two curule, were annually elected. The distinctive honours of the curule aediles were, the sella curulis, from whence their title is derived, the toga praetexta, precedence in speaking in the senate, and the jus imaginum. Only the curule aediles had the jus edicendi, or the right of promulgating edicta; but the rules comprised in their edicta served for the guidance of all the aediles. The edicta of the curule aediles were founded on their authority as superintendents of the markets, and of buying and selling in general. Accordingly, their edicts had mainly, or perhaps solely, reference to the rules as to buying and selling, and contracts for bargain and sale. The persons both of the plebeian and curule aediles were sacrosancti. It seems that after the appointment of the curule aediles, the functions formerly exercised by the plebeian aediles were exercised, with some few exceptions, by all the aediles indifferently. Within five days after being elected, or entering on office, they were required to determine by lot, or by agreement among themselves, what parts of the city each should take under his superintendence; and each aedile alone had the care of looking after the paving and cleansing of the streets, and other matters, it may be presumed, of the same local character within his district. The other duties of the office seem to have been exercised by them jointly. In the superintendence of the public festivals or solemnities, there was a further distinction between the two sets of aediles. Many of these festivals, such as those of Flora and Ceres, were superintended by either set of aediles indifferently; but the plebeian games were under the superintendence of the plebeian aediles, who had an allowance of money for that purpose; and the fines levied on the pecuarii, and others, seem to have been appropriated to these among other public purposes. The celebration of the Ludi Magni or Romani, of the Ludi Scenici, or dramatic representations, and the Ludi Megalesii, belonged specially to the curule aediles, and it was on such occasions that they often incurred a prodigious expense, with a view of pleasing the people, and securing their votes in future elections. This extravagant expenditure of the aediles arose after the close of the second Punic war, and increased with the opportunities which individuals had of enriching themselves after the Roman arms were carried into Greece, Africa, and Spain. Even the prodigality of the emperors hardly surpassed that of individual curule aediles under the republic; such as C. Julius Caesar, the dictator, P. Cornelius Lentulus Spinther, and, above all, M. Aemilius Scaurus, whose expenditure was not limited to bare show, but comprehended objects of public utility, as the reparation of walls, dock-yards, ports, and aquaeducts. In B. C. 45, Julius Caesar caused two curule aediles and four plebeian aediles to be elected; and thenceforward, at least so long as the office of aedile was of any importance, six aediles were annually elected. The two new plebeian aediles were called Cereales, and their duty was to look after the supply of corn. Though their office may not have been of any great importance after the institution of a praefectus annonae by Augustus, there is no doubt that it existed for several centuries, and at least as late as the time of the emperor Gordian. The aediles belonged to the class of the minores magistratus. The plebeian aediles were originally chosen at the comitia centuriata, but afterwards at the comitia tributa, in which comitia the curule aediles also were chosen. It appears that until the lex annalis was passed (B. c. 180) a Roman citizen might be a candidate for any office after completing his twenty-seventh year. This law fixed the age at which each office might be enjoyed, and it seems that the age fixed for the aedileship was thirty-six. The aediles existed under the emperors; but their powers were gradually diminished, and their functions exercised by new officers created by the emperors. After the battle of Actium, Augustus appointed a Praefectus urbi, who exercised the general police, which had formerly been one of the duties of the aediles. Augustus also took from the aediles, or exercised himself, the office of superintending the religious rites, and the banishing from the city of all foreign ceremonials; he also assumed the superintendence of the temples, and thus may be said to have destroyed the aedileship by depriving it of its old and original function. The last recorded instance of the splendours of the aedileship is the administration of Agrippa, who volunteered to take the office, and repaired all the public buildings and all the roads at his own expense, without drawing anything from the treasury. The aedileship had, however, lost its true character before this time. Agrippa had already been consul before he accepted the office of aedile, and his munificent expenditure in this nominal office was the close of the splendour of the aedileship. Augustus appointed the curule aediles specially to the office of putting out fires, and placed a body of 600 slaves at their command; but the praefecti vigilum afterwards performed this duty. They retained, under the early emperors, a kind of police, for the purpose of repressing open licentiousness and disorder. The coloniae, and the municipia of the later period, had also their aediles, whose numbers and functions varied in different places. They seem, however, as to their powers and duties, to have resembled the aediles of Rome. They were chosen annually.

AEDĬTŬI, AEDĬTŬMI, AEDĬTĬMI (called by the Greeks νεωκόροι, ζάκοροι, and ὑποζάκοροι), were persons who took care of the temples, attended to the cleaning of them, &c. They appear to have lived in the temples, or near them, and to have acted as ciceroni to those persons who wished to see them. Subsequently among the Greeks, the menial services connected with this office were left to slaves, and the persons called *neocori* became priestly officers of high rank, who had the chief superintendence of temples, their treasures, and the sacred rites observed in them.

AEGIS (αἰγίς) signifies, literally, a goat-skin. According to ancient mythology, the aegis worn by Zeus was the hide of the goat Amaltheia, which had suckled him in his infancy. Homer always represents it as part of the armour of Zeus, whom on this account he distinguishes by the epithet *aegis-bearing* (αἰγίοχος). He, however, asserts, that it was borrowed on different occasions both by Apollo and Athena. The aegis was connected with the shield of Zeus, either serving as a covering over it, or as a belt by which it was suspended from the right shoulder. Homer accordingly uses the word to denote not only the goat-skin, which it properly signified, but also the shield to which it belonged. The aegis was adorned in a style corresponding to the might and majesty of the father of the gods. In the middle of it was fixed the appalling Gorgon's head, and its border was surrounded with golden tassels (θύσανοι), each of which was worth a hecatomb. The aegis is usually seen on the statues of Athena, in which it is a sort of scarf falling obliquely over the right shoulder, so as to pass round the body under the left arm. The serpents of the Gorgon's head are transferred to the border of the skin. (See the left-hand figure

Aegis worn by Athena.
From Torso at Dresden. From Ancient Statues.

in the cut.) The later poets and artists represent the aegis as a breast-plate covered with metal in the form of scales. (See the right-hand figure.)

AENEĀTŌRES, were those who blew upon wind instruments in the Roman army; namely, the *buccinatores*, *cornicines*, and *tubicines*. They were also employed in the public games.

AENIGMA (αἴνιγμα), a riddle. It was an ancient custom among the Greeks to amuse themselves by proposing riddles at their symposia, or drinking parties. Those who were successful in solving them received a prize, which usually consisted of wreaths, cakes, &c., while those who were unsuccessful were condemned to drink in one breath a certain quantity of wine, sometimes mixed with salt water. Those riddles which have come down to us are mostly in hexameter verse. The Romans seem to have been too serious to find any great amusement in riddles.

AENUM, or AHENUM (sc. *vas*), a brazen vessel, used for boiling. The word is also frequently used in the sense of a dyer's copper; and, as purple was the most celebrated dye of antiquity, we find the expressions *Sidonium aënum*, *Tyrium aënum*, &c.

AEORA, or EORA (αἰώρα, ἐώρα), a festival at Athens, accompanied with sacrifices and banquets, whence it is sometimes called εὐδειπνος. It was probably instituted in honour of Icarius and his daughter Erigone.

AERA. [CHRONOLOGIA.]

AERARII, a class of Roman citizens, who were not included in the thirty tribes instituted by Servius Tullius. Although citizens, they did not possess the suffragium, or right of voting in the comitia. They were *cives sine suffragio*. They also paid the tribute in a different manner from the other citizens. The Aerarians were chiefly artisans and freedmen. The Caerites, or inhabitants of the Etruscan town of Caere, who obtained the franchise in early times, but without the suffragium, were probably the first body of aerarians. Any Roman citizen guilty of a crime punishable by the censors, might be degraded to the rank of an aerarian; so that his civic rights were suspended, at least for the time that he was an aerarian. All citizens so degraded were classed among the Caerites; whence we find the expressions *aerarium facere* and *in tabulas Caeritum referre* used as synonymous. Persons who were made *infames* likewise became aerarians, for they lost the jus honorum and the suffragium. The aerarians had to pay a tributum pro capite which was considerably higher than that paid by the other citizens. They were not allowed to serve in the legions.

AERARII TRIBŪNI. [AES EQUESTRE.]

AERĀRIUM (τὸ δημόσιον), the public treasury at Rome, and hence the public money itself. After the banishment of the kings the temple of Saturn was employed as the place for keeping the public money, and it continued to be so used till the later times of the empire. Besides the public money and the accounts connected with it, various other things were preserved in the treasury; of these, the most important were:—1. The standards of the legions. 2. The various laws passed from time to time, engraven on brazen tables. 3. The decrees of the senate, which were entered there in books kept for the purpose, though the original documents were preserved in the temple of Ceres under the custody of the aediles. 4. Various other public documents, the reports and despatches of all generals and governors of provinces, the names of all foreign ambassadors that came to Rome, &c. Under the republic the aerarium was divided into two parts: the *common* treasury, in which were deposited the regular taxes, and from which were taken the sums of money needed for the ordinary expenditure of the state; and the *sacred* treasury (*aerarium sanctum* or *sanctius*), which was never touched except in cases of extreme peril. Both of these treasuries were in the temple of Saturn, but in distinct parts of the temple. The produce of a tax of five per cent. (*vicesima*) upon the value of every manumitted slave, called *aurum vicesimarium*, was paid into the sacred treasury, as well as a portion of the immense wealth obtained by the Romans in their conquests in the East. Under Augustus the provinces and the administration of the government were divided between the senate, as the representative of the old Roman people, and the Caesar: all the property of the former continued to be called *aerarium*, and that of the latter received the name of *fiscus*. Augustus also established a third treasury, to provide for the pay and support of the army, and this received the name of *aerarium militare*. He also imposed several new taxes to be paid into this aerarium. In the time of the republic, the entire management of the revenues of the state belonged to the senate; and under the superintendence and control of the senate the quaestors had the charge of the aerarium. In B.C. 28, Augustus deprived the quaestors of the charge of the treasury and gave it to two praefects, whom he allowed the senate to choose from among the praetors at the end of their year of office. Various other changes were made with respect to the charge of the aerarium, but it was eventually entrusted, in the reign of Trajan, to praefects, who appear to have held their office for two years.

AES (χαλκός), properly signifies a compound of copper and tin, corresponding to what we call *bronze*. It is incorrect to translate it *brass*, which is a combination of copper and zinc, since all the specimens of ancient objects, formed of the material called aes, are found upon analysis to contain no zinc. The employment of aes was very general among the ancients; money, vases, and utensils of all sorts, being made of it. All the most ancient coins in Rome and the old Italian states were made of aes, and hence money in general was called by this name. For the same reason we have *aes alienum*, meaning debt, and *aera* in the plural, pay to the soldiers. The Romans had no other coinage except bronze or copper (*aes*), till B. C. 269, five years before the first Punic war, when silver was first coined; gold was not coined till sixty-two years after silver. The first coinage of aes is usually attributed to Servius Tullius, who is said to have stamped the money with the image of cattle (*pecus*), whence it is called *pecunia*. According to some accounts, it was coined from the commencement of the city, and we know that the old Italian states possessed a bronze or copper coinage from the earliest times. The first coinage was the *as* [As], which originally was a pound weight; but as in course of time the weight of the *as* was reduced not only in Rome, but in the other Italian states, and this reduction in weight was not uniform in the different states, it became usual in all bargains to pay the asses according to their weight, and not according to their nominal value. The *aes grave* was not the old heavy coins as distinguished from the lighter modern; but it signified any number of copper coins reckoned according to the old style, by weight. There was, therefore, no occasion for the state to suppress the circulation of the old copper coins, since in all bargains the asses were not reckoned by tale, but by weight.—Bronze or copper (χαλκός) was very little used by the Greeks for money in early times. Silver was originally the universal currency, and copper appears to have been seldom coined till after the time of Alexander the Great. The copper coin was called *Chalcous* (χαλκούς). The smallest silver coin at Athens was the quarter-obol, and the chalcous was the half of that, or the eighth of an obol. In later times, the obol was coined of copper as well as silver.

AES CIRCUMFORANEUM, money borrowed from the Roman bankers (*argentarii*), who had shops in porticoes round the forum.

AES EQUESTRE, AES HORDEARIUM, and AES MILITARE, were the ancient terms for the pay of the Roman soldiers, before the regular *stipendium* was introduced. The *aes equestre* was the sum of money given for the purchase of the horse of an eques; the *aes hordearium*, the sum paid yearly for its keep, in other words the pay of an eques; and the *aes militare*, the pay of a foot soldier. None of this money seems to have been taken from the public treasury, but to have been paid by certain private persons, to whom this duty was assigned by the state. The *aes hordearium*, which amounted to 2000 asses, had to be paid by single women (*viduae*, i. e. both maidens and widows) and orphans (*orbi*), provided they possessed a certain amount of property. The *aes equestre*, which amounted to 10,000 asses, was probably also paid by the same class of persons. The *aes militare*, the amount of which is not expressly mentioned, had to be paid by the *tribuni aerarii*, and if not paid, the foot soldiers had a right of distress against them. It is generally assumed that these *tribuni aerarii* were magistrates connected with the treasury, and that they were the assistants of the quaestors; but there are good reasons for believing that the *tribuni aerarii* were private persons, who were liable to the payment of the *aes militare*, and upon whose property a distress might be levied, if the money were not paid. They were probably persons whose property was rated at a certain sum in the census, and we may conjecture that they obtained the name of *tribuni aerarii* because they levied the *tributum*, which was imposed for the purpose of paying the army, and then paid it to the soldiers. These *tribuni aerarii* were no longer needed when the state took into its own hands the payment of the troops; but they were revived in B.C. 70, as a distinct class in the commonwealth, by the Lex Aurelia, which gave the judicia to the senators, equites and tribuni aerarii.

AES UXORIUM, was a tax paid by men who reached old age without having married. It was first imposed by the censors in B. C. 403. [LEX JULIA ET PAPIA POPPAEA.]

AESYMNETES (αἰσυμνήτης), a person who was sometimes invested with unlimited power in the Greek states. His power partook in some degree of the nature both of kingly and tyrannical authority; since he was appointed legally, and did not usurp the government, but at the same time was not bound by any laws in his public administration. The office was not hereditary, nor was it held for life; but it only continued for a limited time, or till some object was accomplished. Thus we read that the inhabitants of Mytilene appointed Pittacus aesymnetes, in order to prevent the return of Alcaeus and the other exiles. Dionysius compares it with the dictatorship of Rome. In some states, such as

Cyme and Chalcedon, it was the title borne by the regular magistrates.

AETAS. [INFANS; IMPUBES.]

AETŌLĬCUM FOEDUS (κοινὸν τῶν Αἰτώλων), the Aetolian league, appears as a powerful political body soon after the death of Alexander the Great, viz. during the Lamian war against Antipater. The characteristic difference between the Aetolian and Achaean leagues was that the former originally consisted of a confederacy of nations or tribes, while the latter was a confederacy of towns. The sovereign power of the confederacy was vested in the general assemblies of all the confederates (κοινὸν τῶν Αἰτώλων, concilium Aetolorum), and this assembly had the right to discuss all questions respecting peace and war, and to elect the great civil or military officers of the league. The ordinary place of meeting was Thermon, but on extraordinary occasions assemblies were also held in other towns belonging to the league, though they were not situated in the country of Aetolia Proper. The questions which were to be brought before the assembly were sometimes discussed previously by a committee, selected from the great mass, and called Apocleti (ἀπόκλητοι). The general assembly usually met in the autumn, when the officers of the league were elected. The highest among them, as among those of the Achaean league, bore the title of *Strategus* (στρατηγός), whose office lasted only for one year. The strategus had the right to convoke the assembly; he presided in it, introduced the subjects for deliberation, and levied the troops. The officers next in rank to the strategus were the hipparchus and the public scribe. The political existence of the league was destroyed in B.C. 189 by the treaty with Rome, and the treachery of the Roman party among the Aetolians themselves caused in B.C. 167 five hundred and fifty of the leading patriots to be put to death, and those who survived the massacre were carried to Rome as prisoners.

AĒTŌMA (ἀέτωμα). [FASTIGIUM.]

AFFĪNES, AFFĪNĬTAS, or **ADFĪNES, ADFĪNĬTAS.** Affines are the *cognati* [COGNATI] of husband and wife, the cognati of the husband becoming the affines of the wife, and the cognati of the wife the affines of the husband. The father of a husband is the *socer* of the husband's wife, and the father of a wife is the *socer* of the wife's husband. The term *socrus* expresses the same affinity with respect to the husband's and wife's mothers. A son's wife is *nurus*, or daughter-in-law to the son's parents; a wife's husband is *gener*, or son-in-law to the wife's parents. Thus the *avus, avia—pater, mater*—of the wife became by the marriage respectively the *socer magnus, prosocrus,* or *socrus magna—socer, socrus*—of the husband, who becomes with respect to them severally *progener* and *gener*. In like manner the corresponding ancestors of the husband respectively assume the same names with respect to the son's wife, who becomes with respect to them *pronurus* and *nurus*. The son and daughter of a husband or wife born of a prior marriage are called *privignus* and *privigna*, with respect to their step-father or step-mother; and with respect to such children, the step-father and step-mother are severally called *vitricus* and *noverca*. The husband's brother becomes *levir* with respect to the wife, and his sister becomes *glos* (the Greek γάλως). Marriage was unlawful among persons who had become such affines as above mentioned.

ĂGALMA (ἄγαλμα) is a general name for a statue or image to represent a god.

ĂGĀSO, a groom, whose business it was to take care of the horses. The word is also used for a driver of beasts of burden, and is sometimes applied to a slave who had to perform the lowest menial duties.

ĂGĂTHOERGI (ἀγαθοεργοί). In time of war the kings of Sparta had a body-guard of three hundred of the noblest of the Spartan youths (ἱππεῖς), of whom the five eldest retired every year, and were employed for one year under the name of *Agathoergi*, in missions to foreign states.

ĂGĒLA (ἀγέλη), an assembly of young men in Crete, who lived together from their eighteenth year till the time of their marriage. An *agela* always consisted of the sons of the most noble citizens, and the members of it were obliged to marry at the same time.

ĂGĒMA (ἄγημα from ἄγω), the name of a chosen body of troops in the Macedonian army, usually consisting of horsemen.

ĂGER PŪBLĬCUS, the public land, was the land belonging to the Roman state. It was a recognised principle among the Italian nations that the territory of a conquered people belonged to the conquerors. Accordingly, the Romans were constantly acquiring fresh territory by the conquest of the surrounding people. The land thus acquired was usually disposed of in the following way. 1. The land which was under cultivation was either distributed among colonists, who were sent to occupy it, or it was sold, or it was let out to farm. 2. The land which was then out of cultivation, and which, owing to war, was by far the greater part, might be occupied by any of the Roman citizens on the payment of a portion of the yearly produce; a tenth of the produce of arable land, and a fifth of the produce of the land planted with the vine, the olive, and other valuable trees.

2. The land which had previously served as the common pasture land of the conquered state, or was suitable for the purpose, continued to be used as pasture land by the Roman citizens, who had, however, to pay a certain sum of money for the cattle which they turned upon it. The occupation of the public land spoken of above under the second head was always expressed by the words *possessio* and *possidere*, and the occupier of the land was called the *possessor*. The land continued to be the property of the state; and accordingly we must distinguish between the terms *possessio*, which merely indicated the use or enjoyment of the land, and *dominium*, which expressed ownership, and was applied to private land, of which a man had the absolute ownership. The right of occupying the public land belonged only to citizens, and consequently only to the patricians originally, as they were the state. The plebeians were only subjects, and consequently had no right to the property of the state; but it is probable that they were permitted to feed their cattle on the public pasture lands. Even when the plebeians became a separate estate by the constitution of Servius Tullius, they still obtained no right to share in the possession of the public land, which continued to be the exclusive privilege of the patricians; but as a compensation, each individual plebeian received an assignment of a certain quantity of the public land as his own property. Henceforth the possession of the public land was the privilege of the patricians, and an assignment of a portion of it the privilege of the plebeians. As the state acquired new lands by conquest, the plebeians ought to have received assignments of part of them, but since the patricians were the governing body, they generally refused to make any such assignment, and continued to keep the whole as part of the ager publicus, whereby the enjoyment of it belonged to them alone. Hence, we constantly read of the plebeians claiming, and sometimes enforcing, a division of such land. With the extension of the conquests of Rome, the ager publicus constantly increased, and thus a large portion of Italy fell into the hands of the patricians, who frequently withheld from the state the annual payments of a tenth and a fifth, which they were bound to pay for the possession of the land, and thus deprived the state of a fund for the expenses of the war. In addition to which they used slaves as cultivators and shepherds, since freemen were liable to be drawn off from field-labour to military service, and slave-labour was consequently far cheaper. In this way the number of free labourers was diminished, and that of slaves augmented. To remedy this state of things several laws were from time to time proposed and carried, which were most violently opposed by the patricians. All laws which related to the *public* land are called by the general title of *Leges Agrariae*, and accordingly all the early laws relating to the possession of the public land by the patricians, and to the assignment of portions of it to the plebeians, were strictly agrarian laws; but the first law to which this name is usually applied was proposed soon after the establishment of the republic by the consul, Sp. Cassius, in B.C. 486. Its object was to set apart the portion of the public land which the patricians were to possess, to divide the rest among the plebeians, to levy the payment due for the possession, and to apply it to paying the army. The first law, however, which really deprived the patricians of the advantages they had previously enjoyed in the occupation of the public land was the agrarian law of C. Licinius Stolo (B.C. 366), which limited each individual's possession of public land to 500 jugera, and declared that no individual should have above 100 large and 500 smaller cattle on the public pastures: it further enacted that the surplus land was to be divided among the plebeians. As this law, however, was soon disregarded, it was revived again by Tib. Sempronius Gracchus (B.C. 133), with some alterations and additions. The details of the other agrarian laws mentioned in Roman history are given under the name of the lex by which they are called. [LEX.]

AGGER (χῶμα), from *ad* and *gero*, used in general for a heap or mound of any kind. It was more particularly applied:—
(1) To a mound, usually composed of earth, which was raised round a besieged town, and which was gradually increased in breadth and height, till it equalled or overtopped the walls. The agger was sometimes made, not only of earth, but of wood, hurdles, &c.; whence we read of the agger being set on fire.—(2) To the earthen wall surrounding a Roman encampment, composed of the earth dug from the ditch (*fossa*), which was usually 9 feet broad and 7 feet deep; but if any attack was apprehended, the depth was increased to 12 feet and the breadth to 13 feet. Sharp stakes, &c., were usually fixed upon the agger, which was then called *vallum*. When both words are used, the agger means the mound of earth, and the vallum the stakes, &c., which were fixed upon the agger.

AGITATORES. [CIRCUS.]
AGMEN. [EXERCITUS.]
AGNATI. [COGNATI.]
AGNOMEN. [NOMEN.]

AGONALIA or AGONIA, one of the most ancient festivals at Rome, its institution being attributed to Numa Pompilius. It was celebrated on the 9th of January, the 21st of May, and the 11th of December; to which we should probably add the 17th of March, the day on which the Liberalia was celebrated, since this festival is also called *Agonia* or *Agonium Martiale*. The object of this festival was a disputed point among the ancients themselves. The victim which was offered was a ram; the person who offered it was the rex sacrificulus; and the place where it was offered was the regia. Now the ram was the usual victim presented to the guardian gods of the state, and the rex sacrificulus and the regia could be employed only for such ceremonies as were connected with the highest gods and affected the weal of the whole state. Regarding the sacrifice in this light, we see a reason for its being offered several times in the year. The etymology of the name was also a subject of much dispute among the ancients; and the various etymologies that were proposed are given at length by Ovid (*Fast.* i. 319-332). None of these, however, are at all satisfactory; and we would therefore suggest that it may have received its name from the sacrifice having been offered on the Quirinal hill, which was originally called *Agonus*.

AGONES (ἀγῶνες), the general term among the Greeks for the contests at their great national games. The word also signified lawsuits, and was especially employed in the phrase ἀγῶνες τιμητοί and ἀτίμητοι. [TIMEMA.]

AGONOTHETAE (ἀγωνοθέται), persons in the Grecian games who decided disputes, and adjudged the prizes to the victors. Originally, the person who instituted the contest and offered the prize was the *Agonothetes*, and this continued to be the practice in those games which were instituted by kings or private persons. But in the great public games, such as the Isthmian, Pythian, &c., the *Agonothetae* were either the representatives of different states, as the Amphictyons at the Pythian games, or were chosen from the people in whose country the games were celebrated. During the flourishing times of the Grecian republics the Eleans were the *Agonothetae* in the Olympic games, the Corinthians in the Isthmian games, the Amphictyons in the Pythian games, and the Corinthians, Argives, and inhabitants of Cleonae in the Nemaean games. The *Agonothetae* were also called *Aesymnetae* (αἰσυμνῆται), *Agonarchae* (ἀγωνάρχαι), *Agonodicae* (ἀγωνοδίκαι), *Athlothetae* (ἀθλοθέται), *Rhabduchi* (ῥαβδοῦχοι), or *Rhabdonomi* (ῥαβδονόμοι, from the staff which they carried as an emblem of authority), *Brabeis* (βραβεῖς), and *Brabeutae* (βραβευταί).

AGORA (ἀγορά) properly means an assembly of any kind, and is usually employed by Homer to designate the general assembly of the people. The Agora seems to have been considered an essential part of the constitution of the early Grecian states. It was usually convoked by the king, but occasionally by some distinguished chieftain, as, for example, by Achilles before Troy. The king occupied the most important seat in these assemblies, and near him sat the nobles, while the people stood or sat in a circle around them. The people appear to have had no right of speaking or voting in these assemblies, but merely to have been called together to hear what had been already agreed upon in the council of the nobles, and to express their feelings as a body. The council of the nobles is called *Boulé* (βουλή) and *Thoöcus* (θόωκος), and sometimes even *Agora*. Among the Athenians, the proper name for the assembly of the people was *Ecclesia* (ἐκκλησία), and among the Dorians *Halia* (ἁλία). The term Agora was confined at Athens to the assemblies of the phylae and demi. The name Agora was early transferred from the assembly itself to the place in which it was held; and thus it came to be used for the market-place, where goods of all descriptions were bought and sold. Hence it answers to the Roman *forum*.

AGORANOMI (ἀγορανόμοι), public functionaries in most of the Grecian states, whose duties corresponded in many respects with those of the Roman aediles. At Athens their number was ten, five for the city, and five for the Peiraeeus, and they were chosen by lot. The principal duty of the Agoranomi was, as their name imports, to inspect the market, and to see that all the laws respecting its regulation were properly observed. They had the inspection of all things that were sold in the market, with the exception of corn, which was subject to the jurisdiction of special officers, called *Sitophylaces* (σιτοφύλακες). They regulated the price and quantity of articles exposed for sale, and punished all persons convicted of cheating, especially by means of false weights and measures. They had the power of fining all citizens who infringed upon the rules of the market, and of whipping all slaves and foreigners guilty of a like offence. They also collected the market dues, and had the care of all the temples and fountains in the market place.

AGRARIAE LEGES. [AGER PUBLICUS; LEX.]

AGRAULIA (ἀγραύλια) was a festival celebrated by the Athenians in honour of Agraulos, the daughter of Cecrops. It was perhaps connected with the solemn oath, which all Athenians, when they arrived at manhood (ἔφηβοι), were obliged to take in the temple of Agraulos, that they would fight for their country, and always observe its laws.

AGRIMENSŌRES, or "land surveyors," a college established under the Roman emperors. Like the jurisconsults, they had regular schools, and were paid handsome salaries by the state. Their business was to measure unassigned lands for the state, and ordinary lands for the proprietors, and to fix and maintain boundaries. Their writings on the subject of their art were very numerous; and we have still scientific treatises on the law of boundaries, such as those by Frontinus and Hyginus.

AGRIŌNĬA (ἀγριώνια), a festival which was celebrated at Orchomenus, in Boeotia, in honour of Dionysus, surnamed Agrionius. A human being used originally to be sacrificed at this festival, but this sacrifice seems to have been avoided in later times. One instance, however, occurred in the days of Plutarch.

AGRONŎMI (ἀγρονόμοι), the country-police, probably in Attica, whose duties corresponded in most respects to those of the astynomi in the city, and who appear to have performed nearly the same duties as the hylori (ὑλωροί).

AGRŌTĔRAS THŪSIA (ἀγροτέρας θυσία), a festival celebrated every year at Athens in honour of Artemis, surnamed Agrotera (from ἄγρα, the chase). It was solemnized on the sixth of the month of Boëdromion, and consisted of a sacrifice of 500 goats, which continued to be offered in the time of Xenophon. Its origin is thus related:—When the Persians invaded Attica, the Athenians made a vow to sacrifice to Artemis Agrotera as many goats as there should be enemies slain at Marathon. But as the number of enemies slain was so great that an equal number of goats could not be found at once, the Athenians decreed that 500 should be sacrificed every year.

AGYRTAE (ἀγύρται), mendicant priests, who were accustomed to travel through the different towns of Greece, soliciting alms for the gods whom they served, and whose images they carried, either on their shoulders or on beasts of burthen. They were, generally speaking, persons of the lowest and most abandoned character.

AHĒNUM. [AENUM.]

AIKĬAS DĬKĒ (αἰκίας δίκη), an action brought at Athens, before the court of the Forty (οἱ τετταράκοντα), against any individual who had struck a citizen. Any citizen who had been thus insulted might proceed against the offending party, either by the αἰκίας δίκη, which was a private action, or by the ὕβρεως γραφή, which was looked upon in the light of a public prosecution.

AITHOUSA (αἴθουσα), a word only used by Homer, is probably for αἴθουσα στοά, a portico exposed to the sun. From the passages in which it occurs, it seems to denote a covered portico, opening on to the court of the house, αὐλή, in front of the vestibule, πρόθυρον.

ĀLA, part of a Roman house. [Domus.]

ĀLA, ĀLĀRES, ĀLĀRĬI. *Ala*, which literally means *a wing*, was from the earliest epochs employed to denote the wing of an army, but in process of time was frequently used in a restricted sense.—(1) When a Roman army was composed of Roman citizens exclusively, the flanks of the infantry when drawn up in battle array were covered on the right and left by the cavalry; and hence *Ala* denoted the body of horse which was attached to and served along with the foot-soldiers of the legion.—(2) When, at a later date, the Roman armies were composed partly of Roman citizens and partly of *Socii*, either *Latini* or *Italici*, it became the practice to marshal the Roman troops in the centre of the battle line and the Socii upon the wings. Hence *ala* and *alarii* denoted the contingent furnished by the allies, both horse and foot, and the two divisions were distinguished as *dextera ala* and *sinistra ala*. —(3) When the whole of the inhabitants of Italy had been admitted to the privileges of Roman citizens the terms *alarii*, *cohortes alariae* were transferred to the *foreign* troops serving along with the Roman armies.— (4) Lastly, under the empire, the term *ala* was applied to regiments of horse, raised it would seem with very few exceptions in the provinces, serving apart from the legions and the cavalry of the legions.

ĀLĂBARCHĒS (ἀλαβάρχης), the chief magistrate of the Jews at Alexandria, whose duties, as far as the government was concerned, chiefly consisted in raising and paying the taxes.

ĀLĂBASTER or ĀLĂBASTRUM, a vessel or pot used for containing perfumes, or rather ointments, made of that species of marble which mineralogists call *gypsum*, and which is usually designated by the name of *alabaster*. When varieties of colour occur in the same stone, and are disposed in bands or horizontal strata, it is often called onyx alabaster; and when dispersed irregularly, as if in clouds, it is distinguished as agate alabaster. The term seems to have been employed to denote vessels appropriated to these uses, even when they were not made of the material from which it is supposed they originally received their name. Thus Theocritus speaks of golden alabastra. These vessels were of a tapering shape, and very often had a long narrow neck, which was sealed; so that when Mary, the sister of Lazarus, is said by St. Mark to break the alabaster box of ointment for the purpose of anointing our Saviour, it appears probable that she only broke the extremity of the neck, which was thus closed.

ĀLĀRII. [ALA.]

ĀLAUDA, a Gaulish word, the prototype of the modern French *Alouette*, denoting a small crested bird of the lark kind. The name alauda was bestowed by Julius Caesar on a legion of picked men, which he raised at his own expense among the inhabitants of Transalpine Gaul, about the year B.C. 55, which he equipped and disciplined after the Roman fashion, and on which he at a subsequent period bestowed the freedom of the state. The designation was, in all probability, applied from a plume upon the helmet, resembling the "apex" of the bird in question, or from the general shape and appearance of the head-piece.

ALBŌGĂLĒRUS. [APEX.]

ALBUM, a tablet of any material on which the praetor's edicts, and the rules relating to actions and interdicts, were written. The tablet was put up in a public place, in order that all the world might have notice of its contents. According to some authorities, the album was so called because it was either a white material or a material whitened, and of course the writing would be of a different colour. According to other authorities, it was so called because the writing was in white letters. Probably the word album originally meant any tablet containing anything of a public nature. We know that it was, in course of time, used to signify a list of any public body; thus we find *album judicum*, or the body out of which judices were to be chosen [JUDEX], and *album senatorium*, or list of senators.

ĀLĒA, gaming, or playing at a game of chance of any kind: hence *aleo*, *aleator*, a gamester, a gambler. Playing with *tali*, or *tesserae*, was generally understood, because this was by far the most common game of chance among the Romans. Gaming was forbidden by the Roman laws, both during the times of the republic and under the emperors, but was tolerated in the month of December at the Saturnalia, which was a period of general relaxation; and old men were allowed to amuse themselves in this manner at all times.

ĀLĪCŬLA (ἀλλιξ or ἀλλῆξ), an upper dress, in all probability identical with the chlamys.

ĀLĪMENTĀRII PŬĔRI ET PUELLAE. In the Roman republic the poorer citizens were assisted by public distributions of corn, oil, and money, which were called *congiaria*. [CONGIARIUM.] The Emperor Nerva was the first who extended them to children, and Trajan appointed them to be made every month, both to orphans and to the children of poor parents. The children who received them were called *pueri et puellae alimentarii*, and also (from the emperor) *pueri puellaeque Ulpiani*.

ĀLĪPĬLUS, a slave, who attended on bathers to remove the superfluous hair from their bodies.

ĀLIPTAE (ἀλείπται), among the Greeks, were persons who anointed the bodies of the athletae preparatory to their entering the palaestra. The chief object of this anointing was to close the pores of the body, in order to prevent much perspiration, and the weakness consequent thereon. The athleta was again anointed after the contest, in order to restore the tone of the strained muscles. He then bathed, and had the dust, sweat, and oil scraped off his body, by means of an instrument similar to the strigil of the Romans, and called *stlengis* (στλεγγίς), and afterwards *xystra* (ξύστρα). The aliptae took advantage of the knowledge they necessarily acquired of the state of the muscles of the athletae, and their general strength or weakness of body, to advise them as to their exercises and mode of life. They were thus a kind of medical trainers. Among the Romans the aliptae were slaves who scrubbed and anointed their masters in the baths. They, too, like the Greek aliptae, appear to have attended to their masters' constitution and mode of life. They were also called *unctores*. They used in their operations a kind of scraper called strigil, towels (*lintea*), a cruise of oil (*guttus*), which was usually of horn, a bottle (*ampulla*), and a small vessel called *lenticula*.

ALLŌCŬTIO, an harangue made by a Roman imperator to his soldiers, to en-

Allocutio. (Coin of Nero.)

courage them before battle, or on other occasions. On coins we frequently find a figure of an imperator standing on a platform and addressing the soldiers below him. Such coins bear the epigraph ADLOCUTIO.

Allocutio. (Coin of Galba.)

ALŌA or HALŌA (ἀλῶα, ἁλῶα), an Attic festival, but celebrated principally at Eleusis, in honour of Demeter and Dionysus, the inventors of the plough and protectors of the fruits of the earth.

ALTĀRE. [ARA.]

ALŪTA. [CALCEUS.]

ALȲTAE (ἀλύται), persons whose business it was to keep order in the public games. They received their orders from an alytarches (ἀλυτάρχης), who was himself under the direction of the agonothetae, or hellenodicae.

AMĀNŪENSIS, or AD MĀNUM SERVUS, a slave, or freedman, whose office it was to write letters and other things under his master's direction. The amanuenses must not be confounded with another sort of slaves, also called ad manum servi, who were always kept ready to be employed in any business.

AMĀRYNTHIA, or AMĀRYSIA (ἀμαρύνθια or ἀμαρύσια), a festival of Artemis Amarynthia or Amarysia, celebrated, as it seems, originally at Amarynthus in Euboea, with extraordinary splendour, but also solemnised in several places in Attica, such as Athmone.

AMBARVĀLIA. [ARVALES FRATRES.]

AMBĬTUS, which literally signifies " a going about," cannot, perhaps, be more nearly expressed than by our word canvassing. After the plebs had formed a distinct class at Rome, and when the whole body of the citizens had become very greatly increased, we frequently read, in the Roman writers, of the great efforts which it was necessary for candidates to make in order to secure the votes of the citizens. At Rome, as in every community into which the element of popular election enters, solicitation of votes, and open or secret influence and bribery, were among the means by which a candidate secured his election to the offices of state. The following are the principal terms occurring in the Roman writers in relation to the canvassing for the public offices:—A candidate was called petitor; and his opponent with reference to him competitor. A candidate (candidatus) was so called from his appearing in the public places, such as the fora and Campus Martius, before his fellow-citizens, in a whitened toga. On such occasions the candidate was attended by his friends (deductores), or followed by the poorer citizens (sectatores), who could in no other manner show their good will or give their assistance. The word assiduitas expressed both the continual presence of the candidate at Rome and his continual solicitations. The candidate, in going his rounds or taking his walk, was accompanied by a nomenclator, who gave him the names of such persons as he might meet; the candidate was thus enabled to address them by their name, an indirect compliment, which could not fail to be generally gratifying to the electors. The candidate accompanied his address with a shake of the hand (prensatio). The term benignitas comprehended generally any kind of treating, as shows, feasts, &c. The ambitus, which was the object of several penal enactments, taken as a generic term, comprehended the two species —ambitus and largitiones (bribery). Liberalitas and benignitas are opposed by Cicero, as things allowable, to ambitus and largitio, as things illegal. Money was paid for votes; and, in order to insure secrecy and secure the elector, persons called interpretes were employed to make the bargain, sequestres to hold the money till it was to be paid, and divisores to distribute it. The offence of ambitus was a matter which belonged to the judicia publica, and the enactments against it were numerous. One of the earliest, though not the earliest of all, the Lex Cornelia Baebia (B.C. 181) was specially directed against largitiones. Those convicted under it were incapacitated from being candidates for ten years. The Lex Cornelia Fulvia (B.C. 159) punished the offence with exile. The Lex Acilia Calpurnia (B.C. 67) imposed a fine on the offending party, with exclusion from the senate and all public offices. The Lex Tullia (B.C. 63), passed in the consulship of Cicero, in addition to the penalty of the Acilian law, inflicted ten years' exsilium on the offender; and, among other things, forbade a person to exhibit gladiatorial shows (gladiatores dare) within any two years in which he was a candidate, unless he was required to do so, on a fixed day, by a testator's will. Two years afterwards the Lex Aufidia was proposed, but not passed; by which, among other things, it was provided that, if a candidate promised (*pronuntiarit*) money to a tribe, and did not pay it, he should be unpunished; but, if he did pay the money, he should further pay to each tribe (annually?) 3000 sesterces as long as he lived. This absurd proposal occasioned the witticism of Cicero, who said that Clodius observed the law by anticipation; for he promised, but did not pay. The Lex Licinia (B.C. 55) was specially directed against the offence of *sodalitium*, or the wholesale bribery of a tribe by gifts and treating; and another lex, passed (B.C. 52) when Pompey was sole consul, had for its object the establishment of a speedier course of proceeding on trials for ambitus. All these enactments failed in completely accomplishing their object. That which no law could suppress, so long as the old popular forms retained any of their pristine vigour, was accomplished by the imperial usurpation. Caesar, when dictator, nominated some of the candidates for public offices: as to the consulship, he managed the appointments to that office just as he pleased. The popular forms of election were observed during the time of Augustus. Tiberius transferred the elections from the comitia to the senate, by which the offence of ambitus, in its proper sense, entirely disappeared. The trials for ambitus were numerous in the time of the republic. The oration of Cicero in defence of L. Murena, who was charged with ambitus, and that in defence of Cn. Plancius, who was charged with *sodalitium*, are both extant.

AMBROSIA (ἀμβροσία), the food of the gods, which conferred upon them eternal youth and immortality, and was brought to Jupiter by pigeons. It was also used by the gods for anointing their body and hair; whence we read of the ambrosial locks of Jupiter.

AMBUBAIAE (probably from the Syriac, *abub aubub*, a pipe), Eastern dancing girls, who frequented chiefly the Circus at Rome, and obtained their living by prostitution and lascivious songs and dances.

AMBURBIUM, a sacrifice which was performed at Rome for the purification of the city.

AMENTUM. [Hasta.]

AMICTORIUM. [Strophium.]

AMICTUS. The verb *amicire* is commonly opposed to *induere*, the former being applied to the putting on of the outer garment, the pallium, laena, or toga (ἱμάτιον, φᾶρος); the latter, to the putting on of the inner garment, the tunic (χιτών). In consequence of this distinction, the verbal nouns *amictus* and *indutus*, even without any further denomination of the dress being added, indicate respectively the outer and inner clothing. In Greek *amicire* is expressed by ἀμφιέννυσθαι, ἀμπέχεσθαι, ἐπιβάλλεσθαι, περιβάλλεσθαι: and *induere* by ἐνδύειν. Hence came ἀμπεχόνη, ἐπίβλημα, and ἐπιβόλαιον, περίβλημα, and περιβόλαιον, an outer garment; a cloak, a shawl; and ἔνδυμα, an inner garment, a tunic, a shirt.

AMPHICTYONES (ἀμφικτύονες). Institutions called amphictyonic appear to have existed in Greece from time immemorial. They seem to have been originally associations of neighbouring tribes, formed for the regulation of mutual intercourse and the protection of a common temple or sanctuary, at which the representatives of the different members met, both to transact business and to celebrate religious rites and games. One of these associations was of much greater importance than all the rest, and was called, by way of eminence, the *Amphictyonic League* or *Council* (ἀμφικτυονία). It differed from other similar associations in having two places of meeting, the sanctuaries of two divinities; which were the temple of Demeter, in the village of Anthela, near Thermopylae, where the deputies met in autumn; and that of Apollo, at Delphi, where they assembled in spring. Its connexion with the latter place not only contributed to its dignity, but also to its permanence. Its early history is involved in obscurity. Most of the ancients suppose it to have been founded by Amphictyon, the son of Deucalion and Pyrrha, from whom they imagined that it derived its name: but this opinion is destitute of all foundation, and arose from the ancients assigning the establishment of their institutions to some mythical hero. There can be little doubt as to the true etymology of the word. It was originally written ἀμφικτίονες, and consequently signified those that dwelt around some particular locality. Its institution, however, is clearly of remote antiquity. It was originally composed of twelve *tribes* (not cities or states, it must be observed), each of which tribes contained various independent cities or states. We learn from Aeschines, that in B. C. 343, eleven of these tribes were as follows:—The Thessalians, Boeotians (not Thebans only), Dorians, Ionians, Perrhaebians, Magnetes, Locrians, Octaeans or Oenianians, Phthiots or Achaeans of Phthia, Malians, and Phocians; other lists leave us in doubt whether the remaining tribe were the Dolopes or Delphians; but as the Delphians could hardly be called a distinct tribe, their nobles appearing to have been Dorians, it seems probable that the Dolopes were originally members, and afterwards supplanted by the Delphians. All the states belonging to each of these tribes were on a footing of perfect equality. Thus Sparta enjoyed no advantages over Dorium and Cytinium, two small towns in Doris: and Athens, an Ionic city, was on a par with Eretria in Euboea, and Priene in Asia Minor, two other Ionic cities. The ordinary council was called *Pylaea* (πυλαία), from its meeting in the neighbourhood of Pylae (Thermopylae), but the name was given to the session at Delphi as well as to that at Thermopylae. The council was composed of two classes of representatives, one called *Pylagorae* (Πυλαγόραι), and the other *Hieromnemones* (Ἱερομνήμονες). Athens sent three Pylagorae and one Hieromnemon; of whom the former were elected apparently for each session, and the latter by lot, probably for a longer period. Respecting the relative duties of the Pylagorae and Hieromnemones we have little information: the name of the latter implies that they had a more immediate connection with the temple. We are equally in the dark respecting the numbers who sat in the council and its mode of proceeding. It would seem that all the deputies had seats in the council, and took part in its deliberations; but if it be true, as appears from Aeschines, that each of the tribes had only two votes, it is clear that all the deputies could not have voted. In addition to the ordinary council, there was an *ecclesia* (ἐκκλησία), or general assembly, including not only the classes above mentioned, but also those who had joined in the sacrifices, and were consulting the god. It was convened on extraordinary occasions by the chairman of the council. Of the duties of the Amphictyons nothing will give us a clearer view than the oath they took, which was as follows:—"They would destroy no city of the Amphictyons, nor cut off their streams in war or peace; and if any should do so, they would march against him, and destroy his cities; and should any pillage the property of the god, or be privy to or plan anything against what was in his temple (at Delphi), they would take vengeance on him with hand and foot, and voice, and all their might." From this oath we see that the main duty of the deputies was the preservation of the rights and dignity of the temple of Delphi. We know, too, that after it was burnt down (B. C. 548), they contracted with the Alcmaeonidae for its rebuilding. History, moreover, teaches that if the council produced any palpable effects, it was from their interest in Delphi; and though they kept up a standing record of what ought to have been the international law of Greece, they sometimes acquiesced in, and at other times were parties to, the most iniquitous acts. Of this case of Crissa is an instance. This town lay on the Gulf of Corinth, near Delphi, and was much frequented by pilgrims from the West. The Crissaeans were charged by the Delphians with undue exactions from these strangers. The council declared war against them, as guilty of a wrong against the god. The war lasted ten years, till, at the suggestion of Solon, the waters of the Pleistus were turned off, then poisoned, and turned again into the city. The besieged drank their fill, and Crissa was soon razed to the ground; and thus, if it were an Amphictyonic city, was a solemn oath doubly violated. Its territory—the rich Cirrhaean plain—was consecrated to the god, and curses imprecated upon whomsoever should till or dwell in it. Thus ended the First Sacred War (B. C. 585), in which the Athenians were the instruments of Delphian vengeance. The second or Phocian war (B. C. 350) was the most important in which the Amphictyons were concerned; and in this the Thebans availed themselves of the sanction of the council to take vengeance on their enemies, the Phocians. To do this, however, it was necessary to call in Philip of Macedon, who readily proclaimed himself the champion of Apollo, as it opened a pathway to his own ambition. The Phocians were subdued (B. C. 346), and the council decreed that all their cities, except Abae, should be razed, and the inhabitants dispersed in villages not containing more than fifty persons. Their two votes were given to Philip, who thereby gained a pretext for interfering with the affairs of Greece; and also obtained the recognition of his subjects as Hellenes. The Third Sacred War arose from the Amphissians tilling the devoted Cirrhaean plain. The Amphictyons called in the assistance of Philip, who soon reduced the Amphissians to subjection. Their submission was immediately followed by the battle of Chaeroneia (B. C. 338), and the extinction of the independence of Greece. In the following year, a congress of the Amphictyonic states was held, in which war was declared as if by united Greece against Persia, and Philip elected commander-in-chief. On this occasion the Amphictyons assumed the character of national representatives as of old, when they set a price upon the head of Ephialtes, for his treason to Greece at Thermopylae. It has been sufficiently shown that the Amphictyons themselves did not observe the oaths they took; and that they did not much alleviate the horrors of war, or enforce what they had sworn to do, is proved by many instances. Thus, for instance, Mycenae was destroyed by Argos (B. C. 535), Thespiae and Plataeae by Thebes, and Thebes herself swept from the face of the earth by Alexander, without the Amphictyons raising one word in opposition. Indeed, a few years before the Peloponnesian war, the council was a passive spectator of what Thucydides calls the Sacred War (ὁ ἱερὸς πόλεμος), when the Lacedaemonians made an expedition to Delphi, and put the temple into the hands of the Delphians, the Athenians, after their departure, restoring it to the Phocians. The council is rarely mentioned after the time of Philip. We are told that Augustus wished his new city, Nicopolis (A. D. 31), to be enrolled among the members. Pausanias, in the second century of our era, mentions it as still existing, but deprived of all power and influence.

AMPHIDROMIA (ἀμφιδρόμια or δρομιάμφιον ἦμαρ), a family festival of the Athenians, at which the newly-born child was introduced into the family, and received its name. The friends and relations of the parents were invited to the festival of the amphidromia, which was held in the evening, and they generally appeared with presents. The house was decorated on the outside with olive branches when the child was a boy, or with garlands of wool when the child was a girl; and a repast was prepared for the guests. The child was carried round the fire by the nurse, and thus, as it were, presented to the gods of the house and to the family, and at the same time received its name, to which the guests were witnesses. The carrying of the child round the hearth was the principal part of the solemnity, from which its name was derived.

AMPHITHEATRUM, an amphitheatre, was a place for the exhibition of public shows of combatants, wild beasts, and naval engagements, and was entirely surrounded with seats for the spectators; whereas, in those for dramatic performances, the seats were arranged in a semicircle facing the stage. An amphitheatre is therefore frequently described as a double theatre, consisting of two such semicircles, or halves, joined together, the spaces allotted to their orchestras becoming the inner inclosure, or area, termed the *arena*. The form, however, of the ancient amphitheatres was not a circle, but invariably an ellipse. Gladiatorial shows and combats of wild beasts (*venationes*) were first exhibited in the forum and the circus; and it appears that the ancient custom was still preserved till the time of Julius Caesar. The first building in the form of an amphitheatre is said to have been erected by C. Scribonius Curio, one of Caesar's partisans; but the account which is given of this building sounds rather fabulous. It is said to have consisted of two wooden theatres, made to revolve on pivots, in such a manner that they could, by means of windlasses and machinery, be turned round face to face, so as to form one building. Soon after Caesar himself erected, in the Campus Martius, a stationary amphitheatre, made of wood; to which building the name of *amphitheatrum* was for the first time given. The first stone amphitheatre was built by Statilius Taurus, in the Campus Martius, at the desire of Augustus. This was the only stone amphitheatre at Rome till the time of Vespasian. One was commenced by Caligula, but was not continued by Claudius. The one erected by Nero in the Campus Martius was only a temporary building, made of wood. The amphitheatre of Statilius Taurus was burnt in the fire of Rome in the time of Nero; and hence, as a new one was needed, Vespasian commenced the celebrated *Amphitheatrum Flavium* in the middle of the city, in the valley between the Caelian, the Esquiline, and the Velia, on the spot originally occupied by the lake or large pond attached to Nero's palace. Vespasian did not live to finish it. It was dedicated by Titus in A. D. 80, but was not completely finished till the reign of Domitian. This immense edifice, which is even yet comparatively entire, covered nearly six acres of ground, and was capable of containing about 87,000 spectators. It is called at the present day the *Colosseum* or *Colisaeum*. The interior of an amphitheatre was divided into three parts, the *arena*, *podium*, and *gradus*. The clear open space in the centre of the amphitheatre was called the *arena*, because it was covered with sand, or sawdust, to prevent the gladiators from slipping, and to absorb the blood. The size of the arena was not always the same in proportion to the size of the amphitheatre, but its average proportion was one third of the shorter diameter of the building. The arena was surrounded by a wall distinguished by the name of *podium*; although such appellation, perhaps, rather belongs to merely the upper part of it, forming the parapet, or balcony, before the first or lowermost seats, nearest to the arena. The arena, therefore, was no more than an open oval court, surrounded by a wall about fifteen feet high; a height considered necessary, in order to render the spectators perfectly secure from the attacks of wild beasts. There were four principal entrances leading into the arena; two at the ends of each axis or diameter of it, to which as many passages led directly from the exterior of the building; besides secondary ones, intervening between them, and communicating with the corridors beneath the seats on the podium. The wall or enclosure of the arena is supposed to have been faced with marble, more or less sumptuous; besides which, there appears to have been, in some instances at least, a sort of net-work affixed to the top of the podium, consisting of railing, or rather open trellis-work of metal. As a further defence, ditches, called *euripi*, sometimes surrounded the arena. The term podium was also applied to the terrace, or gallery itself, immediately above the arena, which was no wider than to be capable of containing two, or at the most, three ranges of moveable seats, or chairs. This, as being by far the best situation for distinctly viewing the sports in the arena, and also more commodiously accessible than the seats higher up, was the place set apart for senators and other persons of distinction, such as foreign ambassadors; and it was here, also, that the emperor himself used to sit, in an elevated place, called *suggestus* or *cubiculum*, and likewise the person who exhibited the games on a place elevated like a pulpit or tribunal *(editoris tribunal)*. Above the podium were the *gradus*, or seats of the other spectators, which were divided into *maeniana*, or stories. The first maenianum, consisting of fourteen rows of stone or marble seats, was appropriated to the equestrian order. The seats appro-

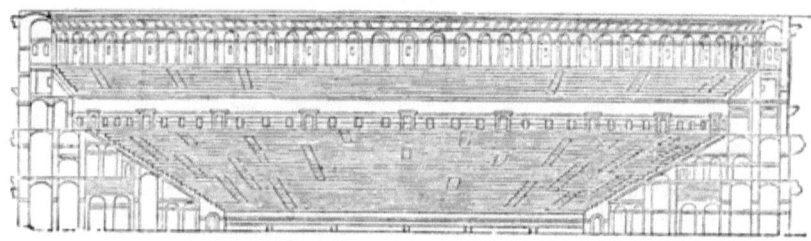

Longitudinal Section of the Flavian Amphitheatre.

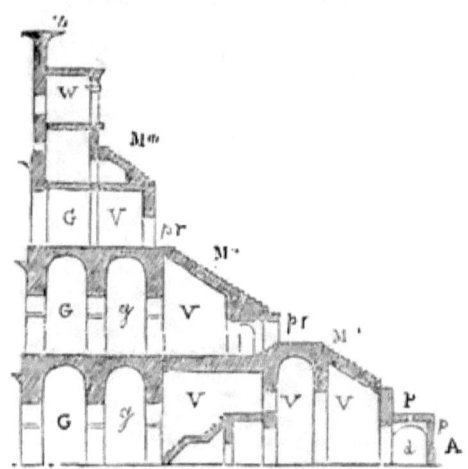

Elevation of one side of the preceding Section.

EXPLANATION.

A, The arena.
p, The wall or podium inclosing it.
r, The podium itself, on which were chairs, or seats, for the senators, &c.
M', The first maenianum, or slope of benches, for the equestrian order.
M'', The second maenianum.
M''', The third maenianum, elevated considerably above the preceding one, and appropriated to the pullati.
w, The colonnade, or gallery, which contained seats for women.
s, The narrow gallery round the summit of the interior, for the attendants who worked the velarium.

pr, pr, The præcinctiones, or landings, at the top of the first and second maenianum; in the pavement of which were grated apertures, at intervals, to admit light into t' vomitoria beneath them.
v v v v, Vomitoria.
G G G, The three external galleries through the circumference of the building, open to the arcades of the exterior.
g g, Inner gallery.

The situation and arrangement of the staircases, &c., are not expressed, as they could not be rendered intelligible without plans at various levels of the building.

priated to the senators and equites were covered with cushions, which were first used in the time of Caligula. Then, after an interval or space, termed a *praecinctio*, and forming a continued landing-place from the several staircases in it, succeeded the second maenianum, where were the seats called *popularia*, for the third class of spectators, or the populus. Behind this was the second praecinctio, bounded by a rather high wall; above which was the third maenianum, where there were only wooden benches for the *pullati*, or common people. The next and last division, namely, that in the highest part of the building, consisted of a colonnade, or gallery, where females were allowed to witness the spectacles of the amphitheatre, but some parts of it were also occupied by the pullati. Each maenianum was not only divided from the other by the praecinctio, but was intersected at intervals by spaces for passages left between the seats, called *scalae*, or *scalaria*; and the portion between two such passages was called *cuneus*, because the space gradually widened like a wedge, from the podium to the top of the building. The entrances to the seats from the outer porticoes were called *vomitoria*. At the very summit was the narrow platform for the men who had to attend to the *velarium*, or awning, by which the building was covered as a defence against the sun and rain. The velarium appears usually to have been made of wool, but more costly materials were sometimes employed. The first of the preceding cuts represents a longitudinal section of the Flavian amphitheatre, and the second, which is on a larger scale, a part of the above section, including the exterior wall, and the seats included between that and the arena. It will serve to convey an idea of the leading form and general disposition of the interior. For an account of the gladiatorial contests, and the shows of wild beasts, exhibited in the amphitheatre, see GLADIATORES, NAUMACHIA, and VENATIO.

AMPHŌRA (ἀμφορεύς), a vessel used for holding wine, oil, honey, &c. The following cut represents amphorae in the British Museum. They are of various forms and sizes; in general they are tall and narrow, with a small neck, and a handle on each side of the neck (whence the name, from ἀμφί, *on both sides*, and φέρω, to carry), and terminating at the bottom in a point, which was let into a stand or stuck in the ground, so that the vessel stood upright: several amphorae have been found in this position in the cellars at Pompeii. Amphorae were commonly made of earthenware. Homer mentions amphorae of gold and stone, and the Egyptians had them of brass; glass vessels of this form have been found at Pompeii. The most common use of the amphora, both among the

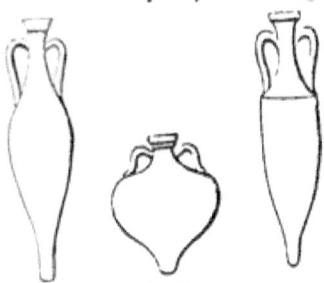

Amphorae. (British Museum.)

Greeks and the Romans, was for keeping wine. The cork was covered with pitch or gypsum, and (among the Romans) on the outside the title of the wine was painted, the date of the vintage being marked by the names of the consuls then in office; or, when the jars were of glass, little tickets (*pittoria, tesserae*) were suspended from them, indicating these particulars.—The Greek amphoreus and the Roman amphora were also names of fixed measures. The amphoreus, which was also called *metretes* (μετρητής) and *cadus* (κάδος), was equal to three Roman urnae = 8 gallons, 7·365 pints, imperial measure. The Roman amphora was two-thirds of the amphoreus, and was equal to 2 urnae = 8 congii = to 5 gallons, 7·577 pints; its solid content was exactly a Roman cubic foot.

AMPLIĀTIO, an adjournment of a trial, which took place when the judices after hearing the evidence of the advocates were unable to come to a satisfactory conclusion. This they expressed by giving in the tablets, on which were the letters N. L. (*non liquet*), and the praetor, by pronouncing the word *amplius*, thereupon adjourned the trial to any day he chose. The defendant and the cause were then said *ampliari*.

AMPULLA (λήκυθος, βομβύλιος), a bottle, usually made among the Romans either of glass or earthenware, rarely of more valuable

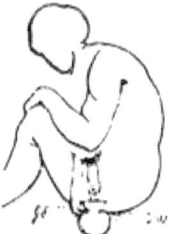

Ampulla. (Sketched by G. Scharf from a relief at Athens, discovered in 1840.)

materials. Ampullae were more or less globular. From their round and swollen shape, the word was used by Horace to indicate grand and turgid but empty language. ("Projicit ampullas et sesquipedalia verba," *Ar. Poet.* 97.) Ampullae are frequently mentioned in connection with the bath, since every Roman took with him to the bath a bottle of oil for anointing the body after bathing. The dealer in bottles was called *ampullarius*.

Ampulla. (From a tomb at Myra in Lycia.)

AMPYX (ἄμπυξ, ἀμπυκτῆρ, Lat. *frontale*), a frontal, a broad band or plate of metal, which ladies of rank wore above the forehead as part of the head-dress. The frontal of a horse was called by the same name. The annexed cut exhibits the frontal on the head of Pegasus, in contrast with the corresponding ornament as shown on the heads of two females.

Ampyces, Frontlets. (From Paintings on Vases.)

AMŪLĒTUM (περίαπτον, περίαμμα, φυλακτήριον), an amulet. This word in Arabic (hamalet) means *that which is suspended*. It was probably brought into Europe by Arabian merchants, together with the articles to which it was applied. An amulet was any object,—a stone, a plant, an artificial production, or a piece of writing,—which was suspended from the neck, or tied to any part of the body, for the purpose of warding off calamities and securing advantages of any kind. Faith in the virtues of amulets was almost universal in the ancient world, so that the art of medicine consisted in a very considerable degree of directions for their application.

AMUSSIS or AMUSSIUM, a carpenter's and mason's instrument, the use of which was to obtain a true plane surface.

ANACEIA (ἀνάκεια, or ἀνάκειον), a festival of the Dioscuri or Anactes (Ἄνακτες), as they were called at Athens. These heroes, however, received the most distinguished honours in the Dorian and Achaean states, where it may be supposed that every town celebrated a festival in their honour, though not under the name of Anaceia.

ANACRĬSIS (ἀνάκρισις), an examination, was used to signify the pleadings preparatory to a trial at Athens, the object of which was to determine, generally, if the action would lie. The magistrates were said ἀνακρίνειν τὴν δίκην or τοὺς ἀντιδίκους, and the parties ἀνακρίνεσθαι. The process consisted in the production of proofs, of which there were five kinds:—1. The laws; 2. Written documents; 3. Testimonies of witnesses present (μαρτυρίαι), or affidavits of absent witnesses (ἐκμαρτυρίαι); 4. Depositions of slaves extorted by the rack; 5. The oath of the parties. All these proofs were committed to writing, and placed in a box secured by a seal (ἐχῖνος) till they were produced at the trial. If the evidence produced at the anacrisis was so clear and convincing that there could not remain any doubt, the magistrate could decide the question without sending the cause to be tried before the dicasts: this was called *diamartyria* (διαμαρτυρία). The archons were the proper officers for holding the anacrisis; they are represented by Athena (Minerva), in the *Eumenides* of Aeschylus, where there is a poetical sketch of the process in the law courts. For an account of the *anacrisis* or examination, which each archon underwent previously to entering on office, see ARCHON.

ANAGLYPHA or ANAGLYPTA (ἀνάγλυφα, ἀνάγλυπτα), chased or embossed vessels made of bronze or of the precious metals, which derived their name from the work on them being in relief, and not engraved.

ANAGNOSTES, a slave, whose duty it was

to read or repeat passages from books during an entertainment, and also at other times.

ANAGOGIA (ἀναγώγια), a festival celebrated at Eryx, in Sicily, in honour of Aphrodite. The inhabitants of the place believed that, during this festival, the goddess went over into Africa.

ANATOCISMUS. [FENUS.]
ANCILE. [SALII.]
ANCORA. [NAVIS.]
ANDABATA. [GLADIATOR.]

ANDROGEONIA (ἀνδρογεώνια), a festival with games, held every year in the Cerameicus at Athens, in honour of the hero Androgeus, son of Minos, who had overcome all his adversaries in the festive games of the Panathenaea, and was afterwards killed by his jealous rivals.

ANDROLEPSIA (ἀνδροληψία or ἀνδρολήψιον), a legal means by which the Athenians were enabled to take vengeance upon a community in which an Athenian citizen had been murdered, by seizing three individuals of that state or city, as hostages, until satisfaction was given.

ANDRONITIS. [DOMUS, GREEK.]

ANGARIA (ἀγγαρεία, Hdt. ἀγγαρήϊον), a word borrowed from the Persians, signifying a system of posting by relays of horses, which was used among that people, and which, according to Xenophon, was established by Cyrus. The term was adopted by the Romans under the empire to signify compulsory service in forwarding the messages of the state. The Roman *angaria*, also called *angariarum exhibitio* or *praestatio*, included the maintenance and supply, not only of horses, but of ships and messengers, in forwarding both letters and burdens; it is defined as a *personale munus*; and there was no ground of exemption from it allowed, except by the favour of the emperor.

ANGIPORTUS, or ANGIPORTUM, a narrow lane between two rows of houses, which might either be what the French call a *cul-de-sac*, or it might terminate at both ends in some public street.

ANGUSTICLAVII. [CLAVUS.]
ANNALES MAXIMI. [PONTIFEX.]

ANNONA (from *annus*, like *pomona* from *pomum*).—(1) The produce of the year in corn, fruit, wine, &c., and hence,—(2) provisions in general, especially the corn, which, in the later years of the republic, was collected in the storehouses of the state, and sold to the poor at a cheap rate in times of scarcity; and which, under the emperors, was distributed to the people gratuitously, or given as pay and rewards;—(3) the price of provisions;—(4) a soldier's allowance of provisions for a certain time. The word is used also in the plural for yearly or monthly distributions of pay in corn, &c.

ANNULUS (δακτύλιος), a ring. It is probable that the custom of wearing rings was very early introduced into Greece from Asia, where it appears to have been almost universal. They were worn not merely as ornaments, but as articles for use, as the ring always served as a seal. A seal was called *sphragis* (σφραγίς), and hence this name was given to the ring itself, and also to the gem or stone for a ring in which figures were engraved. Rings in Greece were mostly worn on the fourth finger (παράμεσος). At Rome, the custom of wearing rings was believed to have been introduced by the Sabines, who were described in the early legends as wearing golden rings with precious stones of great beauty. But, whenever introduced at Rome, it is certain that they were at first always of iron; that they were destined for the same purpose as in Greece, namely, to be used as seals; and that every free Roman had a right to use such a ring. This iron ring was worn down to the last period of the republic by such men as loved the simplicity of the good old times. In the course of time, however, it became customary for all the senators, chief magistrates, and at last for the equites also, to wear a golden seal-ring. The right of wearing a gold ring, which was subsequently called the *jus annuli aurei*, or the *jus annulorum*, remained for several centuries at Rome the exclusive privilege of senators, magistrates, and equites, while all other persons continued to wear iron ones. During the empire the right of granting the annulus aureus belonged to the emperors, and some of them were not very scrupulous in conferring this privilege. Augustus gave it to Mena, a freedman, and to Antonius Musa, a physician. The emperors Severus and Aurelian conferred the right of wearing golden rings upon all Roman soldiers; and Justinian at length allowed all the citizens of the empire, whether ingenui or libertini, to wear such rings. The ring of a Roman emperor was a kind of state seal, and the emperor sometimes allowed the use of it to such persons as he wished to be regarded as his representatives. During the republic and the early times of the empire the jus annuli seems to have made a person ingenuus (if he was a libertus), and to have raised him to the rank of eques, provided he had the requisite equestrian census, and it was probably never granted to any one who did not possess this census. Those who lost their property, or were found guilty of a criminal offence, lost the jus annuli. The principal value of a ring consisted in the gem set in it, or rather in the workmanship of the engraver. The stone most frequently used was the onyx (σαρδῶνος, σαρδόνυξ), on account of its various colours, of which the artist made the most skilful use. In the art of engraving upon gems the ancients far surpassed anything that modern times can boast of. The devices engraved upon rings were very various: they were portraits of ancestors or of friends, subjects connected with mythology; and in many cases a person had engraved upon his seal some symbolical allusion to the real or mythical history of his family. The bezel or part of the ring which contained the gem was called *pala*. With the increasing love of luxury and show, the Romans, as well as the Greeks, covered their fingers with rings. Some persons also wore rings of immoderate size, and others used different rings for summer and winter. Much superstition appears to have been connected with rings, especially in the East and in Greece. Some persons made it a lucrative trade to sell rings which were believed to possess magic powers, and to preserve the wearers from external danger.

ANNUS. [CALENDARIUM.]

ANQUISĪTĬO, signified, in criminal trials at Rome, the investigation of the facts of the case with reference to the penalty that was to be imposed: accordingly the phrases *pecunia capitis* or *capitis anquirere* are used. Under the emperors the term *anquisitio* lost its original meaning, and was employed to indicate an accusation in general; in which sense it also occurs even in the times of the republic.

ANTAE (παραστάδες), square pillars, which were commonly joined to the side-walls of a building, being placed on each side of the door, so as to assist in forming the portico.

Temple in Antis. (Temple of Artemis at Eleusis.)

These terms are seldom found except in the plural; because the purpose served by antae required that they should be erected corresponding to each other and supporting the extremities of the same roof. The temple *in antis* was one of the simplest kind. It had in front antae attached to the walls which inclosed the cella; and in the middle, between the antae, two columns supporting the architrave.

ANTĔAMBŬLŌNES, slaves who were accustomed to go before their masters, in order to make way for them through the crowd. The term *anteambulones* was also given to the clients, who were accustomed to walk before their patroni, when the latter appeared in public.

ANTĔCESSŌRES, called also ANTĔCURSŌRES, horse-soldiers, who were accustomed to precede an army on march, in order to choose a suitable place for the camp, and to make the necessary provisions for the army. They do not appear to have been merely scouts, like the *speculatores*.

ANTĔCOENA. [COENA.]

ANTĔFIXA, terra-cottas, which exhibited various ornamental designs, and were used in architecture to cover the frieze (*zophorus*) of the entablature. These terra-cottas do not appear to have been used among the Greeks, but were probably Etruscan in their origin, and were thence taken for the decoration of Roman buildings. The name *antefixa* is evidently derived from the circumstance that they were *fixed before* the buildings which they adorned. Cato, the censor, complained that the Romans of his time began to despise ornaments of this description, and to prefer the marble friezes of Athens and Corinth. The rising taste which Cato deplored may account for the superior beauty of the antefixa preserved in the British Museum, which were discovered at Rome.

ANTENNA. [NAVIS.]
ANTĔPĪLĀNI. [EXERCITUS.]
ANTĔSIGNĀNI. [EXERCITUS.]

ANTHESPHŎRIA (ἀνθεσφόρια), a flower-festival, principally celebrated in Sicily, in honour of Demeter and Persephone, in commemoration of the return of Persephone to her mother in the beginning of spring.

ANTHESTĔRĬA. [DIONYSIA.]

ANTĬDŌSIS (ἀντίδοσις), in its literal and general meaning, "an exchange," was, in the language of the Attic courts, peculiarly applied to proceedings under a law which is said to have originated with Solon. By this a citizen nominated to perform a leiturgia such as a trierarchy or choregia, or to rank among the property-tax payers, in a class disproportioned to his means, was empowered to call upon any qualified person not so charged to take the office in his stead, or submit to a complete exchange of property, the charge in question of course attaching to the first party, if the exchange were finally effected. For the proceedings the courts were opened at a stated time every year by the magistrates that had official cognisance of the particular subject; such as the strategi in cases of trierarchy and rating to the property-taxes, and the archon in those of choregia.

ANTIGRAPHE (ἀντιγραφή) originally signified the writing put in by the defendant, his "plea" in all causes whether public or private, in answer to the indictment or bill of the prosecutor. It is, however, also applied to the bill or indictment of the plaintiff or accuser.

ANTLIA (ἀντλία), any machine for raising water, a pump. The most important of these machines were:—(1) The tympanum; a tread-wheel, worked by men treading on it.—(2) A wheel having wooden boxes or buckets, so arranged as to form steps for those who trod the wheel.—(3) The chain pump.—(4) The *cochlea*, or Archimedes's screw.—(5) The *ctesibica machina*, or forcing-pump.—Criminals were condemned to the *antlia* or tread-mill. The antlia with which Martial (ix. 19) watered his garden, was probably the pole and bucket universally employed in Italy, Greece, and Egypt. The pole is curved, as shown in the annexed figure; because it is the stem of a fir or some other tapering tree.

Antlia.

ANTYX (ἄντυξ), the rim or border of anything, especially of a shield or chariot. The rim of the large round shield of the ancient Greeks was thinner than the part which it enclosed; but on the other hand, the antyx of a chariot must have been thicker than the body to which it gave both form and strength. In front of the chariot the antyx was often raised above the body, into the form of a curvature, which served the purpose of a hook to hang the reins upon.

Antyx. (From an Etruscan tomb.)

APAGOGE (ἀπαγωγή), a summary process, allowed in certain cases by the Athenian law. The term denotes not merely the act of apprehending a culprit caught *in ipso facto*, but also the written information delivered to the magistrate, urging his apprehension. The cases in which the *apagoge* was most generally allowed were those of theft, murder, ill-usage of parents, &c.

APATURIA (ἀπατούρια) was a political festival, which the Athenians had in common with all the Greeks of the Ionian name, with the exception of those of Colophon and Ephesus. It was celebrated in the month of Pyanepsion, and lasted for three days. The name ἀπατούρια is not derived from ἀπατᾶν, to deceive, but is composed of ἅ=ἅμα and πατύρια, which is perfectly consistent with what Xenophon says of the festival, that when it is celebrated the fathers and relations assemble together. According to this derivation, it is the festival at which the phratriae met to discuss and settle their own affairs. But, as every citizen was a member of a phratria, the festival extended over the whole nation, who assembled *according to phratriae*. The festival lasted three days. The third day was the most important; for on that day, children born in that year, in the families of the phratriae, or such as were not yet registered, were taken by their fathers, or in their absence by their representatives (κύριοι), before the assembled members of the phratria. For every child a sheep or a goat was sacrificed. The father, or he who supplied his place, was obliged to establish by oath that the child was the offspring of free-born parents, and citizens of Athens. After the victim was sacrificed, the phratores gave their votes, which they took from the altar of Zeus Phratrius. When the majority voted against the reception, the cause might be tried before one of the courts of Athens; and if the claims of the child were found unobjectionable, its name, as well as that of the father, was entered into the register of the phratria, and those who had wished to effect the exclusion of the child were liable to be punished.

APERTA NAVIS. [NAVIS.]

APEX, a cap worn by the flamines and salii at Rome. The essential part of the apex, to which alone the name properly belonged, was a pointed piece of olive-wood, the base of which was surrounded with a lock of wool. This was worn on the top of the head, and was held there either by fillets only, or, as was more commonly the case, by the aid of a cap which fitted the head, and was also fastened by means of two strings or bands. The albogalerus, a white cap made of the skin of a white victim sacrificed to Jupiter, and worn by the flamen dialis, had the apex fastened to it by means of an olive twig.

Apices, caps worn by the Salii. (From bas-reliefs and coins.)

APHLASTON (ἄφλαστον). [NAVIS.]
APHRACTUS. [NAVIS.]
APHRODISIA (ἀφροδίσια) were festivals celebrated in honour of Aphrodité, in a great number of towns in Greece, but particularly in the island of Cyprus. Her most ancient temple was at Paphos. No bloody sacrifices were allowed to be offered to her, but only pure fire, flowers, and incense.

APLUSTRE. [NAVIS.]
APOCLETI (ἀπόκλητοι). [AETOLICUM FOEDUS.]

APODECTAE (ἀποδέκται), public officers at Athens, who were introduced by Cleisthenes in the place of the ancient colacretae (κωλακρέται). They were ten in number, one for each tribe, and their duty was to collect all the ordinary taxes, and distribute them among the separate branches of the administration which were entitled to them.

APOGRAPHE (ἀπογραφή), literally, "a list, or register;" signified also, (1) An accusation in public matters, more particularly when there were several defendants. It differed but little, if at all, from the ordinary graphe.—(2) A solemn protest or assertion in writing before a magistrate, to the intent that it might be preserved by him till it was required to be given in evidence.—(3) A specification of property, said to belong to the state, but actually in the possession of a private person; which specification was made with a view to the confiscation of such property to the state.

APOLLINARES LUDI. [LUDI APOLLINARES.]

APOLLONIA (ἀπολλώνια), the name of a propitiatory festival solemnized at Sicyon, in honour of Apollo and Artemis.

APOPHORETA (ἀποφόρητα) were presents, which were given to friends at the end of an entertainment to take home with them. These presents appear to have been usually given on festival days, especially during the Saturnalia.

APORRHETA (ἀπόρρητα), literally "things forbidden," has two peculiar, but widely different, acceptations in the Attic dialect. In one of these it implies contraband goods; in the other, it denotes certain contumelious epithets, from the application of which both the living and the dead were protected by special laws.

APOSTOLEUS (ἀποστολεύς), the name of a public officer at Athens. There were ten magistrates of this name, and their duty was to see that the ships were properly equipped and provided by those who were bound to discharge the trierarchy. They had the power, in certain cases, of imprisoning the trierarchs who neglected to furnish the ships properly.

APOTHECA (ἀποθήκη), a place in the upper part of the house, in which the Romans frequently placed the earthen amphorae in which their wines were deposited. This place, which was quite different from the cella vinaria, was above the fumarium; since it was thought that the passage of the smoke through the room tended greatly to increase the flavour of the wine. The position of the apotheca explains the expression in Horace (Carm. ii. 21, 7), Descende, testa.

APOTHEOSIS (ἀποθέωσις), the enrolment of a mortal among the gods. The mythology of Greece contains numerous instances of the deification of mortals; but in the republican times of Greece we find few examples of such deification. The inhabitants of Amphipolis however, offered sacrifices to Brasidas after his death. In the Greek kingdoms, which arose in the East on the dismemberment of the empire of Alexander, it appears to have been no uncommon for the successor to the throne to offer divine honours to the former sovereign. Such an apotheosis of Ptolemy, king of Egypt, is described by Theocritus in his 17th Idyl. The term apotheosis, among the Romans, properly signified the elevation of a deceased emperor to divine honours. This practice, which was common upon the death of almost all the emperors, appears to have arisen from the opinion which was generally entertained among the Romans, that the souls or manes of their ancestors became deities; and as it was common for children to worship the manes of their fathers, so it was natural for divine honours to be publicly paid to a deceased emperor, who was regarded as the parent of his country. This apotheosis of an emperor was usually called *consecratio;* and the emperor who received the honour of an apotheosis was usually said *in deorum numerum referri,* or *consecrari,* and whenever he is spoken of after his death, the title of *divus* is prefixed to his name. The funeral pile on which the body of the deceased emperor was burnt, was constructed of several stories in the form of chambers rising one above another, and in the highest an eagle was placed, which was let loose as the fire began to burn, and which was supposed to carry the soul of the emperor from earth to heaven.

APPĂRĬTOR, the general name for a public servant of the magistrates at Rome, namely, the ACCENSUS, CARNIFEX, COACTOR, INTERPRES, LICTOR, PRAECO, SCRIBA, STATOR, VIATOR, of whom an account is given in separate articles. They were called apparitores because they were at hand to execute the commands of the magistrates (*quod iis apparebant*). Their service or attendance was called *apparitio.*

APPELLĀTĬO, appeal.—(1) GREEK (ἔφεσις or ἀναδικία.) Owing to the constitution of the Athenian tribunals, each of which was generally appropriated to its peculiar subjects of cognisance, and therefore could not be considered as homogeneous with or subordinate to any other, there was little opportunity for bringing appeals properly so called. It is to be observed also, that in general a cause was finally and irrevocably decided by the verdict of the dicasts (δίκη αὐτοτελής). There were only a few exceptions in which appeals and new trials might be resorted to. —(2) ROMAN. The word *appellatio,* and the corresponding verb *appellare,* are used in the early Roman writers to express the application of an individual to a magistrate, and particularly to a tribune, in order to protect himself from some wrong inflicted, or threatened to be inflicted. It is distinguished from *provocatio,* which in the early writers is used to signify an appeal to the populus in a matter affecting life. It would seem that the provocatio was an ancient right of the Roman citizens. The surviving Horatius, who murdered his sister, appealed from the duumviri to the populus. The decemviri took away the provocatio; but it was restored by the *Lex Valeria et Horatia,* B.C. 449, in the year after the decemvirate, and it was at the same time enacted, that in future no magistrate should be made from whom there should be no appeal. On this Livy remarks, that the plebs were now protected by the *provocatio* and the *tribunicium auxilium;* this latter term has reference to the appellatio properly so called. The complete phrase to express the provocatio is *provocare ad populum;* and the phrase which expresses the appellatio is *appellare ad,* &c.

APSIS or ABSIS (ἀψίς), in architecture, signified first, any building or portion of a building of a circular form or vaulted, and more especially the circular and vaulted end of a Basilica.

AQUAE DUCTUS (ὑδραγωγία), literally, a water-conduit, but the word is used especially for the magnificent structures by means of which Rome and other cities of the Roman empire were supplied with water. A Roman aqueduct, often called simply *aqua,* may be described in general terms as a channel, constructed as nearly as possible with a regular declivity from the source whence the water was derived to the place where it was delivered, carried through hills by means of tunnels, and over valleys upon a substruction of solid masonry or arches. The aqueduct is mentioned by Strabo as among the structures which were neglected by the Greeks, and first brought into use by the Romans. Springs (κρῆναι, κρουνοί) were sufficiently abundant in Greece to supply the great cities with water; and they were frequently converted into public fountains by the formation of a head for their waters, and the erection of an ornamental superstructure. Of this we have an example in the *Enneacrunos* at Athens, which was constructed by Peisistratus and his sons. The Romans were in a very different position, with respect to the supply of water, from most of the Greek cities. They, at first, had recourse to the Tiber, and to wells sunk in the city; but the water obtained from those sources was very unwholesome, and must soon have proved insufficient, from the growth of the population. It was this necessity that led to the invention of aqueducts, in order to bring pure water from the hills which surround the Campagna. The number of aqueducts was gradually increased, partly at the public expense, and partly by the munificence of individuals, till, in the fourth century of the Christian era, they amounted to fourteen. Of these only four belong to the time of the republic, while five were built in the reigns of Augustus and Claudius.—1. The *Aqua Appia*, begun by the censor Appius Claudius Caecus in B.C. 313. Its sources were near the *Via Praenestina*, between the seventh and eighth milestones.—2. The *Anio Vetus* was commenced forty years later, B.C. 273, by the censor M. Curius Dentatus, and was finished by M. Fulvius Flaccus. The water was derived from the river Anio, above Tibur, at a distance of 20 Roman miles from the city; but, on account of its windings, its actual length was 43 miles.—3. The *Aqua Marcia*, one of the most important of the whole, was built by the praetor Q. Marcius Rex, by command of the senate, in B.C. 144. It commenced at the side of the *Via Valeria*, 36 miles from Rome.—4. The *Aqua Tepula*, built by the censors Cn. Servilius Caepio and L. Cassius Longinus in B.C. 127, began at a spot in the Lucullan or Tusculan land, two miles to the right of the tenth milestone on the *Via Latina*. It was afterwards connected with—5. The *Aqua Julia*, built by Agrippa in his aedileship, B.C. 33. It was conducted from a source two miles to the right of the twelfth milestone on the *Via Latina*, first to the *Aqua Tepula*, in which it was merged as far as the reservoir (*piscina*) on the *Via Latina*, seven miles from Rome. From this reservoir the water was carried along two distinct channels, on the same substructions; the lower channel being called the *Aqua Tepula*, and the upper the *Aqua Julia*; and this double aqueduct again was united with the *Aqua Marcia*, over the watercourse of which the other two were carried.—6. The *Aqua Virgo*, built by Agrippa, to supply his baths. From a source in a marshy spot by the 8th milestone on the *Via Collatina*, it was conducted by a very circuitous route.—7. The *Aqua Alsietina* (sometimes called also *Aqua Augusta*), on the other side of the Tiber, was constructed by Augustus from the *Lacus Alsietinus* (*Lago di Martignano*), which lay 6500 *passus* to the right of the 14th milestone on the *Via Claudia*.—8, 9. The two most magnificent aqueducts were the *Aqua Claudia* and the *Anio Novus* (or *Aqua Aniena Nova*), both commenced by Caligula in A.D. 36, and finished by Claudius in A.D. 50. The water of the *Aqua Claudia* was derived from two copious and excellent springs, near the 38th milestone on the *Via Sublacensis*. Its length was nearly 46½ miles. The *Anio Novus* began at the 42nd milestone. It was the longest and the highest of all the aqueducts, its length being nearly 59 miles, and some of its arches 109 feet high. In the neighbourhood of the city these two aqueducts were united, forming two channels on the same arches, the *Claudia* below and the *Anio Novus* above. These nine aqueducts were all that existed in the time of Frontinus, who was the *curator* of the aqueducts in the reigns of Nerva and Trajan. There was also another aqueduct, not reckoned with the nine, because its waters were no longer brought all the way to Rome, viz.: 10. The *Aqua Crabra*.—The following were of later construction. 11. The *Aqua Trajana*, brought by Trajan from the *Lacus Sabatinus* (now *Bracciano*).—12. The *Aqua Alexandrina*, constructed by Alexander Severus; its source was in the lands of Tusculum, about 14 miles from Rome.—13. The *Aqua Septimiana*, built by Septimius Severus, was perhaps only a branch of the *Aqua Julia*.—14. The *Aqua Algentia* had its source at M. *Algidus* by the *Via Tusculana*. Its builder is unknown.—Great pains were taken by successive emperors to preserve and repair the aqueducts. From the Gothic wars downwards, they have for the most part shared the fate of the other great Roman works of architecture; their situation and purpose rendering them peculiarly exposed to injury in war; but still their remains form the most striking features of the Campagna, over which their lines of ruined arches, clothed with ivy and the wild fig-tree, radiate in various directions. Three of them still serve for their ancient use. They are—(1.) The *Acqua Vergine*, the ancient *Aqua Virgo*. (2.) The *Acqua Felice*, named after the conventual name of its restorer Sixtus V. (Fra Felice), is, probably, a part of the ancient *Aqua Claudia*, though some take it for the *Alexandrina*. (3.) The *Acqua Paola*, the ancient *Alsietina*. — The following woodcut represents a restored section of the triple aqueduct of Agrippa:—*a.* the *Aqua Marcia*; *b.* the *Aqua Tepula*; *c.* the *Aqua Julia*. The two latter are of brick and vaulted over. The air-vents are also shown.—The channel of an aqueduct (*specus*, *canalis*) was a trough of brick or stone, lined with cement, and covered with a coping, which was almost always arched;

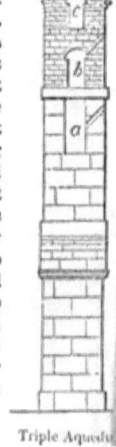

Triple Aqueduct

and the water either ran directly through this trough, or it was carried through pipes laid along the trough. These pipes were of lead, or terra-cotta (*fictiles*), and sometimes, for the sake of economy, of leather. At convenient points on the course of the aqueduct, and especially near the middle and end, there was generally a reservoir (*piscina, piscina limosa*) in which the water might deposit any sediment that it contained. The water was received, when it reached the walls of the city, in a vast reservoir called *castellum*, which formed the *head of water* and also served the purpose of a *meter*. From this principal *castellum* the water flowed into other *castella*, whence it was distributed for public and private use. The term *castellum* is sometimes also applied to the intermediate reservoirs already mentioned. During the republic, the censors and aediles had the superintendence of the aqueducts. Augustus first established *curatores* (or *praefecti*) *aquarum*, who were invested with considerable authority. They were attended outside the city by two lictors, three public slaves, a secretary, and other attendants. In the time of Nerva and Trajan, 460 slaves were constantly employed under the orders of the *curatores aquarum* in attending to the aqueducts. They consisted of:—1. The *villici*, whose duty it was to attend to the pipes and *calices*. 2. The *castellarii*, who had the superintendence of all the *castella*, both within and without the city. 3. The *circuitores*, so called because they had to go from post to post, to examine into the state of the works, and also to keep watch over the labourers employed upon them. 4. The *silicarii*, or paviours. 5. The *tectores*, or masons. These and other workmen appear to have been included under the general term of AQUARII.

AQUAE ET IGNIS INTERDICTIO. [EXSILIUM.]

AQUARII, slaves who carried water for bathing, &c., into the female apartments. The aquarii were also public officers who attended to the aqueducts. [AQUAE DUCTUS.]

AQUILA. [SIGNA MILITARIA.]

ARA (βωμός, θυτήριον), an altar. *Ara* was a general term denoting any structure elevated above the ground, and used to receive upon it offerings made to the gods. *Altare*, probably contracted from *alta ara*, was properly restricted to the larger, higher, and more expensive structures. Four specimens of ancient altars are given below; the two in the former woodcut are square, and those in the latter round, which is the less common form. At the top of three of the above altars we see the hole intended to receive the fire (ἐσχαρίς, ἐσχάρα): the fourth was probably intended for the offering of fruits or other gifts, which were presented to the gods without fire. When the altars were prepared for

Arae, Altars.

sacrifice, they were commonly decorated with garlands or festoons. These were composed of certain kinds of leaves and flowers, which

Arae, Altars.

were considered consecrated to such uses, and were called *verbenae*. The altars constructed with most labour and skill belonged to temples; and they were erected either before the temple or within the cella of the temple, and principally before the statue of the divinity to whom it was dedicated. The altars in the area before the temple were altars of burnt-offerings, at which animal sacrifices (*victimae*, σφάγια, ἱερεῖα) were presented: only incense was burnt, or cakes and bloodless sacrifices offered on the altars within the building.

ARATRUM (ἄροτρον), a plough. Among the Greeks and Romans the three most essential parts of the plough were,—the ploughtail (γύης, *buris, bura*), the share-beam (ἔλυμα, *dens, dentale*), that is, the piece of wood to which the share is fixed, and the pole (ῥυμός, ἱστοβοεύς, *temo*). In the time and country of Virgil it was the custom to force a tree into the crooked form of the *buris*, on plough-tail. The upper end of the *buris* being held by the ploughman, the lower part, below its junction with the pole, was used to hold the *dentale* or share-beam, which was either sheathed with metal, or driven bare into the ground, according to circumstances. The term *romer* was sometimes applied to the end of the *dentale*. To these three parts, the two following are added in the description of the plough by Virgil:—1. The *earth-boards*, or *mould-boards* (*aures*), rising on each side, bending outwardly in such a manner as to throw on either hand the soil which had been previously loosened and raised by the share, and adjusted to the share-beam (*dentale*), which was made double for the purpose of receiving them. 2. The *handle* (*stiva*). Virgil describes this part as used to turn the plough at the end of the furrow; and it is defined by an ancient commentator on Virgil as the "handle by which the plough is directed." It is probable that as the *dentalia*, the two share-beams, were in the form of the Greek letter Λ, which Virgil describes by *duplici dorso*, the *buris* was fastened to the left share-beam and the *stiva* to the right, so that the plough of Virgil was more like the modern Lancashire plough, which is commonly held behind with both hands. Sometimes, however, the *stiva* was used alone and instead of the *buris* or tail. In place of *stiva* the term *capulus* is sometimes employed. The only other part of the plough requiring notice is the coulter (*culter*), which was used by the Romans as it is with us. It was inserted into the pole so as to depend vertically before the share, cutting through the roots which came in its way, and thus preparing for the more complete overturning of the soil by the share. Two small wheels were also added to some ploughs. The plough, as described by Virgil, corresponds in all essential particulars with the plough now used about Mantua and Venice. The Greeks and Romans usually ploughed their land three times for each crop. The first ploughing was called *proscindere*, or *novare* (νεοῦσθαι, νεάζεσθαι); the second *offringere*, or *iterare*; and the third, *lirare*, or *tertiare*. The field which underwent the "proscissio" was called *vervactum* or *novale* (νεός), and in this process the coulter was employed, because the fresh surface was entangled with numberless roots which required to be divided before the soil could be turned up by the share. The term "*offringere*," from *ob* and *frangere*, was applied to the second ploughing; because the long parallel clods already turned up were broken and cut across, by drawing the plough through them at right angles to its former direction. The field which underwent this process was called *ager iteratus*. After the second ploughing the sower cast his seed. Also the clods were often, though not always, broken still further by a wooden mallet, or by harrowing (*occatio*). The Roman ploughman then, for the first time, attached the earth-boards to his share. The effect of this adjustment was to divide the level surface of the "*ager iteratus*" into ridges. These were called *porcae*, and also *lirae*, whence came the verb *lirare*, to make ridges, and also *delirare*, to decline from the straight line. The earth-boards, by throwing the earth to each side in the manner already explained, both covered the newly-scattered seed, and formed between the ridges furrows (αὔλακες, *sulci*) for carrying off the water. In this state the field was called *seges* and τρίπολος. When the ancients ploughed three times only, it was done in the spring, summer, and autumn of the same year. But in order to obtain a still heavier crop, both the Greeks and the Romans ploughed four times, the proscissio being performed in the latter part of the preceding year, so that between one crop and another two whole years intervened.

ARBĬTER. [JUDEX.]

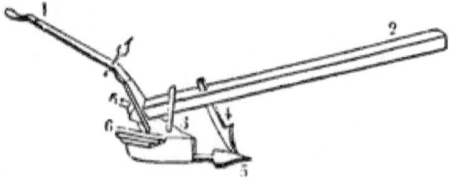

Aratrum, Plough (now used at Mantua).

1. Buris. 2. Temo. 3. Dentale. 4. Culter. 5. Vomer. 6 6. Aures.

ARCA (κιβωτός). (1) A chest, in which the Romans were accustomed to place their money; and the phrase *ex arca solvere* had the meaning of paying in ready money. The term *arcae* was usually applied to the chest in which the rich kept their money, and was opposed to the smaller *loculi*, *sacculus*, and *crumena*.—(2) The coffin in which person were buried, or the bier on which the corpse was placed previously to burial.—(3) A strong cell made of oak, in which criminals and slaves were confined.

ARCĒRA, a covered carriage or litter, spread with cloths, which was used in ancient times in Rome, to carry the aged and infirm. It is said to have obtained the name of arcera on account of its resemblance to an area, or chest.

Arcera. (Ginzrot, Wagen, Tav. 19, fig. 3.)

ARCHEION (ἀρχεῖον) properly means any public place belonging to the magistrates, but is more particularly applied to the archive office, where the decrees of the people and other state documents were preserved. This office is sometimes merely called τὸ δημόσιον. At Athens the archives were kept in the temple of the mother of the gods (μητρῷον), and the charge of it was entrusted to the president (ἐπιστάτης) of the senate of the Five-hundred.

ARCHIĀTER (ἀρχίατρος), a medical title under the Roman emperors, the exact signification of which has been the subject of much discussion, but which most probably means "the chief of the physicians." The first person whom we find bearing this title is Andromachus, physician to Nero. In after times the order appears to have been divided, and we find two distinct classes of archiatri, viz., those of the palace and those of the people.

ARCHIMIMUS. [MIMUS.]

ARCHITECTŪRA (ἀρχιτεκτονία, ἀρχιτεκτονική), architecture. The necessity for a habitation, and the attempt to adorn those habitations which were intended for the gods, are the two causes from which the art derives its existence. In early times little attention was paid to domestic architecture. The resources of the art were lavished upon the temples of the gods; and hence the greater part of the history of Grecian architecture is inseparably connected with that of the temple, and has its proper place under TEMPLUM, and the subordinate headings, such as COLUMNA, &c. But, though the first rise of architecture, as a fine art, is connected with the temple, yet, viewed as the science of construction, it must have been employed,

even earlier, for other purposes, such as the erection of fortifications, palaces, treasuries, and other works of utility. Accordingly, it is the general opinion of antiquaries, that the very earliest edifices, of which we have any remains, are the so-called Cyclopean works, in which we see huge unsquared blocks of stone built together in the best way that their shapes would allow. [MURUS.] In addition to these, however, there are other purposes for which architecture, still using the term in its lower sense, would be required in a very early stage of political society; such as the general arrangement of cities, the provision of a place for the transaction of public business, with the necessary edifices appertaining to it [AGORA, FORUM], and the whole class of works which we embrace under the head of civil engineering, such as those for drainage [CLOACA, EMISSARIUS], for communication [VIA, PONS], and for the supply of water [AQUAE DUCTUS]. Almost equally necessary are places devoted to public exercise, health, and amusement, GYMNASIUM, STADIUM, HIPPODROMUS, CIRCUS, BALNEUM, THEATRUM, AMPHITHEATRUM. Lastly, the skill of the architect has been from the earliest times employed to preserve the memory of departed men and past events; and hence we have the various works of monumental and triumphal architecture, which are described under the heads FUNUS, ARCUS, COLUMNA. The history of architecture may be divided into five periods. The first, which is chiefly mythical, comes down to the time of Cypselus, Ol. 30, B.C. 660: the second period comes down to the termination of the Persian war, Ol. 75. 2, B.C. 478: the third is the brilliant period from the end of the Persian war to the death of Alexander the Great, Ol. 114, B.C. 323: the fourth period extends to the battle of Actium, B.C. 31: the fifth period embraces the architecture of the Roman empire till it became mingled with the Gothic. Strongly fortified cities, palaces, and treasuries are the chief works of the earlier part of the first period; and to it may be referred most of the so-called Cyclopean remains; while the era of the Dorian invasion marks, in all probability, the commencement of the Dorian style of temple architecture. In the second period the art made rapid advances under the powerful patronage of the aristocracies in some cities, as at Sparta, and of the tyrants in others, as Cypselus at Corinth, Theagnes at Megara, Cleisthenes at Sicyon, the Peisistratids at Athens, and Polycrates at Samos. Architecture now assumed decidedly the character of a fine art, and became associated with the sister arts of sculpture and painting, which are essential

D

to its development. Magnificent temples sprung up in all the principal Greek cities; and while the Doric order was brought almost, if not quite, to perfection, in Greece Proper, in the Doric colonies of Asia Minor, and in Central Italy and Sicily, the Ionic order appeared, already perfect at its first invention, in the great temple of Artemis at Ephesus. The ruins still existing at Paestum, Syracuse, Agrigentum, Selinus, Aegina, and other places, are imperishable monuments of this period. To it also belong the great works of the Roman kings. The commencement of the third and most brilliant period of the art was signalized by the rebuilding of Athens, the establishment of regular principles for the laying out of cities by Hippodamus of Miletus, and the great works of the age of Pericles, by the contemporaries of Phidias, at Athens, Eleusis, and Olympia. The first part of the fourth period saw the extension of the Greek architecture over the countries conquered by Alexander, and, in the West, the commencement of the new style, which arose from the imitation, with some alterations, of the Greek forms by Roman architects, to which the conquest of Greece gave, of course, a new impulse. By the time of Augustus, Rome was adorned with every kind of public and private edifice, surrounded by villas, and furnished with roads and aqueducts; and these various erections were adorned by the forms of Grecian art; but already Vitruvius begins to complain that the purity of that art is corrupted by the intermixture of heterogeneous forms. This process of deterioration went on rapidly during the fifth period, though combined at first with increasing magnificence in the scale and number of the buildings erected. The early part of this period is made illustrious by the numerous works of Augustus and his successors, especially the Flavii, Nerva, Trajan, Hadrian, and the Antonines, at Rome and in the provinces; but from the time of the Antonines the decline of the art was rapid and decided. In one department a new impulse was given to architecture by the rise of Christian churches, which were generally built on the model of the Roman Basilica. One of the most splendid specimens of Christian architecture is the church of S. Sophia at Constantinople, built in the reign of Justinian, A.D. 537, and restored, after its partial destruction by an earthquake, in 554. But, long before this time, the Greco-Roman style had become thoroughly corrupted, and that new style, which is called the Byzantine, had arisen out of the mixture of Roman architecture with ideas derived from the Northern nations.

ARCHITHEŌRUS (ἀρχιθέωροσ). [L'ELIA.]

ARCHON (ἄρχων). The government of Athens began with monarchy, and, after passing through a dynasty* and aristocracy, ended in democracy. Of the kings of Athens, considered as the capital of Attica, Theseus may be said to have been the first; for to him, whether as a real individual or a representative of a certain period, is attributed the union of the different and independent states of Attica under one head. The last was Codrus; in acknowledgment of whose patriotism in meeting death for his country, the Athenians are said to have determined that no one should succeed him with the title of king (βασιλεύς). It seems, however, equally probable that it was the nobles who availed themselves of the opportunity to serve their own interests, by abolishing the kingly power for another, the possessors of which they called *Archontes* (ἄρχοντες) or rulers. These for some time continued to be like the kings of the house of Codrus, appointed for life: still an important point was gained by the nobles, the office being made accountable (ὑπεύθυνος), which of course implies that the nobility had some control over it. This state of things lasted for twelve reigns of archons. The next step was to limit the continuance of the office to ten years, still confining it to the Medontidae, or house of Codrus, so as to establish what the Greeks called a dynasty, till the archonship of Eryxias, the last archon of that family elected as such. At the end of his ten years (B.C. 684), a much greater change took place: the archonship was made annual, and its various duties divided among a college of nine, chosen by suffrage (χειροτονία) from the Eupatridae, or Patricians, and no longer elected from the Medontidae exclusively. This arrangement lasted till the time of Solon, who still continued the election by suffrage, but made the qualification for office depend, not on birth, but property. The election by lot is believed to have been introduced by Cleisthenes (B.C. 508). The last change is supposed to have been made by Aristides, who after the battle of Plataeae (B.C. 479) abolished the property qualification, throwing open the archonship and other magistracies to all the citizens; that is, to the Thetes, as well as the other classes, the former of whom were not allowed by Solon's laws to hold any magistracy at all. Still, after the removal of the old restrictions, some security was left to insure respectability; for, previously to an archon entering on office, he underwent an examination, called the *anacrisis* (ἀνάκρισις), as to his being a legitimate and a good citizen,

* By this is meant that the supreme power, though not monarchical, was confined to one family.

a point of property,			certain sacrifices, and therefore it was re-
as either done away			quired that she should be a citizen of pure
n became obsolete.			blood, without stain or blemish. The *Pole-*
a satisfactory ana-			*march* was originally, as his name denotes,
s, in common with			the commander-in-chief, and we find him
le to be deposed on			discharging military duties as late as the
made before the				battle of Marathon, in conjunction with the
r assembly in each			ten *Strategi;* he there took, like the kings of
asion the *epicheiro-*			old, the command of the right wing of the
t was called, took			army. This, however, seems to be the last
one case the whole			occasion on record of this magistrate ap-
deprived of office			pointed by lot being invested with such im-
onsequence of the			portant functions; and in after ages we find
the assembly and			that his duties ceased to be military, having
aed by Solon, the			been, in a great measure, transferred to the
litical power which			protection and superintendence of the resident
. They became, in			aliens, so that he resembled in many respects
of the government,			the praetor peregrinus at Rome. Thus, all
istrates, exercising			actions affecting aliens, the isoteles and
es described below.			proxeni were brought before him previously
that the duties of			to trial. Moreover, it was the polemarch's
ared by a college of			duty to offer the yearly sacrifice to Artemis,
dent of this body,			in commemoration of the vow made by Calli-
y of pre-eminence,			machus, at Marathon, and to arrange the
ων ἐπώνυμος), from			funeral games in honour of those who fell in
hed by and regis-			war. The six *Thesmothetae* were extensively
second was styled			connected with the administration of justice,
βασιλεύς), or the			and appear to have been called legislators,
Polemarchus (πολέ-			because, in the absence of a written code,
chief; the remain-			they might be said to make laws, or *thesmi*
τμοθέται), or legis-			(θεσμοί), in the ancient language of Athens,
ties of the archons,			though in reality they only explained them.
o distinguish what			They were required to review, every year,
ally, and what col-			the whole body of laws, that they might
a considerable por-			detect any inconsistencies or superfluities,
ons of the ancient			and discover whether any laws which were
Archon Eponymus,			abrogated were in the public records amongst
a sort of state pro-			the rest. Their report was submitted to the
: unable to defend			people, who referred the necessary alterations
as to superintend			to a legislative committee chosen for the pur-
losing their repre-			pose, and called *Nomothetae* (νομοθέται). The
egnant, and to see			chief part of the duties of the thesmothetae
nged in any way.			consisted in receiving informations, and bring-
le superintendence			ing cases to trial in the courts of law, of the
and the Thargelia.			days of sitting in which they gave public
Archon were almost			notice. They did not try them themselves,
; his distinguishing			but seem to have constituted a sort of grand
onsidered a repre-			jury, or inquest. The trial itself took place
in their capacity of			before the Dicastae. [DICASTAE.] It is ne-
Sacrificulus was at			cessary to be cautious in our interpretation of
at the Lenaea, or			the words ἀρχή and ἄρχοντες, since they have
nded the mysteries			a double meaning in the Attic orators, some-
mpadephoriae, and			times referring to the archons peculiarly so
and prayers in the			called, and sometimes to any other magistracy.
thens and Eleusis.			The archons had various privileges and ho-
impiety, and con-			nours. The greatest of the former was the
hood, were laid be-			exemption from the trierarchies—a boon not
murder, he brought			allowed even to the successors of Harmodius
the areiopagus, and			and Aristogeiton. As a mark of their office,
His wife, also, who			they wore a chaplet or crown of myrtle; and
λισσα), had to offer			if any one struck or abused one of the archons,

when wearing this badge of office, he became *atimus* (ἄτιμος), or infamous in the fullest extent, thereby losing his civic rights. The archons, at the close of their year of service, were admitted among the members of the areiopagus. [AREIOPAGUS.]

ARCUS (also fornix), an arch. A true arch is formed of a series of wedge-like stones, or of bricks, supporting each other, and all bound firmly together by their mutual pressure. It would seem that the arch, as thus defined, and as used by the Romans, was not known to the Greeks in the early periods of their history. But they made use of a contrivance, even in the heroic age, by which they were enabled to gain all the advantages of our archway in making corridors, or hollow galleries, and which in appearance resembled the pointed arch, such as is now termed Gothic. This was effected by cutting away the superincumbent stones in the manner already described, at an angle of about 45° with the horizon. The mode of construction and appearance of such arches is represented in the annexed drawing of the walls of Tiryns. The gate of Signia (*Segni*) in Latium exhibits a similar example. The principle of the true arch seems to have been known to the Romans from the earliest period; it is used in the *Cloaca Maxima*. It is most probably an Etruscan invention. The use of it constitutes one leading distinction between Greek and Roman architecture, for by its application the Romans were enabled to exe-

Arch of Tiryns. (Gell's Itinerary, pl. 16.)

cute works of far bolder construction than those of the Greeks. The Romans, however, never used any other form of arch than the semicircle. The arcus triumphalis, triumphal arch, was a structure peculiar to the Romans, erected in honour of an individual, or in commemoration of a conquest. Triumphal arches were built across the principal streets of Rome, and, according to the space of their respective localities, consisted of a single archway, or a central one for carriages, and two smaller ones on each side for foot-pas-

Arch of Drusus at Rome.

sengers. Those actually made use of on the occasion of a triumphal entry and procession were merely temporary and hastily erected; and, having served their purpose, were taken down again, and sometimes replaced by others of more durable materials. Stertinius is the first upon record who erected anything of the kind. He built an arch in the Forum Boarium, about B. C. 196, and another in the Circus Maximus, each of which was surmounted by gilt statues. There are twenty-one arches recorded by different writers, as having been erected in the city of Rome, five of which now remain:—1. *Arcus Drusi*, which was erected to the honour of Claudius Drusus on the Appian way. 2. *Arcus Titi*, at the foot of the Palatine, which was erected to the honour of Titus, after his conquest of Judaea; the bas-reliefs of this arch represent the spoils from the temple of Jerusalem carried in triumphal procession. 3. *Arcus Septimii Severi*, which was erected by the senate (A. D. 207) at the end of the Via Sacra, in honour of that emperor and his two sons, Caracalla and Geta, on account of his conquest of the Parthians and Arabians. 4. *Arcus Gallieni*, erected to the honour of Gallienus by a private individual, M. Aurelius Victor. 5. *Arcus Constantini*, which was larger than the arch of Titus. As a specimen of the triumphal arches, a drawing of the arch of Drusus is given in the preceding page.

ARCUS (βιός, τόξον), the bow used for shooting arrows, is one of the most ancient of all weapons, but is characteristic of Asia rather than of Europe. In the Roman armies it was scarcely ever employed except by auxiliaries; and these auxiliaries, called *sagittarii*, were chiefly Cretes and Arabians. The upper of the two figures below shows the Scythian or Parthian bow unstrung; the lower one represents the usual form of the Grecian bow, which had a double curvature, consisting of two circular portions united by the handle. When not used, the bow was put into a case (τοξοθήκη, γωρυτός, corytus), which was made of leather, and sometimes ornamented. It frequently held the arrows as well as the bow, and on this account is often confounded with the *pharetra* or quiver.

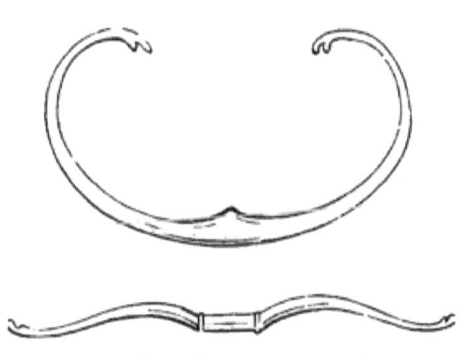

Arcus, Bow. (From paintings on vases.)

Corytus, Bow-case. (From a Relief in the Vatican, Visconti, iv. tav. 43.)

ĀRĔA (ἅλως, or ἀλωά), the threshing-floor, was a raised place in the field, open on all sides to the wind. Great pains were taken to make this floor hard; it was sometimes paved with flint stones, but more usually covered with clay and smoothed with a roller.

ĀREIOPĂGUS (ὁ Ἄρειος πάγος, or hill of Ares) was a rocky eminence, lying to the west of, and not far from the Acropolis at Athens. It was the place of meeting of the council (Ἡ ἐν Ἀρείῳ πάγῳ βουλή), which was sometimes called *The Upper Council* (Ἡ ἄνω βουλή), to distinguish it from the senate of Five-hundred, which sat in the Cerameicus within the city. It was a body of very remote antiquity, acting as a criminal tribunal, and existed long before the time of Solon, but he so far modified its constitution and sphere of duty, that he may almost be called its founder. What that original constitution was, must in some degree be left to conjecture, though there is every reason to suppose that it was aristocratical, the members being taken, like the ephetae, from the noble patrician families. [EPHETAE.] By the legislation of Solon the Areiopagus was composed of the ex-archons, who, after an unexceptionable discharge of their duties, "went up" to the Areiopagus, and became members of it for life, unless expelled for misconduct. As Solon made the qualification for the office of archon to depend not on birth but on property, the council after his time ceased to be aristocratic in constitution; but, as we learn from Attic writers, continued so in spirit. In fact, Solon is said to have formed the two councils, the senate and the Areiopagus, to be a check upon the democracy; that, as he himself expressed it, "the state riding upon them as anchors might be less tossed by storms." Nay, even after the archons were no longer elected by suffrage, but by lot, and the office was thrown open by Aristides to all the Athenian citizens, the "upper council" still retained its former tone of feeling. Moreover, besides these changes in its constitution, Solon altered and extended its functions. Before his time it was only a criminal court, trying cases of "wilful murder and wounding, of arson and poisoning," whereas he gave it extensive powers of a censorial and political nature. Thus we learn that he made the council an "overseer of everything, and the guardian of the laws," empowering it to inquire how any one got his living and to punish the idle; and we are also told that the Areiopagites were "superintendents of good order and decency," terms as unlimited and undefined as Solon not improbably wished to leave their authority. When heinous crimes had notoriously been committed, but the guilty parties were not known, or no accuser appeared, the Areiopagus inquired into the subject, and reported to the demus. The report or information was called *apophasis*. This was a duty which they sometimes undertook on their own responsibility, and in the exercise of an old established right, and sometimes on the order of the demus. Nay, to such an extent did they carry their power, that on one occasion they apprehended an individual (Antiphon), who had been acquitted by the general assembly, and again brought him to a trial, which ended in his condemnation and death. Again, we find them revoking an appointment whereby Aeschines was made the advocate of Athens before the Amphictyonic council, and substituting Hyperides in his room. They also had duties connected with religion, one of which was to superintend the sacred olives growing about Athens, and try those who were charged with destroying them; and in general it was their office to punish the impious and irreligious. Independent, then, of its jurisdiction as a criminal court in cases of wilful murder, which Solon continued to the Areiopagus, its influence must have been sufficiently great to have been a considerable obstacle to the aggrandisement of the democracy at the expense of the other parties in the state. Accordingly, we find that Pericles, who was opposed to the aristocracy, resolved to diminish its power and circumscribe its sphere of action. His coadjutor in this work was Ephialtes, a statesman of inflexible integrity, and also a military commander. They experienced much opposition in their attempts, not only in the assembly, but also on the stage, where Aeschylus produced his tragedy of the Eumenides, the object of which was to impress upon the Athenians the dignity, sacredness, and constitutional worth of the institution which Pericles and Ephialtes wished to reform. Still the opposition failed: a decree was carried by which, as Aristotle says, the Areiopagus was "mutilated," and many of its hereditary rights abolished, though it is difficult to ascertain the precise nature of the alterations which Pericles effected. The jurisdiction of the Areiopagus in cases of murder was still left to them. In such cases the process was as follows:—The king archon brought the case into court, and sat as one of the judges, who were assembled in the open air, probably to guard against any contamination from the criminal. The accuser first came forwards to make a solemn oath that his accusation was true, standing over the slaughtered victims, and imprecating extirpation upon himself and his whole family were it not so. The accused then denied the charge with the same solemnity and form of oath. Each party then stated his case with all possible plainness, keeping strictly to the subject, and not being allowed to appeal in any way to the feelings or passions of the judges. After the first speech, a criminal accused of murder might remove from Athens, and thus avoid the capital punishment fixed by Draco's *Thesmi*, which on this point were still in force. Except in cases of parricide, neither the accuser nor the court had power to prevent this; but the party who thus evaded the extreme punishment was not allowed to return home, and when any decree was passed at Athens to legalize the return of exiles, an exception was always made against those who had thus left their country. The Areiopagus continued to exist, in name at least, till a very late period. Thus we find Cicero mentioning the council in his letters; and an individual is spoken of as an Areiopagite under the emperors Gratian and Theodosius (A. D. 380). The case of St. Paul is generally quoted as an instance of the authority of the Areiopagus in religious matters; but the words of the sacred historian do not necessarily imply that he was brought before the council. It may, however, be remarked, that the Areiopagites certainly took cognizance of the introduction of new and unauthorized forms of religious worship, called ἐπίθετα ἱερά, in contradistinction to the πάτρια or older rites of the state.

ĀRĒNA. [AMPHITHEATRUM.]

ĀRĒTĀLOGI, persons who amused the company at the Roman dinner tables.

ARGEI, the name given by the pontifices to the places consecrated by Numa for the celebration of religious services. Varro calls them the chapels of the argei, and says they were twenty-seven in number, distributed in the different districts of the city. There was a tradition that these argei were named from the chieftains who came with Hercules, the Argive, to Rome, and occupied the Capitoline, or, as it was anciently called, Saturnian hill. It is impossible to say what is the historical value or meaning of this legend; we may, however, notice its conformity with the statement that Rome was founded by the Pelasgians, with whom the name of Argos was connected. The name argei was also given to certain figures thrown into the Tiber from the Sublician bridge, on the Ides of May in every year. This was done by the pontifices, the vestals, the praetors, and other citizens, after the performance of the customary sacrifices. The images were thirty in number, made of bulrushes, and in the form of men. Ovid makes various suppositions to account for the origin of this rite; we can only conjecture that it was a symbolical offering, to propitiate the gods, and that the number was a representative either of the thirty patrician curiae at Rome, or perhaps of the thirty Latin townships.

ARGENTĀRII, bankers or money changers.
(1) GREEK. The bankers at Athens were called *Trapezitae* (τραπεζίται), from their tables (τραπεζαι) at which they sat, while carrying on their business, and which were in the market place. Their principal occupation was that of changing money; but they frequently took money, at a moderate premium, from persons who did not like to occupy themselves with the management of their own affairs, and placed it out at interest. Their usual interest was 36 per cent.; a rate that at present scarcely occurs except in cases of money lent on bottomry. The only instance of a bank recognized and conducted on behalf of the state occurs at Byzantium, where at one time it was let by the republic to capitalists to farm. Yet the state probably exercised some kind of superintendence over the private bankers, since it is hardly possible otherwise to account for the unlimited confidence which they enjoyed.
—(2) ROMAN. The *Argentarii* at Rome must be distinguished from the *mensarii* and *nummularii*, or public bankers. [MENSARII.] The argentarii were private persons, who carried on business on their own responsibility, and were not in the service of the republic; but the shops or *tabernae* about the forum, which they occupied, and in which they transacted their business, were state property. The business of the argentarii may be divided into the following branches. 1. *Permutatio*, or the exchange of foreign coin for Roman, and in later times the giving of bills of exchange payable in foreign towns. 2. The keeping of sums of money for other persons. Such money might be deposited by the owner merely to save himself the trouble of keeping it and making payments, and in this case it was called *depositum*; the argentarius then paid no interest, and the money was called *vacua pecunia*. Or the money was deposited on condition of the argentarius paying interest; in this case the money was called *creditum*. A payment made through a banker was called *per mensam*, *de mensa*, or *per mensae scripturam*, while a payment made by the debtor in person was a payment *ex arca* or *de domo*. An argentarius never paid away any person's money without being either authorised by him in person or receiving a cheque which was called *perscriptio*. The argentarii kept accurate accounts in books called *codices*, *tabulae*, or *rationes*, and there is every reason for believing that they were acquainted with what is called in book-keeping double entry. When a party found to be in debt paid what he owed, he had his name effaced (*nomen expedire* or *expungere*) from the banker's books. 3. Their connection with commerce and public auctions. In private sales and purchases, they sometimes acted as agents for either party (*interpretes*), and sometimes they undertook to sell the whole estate of a person, as an inheritance. At public auctions they were almost invariably present, registering the articles sold, their prices, and purchasers, and receiving the payment from the purchasers. 4. The testing of the genuineness of coins (*probatio nummorum*). This, however, seems originally to have been a part of the duty of public officers, the mensarii or nummularii, until in the course of time the opinion of an argentarius also came to be looked upon as decisive. 5. The *solidorum venditio*, that is, the obligation of purchasing from the mint the newly coined money, and circulating it among the people. This branch of their functions occurs only under the empire. The argentarii formed a collegium, divided into *societates* or corporations, which alone had the right to admit new members of their guild. None but free men could become members of such a corporation. It has already been observed that the argentarii had their shops round the forum: hence to become bankrupt was expressed by *foro cedere*, or *abire*, or *foro mergi*,

ARGENTUM (ἄργυρος), silver. The relative value of gold and silver differed considerably at different periods in Greek and Roman history. Herodotus mentions it as 13 to 1; Plato, as 12 to 1; Menander, as 10 to 1; and Livy as 10 to 1, about B. C. 189. According to Suetonius, Julius Caesar, on one occasion, exchanged silver for gold in the proportion of 9 to 1; but the most usual proportion under the early Roman emperors was about 12 to 1. The proportion in modern times, since the discovery of the American mines, has varied between 17 to 1 and 14 to 1. In the earliest times the Greeks obtained their silver chiefly as an article of commerce from the Phocaeans and the Samians; but they soon began to work the rich mines of their own country and its islands. The chief mines were in Siphnos, Thessaly, and Attica. In the last-named country, the silver mines of Laurion furnished a most abundant supply, and were generally regarded as the chief source of the wealth of Athens. The Romans obtained most of their silver from the very rich mines of Spain, which had been previously worked by the Phoenicians and Carthaginians, and which, though abandoned for those of Mexico, are still not exhausted. By far the most important use of silver among the Greeks was for money. There are sufficient reasons for believing that, until some time after the end of the Peloponnesian war, the Athenians had no gold currency. [AURUM.] It may be remarked that all the words connected with money are derived from ἄργυρος, and not from χρυσός, as καταργυρόω, "to bribe with money;" ἀργυραμοιβός, "a money changer," &c.; and ἄργυρος is itself not unfrequently used to signify money in general, as aes is in Latin. At Rome, on the contrary, silver was not coined till B. C. 269, before which period Greek silver was in circulation at Rome; and the principal silver coin of the Romans, the *denarius*, was borrowed from the Greek *drachma*. For further details respecting silver money, see DENARIUS, DRACHMA. From a very early period, silver was used also in works of art; and the use of it for mere purposes of luxury and ostentation, as in plate, was very general both in Greece and Rome.

ARGYRASPIDES (ἀργυράσπιδες), a division of the Macedonian army, who were so called because they carried shields covered with silver plates.

ARGYROCOPEION (ἀργυροκοπεῖον), the place where money was coined, the mint, at Athens.

ARIES (κριός), the battering-ram, was used to batter down the walls of besieged cities. It consisted of a large beam, made of the trunk of a tree, especially of a fir or an ash. To one end was fastened a mass of bronze or iron (κεφαλή, ἐμβολή, προτομή), which resembled in its form the head of a ram. The aries in its simplest state was borne and impelled by human hands, without other assistance. In an improved form, the ram

Aries, Battering Ram. (From Column of Trajan.)

was surrounded with iron bands, to which rings were attached for the purpose of suspending it by ropes or chains from a beam fixed transversely over it. By this contrivance the soldiers were relieved from the necessity of supporting the weight of the ram, and could with ease give it a rapid and forcible motion backwards and forwards. The use of this machine was further aided by placing the frame in which it was suspended upon wheels, and also by constructing over it a wooden roof, so as to form a "testudo," which protected the besieging party from the defensive assaults of the besieged.

ARISTOCRATIA (ἀριστοκρατία), signifies literally "the government of the best men," and as used by Plato, Aristotle, Polybius, &c., it meant the government of a class whose supremacy was founded not on wealth merely, but on personal distinction. That there should be an aristocracy, moreover, it was essential that the administration of affairs should be conducted with a view to the promotion of the general interests, not for the exclusive or predominant advantage of the privileged class.

As soon as the government ceased to be thus conducted, or whenever the only title to political power in the dominant class was the possession of superior wealth, the constitution was termed an oligarchy (ὀλιγαρχία), which, in the technical use of the term, was always looked upon as a corruption (παρέκβασις) of an aristocracy. In the practical application of the term aristocracy, however, the personal excellence which was held to be a necessary element was not of a higher kind than what, according to the deeply-seated ideas of the Greeks, was commonly hereditary in families of noble birth, and in early times would be the ordinary accompaniments of noble rank, namely, wealth, military skill, and superior education and intelligence. It is to be noted that the word ἀριστοκρατία is never, like the English term *aristocracy*, the name of a class, but only of a particular political constitution.

ARMA, ARMATŪRA (ἔντεα, τεύχεα, Hom.; ὅπλα), arms, armour. Homer describes in various passages an entire suit of armour, and we observe that it consisted of the same portions which were used by the Greek soldiers ever after. Moreover, the order of putting them on is always the same. The heavy-armed warrior, having already a tunic around his body, and preparing for combat, puts on— 1. his greaves (κνημῖδες, *ocreae*); 2. his cuirass (θώραξ, *lorica*), to which belonged the μίτρη underneath, and the zone (ζώνη, ζωστήρ, *cingulum*), above; 3. his sword, (ξίφος, *ensis, gladius*), hung on the left side of his body by means of a belt which passed over the right shoulder; 4. the large round shield (σάκος, ἀσπίς, *clipeus, scutum*), supported in the same manner; 5. his helmet (κόρυς, κυνέη, *cassis, galea*); 6. he took his spear (ἔγχος, δόρυ, *hasta*), or in many cases, two spears. The form and use of these portions are described in separate articles, under their Latin names. The annexed cut exhibits them all. Those who were defended in the manner which has now been represented are called by Homer *aspistae* (ἀσπισταί), from their great shield (ἀσπίς); also *anchemachi* (ἀγχεμάχοι), because they fought hand to hand with their adversaries; but much more commonly *promachi* (πρόμαχοι), because they occupied the front of the army. In later times, the heavy-armed soldiers were called *hoplitae* (ὁπλῖται), because the term *hopla* (ὅπλα) more especially denoted the defensive armour, the shield and thorax. By wearing these they were distinguished from the light-armed (ψιλοί, ἄνοπλοι, γυμνοί, γυμνῆται, γυμνῆτες), who, instead of being defended by the shield and thorax, had a much slighter covering, sometimes consisting of skins, and sometimes of leather or cloth; and instead of the sword or lance, they commonly fought with darts, stones, bows and arrows, or slings. Besides the heavy and light-armed soldiers, another description of men, the *peltastae*

Greek Soldier. (From an ancient vase.)

Roman Soldiers. (From Column of Trajan.)

(πελτασταί), also formed a part of the Greek army, though we do not hear of them in early times. Instead of the large round shield, they carried a smaller one called the *peltè* (πέλτη), and in other respects their armour, though heavier and more effective than that of the psili, was much lighter than that of the hoplites. The weapon on which they principally depended was the spear. The Roman legions consisted, as the Greek infantry for the most part did, of heavy and light-armed troops (*gravis et levis armatura*). The preceding figure represents two heavy-armed Roman soldiers. All the essential parts of the Roman heavy armour (*lorica, ensis, clipeus, galea, hasta*) are mentioned together, except the spear, in a well-known passage of St. Paul (*Eph.* vi. 17).

ARMĀRIUM, originally a place for keeping arms, afterwards a cupboard, in which were kept not only arms, but also clothes, books, money, and other articles of value. The armarium was generally placed in the atrium of the house.

ARMILLA (ψάλιον, ψέλιον, or ψέλλιον, χλιδών, ἀμφιδεᾶ), a bracelet or armlet, worn both by men and women. It was a favourite ornament of the Medes and Persians. Bracelets do not appear to have been worn among the Greeks by the male sex, but Greek ladies had bracelets of various materials, shapes, and styles of ornament. They frequently exhibited the form of snakes, and were in such cases called snakes (ὄφεις) by the Athenians. According to their length, they went once, twice, or thrice round the arm, or even a greater number of times. The Roman generals frequently bestowed armillae upon soldiers for deeds of extraordinary merit.

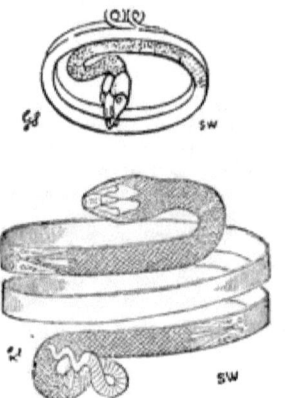

Armillae, Bracelets. (Museo Borbonico, vo. ii. tav. 14 vol. vii. tav. 46.)

Armilla, Bracelet. (On Statue of Sleeping Ariadne in Vatican.)

ARMILUSTRIUM, a Roman festival for the purification of arms. It was celebrated every year on the 19th of October, when the citizens assembled in arms, and offered sacrifices in the place called Armilustrum, or Vicus Armilustri.

ARRA, ARRĀBO, or ARRHA, ARRHABO, was the thing which purchasers and vendors gave to one another, whether it was a sum of money or anything else, as an evidence of the contract being made: it was no essential part of the contract of buying and selling, but only evidence of agreement as to price. The term arrha, in its general sense of an evidence of agreement, was also used on other occasions, as in the case of betrothment (*sponsalia*). Sometimes the word arrha is used as synonymous with *pignus*, but this is not the legal meaning of the term.

ARRHĒPHŎRĬA (ἀῤῥηφόρια), a festival celebrated at Athens in honour of Athena (Minerva). Four girls, of between seven and eleven years (ἀῤῥηφόροι, ἐρσηφόροι, ἐῤῥηφόροι), were selected every year by the king archon from the most distinguished families, two of whom superintended the weaving of the sacred peplus of Athena; the two others had to carry the mysterious and sacred vessels of the goddess. These latter remained a whole year on the Acropolis; and when the festival commenced, the priestess of the goddess placed vessels upon their heads, the contents of which were neither known to them nor to the priestess. With these they descended to a natural grotto within the district of Aphrodite in the gardens. Here they deposited the sacred vessels, and carried back something else, which was covered and like

a duty of the priesthood to invoke a blessing on the whole territory of Rome. There were also the private *ambarvalia*, which were so called from the victim (*hostia ambarvalis*) that was slain on the occasion being led three times round the corn-fields, before the sickle was put to the corn. This victim was accompanied by a crowd of merry-makers, the reapers and farm-servants dancing and singing, as they marched, the praises of Ceres, and praying for her favour and presence, while they offered her the libations of milk, honey, and wine. This ceremony was also called a *lustratio*, or purification.

ARX signifies a height within the walls of a city, upon which a citadel was built, and thus came to be applied to the citadel itself. Thus one of the summits of the Capitoline hill at Rome is called *Arx*. The *Arx* was the regular place at Rome for taking the auspices, and was hence likewise called *auguraculum*: or, more probably, the auguraculum was a place in the Arx.

AS, or *Libra*, a pound, the unit of weight among the Romans. [LIBRA.]

AS, the unit of value in the Roman and old Italian coinages, was made of copper, or of the mixed metal called AES. It was originally of the weight of a pound of twelve ounces, whence it was called *as libralis* and *aes grave*. The oldest form of the *as* is that which bears the figure of an animal (a bull, ram, boar, or sow). The next and most common form is that which has the two-faced head of Janus on one side, and the prow of a ship on the other (whence the expression used by Roman boys in tossing up, *Capita aut navim*.) Pliny informs us, that in the time of the first Punic war (B.C. 264-241), in order to meet the expenses of the state, this weight of a pound was diminished, and asses were struck of the same weight as the sextans (that is, two ounces, or one sixth of the ancient weight); and that thus the republic paid off its debts, gaining five parts in six; that afterwards, in the second Punic war, in the dictatorship of Q. Fabius Maximus (B.C. 217), asses of one ounce were made, and the denarius was decreed to be equal to sixteen asses, the republic thus gaining one half; but that in military pay the denarius was always given for ten asses; and that soon after, by the Papirian law (about B.C. 191), asses of half an ounce were made. The value of the as, of course, varied with its weight. Before the reduction to two ounces, ten asses were equal to the denarius = about $8\frac{1}{2}$ pence English [DENARIUS]. Therefore the as = $3 \cdot 4$ farthings. By the reduction the denarius was made equal to sixteen asses; therefore the as = $2\frac{1}{8}$ farthings. The as was divided into parts, which were named according to the number of ounces they contained. They were the *deunx, dextans, dodrans, bes, septunx, semis, quincunx, triens, quadrans* or *teruncius, sextans, sescunx* or *sesenncia,* and *uncia,* consisting respectively of 11, 10, 9, 8, 7, 6, 5, 4, 3, 2, 1½, and 1 ounces. Of these divisions the following were represented by coins; namely, the *semis, quincunx, triens, quadrans, sextans,* and *uncia.* After the reduction in the weight of the as, coins were struck of the value of 2, 3, 4, and even 10 asses, which were called respectively *dussis* or *dupondius, tressis, quadrussis,* and *decussis.* Other multiples of the *as* were denoted by words of similar formation, up to *centussis,* 100 asses; but most of them do not exist as coins. In certain forms of expression, in which *aes* is used for money without specifying the denomination, we must understand the as. Thus *deni aeris, mille aeris, decies aeris,* mean respectively 10, 1000, 1,000,000 *asses.* The word *as* was used also for any whole which was to be divided into equal parts; and those parts were called *unciae.* Thus these words were applied not only to weight and money, but to measures of length, surface, and capacity, to inheritances, interest, houses, farms, and many other things. Hence the phrases *haeres ex asse,* the heir to a whole estate; *haeres ex dodrante,* the heir to three-fourths. The *as* was also called in ancient times *assarius* (sc. nummus), and in Greek τὸ ἀσσάριον. According to Polybius, the assarius was equal to half the obolus.

ASCIA (σκέπαρνον), an adze. The annexed cut shows two varieties of the adze.

The instrument at the bottom was called *acisculus,* and was chiefly used by masons.

Asciae, adzes. (From ancient monuments and a coin.)

ASCLEPIEIA (ἀσκληπίεια), the name of festivals which were probably celebrated in all places where temples of Asclepius (Aesculapius) existed. The most celebrated, however, was that of Epidaurus, which took place every five years, and was solemnized with contests of rhapsodists and musicians, and with solemn processions and games.

ASCOLIASMUS (ἀσκωλιασμός, the leaping upon the leathern bag, ἀσκός) was one of the many kinds of amusements in which the Athenians indulged during the Anthesteria and other festivals in honour of Dionysus. Having sacrificed a he-goat to the god, they made a bag out of the skin, smeared it with oil, and then tried to dance upon it.

Ascoliasmus. (From an ancient gem.)

ASEBEIAS GRAPHE (ἀσεβείας γραφή), one of the many forms prescribed by the Attic laws for the impeachment of impiety. Any citizen not incapacitated by disfranchisement (ἀτιμία) seems to have been a competent accuser; and citizens, resident aliens, and strangers, were equally liable to the accusation. Whether the causes were brought into the areiopagus, or the common heliastic court, seems to have been determined by the form of action adopted by the prosecutor, or the degree of competency to which the areio-

different periods of larly in the capital, as shown in the following woodcut.

) were, in the Ro-
chief presidents of
office it was to ex-
amusements every
gods and the Roman
pense, like the Ro-
re ten in number,
different towns of
the Roman procon-
e chief asiarch, and
rs, resided at Ephe-

Astragalus. (Capital of an Ionic Column. Dilettanti Society, Ionian Antiquities.)

[As.]
ITOR, contains the
severe, which, when
inu, signifies to lay
:owards one. Hence
ibertatem, or *liberali*
him who lays his
'd to be a slave, and
reedom. The person
freedom of a reputed

The person whose
l was said to be *ad-
liberalis causa*, and
ccur in connection
ill easily be under-
n said. Sometimes
was used as equiva-
atem. The expres-
), to claim a person

SSOR, literally one
another. Since the
nors of provinces,
ften imperfectly ac-
and forms of pro-
y that they should
o had made the law
rs sat on the tribu-
Their advice or aid
ceedings as well as
never pronounced a

rs.]
γαλος), literally, that
kles of certain quad-
s, as well as the Ro-
d other purposes.
it signifies a certain
which seems to have
its resemblance to a
d it is in fact always
t seems intended to
o which it is applied.
the more highly de-
ic order, in which it
to the larger mould-
us (ovolo), particu-

ASTRATEIAS GRAPHE (ἀστρατείας γραφή), the accusation instituted at Athens against persons who failed to appear among the troops after they had been enrolled for a campaign by the generals. The defendant, if convicted, incurred disfranchisement (ἀτιμία) both in his own person and that of his descendants.

ASTROLOGIA, astrology. A belief very early arose, which still prevails unshaken in the East, that a close connection subsisted between the position and movements of the heavenly bodies and the fate of man. Few doubted that the destiny of a child might be predicted with certainty by those who were skilled to interpret the position of the stars at the moment of his birth, and that the result of any undertaking might be foretold from the aspect of the firmament when it was commenced. Hence a numerous and powerful class of men arose who were distinguished by various designations. From the country where their science was first developed, they were called *Chaldaei* or *Babylonii*; from observing the stars, *astronomi, astrologi, planetarii*; from employing diagrams such as were used by geometricians, *mathematici*; from determining the lot of man at his natal hour, *genethliaci*; from prophesying the consummation of his struggles, ἀποτελεσματικοί; while their art was known as ἀστρολογία, μετεωρολογία, γενεθλιαλογία, ἀποτελεσματική, *Ars Chaldaeorum, Mathesis*, or, from the tables they consulted, πινακική. Their calculations were termed *Babylonii numeri*, Χαλδαίων μέθοδοι, Χαλδαίων ψηφίδες, *Rationes Chaldaicae*; their responses when consulted *Chaldaeorum monita, Chaldaeorum natalicia praedicta, Astrologorum praedicta*. The stars and constellations to which attention was chiefly directed were the planets and the signs of the zodiac, some of which were supposed to exert uniformly a benign influence (ἀγαθοποιοὶ ἀστέρες), such as Venus, Jupiter, Luna, Virgo, Libra, Taurus; others to be uniformly malign (κακοποιοὶ ἀστέρες), such as Saturnus, Mars, Scorpio, Capricornus; others to be doubtful (ἐπίκοινοι ἀστέρες), such as Mercurius. The exact period of birth (*hora genitalis*) being the critical moment, the computations founded upon it were styled γένεσις (*genitura*), ὡροσκόπος (*horoscopus*), or simply θέμα, and the star or stars in the ascendant *sidus natalitium*, *sidera natalitia*. Astrologers seem to have found their way very early into Italy. In B.C. 139 an edict was promulgated by C. Cornelius Hispallus, at that time praetor, by which the Chaldaeans were ordered to quit Italy within ten days, and they were again banished from the city in B.C. 33, by M. Agrippa, who was then aedile. Another severe ordinance was levelled by Augustus against this class, but the frequent occurrence of such phrases as "expulit et mathematicos," "pulsis Italia mathematicis," in the historians of the empire prove how firm a hold these pretenders must have obtained over the public mind, and how profitable the occupation must have been which could induce them to brave disgrace, and sometimes a cruel death.

ASTYNOMI (ἀστυνόμοι), or street-police of Athens, were ten in number, five for the city, and as many for the Peiraeeus. The *astynomi* and *agoranomi* divided between them most of the functions of the Roman aediles. [AGORANOMI.]

ASYLUM (ἄσυλον). In the Greek states the temples, altars, sacred groves, and statues of the gods, generally possessed the privilege of protecting slaves, debtors, and criminals, who fled to them for refuge. The laws, however, do not appear to have recognised the right of all such sacred places to afford the protection which was claimed, but to have confined it to a certain number of temples, or altars, which were considered in a more especial manner to have the ἀσυλία, or *jus asyli*. There were several places in Athens which possessed this privilege; of which the best known was the Theseium, or temple of Theseus, in the city, near the gymnasium, which was chiefly intended for the protection of ill-treated slaves, who could take refuge in this place, and compel their masters to sell them to some other person. In the time of Tiberius, the number of places possessing the jus asyli in the Greek cities in Greece and Asia Minor became so numerous, as seriously to impede the administration of justice; and, consequently, the senate, by the command of the emperor, limited the jus asyli to a few cities. The asylum, which Romulus is said to have opened at Rome to increase the population of the city, was a place of refuge for the inhabitants of other states, rather than a sanctuary for those who had violated the laws of the city. In the republican and early imperial times, a right of asylum, such as existed in the Greek states, does not appear to have been recognised by the Roman law; but it existed under the empire, and a slave could fly to the temples of the gods, or the statues of the emperors, to avoid the ill-usage of his master.

ATELEIA (ἀτέλεια), immunity from public burthens, was enjoyed at Athens by the archons for the time being; by the descendants of certain persons, on whom it had been conferred as a reward for great services, as in the case of Harmodius and Aristogeiton; and by the inhabitants of certain foreign states. It was of several kinds : it might be a general immunity (ἀτέλεια ἁπάντων); or a more special exemption, as from custom-duties, from the liturgies, or from providing sacrifices.

ATELLANAE FABULAE were a species of farce or comedy, so called from Atella, a town of the Osci, in Campania. From this circumstance, and from being written in the Oscan dialect, they were also called *Ludi Osci*. These Atellane plays were not *praetextatae*, *i. e.* comedies in which magistrates and persons of rank were introduced, nor *tabernariae*, the characters in which were taken from low life; they rather seem to have been a union of high comedy and its parody. They were also distinguished from the mimes by the absence of low buffoonery and ribaldry, being remarkable for a refined humour, such as could be understood and appreciated by educated people. They were not performed by regular actors (*histriones*), but by Roman citizens of noble birth, who were not on that account subjected to any degradation, but retained their rights as citizens, and might serve in the army. The Oscan or Opican language, in which these plays were written, was spread over the whole of the south of Italy, and from its resemblance to the Latin could easily be understood by the more educated Romans.

ATHENAEUM (ἀθήναιον), a school (*ludus*) founded by the Emperor Hadrian at Rome, for the promotion of literary and scientific studies (*ingenuarum artium*), and called Athenaeum from the town of Athens, which was still regarded as the seat of intellectual refinement. The Athenaeum was situated on the Capitoline hill. It was a kind of university, with a staff of professors, for the various branches of study. Besides the instruction given by these magistri, poets, orators, and critics were accustomed to recite their compositions there, and these prelections were sometimes honoured with the presence of the emperors themselves. The Athenaeum seems to have continued in high repute till the fifth century.

ATHLETAE.

(ἀθληταί, ἀθλητῆρες), persons in the public games of the ...ans for prizes (ἄθλα, whence ...ηταί), which were given to ...uered in contests of agility. The name was in the later ...n history, and among the ...ly confined to those persons ...oted themselves to a course ...h might fit them to excel in ...d who, in fact, made athletic ... profession. The athletae ...re, from the *agonistae* (ἀγω-...ly pursued gymnastic exer-...ke of improving their health ...gth, and who, though they ...nded for the prizes in the ...did not devote their whole ...hletae, to preparing for these ...tae were first introduced at ..., in the games exhibited by ...he conclusion of the Aetolian Paullus, after the conquest of ...7, is said to have exhibited ...polis, in which athletae con-... the Roman emperors, and Nero, who was passionately ...cian games, the number of ...ed greatly in Italy, Greece, ... Those athletae who con-...f the great national festivals were called *Hieronicae* (ἱερο-...ved the greatest honours and a conqueror was considered ...r upon the state to which he ...tered his native city through ...n the walls for his reception, ...wn by four white horses, and principal street of the city to ...e guardian deity of the state. ...hich gave the conquerors the ... entrance into the city, were (from εἰσελαύνειν). This ...lly confined to the four great ...s, the Olympian, Isthmian, ...ythian, but was afterwards public games. In the Greek ...ors in these games not only ...eatest glory and respect, but ... rewards. They were gene-...om the payment of taxes, and ...e first seat (προεδρία) in all ...nd spectacles. Their statues ... erected at the cost of the ...st frequented part of the city, ...place, the gymnasia, and the ...of the temples. At Athens, ...w of Solon, the conquerors in ...mes were rewarded with a ...achmae ; and the conquerors Nemean, and Isthmian, with

ATLANTES.

one of 100 drachmae ; and at Sparta they had the privilege of fighting near the person of the king. The privileges of the athletae were secured, and in some respects increased, by the Roman emperors. The term athletae, though sometimes applied metaphorically to other combatants, was properly limited to those who contended for the prize in the five following contests :— 1. *Running* (δρόμος, *cursus*). [STADIUM.] 2. *Wrestling* (πάλη, *lucta*). 3. *Boxing* (πυγμή, *pugilatus*). 4. The *pentathlum* (πένταθλον), or, as the Romans called it, *quinquertium*. 5. The *pancratium* (παγκράτιον). Of all these an account is given in separate articles. Great attention was paid to the training of the athletae. They were generally trained in the *palaestrae*, which, in the Grecian states, were distinct places from the gymnasia. Their exercises were superintended by the gymnasiarch, and their diet was regulated by the aliptes. [ALIPTAE.]—The athletae were accustomed to contend naked. In the descriptions of the games given in the Iliad, the combatants are represented with a girdle about their loins ; and the same practice, as we learn from Thucydides, anciently prevailed at the Olympic games, but was discontinued afterwards.

ATĪMĬA (ἀτιμία), the forfeiture of a man's civil rights at Athens. It was either total or partial. A man was totally deprived of his rights, both for himself and for his descendants (καθάπαξ ἄτιμος), when he was convicted of murder, theft, false witness, partiality as arbiter, violence offered to a magistrate, and so forth. This highest degree of atimia excluded the person affected by it from the forum, and from all public assemblies ; from the public sacrifices, and from the law courts ; or rendered him liable to immediate imprisonment, if he was found in any of these places. It was either temporary or perpetual, and either accompanied or not with confiscation of property. Partial atimia only involved the forfeiture of some few rights, as, for instance, the right of pleading in court. Public debtors were suspended from their civic functions till they discharged their debt to the state. People who had once become altogether atimi were very seldom restored to their lost privileges. The converse term to atimia was *epitimia* (ἐπιτιμία).

ATLANTES (ἄτλαντες) and TĔLĂMŌNES (τελαμῶνες), terms used in architecture, the former by the Greeks, the latter by the Romans, to designate those male figures which are sometimes fancifully used, like the female *Caryatides*, in place of columns. Both words are derived from τλῆναι, and the former evidently refers to the fable of Atlas, who supported the vault of heaven, the latter *perhaps* to the strength of the Telamonian Ajax.

Atlantes. (From Temple at Agrigentum: Professor Cockerell.)

ĀTRĀMENTUM, a term applicable to any black colouring substance, for whatever purpose it may be used, like the *melan* (μέλαν) of the Greeks. There were, however, three principal kinds of atramentum: one called *librarium*, or *scriptorium* (in Greek, γραφικὸν μέλαν), writing-ink; another called *sutorium*, which was used by the shoemakers for dyeing leather; the third *tectorium*, or *pictorium*, which was used by painters for some purposes, apparently as a sort of varnish. The inks of the ancients seem to have been more durable than our own; they were thicker and more unctuous, in substance and durability more resembling the ink now used by printers. An inkstand was discovered at Herculaneum, containing ink as thick as oil, and still usable for writing. The ancients used inks of various colours. Red ink, made of *minium* or vermilion, was used for writing the titles and beginning of books. So also was ink made of *rubrica*, "red ochre;" and because the headings of *laws* were written with rubrica, the word rubric came to be used for the civil law. So *album*, a white or whited table, on which the praetors' edicts were written, was used in a similar way. A person devoting himself to *album* and *rubrica*, was a person devoting himself to the law. [ALBUM.]

ĀTRIUM (called αὐλή by the Greeks and by Virgil, and also μεσαύλιον, περίστυλον, περίστῳον) is used in a distinctive as well as collective sense, to designate a particular part in the private houses of the Romans [DOMUS], and also a class of public buildings, so called from their general resemblance in construc-

tion to the atrium of a private house. An atrium of the latter description was a building by itself, resembling in some respects the open basilica [BASILICA], but consisting of three sides. Such was the Atrium Publicum in the capitol, which, Livy informs us, was struck with lightning, B.C. 216. It was at other times attached to some temple or other edifice, and in such case consisted of an open area and surrounding portico in front of the structure. Several of these buildings are mentioned by the ancient historians, two of which were dedicated to the same goddess, Libertas. The most celebrated, as well as the most ancient, was situated on the Aventine Mount. In this atrium there was a tabularium, where the legal tablets (*tabulae*) relating to the censors were preserved. The other Atrium Libertatis was in the neighbourhood of the Forum Caesaris, and was immediately behind the Basilica Paulli or Aemilia.

AUCTIO signifies generally "an increasing, an enhancement," and hence the name is applied to a public sale of goods, at which persons bid against one another. The sale was sometimes conducted by an *argentarius*, or by a *magister auctionis*; and the time, place, and conditions of sale, were announced either by a public notice (*tabula, album*, &c.), or by a crier (*praeco*). The usual phrases to express the giving notice of a sale were, *auctionem proscribere, praedicare*; and to determine on a sale, *auctionem constituere*. The purchasers (*emtores*), when assembled, were sometimes said *ad tabulam adesse*. The phrases signifying to bid are, *liceri, licitari*, which was done either by word of mouth, or by such significant hints as are known to all people who have attended an auction. The property was said to be knocked down (*addici*) to the purchaser. The praeco, or crier, seems to have acted the part of the modern auctioneer, so far as calling out the biddings, and amusing the company. Slaves, when sold by auction, were placed on a stone, or other elevated thing, as is the case when slaves are sold in the United States of North America; and hence the phrase *homo de lapide emtus*. It was usual to put up a spear (*hasta*) in auctions; a symbol derived, it is said, from the ancient practice of selling under a spear the booty acquired in war.

AUCTOR, a word which contains the same element as *aug-eo*, and signifies generally one who enlarges, confirms, or gives to a thing its completeness and efficient form. The numerous technical significations of the word are derivable from this general notion. As he who gives to a thing that which is necessary for its completeness may in this sense be viewed as the chief actor or doer, the word auctor is also used in the sense of one who originates or proposes a thing; but this cannot be viewed as its primary meaning. Accordingly, the word auctor, when used in connection with lex or senatus consultum, often means him who originates and proposes.—The expressions *patres auctores fiunt*, *patres auctores facti*, have given rise to much discussion. In the earlier periods of the Roman state, the word *patres* was equivalent to *patricii*; in the later period, when the patricians had lost all importance as a political body, the term *patres* signified the senate. Hence some ambiguity has arisen. The expression *patres auctores fiunt*, when used of the early period of Rome, means that the determinations of the populus in the comitia centuriata were confirmed by the patricians in the comitia curiata. Till the time of Servius Tullius there were only the comitia curiata, and this king first established the comitia centuriata, in which the plebs also voted, and consequently it was not till after this time that the phrase *patres auctores fiunt* could be properly applied. Livy, however, uses it of an earlier period. The comitia curiata first elected the king, and then by another vote conferred upon him the imperium. The latter was called *lex curiata de imperio*, an expression not used by Livy, who employs instead the phrase *patres auctores fiunt* (Liv. i. 17, 22, 32).—After the exile of the last Tarquin, the patres, that is the patricians, had still the privilege of confirming at the comitia curiata the vote of the comitia centuriata, that is, they gave to it the *patrum auctoritas*; or, in other words, the *patres* were *auctores facti*. In the fifth century of the city a change was made. By one of the laws of the plebeian dictator Q. Publilius Philo, it was enacted that in the case of leges to be enacted at the comitia centuriata, the *patres* should be *auctores*, that is, the curiae should give their assent before the vote of the comitia centuriata. By a lex Maenia of uncertain date the same change was made as to elections.—But both during the earlier period and afterwards no business could be brought before the comitia without first receiving the sanction of the senate; and accordingly the phrase *patres auctores fiunt* came now to be applied to the approval of a measure by the senate before it was confirmed by the votes of the people. This preliminary approval was also termed *senatus auctoritas*.—When the word auctor is applied to him who recommends but does not originate a legislative measure, it is equivalent to *suasor*. Sometimes both auctor and suasor are used in the same sentence, and the meaning of each is kept distinct. With reference to dealings between individuals, auctor has the sense of owner. In this sense auctor is the seller (*venditor*), as opposed to the buyer (*emtor*): and hence we have the phrase *a malo auctore emere*. Auctor is also used generally to express any person under whose authority any legal act is done. In this sense, it means a tutor who is appointed to aid or advise a woman on account of the infirmity of her sex.

AUCTŌRĀMENTUM, the pay of gladiators. [GLADIATORES.]

AUCTŌRĬTAS. The technical meanings of this word correlate with those of auctor. The auctoritas senatus was not a senatusconsultum; it was a measure, incomplete in itself, which received its completion by some other authority. Auctoritas, as applied to property, is equivalent to legal ownership, being a correlation of auctor.

AUDĪTŌRĬUM, as the name implies, is any place for hearing. It was the practice among the Romans for poets and others to read their compositions to their friends, who were sometimes called the auditorium; but the word was also used to express any place in which any thing was heard, and under the empire it was applied to a court of justice. Under the republic the place for all judicial proceedings was the comitium and the forum. But for the sake of shelter and convenience it became the practice to hold courts in the Basilicae, which contained halls, which were also called auditoria. It is first under M. Aurelius that the auditorium principis is mentioned, by which we must understand a hall or room in the imperial residence; and in such a hall Septimius Severus and the later emperors held their regular sittings when they presided as judges. The latest jurists use the word generally for any place in which justice was administered.

AUGUR, AUGŬRĬUM; AUSPEX, AUSPĬCĬUM. *Augur* or *auspex* meant a diviner by birds, but came in course of time, like the Greek οἰωνός, to be applied in a more extended sense: his art was called *augurium* or *auspicium*. Plutarch relates that the *augures* were originally termed *auspices*. The word *auspex* was supplanted by *augur*, but the scientific term for the observation continued on the contrary to be *auspicium* and not *augurium*. By Greek writers on Roman affairs, the augurs are called οἰωνοπόλοι, οἰωνοσκόποι, οἰωνισταί, οἱ ἐπ' οἰωνοῖς ἱερεῖς. The belief that the flight of birds gave some intimation of the will of the gods seems to have been prevalent among many nations of antiquity, and was common to the Greeks, as well as the Romans; but it was only among the latter people that it was reduced to a complete system, governed by fixed rules, and handed down from generation to generation. In Greece, the oracles supplanted the birds, and the future was learnt from Apollo and other gods, rarely from Zeus, who possessed very few oracles in Greece. The contrary was the case at Rome: it was from Jupiter that the future was learnt, and the birds were regarded as his messengers. It must be remarked in general, that the Roman auspices were essentially of a practical nature; they gave no information respecting the course of future events, they did not inform men *what was to happen*, but simply taught them *what they were to do, or not to do;* they assigned no reason for the decision of Jupiter—they simply announced, yes or no. The words *augurium* and *auspicium* came to be used in course of time to signify the observation of various kinds of signs. They were divided into five sorts: *ex caelo, ex avibus, ex tripudiis, ex quadrupedibus, ex diris.* Of these, the last three formed no part of the ancient auspices.—1. *Ex caelo.* This included the observation of the various kinds of thunder and lightning, and was regarded as the most important, *maximum auspicium.* Whenever it was reported by a person authorised to take the auspices, that Jupiter thundered or lightened, the comitia could not be held.—2. *Ex avibus.* It was only a few birds which could give auguries among the Romans. They were divided into two classes: *Oscines,* those which gave auguries by singing, or their voice, and *Alites,* those which gave auguries by their flight. To the former class belonged the raven (*corvus*) and the crow (*cornix*), the first of these giving a favourable omen (*auspicium ratum*) when it appeared on the right, the latter, on the contrary, when it was seen on the left: likewise the owl (*noctua*) and the hen (*gallina*). To the *aves alites* belonged first of all the eagle (*aquila*), which is called pre-eminently the bird of Jupiter (*Jovis ales*), and next the vulture (*vultur*). Some birds were included both among the *oscines* and the *alites:* such were the *Picus Martius,* and *Feronius,* and the *Parra.* These were the principal birds consulted in the auspices. When the birds favoured an undertaking, they were said *addicere, admittere* or *secundare,* and were then called *addictivae, admissivae, secundae,* or *praepetes:* when unfavourable they were said *abdicere, arcere, refragari,* &c., and were then called *adversae* or *alterae.* The birds which gave unfavourable omens were termed *funebres, inhibitae, lugubres, malae,* &c., and such auspices were called *elivia* and *clamatoria.*—3. *Ex tripudiis.* These auspices were taken from the feeding of chickens, and were especially employed on military expeditions. The chickens were kept in a cage, under care of a person called *pullarius;* and when the auspices were to be taken, the pullarius opened the cage and threw to the chickens pulse or a kind of soft cake. If they refused to come out or to eat, or uttered a cry (*occinerent*), or beat their wings, or flew away, the signs were considered unfavourable. On the contrary, if they ate greedily, so that something fell from their mouth and struck the earth, it was called *tripudium solistimum* (*tripudium* quasi *terripavium, solistimum,* from *solum,* according to the ancient writers), and was held a favourable sign.—4. *Ex quadrupedibus.* Auguries could also be taken from four-footed animals; but these formed no part of the original science of the augurs, and were never employed by them in taking auspices on behalf of the state, or in the exercise of their art properly so called. They must be looked upon simply as a mode of private divination. When a fox, a wolf, a horse, a dog, or any other kind of quadruped ran across a person's path or appeared in an unusual place, it formed an augury.—5. *Ex diris,* sc. *signis.* Under this head was included every kind of augury which does not fall under any of the four classes mentioned above, such as sneezing, stumbling, and other accidental things. There was an important augury of this kind connected with the army, which was called *ex acuminibus,* that is, the flames appearing at the points of spears or other weapons. The ordinary manner of taking the auspices, properly so called (i. e. *ex caelo* and *ex avibus*), was as follows: The person who was to take them first marked out with a wand (*lituus*) a division in the heavens called *templum* or *tescum,* within which he intended to make his observations. The station where he was to take the auspices was also separated by a solemn formula from the rest of the land, and was likewise called *templum* or *tescum.* He then proceeded to pitch a tent in it (*tabernaculum capere*), and this tent again was also called *templum,* or, more accurately, *templum minus.* [TEMPLUM.] Within the walls of Rome, or, more properly speaking, within the pomoerium, there was no occasion to select a spot and pitch a tent on it, as there was a place on the Arx on the summit of the Capitoline hill, called *Auguraculum,* which had been consecrated once for all for this purpose. In like manner there was in every Roman camp a place called *augurale,* which answered the same purpose; but on all other occasions a place had to be consecrated, and a tent to be pitched, as, for instance, in the

Campus Martius, when the comitia centuriata were to be held. The person who was then taking the auspices waited for the favourable signs to appear; but it was necessary during this time that there should be no interruption of any kind whatsoever (*silentium*), and hence the word *silentium* was used in a more extended sense to signify the absence of every thing that was faulty. Every thing, on the contrary, that rendered the auspices invalid was called *vitium*; and hence we constantly read in Livy and other writers of *vitio magistratus creati, vitio lex lata*, &c. The watching for the auspices was called *spectio* or *servare de coelo*, the declaration of what was observed *nuntiatio*, or, if they were unfavourable, *obnuntiatio*. In the latter case, the person who took the auspices seems usually to have said *alio die*, by which the business in hand, whether the holding of the *comitia* or any thing else, was entirely stopped.—In ancient times no one but a patrician could take the auspices. Hence the possession of the auspices (*habere auspicia*) is one of the most distinguished prerogatives of the patricians; they are said to be *penes patrum*, and are called *auspicia patrum*. It would further appear that every patrician might take the auspices; but here a distinction is to be observed between the *auspicia privata* and *auspicia publica*. One of the most frequent occasions on which the *auspicia privata* were taken, was in case of a marriage: and this was one great argument used by the patricians against *connubium* between themselves and the plebeians, as it would occasion, they urged, *perturbationem auspiciorum publicorum privatorumque*. In taking these private auspices, it would appear that any patrician was employed who knew how to form *templa* and was acquainted with the art of augury. The case, however, was very different with respect to the *auspicia publica*, generally called *auspicia* simply, or those which concerned the state. The latter could only be taken by the persons who represented the state, and who acted as mediators between the gods and the state; for though all the patricians were eligible for taking the auspices, yet it was only the magistrates who were in actual possession of them. In case, however, there was no patrician magistrate, the auspices became vested in the whole body of the patricians (*auspicia ad patres redeunt*), who had recourse to an *interregnum* for the renewal of them, and for handing them over in a perfect state to the new magistrates: hence we find the expressions *repetere de integro auspicia*, and *renovare per interregnum auspicia*.—The distinction between the duties of the magistrates and the augurs in taking the auspices is one of the most difficult points connected with this subject, but perhaps a satisfactory solution of these difficulties may be found by taking an historical view of the question. We are told not only that the kings were in possession of the auspices, but that they themselves were acquainted with the art and practised it. Romulus is stated to have appointed three augurs, but only as his assistants in taking the auspices, a fact which it is important to bear in mind. Their dignity gradually increased in consequence of their being employed at the inauguration of the kings, and also in consequence of their becoming the preservers and depositaries of the science of augury. Formed into a collegium, they handed down to their successors the various rules of the science, while the kings, and subsequently the magistrates of the republic, were liable to change. Their duties thus became twofold, to assist the magistrates in taking the auspices, and to preserve a scientific knowledge of the art. As the augurs were therefore merely the assistants of the magistrates, they could not take the auspices without the latter, though the magistrates on the contrary could dispense with their assistance. At the same time it must be borne in mind, that as the augurs were the interpreters of the science, they possessed the right of declaring whether the auspices were valid or invalid. They thus possessed in reality a veto upon every important public transaction; and they frequently exercised this power as a political engine to vitiate the election of such parties as were unfavourable to the exclusive privileges of the patricians. But although the augurs could declare that there was some fault in the auspices, yet, on the other hand, they could not, by virtue of their office, declare that any unfavourable sign had appeared to them, since it was not to them that the auspices were sent. Thus we are told that the augurs did not possess the *spectio*. This *spectio* was of two kinds, one more extensive and the other more limited. In the one case the person who exercised it could put a stop to the proceedings of any other magistrate by his obnuntiatio: this was called *spectio et nuntiatio* (perhaps also *spectio cum nuntiatione*), and belonged only to the highest magistrates, the consuls, dictators, interreges, and, with some modifications, to the praetors. In the other case, the person who took the auspices only exercised the *spectio* in reference to the duties of his own office, and could not interfere with any other magistrate: this was called *spectio sine nuntiatione*, and belonged to the other magistrates, the censors, aediles, and quaestors. Now as the augurs did not possess the auspices, they consequently could not possess the spectio (*habere spectionem*); but as the augurs were constantly employed by the magistrates to take the auspices, they *exercised* the spectio, though they did not *possess* it in virtue of their office. When they were employed by the magistrates in taking the auspices, they possessed the right of the *nuntiatio*, and thus had the power, by the declaration of unfavourable signs (*obnuntiatio*), to put a stop to all important public transactions.—The auspices were not conferred upon the magistrates in any special manner. It was the act of their election which made them the recipients of the auspices, since the comitia, in which they were appointed to their office, were held *auspicato*, and consequently their appointment was regarded as ratified by the gods. The auspices, therefore, passed immediately into their hands upon the abdication of their predecessors in office.—The auspices belonging to the different magistrates were divided into two classes, called *auspicia maxima* or *majora* and *minora*. The former, which belonged originally to the kings, passed over to the consuls, censors, and praetors, and likewise to the extraordinary magistrates, the dictators, interreges, and consular tribunes. The quaestors and the curule aediles, on the contrary, had only the *auspicia minora*.—It was a common opinion in antiquity that a college of three augurs was appointed by Romulus, answering to the number of the early tribes, the Ramnes, Tities, and Lucerenses, but the accounts vary respecting their origin and number. At the passing of the Ogulnian law (B.C. 300) the augurs were four in number. This law increased the number of pontiffs to eight, by the addition of four plebeians, and that of the augurs to nine by the addition of five plebeians. The number of nine augurs lasted down to the dictatorship of Sulla, who increased them to fifteen, a multiple of the original three, probably with a reference to the early tribes. A sixteenth was added by Julius Caesar after his return from Egypt. The members of the college of augurs possessed the right of self-election (*cooptatio*) until B.C. 103, the year of the Domitian law. By this law it was enacted that vacancies in the priestly colleges should be filled up by the votes of a minority of the tribes, *i.e.* seventeen out of thirty-five chosen by lot. The Domitian law was repealed by Sulla B.C. 81, but again restored B.C. 63, during the consulship of Cicero, by the tribune T. Annius Labienus, with the support of Caesar. It was a second time abrogated by Antony B.C. 44; whether again restored by Hirtius and Pansa in their general annulment of the acts of Antony, seems uncertain. The emperors possessed the right of electing augurs at pleasure. The augurs were elected for life, and even if capitally convicted, never lost their sacred character. When a vacancy occurred, the candidate was nominated by two of the elder members of the college, the electors were sworn, and the new member was then solemnly inaugurated. On such occasion there was always a splendid banquet given, at which all the augurs were expected to be present. The only distinction in the college was one of age; an elder augur always voted before a younger, even if the latter filled one of the higher offices in the state. The head of the college was called *magister collegii*. As insignia of their office the augurs wore the *trabea*, or public dress, and carried in their hand the *lituus* or curved wand. [LITUUS.] On the coins of the Romans, who filled the office of augur, we constantly find the *lituus*, and along with it, not unfrequently, the *capis*, an earthen vessel which was used by them in sacrifices. The

Coin representing the lituus and capis on the reverse.

science of the augurs was called *jus augurum* and *jus augurium*, and was preserved in books (*libri augurales*), which are frequently mentioned in the ancient writers. The expression for consulting the augurs was *referre ad augures*, and their answers were called *decreta* or *responsa augurum*. The science of augury had greatly declined in the time of Cicero; and although he frequently deplores its neglect in his *De Divinatione*, yet neither he nor any of the educated classes appears to have had any faith in it.

AUGURĀCŬLUM. [ARX; AUGUR, p. 50, b.]
AUGURĀLE. [AUGUR, p. 50, b.]
AUGURIUM. [AUGUR.]

AUGUSTĀLES—(1) (sc. *ludi*, also called *Augustalia*, sc. *certamina*, *ludicra*), games celebrated in honour of Augustus, at Rome and in other parts of the Roman empire. After the battle of Actium, a quinquennial festival was instituted; and the birthday of Augustus, as well as that on which the victory was announced at Rome, were regarded as festival days. It was not, however, till B.C. 11 that the festival on the birthday of Augustus was formally established by a decree of the senate, and it is this festival which is usually meant when the Augustales or Augustalia are mentioned. It was celebrated iv. Id. Octobr. At the death of Augustus, this festival assumed a more solemn character, was added to the Fasti, and celebrated by his honour as a god. It was henceforth exhibited annually in the circus, at first by the tribunes of the plebs, at the commencement of the reign of Tiberius, but afterwards by the praetor peregrinus.—(2) The name of two classes of priests, one at Rome and the other in the municipia. The *Augustales* at Rome, properly called *sodales Augustales*, were an order of priests instituted by Tiberius to attend to the worship of Augustus and the Julia gens. They were chosen by lot from among the principal persons of Rome, and were twenty-one in number, to which were added Tiberius, Drusus, Claudius, and Germanicus, as members of the imperial family. They were also called *sacerdotes Augustales*, and sometimes simply *Augustales*. The *Augustales* in the municipia are supposed by most modern writers to have been a class of priests selected by Augustus from the libertini to attend to the religious rites connected with the worship of the Lares, which that emperor was said to have put up in places where two or more ways met; but there are good reasons for thinking that they were instituted in imitation of the Augustales at Rome, and for the same object, namely, to attend to the worship of Augustus. They formed a collegium and were appointed by the *decuriones*, or senate of the municipia. The six principal members of the college were called *Seviri*, a title which seems to have been imitated from the *Seviri* in the equestrian order at Rome.

AUGUSTUS, a name bestowed upon Octavianus in B.C. 27, by the senate and the Roman people. It was a word used in connection with religion, and designated a person as sacred and worthy of worship; hence the Greek writers translate it by Σεβαστός. It was adopted by all succeeding emperors, as if descended, either by birth or adoption, from the first emperor of the Roman world. The name of *Augusta* was frequently bestowed upon females of the imperial family, but *Augustus* belonged exclusively to the reigning emperor till towards the end of the second century of the Christian aera, when M. Aurelius and L. Verus both received this surname. From this time we frequently find two or even a greater number of *Augusti*. From the time of Probus the title became *perpetuus Augustus*, and from Philippus or Claudius Gothicus *semper Augustus*, the latter of which titles was borne by the so-called Roman emperors in Germany. [CAESAR.]

AULAEUM. [SIPARIUM.]
AUREUS. [AURUM.]
AURIGA. [CIRCUS.]
AURUM (χρυσός), gold. Gold was scarce in Greece. The chief places from which the Greeks procured their gold were India, Arabia, Armenia, Colchis, and Troas. It was found mixed with the sands of the Pactolus and other rivers. Almost the only method of purifying gold, known to the ancients, seems to have been that of grinding and then roasting it, and by this process they succeeded in getting it very pure. This is what we are to understand by the phrase χρυσίον ἄπεφθον in Thucydides, and by the word *obrussa* in Pliny. The art of gilding was known to the Greeks from the earliest times of which we have any information. The time when gold was first coined at Athens is very uncertain, but on the whole it appears most probable that gold money was not coined there, or in Greece Proper generally, till the time of Alexander the Great, if we except a solitary issue of debased gold at Athens in B.C. 407. But from a very early period the Asiatic nations, and the Greek cities of Asia Minor and the adjacent islands, as well as Sicily and Cyrene, possessed a gold coinage, which was more or less current in Greece. Herodotus says that the Lydians were the first who coined gold, and the stater of Croesus appears to have been the earliest gold coin known to the Greeks. The Daric was a Persian coin. Staters of Cyzicus and Phocaea had a considerable currency in Greece. There was a gold coinage in Samos as early as the time of Polycrates. The islands of Siphnos and Thasos, which possessed gold mines, appear to have had a gold coinage at an early period. The Macedonian gold coinage came into circulation in Greece in the time of Philip, and continued in use till the subjection of Greece to the Romans. [DARICUS; STATER.] The standard gold coin of Rome was the *aureus nummus*, or *denarius aureus*, which, according to Pliny, was first coined 62 years after the first silver coinage [ARGENTUM], that is, in the year 207 B.C. The lowest denomination was the *scrupulum*, which was made equal to 20 sestertii. The weight of the scrupulum was 18·06 grains. The annexed cut represents a gold coin of 60 sestertii. Pliny adds that afterwards aurei were coined

Aureus Nummus   (British Museum.)

of 40 to the pound, which weight was diminished, till under Nero they were 45 to the pound. The average weight of the aurei of Augustus, in the British Museum, is 121·26 grains: and as the weight was afterwards diminished, we may take the average at 120 grains. The value of the aureus in terms of

Aureus of Augustus. (British Museum.)

the sovereign = 1*l*. 1*s*. 1*d*. and a little more than a halfpenny. This is its value according to the present worth of gold; but its current value in Rome was different from this, on account of the difference in the worth of the metal. The aureus passed for 25 denarii; therefore, the denarius being 8½*d*., it was worth 17*s*. 8½*d*. The ratio of the value of gold to that of silver is given in the article ARGENTUM. Alexander Severus coined pieces of one-half and one-third of the aureus, called *Semissis* and *tremissis*, after which time the aureus was called *solidus*. Constantine the Great coined aurei of 72 to the pound; at which standard the coin remained to the end of the empire.

AURUM CŎRŌNĀRĬUM. When a general in a Roman province had obtained a victory, it was the custom for the cities in his own provinces, and for those from the neighbouring states, to send golden crowns to him, which were carried before him in his triumph at Rome. In the time of Cicero it appears to have been usual for the cities of the provinces, instead of sending crowns on occasion of a victory, to pay money, which was called *aurum coronarium*. This offering, which was at first voluntary, came to be regarded as a regular tribute, and was sometimes exacted by the governors of the provinces, even when no victory had been gained.

AURUM VĪCĔSĪMĀRĬUM. [AERARIUM.]
AUSPEX. [AUGUR.]
AUSPĬCĬUM. [AUGUR.]
AUTHEPSA (αὐθέψης), which literally means "self-boiling," or "self-cooking," was the name of a vessel which is supposed to have been used for heating water, or for keeping it hot.

AUTŎNŎMI (αὐτονόμοι), the name given by the Greeks to those states which were governed by their own laws, and were not subject to any foreign power. This name was also given to those cities subject to the Romans, which were permitted to enjoy their own laws and elect their own magistrates.

AUXĪLĬA. [SOCII.]
AXĀMENTA. [SALII.]
AXĪNĒ. [SECURIS.]
AXIS. [CURRUS.]
AXŎNES (ἄξονες), also called *kurbeis* (κύρβεις), wooden tablets of a square or pyramidal form, made to turn on an axis, on which were written the laws of Solon. According to some writers the *Axones* contained the civil, and the *Kurbeis* the religious laws; according to others the *Kurbeis* had four sides and the *Axones* three. But at Athens, at all events, they seem to have been identical. They were at first preserved in the Acropolis, but were afterwards placed in the agora, in order that all persons might be able to read them.

BĀLISTA, BALLISTA. [TORMENTUM.]
BALNĔUM or BĂLĬNĔUM (λουτρόν or λουτρόν, βαλανεῖον, also *balneae* or *balineae*), a bath. *Balneum* or *balineum* signifies, in its primary sense, a bath or bathing vessel, such as most Romans possessed in their own houses; and from that it came to mean the chamber which contained the bath. When the baths of private individuals became more sumptuous, and comprised many rooms, the plural *balnea* or *balinea* was adopted, which still, in correct language, had reference only to the baths of private persons. *Balneae* and *balineae*, which have no singular number, were the public baths. But this accuracy of diction is neglected by many of the later writers. *Thermae* (from θέρμη, warmth) means properly warm springs, or baths of warm water, but was afterwards applied to the structures in which the baths were placed, and which were both hot and cold. There was, however, a material distinction between the *balneae* and *thermae*, inasmuch as the former was the term used under the republic, and referred to the public establishments of that age, which contained no appliances for luxury beyond the mere convenience of hot and cold baths, whereas the latter name was given to those magnificent edifices which grew up under the empire, and which comprised within their range of buildings all the appurtenances belonging to the Greek gymnasia, as well as a regular establishment appropriated for bathing.—Bathing was a practice familiar to the Greeks of both sexes from the earliest times. The artificial warm bath was taken in a vessel called *asaminthus* (ἀσάμινθος) by Homer, and *puelus* (πύελος) by the later Greeks. It did not contain water itself, but

was only used for the bather to sit in, while the warm water was poured over him. On Greek vases, however, we never find anything corresponding to a modern bath in which persons can stand or sit; but there is always a round or oval basin (λουτήρ or λουτήριον), resting on a stand, by the side of which those who are bathing are standing undressed and washing themselves. In the Homeric times it was customary to take first a cold and afterwards a warm bath; but in later times it was the usual practice of the Greeks to take first a warm or vapour, and afterwards a cold bath. At Athens the frequent use of the public baths, most of which were warm baths (βαλανεῖα, called by Homer θερμὰ λοετρά), was regarded in the time of Socrates and Demosthenes as a mark of luxury and effeminacy. Accordingly, Phocion was said to have never bathed in a public bath, and Socrates to have used it very seldom. After bathing both sexes anointed themselves, in order that the skin might not be left harsh and rough, especially after warm water. Oil (ἔλαιον) is the only ointment mentioned by Homer, but in later times precious unguents (μύρα) were used for this purpose. The bath was usually taken before the principal meal of the day (δεῖπνον). The Lacedaemonians, who considered warm water as enervating, used two kinds of baths; namely, the cold daily bath in the Eurotas, and a dry sudorific bath in a chamber heated with warm air by means of a stove, and from them the chamber used by the Romans for a similar purpose was termed *Laconicum*. A sudorific or vapour bath (πυρία or πυριατήριον) is mentioned as early as the time of Herodotus. At what period the use of the warm bath was introduced among the Romans is not recorded; but we know that Scipio had a warm bath in his villa at Liternum, and the practice of heating an apartment with warm air by flues placed immediately under it, so as to produce a vapour bath, is stated to have been invented by Sergius Orata, who lived in the age of Crassus, before the Marsic war. By the time of Cicero the use of baths of warm water and hot air had become common, and in his time there were baths at Rome which were open to the public upon payment of a small fee. In the public baths at Rome the men and women used originally to bathe in separate sets of chambers; but under the empire it became the common custom for both sexes to bathe indiscriminately in the same bath. This practice was forbidden by Hadrian and M. Aurelius; and Alexander Severus prohibited any baths, common to both sexes, from being opened in Rome. The price of a bath was a quadrant, the smallest piece of coined money, from the age of Cicero downwards, which was paid to the keeper of the bath (*balneator*). Children below a certain age were admitted free. It was usual with the Romans to take the bath after exercise, and before the principal meal (*coena*) of the day; but the debauchees of the empire bathed also after eating as well as before, in order to promote digestion, and to acquire a new appetite for fresh delicacies. Upon quitting the bath the Romans as well as the Greeks

Roman Bath. (Fresco from the Thermae of Titus.)

were anointed with oil. The Romans did not content themselves with a single bath of hot or cold water; but they went through a course of baths in succession, in which the agency of air as well as water was applied. It is difficult to ascertain the precise order in which the course was usually taken; but it appears to have been a general practice to close the pores, and brace the body after the excessive perspiration of the vapour bath, either by pouring cold water over the head, or by plunging at once into the *piscina*. To render the subjoined remarks more easily intelligible, the preceding woodcut is inserted, which is taken from a fresco painting upon the walls of the thermae of Titus at Rome. The chief parts of a Roman bath were as follow:—1. *Apodyterium*. Here the bathers were expected to take off their garments, which were then delivered to a class of slaves, called *capsarii*, whose duty it was to take charge of them. These men were notorious for dishonesty, and were leagued with all the thieves of the city, so that they connived at the robberies which they were placed to prevent. There was probably an *Elaeothesium* or *Unctorium*, as appears from the preceding cut, in connection with the apodyterium, where the bathers might be anointed with oil.—2. *Frigidarium* or *Cella Frigidaria*, where the cold bath was taken. The cold bath itself was called *Natatio*, *Natatorium*, *Piscina*, *Baptisterium*, or *Puteus*.—3. *Tepidarium* would seem from the preceding cut to have been a bathing room, for a person is there apparently represented pouring water over a bather. But there is good reason for thinking that this was not the case. In most cases the tepidarium contained no water at all, but was a room merely heated with warm air of an agreeable temperature, in order to prepare the body for the great heat of the vapour and warm baths, and upon returning from the latter, to obviate the danger of a too sudden transition to the open air.—4. The *Caldarium* or *Concamerata Sudatio* contained at one extremity the vapour bath (*Laconicum*), and at the other the warm bath (*balneum* or *calda lavatio*), while the centre space between the two ends was termed *sudatio* or *sudatorium*. In larger establishments the vapour bath and warm bath were in two separate cells, as we see in the preceding cut: in such cases the former part *alone* was called *concamerata sudatio*. The whole rested on a suspended pavement (*suspensura*), under which was a fire (*hypocaustum*), so that the flames might heat the whole apartment. (See cut.) The warm water bath (*balneum* or *calda lavatio*), which is also called *piscina* or *calida piscina*, *labrum* and *solium*, appears to have been a capacious marble vase, sometimes standing upon the floor, like that in the preceding cut, and sometimes either partly elevated above the floor, as it was at Pompeii, or entirely sunk into it. After having gone through the regular course of perspiration, the Romans made use of instruments called *strigiles* or *strigles*, to scrape off the perspiration. The strigil was also used by the Greeks,

Strigil. (From a Relief at Athens.)

who called it *stlengis* (στλεγγίς) or *xystra* (ξύστρα). The figure in the cut on p. 24 is represented with a strigil in his hand. As the strigil was not a blunt instrument, its edge was softened by the application of oil, which was dropped upon it from a small vessel called *guttus* or *ampulla*, which had a narrow neck, so as to discharge its contents drop by drop, from whence the name is taken.

Strigil and Guttus. (From a Statue in the Vatican.)

In the *Thermae*, spoken of above, the baths were of secondary importance. They were a Roman adaptation of the Greek gymnasium, contained exedrae for the philosophers and rhetoricians to lecture in, porticoes for the idle, and libraries for the learned, and were adorned with marbles, fountains, and shaded walks and plantations. M. Agrippa, in the reign of Augustus, was the first who afforded these luxuries to his countrymen, by bequeathing to them the thermae and gardens which he had erected in the Campus Martius. The example set by Agrippa was followed by Nero, and afterwards by Titus, the ruins of whose thermae are still visible, covering a vast extent, partly under ground and partly above the Esquiline hill. Thermae were also erected by Trajan, Caracalla, and Diocletian, of the two last of which ample remains still exist. Previously to the erection of these establishments for the use of the population, it was customary for those who sought the favour of the people to give them a day's bathing free of expense. From thence it is fair to infer that the quadrant paid for admission into the *balneae* was not exacted at the *thermae*, which, as being the works of the emperors, would naturally be opened with imperial generosity to all, and without any charge.

BALTĔUS (τελαμών), a belt, a shoulder celt, was used to suspend the sword. See the figs. on p. 41. In the Homeric times the Greeks used a belt to support the shield. The balteus was likewise employed to suspend the quiver, and sometimes together with it the bow. More commonly the belt, whether employed to support the sword, the shield, or the quiver, was made of leather, and was frequently ornamented with gold, silver, and precious stones. In a general sense *balteus* was applied not only to the belt which passed over the shoulder, but also to the girdle (*cingulum*), which encompassed the waist. In architecture, Vitruvius applies the term *Baltei* to the bands surrounding the volute on each side of an Ionic capital. Other writers apply it to the praecinctiones of an amphitheatre. [AMPHITHEATRUM.]

BARATHRON (βάραθρον), also called ORYGMA (ὄρυγμα), a deep cavern or chasm, like the Ceadas at Sparta, behind the Acropolis at Athens, into which criminals were thrown. [CEADAS.]

BARBA (πώγων, γένειον, ὑπήνη), the beard. The Greeks seem generally to have worn the beard till the time of Alexander the Great; and a thick beard was considered as a mark of manliness. The Greek philosophers in particular were distinguished by their long beards as a sort of badge. The Romans in early times wore the beard uncut, and the Roman beards are said not to have been shaved till B.C. 300, when P. Ticinius Maena brought over a barber from Sicily; and Pliny adds, that the first Roman who is said to have been shaved every day was Scipio Africanus. His custom, however, was soon followed, and shaving became a regular thing.

In the later times of the republic there were many who shaved the beard only partially, and trimmed it, so as to give it an ornamental form; to them the terms *bene barbati* and *barbatuli* are applied. In the general way at Rome, a long beard (*barba promissa*) was considered a mark of slovenliness and *squalor*. The first time of shaving was regarded as the beginning of manhood, and the day on which this took place was celebrated as a festival. There was no particular time fixed for this to be done. Usually, however, it was done when the young Roman assumed the toga virilis. The hair cut off on such occasions was consecrated to some god. Thus Nero put his up in a gold box, set with pearls, and dedicated it to Jupiter Capitolinus. Under the emperor Hadrian the beard began to revive. Plutarch says that the emperor wore it to hide some scars on his face. The practice afterwards became common, and till the time of Constantine the Great, the emperors appear in busts and coins with beards. The Romans let their beards grow in time of mourning; the Greeks, on the other hand, on such occasions shaved the beard close.

BARBĬTUS (βάρβιτος), or BARBĬTON (βάρβιτον), a stringed instrument, the original form of which is uncertain. Later writers use it as synonymous with the lyra. [LYRA.]

BASCAUDA, a British basket. This term, which remains with very little variation in the Welsh "basgawd" and the English "basket," was conveyed to Rome together with the articles denoted by it.

BASĬLĬCA (sc. *aedes, aula, porticus —* βασιλική, also *regia*), a building which served as a court of law and an exchange, or place of meeting for merchants and men of business. The word was adopted from the Athenians, whose second archon was styled *archon basileus* (ἄρχων βασιλεύς), and the tribunal where he adjudicated *stoa basileios* (ἡ βασίλειος στοά), the substantive *aula* or *porticus* in Latin being omitted for convenience, and the distinctive epithet converted into a substantive. The first edifice of this description at Rome was not erected until B.C. 182. It was situated in the forum adjoining the curia, and was denominated Basilica Portia, in commemoration of its founder, M. Porcius Cato. Besides this there were twenty others erected at different periods, within the city of Rome. The forum, or, where there was more than one, the one which was in the most frequented and central part of the city, was always selected for the site of a basilica; and hence it is that the classic writers not unfrequently use the terms *forum* and *basilica* synonymously. The ground plan of all these buildings is rectangular, and their width not more than half, nor less than one-third of the length. This area was divided into three naves, consisting of a centre (*media porticus*), and two side aisles, separated from the centre one, each by a single row of columns. At one end of the centre aisle was the tribunal of the judge, in form either rectangular or circular, as is seen in the annexed plan of the basilica at Pompeii. In the centre of the tribunal was

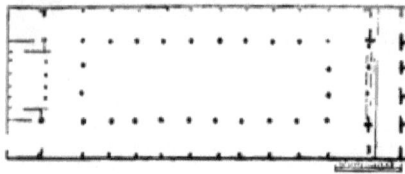

Ground Plan of a Basilica.

placed the curule chair of the praetor, and seats for the judices and the advocates. The two side aisles, as has been said, were separated from the centre one by a row of columns, behind each of which was placed a square pier or pilaster (*parastata*), which supported the flooring of an upper portico, similar to the gallery of a modern church. The upper gallery was in like manner decorated with columns, of lower dimensions than those below; and these served to support the roof, and were connected with one another by a parapet-wall or balustrade (*pluteus*), which served as a defence against the danger of falling over, and screened the crowd of loiterers above (*sub-basilicani*) from the people of business in the area below. Many of these edifices were afterwards used as Christian churches, and many churches were built after the model above described. Such churches were called *basilicae*, which name they retain to the present day, being still called at Rome *basiliche*.

BASTERNA, a kind of litter (*lectica*) in which women were carried in the time of the Roman emperors. It appears to have resembled the Lectica [LECTICA] very closely; and the only difference apparently was, that the lectica was carried by slaves, and the basterna by two mules.

BAXA, or BAXEA, a sandal made of vegetable leaves, twigs, or fibres, worn on the stage by comic actors.

BĒMA (βῆμα). [ECCLESIA.]

BENDIDEIA (βενδίδεια), a Thracian festival in honour of the goddess Bendis, who is said to be identical with the Grecian Artemis and with the Roman Diana. The festival was of a bacchanalian character. From Thrace it was brought to Athens, where it was celebrated in the Peiraeeus, on the 19th or 20th of the month Thargelion, before the Panathenae Minora. The temple of Bendis was called Bendideion.

BENĒFĬCĬUM, BENĒFĬCĬĀRĬUS. The term *beneficium* is of frequent occurrence in the Roman law, in the sense of some special privilege or favour granted to a person in respect of age, sex, or condition. But the word was also used in other senses. In the time of Cicero it was usual for a general, or a governor of a province, to report to the treasury the names of those under his command who had done good service to the state: those who were included in such report were said *in beneficiis ad aerarium deferri*. *In beneficiis* in these passages may mean that the persons so reported were considered as persons who had deserved well of the state; and so the word *beneficium* may have reference to the services of the individuals; but as the object for which their services were reported was the benefit of the individuals, it seems that the term had reference also to the reward, immediate or remote, obtained for their services. The honours and offices of the Roman state, in the republican period, were called the *beneficia* of the Populus Romanus. Beneficium also signified any promotion conferred on or grant made to soldiers, who were thence called *beneficiarii*.

BESTIĀRĬI (θηριομάχοι), persons who fought with wild beasts in the games of the circus. They were either persons who fought for the sake of pay (*auctoramentum*), and who were allowed arms, or they were criminals, who were usually permitted to have no means of defence against the wild beasts.

BIBLIŎPŌLA (βιβλιοπώλης), also called *librarius*, a bookseller. The shop was called *apotheca* or *taberna libraria*, or merely *libraria*. The Romans had their Paternoster-row; for the bibliopolae or librarii lived mostly in one street, called Argiletum. Another favourite quarter of the booksellers was the Vicus Sandalarius. There seems also to have been a sort of bookstalls by the temples of Vertumnus and Janus.

BIBLIŎTHĒCA (βιβλιοθήκη, or ἀποθήκη βιβλίων), primarily, the place where a collection of books was kept; secondarily, the collection itself. Public collections of books appear to have been very ancient. That of Peisistratus (B.C. 550) was intended for public use; it was subsequently removed to Persia by Xerxes. About the same time Polycrates, tyrant of Samos, is said to have founded a library. In the best days of Athens, even private persons had large collections of books; but the most important and splendid public library of antiquity was that founded by the

Ptolemies at Alexandria, begun under Ptolemy Soter, but increased and re-arranged in an orderly and systematic manner by Ptolemy Philadelphus, who also appointed a fixed librarian, and otherwise provided for the usefulness of the institution. A great part of this splendid library was consumed by fire in the siege of Alexandria by Julius Caesar; but it was soon restored, and continued in a flourishing condition till it was destroyed by the Arabs, A.D. 640. The Ptolemies were not long without a rival in zeal. Eumenes, king of Pergamus, became a patron of literature and the sciences, and established a library, which, in spite of the prohibition against exporting papyrus issued by Ptolemy, who was jealous of his success, became very extensive, and perhaps next in importance to the library of Alexandria. The first public library in Rome was that founded by Asinius Pollio, and was in the atrium Libertatis on Mount Aventine. The library of Pollio was followed by that of Augustus in the temple of Apollo on Mount Palatine and by another, bibliothecae Octavianae, in the theatre of Marcellus. There were also libraries on the Capitol, in the temple of Peace, in the palace of Tiberius, besides the Ulpian library, which was the most famous, founded by Trajan. Libraries were also usually attached to the Thermae. [BALNEUM.] Private collections of books were made at Rome soon after the second Punic war. The zeal of Cicero, Atticus, and others, in increasing their libraries is well known. It became, in fact, the fashion to have a room elegantly furnished as a library, and reserved for that purpose. The charge of the libraries in Rome was given to persons called *librarii*.

BĪCOS (βῖκος), the name of an earthen vessel in common use among the Greeks, for holding wine, and salted meat and fish.

BIDENTAL, the name given to a place where any one had been struck by lightning, or where any one had been killed by lightning and buried. Such a place was considered sacred. Priests, who were called *bidentales*, collected the earth which had been torn up by lightning, and every thing that had been scorched, and burnt it in the ground with a sorrowful murmur. The officiating priest was said *condere fulgur*; he further consecrated the spot by sacrificing a two-year-old sheep (*bidens*), whence the name of the place and of the priest, and he also erected an altar, and surrounded it with a wall or fence. To move the bounds of a bidental, or in any way to violate its sacred precincts, was considered as sacrilege.

BIDIAEI (βιδιαῖοι), magistrates in Sparta, whose business was to inspect the gymnastic exercises. They were either five or six in number.

BĪGA or BĪGAE. [CURRUS.]
BĪGĀTUS. [DENARIUS.]
BĪPENNIS. [SECURIS.]
BIRĒMIS. (1.) A ship with two banks of oars. [NAVIS.] Such ships were called *dicrota* by the Greeks, which term is also used by Cicero.—(2.) A boat rowed by two oars.

BISSEXTUS ANNUS. [CALENDARIUM, ROMAN.]

BOĒDROMĬA (Βοηδρόμια), a festival celebrated at Athens on the seventh day of the month Boëdromion, in honour of Apollo Boëdromius. The name Boëdromius, by which Apollo was called in Boeotia and many other parts of Greece, seems to indicate that by this festival he was honoured as a martial god, who, either by his actual presence or by his oracles, afforded assistance in the dangers of war.

BOEŌTARCHĒS (Βοιωτάρχης, or βοιωτάσχος), the name of the chief magistrates of the Boeotian confederacy, chosen by the different states. Their duties were chiefly of a military character. Each state of the confederacy elected one boeotarch, the Thebans two. The total number from the whole confederacy varied with the number of the independent states, but at the time of the Peloponnesian war they appear to have been ten or twelve. The boeotarchs, when engaged in military service, formed a council of war, the decisious of which were determined by a majority of votes, the president being one of the two Theban boeotarchs, who commanded alternately. Their period of service was a year, beginning about the winter solstice; and whoever continued in office longer than his time was punishable with death, both at Thebes and in other cities.

BONA, property. The phrase *in bonis* is frequently used as opposed to *dominium* or *Quiritarian ownership* (*ex jure Quiritium*). The ownership of certain kinds of things among the Romans could only be transferred from one person to another with certain formalities, or acquired by usucapion (that is, the uninterrupted possession of a thing for a certain time). But if it was clearly the intention of the owner to transfer the ownership, and the necessary forms only were wanting, the purchaser had the thing *in bonis*, and he had the enjoyment of it, though the original owner was still *legally* the owner, and was said to have the thing *ex jure Quiritium*, notwithstanding he had parted with the thing. The person who possessed a thing *in bonis* was protected in the enjoyment of it by the praetor, and consequently after a time would obtain the Quiritarian ownership of it by usucapion. [USUCAPIO.]

BONA CADUCA. *Caducum* literally signifies that which falls: thus *glans caduca* is the mast which falls from a tree. The strict legal sense of *caducum* and *bona caduca* is as follows:—If a thing is left by testament to a person, so that he can take it by the jus civile, but from some cause has not taken it, that thing is called *caducum*, as if it had *fallen* from him. Or if a *heres ex parte*, or a legatee, died before the opening of the will, the thing was *caducum*. That which was caducum came, in the first place, to those among the heredes who had children; and if the heredes had no children, it came among those of the legatees who had children. In case there was no prior claimant the caducum belonged to the aerarium; and subsequently to the fiscus. [AERARIUM.]

BONA FIDES implies, generally speaking, the absence of all fraud and unfair dealing or acting. In various actions arising out of mutual dealings, such as buying and selling, lending and hiring, partnership and others, bona fides is equivalent to aequum and justum; and such actions were sometimes called bonae fidei actiones. The formula of the praetor, which was the authority of the judex, empowered him in such cases to inquire and determine *ex bona fide*, that is, according to the real merits of the case: sometimes acquius melius was used instead of ex bona fide.

BONORUM CESSIO. There were two kinds of bonorum cessio, *in jure* and *extra jus*. The *in jure cessio* was a mode of transferring ownership by means of a fictitious suit. The *bonorum cessio extra jus* was introduced by a Julian law, passed either in the time of Julius Caesar or Augustus, which allowed an insolvent debtor to give up his property to his creditors. The debtor thus avoided the infamia consequent on the bonorum emtio, which was involuntary, and he was free from all personal execution. He was also allowed to retain a small portion of his property for his support. The property thus given up was sold, and the proceeds distributed among the creditors.

BONORUM COLLATIO. By the strict rules of the civil law an emancipated son had no right to the inheritance of his father, whether he died testate or intestate. But, in course of time, the praetor granted to emancipated children the privilege of equal succession with those who remained in the power of the father at the time of his death; but only on condition that they should bring into one common stock with their father's property, and for the purpose of an equal division among all the father's children, whatever property they had at the time of the father's death, and which would have been acquired for the father in case they had still remained in his power. This was called bonorum collatio.

BONORUM EMTIO ET EMTOR. The expression bonorum emtio applies to a sale of the property either of a living or of a dead person. It was in effect, as to a living debtor, an execution. In the case of a dead person, his property was sold when it was ascertained that there was neither heres nor bonorum possessor, nor any other person entitled to succeed to it. In the case of the property of a living person being sold, the praetor, on the application of the creditors, ordered it to be possessed (*possideri*) by the creditors for thirty successive days, and notice to be given of the sale. This explains the expression in Livy (ii. 24): "ne quis militis, donec in castris esset, bona *possideret* aut venderet."

BONORUM POSSESSIO was the right of suing for or retaining a patrimony or thing which belonged to another at the time of his death. The bonorum possessio was given by the edict both *contra tabulas*, *secundum tabulas*, and *intestati*. 1. An emancipated son had no legal claim on the inheritance of his father; but if he was omitted in his father's will, or not expressly exheredated, the praetor's edict gave him the bonorum possessio contra tabulas, on condition that he would bring into hotchpot (*bonorum collatio*) with his brethren who continued in the parent's power, whatever property he had at the time of the parent's death. 2. The *bonorum possessio secundum tabulas* was that possession which the praetor gave, conformably to the words of the will, to those named in it as heredes, when there was no person intitled to make a claim against the will, or none who chose to make such a claim. 3. In the case of intestacy (*intestati*) there were seven degrees of persons who might claim the bonorum possessio, each in his order, upon there being no claim of a prior degree. The first three degrees were children, *legitimi heredes*, and *proximi cognati*. Emancipated children could claim as well as those who were not emancipated, and adoptive as well as children of the blood; but not children who had been adopted into another family. If a freedman died intestate, leaving only a wife (in manu) or an adoptive son, the patron was entitled to the bonorum possessio of one half of his property.

BOÖNAE (βοῶναι), persons in Athens who purchased oxen for the public sacrifices and feasts. They are spoken of by Demosthenes in conjunction with the ἱεροποιοί and those who presided over the mysteries.

BORÉASMUS (Βορεασμός or Βορεασμοί), a festival celebrated by the Athenians in honour of Boreas, which, as Herodotus seems to think, was instituted during the Persian war, when the Athenians, being commanded by an oracle to invoke their γαμβρὸς ἐπίκουρος, prayed to Boreas. But considering that Boreas was intimately connected with the early history of Attica, we have reason to suppose that even previous to the Persian wars certain honours were paid to him, which were perhaps only revived and increased after the event recorded by Herodotus. The festival, however, does not seem ever to have had any great celebrity.

BOULÉ (βουλή—ἡ τῶν πεντακοσίων). In the heroic ages, represented to us by Homer, the *boulé* is simply an aristocratical council of the elders amongst the nobles, sitting under their king as president, which decided on public business and judicial matters, frequently in connection with, but apparently not subject to an *agora*, or meeting of the freemen of the state. [AGORA.] This form of government, though it existed for some time in the Ionian, Aeolian, and Achaean states, was at last wholly abolished in these states. Among the Dorians, however, especially among the Spartans, this was not the case, for they retained the kingly power of the Heracleidae, in conjunction with the *Gerousia* or assembly of elders, of which the kings were members. [GEROUSIA.] At Athens on the contrary, the *boulé* was a representative, and in most respects a popular body (δημοτικόν). The first institution of the Athenian *boulé* is generally attributed to Solon; but there are strong reasons for supposing that, as in the case of the *Areiopagus*, he merely modified the constitution of a body which he found already existing. But be this as it may, it is admitted that Solon made the number of his *boulé* 400, 100 from each of the four tribes. When the number of the tribes was raised to ten by Cleisthenes (B. C. 510), the council also was increased to 500, fifty being taken from each of the ten tribes. The *bouleutae* (βουλευταί) or councillors were appointed by lot, and hence they are called councillors made by the bean (οἱ ἀπὸ τοῦ κυάμου βουλευταί), from the use of beans in drawing lots. They were required to submit to a scrutiny or *docimasia*, in which they gave evidence of being genuine citizens, of never having lost their civic rights by *atimia*, and also of being above 30 years of age. They remained in office for a year, receiving a drachma (μισθὸς βουλευτικός) for each day on which they sat: and independent of the general account (εὔθυνα), which the whole body had to give at the end of the year, any single member was liable to expulsion for misconduct by his colleagues. The senate of 500 was divided into ten sections of fifty each, the members of which were called *prytanes* (πρυτάνεις), and were all of the same tribe; they acted as presidents both of the council and the assemblies during thirty-five or thirty-six days, as the case might be, so as to complete the lunar year of 354 days (12×29½). Each tribe exercised these functions in turn; the period of office was called a *prytany* (πρυτανεία), and the tribe that presided the *presiding tribe;* the order in which the tribes presided was determined by lot, and the four supernumerary days were given to the tribes which came last in order. Moreover, to obviate the difficulty of having too many in office at once, every fifty was subdivided into five bodies of ten each; its prytany also being portioned out into five periods of seven days each; so that only ten senators presided for a week over the rest, and were thence called *proedri* (πρόεδροι). Again, out of these proedri an *epistates* (ἐπιστάτης) was chosen for one day to preside as a chairman in the senate, and the assembly of the people; during his day of office he kept the public records and seal. The prytanes had the right of convening the council and the assembly (ἐκκλησία). The duty of the proedri and their president was to propose subjects for discussion, and to take the votes both of the councillors and the people, for neglect of their duty they were liable to a fine. Moreover, whenever a meeting, either of the council or of the assembly, was convened, the chairman of the proedri selected by lot nine others, one from each of the non-presiding tribes; these also were called proedri, and possessed a chairman of their own, likewise appointed by lot from among themselves. But the proedri who proposed the subject for discussion to the assembly belonged to the presiding tribe. It is observed, under AREIOPAGUS, that the chief object of Solon, in forming the senate and the areiopagus, was to control the democratical powers of the state for this purpose he ordained that the senate should discuss and vote upon all matters before they were submitted to the assembly, so that nothing could be laid before the people on which the senate had not come to a previous decision. This decision, or bill, was called *probouleuma* (προβούλευμα); but then not only might this *probouleuma* be rejected or modified by the assembly, but the latter also possessed and exercised the power of coming to a decision completely different from the will of the senate. In addition to the bills which it was the duty of the senate to propose of their own accord, there were others of a different character, viz. such as any private individual might wish to have submitted to the people. To accomplish this, it was first necessary for the party to obtain, by petition, the privilege of access to the senate, and leave to propose his motion; and if the measure met with their approbation, he could then submit it to the assembly. A proposal of this kind, which had the sanction of the senate, was also called *probouleuma*, and frequently related to the conferring of some particular honour or privilege upon an individual. Thus the proposal of Ctesiphon for crowning Demosthenes is so styled. In the assembly the bill of the senate was first read, perhaps by the crier, after the introductory ceremonies were over; and then the proedri put the question to the people, whether they approved of it. The people declared their will by a show of hands (προχειροτονία). If it was confirmed it became a *psephisma* (ψήφισμα), or decree of the people, binding upon all classes. The form for drawing up such decrees varied in different ages. In the time of Demosthenes the decrees commence with the name of the archon; then come the day of the month, the tribe in office, and, lastly, the name of the proposer. The motive for passing the decree is next stated; and then follows the decree itself, prefaced with the formula δεδόχθαι τῇ βουλῇ καὶ τῷ δήμῳ. The senate house was called *Bouleuterion* (βουλευτήριον). The prytanes also had a building to hold their meetings in, where they were entertained at the public expense during their prytany. This was called the *Prytaneion*, and was used for a variety of purposes. [PRYTANEION.]

BRĀCAE, or BRACCAE (ἀναξυρίδες), trowsers, pantaloons, were common to all the nations which encircled the Greek and Roman population, extending from the Indian to the Atlantic ocean, but were not worn by the Greeks and Romans themselves. Accordingly the monuments containing representations of people different from the Greeks and Romans exhibit them in trowsers, thus distinguishing them from the latter people.

BRAURŌNIA (βραυρώνια), a festival celebrated in honour of Artemis Brauronia, in the Attic town of Brauron, where Orestes and Iphigeneia, on their return from Tauris, were supposed by the Athenians to have landed, and left the statue of the Taurian goddess. It was held every fifth year, and the chief solemnity consisted in the Attic girls between the ages of five and ten years going in solemn procession to the sanctuary, where they were consecrated to the goddess. During this act the priests sacrificed a goat, and the girls performed a propitiatory rite, in which they imitated bears. This rite may have simply risen from the circumstance that the bear was sacred to Artemis, especially in Arcadia. There was also a quinquennial festival called Brauronia, which was celebrated by men and dissolute women, at Brauron, in honour of Dionysus.

BRUTTIĀNI, slaves whose duty it was to wait upon the Roman magistrates. They are said to have been originally taken from among the Bruttians.

BUCCĪNA (βυκάνη), a kind of horn trumpet, anciently made out of a shell (*buccinum*), the form of which is exhibited in the specimen annexed. The *buccina* was distinct from the

Buccina, Trumpet. (Blanchini, De Mus. Instrum. Vet.)

cornu; but it is often confounded with it. The buccina seems to have been chiefly distinguished by the twisted form of the shell, from which it was originally made. In later times it was carved from horn, and perhaps from wood or metal, so as to imitate the shell. The *buccina* was chiefly used to proclaim the watches of the day and of the night, hence called *buccina prima, secunda*, &c. It was also blown at funerals, and at festive entertainments both before sitting down to table and after.

BULLA, a circular plate or boss of metal, so called from its resemblance in form to a bubble floating upon water. Bright studs of this description were used to adorn the sword

Bulla. (From the Collection of Mr. Rogers: the gold chain added from a specimen in the Brit. Mus.)

belt; but we most frequently read of *bullae* as ornaments worn by children, suspended from the neck, and especially by the sons of the noble and wealthy. Such an one is called *heres bullatus* by Juvenal. The bulla was usually made of thin plates of gold. The use of the bulla, like that of the praetexta, was derived from the Etruscans. It was originally worn only by the children of the patricians, but subsequently by all of free birth.

BŪRIS. [ARATRUM.]

BUSTUM. It was customary among the Romans to burn the bodies of the dead before burying them. When the spot appointed for that purpose adjoined the place of sepulture, it was termed *bustum*; when it was separate from it, it was called *ustrina*. From this word the gladiators, who were hired to fight round the burning pyre of the deceased, were called *bustuarii*.

BUXUM or BUXUS, probably means the wood of the box-tree, but was given as a name to many things made of this wood. The tablets used for writing on, and covered with wax (*tabulae ceratae*), were usually made of box. In the same way the Greek πυξίον, formed from πύξος, "box-wood," came to be applied to any tablets, whether they were made of this wood or any other substance. Tops and combs were made of box-wood, and also all wind instruments, especially the flute.

BYSSUS (βύσσος), linen, and not cotton. The word byssus appears to come from the Hebrew *butz*, and the Greeks probably got it through the Phoenicians.

CABEIRIA (καβείρια), mysteries, festivals, and orgies, solemnised in all places in which the Pelasgian Cabeiri were worshipped, but especially in Samothrace, Imbros, Lemnos, Thebes, Anthedon, Pergamus, and Berytos. Little is known respecting the rites observed in these mysteries, as no one was allowed to divulge them. The most celebrated were those of the island of Samothrace, which, if we may judge from those of Lemnos, were solemnised every year, and lasted for nine days. Persons on their admission seem to have undergone a sort of examination respecting the life they had led hitherto, and were then purified of all their crimes, even if they had committed murder.

CADUCEUS (κηρύκειον, κηρύκιον), the staff or mace carried by heralds and ambassadors in time of war. This name is also given to the staff with which Hermes or Mercury is usually represented, as is shown in the following figure of that god. From *caduceus* was formed the word *caduceator*, which signified a person sent to treat of peace. The persons of the caduceatores were considered sacred.

Hermes bearing the Caduceus. (Museo Borbonico, vol. vi. pl. 2.)

CADŪCUM. [BONA CADUCA.]

CADUS (κάδος, κάδδος), a large vessel usually made of earthenware, which was used for keeping wine, drawing water, &c. The name of cadus was sometimes given to the vessel or urn in which the counters or pebbles of the dicasts were put, when they gave their vote on a trial, but the diminutive καδίσκος was more commonly used in this signification.

CAELĀTŪRA (τορευτική), a branch of the fine arts, under which all sorts of ornamental work in metal, except actual statues, appear to be included. The principal processes, which these words were used to designate, seem to have been of three kinds: hammering metal plates into moulds or dies, so as to bring out a raised pattern; engraving the surface of metals with a sharp tool; and working a pattern of one metal upon or into the surface of another: in short, the various processes which we describe by the words *chasing*, *damascening*, &c. The objects on which the *caelator* exercised his art were chiefly weapons and armour — especially shields, chariots, tripods, and other votive offerings, quoits, candelabra, thrones, curule chairs, mirrors, goblets, dishes, and all kinds of gold and silver plate. The ornamental work with which the chaser decorated such objects consisted either of simple running patterns, chiefly in imitation of plants and flowers, or of animals, or of mythologica subjects, and, for armour, of battles. The mythological subjects were reserved for the works of the greatest masters of the art: they were generally executed in very high relief (*anaglypha*). In the finest works, the ornamental pattern was frequently distinct from the vessel, to which it was either fastened permanently, or so that it could be removed at pleasure, the vessel being of silver, and the ornaments of gold, *crustae aut emblemata*. The art of ornamental metal-work was in an advanced stage of progress among the Greeks of the heroic period, as we see from numerous passages of Homer: but its origin, in the high artistic sense, is to be ascribed to Phidias, and its complete development to Polycletus. In the last age of the Roman Republic, the prevailing wealth and luxury, and the presence of Greek artists at Rome, combined to bring the art more than ever into requisition. After this period it suddenly fell into disuse.

CAELĪBĀTUS. [AES UXORIUM; LEX JULIA et PAPIA POPPAEA.]

CAERĪTUM TĂBŬLAE. [AERARII.]

CAESAR, a title of the Roman emperors, was originally a family name of the Julia gens; it was assumed by Octavianus as the adopted son of the great dictator, C. Julius Caesar, and was by him handed down to his adopted son Tiberius. It continued to be used by Caligula, Claudius, and Nero, as members either by adoption or female descent of Caesar's family; but although the family became extinct with Nero, succeeding emperors still retained the name as part of their titles, and it was the practice to prefix it to their own names, as for instance, *Imperator Caesar Domitianus Augustus*. When Hadrian adopted Aelius Varus, he allowed the latter to take the title of Caesar; and from this time, though the title of *Augustus* continued to be confined to the reigning emperor, that of *Caesar* was also granted to the second person in the state and the heir presumptive to the throne. [AUGUSTUS.]

CALAMISTRUM, an instrument made of iron, and hollow like a reed (*calamus*), used for curling the hair. For this purpose it was heated, the person who performed the office of heating it in wood ashes (*cinis*) being called *ciniflo*, or *cincrarius*.

CĂLĂMUS, a sort of reed which the ancients used as a pen for writing. The best sorts were got from Aegypt and Cnidus.

CĂLANTĪCA. [COMA.]

CĂLĂTHUS (κάλαθος, also called τάλαρος), usually signified the basket in which women placed their work, and especially the materials for spinning. In the following cut a slave, belonging to the class called *quasilla-*

riae, is presenting her mistress with the calathus. Baskets of this kind were also used for other purposes, such as for carrying fruits,

Slave presenting a Calathus. (From a Painting on a Vase.)

flowers, &c. The name of calathi was also given to cups for holding wine. Calathus was properly a Greek word, though used by the Latin writers. The Latin word corresponding to it was *qualus* or *quasillus*. From *quasillus* came *quasillaria*, the name of the slave who spun, and who was considered the meanest of the female slaves.

CALCĔUS, CALCĔĀMEN, CALCĔĀMENTUM (ὑπόδημα, πέδιλον), a shoe or boot, anything adapted to cover and preserve the feet in walking. The use of shoes was by no means universal among the Greeks and Romans. The Homeric heroes are represented without shoes when armed for battle. Socrates, Phocion, and Cato, frequently went barefoot. The Roman slaves had no shoes. The covering of the feet was removed before reclining at meals. People in grief, as for instance at funerals, frequently went barefooted. Shoes may be divided into those in which the mere sole of a shoe was attached to the sole of the foot by ties or bands, or by a covering for the toes or the instep [SOLEA; CREPIDA; SOCCUS]; and those which ascended higher and higher, according as they covered the ankles, the calf, or the whole of the leg. To calceamenta of the latter kind, *i. e.* to shoes and boots, as distinguished from sandals and slippers, the term *calceus* was applied in its proper and restricted sense. There were also other varieties of the *calceus* according to its adaptation to particular professions or modes of life. Thus the CALIGA was principally worn by soldiers; the PERO by labourers and rustics; and the COTHURNUS by tragedians, hunters, and horsemen. The *calcei* probably did not much differ from our shoes, and are exemplified in a painting at Herculaneum, which represents a female wearing bracelets, a wreath of ivy, and a panther's skin, while she is in the attitude of dancing and playing on the cymbals. The form and colour of the calceus indicated rank and office. Roman senators wore high shoes like buskins, fastened in front with four black thongs. They were also sometimes adorned with a small crescent: we do not find on any ancient statues the crescent, but we may regard the bottom right hand figure in the annexed cut as representing the shoe of a senator. Among the calcei worn by senators, those called *mullei*, from their resemblance to the scales of the red mullet, were particularly admired; as well as others called *alutae*, because the leather was softened by the use of alum.

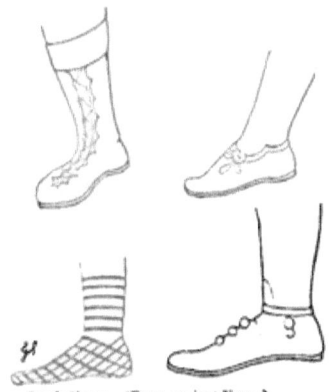

Greek Shoes. (From ancient Vases.)

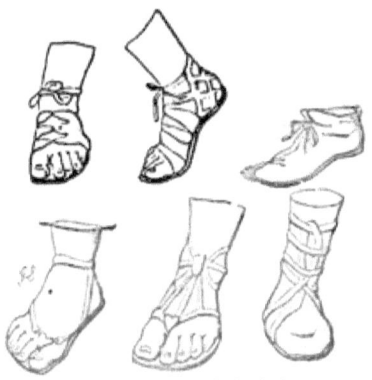

Roman Shoes. (Museo Borbonico.)

CALCŬLĀTOR (λογιστής), a keeper of accounts in general, and also a teacher of arithmetic. In Roman families of importance there was a *calculator* or account-keeper, who is, however, more frequently called by the name of *dispensator*, or *procurator*: he was a kind of steward.

CALCŬLI, little stones or pebbles, used for various purposes, as, for instance, among the Athenians for voting. Calculi were used in playing a sort of draughts. Subsequently, instead of pebbles, ivory, or silver, or gold, or other men (as we call them) were used; but they still bore the name of calculi. Calculi were also used in reckoning; and hence the phrases *calculum ponere*, *calculum subducere*.

CALDĀRĬUM. [BALNEUM.]

CĂLENDAE or KĂLENDAE. [CALENDARIUM.]

CĂLENDĀRĬUM or KĂLENDĀRĬUM, generally signified an account-book, in which were entered the names of a person's debtors, with the interest which they had to pay, and it was so called because the interest had to be paid on the calends of each month. The word, however, was also used in the signification of a modern calendar or almanac. (1) GREEK CALENDAR. The Greek year was divided into twelve lunar months, depending on the actual changes of the moon. The first day of the month (νουμηνία) was not the day of the conjunction, but the day on the evening of which the new moon appeared; consequently full moon was the middle of the month. The lunar month consists of twenty-nine days and about thirteen hours; accordingly some months were necessarily reckoned at twenty-nine days, and rather more of them at thirty days. The latter were called *full* months (πλήρεις), the former *hollow* months (κοῖλοι). As the twelve lunar months fell short of the solar year, they were obliged every other year to interpolate an intercalary month (μὴν ἐμβολιμαῖος) of thirty or twenty-nine days. The ordinary year consisted of 354 days, and the interpolated year, therefore, of 384 or 383. This interpolated year (τριέτηρις) was seven days and a half too long, and to correct the error, the intercalary month was from time to time omitted. The Attic year began with the summer solstice : the following is the sequence of the Attic months and the number of days in each:—Hecatombaeon (30), Metageitnion (29), Boedromion (30), Pyanepsion (29), Maemacterion (30), Poseideon (29), Gamelion (30), Anthesterion (29), Elaphebolion (30), Munychion (29), Thargelion (30), Scirophorion (29). The intercalary month was a second Poseideon inserted in the middle of the year. Every Athenian month was divided into three decads. The days of the first decad were designated as ἱσταμένου or ἀρχομένου μηνός, and were counted on regularly from one to ten ; thus, δευτέρα ἀρχομένου or ἱσταμένου is "the

F

second day of the month." The days of the second decad were designated as ἐπὶ δέκα or μεσοῦντος, and were counted on regularly from the 11th to the 20th day, which was called εἰκάς. There were two ways of counting the days of the last decad; they were either reckoned onwards from the 20th (thus, πρώτη ἐπὶ εἰκάδι was the 21st), or backwards from the last day, with the addition φθίνοντος, παυομένου, λήγοντος, or ἀπίοντος; thus, the twenty-first day of a hollow month was ἐνάτη φθίνοντος; of a full month, δεκάτη φθίνοντος. The last day of the month was called ἔνη καὶ νέα, "the old and new," because as the lunar month really consisted of more than twenty-nine and less than thirty days, the last day might be considered as belonging equally to the old and new month. Separate years were designated at Athens by the name of the chief archon, hence called *archon eponymus* (ἄρχων ἐπώνυμος), or "the name giving archon;" at Sparta, by the first of the ephors; at Argos, by the priestess of Juno, &c.— (2) ROMAN CALENDAR. The old Roman, frequently called the Romulian year, consisted of only ten months, which were called Martius, Aprilis, Maius, Junius, Quinctilis, Sextilis, September, October, November, December. That March was the first month in the year is implied in the last six names. Of these months, four, namely, Martius, Maius, Quinctilis, and October, consisted of thirty-one days, the other six of thirty. The four former were distinguished in the latest form of the Roman calendar by having their nones two days later than any of the other months. The symmetry of this arrangement will appear by placing the numbers in succession :— 31, 30; 31, 30; 31, 30, 30; 31, 30, 30. The Romulian year therefore consisted of 304 days, and contained thirty-eight nundinae or weeks; every eighth day, under the name of *nonae*, or *nundinae*, being especially devoted to religious and other public purposes. Hence we find that the number of *dies fasti* afterwards retained in the Julian calendar tally exactly with these thirty-eight nundines; besides which, it may be observed that a year of 304 days bears to a solar year of 365 days nearly the ratio of five to six, six of the Romulian years containing 1824, five of the solar years 1825 days; and hence we may explain the origin of the well-known quinquennial period called the lustrum, which ancient writers expressly call an *annus magnus*; that is, in the modern language of chronology, a cycle. It was consequently the period at which the Romulian and solar years coincided. The next division of the Roman year was said to have been made by Numa Pompilius, who instituted a lunar year of 12 months and 355 days. Livy says that Numa so regulated his lunar year of twelve months by the insertion of intercalary months, that at the end of every *nineteenth* year (*vicesimo anno*) it again coincided with the same point in the sun's course from which it started. It is well known that 19 years constitute a most convenient cycle for the junction of a lunar and solar year. It seems certain that the Romans continued to use a lunar year for some time after the establishment of the republic; and it was probably at the time of the decemviral legislation that the lunar year was abandoned. By the change which was then made the year consisted of 12 months, the length of each of which was as follows :—

Martius,	31 days.	September,	29 days.	
Aprilis,	29 ,,	October,	31	,,
Maius,	31 ,,	November,	29	,,
Junius,	29 ,,	December,	29	,,
Quinctilis,	31 ,,	Januarius,	29	,,
Sextilis,	29 ,,	Februarius,	28	,,

The year thus consisted of 355 days, and this was made to correspond with the solar year by the insertion of an intercalary month (*mensis intercalaris* or *intercalarius*), called *Mercedonius* or *Mercidonius*. This month of 22 or 23 days seems to have been inserted in alternate years. As the festivals of the Romans were for the most part dependent upon the calendar, the regulation of the latter was entrusted to the college of pontifices, who in early times were chosen exclusively from the body of patricians. It was therefore in the power of the college to add to their other means of oppressing the plebeians, by keeping to themselves the knowledge of the days on which justice could be administered, and assemblies of the people could be held. In the year 304 B.C., one Cn. Flavius, a secretary (*scriba*) of Appius Claudius, is said fraudulently to have made the *Fasti* public. The other privilege of regulating the year by the insertion of the intercalary month gave the pontiffs great political power, which they were not backward to employ. Every thing connected with the matter of intercalation was left to their unrestrained pleasure; and the majority of them, on personal grounds, added to or took from the year by capricious intercalations, so as to lengthen or shorten the period during which a magistrate remained in office, and seriously to benefit or injure the farmer of the public revenue. The calendar was thus involved in complete confusion, and accordingly we find that in the time of Cicero the year was three months in advance of the real solar year. At length, in the year B.C. 46, Caesar, now master of the Roman world, employed his authority, as pontifex maximus, in the correction of this serious evil. The account of the way in which he effected this is given by Censorinus:—"The confusion was at last carried so far that C. Caesar, the pontifex maximus, in his third consulate, with Lepidus for his colleague, inserted between November and December two intercalary months of 67 days, the month of February having already received an intercalation of 23 days, and thus made the whole year to consist of 445 days. At the same time he provided against a repetition of similar errors, by casting aside the intercalary month, and adapting the year to the sun's course. Accordingly, to the 355 days of the previously existing year he added ten days, which he so distributed between the seven months having 29 days that January, Sextilis, and December received two each, the others but one; and these additional days he placed at the end of the several months, no doubt with the wish not to remove the various festivals from those positions in the several months which they had so long occupied. Hence in the present calendar, although there are seven months of 31 days, yet the four months, which from the first possessed that number, are still distinguishable by having their nones on the seventh, the rest having them on the fifth of the month. Lastly, in consideration of the quarter of a day, which he regarded as completing the true year, he established the rule that, at the end of every four years, a single day should be intercalated, where the month had been hitherto inserted, that is, immediately after the terminalia; which day is now called the bissextum." The mode of denoting the days of the month will cause no difficulty, if it be recollected that the kalends always denote the first of the month; that the nones occur on the seventh of the four months of March, May, Quinctilis or July, and October, and on the fifth of the other months; that the ides always fall eight days later than the nones; and lastly, that the intermediate days are in all cases reckoned backwards upon the Roman principle of counting both extremes. For the month of January the notation will be as follows:—

1. Kal. Jan.
2. a. d. IV. Non. Jan.
3. a. d. III. Non. Jan.
4. Prid. Non. Jan.
5. Non. Jan.
6. a. d. VIII. Id. Jan.
7. a. d. VII. Id. Jan.
8. a. d. VI. Id. Jan.
9. a. d. V. Id. Jan.
10. a. d. IV. Id. Jan.
11. a. d. III. Id. Jan.
12. Prid. Id. Jan.
13. Id. Jan.
14. a. d. XIX. Kal. Feb.
15. a. d. XVIII. Kal. Feb.
16. a. d. XVII. Kal. Feb.
17. a. d. XVI. Kal. Feb.
18. a. d. XV. Kal. Feb.
19. a. d. XIV. Kal. Feb.
20. a. d. XIII. Kal. Feb.
21. a. d. XII. Kal. Feb.
22. a. d. XI. Kal. Feb.
23. a. d. X. Kal. Feb.
24. a. d. IX. Kal. Feb.
25. a. d. VIII. Kal. Feb.
26. a. d. VII. Kal. Feb.
27. a. d. VI. Kal. Feb.
28. a. d. V. Kal. Feb.
29. a. d. IV. Kal. Feb.
30. a. d. III. Kal. Feb.
31. Prid. Kal. Feb.

The letters *a d* are often, through error, written together, and so confounded with the preposition *ad* which would have a different meaning, for *ad kalendas* would signify *by*, i. e. *on or before the kalends*. The letters are in fact an abridgment of *ante diem*, and the full phrase for "on the second of January," would be *ante diem quartum nonas Januarias*. The word *ante* in this expression seems really to belong in sense to *nonas*, and to be the cause why *nonas* is an accusative. Whether the phrase *kalendae Januarii* was ever used by the best writers is doubtful. The words are commonly abbreviated; and those passages where Aprilis, Decembris, &c. occur are of no avail, as they are probably accusatives. The *ante* may be omitted, in which case the phrase will be *die quarto nonarum*. In the leap year (to use a modern phrase), the last days of February were called,—

Feb. 23. a. d. VII. Kal. Mart.
Feb. 24. a. d. VI. Kal. Mart. posteriorem.
Feb. 25. a. d. VI. Kal. Mart. priorem.
Feb. 26. a. d. V. Kal. Mart.
Feb. 27. a. d. IV. Kal. Mart.
Feb. 28. a. d. III. Kal. Mart.
Feb. 29. Prid. Kal. Mart.

In which the words *prior* and *posterior* are used in reference to the retrograde direction of the reckoning. From the fact that the intercalated year has two days called *ante diem sextum*, the name bissextile has been applied to it. The term *annus bissextilis*, however, does not occur in any classical writer, but in place of it the phrase *annus bissextus*.—The names of two of the months were changed in honour of Julius Caesar and Augustus. Julius was substituted for Quinctilis, the month in which Caesar was born, in the second Julian year, that is, the year of the dictator's death, for the first Julian year was the first year of the *corrected* Julian calendar, that is, B.C. 45. The name Augustus in place of Sextilis was introduced by the emperor himself in B.C. 27. The month of September in like manner received the name of Germanicus from the general so called, and the appellation appears to have existed even in the time of Macrobius. Domitian, too, conferred his name upon October; but the old word was restored upon the death of the tyrant.—The Julian calendar supposes the mean tropical year to be 365 d. 6 h.; but this exceeds the real amount by 11′ 12″, the accumulation of which, year after year, caused at last considerable inconvenience. Accordingly, in the year 1582, Pope Gregory XIII. again reformed the calendar. The ten days by which the year had been unduly retarded were struck out by a regulation that the day after the fourth of October in that year should be called the fifteenth; and it was ordered that whereas hitherto an intercalary day had been inserted every four years, for the future three such intercalations in the course of four hundred years should be omitted, viz., in those years which are divisible without remainder by 100, but not by 400. Thus, according to the Julian calendar, the years 1600, 1700, 1800, 1900, 2000, were to be bissextile as before. The bull which effected this change was issued Feb. 24th, 1582. The Protestant parts of Europe resisted what they called a papistical invention for more than a century. In England the Gregorian calendar was first adopted in 1752. In Russia, and those countries which belonged to the Greek church, the Julian year, or *old style*, as it is called, still prevails. In the ancient calendars the letters A, B, C, D, E, F, G, H, were used for the purpose of fixing the nundines in the week of eight days; precisely in the same way in which the first seven letters are still employed in ecclesiastical calendars, to mark the days of the Christian week.

CĂLIGA, a strong and heavy sandal worn by the Roman soldiers, but not by the superior officers. Hence the common soldiers, including centurions, were distinguished by the name of *caligati*. The emperor Caligula received that cognomen when a boy, in consequence of wearing the caliga, and being inured to the life of a common soldier. The cuts on pp. 1, 41, show the difference between the caliga of the common soldier and the calceus worn by men of higher rank.

CĂLIX (κύλιξ). (1) a drinking-cup used at symposia and on similar occasions.—(2) A vessel used in cooking.—(3) A tube in the aquaeducts attached to the extremity of each pipe, where it entered the castellum.

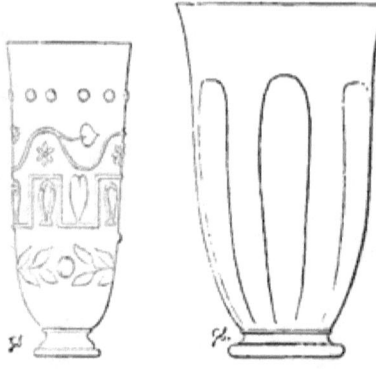

Calices, Drinking-cups. (Museo Borbonico, vol. v. pl. 13.)

CALLIS, a beaten path or track made by the feet of cattle. The sheep-walks in the mountainous parts of Campania and Apulia were the property of the Roman state; and as they were of considerable value, one of the quaestors usually had these *calles* assigned to him as his province, whence we read of the *Callium provincia*. His principal duties were to receive the *scriptura*, or tax paid for the pasturage of the cattle, and to protect life and property in these wild and mountainous districts. When the senate wished to put a slight upon the consuls on one occasion they endeavoured to assign to them as their provinces, the care of the woods (*silvae*) and sheep-walks (*calles*).

CALLISTEIA (καλλιστεῖα), a festival, or perhaps merely a part of one, held by the women of Lesbos; at which they assembled in the sanctuary of Hera, and the fairest received the prize of beauty. Similar contests of beauty are said to have been held in other places.

CĂLŌNES, the slaves or servants of the Roman soldiers, so called from carrying wood (κᾶλα) for their use. The word *calo*, however, was also applied to farm-servants. The *calones* and *lixae* are frequently spoken of together, but they were not the same : the latter were freemen, who merely followed the camp for the purposes of gain and merchandise, and were so far from being indispensable to an army, that they were sometimes forbidden to attend it.

CĂLUMNIA. When an accuser failed in his proof, and the accused party was acquitted, there might be an inquiry into the conduct and motives of the accuser. If the person who made this judicial inquiry found that the accuser had merely acted from error of judgment, he acquitted him in the form *non probasti;* if he convicted him of evil intention, he declared his sentence in the words *calumniatus es,* which sentence was followed by the legal punishment. The punishment for *calumnia* was fixed by the lex Remmia, or as it is sometimes, perhaps incorrectly, named, the lex Memmia. But it is not known when this lex was passed, nor what were its penalties. It appears from Cicero, that the false accuser might be branded on the forehead with the letter K, the initial of Kalumnia. The punishment for calumnia was also *exsilium, relegatio in insulam,* or loss of rank (*ordinis amissio*); but probably only in criminal cases, or in matters relating to status.

CĂMĂRA (καμάρα), or CĂMĒRA. (1) A particular kind of arched ceiling, formed by semicircular bands or beams of wood, arranged at small lateral distances, over which a coating of lath and plaster was spread, and the whole covered in by a roof, resembling in construction the hooped awnings in use amongst us.—(2) A small boat used in early times by the people who inhabited the shores of the Palus Maeotis, capable of containing from twenty-five to thirty men. These boats were made to work fore and aft, like the fast-sailing proas of the Indian seas, and continued in use until the age of Tacitus.

CĂMILLI, CĂMILLAE, boys and girls employed in the religious rites and ceremonies of the Romans. They were required to be perfect in form, and sound in health, free born, and with both their parents alive; or, in other words, according to the expression of the Romans, *pueri seu puellae ingenui, felicissimi, patrimi matrimique.*

CĂMĪNUS. [Domus.]

CAMPESTRE (sc. *subligar*), a kind of girdle or apron, which the Roman youths wore around their loins, when they exercised naked in the Campus Martius. The campestre was sometimes worn in warm weather, in place of the tunic under the toga.

CAMPUS MARTIUS. [See CLASSICAL DICTIONARY.]

CĂNĂBUS (κάναβος), a figure of wood in the form of a skeleton, round which the clay or plaster was laid in forming models. Figures of a similar kind, formed to display the muscles and veins, were studied by painters in order to acquire some knowledge of anatomy.

CĂNATHRON (κάναθρον), a carriage, the upper part of which was made of basket-work, or more properly the basket itself, which was fixed in the carriage.

CANCELLĀRIUS. [CANCELLI.]

CANCELLI, lattice-work, placed before a window, a door-way, the tribunal of a judge, or any other place. Hence was derived the word *Cancellarius,* which originally signified a porter, who stood at the latticed or grated door of the emperor's palace. The cancellarius also signified a legal scribe or secretary, who sat within the cancelli or lattice-work. The chief scribe or secretary was called Cancellarius κατ' ἐξοχήν, and was eventually invested with judicial power at Constantinople. From this word has come the modern Chancellor.

CANDĒLA, a candle, made either of wax (*cera*), or tallow (*sebacea*), was used universally by the Romans before the invention of oil lamps (*lucernae*). In later times candelae were only used by the poorer classes; the houses of the more wealthy were always lighted by lucernae.

CANDĒLABRUM, originally a candlestick, but afterwards the name of a stand for sup-

Candelabrum in the Vatican. (Visconti vol. iv. tav. 5.)

porting lamps (λυχνοῦχοι), in which signification it most commonly occurs. The candelabra of this kind were usually made to stand upon the ground, and were of a considerable height. The most common kind were made of wood; but those which have been found in Herculaneum and Pompeii are mostly of bronze. Sometimes they were made of the more precious metals, and even of jewels. The candelabra did not always stand upon the ground, but were also placed upon the table. Such candelabra usually consisted of pillars, from the capitals of which several lamps hung down, or of trees, from whose branches lamps also were suspended.

CANDĪDĀTUS. [AMBITUS.]

CANDYS (κάνδυς), a robe worn by the Medes and Persians over their trowsers and other garments. It had wide sleeves, and was made of woollen cloth, which was either purple or of some other splendid colour. In the Persepolitan sculptures, from which the annexed figures are taken, nearly all the principal personages wear it.

Candys, Persian Cloak. (From Bas-relief at Persepolis.)

CĂNĒPHŎROS (κανηφόρος), a virgin who carried a flat circular basket (κάνεον, canistrum) at sacrifices, in which the chaplet of flowers, the knife to slay the victim, and sometimes the frankincense were deposited. The name, however, was more particularly applied to two virgins of the first Athenian families who were appointed to officiate as canephori at the Panathenaea. The preceding cut represents the two canephori approaching a candelabrum. Each of them elevates one arm to support the basket while she slightly raises her tunic with the other.

CANTHĂRUS (κάνθαρος), a kind of drinking cup, furnished with handles. It was the cup sacred to Bacchus, who is frequently represented on ancient vases holding it in his hand.

Cantharus (From an ancient Vase.)

CANTĬCUM, an interlude between the acts of a Roman comedy, and sometimes, perhaps, of a tragedy. It consisted of flute music, accompanied by a kind of recitative performed by a single actor, or if there were two, the second was not allowed to speak with the first. In the canticum, as violent gesticulation was required, it appears to have been the custom, from the time of Livius Andronicus, for the actor to confine himself to the gesticulation, while another person sang the recitative.

CĂPILLUS. [COMA.]

CĂPISTRUM (φορβειά), a halter, or tie for horses, asses, or other animals, placed round the head or neck, and made of osiers or other fibrous materials. The Greek word φορβειά was also applied to a contrivance used by pipers and trumpeters to compress their mouths and cheeks, and thus to aid them in blowing. It is often seen in works of ancient art, and was said to be the invention of Marsyas. [TIBIA.]

CĂPĬTE CENSI. [CAPUT.]
CĂPĬTIS DĒMĬNŪTĬO. [CAPUT.]
CĂPĬTŌLĪNI LŪDI. [LUDI.]
CĂPĬTŌLIUM. [See CLASS. DICTIONARY.]
CĂPĬTŬLUM. [COLUMNA.]

CAPSA, or SCRĪNIUM, a box for holding books among the Romans. These boxes were of a cylindrical form. There does not appear to have been any difference between the *capsa* and *scrinium*, except that the latter word was usually applied to those boxes which held a considerable number of rolls. The slaves who had the charge of these book-

Canephori. (British Museum.)

chests were called *capsarii*, and also *custodes scriniorum*; and the slaves who carried in a *capsa* behind their young masters the books, &c. of the sons of respectable Romans, when they went to school, were called by the same name.

The Muse Clio with a Capsa. (Pitture d'Ercolano, vol. ii. pl. 2.)

CAPSĀRII, the name of three different classes of slaves. [BALNEUM; CAPSA.]

CĂPUT, the head. The term "head" is often used by the Roman writers as equivalent to "person," or "human being." By an easy transition it was used to signify "life:" thus, *capite damnari, plecti*, &c., are equivalent to capital punishment. *Caput* is also used to express a man's *status*, or civil condition; and the persons who were registered in the tables of the censor are spoken of as *capita*, sometimes with the addition of the word *civium*, and sometimes not. Thus to be registered in the census was the same thing as *caput habere*: and a slave and a *filius familias*, in this sense of the word, were said to have no *caput*. The sixth class of Servius Tullius comprised the *proletarii* and the *capite censi*, of whom the latter, having little or no property, were barely rated as so many *head* of citizens.—He who lost or changed his status was said to be *capite minutus, deminutus*, or *capitis minor*. *Capitis minutio* or *deminutio* was a change of a person's status or civil condition, and consisted of three kinds.—A Roman citizen possessed freedom (*libertas*), citizenship (*civitas*), and family (*familias*) the loss of all three constituted the *maxima capitis deminutio*. This *capitis deminutio* was sustained by those who refused to be registered at the census, or neglected the registration, and were thence called *incensi*. The *incensus* was liable to be sold, and so to lose his liberty. Those who refused to perform military service might also be sold.—The loss of citizenship and family only, as when a man was interdicted from fire and water, was the *media capitis deminutio*. [EXSILIUM.]—The change of family by adoption, and by the in manum conventio, was the *minima capitis deminutio*.—A *judicium capitale*, or *poena capitalis*, was one which affected a citizen's caput.

CĂPUT. [FENUS.]

CĂPUT EXTŌRUM. The Roman soothsayers (*haruspices*) pretended to a knowledge of coming events from the inspection of the entrails of victims slain for that purpose. The part to which they especially directed their attention was the liver, the convex upper portion of which seems to have been called the *caput extorum*. Any disease or deficiency in this organ was considered an unfavourable omen; whereas, if healthy and perfect, it was believed to indicate good fortune. If no caput was found, it was a bad sign (*nihil tristius accidere potuit*); if well defined or double, it was a lucky omen.

CĂRĀCALLA, an outer garment used in Gaul, and not unlike the Roman *lacerna*. It was first introduced at Rome by the emperor Aurelius Antoninus Bassianus, who compelled all the people that came to court to wear it, whence he obtained the surname of Caracalla. This garment, as worn in Gaul, does not appear to have reached lower than the knee, but Caracalla lengthened it so as to reach the ankle.

CARCER (*kerker*, German; γοργύρα, Greek), a prison, is connected with ἕρκος and εἴργω, the guttural being interchanged with the aspirate. (1) GREEK. Imprisonment was seldom used amongst the Greeks as a legal punishment for offences; they preferred banishment to the expense of keeping prisoners in confinement. The prisons in different countries were called by different names; thus there was the *Ceadas* (Κεάδας), at Sparta; and, among the Ionians, the *Gorgyra* (γοργύρα), as at Samos. The prison at Athens was in former times called *Desmoterion* (δεσμωτήριον), and afterwards, by a sort of euphemism, οἴκημα. It was chiefly used as a guard-house or place of execution, and was under the charge of the public officers called the Eleven. —(2) ROMAN. A prison was first built at Rome by Ancus Martius, overhanging the forum. This was enlarged by Servius Tullius, who added to it a souterrain, or dungeon, called from him the *Tullianum*. Sallust describes this as being twelve feet under ground, walled on each side, and arched over with stone work. For a long time this was the only prison at Rome, being, in fact, the "Tower," or state prison of the city, which was sometimes doubly guarded in times of alarm, and was the chief object of attack in many conspiracies. There were, however, other prisons besides this, though, as we might expect, the words of Roman historians generally refer to this alone. In the *Tullianum* prisoners were generally executed, and this part of the prison was also called *robur*.

CARCĔRES. [CIRCUS.]

CARCHĒSĬUM (καρχήσιον). (1) A beaker or drinking-cup, which was used by the Greeks in very early times. It was slightly contracted in the middle, and its two handles extended from the top to the bottom. It was much employed in libations of wine, milk, and honey.—(2) The upper part of the mast of a ship. [NAVIS.]

CARMENTALIA, a festival celebrated in honour of Carmenta or Carmentis, who is fabled to have been the mother of Evander, who came from Pallantium in Arcadia, and settled in Latium: he was said to have brought with him a knowledge of the arts, and the Latin alphabetical characters as distinguished from the Etruscan. This festival was celebrated annually on the 11th of January. A temple was erected to the same goddess, at the foot of the Capitoline hill, near the Porta Carmentalis, afterwards called Scelerata. The name Carmenta is said to have been given to her from her prophetic character, carmens or carmentis being synonymous with vates. The word is, of course, connected with *carmen*, as prophecies were generally delivered in verse.

CARNEIA (καρνεῖα), a great national festival, celebrated by the Spartans in honour of Apollo Carneios. The festival began on the seventh day of the month of Carneios = Metageitnion of the Athenians, and lasted for nine days. It was of a warlike character, similar to the Attic Boëdromia. During the time of its celebration nine tents were pitched near the city, in each of which nine men lived in the manner of a military camp, obeying in everything the commands of a herald. The priest conducting the sacrifices at the Carneia was called *Agetes* (Ἀγητής), whence the festival was sometimes designated by the name *Agetoria* or *Agetoreion* (Ἀγητόρια or Ἀγητόρειον), and from each of the Spartan tribes five men (Καρνεᾶται) were chosen as his ministers, whose office lasted four years, during which period they were not allowed to marry. When we read in Herodotus and Thucydides that the Spartans during the celebration of this festival were not allowed to take the field against an enemy, we must remember that this restriction was not peculiar to the Carneia, but common to all the great festivals of the Greeks: traces of it are found even in Homer.

CARNĬFEX, the public executioner at Rome, who executed slaves and foreigners, but not citizens, who were punished in a manner different from slaves. It was also his business to administer the torture. This office was considered so disgraceful, that he was not allowed to reside within the city, but lived without the Porta Metia or Esquilina, near the place destined for the punishment of slaves, called Sestertium under the emperors.

CARPENTUM, a cart; also a two-wheeled carriage, enclosed, and with an arched or sloping cover overhead. The carpentum was used to convey the Roman matrons in the public festal processions; and this was a high distinction, since the use of carriages in the city was entirely forbidden during the whole of the republican period. Hence the privilege of riding in a carpentum in the public festivals was sometimes granted to females of the imperial family. This carriage contained seats for two, and sometimes for three persons, besides the coachman. It was commonly drawn by a pair of mules, but more rarely by oxen or horses, and sometimes by four horses like a quadriga.—Carpenta, or covered carts, were much used by the Britons, the Gauls, and other northern nations. These, together with the carts of the more common form, including baggage-waggons, appear to have been comprehended under the term *carri*, or *carra*, which is the Celtic name with a Latin termination. The Gauls took a great multitude of them on their military expeditions, and when they were encamped, arranged them in close order, so as to form extensive lines of circumvallation.

CARRĀGO, a kind of fortification, consisting of a great number of waggons placed round an army. It was employed by barbarous nations, as, for instance, the Scythians, Gauls, and Goths. Carrago also signifies sometimes the baggage of an army.

CARRŪCA, a carriage, the name of which only occurs under the emperors. It appears to have been a species of rheda [RHEDA], had four wheels, and was used in travelling. These carriages were sometimes used in Rome by persons of distinction, like the carpenta; in which case they appear to have been covered with plates of bronze, silver, and even gold, which were sometimes ornamented with embossed work.

CARRUS. [CARPENTUM.]

CĂRYA or CĂRYĀTIS (καρύα, καρυατίς), a festival celebrated at Caryae, in Laconia, in honour of Artemis Caryatis. It was celebrated every year by Lacedaemonian maidens with national dances of a very lively kind.

CĂRYĀTĬDES, female figures used in architecture instead of columns. Their name is usually derived from Caryae, a city in Arcadia, near the Laconian border, the women of which are said to have been reduced to slavery by the Greeks, because Caryae had joined the Persians at the invasion of Greece. But this tale is probably apocryphal. One of the porticos of the Erechtheum at Athens is supported by Caryatides.

CASSIS. [GALEA.]

CASTELLUM ĂQUAE. [AQUAE DUCTUS.]

CASTRA. Roman armies never halted for a single night without forming a regular entrenchment, termed *castra*, capable of receiving within its limits the whole body of fighting men, their beasts of burden, and the baggage. So completely was this recognised as a part of the ordinary duties of each march, that *pervenire ad locum tertiis . . . quartis . . . septuagesimis castris* are the established phrases for expressing the number of days occupied in passing from one point to another. Whenever circumstances rendered it expedient for a force to occupy the same ground for any length of time, then the encampment was distinguished as *castra stativa*. In wild and barbarian lands, where there were no large towns and no tribes on whose faith reliance could be placed, armies, whether of invasion or occupation, were forced to remain constantly in camps. They usually, however, occupied different ground in summer and in winter, whence arose the distinction between *castra aestiva* and *castra hiberna*, both alike being *stativa*. But whether a camp was temporary or permanent, whether tenanted in summer or in winter, the main features of the work were always the same for the same epoch. In hiberna, huts of turf or stone would be substituted for the open tents of the aestiva (hence *aedificare hiberna*), and in stativa held for long periods the defences would present a more substantial and finished aspect, but the general outline and disposition of the parts were invariable. Polybius has transmitted to us a description of a Roman camp, from which the annexed plan has been drawn up. It is such as would be formed at the close of an ordinary day's march by a regular consular army consisting of two Roman legions with the full contingent of Socii. Each legion is calculated at 4200 infantry and 300 cavalry; the Socii furnished an equal number of infantry, and twice as many cavalry, so that the whole force would amount to 16,800 foot and 1800 horse. Skill in the selection of a spot for a camp (*capere locum castris*) was ever considered as a high quality in a general, and we find it recorded among the praises of the most renowned commanders that they were wont in person to perform this duty. Under ordinary circumstances, however, the task was devolved upon one of the military tribunes, and a certain number of centurions appointed from time to time for the purpose. These having gone forward in advance of the army until they reached the place near which it was intended to halt, and having taken a general survey of the ground, selected a spot from whence a good view of the whole proposed area might be obtained. This spot was considerably within the limits of the contemplated enclosure, and was marked by a small white flag. The next object was to ascertain in what direction water and fodder might be most easily and securely provided. These two preliminary points being decided, the business of measuring out the ground (*metari castra*) commenced, and was executed, as we learn from various sources, with graduated rods (*decempedae*) by persons denominated *metatores*. In practice the most important points were marked by white poles, some of which bore flags of various colours, so that the different battalions on reaching the ground could at once discover the place assigned to them. The white flag A, which served as the starting point of the whole construction, marked the position of the consul's tent, or *praetorium*, so called because *praetor* was the ancient term for any one invested with supreme command. A square area was left open, extending a hundred feet each way from the praetorium. The camp was divided into two parts, the upper and the lower. The upper part formed about a third of the whole. In it was the *praetorium* (A) or general's tent. A part of the praetorium was called the *Augurale*, as the auguries were there taken by the general. On the right and left of the praetorium were the *forum* and *quaestorium*; the former a sort of market-place, the latter appropriated to the quaestor and the camp stores under his superintendence. On the sides of and facing the forum and quaestorium, were stationed select bodies of horse

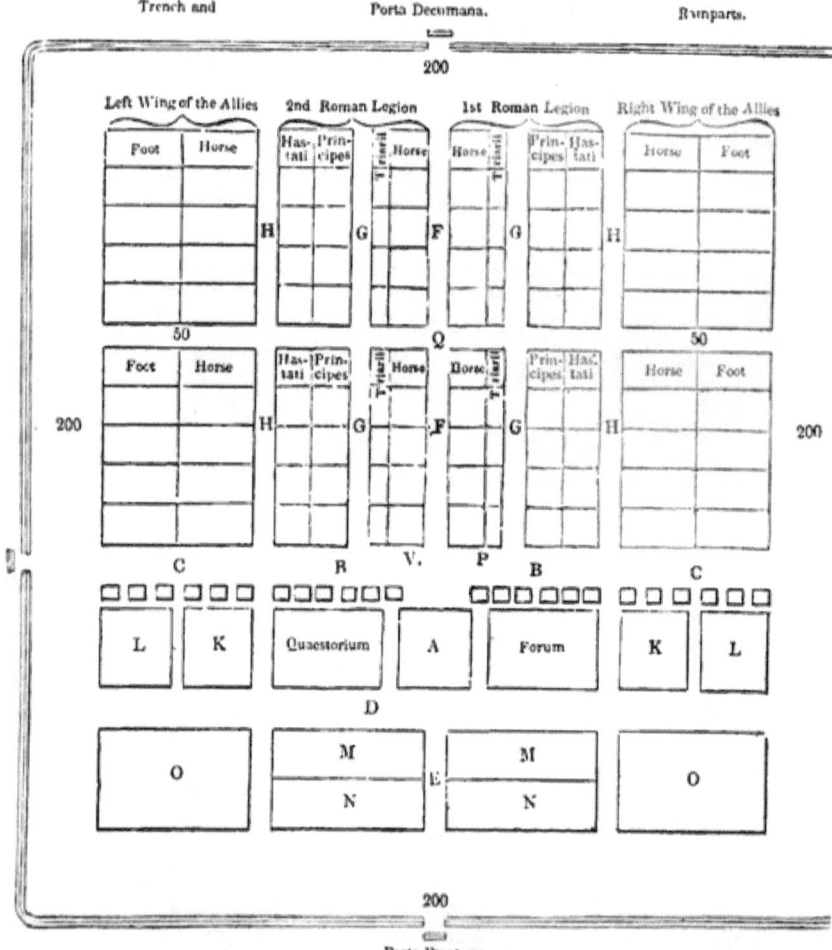

A, praetorium.—B, tents of the tribunes.—C, tents of the praefecti sociorum.—D, street 100 feet wide.—E, F, G, and H, streets 50 feet wide.—L, select foot and volunteers.—K, select horse and volunteers.—M, extraordinary horse of the allies.—N, extraordinary foot of the allies.—O, reserved for occasional auxiliaries.—Q, the street called Quintana, 50 feet wide.—V P, via principalis, 100 feet wide.

(K) taken from the extraordinaries, with mounted volunteers, who served out of respect to the consul, and were stationed near him. And parallel to these were posted similar bodies of foot-soldiers (L). Before the quaestorium and the forum were the tents of the twelve tribunes of the two legions (B), and before the select bodies of horse and infantry the tents of the praefecti sociorum were probably placed (C). Again, behind the praetorium, the quaestorium, and the forum, ran a street or *via* (D), 100 feet broad, from one side of the camp to the other. Along the upper side of this street was ranged the main body of the "extraordinary" horse (M): they were separated into two equal parts by a street fifty feet broad (E). At the back of this body of cavalry was posted a similar body of infantry (N), selected from the allies, and facing the opposite way, *i. e.* towards the ramparts of the camp. The vacant spaces (O) on each side of these troops were reserved for foreigners and occasional auxiliaries. The lower part of the camp was divided from the upper by a street, called the *Via Principalis* (V P), or *Principia*, a hundred feet broad. Here the tribunal of the general was erected, from which he harangued the soldiers, and here the tribunes administered justice. Here also the principal standards, the altars of the gods, and the images of the emperors were placed. The lower part of the camp was occupied by the two legions and the troops of the allies according to the arrangement of the preceding cut. Between the ramparts and the tents was left a vacant space of 200 feet on every side, which was useful for many purposes: thus it served for the reception of any booty that was taken, and facilitated the entrance and exit of the army. The camp had four gates, one at the top and bottom, and one at each of the sides; the top or back-gate, which was the side most away from the enemy, was called the *decumana*. The bottom or the front gate was the *praetoria*, the gates of the sides were the *porta principalis dextra*, and the *porta principalis sinistra*. The whole camp was surrounded by a trench (*fossa*), generally nine feet deep and twelve broad, and a rampart (*vallum*) made of the earth that was thrown up (*agger*), with stakes (*valli*) fixed at the top of it. The labour of this work was so divided, that the allies completed the two sides of the camp alongside of which they were stationed, and the two Roman legions the rest.—In describing the Roman camp and its internal arrangements, we have confined ourselves to the information given by Polybius, which, of course, applies only to his age, and to armies constituted like those he witnessed. When the practice of drawing up the army according to cohorts, ascribed to Marius or Caesar [EXERCITUS], had superseded the ancient division into maniples, and the distinction of triarii, &c., the internal arrangements of the camp must have been changed accordingly. In each legion the tribunes divided themselves into three sections of two each, and each section in turn undertook for two months the superintendence of all matters connected with the camp. Out of the twenty maniples of Principes and Triarii in each legion, two were appointed to take charge of the broad passage or street called *Principia*, extending right across the camp in front of the tents of the tribunes. Of the remaining eighteen maniples of Principes and Hastati in each legion, three were assigned by lot to each of the six tribunes, and of these three maniples one in turn rendered each day certain services to the tribune to whom it was specially attached. One maniple was selected each day from the whole legionary force, to keep guard beside the tent of the general. Three sentinels were usually posted at the tents of the quaestor and of the legati: and by night sentinels kept watch at every maniple, being chosen out of the maniple which they guarded. The Velites mounted guard by day and by night along the whole extent of the vallum: to them also in bodies of ten was committed the charge of the gates, while strong bodies of infantry and cavalry were thrown forward in advance of each gate, to resist any sudden onset, and give timely notice of the approach of the enemy.—*Excubiae; excubias agere; excubare;* are the general terms used with reference to mounting guard whether by night or by day. *Vigiliae; vigilias agere; vigilare;* are restricted to night duty: *Excubiae* and *Vigiliae* frequently denote not only the service itself, but also the individuals who performed it. *Stationes* is used specially to denote the advanced posts thrown forward in front of the gates. *Custodes* or *Custodiae* the parties who watched the gates themselves, *Praesidia* the sentinels on the ramparts, but all these words are employed in many other significations also. The duty of going the rounds (*Vigilias circuire s. circumire*) was committed to the Equites, and for this purpose each legion supplied daily four, picked out from each turma in rotation by the commander of the troop. The eight persons thus selected decided by lot in which watch they should make their rounds, two being assigned to each watch. They then repaired to the tribune, and each individual received a written order specifying the posts which he was to visit, every post being visited in each watch by one or other of the two to whom the watch belonged. Sometimes we find centurions, tribunes, and even the general in chief represented as going the rounds, but, under ordinary circumstances, the duty was performed as we have described. The watchword for the night was not communicated verbally, but by means of a small rectangular tablet of wood (πλατεῖον ἐπιγεγραμμένον—tessera) upon which it was written.—*Breaking up a Camp.* On the first signal being given by the trumpet, the tents were all struck and the baggage packed, the tents of the general and the tribunes being disposed of before the others were touched. At the second signal the baggage was placed upon the beasts of burden; at the third, the whole army began to move.

CATĂLŎGUS (κατάλογος), the catalogue of those persons in Athens who were liable to regular military service. At Athens, those persons alone who possessed a certain amount of property were allowed to serve in the regular infantry, whilst the lowest class, the thetes, had not this privilege. [CENSUS.] Thus the former are called οἱ ἐκ καταλόγου στρατεύοντες, and the latter οἱ ἔξω τοῦ καταλόγου.

CATĂPHRACTA. [LORICA.]

CATĂPHRACTI (κατάφρακτοι). (1) Heavy-armed cavalry, the horses of which were also covered with defensive armour. Among many of the Eastern nations, who placed their chief dependence upon their cavalry, we find horses protected in this manner; but among the Romans we do not read of any troops of this description till the later times of the empire, when the discipline of the legions was destroyed, and the chief dependence began to be placed on the cavalry. This species of troops was common among the Persians from the earliest times, from whom it was adopted by their Macedonian conquerors. They were called by the Persians *clibanarii.*—(2) Decked vessels, in opposition to *Aphracti.*

CATĂPĪRĀTĒR (καταπειρατηρία, βολίς), the lead used in sounding (ἐν τῷ βολίζειν), or fathoming the depth of water in navigation. The mode of employing this instrument appears to have been precisely the same as that now in use.

CATĂPULTA. [TORMENTUM.]

CATĂRACTA (καταρράκτης), a portcullis, so called because it fell with great force and a loud noise. It was an additional defence, suspended by iron rings and ropes, before the gates of a city, in such a manner that, when the enemy had come up to the gates, the portcullis might be let down so as to shut them in, and to enable the besieged to assail them from above.

CĀTEIA, a missile used in war by the Germans, Gauls, and some of the Italian nations, supposed to resemble the ACLIS.

CATĒNA, dim. CATELLA (ἅλυσις, dim. ἁλύσιον, ἁλυσίδιον), a chain. The chains which were of superior value, either on account of the material or the workmanship, are commonly called *catellae* (ἁλύσια), the diminutive expressing their fineness and delicacy as well as their minuteness. The specimens of ancient chains which we have in bronze lamps, in scales, and in ornaments for the person, especially necklaces, show a great variety of elegant and ingenious patterns. Besides a plain circle or oval, the separate link is often shaped like the figure 8, or is a bar with a circle at each end, or assumes other forms, some of which are here shown. The

Ancient Chains.

links are also found so closely entwined, that the chain resembles platted wire or thread, like the gold chains now manufactured at Venice. This is represented in the lowest figure of the woodcut.

CATERVĀRĬI. [GLADIATORES.]

CATHEDRA, a seat or chair, was more particularly applied to a soft seat used by

Cathedra. (From a Painting on a Vase.)

women, whereas *sella* signified a seat common to both sexes. The cathedrae were, no doubt, of various forms and sizes; but they usually appear to have had backs to them. On the cathedra in the annexed cut is seated a bride, who is being fanned by a female slave with a fan made of peacock's feathers. Women were also accustomed to be carried abroad in these cathedrae instead of in lecticae, which practice was sometimes adopted by effeminate persons of the other sex. The word cathedra was also applied to the chair or pulpit from which lectures were read.

CĀTĪNUS, or CĀTĪNUM, a large dish, on which fish and meat were served up at table. Hence Horace speaks of an *angustus catinus* as an indication of niggardliness on the part of the host.

CĂVAEDĪUM. [DOMUS.]
CĂVĔA. [THEATRUM.]
CAUPŌNA. (1) An inn, where travellers obtained food and lodging; in which sense it answered to the Greek words πανδοκεῖον, καταγώγιον, and κατάλυσις. Inns for the accommodation of persons of all classes existed among the Greeks and Romans, although they were not equal either in size or convenience to similar places in modern times. An inn was also called *taberna* and *taberna diversoria*, or simply *diversorium* or *deversorium*.—(2) A shop, where wine and ready-dressed meat were sold, thus corresponding to the Greek καπηλεῖον. The person who kept a caupona was called *caupo*. In Greek κάπηλος signifies in general a retail trader, who sold goods in small quantities; but the word is more particularly applied to a person who sold ready-dressed provisions, and especially wine in small quantities. In these καπηλεῖα only persons of the very lowest class were accustomed to eat and drink. In Rome itself there were, no doubt, inns to accommodate strangers; but these were probably only frequented by the lower classes, since all persons in respectable society could easily find accommodation in the houses of their friends. There were, however, in all parts of the city, numerous houses where wine and ready-dressed provisions were sold. The houses where persons were allowed to eat and drink were usually called *popinae* and not *cauponae*; and the keepers of them, *popae*. They were principally frequented by slaves and the lower classes, and were consequently only furnished with stools to sit upon instead of couches. The *Thermopolia*, where the *calida* or warm wine and water was sold, appear to have been the same as the *popinae*. Many of these popinae were little better than the *lupanaria* or brothels; whence Horace calls them *immundas popinas*. The *ganeae*, which are sometimes mentioned in connection with the *popinae*, were brothels, whence they are often classed with the *lustra*. Under the emperors many attempts were made to regulate the popinae, but apparently with little success. All persons who kept inns or houses of public entertainment of any kind were held in low estimation both among the Greeks and Romans. They appear to have fully deserved the bad reputation which they possessed, for they were accustomed to cheat their customers by false weights and measures, and by all the means in their power.

CAUSĬA (καυσία), a hat with a broad brim, which was made of felt, and worn by the Macedonian kings. Its form is seen in the annexed figure. The Romans adopted it from the Macedonians.

Causia, Hat. (From a Painting on a Vase.)

CAUTIO, CĂVĒRE. These words are of frequent occurrence, and have a great variety of significations, according to the matter to which they refer. Their general signification is that of security given by one person to another, or security which one person obtains by the advice or assistance of another. The *cautio* was most frequently a writing, which expressed the object of the parties to it; accordingly the word cautio came to signify both the instrument (*chirographum* or *instrumentum*) and the object which it was the purpose of the instrument to secure. Cicero uses the expression *cautio chirographi mei*. The phrase *cavere aliquid alicui* expressed the fact of one person giving security to another as to some particular thing or act. The word *cautio* was also applied to the release which a debtor obtained from his creditor on satisfying his demand; in this sense *cautio* is equivalent to a modern receipt; it is the debtor's security against the same demand being made a second time. Thus *cavere ab aliquo* signifies to obtain this kind of security. *Cavere* is also applied to express the professional advice and assistance of a lawyer to his client for his conduct in any legal matter. *Cavere* and its derivatives are also used to express the provisions of a law, by which any thing is forbidden or ordered, as in the phrase, *Cautum est lege*, &c. It is also used to express the words in a will, by which a testator declares his wish that certain things should be done after his death.

CEADAS or CAEADAS (κεάδας or καιάδας), a deep cavern or chasm, like the Barathron at Athens, into which the Spartans were accustomed to thrust persons condemned to death.

CELERES, are said by Livy to have been three hundred horsemen, who formed the body-guard of Romulus both in peace and war. There can, however, be little doubt that these Celeres were not simply the body-guard of the king, but were the same as the equites, or horsemen, a fact which is expressly stated by some writers. [EQUITES.] The etymology of Celeres is variously given. Some writers derived it from their leader Celer, who was said to have slain Remus, but most writers connected it with the Greek κέλης, in reference to the quickness of their service. The Celeres were under the command of a *Tribunus Celerum*, who stood in the same relation to the king as the magister equitum did in a subsequent period to the dictator. He occupied the second place in the state, and in the absence of the king had the right of convoking the comitia. Whether he was appointed by the king, or elected by the comitia, has been questioned, but the former is the more probable.

CELLA, in its primary sense, means a store-room of any kind. Of these there were various descriptions, which took their distinguishing denominations from the articles they contained, as, for instance, the *cella penuaria* or *penaria*, the *cella olearia* and *cella vinaria*. The slave to whom the charge of these stores was intrusted, was called *cellarius*, or *promus*, or *condus*, "quia promit quod *conditum est*," and sometimes *promus condus* and *procurator peni*. This answers to our butler and housekeeper. Any number of small rooms clustered together like the cells of a honeycomb were also termed *cellae*; hence the dormitories of slaves and menials are called *cellae*, and *cellae familiaricae*, in distinction to a bed-chamber, which was *cubiculum*. Thus a sleeping-room at a public-house is also termed *cella*. *Cella ostiarii*, or *janitoris*, is the porter's lodge. In the baths the *cella caldaria*, *tepidaria*, and *frigidaria*, were those which contained respectively the warm, tepid, and cold bath. [BALNEAE.] The interior of a temple, that is the part included within the outside shell (σηκός), was also called *cella*. There was sometimes more than one *cella* within the same peristyle or under the same roof, in which case each cell took the name of the deity whose statue it contained, as *cella* Jovis, *cella* Junonis, *cella* Minervae, as in the temple of Jupiter on the Capitoline.

CENOTAPHIUM, a cenotaph (κενός and τάφος), was an empty or honorary tomb, erected as a memorial of a person whose body was buried elsewhere, or not found for burial at all.

CENSOR (τιμητής), the name of two magistrates of high rank in the Roman republic. Their office was called *Censura* (τιμητεία or τιμητία). The *Census*, which was a register of Roman citizens and of their property, was first established by Servius Tullius, the fifth king of Rome. After the expulsion of the kings it was taken by the consuls; and special magistrates were not appointed for the purpose of taking it till the year B.C. 443. The reason of this alteration was owing to the appointment in the preceding year of tribuni militum with consular power in place of the consuls; and as these tribunes might be plebeians, the patricians deprived the consuls, and consequently their representatives, the tribunes, of the right of taking the census, and entrusted it to two magistrates, called *Censores*, who were to be chosen exclusively from the patricians. The magistracy continued to be a patrician one till B.C. 351, when C. Marcius Rutilus was the first plebeian censor. Twelve years afterwards, B.C. 339, it was provided by one of the Publilian laws, that one of the censors must necessarily be a plebeian, but it was not till B.C. 280 that a plebeian censor performed the solemn purification of the people (*lustrum condidit*). In B.C. 131 the two censors were for the first time plebeians.—The censors were elected in the comitia centuriata held under the presidency of a consul. As a general principle, the only persons eligible to the office were those who had previously been consuls; but a few exceptions occur. At first there was no law to prevent a person being censor a second time; but the only person, who was twice elected to the office, was C. Marcius Rutilus in B.C. 265; and he brought forward a law in this year, enacting that no one should be chosen censor a second time, and received in consequence the surname of Censorinus.—The censorship is distinguished from all other Roman magistracies by the length of time during which it was held The censors were originally chosen for a whole lustrum, that is, a period of five years; but their office was limited to eighteen months as early as ten years after its institution (B.C. 433), by a law of the dictator Mam. Aemilius Mamercinus. The censors also held a very peculiar position with respect to rank and dignity. No imperium was bestowed upon them, and accordingly they had no lictors. The *jus censurae* was granted to them by a *lex centuriata*, and not by the curiae, and in that respect they were inferior in power to the consuls and praetors. But notwithstanding this, the censorship was regarded as the highest dignity in the state, with the exception of the dictatorship; it was a *sanctus magistratus*, to which the deepest reverence was due. They possessed of course the sella curulis. The funeral of a censor was always conducted with great pomp and splendour, and hence a *funus censorium* was voted even to the emperors.—The censorship continued in existence for 421 years, namely, from B.C. 443 to B.C. 22; but during this period many lustra passed by without any censor being chosen at all. Its power was limited by one of the laws of the tribune Clodius (B.C. 58). After the year B.C. 22 the emperors discharged the duties of the censorship under the name of *Praefectura Morum*.—The duties of the censors may be divided into three classes, all of which were however closely connected with one another: I. *The Census*, or register of the citizens and of their property, in which were included the *lectio senatus*, and the *recognitio equitum*; II. *The Regimen Morum*; and III. *The administration of the finances of the state*, under which were classed the superintendence of the public buildings and the erection of all new public works.—1. The Census, the first and principal duty of the censors, for which the proper expression is *censum agere*, was always held in the Campus Martius, and from the year B.C. 435 in a special building called *Villa Publica*. After the auspicia had been taken, the citizens were summoned by a public crier (*praeco*) to appear before the censors. Each tribe was called up separately, and every paterfamilias had to appear in person before the censors, who were seated in their curule chairs. The census was conducted *ad arbitrium censoris*; but the censors laid down certain rules, sometimes called *leges censui censendo*, in which mention was made of the different kinds of property subject to the census, and in what way their value was to be estimated. According to these laws each citizen had to give an account of himself, of his family, and of his property upon oath, *ex animi sententia*. First he had to give his full name (*praenomen, nomen*, and *cognomen*) and that of his father, or if he were a freedman that of his patron, and he was likewise obliged to state his age. He was then asked, *Tu, ex animi tui sententia, uxorem habes?* and if married he had to give the name of his wife, and likewise the number, names, and ages of his children, if any. Single women (*viduae*) and orphans (*orbi orbaeque*) were represented by their tutores; their names were entered in separate lists, and they were not included in the sum total of capita. After a citizen had stated his name, age, family, &c., he then had to give an account of all his property, so far as it was subject to the census. In making this statement he was said *censere* or *censeri*, as a deponent, "to value or estimate himself," or as a passive "to be valued or estimated:" the censor, who received the statement, was also said *censere*, as well as *accipere censum*. Only such things were liable to the census (*censui censendo*) as were property *ex jure Quiritium*. Land formed the most important article in the census; next came slaves and cattle. The censors also possessed the right of calling for a return of such objects as had not usually been given in, such as clothing, jewels, and carriages. We can hardly doubt that the censors possessed the power of setting a higher valuation on the property than the citizens themselves had put. The tax (*tributum*) was usually one per thousand upon the property entered in the books of the censors; but on one occasion the censors, as a punishment, compelled a person to pay eight per thousand (*octuplicato censu*, Liv. iv. 24). A person who voluntarily absented himself from the census, and thus became *incensus*, was subject to the severest punishment. It is probable that service in the army was a valid excuse for absence. After the censors had received the names of all the citizens with the amount of their property, they then had to make out the lists of the tribes, and also of the classes and centuries; for by the legislation of Servius Tullius the position of each citizen in the state was determined by the amount of his property. [COMITIA CENTURIATA.] These lists formed a most important part of the *Tabulae Censoriae*, under which name were included all the documents connected in any way with the discharge of the censors' duties. These lists, as far at least as they were connected with the finances of the state, were deposited in the aerarium, which was the temple of Saturn; but the regular depository for all the archives of the censors was in earlier times the Atrium Libertatis, near the Villa publica, and in later times the temple of the Nymphs. The censors had also to make out the lists of the senators for the ensuing lustrum, or till new censors were appointed; striking out the names of such as they considered unworthy, and making additions to the body from those who were qualified. [SENATUS.] In the same manner they held a review of the equites equo publico, and added and removed names as they judged proper. [EQUITES.] After the lists had been completed, the number of citizens was counted up, and the sum total announced; and accordingly we find that, in the account of a census, the number of citizens is likewise usually given. They are in such cases spoken of as *capita*, sometimes with the addition of the word *civium*, and sometimes not; and hence to be registered in the census was the same thing as *caput habere*. [CAPUT.]—II. REGIMEN MORUM. This was the most important branch of the censors' duties, and the one which caused their office to be the most revered and the most dreaded in the Roman state. It naturally grew out of the right which they possessed of excluding unworthy persons from the lists of citizens. They were constituted the conservators of public and private virtue and morality; they were not simply to prevent crime or particular acts of immorality, but their great object was to maintain the old Roman character and habits, the *mos majorum*. The proper expression for this branch of their power was *regimen morum*, which was called in the times of the empire *cura* or *praefectura morum*. The punishment inflicted by the censors in the exercise of this branch of their duties was called *Nota* or *Notatio*, or *Animadversio Censoria*. In inflicting it they were guided only by their conscientious convictions of duty; they had to take an oath that they would act neither through partiality nor favour; and in addition to this, they were bound in every case to state in their lists, opposite the name of the guilty citizen, the cause of the punishment inflicted on him,—*Subscriptio censoria*. The consequence of such a nota was only *ignominia* and not *infamia* [INFAMIA], and the censorial verdict was not a *judicium* or *res judicata*, for its effects were not lasting, but might be removed by the following censors, or by a lex. A nota censoria was moreover not valid, unless both censors agreed. The ignominia was thus only a transitory capitis deminutio, which does not appear even to have deprived a magistrate of his office, and certainly did not disqualify persons labouring under it for obtaining a magistracy, for being appointed as judices by the praetor, or for serving in the Roman armies. This superintendence of the conduct of Roman citizens extended so far, that it embraced the whole of the public and private life of the citizens. Thus we have instances of their censuring or punishing persons for not marrying, for breaking a promise of marriage, for divorce, for bad conduct during marriage, for improper education of children, for living in an extravagant and luxurious manner, and for many other irregularities in private life. Their influence was still more powerful in matters connected with the public life of the citizens. Thus we find them censuring or punishing magistrates who were forgetful of the dignity of their office or guilty of bribery, as well as persons who were guilty of improper conduct towards magistrates, of perjury, and of neglect of their duties both in civil and military life. The punishments inflicted by the censors are generally divided into four classes :—1. *Motio* or *ejectio e senatu*, or the exclusion of a man from the number of senators. This punishment might either be a simple exclusion from the list of senators, or the person might at the same time be excluded from the tribes and degraded to the rank of an aerarian. The censors in their new lists omitted the names of such senators as they wished to exclude, and in reading these new lists in public, passed over the names of those who were no longer to be senators. Hence the expression *praeteriti senatores* is equivalent to *e senatu ejecti*. 2. The *ademptio equi*, or the taking away the equus publicus from an eques. This punishment might likewise be simple, or combined with the exclusion from the tribes and the degradation to the rank of an aerarian. [EQUITES.] 3. The *motio e tribu*, or the exclusion of a person from his tribe. If the further degradation to the rank of an aerarian was combined with the motio e tribu, it was always expressly stated. 4. The fourth punishment was called *referre in aerarios* or *facere aliquem aerarium*, and might be inflicted on any person who was thought by the censors to deserve it. [AERARII.]—III. THE ADMINISTRATION OF THE FINANCES OF THE STATE, was another part of the censors' office. In the first place the *tributum*, or property-tax, had to be paid by each citizen according to the amount of his property registered in the census, and, accordingly, the regulation of this tax naturally fell under the jurisdiction of the censors. [TRIBUTUM.] They also had the superintendence of all the other revenues of the state, the *vectigalia*, such as the tithes paid for the public lands, the salt works, the mines, the customs, &c. [VECTIGALIA.] All these branches of the revenue the censors were accustomed to let out to the highest bidder for the space of a lustrum or five years. The act of letting was called *venditio* or *locatio*, and seems to have taken place in the month of March. The censors also possessed the right, though probably not without the concurrence of the senate, of imposing new vectigalia, and even of selling the land belonging to the state.

The censors, however, did not receive the revenues of the state. All the public money was paid into the aerarium, which was entirely under the jurisdiction of the senate; and all disbursements were made by order of this body, which employed the quaestors as its officers. [AERARIUM; SENATUS.]—In one important department the censors were entrusted with the expenditure of the public money; though the actual payments were no doubt made by the quaestors. The censors had the general superintendence of all the public buildings and works (*opera publica*); and to meet the expenses connected with this part of their duties, the senate voted them a certain sum of money or certain revenues, to which they were restricted, but which they might at the same time employ according to their discretion. They had to see that the temples and all other public buildings were in a good state of repair (*aedes sacras tueri* and *sarta tecta exigere*), that no public places were encroached upon by the occupation of private persons (*loca tueri*), and that the aqueducts, roads, drains, &c. were properly attended to. The repairs of the public works and the keeping of them in proper condition were let out by the censors by public auction to the lowest bidder. The persons who undertook the contract were called *conductores, mancipes, redemptores, susceptores*, &c.; and the duties they had to discharge were specified in the *Leges Censoriae*. The censors had also to superintend the expenses connected with the worship of the gods. In these respects it is not easy to define with accuracy the respective duties of the censors and aediles: but it may be remarked in general that the superintendence of the aediles had more of a police character, while that of the censors had reference to all financial matters.—After the censors had performed their various duties and taken the census, the *lustrum* or solemn purification of the people followed. When the censors entered upon their office, they drew lots to see which of them should perform this purification (*lustrum facere* or *condere*), but both censors were obliged of course to be present at the ceremony. [LUSTRUM.]—In the Roman and Latin colonies and in the municipia there were censors, who likewise bore the name of *quinquennales*. They are spoken of under COLONIA. A census was sometimes taken in the provinces, even under the republic; but there seems to have been no general census taken in the provinces till the time of Augustus. At Rome the census still continued to be taken under the empire, but the old ceremonies connected with it were no longer continued, and the ceremony of the lustration was not performed after the time of Vespasian.—The word *census*, besides the meaning of "valuation" of a person's estate, has other significations, which must be briefly mentioned: 1. It signified the amount of a person's property, and hence we read of *census senatorius*, the estate of a senator; *census equestris*, the estate of an eques. 2. The lists of the censors. 3. The tax which depended upon the valuation in the census.

CENSUS.—(1) GREEK.—The Greek term for a man's property as ascertained by the census, as well as for the act of ascertaining it, is τίμημα. The only Greek state concerning whose arrangement of the census we have any satisfactory information, is Athens. Previous to the time of Solon no census had been instituted at Athens. According to his census, all citizens were divided into four classes: 1. *Pentacosiomedimni* (Πεντακοσιομέδιμνοι), or persons possessing landed property which yielded an annual income of at least 500 medimni of dry or liquid produce. 2. *Hippeis* ('Ιππεῖς), i. e. knights or persons able to keep a war-horse, were those whose lands yielded an annual produce of at least 300 medimni, whence they are also called τριακοσιομέδιμνοι. 3. *Zeugitae* (Ζευγῖται), i. e. persons able to keep a yoke of oxen (ζεῦγος), were those whose annual income consisted of at least 150 medimni. 4. The *Thetes* (Θῆτες) contained all the rest of the free population, whose income was below that of the Zeugitae. The constitution of Athens, so long as it was based upon these classes, was a timocracy (τιμοκρατία, or ἀπὸ τιμημάτων πολιτεία). The highest magistracy at Athens, or the archonship, was at first accessible only to persons of the first class, until Aristides threw all the state offices open to all classes indiscriminately. The maintenance of the republic mainly devolved upon the first three classes, the last being exempted from all taxes. As the land in the legislation of Solon was regarded as the capital which yielded an annual income, he regulated his system of taxation by the value of the land, which was treated as the taxable capital. Lists of this taxable property (ἀπογραφαί) were kept at first by the naucrari, who also had to conduct the census, and afterwards by the demarchi.—As property is a fluctuating thing, the census was repeated from time to time, but the periods differed in the various parts of Greece, for in some a census was held every year, and in others every two or four years. At Athens every person had to state the amount of his property, and if there was any doubt about his honesty, it seems that a counter-valuation (ἀντιτίμησις) might be made.

G

This system of taxation according to classes, and based upon the possession of productive estates, underwent a considerable change in the time of the Peloponnesian war, though the divisions into classes themselves continued to be observed for a considerable time after. As the wants of the republic increased, and as many citizens were possessed of large property, without being landed proprietors, the original land-tax was changed into a property-tax. This property-tax was called εἰσφορά, concerning which see FISPHORA. Compare LEITURGIAE; and for the taxes paid by resident aliens, METOICI.—(2) ROMAN. [CENSOR.]

CENTESIMA, namely *pars*, or the hundredth part, also called *vectigal rerum venalium*, or *centesima rerum venalium*, was a tax of one per cent. levied at Rome and in Italy upon all goods that were exposed for public sale at auctions. It was collected by persons called *coactores*. This tax was perhaps introduced after the civil war between Marius and Sulla. Its produce was assigned by Augustus to the *aerarium militare*. Tiberius reduced the tax to one half per cent. (*ducentesima*), after he had changed Cappadocia into a province, and had thereby increased the revenue of the empire. Caligula in the beginning of his reign abolished the tax altogether for Italy.

CENTUMVIRI, were judices, who resembled other judices in this respect, that they decided cases under the authority of a magistratus; but they differed from other judices in being a definite body or collegium. This collegium seems to have been divided into four parts, each of which sometimes sat by itself. The origin of the court is unknown. According to an ancient writer, three were chosen out of each tribe, and consequently the whole number out of the 35 tribes would be 105, who, in round numbers, were called the hundred men. If the centumviri were chosen from the tribes, this seems a strong presumption in favour of the high antiquity of the court. It was the practice to set up a spear in the place where the centumviri were sitting, and accordingly the word *hasta*, or *hasta centumviralis*, is sometimes used as equivalent to the words *judicium centumvirale*. The praetor presided in this court. The jurisdiction of the centumviri was chiefly confined to civil matters, but it appears that crimina sometimes came under their cognizance. The younger Pliny, who practised in this court, makes frequent allusions to it in his letters.

CENTURIA. [EXERCITUS; COMITIA.]
CENTURIATA COMITIA. [COMITIA.]
CENTURIO. [EXERCITUS.]

CENTUSSIS. [As.]

CERA (κηρός), wax. For its employment in painting, see PICTURA; and for its application as a writing material, see TABULAE and TESTAMENTUM.

CEREALIA, a festival celebrated at Rome in honour of Ceres, whose wanderings in search of her lost daughter Proserpine were represented by women, clothed in white, running about with lighted torches. During its continuance, games were celebrated in the Circus Maximus, the spectators of which appeared in white; but on any occasion of public mourning the games and festivals were not celebrated at all, as the matrons could not appear at them except in white. The day of the Cerealia is doubtful; some think it was the ides or 13th of April, others the 7th of the same month.

CEREVISIA, CERVISIA (ζῦθος), ale or beer, was almost or altogether unknown to the Greeks and Romans; but it was used very generally by the surrounding nations, whose soil and climate were less favourable to the growth of vines. According to Herodotus, the Egyptians commonly drank "barley wine;" and Diodorus Siculus says that the Egyptian beer was nearly equal to wine in strength and flavour. The Iberians and Thracians, and the people in the north of Asia Minor, instead of drinking their beer out of cups, placed it before them in a large bowl or vase, which was sometimes of gold or silver. This being full to the brim with the grains, as well as the fermented liquor, the guests, when they pledged one another, drank together out of the same bowl by stooping down to it, although, when this token of friendship was not intended, they adopted the more refined method of sucking up the fluid through tubes of cane. The Suevi and other northern nations offered to their gods libations of beer, and expected that to drink it in the presence of Odin would be among the delights of Valhalla.

CEROMA (κήρωμα), the oil mixed with wax (κηρός) with which wrestlers were anointed; also the place where they were anointed, and, in later times, the place where they wrestled.

CERUCHI. [NAVIS.]
CESTRUM. [PICTURA.]

CESTUS. (1) The thongs or bands of leather, which were tied round the hands of boxers, in order to render their blows more powerful (ἱμάντες, or ἱμάντες πυκτικοί). The cestus was used by boxers in the earliest times, and is mentioned in the Iliad; but in the heroic times it consisted merely of thongs of leather, and differed from the cestus used in later times in the public games, which was a most formidable weapon, being frequently covered with knots and nails, and loaded with lead and iron.—(2) A band or tie of any

Cestus. (Fabretti, de Col. Traj., p. 261.)

kind, but more particularly the zone or girdle of Venus, on which was represented every thing that could awaken love.

CETRA, or CAETRA, a target, *i. e.* a small round shield, made of the hide of a quadruped. It formed part of the defensive armour of the Osci, and of the people of Spain, Mauritania, and Britain, and seems to have been much the same as the target of the Scotch Highlanders. The Romans do not appear to have used the cetra; but we find mention of *cetratae cohortes* levied in the provinces. Livy compares it to the *pelta* of the Greeks and Macedonians, which was also a small light shield.

CHALCIOECIA (χαλκιοίκια), an annual festival, with sacrifices, held at Sparta in honour of Athena, surnamed *Chalcioecus* (Χαλκίοικος), i. e. the goddess of the brazen-house. Young men marched on the occasion in full armour to the temple of the goddess; and the ephors, although not entering the temple, but remaining within its sacred precincts, were obliged to take part in the sacrifice.

CHALCUS (χαλκοῦς), a denomination of Greek copper-money. Bronze or copper (χαλκός) was very little used by the Greeks for money till after the time of Alexander the Great. The χαλκία πονηρά at Athens issued in B. C. 406 were a peculiar exception; and they were soon afterwards called in, and the silver currency restored. It is not improbable, however, that the copper coin called χαλκοῦς was in circulation in Athens still earlier. The smallest silver coin at Athens was the quarter obol, and the χαλκοῦς was the half of that, or the eighth of an obol. Its value was somewhat more than 3-4ths of a farthing. The χαλκοῦς in later times was divided into *lepta*, of which it contained seven. In later times the obol was coined of copper as well as silver.

CHARISTIA (from χαρίζομαι, to grant a favour or pardon), a solemn feast among the Romans, to which none but relations and members of the same family were invited, in order that any quarrel or disagreement which had arisen amongst them might be made up. The day of celebration was the 19th of February.

CHEIRONOMIA (χειρονομία), a mimetic movement of the hands, which formed a part of the art of dancing among the Greeks and Romans. In gymnastics it was applied to the movements of the hands in pugilistic combat.

CHEIROTONIA (χειροτονία). In the Athenian assemblies two modes of voting were practised, the one by pebbles (ψηφίζεσθαι), the other by a show of hands (χειροτονεῖν). The latter was employed in the election of those magistrates who were chosen in the public assemblies, and who were hence called χειροτονητοί, in voting upon laws, and in some kinds of trials on matters which concerned the people. We frequently find, however, the word ψηφίζεσθαι used where the votes were really given by show of hands. The manner of voting by a show of hands was as follows:—The herald said: "Whoever thinks that Meidias is guilty, let him lift up his hand." Then those who thought so stretched forth their hands. Then the herald said again: "Whoever thinks that Meidias is not guilty, let him lift up his hand;" and those who were of this opinion stretched forth their hands. The number of hands was counted each time by the herald; and the president, upon the herald's report, declared on which side the majority voted. It is important to understand clearly the compounds of this word. A vote condemning an accused person is καταχειροτονία; one acquitting him, ἀποχειροτονία; ἐπιχειροτονεῖν is to confirm by a majority of votes: ἐπιχειροτονία τῶν νόμων was a revision of the laws, which took place at the beginning of every year: ἐπιχειροτονία τῶν ἀρχῶν was a vote taken in the first assembly of each prytany on the conduct of the magistrates; in these cases, those who voted for the confirmation of the law, or for the continuance in office of the magistrate, were said ἐπιχειροτονεῖν, those on the other side ἀποχειροτονεῖν: διαχειροτονία is a vote for one of two alternatives: ἀντιχειροτονεῖν, to vote against a proposition. The compounds of ψηφίζεσθαι have similar meanings.

CHIROGRAPHUM (χειρόγραφον), meant first, as its derivation implies, a hand-writing or autograph. In this its simple sense, χείρ in Greek and *manus* in Latin are often substituted for it. From this meaning was easily derived that of a signature to a will or other instrument, especially a note of hand given by a debtor to his creditor.

CHITON (χιτών). [TUNICA.]

CHLAENA (χλαῖνα). [PALLIUM.]

CHLĂMYS (χλαμύς, dim. χλαμύδιον), a scarf, denoted an article of the *amictus*, or outer raiment of the Greeks. It was for the most part woollen; and it differed from the *himation* (ἱμάτιον), or cloak, the usual amictus of the male sex, in being smaller, finer, and oblong instead of square, its length being generally about twice its breadth. The scarf does not appear to have been much worn by children. It was generally assumed on reaching adolescence, and was worn by the ephebi from about seventeen to twenty years of age, and hence was called χλαμὺς ἐφηβηκή. It was also worn by the military, especially of high rank, over their body armour, and by hunters and travellers, more particularly on horseback. The usual mode of wearing the scarf was to pass one of its shorter sides round the neck, and to fasten it by means of a brooch (*fibula*), either over the breast (cut, HASTA), in which case it hung down the back, or over the right shoulder, so as to cover the left arm (cut, CAUSIA). In the following cut it is worn again in another way. The apti-

Chlamys. (Neptune from a Coin, and Diana from a Statue in the Vatican.)

scarf came more into use under the emperors. Caligula wore one enriched with gold. Severus, when he was in the country or on an expedition, wore a scarf dyed with the coccus.

CHOENIX (χοῖνιξ), a Greek measure of capacity, the ze of which is differently given; it was probably of different sizes in the several states. Some writers make it equal to three cotylae (nearly 1½ pints English); others to four cotylae (nearly 2 pints English); others again make it eight cotylae (nearly 4 pints English).

CHŎRĒGUS (χορηγός), a person who had to bear the expenses of the choregia (χορηγία), one of the regularly recurring state burthens (ἐγκύκλιοι λειτουργίαι) at Athens. The choregus was appointed by his tribe, though we are not informed according to what order. The same person might serve as choregus for two tribes at once; and after B.C. 412 a decree was passed allowing two persons to unite and undertake a choregia together. The duties of the choregia consisted in providing the choruses for tragedies and comedies, the lyric choruses of men and boys, the pyrrhicists, the cyclic choruses, and the choruses of flute-players for the different religious festivals at Athens. When a poet intended to bring out a play, he had to get a chorus assigned him by the archon [CHORUS], who nominated a choregus to fulfil the requisite duties. He had first to collect his chorus, and then to procure a teacher (χοροδιδάσκαλος), whom he paid for instructing the choreutae. The chorus were generally maintained, during the period of their instruction, at the expense of the choregus. The choregus who exhi-

Chlamys. (The Figure on the left from a Painting on a Vase; that on the right from the Brit. Mus.)

tude of the scarf to be turned in every possible form around the body, made it useful even for defence. The hunter used to wrap his chlamys about his left arm when pursuing wild animals, and preparing to fight with them. The annexed woodcut exhibits a figure of Neptune armed with the trident in his right hand, and having a chlamys to protect the left. When Diana goes to the chase, as she does not require her scarf for purposes of defence, she draws it from behind over her shoulders, and twists it round her

bited the best musical or theatrical entertainment received as a prize a tripod, which he had the expense of consecrating, and sometimes he had also to build the monument on which it was placed. There was a whole street at Athens formed by the line of these tripod-temples, and called "The Street of the Tripods."

CHŌRUS (χορός) probably signified originally a company of dancers dancing in a ring. In later times, a choric performance always implies the singing or musical recitation of a poetical composition, accompanied by appropriate dancing and gesticulation, or at least by a measured march. In all the Dorian states, especially among the Spartans, choral performances were cultivated with great assiduity. Various causes contributed to this, as, for example, their universal employment in the worship of Apollo, the fact that they were not confined to the men, but that women also took part in them, and that many of the dances had a gymnastic character given them, and were employed as a mode of training to martial exercises. [SALTATIO.] Hence Doric lyric poetry became almost exclusively choral, which was not the case with the other great school of Greek lyric poetry, the Aeolian ; so that the Doric dialect came to be looked upon as the appropriate dialect for choral compositions, and Doric forms were retained by the Athenians even in the choral compositions which were interwoven with their dramas. The instrument commonly used in connection with the Doric choral poetry was the cithara. A great impetus was given to choral poetry by its application to the dithyramb. This ancient Bacchanalian performance seems to have been a hymn sung by one or more of an irregular band of revellers, to the music of the flute. Arion, a contemporary of Periander, was the first who gave a regular choral form to the dithyramb. This chorus, which ordinarily consisted of fifty men or youths, danced in a ring round the altar of Dionysus. Hence such choruses were termed *cyclic* (κύκλιοι χοροί). With the introduction of a regular choral character, Arion also substituted the cithara for the flute. It was from the dithyramb that the Attic tragedy was developed. For details see TRAGOEDIA. From the time of Sophocles onwards the regular number of the chorus in a tragedy was 15 ; but it is impossible to arrive at any definite conclusion with regard to the number of the chorus in the early dramas of Aeschylus. The fact that the number of the dithyrambic chorus was 50, and that the mythological number of the Oceanides and Danaides was the same, tempts one to suppose that the chorus in the Prometheus and the Supplices consisted of 50. Most writers, however, agree in thinking that such a number was too large to have been employed. The later chorus of 15 was arranged in a quadrangular form (τετράγωνος). It entered the theatre by the passage to the right of the spectators. [THEATRUM.] Its entrance was termed πάροδος ; its leaving the stage in the course of the play μετάστασις ; its re-entrance ἐπιπάροδος ; its exit ἄφοδος. As it entered in three lines, with the spectators on its left, the stage on its right, the middle choreutes of the left row (τρίτος ἀριστέρου) was the Coryphaeus or Hegemon, who in early times at least was not unfrequently the choregus himself. Of course the positions first taken up by the choreutae were only retained till they commenced their evolutions. To guide them in these, lines were marked upon the boards with which the orchestra was floored. The flute as well as the cithara was used as an accompaniment to the choric songs. The dance of the tragic chorus was called ἐμμέλεια.—The ordinary number of the chorus in a comedy was 24. Like the tragic chorus it was arranged in a quadrangular form, and entered the orchestra from opposite sides, according as it was supposed to come from the city or from the country. It consisted sometimes half of male and half of female choreutae. The dance of the comic chorus was the κόρδαξ. In the Satyric drama the chorus consisted of Satyrs : its number is quite uncertain. Its dance was called σίκιννις. When a poet intended to bring forward a play, he had to apply for a chorus (χορὸν αἰτεῖν) to the archons, to the king archon if the play was to be brought forward at the Lenaea, to the archon eponymus if at the great Dionysia. If the play were thought to deserve it, he received a chorus (χορὸν λαμβάνειν), the expenses of which were borne by a choregus. [CHOREGUS.] The poet then either trained (διδάσκειν) the chorus himself, or entrusted that business to a professed chorus trainer (χοροδιδάσκαλος), who usually had an assistant (ὑποδιδάσκαλος). For training the chorus in its evolutions there was also an ὀρχηστοδιδάσκαλος.

CHOUS, or CHOEUS (χοῦς or χοεύς), was equal to the Roman congius, and contained six ξέσται, or sextarii (nearly six pints English). It seems that there was also a smaller measure of the same name, containing two sextarii (nearly two pints English).

CHRŌNŎLŎGĬA (χρονολογία), chronology. The Greeks reckoned their years generally according to their magistrates, in the early times according to the years of the reign of their kings, and afterwards according to their annual magistrates. At Athens the year was called by the name of one of the nine archons, who from this circumstance was called ἄρχων ἐπώνυμος, or the archon par excellence; and at Sparta the years were called after one of the five ephors, who for this reason was likewise termed ἐπώνυμος. In Argos time was counted according to the years of the nigh priestess of Hera, who held her office for life (ἡρεσίς); and the inhabitants of Elis probably reckoned according to the Olympic games, which were celebrated every fifth year during the first full moon which followed after the summer solstice. Thus there was no era which was used by *all* the Greeks in common for the ordinary purposes of life.—Timaeus, who flourished about B.C. 260, was the first historian who counted the years by Olympiads, each of which contained four years. The beginning of the Olympiads is commonly fixed in the year 3938 of the Julian period, or in B.C. 776. If we want to reduce any given Olympiad to years before Christ, *e. g.* Ol. 87, we take the number of the Olympiads actually elapsed, that is, 86, multiply it by 4, and deduct the number obtained from 776, so that the first year of the 87th Ol. will be the same as the year 432 B.C. If the number of Olympiads amounts to more than 776 years, that is, if the Olympiad falls after the birth of Christ, the process is the same as before, but from the sum obtained by multiplying the Olympiads by 4, we must deduct the number 776, and what remains is the number of the years after Christ. As the Olympic games were celebrated 293 times, we have 293 Olympic cycles, that is, 1172 years, 776 of which fall before, and 396 after Christ.—Some writers also adopted the Trojan era, the fall of Troy being placed by Eratosthenes and those who adopted this era, in the year B.C. 1184. After the time of Alexander the Great, several other eras were introduced in the kingdoms that arose out of his empire. The first was the Philippic era, sometimes also called the era of Alexander or the era of Edessa; it began on the 12th of November B.C. 324, the date of the accession of Philip Arrhidaeus. The second was the era of the Seleucidae, beginning on the 1st of October B.C. 312, the date of the victory of Seleucus Nicator at Gaza, and of his re-conquest of Babylonia. This era was used very extensively in the East. The Chaldaean era differed from it only by six months, beginning in the spring of B.C. 311. Lastly, the eras of Antioch, of which there were three, but the one most commonly used began in November B.C. 49.—The Romans during the time of the republic reckoned their years by the names of the consuls, which were registered in the Fasti. Along with this era there existed another, used only by the historians. It reckoned the years from the foundation of the city (*ab urbe condita*); but the year of the foundation of the city was a question of uncertainty among the Romans themselves. M. Terentius Varro placed it on the 21st of April in the third year of the 6th Olympiad, that is, B.C. 753; and this is the era most commonly used. To find out the year B.C. corresponding to the year A.U.C., subtract the year A.U.C. from 754; thus 605 A.U.C. = 149 B.C. To find out the year A.D. corresponding to the year A.U.C., subtract 753 from the year A.U.C.; thus 767 A.U.C. = 14 A.D.

CHRYSENDETA, costly dishes used by the Romans at their entertainments, apparently made of silver, with golden ornaments.
CIDĀRIS. [TIARA.]
CINCTUS GABĪNUS. [TOGA.]
CINGŬLUM. [ZONA.]
CINĒRĀRIUS. [CALAMISTRUM.]
CINĔRES. [FUNUS.]
CINĬFLO. [CALAMISTRUM.]
CIPPUS, a low column, sometimes round, but more frequently rectangular. Cippi were used for various purposes; the decrees of the senate were sometimes inscribed upon them; and with distances engraved upon them, they also served as milestones. They were, however, more frequently employed as sepulchral monuments. It was also usual to place at one corner of the burying-ground a cippus, on which the extent of the burying-ground was marked, towards the road (*in fronte*), and backwards to the fields (*in agrum*).

Cippus, in the Vatican.

CIRCENSES LŪDI. [Circus.]
CIRCĬTŌRES, or CIRCŬITŌRES. [Castra.]

CIRCUS. When Tarquinius Priscus had taken the town of Apiolae from the Latins, he commemorated his success by an exhibition of races and pugilistic contests in the Murcian valley, between the Palatine and Aventine hills, around which a number of temporary platforms were erected by the patres and equites, called *spectacula, fori*, or *foruli*, from their resemblance to the deck of a ship; each one raising a stage for himself, upon which he stood to view the games. This course, with its surrounding scaffoldings, was termed circus; either because the spectators stood round to see the shows, or because the procession and races went round in a circuit. Previously, however, to the death of Tarquin, a permanent building was constructed for the purpose, with regular tiers of seats in the form of a theatre. To this the name of Circus Maximus was subsequently given, as a distinction from the Flaminian and other similar buildings, which it surpassed in extent and splendour; and hence it is often spoken of as *the* Circus, without any distinguishing epithet. Of the Circus Maximus scarcely a vestige now remains; but this loss is fortunately supplied by the remains of a small circus on the Via Appia, the ground-plan of which is in a state of considerable preservation: it is represented in the annexed cut, and may be taken as a mo-

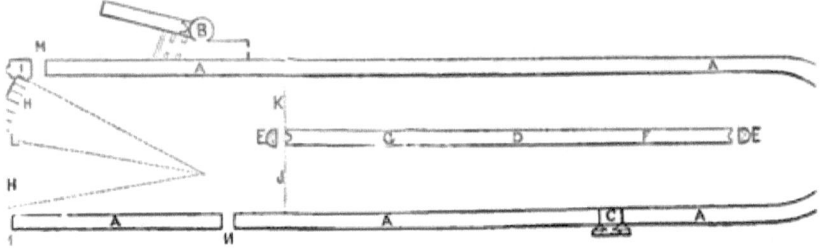

Ground Plan of the Circus.

del of all others. Around the double lines (A, A) were arranged the seats (*gradus, sedilia, subsellia*), as in a theatre, termed collectively the *cavea*; the lowest of which were separated from the ground by a *podium*, and the whole divided longitudinally by *praecinctiones*, and diagonally into *cunei*, with their *vomitoria* attached to each. [Amphitheatrum.] Towards the extremity of the upper branch of the *cavea*, the general outline is broken by an outwork (B), which was probably the *pulvinar*, or station for the emperor, as it is placed in the best situation for seeing both the commencement and end of the course, and in the most prominent part of the circus. In the opposite branch is observed another interruption to the uniform line of seats (C), betokening also, from its construction, a place of distinction; which might have been assigned to the person at whose expense the games were given (*editor spectaculorum*). In the centre of the area was a low wall (D) running lengthways down the course, which, from its resemblance to the position of the dorsal bone in the human frame, was termed *spina*. At each extremity of the spina were placed, upon a base (E, E), three wooden cylinders, of a conical shape, like cypress trees, which were called *metae*—the goals. Their situation is distinctly seen in the cut on p. 89. The most remarkable objects upon the *spina* were two columns (F) supporting seven conical balls, which, from their resemblance to eggs, were called *ova*. Their use was to enable the spectators to count the number of rounds which had been run; and they were seven in number, because seven was the number of the circuits made in each race. As each round was run, one of the *ova* was either put up or taken down. An egg was adopted for this purpose, in honour of Castor and Pollux. At the other extremity of the spina were two similar columns (G), sustaining dolphins, termed *delphinae*, or *delphinarum columnae*, which do not appear to have been intended to be removed, but only placed there as corresponding ornaments to the *ova*; and the figure of the dolphin was selected in honour of Neptune. These figures are also seen in the cut on p. 89. At the extremity of the circus in which the two horns of the *cavea* terminate, were placed the stalls for the horses and chariots (H, H), commonly called *carceres*, but more anciently the whole line of building at this end of the circus was termed *oppidum*: hence in the circus, of which the plan is given above, we find two towers (I, I) at each end of the *carceres*. The number of *carceres* is supposed to have been usually twelve, as in this plan. They were vaults, closed in front by gates of open wood-work (*cancelli*), which were opened simultaneously upon the signal being given, by removing a rope attached to pilasters of the kind called *Hermae*, placed for that purpose between each stall, upon which the gates were immediately thrown open by a number of men, as

Carceres opening of the Gates. (From a marble at Velletri.)

represented in the preceding woodcut. The cut below represents a set of four *carceres*, with their *Hermae*, and *cancelli* open, as left after the chariots had started; in which the gates are made to open inwards. The preceding account and woodcuts will be sufficient to explain the meaning of the various words by which the *carceres* were designated in poetical language, namely, *claustra, crypta, fauces, ostia, fores carceris, repagula, limina equorum*. There were five entrances to the circus; one (L) in the centre of the carceres, called *porta pompae*, because it was the one through which the Circensian procession entered, and the others at M, M, N, and O. At the entrance of the course, exactly in the direction of the line (J, K), were two small pedestals (*hermuli*) on each side of the *podium*, to which was attached a chalked rope (*alba linea*), for the purpose of making the start fair, precisely as is practised at Rome for the horse-races during Carnival. Thus, when the doors of the *carceres* were thrown open, if any of the horses rushed out before the others, they were brought up by this rope until the whole were fairly abreast, when it was loosened from one side, and all poured into the course at once. This line was also called *calx*, and *creta*. The *metae* served only to regulate the turnings of the course, the *alba linea* answered to the starting and winning post of modern days.—From this description the Circus Maximus differed little, except in size and magnificence of embellishment. The numbers which the Circus Maximus was capable of containing are computed at 150,000 by Dionysius, 260,000 by Pliny, and 385,000 by P. Victor, all of which are probably correct, but have reference to different periods of its history. Its length, in the time of Julius Caesar, was three stadia, the width one, and the depth of the buildings occupied half a stadium. When the Circus Maximus was permanently formed by Tarquinius Priscus, each of the thirty curiae had a particular place assigned to it; but as no provision was made for the plebeians in this circus, it is supposed that the Circus Flaminius was designed for the games of the commonalty, who in early times chose their tribunes there, on the Flaminian field. However, in the latter days of the republic, these invidious distinctions were lost, and all classes sat promiscuously in the circus. The seats were then marked off at intervals by a line or groove drawn across them (*linea*), so that the space included between two lines afforded sitting room for a certain number of spectators. Under the empire, however, the senators and equites were separated from the

Carceres, with Gates open. (Marble in British Museum.)

common people. The seat of the emperor (*pulvinar* or *cubiculum*) was most likely in the same situation in the Circus Maximus as in the one above described.—The Circensian games (*Ludi Circenses*) were first instituted by Romulus, according to the legends, when he wished to attract the Sabine population to Rome, for the purpose of furnishing his own people with wives, and were celebrated in honour of the god Consus, or Neptunus Equestris, from whom they were styled *Consuales*. But after the construction of the Circus Maximus they were called indiscriminately *Circenses*, *Romani*, or *Magni*. They embraced six kinds of games:—I. CURSUS; II. LUDUS TROJAE; III. PUGNA EQUESTRIS; IV. CERTAMEN GYMNICUM; V. VENATIO; VI. NAUMACHIA. The two last were not peculiar to the circus, but were exhibited also in the amphitheatre, or in buildings appropriated for them. The games commenced with a grand procession (*Pompa Circensis*), in which all those who were about to exhibit in the circus, as well as persons of distinction, bore a part. The statues of the gods formed the most conspicuous feature in the show, which

Chariot Race in the Circus. (Florentine Gem.)

were paraded upon wooden platforms, called *fercula* and *thensae*. The former were borne upon the shoulders, as the statues of saints are carried in modern processions; the latter were drawn along upon wheels.—1. CURSUS, the races. The carriage usually employed in the circus was drawn by two or four horses (*bigae*, *quadrigae*). [CURRUS.] The usual number of chariots which started for each race was four. The drivers (*aurigae*, *agitatores*) were also divided into four companies, each distinguished by a different colour, to represent the four seasons of the year, and called a *factio*: thus *factio prasina*, the green, represented the spring; *factio russata*, red, the summer; *factio veneta*, azure, the autumn; and *factio alba* or *albata*, white, the winter. Originally there were but two factions, *albata* and *russata*, and consequently only two chariots started at each race. The driver stood in his car within the reins, which went round his back. This enabled him to throw all his weight against the horses, by leaning backwards; but it greatly enhanced his danger in case of an upset. To avoid this peril, a sort of knife or bill-hook was carried at the waist, for the purpose of cutting the reins in a case of emergency. When all was ready, the doors of the *carceres* were flung open, and the chariots were formed abreast of the *alba linea* by men called *moratores* from their duty; the signal for the start was then given by the person who presided at the games, sometimes by sound of trumpet, or more usually by letting fall a napkin; whence the Circensian games are called *spectacula mappae*. The *alba linea* was then cast off, and the race commenced, the extent of which was seven times round the *spina*, keeping it always on the left. A course of seven circuits was termed *unus missus*, and twenty-five was the number of races run in each day, the last of which was called *missus aerarius*, because in early times the expense of it was defrayed by a collection of money (*aes*) made amongst the people. The victor descended from his car at the conclusion of the race, and ascended the *spina*, where he received his reward (*bravium*, from the Greek βραβεῖον), which consisted in a considerable sum of money. The horse-racing followed the same rules as the chariots. The enthusiasm of the Romans for these races exceeded all bounds. Lists of the horses (*libella*), with their names and colours, and those of the drivers, were handed about, and heavy bets made upon each faction; and sometimes the contests between two parties broke out into open violence and bloody quarrels, until at last the disputes which originated in the circus had nearly lost the Emperor Justinian his crown.—II. LUDUS TROJAE, a sort of sham-fight, said to have been invented by Aeneas, performed by young men of rank on horseback, and often exhibited by the emperors.— III. PUGNA EQUESTRIS ET PEDESTRIS, a representation of a battle, upon which occasions a camp was formed in the circus.—IV. CERTAMEN GYMNICUM. See ATHLETAE, and the references to the articles there given.—V. [VENATIO.]—VI. [NAUMACHIA.]

CISIUM, a light open carriage with two wheels, adapted to carry two persons rapidly from place to place. The cisia were quickly drawn by mules. Cicero mentions the case of a messenger who travelled 56 miles in 10 hours in such vehicles, which were kept for hire at the stations along the great roads; a proof that the ancients considered six Roman miles per hour as an extraordinary speed.

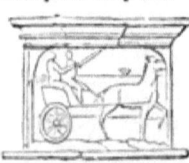
Cisium. (From monument at Igel, near Treves.)

CISTA (κίστη). (1) A small box or chest, in which anything might be placed, but more particularly applied to the small boxes which were carried in procession in the festivals of Demeter and Dionysus. These boxes, which were always kept closed in the public processions, contained sacred things connected with the worship of these deities. In the representations of Dionysiac processions on ancient vases women carrying cistae are frequently introduced.—(2) The ballot-box, into which

Cista. (From a Painting on a Vase.)

those who voted in the comitia and in the courts of justice cast their tabellae. It is represented in the annexed cut, and should not be confounded with the *situla* or *sitella*, into which sortes or lots were thrown. [SITULA.]

CISTOPHORUS (κιστοφόρος), a silver coin, which is supposed to belong to Rhodes, and which was in general circulation in Asia Minor at the time of the conquest of that country by the Romans. It took its name from the device upon it, which was either the sacred chest (*cista*) of Bacchus, or more probably a flower called κιστός. Its value is extremely uncertain: some writers suppose it to have been worth in our money about $7\frac{3}{4}d$.

CITHARA. [LYRA.]

CIVIS. [CIVITAS.]

CIVITAS, citizenship. (1) GREEK (πολιτεία). Aristotle defines a citizen (πολίτης) to be one who is a partner in the legislative and judicial power (μέτοχος κρίσεως καὶ ἀρχῆς). No definition will equally apply to all the different states of Greece, or to any single state at different times; the above seems to comprehend more or less properly all those whom the common use of language entitled to the name. A state in the heroic ages was the government of a prince; the citizens were his subjects, and derived all their privileges, civil as well as religious, from their nobles and princes. The shadows of a council and assembly were already in existence, but their business was to obey. Upon the whole the

notion of citizenship in the heroic ages only existed so far as the condition of aliens or of domestic slaves was its negative. The rise of a dominant class gradually overthrew the monarchies of ancient Greece. Of such a class, the chief characteristics were good birth and the hereditary transmission of privileges, the possession of land, and the performance of military service. To these characters the names *gamori* (γάμοροι), *knights* (ἱππεῖς), *eupatridae* (εὐπατρίδαι), &c. severally correspond. Strictly speaking, these were the only citizens; yet the lower class were quite distinct from bondmen or slaves. It commonly happened that the nobility occupied the fortified towns, while the *demus* (δῆμος) lived in the country and followed agricultural pursuits: whenever the latter were gathered within the walls, and became seamen or handicraftsmen, the difference of ranks was soon lost, and wealth made the only standard. The quarrels of the nobility among themselves, and the admixture of population arising from immigrations, all tended to raise the lower orders from their political subjection. It must be remembered, too, that the possession of domestic slaves, if it placed them in no new relation to the governing body, at any rate gave them leisure to attend to the higher duties of a citizen, and thus served to increase their political efficiency. During the convulsions which followed the heroic ages, naturalisation was readily granted to all who desired it; as the value of citizenship increased, it was, of course, more sparingly bestowed. The ties of hospitality descended from the prince to the state, and the friendly relations of the Homeric heroes were exchanged for the προξενίαι of a later period. In political intercourse, the importance of these last soon began to be felt, and the *Proxenus* at Athens, in after times, obtained rights only inferior to actual citizenship. [HOSPITIUM.] The isopolite relation existed, however, on a much more extended scale. Sometimes particular privileges were granted: as ἐπιγαμία, the right of intermarriage; ἔγκτησις, the right of acquiring landed property; ἀτέλεια, immunity from taxation, especially ἀτέλεια μετοικίου, from the tax imposed on resident aliens. All these privileges were included under the general term ἰσοτέλεια, or ἰσοπολίτεια, and the class who obtained them were called ἰσοτελεῖς. They bore the same burthens with the citizens, and could plead in the courts or transact business with the people, without the intervention of a προστάτης, or patron. Respecting the division of the Athenian citizens into tribes, phratriae and demes, see the articles TRIBUS and DEMUS.—If we would picture to ourselves the true notion which the Greeks embodied in the word *polis* (πόλις), we must lay aside all modern ideas respecting the nature and object of a state. With us practically, if not in theory, the *essential* object of a state hardly embraces more than the protection of life and property. The Greeks, on the other hand, had the most vivid conception of the state as a whole, every part of which was to co-operate to some great end to which all other duties were considered as subordinate. Thus the aim of democracy was said to be liberty; wealth, of oligarchy; and education, of aristocracy. In all governments the endeavour was to draw the social union as close as possible, and it seems to have been with this view that Aristotle laid down a principle which answered well enough to the accidental circumstances of the Grecian states, that a *polis* must be of a certain size. This unity of purpose was nowhere so fully carried out as in the government of Sparta. The design of Spartan institutions was evidently to unite the governing body among themselves against the superior numbers of the subject population. The division of lands, the syssitia, the education of their youth, all tended to this great object. [HELOTES; PERIOECI.] In legal rights all Spartans were equal but there were yet several gradations, which, when once formed, retained their hold on the aristocratic feelings of the people. First, there was the dignity of the Heraclide families; and, connected with this, a certain pre-eminence of the Hyllean tribe. Another distinction was that between the *Homoioi* (ὅμοιοι) and *Hypomeiones* (ὑπομείονες), which, in later times, appears to have been considerable. The latter term probably comprehended those citizens who, from degeneracy of manners or other causes, had undergone some kind of civil degradation. To these the *Homoioi* were opposed, although it is not certain in what the precise difference consisted. All the Spartan citizens were included in the three tribes, Hylleans, Dymanes or Dymanatae, and Pamphilians, each of which was divided into ten obes or phratries. The citizens of Sparta, as of most oligarchical states, were landowners, although this does not seem to have been looked upon as an essential of citizenship.—
(2) ROMAN. *Civitas* means the whole body of *cives*, or members, of any given state, and the word is frequently used by the Roman writers to express the rights of a Roman citizen, as distinguished from those of other persons not Roman citizens, as in the phrases, *dare civitatem, donare civitate, usurpare civitatem.* Some members of a political community (*cives*) may have more political rights than others; and this was the case at Rome under the republic, in which we find a dis-

tinction made between two great classes of Roman citizens, one that had, and another that had not, a share in the sovereign power (*optimo jure, non optimo jure cives*). That which peculiarly distinguished the higher class, or the *optimo jure cives*, was the right to vote in a tribe (*jus suffragiorum*), and the capacity of enjoying magistracy (*jus honorum*). The inferior class, or the *non optimo jure cives*, did not possess the above rights, which the Romans called *jus publicum*, but they only had the *jus privatum*, which comprehended the *jus connubii* and *jus commercii*, and those who had not these had no citizenship.—Under the empire we find the free persons who were within the political limits of the Roman state divided into three great classes. The same division probably existed in an early period of the Roman state, and certainly existed in the time of Cicero. These classes were, *Cives*, *Latini*, and *Peregrini*. *Civis* is he who possesses the complete rights of a Roman citizen. *Peregrinus* was incapable of exercising the rights of *commercium* and *connubium*, which were the characteristic rights of a Roman citizen; but he had a capacity for making all kinds of contracts which were allowable by the jus gentium. The *Latinus* was in an intermediate state; he had not the *connubium*, and consequently he had not the *patria potestas* nor rights of agnatio; but he had the *commercium* or the right of acquiring quiritarian ownership, and he had also a capacity for all acts incident to quiritarian ownership, as the power of making a will in Roman form, and of becoming heres under a will. The rights of a Roman citizen were acquired in several ways, but most commonly by a person being born of parents who were Roman citizens. A slave might obtain the civitas by manumission (*vindicta*), by the census, and by a testamentum, if there was no legal impediment; but it depended on circumstances whether he became a *civis Romanus*, a *Latinus*, or in the number of the *peregrini dediticii*. [MANUMISSIO.] The civitas could be conferred on a foreigner by a lex, as in the case of Archias, who was a civis of Heraclea, a civitas which had a foedus with Rome, and who claimed the civitas Romana under the provisions of a lex of Silvanus and Carbo, B. c. 89. By the provisions of this lex, the person who chose to take the benefit of it was required, within sixty days after the passing of the lex, to signify to the praetor his wish and consent to accept the civitas (*profiteri*). This lex was intended to give the civitas, under certain limitations, to foreigners who were citizens of foederate states (*foederatis civitatibus adscripti*). [FOEDERATAE CIVITATES.] Thus the great mass of the Italians obtained the civitas, and the privileges of the former civitates foederatae were extended to the provinces, first to part of Gaul, and then to Sicily, under the name of Jus Latii or Latinitas. This Latinitas gave a man the right of acquiring the Roman citizenship by having exercised a magistratus in his own civitas; a privilege which belonged to the foederatae civitates of Italy before they obtained the Roman civitas.

CLĀRIGĀTIO. [FETIALES.]

CLASSĬCUM. [CORNU.]

CLĀVUS ANNĀLIS. In the early ages of Rome, when letters were yet scarcely in use, the Romans kept a reckoning of their years by driving a nail (*clavus*), on the ides of each September, into the side walls of the temple of Jupiter Optimus Maximus, which ceremony was performed by the consul or a dictator.

CLĀVUS GŬBERNĀCŬLI. [NAVIS.]

CLĀVUS LĀTUS, CLĀVUS ANGUSTUS. The *clavus*, as an article of dress, seems to have been a purple band worn upon the tunic and toga, and was of two fashions, one broad and the other narrow, denominated respectively *clavus latus* and *clavus angustus*. The former was a single broad band of purple, extending perpendicularly from the neck down the centre of the tunic; the latter probably consisted of two narrow purple slips, running parallel to each from the top to the bottom of the tunic, one from each shoulder. The *latus clavus* was a distinctive badge of the senatorial order; and hence it is used to signify the senatorial dignity, and *laticlavius*, the person who enjoys it. The *angustus clavus* was the decoration of the equestrian order; but the right of wearing the latus clavus was also given to the children of equestrians, at least in the time of Augustus, as a prelude to entering the senate-house. This, however, was a matter of personal indulgence, and was granted only to persons of very ancient family and corresponding wealth, and then by special favour of the emperor. In such cases the latus clavus was assumed with the toga virilis, and worn until the age arrived at which the young equestrian was admissible into the senate, when it was relinquished and the angustus clavis resumed, if a disinclination on his part, or any other circumstances, prevented him from entering the senate, as was the case with Ovid. But it seems that the latus clavus could be again resumed if the same individual subsequently wished to become a senator, and hence a fickle character is designated as one who is always changing his clavus. The latus clavus is said to have been introduced at Rome by Tullus Hostilius, and to have been adopted by him after his conquest of the Etruscans; nor does it appear to have been confined to any particular class during the earlier periods, but to have been worn by all ranks promiscuously. It was laid aside in public mourning.

CLEPSÝDRA. [HOROLOGIUM.]

CLĒRŪCHI (κληροῦχοι), the name of Athenian citizens who occupied conquered lands; their possession was called *cleruchia* (κληρουχία). The Athenian Cleruchi differed from the ἄποικοι or ordinary colonists. The only object of the earlier colonies was to relieve surplus population, or to provide a home for those whom internal quarrels had exiled from their country. Most usually they originated in private enterprise, and became independent of, and lost their interest in, the parent state. On the other hand, it was essential to the very notion of a *cleruchia* that it should be a public enterprise, and should always retain a connection more or less intimate with Athens herself. The connection with the parent state subsisted in all degrees. Sometimes, as in the case of Lesbos, the holders of land did not reside upon their estates, but let them to the original inhabitants, while themselves remained at Athens. The condition of these cleruchi did not differ from that of Athenian citizens who had estates in Attica. All their political rights they not only retained, but exercised as Athenians. Another case was where the cleruchi resided on their estates, and either with or without the old inhabitants, formed a new community. These still retained the rights of Athenian citizens, which distance only precluded them from exercising: they used the Athenian courts; and if they or their children wished to return to Athens, naturally and of course they regained the exercise of their former privileges. Sometimes, however, the connection might gradually dissolve, and the cleruchi sink into the condition of mere allies, or separate wholly from the mother country. It was to Pericles that Athens was chiefly indebted for the extension and permanence of her colonial settlements. His principal object was to provide for the redundancies of population, and raise the poorer citizens to a fortune becoming the dignity of Athenian citizens. It was of this class of persons that the settlers were chiefly composed; the state provided them with arms, and defrayed the expenses of their journey. The Cleruchiae were lost by the battle of Aegospotami, but partially restored on the revival of Athenian power.

CLĒTĒRES or CLĒTORES (κλητῆρες, κλήτορες), summoners, were at Athens not official persons, but merely witnesses to the prosecutor that he had served the defendant with a notice of the action brought against him, and the day upon which it would be requisite for him to appear before the proper magistrate.

CLĪBĂNĀRĪI. [CATAPHRACTI.]

CLIENS is said to contain the same element as the verb *cluere*, to "hear" or "obey," and may be accordingly compared with the German word *höriger*, "a dependant," from *hören*, "to hear." In the earliest times of the Roman state we find a class of persons called *clientes*, who must not be confounded with the plebeians, from whom they were distinct. The clients were not slaves: they had property of their own and freedom, and appear to have had votes in the comitia centuriata, but they did not possess the full rights of Roman citizens; and the peculiarity of their condition consisted in every client being in a state of dependence upon or subjection to some patrician, who was called his *patronus*, and to whom he owed certain rights and duties. The patronus, on the other hand, likewise incurred certain obligations towards his client. This relationship between patronus and cliens was expressed by the word *clientela*, which also expressed the whole body of a man's clients. The relative rights and duties of the patrons and the clients were, according to Dionysius, as follows:—The patron was the legal adviser of the cliens; he was the client's guardian and protector, as he was the guardian and protector of his own children; he maintained the client's suit when he was wronged, and defended him when another complained of being wronged by him: in a word, the patron was the guardian of the client's interests, both private and public. The client contributed to the marriage portion of the patron's daughter, if the patron was poor; and to his ransom, or that of his children, if they were taken prisoners; he paid the costs and damages of a suit which the patron lost, and of any penalty in which he was condemned; he bore a part of the patron's expenses incurred by his discharging public duties, or filling the honourable places in the state. Neither party could accuse the other, or bear testimony against the other, or give his vote against the other. This relationship between patron and client subsisted for many generations, and resembled in all respects the relationship by blood. The relation of a master to his liberated slave (*libertus*) was expressed by the word *patronus*, and the libertus was the cliens of his patronus. Distinguished Romans were also the protectors of states and cities, which were in a certain relation of subjection or dependence to Rome. In the time of Cicero we also find *patronus* in the sense of adviser, advocate, or defender, opposed to *cliens* in the sense of the person defended or the consultor,—a use of the word which must be referred to the original character of the patronus.

CLIENTELA. [CLIENS.]

CLIPEUS (ἀσπίς), the large shield worn by the Greeks and Romans, which was originally of a circular form, and is said to have been first used by Proetus and Acrisius of Argos, and therefore is called *clipeus Argolicus*, and likened to the sun. But the clipeus is often represented in Roman sculpture of an oblong oval, which makes the distinction between the common buckler and that of Argos. The outer rim was termed ἄντυξ by the Greeks; and in the centre was a projection called ὀμφάλος or *umbo*, which served as a sort of weapon by itself, or caused the missiles of the enemy to glance off from the shield. In the Homeric times, the Greeks merely used a leather strap (τελαμών) to support the shield, but subsequently a handle (ὄχανον or ὀχάνη). The usual form of the clipeus is exhibited in the figure of the Greek warrior on p. 41. When the census was instituted by Servius Tullius at Rome, the first class only used the *clipeus*, and the second were armed with the *scutum* [SCUTUM]; but after the Roman soldiery received pay, the *clipeus* was discontinued altogether for the *scutum*.

CLITELLAE, a pair of panniers, and therefore only used in the plural number.

CLOACA, a sewer, a drain. Rome was intersected by numerous sewers, some of which were of an immense size: the most celebrated of them was the *cloaca maxima*,

Cloaca Maxima at Rome.

the construction of which is ascribed to Tarquinius Priscus. It was formed by three tiers of arches, one within the other, the innermost of which is a semicircular vault of 14 feet in diameter. The manner of its construction is shown in the preceding cut. Under the republic, the administration of the sewers was entrusted to the censors: but under the empire, particular officers were appointed for that purpose, called *cloacarum*

curatores, who employed condemned criminals in cleansing and repairing them.

COA VESTIS, the Coan robe, was a transparent dress, chiefly worn by women of loose reputation. It has been supposed to have been made of silk, because in Cos silk was spun and woven at a very early period.

Coa Vestis. (From a Painting at Herculaneum.)

COACTOR, the name of collectors of various sorts, e. g. the servants of the publicani, or farmers of the public taxes, who collected the revenues for them, and those who collected the money from the purchasers of things sold at a public auction. Horace informs us that his father was a coactor of this kind. Moreover, the servants of the money-changers were so called, from collecting their debts for them. The "coactores agminis" were the soldiers who brought up the rear of a line of march.

COCHLEA (κοχλίας), which properly means a snail, was also used to signify other things of a spiral form. (1) A screw, used in working clothes-presses, and oil and wine presses.—(2) A spiral pump for raising water, invented by Archimedes, from whom it has ever since been called the Archimedean screw.—(3) A peculiar kind of door through which the wild beasts passed from their dens into the arena of the amphitheatre.

COCHLEAR (κοχλιάριον), a kind of spoon, which appears to have terminated with a point at one end, and at the other was broad and hollow like our own spoons. The pointed end was used for drawing snails (*cochleae*) out of their shells, and eating them, whence it derived its name; and the broader part for eating eggs, &c. Cochlear was also the name given to a small measure like our spoonful.

CODEX, identical with *caudex*, as *Claudius* and *Clodius*, *claustrum* and *clostrum*, *cauda* and *coda*, originally signified the trunk or stem of a tree. The name codex was especially applied to wooden tablets bound together and lined with a coat of wax, for the purpose of writing upon them, and when, at a later age, parchment or paper, or other materials were substituted for wood, and put together in the shape of a book, the name of codex was still given to them. In the time of Cicero we find it also applied to the tablet on which a bill was written. At a still later period, during the time of the emperors, the word was used to express any collection of laws or constitutions of the emperors, whether made by private individuals or by public authority, as the *Codex Gregorianus*, *Codex Theodosianus*, and *Codex Justinianëus*.

COEMPTIO. [MATRIMONIUM.]

COENA (δεῖπνον), the principal meal of the Greeks and Romans, dinner. (1) GREEK. Three names of meals occur in the Iliad and Odyssey—*ariston* (ἄριστον), *deipnon* (δεῖπνον), *dorpon* (δόρπον). The word *ariston* uniformly means the early, as *dorpon* does the late meal; but *deipnon*, on the other hand, is used for either, apparently without any reference to time. In the Homeric age it appears to have been usual to sit during mealtimes. Beef, mutton, and goat's flesh were the ordinary meats, usually eaten roasted. Cheese, flour, and occasionally fruits, also formed part of the Homeric meals. Bread, brought on in baskets, and salt (ἅλς, to which Homer gives the epithet θεῖος), are mentioned. The Greeks of a later age usually partook of three meals, called *acratisma* (ἀκράτισμα), *ariston*, and *deipnon*. The last, which corresponds to the *dorpon* of the Homeric poems, was the evening meal or dinner; the *ariston* was the luncheon; and the *acratisma*, which answers to the *ariston* of Homer, was the early meal or breakfast. The *acratisma* was taken immediately after rising in the morning. It usually consisted of bread, dipped in unmixed wine (ἄκρατος), whence it derived its name. Next followed the *ariston* or luncheon; but the time at which it was taken is uncertain. It is frequently mentioned in Xenophon's Anabasis, and appears to have been taken at different times, as would naturally be the case with soldiers in active service. We may conclude from many circumstances that this meal was taken about the middle of the day, and that it answered to the Roman *prandium*. The *ariston* was usually a simple meal, but of course varied according to the habits of individuals. The principal meal was the *deipnon*. It was usually taken rather late in the day, frequently not before sunset. The Athenians were a social people, and were very fond of dining in company. Entertainments were usually given, both in the heroic ages and later times, when sacrifices were offered to the gods, either on public or private occasions; and also on the anniversary of the birthdays of members of the family, or of illustrious persons, whether living or dead. When young men wished to dine together they frequently contributed each a certain sum of money, called *symbole* (συμβολή), or brought their own provisions with them. When the first plan was adopted, they were said ἀπὸ συμβολῶν δειπνεῖν, and one individual was usually entrusted with the money to procure the provisions, and make all the necessary preparations. This kind of entertainment, in which each guest contributed to the expense, is mentioned in Homer under the name of ἔρανος. An entertainment in which each person brought his own provisions with him, or at least contributed something to the general stock, was called a δεῖπνον ἀπὸ σπυρίδος, because the provisions were brought in baskets.—The most usual kind of entertainments, however, were those in which a person invited his friends to his own house. It was expected that they should come dressed with more than ordinary care, and also have bathed shortly before. As soon as the guests arrived at the house of their host, their shoes or sandals were taken off by the slaves and their feet washed. After their feet had been washed, the guests reclined on the couches. It has already been remarked that Homer never describes persons as reclining, but always as sitting at their meals; but at what time the change was introduced is uncertain. The Dorians of Crete always sat; but the other Greeks reclined. The Greek women and children, however, like the Roman, continued to sit at their meals. [ACCUBATIO.] It was usual for only two persons to recline on each couch. After the guests had placed themselves on the couches, the slaves brought in water to wash their hands. The dinner was then served up; whence we read of τὰς τραπέζας εἰσφέρειν, by which expression we are to understand not merely the dishes, but the tables themselves, which were small enough to be moved with ease. In eating, the Greeks had no knives or forks, but made use of their fingers only, except in eating soups or other liquids, which they partook of by means of a spoon, called μυστίλη, μύστρον, or μύστρος. It would exceed the limits of this work to give an account of the different dishes which were introduced at a Greek dinner, though their number is far below those which were usually partaken of at a Roman entertainment. The most common food among the Greeks was the μᾶζα, a kind of frumenty or soft cake, which was prepared in different ways. Wheaten or barley bread was the second most usual species of food; it was sometimes made at home, but more usually bought at the market of the ἀρτοπῶλαι or ἀρτοπώλιδες. The vegetables ordinarily eaten were mallows (μαλάχη), lettuces (θρίδαξ), cabbages (ῥάφανοι), beans (κύαμοι), lentils (φακαῖ), &c. Pork was the most favourite animal food, as was the case among the Romans. It is a curious fact, which Plato has remarked, that we never read in Homer of the heroes partaking of fish. In later times, however, fish was one of the most favourite foods of the Greeks. A dinner given by an opulent Athenian usually consisted of two courses, called respectively πρῶται τράπεζαι and δεύτεραι τράπεζαι. The first course embraced the whole of what we consider the dinner, namely, fish, poultry, meat, &c.; the second, which corresponds to our dessert and the Roman *bellaria*, consisted of different kinds of fruit, sweetmeats, confections, &c. When the first course was finished, the tables were taken away, and water was given to the guests for the purpose of washing their hands. Crowns made of garlands of flowers were also then given to them, as well as various kinds of perfumes. Wine was not drunk till the first course was finished; but as soon as the guests had washed their hands, unmixed wine was introduced in a large goblet, of which each drank a little, after pouring out a small quantity as a libation. This libation was said to be made to the "good spirit" (ἀγαθοῦ δαίμονος), and was usually accompanied with the singing of the paean and the playing of flutes. After this libation mixed wine was brought in, and with their first cup the guests drank to Διὸς Σωτῆρος. With the libations the *deipnon* closed; and at the introduction of the dessert (δεύτεραι τράπεζαι) the πότος, συμπόσιον, or κῶμος commenced, of which an account is given under SYMPOSIUM. —(2) ROMAN. As the Roman meals are not always clearly distinguished, it will be convenient to treat of all under the most important one; and we shall confine ourselves to the description of the ordinary life of the middle ranks of society in the Augustan age, noticing incidentally the most remarkable deviations. The meal with which the Roman sometimes began the day was the *jentaculum*, which was chiefly taken by children, or sick persons, or the luxurious. An irregular meal (if we may so express it) was not likely to have any very regular time: two epigrams of Martial, however, seem to fix the hour at about three or four o'clock in the morning. Bread formed the substantial part of this early breakfast, to which cheese, or dried fruit, as dates and raisins, were sometimes added. Next followed the *prandium* or luncheon, with persons of simple habits a frugal meal, usually taken about twelve or one o'clock. The *coena*, or principal meal of the day, corresponding to our "dinner," was usually taken about three o'clock in the time of Cicero and Augustus, though we read of some persons not dining till near sunset. A Roman dinner at the house of a wealthy man usually consisted of three courses. The first was called *promulsis, antecoena*, or *gustatio*, and was made up of all sorts of stimulants to the appetite. Eggs also were so indispensable to the first course that they almost gave a name to it (*ab ovo usque ad mala*). The frugality of Martial only allowed of lettuce and Sicenian olives; indeed he himself tells us that the *promulsis* was a refinement of modern luxury. It would far exceed our limits to mention all the dishes which formed the second course of a Roman dinner. Of birds, the Guinea hen (*Afra avis*), the pheasant (*phasiana*, so called from Phasis, a river of Colchis), and the thrush, were most in repute; the liver of a capon steeped in milk, and beccaficos (*ficedulae*) dressed with pepper, were held a delicacy. The peacock, according to Macrobius, was first introduced by Hortensius the orator, at an inaugural supper, and acquired such repute among the Roman gourmands as to be commonly sold for fifty denarii. Other birds are mentioned, as the duck (*anas*), especially its head and breast; the woodcock (*attagen*), the turtle, and flamingo (*phoenicopterus*), the tongue of which, Martial tells us, particularly commended itself to the delicate palate. Of fish, the variety was perhaps still greater; the charr (*scarus*), the turbot (*rhombus*), the sturgeon (*acipenser*), the mullet (*mullus*), were highly prized, and dressed in the most various fashions. Of solid meat, pork seems to have been the favourite dish, especially sucking pig. Boar's flesh and venison were also in high repute: the former is described by Juvenal as *animal propter convivia natum*. Condiments were added to most of these dishes: such were the *muria*, a kind of pickle made from the tunny fish; the *garum sociorum*, made from the intestines of the mackerel (*scomber*), so called because brought from abroad; *alec*, a sort of brine; *faex*, the sediment of wine, &c. Several kinds of *fungi* are mentioned, truffles (*boleti*), mushrooms (*tuberes*), which either made dishes by themselves, or formed the garniture for larger dishes. It must not be supposed that the *artistes* of imperial Rome were at all behind ourselves in the preparation and arrangements of the table. In a large household, the functionaries to whom this important duty was entrusted were four, the butler (*promus*), the cook (*archimagirus*), the arranger of the dishes (*structor*), and the carver (*carptor* or *scissor*). Carving was taught as an art, and performed to the sound of music, with appropriate gesticulations.

<blockquote>—— " minimo sane discrimine refert,
Quo vultu lepores, et quo gallina secetur."</blockquote>

In the supper of Petronius, a large round tray (*ferculum, repositorium*) is brought in, with the signs of the zodiac figured all round it, upon each of which the *artiste* (*structor*) had placed some appropriate viand, a goose on Aquarius, a pair of scales with tarts (*scriblitae*) and cheesecakes (*placentae*) in each scale on Libra, &c. In the middle was placed a hive supported by delicate herbage. Presently four slaves come forward dancing to the sound of music, and take away the upper part of the dish; beneath appear all kinds of dressed meats; a hare with wings to imitate Pegasus, in the middle; and four figures of Marsyas at the corners, pouring hot sauce (*garum piperatum*) over the fish, that were swimming in the Euripus below. So entirely had the Romans lost all shame of luxury, since the days when Cincius, in supporting the Fannian law, charged his own age with the enormity of introducing the *porcus Trojanus*, a sort of pudding stuffed with the flesh of other animals.—The third course was the *bellaria* or dessert, to which Horace alludes when he says of Tigellius *ab ovo usque ad mala citaret*; it consisted of fruits (which the Romans usually ate uncooked), such as almonds (*amygdalae*), dried grapes (*urae passae*), dates (*palmulae, caryotae, dactyli*); of sweetmeats and confections, called *edulia mellita, dulciaria*, such as cheesecakes (*cupediae, crustula, liba, placentae, artolagani*), almond cakes (*coptae*), tarts (*scriblitae*), whence the maker of them was called *pistor dulciarius, placentarius, libarius*, &c. We will now suppose the table spread and the guests assembled, each with his *mappa* or napkin, and in his dinner dress, called *coenatoria* or *cubitoria*, usually of a bright colour, and variegated with flowers. First they took off their shoes, for fear of soiling the couch, which was often inlaid with ivory or tortoiseshell, and covered with cloth of gold. Next they lay down to eat, the head resting on the left elbow and supported by cushions. There were usually, but not always, three on the same couch, the middle place being esteemed the most honourable. Around the tables stood the servants (*ministri*) clothed in a tunic, and girt with napkins; some removed the dishes and wiped the tables with a rough cloth, others gave the guests water for their hands, or cooled the room with fans. Here stood an eastern youth behind his master's couch, ready to answer the noise of the fingers, while others bore a large platter of different kinds of meat to the guests. Dinner was set out in a room called *coenatio* or *diaeta* (which two words perhaps conveyed to a Roman ear nearly the same distinction as our dining-room and parlour). The *coenatio*, in rich men's houses, was fitted up with great magnificence. Suetonius mentions a supper-room in the golden palace of Nero, constructed like a theatre, with shifting scenes to change with every course. In the midst of the coenatio were set three couches

A Feast. (Vatican Virgil MS.)

(*triclinia*), answering in shape to the square, as the long semicircular couches (*sigmata*) did to the oval tables. An account of the disposition of the couches, and of the place which each guest occupied, is given in the article TRICLINIUM.

COENACULUM. [DOMUS.]
COENATIO. [COENA.]
COGNATI, COGNATIO. The *cognatio* was the relationship of blood which existed between those who were sprung from a common pair; and all persons so related were called *cognati*. The foundation of *cognatio* is a legal marriage. The term *cognatus* (with some exceptions) comprehends *agnatus*; an *agnatus* may be a *cognatus*, but a *cognatus* is only an *agnatus* when his relationship by blood is traced through males. Those who were of the same blood by both parents were sometimes called *germani*; *consanguinei* were those who had a common father only; and *uterini* those who had a common mother only.

COGNITOR. [ACTIO.]
COGNOMEN. [NOMEN.]
COHORS. [EXERCITUS.]
COLACRETAE (κωλακρέται, also called κωλαγρέται), the name of very ancient magistrates at Athens, who had the management of all financial matters in the time of the kings. Cleisthenes deprived them of the charge of the finances, which he transferred to the Apodectae. [APODECTAE.] From this time the Colacretae had only to provide for the meals in the Prytaneium, and subsequently to pay the fees to the dicasts, when the practice of paying the dicasts was introduced by Pericles.

COLLEGIUM. The persons who formed a collegium were called *collegae* or *sodales*. The word collegium properly expressed the notion of several persons being united in any office or for any common purpose; it afterwards came to signify a body of persons, and the union which bound them together. The collegium was the ἑταιρία of the Greeks. The legal notion of a collegium was as follows:—A collegium or corpus, as it was also called, must consist of three persons at least. Persons who legally formed such an association were said *corpus habere*, which is equivalent to our phrase of being incorporated; and in later times they were said to be *corporati*, and the body was called a *corporatio*. Associations of individuals, who were entitled to have a corpus, could hold property in common. Such a body, which was sometimes also called a *universitas*, was a legal unity. That which was due to the body, was not due to the individuals of it; and that which the body owed, was not the debt of the individuals. The common property of the body was liable to be seized and sold for the debts of the body. It does not appear how collegia were formed, except that some were specially established by legal authority. Other collegia were probably formed by voluntary associations of individuals under the provisions of some general legal authority, such as those of the publicani. Some of these corporate bodies resembled our companies or guilds; such were the *fabrorum*, *pistorum*, &c. *collegia*. Others were of a religious character; such as the *pontificum*, *augurum*, *fratrum arvalium collegia*. Others were bodies concerned about government and administration; as *tribunorum plebis*, *quaestorum*, *decurionum collegia*. According to the definition of a collegium, the consuls being only two in number were not a collegium, though each was called collega with respect to the other, and their union in office was called collegium. When a new member was taken into a collegium, he was said *co-optari*, and the old members were said with respect to him, *recipere in collegium*. The mode of filling up vacancies would vary in different collegia. The statement of their rules belongs to the several heads of AUGUR, PONTIFEX, &c.

COLONIA, a colony, contains the same element as the verb *colere*, "to cultivate," and as the word *colonus*, which probably originally signified a "tiller of the earth." (1) GREEK. The usual Greek words for a colony are ἀποικία and κληρουχία. The latter word, which signified a division of conquered lands among Athenian citizens, and which corresponds in some respects to the Roman *colonia*, is explained in the article CLERUCHI. The earlier Greek colonies, called ἀποικίαι, were usually composed of mere bands of adventurers, who left their native country, with their families and property, to seek a new home for themselves. Some of the colonies, which arose in consequence of foreign invasion or civil wars, were undertaken without any formal consent from the rest of the community; but usually a colony was sent out with the approbation of the mother country, and under the management of a leader (οἰκιστής) appointed by it. But whatever may have been the origin of the colony, it was always considered in a political point of view independent of the mother country, called by the Greeks *metropolis* (μητρόπολις), the "mother-city," and entirely emancipated from its control. At the same time, though a colony was in no political subjection to its parent state, it was united to it by the ties of filial affection; and, according to the generally received opinions of the Greeks, its duties to the parent state corresponded to those of a daughter to her mother. Hence, in all matters of common interest, the colony gave precedence to the mother state ; and the founder of the colony (οἰκιστής), who might be considered as the representative of the parent state, was usually worshipped, after his death, as a hero. Also, when the colony became in its turn a parent, it usually sought a leader for the colony which it intended to found from the original mother country ; and the same feeling of respect was manifested by embassies which were sent to honour the principal festivals of the parent state, and also by bestowing places of honour and other marks of respect upon the ambassadors and other members of the parent state, when they visited the colony at festivals and on similar occasions. The colonists also worshipped in their new settlement the same deities as they had been accustomed to honour in their native country : the sacred fire, which was constantly kept burning on their public hearth, was taken from the Prytaneium of the parent city ; and sometimes the priests also were brought from the mother state. In the same spirit, it was considered a violation of sacred ties for a mother country and a colony to make war upon one another. The preceding account of the relations between the Greek colonies and the mother country is supported by the history which Thucydides gives us of the quarrel between Corcyra and Corinth. Corcyra was a colony of Corinth, and Epidamnus a colony of Corcyra ; but the leader (οἰκιστής) of the colony of Epidamnus was a Corinthian who was invited from the metropolis Corinth. In course of time, in consequence of civil dissensions, and attacks from the neighbouring barbarians, the Epidamnians apply for aid to Corcyra, but their request is rejected. They next apply to the Corinthians, who took Epidamnus under their protection, thinking, says Thucydides, that the colony was no less theirs than the Corinthians' : and also induced to do so through hatred of the Corcyraeans, because they neglected them though they were colonists; for they did not give to the Corinthians the customary honours and deference in the public solemnities and sacrifices, which the other colonies were wont to pay to the mother country. The Corcyraeans, who had become very powerful by sea, took offence at the Corinthians receiving Epidamnus under their protection, and the result was a war between Corcyra and Corinth. The Corcyraeans sent ambassadors to Athens to ask assistance ; and in reply to the objection that they were a colony of Corinth, they said, "that every colony, as long as it is treated kindly, respects the mother country but when it is injured, is alienated from it ; for colonists are not sent out as subjects, but that they may have equal rights with those that remain at home." It is true that ambitious states, such as Athens, sometimes claimed dominion over other states on the ground of relationship ; but as a general rule, colonies may be regarded as independent states, attached to their metropolis by ties of sympathy and common descent, but no further. The case of Potidaea, to which the Corinthians sent annually the chief magistrates (δημιουργοί), appears to have been an exception to the general rule.—(2) ROMAN. A kind of colonisation seems to have existed among the oldest Italian nations, who, on certain occasions, sent out their superfluous male population, with arms in their hands, to seek for a new home. But these were apparently mere bands of adventurers, and such colonies rather resembled the old Greek colonies, than those by which Rome extended her dominion and her name. Colonies were established by the Romans as far back as the annals or traditions of the city extend, and the practice was continued, without intermission, during the republic and under the empire. Colonies were intended to keep in check a conquered people, and also to repress hostile incursions ; and their chief object was originally the extension and preservation of the Roman dominion in Italy. Cicero calls the old Italian colonies the *propugnacula imperii*. Another object was to increase the power of Rome by increasing the population. Sometimes the immediate object of a colony was to carry off a number of turbulent and discontented persons. Colonies were also established for the purpose of providing for veteran soldiers, a practice which was begun by Sulla, and continued under the emperors ; these coloniae were called militares. The old Roman colonies were in the nature of garrisons planted in conquered towns, and the colonists had a portion of the conquered territory (usually a third part) assigned to them. The inhabitants retained the rest of their lands, and lived together with the new settlers, who alone composed the proper colony. The conquered people must at first have been quite a distinct class from, and inferior to, the colonists. No colonia was established without a lex, plebiscitum, or senatusconsultum ; a fact which shows that a Roman colony was never a mere body of adventurers, but had a regular organisation by the parent state. When a law was passed for founding a colony, persons were appointed to superintend its formation (*coloniam deducere*). These persons varied in number, but three was a common number (*triumviri ad colonos deducendos*). We also read of *duumviri, quinqueviri, vigintiviri* for the same purpose. The law fixed the quantity of land that was to be distributed, and how much was to be assigned to each person. No Roman could be sent out as a colonist without his free consent, and when the colony was not an inviting one, it was difficult to fill up the number of volunteers. The colonia proceeded to its place of destination in the form of an army (*sub vexillo*), which is indicated on the coins of some coloniae. An urbs, if one did not already exist, was a necessary part of a new colony, and its limits were marked out by a plough, which is also indicated on ancient coins. The colonia had also a territory, which, whether marked out by the plough or not, was at least marked out by metes and bounds. Thus the urbs and territory of the colonia respectively corresponded to the urbs Roma and its territory. Religious ceremonies always accompanied the foundation of the colony, and the anniversary was afterwards observed. It is stated that a colony could not be sent out to the same place to which a colony had already been sent in due form (*auspicato deducta*). This merely means, that so long as the colony maintained its existence, there could be no new colony in the same place; a doctrine that would hardly need proof, for a new colony implied a new assignment of lands; but new settlers (*novi adscripti*) might be sent to occupy colonial lands not already assigned. Indeed it was not unusual for a colony to receive additions, and a colony might be re-established, if it seemed necessary, from any cause. The commissioners appointed to conduct the colony had apparently a profitable office, and the establishment of a new settlement gave employment to numerous functionaries, among whom Cicero enumerates—*apparitores, scribae, librarii, praecones, architecti*. The foundation of a colony might then, in many cases, not only be a mere party measure, carried for the purpose of gaining popularity, but it would give those in power an opportunity of providing places for many of their friends.—The colonies founded by the Romans were divided into two great classes of colonies of Roman citizens and Latin colonies; names which had no reference to the persons who formed the colonies, but merely indicated their political rights with respect to Rome as members of the colony. The members of a Roman colony (*colonia civium Romanorum*) preserved all the rights of Roman citizens. The members of a Latin colony (*colonia Latina*) ceased to have the full rights of Roman citizens. Probably some of the old Latin colonies were established by the Romans in conjunction with other Latin states. After the conquest of Latium, the Romans established colonies, called Latin colonies, in various parts of Italy. Roman citizens, who chose to join such colonies, gave up their civic rights for the more solid advantage of a grant of land, and became LATINI. [CIVITAS.] Such colonies were subject to, and part of, the Roman state; but they did not possess the Roman franchise, and had no political bond among themselves.—The lex Julia, passed B. C. 90, gave the Roman franchise to the members of the Latin colonies and the Socii; and such Latin colonies and states of the Socii were then called *municipia*, and became complete members of the Roman state. Thus there was then really no difference between these municipia and the Roman coloniae, except in their historical origin: the members of both were Roman citizens, and the Roman law prevailed in both.—In the colonies, as at Rome, the popular assembly had originally the sovereign power; they chose the magistrates, and could even make laws. When the popular assemblies became a mere form in Rome, and the elections were transferred by Tiberius to the senate, the same thing happened in the colonies, whose senates then possessed whatever power had once belonged to the community. The common name of this senate was *ordo decurionum*; in later times, simply *ordo* and *curia*; the members of it were *decuriones* or *curiales*. Thus, in the later ages, *curia* is opposed to *senatus*, the former being the senate of a colony, and the latter the senate of Rome. But the terms senatus and senator were also applied to the senate and members of the senate of a colony. After the decline of the popular assemblies, the senate had the whole internal administration of a city, conjointly with the magistratus; but only a decurio could be a magistratus, and the choice was made by the decuriones. The highest magistratus of a colonia were the *duumviri* or *quattuorviri*, so called, as the members might vary, whose functions may be compared with those of the consulate at Rome before the establishment of the praetorship. The name *duumviri* seems to have been the most common. Their principal duties were the administration of justice, and accordingly we find on inscriptions "Duumviri J. D." (*juri dicundo*), "Quattuorviri J. D." The name consul also occurs in inscriptions to denote this chief magistracy; and even dictator and praetor occur under the empire and under the republic. The office of the duumviri lasted a year.—In some Italian towns there was a *praefectus juri dicundo*; he was in the place of, and not co-existent with, the duumviri. The duumviri were, as we have seen, originally chosen by the people;

but the praefectus was appointed annually in Rome, and sent to the town called a *praefectura*, which might be either a municipium or a colonia, for it was only in the matter of the praefectus that a town called a praefectura differed from other Italian towns. Arpinum is called both a municipium and a praefectura; and Cicero, a native of this place, obtained the highest honours that Rome could confer.—The *censor, curator*, or *quinquennalis*, all which names denote the same functionary, was also a municipal magistrate, and corresponded to the censor at Rome, and in some cases, perhaps, to the quaestor also. Censors are mentioned in Livy as magistrates of the twelve Latin colonies. The quinquennales were sometimes duumviri, sometimes quattuorviri; but they are always carefully distinguished from the duumviri and quattuorviri J. D.; and their functions were those of censors. They held their office for one year, and during the four intermediate years the functions were not exercised. The office of censor or quinquennalis was higher in rank than that of the duumviri J. D., and it could only be filled by those who had discharged the other offices of the municipality.

CŎLOSSUS (κολοσσός) is used both by the Greeks and Romans to signify a statue larger than life; but as such statues were very common, the word was more frequently applied to designate figures of gigantic dimensions. Such figures were first executed in Egypt, and were afterwards made by the Greeks and Romans. Among the colossal statues of Greece, the most celebrated was the bronze *colossus* at Rhodes, dedicated to the sun, the height of which was about 90 feet.

CŌLUM (ἠθμός), a strainer or colander, was used for straining wine, milk, olive-oil,

and other liquids. Those that were used as articles of luxury for straining wine were frequently made of some metal, such as bronze or silver. Occasionally a piece of linen cloth (σάκκος, *saccus*) was placed over the τρύγοιπος or *colum*, and the wine (σακκίας, *saccatus*) filtered through. The use of the *saccus* was considered objectionable for all delicate wines, since it was believed to injure, if not entirely to destroy their flavour, and in every instance to diminish the strength of the liquor. For this reason it was employed by the dissipated in order that they might be able to swallow a greater quantity without becoming intoxicated. The double purpose of cooling and weakening was effectually accomplished by placing ice or snow in the filter, which under such circumstances became a *colum nivarium*, or *saccus nivarius*. The preceding woodcut shows the plan and profile of a silver colum.

CŎLUMBĀRĬUM, a dovecot or pigeonhouse, also signified a sepulchral chamber formed to receive the ashes of the lower orders, or dependants of great families; and in the plural, the niches in which the cinerary urns (*ollae*) were deposited.

CŎLUMNA (κίων, στῦλος), a pillar or column. The use of the trunks of trees placed upright for supporting buildings, unquestionably led to the adoption of similar supports wrought in stone. As the tree required to be based upon a flat square stone, and to have a stone or tile of similar form fixed on its summit to preserve it from decay, so the column was made with a square base, and was covered with an *abacus*. [ABACUS.] Hence the principal parts of which every column consists are three, the base (*basis*), the shaft (*scapus*), and the capital (*capitulum*). In the Doric, which is the oldest style of Greek architecture, we must consider all the columns in the same row as having one common base (*podium*), whereas in the Ionic and Corinthian each column has a separate base, called *spira*. The capitals of these two latter orders show, on comparison with the Doric, a much richer style of ornament; and the character of lightness and elegance is further obtained in them by their more slender shaft, its height being much greater in proportion to its thickness. Of all these circumstances some idea may be formed by the inspection of the three accompanying specimens of pillars. The first on the left hand is Doric, the second Ionic, and the third Corinthian. In all the orders the shaft tapers from the bottom towards the top. The shaft was, however, made with a slight swelling in the middle, which was called the *entasis*. It was, moreover, almost universally channelled or fluted.

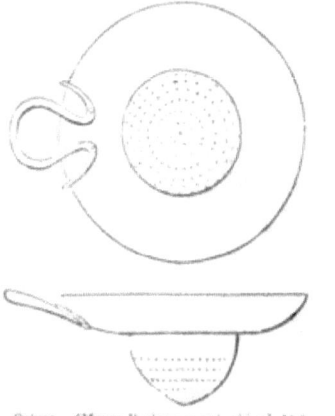

Colum. (Museo Borbonico, vol. viii. pl. 14.)

Columns were used in the interior of buildings, to sustain the beams which supported

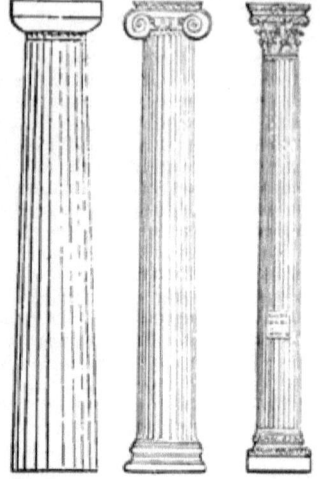

Ancient Columns.

the ceiling. Rows of columns were often employed within a building, to enclose a space open to the sky. Beams supporting ceilings passed from above the columns to the adjoining walls, so as to form covered passages or ambulatories (στοαί). Such a circuit of columns was called a *peristyle* (περίστυλον), and the Roman *atrium* was built upon this plan. The largest and most splendid temples enclosed an open space like an atrium, which was accomplished by placing one peristyle upon another. In such cases, the lower rows of columns being Doric, the upper were sometimes Ionic or Corinthian, the lighter being properly based upon the heavier. A temple so constructed was called *hypaethral* (ὕπαιθρος). But it was on the exterior of public buildings, and especially of temples, that columns were displayed in the most beautiful combinations, either surrounding the building entirely, or arranged in porticoes on one or more of its fronts. [TEMPLUM.] Their original and proper use was, of course, to support the roof of the building; and, amidst all the elaborations of architectural design, this object was still kept in view. On the summit of the row of columns rests the *architrave*, i. e. *chief beam* (ἐπιστύλιον, *epistylium*): above this is the *frieze* (ζωοφόρος, ζωφόρος, *zophorus*), in which the most ancient order, namely the Doric, shows, in its triglyphs, what were originally the ends of the cross-beams: in the other orders these ends are generally concealed, and the frieze forms a flat surface, which is frequently ornamented by figures in relief, whence its Greek name. Above the frieze projects the cornice (κορωνίς, *coronis* or *corona*), forming a handsome finish to the entablature (for so these three members taken together are called), and also, on the sides of the building, serving to unite the ends of the rafters of the roof. The triangular gable-end of the roof, above the entablature, is called the *pediment*. [FASTIGIUM.]—Columns in long rows were used in aquaeducts, and single pillars were fixed in harbours for mooring ships.—Single columns were also erected to commemorate persons or events. Among these, some of the most remarkable were the *columnae rostratae*, called by that name because three ship-beaks proceeded from each

Columna Rostrata.   Columna Trajana.

side of them, designed to record successful engagements at sea. The most important and celebrated of those which yet remain, is one erected in honour of the consul C. Duillius, on occasion of his victory over the Carthaginian fleet, B.C. 261. Columns were also employed to commemorate the dead. The column on the right hand in the last woodcut exhibits that which the senate erected to the honour of the Emperor Trajan. Similar columns were erected to the memory of many of the Roman emperors.

COLUMNĀRĬUM, a tax imposed in the time of Julius Caesar upon the pillars that supported a house. The *Ostiarium* was a similar tax. [OSTIARIUM.] The *columnarium* levied by Metellus Scipio in Syria in B.C. 49-48, was a tax of a similar kind, but was simply an illegal means of extorting money from the provincials.

COLUS, a distaff. [FUSUS.]

COMA (κόμη, κουρά), the hair. (1) GREEK. In the earliest times the Greeks wore their hair long, and thus they are constantly called in Homer καρηκομόωντες Ἀχαιοί. The Spartan boys always had their hair cut quite short (ἐν χρῷ κείροντες); but as soon as they reached the age of puberty (ἔφηβοι), they let it grow long. Before going to battle they combed and dressed it with especial care. It seems that both Spartan men and women tied their hair in a knot over the crown of the head. The custom of the Athenians was different. They wore their hair long in childhood, and cut it off when they reached the age of puberty. The cutting off of the hair, which was always done when a boy became an ἔφηβος, was a solemn act, attended with religious ceremonies. A libation was first offered to Hercules, which was called οἰνιστήρια or οἰνιαστήρια, and the hair after being cut off was dedicated to some deity, usually a river-god. But when the Athenians passed into the age of manhood, they again let their hair grow. In ancient times at Athens the hair was rolled up into a kind of knot on the crown of the head, and fastened with golden clasps in the shape of grasshoppers. This fashion of wearing the hair was called κρωβύλος, and in the case of females κόρυμβος. The heads of females were frequently covered with a kind of band or a coif of net-work. Of these coiffures one was called σφενδόνη, which was a broad band across the forehead, sometimes made of metal, and sometimes of leather, adorned with gold. But the most common kind of head-dress for females was called by the general name of κεκρύφαλος, and this was divided into the three species of κεκρύφαλος, σάκκος, and μίτρα. The κεκρύφαλος, in its narrower sense, was a caul or coif of net-work, corresponding to the Latin *reticulum*. These hair-nets were frequently made of gold threads, sometimes of silk, or the Elean byssus, and probably of other materials. The σάκκος and the μίτρα were, on the contrary, made of close materials. The σάκκος covered the head entirely like a sack or bag; it was made of various materials, such as silk, byssus, and wool. The μίτρα was a broad band of cloth of different colours, which was wound round the hair, and was worn in various ways. It was originally an Eastern head-dress, and may, therefore, be compared to the modern turban. The Roman *calautica* or *calvatica* is said by Servius to have been the same as the *mitra*, but in a passage in the Digest they are mentioned as if they were distinct.—With respect to the colour of the hair, black was the most frequent, but *blonde* (ξανθὴ κόμη) was the most prized. In Homer,

Greek Head-dresses. (From Ancient Vases.)

The left-hand figure on the top wears a κεκρύφαλος proper (*reticulum*). Of the two bottom figures, the one on the left-hand wears a μίτρα, and the one on the right a σάκκος.

Achilles, Ulysses, and other heroes are represented with blonde hair. At a later time it seems to have been not unfrequent to dye hair, so as to make it either black or blonde, and this was done by men as well as by women, especially when the hair was growing gray.—(2) ROMAN. Besides the generic *coma* we also find the following words signifying the hair: *capillus*, *caesaries*, *crines*, *cincinnus*, and *cirrus*, the two last words being used to signify curled hair. In early times the Romans wore their hair long, and hence the Romans of the Augustan age designated their ancestors *intonsi* and *capillati*. But after the introduction of barbers into Italy about B. C. 300, it became the practice to wear the hair short. The women, too, originally dressed their hair with great simplicity, but in the Augustan period a variety of different head-dresses came into fashion. Sometimes these head-dresses were raised to a great height by rows of false curls. So much attention did the Roman ladies devote to the dressing of the hair, that they kept slaves especially for this purpose, called *ornatrices*, and had them instructed by a master in the art. Most of the Greek head-dresses mentioned above were also worn by the Roman ladies; but the *mitrae* appear to have been confined to prostitutes. One of the simplest modes of wearing the hair was allowing it to fall down in tresses behind, and only confining it by a band encircling the head. [VITTA.] Another favourite plan was platting the hair, and then fastening it behind with a large pin. Blonde hair was as much prized by the Romans as by the Greeks, and hence the Roman ladies used a kind of composition or wash to make it appear this colour (*spuma caustica*). False hair or wigs (φενάκη, πηνίκη, *galerus*) were worn both by Greeks and Romans. Among both people likewise in ancient times the hair was cut close in mourning [FUNUS]; and among both the slaves had their hair cut close as a mark of servitude.

COMISSATIO (derived from κῶμος), the name of a drinking entertainment, which took place after the coena, from which, however, it must be distinguished. The comissatio was frequently prolonged to a late hour at night, whence the verb *comissari* means "to revel," and the substantive *comissator* a "reveller," or "debauchee."

COMITIA. This word is formed from *co*, *cum*, or *con*, and *ire*, and therefore *comitium* is a place of meeting, and *comitia* the meeting itself, or the assembled people. In the Roman constitution the comitia were the ordinary and legal meetings or assemblies of the people, and distinct from the *contiones* and *concilia*. All the powers of government were divided at Rome between the senate, the magistrates, and the people in their assemblies. Properly speaking, the people alone (the *populus*) was the real sovereign by whom the power was delegated to the magistrates and the senate. The sovereign people or populus, however, was not the same at all times. In the earliest times of Rome the populus consisted of the patricians (or patres) only, the plebs and the clients forming no part of the populus, but being without the pale of the state. The original populus was divided into thirty *curiae*, and the assembly of these curiae (the *comitia curiata*) was the only assembly in which the populus was represented. A kind of amalgamation of the patricians and the plebs afterwards appeared in the comitia of the centuries, instituted by king Servius Tullius, and henceforth the term populus was applied to the united patricians and plebeians assembled in the *comitia centuriata*. But Servius had also made a local division of the whole Roman territory into thirty tribes, which held their meetings in assemblies called *comitia tributa*, which, in the course of time, acquired the character of national assemblies, so that the people thus assembled were likewise designated by the term populus.

We shall examine in order the nature, power, and business of each of these different comitia. (1) COMITIA CURIATA consisted of the members of the thirty curiae, that is, the patricians, who formed exclusively the populus in the early times. They were convened, in the kingly period, by the king himself, or by his tribunus celerum, and in the king's absence by the praefectus urbi. After the death of a king the comitia were held by the interrex. In the republican period, the president was always one of the high patrician magistrates, viz. a consul, praetor, or dictator. They were called together by lictors or heralds. The votes were given by curiae, each curia having one collective vote; but within a curia each citizen belonging to it had an independent vote, and the majority of the members of a curia determined the vote of the whole curia. The meeting was always held in the comitium. The comitia curiata did not possess much power in the kingly period. They could only be called together when the king (or his representative) chose, and could only determine upon matters which the king submitted to them. The main points upon which the populus had to decide were the election of the king, the passing of laws, declarations of war, the capital punishment of Roman citizens, and, lastly, certain affairs of the curiae and gentes. The priestly officers, such as the Curiones, Flamines Curiales, were likewise either elected by the curiae, or at least inaugurated by them. The right of finally deciding upon the life of Roman citizens (*judicia de capite civis Romani*) is said to have been given to the populus by king Tullus Hostilius. It must further be remarked, that when the king had been elected, the populus held a second meeting, in which he was formally inducted into his new office. This formality was called *lex curiata de imperio*, whereby the king received his *imperium*, together with the right of holding the comitia. Down to the time of Servius Tullius, the comitia curiata were the only popular assemblies of Rome, and remained of course in the undiminished possession of the rights above described; but the constitution of that king brought about a great change, by transferring the principal rights which had hitherto been enjoyed by the curiae to a new national assembly or the comitia centuriata. But while the patricians were obliged to share their rights with the plebeians, they reserved for themselves the very important right of sanctioning or rejecting any measure which had been passed by the centuries. The sanction of decrees passed by the centuries is often expressed by *patres auctores fiunt*, and down to

the time of the Publilian law no decree of the centuries could become law without this sanction. By the Publilian law (B.C. 339) it was enacted that the curiae should give their assent before the vote of the comitia centuriata; so that the veto of the curiae was thus virtually abolished. The comitia curiata thus became a mere formality, and, instead of the thirty curiae themselves giving their votes, the ceremony was performed by thirty lictors. The comitia of the curiae were also called COMITIA CALATA or "the summoned comitia" (from *calare*, i. e. *vocare*), when summoned for the purposes mentioned below:—
1. On the calends it was proclaimed to the comitia calata on what day of the new month the nones fell, and perhaps also the ides as well as the nature of the other days, namely, whether they were fasti or nefasti, comitiales, feriae, &c., because all these things were known in the early times to the pontiffs exclusively. 2. The inauguration of the flamines, and after the banishment of the kings, also that of the rex sacrorum. 3. The *testamenti factio*, or the making of a will. 4. The *detestatio sacrorum*, which was in all probability an act connected with the testamenti factio, that is, a solemn declaration, by which the heir was enjoined to undertake the sacra privata of the testator along with the reception of his property. The comitia calata were summoned by the college **of pontiffs,** who also presided in them.

(2) COMITIA CENTURIATA. The object of the legislation of Servius Tullius was to unite the different elements of which **the** Roman people consisted, into one great political body, in which power and influence were to be determined by property and age. The whole people was conceived as an army (*exercitus*), and was therefore divided into two parts, **the cavalry** (*equites*), and infantry (*pedites*). **The infantry was divided into five classes, or,** as Dionysius has it, into six classes, for **he regards the whole** body of people, whose **property did not come up** to the census of the **fifth class, as a sixth.** The class to which a **citizen belonged determined** the *tributum*, or **war tax, he had to pay, as** well as the kind **of service he had to perform** in the army and **the armour in which he had** to serve. But for the purpose of voting in **the** comitia, each class was subdivided into a number of centuries (*centuriae*, probably because each was conceived to contain 100 men, though the centuries may have greatly differed in the number of men they contained). Hence the name of *Comitia Centuriata*. Each century was divided into the *seniores* and the *juniores*. **Each century, further,** was counted **as one vote, so that a class had as many votes as it** contained centuries. **In like manner, the** equites **were divided into a number of centuries** or votes. **The two principal authorities on these subdivisions are Livy and Dionysius. The annexed table will show the** census as well as the number of **centuries or** votes assigned to each class.

According to Livy.

I. CLASSIS. Census: 100,000 asses.
  40 centuriae seniorum.
  40 centuriae juniorum.
  2 centuriae fabrum.

II. CLASSIS. Census: 75,000 asses.
  10 centuriae seniorum.
  10 centuriae juniorum.

III. CLASSIS. Census: 50,000 asses.
  10 centuriae seniorum.
  10 centuriae juniorum.

IV. CLASSIS. Census: 25,000 asses.
  10 centuriae seniorum.
  10 centuriae juniorum.

V. CLASSIS. Census: 11,000 asses.
  15 centuriae seniorum.
  15 centuriae juniorum.
  3 centuriae accensorum, cornicinum, tubicinum.
  1 centuria capite censorum.

According to Dionysius.

I. CLASSIS. Census: 100 minae.
  40 centuriae seniorum.
  40 centuriae juniorum.

II. CLASSIS. Census: 75 minae.
  10 centuriae seniorum.
  10 centuriae juniorum.
  2 centuriae fabrum (one voting with the seniores and the other with the juniores).

III. CLASSIS. Census: 50 minae.
  10 centuriae **seniorum.**
  10 centuriae juniorum.

IV. CLASSIS. Census: 25 minae.
  10 centuriae seniorum.
  10 centuriae juniorum.
  2 centuriae cornicinum **and** tubicinum (one voting with the seniores, and the other with the juniores).

V. CLASSIS. Census: 12½ minae.
  15 centuriae seniorum.
  15 centuriae juniorum.

VI. CLASSIS. Census: below 12½ minae.
  1 centuria capite censorum.

According to both Dionysius and Livy, the equites voted in eighteen centuries before the seniores of the first class; and hence there were, according to Livy, 194, and, according to Dionysius, 193 centuries or votes. The latter number is the more probable, since Livy's even number of 194 centuries would have rendered it impossible to obtain an absolute majority. In this manner all Roman citizens, whether patricians or plebeians, who had property to a certain amount, were privileged to take part and vote in the centuriata comitia, and none were excluded except slaves, peregrini, women and the aerarii. The juniores were all men from the age of seventeen to that of forty-six, and the seniores all men from the age of forty-six upwards. The order of voting was arranged in such a manner, that if the eighteen centuries of the equites and the eighty centuries of the first class were agreed upon a measure, the question was decided at once, there being no need for calling upon the other classes to vote. Hence, although all Roman citizens appeared in these comitia on a footing of equality, yet by far the greater power was thrown into the hands of the wealthy.—As regards the functions of the comitia centuriata, they were— (a.) *The election of magistrates.* The magistrates that were elected by the centuries are the consuls (whence the assembly is called *comitia consularia*), the praetors (hence *comitia praetoria*), the military tribunes with consular power, the censors, and the decemvirs. (b.) *Legislation.* The legislative power of the centuries at first consisted in their passing or rejecting a measure which was brought before them by the presiding magistrate in the form of a senatus consultum, so that the assembly had no right of originating any legislative measure, but voted only upon such as were brought before them as resolutions of the senate. (c.) *The decision upon war,* on the ground of a senatus consultum, likewise belonged to the centuries. Peace was concluded by a mere senatus consultum, and without any co-operation of the people. (d.) *The highest judicial power.* The comitia centuriata were in the first place the highest court of appeal, and in the second, they had to try all offences committed against the state; hence, all cases of *perduellio* and *majestas*: and no case involving the life of a Roman citizen could be decided by any other court. The sanction of the curiae to the measures of the centuriae has been already explained.—The comitia centuriata could be held only on *dies comitiales* or *fasti*, on which it was lawful to transact business with the people, and the number of such days in every year was about 190; but on *dies nefasti* (that is, *dies festi, feriati*, comp. DIES), and, at first also on the nundinae, no comitia could be held, until in B.C. 287 the Hortensian law ordained that the nundinae should be regarded as dies fasti.— The place where the centuries met was the Campus Martius, which contained the septa for the voters, a tabernaculum for the president, and the villa publica for the augurs.—The president at the comitia was the same magistrate who convoked them, and this right was a privilege of the consuls, and, in their absence, of the practors. An interrex and dictator also, or his representative, the magister equitum, might likewise convene and preside at the comitia. One of the main duties devolving upon the president, and which he had to perform before holding the comitia, was to consult the auspices (*auspicari*). When the auspices were favourable, the people were called together, which was done by three successive and distinct acts: the first was quite a general invitation to come to the assembly (*inlicium*). At the same time when this invitation was proclaimed *circum moeros* or *de moeris*, a horn was blown, which being the more audible signal, is mentioned by some writers alone, and without the inlicium. When upon this signal the people assembled in irregular masses, there followed the second call by the accensus, or the call *ad contionem* or *conventionem;* that is, to a regular assembly, and the crowd then separated, grouping themselves according to their classes and ages. Hereupon the consul appeared, ordering the people to come *ad comitia centuriata;* and led the whole *exercitus*—for, in these comitia, the Roman people are always conceived as an exercitus—out of the city, to the Campus Martius.— It was customary from the earliest times for an armed force to occupy the Janiculum, when the people were assembled in the Campus Martius, for the purpose of protecting the city against any sudden attack of the neighbouring people; and on the Janiculum a vexillum was hoisted during the whole time that the assembly lasted. This custom continued to be observed even at the time when Rome had no longer anything to fear from the neighbouring tribes.—When the people were thus regularly assembled, the business was commenced with a solemn sacrifice, and a prayer of the president, who then took his seat on his tribunal. The president then opened the business by explaining to the people the subject for which they had been convened, and concluded his exposition with the words, *velitis, jubeatis Quirites,* e. g. *bellum indici,* or *ut M. Tullio aqua igni interdictum sit,* or whatever the subject might be. This formula was the standing one in all comitia, and the whole exposition of the president was called *rogatio*. When the comitia were assembled for the purpose of an election, the presiding magistrate had to read out the names of the candidates, and might exercise his influence by recommending the one whom he thought most fit for the office in question. If the assembly had been convened for the purpose of passing a legislative measure, the president usually recommended the proposal, or he might grant to others, if they desired it, permission to speak about the measure, either in its favour or against it (*Contionem dare*). When the comitia acted as a court of justice, the president stated the crime, proposed the punishment to be inflicted upon the offender, and then allowed others to speak either in defence of the accused or against him. When the subject brought before the assembly was sufficiently discussed, the president called upon the people to prepare for voting by the words, *ite in suffragium, bene juvantibus diis*. He then passed the stream Petronia, and went to the *septa*.—Respecting the mode of voting, it is commonly supposed that the people were always polled by word of mouth, till the passing of the *leges tabellariae* about the middle of the second century before Christ, when the ballot by means of tabellae was introduced. [LEGES TABELLARIAE.] It appears, however, that the popular assemblies voted by ballot, as well as by word of mouth, long before the passing of the *leges tabellariae*, but that instead of using tabellae, they employed stones or pebbles (the Greek ψῆφοι), and that each voter received two stones, one white and the other black, the former to be used in the approval and the latter in the condemnation of a measure. The voting by word of mouth seems to have been adopted in elections and trials, and the use of pebbles to have been confined to the enactment and repeal of laws. Previous to the *leges tabellariae*, the rogatores, who subsequently collected the written votes, stood at the entrance of the septa, and asked every citizen for his vote, which was taken down, and used to determine the vote of each century. After the introduction of the ballot, if the business was the passing of a law, each citizen was provided with two tabellae, one inscribed V. R. *i. e. Uti Rogas*, "I vote for the law," the other inscribed A. *i. e. Antiquo*, "I am for the old law." If the business was the election of a magistrate, each citizen was supplied with only one tablet, on which the names of the candidates were written, or the initials of their names; the voter then placed a mark (*punctum*) against the one for whom he voted, whence *puncta* are spoken of

in the sense of votes. For further particulars respecting the voting in the comitia, see DIRIBITORES and SITULA. In judicial assemblies every citizen was provided with three tabellae, one of which was marked with A. *i. e. Absolvo*, "I acquit;" the second with C. *i. e. Condemno*, "I condemn;" and the third with N. L. *i. e. Non Liquet*, "It is not clear to me." The first of these was called *Tabella absolutoria* and the second *Tabella damnatoria*, and hence Cicero calls the former *litera salutaris*, and the latter *litera tristis*.—There were in the Campus Martius septa or inclosures (whether they existed from the earliest times is unknown), into which one class of citizens was admitted after another for the purpose of voting. The first that entered were the eighteen centuries of the equites, then followed the first class and so on. It very rarely happened that the lowest class was called upon to vote, as there was no necessity for it, unless the first class did not agree with the equites. After the time when the comitia of the centuries became amalgamated with those of the tribes, a large space near the villa publica was surrounded with an enclosure, and divided into compartments for the several tribes. The whole of this enclosure was called *ovile*, *septa*, *carceres*, or *cancelli*; and in later times a stone building, containing the whole people, was erected; it was divided into compartments for the classes as well as the tribes and centuries; the access to these compartments was formed by narrow passages called *pontes* or *ponticuli*. On entering, the citizens received their tablets, and when they had consulted within the enclosures, they passed out of them again by a *pons* or *ponticulus*, at which they threw their vote into a chest (*cista*) which was watched by *rogatores*. Hereupon the *rogatores* collected the tablets, and gave them to the *diribitores*, who classified and counted the votes, and then handed them over to the *custodes*, who again checked them off by points marked on a tablet. The order in which the centuries voted was determined in the Servian constitution, in the manner described above; but after the union of the centuries and tribes, the order was determined by lot; and this was a matter of no slight importance, since it frequently happened that the vote of the first determined the manner in which subsequent ones voted. In the case of elections, the successful candidate was proclaimed twice, first by the praeco, and then by the president, and without this renuntiatio the election was not valid. After all the business was done, the president pronounced a prayer, and dismissed the assembly with the word *discedite*.—Cases are frequently mentioned in which the proceedings of the assembly were disturbed, so that it was necessary to defer the business till another day. This occurred—1, when it was discovered that the auspices had been unfavourable, or when the gods manifested their displeasure by rain, thunder, or lightning; 2, when a tribune interceded; 3, when the sun set before the business was over, for it was a principle that the auspices were valid only for one day from sunrise to sunset; 4, when a *morbus comitialis* occurred, *i. e.* when one of the assembled citizens was seized with an epileptic fit; 5, when the vexillum was taken away from the Janiculum, this being a signal which all citizens had to obey; 6, when any tumult or insurrection broke out in the city.

(3) COMITIA TRIBUTA. These assemblies likewise were called into existence by the constitution of Servius Tullius, who divided the Roman territory into thirty local tribes. It is a disputed question whether the patricians were originally included in these tribes; but, whether they were or not, it is certain, that by far the majority of the people in the tribes were plebeians, and that, consequently, the character of these assemblies was essentially plebeian. After the decemvirate, the patricians had certainly the right of voting in the assemblies of the tribes, which were then also convened by the higher magistrates. The assemblies of the tribes had originally only a local power; they were intended to collect the tributum, and to furnish the contingents for the army; they may further have discussed the internal affairs of each tribe, such as the making or keeping up of roads, wells, and the like. But their influence gradually increased, and they at length acquired the following powers:—
1. *The election of the inferior magistrates,* whose office it was to protect the commonalty or to superintend the affairs of the tribes. Hence the tribunes of the plebs were elected in the comitia tributa. In like manner, the aediles were elected by them, though the curule aediles were elected at a different time from the plebeian aediles and under the presidency of a consul. At a still later time, the quaestors and tribunes of the soldiers, who had before been appointed by the consuls, were appointed in the assemblies of the tribes. The proconsuls to be sent into the provinces, and the prolongation of the imperium for a magistrate who was already in a province, were likewise points which were determined by the tribes in later times. The inferior magistrates elected by the tribes are:—the triumviri capitales, triumviri monetales, the curatores viarum, decemviri litibus judicandis, tribuni aerarii, magistri vicorum et pagorum, praefecti annonae, duumviri navales, quinqueviri muris turribusque reficiendis, triumviri coloniae deducendae, triumviri, quatuorviri, &c., mensarii, and lastly, after the Domitian law, B. C. 104, also the members of colleges of priests. The pontifex maximus had been elected by the people from an earlier time. 2. *The legislative power* of the comitia tributa was at first very insignificant, for all they could do was to make regulations concerning the local affairs of the tribes. But after a time, when the tribes began to be the real representatives of the people, matters affecting the whole people also were brought before them by the tribunes, which, framed as resolutions, were laid before the senate, where they might either be sanctioned or rejected. This practice of the tributa comitia gradually acquired for them the right of taking the initiative in any measure, or the right of originating measures, until, in B. C. 449, this right was recognised and sanctioned by a law of L. Valerius Publicola and M. Horatius Barbatus. This law gave to the decrees passed by the tribes the power of a real *lex*, binding upon the whole people, provided they obtained the sanction of the senate and the populus, that is, the people assembled in the comitia curiata or in the comitia centuriata. In B. C. 339, the Publilian law enacted *ut plebiscita omnes Quirites tenerent*. This law was either a re-enactment of the one passed in B. C. 449, or contained a more detailed specification of the cases in which plebiscita should be binding upon the whole nation, or, lastly, it made their validity independent of the sanction of other comitia, so that nothing would be required except the assent of the senate. In B. C. 287, the Hortensian law was passed, which seems to have been only a revival and a confirmation of the two preceding laws, for it was framed in almost the same terms; but it may also be, that the Hortensian law made the plebiscita independent of the sanction of the senate, so that henceforth the comitia tributa were quite independent in their legislative character. 3. *The judicial power* of the comitia tributa was much more limited than that of the comitia centuriata, inasmuch as they could take cognizance only of offences against the majesty of the people, while all crimes committed against the state were brought before the centuries. Even patricians, when they had offended against the commonalty or its members, were tried and fined by the tribes. This again constitutes a difference between the judicial power of the centuries and that of the tribes, for the former could inflict capital punishment, but the latter only fines. The comitia tri-

buta might assemble either within or without the city, but not farther from it than 1000 paces, because the power of the tribunes did not extend farther. For elections the Campus Martius was usually chosen, but sometimes also the forum, the Capitol, or the Circus Flaminius. The presidents were commonly the tribunes, who were supported by the aediles, and no matter could be brought before the tribes without the knowledge and consent of the tribunes. As the comitia tributa, however, more and more assumed the character of national assemblies, the higher magistrates also sometimes acted as presidents, though perhaps not without previously obtaining the permission of the tribunes. The preparations for the comitia tributa were less formal and solemn than for those of the centuries. In the case of elections, the candidates had to give in their names, and the president communicated them to the people. When a legislative measure was to be brought before the assembly, a tribune made the people acquainted with it in contiones, and that on the three preceding nundines. The same was the case when the people were to meet as a court of justice. The auspicia were not consulted for the comitia of the tribes, but the spectio alone was sufficient, and the tribunes had the right of obnuntiatio. In the comitia the tribune who had been chosen to preside sat on the tribunal supported by his colleagues, and laid before the people the subject of the meeting, concluding with the words velitis, jubeatis Quirites. The bill was never read by the tribune himself, but by a praeco, and then began the debates, in which persons might either oppose or recommend the measure, though private persons had to ask the tribunes for permission to speak. When the discussion was over the president called upon the people ite in suffragium, as at the comitia centuriata. They then formed themselves into their tribes, which, like the centuries, ascertained their own votes in enclosures (septa). Which of the 35 tribes was to give its vote first, was determined by lot, and that tribe was called praerogativa or principium (the others were termed jure vocatae). The vote of the first tribe was given by some person of distinction whose name was mentioned in the plebiscitum, if it was of a legislative nature. The manner of collecting the votes was, on the whole, the same as in the comitia centuriata. The announcing of the result of the votes was the renuntiatio. If it so happened that two candidates had the same number of votes, the question was decided by drawing lots. The circumstances which might cause the meeting to break up and defer its business till another day, are the same as those which put an end to the comitia centuriata.

(4) *The comitia centuriata mixed with the comitia tributa.*—The Servian constitution was retained unaltered so long as no great change took place in the republic; but when the coinage and the standard of property had become altered, when the constitution of the army had been placed on a different footing, and, above all, when the plebeians began to be recognized as a great and essential element in the Roman state, it must have been found inconvenient to leave to the equites and the first class so great a preponderance in the comitia of the centuries, and it became necessary to secure more power and influence to the democratic element. A change, therefore, took place, and the comitia centuriata became mixed with the comitia tributa; but neither the time nor the exact nature of this change is accurately ascertained. Some refer it to the censorship of C. Flaminius, B. c. 220, others to that of Q. Fabius and P. Decius, B. c. 304. But there is evidence that it must be assigned to even an earlier date than this, for the (tribus) praerogativa is mentioned as early as B. c. 396 in the election of the consular tribunes, where the pure comitia tributa cannot be meant, and a centuria praerogativa is a thing unknown. With regard to the manner of the change, the most probable opinion is, that the citizens of each tribe were divided into five property classes, each consisting of seniores and juniores, so that each of the 35 tribes contained ten centuries, and all the tribes together 350 centuries. According to this new arrangement, the five ancient classes, divided into seniores and juniores, continued to exist as before, but henceforth they were most closely united with the tribes, whereas before the tribes had been mere local divisions and entirely independent of property. The union now effected was that the classes became subdivisions of the tribes, and that accordingly centuries occur both in the classes and in the tribes. Each tribe contained ten centuries, two of the first class (one of the seniores and one of the juniores), two of the second (likewise seniores and juniores), two of the third, two of the fourth, and two of the fifth class. The equites were likewise divided according to tribes and centuries, and they seem to have voted with the first class, and to have been in fact included in it, so as to be called centuries of the first class. The centuries of the cornicines, tubicines and fabri, which are no longer mentioned, probably ceased to exist as distinct centuries. The voting by tribes can hardly be conceived, except in those cases in which the ten centuries of every tribe were unani-

mous; this may have been the case very often, and when it was so, the tribus praerogativa was certainly the tribe chosen by lot to give its unanimous vote first. But if there was any difference of opinion among the centuries making up a tribe, the true majority could only be ascertained by choosing by lot one of the 70 centuriae of the first class to give its vote first, or rather it was decided by lot from which tribe the two centuries of the first class were to be taken to give their vote first. (Hence the plural *praerogativae*.) The tribe, moreover, to which those centuries belonged which voted first, was itself likewise called tribus praerogativa. Of the two centuries, again, that of seniores gave its vote before the juniores, and in the documents both were called by the name of their tribe, as *Galeria juniorum*, *i. e.* the juniores of the first class in the tribus Galeria, *Aniensis juniorum*, *Veturia juniorum*. As soon as the praerogativa had voted, the renuntiatio took place, and the remaining centuries then deliberated whether they should vote the same way or not. When this was done all the centuries of the first tribe proceeded to vote at once, for there would not have been time for the 350 centuries to vote one after another, as was done by the 193 centuries in the comitia centuriata.—These comitia of the centuries combined with the tribes were far more democratical than the comitia of the centuries; they continued to be held, and preserved their power along with the comitia tributa, even after the latter had acquired their supreme importance in the republic. During the time of the moral and political corruption of the Romans, the latter appear to have been chiefly attended by the populace, which was guided by the tribunes, and the wealthier and more respectable citizens had little influence in them. When the libertini and all the Italians were incorporated in the old thirty-five tribes, and when the political corruption had reached its height, no trace of the sedate and moderate character was left by which the comitia tributa had been distinguished in former times. Under Augustus the comitia still sanctioned new laws and elected magistrates, but their whole proceedings were a mere farce, for they could not venture to elect any other persons than those recommended by the emperor. Tiberius deprived the people even of this shadow of their former power, and conferred the power of election upon the senate. When the elections were made by the senate the result was announced to the people assembled as comitia centuriata or tributa. Legislation was taken away from the comitia entirely, and was completely in the hands of the senate and the emperor. From this time the comitia may be said to have ceased to exist, as all the sovereign power formerly possessed by the people was conferred upon the emperor by the lex regia. [LEX REGIA.]

COMMEĀTUS, a furlough, or leave of absence from the army for a certain time.

COMMENTĀRĬUS or COMMENTĀRĬUM, a book of memoirs or memorandum-book, whence the expression *Caesaris Commentarii*. It is also used for a lawyer's brief, the notes of a speech, &c.

COMMERCĬUM. [CIVITAS (ROMAN).]

CŌMOEDĬA (κωμῳδία), comedy. (1) GREEK. Comedy took its rise at the vintage festivals of Dionysus. It originated with those who led off the phallic songs of the band of revellers (κῶμος), who at the vintage festivals of Dionysus gave expression to the feelings of exuberant joy and merriment which were regarded as appropriate to the occasion, by parading about, partly on foot, partly in waggons, with the symbol of the productive powers of nature, singing a wild, jovial song in honour of Dionysus and his companions. These songs were commonly interspersed with, or followed by petulant, extemporal witticisms with which the revellers assailed the bystanders. This origin of comedy is indicated by the name κωμῳδία, which undoubtedly means "the song of the κῶμος," though it has sometimes been derived from κώμη, as if the meaning were "a village song." It was among the Dorians that comedy first assumed any thing of a regular shape. The Megarians, both in the mother country and in Sicily, claimed to be considered as its originators, and so far as the comedy of Athens is concerned, the claim of the former appears well founded. Among the Athenians the first attempts at comedy were made at Icaria by Susarion, a native of Megara, about B. C. 578. Susarion no doubt substituted for the more ancient improvisations of the chorus and its leader premeditated compositions. There would seem also to have been some kind of poetical contest, for we learn that the prize for the successful poet was a basket of figs and a jar of wine. It was also the practice of those who took part in the comus to smear their faces with wine-lees, either to prevent their features from being recognised, or to give themselves a more grotesque appearance. Hence comedy came to be called τρυγῳδία, or lee-song. Others connected the name with the circumstance of a jar of new wine (τρύξ) being the prize for the successful poet. It was, however, in Sicily, that comedy was earliest brought to something like perfection. Epicharmus was the first writer who gave it new form, and introduced a regular plot. In his efforts he appears to have been associated with Phormis, a somewhat older contemporary. The Megarians in Sicily claimed the honour of the invention of comedy, on account of Epicharmus having lived in Megara before he went to Syracuse. In Attica, the first comic poet of any importance whom we hear of after Susarion is Chionides, who is said to have brought out plays in B. C. 488. Euetes, Euxenides, and Myllus were probably contemporaries of Chionides; he was followed by Magnes and Ecphantides. Their compositions, however, seem to have been little but the reproduction of the old Megaric farce of Susarion, differing, no doubt, in form, by the introduction of an actor or actors, separate from the chorus, in imitation of the improvements that had been made in tragedy.—That branch of the Attic drama which was called the *Old Comedy*, begins properly with Cratinus, who was to comedy very much what Aeschylus was to tragedy. The old comedy has been described as the comedy of caricature, and such indeed it was, but it was also a great deal more. As it appeared in the hands of its great masters Cratinus, Hermippus, Eupolis, and especially Aristophanes, its main characteristic was that it was throughout *political*. Everything that bore upon the political or social interests of the Athenians furnished materials for it. The old Attic comedy lasted from Ol. 80 to Ol. 94 (B. C. 458-404). From Cratinus to Theopompus there were forty-one poets, fourteen of whom preceded Aristophanes. The later pieces of Aristophanes belong to the Middle rather than to the Old Comedy. The chorus in a comedy consisted of twenty-four. Chorus.] The dance of the chorus was the κόρδαξ, the movements of which were capricious and licentious, consisting partly in a reeling to and fro, in imitation of a drunken man, and in various unseemly and immodest gestures. Comedies have choric songs, but no στάσιμα, or songs between acts. The most important of the choral parts was the Parabasis, when the actors having left the stage, the chorus, which was ordinarily divided into four rows, containing six each, and was turned towards the stage, turned round, and advancing towards the spectators delivered an address to them in the name of the poet, either on public topics of general interest, or on matters which concerned the poet personally, criticising his rivals and calling attention to his merits; the address having nothing whatever to do with the action of the play. The parabasis was not universally introduced: three plays of Aristophanes, the Ecclesiazusae, Lysistrata, and Plutus, have

none. As the old Attic comedy was the offspring of the political and social vigour and freedom of the age during which it flourished, it naturally declined and ceased with the decline and overthrow of the freedom and vigour which were necessary for its development.—It was replaced by a comedy of a somewhat different style, which was known as the *Middle Comedy*, the age of which lasted from the end of the Peloponnesian war to the overthrow of liberty by Philip of Macedon. (Ol. 94-110.) The comedy of this period found its materials in satirizing classes of people instead of individuals, in criticising the systems and merits of philosophers and literary men, and in parodies of the compositions of living and earlier poets, and travesties of mythological subjects. It formed a transition from the old to the new comedy, and approximated to the latter in the greater attention to the construction of plots which seem frequently to have been founded on amorous intrigues, and in the absence of that wild grotesqueness which marked the old comedy. As regards its external form, the plays of the middle comedy, generally speaking, had neither parabasis nor chorus. The most celebrated authors of the middle comedy were Antiphanes and Alexis.—The *New Comedy* was a further development of the last mentioned kind. It answered as nearly as may be to the modern comedy of manners or character. Dropping, for the most part personal allusions, caricature, ridicule, and parody, which, in a more general form than in the old comedy, had maintained their ground in the middle comedy, the poets of the new comedy made it their business to reproduce in a generalized form a picture of the every-day life of those by whom they were surrounded. There were various standing characters which found a place in most plays, such as we find in the plays of Plautus and Terence, the *leno perjurus, amator ferridus, serculus callidus, amica illudens, sodalis opitulator, miles proeliator, parasitus edax, parentes tenaces, meretrices procaces*. In the new comedy there was no chorus. It flourished from about B. C. 340 to B. C. 260. The poets of the new comedy amounted to 64 in number. The most distinguished was Menander.—(2) ROMAN.—The accounts of the early stages of comic poetry among the Romans are scanty. Scenic entertainments were introduced at Rome in B. C. 363 from Etruria, where it would seem they were a familiar amusement. Tuscan players (*ludiones*), who were fetched from Etruria, exhibited a sort of pantomimic dance to the music of a flute, without any song accompanying their dance, and without regular dramatic gesticulation. The amusement became popular, and was imitated by the young Romans, who improved upon the original entertainment by uniting with it extemporaneous mutual raillery, composed in a rude irregular measure, a species of diversion which had been long known among the Romans at their agrarian festivals under the name of *Fescennina* [FESCENNINA]. It was 123 years after the first introduction of these scenic performances before the improvement was introduced of having a regular plot. This advance was made by Livius Andronicus, a native of Magna Graecia, in B.C. 240. His pieces, which were both tragedies and comedies, were merely adaptations of Greek dramas. The representation of regular plays of this sort was now left to those who were histriones by profession, and who were very commonly either foreigners or slaves; the free-born youth of Rome confined their own scenic performances to the older, irregular farces, which long maintained their ground, and were subsequently called *exodia*. [EXODIA; SATURA.] Livius, as was common at that time, was himself an actor in his own pieces. The first imitator of the dramatic works of Livius Andronicus was Cn. Naevius, a native of Campania. He composed both tragedies and comedies, which were either translations or imitations of those of Greek writers. The most distinguished successors of Naevius were Plautus, who chiefly imitated Epicharmus, and Terence, whose materials were drawn mostly from Menander, Diphilus, Philemon, and Apollodorus. The comedy of the Romans was throughout but an imitation of that of the Greeks, and chiefly of the new comedy. Where the characters were ostensibly Greek, and the scene laid in Athens or some other Greek town, the comedies were termed *palliatae*. All the comedies of Terence and Plautus belong to this class. When the story and characters were Roman, the plays were called *togatae*. But the fabulae togatae were in fact little else than Greek comedies clothed in a Latin dress.

The togatae were divided into two classes, the *trabeatae* and *tabernariae*, according as the subject was taken from high or from low life. In the comediae palliatae, the costume of the ordinary actors was the Greek pallium. The plays which bore the name of *praetextatae*, were not so much tragedies as historical plays. It is a mistake to represent them as comedies. There was a species of tragicomedy, named from the poet who introduced that style *Rhinthonica*. A tragedy the argument of which was Greek was termed *crepidata*. The mimes are sometimes classed with the Latin comedies. [MIMUS.] The mimes differed from the comedies in little more than the predominance of the mimic representation over the dialogue. Latin comedies had no chorus, any more than the dramas of the new comedy, of which they were for the most part imitations. Like them, too, they were introduced by a prologue, which answered some of the purposes of the parabasis of the old comedy, so far as bespeaking the good will of the spectators, and defending the poet against his rivals and enemies. It also communicated so much information as was necessary to understand the story of the play. The prologue was commonly spoken by one of the players, or, perhaps, by the manager of the troop. Respecting the *Atellanae fabulae* see that article.

COMPITĀLIA, also called LŪDI COMPITĀLICII, a festival celebrated once a year in honour of the lares compitales, to whom sacrifices were offered at the places where two or more ways met. In the time of Augustus, the ludi compitalicii had gone out of fashion, but were restored by him. The compitalia belonged to the *feriae conceptivae*, that is, festivals which were celebrated on days appointed annually by the magistrates or priests. The exact day on which this festival was celebrated appears to have varied, though it was always in the winter, generally at the beginning of January.

COMPLŬVĬUM. [DOMUS.]

CONCĬLĬUM generally has the same meaning as *conventus* or *conventio*, but the technical import of concilium in the Roman constitution was an assembly of a *portion* of the people as distinct from the general assemblies or comitia. Accordingly, as the comitia tributa embraced only a portion of the Roman people, viz. the plebeians, these comitia are often designated by the term *concilia plebis*. Concilium is also used by Latin writers to denote the assemblies or meetings of confederate towns or nations, at which either their deputies alone or any of the citizens met who had time and inclination, and thus formed a representative assembly. Such an assembly or diet is commonly designated as *commune concilium*, or τὸ κοινόν, e.g. *Achaeorum, Aetolorum, Boeotorum, Macedoniae*, and the like.

CONFARRĒĀTĬO. [MATRIMONIUM.]

CONGĬĀRĬUM (*scil. vas*, from *congius*), a vessel containing a *congius*. [CONGIUS.] In the early times of the Roman republic the *congius* was the usual measure of oil or wine which was, on certain occasions, distributed among the people; and thus *congiarium* became a name for liberal donations to the people, in general, whether consisting of oil, wine, corn, money, or other things, while donations made to the soldiers were called *donativa*, though they were sometimes also termed *congiaria*. Many coins of the Roman emperors were struck in commemoration of such congiaria. *Congiarium* was, moreover, occasionally used simply to designate a present or a pension given by a person of high rank, or a prince, to his friends.

Congiarium. (Coin of Trajan.)

CONGĬUS, a Roman liquid measure, which contained six sextarii, or the eighth part of the amphora (nearly six pints Eng.) It was equal to the larger *chous* of the Greeks.

CONNUBIUM. [MATRIMONIUM.]

CŌNŌPĔUM (κωνωπειον), a gnat or musquito-curtain, *i. e.* a covering made to be expanded over beds and couches to keep away gnats and other flying insects, so called from κωνωψ, a gnat. *Conopeum* is the origin of the English word *canopy*.

CONQUĪSĪTŌRES, persons employed to go about the country and impress soldiers, when there was a difficulty in completing a levy. Sometimes commissioners were appointed by a decree of the senate for the purpose of making a conquisitio.

CONSANGUĬNĔI. [COGNATI.]

CONSECRĀTIO. [APOTHEOSIS.]

CONSĬLĬUM. [CONVENTUS.]

CONSUĀLĬA, a festival, with games, celebrated by the Romans, according to Ovid and others, in honour of Consus, the god of secret deliberations, or, according to Livy, of Neptunus Equestris. Some writers, however, say that Neptunus Equestris and Consus were only different names for one and the same deity. It was solemnised every year in the circus, by the symbolical ceremony of uncovering an altar dedicated to the god, which was buried in the earth. For Romulus, who was considered as the founder of the festival, was said to have discovered an altar in the earth on that spot. The solemnity took place on the 21st of August with horse and chariot races, and libations were poured into the flames which consumed the sacrifices. During these festive games horses and mules were not allowed to do any work, and were adorned with garlands of flowers. It was at their first celebration that, according to the ancient legend, the Sabine maidens were carried off.

CONSUL (ὕπατος), the title of the two chief officers or magistrates of the Roman republic. The word is probably composed of *con* and *sul*, which contains the same root as the verb *salio*, so that consules signifies "those who come together," just as *praesul* means "one who goes before," and *exsul*, "one who goes out." The consulship is said to have been instituted upon the expulsion of the kings in B.C. 509, when the kingly power was transferred to two magistrates, whose office lasted only for one year, that it might not degenerate into tyranny by being vested longer in the same persons; and for the same reason two were appointed instead of one king, as neither could undertake anything unless it was sanctioned and approved by his colleague. Their original title was *praetores*, or commanders of the armies, but this was changed into that of *consules* in B.C. 449, and the latter title remained in use until the latest periods of the Roman empire.—The consuls were at first elected from the patricians exclusively. Their office was suspended in B.C. 451, and its functions were performed by ten high commissioners (*decemviri*), appointed to frame a code of laws. On the re-establishment of the consulship in B.C. 449, the tribunes proposed that one of the consuls should be chosen from the plebeians, but this was strenuously resisted by the patricians, and a compromise effected by suspending the consular office, and creating in its stead military tribunes (*tribuni militum*) with consular power, who might be elected indifferently both from the patricians and plebeians. They were first appointed in B.C. 444. The plebeians, however, were not satisfied with this concession, and still endeavoured to attain the higher dignity of the consulship. At length, after a serious and long-protracted struggle between the two orders, it was enacted by the Licinian law, in B.C. 367, that henceforth the consulship should be divided between the patricians and plebeians, and that one of the consuls should always be a plebeian. Accordingly, in B.C. 366 L. Sextius was elected the first plebeian consul. This law, however, was not always observed, and it still frequently happened that both consuls were patricians, until, in later times, when the difference between the two orders had entirely ceased, and the plebeians were on a footing of perfect equality with the patricians, the consuls were elected from both orders indiscriminately.—During the later periods of the republic it was customary for persons to pass through several subordinate magistracies before they were elected consuls, though this rule was departed from in many particular cases. The age at which a person was eligible to the consulship was fixed in B.C. 180, by the lex annalis (LEX ANNALIS), at 43.—The election of the consuls always took place in the comitia of the centuries, some time before the expiration of the official year of the actual consuls, and the election was conducted either by the actual consuls themselves, or by an interrex or a dictator, and the persons elected, until they entered upon their office, were called *consules designati*. While they were *designati*, they were in reality no more than private persons, but still they might exercise considerable influence upon public affairs, for in the senate they were asked for their opinion first. If they had been guilty of any illegal act, either before or during their election, such as bribery (*ambitus*), they were liable to prosecution, and the election might be declared void.—The time at which the old consuls laid down their office and the consules designati entered upon theirs, differed at different times. The first consuls are said to have entered upon their office in October, then we find mention of the 1st of August, of the ides of December, the 1st of July, and very frequently of the ides of March, until, in B.C. 153, it became an established rule for the consuls to enter upon their duties on the 1st of January; and this custom remained down to the end of the republic. On that day the senators, equites, and citizens of all classes conducted in a procession (*deductio* or *processus consularis*) the new magistrates from their residence to the capitol, where, if the auspices were favourable, the consuls offered up sacrifices, and were inaugurated. From thence the procession went to the curia, where the senate assembled, and where the consuls returned thanks for their election. There they might also speak on any subject that was of importance to the republic, such as peace and war, the distribution of provinces, the general condition of the state, the *feriae Latinae*, and the like. During the first five days of their office they had to convoke a *contio*, and publicly to take a solemn oath, by which, in the earliest times, they pledged themselves not to allow any one to assume regal power at Rome, but afterwards only to maintain the laws of the republic (*in leges jurare*). On the expiration of their office they had to take another oath, stating that they had faithfully obeyed the laws, and not done anything against the constitution. The new consuls on entering upon their office usually invited their friends to a banquet. When a consul died during his year of office, his colleague immediately convoked the comitia to elect a new one. A consul thus elected to fill a vacancy was called *consul suffectus*, but his powers were not equal to those of an ordinary consul, for he could not preside at the elections of other magistrates, not even in the case of the death of his colleague. In the latter case, as well as when the consuls were prevented by illness or other circumstances, the comitia were held by an interrex or a dictator.—The outward distinctions of the consuls were, with few exceptions, the same as those which had formerly belonged to the kings. The principal distinction was the twelve lictors with the *fasces*, who preceded the consuls; but the axes did not appear in the fasces within the city. This outward sign of their power was taken by the consuls in turn every month, and while one consul was preceded by the twelve lictors with their fasces, the other was during the same month preceded by an *accensus*, and followed by the lictors; and the one was called during that month *consul major*, and the other *consul minor*. Other distinctions of the consuls were the curule chair (*sella curulis*), and the toga with the purple hem (*toga praetexta*). The ivory sceptre (*scipio* or *sceptrum*) and purple toga were not distinctions of the consuls in general, but only when they celebrated a triumph. Under the empire a consul was sometimes distinguished by the senate with a sceptre bearing an eagle on the top, but his regular ensigns consisted of the *toga picta*, the *trabea*, and the fasces, both within and without the city.—The consuls were the highest ordinary magistrates at Rome. Their power was at first quite equal to that of the kings, except that it was limited to one year, and that the office of high priest, which had been vested in the king, was at the very beginning detached from the consulship, and given to the *rex sacrorum* or *rex sacrificulus*. Yet the *auspicia majora* continued to belong to the consuls. This regal power of the consuls, however, was gradually curtailed by various laws, especially by the institution of the tribunes of the plebs, whose province it was to protect the plebeians against the unjust or oppressive commands of the patrician magistrates. Nay, in the course of time, whole branches of the consular power were detached from it; the reason for which was, that, as the patricians were compelled to allow the plebeians a share in the highest magistracy, they stripped it of as much of its original power as they could, and reserved these detached portions for themselves. In this manner the censorship was detached from the consulship in B.C. 443, and the praetorship in B.C. 367. But notwithstanding all this, the consuls remained the highest magistrates, and all other magistrates, except the tribunes of the plebs, were obliged to obey their commands, and show them great outward respect. The functions of the consuls during the time of the republic may be conveniently described under the following heads:—1. They were in all civil matters the heads of the state, being invested with the imperium, which emanated from the sovereign people, and which they held during the time of their office. In this capacity they had the right of convoking both the senate and the assembly of the people; they presided in each (in the comitia of the curies as well as in those of the centuries), and they took care that the resolutions of the senate and people were carried into effect. They might also convoke *contiones*, whenever they thought it necessary. In the senate they conducted the discussions, and put the questions to the vote, thus exercising the greatest influence upon all matters which were brought before the senate either by themselves or by others. When a decree was passed by the senate, the consuls were usually commissioned to see that it was carried into effect; though there are also instances of the consuls opposing a decree of the senate. 2. The supreme command of the armies belonged to the consuls alone by virtue of their imperium. Accordingly, when a war was decreed, they were ordered by a senatus consultum to levy the troops, whose number was determined by the senate, and they appointed most of the other military officers. While at the head of their armies they had full power of life and death over their soldiers, who, on their enrolment, had to take an oath (*sacramentum*) to be faithful and obedient to the commands of the consuls. When the consuls had entered upon their office, the senate assigned them their provinces, that is, their spheres of action, and the consuls either settled between themselves which province each was to have, or, which was more common, they drew lots. Usually one consul remained at Rome, while the other went out at the head of the army: sometimes both left the city, and carried on war in different quarters; and sometimes, when the danger was very pressing, both consuls commanded the armies against one and the same enemy. If it was deemed advisable, the imperium of one or of both consuls was prolonged for the particular province in which they were engaged, in which case they had the title of proconsuls [PROCONSUL], and their successors either remained at Rome, or were engaged in other quarters. During the latter period of the republic the consuls remained at Rome during the time of their office, and on its expiration they had a foreign province (in the real sense of the word) assigned to them, where they undertook either the peaceful administration, or carried on war against internal or external enemies. While in their provinces, both the consuls and proconsuls had the power of life and death over the provincials, for they were looked upon there as the chief military commanders; and the provincials, being *peregrini*, did not enjoy the privileges of Roman citizens. 3. The supreme jurisdiction was part of the consular imperium, and as such vested in the consuls so long as there were no praetors. In civil cases they administered justice to the patricians as well as plebeians, either acting themselves as *judices*, or appointing others as *judices* and *arbitri*. In criminal cases there appears from early times to have been this difference: that patricians charged with capital offences were tried by the curies, while the plebeians came under the jurisdiction of the consuls, whose power, however, was in this case rather limited, partly by the intercession of the tribunes of the people, and partly by the right of appeal (*provocatio*) from the sentence of the consuls. The consuls might, further, summon any citizen before their tribunal, and, in case of disobedience, seize him (*prendere*), and fine him up to a certain amount. After the institution of the praetorship, the consuls no longer possessed any regular ordinary jurisdiction; and whenever they exercised it, it was an exception to the general custom, and only by a special command of the senate. 4. Previous to the institution of the censorship the consuls had to perform all the functions which afterwards belonged to the censors: they were accordingly the highest officers of finance, held the census, drew up the lists of the senators, equites, &c. After the establishment of the censorship they still retained the general superintendence of the public economy, inasmuch as they had the keys of the *aerarium*, and as the quaestors or paymasters were dependent on them. But still in the management of the finances the consuls were at all times under the control of the senate. 5. In all relations with foreign states the consuls were the representatives of the Roman republic. Hence they might conclude peace or treaties with foreign nations, which had, however, to be sanctioned by the senate and people at Rome; and unless this sanction was obtained a treaty

I 2

was void. They received foreign ambassadors, and introduced them into the senate, and in short all negotiations with foreign princes or nations passed through their hands. 6. In matters connected with their own official functions, the consuls, like all other magistrates, had the power of issuing proclamations or orders (*edicta*), which might be binding either for the occasion only, or remain in force permanently.—Although the consular power had been gradually diminished, it was in cases of imminent danger restored to its original and full extent, by a decree of the senate calling upon the consuls *videant ne quid res publica detrimenti capiat*. In such cases the consuls received sovereign power, but they were responsible for the manner in which they had exercised it.—It has already been observed, that to avoid collision and confusion, the two consuls did not possess the same power at the same time, but that each had the imperium every other month. The one who possessed it, as the *consul major*, exercised all the rights of the office, though he always consulted his colleague. In the earliest times it was customary for the elder of the two consuls to take the imperium first, afterwards the one who had had the greater number of votes at the election, and had therefore been proclaimed (*renuntiare*) first. In the time of Augustus it was enacted that the consul who had most children should take precedence of the other; and some distinction of rank continued to be observed down to the latest times of the empire.—Towards the end of the republic the consulship lost its power and importance. The first severe blow it received was from Julius Caesar, the dictator, for he received the consulship in addition to his dictatorship, or he arbitrarily ordered others to be elected, who were mere nominal officers, and were allowed to do nothing without his sanction. He himself was elected consul at first for five, then for ten years, and at last for life. Under Augustus the consulship was a mere shadow of what it had been: the consuls no longer held their office for a whole year, but usually for a few months only; and hence it happened that sometimes one year saw six, twelve, or even twenty-five consuls. Those who were elected the first in the year ranked higher than the rest, and their names alone were used to mark the year, according to the ancient custom of the Romans of marking the date of an event by the names of the consuls of the year in which the event occurred. During the last period of the empire it became the practice to have titular or honorary consuls, who were elected by the senate and confirmed by the emperor. Constantine appointed two consuls, one for Rome and another for Constantinople, who held their office for a whole year, and whose functions were only those of chief justices. All the other consuls were designated as *honorarii* or *consulares*. But though the consulship had thus become almost an empty title, it was still regarded as the highest dignity in the empire, and as the object of the greatest ambition. It was connected with very great expenses, partly on account of the public games which a consul had to provide, and partly on account of the large donations he had to make to the people. The last consul at Rome was Decimus Theodorus Paulinus, A.D. 536, and at Constantinople, Flavius Basilius junior, A.D. 541.

CONSULARIS, signified, under the republic, a person who had held the office of consul; but under the empire, it was the title of many magistrates and public officers, who enjoyed the insignia of consular dignity, without having filled the office of consul. Thus we find commanders of armies and governors of provinces called *Consulares* under the empire.

CONTIO, a contraction for *conventio*, that is, a meeting, or a *conventus*. In the technical sense, however, a contio was an assembly of the people at Rome convened by a magistrate for the purpose of making the people acquainted with measures which were to be brought before the next comitia, and of working upon them either to support or oppose the measure. But no question of any kind could be decided by a contio, and this constitutes the difference between contiones and comitia. Still contiones were also convened for other purposes, e. g. of persuading the people to take part in a war, or of bringing complaints against a party in the republic. Every magistrate had the right to convene contiones, but it was most frequently exercised by the consuls and tribunes, and the latter more especially exercised a great influence over the people in and through these contiones. A magistrate who was higher in rank than the one who had convened a contio, had the right to order the people to disperse, if he disapproved of the object. It should be remarked, that the term contio is also used to designate the speeches and harangues addressed to the people in an assembly, and that in a loose mode of speaking, contio denotes any assembly of the people.

CONTUBERNALES (σύσκηνοι), signified originally men who served in the same army and lived in the same tent. The word is derived from *taberna* (afterwards *tabernaculum*), which was the original name for a military tent, as it was made of boards (*ta-*

bulae). Each tent was occupied by ten soldiers (*contubernales*), with a subordinate officer at their head, who was called *decanus*, and in later times *caput contubernii*. Young Romans of illustrious families used to accompany a distinguished general on his expeditions, or to his province, for the purpose of gaining under his superintendence a practical training in the art of war, or in the administration of public affairs, and were, like soldiers living in the same tent, called his *contubernales*. In a still wider sense, the name *contubernales* was applied to persons connected by ties of intimate friendship, and living under the same roof; and hence, when a free man and a slave, or two slaves, who were not allowed to contract a legal marriage, lived together as husband and wife, they were called *contubernales*; and their connection, as well as their place of residence, *contubernium*.

CONTŪBERNĬUM. [CONTUBERNALES.]
CONVĔNĪRE IN MĀNUM. [MATRIMONIUM.]
CONVENTUS, was the name applied to the whole body of Roman citizens who were either permanently or for a time settled in a province. In order to facilitate the administration of justice, a province was divided into a number of districts or circuits, each of which was called *conventus*, *forum*, or *jurisdictio*. Roman citizens living in a province were entirely under the jurisdiction of the proconsul; and at certain times of the year, fixed by the proconsul, they assembled in the chief town of the district, and this meeting bore the name of *conventus* (σύνοδος). Hence the expressions—*conventus agere*, *peragere*, *convocare*, *dimittere*. At this conventus litigant parties applied to the proconsul, who selected a number of judges from the conventus to try their causes. The proconsul himself presided at the trials, and pronounced the sentence according to the views of the judges, who were his assessors (*consilium* or *consiliarii*). These conventus appear to have been generally held after the proconsul had settled the military affairs of the province; at least, when Caesar was proconsul of Gaul, he made it a regular practice to hold the conventus after his armies had retired to their winter quarters.

CONVĪVĬUM. [SYMPOSIUM.]
CŎPHĬNUS (κόφινος, Engl. *coffin*), a large kind of wicker basket, made of willow branches. It would seem that it was used by the Greeks as a basket or cage for birds. The Romans used it for agricultural purposes, and it sometimes formed a kind of portable hot-bed. Juvenal, when speaking of the Jews, uses the expression *cophinus et foenum* (a truss of hay), figuratively to designate their poverty.

CORBIS, *dim.* CORBŬLA, CORBĪCŬLA, a basket of very peculiar form and common use among the Romans, both for agricultural and other purposes. It was made of osiers twisted together, and was of a conical or pyramidal shape. A basket answering precisely to this description, both in form and material, is still to be seen in everyday use among the Campanian peasantry, which is called in the language of the country "la corbella."

CORBĪTAE, merchantmen of the larger class, so called because they hung out a *corbis* at the mast-head for a sign. They were also termed *onerariae*; and hence Plautus, in order to designate the voracious appetites of some women, says, "Corbitam cibi comesse possunt."

CORNU, a wind instrument, anciently made of horn, but afterwards of brass. Like

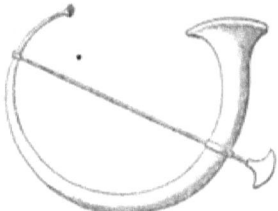

Cornu. (Bartholini de Tibiis.)

the *tuba*, it differed from the *tibia* in being a larger and more powerful instrument, and

Altar of Julius Victor. (Bartoli, Pict. Ant., p. 76.)

from the *tuba* itself, in being curved nearly in the shape of a C, with a cross-piece to steady the instrument for the convenience of the performer. Hence Ovid says (*Met.* i. 98):

"Non tuba directi, non aeris cornua flexi."

The *classicum*, which originally meant a signal, rather than the musical instrument which gave the signal, was usually sounded with the *cornu*.

"Sonuit reflexo classicum cornu,
Lituusque adunco stridulos cantus
Elisit aere." (Sen. *Oed.* 734.)

The *Cornicines* and *Liticines*, the persons who blew the *Cornu* and *Lituus*, formed a collegium. In the preceding cut, M. Julius Victor, a member of the Collegium, holds a lituus in his right hand, and touches with his left a cornu on the ground. See engraving under TUBA.

CŎRŌNA (στέφανος), a crown, that is, a circular ornament of metal, leaves, or flowers, worn by the ancients round the head or neck, and used as a festive as well as funereal decoration, and as a reward of talent, military or naval prowess, and civil worth. Its first introduction as an honorary reward is attributable to the athletic games, in some of which it was bestowed as a prize upon the victor. It was the only reward contended for by the Spartans in their gymnic contests, and was worn by them when going to battle. The Romans refined upon the practice of the Greeks, and invented a great variety of crowns formed of different materials, each with a separate appellation, and appropriated to a particular purpose.—I. CORONA OBSIDIONALIS. Amongst the honorary crowns bestowed by the Romans for military achievements, the most difficult of attainment, and the one which conferred the highest honour, was the *corona obsidionalis*, presented by a beleaguered army after its liberation to the general who broke up the siege. It was made of grass, or weeds and wild flowers, thence called *corona graminea*, and *graminea obsidionalis*, gathered from the spot on which the beleaguered army had been enclosed.— II. CORONA CIVICA, the second in honour and importance, was presented to the soldier who had preserved the life of a Roman citizen in battle. It was made of the leaves of the oak.

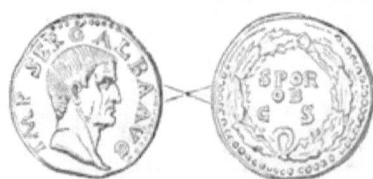

Corona Civica, on a Coin of the Emperor Galba.
SPQR OB CS = Senatus Populusque Romanus ob civem servatum.

The soldier who had acquired this crown had a place reserved next to the senate at all the public spectacles; and they, as well as the rest of the company, rose up upon his entrance. He was freed from all public burthens, as were also his father, and his paternal grandfather; and the person who owed his life to him was bound, ever after, to cherish his preserver as a parent, and afford him all such offices as were due from a son to his father.—III. CORONA NAVALIS or ROSTRATA, called also CLASSICA. It is difficult to determine whether these were two distinct crowns, or only two denominations for the same one. It seems probable that the *navalis corona*, besides being a generic term, was inferior in dignity to the latter, and given to the sailor who first boarded an enemy's ship; whereas the *rostrata* was given to a commander who destroyed the whole fleet, or gained any very signal victory. At all events, they were both made of gold; and one at least (*rostrata*) decorated with the beaks of ships like the *rostra* in the forum. The Athenians likewise bestowed golden crowns for naval services; sometimes upon the person who got his trireme first equipped, and at others upon the captain who had his vessel in the best order.—IV. CORONA MURALIS, was presented by the general to the first man who scaled the wall of a besieged city. It was made of gold, and decorated with turrets.—V. CORONA CASTRENSIS or VALLARIS, was presented to the first soldier who surmounted the *vallum*, and forced an entrance into the enemy's camp. This crown was made of gold, and ornamented with the palisades (*ralli*) used in forming an entrenchment.—VI. CORONA TRIUMPHALIS. There were three sorts of triumphal crowns: the first was made of laurel or bay leaves, and was worn round the head of the commander during his triumph; the second was of gold, which, being too large and massive to be worn, was held over the head of the general during his triumph, by a public officer. This crown, as well as the former one, was presented to the victorious general by his army. The third kind, likewise of gold and of great value, was sent as a present from the provinces to the commander. [AURUM CORONARIUM.]—VII. CORONA OVALIS, was given to a commander who obtained only an ovation. It was made of myrtle.—VIII. CORONA OLEAGINA, was made of the olive leaf, and conferred upon the soldiers as well as their commanders.—The Greeks in general made but little use of crowns as rewards of valour in the earlier periods of their history, except as prizes in the athletic contests; but previous to the time of Alexander, crowns of gold were profusely distributed, amongst the Athenians at least, for every trifling feat, whether civil, naval, or military, which, though lavished without much discrimination as far as regards the character of the receiving parties, were still subjected to certain legal restrictions in respect of the time, place, and mode in which they were conferred. They could not be presented but in the public assemblies, and with the consent, that is by suffrage, of the people, or by the senators in their council, or by the tribes to their own members, or by the δημόται to members of their own δῆμος. According to the statement of Aeschines, the people could not lawfully present crowns in any place except in their assembly, nor the senators except in the senate-house; nor, according to the same authority, in the theatre, which is, however, denied by Demosthenes; nor at the public games, and if any crier there proclaimed the crowns he was subject to *atimia*. Neither could any person holding an office receive a crown whilst he was ὑπεύθυνος, that is, before he had passed his accounts.—The second class of crowns were emblematical and not honorary, and the adoption of them was not regulated by law, but custom. Of these there were also several kinds.—I. CORONA SACERDOTALIS, was worn by the priests (*sacerdotes*), with the exception of the pontifex maximus and his minister (*camillus*), as well as the bystanders, when officiating at the sacrifice. It does not appear to have been confined to any one material.—II. CORONA FUNEBRIS and SEPULCHRALIS. The Greeks first set the example of crowning the dead with chaplets of leaves and flowers, which was imitated by the Romans. Garlands of flowers were also placed upon the bier, or scattered from the windows under which the procession passed,

Females with Crowns. (From an ancient Painting.)

or entwined about the cinerary urn, or as a decoration to the tomb. In Greece these crowns were commonly made of parsley.— III. CORONA CONVIVIALIS. The use of chaplets at festive entertainments sprung likewise from Greece. They were of various shrubs and flowers, such as roses (which were the choicest), violets, myrtle, ivy, *philyra*, and even parsley.—IV. CORONA NUPTIALIS. The bridal wreath was also of Greek origin, among whom it was made of flowers plucked by the bride herself, and not bought, which was of lil omen. Amongst the Romans it was made of *verbena*, also gathered by the bride herself, and worn under the *flammeum*, with which the bride was always enveloped. The bridegroom also wore a chaplet. The doors of his house were likewise decorated with garlands, and also the bridal couch.—V. CORONA NATALITIA, the chaplet suspended over the door of the vestibule, both in the houses of Athens and Rome, in which a child was born. At Athens, when the infant was male, the crown was made of olive; when female, of wool. At Rome it was of laurel, ivy, or parsley.

CORŌNIS (κορωνίς), the cornice of an entablature, is properly a Greek word signifying anything curved. It is also used by Latin writers, but the genuine Latin word for a *cornice* is *corona* or *coronix*.

CORTĪNA, the name of the table or hollow slab, supported by a tripod, upon which the priestess at Delphi sat to deliver her responses; and hence the word is used for the oracle itself. The Romans made tables of marble or bronze after the pattern of the Delphian tripod, which they used as we do our sideboards, for the purpose of displaying their plate at an entertainment. These were termed *cortinae Delphicae*, or *Delphicae* simply.

CORYBANTĬCA (κορυβαντικά), a festival and mysteries celebrated at Cnossus in Crete, by the Corybantes. (See *Class. Dict.*, CORYBANTES.)

CŎRYMBUS (κόρυμβος). [COMA.]

CORVUS, a sort of crane, used by C. Duilius against the Carthaginian fleet in the battle fought off Mylae, in Sicily (B. C. 260). The Romans, we are told, being unused to the sea, saw that their only chance of victory was by bringing a sea-fight to resemble one on land. For this purpose they invented a machine, of which Polybius has left a minute description. In the fore part of the ship a round pole was fixed perpendicularly, twenty-four feet in height and about nine inches in diameter; at the top of this was a pivot, upon which a ladder was set, thirty-six feet in length and four in breadth. The ladder was guarded by cross-beams, fastened to the upright pole by a ring of wood, which turned with the pivot above. Along the ladder a rope was passed, one end of which took hold of the *corvus* by means of a ring. The *corvus* itself was a strong piece of iron, with a spike at the end, which was raised or lowered by drawing in or letting out the rope. When an enemy's ship drew near, the machine was turned outwards, by means of the pivot, in the direction of the assailant. Another part of the machine was a breastwork, let down from the ladder, and serving as a bridge, on which to board the enemy's vessel. By means of these cranes the Carthaginian ships were either broken or closely locked with the Roman, and Duilius gained a complete victory.

CŎRȲTOS or CŎRȲTUS (γωρυτός, κωρυτός). [ARCUS.]

COSMĒTAE, a class of slaves among the Romans, whose duty it was to dress and adorn ladies.

COSMI (κοσμοί), the supreme magistrates in Crete, were ten in number, and were chosen, not from the body of the people, but from certain γένη or houses, which were probably of more pure Doric or Achaean descent than their neighbours. The first of them in rank was called *protocosmus*, and gave his name to the year. They commanded in war, and also conducted the business of the state with the representatives and ambassadors of other cities. Their period of office was a year; but any of them during that time might resign, and was also liable to deposition by his colleagues. In some cases, too, they might be indicted for neglect of their duties. On the whole, we may conclude that they formed the executive and chief power in most of the cities of Crete.

CŎTHURNUS (κόθορνος), a boot. Its essential distinction was its height; it rose above the middle of the leg, so as to surround the calf, and sometimes it reached as high as the knees. It was worn principally by horsemen, by hunters, and by men of rank and authority. The sole of the cothurnus was commonly of the ordinary thickness; but it was sometimes made much thicker than usual, probably by the insertion of slices of cork.

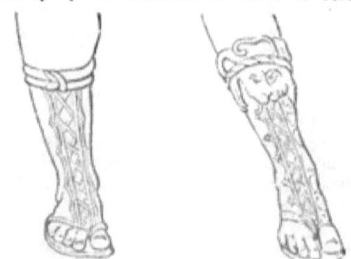

Cothurnus. (From Statue of Artemis—Diana.)

The object was, to add to the apparent stature of the wearer; and this was done in the case of the actors in Athenian tragedy, who had the soles made unusually thick as one of the methods adopted in order to magnify their whole appearance. Hence tragedy in general was called *cothurnus*. As the cothurnus was commonly worn in hunting, it is represented as part of the costume of Artemis (Diana).

COTTĂBUS (κότταβος), a social game which was introduced from Sicily into Greece, where it became one of the favourite amusements of young people after their repasts. The simplest way in which it originally was played was this:—One of the company threw out of a goblet a certain quantity of wine, at a certain distance, into a metal basin. While he was doing this, he either thought of or pronounced the name of his mistress; and if all the wine fell in the basin, and with a full sound, it was a good sign for the lover. This simple amusement soon assumed a variety of different characters, and became, in some instances, a regular contest, with prizes for the victor. One of the most celebrated modes in which it was carried on is called δἰ ὀξυβάφων. A basin was filled with water, with small empty cups (ὀξύβαφα) swimming upon it. Into these the young men, one after another, threw the remnant of the wine from their goblets, and he who had the good fortune to drown most of the bowls obtained the prize, consisting either of simple cakes, sweetmeats, or sesame-cakes.

COTYTTIA (κοττύτια), a festival which was originally celebrated by the Edonians of Thrace, in honour of a goddess called Cotys, or Cotytto. It was held at night. The worship of Cotys, together with the festival of the Cotyttia, was adopted by several Greek states, chiefly those which were induced by their commercial interest to maintain friendly relations with Thrace. The festivals of this goddess were notorious among the ancients for the dissolute manner and the debaucheries with which they were celebrated.

CŎTŬLA (κοτύλη), a measure of capacity among the Romans and Greeks: by the former it was also called *hemina*; by the latter, τρυβλίον and ἡμίνα or ἡμίμνα. It was the half of the sextarius or ξέστης, and contained 6 cyathi, or nearly half a pint English.

CŎVĬNUS (Celtic, *kowain*), a kind of car, the spokes of which were armed with long sickles, and which was used as a scythe-chariot chiefly by the ancient Belgians and Britons. The Romans designated, by the name of covinus, a kind of travelling carriage, which seems to have been covered on all sides with the exception of the front. It had no seat for a driver, but was conducted by the traveller himself, who sat inside. The *corinarii* (this word occurs only in Tacitus) seem to have constituted a regular and distinct part of a British army. Compare ESSEDUM.

CRATER (κρατήρ, Ionic κρητήρ, from κεράννυμι, I mix), a vessel in which the wine, according to the custom of the ancients, who very seldom drank it pure, was mixed with water, and from which the cups were filled. Craters were among the first things on the embellishment of which the ancient artists exercised their skill; and the number of craters dedicated in temples seems everywhere to have been very great.

CREPIDA (κρηπίς), a slipper. Slippers were worn with the pallium, not with the toga, and were properly characteristic of the Greeks, though adopted from them by the Romans.

CRIMEN. Though this word occurs so frequently, it is not easy to fix its meaning. *Crimen* is often equivalent to *accusatio* (κατηγορία); but it frequently means an act which is legally punishable. Those delicta which were punishable according to special leges, senatus consulta, and constitutiones, and were prosecuted in judicia publica by an accusatio publica, were more especially called crimina; and the penalties in case of conviction were loss of life, of freedom, of civitas, and the consequent infamia, and sometimes pecuniary penalties also.

CRISTA. [GALEA.]

CRITES (κριτής), a judge, was the name applied by the Greeks to any person who did not judge of a thing like a δικαστής, according to positive laws, but according to his own sense of justice and equity. But at Athens a number of κριταί was chosen by ballot from a number of selected candidates at every celebration of the Dionysia: they were called οἱ κριταί, κατ' ἐξοχήν. Their office was to judge of the merit of the different choruses and dramatic poems, and to award the prizes to the victors. Their number was five for comedy and the same number for tragedy, one being taken from every tribe.

CROBYLUS. [COMA.]

CROCOTA (sc. *vestis*, κροκωτὸν sc. ἱμάτιον, or κροκωτὸς sc. χιτών), was a kind of gala-dress, chiefly worn by women on solemn occasions, and in Greece especially, at the festival of the Dionysia. Its name was derived from *crocus*, one of the favourite colours of the Greek ladies.

CROTALUM. [CYMBALUM.]

CRUSTA. [CAELATURA.]

CRUX (σταυρός, σκόλοψ), an instrument of capital punishment, used by several ancient nations, especially the Romans and Carthaginians. Crucifixion was of two kinds, the less usual sort being rather impalement than what we should describe by the word crucifixion, as the criminal was transfixed by a pole, which passed through the back and spine and came out at the mouth. The cross was of several kinds; one in the shape of an X, called *crux Andreana*, because tradition reports St. Andrew to have suffered upon it; another was formed like a T. The third, and most common sort, was made of two pieces of wood crossed, so as to make four right angles. It was on this, according to the unanimous testimony of the fathers, that our Saviour suffered. The punishment, as is well known, was chiefly inflicted on slaves, and the worst kind of malefactors. The criminal, after sentence pronounced, carried his cross to the place of execution; a custom mentioned in the Gospels. Scourging appears to have formed a part of this, as of other capital punishments among the Romans; but the scourging of our Saviour is not to be regarded in this light, for it was inflicted before sentence was pronounced. The criminal was next stripped of his clothes and nailed or bound to the cross. The latter was the more painful method, as the sufferer was left to die of hunger. Instances are recorded of persons who survived nine days. It was usual to leave the body on the cross after death. The breaking of the legs of the thieves, mentioned in the Gospels, was accidental; because, by the Jewish law, it is expressly remarked, the bodies could not remain on the cross during the Sabbath-day.

CRYPTA (from κρύπτειν, to conceal), a crypt. Amongst the Romans, any long narrow vault, whether wholly or partially below the level of the earth, is expressed by this term. The specific senses of the word are:—(1) A covered portico or arcade; called more definitely *crypto-porticus*, because it was not supported by open columns like the ordinary portico, but closed at the sides, with windows only for the admission of light and air.—(2) A grotto, particularly one open at both extremities, forming what in modern language is denominated a "tunnel." A subterranean vault used for any secret worship was also called *crypta*.—(3) When the practice of consuming the body by fire was relinquished [FUNUS], and a number of bodies was consigned to one place of burial, as the catacombs for instance, this common tomb was called *crypta*.

CRYPTEIA (κρυπτεία), the name of an atrocious practice at Sparta, said to have been introduced by Lycurgus. The following is the description given of the crypteia. The ephors, at intervals, selected from among the young Spartans; those who appeared to be best qualified for the task, and sent them in various directions all over the country, provided with daggers and their necessary food. During the day-time, these young men concealed themselves; but at night they broke forth into the high-roads, and massacred those of the helots whom they met, or whom they thought proper.

CUBICULARII, slaves who had the care of the sleeping and dwelling rooms. Faithful slaves were always selected for this office, as they had, to a certain extent, the care of their master's person. It was the duty of the cubicularii to introduce visitors to their master.

CUBICULUM usually means a sleeping and dwelling room in a Roman house [DOMUS], but it is also applied to the pavilion or tent in which the Roman emperors were accustomed to witness the public games. It appears to have been so called, because the emperors were accustomed to recline in the cubicula, instead of sitting, as was anciently the practice, in a sella curulis.

CUBITUS (πῆχυς), a Greek and Roman measure of length, originally the length of the human arm from the elbow to the wrist, or to the knuckle of the middle finger. It was equal to a foot and a half, which gives 1 foot 5·4744 inches Eng. for the Roman, and 1 foot 6·2016 inches for the Greek cubit.

CUCULLUS, a cowl. As the cowl was intended to be used in the open air, and to be drawn over the head to protect it from the injuries of the weather, instead of a hat or cap, it was attached only to garments of the coarsest kind. The cucullus was also used by persons in the higher circles of society, when they wished to go abroad without being known.

CUDO or CUDON, a skull-cap made of leather or of the rough shaggy fur of any wild animal, such as were worn by the *velites* of the Roman armies, and apparently synonymous with *galerus* or *galericulus*.

CULEUS, or CULLEUS, a Roman measure, which was used for estimating the produce of vineyards. It was the largest liquid measure used by the Romans, containing 20 amphorae, or 118 gallons, 7·546 pints.

CULINA. [DOMUS, p. 143.]

CULTER (μάχαιρα, κοπίς, or σφαγίς), a knife with only one edge, which formed a straight line. The blade was pointed, and its back curved. It was used for a variety of purposes, but chiefly for killing animals either in the slaughter-house, or in hunting, or at the altars of the gods. The priest who conducted a sacrifice never killed the victim himself; but one of his ministri, appointed for that purpose, who was called either by the general name *minister*, or the more specific *popa* or *cultrarius*.

CULTRARIUS. [CULTER.]

CUNEUS was the name applied to a body of foot soldiers, drawn up in the form of a wedge, for the purpose of breaking through an enemy's line. The common soldiers called it a *caput porcinum*, or pig's head. The name *cuneus* was also applied to the compartments of seats in circular or semi-circular theatres, which were so arranged as to converge to the centre of the theatre, and diverge towards the external walls of the building, with passages between each compartment.

CUNICULUS (ὑπόνομος), a mine or passage underground, was so called from its resemblance to the burrowing of a rabbit. Fidenae and Veii are said to have been taken by mines, which opened, one of them into the citadel, the other into the temple of Juno.

CUPA, a wine-vat, a vessel very much like the *dolium*, and used for the same purpose, namely, to receive the fresh must, and to contain it during the process of fermentation. The inferior wines were drawn for drinking from the *cupa*, without being bottled in *amphorae*, and hence the term *vinum de cupa*. The *cupa* was either made of earthenware, like the *dolium*, or of wood, and covered with pitch. It was also used for fruits and corn, forming rafts, and containing combustibles in war, and even for a sarcophagus.

CURATOR. Till a Roman youth attained the age of puberty, which was generally fixed at fourteen years of age, he was incapable of any legal act, and was under the authority of a *tutor* or guardian; but with the attainment of the age of puberty, he became capable of performing every legal act, and was freed from the control of his *tutor*. As, however, a person of that tender age was liable to be imposed upon, the lex Plaetoria enacted that every person between the time of puberty and twenty-five years of age should be under the protection of a *curator*. The date of this lex is not known, though it is certain that the law existed when Plautus wrote (about B. C. 200), who speaks of it as the *lex quina vicenaria*. This law established a distinction of age, which was of great practical importance, by forming the citizens into

Culm (From Tombstone of a Cultrarius.)

two classes, those above and those below twenty-five years of age (*minores viginti quinque annis*). A person under the last-mentioned age was sometimes simply called *minor*. The object of the lex was to protect persons under twenty-five years of age against all fraud (*dolus*). A person who wasted his property (*prodigus*), and a person of unsound mind (*furiosus, demens*), were also placed under the care of a *curator*.

CURATORES were public officers of various kinds under the Roman empire, such as the *curatores annonae*, the *curatores ludorum*, the *curatores regionum*, &c.

CURIA, signifies both a division of the Roman people and the place of assembly for such a division. Each of the three ancient Romulian tribes, the Ramnes, Tities, and Luceres, was subdivided into 10 curiae, so that the whole body of the populus or the patricians was divided into 30 curiae. The plebeians had no connection whatever with the curiae. All the members of the different gentes belonging to one curia were called, in respect of one another, *curiales*. The division into curiae was of great political importance in the earliest times of Rome, for the curiae alone contained the citizens, and their assembly alone was the legitimate representative of the whole people. [COMITIA CURIATA.] Each curia as a corporation had its peculiar sacra, and besides the gods of the state, they worshipped other divinities and with peculiar rites and ceremonies. For such religious purposes each curia had its own place of worship, called curia, in which the curiales assembled for the purpose of discussing political, financial, religious and other matters. The religious affairs of each curia were taken care of by a priest, *Curio*, who was assisted by another called curialis Flamen. As there were 30 curiae, there were likewise 30 curiones, who formed a college of priests, presided over by one of them, called *Curio Maximus*. The 30 curiae had each its distinct name, which are said to have been derived from the names of the Sabine women who had been carried off by the Romans, though it is evident that some derived their names from certain districts or from ancient eponymous heroes. Curia is also used to designate the place in which the senate held its meetings, such as curia Hostilia, curia Julia, curia Pompeii, and from this there gradually arose the custom of calling the senate itself in the Italian towns curia, but never the senate of Rome. The official residence of the Salii, which was dedicated to Mars, was likewise styled curia.

CURIATA COMITIA. [COMITIA.]

CURIO. [CURIA.]

CURIUS (κύριος), signified generally at Athens the person responsible for the welfare of such members of a family as the law presumed to be incapable of protecting themselves; as, for instance, minors and slaves, and women of all ages.

CURRUS (ἅρμα), a chariot, a car. These terms appear to have denoted those two-wheeled vehicles for the carriage of persons, which were open overhead, thus differing from the *carpentum*, and closed in front, in which they differed from the *cisium*. The most essential articles in the construction of

Currus. (Ancient Chariot preserved in the Vatican.)

the currus were, 1. The rim (ἄντυξ) [ANTYX]. 2. The axle (ἄξων, *axis*). 3. The wheels (κύκλα, τροχοί, *rotae*), which revolved upon the axle, and were prevented from coming off by the insertion of pins (ἔμβολοι) into the extremities of the axles. The parts of the wheel were :—(*a*) The nave (πλήμνη, *modiolus*). (*b*) The spokes (κνῆμαι, literally, the *legs*, *radii*.) (*c*) The felly (ἴτυς). (*d*) The tire (ἐπίσωτρον, *canthus*). 4. The pole (ῥυμός, *temo*). All the parts above mentioned are seen in the preceding cut of an ancient chariot. The Greeks and Romans appear never to have used more than one pole and one yoke, and the currus thus constructed was commonly drawn by two horses, which were attached to it by their necks, and therefore called δίζυγες ἵπποι, συνωρίς, *gemini jugales*, *equi bijuges*, &c. If a third horse was added, as was not unfrequently the case, it was fastened by traces. The horse so attached was called παρήορος, παράσειρος, σειραφόρος, in Latin, *funalis*, and is opposed to the ζυγῖται or ζύγιοι, the yoke-horses. The ἵππος παρήορος is placed on the right of the two yoke-horses. (See woodcut.) The Latin name for a chariot and

Triga. (From a Painting on a Vase.)

pair was *biga*, generally *bigae*. When a third horse was added, it was called *triga*. A chariot and four was called *quadriga*, generally *quadrigae* ; in Greek, τετραορία or τέθριππος. The horses were commonly harnessed in a quadriga after the manner already represented, the two strongest horses being placed under the yoke, and the two others fastened on each side by means of ropes. This is clearly seen in the two quadrigae figured below, especially in the one on the right hand. It represents a chariot overthrown in passing the goal at the circus. The charioteer having fallen backwards, the pole and yoke are thrown upwards into the air; the two trace-horses have fallen on their knees, and the two yoke-horses are prancing on their hind legs.—The currus was adapted to carry two persons, and on this account was called in Greek δίφρος. One of the two was of course the driver. He was called ἡνίοχος, because he held the reins, and his companion παραβάτης, from going by his side or near him. In the Homeric ages, chariots were commonly employed on the field of battle. The men of rank all took their chariots with

Quadriga. (From Paintings on a Vase and a Terra-cotta.)

them, and in an engagement placed themselves in front. Chariots were not much used by the Romans. The most splendid kind were the quadrigae, in which the Roman generals and emperors rode when they triumphed. The body of the triumphal car was cylindrical, as we often see it represented on medals. It was enriched with gold and ivory. The utmost skill of the painter and the sculptor was employed to enhance its beauty and splendour. The triumphal car had in general no pole, the horses being led by men who were stationed at their heads.

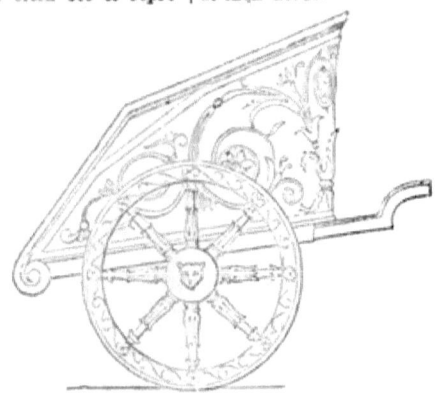

Marble Chariot in the Vatican.

CURSORES, slaves whose duty it was to run before the carriage of their masters. They first came into fashion in the first century of the Christian aera. The word *cursores* was also applied to all slaves whom their masters employed in carrying letters, messages, &c.

CURSUS. [CIRCUS.]
CURULIS SELLA. [SELLA CURULIS.]
CUSTODES. [COMITIA.]
CUSTODES, CUSTODIAE. [CASTRA.]
CUSTOS URBIS. [PRAEFECTUS URBI.]
CYATHUS (κύαθος), a Greek and Roman liquid measure, containing one-twelfth of the sextarius, or ·0825 of a pint English. The form of the cyathus used at banquets was that of a small ladle, by means of which the wine was conveyed into the drinking-cups from the large vessel (*crater*) in which it was mixed. Two of these cyathi are represented in the preceding woodcut. The cyathus was also the name given to a cup holding the same quantity as the measure. Hence Horace says (*Carm.* iii. 8. 13):

" Sume, Maecenas, cyathos amici
Sospitis centum."

CYCLAS (κυκλάς), a circular robe worn by women, to the bottom of which a border was affixed, inlaid with gold. It appears to have been usually made of some thin material.

CYMA (κῦμα), in architecture, an *ogee*, a wave-shaped moulding, consisting of two curves, the one concave and the other convex. There were two forms, the *cyma recta*, which was concave above, and convex below, thus, ⌒, and the *cyma reversa*, which was convex above and concave below, thus ⌒. The diminutive *cymatium* or *cumatium* (κυμάτιον) is also used, and is indeed the more common name.

CYMBA (κύμβη) is derived from τύμβος, a hollow, and is employed to signify any small kind of boat used on lakes, rivers, &c. It appears to have been much the same as the *acatium* and *scapha*.

CYMBALUM (κύμβαλον), a musical instrument, in the shape of two half globes, which were held one in each hand by the performer,

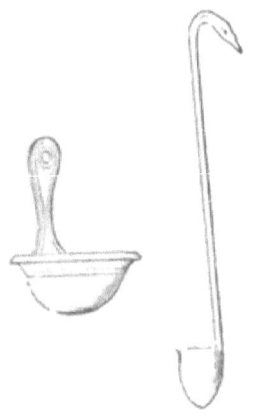

Cyathu. (Museo Barberino, vol. iv. pl. 12.)

and played by being struck against each other. The word is derived from κύμβος, a hollow. The cymbal was a very ancient instrument, being used in the worship of Cybelé, Bacchus, Juno, and all the earlier deities of the Grecian and Roman mythology. It probably came from the East. The crotalum (κρόταλον) was a kind of cymbal. It appears to have

Cymbala. (From a Bas-relief in the Vatican.)

been a split reed or cane, which clattered when shaken with the hand. Women who played on the crotalum were termed *crotalistriae*. Such was Virgil's Copa :

"Crispum sub crotalo docta movere latus."

The line alludes to the dance with crotala (similar to castanets).—For *sistrum*, which some have referred to the class of *cymbala*, see SISTRUM.

Crotala. (Borghese Vase now in the Louvre.)

DACTYLUS (δάκτυλος), a Greek measure, answering to the Roman *digitus*, each signifying a *finger-breadth*, and being the sixteenth part of a foot. [PES.]

DAEDALA or DAEDALEIA (δαίδαλα, δαιδάλεια), names used by the Greeks to signify those early works of art which were ascribed to the age of Daedalus, and especially the ancient wooden statues, ornamented with gilding and bright colours and real drapery, which were the earliest known forms of the images of the gods, after the mere blocks of wood or stone, which were at first used for symbols of them.

DAEDALA (δαίδαλα), the name of two festivals, celebrated in Boeotia in honour of Hera, and called respectively the *Great* and the *Lesser Daedala*. The latter were celebrated by the Plataeans alone ; in the celebration of the former, which took place only every sixtieth year, the Plataeans were joined by the other Boeotians.

DAMARETION (δαμαρέτειον χρύσιον), a Sicilian coin, respecting which there is much dispute ; but it was probably a gold coin, equal in value to fifty litrae or ten Attic drachmae of silver ; that is, a half stater.

DAMIURGI. [DEMIURGI.]

DAMOSIA. [EXERCITUS.]

DANACE (δανάκη), properly the name of a foreign coin, was also the name given to the obolos, which was placed in the mouth of the dead to pay the ferryman in Hades.

DAPHNEPHORIA (δαφνηφόρια), a festival celebrated every ninth year at Thebes in honour of Apollo, surnamed Ismenius or Galaxius. Its name was derived from the laurel branches (δάφναι) which were carried by those who took part in its celebration.

DAREICUS (δαρεικός), or to give the name in full, the Stater of Dareius, a gold coin of Persia, stamped on one side with the figure of an archer crowned and kneeling upon one knee, and on the other with a sort of quadrata incusa or deep cleft. It is supposed to have derived its name from the first Dareius king of Persia. It is equal to about 1*l*. 1*s*. 10*d*. 1·76 farthings.

Dareicus. (British Museum.)

DĒCĀDŪCHI (δεκαδοῦχοι), the members of a council of Ten, who succeeded the Thirty in the supreme power at Athens, B. C. 403. They were chosen from the ten tribes, one from each; but, though opposed to the Thirty, they sent ambassadors to Sparta to ask for assistance against Thrasybulus and the exiles. They remained masters of Athens till the party of Thrasybulus obtained possession of the city and the democracy was restored.

DĒCARCHĪA or DĒCĀDARCHĪA (δεκαρχία, δεκαδαρχία), a supreme council established in many of the Grecian cities by the Lacedaemonians, who entrusted to it the whole government of the state under the direction of a Spartan harmost. It always consisted of the leading members of the aristocratical party.

DĒCASMUS (δεκασμός), bribery. There were two actions for bribery at Athens: one, called δεκασμοῦ γραφή, lay against the person who gave the bribe; and the other, called δώρων or δωροδοκίας γραφή, against the person who received it. These actions applied to the bribery of citizens in the public assemblies of the people (συνδεκάζειν τὴν ἐκκλησίαν), of the Heliaea or any of the courts of justice, of the βουλή, and of the public advocates. Actions for bribery were under the jurisdiction of the thesmothetae. The punishment on conviction of the defendant was death, or payment of ten times the value of the gift received, to which the court might add a further punishment (προστίμημα).

DĒCĀTE (δεκάτη). [DECUMAE.]

DĒCEMPĒDA, a pole ten feet long, used by the agrimensores [AGRIMENSORES] in measuring land. Thus we find that the agrimensores were sometimes called *decempedatores*.

DĒCEMPRĪMI. [SENATUS.]

DĒCEMVĪRI, or the "ten-men," the name of various magistrates and functionaries at Rome, of whom the most important were:—
(1) DECEMVIRI LEGIBUS SCRIBENDIS, ten commissioners, who were appointed to draw up a code of laws. They were entrusted with supreme power in the state, and all the other magistracies were suspended. They entered upon their office at the beginning of the year B. C. 451; and they discharged their duties with diligence, and dispensed justice with impartiality. Each administered the government day by day in succession as during an interregnum; and the fasces were only carried before the one who presided for the day. They drew up a body of laws, distributed into ten sections; which, after being approved of by the senate and the comitia, were engraven on tables of metal, and set up in the comitium. On the expiration of their year of office, all parties were so well satisfied with the manner in which they had discharged their duties, that it was resolved to continue the same form of government for another year; more especially as some of the decemvirs said that their work was not finished. Ten new decemvirs were accordingly elected, of whom App. Claudius alone belonged to the former body. These magistrates framed several new laws, which were approved of by the centuries, and engraven on two additional tables. They acted, however, in a most tyrannical manner. Each was attended by twelve lictors, who carried not the rods only, but the axes, the emblem of sovereignty. They made common cause with the patrician party, and committed all kinds of outrages upon the persons and property of the plebeians and their families. When their year of office expired they refused to resign or to appoint successors. At length, the unjust decision of App. Claudius, in the case of Virginia, which led her father to kill her with his own hands to save her from prostitution, occasioned an insurrection of the people. The decemvirs were in consequence obliged to resign their office, B.C. 449; after which the usual magistracies were re-established. The ten tables of the former, and the two tables of the latter decemvirs, form together the laws of the Twelve Tables, which were the groundwork of the Roman laws. This, the first attempt to make a code, remained also the only attempt for near one thousand years, until the legislation of Justinian.—(2) DECEMVIRI LITIBUS or STLITIBUS JUDICANDIS, were magistrates forming a court of justice, which took cognizance of civil cases. The history as well as the peculiar jurisdiction of this court during the time of the republic is involved in inextricable obscurity. In the time of Cicero it still existed, and the proceedings in it took place in the ancient form of the sacramentum. Augustus transferred to these decemvirs the presidency in the courts of the centumviri. During the empire, this court had jurisdiction in capital matters, which is expressly stated in regard to the decemvirs.—(3) DECEMVIRI SACRIS FACIUNDIS, sometimes called simply DECEMVIRI SACRORUM, were the members of an ecclesiastical collegium, and were elected for life. Their chief duty was to take care of the Sibylline books, and to inspect them on all important occasions by command of the senate. Under the kings the care of the Sibylline books was committed to two men (*duumviri*) of high rank. On the expulsion of the kings, the care of these books was entrusted to the noblest of the patricians, who were exempted from all military and civil duties. Their number was increased about the year 367 B. C. to ten, of whom five were

chosen from the patricians and five from the plebeians. Subsequently their number was still further increased to fifteen (*quindecemviri*), probably by Sulla. It was also the duty of the decemviri to celebrate the games of Apollo, and the secular games.

DECENNĀLIA or DECENNIA, a festival celebrated with games every ten years by the Roman emperors. This festival owed its origin to the fact that Augustus refused the supreme power when offered to him for his life, and would only consent to accept it for ten years, and when these expired, for another period of ten years, and so on to the end of his life.

DECIMĀTIO, the selection, by lot, of every tenth man for punishment, when any number of soldiers in the Roman army had been guilty of any crime. The remainder usually had barley allowed to them instead of wheat. This punishment appears not to have been inflicted in the early times of the republic.

DECRĒTUM seems to mean that which is determined in a particular case after examination or consideration. It is sometimes applied to a determination of the consuls, and sometimes to a determination of the senate. A *decretum* of the senate would seem to differ from a *senatus-consultum*, in the way above indicated: it was limited to the special occasion and circumstances, and this would be true whether the decretum was of a judicial or a legislative character. But this distinction in the use of the two words, as applied to an act of the senate, was, perhaps, not always observed.

DECŪMAE (sc. *partes*) formed a portion of the *vectigalia* of the Romans, and were paid by subjects whose territory, either by conquest or *deditio*, had become the property of the state (*ager publicus*). They consisted, as the name denotes, of a tithe or tenth of the produce of the soil, levied upon the cultivators (*aratores*) or occupiers (*possessores*) of the lands, which, from being subject to this payment, were called *agri decumani*. The tax of a tenth was, however, generally paid by corn lands: plantations and vineyards, as requiring no seed and less labour, paid a fifth of the produce. A similar system existed in Greece also. Peisistratus, for instance, imposed a tax of a tenth on the lands of the Athenians, which the Peisistratidae lowered to a twentieth. At the time of the Persian war the confederate Greeks made a vow, by which all the states who had surrendered themselves to the enemy were subjected to the payment of tithes for the use of the god at Delphi. The tithes of the public lands belonging to Athens were farmed out as at Rome to contractors, called δεκατῶναι: the term δεκατηλόγοι was applied to the collectors; but the callings were, as we might suppose, often united in the same person. The title δεκατευταί is applied to both. A δεκάτη, or tenth of a different kind, was the arbitrary exaction imposed by the Athenians (B. c. 410) on the cargoes of all ships sailing into or out of the Pontus. They lost it by the battle of Aegospotami (B. c. 405); but it was re-established by Thrasybulus about B. c. 391. The tithe was let out to farm.

DECUNCIS, another name for the Dextans. [As.]

DECŬRIA. [Exercitus.]

DECŬRIŌNES. [Colonia: Exercitus.]

DECUSSIS. [As.]

DEDICĀTIO. [Inauguratio.]

DEDITICII, were those who had taken up arms against the Roman people, and being conquered, had surrendered themselves. Such people did not individually lose their freedom, but as a community all political existence, and of course had no other relation to Rome than that of subjects.

DEDUCTŌRES. [Ambitus.]

DEIGMA (δεῖγμα), a particular place in the Peiraceus, as well as in the harbours of other states, where merchants exposed samples of their goods for sale. The samples themselves were also called *deigmata*.

DEIPNON. [Coena.]

DELĀTOR, an informer. The delatores, under the emperors, were a class of men who gained their livelihood by informing against their fellow-citizens. They constantly brought forward false charges to gratify the avarice or jealousy of the different emperors, and were consequently paid according to the importance of the information which they gave.

DELECTUS. [Exercitus.]

DELIA (Δήλια), the name of festivals and games celebrated in the island of Delos, to which the Cyclades and the neighbouring Ionians on the coasts belonged. The Delia had existed from very early times, and were celebrated every fifth year. That the Athenians took part in these solemnities at a very early period, is evident from the *Deliastae* (afterwards called θεωροί) mentioned in the laws of Solon; the sacred vessel (θεωρίς), moreover, which they sent to Delos every year, was said to be the same which Theseus had sent after his return from Crete. In the course of time the celebration of this ancient panegyris in Delos had ceased, and it was not revived until B. c. 426, when the Athenians, after having purified the island in the winter of that year, restored the ancient solemnities, and added horse-races, which had never before taken place at the Delia. After this restoration, Athens, being at the head of the

Ionian confederacy, took the most prominent part in the celebration of the Delia; and though the islanders, in common with Athens, provided the choruses and victims, the leader (ἀρχιθέωρος), who conducted the whole solemnity, was an Athenian, and the Athenians had the superintendence of the common sanctuary. From these solemnities, belonging to the great Delian panegyris, we must distinguish the *lesser Delia*, which were mentioned above, and which were celebrated every year, probably on the 6th of Thargelion. The Athenians on this occasion sent the sacred vessel (θεωρίς), which the priest of Apollo adorned with laurel branches, to Delos. The embassy was called θεωρία; and those who sailed to the island, θεωροί; and before they set sail a solemn sacrifice was offered in the Delion, at Marathon, in order to obtain a happy voyage. During the absence of the vessel the city of Athens was purified, and no criminal was allowed to be executed.

DELPHINIA (δελφίνια), a festival of the same expiatory character as the Apollonia, which was celebrated in various towns of Greece, in honour of Apollo, surnamed Delphinius.

DELPHIS (δελφίς), an instrument of naval warfare. It consisted of a large mass of iron or lead suspended on a beam, which projected from the mast of the ship like a yardarm. It was used to sink, or make a hole in, an enemy's vessel, by being dropped upon it when alongside.

DELUBRUM. [TEMPLUM.]

DEMARCHI (δήμαρχοι), officers, who were the head-boroughs or chief magistrates of the demi in Attica, and are said to have been first appointed by Cleisthenes. Their duties were various and important. Thus, they convened meetings of the demus, and took the votes upon all questions under consideration; they made and kept a register of the landed estates in their districts, levied the monies due to the demus for rent, &c. They succeeded to the functions which had been discharged by the *naucrari* of the old constitution.

DEMENSUM, an allowance of corn, given to Roman slaves monthly or daily. It usually consisted of four or five modii of corn a month.

DEMINUTIO CĀPĪTIS. [CAPUT.]

DEMIURGI (δημιουργοί), magistrates, whose title is expressive of their doing the service of the people, existed in several of the Peloponnesian states. Among the Eleans and Mantineans they seem to have been the chief executive magistracy. We also read of *demiurgi* in the Achaean league, who probably ranked next to the *strategi*, and put questions to the vote in the general assembly of the confederates. Officers named *epidemiurgi*, or upper demiurgi, were sent by the Corinthians to manage the government of their colony at Potidaea.

DEMOCRATIA (δημοκρατία), that form of constitution in which the sovereign political power is in the hands of the demus (δῆμος) or commonalty. In a passage of Herodotus (iii. 80), the characteristics of a democracy are specified to be—1. Equality of legal rights (ἰσονομίη). 2. The appointment of magistrates by lot. 3. The accountability of all magistrates and officers. 4. The reference of all public matters to the decision of the community at large. Aristotle remarks— "The following points are characteristic of a democracy; that all magistrates should be chosen out of the whole body of citizens; that all should rule each, and each in turn rule all; that either all magistracies, or those not requiring experience and professional knowledge, should be assigned by lot; that there should be no property qualification, or but a very small one, for filling any magistracy; that the same man should not fill the same office twice, or should fill offices but few times, and but few offices, except in the case of military commands; that all, or as many as possible of the magistracies, should be of brief duration; that all citizens should be qualified to serve as dicasts; that the supreme power in everything should reside in the public assembly, and that no magistrate should be entrusted with irresponsible power except in very small matters." It is somewhat curious that neither in practice nor in theory did the representative system attract any attention among the Greeks. That diseased form of a democracy, in which from the practice of giving pay to the poorer citizens for their attendance in the public assembly, and from other causes, the predominant party in the state came to be in fact the lowest class of the citizens, was by later writers termed an *Ochlocracy* (ὀχλοκρατία— the dominion of the mob).

DEMOSII (δημόσιοι), public slaves at Athens, who were purchased by the state. The public slaves, most frequently mentioned, formed the city guard; it was their duty to preserve order in the public assembly, and to remove any person whom the prytaneis might order. They are generally called bowmen (τοξόται); or from the native country of the majority, Scythians (Σκύθαι); and also Speusinians, from the name of the person who first established the force. They originally lived in tents in the market-place, and afterwards upon the Areiopagus. Their officers had the name of toxarchs (τόξαρχοι).

k

Their number was at first 300, purchased soon after the battle of Salamis, but was afterwards increased to 1200.

DĒMUS (δῆμος), originally indicated a district or tract of land; and in this meaning of a country district, inhabited and under cultivation, it is contrasted with πόλις. When Cleisthenes, at Athens, broke up the four tribes of the old constitution, he substituted in their place ten local tribes (φυλαὶ τοπικαί), each of which he subdivided into ten *demi* or country parishes, possessing each its principal town; and in some one of these demi were enrolled all the Athenian citizens resident in Attica, with the exception, perhaps, of those who were natives of Athens itself. These subdivisions corresponded in some degree to the *naucrariae* (ναυκραρίαι) of the old tribes, and were originally one hundred in number. These demi formed independent corporations, and had each their several magistrates, landed and other property, with a common treasury. They had likewise their respective convocations or "parish meetings," convened by the *demarchi*, in which was transacted the public business of the demus, such as the leasing of its estates, the elections of officers, the revision of the registers or lists of δημόται, and the admission of new members. Independent of these bonds of union, each demus seems to have had its peculiar temples and religious worship. There were likewise judges, called δικασταὶ κατὰ δήμους, who decided cases where the matter in dispute was of less value than ten drachmae. Admission into a demus was necessary before any individual could enter upon his full rights and privileges as an Attic citizen. The register of enrolment was called ληξιαρχικὸν γραμματεῖον.

DĒNĀRĪUS, the principal silver coin among the Romans, was so called because it was originally equal to ten asses; but on the reduction of the weight of the as [As], it was made equal to sixteen asses, except in military pay, in which it was still reckoned as equal to ten asses. The denarius was first coined five years before the first Punic war, B.C. 269. [ARGENTUM.] The average value of the denarii coined at the end of the commonwealth is about 8½d., and those under the empire about 7½d. If the denarius be reckoned in value 8½d., the other Roman coins of silver will be of the following value:

				Pence.	Farth.
Teruncius	-	-	-	—	·53125
Sembella	-	-	-	—	1·0625
Libella	-	-	-	—	2·125
Sestertius	-	-	-	2	·5
Quinarius or Victoriatus	-	4	1
Denarius	-	-	-	8	2

Some denarii were called *serrati*, because their edges were notched like a saw, which

Denarius. (British Museum.)

appears to have been done to prove that they were solid silver, and not plated; and others *bigati* and *quadrigati*, because on their reverse were represented chariots drawn by two and four horses respectively.

DĒSIGNĀTOR. [FUNUS.]

DĒSULTOR, a rider in the Roman games, who generally rode two horses at the same time, sitting on them without a saddle, and vaulting upon either of them at his pleasure.

DEUNX. [As, LIBRA.]

DEXTANS. [As, LIBRA.]

DIĀDĒMA, originally a white fillet, used to encircle the head. It is represented on the head of Dionysus, and was, in an ornamented form, assumed by kings as an emblem of sovereignty.

DIAETĒTAE (διαιτηταί), or arbitrators, at Athens, were of two kinds; the one public and appointed by lot (κληρωτοί), the other private, and chosen (αἱρετοί) by the parties who referred to them the decision of a disputed point, instead of trying it before a court of justice; the judgments of both, according to Aristotle, being founded on equity rather than law. The number of public arbitrators seems to have been 40, four for each tribe. Their jurisdiction was confined to civil cases.

DIĀLIS FLĀMEN. [FLAMEN.]

DIĀMASTĪGŌSIS (διαμαστίγωσις), a solemnity performed at Sparta at the festival of Artemis Orthia. Spartan youths were scourged on the occasion at the altar of Artemis, by persons appointed for the purpose, until their blood gushed forth and covered the altar. Many anecdotes are related of the courage and intrepidity with which young Spartans bore the lashes of the scourge; some even died without uttering a murmur at their sufferings, for to die under the strokes was considered as honourable a death as that on the field of battle.

DIĀPSĒPHISIS (διαψήφισις), a political institution at Athens, the object of which was to prevent aliens, or such as were the offspring of an unlawful marriage, from assuming the rights of citizens. By this method a trial of spurious citizens was to be held by the demotae, within whose deme intruders were suspected to exist.

DIASIA (διάσια), a great festival celebrated at Athens, without the walls of the city, in honour of Zeus, surnamed Μειλίχιος. The whole people took part in it, and the wealthier citizens offered victims, while the poorer classes burnt such incense as their country furnished. The diasia took place in the latter half of the month of Anthesterion with feasting and rejoicings, and was, like most other festivals, accompanied by a fair.

DICASTES (δικαστής), the name of a judge, or rather juryman, at Athens. The conditions of his eligibility were, that he should be a free citizen, in the enjoyment of his full franchise (ἐπιτιμία), and not less than thirty years of age, and of persons so qualified 6,000 were selected by lot for the service of every year. Their appointment took place annually under the conduct of the nine archons and their official scribe; each of these ten personages drew by lot the names of 600 persons of the tribe assigned to him; the whole number so selected was again divided by lot into ten sections of 500 each, together with a supernumerary one, consisting of 1000 persons, from among whom the occasional deficiencies in the sections of 500 might be supplied. To each of the ten sections one of the ten first letters of the alphabet was appropriated as a distinguishing mark, and a small tablet (πινάκιον), inscribed with the letter of the section and the name of the individual, was delivered as a certificate of his appointment to each dicast. Before proceeding to the exercise of his functions, the dicast was obliged to swear the official oath. This oath being taken, and the divisions made as above mentioned, it remained to assign the courts to the several sections of dicasts in which they were to sit. This was not, like the first, an appointment intended to last during the year, but took place under the conduct of the thesmothetae, de novo, every time that it was necessary to impanel a number of dicasts. As soon as the allotment had taken place, each dicast received a staff, on which was painted the letter and the colour of the court awarded him, which might serve both as a ticket to procure admittance, and also to distinguish him from any loiterer that might endeavour clandestinely to obtain a sitting after business had begun. While in court, and probably from the hand of the presiding magistrate (ἡγεμὼν δικαστηρίου), he received the token or ticket that entitled him to receive his fee (δικαστικόν). This payment is said to have been first instituted by Pericles, and

was originally a single obolus; it was increased by Cleon to thrice that amount about the 88th Olympiad.

DICE (δίκη), signifies generally any proceedings at law by one party directly or mediately against others. The object of all such actions is to protect the body politic, or one or more of its individual members, from injury and aggression; a distinction which has in most countries suggested the division of all causes into two great classes, the public and the private, and assigned to each its peculiar form and treatment. At Athens the first of these was implied by the terms public, δίκαι, or ἀγῶνες, or still more peculiarly by γραφαί; causes of the other class were termed private δίκαι, or ἀγῶνες, or simply δίκαι in its limited sense. In a δίκη, only the person whose rights were alleged to be affected, or the legal protector (κύριος) of such person, if a minor or otherwise incapable of appearing suo jure, was permitted to institute an action as plaintiff; in public causes, with the exception of some few in which the person injured or his family were peculiarly bound and interested to act, any free citizen, and sometimes, when the state was directly attacked, almost any alien, was empowered to do so. The court fees, called prytaneia, were paid in private but not in public causes, and a public prosecutor that compromised the action with the defendant was in most cases punished by a fine of a thousand drachmae and a modified disfranchisement, while there was no legal impediment at any period of a private lawsuit to the reconciliation of the litigant parties.—The proceedings in the δίκη were commenced by a summons (πρόσκλησις) to the defendant to appear on a certain day before the proper magistrate (εἰσαγωγεύς), and there answer the charges preferred against him. This summons was often served by the plaintiff in person, accompanied by one or two witnesses (κλητῆρες), whose names were endorsed upon the declaration (λῆξις or ἔγκλημα). Between the service of the summons and appearance of the parties before the magistrate, it is very probable that the law prescribed the intervention of a period of five days. If both parties appeared, the proceedings commenced by the plaintiff putting in his declaration, and at the same time depositing his share of the court fees (πρυτανεία), which were trifling in amount, but the non-payment of which was a fatal objection to the further progress of a cause When these were paid, it became the duty of the magistrate, if no manifest objection appeared on the face of the declaration, to cause it to be written out on a tablet, and exposed for the inspection of the public on the wall or other place that served as the cause list of his court. The magistrate then appointed a day for the further proceedings of the *anacrisis* [ANACRISIS]. If the plaintiff failed to appear at the anacrisis, the suit, of course, fell to the ground; if the defendant made default, judgment passed against him. An affidavit might at this, as well as at other periods of the action, be made in behalf of a person unable to attend upon the given day, and this would, if allowed, have the effect of postponing further proceedings (ὑπωμοσία); it might, however, be combated by a counter-affidavit, to the effect that the alleged reason was unfounded or otherwise insufficient (ἀνθυπωμοσία); and a question would arise upon this point, the decision of which, when adverse to the defendant, would render him liable to the penalty of contumacy. The plaintiff was in this case said ἐρήμην ἑλεῖν; the defendant, ἐρήμην ὀφλεῖν, δίκην being the word omitted in both phrases. The anacrisis began with the affidavit of the plaintiff (προωμοσία), then followed the answer of the defendant (ἀντωμοσία or ἀντιγραφή), then the parties produced their respective witnesses, and reduced their evidence to writing, and put in originals, or authenticated copies, of all the records, deeds, and contracts that might be useful in establishing their case, as well as memoranda of offers and requisitions then made by either side (προκλήσεις). The whole of the documents were then, if the cause took a straightforward course (εὐθυδικία), enclosed on the last day of the anacrisis in a casket (ἐχῖνος), which was sealed, and entrusted to the custody of the presiding magistrate, till it was produced and opened at the trial. During the interval no alteration in its contents was permitted, and accordingly evidence that had been discovered after the anacrisis was not producible at the trial.—In some causes, the trial before the dicasts was by law appointed to come on within a given time; in such as were not provided for by such regulations, we may suppose that it would principally depend upon the leisure of the magistrate. Upon the court being assembled, the magistrate called on the cause, and the plaintiff opened his case. At the commencement of the speech, the proper officer (ὁ ἐφ' ὕδωρ) filled the clepsydra with water. As long as the water flowed from this vessel the orator was permitted to speak; if, however, evidence was to be read by the officer of the court, or a law recited, the water was stopped till the speaker recommenced. The quantity of water, or, in other words, the length of the speeches, was different in different causes. After the speeches of the advocates, which were in general two on each side, and the incidental reading of the documentary and other evidence, the dicasts proceeded to give their judgment by ballot.—When the principal point at issue was decided in favour of the plaintiff, there followed in many cases a further discussion as to the fine or punishment to be inflicted on the defendant (παθεῖν ἢ ἀποτῖσαι). All actions were divided into two classes,—ἀγῶνες ἀτίμητοι, *suits not to be assessed*, in which the fine, or other penalty, was determined by the laws; and ἀγῶνες τιμητοί, *suits to be assessed*, in which the penalty had to be fixed by the judges. If the suit was an ἀγὼν τιμητός, the plaintiff generally mentioned in the pleadings the punishment which he considered the defendant deserved (τίμημα); and the defendant was allowed to make a counter-assessment (ἀντιτιμᾶσθαι or ὑποτιμᾶσθαι), and to argue before the judges why the assessment of the plaintiff ought to be changed or mitigated. In certain causes, which were determined by the laws, any of the judges was allowed to propose an additional assessment (προστίμημα); the amount of which, however, appears to have been usually fixed by the laws. Thus, in certain cases of theft, the additional penalty was fixed at five days' and nights' imprisonment. Upon judgment being given in a private suit, the Athenian law left its execution very much in the hands of the successful party, who was empowered to seize the moveables of his antagonist as a pledge for the payment of the money, or institute an action of ejectment (ἐξούλης) against the refractory debtor. The judgment of a court of dicasts was in general decisive (δίκη αὐτοτελής); but upon certain occasions, as, for instance, when a gross case of perjury or conspiracy could be proved by the unsuccessful party to have operated to his disadvantage, the cause, upon the conviction of such conspirators or witnesses, might be commenced *de novo*.

DICTATOR, an extraordinary magistrate at Rome. The name is of Latin origin, and the office probably existed in many Latin towns before it was introduced into Rome. We find it in Lanuvium even in very late times. At Rome this magistrate was originally called *magister populi* and not *dictator*, and in the sacred books he was always designated by the former name down to the latest times. On the establishment of the Roman republic the government of the state was entrusted to *two* consuls, that the citizens might be the better protected against the tyrannical exercise of the supreme power. But it was soon felt that circumstances might arise in which it was of importance for the safety of the state that the government should be vested in the hands of a single person, who should possess for a season absolute power, and from whose decision there should be no appeal to any other body. Thus it came to pass that in B.C. 501, nine years after the expulsion of the Tarquins, the dictatorship (*dictatura*) was instituted. By the original law respecting the appointment of a dictator (*lex de dictatore creando*) no one was eligible for this office unless he had previously been consul. We find, however, a few instances in which this law was not observed.—When a dictator was considered necessary, the senate passed a senatus consultum, that one of the consuls should nominate (*dicere*) a dictator; and without a previous decree of the senate the consuls had not the power of naming a dictator. The nomination or proclamation of the dictator was always made by the consul, probably without any witnesses, between midnight and morning, and with the observance of the auspices (*surgens* or *oriens nocte silentio dictatorem dicebat*). The technical word for this nomination or proclamation was *dicere* (seldom *creare* or *facere*). Originally the dictator was of course a patrician. The first plebeian dictator was C. Marcius Rutilus, nominated in B.C. 356 by the plebeian consul M. Popillius Laenas. The reasons which led to the appointment of a dictator, required that there should be only one at a time. The dictators that were appointed for carrying on the business of the state were said to be nominated *rei gerundae causa*, or sometimes *seditionis sedandae causa*; and upon them, as well as upon the other magistrates, the imperium was conferred by a *Lex Curiata*. The dictatorship was limited to six months, and no instances occur in which a person held this office for a longer time, for the dictatorships of Sulla and Caesar are of course not to be taken into account. On the contrary, though a dictator was appointed for six months, he often resigned his office long previously, immediately after he had dispatched the business for which he had been appointed. As soon as the dictator was nominated, a kind of suspension took place with respect to the consuls and all the other magistrates, with the exception of the tribuni plebis. The regular magistrates continued, indeed, to discharge the duties of their various offices under the dictator, but they were no longer independent officers, but were subject to the higher imperium of the dictator, and obliged to obey his orders in every thing. The superiority of the dictator's power to that of the consuls consisted chiefly in the three following points—greater independence of the senate, more extensive power of punishment without any appeal (*provocatio*) from their sentence to the people, and irresponsibility. To these three points, must of course be added that he was not fettered by a colleague. We may naturally suppose that the dictator would usually act in unison with the senate; but it is expressly stated that in many cases where the consuls required the co-operation of the senate, the dictator could act on his own responsibility. That there was originally no appeal from the sentence of the dictator is certain, and accordingly the lictors bore the axes in the fasces before them even in the city, as a symbol of their absolute power over the lives of the citizens, although by the Valerian law the axes had disappeared from the fasces of the consuls. Whether, however, the right of *provocatio* was afterwards given cannot be determined. It was in consequence of the great and irresponsible power possessed by the dictatorship, that we find it frequently compared with the regal dignity, from which it only differed in being held for a limited time.—There were however a few limits to the power of the dictator. 1. The most important was that which we have mentioned above, that the period of his office was only six months. 2. He had not power over the treasury, but could only make use of the money which was granted him by the senate. 3. He was not allowed to leave Italy, since he might thus easily become dangerous to the republic; though the case of Atilius Calatinus in the first Punic war forms an exception to this rule. 4. He was not allowed to ride on horseback at Rome, without previously obtaining the permission of the people; a regulation apparently capricious, but perhaps adopted that he might not bear too great a resemblance to the kings, who were accustomed to ride.—The insignia of the dictator were nearly the same as those of the kings in earlier times; and of the consuls subsequently. Instead however of having only twelve lictors, as was the case with the consuls, he was preceded by twenty-four bearing the secures as well as the fasces. The *sella curulis* and *toga praetexta* also belonged to the dictator.—The preceding account of the dictatorship applies more particularly to the dictator rei gerundae causa; but dictators were also frequently appointed, especially when the consuls were absent from the city, to perform certain acts, which could not be done by any inferior magistrate. These dictators had little more than the name; and as they were only appointed to discharge a particular duty, they had to resign immediately that duty was performed. The occasions on which such dictators were appointed, were principally:—1. For the purpose of holding the comitia for the elections (*comitiorum habendorum causa*). 2. For fixing the *clavus annalis* in the temple of Jupiter (*clavi figendi causa*) in times of pestilence or civil discord, because the law said that this ceremony was to be performed by the *praetor maximus*, and after the institution of the dictatorship the latter was regarded as the highest magistracy in the state. 3. For appointing holidays (*feriarum constituendarum causa*) on the appearance of prodigies, and for officiating at the public games (*ludorum faciendorum causa*), the presidency of which belonged to the consuls or praetors. 4. For holding trials (*quaestionibus exercendis*.) 5. And on one occasion, for filling up vacancies in the senate (*legendo senatui*).—Along with the dictator there was always a *magister equitum*, the nomination of whom was left to the choice of the dictator, unless the senatus consultum specified, as was sometimes the case, the name of the person who was to be appointed. The magister equitum had, like the dictator, to receive the imperium by a lex curiata. The dictator could not be without a magister equitum, and, consequently, if the latter died during the six months of the dictatorship, another had to be nominated in his stead. The magister equitum was subject to the imperium of the dictator, but in the absence of his superior he became his representative, and exercised the same powers as the dictator. The magister equitum was originally, as his name imports, the commander of the cavalry, while the dictator was at the head of the legions, the infantry; and the relation between them was in this respect similar to that which subsisted between the king and the tribunus celerum. Dictators were only appointed so long as the Romans had to carry on wars in Italy. A solitary instance of the nomination of a dictator for the purpose of carrying on war out of Italy has been already mentioned. The last dictator rei gerundae causa was M. Junius Pera, in B. C. 216. From that time dictators were frequently appointed for holding the elections down to B.C. 202, but after that year the dictatorship disappears altogether.—After a lapse of 120 years, Sulla caused himself to be appointed dictator in B.C. 82, *reipublicae constituendae causa*, but neither his dictatorship nor that of Caesar is to be compared with the genuine office. Soon after Caesar's death the dictatorship was abolished for ever by a lex proposed by the consul Antonius. During the time, however, that the dictatorship was in abeyance, a substitute was invented for it, whenever the circumstances of the republic required the adoption of extraordinary measures, by the senate investing the consuls with dictatorial power. This was done by the well-known formula, *Videant or dent operam consules, ne quid respublica detrimenti capiat.*

DICTYNNIA (δικτύννια), a festival with sacrifices, celebrated at Cydonia in Crete, in honour of Artemis, surnamed Δίκτυννα or Δικτύνναια, from δίκτυον, a hunter's net.

DIES (ἡμέρα), a day. The name *dies* was applied, like our word day, to the time during which, according to the notions of the ancients, the sun performed his course around the earth, and this time they called the civil day (*dies civilis*, in Greek νυχθήμερον, because it included both night and day). The natural day (*dies naturalis*), or the time from the rising to the setting of the sun, was likewise designated by the name dies. The civil day began with the Greeks at the setting of the sun, and with the Romans at midnight. At the time of the Homeric poems the natural day was divided into three parts. The first, called ἠώς, began with sunrise, and comprehended the whole space of time during which light seemed to be increasing, *i. e.* till midday. The second part was called μέσον ἦμαρ or mid-day, during which the sun was thought to stand still. The third part bore the name of δείλη or δείελον ἦμαρ, which derived its name from the increased warmth of the atmosphere. Among the Athenians the first and last of the divisions made at the time of Homer were afterwards subdivided into two parts. The earlier part of the morning was termed πρωί or πρῷ τῆς ἡμέρας: the latter, πληθούσης τῆς ἀγορᾶς, or περὶ πλήθουσαν ἀγοράν. The μέσον ἦμαρ of Homer was afterwards expressed by μεσημβρία, μέσον ἡμέρας, or μέση ἡμέρα, and comprehended, as before, the middle of the day, when the sun seemed neither to rise nor to decline. The two parts of the afternoon were called δείλη πρωίη or πρωία, and δείλη ὀψίη or ὀψία. This division continued to be observed down to the latest period of Grecian history, though another more accurate division was introduced at an early period; for Anaximander, or, according to others, his disciple Anaximenes, is said to have made the Greeks acquainted with the use of the Babylonian chronometer or sun-dial (called πόλος, or ὡρολόγιον), by means of which the natural day was divided into twelve equal spaces of time. The division of the day most generally observed by the Romans, was that into *tempus antemeridianum* and *pomeridianum*, the *meridies* itself being only considered as a point at which the one ended and the other commenced. But as it was of importance that this moment should be known, an especial officer [ACCENSUS] was appointed, who proclaimed the time of mid-day. The division of the day into twelve equal spaces, which were shorter in winter than in summer, was first adopted when artificial means of measuring time were introduced among the Romans from Greece. This was about the year B. C. 291, when L. Papirius Cursor, after the war with Pyrrhus in southern Italy, brought to Rome an instrument called *solarium horologium*, or simply *solarium*. But as the solarium had been made for a different latitude, it showed the time at Rome very incorrectly. Scipio Nasica, therefore, erected in B. C. 159 a public clepsydra, which indicated the hours of the night as well as of the day. Even after the erection of this clepsydra it was customary for one of the subordinate officers of the praetor to proclaim the third, sixth, and ninth hours; which shows that the day was, like the night, divided into four parts, each consisting of three hours.— All the days of the year were, according to different points of view, divided by the Romans into different classes. For the purpose of the administration of justice all days were divided into *dies fasti* and *dies nefasti*. DIES FASTI were the days on which the praetor was allowed to administer justice in the public courts; they derived their name from *fari* (*fari tria verba*; *do, dico, addico*). On some of the dies fasti comitia could be held, but not on all. The regular *dies fasti* were marked in the Roman calendar by the letter F, and their number in the course of the year was 38.—Besides these there were certain days called *dies intercisi*, on which the praetor might hold his courts, but not at all hours, so that sometimes one half of such a day was *fastus*, while the other half was *nefastus*. Their number was 65 in the year. —DIES NEFASTI were days on which neither courts of justice nor comitia were allowed to be held, and which were dedicated to other purposes. The term *dies nefasti*, which originally had nothing to do with religion, but simply indicated days on which no courts were to be held, was in subsequent times applied to religious days in general, as *dies nefasti* were mostly dedicated to the worship of the gods.—In a religious point of view all days of the year were either *dies festi*, or *dies profesti*, or *dies intercisi*. According to the definition given by Macrobius, *dies festi* were dedicated to the gods, and spent with sacrifices, repasts, games, and other solemnities; *dies profesti* belonged to men for the administration of their private and public affairs. *Dies intercisi* were common between gods and men, that is, partly devoted to the worship of the gods, partly to the transaction of ordinary business. *Dies profesti* were either *dies fasti*, or *dies comitiales*, that is, days on which comitia were held, or *dies comperendini*, that is, days to which any action was allowed to be transferred; or *dies stati*, that is, days set apart for causes between Roman citizens and foreigners; or *dies proeliales*, that is, all days on which religion did not forbid the commencement of a war.

DIFFARREATIO. [DIVORTIUM.]

DIIPOLEIA (διιπόλεια), also called Διπόλεια or Διπόλια, a very ancient festival celebrated every year on the acropolis of Athens in honour of Zeus, surnamed Πολιεύς.

DIMACHAE (διμάχαι), Macedonian horse-soldiers, who also fought on foot when occasion required, like our dragoons.

DIMINUTIO CAPITIS. [CAPUT.]

DIOCLEIA (διόκλεια), a festival celebrated by the Megarians in honour of an ancient Athenian hero, Diocles, around whose grave young men assembled on the occasion, and amused themselves with gymnastic and other contests. We read that he who gave the sweetest kiss obtained the prize, consisting of a garland of flowers.

DIONYSIA (διονύσια), festivals celebrated in various parts of Greece in honour of Dionysus, and characterised by extravagant merriment and enthusiastic joy. Drunkenness, and the boisterous music of flutes, cymbals, and drums, were likewise common to all Dionysiac festivals. In the processions called θίασοι (from θειάζω), with which they were celebrated, women also took part in the disguise of Bacchae, Lenae, Thyades, Naiades, Nymphs, &c., adorned with garlands of ivy, and bearing the thyrsus in their hands, so that the whole train represented a population inspired, and actuated by the powerful presence of the god. The choruses sung on the occasion were called dithyrambs, and were hymns addressed to the god in the freest metres and with the boldest imagery, in which his exploits and achievements were extolled. [CHORUS.] The phallus, the symbol of the fertility of nature, was also carried in these processions. The indulgence in drinking was considered by the Greeks as a duty of gratitude which they owed to the giver of the vine; hence in some places it was thought a crime to remain sober at the Dionysia. The Attic festivals of Dionysus were four in number: the *Rural* or *Lesser Dionysia* (Διονύσια κατ' ἀγρούς, or μικρά), the *Lenaea* (Λήναια), the *Anthesteria* (Ἀνθεστήρια), and the *City* or *Great Dionysia* (Διονύσια ἐν ἄστει, ἀστικά, or μεγάλα). The season of the year sacred to Dionysus was during the months nearest to the shortest day; and the Attic festivals were accordingly celebrated in Poseideon, Gamelion, Anthesterion, and Elaphebolion.—The *Rural* or *Lesser Dionysia*, a vintage festival, were celebrated in the various demes of Attica in the month of Poseideon, and were under the superintendence of the several local magistrates, the demarchs. This was doubtless the most ancient of all, and was held with the highest degree of merriment and freedom; even slaves enjoyed full freedom during its celebration, and their boisterous shouts on the occasion were almost intolerable. It is here that we have to seek for the origin of comedy, in the jests and the scurrilous abuse with which the peasants assailed the bystanders from a waggon in which they rode about. The Dionysia in the Peiraeeus, as well as those of the other demes of Attica, belonged to the lesser Dionysia.—The second festival, the *Lenaea* (from ληνός, the wine-press, from which also the month of Gamelion was called by the Ionians Lenaeon), was celebrated in the month of Gamelion; the place of its celebration was the ancient temple of Dionysus Limnaeus (from λίμνη, as the district was originally a swamp). This temple was called the Lenaeon. The Lenaea were celebrated with a procession and scenic contests in tragedy and comedy. The procession probably went to the Lenaeon, where a goat (τράγος, whence the chorus and tragedy which arose out of it were called τραγικὸς χορός, and τραγῳδία) was sacrificed, and a chorus standing around the altar sang the dithyrambic ode to the god. As the dithyramb was the element out of which, by the introduction of an actor, tragedy arose [CHORUS], it is natural that, in the scenic contests of this festival, tragedy should have preceded comedy. The poet who wished his play to be brought out at the Lenaea applied to the second archon, who had the superintendence of this festival, and who gave him a chorus if the piece was thought to deserve it.—The third festival, the *Anthesteria*, was celebrated on the 11th, 12th, and 13th days of the month of Anthesterion. The second archon likewise superintended the celebration of the Anthesteria, and distributed the prizes among the victors in the various games which were carried on during the season. The first day was called πιθοιγία: the second, χόες: and the third, χύτροι. The first day derived its name from the opening of the casks to taste the wine of the preceding year; the second from χοῦς, the cup, and seems to have been the day devoted to drinking. The third day had its name from χύτρος, a pot, as on this day persons offered pots with flowers, seeds, or cooked vegetables, as a sacrifice to Dionysus and Hermes Chthonius. It is uncertain whether dramas were performed at the Anthesteria; but it is supposed that comedies were represented, and that tragedies which were to be brought out at the great Dionysia were perhaps rehearsed at the Anthesteria. The mysteries connected with the celebration of the Anthesteria were held at night.—The fourth festival, the *City* or *Great Dionysia*, was celebrated about the 12th of the month of Elaphebolion; but we do not know whether they lasted more than one day or not. The order in which the solemnities took place was as follows:—the great public procession, the chorus of boys, the *comus* [CHORUS], comedy, and, lastly, tragedy. Of the dramas which were performed at the great Dionysia, the tragedies at least were generally new pieces; repetitions do not, however, seem to have been excluded from any Dionysiac festival. The first archon had the superintendence, and gave the chorus to the dramatic poet who wished to bring out his piece at this festival. The prize awarded to the dramatist for the best play consisted of a crown, and his name was proclaimed in the theatre of Dionysus. As the great Dionysia were celebrated at the beginning of spring, when the navigation was re-opened, Athens was not only visited by numbers of country people, but also by strangers from other parts of Greece, and the various amusements and exhibitions on this occasion were not unlike those of a modern fair.—The worship of Dionysus, whom the Romans called Bacchus, or rather the Bacchic mysteries and orgies (*Bacchanalia*), are said to have been introduced from southern Italy into Etruria, and from thence to Rome, where for a time they were carried on in secret, and, during the latter period of their existence, at night. The initiated, according to Livy, not only indulged in feasting and drinking at their meetings, but when their minds were heated with wine they indulged in the coarsest excesses and the most unnatural vices. The time of initiation lasted ten days; on the tenth, the person who was to be initiated took a solemn meal, underwent a purification by water, and was led into the sanctuary (*Bacchanal*). At first only women were initiated, and the orgies were celebrated every year during three days. But Pacula Annia, a Campanian matron, pretending to act under the direct influence of Bacchus, changed the whole method of celebration: she admitted men to the initiation, and transferred the solemnisation, which had hitherto taken place during the daytime, to the night. Instead of three days in the year, she ordered that the Bacchanalia should be held during five days in every month. It was from that time that these orgies were carried on with frightful licentiousness and excesses of every kind. The evil at length became so alarming, that, in B. c. 186, the consuls, by the command of the senate, instituted an investigation into the nature and object of these new rites. The result was that numerous persons were arrested, and some put to death ; and that a decree of the senate was issued, commanding that no Bacchanalia should be held either in Rome or Italy; that if any one should think such ceremonies necessary, or if he could not neglect them without scruples or making atonements, he should apply to the praetor urbanus, who might then consult the senate. If the permission should be granted to him in an assembly of the senate, consisting of not less than one hundred members, he might solemnise the Bacchic sacra ; but no more than five persons were to be present at the celebration ; there should be no common fund, and no master of the sacra or priest. A brazen table containing this important document was discovered near Bari, in southern Italy, in the year 1640, and is at present in the imperial Museum of Vienna. While the *Bacchanalia* were thus suppressed, another more simple and innocent festival of Bacchus, the *Liberalia* (from *Liber*, or *Liber Pater*, a name of Bacchus), continued to be celebrated at Rome every year on the 16th of March. Priests and aged priestesses, adorned with garlands of ivy, carried through the city wine, honey, cakes, and sweetmeats, together with an altar with a handle (*ansata ara*), in the middle of which there was a small fire-pan (*foculus*), in which from time to time sacrifices were burnt. On this day Roman youths who had attained their sixteenth year received the *toga virilis*.

DIOSCURIA (διοσκούρια), festivals celebrated in various parts of Greece in honour of the Dioscuri (Castor and Pollux). Their worship was very generally adopted in Greece, especially in the Doric and Achaean states ; but little is known of the manner in which their festivals were celebrated. At Athens the festival was called Anaceia.

DIOTA, a vessel having two ears (ὦτα) or handles, used for holding wine. It appears to have been much the same as the amphora. [AMPHORA.]

DIPHTHERA (διφθέρα), a kind of cloak made of the skins of animals, and worn by herdsmen and country people. It had a covering for the head (ἐπικράνον), in which respect it would correspond to the Roman *cucullus*.

DIPLOMA, a writ or public document, which conferred upon a person any right or privilege. During the republic, it was granted by the consuls and senate, and under the empire, by the emperor and the magistrates whom he authorised to do so. It consisted of two leaves, whence it derived its name.

DIPTYCHA (δίπτυχα), two writing tablets, which could be folded together. They were commonly made of wood and covered over with wax.

DIRIBITORES. [COMITIA.]

DISCUS (δίσκος), a circular plate of stone, or metal, made for throwing to a distance as an exercise of strength and dexterity. It was one of the principal gymnastic exercises of the ancients, being included in the *Pentathlum*.

Discobolus. (Osterley, Denk. der alt Kunst, vol. I. No. 139

DISPENSATOR. [CALCULATOR.]
DITHYRAMBUS. [CHORUS.]
DIVERSORIUM. [CAUPONA.]

DIVINATIO (μαντική), a power in man which foresees future things by means of those signs which the gods throw in his way. Among the Greeks the *manteis* (μάντεις), or seers, who announced the future, were supposed to be under the direct influence of the gods, chiefly that of Apollo. In many families of seers the inspired knowledge of the future was considered to be hereditary, and to be transmitted from father to son. To these families belonged the Iamids, who from Olympia spread over a considerable part of Greece ; the Branchidae, near Miletus ; the Eumolpids, at Athens and Eleusis ; the Telliads, the Acarnanian seers, and others. Along with the seers we may also mention the Bacides and the Sibyllae. Both existed from a very remote time, and were distinct from the manteis so far as they pretended to derive their knowledge of the future from sacred books (χρησμοί) which they consulted, and which were in some places, as at Athens and Rome, kept by the government or some especial officers, in the acropolis and in the most revered sanctuary. The Bacides are said to have been descended from one or more prophetic nymphs of the name of Bacis. The Sibyllae were prophetic women, probably of Asiatic origin, whose peculiar custom seems to have been to wander with their sacred books from place to place. The Sibylla, whose books gained so great an importance at Rome, is reported to have been the Erythraean: the books which she was said to have sold to one of the Tarquins were carefully concealed from the public, and only accessible to the duumvirs. Besides these more respectable prophets and prophetesses, there were numbers of diviners of an inferior order (χρησμολόγοι), who made it their business to explain all sorts of signs, and to tell fortunes. They were, however, more particularly popular with the lower orders, who are everywhere most ready to believe what is most marvellous and least entitled to credit. No public undertaking of any consequence was ever entered upon by the Greeks and Romans without consulting the will of the gods, by observing the signs which they sent, especially those in the sacrifices offered for the purpose, and by which they were thought to indicate the success or the failure of the undertaking. For this kind of divination no divine inspiration was thought necessary, but merely experience and a certain knowledge acquired by routine; and although in some cases priests were appointed for the purpose of observing and explaining signs [AUGUR; HARUSPEX], yet on any sudden emergency, especially in private affairs, any one who met with something extraordinary, might act as his own interpreter. The principal signs by which the gods were thought to declare their will, were things connected with the offering of sacrifices, the flight and voice of birds, all kinds of natural phenomena, ordinary as well as extraordinary, and dreams.—The interpretation of signs of the first class (ἱερομαντεία or ἱεροσκοπία, haruspicium or ars haruspicina) was, according to Aeschylus, the invention of Prometheus. It seems to have been most cultivated by the Etruscans, among whom it was raised into a complete science, and from whom it passed to the Romans. Sacrifices were either offered for the special purpose of consulting the gods, or in the ordinary way; but in both cases the signs were observed, and when they were propitious, the sacrifice was said καλλιερεῖν. The principal points that were generally observed were, 1. The manner in which the victim approached the altar. 2. The nature of the intestines with respect to their colour and smoothness; the liver and bile were of particular importance. 3. The nature of the flame which consumed the sacrifice. Especial care was also taken during a sacrifice, that no inauspicious or frivolous words were uttered by any of the bystanders: hence the admonitions of the priests, εὐφημεῖτε and εὐφημία, or σιγᾶτε, σιωπᾶτε, favete linguis, and others; for improper expressions were not only thought to pollute and profane the sacred act, but to be unlucky omens.—The art of interpreting signs of the second class was called οἰωνιστική, augurium, or auspicium. It was, like the former, common to Greeks and Romans, but never attained the same degree of importance in Greece as it did in Rome. [AUSPICIUM.] The Greeks, when observing the flight of birds, turned their face toward the north, and then a bird appearing to the right (east), especially an eagle, a heron, or a falcon, was a favourable sign; while birds appearing to the left (west) were considered as unlucky signs. Of greater importance than the appearance of animals, at least to the Greeks, were the phenomena in the heavens, particularly during any public transaction. Among the unlucky phenomena in the heavens (διοσημεία, signa, or portenta) were thunder and lightning, an eclipse of the sun or moon, earthquakes, rain of blood, stones, milk, &c. Any one of these signs was sufficient at Athens to break up the assembly of the people.—In common life, things apparently of no importance, when occurring at a critical moment, were thought by the ancients to be signs sent by the gods, from which conclusions might be drawn respecting the future. Among these common occurrences we may mention sneezing, twinkling of the eyes, tinkling of the ears, &c.—The art of interpreting dreams (ὀνειροπολία), which had probably been introduced into Europe from Asia, where it is still a universal practice, seems in the Homeric age to have been held in high esteem, for dreams were said to be sent by Zeus. In subsequent times, that class of diviners who occupied themselves with the interpretation of dreams, seems to have been very numerous and popular; but they never enjoyed any protection from the state, and were chiefly resorted to by private individuals.—The subject of oracles is treated in a separate article. [ORACULUM.]—The word *divinatio* was used in a particular manner by the Romans as a law term. If in any case two or more accusers came forward against one and the same individual, it was, as the phrase ran, *decided by divination*, who should be the chief or real accuser, whom the others then joined as *subscriptores*; *i. e.* by putting their names to the charge brought against the offender. This transaction, by which one of several accusers was selected to conduct the accusation, was called *divinatio*, as the question here was not about facts, but about something which was to be done, and which could not be found out by witnesses or written documents; so that the judices had, as it were, to divine the course which they had to take. Hence the oration of Cicero, in which he tries to show that he, and not Q. Caecilius Niger, ought to conduct the accusation against Verres, is called *Divinatio in Caecilium*.

DĪVĪSOR. [Ambitus.]

DĪVORTĬUM (ἀπόλειψις, ἀπόπεμψις), divorce. (1) Greek. The laws of Athens permitted either the husband or the wife to call for and effect a divorce. If it originated with the wife, she was said to leave her husband's house (ἀπολείπειν); if otherwise, to be dismissed from it (ἀποπεμπέσθαι). After divorce, the wife resorted to her male relations, with whom she would have remained if she had never quitted her maiden state; and it then became their duty to receive or recover from her late husband all the property that she had brought to him in acknowledged dowry upon their marriage. If, upon this, both parties were satisfied, the divorce was final and complete: if otherwise, an action ἀπολείψεως, or ἀποπέμψεως, would be instituted, as the case might be, by the party opposed to the separation. A separation, however, whether it originated from the husband or the wife, was considered to reflect discredit on the latter.—(2) Roman. Divorce always existed in the Roman polity. As one essential part of a marriage was the consent and conjugal affection of the parties, it was considered that this affection was necessary to its continuance, and accordingly either party might declare his or her intention to dissolve the connection. No judicial decree, and no interference of any public authority, was requisite to dissolve a marriage. The first instance of divorce at Rome is said to have occurred about B. C. 234, when Sp. Carvilius Ruga put away his wife, on the ground of barrenness: it is added, that his conduct was generally condemned. Towards the latter part of the republic, and under the empire, divorces became very common. Pompey divorced his wife Mucia for alleged adultery;

and Cicero divorced his wife Terentia, after living with her thirty years, and married a young woman. Cato the younger divorced his wife Marcia, that his friend Hortensius might marry her, and have children by her; for this is the true meaning of the story that he lent his wife to Hortensius. If a husband divorced his wife, the wife's dowry, as a general rule, was restored; and the same was the case when the divorce took place by mutual consent. Corresponding to the forms of marriage by *confarreatio* and *coemtio*, there were the forms of divorce by *diffarreatio* and *remancipatio*. In course of time, less ceremony was used; but still some distinct notice or declaration of intention was necessary to constitute a divorce. The term *repudium*, it is said, properly applies to a marriage only contracted, and *divortium* to an actual marriage; but sometimes divortium and repudium appear to be used indifferently. The phrases to express a divorce are, *nuntium remittere, divortium facere*; and the form of words might be as follows—*Tuas res tibi habeto, tuas res tibi agito*. The phrases used to express the renunciation of a marriage contract were, *renuntiare repudium, repudium remittere, dicere*, and *repudiare*; and the form of words might be, *Conditione tua non utor*.

DŎCĂNA (τὰ δόκανα, from δοκός, a beam) was an ancient symbolical representation of the Dioscuri (Castor and Pollux), at Sparta. It consisted of two upright beams with others laid across them transversely.

DŎCĬMĂSĬA (δοκιμασία). When any citizen of Athens was either appointed by lot, or chosen by suffrage, to hold a public office, he was obliged, before entering on its duties, to submit to a *docimasia*, or scrutiny into his previous life and conduct, in which any person could object to him as unfit. The *docimasia*, however, was not confined to persons appointed to public offices; for we read of the denouncement of a scrutiny against orators who spoke in the assembly while leading profligate lives, or after having committed flagitious crimes.

DODRANS. [As.]

DŎLĀBRA, *dim.* DŎLĀBELLA (σμίλη, *dim.* σμιλίον), a chisel, a celt, was used for a variety of purposes in ancient as in modern times. *Celtes* is an old Latin word for a chisel, probably derived from *coelo*, to engrave. Celts, or chisels, were frequently employed in making entrenchments and in destroying fortifications; and hence they are often found in ancient earth-works and encampments. They are for the most part of bronze, more rarely of hard stone. The sizes and forms which they present, are as various as the uses to which they were applied. The annexed woodcut is designed to show a few of the most remarkable varieties.

DŌLĬUM, a cylindrical vessel, somewhat resembling our tubs or casks, into which new wine was put to let it ferment.

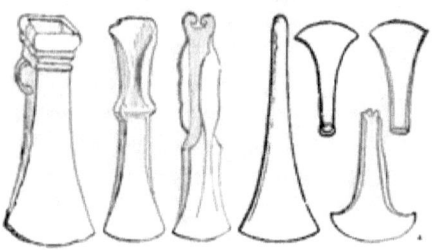

Dolabrae, Celts. (From different Collections in Great Britain.)

DŎLO (δόλων). (1) A secret poniard or dagger contained in a case, used by the Italians. It was inserted in the handles of whips, and also in walking sticks, thus corresponding to our sword-stick.—(2) A small top-sail.

DŎMĬNĬUM signifies quiritarian ownership, or property in a thing; and *dominus*, or *dominus legitimus*, is the owner. The *dominus* has the power of dealing with a thing as he pleases, and differs from the bare *possessor*, who has only the right of possession, and has not the absolute ownership of the thing.

DŎMUS (οἶκος), a house.—(1) GREEK. A Greek house was always divided into two distinct portions, the *Andronitis*, or men's apartments (ἀνδρωνῖτις), and the *Gynaeconitis*, or women's apartments (γυναικωνῖτις). In the earliest times, as in the houses referred to by Homer, and in some houses at a later period, the women's apartments were in the upper story (ὑπερῷον), but usually at a later time the gynaeconitis was on the same story with the andronitis, and behind it. The front of the house towards the street was not large, as the apartments extended rather in the direction of its depth than of its width. In towns the houses were often built side by side, with party-walls between. The exterior wall was plain, being composed generally of stone, brick, and timber, and often covered with stucco. There was no open space between the street and the house-door, like the Roman *vestibulum*. The πρόθυρα, which is sometimes mentioned, seems to be merely the space in front of the house, where there was generally an altar of Apollo Agyieus, or a rude obelisk emblematical of the god. Sometimes there was a laurel tree in the same position, and sometimes a head of the god Hermes. A few steps (ἀναβαθμοί) led up to the house-door, which generally bore some inscription, for the sake of a good omen, or as a charm. The door sometimes opened outwards; but this seems to have been an exception to the general rule, as is proved by the expressions used for opening, ἐνδοῦναι, and shutting it, ἐπισπάσασθαι and ἐφελκύσασθαι. The handles were called ἐπισπαστῆρες. The house-door was called αὔλειος or αὔλεια θύρα, because it led to the αὐλή. It gave admittance to a narrow passage (θυρωρεῖον, πυλών, θυρών), on one side of which, in a large house, were the stables, on the other the porter's lodge. The duty of the porter (θυρωρός) was to admit visitors and to prevent anything improper from being carried into or out of the house. The porter was attended by a dog. Hence the phrase εὐλαβεῖσθαι τὴν κύνα, corresponding to the Latin *Cave canem*. From the θυρωρεῖον we pass into the peristyle or court (περιστύλιον, αὐλή) of the andronitis, which was a space open to the sky in the centre (ὕπαιθρον), and surrounded on all four sides by porticoes (στοαί), of which one, probably that nearest the entrance, was called προστόον. These porticoes were used for exercise, and sometimes for dining in. Here was commonly the altar on which sacrifices were offered to the household gods. In building the porticoes the object sought was to obtain as much sun in winter, and as much shade and air in summer as possible. Round the peristyle were arranged the chambers used by the men, such as banqueting rooms (οἶκοι, ἀνδρῶνες), which were large enough to contain several sets of couches (τρίκλινοι, ἑπτάκλινοι, τριακοντάκλινοι), and at the same time to allow abundant room for attendants, musicians, and performers of games; parlours or sitting rooms (ἐξέδραι), and smaller chambers and sleeping rooms (δωμάτια, κοιτῶνες, οἰκήματα); picture-galleries and libraries, and sometimes store-rooms; and in the arrangement of these apartments attention was paid to their aspect. The peristyle of the andronitis was connected with that of the gynaeconitis by a door called μέταυλος, μέσαυλος, or μεσαύλιος, which was in the middle of the portico of the peristyle opposite to the entrance. By means of this door all communication between the andronitis and gynaeconitis could be shut off. Accordingly Xenophon calls it θύρα βαλανωτός. Its name μέσαυλος is evidently derived from μέσος, and means the door *between* the two αὐλαί or peristyles. This door gave admittance to the peristyle of the gynaeconitis, which differed from that of the andronitis in having porticoes round only three of its sides. On the fourth side were placed two antae [ANTAE], at a considerable distance from each other. A third of the distance between these antae was set off inwards, thus forming a chamber or vestibule, which was called προστάς, παραστάς, and πρόδρομος. On the right and left of this προστάς were two bed chambers, the θάλαμος and ἀμφιθάλαμος, of which the former was the principal bed-chamber of the house, and here also seem to have been kept the vases, and other valuable articles of ornament. Beyond these rooms were large apartments (ἱστῶνες) used for working in wool. Round the peristyle were the eating-rooms, bed-chambers, store-rooms, and other apartments in common use. Besides the αὔλειος θύρα and the μέσαυλος θύρα, there was a third door (κηπαία θύρα) leading to the garden. The preceding is a conjectural plan of the ground-floor of a Greek house of the larger size. There was usually, though not always, an upper story (ὑπερῷον, διήρες), which seldom extended over the whole space occupied by the lower story. The principal use of the upper story was for the lodging of the slaves. The access to the upper floor seems to have been sometimes by stairs on the outside of the house, leading up from the street. Guests were also lodged in the upper story. But in some large houses there were rooms set apart for their reception (ξενῶνες) on the ground-floor. The roofs were generally flat, and it was customary to walk about upon them. In the interior of the house the place of doors was sometimes supplied by curtains (παραπετάσματα), which were either plain, or dyed, or embroidered. The principal openings for the admission of light and air were in the roofs of the peristyles; but it is incorrect to suppose that the houses had no windows (θυρίδες), or at least none overlooking the street. They were not at all uncommon. Artificial warmth was procured partly by means of fire-places. It is supposed that chimneys were altogether unknown, and that the smoke escaped through an opening in the roof (καπνοδόκη), but it is not easy to understand how this could be the case when there was an upper story. Little portable stoves (ἐσχάραι, ἐσχαρίδες) or chafing-dishes (ἀνθράκια) were frequently used. The houses of the wealthy in the country, at least in Attica, were much larger and more magnificent than those in the towns. The latter seem to have been generally small and plain, especially in earlier times, when the Greeks preferred expending the resources of art and wealth on their temples and public buildings; but the private houses became more magnificent as the public buildings began to be neglected. The decorations of the interior were very plain at the period to which our description refers. The floors were of stone. At a late period coloured stones were used. Mosaics are first mentioned under the kings of Pergamus. The walls, up to the 4th century B. C., seem to

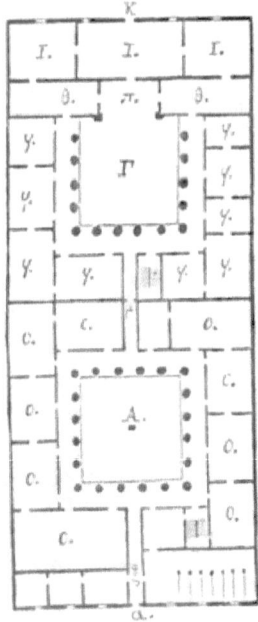

Ground-plan of a Greek House.

a. House-door, αὔλειος θύρα : θυρ., passage, θυρωρεῖον or θυρών : A, peristyle, or αὐλή of the andronitis ; o, the halls and chambers of the andronitis ; μ, μέταυλος or μέσαυλος θύρα : Γ, peristyle of the gynaeconitis , γ. chambers of the gynaeconitis ; π, προστας or παραστάς : θ. θάλαμος and ἀμφιθάλαμος : I. rooms for working in wool (ἱστῶνες) ; K, garden-door, κηπαία θύρα.

have been only whited. The first instance of painting them is that of Alcibiades. This innovation met with considerable opposition. We have also mention of painted ceilings at the same period. At a later period this mode of decoration became general.—(2) ROMAN. The houses of the Romans were poor and mean for many centuries after the foundation of the city. Till the war with Pyrrhus the houses were covered only with thatch or shingles, and were usually built of wood or unbaked bricks. It was not till the latter times of the republic, when wealth had been acquired by conquests in the East, that houses of any splendour began to be built; but it then became the fashion not only to build houses of an immense size, but also to adorn them with columns, paintings, statues, and costly works of art. Some idea may be formed of the size and magnificence of the houses of the Roman nobles during the later times of the republic by the price which they fetched. The consul Messalla bought the house of Autronius for 3700 sestertia (nearly 33,000*l*.), and Cicero the house of Crassus, on the Palatine, for 3500 sestertia (nearly 31,000*l*.). The house of Publius Clodius, whom Milo killed, cost 14,800 sestertia (about 131,000*l*.); and the Tusculan villa of Scaurus was fitted up with such magnificence, that when it was burnt by his slaves, he lost 100,000 sestertia, upwards of 885,000*l*.—Houses were originally only one story high; but as the value of ground increased in the city they were built several stories in height, and the highest floors were usually inhabited by the poor. Till the time of Nero, the streets in Rome were narrow and irregular, and bore traces of the haste and confusion with which the city was built after it had been burnt by the Gauls; but after the great fire in the time of that emperor, by which two-thirds of Rome was burnt to the ground, the city was built with great regularity. The streets were made straight and broad; the height of the houses was restricted, and a certain part of each was required to be built of Gabian or Alban stone, which was proof against fire. The principal parts of a Roman house were the, 1. *Vestibulum*, 2. *Ostium*, 3. *Atrium* or *Cavum Aedium*, 4. *Alae*, 5. *Tablinum*, 6. *Fauces*, 7. *Peristylium*. The parts of a house which were considered of less importance, and of which the arrangement differed in different houses, were the, 1. *Cubicula*, 2. *Triclinia*, 3. *Oeci*, 4. *Exedrae*, 5. *Pinacotheca*, 6. *Bibliotheca*, 7. *Balineum*, 8. *Culina*, 9. *Coenacula*, 10. *Diaeta*, 11. *Solaria*. We shall speak of each in order.—1. VESTIBULUM did not properly form part of the house, but was a vacant space before the door, forming a court, which was surrounded on three sides by the house, and was open on the fourth to the street.—2. OSTIUM, which is also called *janua* and *fores*, was the entrance to the house. The street-door admitted into a hall, to which the name of ostium was also given, and in which there was frequently a small room (*cella*) for the porter (*janitor* or *ostiarius*), and also for a dog, which was usually kept in the hall to guard the house. Another door (*janua interior*) opposite the street-door led into the atrium. —3. ATRIUM or CAVUM AEDIUM, also written *Cavaedium*, are probably only different names of the same room. The Atrium or Cavum Aedium was a large apartment roofed over with the exception of an opening in the centre, called *compluvium*, towards which the roof sloped so as to throw the rain-water into a cistern in the floor, termed *impluvium*, which was frequently ornamented with statues, columns, and other works of art. The word *impluvium*, however, is also employed to denote the aperture in the roof. The atrium was the most important room in the house, and among the wealthy was usually fitted up with much splendour and magnificence. Originally it was the only sitting-room in the house; but in the houses of the wealthy it was distinct from the private apartments, and was used as a reception-room, where the patron received his clients, and the great and noble the numerous visitors who were accustomed to call every morning to pay their respects or solicit favours. But though the atrium was not used by the wealthy as a sitting-room for the family, it still continued to be employed for many purposes which it had originally served. Thus the nuptial couch was placed in the atrium opposite the door, and also the instruments and materials for spinning and weaving, which were formerly carried on by the women of the family in this room. Here also the images of their ancestors were placed, and the focus or fire-place, which possessed a sacred character, being dedicated to the Lares of each family.—4. ALAE, wings, were small apartments or recesses on the left and right sides of the atrium.—5. TABLINUM was in all probability a recess or room at the further end of the atrium opposite the door leading into the hall, and was regarded as part of the atrium. It contained the family records and archives. With the tablinum the Roman house appears to have originally ceased; and the sleeping-rooms were probably arranged on each side of the atrium. But when the atrium and its surrounding rooms were used for the reception of clients and other public visitors, it became necessary to increase the size of the house; and the fol-

lowing rooms were accordingly added:—
—6. FAUCES appear to have been passages, which passed from the atrium to the peristylium or interior of the house.—7. PERISTYLIUM was in its general form like the atrium, but it was one-third greater in breadth, measured transversely, than in length. It was a court open to the sky in the middle; the open part, which was surrounded by columns, was larger than the impluvium in the atrium, and was frequently decorated with flowers and shrubs.—The arrangement of the rooms, which are next to be noticed, varied according to the taste and circumstances of the owner. It is therefore impossible to assign to them any regular place in the house.—1. CUBICULA, bed-chambers, appear to have been usually small. There were separate cubicula for the day and night; the latter were also called *dormitoria*.—2. TRICLINIA are treated of in a separate article. [TRICLINIUM.]—3. OECI, from the Greek οἶκος, were spacious halls or saloons borrowed from the Greeks, and were frequently used as triclinia. They were to have the same proportions as triclinia, but were to be more spacious on account of having columns, which triclinia had not.—4. EXEDRAE were rooms for conversation and the other purposes of society.—5. PINACOTHECA, a picture-gallery. —6, 7. BIBLIOTHECA and BALINEUM are treated of in separate articles.—8. CULINA, the kitchen. The food was originally cooked in the atrium; but the progress of refinement afterwards led to the use of another part of the house for this purpose. In the kitchen of Pansa's house at Pompeii, a stove for stews and simi-

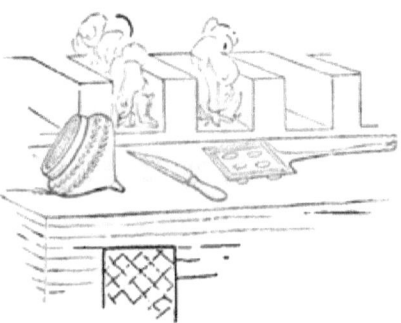

Kitchen of the House of Pansa at Pompeii.

lar preparations was found, very much like the charcoal stoves used in the present day. Before it lie a knife, a strainer, and a kind of frying-pan with four spherical cavities, as if it were meant to cook eggs.—9. COENACULA, properly signified rooms to dine in; but after it became the fashion to dine in the upper part of the house, the whole of the rooms above the ground-floor were called *coenacula*.—10. DIAETA, an apartment used for dining in, and for the other purposes of life. It appears to have been smaller than the triclinium. *Diaeta* is also the name given by Pliny to rooms containing three or four bed-chambers (*cubicula*). Pleasure-houses or summer-houses are also called *diaetae*.

Atrium of the House of Ceres at Pompeii.

—11. SOLARIA, properly places for basking in the sun, were terraces on the tops of houses. The preceding cut represents the atrium of a house at Pompeii. In the centre is the impluvium, and the passage at the further end is the ostium or entrance hall.—The preceding account of the different rooms, and especially of the arrangement of the atrium, tablinum, peristyle, &c., is best illustrated by the houses which have been disinterred at Pompeii. The ground-plan of one is accordingly subjoined. Like most of the other houses at Pompeii, it had no vestibulum according to the meaning given above. 1. The *ostium* or entrance-hall, which is six

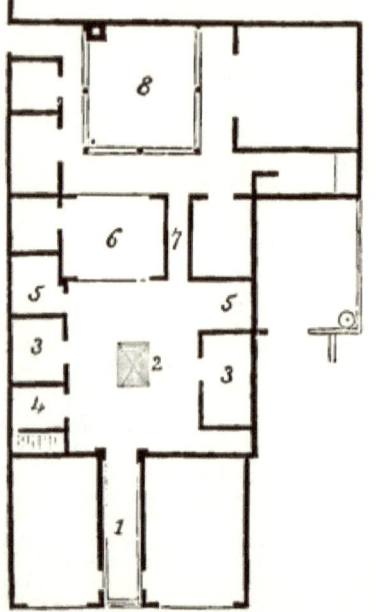

Ground-plan of a House at Pompeii.

feet wide and nearly thirty long. Near the street-door there is a figure of a large fierce dog worked in mosaic on the pavement, and beneath it is written *Cave Canem*. The two large rooms on each side of the vestibule appear from the large openings in front of them to have been shops; they communicate with the entrance-hall, and were therefore probably occupied by the master of the house. 2. The *atrium*, which is about twenty-eight feet in length and twenty in breadth; its *impluvium* is near the centre of the room, and its floor is paved with white tesserae, spotted with black. 3. Chambers for the use of the family, or intended for the reception of guests, who were entitled to claim hospitality. 4. A small room with a staircase leading up to the upper rooms. 5. *Alae.* 6. The *tablinum*. 7. The *fauces*. 8. Peristyle, with Doric columns and garden in the centre. The large room on the right of the peristyle is the triclinium; beside it is the kitchen; and the smaller apartments are cubicula and other rooms for the use of the family.—Having given a general description of the rooms of a Roman house, it remains to speak of the (1) floors, (2) walls, (3) ceilings, (4) windows, and (5) the mode of warming the rooms. For the doors, see JANUA.—(1.) The floor (*solum*) of a room was seldom boarded: it was generally covered with stone or marble, or mosaics. The common floors were paved with pieces of bricks, tiles, stones, &c., forming a kind of composition called *ruderatio*. Sometimes pieces of marble were imbedded in a composition ground, and these probably gave the idea of mosaics. As these floors were beaten down (*parita*) with rammers (*fistucae*), the word *parimentum* became the general name for a floor. Mosaics, called by Pliny *lithostrota* (λιθόστρωτα), though this word has a more extensive meaning, first came into use in Sulla's time, who made one in the temple of Fortune at Praeneste. Mosaic work was afterwards called *Musivum opus*, and was most extensively employed. —(2.) The inner walls (*parietes*) of private rooms were frequently lined with slabs of marble, but were more usually covered by paintings, which in the time of Augustus were made upon the walls themselves. This practice was so common that we find even the small houses in Pompeii have paintings upon their walls.—(3.) The ceilings seem originally to have been left uncovered, the beams which supported the roof or the upper story being visible. Afterwards planks were placed across these beams at certain intervals, leaving hollow spaces, called *lacunaria* or *laquearia*, which were frequently covered with gold and ivory, and sometimes with paintings. There was an arched ceiling in common use, called CAMARA.—(4.) The Roman houses had few windows (*fenestrae*). The principal apartments, the atrium, peristyle, &c., were lighted from above, and the cubicula and other small rooms generally derived their light from them, and not from windows looking into the street. The rooms only on the upper story seem to have been usually lighted by windows. The windows appear originally to have been merely openings in the wall, closed by means of shutters, which frequently had two leaves (*bifores fenestrae*). Windows were also sometimes covered by a kind of lattice or trellis work (*clathri*), and sometimes by net-work, to prevent serpents and other noxious reptiles from getting in. Afterwards, however, windows were made of a transparent stone, called *lapis specularis* (mica); such windows were called *specularia*. Windows made of glass (*vitrum*) are first mentioned by Lactantius, who lived in the fourth century of the Christian era; but the discoveries at Pompeii prove that glass was used for windows under the early emperors.—(5.) The rooms were heated in winter in different ways; but the Romans had no stoves like ours. The cubicula, triclinia, and other rooms, which were intended for winter use, were built in that part of the house upon which the sun shone most; and in the mild climate of Italy this frequently enabled them to dispense with any artificial mode of warming the rooms. Rooms exposed to the sun in this way were sometimes called *heliocamini*. The rooms were sometimes heated by hot air, which was introduced by means of pipes from a furnace below, but more frequently by portable furnaces or braziers (*foculi*), in which coal or charcoal was burnt. The *caminus* was also a kind of stove, in which wood appears to have been usually burnt, and probably only differed from the *foculus* in being larger and fixed to one place. The rooms usually had no chimneys for carrying off the smoke, which escaped through the windows, doors, and openings in the roof; still chimneys do not appear to have been entirely unknown to the ancients, as some are said to have been found in the ruins of ancient buildings.

DŌNĀRĬA (ἀναθήματα or ἀνακείμενα), presents made to the gods, either by individuals or communities. Sometimes they are also called *dona* or δῶρα. The belief that the gods were pleased with costly presents was as natural to the ancients as the belief that they could be influenced in their conduct towards men by the offering of sacrifices; and, indeed, both sprang from the same feeling. Presents were mostly given as tokens of gratitude for some favour which a god had bestowed on man; as, for instance, by persons who had recovered from illness or escaped from shipwreck; but some are also mentioned, which were intended to induce the deity to grant some especial favour. Almost all presents were dedicated in temples, to which in some places an especial building was added, in which these treasures were preserved. Such buildings were called θησαυροί (treasuries), and in the most frequented temples of Greece many states had their separate treasuries. The act of dedication was called ἀνατιθέναι, *donare*, *dedicare*, or *sacrare*.

DŌNĀTĪVUM. [CONGIARIUM.]
DORMĪTŌRĬA. [DOMUS.]
DOS (φερνή, προίξ), dowry. (1) GREEK. In the Homeric times it was customary for the husband to purchase his wife from her relations, by gifts called ἕδνα or ἔεδνα. But at Athens, during the historical period, the contrary was the case; for every woman had to bring her husband some dowry, and so universal was the practice, that one of the chief distinctions between a wife and a παλλακή, or concubine, consisted in the former having a portion, whereas the latter had not; hence, persons who married wives without portions appear to have given them or their guardians an acknowledgment in writing by which the receipt of a portion was admitted. Moreover, poor heiresses were either married or portioned by their next of kin, according to a law, which fixed the amount of portion to be given at five minae by a Pentacosiomedimnus, three by a Horseman, and one and a half by a Zeugites. The husband had to give to the relatives or guardians of the wife security (ἀποτίμημα) for the dowry, which was not considered the property of the husband himself, but rather of his wife and children. The portion was returned to the wife in case of a divorce.—(2) ROMAN. The *dos* among the Romans was every thing which on the occasion of a woman's marriage was transferred by her, or by another person, to the husband. All the property of the wife which was not made dos continued to be her own, and was comprised under the name of *parapherna*. The dos upon its delivery became the husband's property, and continued to be his so long as the marriage relation existed. In the case of divorce, the woman, or her relations, could bring an action for the restitution of the dos; and, accordingly, a woman whose dos was large (*dotata uxor*) had some influence over her husband, inasmuch as she had the power of divorcing herself, and thus of depriving him of the enjoyment of her property.

DRACHMA (δραχμή), the principal silver coin among the Greeks. The two chief standards in the currencies of the Greek states were the Attic and Aeginetan. The average value of the Attic drachma was 9¾d. of our money. It contained six obols (ὀβολοί); and the Athenians had separate silver coins, from four drachmae to a quarter of an obol. There were also silver pieces of two drachmae and four drachmae. (See tables.) The tetradrachm in later times was called *stater*. The latter word also signifies a gold coin, equal in value to twenty drachmae [STATER]. The obolos, in later times, was of bronze: but in the best times of Athens we only read of silver obols. The χαλκοῦς was a copper coin, and the eighth part of an obol. The Attic

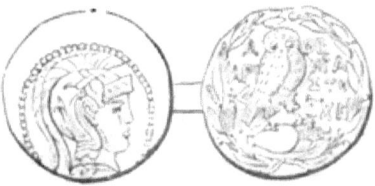

Attic Drachma. (British Museum.)

standard prevailed most in the maritime and commercial states. It was the standard of Philip's gold, and was introduced by Alexander for silver also.—The Aeginetan standard appears to have been the prevalent one in early times: we are told that money was first coined at Aegina by order of Pheidon of Argos. In later times the Aeginetan standard was used in almost all the states of the Peloponnesus, except Corinth. The average value of the Aeginetan drachma was $1s. 1\frac{3}{4}d.$ in our money; and the values of the different coins of this standard are as follows:—

	Shill.	Pence.	Farth.
½ Obol	—	1	0·583
Obol	—	2	1·166
Diobolus	—	4	2·33
Triobolus	—	6	2·5
Drachma	1	1	3
Didrachm	2	3	2

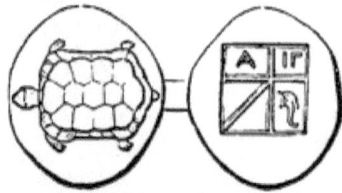

Aeginetan Drachma. (British Museum.)

As the Romans reckoned in sesterces, so the Greeks generally reckoned by drachmae; and when a sum is mentioned in the Attic writers, without any specification of the unit, drachmae are usually meant.

DRACO. [SIGNA MILITARIA.]

DUCENARII.—(1) The name given to the Roman procuratores, who received a salary of 200 sestertia. The procuratores first received a salary in the time of Augustus.—(2) A class or decuria of judices, first established by Augustus. They were so called because their property, as valued in the census, amounted only to 200 sestertia. They appear to have tried causes of small importance.

DUCENTESIMA. [CENTESIMA.]

DUODECIM SCRIPTA. [LATRUNCULI.]

DUODECIM TABULARUM LEX. [LEX.]

DUPLARII or DUPLICARII, were soldiers who received on account of their good conduct double allowance (*duplicia cibaria*), and perhaps in some cases double pay likewise.

DUPONDIUS. [AS.]

DUSSIS. [AS.]

DUUMVIRI, or the two men, the name of various magistrates and functionaries at Rome, and in the coloniae and municipia. (1) DUUMVIRI JURI DICUNDO were the highest magistrates in the municipal towns. [COLONIA.]—(2) DUUMVIRI NAVALES, extraordinary magistrates, who were created, whenever occasion required, for the purpose of equipping and repairing the fleet. They appear to have been originally appointed by the consuls and dictators, but were first elected by the people, B.C. 311.—(3) DUUMVIRI PERDUELLIONIS. [PERDUELLIO.]—(4) DUUMVIRI QUINQUENNALES, were the censors in the municipal towns, and must not be confounded with the *duumviri juri dicundo*. [COLONIA.]—(5) DUUMVIRI SACRORUM originally had the charge of the Sibylline books. Their duties were afterwards discharged by the *decemviri sacris faciundis*. [DECEMVIRI.]—(6) DUUMVIRI were also appointed for the purpose of building or dedicating a temple.

ECCLESIA (ἐκκλησία), the name of the general assembly of the citizens at Athens, in which they met to discuss and determine upon matters of public interest, and which was therefore the sovereign power in the state. These assemblies were either *ordinary* (νόμιμοι or κύριαι), and held four times in each prytany, or *extraordinary*, that is, specially convened, upon any sudden emergency, and therefore called σύγκλητοι. The place in which they were anciently held was the *agora*. Afterwards they were transferred to the Pnyx, and at last to the great theatre of Dionysus, and other places. The most usual place, however, was the Pnyx, which was situated to the west of the Areiopagus, on a slope connected with Mount Lycabettus, and partly at least within the walls of the city. It was semicircular in form, with a boundary wall part rock and part masonry, and an area of about 12,000 square yards. On the north the ground was filled up and paved with large stones, so as to get a level surface on the slope. Towards this side, and close to the wall, was the *bema* (βῆμα), a stone platform or hustings ten or eleven feet high, with an ascent of steps. The position of the *bema* was such as to command a view of the sea from behind, and of the Propylaea and Parthenon in front, and we may be sure that the Athenian orators would often rouse the national feelings of their hearers by pointing to the assemblage of magnificent edifices, "monuments of Athenian gratitude and glory," which they had in view from the Pnyx.—The right of convening the people was generally vested in the prytanes or presidents of the council of Five Hundred [see BOULÉ], but in cases of sudden emergency, and especially during wars, the strategi also had the power of calling extraordinary meetings, for which, however, the consent of the senate appears to have been necessary.

The prytanes not only gave a **previous notice of the day of assembly, and published a programme of the subjects to be discussed, but** also, it appears, sent a crier **round to collect the citizens. All persons who did not obey the call were subject to a fine, and six magistrates called lexiarchs were appointed,** whose duty it was **to take care that the people attended the meetings, and to levy fines on those who refused to do so. With a** view to this, whenever an assembly was to be held, certain public **slaves** (Σκύθαι or τοξόται) were sent round to sweep **the agora,** and other places of public resort, **with a rope coloured with vermilion. The different persons whom these ropemen met, were driven by them towards the ecclesia, and those who refused to go were marked by the rope and fined.** An additional inducement **to attend,** with the poorer classes, was the μισθὸς ἐκκλησιαστικός, or pay which they received for it. The payment was originally **an obolus,** but was afterwards raised to three. The right of attending was enjoyed **by all legitimate citizens who were** of **the proper age (generally supposed to be twenty, certainly not less than eighteen), and not labouring under any** *atimia*, **or loss of civil rights.**—In the article BOULÉ it is explained who the prytanes and the proedri were; and we may here remark, **that** it was **the duty of the proedri of the same** tribe, **under the presidency of their chairman** (ὁ ἐπιστάτης), **to lay before the people** the subjects to be discussed; to read, or cause to be read, **the previous bill** (τὸ προβούλευμα) of the senate, without which no measure could be brought **before the ecclesia, and to give permission to the** speakers to address the people. The **officers who acted under them, were the crier** (ὁ κῆρυξ), and the Scythian bowmen.—Previous, however, to the commencement **of any business, the place was purified by the offering of sacrifices, and then the gods were** implored in a prayer to bless the proceedings of the meeting. The privilege of addressing the assembly was not confined to any class or age **among** those who had the right to be present: all, without any distinction, were invited to do so by the proclamation, Τίς ἀγορεύειν βούλεται, **which** was made by the crier after the proedri had gone through the necessary preliminaries, and laid the subject of discussion before the meeting; for though, according to the institutions of Solon, those persons who were above fifty years of **age ought to have been called upon to speak first,** this regulation had in later times become quite obsolete. The speakers are sometimes simply called οἱ παριόντες, and appear to have worn a crown of myrtle on their heads while addressing the assembly. The most influential and practised speakers of the assembly were generally distinguished by the name of ῥήτορες. **After the** speakers had concluded, any one **was at** liberty to propose **a** decree, whether drawn up beforehand **or** framed in **the** meeting, which, however, **it was necessary to present to the proedri, that they** might see, **in conjunction with the** *nomophylaces*, whether there was contained in it anything injurious to the state, or contrary to the existing laws. If not, it was read by **the crier; though,** even after the **reading, the chairman could prevent** it being put to **the vote, unless his opposition was overborne by threats and clamours.** Private individuals also could do the same, **by engaging upon oath** (ὑπωμοσία) **to bring against the author of any measure they might object to, an accusation called** a γραφὴ παρανόμων. **If, however, the chairman refused to submit any question to the decision of the people, he might be proceeded against by** *endeixis;* **and if he allowed the people to vote upon a proposal which was contrary to existing constitutional laws, he was in some cases liable to** *atimia.* **If, on the contrary, no opposition of this sort was offered to a proposed decree, the votes of the people were taken, by the permission of the chairman and with the consent of the rest of the proedri. The decision of the people was given either by show of hands, or by ballot,** *i. e.* **by casting pebbles into urns (**καδίσκοι**);** the former was expressed by the word χειροτονεῖν, the latter **by** ψηφίζεσθαι, although **the two** terms are frequently confounded. The more usual method of voting was by show of hands, **as being** more expeditious and convenient (χειροτονία). **Vote by** ballot, **on** the other hand, was only **used in a few** special cases determined by **law; as, for** instance, when a proposition **was made for** allowing those who had suffered *atimia* to appeal to the people for restitution of their former rights; or for inflicting extraordinary punishments on atrocious offenders, **and generally, upon any matter which** affected **private persons.** In cases of this sort **it was settled by law, that** a decree **should not be valid unless six** thousand **citizens at least voted in favour of it.** This **was by far the majority of those** citizens who **were in the habit of attending;** for, in time **of war, the number** never amounted to five thousand, **and in time of peace** seldom to ten thousand.—The determination or decree of **the people was called** a ψήφισμα, **which** properly signifies a law proposed to an assembly, and approved of by the people. Respecting the form for drawing up a ψήφισμα, see BOULÉ.—When the business was over, the order for the dismissal of the assembly was given by the prytanes, through the proclamation of the crier; and as it was not customary to continue meetings, which usually began early in the morning, till after sunset, if one day were not sufficient for the completion of any business, it was adjourned to the next. But an assembly was sometimes broken up, if any one, whether a magistrate or private individual, declared that he saw an unfavourable omen, or perceived thunder and lightning. The sudden appearance of rain also, or the shock of an earthquake, or any natural phenomenon of the kind called διοσημίαι, was a sufficient reason for the hasty adjournment of an assembly.

ECCLETI. [ΗΟΜΟΕΙ.]

ECDICUS (ἔκδικος), the name of an officer in many of the towns of Asia Minor during the Roman dominion, whose principal duty was the care of the public money, and the prosecution of all parties who owed money to the state.

ECMARTYRIA (ἐκμαρτυρία), signifies the deposition of a witness at Athens, who, by reason of absence abroad, or illness, was unable to attend in court. His statement was taken down in writing, in the presence of persons expressly appointed to receive it, and afterwards, upon their swearing to its identity, was read as evidence in the cause.

EDICTUM. The *Jus Edicendi*, or power of making edicts, belonged to the higher *magistratus populi Romani*, but it was principally exercised by the two praetors, the praetor urbanus, and the praetor peregrinus, whose jurisdiction was exercised in the provinces by the praeses. The curule aediles likewise made many edicts; and tribunes, censors, and pontifices also promulgated edicts relating to the matters of their respective jurisdictions. The edicta were among the sources of Roman law. The edictum may be described generally as a rule promulgated by a magistratus on entering on his office, which was done by writing it on an album and exhibiting it in a conspicuous place. As the office of a magistratus was annual, the rules promulgated by a predecessor were not binding on a successor, but he might confirm or adopt the rules of his predecessor, and introduce them into his own edict, and hence such adopted rules were called *edictum tralatitium*, or *vetus*, as opposed to *edictum novum*. A *repentinum edictum* was that rule which was made (*prout res incidit*) for the occasion. A *perpetuum edictum* was that rule which was made by the magistratus on entering upon office, and which was intended to apply to all cases to which it was applicable during the year of his office: hence it was sometimes called also *annua lex*. Until it became the practice for magistratus to adopt the edicta of their predecessors, the edicta could not form a body of permanent binding rules; but when this practice became common, the edicta (*edictum tralatitium*) soon constituted a large body of law, which was practically of as much importance as any other part of the law.

EICOSTE (εἰκοστή), a tax or duty of one-twentieth (five per cent.) upon all commodities exported or imported by sea in the states of the allies subject to Athens. This tax was first imposed B.C. 413, in the place of the direct tribute which had up to this time been paid by the subject allies; and the change was made with the hope of raising a greater revenue. This tax, like all others, was farmed, and the farmers of it were called εἰκοστολόγοι.

EIREN or IREN (εἴρην or ἴρην), the name given to the Spartan youth when he attained the age of twenty. At the age of eighteen he emerged from childhood, and was called μελλείρην. When he had attained his twentieth year, he began to exercise a direct influence over his juniors, and was entrusted with the command of troops in battle. The word appears to have originally signified a commander. The ἰρένες mentioned in Herodotus, in connection with the battle of Plataeae, were certainly not youths, but commanders.

EISANGELIA (εἰσαγγελία), signifies, in its primary and most general sense, a denunciation of any kind, but, much more usually, an information laid before the council or the assembly of the people, and the consequent impeachment and trial of state criminals at Athens under novel or extraordinary circumstances. Among these were the occasions upon which manifest crimes were alleged to have been committed, and yet of such a nature as the existing laws had failed to anticipate, or at least describe specifically (ἄγραφα ἀδικήματα), the result of which omission would have been, but for the enactment by which the accusations in question might be preferred (νόμος εἰσαγγελτικός), that a prosecutor would not have known to what magistrate to apply; that a magistrate, if applied to, could not with safety have accepted the indictment or brought it into court; and that, in short, there would have been a total failure of justice.

EISITERIA (εἰσιτήρια, scil. ἱερά), sacrifices offered at Athens by the senate before the session began, in honour of the Θεοὶ Βουλαῖοι, i. e. Zeus and Athena.

EISPHORA (εἰσφορά), an extraordinary tax on property, raised at Athens, whenever the means of the state were not sufficient to carry on a war. It is not quite certain when this property-tax was introduced; but it seems to have come first into general use about B. C. 428. It could never be raised without a decree of the people, who also assigned the amount required; and the *strategi*, or generals, superintended its collection, and presided in the courts where disputes connected with, or arising from, the levying of the tax were settled. The usual expressions for paying this property-tax are: εἰσφέρειν χρήματα, εἰσφέρειν εἰς τὸν πόλεμον, εἰς τὴν σωτηρίαν τῆς πόλεως, εἰσφορὰς εἰσφέρειν, and those who paid it were called οἱ εἰσφέροντες. The census of Solon was at first the standard according to which the *eisphora* was raised, until in B. C. 377 a new census was instituted, in which the people, for the purpose of fixing the rates of the property-tax, were divided into a number of symmoriae (συμμορίαι) or classes, similar to those which were afterwards made for the trierarchy. Each of the ten tribes or phylae, appointed 120 of its wealthier citizens; and the whole number of persons included in the symmoriae was thus 1200, who were considered as the representatives of the whole republic. This body of 1200 was divided into four classes, each consisting of 300. The first class, or the richest, were the leaders of the symmoriae (ἡγεμόνες συμμοριῶν), and are often called the three hundred. They probably conducted the proceedings of the symmoriae, and they, or, which is more likely, the demarchs, had to value the taxable property. Other officers were appointed to make out the lists of the rates, and were called ἐπιγραφεῖς, διαγραφεῖς or ἐκλογεῖς. When the wants of the state were pressing, the 300 leaders advanced the money to the others, who paid it back to the 300 at the regular time. The first class probably consisted of persons who possessed property from 12 talents upwards; the second class, of persons who possessed property from 6 talents and upwards, but under 12; the third class, of persons who possessed property from 2 talents upwards, but under 6; the fourth class, of persons who possessed property from 25 minae upwards, but under 2 talents. The rate of taxation was higher or lower according to the wants of the republic at the time; we have accounts of rates of a 12th, a 50th, a 100th, and a 500th part of the taxable property. If any one thought that his property was taxed higher than that of another man on whom juster claims could be made, he had the right to call upon this person to take the office in his stead, or to submit to a complete exchange of property. [ANTIDOSIS.] No Athenian, on the other hand, if belonging to the tax-paying classes, could be exempt from the *eisphora*, not even the descendants of Harmodius and Aristogeiton.

ELECTRUM (ἤλεκτρος and ἤλεκτρον), is used by the ancient writers in two different senses, either for *amber* or for a mixture of metals composed of gold and silver. In Homer and Hesiod, it has, in all probability, the former meaning. The earliest passage of any Greek writer, in which the word is *certainly* used for the metal, is in the *Antigone* of Sophocles (1038). This alludes to *native electrum*; but the compound was also made artificially. Pliny states that when gold contains a fifth part of silver, it is called *electrum*; that it is found in veins of gold; and that it is also made by art: if, he adds, it contains more than a fifth of silver, it becomes too brittle to be malleable. But Isidorus mentions electrum composed of *three* parts gold, and *one* of silver. Electrum was used for plate, and the other similar purposes for which gold and silver were employed. It was also used as a material for money. Lampridius tells us, that Alexander Severus struck coins of it; and coins are in existence, of this metal, struck by the kings of Bosporus, by Syracuse, and by other Greek states.

ELEUSINIA (ἐλευσίνια), a festival and mysteries, originally celebrated only at Eleusis in Attica, in honour of Demeter and Persephone. The Eleusinian mysteries, or *the* mysteries, as they were sometimes called, were the holiest and most venerable of all that were celebrated in Greece. Various traditions were current among the Greeks respecting the author of these mysteries: for, while some considered Eumolpus or Musaeus to be their founder, others stated that they had been introduced from Egypt by Erechtheus, who at a time of scarcity provided his country with corn from Egypt, and imported from the same quarter the sacred rites and mysteries of Eleusis. A third tradition attributed the institution to Demeter herself, who, when wandering about in search of her daughter, Persephone, was believed to have come to Attica, in the reign of Erechtheus, to have supplied its inhabitants with corn, and to have instituted the mysteries at Eleusis. This last opinion seems to have been the most common among the ancients, and in subsequent times a stone was shown near the well Callichoros at Eleusis, on which the goddess, overwhelmed with grief and fatigue, was believed to have rested on her arrival in Attica. All the accounts and allusions in ancient writers seem to warrant the conclusion, that the legends concerning the introduction of the Eleusinia are descriptions of a period when the inhabitants of Attica were becoming acquainted with the benefits of agriculture, and of a regularly constituted form of society.—In the reign of Erechtheus a war is said to have broken out between the Athenians and Eleusinians; and when the latter were defeated, they acknowledged the supremacy of Athens in everything except the mysteries, which they wished to conduct and regulate for themselves. Thus the superintendence remained with the descendants of Eumolpus [EUMOLPIDAE], the daughters of the Eleusinian king Celeus, and a third class of priests, the Ceryces, who seem likewise to have been connected with the family of Eumolpus, though they themselves traced their origin to Hermes and Aglauros.—At the time when the local governments of the several townships of Attica were concentrated at Athens, the capital became also the centre of religion, and several deities who had hitherto only enjoyed a local worship, were now raised to the rank of national gods. This seems also to have been the case with the Eleusinian goddess, for in the reign of Theseus we find mention of a temple at Athens, called Eleusinion, probably the new and national sanctuary of Demeter. Her priests and priestesses now became naturally attached to the national temple of the capital, though her original place of worship at Eleusis, with which so many sacred associations were connected, still retained its importance and its special share in the celebration of the national solemnities.—We must distinguish between the greater Eleusinia, which were celebrated at Athens and Eleusis, and the lesser, which were held at Agrae on the Ilissus. The lesser Eleusinia were only a preparation (προκάθαρσις or προάγνευσις) for the real mysteries. They were held every year in the month of Anthesterion, and, according to some accounts, in honour of Persephone alone. Those who were initiated in them bore the name of *Mystae* (μύσται), and had to wait at least another year before they could be admitted to the great mysteries. The principal rites of this first stage of initiation consisted in the sacrifice of a sow, which the mystae seem to have first washed in the Cantharus, and in the purification by a priest, who bore the name of *Hydranos* ('Υδρανός). The mystae had also to take an oath of secrecy, which was administered to them by the *Mystagogus* (μυσταγωγός, also called ἱεροφάντης or προφήτης), and they received some kind of preparatory instruction, which enabled them afterwards to understand the mysteries which were revealed to them in the great Eleusinia.—The great mysteries were celebrated every year in the month of Boedromion, during nine days, from the 15th to the 23rd, both at Athens and Eleusis. The initiated were called ἐπόπται or ἔφυροι. On the first day, those who had been initiated in the lesser Eleusinia, assembled at Athens. On the second day the mystae went in solemn procession to the sea-coast, where they underwent a purification. Of the third day scarcely anything is known with certainty; we are only told that it was a day of fasting, and that in the evening a frugal meal was taken, which consisted of cakes made of sesame and honey. On the fourth day the καλάθος κάθοδος seems to have taken place. This was a procession with a basket containing pomegranates and poppy-seeds; it was carried on a waggon drawn by oxen, and women followed with small mystic cases in their hands. On the fifth day, which appears to have been called the torch day (ἡ τῶν λαμπάδων ἡμέρα), the mystae, led by the δᾳδοῦχος, went in the evening with torches to the temple of Demeter at Eleusis, where they seem to have remained during the following night. This rite was probably a symbolical representation of Demeter wandering about in search of Persephone. The sixth day, called *Iacchos*, was the most solemn of all. The statue of Iacchos, son of Demeter, adorned with a garland of myrtle and bearing a torch in his hand, was carried along the sacred road amidst joyous shouts and songs, from the Cerameicus to Eleusis. This solemn procession was accompanied by great numbers of followers and spectators. During the night from the sixth to the seventh day the mystae remained at Eleusis, and were initiated into the last mysteries (ἐποπτεία). Those who were neither ἐπόπται nor μύσται were sent away by a herald. The mystae now repeated the oath of secrecy which had been administered to them at the lesser Eleusinia, underwent a new purification, and then they were led by the mystagogus in the darkness of night into the lighted interior of the sanctuary (φωταγωγία), and were allowed to see (αὐτοψία) what none except the epoptae ever beheld. The awful and horrible manner in which the initiation is described by later, especially Christian writers, seems partly to proceed from their ignorance of its real character, partly from their horror and aversion to these pagan rites. The more ancient writers always abstained from entering upon any description of the subject. Each individual, after his initiation, is said to have been dismissed by the words κόγξ, ὄμπαξ, in order to make room for other mystae. On the seventh day the initiated returned to Athens amid various kinds of raillery and jests, especially at the bridge over the Cephisus, where they sat down to rest, and poured forth their ridicule on those who passed by. Hence the words γεφυρίζειν and γεφυρισμός. These σκώμματα seem, like the procession with torches to Eleusis, to have been dramatical and symbolical representations of the jests by which, according to the ancient legend, Iambe or Baubo had dispelled the grief of the goddess and made her smile. We may here observe, that probably the whole history of Demeter and Persephone was in some way or other symbolically represented at the Eleusinia. The eighth day, called *Epidauria* ('Επιδαύρια), was a kind of additional day for those who by some accident had come too late, or had been prevented from being initiated on the sixth day. It was said to have been added to the original number of days, when Asclepius, coming over from Epidaurus to be initiated, arrived too late, and the Athenians, not to disappoint the god, added an eighth day. The ninth and last day bore the name of πλημοχοαί, from a peculiar kind of vessel called πλημοχοή, which is described as a small kind of κότυλος. Two of these vessels were on this day filled with water or wine, and the contents of the one thrown to the east, and those of the other to the west, while those who performed this rite uttered some mystical words.—The Eleusinian mysteries long survived the independence of Greece. Attempts to suppress them were made by the emperor Valentinian, but he met with strong opposition, and they seem to have continued down to the time of the elder Theodosius. Respecting the secret doctrines which were revealed in them to the initiated, nothing certain is known. The general belief of the ancients was, that they opened to man a comforting prospect of a future state. But this feature does not seem to have been originally connected with these mysteries, and was probably added to them at the period which followed the opening of a regular intercourse between Greece and Egypt, when some of the speculative doctrines of the latter country, and of the East, may have been introduced into the mysteries, and hallowed by the names of the venerable bards of the mythical age. This supposition would also account, in some measure, for the legend of their introduction from Egypt. In modern times many attempts have been made to discover the nature of the mysteries revealed to the initiated, but the results have been as various and as fanciful as might be expected. The most sober and probable view is that, according to which, " they were the remains of a worship which preceded the rise of the Hellenic mythology and its attendant rites,

grounded on a view of nature, less fanciful, more earnest, and better fitted to awaken both philosophical thought and religious feeling."

ELEUTHĔRĬA (ἐλευθέρια), the feast of liberty, a festival which the Greeks, after the battle of Plataeae (479 B. C.), instituted in honour of Zeus Eleutherios (the deliverer). It was intended not merely to be a token of their gratitude to the god to whom they believed themselves to be indebted for their victory over the barbarians, but also as a bond of union among themselves; for, in an assembly of all the Greeks, Aristeides carried a decree that delegates (πρόβουλοι καὶ θεωροί) from all the Greek states should assemble every year at Plataeae for the celebration of the Eleutheria. The town itself was at the same time declared sacred and inviolable, as long as its citizens offered the annual sacrifices which were then instituted on behalf of Greece. Every fifth year these solemnities were celebrated with contests, in which the victors were rewarded with chaplets.

ELLŌTĬA or HELLŌTĬA (ἐλλώτια or ἑλλώτια), a festival with a torch race celebrated at Corinth in honour of Athena as a goddess of fire.

EMANCĬPĀTĬO, was an act by which the *patria potestas* was dissolved in the lifetime of the parent, and it was so called because it was in the form of a sale (*mancipatio*). By the laws of the Twelve Tables it was necessary that a son should be sold three times in order to be released from the paternal power, or to be *sui juris*. In the case of daughters and grandchildren, one sale was sufficient. The father transferred the son by the form of a sale to another person, who manumitted him, upon which he returned into the power of the father. This was repeated, and with the like result. After a third sale, the paternal power was extinguished, but the son was re-sold to the parent, who then manumitted him, and so acquired the rights of a patron over his emancipated son, which would otherwise have belonged to the purchaser who gave him his final manumission.

EMBAS (ἐμβάς), a shoe worn by men, and which appears to have been the most common kind of shoe worn at Athens. Pollux says that it was invented by the Thracians, and that it was like the low cothurnus. The *embas* was also worn by the Boeotians, and probably in other parts of Greece.

EMBĂTEIA (ἐμβατεία). In Attic law this word (like the corresponding English one, *entry*), was used to denote a formal taking possession of real property. Thus, when a son entered upon the land left him by his father, he was said ἐμβατεύειν or βαδίζειν εἰς τὰ πατρῷα, and thereupon he became *seised*, or possessed of his inheritance. If any one disturbed him in the enjoyment of this property, with an intention to dispute the title, he might maintain an action of ejectment, ἐξούλης δίκη. Before entry he could not maintain such action.

EMBLEMA (ἔμβλημα, ἐμπαισμα), an inlaid ornament. The art of inlaying was employed in producing beautiful works of two descriptions, viz. ;—1st, those which resembled our marquetry, buhl, and Florentine mosaics; and 2dly, those in which crusts (*crustae*), exquisitely wrought in bas-relief and of precious materials, were fastened upon the surface of vessels or other pieces of furniture. To the latter class of productions belonged the cups and plates which Verres obtained by violence from the Sicilians, and from which he removed the emblems for the purpose of having them set in gold instead of silver.

EMERITI, the name given to those Roman soldiers who had served out their time, and had exemption (*vacatio*) from military service. The usual time of service was twenty years for the legionary soldiers, and sixteen for the praetorians. At the end of their period of service they received a bounty or reward (*emeritum*), either in lands or money, or in both.

EMISSARIUM (ὑπόνομος), a channel, natural or artificial, by which an outlet is formed to carry off any stagnant body of water. Such channels may be either open or underground; but the most remarkable works of the kind are of the latter description, as they carry off the waters of lakes surrounded by hills. In Greece, the most striking example is presented by the subterraneous channels which carry off the waters of the lake Copais in Boeotia, which were partly natural and partly artificial. Some works of this kind are among the most remarkable efforts of Roman ingenuity. Remains still exist to show that the lakes Trasimene, Albano, Nemi, and Fucino, were all drained by means of *emissaria*, the last of which is still nearly perfect, and open to inspection, having been partially cleared by the present king of Naples. Julius Caesar is said to have first conceived the idea of this stupendous undertaking, which was carried into effect by the Emperor Claudius.

EMMĒNI DĪKAE (ἔμμηνοι δίκαι), suits in the Athenian courts, which were not allowed to be pending above a month. This regulation was confined to those subjects which required a speedy decision; and of these the most important were disputes respecting commerce (ἐμπορικαὶ δίκαι). All causes relating to mines (μεταλλικαὶ δίκαι) were also ἔμμηνοι δίκαι, as well as those relating to ἔρανοι. [ERANI.]

EMPORĬUM (τὸ ἐμπόριον), a place for wholesale trade in commodities carried by sea. The name is sometimes applied to a sea-port town, but it properly signifies only a particular place in such a town. The word is derived from ἔμπορος, which signifies in Homer a person who sails as a passenger in a ship belonging to another person; but in later writers it signifies the merchant or wholesale dealer, and differs from κάπηλος, the retail dealer. The emporium at Athens was under the inspection of certain officers, who were elected annually (ἐπιμεληταὶ τοῦ ἐμπορίου).

ENCAUSTĬCA. [PICTURA.]

ENCTĒSIS (ἔγκτησις), the right of possessing landed property and houses (ἔγκτησις γῆς καὶ οἰκίας) in a foreign country, which was frequently granted by one Greek state to another, or to separate individuals of another state. Ἐγκτήματα were such possessions in a foreign country, or in a different δῆμος from that to which an Athenian belonged by birth.

ENDEIXIS (ἔνδειξις), properly denotes a prosecution instituted against such persons as were alleged to have exercised rights or held offices while labouring under a peculiar disqualification. The same form of action was available against the chairman of the proedri (ἐπιστάτης), who wrongly refused to take the votes of the people in the assembly; against malefactors, especially murderers; traitors, ambassadors accused of malversation, and persons who furnished supplies to the enemy during war. The first step taken by the prosecutor was to lay his information in writing, also called *endeixis*, before the proper magistrate, who then arrested, or held to bail, the person criminated, and took the usual steps for bringing him to trial. There is great obscurity with respect to the punishment which followed condemnation. The accuser, if unsuccessful, was responsible for bringing a malicious charge (ψευδοῦς ἐνδείξεως ὑπεύθυνος).

ENDROMIS (ἐνδρομίς), a thick, coarse blanket, manufactured in Gaul, and called "endromis" because those who had been exercising in the stadium (ἐν δρόμῳ) threw it over them to obviate the effects of sudden exposure when they were heated. Notwithstanding its coarse and shaggy appearance, it was worn on other occasions as a protection from the cold by rich and fashionable persons at Rome.

ENSIS. [GLADIUS.]

ENTĂSIS (ἔντασις). The most ancient columns now existing, diminish immediately and regularly from the base to the neck, so that the edge forms a straight line—a mode of construction which is wanting in grace and apparent solidity. To correct this, a swelling outline, called *entasis*, was given to the shaft, which seems to have been the first step towards combining grace and grandeur in the Doric column.

EPANGELIA (ἐπαγγελία). If a citizen of Athens had incurred *atimia*, the privilege of taking part or speaking in the public assembly was forfeited. But as it sometimes might happen that a person, though not formally declared *atimus*, had committed such crimes as would, on accusation, draw upon him this punishment, it was of course desirable that such individuals, like real *atimi*, should be excluded from the exercise of the rights of citizens. Whenever, therefore, such a person ventured to speak in the assembly, any Athenian citizen had the right to come forward in the assembly itself and demand of him to establish his right to speak by a trial or examination of his conduct (δοκιμασία τοῦ βίου), and this demand, denouncement, or threat, was called *epangelia*, or *epangelia docimasias* (ἐπαγγελία δοκιμασίας). The impeached individual was then compelled to desist from speaking, and to submit to a scrutiny into his conduct, and, if he was convicted, a formal declaration of *atimia* followed.

EPARITI (ἐπάριτοι), the name of the standing army in Arcadia, which was formed to preserve the independence of the Arcadian towns, when they became united as one state after the defeat of the Spartans at Leuctra. They were 5000 in number, and were paid by the state.

EPHEBUS (ἔφηβος), the name of Athenian youths after they had attained the age of 18. The state of *ephebeia* (ἐφηβεία) lasted for two years, till the youths had attained the age of 20, when they became men, and were admitted to share all the rights and duties of citizens, for which the law did not prescribe a more advanced age. Before a youth was enrolled among the ephebi, he had to undergo a *docimasia* (δοκιμασία), the object of which was partly to ascertain whether he was the son of Athenian citizens, or adopted by a citizen, and partly whether his body was sufficiently developed and strong to undertake the duties which now devolved upon him. After the *docimasia* the young men received in the assembly a shield and a lance; but those whose fathers had fallen in the defence of their country received a complete suit of armour in the theatre. It seems to have been on this occasion that the ephebi took an oath in the temple of Artemis Aglauros, by which they pledged themselves never to disgrace their arms or to desert their comrades; to fight to the last in the defence of their country, its altars and hearths; to leave their country not in a worse but in a better state than they found it; to obey the magistrates and the laws; to resist all attempts to subvert the institutions of Attica; and finally, to respect the religion of their forefathers. This solemnity took place towards the close of the year, and the festive season bore the name of *ephebia* (ἐφήβια). The external distinction of the ephebi consisted in the chlamys and the petasus. During the two years of the ephebeia, which may be considered as a kind of apprenticeship in arms, and in which the young men prepared themselves for the higher duties of full citizens, they were generally sent into the country, under the name of *peripoli* (περίπολοι), to keep watch in the towns and fortresses, on the coast and frontier, and to perform other duties which might be necessary for the protection of Attica.

EPHEGESIS (ἐφήγησις), denotes the method of proceeding against such criminals as were liable to be summarily arrested by a private citizen [APAGOGE] when the prosecutor was unwilling to expose himself to personal risk in apprehending the offender. Under these circumstances he made an application to the proper magistrate, and conducted him and his officers to the spot where the capture was to be effected.

EPHETAE (ἐφέται), the name of certain judges at Athens, who tried cases of homicide. They were fifty-one in number, selected from noble families, and more than fifty years of age. They formed a tribunal of great antiquity, and were in existence before the legislation of Solon, but, as the state became more and more democratical, their duties became unimportant and almost antiquated. The Ephetae once sat in one or other of the five courts, according to the nature of the causes they had to try. In historical times, however, they sat in *four* only, called respectively the court by the Palladium (τὸ ἐπὶ Παλλαδίῳ), by the Delphinium (τὸ ἐπὶ Δελφινίῳ), by the Prytaneium (τὸ ἐπὶ Πρυτανείῳ), and the court at Phreatto or Zea (τὸ ἐν Φρεαττοῖ). At the first of these courts they tried cases of unintentional, at the second, of intentional but justinable homicide. At the Prytaneium, by a strange custom, somewhat analogous to the imposition of a deodand, they passed sentence upon the instrument of murder when the perpetrator of the act was not known. In the court at Phreatto, on the sea shore at the Peiraeeus, they tried such persons as were charged with wilful murder during a temporary exile for unintentional homicide.

EPHIPPIUM (ἀστράβη, ἐφίππιον, ἐφίππειον), a saddle. Although the Greeks occasionally rode without any saddle, yet they commonly used one, and from them the name, together with the thing, was borrowed by the Romans. The ancient saddles appear, indeed, to have been thus far different from ours, that the cover stretched upon the hard frame was probably of stuffed or padded cloth rather than leather, and that the saddle was, as it were, a cushion fitted to the horse's back. Pendent cloths (στρώματα, strata) were always attached to it so as to cover the sides of the animal; but it was not provided with stirrups. The saddle with the pendent cloths is exhibited in the annexed coin. The term

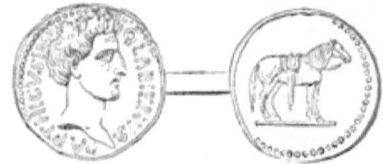

Ephippium, Saddle. (Coin of Labienus.)

"Ephippium" was in later times in part supplanted by the word "sella," and the more specific expression "sella equestris."

EPHORI (ἔφοροι). Magistrates called *Ephori* or overseers were common to many Dorian constitutions in times of remote antiquity; but the Ephori of Sparta are the most celebrated of them all. The origin of the Spartan ephori is quite uncertain, but their office in the historical times was a kind of counterpoise to the kings and council, and in that respect peculiar to Sparta alone of the Dorian states. Their number, five, appears to have been always the same, and was probably connected with the five divisions of the town of Sparta, namely, the four κῶμαι, Limnae, Mesoa, Pitana, Cynosura, and the Πόλις or city properly so called, around which the κῶμαι lay. They were elected from and by the people, without any qualification of age or property, and without undergoing any scrutiny; so that the people enjoyed through them a participation in the highest magistracy of the state. They entered upon office at the autumnal solstice, and the first in rank of the five gave his name to the year, which was called after him in all civil transactions. They possessed judicial authority in civil suits, and also a general superintendence over the morals and domestic economy of the nation, which in the hands of able men would soon prove an instrument of unlimited power. Their jurisdiction and power were still further increased by the privilege of instituting scrutinies (εὔθυναι) into the conduct of all the magistrates. Even the kings themselves could be brought before their tribunal (as Cleomenes was for bribery). In extreme cases, the ephors were also competent to lay an accusation against the kings as well as the other magistrates, and bring them to a capital trial before the great court of justice. In later times the power of the ephors was greatly increased; and this increase appears to have been principally owing to the fact, that they put themselves in connection with the assembly of the people, convened its meetings, laid measures before it, and were constituted its agents and representatives. When this connection arose is matter of conjecture. The power which such a connection gave would, more than anything else, enable them to encroach on the royal authority, and make themselves virtually supreme in the state. Accordingly, we find that they transacted business with foreign ambassadors; dismissed them from the state; decided upon the government of dependent cities; subscribed in the presence of other persons to treaties of peace; and in time of war sent out troops when they thought necessary. In all these capacities the ephors acted as the representatives of the nation, and the agents of the public assembly, being in fact the executive of the state. In course of time the kings became completely under their control. For instance, they fined Agesilaus on the vague charge of trying to make himself popular, and interfered even with the domestic arrangements of other kings. In the field the kings were followed by two ephors, who belonged to the council of war; the three who remained at home received the booty in charge, and paid it into the treasury, which was under the superintendence of the whole College of Five. But the ephors had still another prerogative, based on a religious foundation, which enabled them to effect a temporary deposition of the kings. Once in eight years, as we are told, they chose a calm and cloudless night to observe the heavens, and if there was any appearance of a falling meteor, it was believed to be a sign that the gods were displeased with the kings, who were accordingly suspended from their functions until an oracle allowed of their restoration. The outward symbols of supreme authority also were assumed by the ephors; and they alone kept their seats while the kings passed; whereas it was not considered below the dignity of the kings to rise in honour of the ephors. When Agis and Cleomenes undertook to restore the old constitution, it was necessary for them to overthrow the ephoralty, and accordingly Cleomenes murdered the ephors for the time being, and abolished the office (B. C. 225); it was, however, restored under the Romans.

EPIBATAE (ἐπιβάται), were soldiers or marines appointed to defend the vessels in the Athenian navy, and were entirely distinct from the rowers, and also from the land soldiers, such as hoplitae, peltasts, and cavalry. It appears that the ordinary number of epibatae on board a trireme was ten. The epibatae were usually taken from the thetes, or fourth class of Athenian citizens. The term is sometimes also applied by the Roman writers to the marines, but they are more usually called *classiarii milites*. The latter term, however, is also applied to the rowers or sailors as well as the marines.

EPIBOLE (ἐπιβολή), a fine imposed by a magistrate, or other official person or body, for a misdemeanour. The various magistrates at Athens had (each in his own department) a summary penal jurisdiction; *i. e.* for certain offences they might inflict a pecuniary mulct or fine, not exceeding a fixed amount; if the offender deserved further punishment, it was their duty to bring him before a judicial tribunal. These *epibolae* are to be distinguished from the penalties awarded by a jury or court of law (τιμήματα) upon a formal prosecution.

EPICLERUS (ἐπίκληρος, heiress), the name given to the daughter of an Athenian citizen, who had no son to inherit his estate. It was deemed an object of importance at Athens to preserve the family name and property of every citizen. This was effected, where a man had no child, by adoption (εἰσποίησις); if he had a daughter, the inheritance was transmitted through her to a grandson, who would take the name of the maternal ancestor. If the father died intestate, the heiress had not the choice of a husband, but was bound to marry her nearest relation, not in the ascending line. When there was but one daughter, she was called ἐπίκληρος ἐπὶ παντὶ τῷ οἴκῳ. If there were more, they inherited equally, like our co-parceners; and were severally married to relatives, the nearest having the first choice.

EPIDOSEIS (ἐπιδόσεις), voluntary contributions, either in money, arms, or ships, which were made by the Athenian citizens in order to meet the extraordinary demands of the state. When the expenses of the state were greater than its revenue, it was usual for the prytaneis to summon an assembly of the people, and after explaining the necessities of the state, to call upon the citizens to contribute according to their means. Those who were willing to contribute then rose and mentioned what they would give; while those who were unwilling to give any thing remained silent, or retired privately from the assembly.

EPIMELETAE (ἐπιμεληταί), the names of various magistrates and functionaries at Athens.—(1) Ἐπιμελητὴς τῆς κοινῆς προσόδου, more usually called ταμίας, the treasurer or manager of the public revenue. [TAMIAS.]— (2) Ἐπιμεληταὶ τῶν μορίων Ἐλαιῶν, were persons chosen from among the Areopagites to take care of the sacred olive trees.—(3) Ἐπιμεληταὶ τοῦ Ἐμπορίου, were the overseers of the emporium. [EMPORIUM.] They were ten in number, and were elected yearly by lot. They had the entire management of the emporium, and had jurisdiction in all breaches of the commercial laws.—(4) Ἐπιμεληταὶ τῶν Μυστηρίων, were, in connection with the king archon, the managers of the Eleusinian mysteries. They were elected by open vote, and were four in number.—(5) Ἐπιμεληταὶ τῶν νεωρίων, the inspectors of the dockyards, were ten in number.—(6) Ἐπιμεληταὶ τῶν φυλῶν, the inspectors of the φυλαί or tribes. [TRIBUS.]

EPISCOPI (ἐπίσκοποι), inspectors, who were sometimes sent by the Athenians to subject states. They were also called φύλακες. It appears that these Episcopi received a salary at the cost of the cities over which they presided.

EPISTATES (ἐπιστάτης).—(1) The chairman of the senate and assembly of the people, respecting whose duties see BOULE and ECCLESIA.—(2) The name of the directors of the public works. (Ἐπιστάται τῶν δημοσίων ἔργων).

EPISTOLEUS (ἐπιστολεύς), the officer second in rank in the Spartan fleet, who succeeded to the command if any thing happened to the *navarchus* (ναύαρχος) or admiral. When the Chians and the other allies of Sparta on the Asiatic coast sent to Sparta to request that Lysander might be again appointed to the command of the navy, he was sent with the title of epistoleus, because the laws of Sparta did not permit the same person to hold the office of navarchus twice.

EPISTYLIUM (ἐπιστύλιον), properly, as the name implies, the architrave, or lower member of an entablature, which lies immediately over the columns. The word is sometimes also used for the whole of the entablature.

EPITROPUS (ἐπίτροπος), the name at Athens of a guardian of orphan children. Of such guardians there were at Athens three kinds: first, those appointed in the will of the deceased father; secondly, the next of kin, whom the law designated as tutores legitimi in default of such appointment, and who required the authorization of the archon to enable them to act; and lastly, such persons as the archon selected if there were no next of kin living to undertake the office. The duties of the guardian comprehended the education, maintenance, and protection of the ward, the assertion of his rights, and the safe custody and profitable disposition of his inheritance during his minority, besides making a proper provision for the widow if she remained in the house of her late husband.

EPŌBĒLIA (ἐπωβελία), as its etymology implies, at the rate of one obolus for a drachma, or one in six, was payable on the assessment (τίμημα) of several private causes, and sometimes in a case of phasis, by the litigant that failed to obtain the votes of one-fifth of the dicasts.

EPŎNȲMUS. [ARCHON.]
EPOPTAE (ἐπόπται). [ELEUSINIA.]
EPŬLŌNES, who were originally three in number (triumviri epulones), were first created in B. C. 196, to attend to the Epulum Jovis, and the banquets given in honour of the other gods; which duty had originally belonged to the pontifices. Their number was afterwards increased to seven, and they were called septemviri epulones or septemviri epulonum. The epulones formed a collegium, and were one of the four great religious corporations at Rome; the other three were those of the Pontifices, Augures, and Quindecemviri.

EPŬLUM JŎVIS. [EPULONES.]
EQUIRIA, horse-races, which are said to have been instituted by Romulus in honour of Mars, and were celebrated in the Campus Martius. There were two festivals of this name; of which one was celebrated A. D. III. Cal. Mart., and the other prid. Id. Mart.

EQUITES, horsemen. Romulus is said to have formed three centuries of equites; and these were the same as the 300 Celeres, whom he kept about his person in peace and war. A century was taken from each of the three tribes, the *Ramnes*, *Titienses*, and *Luceres*. Tarquinius Priscus added three more, under the title of Ramnes, Titienses, and Luceres *posteriores*. These were the six patrician centuries of equites, often referred to under the name of the *sex suffragia*. To these Servius Tullius added twelve more centuries, for admission into which, property and not birth was the qualification. These twelve centuries might therefore contain plebeians, but they do not appear to have been restricted to plebeians, since we have no reason for believing that the six old centuries contained the *whole* body of patricians. A property qualification was apparently also necessary by the Servian constitution for admission into the six centuries. We may therefore suppose that those patricians who were included in the six old centuries were allowed by the Servian constitution to continue in them, if they possessed the requisite property; and that all other persons in the state, whether patricians or plebeians, who possessed the requisite property, were admitted into the twelve new centuries. We are not told the amount of property necessary to entitle a person to a place among the equites, but it was probably the same as in the latter times of the republic, that is, four times that of the first class. [COMITIA, p. 105.] Property, however, was not the only qualification; for in the ancient times of the republic no one was admitted among the equestrian centuries unless his character was unblemished, and his father and grandfather had been born freemen. Each of the equites received a horse from the state (*equus publicus*), or money to purchase one, as well as a sum of money for its annual support; the expense of its support was defrayed by the orphans and unmarried females; since, in a military state, it could not be esteemed unjust, that the women and the children were to contribute largely for those who fought in behalf of them and of the commonwealth. The purchase-money for a knight's horse was called *aes equestre*, and its annual provision *aes hordearium*. The former amounted, according to Livy, to 10,000 asses, and the latter to 2000.—All the equites, of whom we have been speaking, received a horse from the state, and were included in the 18 equestrian centuries of the Servian constitution; but in course of time, we read of another class of equites in Roman history, who did not receive a horse from the state, and who were not included in the 18 centuries. This latter class is first mentioned by Livy, in his account of the siege of Veii, B. C. 403. He says that during the siege, when the Romans had at one time suffered great disasters, all those citizens who had an equestrian fortune, and no horse allotted to them, volunteered to serve with their own horses; and he adds, that from this time equites first began to serve with their own horses. The state paid them, as a kind of compensation for serving with their own horses. The foot soldiers had received pay a few years before; and two years afterwards, B. C. 401, the pay of the equites was made three-fold that of the infantry. From the year B. C. 403, there were therefore two classes of Roman knights: one who received horses from the state, and are therefore frequently called *equites equo publico*, and sometimes *Flexumines* or *Trossuli*, and **another** class, who served, **when they were required, with their own horses, but were not classed among the 18 centuries. As they served on horseback they were called** *equites*; **and when spoken of in opposition to cavalry, which did not consist of Roman citizens, they were also called** *equites Romani*; **but they had no legal claim to the name of equites, since in ancient times this title was strictly confined to those who received horses from the state.—The reason of this distinction of two classes arose from the fact, that the number of equites in the 18 centuries was fixed from the time of Servius Tullius. As vacancies occurred in them, the descendants of those who were originally enrolled succeeded to their places, provided they had not dissipated their property.** But in course of time, **as population and wealth increased, the number of persons who** possessed an equestrian **fortune, also increased greatly; and as the ancestors of these persons had not been enrolled in the 18 centuries, they could not receive horses from the state, and were therefore allowed the privilege of serving with their own horses among the cavalry, instead of the infantry, as they would otherwise have been obliged to have done.—The inspection of the equites who received horses from the state belonged to the censors, who had the power of depriving an eques of his horse, and reducing him to the condition of an aerarian, and also of giving the vacant horse to the most distinguished of the equites who had previously served at their own expense. For these purposes they made during their censorship a public inspection, in the forum, of all the knights who possessed public horses (***equitatum recognoscere***). The tribes were taken in order, and each knight was summoned by name. Every one, as his name was called, walked past the censors, leading his horse. If the censors had no fault to find either with the character of the knight or the equipments of his horse, they ordered him to pass on (***traduc equum***); but if on the contrary they considered him unworthy of his rank, they struck him out of the list of knights, and deprived him of his horse, or ordered him to sell it, with the intention no** doubt **that the person thus degraded should** refund to the **state the money which had been** advanced to him for its purchase.—This **review of the equites by the censors must not** be confounded **with the** *Equitum Transvectio*, **which was a** soleman procession of the **body** every year on the Ides of Quintilis (July). The procession started from the temple of Mars outside the city, and passed through the city over the forum, and by the temple of the Dioscuri. On this occasion the equites were always crowned with olive chaplets, and wore their state dress, the trabea, **with all the honourable** distinctions which **they had gained in battle.** According to Livy, this annual procession was first established by **the censors Q. Fabius and P.** Decius, B.C. 304; **but according to Dionysius it was instituted after the defeat of the Latins near the lake Regillus, of which** an account was brought to Rome **by the Dioscuri.—It** may be asked **how long did the knight retain** his public horse, **and a vote in the equestrian century to which he** belonged? **On this subject we have no positive** information; **but as those equites, who** served with their **own horses, were only** obliged **to serve for ten years (***stipendia***) under the age of 46, we may presume that** the **same rule extended to those who served with the public horses, provided they** *wished* **to give up the service. For it is certain that in the ancient times of the republic a knight might retain his horse as long as he pleased, even after he had entered the senate, provided he continued able to discharge the duties of a knight. Thus the two censors, M. Livius Salinator and C. Claudius Nero, in B.C. 204, were also equites, and L. Scipio Asiaticus, who was deprived of his horse by the censors in B.C. 185, had himself been censor in B.C. 191. But during the later times of the** republic **the knights were obliged to** give up their horses **on** entering **the senate, and** consequently ceased to belong **to the** equestrian centuries. It thus naturally came **to** pass, **that the greater number of the equites equo publico, after the exclusion of** senators from the **equestrian centuries, were young men.—The equestrian centuries, of which we have hitherto been treating, were only regarded as a division of the army: they did not form a distinct class or ordo in the constitution. The community, in a political point of view, was divided only into patricians and plebeians, and the equestrian centuries were composed of both.** But in the year B.C. 123, a new **class, called** the *Ordo Equestris*, was formed **in the** state by the Lex Sempronia, which was introduced by C. Gracchus. By **this** law, or one passed a few years afterwards, every person **who was to** be chosen judex **was** required to be **above 30 and under** 60 **years of age, to have either an equus publicus, or to be qualified by his fortune to possess one, and *not* to be a senator. The number of judices, who were required yearly, was chosen from this class by the praetor urbanus. As the name of** equites **had been originally extended from those** who possessed **the public horses to those who** served with their **own horses, it now came to be applied to all those persons who were qualified by their fortune to act as judices, in which sense the word is usually used by Cicero. After the reform of Sulla, which entirely deprived the equestrian order of the right of being chosen as judices, and the passing of the Lex Aurelia (B.C. 70), which ordained that the judices should be chosen from the senators, equites, and tribuni aerarii, the influence of the order, says Pliny, was still maintained by the *publicani*, or farmers of the public taxes. We find that the publicani were almost always called equites, not because any particular rank was necessary in order to obtain from the state the farming of the taxes, but because the state was not accustomed to let them to any one who did not possess a considerable fortune. Thus the publicani are frequently spoken of by Cicero as identical with the equestrian order. The consulship of Cicero, and the active part which the knights then took in suppressing the conspiracy of Catiline, tended still further to increase the power and influence of the equestrian order; and "from that time," says Pliny, "it became a third body (*corpus*) in the state, and, to the title of *Senatus Populusque Romanus*, there began to be added *Et Equestris Ordo*." In B.C. 63, a distinction was conferred upon them, which tended to separate them still further from the plebs. By the Lex Roscia Othonis, passed in that year, the first fourteen seats in the theatre behind the orchestra were given to the equites. They also possessed the right of wearing the Clavus Angustus [CLAVUS], and subsequently obtained the privilege of wearing a gold ring, which was originally confined to the equites equo publico. The number of equites increased greatly under the early emperors, and all persons were admitted into the order, provided they possessed the requisite property, without any inquiry into their character, or into the free birth of their father and grandfather. The order in consequence gradually began to lose all the consideration which it had acquired during the later times of the republic.—Augustus formed a select class of equites, consisting of those equites who possessed the property of a senator, and the old requirement of free birth up to the grandfather. He permitted this class to wear the *latus clavus*; and also allowed the tribunes of the plebs to be chosen from them, as well as the senators, and gave them the option, at the termination of their office, to remain in the senate or return to the equestrian order. This class of knights was distinguished by the special title *illustres* (sometimes *insignes* and *splendidi*) *equites Romani*. The formation of this distinct class tended to lower the others still more in public estimation. In the ninth year of the reign of Tiberius, an attempt was made to improve the order by requiring the old qualifications of free birth up to the grandfather, and by strictly forbidding any one to wear the gold ring unless he possessed this qualification. This regulation, however, was of little avail, as the emperors frequently admitted freedmen into the equestrian order. When private persons were no longer appointed judices, the necessity for a distinct class in the community, like the equestrian order, ceased entirely; and the gold ring came at length to be worn by all free citizens. Even slaves, after their manumission, were allowed to wear it by special permission from the emperor, which appears to have been usually granted provided the patronus consented.— Having thus traced the history of the equestrian order to its final extinction as a distinct class in the community, we must now return to the equites equo publico, who formed the 18 equestrian centuries. This class still existed during the latter years of the republic, but had entirely ceased to serve as horse-soldiers in the army. The cavalry of the Roman legions no longer consisted, as in the time of Polybius, of Roman equites, but their place was supplied by the cavalry of the allied states. It is evident that Caesar in his Gallic wars possessed no Roman cavalry. When he went to an interview with Ariovistus, and was obliged to take cavalry with him, we are told that he did not dare to trust his safety to the Gallic cavalry, and therefore mounted his legionary soldiers upon their horses. The Roman equites are, however, frequently mentioned in the Gallic and civil wars, but never as common soldiers; they were officers attached to the staff of the general, or commanded the cavalry of the allies, or sometimes the legions.—After the year B.C. 50, there were no censors in the state, and it would therefore follow that for some years no review of the body took place, and that the vacancies were not filled up. When Augustus, however, took upon himself, in B.C. 29, the praefectura morum, he frequently reviewed the troops of equites, and restored the long neglected custom of the solemn procession (*transvectio*). From this time these equites formed an honourable corps, from which all the higher officers in the army and the chief magistrates in the state were chosen. Admission into this body was equivalent to an introduction into public life, and was therefore esteemed a great privilege. If a young man was not admitted into this body, he was excluded from all civil offices of any importance, except in municipal towns;

and also from all rank in the army, with the exception of centurion. All those equites, who were not employed in actual service, were obliged to reside at Rome, where they were allowed to fill the lower magistracies, which entitled a person to admission into the senate. They were divided into six turmae, each of which was commanded by an officer, who is frequently mentioned in inscriptions as *Sevir equitum Rom. turmae* I. II., &c., or commonly *Sevir turmae* or *Sevir turmarum equitum Romanorum*. From the time that the equites bestowed the title of *principes juventutis* upon Caius and Lucius Caesar, the grandsons of Augustus, it became the custom to confer this title, as well as that of sevir, upon the probable successor to the throne, when he first entered into public life, and was presented with an equus publicus. The practice of filling all the higher offices in the state from these equites appears to have continued as long as Rome was the centre of the government and the residence of the emperor. After the time of Diocletian, the equites became only a city guard, under the command of the praefectus vigilum; but they still retained, in the time of Valentinianus and Valens, A. D. 364, the second rank in the city, and were not subject to corporal punishment. Respecting the *Magister Equitum*, see DICTATOR.

EQUŬLĔUS or ĔCŬLĔUS, an instrument of torture, which is supposed to have been so called because it was in the form of a horse.

ĔRĀNI (ἔρανοι), were clubs or societies, established for charitable, convivial, commercial, or political purposes. Unions of this kind were called by the general name of ἑταιρίαι, and were often converted to mischievous ends, such as bribery, overawing the public assembly, or influencing the courts of justice. In the days of the Roman empire friendly societies, under the name of *erani*, were frequent among the Greek cities, but were looked on with suspicion by the emperors, as leading to political combinations. The *gilds*, or fraternities for mutual aid, among the ancient Saxons, resembled the *erani* of the Greeks.

ERGASTŬLUM, a private prison attached to most Roman farms, where the slaves were made to work in chains. The slaves confined in an ergastulum were also employed to cultivate the fields in chains. Slaves who had displeased their masters were punished by imprisonment in the ergastulum; and in the same place all slaves, who could not be depended upon or were barbarous in their habits, were regularly kept.

ERĪCIUS, a military engine full of sharp spikes, which was placed by the gate of the camp to prevent the approach of the enemy.

ERŌTĬA or ERŌTĬDĬA (ἐρώτια or ἐρωτίδια), the most solemn of all the festivals celebrated in the Boeotian town of Thespiae. It took place every fifth year, and in honour of Eros, the principal divinity of the Thespians. Respecting the particulars nothing is known, except that it was solemnised with contests in music and gymnastics.

ESSĔDĀRĬI. [ESSEDUM.]

ESSĔDA, or ESSĔDUM (from the Celtic *Ess*, a carriage), the name of a chariot used, especially in war, by the Britons, the Gauls, and the Germans. It was built very strongly, was open before instead of behind, like the Greek war-chariot, and had a wide pole, so that the owner was able, whenever he pleased, to run along the pole, and even to raise himself upon the yoke, and then to retreat with the greatest speed into the body of the car, which he drove with extraordinary swiftness and skill. It appears also that these cars were purposely made as noisy as possible, probably by the creaking and clanging of the wheels; and that this was done in order to strike dismay into the enemy. The warriors who drove these chariots were called *essedarii*. Having been captured, they were sometimes exhibited in the gladiatorial shows at Rome, and seem to have been great favourites with the people. The essedum was adopted for purposes of convenience and luxury among the Romans. As used by the Romans, the essedum may have differed from the cisium in this; that the cisium was drawn by one horse (see cut, p. 90), the essedum always by a pair.

EUMOLPĬDAE (εὐμολπίδαι), the most distinguished and venerable among the priestly families in Attica. They were devoted to the service of Demeter at Athens and Eleusis, and were said to be the descendants of the Thracian bard Eumolpus, who, according to some legends, had introduced the Eleusinian mysteries into Attica. The high priest of the Eleusinian goddess (ἱεροφάντης or μυσταγωγός), who conducted the celebration of her mysteries and the initiation of the mystae, was always a member of the family of the Eumolpidae, as Eumolpus himself was believed to have been the first hierophant. The hierophant was attended by four ἐπιμεληταί (ἐπιμεληταί), one of whom likewise belonged to the family of the Eumolpidae. The Eumolpidae had on certain occasions to offer up prayers for the welfare of the state. They had likewise judicial power in cases where religion was violated. The law according to which they pronounced their sentence, and of which they had the exclusive possession, was not written, but handed down by tradition; and the Eumolpidae alone had the right to interpret it, whence they are sometimes called *Exegetae* (ἐξηγηταί). In cases for which the law had made no provisions, they acted according to their own discretion. In some cases, when a person was convicted of gross violation of the public institutions of his country, the people, besides sending the offender into exile, added a clause in their verdict that a curse should be pronounced upon him by the Eumolpidae. But the Eumolpidae could pronounce such a curse only at the command of the people, and might afterwards be compelled by the people to revoke it, and purify the person whom they had cursed before.

EUPATRIDAE (εὐπατρίδαι), descended from noble ancestors, is the name by which in early times the nobility of Attica was designated. In the division of the inhabitants of Attica into three classes, which is ascribed to Theseus, the Eupatridae were the first class, and thus formed a compact order of nobles, united by their interests, rights, and privileges. They were in the exclusive possession of all the civil and religious offices in the state, ordered the affairs of religion, and interpreted the laws human and divine. The king was thus only the first among his equals, and only distinguished from them by the duration of his office. By the legislation of Solon, the political power and influence of the Eupatridae as an order was broken, and property instead of birth was made the standard of political rights. But as Solon, like all ancient legislators, abstained from abolishing any of the religious institutions, those families of the Eupatridae, in which certain priestly offices and functions were hereditary, retained these distinctions down to a very late period of Grecian history.

EURIPUS. [AMPHITHEATRUM.]

EUTHYNE (εὐθύνη). All public officers at Athens were accountable for their conduct and the manner in which they acquitted themselves of their official duties. The judges in the popular court seem to have been the only authorities who were not responsible, for they were themselves the representatives of the people, and would therefore, in theory, have been responsible to themselves. This account, which officers had to give after the time of their office was over, was called εὐθύνη, and the officers subject to it, ὑπεύθυνοι, and after they had gone through the *euthyne*, they became ἀνεύθυνοι. Every public officer had to render his account within thirty days after the expiration of his office, and at the time when he submitted to the *euthyne* any citizen had the right to come forward and impeach him. The officers before whom the accounts were given were at Athens ten in number, called εὔθυνοι or λογισταί, in other places ἐξετασταί or συνήγοροι.

EVOCATI. [EXERCITUS.]
EXAUCTORITAS. [EXERCITUS.]
EXAUGURATIO, the act of changing a sacred thing into a profane one, or of taking away from it the sacred character which it had received by inauguratio, consecratio, or dedicatio. Such an act was performed by the augurs, and never without consulting the pleasure of the gods, by augurium.

EXCUBIAE. [CASTRA.]
EXCUBITORES, which properly means watchmen or sentinels of any kind, was the name more particularly given to the soldiers of the cohort who guarded the palace of the Roman emperor.

EXEDRA (ἐξέδρα), which properly signifies a seat out of doors, came to be used for a chamber furnished with seats, and opening into a portico, where people met to enjoy conversation; such as the rooms attached to a gymnasium, which were used for the lectures and disputations of the rhetoricians and philosophers. In old Greek the word λέσχη appears to have had a similar meaning; but the ordinary use of the word is for a larger and more public place of resort than the ἐξέδρα. [LESCHE.] Among the Romans the word had a wider meaning, answering to both the Greek terms, ἐξέδρα and λέσχη.

EXEGETAE (ἐξηγηταί, interpreters) is the name of the Eumolpidae, by which they were designated as the interpreters of the laws relating to religion and of the sacred rites. [EUMOLPIDAE.] The name ἐξηγητής was also applied to those persons who served as guides (ciceroni) to the visitors in the most remarkable towns and places of Greece.

EXERCITORIA ACTIO, an action granted by the edict against the exercitor navis. By the term navis was understood any vessel, whether used for the navigation of rivers, lakes, or the sea. The exercitor navis is the person to whom all the ship's gains and earnings (*obventiones et reditus*) belong, whether he is the owner, or has hired the ship (*per aversionem*) from the owner for a time definite or indefinite.

EXERCITUS (στρατός), army. (1) GREEK.
1. *Spartan Army.*—In all the states of Greece, in the earliest as in later times, the general type of their military organisation was the *phalanx*, a body of troops in close array with a long spear as their principal weapon. It was among the Dorians, and especially among the Spartans, that this type was most rigidly adhered to. The strength

of their military array consisted in the heavy-armed infantry (ὁπλῖται). They attached comparatively small importance to their cavalry, which was always inferior. Indeed, the Thessalians and Boeotians were the only Greek people who distinguished themselves much for their cavalry; scarcely any other states had territories adapted for the evolutions of cavalry. The whole life of a Spartan was little else than either the preparation for or the practice of war. The result was, that in the strictness of their discipline, the precision and facility with which they performed their military evolutions, and the skill and power with which they used their weapons, the Spartans were unrivalled among the Greeks. The heavy-armed infantry of the Spartan armies was composed partly of genuine Spartan citizens, partly of Perioeci. Every Spartan citizen was liable to military service (ἔμφρουρος) from the age of twenty to the age of sixty years. They were divided into six divisions called μόραι, under the command or superintendence of a polemarch, each mora being subdivided into four λόχοι (commanded by λοχαγοί), each λόχος into two πεντηκοστύες (headed by πεντηκοστῆρες), each πεντηκοστύς into two ἐνωμοτίαι (headed by enomotarchs). The ἐνωμοτίαι were so called from the men composing them being bound together by a common oath. These were not merely divisions of troops engaged in actual military expeditions. The whole body of citizens at all times formed an army, whether they were congregated at head-quarters in Sparta, or a portion of them were detached on foreign service. The strength of a mora on actual service, of course, varied, according to circumstances. To judge by the name pentecostys, the normal number of a mora would have been 400; but 500, 600, and 900 are mentioned as the number of men in a mora on different occasions. When in the field, each mora of infantry was attended by a mora of cavalry, consisting at the most of 100 men, and commanded by an hipparmost (ἱππαρμοστής). Plutarch mentions squadrons (οὐλαμοί) of fifty, which may possibly be the same divisions. The cavalry seems merely to have been employed to protect the flanks, and but little regard was paid to it. The corps of 300 ἱππεῖς formed a sort of body-guard for the king, and consisted of the flower of the young soldiers. Though called horsemen, they fought on foot. A Spartan army, divided as above described, was drawn up in the dense array of the phalanx, the depth of which depended upon circumstances. An ἐνωμοτία sometimes made but a single file, sometimes was drawn up in three or six files (ζυγά). The enomotarch stood at the head of his file (πρωτοστάτης), or at the head of the right-hand file, if the enomotia was broken up into more than one. The last man was called οὐραγός. It was a matter of great importance that he, like the enomotarch, should be a man of strength and skill, as in certain evolutions he would have to lead the movements. The commander-in-chief, who was usually the king, had his station sometimes in the centre, more commonly on the right wing. The commands of the general were issued in the first place to the polemarchs, by these to the lochagi, by these again to the pentecosteres, by the latter to the enomotarchs, and by these last to their respective divisions. From the orderly manner in which this was done, commands were transmitted with great rapidity: every soldier, in fact, regulating the movements of the man behind him, every two being connected together as πρωτοστάτης and ἐπιστάτης. In later times the king was usually accompanied by two ephors, as controllers and advisers. These, with the polemarchs, the four Pythii, three peers (ὅμοιοι), who had to provide for the necessities of the king in war, the laphyropolae and some other officers, constituted what was called the damosia of the king. The Spartan hoplites were accompanied in the field by helots, partly in the capacity of attendants, partly to serve as light-armed troops. The number attached to an army was probably not uniform. At Plataeae each Spartan was accompanied by seven helots; but that was probably an extraordinary case. One helot in particular of those attached to each Spartan was called his θεράπων, and performed the functions of an armourer or shieldbearer. Xenophon calls them ὑπασπισταί. In extraordinary cases, helots served as hoplites, and in that case it was usual to give them their liberty. A separate troop in the Lacedaemonian army was formed by the Sciritae (Σκιρῖται), originally, no doubt, inhabitants of the district Sciritis. The arms of the phalanx consisted of the long spear and a short sword (ξυήλη). The chief part of the defensive armour was the large brazen shield, which covered the body from the shoulder to the knee, suspended, as in ancient times, by a thong round the neck, and managed by a simple handle or ring (πόρπαξ). Besides this, they had the ordinary armour of the hoplite [ARMA.] The heavy-armed soldiers wore a scarlet uniform. The Spartan encampments were circular. Only the heavy-armed were stationed within them, the cavalry being placed to look out, and the helots being kept as much as possible outside. Preparatory to a battle the Spartan soldier dressed his hair and crowned himself as others would do for a feast. The signal for attack was given not by the trumpet, but by the music of flutes, and sometimes also of the lyre and cithara, to which the men sang the battle song (παιάν ἐμβατήριος). The object of the music was not so much to inspirit the men, as simply to regulate the march of the phalanx. This rhythmical regularity of movement was a point to which the Spartans attached great importance.

2. *Athenian Army.*—In Athens, the military system was in its leading principles the same as among the Spartans, though differing in detail, and carried out with less exactness; inasmuch as when Athens became powerful, greater attention was paid to the navy. Of the four classes into which the citizens were arranged by the constitution of Solon, the citizens of the first and second served as cavalry, or as commanders of the infantry (still it need not be assumed that the ἱππεῖς never served as heavy-armed infantry), those of the third class (ζευγῖται) formed the heavy-armed infantry. The Thetes served either as light-armed troops on land, or on board the ships. The same general principles remained when the constitution was remodelled by Cleisthenes. The cavalry service continued to be compulsory on the wealthier class. Every citizen was liable to service from his eighteenth to his sixtieth year. On reaching their eighteenth year, the young citizens were formally enrolled εἰς τὴν ληξιαρχικὸν γραμματεῖον, and received a shield and spear in a public assembly of the people, binding themselves by oath to perform rightly the duties of a citizen and a soldier. During the first two years, they were only liable to service in Attica itself, chiefly as garrison soldiers in the different fortresses in the country. During this period, they were called περίπολοι. Members of the senate during the period of their office, farmers of the revenue, choreutae at the Dionysia during the festival, in later times, traders by sea also, were exempted from military service. Any one bound to serve who attempted to avoid doing so, was liable to a sentence of ἀτιμία. The resident aliens commonly served as heavy-armed soldiers, especially for the purpose of garrisoning the city. They were prohibited from serving as cavalry. Slaves were only employed as soldiers in cases of great necessity. Of the details of the Athenian military organisation, we have no distinct accounts as we have of those of Sparta. The heavy-armed troops, as was the universal practice in Greece, fought in phalanx order. They were arranged in bodies in a manner dependent on the political divisions of the citizens. The soldiers of each tribe (φυλή) formed a separate body in the army, also called a tribe, and these bodies stood in some preconcerted order. It seems that the name of one division was τάξις, and of another λόχος, but in what relations these stood to the φυλή, and to each other, we do not learn. Every hoplite was accompanied by an attendant (ὑπηρέτης) to take charge of his baggage, and carry his shield on a march. Each horseman also had a servant, called ἱπποκόμος, to attend to his horse. For the command of the army, there were chosen every year ten generals [STRATEGI], and ten taxiarchs [TAXIARCHI], and for the cavalry, two hipparchs (ἵππαρχοι) and ten phylarchs (φύλαρχοι). Respecting the military functions of the ἄρχων πολέμαρχος, see the article ARCHON. The number of strategi sent with an army was not uniform. Three was a common number. Sometimes one was invested with the supreme command; at other times, they either took the command in turn (as at Marathon), or conducted their operations by common consent (as in the Sicilian expedition). The practice of paying the troops when upon service was first introduced by Pericles. The pay consisted partly of wages (μισθός), partly of provisions, or, more commonly, provision-money (σιτηρέσιον). The ordinary μισθός of a hoplite was two obols a day. The σιτηρέσιον amounted to two obols more. Hence, the life of a soldier was called, proverbially, τετρωβόλου βίος. Officers received twice as much; horsemen, three times; generals, four times as much. The horsemen received pay even in time of peace, that they might always be in readiness, and also a sum of money for their outfit (κατάστασις). As regards the military strength of the Athenians, we find 10,000 heavy-armed soldiers at Marathon, 8,000 heavy armed, and as many light armed at Plataeae; and at the beginning of the Peloponnesian war there were 18,000 heavy armed ready for foreign service, and 16,000 consisting of those beyond the limits of the ordinary military age and of the metoeci, for garrison service. It was the natural result of the national character of the Athenians and their democratical constitution, that military discipline was much less stringent among them than among the Spartans, and after defeat especially it was often found extremely difficult to maintain it. The generals had some power of punishing military offences on the spot, but for the greater number of such offences a species of court-martial was held, consisting of persons who had served in the army to which the offender belonged, and presided over by the strategi. Various rewards also were held out for those who especially distinguished themselves in

their courage or conduct, in the shape of chaplets, statues, &c. The Peltastae (πελτασταί), so called from the kind of shield which they wore (PELTA), were a class of troops of which we hear very little before the end of the Peloponnesian war. The Athenian general Iphicrates introduced some important improvements in the mode of arming them, combining as far as possible the peculiar advantages of heavy (ὁπλῖται) and light armed (ψιλοί) troops. He substituted a linen corslet for the coat of mail worn by the hoplites, and lessened the shield, while he doubled the length of the spear and sword. He even took the pains to introduce for them an improved sort of shoe, called after him Ἰφικρατίδες. This equipment proved very effective. The almost total destruction of a mora of Lacedaemonian heavy-armed troops by a body of peltastae under the command of Iphicrates was an exploit that became very famous. When the use of mercenary troops became general, Athenian citizens seldom served except as volunteers, and then in but small numbers. The employment of mercenaries led to considerable alterations in the military system of Greece. War came to be studied as an art, and Greek generals, rising above the old simple rules of warfare, became tacticians. Epaminondas was the first who adopted the method of charging in column, concentrating his attack upon one point of the hostile line, so as to throw the whole into confusion by breaking through it.

3. *Macedonian Army*.—Philip, king of Macedonia, made several improvements in the arms and arrangement of the phalanx. The spear (σάρισσα or σάρισα), with which the soldiers of the Macedonian phalanx were armed, was 24 feet long; but the ordinary length was 21 feet, and the lines were arranged at such distances that the spears of the fifth rank projected three feet beyond the first, so that every man in the front rank was protected by five spears. Besides the spear they carried a short sword. The shield was very large and covered nearly the whole body, so that on favourable ground an impenetrable front was presented to the enemy. The soldiers were also defended by helmets, coats of mail, and greaves; so that any thing like rapid movement was impossible. The ordinary depth of the phalanx was sixteen files, though depths of eight and of thirty-two are also mentioned. Each file of sixteen was called λόχος. Two lochi made a *dilochia*; two dilochiae made a τετραρχία, consisting of sixty-four men; two tetrarchies made a τάξις; two τάξεις a σύνταγμα or ξεναγία, to which were attached five supernumeraries, a herald, an ensign, a trumpeter, a servant, and an officer to bring up the rear (οὐραγός); two syntagmata formed a pentacosiarchia, two of which made a χιλιαρχία, containing 1024 men; two chiliarchies made a τέλος, and two τέλη made a phalangarchia or phalanx in the narrower sense of the word, the normal number of which would therefore be 4096. It was commanded by a polemarch or strategus; four such bodies formed the larger phalanx, the normal number of which would be 16,384. When drawn up, the two middle sections constituted what was termed the ὀμφαλός, the others being called κέρατα or wings. The phalanx soldiers in the army of Alexander amounted to 18,000, and were divided not into four, but into six divisions, each named after a Macedonian province, from which it was to derive its recruits. These bodies are oftener called τάξεις than φάλαγγες by the historians, and their leaders taxiarchs or strategi. The phalanx of Antiochus consisted of 16,000 men, and was formed into ten divisions (μέρη) of 1600 each, arranged 50 broad and 32 deep. The phalanx, of course, became all but useless, if its ranks were broken. It required, therefore, level and open ground, so that its operations were restricted to very narrow limits; and being incapable of rapid movement, it became almost helpless in the face of an active enemy, unless accompanied by a sufficient number of cavalry and light troops. The light armed troops were arranged in files (λόχοι) eight deep. Four lochi formed a σύστασις, and then larger divisions were successively formed, each being the double of the one below it; the largest (called ἐπίταγμα), consisting of 8192 men. The cavalry (according to Aelianus), were arranged in an analogous manner, the lowest division or squadron (ἴλη), containing 64 men, and the successive larger divisions being each the double of that below it; the highest (ἐπίταγμα) containing 4096. Both Philip and Alexander attached great importance to the cavalry, which, in their armies, consisted partly of Macedonians, and partly of Thessalians. The Macedonian horsemen were the flower of the young nobles. They amounted to about 1200 in number, forming eight squadrons, and, under the name ἑταῖροι, formed a sort of body-guard for the king. The Thessalian cavalry consisted chiefly of the élite of the wealthier class of the Thessalians, but included also a number of Grecian youth from other states. There was also a guard of foot soldiers (ὑπασπισταί), whom we find greatly distinguishing themselves in the campaigns of Alexander. They seem to be identical with the πεζέταιροι, of whom we find mention. They amounted to about 3000 men, arranged in six battalions (τάξεις). There was also a

troop called Argyraspids, from the silver with which their shields were ornamented. They seem to have been a species of peltastae. Alexander also organised a kind of troops called διμάχαι, who were something intermediate between cavalry and infantry, being designed to fight on horseback or on foot, as circumstances required. It is in the time of Alexander the Great, that we first meet with artillery in the train of a Grecian army. His *balistae* and *catapeltae* were frequently employed with great effect, as, for instance, at the passage of the Jaxartes.

(2) ROMAN. *General Remarks on the Legion.*—The name *Legio* is coeval with the foundation of Rome, and denoted a body of troops, which, although subdivided into several smaller bodies, was regarded as forming an organised whole. It was not equivalent to what we call a *regiment*, inasmuch as it contained troops of all arms, infantry, cavalry, and, when military engines were extensively employed, artillery also; it might thus, so far, be regarded as a complete *army*, but on the other hand the number of soldiers in a legion was fixed within certain limits, never much exceeding 6000, and hence when war was carried on upon a large scale, a single army, under the command of one general, frequently contained two, three, or more legions, besides a large number of auxiliaries of various denominations. The legion for many centuries was composed exclusively of Roman citizens. By the ordinances of Servius Tullius those alone who were enrolled in the five classes were eligible, and one of the greatest changes introduced by Marius (B.C. 107) was the admission of all orders of citizens, including the lowest, into the ranks. Up to the year B.C. 107, no one was permitted to serve among the regular troops of the state, except those who were regarded as possessing a strong personal interest in the stability of the commonwealth; but the principle having been at this period abandoned, the privilege was extended after the close of the Social War (B.C. 87) to nearly the whole of the free population of Italy, and by the famous edict of Caracalla (or perhaps of M. Aurelius), to the whole Roman world. Long before this, however, the legions were raised chiefly in the provinces; but it does not appear that the admission of foreigners not subjects was ever practised upon a large scale until the reign of the second Claudius (A.D. 268—270), who incorporated a large body of vanquished Goths, and of Probus (A.D. 276—282), who distributed 16,000 Germans among legionary and frontier battalions. From this time forward what had originally been the leading characteristic of the legion was rapidly obliterated, so that under Diocletian, Constantine, and their successors, the best soldiers in the Roman armies were barbarians. The practice of granting pensions for long service in the shape of donations of land was first introduced upon a large scale after the Mithridatic wars. Hence, when Augustus, in compliance with the advice of Maecenas, determined to provide for the security of the distant provinces, and for tranquil submission at home by the establishment of a powerful standing army, he found the public mind in a great degree prepared for such a measure, and the distinction between soldier and civilian unknown, or at least not recognised before, became from this time forward as broadly marked as in the most pure military despotisms of ancient or modern times. The legions were originally numbered according to the order in which they were raised. As they became permanent, the same numbers remained attached to the same corps, which were moreover distinguished by various epithets of which we have early examples in the *Legio Martia*, and the *Legio Quinta Alauda*. [ALAUDA.] Several legions bore the same number: thus there were four *Firsts*, five *Seconds*, and five *Thirds*. The total number of legions under Augustus was twenty-five, under Alexander Severus thirty-two, but during the civil wars the number was far greater.—The number of soldiers who, at different periods, were contained in a legion, does not appear to have been absolutely fixed, but to have varied within moderate limits. Under Romulus the legion contained 3000 foot soldiers. It is highly probable that some change may have been introduced by Servius Tullius, but, in so far as numbers are concerned, we have no evidence. From the expulsion of the Kings until the second year of the second Punic War, the regular number may be fixed at 4000 or 4200 infantry. From the latter period until the consulship of Marius the ordinary number may be fixed at from 5000 to 5200. For some centuries after Marius the numbers varied from 5000 to 6200, generally approaching to the higher limit. Amid all the variations with regard to the infantry, 300 horsemen formed the regular complement (*justus equitatus*) of the legion. When troops were raised for a service which required special arrangements, the number of horsemen was sometimes increased beyond 300. It must be observed, however, that these remarks with regard to the cavalry apply only to the period before Marius. We now proceed to consider the organisation of the legion at five different periods.

First Period. Servius Tullius. The legion of Servius is so closely connected with the Comitia Centuriata that it has already been discussed in a former article [COMITIA], and it is only necessary to repeat here that it was a phalanx equipped in the Greek fashion, the front ranks being furnished with a complete suit of armour, their weapons being long spears, and their chief defence the round Argolic shield (*clipeus*).

Second Period. The Great Latin War, B.C. 340. Our authority for this period is Livy (viii. 8). The legion in B.C. 340 had almost entirely discarded the tactics of the phalanx. It was now drawn up in three, or perhaps we ought to say, in five lines. The soldiers of the first line, called *Hastati*, consisted of youths in the first bloom of manhood distributed into 15 companies or maniples (*manipuli*), a moderate space being left between each. The maniple contained 60 privates, 2 centurions (*centuriones*), and a standard bearer (*vexillarius*); two thirds were heavily armed and bore the *scutum* or large oblong shield, the remainder carried only a spear (*hasta*) and light javelins (*gaesa*). The second line, the *Principes*, was composed of men in the full vigour of life, divided in like manner into 15 maniples, all heavily armed (*scutati omnes*). The two lines of the *Hastati* and *Principes* taken together amounted to 30 maniples, and formed the *Antepilani*. The third line, the *Triarii*, composed of tried veterans, was also in 15 divisions, but each of these was triple, containing 3 manipuli, 180 privates, 6 centurions, and 3 vexillarii. In these triple manipuli the veterans or *triarii* proper formed the front ranks; immediately behind them stood the *Rorarii*, inferior in age and prowess, while the *Accensi* or supernumeraries, less trustworthy than either, were posted in the extreme rear. The battle array may be thus represented. The fight was commenced by the *Rorarii*, so

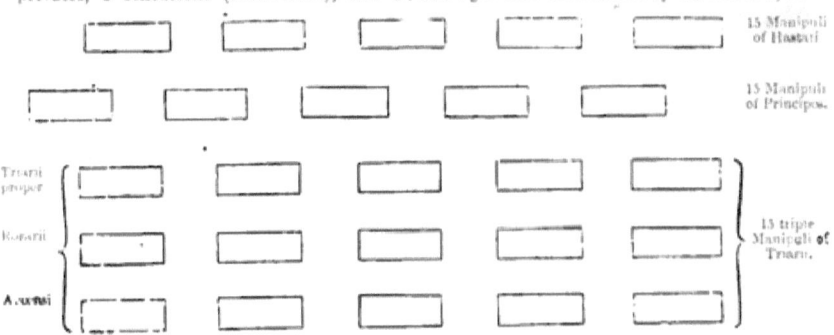

called because the light missiles which they sprinkled among the foe were like the drops which are the forerunners of the thunder shower, who, running forwards between the ranks of the antepilani, acted as tirailleurs; when they were driven in they returned to their station behind the triarii, and the battle began in earnest by the onset of the hastati; if they were unable to make any impression they retired between the ranks of the principes, who now advanced and bore the brunt of the combat, supported by the hastati, who had rallied in their rear. If the principes also failed to make an impression, they retired through the openings between the maniples of the triarii, who up to this time had been crouched on the ground (hence called *subsidiarii*), but now arose to make the last effort (whence the phrase *rem ad triarios redisse*). No longer retaining the open order of the two first lines, they closed up their ranks so as to present an unbroken line of heavy-armed veterans in front, while the rorarii and accensi, pressing up from behind, gave weight and consistency to the mass,—an arrangement bearing evidence to a lingering predilection for the principle of the phalanx, and exhibiting, just as we might expect at that period, the Roman tactics in their transition state. It must be observed that the words *ordo*, *manipulus*, *vexillum*, although generally kept distinct, are throughout the chapter used as synonymous. Livy concludes by saying, that four legions were commonly levied, each consisting of 5000 infantry and 300 horse. We must suppose that he speaks in round numbers in so far as the infantry are concerned, for according to his own calculations the numbers will stand thus:—

Hastati	15 × 60	= 900
Principes	15 × 60	= 900
Triarii, &c.	15 × 3 × 60	= 2700
Centuriones	. . .	= 150
Vexillarii	. . .	= 75
		4725

Third Period. During the wars of the younger Scipio. Polybius describes minutely the method pursued in raising the four legions during this period. Under ordinary circumstances they were levied yearly, two being assigned to each consul. It must be observed that a regular consular army (*justus consularis exercitus*) no longer consisted of Roman legions only, but as Italy became gradually subjugated, the various states under the dominion of Rome were bound to furnish a contingent, and the number of allies (*socii*) usually exceeded that of citizens. They were, however, kept perfectly distinct, both in the camp and in the battle field. After the election of consuls was concluded, the first step was to choose the 24 chief officers of the legions, named *tribuni militum*. The consuls then summoned to the Capitol all citizens eligible for military service. They first divided the 24 tribunes into 4 parties of 6, and the tribes were next summoned in succession by lot. The tribe whose lot came out first being called up, they picked out from it four youths, as nearly matched as possible in age and form; out of these four, the tribunes of the first legion chose one, the tribunes of the second legion one of the remaining three; the tribunes of the third legion, one of the remaining two, and the last fell to the fourth legion. Upon the next tribe being called up, the first choice was given to the tribunes of the second legion, the second choice to those of the third, and the last man fell to the first legion. On the next tribe being called up, the tribunes of the third legion had the first choice, and so on in succession, the object in view being that the four legions should be as nearly alike as possible, not in the number only, but in the quality of the soldiers. This process was continued until the ranks were complete. In ancient times, the cavalry were not chosen until after the infantry levy was concluded, but when Polybius wrote, the cavalry were picked in the first place from the list on which they were enrolled by the censor according to their fortune, and 300 were apportioned to each legion. The levy being completed, the tribunes collected the men belonging to their respective legions, and making one individual stand out from the rest administered to him an oath "that he would obey orders and execute to the best of his ability the command of his officers." (*Sacramento milites adigere* s. *rogare, sacramentum* s. *sacramento dicere.*) The rest of the soldiers then came forward one by one, and swore to do what the first had bound himself to perform. At the same time the consuls gave notice to the magistrates of those towns in Italy in alliance with Rome, from whom they desired to receive a contingent, of the number which each would be required to furnish, and of the day and place of gathering. The allied cities levied their troops and administered the oath much in the same manner as the Romans, and then sent them forth after appointing a commander and a paymaster. The soldiers having again assembled, the men belonging to each legion were separated into four divisions. 1. 1000 of the youngest and poorest were set apart to form the *Velites*, the light-armed troops, or skirmishers of the legion. 2. 1200 who came next in age (or who were of the same age with the preceding but more wealthy), formed the *Hastati*. 3. 1200, consisting of those in the full vigour of manhood, formed the *Principes*. 4. 600, consisting of the oldest and most experienced, formed the *Triarii*. When the number of soldiers in the legion exceeded 4000, the first three divisions were increased proportionally, but the number of the Triarii remained always the same. The Hastati, Principes, and Triarii were each divided into ten companies, called *Manipuli*. The Velites were not divided into companies, but were distributed equally among the Hastati, Principes, and Triarii. Before the division of the three classes into maniples, officers were appointed inferior to the tribunes. 30 men were chosen by merit, 10 from the Hastati, 10 from the Principes, and 10 from the Triarii; and this first choice being completed, 30 more in like manner. These 60 officers, of whom 20 were assigned to each of the three classes, and distributed equally among the maniples, were named *centuriones*, or *ordinum ductores*, and each of the 60 chose for himself a Lieutenant (*optio*), who, being posted in the rear of the company while the centurion was at the head, was named οὐραγός (i. e. *Tergiductor*) by the Greeks, so that in each maniple there were two centurions and two optiones. Further, the centurions selected out of each maniple two of the bravest and most vigorous men as standard bearers (*vexillarii, signiferi*). The first elected centurion of the whole had a seat in the military council, and in each maniple the first chosen commanded the right division of the maniple, and the other the left. Each of these subdivisions of the maniple was called *centuria*. The cavalry were divided into 10 troops (*turmae*), and out of each of these 3 officers were chosen, named *decuriones*, who named 3 lieutenants (*optiones*). In each troop the decurio first chosen commanded the whole troop, and failing him, the second. The infantry furnished by the *socii* was for the most part equal in number to the Roman legions, the cavalry twice or thrice as numerous, and the whole were divided equally between the two consular armies. Each consul named twelve superior officers, who were termed *Praefecti Sociorum*, and corresponded to the legionary tribunes. A selection was then made of the best men, to the extent of one-fifth of the infantry and one-third of the cavalry ; these were formed into a separate corps under the name of *extraordinarii*, and on the march and in the camp were always near the person of the consul. The remainder were divided into two equal portions, and were styled respectively the *Dextera Ala* and the *Sinistra Ala* [ALA].—*Agmen* or *Line of March*. The Extraordinarii Pedites led the van followed by the right wing of the infantry of the allies and the baggage of these two divisions ; next came one of the Roman legions with its baggage following ; next the other Roman legion with its own baggage, and that of the left wing of the allies, who brought up the rear. The different corps of cavalry sometimes followed immediately behind the infantry to which they were attached, sometimes rode on the flanks of the beasts of burden, at once protecting them and preventing them from straggling. Generally, when advancing through a country in which it was necessary to guard against a sudden onset, the troops, instead of proceeding in a loose straggling column, were kept together in close compact bodies ready to act in any direction at a moment's warning, and hence an army under these circumstances was said *agmine quadrato incedere*. Some doubt exists with regard to the force of the term *Agmen Pilatum* as distinguished from *Agmen Quadratum*. Varro defines the *agmen pilatum* as a compact body marching without beasts of burthen. Where the phrase occurs in poetry, it probably denotes merely "columns bristling with spears." To the preceding particulars from Polybius, the following may be added.

1. *The levy (delectus.)* According to the principles of the constitution, none were enrolled in the legion, except freeborn citizens (*ingenui*) above the age of 17, and under the age of 60, possessing not less than 4000 asses ; but in times of peculiar difficulty, these conditions were not insisted upon. In such times all formalities were dispensed with, and every man capable of bearing arms was summoned to join in warding off the threatened danger, a force raised under such circumstances being termed *subitarius s. tumultuarius exercitus*. If citizens between the ages of 17 and 46 did not appear and answer to their names, they might be punished in various ways,—by fine, by imprisonment, by stripes, by confiscation of their property, and even, in extreme cases, by being sold as slaves. At the same time, causes might be alleged which were recognised as forming a legitimate ground for exemption (*vacatio justa militiae*). Thus, all who had served for the full period of 20 years were relieved from further service, although they might still be within the regular age ; and so, in like manner, when they were afflicted by any grievous malady, or disabled by any personal defect, or engaged in any sacred or civil offices which required their constant attendance ; but these and similar pleas, although sustained under ordinary circumstances, might be rendered void by a decree of the senate "ne vacationes valerent." While those who had served for the stipulated period were entitled to immunity for the future, even although within the legal age, and were styled *Emeriti*, so on the other hand, it appears from some passages in the classics, that persons who had not completed their regular term within the usual limits, might be forced, if required, to serve between the ages of 45 and 50. Towards the close of the republic, and under the empire, when the legions became permanent, the soldier who had served his full time received a regular discharge (*missio*), together with a bounty (*praemium*) in money or an allotment of land. The jurists distinguish three kinds of discharge :—1. *Missio honesta*, granted for length of service. 2. *Missio causaria*, in consequence of bad health. 3. *Missio ignominiosa*, when a man was drummed out for bad conduct. It frequently happened that *emeriti* were induced to continue in the ranks, either from attachment to the person of the general, or from hopes of profit or promotion, and were then called *veterani*, or when they joined an army, in consequence of a special invitation, *evocati*.

2. The division of the legion into *Cohortes, Manipuli, Centuriae, Signa, Ordines, Contubernia*.—(i.) *Cohortes*. Polybius takes no notice of the *Cohort*, a division of the legion often mentioned in the Roman writers. When the soldiers of the legion were classified as Velites, Hastati, Principes and Triarii, the cohort contained one maniple of each of the three latter denominations, together with their complement of Velites, so that when the legion contained 4000, each cohort would consist of 60 Triarii, 120 Principes, 120 Hastati, and 100 Velites, in all 400 men. The number of cohorts in a legion being always 10, and the cohorts, during the republic, being all equal to each other, the strength of the cohort varied from time to time with the strength of the legion, and thus at different periods ranged between the

limits of 300 and 600. They were regularly numbered from 1 to 10, the centurion of the first century of the first maniple of the first cohort was the guardian of the eagle, and hence the first cohort seems always to have been regarded as superior in dignity to the rest. Late writers, instead of *cohortes*, prefer the somewhat vague term *numeri*, which appears in Tacitus and Suetonius, and perhaps even in Cicero. *Numeri* seems to have signified strictly the muster roll, whence the phrases *referre in numeros, distribuere in numeros*, and thus served to denote any body of legionaries. Whenever *Cohors* occurs in the Latin classics in connection with the legion, it always signifies a specific division of the legion; but it is very frequently found, in the general sense of *battalion*, to denote troops altogether distinct from the legion.—(ii.) *Manipulus*. The original meaning of this word, which is derived from *manus*, was *a handful or wisp of hay*, straw, fern, *or the like*, and this, according to Roman tradition, affixed to the end of a pole, formed the primitive military standard in the days of Romulus. Hence it was applied to a body of soldiers serving under the same ensign. When the phalanx was resolved into small companies marshalled in open order, these were termed *manipuli*, and down to a very late period the common soldiers of the legion were designated as *manipulares* or *manipularii*, terms equivalent to *gregarii milites*. When the phalanx was first broken up, it appears that each of the three classes of Hastati, Principes, and Triarii, contained 15 maniples; but before the second Punic war the number of maniples in each of these classes was reduced to 10. Hence it is easy to calculate the number of soldiers in each maniple, according to the varying numbers in the legion, it being always borne in mind that the Triarii never exceeded 600, and that the Velites were not divided into maniples, but distributed equally among the heavy-armed companies.—(iii.) *Centuriae*. The distribution of soldiers into *centuriae* must be regarded as coeval with the origin of Rome. Plutarch speaks of the force led by Romulus against Amulius as formed of centuries; and from the close connections between the centuries of Servius Tullius, and the organization of the military force, we cannot hesitate to believe that the term was communicated to the ranks of the phalanx. For a long period after the establishment of the manipular constitution, the legion contained 60 centuries.—(iv.) *Signum*. This word is used to denote a division of the legion, but it is doubtful whether it signifies a maniple or a century.—(v.) *Ordo* generally signifies a century, and *ordinum ductor* is synonymous with *centurio*, and *ducere honestum ordinem* means to be one of the principal centurions in a legion.—(vi.) *Contubernium*. This was the name given under the empire to the body of soldiers who were quartered together in the same tent.

3. *Hastati, Principes, Triarii, Pilani, Antepilani, Antesignani, Principia*.— The *Hastati* were so called, from having been armed with a *hasta*, the *Principes* from having occupied the front line, the *Triarii*, otherwise named *Pilani*, from having been ranged behind the first two lines as a body of reserve and armed with the *pilum*, while the first two lines were termed collectively *Antepilani*, from standing in front of the *Pilani*. In process of time, it came to pass, that these designations no longer expressed the actual condition of the troops to which they were attached. When Polybius wrote, and long before that period, the *Hastati* were not armed with *hastae*, but in common with the *Principes* bore the heavy *pilum:* on the other hand, the *pilani* carried *hastae* and not *pila*, while the *Principes* were not drawn up in the front, but formed the second line.—*Antesignani*. While the Hastati and Principes, taken together, were sometimes termed *Antepilani*, in contradistinction to the Triarii, so the Hastati alone were sometimes termed *Antesignani*, in contradistinction to the Principes and Triarii taken together. The term *Antesignani* having become established as denoting the front ranks in a line of battle, was retained in this general sense long after the Hastati, Principes, and Triarii had disappeared.—Another term employed to denote the front ranks of an army in battle array is *Principia*, and in this sense must be carefully distinguished from the *Principia* or chief street in the camp, and from *Principia*, which in the later writers, such as Ammianus and Vegetius, is equivalent to *principales milites*. *Postsignani* does not occur in any author earlier than Ammianus Marcellinus, and therefore need not be illustrated here; the *Subsignanus miles* of Tacitus seems to be the same with the *Vexillarii*.

4. *Rorarii, Accensi, Ferentarii, Velites, Procubitores*.—When the Hastati had, in a great measure, ceased to act as tirailleurs, their place was supplied by the *Rorarii*, whose method of fighting has been described above (p. 165). The *Accensi*, as described by Livy, were inferior in equipment to the rorarii, although employed in a similar manner, and seem to have been camp-followers or servants, and hence the name is given to those also who attended upon magistrates or other officials. At a later period the *accensi*

were supernumeraries, who served to fill up any vacancies which occurred in the course of a campaign. Another ancient term for light-armed soldiers was *Ferentarii*. The *Velites*, called also *Procubitores*, because they were employed on outpost duty when the Romans were encamped before an enemy, were first formed into a corps at the siege of Capua, B.C. 211.

5. *Officers of the Legion.*—*Tribuni Militum* were the chief officers of the legion. Their number (six) did not vary for many centuries. They were originally chosen by the commanders-in-chief, that is, by the kings in the first instance, and afterwards by the consuls, or a dictator, as the case might be. In B.C. 361 the people assumed to themselves the right of electing either the whole or a certain number; and in B.C. 311 it was ordained that they should choose sixteen for the four legions. In subsequent times the choice of the tribunes was divided between the consuls and the people; but the proportion chosen by each differed at various periods. No one was eligible to the office of tribune who had not served for ten years in the infantry or five in the cavalry; but this rule admitted of exceptions. Augustus introduced certain regulations altogether new. He permitted the sons of senators to wear the *tunica laticlavia* as soon as they assumed the manly gown, and to commence their military career as tribunes, or as commanders (*praefecti*) of cavalry. Such persons were the *Tribuni Laticlarii.*—*Centuriones.* Next in rank to the Tribunus was the *Centurio*, who, as the name implies, commanded a century; and the century, being termed also *ordo*, the centurions were frequently designated *ordinum ductores* (hence, *adimere ordines, offerre ordines, ordines impetrare, ducere honestum ordinem*, to be one of the principal centurions, &c.). The chief ordinary duties of the centurions were to drill the soldiers, to inspect their arms, clothing, and food, to watch the execution of the toils imposed, to visit the centinels, and to regulate the conduct of their men, both in the camp and in the field. They also sat as judges in minor offences, and had the power of inflicting corporal punishment, whence their badge of office was a vine sapling, and thus *vitis* is frequently used to denote the office itself. Of the two centurions in each maniple the one first chosen took the command of the right division, the other of the left. The century to the right was considered as the first century of the maniple, and its commander took precedence probably with the title *Prior*, his companion to the left being called *Posterior*, the *priores* in each of the three divisions of Triarii, Principes, and Hastati being the ten centurions first chosen. So long as these divisions were recognised, all the centurions of the Triarii appear to have ranked before those of the Principes, and all the centurions of the Principes before those of the Hastati. Moreover, since the maniples were numbered in each division from 1 to 10, there was probably a regular progression from the first centurion of the first maniple down to the second centurion of the tenth maniple. The first centurion of the first maniple of the Triarii, originally named *Centurio Primus*, and afterwards *Centurio Primipili*, or simply *Primipilus*, occupied a very conspicuous position. He stood next in rank to the Tribuni militum; he had a seat in the military council; to his charge was committed the eagle of the legion, whence he is sometimes styled *Aquilifer*, and, under the empire at least, his office was very lucrative. A series of terms connected with these arrangements are furnished by the narrative which Sp. Ligustinus gives of his own career (Liv. xlii. 34). He thus enumerates the various steps of his promotion:—" Mihi T. Quinctius Flamininus *decumum ordinem hastatum* adsignavit . . . me imperator dignum judicavit cui *primum hastatum prioris centuriae* adsignaret . . . a M'. Acilio mihi *primus princeps prioris centuriae* est adsignatus . . . quater intra paucos annos *primum pilum duxi.*" The gradual ascent from the ranks being to the post of centurion:—1. In the tenth maniple of the Hastati. 2. In the first century of the first maniple of the Hastati. 3. In the first century of the first maniple of the Principes. 4. In the first century of the first maniple of the Triarii.—But even after the distinction between Hastati, Principes, and Triarii was altogether abolished, and they were all blended together in the cohorts, the same nomenclature with regard to the centuries and their commanders was retained, although it is by no means easy to perceive how it was applied. That great differences of rank existed among the centurions is evident from the phrases *primores centurionum, primi ordines* (i.e. chief centurions), as opposed to *inferiores ordines*, and *infimi ordines*, and that promotion from a lower to a higher grade frequently took place, is evident from many passages in ancient authors. The election of *optiones*, or lieutenants, by the centurions, has been already described.

Fourth Period. From the times of the Gracchi until the downfall of the Republic. After the times of the Gracchi the following changes in military affairs may be noticed:—In the first consulship of Marius the legions were thrown open to citizens of all grades, without distinction of fortune. The whole of the legionaries were armed and equipped in the same manner, all being now furnished with the pilum; and hence we see in Tacitus the *pila* and *gladii* of the legionaries, opposed to the *hastae* and *spathae* of the auxiliaries. The legionaries when in battle order were no longer arranged in three lines, each consisting of ten maniples, with an open space between each maniple, but in two lines, each consisting of five cohorts, with a space between each cohort. The younger soldiers were no longer placed in the front, but in reserve, the van being composed of veterans, as may be seen from various passages in Caesar. As a necessary result of the above arrangements, the distinction between Hastati, Principes, and Triarii ceased to exist. These names, as applied to particular classes of soldiers, are not found in Caesar, in Tacitus, nor in any writer upon military affairs after the time of Marius. The Velites disappeared. The skirmishers, included under the general term *levis armatura*, consisted for the most part of foreign mercenaries possessing peculiar skill in the use of some national weapon, such as the Balearic slingers, (*funditores*), the Cretan archers (*sagittarii*), and the Moorish dartmen (*jaculatores*). Troops of this description had, it is true, been employed by the Romans even before the second Punic war, and were denominated *levium armatorum* (s. *armorum*) *auxilia*; but now the *levis armatura* consisted exclusively of foreigners, were formed into a regular corps under their own officers, and no longer entered into the constitution of the legion. When operations requiring great activity were undertaken, such as could not be performed by mere skirmishers, detachments of legionaries were lightly equipped, and marched without baggage, for these special services; and hence the frequent occurrence of such phrases as *expediti, expediti milites, expeditae cohortes*, and even *expeditae legiones*. The cavalry of the legion underwent a change in every respect analogous to that which took place in regard of the light armed troops. It is evident, from the history of Caesar's campaigns in Gaul, that the number of Roman equites attached to his army was very small, and that they were chiefly employed as aides-de-camp, and on confidential missions. The bulk of Caesar's cavalry consisted of foreigners, a fact which becomes strikingly apparent when we read that Ariovistus having stipulated that the Roman general should come to their conference attended by cavalry alone, Caesar, feeling no confidence in his Gaulish horse, dismounted them, and supplied their place by soldiers of the tenth legion. In like manner they ceased to form part of the legion, and from this time forward we find the legions and the cavalry spoken of as completely distinct from each other. After the termination of the Social War, when most of the inhabitants of Italy became Roman citizens, the ancient distinction between the *Legiones* and the *Socii* disappeared, and all who had served as *Socii* became incorporated with the legiones. An army during the last years of the republic and under the earlier emperors consisted of *Romanae Legiones et Auxilia* s. *Auxiliares*, the latter term comprehending troops of all kinds, except the legions. Whenever the word *socii* is applied to troops after the date of the Social War, it is generally to be regarded as equivalent to *auxiliares*. But the most important change of all was the establishment of the military *profession*, and the distinction now first introduced between the civilian and the soldier.

Fifth Period. From the establishment of the empire until the age of the Antonines, B.C. 31—A.D. 150. Under the empire a regular army consisted of a certain number of *Legiones* and of *Supplementa*, the Supplementa being again divided into the imperial guards, which appear under several different forms, distinguished by different names; and the *Auxilia*, which were subdivided into *Sociae Cohortes* and *Nationes*, the latter being for the most part barbarians. The *Legiones*, as already remarked, although still composed of persons who enjoyed the privileges of Roman citizens, were now raised almost exclusively in the provinces. The legion was divided into 10 cohorts, and each cohort into 6 centuries; the first cohort, which had the custody of the eagle, was double the size of the others, and contained 960 men, the remaining cohorts contained each 480 men; and consequently each ordinary century 80 men, the total strength of the legion being thus 5280 men.—It is during this period that we first meet with the term *Vexillarii* or *Vexilla*, which occurs repeatedly in Tacitus. The *vexillarii*, or *vexilla legionum*, were those soldiers who, after having served in the legion for sixteen years, became *exauctorati*, but continued to serve in company with that legion, under a vexillum of their own, until they received their full discharge. The number attached to each legion was usually about five or six hundred.—The term *exauctorare* also meant *to discharge from military service*, but does not appear to have been in use before the Augustan period. It signified both a simple discharge, and a cashiering on account of some crime. During the later period of the empire the latter signification began almost exclusively to prevail.—As to the Praetorian troops, see PRAETORIANI.—From the time when the cavalry were separated from the legion they were formed into bodies called *alae*, which varied in number according to circumstances. The *Alae* were raised in the Roman provinces and consisted, probably, for the most part, of citizens, or at least subjects. But in addition to these every army at this period was attended by squadrons of light horse composed entirely of barbarians; and the chief duty performed by those named above was guiding the pioneers as they performed their labours in advance of the army.—*Cohortes peditatae*, were battalions raised chiefly in the provinces, composed of Roman citizens, of subjects and allies, or of citizens, allies, and subjects indiscriminately. To this class of troops belonged the *cohortes auxiliares*, the *auxilia cohortium*, and the *sociorum cohortes*, of whom we read in Tacitus, together with a multitude of others recorded in inscriptions and named for the most part from the nations of which they were composed. These cohorts were numbered regularly like the legions.—*Cohortes Equitatae* differed from the *Peditatae* in this only, that they were made up of infantry combined with cavalry.—*Classici*, which we may fairly render *Marines*, were employed, according to Hyginus, as pioneers. They corresponded to the *Navales Socii*, under the republic, who were always regarded as inferior to regular soldiers. After the establishment by Augustus of regular permanent fleets at Misenum, Ravenna, and on the coast of Gaul, a large body of men must have been required to man them, who were sometimes called upon to serve as ordinary soldiers.—*Nationes* were battalions composed entirely of barbarians, or of the most uncivilised among the subjects of Rome, and were probably chiefly employed upon outpost duties. —*Urbanae Cohortes*. Augustus, in addition to the praetorian cohorts, instituted a force of city guards, amounting to 6000 men divided into four battalions. They are usually distinguished as *Cohortes Urbanae* or *Urbana militia*, their quarters, which were within the city, being the *Urbana Castra*.—*Cohortes Vigilum*. Augustus also organised a large body of night-watchers, whose chief duty was to act as firemen. They were divided into seven cohorts, in the proportion of one cohort to each two *Regiones*, were stationed in fourteen guardhouses (*excubitoria*), and called *Cohortes Vigilum*. They were commanded by a *Praefectus*, who was of equestrian rank.

EXĪLIUM. [EXSILIUM.]

EXŎDĬA (ἐξόδια, from ἐξ and ὁδός) were old-fashioned and laughable interludes in verse, inserted in other plays, but chiefly in the Atellanae. The exodium seems to have been introduced among the Romans from Italian Greece; but after its introduction it became very popular among the Romans, and continued to be played down to a very late period.

EXŌMIS (ἐξωμίς), a dress which had only a sleeve for the left arm, leaving the right with the shoulder and a part of the breast free, and was for this reason called *exomis*. The exomis was usually worn by slaves and working people.

Exomis (Bronze in British Museum).

EXŌMŎSĬA (ἐξωμοσία). Any Athenian citizen when called upon to appear as a witness in a court of justice (κλητεύειν or ἐκκλητεύειν), was obliged by law to obey the summons, unless he could establish by oath that he was unacquainted with the case in question. This oath was called ἐξωμοσία, and the act of taking it was expressed by ἐξόμνυσθαι. A person appointed to a public office was at liberty to decline it, if he could take an oath that the state of his health or other circumstances rendered it impossible for him to fulfil the duties connected with it (ἐξόμνυσθαι τὴν ἀρχὴν, or τὴν χειροτονίαν): and this oath was likewise called ἐξωμοσία, or sometimes ἀπωμοσία.

EXOSTRA (ἔξωστρα, from ἐξωθέω), a theatrical machine, by means of which things which had been concealed behind the curtain on the stage were pushed or rolled forward from behind it, and thus became visible to the spectators.

EXPĔDĪTUS is opposed to *impeditus*, and signifies unincumbered with armour or with baggage (*impedimenta*). Hence the epithet was often applied to any portion of the Roman army, when the necessity for haste, or the desire to conduct it with the greatest facility from place to place, made it desirable to leave behind every weight that could be spared.

EXPLŌRĀTŌRES. [SPECULATORES.]

EXSEQUIAE. [FUNUS.]

EXSILIUM (φυγή), banishment. (1) GREEK. Banishment among the Greek states seldom, if ever, appears as a punishment appointed by law for particular offences. We might, indeed, expect this, for the division of Greece into a number of independent states would neither admit of the establishment of penal colonies, as among us, nor of the various kinds of exile which we read of under the Roman emperors. The general term φυγή (flight) was for the most part applied in the case of those who, in order to avoid some punishment or danger, removed from their own country to another. At Athens it took place chiefly in cases of homicide, or murder. An action for wilful murder was brought before the Areiopagus, and for manslaughter before the court of the Ephetae. The accused might, in either case, withdraw himself (φεύγειν) before sentence was passed; but when a criminal evaded the punishment to which an act of murder would have exposed him had he remained in his own land, he was then banished for ever (φεύγει ἀειφυγίαν), and not allowed to return home even when other exiles were restored upon a general amnesty. Demosthenes says, that the word φεύγειν was properly applied to the exile of those who committed murder with malice aforethought, whereas the term μεθίστασθαι was used where the act was not intentional. The property also was confiscated in the former case, but not in the latter. When a verdict of manslaughter was returned, it was usual for the convicted party to leave his country by a certain road, and to remain in exile till he induced some one of the relatives of the slain man to take compassion on him. We are not informed what were the consequences if the relatives of the slain man refused to make a reconciliation; supposing that there was no compulsion, it is reasonable to conclude that the exile was allowed to return after a fixed time. Plato, who is believed to have copied many of his laws from the constitution of Athens, fixes the period of banishment for manslaughter at one year.—Under φυγή, or banishment, as a general term, is comprehended *Ostracism* (ὀστρακισμός). Those that were ostracised did not lose their property, and the time, as well as place of their banishment, was fixed.

This ostracism is supposed by some to have been instituted by Cleisthenes, after the expulsion of the Peisistratidae; its nature and object are thus explained by Aristotle:— "Democratical states (he observes) used to ostracise, and remove from the city for a definite time, those who appeared to be preeminent above their fellow-citizens, by reason of their wealth, the number of their friends, or any other means of influence." Ostracism, therefore, was not a punishment for any crime, but rather a precautionary removal of those who possessed sufficient power in the state to excite either envy or fear. Thus Plutarch says, it was a good-natured way of allaying envy by the humiliation of superior dignity and power. The manner of effecting it at Athens was as follows:—A space in the *agora* was enclosed by barriers, with ten entrances for the ten tribes. By these the tribesmen entered, each with his *ostracon* (ὄστρακον), or piece of tile (whence the name *ostracism*), on which was written the name of the individual whom he wished to be ostracised. The nine archons and the senate, *i. e.* the presidents of that body, superintended the proceedings, and the party who had the greatest number of votes against him, supposing that this number amounted to 6000, was obliged to withdraw (μεταστῆναι) from the city within ten days; if the number of votes did not amount to 6000, nothing was done. Some of the most distinguished men at Athens were removed by ostracism, but recalled when the city found their services indispensable. Among these were Themistocles, Aristeides, and Cimon, son of Miltiades. The last person against whom it was used at Athens was Hyperbolus, a demagogue of low birth and character; but the Athenians thought their own dignity compromised, and ostracism degraded by such an application of it, and accordingly discontinued the practice.—From the ostracism of Athens was copied the *Petalism* (πεταλισμός) of the Syracusans, so called from the πέταλον, or leaf of the olive, on which was written the name of the person whom they wished to remove from the city. The removal, however, was only for five years; a sufficient time, as they thought, to humble the pride and hopes of the exile. In connection with petalism it may be remarked, that if any one were falsely registered in a demus, or ward, at Athens, his expulsion was called ἐκφυλλοφορία, from the votes being given by leaves. Besides those exiled by law, or ostracised, there was frequently a great number of political exiles in Greece; men who, having distinguished themselves as the leaders of one party, were expelled, or obliged to remove from their native city, when the opposite faction became predominant. They are spoken of as οἱ φεύγοντες or οἱ ἐκπεσόντες, and as οἱ κατελθόντες after their return (ἡ κάθοδος) the word κατάγειν being applied to those who were instrumental in effecting it.—(2) ROMAN. Banishment as a punishment did not exist in the old Roman state. The *aquae et ignis interdictio*, which we so frequently read of in the republican period, was in reality not banishment, for it was only a ban, pronounced by the people (by a *lex*), or by a magistrate in a criminal court, by which a person was deprived of water and of fire; that is, of the first necessaries of life; and its effect was to incapacitate a person from exercising the rights of a citizen; in other words, to deprive him of his citizenship. Such a person might, if he chose, remain at Rome, and submit to the penalty of being an outcast, incapacitated from doing any legal act, and liable to be killed by any one with impunity. To avoid these dangers, a person suffering under such an interdict would naturally withdraw from Rome, and in the earlier republican period, if he withdrew to a state between which and Rome isopolitical relations existed, he would become a citizen of that state. This right was called *jus exsulandi* with reference to the state to which the person came; with respect to his own state, which he left, he was *exsul*, and his condition was *exsilium*; and with respect to the state which he entered, he was *inquilinus*.* In the same way a citizen of such a state had a right of going into exsilium at Rome; and at Rome he might attach himself (*applicare se*) to a quasi-patronus. Exsilium, instead of being a punishment, would thus rather be a mode of evading punishment; but towards the end of the republic the *aquae et ignis interdictio* became a regular banishment, since the sentence usually specified certain limits, within which a person was interdicted from fire and water. Thus Cicero was interdicted from fire and water within 400 miles from the city. The punishment was inflicted for various crimes, as *vis publica, peculatus, veneficium,* &c. Under the empire there were two kinds of exsilium; *exsilium* properly so called, and *relegatio*; the great distinction between the two was, that the former deprived a person of his citizenship, while the latter did not. The distinction between *exsilium* and *relegatio* existed under the republic. Ovid also describes himself, not as *exsul*, which he considers a term of reproach, but as *relegatus*. The chief species of exsilium was the *deportatio in insulam* or *deportatio* simply, which was introduced under the emperors in place of the *aquae et ignis interdictio*. The *relegatio* merely confined the person within, or excluded him from particular places. In the latter case it was called *fuga lata*, **fuga libera**, or *liberum exsilium*. The **relegatus** went into banishment; the *deportatus* was conducted to his place of banishment, sometimes in chains.

EXTISPEX. [HARUSPEX.]
EXTRAORDINARII. [EXERCITUS, p. 167.]

FABRI are workmen who make anything out of hard materials, as *fabri tignarii*, carpenters, *fabri aerarii*, smiths, &c. The different trades were divided by Numa into nine collegia, which correspond to our companies or guilds. In the constitution of Servius Tullius, the *fabri tignarii* and the *fabri aerarii* or *ferrarii* were formed into two centuries, which were called the centuriae *fabrûm* (not *fabrorum*). They did not belong to any of the five classes into which Servius divided the people; but the *fabri tign.* probably voted with the first class, and the *fabri aer.* with the second. The fabri in the army were under the command of an officer called *praefectus fabrûm*.

FABULA. [COMOEDIA.]
FALARICA. [HASTA.]
FALSUM. The oldest legislative provision at Rome against Falsum was that of the Twelve Tables against false testimony. The next legislation on Fulsum, so far as we know, was a Lex Cornelia, passed in the time of the Dictator Sulla against forging, concealing, destroying, or committing any other fraudulent act respecting a will or other instrument. The offence was a Crimen Publicum, and, under the emperors, the punishment was deportatio in insulam for the "honestiores;" and the mines or crucifixion for the "humiliores."

FALX, dim. FALCULA (ἄρπη, δρέπανον, poet. δρεπάνη, dim. δρεπάνιον), a sickle; a scythe; a pruning-knife; a falchion, &c. As *Culter* denoted a knife with one straight edge, *falx* signified any similar instrument, the single edge of which was curved. Some of its forms are given in the annexed cut. One represents Perseus with the falchion in his right hand, and the head of Medusa in his left. The two smaller figures are heads

---

* This word appears, by its termination *inus*, to denote a person who was one of a class, like the word *libertinus*. The prefix *in* appears to be the correlative of *ex* in *exsul*, and the remaining part *quil* is probably related to *col* in *incola* and *colonus*.

of Saturn with the falx in its original form; and the fourth represents the same divinity at full length.

Falx. (From ancient Cameos.)

FĂMĬLĬA. The word *familia* contains the same element as the word *famulus*, a slave, and the verb *famulari*. In its widest sense it signifies the totality of that which belongs to a Roman citizen who is sui juris, and therefore a paterfamilias. Thus, in certain cases of testamentary disposition, the word *familia* is explained by the equivalent *patrimonium*; and the person who received the familia from the testator was called *familiae emptor*. But the word *familia* is sometimes limited to signify "persons," that is, all those who are in the power of a paterfamilias, such as his sons (*filii-familias*), daughters, grand-children, and slaves. Sometimes *familia* is used to signify the slaves belonging to a person, or to a body of persons (*societas*).

FĀNUM. [TEMPLUM.]

FARTOR, a slave who fattened poultry.

FASCES, rods bound in the form of a bundle, and containing an axe (*securis*) in the middle, the iron of which projected from them. They were usually made of birch, but sometimes also of the twigs of the elm. They are said to have been derived from Vetulonia, a city of Etruria. Twelve were carried before each of the kings by twelve lictors; and on the expulsion of the Tarquins, one of the consuls was preceded by twelve lictors with the fasces and secures, and the other by the same number of lictors with the fasces only, or, according to some accounts, with crowns around them. But P. Valerius Publicola, who gave to the people the right of provocatio, ordained that the secures should be removed from the fasces, and allowed only one of the consuls to be preceded by the lictors while they were at Rome. The other consul was attended only by a single accensus [ACCENSUS]. When they were out of Rome, and at the head of the army, each of the consuls retained the axe in the fasces, and was preceded by his own lictors, as before the time of Valerius. The fasces and secures were, however, carried before the dictator even in the city, and he was also preceded by twenty-four lictors, and the magister equitum by six. The practors were preceded in the city by two lictors with the fasces; but out of Rome and at the head of an army by six, with the fasces and secures. The tribunes of the plebs, the aediles and quaestors, had no lictors in the city, but in the provinces the quaestors were permitted to have the fasces. The lictors carried the fasces on their shoulders; and when an inferior magistrate met one who was higher in rank, the lictors lowered their fasces to him. This was done by Valerius Publicola, when he addressed the people, and hence came the expression *submittere fasces* in the sense of to yield, to confess one's self inferior to another. When a general had gained a victory, and had been saluted as Imperator by his soldiers, he usually crowned his fasces with laurel.

Fasces. (From the original in the Capitol at Rome.)

FASCIA, a band or fillet of cloth, worn, (1) round the head as an ensign of royalty; —(2) by women over the breast;—(3) round the legs and feet, especially by women. When the toga had fallen into disuse, and the shorter pallium was worn in its stead, so that the legs were naked and exposed, *fasciae crurales* became common even with the male sex.

FASCINUM (βασκανία), fascination, enchantment. The belief that some persons had the power of injuring others by their looks, was prevalent among the Greeks and Romans. The evil eye was supposed to injure children particularly, but sometimes cattle also; whence Virgil (*Ecl.* iii. 103) says,

"Nescio quis teneros oculos mihi fascinat agnum."

Various amulets were used to avert its influence.

FASTI. *Fas* signifies *divine law:* the epithet *fastus* is properly applied to anything in accordance with divine law; and hence those days upon which legal business might, without impiety (*sine piaculo*), be transacted before the praetor, were technically denominated *fasti dies*, i. e. *lawful days*. The sacred books in which the *fasti dies* of the year were marked were themselves denominated *fasti*; the term, however, was employed to denote registers of various descriptions. Of these the two principal are the *Fasti Sacri* or *Fasti Kalendares*, and *Fasti Annales* or *Fasti Historici*.—1. FASTI SACRI or KALENDARES. For nearly four centuries and a half after the foundation of the city a knowledge of the calendar was possessed exclusively by the priests. One of the pontifices regularly proclaimed the appearance of the new moon, and at the same time announced the period which would intervene between the Kalends and the Nones. On the Nones the country people assembled for the purpose of learning from the *rex sacrorum* the various festivals to be celebrated during the month, and the days on which they would fall. In like manner all who wished to go to law were obliged to inquire of the privileged few on what day they might bring their suit, and received the reply as if from the lips of an astrologer. The whole of this lore, so long a source of power and profit, and therefore jealously enveloped in mystery, was at length made public by a certain Cn. Flavius, scribe to App. Claudius; who, having gained access to the pontifical books, copied out all the requisite information, and exhibited it in the forum for the use of the people at large. From this time forward such tables became common, and were known by the name of *Fasti*. They usually contained an enumeration of the months and days of the year; the Nones, Ides, Nundinae, Dies Fasti, Nefasti, Comitiales, Atri, &c., together with the different festivals, were marked in their proper places: astronomical observations on the risings and settings of the fixed stars, and the commencement of the seasons were frequently inserted. [CALENDARIUM; DIES.]—II. FASTI ANNALES or HISTORICI. Chronicles such as the *Annales Maximi*, containing the names of the chief magistrates for each year, and a short account of the most remarkable events noted down opposite to the days on which they occurred, were, from the resemblance which they bore in arrangement to the sacred calendars, denominated *fasti*; and hence this word is used, especially by the poets, in the general sense of *historical records*. In prose writers *fasti* is commonly employed as the technical term for the registers of consuls, dictators, censors, and other magistrates, which formed part of the public archives. Some most important *fasti* belonging to this class, executed probably at the beginning of the reign of Tiberius, have been partially preserved, and are deposited in the Capitol in Rome, where they are known by the name of the *Fasti Capitolini*.

FASTIGIUM. An ancient Greek or Roman temple, of rectangular construction, is terminated at its upper extremity by a triangular figure, both in front and rear, which rests upon the cornice of the entablature as a base, and has its sides formed by the cornices which terminate the roof. The whole of this triangle above the trabeation is implied in the term *fastigium*, called ἀέτωμα by the Greeks, pediment by our architects.

Fastigium. (From a Coin.)

The dwelling-houses of the Romans had no gable ends; consequently when the word is applied to them, it is not in its strictly technical sense, but designates the roof simply, and is to be understood of one which rises to an apex, as distinguished from a flat one. The fastigium, properly so called, was appropriated to the temples of the gods; therefore, when the Romans began to bestow divine honours upon Julius Caesar, amongst other privileges which they decreed to him, was the liberty of erecting a fastigium to his house, that is, a portico and pediment towards the street, like that of a temple.

FAX (φανός), a torch. As the principal use of torches was to give light to those who went abroad after sunset, the portion of the Roman day immediately succeeding sun-set was called *fax* or *prima fax*. The use of torches after sun-set, and the practice of celebrating marriages at that time, probably led to the consideration of the torch as one of the necessary accompaniments and symbols of marriage. Among the Romans the *fax nuptialis* having been lighted at the parental hearth, was carried before the bride by a boy whose parents were alive. The torch was also carried at funerals (*fax sepulchralis*), both because these were often nocturnal ceremonies, and because it was used to set fire to the pile.

FECIĀLES. [FETIALES.]

FEMINĀLIA, worn in winter by Augustus Caesar, who was very susceptible of cold. It seems probable that they were breeches resembling ours.

FENESTRA. [DOMUS.]

FENUS or FOENUS (τόκος), interest of money.—(1) GREEK. At Athens there was no restriction upon the rate of interest. A rate might be expressed or represented in two different ways: (1.) by the number of oboli or drachmae paid by the *month* for every *mina*; (2) by the part of the principal (τὸ ἀρχαῖον or κεφάλαιον) paid as interest either annually or for the whole period of the loan. According to the former method, which was generally used when money was lent upon real security (τόκοι ἔγγυοι or ἔγγειοι), different rates were expressed as follows:—10 per cent. by ἐπὶ πέντε ὀβολοῖς, *i. e.* 5 oboli per month for every mina, or 60 oboli a year = 10 drachmae = $\frac{1}{10}$ of a mina. Similarly,

12 per cent. by ἐπὶ δραχμῇ   per month.
16 per cent. ,, ἐπ' ὀκτὼ ὀβολοῖς   ,,
18 per cent. ,, ἐπ' ἐννέα ὀβολοῖς   ,,
24 per cent. ,, ἐπὶ δυσὶ δραχμαῖς   ,,
36 per cent. ,, ἐπὶ τρισὶ δραχμαῖς   ,,
5 per cent. ,, ἐπὶ τρίτῳ ἡμιοβολίῳ, probably.

Another method was generally adopted in cases of bottomry (τὸ ναυτικόν, τόκοι ναυτικοί, or ἔκδοσις), where money was lent upon the ship's cargo or freightage (ἐπὶ τῷ ναύλῳ), or the ship itself, for a specified time, commonly that of the voyage. By this method the following rates were thus represented:— 10 per cent. by τόκοι ἐπιδέκατοι, *i. e.* interest at the rate of a tenth; 12½, 16⅔, 20, 33⅓, by τόκοι ἐπόγδοοι, ἔφεκτοι, ἐπίπεμπτοι, and ἐπίτριτοι, respectively. The usual rates of interest at Athens about the time of Demosthenes varied from 12 to 18 per cent.—(2) ROMAN. Towards the close of the republic, and also under the emperors, 12 per cent. was the legal rate of interest. The interest became due on the first of every month hence the phrases *tristes* or *celeres calendae* and *calendarium*, the latter meaning a debt-book or book of accounts. The rate of interest was expressed in the time of Cicero, and afterwards, by means of the as and its divisions, according to the following table:—

Asses usurae, or one as per month for the use of one hundred		= 12 per cent.
Deunces usurae	 11	,,
Dextantes ,,	 10	,,
Dodrantes ,,	 9	,,
Besses ,,	 8	,,
Septunces ,,	 7	,,
Semisses ,,	 6	,,
Quincunces ,,	 5	,,
Trientes ,,	 4	,,
Quadrantes ,,	 3	,,
Sextantes ,,	 2	,,
Unciae ,,	 1	,,

Instead of the phrase *asses usurae*, a synonyme was used, viz. *centesimae usurae*, inismuch as at this **rate of** interest there was **paid in a hundred months a sum equal to the whole principal.** Hence *binae centesimae* = 24 per cent., and *quaternae centesimae* = 48 per cent. The monthly rate of **the centesimae** was of foreign origin, **and first** adopted at Rome in the time of Sulla. The old *yearly* rate established **by the Twelve** Tables (B. C. 450) was the *unciarium fenus*. The *uncia* was the twelfth part **of the as,** and since the full (12 oz.) copper coinage was still in use at Rome when the Twelve Tables became law, the **phrase** *unciarium* **fenus** would be a **natural expression for interest of** one ounce **in the pound**; *i.e.* **a twelfth part** of the **sum borrowed, or** $8\frac{1}{3}$ **per cent., not per** month, **but per year. This rate, if calculated** for the old **Roman year** of ten **months, would** give **10 per cent. for the civil year of twelve months, which was in common use in the** time of the decemvirs. **If a debtor could** not pay the principal and **interest at the end** of the year, he used to **borrow money from a fresh creditor, to pay off his old debt. This proceeding was** very frequent, and **called a** *versura*. It amounted **to little short of paying** compound interest, **or an** *anatocismus anniversarius*, **another phrase for which was** *usurae renovatae*; *e.g. centesimae renovatae* **is 12** per cent. compound **interest, to which Cicero** opposes *centesimae perpetuo fenore* = 12 per cent. simple interest. **The following** phrases are of common occurrence **in connection with borrowing and lending money at interest:**—*Pecuniam apud aliquem collocare*, to lend money at interest; *relegere*, **to** call it in again; *cavere*, to give security **for** it; *opponere* or *opponere pignori*, to give **as a** pledge or mortgage. The word *nomen* is also of extensive use in money transactions. Properly it denoted the name of a **debtor,** registered in a banker's or any other account-book: hence it came to signify the articles of an account, a debtor, or a debt itself. Thus **we have** *bonum nomen*, a good **debt;** *nomina facere*, to lend monies, **and also to borrow** money.

FĒRĀLIA. [FUNUS, p. 191, a.]

FERCŬLUM (from *fer-o*) is applied to any kind of tray **or** platform used for carrying anything. Thus **it** is used to signify the tray or frame **on which** several dishes were brought in **at once at** dinner; and **hence** *fercula* came **to mean the number of courses** at dinner, and **even the** dishes themselves. The ferculum was **also** used for carrying the images of the gods **in the** procession of **the** circus, the ashes **of the dead** in a funeral, and the spoils **in a triumph; in all which** cases it appears **to have** been carried on the shoulders or in the hands of men.

FĒRĒTRUM. [FUNUS.]

FĒRIAE, holidays, were, generally speaking, **days or seasons during which free-born Romans suspended their political transactions and their law-suits, and during which slaves enjoyed a cessation from labour. All feriae** were **thus** *dies nefasti*. The **feriae included** all days consecrated to any **deity; consequently** all **days on** which public festivals **were celebrated** were feriae or dies feriati. **But some of** them, such as the feria **vindemialis, and the** feriae aestivae, seem to have **had no direct connection** with the **worship of the gods. The** nundinae, however, **during the time of the kings and the** early period **of the republic, were feriae only** for the **populus, and days of** business **for the plebeians, until, by the Hortensian law, they became fasti or days of business for both orders. All** *feriae publicae, i. e.* those **which were observed by the whole nation, were divided into** *feriae* **stativae,** *feriae conceptivae*, **and** *feriae imperativae*. *Feriae stativae* or *statae* were those **which were held** regularly, **and on certain days marked in the calendar. To these belonged some of the great** festivals, **such as the Agonalia, Carmentalia,** Lupercalia, **&c.** *Feriae conceptivae* or *conceptae* **were held every year, but not on certain or fixed days, the time being every year appointed by the magistrates or priests. Among these** we may **mention the feriae Latinae, feriae** Sementivae, Paganalia, **and Compitalia.** *Feriae imperativae* **were those which were** held on certain **emergencies at** the **command of the** consuls, **praetors, or** of a **dictator. The manner in which all public feriae were kept** bears great analogy to the observance **of** our Sunday. The people visited **the temples of** the gods, and offered up their **prayers and** sacrifices. The most serious and solemn seem to have been the feriae **imperativae, but all** the others were generally **attended with** rejoicings and feasting. **All kinds of** business, especially law-suits, **were suspended during the public feriae, as** they were considered to pollute the sacred season. The most important of the holidays designated by the name of feriae, are the *Feriae Latinae*, **or simply** *Latinae* **(the** original **name** was *Latiar*), **which were said to have been** instituted by the last Tarquin in commemoration **of the alliance between the Romans** and Latins. **This festival, however, was** of much **higher antiquity; it was a** panegyris, or a **festival, of the whole Latin** nation, celebrated on the Alban **mount; and** all that the last Tarquin did was **to convert the** original Latin festival into a Roman one, and to make it the means of hallowing and cementing the alliance between the two nations. Before the union, the chief magistrate of the Latins had presided at the festival; but Tarquin now assumed this distinction, which subsequently, after the destruction of the Latin commonwealth, remained with the chief magistrates of Rome. The object of this panegyris on the Alban mount was the worship of Jupiter Latiaris, and, at least as long as the Latin republic existed, to deliberate and decide on matters of the confederacy, and to settle any disputes which might have arisen among its members. As the feriae Latinae belonged to the conceptivae, the time of their celebration greatly depended on the state of affairs at Rome, since the consuls were never allowed to take the field until they had held the Latinae. This festival was a great engine in the hands of the magistrates, who had to appoint the time of its celebration (*concipere, edicere,* or *indicere Latinas*); as it might often suit their purpose either to hold the festival at a particular time or to delay it, in order to prevent or delay such public proceedings as seemed injurious and pernicious, and to promote others to which they were favourably disposed. The festival lasted six days.

FESCENNINA, scil. *carmina*, one of the earliest kinds of Italian poetry, which consisted of rude and jocose verses, or rather dialogues of extempore verses, in which the merry country folks assailed and ridiculed one another. This amusement seems originally to have been peculiar to country people, but it was also introduced into the towns of Italy and at Rome, where we find it mentioned as one of those in which young people indulged at weddings.

FETIALES or FECIALES, a college of Roman priests, who acted as the guardians of the public faith. It was their province, when any dispute arose with a foreign state, to demand satisfaction, to determine the circumstances under which hostilities might be commenced, to perform the various religious rites attendant on the solemn declaration of war, and to preside at the formal ratification of peace. When an injury had been received from a foreign state, four fetiales were deputed to seek redress, who again elected one of their number to act as their representative. This individual was styled the *pater patratus populi Romani*. A fillet of white wool was bound round his head, together with a wreath of sacred herbs gathered within the inclosure of the Capitoline hill (*Verbenae; Sagmina*), whence he was sometimes named *Verbenarius*. Thus equipped, he proceeded to the confines of the offending tribe, where he halted, and addressed a prayer to Jupiter, calling the god to witness, with heavy imprecations, that his complaints were well founded and his demands reasonable. He then crossed the border, and the same form was repeated in nearly the same words to the first native of the soil whom he might chance to meet; again a third time to the sentinel or any citizen whom he encountered at the gate of the chief town; and a fourth time to the magistrates in the forum in presence of the people. If a satisfactory answer was not returned within thirty days, after publicly delivering a solemn denunciation of what might be expected to follow, he returned to Rome, and, accompanied by the rest of the fetiales, made a report of his mission to the senate. If the people, as well as the senate, decided for war, the pater patratus again set forth to the border of the hostile territory, and launched a spear tipped with iron, or charred at the extremity and smeared with blood (emblematic doubtless of fire and slaughter), across the boundary, pronouncing at the same time a solemn declaration of war. The demand for redress, and the proclamation of hostilities, were alike termed *clarigatio*. The whole system is said to have been borrowed from the Aequicolae or the Ardeates, and similar usages undoubtedly prevailed among the Latin states. The number of the fetiales cannot be ascertained with certainty, but they were probably twenty. They were originally selected from the most noble families, and their office lasted for life.

FIBULA (περόνη, πόρπη), a brooch or buckle, consisting of a pin (*acus*), and of a curved portion furnished with a hook (κλείς).

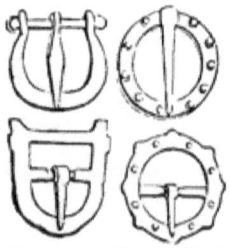

Fibulae, brooches or buckles. (British Museum.)

FICTILE (κέραμος, κεράμιον, ὄστρακον, ὀστράκινον), earthenware, a vessel or other article made of baked clay. The instruments used in pottery (*ars figulina*) were the following:—1. The wheel (τροχός, *urbis, rota, rota figularis*). 2. Pieces of wood or bone, which the potter (κεραμεύς, *figulus*) held in his right hand, and applied occasionally to the surface of the clay during its revolution. 3. Moulds (*formae*, τύποι), used either to decorate with figures in relief vessels which had been thrown on the wheel, or to produce foliage, animals, or any other appearances, on Antefixa, on cornices of terra cotta, and imitative or ornamental pottery of all other kinds, in which the wheel was not adapted to give the first shape. 4. Gravers or scalpels, used by skilful modellers in giving to figures of all kinds a more perfect finish and a higher relief than could be produced by the use of moulds. The earth used for making pottery (κεράμικη γῆ), was commonly red, and often of so lively a colour as to resemble coral. Other pottery is brown or cream-coloured, and sometimes white. Some of the ancient earthenware is throughout its substance black, an effect produced by mixing the earth with comminuted asphaltum (*gagates*), or with some other bituminous or oleaginous substance. It appears also that asphaltum, with pitch and tar, both mineral and vegetable, was used to cover the surface like a varnish. The best pottery was manufactured at Athens, in the island of Samos, and in Etruria. A quarter of Athens was called Cerameicus, because it was inhabited by potters. Vessels, before being sent for the last time to the furnace, were sometimes immersed in that finely prepared mud, now technically called "slip," by which the surface is both smoothed and glazed, and at the same time receives a fresh colour. Ruddle, or red ochre (μίλτος, *rubrica*), was principally employed for this purpose. To produce a further variety in the paintings upon vases the artists employed a few brightly coloured earths and metallic ores. [PICTURA.]

FIDEICOMMISSUM may be defined to be a testamentary disposition, by which a person who gives a thing to another imposes on him the obligation of transferring it to a third person. The obligation was not created by words of legal binding force (*civilia verba*), but by words of request (*precativè*), such as *fideicommitto, peto, volo dari*, and the like; which were the operative words (*verba utilia*).

FIDUCIA. If a man transferred his property to another, on condition that it should be restored to him, this contract was called Fiducia, and the person to whom the property was so transferred was said *fiduciam accipere*. The trustee was bound to discharge his trust by restoring the thing: if he did not, he was liable to an actio fiduciae or fiduciaria, which was an actio bonae fidei. If the trustee was condemned in the action, the consequence was infamia.

FISCUS, the imperial treasury. Under the republic the public treasury was called *Aerarium*. [AERARIUM.] On the establishment of the imperial power, there was a division of the provinces between the senate, as the representative of the old republic, and the Caesar or emperor; and there was consequently a division of the most important branches of public income and expenditure. The property of the senate retained the name of *Aerarium*, and that of the Caesar, as such, received the name of *Fiscus*. The private property of the Caesar (*res privata principis, ratio Caesaris*) was quite distinct from that of the fiscus. The word fiscus signified a wicker-basket, or pannier, in which the Romans were accustomed to keep and carry about large sums of money; and hence fiscus came to signify any person's treasure or money chest. The importance of the imperial fiscus soon led to the practice of appropriating the name to that property which the Caesar claimed as Caesar, and the word fiscus, without any adjunct, was used in this sense. Ultimately the word came to signify generally the property of the state, the Caesar having concentrated in himself all the sovereign power, and thus the word fiscus finally had the same signification as aerarium in the republican period. Various officers, as Procuratores, Advocati, Patroni, and Praefecti, were employed in the administration of the fiscus.

FLABELLUM, *dim*. FLABELLULUM, (ῥιπίς), a fan. Fans were of elegant forms, of delicate colours, and sometimes of costly and splendid materials, such as peacock's feathers; but they were stiff and of a fixed shape, and were held by female slaves (*flabelliferae*), by beautiful boys, or by eunuchs, whose duty it was to wave them so as to produce a cooling breeze. Besides separate feathers the ancient fan was sometimes made of linen, extended upon a light frame.

FLAGRUM, *dim*. FLAGELLUM (μάστιξ), a whip, a scourge, to the handle of which was fixed a lash made of cords (*funibus*), or thongs of leather (*loris*), especially thongs made from the ox's hide (*bubulis exuviis*). The *flagellum* properly so called was a dread-

Flagellum, Scourge. (From a Bas-relief at Rome, and from a Coin.)

ful instrument, and is thus put in opposition to the *scutica*, which was a simple whip. (Hor. *Sat.* i. 3. 119.) Cicero in like manner contrasts the severe *flagella* with the *virgae*. The flagellum was chiefly used in the punishment of slaves. It was knotted with bones or heavy indented circles of bronze or terminated by hooks, in which case it was aptly denominated a *scorpion*. We likewise find that some gladiators fought with the flagella, as in the coin here introduced.

FLAMEN, the name for any Roman priest who was devoted to the service of one particular god, and who received a distinguishing epithet from the deity to whom he ministered. The most dignified were those attached to Dijovis, Mars, and Quirinus, the *Flamen Dialis*, *Flamen Martialis*, and *Flamen Quirinalis*. They are said to have been established by Numa. The number was eventually increased to fifteen: the three original flamens were always chosen from among the patricians, and styled *Majores*; the rest from the plebeians, with the epithet *Minores*. Among the minores, we read of the *Flamen Floralis*, the *Flamen Carmentalis*, &c. The flamens were elected originally at the Comitia Curiata, but it is conjectured that subsequently to the passing of the *Lex Domitia* (B. C. 104) they were chosen in the Comitia Tributa. After being nominated by the people, they were received (*capti*) and installed (*inaugurabantur*) by the pontifex maximus, to whose authority they were at all times subject. The office was understood to last for life; but a flamen might be compelled to resign (*flaminio abire*) for a breach of duty, or even on account of the occurrence of an ill-omened accident while discharging his functions. Their characteristic dress was the *apex* [APEX], the *laena* [LAENA], and a laurel wreath. The most distinguished of all the flamens was the *Dialis*; the lowest in rank the *Pomonalis*. The former enjoyed many peculiar honours. When a vacancy occurred, three persons of patrician descent, whose parents had been married according to the ceremonies of *confarreatio*, were nominated by the Comitia, one of whom was selected (*captus*), and consecrated (*inaugurabatur*) by the pontifex maximus. From that time forward he was emancipated from the control of his father, and became sui juris. He alone of all priests wore the *albogalerus*; he had a right to a *lictor*, to the *toga praetexta*, the *sella curulis*, and to a seat in the senate in virtue of his office. If one in bonds took refuge in his house, his chains were immediately struck off. To counterbalance these high honours, the dialis was subjected to a multitude of restrictions. It was unlawful for him to be out of the city for a single night; and he was forbidden to sleep out of his own bed for three nights consecutively. He might not mount upon horseback, nor even touch a horse, nor look upon an army marshalled without the pomoerium, and hence was seldom elected to the consulship. The object of the above rules was manifestly to make him literally *Jovi adsiduum sacerdotem*; to compel constant attention to the duties of the priesthood. *Flaminica* was the name given to the wife of the dialis. He was required to wed a virgin according to the ceremonies of *confarreatio*, which regulation also applied to the two other flamines majores; and he could not marry a second time. Hence, since her assistance was essential in the performance of certain ordinances, a divorce was not permitted, and if she died, the dialis was obliged to resign. The municipal towns also had their flamens. Thus the celebrated affray between Milo and Clodius took place while the former was on his way to Lanuvium, of which he was then dictator, to declare the election of a flamen (*ad flaminem prodendum*).

FLAMMEUM. [MATRIMONIUM.]

FLORALIA, or Florales Ludi, a festival which was celebrated at Rome in honour of Flora or Chloris, during five days, beginning on the 28th of April and ending on the 2nd of May. It was said to have been instituted at Rome in 238 B. C., at the command of an oracle in the Sibylline books, for the purpose of obtaining from the goddess the protection of the blossoms. The celebration was, as usual, conducted by the aediles, and was carried on with excessive merriment, drinking, and lascivious games.

FOCALE, a covering for the ears and neck, made of wool, and worn by infirm and delicate persons.

FOCUS, dim. FOCULUS (ἑστία, ἐσχάρα, ἐσχαρίς), a fire-place; a hearth; a brazier. The fire-place possessed a sacred character, and was dedicated among the Romans to the Lares of each family. Moveable hearths, or braziers, properly called *foculi*, were frequently used.

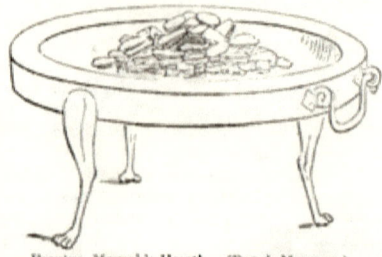

Foculus, Moveable Hearth. (British Museum.)

FOEDERĀTAE CĪVITĀTES, FOEDERĀTI, SŎCĪI. In the seventh century of Rome these names expressed those Italian states which were connected with Rome by a treaty (*foedus*). These names did not include Roman colonies or Latin colonies, or any place which had obtained the Roman civitas or citizenship. Among the *foederati* were the *Latini*, who were the most nearly related to the Romans, and were designated by this distinctive name; the rest of the foederati were comprised under the collective name of *Socii* or *Foederati*. They were independent states, yet under a general liability to furnish a contingent to the Roman army. Thus they contributed to increase the power of Rome, but they had not the privileges of Roman citizens. The discontent among the foederati, and their claims to be admitted to the privileges of Roman citizens, led to the Social War. The Julia Lex (B. C. 90) gave the civitas to the Socii and Latini; and a lex of the following year contained, among other provisions, one for the admission to the Roman civitas of those peregrini who were entered on the lists of the citizens of federate states, and who complied with the provisions of the lex. [CIVITAS.]

FOENUS. [FENUS.]

FOLLIS—(1) An inflated ball of leather, which boys and old men among the Romans threw from one to another as a gentle exercise of the body.—(2) A leather purse or bag.—(3) A pair of bellows, consisting of two inflated skins, and having valves ad-

Folles, Bellows. (From a Roman Lamp.)

justed to the natural apertures at one part for admitting the air, and a pipe inserted into another part for its emission.

FONS (κρήνη), a spring of water, and also an artificial fountain, made either by covering and decorating a spring with buildings and sculpture, or by making a jet or stream of water, supplied by an elevated cistern, play into an artificial basin. Such fountains served the double purpose of use and ornament. They were covered to keep them pure and cool, and the covering was frequently in the form of a monopteral temple: there were also statues, the subjects of which were suggested by the circumstance that every fountain was sacred to some divinity, or they were taken from the whole range of mythological legends. A very large proportion of

Fountain of Perseus at Corinth.

the immense supply of water brought to Rome by the aqueducts was devoted to the public fountains, which were divided into two classes; namely, *lacus*, ponds or reservoirs, and *salientes*, jets of water, besides which many of the castella were so constructed as to be also fountains. There were also many small private fountains in the houses and villas of the wealthy.

Fountain. (From a Painting at Pompeii.)

FŎRES. [DOMUS.]

FORNACĀLIA, a festival in honour of Fornax, the goddess of furnaces, in order that the corn might be properly baked. This ancient festival is said to have been instituted by Numa. The time for its celebration was proclaimed every year by the curio maximus, who announced in tablets, which were placed in the forum, the different part which each curia had to take in the celebration of the festival. Those persons who did not know to what curia they belonged performed the sacred rites on the *Quirinalia*, called from this circumstance the *Stultorum feriae*, which fell on the last day of the Fornacalia.

FORNIX, in its primary sense, is synonymous with ARCUS, but more commonly implies an arched vault, constituting both roof and ceiling to the apartment which it encloses.

FŎRUM. [See CLASSICAL DICT.]

FRĀMĔA. [HASTA.]

FRĀTRES ARVĀLES. [ARVALES FRATRES.]

FRĒNUM (χαλινός), a bridle. That Bellerophon might be enabled to perform the exploits required of him by the king of Lycia, he was presented by Athena with a bridle as the means of subduing the winged horse Pegasus, who submitted to receive it whilst he was slaking his thirst at the fountain Peirene. Such was the Grecian account of the invention of the bridle, and in reference to it

Athena was worshipped at Corinth under the titles Ἱππία and Χαλινῖτις. The bit (*orea*, δῆγ-

Pegasus receiving the Bridle.

μα, στόμιον), was commonly made of several pieces, and flexible, so as not to hurt the horse's mouth; although there was likewise a bit which was armed with protuberances resembling wolves' teeth, and therefore called *lupatum*.

FRĪGĬDĀRĬUM. [BALNEUM.]

FRĪTILLUS (φιμός), a dice-box of a cylindrical form, and therefore called also *turricula*, or *pyrgus*, and formed with parallel indentations (*gradus*) on the inside, so as to make a rattling noise when the dice were shaken in it.

FRŪMENTĀRĬAE LEGES. The supply of corn at Rome was considered one of the duties of the government. The superintendence of the corn-market belonged in ordinary times to the aediles, but when great scarcity prevailed, an extraordinary officer was appointed for the purpose under the title of *Praefectus Annonae*. Even in early times it had been usual for the state on certain occasions, and for wealthy individuals, to make occasional donations of corn to the people (*donatio, largitio, divisio*; subsequently called *frumentatio*). But such donations were only casual; and it was not till B. C. 123, that the first legal provision was made for supplying the poor at Rome with corn at a price much below its market value. In that year C. Sempronius Gracchus brought forward the first *Lex Frumentaria*, by which each citizen was entitled to receive every month a certain quantity of wheat (*triticum*) at the price of 6½ asses for the modius, which was equal to 1 gallon and nearly 8 pints English. This was only a trifle more than half the market price. Each person probably received five modii monthly, as in later times. About B. C. 91, the tribune M. Octavius brought forward the *Lex Octavia*, which modified the law of Gracchus to some extent, so that the public treasury did not suffer so much. Sulla went still further, and by his *Lex Cornelia*, B. C. 82, did away altogether with these distributions of corn; but in B. C. 73, the Lex Sempronia was renewed by the *Lex Terentia Cassia*, which enacted that each Roman citizen should receive 5 modii a month at the price of 6½ asses for each modius. The Leges Frumentariae had *sold* corn to the people; but by the *Lex Clodia* of the tribune Clodius, B. C. 58, the corn was distributed without any payment; the abolition of the payment cost the state a fifth part of its revenues. When Caesar became master of the Roman world, he resolved to remedy the evils attending the system, so far as he was able. He did not venture to abolish altogether these distributions of corn, but he did the next best thing in his power, which was reducing the number of the recipients. During the civil wars numbers of persons, who had no claim to the Roman franchise, had settled at Rome in order to obtain a share in the distributions. Caesar excluded from this privilege every person who could not prove that he was a Roman citizen; and thus the 320,000 persons, who had previously received the corn, were at once reduced to 150,000. The useful regulations of Caesar fell into neglect after his death; and in B.C. 5, the number of recipients had amounted to 320,000. But in B. C. 2, Augustus reduced the number of recipients to 200,000, and renewed many of Caesar's regulations. The chief of them seem to have been: 1. That every citizen should receive monthly a certain quantity of corn (probably 5 modii) on the payment of a certain small sum. Occasionally, in seasons of scarcity, or in order to confer a particular favour, Augustus made these distributions quite gratuitous; they then became *congiaria*. [CONGIARIUM.] 2. That those who were completely indigent should receive the corn gratuitously, and should be furnished for the purpose with *tesserae nummariae* or *frumentariae*, which entitled them to the corn without payment. The system which had been established by Augustus, was followed by his successors; but as it was always one of the first maxims of the state policy of the Roman emperors to prevent any disturbance in the capital, they frequently lowered the price of the public corn, and also distributed it gratuitously as a *congiarium*. Hence, the cry of the populace *panem et circenses*. In course of time, the sale of the corn by the state seems to have ceased altogether, and the distribution became altogether gratuitous. Every corn-receiver was therefore now provided with a *tessera*, and this tessera, when once granted to him, became his property. Hence it came to pass, that he was not only allowed to keep the tessera for life, but even to dispose of it by sale, and bequeath it by will. Every citizen was competent to hold a tessera, with the exception of senators. Further, as the corn had been originally distributed to the people according to the thirty-five tribes into which they were divided, the corn-receivers in each tribe formed a kind of corporation, which came eventually to be looked upon as the tribe, when the tribes had lost all political significance. Hence, the purchase of a tessera became equivalent to the purchase of a place in a tribe; and, accordingly, we find in the Digest the expressions *emere tribum* and *emere tesseram* used as synonymous. Another change was also introduced at a later period, which rendered the bounty still more acceptable to the people. Instead of distributing the corn every month, wheaten bread, called *annona civica*, was given to the people. It is uncertain at what time this change was introduced, but it seems to have been the custom before the reign of Aurelian (A. D. 270-275).

FRŪMENTĀRII, officers under the Roman empire, who acted as spies in the provinces, and reported to the emperors anything which they considered of importance. They appear to have been called *Frumentarii* because it was their duty to collect information in the same way as it was the duty of other officers, called by the same name, to collect corn.

FŪCUS (φῦκος), the paint which the Greek and Roman ladies employed in painting their cheeks, eye-brows, and other parts of their faces. The practice of painting the face was very general among the Greek ladies, and probably came into fashion in consequence of their sedentary mode of life, which robbed their complexions of their natural freshness, and induced them to have recourse to artificial means for restoring the red and white of nature. The eye-brows and eye-lids were stained black with στίμμι or στίμμις, a sulphuret of antimony, which is still employed by the Turkish ladies for the same purpose. The eye-brows were likewise stained with ἄσβολος, a preparation of soot. Among the Romans the art of painting the complexion was carried to a still greater extent than among the Greeks, and even Ovid did not disdain to write a poem on the subject, which he calls (*de Art. Am.* iii. 206) "parvus, sed cura grande, libellus, opus;" though the genuineness of the fragment of the *Medicamina faciei*, ascribed to this poet, is doubtful. The Roman ladies even went so far as to paint with blue the veins on the temples,

The ridiculous use of patches (*splenia*), which were common among the English ladies in the reign of Queen Anne and the first Georges, was not unknown to the Roman ladies. The more effeminate of the male sex at Rome, and likewise in Greece, also employed paint.

Girl painting herself. (From a Gem.)

FŬGA LĀTA. [EXSILIUM.]
FŬGA LĪBĚRA. [EXSILIUM.]
FŬGĬTĪVUS. [SERVUS.]

FULLO (κναφεύς, γναφεύς), also called NACCA, a fuller, a washer or scourer of cloth and linen. The fullones not only received the cloth as it came from the loom in order to scour and smooth it, but also washed and cleansed garments which had been already worn. The clothes were first washed, which was done in tubs or vats, where they were trodden upon and stamped by the feet of the fullones, whence Seneca speaks of *saltus fullonicus*. The ancients were not acquainted with soap, but they used in its stead different kinds of alkali, by which the dirt was more easily separated from the clothes. Of these, by far the most common was the urine of men and animals, which was mixed with the water in which the clothes were washed. When the clothes were dry, the wool was brushed and carded to raise the nap, sometimes with the skin of a hedgehog, and sometimes with some plants of the thistle kind. The clothes were then hung on a vessel of basket-work (*viminea cavea*), under which sulphur was placed in order to whiten the cloth. A fine white earth, called Cimolian by Pliny, was often rubbed into the cloth to increase its whiteness. The establishment or workshop of the fullers was called *Fullonica*, *Fullonicum*, or *Fullonium*. The Greeks were also accustomed to send their garments to fullers to be washed and scoured. The word πλύνειν denoted the washing of linen, and κναφεύειν or γναφεύειν the washing of woollen clothes.

FŬNAMBŬLUS (καλοβάτης σχοινοβάτης), a rope-dancer. The art of dancing on the tight rope was carried to as great perfection among the Romans as it is with us. The performers placed themselves in an endless variety of graceful and sportive attitudes, and represented the characters of bacchanals, satyrs, and other imaginary beings. One of the most difficult exploits was running down the rope at the conclusion of the performance. It was a strange attempt of Germanicus and of the emperor Galba to exhibit elephants walking on the rope.

FUNDA (σφενδόνη), a sling. Slingers are not mentioned in the Iliad; but the light troops of the Greek and Roman armies consisted in great part of slingers (*funditores*, σφενδονῆται). The most celebrated slingers were the inhabitants of the Balearic islands. Besides stones, plummets, called *glandes* (μολυβδίδες), of a form between acorns and almonds, were cast in moulds to be thrown with slings. The manner in which the sling was wielded may be seen in the annexed figure of a soldier with a provision of stones in the sinus of his pallium, and with his arm extended in order to whirl the sling about his head.

Funda, Sling. (Column of Trajan.)

FUNDĬTŌRES. [FUNDA.]

FŪNUS, a funeral.—(1) GREEK. The Greeks attached great importance to the burial of the dead. They believed that souls could not enter the Elysian fields till their bodies had been buried; and so strong was this feeling among the Greeks, that it was considered a religious duty to throw earth upon a dead body, which a person might happen to find unburied; and among the Athenians, those children who were released from all other obligations to unworthy parents, were nevertheless bound to bury them by one of Solon's laws. The neglect of burying one's relatives is frequently mentioned by the orators as a grave charge against the moral character of a man; in fact, the burial of the body by the relations of the dead was considered one of the most sacred duties by the universal law of the Greeks. Sophocles represents Antigone as disregarding all consequences in order to bury the dead body of her brother Polyneices, which Creon, the king of Thebes, had commanded to be left unburied. The common expressions for the funeral rites, τὰ δίκαια, νόμιμα or νομιζόμενα, προσήκοντα, show that the dead had, as it were, a legal and moral claim to burial. After a person was dead, it was the custom first to place in his mouth an obolus, called danace (δανάκη), with which he might pay the ferryman in Hades. The body was then washed and anointed with perfumed oil, the head was crowned with the flowers which happened to be in season, and the body dressed in as handsome a robe as the family could afford. These duties were not performed by hired persons, like the *pollinctores* among the Romans, but by the women of the family, upon whom the care of the corpse always devolved. The corpse was then laid out (πρόθεσις, προτίθεσθαι) on a bed, which appears to have been of the ordinary kind, with a pillow for supporting the head and back. By the side of the bed there were placed painted earthen vessels, called λήκυθοι, which were also buried with the corpse. Great numbers of these painted vases have been found in modern times; and they have been of great use in explaining many matters connected with antiquity. A honey-cake, called μελιττοῦτα, which appears to have been intended for Cerberus, was also placed by the side of the corpse. Before the door a vessel of water was placed, called ὄστρακον, ἀρδάλιον or ἀρδάνιον, in order that persons who had been in the house might purify themselves by sprinkling water on their persons. The relatives stood around the bed, the women uttering great lamentations, rending their garments, and tearing their hair. On the day after the πρόθεσις, or the third day after death, the corpse was carried out (ἐκφορά,

ἐκκομιδή) for burial, early in the morning and before sunrise. A burial soon after death was supposed to be pleasing to the dead. In some places it appears to have been usual to bury the dead on the day following death. The men walked before the corpse, and the women behind. The funeral procession was preceded or followed by hired mourners (θρηνῳδοί), who appear to have been usually Carian women, playing mournful tunes on the flute. The body was either buried or burnt. The word θάπτειν is used in connection with either mode; it is applied to the collection of the ashes after burning, and accordingly we find the words καίειν and θάπτειν used together. The proper expression for interment in the earth is κατορύττειν. In Homer the bodies of the dead are burnt; but interment was also used in very ancient times. Cicero says that the dead were buried at Athens in the time of Cecrops; and we also read of the bones of Orestes being found in a coffin at Tegea. The dead were commonly buried among the Spartans and the Sicyonians, and the prevalence of this practice is proved by the great number of skeletons found in coffins in modern times, which have evidently not been exposed to the action of fire. Both burning and burying appear to have been always used to a greater or less extent at different periods; till the spread of Christianity at length put an end to the former practice. The dead bodies were usually burnt on piles of wood, called *pyres* (πυραί). The body was placed on the top; and in the heroic times it was customary to burn with the corpse animals and even captives or slaves. Oils and perfumes were also thrown into the flames. When the pyre was burnt down, the remains of the fire were quenched with wine, and the relatives and friends collected the bones. The bones were then washed with wine and oil, and placed in urns, which were sometimes made of gold. The corpses which were not burnt were buried in coffins, which were called by various names, as σοροί, πύελοι, ληνοί, λάρνακες, δροῖται, though some of these names are also applied to the urns in which the bones were collected. They were made of various materials, but were usually of baked clay or earthenware. The following woodcut contains two of the most ancient kind; the figure in the middle is the section

Coffins. (Stackelberg, 'Die Gräber der Hellenen,' pl. 7, 8.)

of one. The dead were usually buried outside the town, as it was thought that their presence in the city brought pollution to the living. At Athens none were allowed to be buried within the city; but Lycurgus, in order to remove all superstition respecting the presence of the dead, allowed of burial in Sparta. Persons who possessed lands in Attica were frequently buried in them, and we therefore read of tombs in the fields. Tombs, however, were most frequently built by the side of roads, and near the gates of the city.

Tomb in Lycia.

At Athens, the most common place of burial was outside of the Itonian gate, near the road leading to the Peiraeeus, which gate was for that reason called the burial gate. Those who had fallen in battle were buried at the public expense in the outer Cerameicus, on the road leading to the Academia. Tombs were called θῆκαι, τάφοι, μνήματα, μνημεῖα, σήματα. Many of these were only mounds of earth or stones (χώματα, κολῶναι, τύμβοι). Others were built of stone, and frequently ornamented with great taste. Some Greek tombs were built under ground, and called *hypogea* (ὑπόγαια or ὑπόγεια). They correspond to the Roman *conditoria*. The monuments erected over the graves of persons were usually of four kinds: 1. στῆλαι, pillars or upright stone tablets; 2. κίονες, columns; 3. ναΐδια or ἡρῷα, small buildings in the form of temples; and 4. τρά-

πεζαι, flat square stones, called by Cicero *mensae*. The term στῆλαι is sometimes applied to all kinds of funeral monuments, but properly designates upright stone tablets, which were usually terminated with an oval heading, called ἐπίθημα. The epithema was fre-

Epithema or Heading of Tombstone. (Stackelberg, pl. 3

quently ornamented with a kind of arabesque work, as in the preceding specimen. The κίονες, or columns, were of various forms, as is shown by the two specimens in the annexed cut.

Sepulchral Columns. (Paintings on Vases.)

The inscriptions upon these funeral monuments usually contain the name of the deceased person, and that of the demus to which he belonged, as well as frequently some account of his life. The following example of an ἡρῷον will give a general idea of monuments of this kind.—Orations in praise of the dead were sometimes pronounced; but Solon ordained that such orations should be confined to persons who were honoured with a public funeral. In the heroic ages games were celebrated at the funeral of a great man, as in the case of Patroclus; but this practice

Sepulchral Heroon. (Painting on Vase.)

does not seem to have been usual in the historical times.—All persons who had been engaged in funerals were considered polluted, and could not enter the temples of the gods till they had been purified. After the funeral was over, the relatives partook of a feast, which was called περίδειπνον or νεκρόδειπνον. This feast was always given at the house of the nearest relative of the deceased. Thus the relatives of those who had fallen at the battle of Chaeroneia partook of the περίδειπνον at the house of Demosthenes, as if he were the nearest relative to them all. On the second day after the funeral a sacrifice to the dead was offered, called τρίτα; but the principal sacrifice to the dead was on the ninth day, called ἔννατα or ἔνατα. The mourning for the dead appears to have lasted till the thirtieth day after the funeral, on which day sacrifices were again offered. At Sparta the time of mourning was limited to eleven days. During the time of mourning it was considered indecorous for the relatives of the deceased to appear in public; they were accustomed to wear a black dress, and in ancient times they cut off their hair as a sign of grief.—The tombs were preserved by the family to which they belonged with the greatest care, and were regarded as among the strongest ties which attached a man to his native land. In the Docimasia of the Athenian archons it was always a subject of inquiry whether they had kept in proper repair the tombs of their ancestors. On certain days the tombs were crowned with flowers, and offerings were made to the dead, consisting of garlands of flowers and various other things. The act of offering these presents was called ἐναγίζειν, and the offerings themselves ἐναγίσματα, or more commonly χοαί. The γενέσια mentioned by Herodotus appear to have consisted in offerings of the same kind, which were presented on the anniversary of the birth-day of the deceased. The νεκύσια were probably offerings on the anniversary of the day of the death; though, according to some writers, the νεκύσια were the same as the γενέσια. Certain criminals, who were put to death by the state, were also deprived of the rights of burial, which was considered as an additional punishment. There were certain places, both at Athens and Sparta, where the dead bodies of such criminals were cast. A person who had committed suicide was not deprived of burial, but the hand with which he had killed himself was cut off and buried by itself.—(2) ROMAN. When a Roman was at the point of death, his nearest relation present endeavoured to catch the last breath with his mouth. The ring was taken off the finger of the dying person; and as soon as he was dead his eyes and mouth were closed by the nearest relation, who called upon the deceased by name, exclaiming have or vale. The corpse was then washed, and anointed with oil and perfumes, by slaves, called pollinctores, who belonged to the libitinarii, or undertakers. The libitinarii appear to have been so called because they dwelt near the temple of Venus Libitina, where all things requisite for funerals were sold. Hence we find the expressions vitare Libitinam and evadere Libitinam used in the sense of escaping death. At this temple an account (ratio, ephemeris) was kept of those who died, and a small sum was paid for the registration of their names. A small coin was then placed in the mouth of the corpse, in order to pay the ferryman in Hades, and the body was laid out on a couch in the vestibule of the house, with its feet towards the door, and dressed in the best robe which the deceased had worn when alive. Ordinary citizens were dressed in a white toga, and magistrates in their official robes. If the deceased had received a crown while alive as a reward for his bravery, it was now placed on his head; and the couch on which he was laid was sometimes covered with leaves and flowers. A branch of cypress was also usually placed at the door of the house, if he was a person of consequence. Funerals were usually called *funera justa* or *exsequiae*; the latter term was generally applied to the funeral procession (*pompa funebris*). There were two kinds of funerals, public and private; of which the former was called *funus publicum* or *indictivum*, because the people were invited to it by a herald; the latter *funus tacitum, translatitium*, or *plebeium*. A person appears to have usually left a certain sum of money in his will to pay the expenses of his funeral; but if he did not do so, nor appoint any one to bury him, this duty devolved upon the persons to whom the property was left, and if he died without a will, upon his relations, according to their order of succession to the property. The expenses of the funeral were in such cases decided by an arbiter, according to the property and rank of the deceased, whence *arbitria* is used to signify the funeral expenses.—The following description of the mode in which a funeral was conducted only applies strictly to the funerals of the great; the same pomp and ceremony could not of course be observed in the case of persons in ordinary circumstances. All funerals in ancient times were performed at night, but afterwards the poor only were buried at night, because they could not afford to have any funeral procession. The corpse was usually carried out of the house (*efferebatur*) on the eighth day after the death. The order of the funeral procession was regulated by a person called *designator* or *dominus funeris*, who was attended by lictors dressed in black. It was headed by musicians of various kinds (*cornicines, siticines*), who played mournful strains, and next came mourning women, called *praeficae*, who were hired to lament and sing the funeral song (*naenia* or *lessus*) in praise of the deceased. These were sometimes followed by players and buffoons (*scurrae, histriones*), of whom one, called *archimimus*, represented the character of the deceased, and imitated his words and actions. Then came the slaves whom the deceased had liberated, wearing the cap of liberty (*pileati*); the number of whom was occasionally very great, since a master sometimes liberated all his slaves, in his will, in order to add to the pomp of his funeral. Before the corpse the images of the deceased and of his ancestors were carried, and also the crowns or military rewards which he had gained. The corpse was carried on a couch (*lectica*), to which the name of *feretrum* or *capulum* was usually given; but the bodies of poor citizens and of slaves were carried on a common kind of bier or coffin, called *sandapila*. The *sandapila* was carried by bearers, called *vespae* or *vespillones*, because they carried out the corpses in the evening (*vespertino tempore*). The couches on which the corpses of the rich were carried were sometimes made of ivory, and covered with gold and purple. They were often carried on the shoulders of the nearest relations of the deceased, and sometimes on those of his freed-men. Julius Caesar was carried by the magistrates, and Augustus by the senators. The relations of the deceased walked behind the corpse in mourning; his sons with their heads veiled, and his daughters with their heads bare and their hair dishevelled, contrary to the ordinary practice of both. They often uttered loud lamentations, and the women beat their breasts and tore their cheeks, though this was forbidden by the Twelve Tables. If the deceased was of illustrious rank, the funeral procession went through the forum, and stopped before the *rostra*, where a funeral oration (*laudatio*) in praise of the deceased was delivered. This practice was of great antiquity among the Romans, and is said by some writers to have been first introduced by Publicola, who pronounced a funeral oration in honour of his colleague Brutus. Women also were honoured by funeral orations. From the Forum the corpse was carried to the place of burning or burial, which, according to a law of the Twelve Tables, was obliged to be outside the city. The Romans in the most ancient times buried their dead, though they also early adopted, to some extent, the custom of burning, which is mentioned in the Twelve Tables. Burning, however, does not appear to have become general till the later times of the republic. Marius was buried, and Sulla was the first of the Cornelian gens whose body was burned. Under the empire burning was almost universally practised, but was gradually discontinued as Christianity spread, so that it had fallen into disuse in the fourth century. Persons struck by lightning were not burnt, but buried on the spot, which was called *Bidental*, and was considered sacred. [BIDENTAL.] Children also, who had not cut their teeth, were not burnt, but buried in a place called *Suggrundarium*. Those who were buried were placed in a coffin (*arca* or *loculus*), which was frequently made of stone, and sometimes of the Assian stone, which came from Assos in Troas, and which consumed all the body, with the exception of the teeth, in 40 days, whence it was called *sarcophagus*. This name was in course of time applied to any kind of coffin or tomb. The corpse was burnt on a pile of wood (*pyra* or *rogus*). This pile was built in the form of an altar, with four equal sides, whence we find it called *ara sepulcri* and *funeris ara*. The sides of the pile were, according to the Twelve Tables, to be left rough and unpolished, but were frequently covered with dark leaves. Cypress trees were sometimes placed before the pile. On the top of the pile the corpse was placed, with the couch on which it had been carried, and the nearest relation then set fire to the pile with his face turned away. When the flames began to rise, various perfumes were thrown into the fire, though this practice was forbidden by the Twelve Tables; cups of oil, ornaments, clothes, dishes of food, and other things, which were supposed to be agreeable to the deceased, were also thrown upon the flames. The place where a person was burnt was called *bustum*, if he was afterwards buried on the same spot, and *ustrina* or *ustrinum* if he was buried at a different place. Sometimes animals were slaughtered at the pile, and in ancient times captives and slaves, since the manes were supposed to be fond of blood; but afterwards gladiators, called bustuarii, were hired to fight round the burning pile. When the pile was burnt down, the embers were soaked with wine, and the bones and ashes of the deceased were gathered by the nearest relatives, who sprinkled them with perfumes, and placed them in a vessel called *urna*, which was made of various materials, according to the circumstances of individuals. The urnae were also of various shapes, but most commonly square or round; and upon them there was usually an inscription or epitaph (*titulus* or *epitaphium*), beginning with the letters D. M. S., or only D. M., that is, Dis MANIBUS SACRUM, followed by the name of the deceased, with the length of his life, &c. The woodcut opposite is a representation of a sepulchral urn in the British Museum. It is of an upright rectangular form, richly ornamented with foliage, and supported at the sides with pilasters. It is to the memory of Cossutia Prima. Its height is 21 inches, and its width at the base 14 inches 6-8ths. Below the inscription an infant genius is represented driving a car drawn by four horses.— After the bones and ashes of the deceased had been placed in the urn, the persons present were thrice sprinkled by a priest with pure water from a branch of olive or laurel for the purpose of purification; after which they were dismissed by the *praefica*, or some other person, by the solemn word *Ilicet*, that is, *ire licet*. At their departure they were accustomed to bid farewell to the deceased by pronouncing the word *Vale*.

The urns were placed in sepulchres, which, as already stated, were outside the city, though in a few cases we read of the dead being buried within the city. Thus Valerius Publicola, Tubertus, and Fabricius, were buried in the city; which right their descendants also possessed, but did not use. The vestal virgins and the emperors were buried in the city.—The verb *sepelire*, like the Greek θάπτειν, was applied to every mode of disposing of the dead; and *sepulcrum* signified any kind of tomb in which the body or bones of a man were placed. The term *humare* was originally used for burial in the earth, but was afterwards applied like *sepelire* to any mode of disposing of the dead: since it appears to have been the custom, after the body was burnt, to throw some earth upon the bones.—The places for burial were either public or private. The public places of burial were of two kinds; one for illustrious citizens, who were buried at the public expense, and the other for poor citizens, who could not afford to purchase ground for the purpose. The former was in the Campus Martius, which was ornamented with the tombs of the illustrious dead, and in the Campus Esquilinus; the latter was also in the Campus Esquilinus, and consisted of small pits or caverns, called *puticuli* or *puticulae*;

Sepulchral Urn in British Museum.

but as this place rendered the neighbourhood unhealthy, it was given to Maecenas, who converted it into gardens, and built a magnificent house upon it. Private places for burial were usually by the sides of the roads leading to Rome; and on some of these roads, such as the Via Appia, the tombs formed an almost uninterrupted street for many miles from the gates of the city. They were frequently built by individuals during their lifetime; thus Augustus, in his sixth consulship, built the Mausoleum for his sepulchre between the Via Flaminia and the Tiber, and planted round it woods and walks for public use. The heirs were often ordered by the will of the deceased to build a tomb for him; and they sometimes did it at their own expense.—Sepulchres were originally called *busta*, but this word was afterwards employed in the manner mentioned under BUSTUM. Sepulchres were also frequently called *monumenta*, but this term was also applied to a monument erected to the memory of a person in a different place from that where he was buried. *Conditoria* or *conditiva* were sepulchres under ground, in which dead bodies were placed entire, in contradistinction to those sepulchres which contained the bones and ashes only.—The tombs of the rich were commonly built of marble, and the ground enclosed with an iron railing or wall, and planted round with trees. The extent of the burying ground was marked by cippi [CIPPUS]. The name of mausoleum, which was originally the name of the magnificent sepulchre erected by Artemisia to the memory of Mausolus, king of Caria, was sometimes given to any splendid tomb. The open space before a sepulchre was called forum, and neither this space nor the sepulchre itself could become the property of a person by usucapion. Private tombs were either built by an individual for himself and the members of his family (*sepulcra familiaria*), or for himself and his heirs (*sepulcra hereditaria*). A tomb, which was fitted up with niches to receive the funeral urns, was called *columbarium*, on account of the resemblance of these niches to the holes of a pigeon-house. In these tombs the ashes of the freedmen and slaves of great families were frequently placed in vessels made of baked clay, called *ollae*, which were let into the thickness of the wall within these niches, the lids only being seen, and the inscriptions placed in front. Tombs were of various sizes and forms, according to the wealth and taste of the owner. A sepulchre, or any place in which a person was buried, was *religiosus*; all things which were left or belonged to the Dii Manes were *religiosae*; those consecrated to the Dii Superi were called *sacrae*. Even the place in which a slave was buried was considered religiosus. Whoever violated a sepulchre was subject to an action termed *sepulcri violati actio*. After the bones had been placed in the urn at the funeral, the friends returned home. They then underwent a further purification, called *suffitio*, which consisted in being sprinkled with water and stepping over a fire. The house itself was also swept with a certain kind of broom; which sweeping or purification was called *exverrae*, and the person who did it *everriator*. The *Denicales Feriae* were also days set apart for the purification of the family. The mourning and solemnities connected with the dead lasted for nine days after the funeral, at the end of which time a sacrifice was performed, called *novendiale*.—A feast was given in honour of the dead, but it is uncertain on what day; it sometimes appears to have been given at the time of the funeral, sometimes on the novendiale, and sometimes later. The name of *silicernium* was given to this feast. Among the tombs at Pompeii there is a funeral triclinium for the celebration of these feasts, which is represented in the annexed woodcut. It is open to the sky, and the walls are ornamented by paintings of animals in the centre of compartments, which have borders of flowers. The triclinium is made of stone, with a pedestal in the centre to receive the table. After the funeral of great men, there was, in addition to the feast for the friends of the deceased, a distribution of raw meat to the people, called *visceratio*, and sometimes a public banquet. Combats of gladiators and other games were also frequently exhibited in honour of the deceased. Thus at the

Funeral Triclinium at Pompeii. (Mazois, Pomp., I, pl. xx.)

funeral of P. Licinius Crassus, who had been Pontifex Maximus, raw meat was distributed to the people, 120 gladiators fought, and funeral games were celebrated for three days, at the end of which a public banquet was given in the forum. Public feasts and funeral games were sometimes given on the anniversary of funerals. At all banquets in honour of the dead, the guests were dressed in white.—The Romans, like the Greeks, were accustomed to visit the tombs of their relatives at certain periods, and to offer to them sacrifices and various gifts, which were called *inferiae* and *parentalia*. The Romans appear to have regarded the manes or departed souls of their ancestors as gods; whence arose the practice of presenting to them oblations, which consisted of victims, wine, milk, garlands of flowers, and other things. The tombs were sometimes illuminated on these occasions with lamps. In the latter end of the month of February there was a festival, called *feralia*, in which the Romans were accustomed to carry food to the sepulchres for the use of the dead. The Romans were accustomed to wear mourning for their deceased friends, which appears to have been black under the republic for both sexes. Under the empire the men continued to wear black in mourning, but the women wore white. They laid aside all kinds of ornaments, and did not cut either their hair or beard. Men appear to have usually worn their mourning for only a few days, but women for a year when they lost a husband or parent. In a public mourning on account of some signal calamity, as, for instance, the loss of a battle, or the death of an emperor, there was a total cessation from business, called *justitium*, which was usually ordained by public appointment. During this period the courts of justice did not sit, the shops were shut, and the soldiers freed from military duties. In a public mourning the senators did not wear the latus clavus and their rings, nor the magistrates their badges of office.

FURCA, which properly means a fork, was also the name of an instrument of punishment. It was a piece of wood in the form of the letter A, which was placed upon the shoulders of the offender, whose hands were tied to it. Slaves were frequently punished in this way, and were obliged to carry about the furca wherever they went; whence the appellation of *furcifer* was applied to a man as a term of reproach. The furca was used in the ancient mode of capital punishment among the Romans; the criminal was tied to it, and then scourged to death. The *patibulum* was also an instrument of punishment, resembling the furca; it appears to have been in the form of the letter II. Both the furca and patibulum were also employed as crosses, to which criminals appear to have been nailed.

FURIOSUS. [CURATOR.]

FUSCINA (τρίαινα), a trident, more commonly called *tridens*, meaning *tridens stimulus*, because it was originally a three-pronged goad, used to incite horses to greater swiftness. Neptune was supposed to be armed with it when he drove his chariot, and it thus became his usual attribute, perhaps with an allusion also to the use of the same instrument in harpooning fish. It is represented in the cut on p. 84. In the contests of gladiators, the *retiarius* was armed with a trident. [GLADIATORES.]

FUSTUARIUM (ξυλοκοπία), was a capital punishment inflicted upon Roman soldiers for desertion, theft, and similar crimes. It was administered in the following manner: —When a soldier was condemned, the tribune touched him slightly with a stick, upon which all the soldiers of the legion fell upon him with sticks and stones, and generally killed him upon the spot. If, however, he escaped, for he was allowed to fly, he could not return to his native country, nor did any of his relatives dare to receive him into their houses.

FUSUS (ἄτρακτος), the spindle, was always, when in use, accompanied by the distaff (*colus*, ἠλακάτη), as an indispensable part of the same apparatus. The wool, flax, or other material, having been prepared for spinning, was rolled into a ball (τολύπη, *glomus*), which was, however, sufficiently loose to allow the fibres to be easily drawn out by the hand of the spinner. The upper part of the distaff was then inserted into this mass of flax or wool, and the lower part was held under the left arm in such a position as was most convenient for conducting the operation. The fibres were drawn out, and at the same time spirally twisted, chiefly by the use of the fore-finger and thumb of the right hand; and the thread (*filum, stamen,* νῆμα) so produced was wound upon the spindle until the quantity was as great as it would carry. The spindle was a stick, 10 or 12 inches long, having at the top a slit or catch (*dens,* ἄγκιστρον) in which the thread was fixed, so that the weight of the spindle might continually carry down the thread as it was formed. Its lower extremity was inserted into a small wheel, called the whorl (*vorticellum*), made of wood, stone, or metal (see woodcut), the use of which was to keep the spindle more steady, and to promote its rotation. The accompanying woodcut shows the operation of spinning, at the moment when the woman has drawn out a sufficient length of yarn to twist it by whirling the spindle with her right thumb and fore-finger, and previously to the act of taking it out of the slit to wind it upon the bobbin (πηνίον) already formed. It was usual to have a basket to hold the distaff and spindle, with the balls of wool prepared for spinning, and the bobbins already spun. [CALATHUS.] The distaff and spindle, with the wool and thread upon them, were carried in bridal processions; and, without the wool and thread, they were often suspended by females as offerings of religious gratitude, especially in old age, or on relinquishing the constant use

Fusus, spindle.

of them. They were most frequently dedicated to Pallas, the patroness of spinning, and of the arts connected with it. They were exhibited in the representations of the three Fates, who were conceived, by their spinning, to determine the life of every man.

GĀBĪNUS CINCTUS. [TOGA.]
GAESUM (γαισός), a term probably of Celtic origin, denoting a kind of javelin which was used by the Gauls wherever their ramifications extended. It was a heavy weapon, the shaft being as thick as a man could grasp, and the iron head barbed, and of an extraordinary length compared with the shaft.

GĂLĔA (κράνος, poet. κόρυς, πήληξ), a helmet; a casque. The helmet was originally made of skin or leather, whence is supposed to have arisen its appellation, κυνέη, meaning properly a helmet of dog-skin, but applied to caps or helmets made of the hide of other animals, and even to those which were entirely of bronze or iron. The leathern basis of the helmet was also very commonly strengthened and adorned by the addition of either bronze or gold. Helmets which had a metallic basis were in Latin properly called cassides, although the terms galea and cassis are often confounded. The additions by which the external appearance of the helmet was varied, and which served both for ornament and protection, were the following:—
1. Bosses or plates (φάλος), proceeding either from the top or the sides, and varying in number from one to four (ἀμφίφαλος, τετράφαλος). The φάλος was often an emblematical figure, referring to the character of the wearer. Thus in the colossal statue of Athena in the Parthenon at Athens, she bore a sphinx on the top of her helmet, and a griffin on each side. 2. The helmet thus adorned was very commonly surmounted by the crest (crista, λόφος), which was often of horse-hair. 3. The two check-pieces (bucculae, παραγναθίδες), which were attached to the helmet by hinges, so as to be lifted up and down. They had buttons or ties at their extremities, for fastening the helmet on the head. 4. The beaver, or visor, a

Galeae, helmets. (From ancient Gems,—size of originals.)

peculiar form of which is supposed to have been the αὐλῶπις τρυφάλεια, *i. e.* the perforated beaver. The gladiators wore helmets of this kind.

GALĒRUS or **GALĒRUM**, originally a covering for the head worn by priests, especially by the *flamen dialis.* It appears to have been a round cap made of leather, with its top ending in an apex or point. [APEX.] In course of time the name was applied to any kind of cap fitting close to the head like a helmet. *Galerus* and its diminutive *Galericulum* are also used to signify a covering for the head made of hair, and hence a wig.

GALLI, the priests of Cybelé, whose worship was introduced at Rome from Phrygia. The Galli were, according to an ancient custom, always castrated, and it would seem that, impelled by religious fanaticism, they performed this operation on themselves. In their wild, enthusiastic, and boisterous rites they resembled the Corybantes. They seem to have been always chosen from a poor and despised class of people, for while no other priests were allowed to beg, the Galli were permitted to do so on certain days. The chief priest among them was called *archigallus.*

GAMĒLIA (γαμηλία). The demes and phratries of Attica possessed various means to prevent intruders from assuming the rights of citizens. Among other regulations, it was ordained that every bride, previous to her marriage, should be introduced by her parents or guardians to the phratria of her husband. This introduction of the young women was accompanied by presents to their new phratores, which were called *gamelia.* The women were enrolled in the lists of the phratries, and this enrolment was also called *gamelia.*

GAUSAPA, GAUSAPE, or GAUSAPUM, a kind of thick cloth, which was on one side very woolly, and was used to cover tables and beds, and by persons to wrap themselves up after taking a bath, or in general to protect themselves against rain and cold. It was worn by men as well as women. The word *gausapa* is also sometimes used to designate a thick wig, such as was made of the hair of Germans, and worn by the fashionable people at Rome at the time of the emperors.

GENĒSIA. [FUNUS.]

GENOS (γένος). [TRIBUS, GREEK.]

GENS. According to the traditional accounts of the old Roman constitution, the *Gentes* were subdivisions of the *curiae,* just as the *curiae* were subdivisions of the three ancient tribes, the Ramnes, Titienses, and Luceres. There were ten gentes in each curia, and consequently one hundred gentes in each tribe, and three hundred in the three tribes. Now if there is any truth in the tradition of this original distribution of the population into tribes, curiae, and gentes, it follows that there was no necessary kinship among those families which belonged to a gens, any more than among those families which belonged to one curia. The name of the gens was always characterised by the termination *ia,* as Julia, Cornelia, Valeria; and the gentiles, or members of a gens, all bore the name of the gens to which they belonged. As the gentes were subdivisions of the three ancient tribes, the populus (in the ancient sense) alone had gentes, so that to be a patrician and to have a gens were synonymous; and thus we find the expressions gens and patricii constantly united. Yet it appears that some gentes contained plebeian familiae, which it is conjectured had their origin in marriages between patricians and plebeians before there was connubium between them. A hundred new members were added to the senate by the first Tarquin. These were the representatives of the *Luceres,* the third and inferior tribe; which is indicated by the gentes of this tribe being called *minores,* by way of being distinguished from the older gentes, *majores,* of the Ramnes and Tities, a distinction which appears to have been more than nominal. [SENATUS.] There were certain sacred rites *(sacra gentilitia)* which belonged to a gens, to which all the members of a gens, as such, were bound. It was the duty of the pontifices to look after the due observance of these gentile sacra, and to see that they were not lost. Each gens seems to have had its peculiar place *(sacellum)* for the celebration of these sacra, which were performed at stated times. By the law of the Twelve Tables the property of a person who died intestate devolved upon the gens to which he belonged.

GEŌMŎRI. [TRIBUS, GREEK.]

GĒROUSĪA (γερουσία), or *assembly of elders,* was the aristocratic element of the Spartan polity. It was not peculiar to Sparta only, but found in other Dorian states, just as a *Boulé* (βουλή) or democratical council was an element of most Ionian constitutions. The *Gerousia* at Sparta, including the two kings, its presidents, consisted of thirty members (γέροντες): a number which seems connected with the divisions of the Spartan people. Every Dorian state, in fact, was divided into three tribes: the Hylleis, the Dymanes, and the Pamphyli. The tribes at Sparta were again subdivided into *obae* (ὠβαί), which were, like the *Gerontes,* thirty in number, so that each oba was represented by its councillor: an inference which leads to the conclusion that two obae at least of the llylean tribe, must have belonged to the royal house of the Heracleids. No one was eligible to the council till he was sixty years of age, and the additional qualifications were strictly of an aristocratic nature. We are told, for instance, that the office of a councillor was the reward and prize of virtue, and that it was confined to men of distinguished character and station. The election was determined by vote, and the mode of conducting it was remarkable for its old-fashioned simplicity. The competitors presented themselves one after another to the assembly of electors; the latter testified their esteem by acclamations, which varied in intensity according to the popularity of the candidates for whom they were given. These manifestations of esteem were noted by persons in an adjoining building, who could judge of the shouting, but could not tell in whose favour it was given. The person whom these judges thought to have been most applauded was declared the successful candidate. The office lasted for life. The functions of the councillors were partly deliberative, partly judicial, and partly executive. In the discharge of the first, they prepared measures and passed preliminary decrees, which were to be laid before the popular assembly, so that the important privilege of initiating all changes in the government or laws was vested in them. As a criminal court, they could punish with death and civil degradation (ἀτιμία). They also appear to have exercised, like the Areiopagus at Athens, a general superintendence and inspection over the lives and manners of the citizens, and probably were allowed a kind of patriarchal authority, to enforce the observance of ancient usage and discipline. It is not, however, easy to define with exactness the original extent of their functions, especially as respects the last-mentioned duty, since the ephors not only encroached upon the prerogatives of the king and council, but also possessed, in very early times, a censorial power, and were not likely to permit any diminution of its extent.

GERRHA (γέῤῥα), in Latin, *Gerrae*, properly signified any thing made of wickerwork, and was especially used as the name of the Persian shields, which were made of wicker-work, and were smaller and shorter than the Greek shields.

GLADIATORES (μονομάχοι) were men who fought with swords in the amphitheatre and other places, for the amusement of the Roman people. They are said to have been first exhibited by the Etrurians, and to have had their origin from the custom of killing slaves and captives at the funeral pyres of the deceased. [BUSTUM; FUNUS.] A show of gladiators was called *munus*, and the person who exhibited (*edebat*) it, *editor, munerator*, or *dominus*, who was honoured during the day of exhibition, if a private person, with the official signs of a magistrate. Gladiators were first exhibited at Rome in B.C. 264, in the Forum Boarium, by Marcus and Decimus Brutus, at the funeral of their father. They were at first confined to public funerals, but afterwards fought at the funerals of most persons of consequence, and even at those of women. Combats of gladiators were also exhibited at entertainments, and especially at public festivals by the aediles and other magistrates, who sometimes exhibited immense numbers, with the view of pleasing the people. Under the empire the passion of the Romans for this amusement rose to its greatest height, and the number of gladiators who fought on some occasions appears almost incredible. After Trajan's triumph over the Dacians, there were more than 10,000 exhibited. Gladiators consisted either of captives, slaves, and condemned malefactors, or of freeborn citizens who fought voluntarily. Freemen, who became gladiators for hire, were called *auctorati*, and their hire *auctoramentum* or *gladiatorium*. Even under the republic, free-born citizens fought as gladiators, but they appear to have belonged only to the lower orders. Under the empire, however, both knights and senators fought in the arena, and even women.—Gladiators were kept in schools (*ludi*), where they were trained by persons called *lanistae*. The whole body of gladiators under one lanista was frequently called *familia*. They sometimes were the property of the lanistae, who let them out to persons who wished to exhibit a show of gladiators; but at other times they belonged to citizens, who kept them for the purpose of exhibition, and engaged lanistae to instruct them. Thus we read of the ludus Aemilius at Rome, and of Caesar's ludus at Capua. The gladiators fought in these ludi with wooden swords, called *rudes*. Great attention was paid to their diet, in order to increase the strength of their bodies.—Gladiators were sometimes exhibited at the funeral pyre, and sometimes in the forum, but more frequently in the amphitheatre. [AMPHITHEATRUM.]—The person who was to exhibit a show of gladiators, published some days before the exhibition bills (*libelli*), containing the number and frequently the names of those who were to fight. When the day came, they were led along the arena in procession, and matched by pairs; and their swords were examined by the editor to see if they were sufficiently sharp. At first there was a kind of sham battle, called *praelusio*, in which they fought with wooden swords, or the like, and afterwards at the sound of the trumpet the real battle began. When a gladiator was wounded, the people called out *habet* or *hoc habet;* and the one who was vanquished lowered his arms in token of submission. His fate, however, depended upon the people, who pressed down their thumbs if they wished him to be saved, but turned them up if they wished him to be killed, and ordered him to receive the sword (*ferrum recipere*), which gladiators usually did with the greatest firmness. If the life of a vanquished gladiator was spared, he obtained his discharge for that day, which was called *missio;* and hence in an exhibition of gladiators *sine missione*, the lives of the conquered were never spared. This kind of exhibition, however, was forbidden by Augustus. Palms were usually given to the victorious gladiators. Old gladiators, and sometimes those who had only fought for a short time, were discharged from the service by the editor, at the request of the people, who presented each of them with a *rudis* or wooden sword; whence those who were discharged were called *Rudiarii.*—Gladiators were divided into different classes, according to their arms and different mode of fighting, or other circumstances. The names of the most important of these classes are given in alphabetical order:—*Andabatae* wore helmets without any aperture for the eyes, so that they were obliged to fight blindfold, and thus excited the mirth of the spectators.—*Catervarii* was the name given to gladiators when they did not fight in pairs, but when several fought together.—*Essedarii* fought from chariots, like the Gauls and Britons. [ESSEDA.]—*Hoplomachi* appear to have been those who fought in a complete suit of armour.—*Laqueatores* were those who used a noose to catch their adversaries.—*Meridiani* were those who fought in the middle of the day, after combats with wild beasts had taken place in the morning. These gladiators were very slightly armed.—*Mirmillones* are said to have been so called from their having the image of a fish (*mormyr*, μορμύρος) on their helmets. Their arms were like those of the Gauls, whence we find that they were also called Galli. They were usually matched with the Retiarii or Thracians.—*Provocatores* fought with the Samnites, but we do not know any thing respecting them except their name.—*Retiarii* carried only a three-pointed lance, called *tridens* or *fuscina* [FUSCINA], and a net (*rete*), which they endeavoured to throw over their adversaries, and they then attacked them with the fuscina while they were entangled. The retiarius was dressed in a short tunic, and wore nothing on his head. If he missed his aim in throwing the net, he betook himself to flight, and endeavoured to prepare his net for a second cast, while his adversary followed him round the arena in order to kill him before he could make a second attempt. His adversary was usually a *secutor* or a *mirmillo*. In the following woodcut a combat is represented between a retiarius and a

A Mirmillo and a Retiarius. (Winckelmann, 'Monum. Ined.,' pl. 197.)

mirmillo; the former has thrown his net over the head of the latter, and is proceeding to attack him with the fuscina. The lanista stands behind the retiarius.—*Samnites* were so called, because they were armed in the same way as that people, and were particularly distinguished by the oblong *scutum*.—*Secutores* are supposed by some writers to be so called because the secutor in his combat with the retiarius pursued the latter when he failed in securing him by his net. Other writers think that they were the same as the *supposititii*, who were gladiators substituted in the place of those who were wearied or were killed.—*Thraces* or *Threces* were armed, like the Thracians, with a round shield or buckler, and a short sword or dagger (*sica*). They were usually matched, as already stated, with the mirmillones. The following woodcut represents a combat between two Thracians. A lanista stands behind each.

Thracians. (Winckelmann, l. c.)

GLĂDĬUS (ξίφος, *poet.* ἄορ, φάσγανον), a sword or glaive, by the Latin poets called *ensis*. The ancient sword had generally a straight two-edged blade, rather broad, and nearly of equal width from hilt to point. The Greeks and Romans wore them on the left side, so as to draw them out of the sheath (*vagina*, κολεός) by passing the right hand in front of the body to take hold of the hilt with the thumb next to the blade. The early Greeks used a very short sword. Iphicrates, who made various improvements in armour about 400 B. C., doubled its length. The Roman sword was larger, heavier, and more formidable than the Greek.

GLANDES. [FUNDA.]

GRAECŎSTĂSIS, a place in the Roman forum, on the right of the Comitium, so called because the Greek ambassadors, and perhaps also deputies from other foreign or allied states, were allowed to stand there to hear the debates. When the sun was seen from the Curia coming out between the Rostra and the Graecostasis, it was mid-day; and an accensus of the consul announced the time with a clear loud voice.

GRAMMĂTEUS (γραμματεύς), a clerk or scribe. Among the great number of scribes employed by the magistrates and government of Athens, there were three of a higher rank, who were real state-officers. One of them was appointed by lot, by the senate, to serve the time of the administration of each prytany, though he always belonged to a different prytany from that which was in power. He was, therefore, called γραμματεὺς κατὰ πρυτανείαν. His province was to keep the public records, and the decrees of the people which were made during the time of his office, and to deliver to the thesmothetae the decrees of the senate.—The second *grammateus* was elected by the senate, by χειροτονία, and was entrusted with the custody of the laws. His usual name was γραμματεὺς τῆς βουλῆς.—A third *grammateus* was called γραμματεὺς τῆς πόλεως, or γραμματεὺς τῆς βουλῆς καὶ τοῦ δήμου. He was appointed by the people, by χειροτονία, and the principal part of his office was to read any laws or documents which were required to be read in the assembly or in the senate.

GRĂPHĒ (γραφή). [DICE.]
GRĂPHIĂRIUM. [STILUS.]
GRĂPHIS. [PICTURA.]
GRĂPHIUM. [STILUS.]
GŬBERNĂCŬLUM (πηδάλιον). [NAVIS.]
GUSTĀTĬO. [COENA.]

GUTTUS, a vessel with a narrow mouth or neck, from which the liquid was poured in drops, whence its name. It was especially used in sacrifices, and hence we find it represented on the Roman coins struck by persons who held any of the priestly offices. The guttus was also used for keeping the oil, with which persons were anointed in the baths. [See p. 56.]

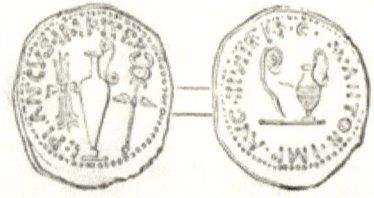

Guttus on Coin of L. Plancus.

GYMNASIUM (γυμνάσιον). The whole education of a Greek youth was divided into three parts,—grammar, music, and gymnastics (γράμματα, μουσική, γυμναστική), to which Aristotle adds a fourth, the art of drawing or painting. Gymnastics, however, were thought by the ancients a matter of such importance, that this part of education alone occupied as much time and attention as all the others put together; and while the latter necessarily ceased at a certain period of life, gymnastics continued to be cultivated by persons of all ages, though those of an advanced age naturally took lighter and less fatiguing exercises than boys and youths. The ancients, and more especially the Greeks, seem to have been thoroughly convinced that the mind could not possibly be in a healthy state, unless the body was likewise in perfect health, and no means were thought, either by philosophers or physicians, to be more conducive to preserve or restore bodily health than well-regulated exercise. The word gymnastics is derived from γυμνός (naked), because the persons who performed their exercises in public or private gymnasia were either entirely naked, or merely covered by the short chiton. Gymnastic exercises among the Greeks seem to have been as old as the Greek nation itself; but they were, as might be supposed, of a rude and mostly of a warlike character. They were generally held in the open air, and in plains near a river, which afforded an opportunity for swimming and bathing. It was about the time of Solon that the Greek towns began to build their regular gymnasia as places of exercise for the young, with baths, and other conveniences for philosophers and all persons who sought intellectual amusements. There was probably no Greek town of any importance which did not possess its gymnasium. Athens possessed three great gymnasia, the Lyceum (Λύκειον), Cynosarges (Κυνόσαργες), and the Academia (Ἀκαδημία); to which, in later times, several smaller ones were added. Respecting the superintendence and administration of the gymnasia at Athens, we know that Solon in his legislation thought them worthy of great attention; and the transgression of some of his laws relating to the gymnasia was punished with death. His laws mention a magistrate, called the gymnasiarch (γυμνασίαρχος or γυμνασιάρχης), who was entrusted with the whole management of the gymnasia, and with everything connected therewith. His office was one of the regular liturgies like the choregia and trierarchy, and was attended with considerable expense. He had to maintain and pay the persons who were preparing themselves for the games and contests in the public festivals, to provide them with oil, and perhaps with the wrestlers' dust. It also devolved upon him to adorn the gymnasium, or the place where the agones were held. The gymnasiarch was a real magistrate, and invested with a kind of jurisdiction over all those who frequented or were connected with the gymnasia. Another part of his duties was to conduct the solemn games at certain great festivals, especially the torch-race (λαμπαδηφορία), for which he selected the most distinguished among the ephebi of the gymnasia. The number of gymnasiarchs was ten, one from every tribe. An office of very great importance, in an educational point of view, was that of the *Sophronistae* (σωφρονίσται). Their province was to inspire the youths with a love of σωφροσύνη, and to protect this virtue against all injurious influences. In early times their number at Athens was ten, one from every tribe, with a salary of one drachma per day. Their duty not only required them to be present at all the games of the ephebi, but to watch and correct their conduct wherever they might meet them, both within and without the gymnasium. The instructions in the gymnasia were given by the *Gymnastae* (γυμνασταί) and the *Paedotribae* (παιδοτρίβαι); at a later period *Hypopaedotribae* were added. The

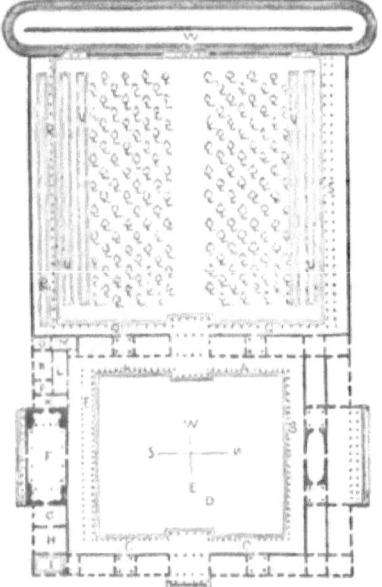

Gymnasium, after the description of Vitruvius.

Paedotribae were required to possess a knowledge of all the various exercises which were performed in the gymnasia; the Gymnastes was the practical teacher, and was expected to know the physiological effects and influences on the constitution of the youths, and therefore assigned to each of them those exercises which he thought most suitable. The anointing of the bodies of the youths and strewing them with dust, before they commenced their exercises, as well as the regulation of their diet, was the duty of the aliptae. [ALIPTAE.]—Among all the different tribes of the Greeks the exercises which were carried on in a Greek gymnasium were either mere games, or the more important exercises which the gymnasia had in common with the public contests in the great festivals. Among the former we may mention, 1. The game at ball (σφαιριστική), which was in universal favour with the Greeks. [PILA.] Every gymnasium contained one large room for the purpose of playing at ball in it (σφαιριστήριον). 2. Παίζειν ἑλκυστίνδα, διελκυστίνδα, or διὰ γραμμῆς, was a game in which one boy, holding one end of a rope, tried to pull the boy who held its other end, across a line marked between them on the ground. 3. The top (βεμβηξ, βέμβιξ, ῥόμβος, στρόβιλος), which was as common an amusement with Greek boys as it is with ours. 4. The πεντάλιθος, which was a game with five stones, which were thrown up from the upper part of the hand and caught in the palm. 5. Σκαπέρδα, which was a game in which a rope was drawn through the upper part of a tree or a post. Two boys, one on each side of the post, turning their backs towards one another, took hold of the ends of the rope and tried to pull each other up. This sport was also one of the amusements at the Attic Dionysia. The more important games, such as running (δρόμος), throwing of the δίσκος and the ἄκων, jumping and leaping (ἄλμα, with and without ἁλτῆρες), wrestling (πάλη), boxing (πυγμή), the pancratium (παγκράτιον), πένταθλος, λαμπαδηφορία, dancing (ὀρχήσις), &c., are described in separate articles. A gymnasium was not a Roman institution. The regular training of boys in the Greek gymnastics was foreign to Roman manners, and even held in contempt. Towards the end of the republic, many wealthy Romans who had acquired a taste for Greek manners, used to attach to their villas small places for bodily exercise, sometimes called gymnasia, sometimes palaestrae, and to adorn them with beautiful works of art. The emperor Nero was the first who built a public gymnasium at Rome.

GYMNĒSII or GYMNĒTES (γυμνήσιοι, or γυμνῆτες), a class of bond-slaves at Argos, who may be compared with the Helots at Sparta. Their name shows that they attended their masters on military service in the capacity of light-armed troops.

GYMNOPAEDĬA (γυμνοπαιδία), the festival of "naked youths," was celebrated at Sparta every year in honour of Apollo Pythaeus, Artemis, and Leto. The statues of these deities stood in a part of the agora called χορός, and it was around these statues that, at the gymnopaedia, Spartan youths performed their choruses and dances in honour of Apollo. The festival lasted for several, perhaps for ten, days, and on the last day men also performed choruses and dances in the theatre; and during these gymnastic exhibitions they sang the songs of Thaletas and Alcman, and the paeans of Dionysodotus. The leader of the chorus (προστάτης or χοροποιός) wore a kind of chaplet in commemoration of the victory of the Spartans at Thyrea. This event seems to have been closely connected with the gymnopaedia, for those Spartans who had fallen on that occasion were always praised in songs at this festival. The boys in their dances performed such rhythmical movements as resembled the exercises of the palaestra and the pancration, and also imitated the wild gestures of the worship of Dionysus. The whole season of the gymnopaedia, during which Sparta was visited by great numbers of strangers, was one of great merriment and rejoicings, and old bachelors alone seem to have been excluded from the festivities. The introduction of the gymnopaedia is generally assigned to the year 665 B.C.

GYNAECONĪTIS. [DOMUS, GREEK.]

GYNAECŎNŎMI or GYNAECŎCOSMI (γυναικονόμοι or γυναικοκοσμοι), magistrates at Athens, originally appointed to superintend the conduct of Athenian women. Their power was afterwards extended in such a manner that they became a kind of police for the purpose of preventing any excesses or indecencies, whether committed by men or by women. Hence they superintended the meetings of friends even in private houses, for instance, at weddings and on other festive occasions.

HALTĒRES (ἁλτῆρες) were certain masses of stone or metal, which were used in the gymnastic exercises of the Greeks and Romans. Persons who practised leaping frequently performed their exercises with halteres in both hands; but they were also frequently used merely to exercise the body in somewhat the same manner as our **dumb-bells.**

Halters. (Tassie, 'Catalogue,' pl. 46.)

HARMĂMAXA (ἁρμάμαξα), a carriage for persons, covered overhead and inclosed with curtains. It was in general large, often drawn by four horses, and attired with splendid ornaments. It occupied among the Persians the same place which the carpentum did among the Romans, being used, especially upon state occasions, for the conveyance of women and children, of eunuchs, and of the sons of the king with their tutors.

HARMOSTAE (ἁρμοσταί, from ἁρμόζω, to fit or join together), the name of the governors whom the Lacedaemonians, after the Peloponnesian war, sent into their subject or conquered towns, partly to keep them in submission, and partly to abolish the democratical form of government, and establish in its stead one similar to their own. Although in many cases they were ostensibly sent for the purpose of abolishing the tyrannical government of a town, and to restore the people to freedom, yet they themselves acted like kings or tyrants.

HARPĂGO (ἁρπάγη: λύκος: κρεάγρα), a grappling-iron, a drag, a flesh-hook. In war the grappling-iron, thrown at an enemy's ship, seized the rigging, and was then used to drag the ship within reach, so that it might be easily boarded or destroyed. These instruments appear to have been much the

Flesh-hook. (British Museum.)

same as the *manus ferreae*. The flesh-hook (κρεάγρα) was an instrument used in cookery, resembling a hand with the fingers bent inwards, used to take boiled meat out of the caldron.

HARPASTUM. [PILA.]

HĂRUSPĬCES, or ĂRUSPĬCES (ἱεροσκόποι), soothsayers or diviners, who interpreted the will of the gods. They originally came to Rome from Etruria, whence haruspices were often sent for by the Romans on important occasions. The art of the haruspices resembled in many respects that of the augurs; but they never acquired that political importance which the latter possessed, and were regarded rather as means for ascertaining the will of the gods than as possessing any religious authority. They did not in fact form any part of the ecclesiastical polity of the Roman state during the republic; they are never called sacerdotes, they did not form a collegium, and had no magister at their head. The art of the haruspices, which was called *haruspicina*, consisted in explaining and interpreting the will of the gods from the appearance of the entrails (*exta*) of animals offered in sacrifice, whence they are sometimes called *extispices*, and their art *extispicium*; and also from lightning, earthquakes, and all extraordinary phenomena in nature, to which the general name of *portenta* was given. Their art is said to have been invented by the Etruscan Tages, and was contained in certain books called *libri haruspicini, fulgurales,* and *tonitruales*. This art was considered by the Romans so important at one time, that the senate decreed that a certain number of young Etruscans, belonging to the principal families in the state, should always be instructed in it. In later times, however, their art fell into disrepute among well-educated Romans; and Cicero relates a saying of Cato, that he wondered that one haruspex did not laugh when he saw another. The name of haruspex is sometimes applied to any kind of soothsayer or prophet.

HASTA (ἔγχος), a spear. The spear is defined by Homer, δόρυ χαλκῆρες, "a pole fitted with bronze," and δόρυ χαλκοβαρές, "a pole heavy with bronze." The bronze, for which iron was afterwards substituted, was indispensable to form the point (αἰχμή, ἀκωκή, Homer; λόγχη, Xenophon; *acies, cuspis, spiculum*) of the spear. Each of these two essential parts is often put for the whole, so that a spear is called δόρυ and δοράτιον, αἰχμή, and λόγχη. Even the more especial term μελία, meaning an ash-tree, is used in the same manner, because the pole of the spear was often the stem of a young ash, stripped of its bark and polished. The bottom of the spear was often inclosed in a pointed cap of bronze, called by the Ionic writers σαυρωτήρ and οὐρίαχος, and in Attic or common Greek στύραξ. By forcing this into the ground the spear was fixed erect. Many of the lancers who accompanied the king of Persia, had, instead of this spike at the bottom of their spears, an apple or a pomegranate, either gilt or silvered. Fig. 1. in the annexed woodcut shows the top and bottom of a spear, which is held by one of the king's guards in the sculptures at Persepolis. The spear was used as a weapon of attack in three different ways:—1. It was thrown from catapults and other engines [TORMENTUM]. 2. It was thrust forward as a pike. 3. It

Hasta with Amentum. (From a Painting on a Vase.)

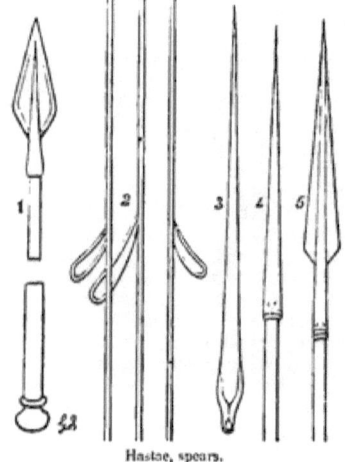

Hastae, spears.

was commonly thrown by the hand. The spear frequently had a leathern thong tied to the middle of the shaft, which was called ἀγκύλη by the Greeks, and amentum by the Romans, and which was of assistance in throwing the spear. The annexed figure represents the amentum attached to the spear at the centre of gravity, a little above the middle. Under the general terms hasta and ἔγχος were included various kinds of missiles, of which the principal were as follow:—Lancea (λόγχη), the lance, a comparatively slender spear commonly used by the Greek horsemen, The appendage shown in woodcut, Fig. 2, enabled them to mount their horses with greater facility.—Pilum (ὑσσός), the javelin, much thicker and stronger than the Grecian lance. Its shaft, often made of cornel, was 4½ feet (three cubits) long, and the barbed iron head was of the same length, but this extended half way down the shaft, to which it was attached with extreme care, so that the whole length of the weapon was about 6 feet 9 inches. It was used either to throw or to thrust with; it was peculiar to the Romans, and gave the name of pilani to the division of the army by which it was adopted. —Whilst the heavy-armed Roman soldiers bore the long lance and the thick and ponderous javelin, the light-armed used smaller missiles, which, though of different kinds, were included under the general term hastae velitares (γρόσφοι). The γρόσφος was a dart, with a shaft about three feet long and an inch in thickness: the iron head was a span long, and so thin and acuminated as to be bent by striking against anything, and thus rendered unfit to be sent back against the enemy. Fig. 3, in the preceding woodcut, shows one which was found in a Roman entrenchment in Gloucestershire.—The light infantry of the Roman army used a similar weapon, called a spit (veru, verutum; σαύνιον). It was adopted by them from the Samnites and the Volsci. Its shaft was 3½ feet long, its point 5 inches. Fig. 4, in the preceding woodcut, represents the head of a dart in the Royal Collection at Naples; it may be taken as a specimen of the verutum, and may be contrasted with fig. 5, which is the head of a lance in the same collection.—The Romans adopted in like manner the gaesum, which was properly a Celtic weapon; it was given as a reward to any soldier who wounded an enemy. [GAESUM.]—Sparus is evidently the same word with the English spar and spear. It was the rudest missile of the whole class. —Besides the terms jaculum and spiculum (ἄκων, ἀκόντιον), which probably denoted darts, resembling in form the lance and javelin, but much smaller, adapted consequently to the light-armed (*jaculatores*), and used in hunting as well as in battle, we find in classical authors the names of various other spears, which were characteristic of particular nations.—Thus, the *sarissa* was the spear peculiar to the Macedonians. This was used both to throw and as a pike. It exceeded in length all other missiles.—The Thracian *romphea*, which had a very long point, like the blade of a sword, was probably not unlike the sarissa.—With these weapons we may also class the Illyrian *sibina*, which resembled a hunting-pole.—The iron head of the German spear, called *framea*, was short and narrow, but very sharp. The Germans used it with great effect either as a lance or a pike: they gave to each youth a framea and a shield on coming of age.—The *Falarica* or *Phalarica* was the spear of the Saguntines, and was impelled by the aid of twisted ropes; it was large and ponderous, having a head of iron a cubit in length, and a ball of lead at its other end; it sometimes carried flaming pitch and tow.—The *matara* and *tragula* were chiefly used in Gaul and Spain: the tragula was probably barbed, as it required to be cut out of the wound.—The *Aclis* and *Cateia* were much smaller missiles. —Among the decorations which the Roman generals bestowed on their soldiers, more especially for saving the life of a fellow-citizen, was a spear without a head, called *hasta pura*. The *celibaris hasta*, having been fixed into the body of a gladiator lying dead on the arena, was used at marriages to part the hair of the bride. A spear was erected at auctions [AUCTIO], and when tenders were received for public offices (*locationes*). It served both to announce, by a conventional sign conspicuous at a distance, that a sale was going on, and to show that it was conducted under the authority of the public functionaries. Hence an auction was called *hasta*, and an auction-room *hastarium*. It was also the practice to set up a spear in the court of the CENTUMVIRI.

HASTATI. [EXERCITUS, p. 168, b.]
HECATOMBE. [SACRIFICIUM.]
HECTE or HECTEUS (ἕκτη, ἑκτεύς), and its half, *Hemiecton* or *Hemiecteon* (ἡμίεκτον, ἡμιεκτέον). In dry measures, the *hecteus* was the sixth part of the *medimnus*, and the *hemiecteon*, of course, the twelfth part. The *hecteus* was equal to the Roman *modius*, as each contained 16 ξέσται or sextarii. The *Hecte* or *Hecteus* and *Hemiecton* were also the names of coins, but the accounts we have of their value are very various. The only consistent explanation is, that there were different *hectae*, **derived from** different units; **in fact, that these coins were** not properly **denominations of money, but** *subdivisions* of the recognised denominations.

HELEPOLIS (ἑλέπολις), "**the taker** of cities," a machine constructed **by** Demetrius Poliorcetes, when he besieged **the city** of Salamis in Cyprus. Its form was **that** of a square tower, each side being 90 **cubits** high **and** 45 wide. It rested **on four** wheels, each eight cubits high. **It was** divided into nine stories, the lower of **which** contained machines for throwing **great** stones, the middle large catapults for throwing spears, **and the highest** other machines for throwing smaller stones, together with smaller catapults. It was manned with 200 soldiers, besides those who **moved it by pushing** the parallel beams at **the bottom. At** the siege of Rhodes, B. C. 306, Demetrius employed an helepolis of still greater dimensions and more complicated construction. In subsequent ages we find the name of "helepolis" applied to moving towers which carried battering rams, as well as machines for throwing spears and stones.

HELLANODICAE (ἑλλανοδίκαι), the judges in the Olympic games, of whom an account is given under OLYMPIA. The same name was also given to the judges or court-martial in the Lacedaemonian army, and they were probably first called by this name when Sparta was at the head of the Greek confederacy.

HELLENOTAMIAE (ἑλληνοταμίαι), or treasurers of the Greeks, were magistrates appointed by the Athenians to receive the contributions of the allied states. They were first appointed B. C. 477, when Athens, in consequence of the conduct of Pausanias, had obtained the command of the allied states. The money paid by the different states, which was originally fixed at 460 talents, was deposited in Delos, which was the place of meeting for the discussion of all common interests; and there can be no doubt that the hellenotamiae not only received, but were also the guardians of, these monies. The office was retained after the treasury was transferred to Athens on the proposal of the Samians, but was of course abolished on the conquest of Athens by the Lacedaemonians.

HELOTES (εἵλωτες), a class of bondsmen peculiar to Sparta. They were Achaeans, who had resisted the Dorian invaders to the last, and had been reduced to slavery as the punishment of their obstinacy. The Helots were regarded as the property of the state, which, while it gave their services to individuals, reserved to itself the power of emancipating them. They were attached to the land, and could not be sold away from it,

They cultivated the land, and paid to their masters as rent a certain measure of corn, the exact amount of which had been fixed at a very early period, the raising of that amount being forbidden under heavy imprecations. Besides being engaged in the cultivation of the land, the Helots attended on their masters at the public meal, and many of them were no doubt employed by the state in public works. In war the Helots served as light-armed troops (ψίλοι), a certain number of them attending every heavy-armed Spartan to the field; at the battle of Plataeae there were seven Helots to each Spartan. These attendants were probably called ἀμπίτταρες (i. e. ἀμφίσταντες), and one of them in particular, the θεράπων, or *servant*. The Helots only served as hoplites in particular emergencies; and on such occasions they were generally emancipated. The first instance of this kind was in the expedition of Brasidas, B. C. 424. The treatment to which the Helots were subjected was marked by the most wanton cruelty; and they were regarded by the Spartans with the greatest suspicion. Occasionally the ephors selected young Spartans for the secret service (κρυπτεία) of wandering over the country, in order to kill the Helots. The Helots might be emancipated, but there were several steps between them and the free citizens, and it is doubtful whether they were ever admitted to all the privileges of citizenship. The following classes of emancipated Helots are enumerated:—ἀφεταί, ἀδεσπότοι, ἐρυκτῆρες, δεσποσιοναῦται, and νεοδαμώδεις. Of these the ἀφεταί were probably released from all service; the ἐρυκτῆρες were those employed in war; the δεσποσιοναῦται served on board the fleet; and the νεοδαμώδεις were those who had been possessed of freedom for some time. Besides these, there were the μόθωνες or μόθακες, who were domestic slaves, brought up with the young Spartans, and then emancipated. Upon being emancipated they received permission to dwell where they wished.

HĒMĒRŎDRŎMI (ἡμεροδρόμοι), couriers in the Greek states, who could keep on running all day, and were often employed to carry news of important events. They were trained for the purpose, and could perform the longest journeys in an almost incredibly short space of time. Such couriers were in times of danger stationed on some eminence in order to observe anything of importance that might happen, and carry the intelligence with speed to the proper quarter. Hence we frequently find them called *Hemeroscopi* (ἡμεροσκόποι).

HĒMĪCYCLIUM (ἡμικύκλιον), a semicircular seat, for the accommodation of persons engaged in conversation; also the semicircular seat round the tribunal in a basilica.

HĒMĪNA (ἡμίνα), the name of a Greek and Roman measure, seems to be nothing more than the dialectic form used by the Sicilian and Italian Greeks for ἡμίσυ. It was therefore applied to the half of the standard fluid measure, the ξέστης, which the other Greeks called κοτύλη, and the word passed into the Roman metrical system, where it is used with exactly the same force, namely for a measure which is half of the *sextarius*, and equal to the Greek *cotylé*.

HENDĔCA (οἱ ἕνδεκα), the Eleven, were magistrates at Athens of considerable importance. They were annually chosen by lot, one from each of the ten tribes, and a secretary (γραμματεύς), who must properly be regarded as their servant (ὑπηρέτης), though he formed one of their number. The principal duty of the Eleven was the care and management of the public prison (δεσμωτήριον), which was entirely under their jurisdiction. The prison, however, was seldom used by the Athenians as a mere place of confinement, serving generally for punishments and executions. When a person was condemned to death he was immediately given into the custody of the Eleven, who were then bound to carry the sentence into execution according to the laws. The most common mode of execution was by hemlock juice (κώνειον), which was drunk after sunset. The Eleven had under them gaolers, executioners, and torturers. When torture was inflicted in causes affecting the state, it was either done in the immediate presence of the Eleven, or by their servant (ὁ δήμιος). The Eleven usually had only to carry into execution the sentence passed in the courts of law and the public assemblies; but in some cases they possessed jurisdiction. This was the case in those summary proceedings called *apagoge*, *ephegesis* and *endeixis*, in which the penalty was fixed by law, and might be inflicted by the court on the confession or conviction of the accused, without appealing to any of the jury courts.

HĒPHAESTEIA. [LAMPADEPHORIA.]

HĒRAEA (ἡραῖα), the name of festivals celebrated in honour of Hera in all the towns of Greece where the worship of this divinity was introduced. The original seat of her worship was Argos; whence her festivals in other places were, more or less, imitations of those which were celebrated at Argos. Her service was performed by the most distinguished priestesses of the place; one of them was the high-priestess, and the Argives counted their years by the date of her office.

The Heraea of Argos were celebrated every fifth year. One of the great solemnities which took place on the occasion, was a magnificent procession to the great temple of Hera, between Argos and Mycenae. A vast number of young men assembled at Argos, and marched in armour to the temple of the goddess. They were preceded by one hundred oxen (ἑκατόμβη), whence the festival is also called ἑκατόμβαια). The high-priestess accompanied this procession, riding in a chariot drawn by two white oxen. The 100 oxen were sacrificed, and their flesh distributed among all the citizens; after which games and contests took place. Of the Heraea celebrated in other countries, those of Samos, which island derived the worship of Hera from Argos, were perhaps the most brilliant of all the festivals of this divinity. The Heraea of Elis, which were celebrated in the fourth year of every Olympiad, were also conducted with considerable splendour.

HERES.—(1) GREEK. To obtain the right of inheritance as well as citizenship at Athens (ἀγχιστεία and πολιτεία), legitimacy was a necessary qualification. When an Athenian died leaving legitimate sons, they shared the inheritance, like our heirs in gavelkind; the only advantage possessed by the eldest son being the first choice in the division. Every man of full age and sound mind, not under durance or improper influence, was competent to make a will; but if he had a son he could not disinherit him, although his will might take effect in case the son did not complete his seventeenth year. If there was but one son, he took the whole estate; but if he had sisters, it was incumbent on him to provide for them, and give them suitable marriage portions; they were then called ἐπίπροικοι. On failure of sons and their issue, daughters and daughters' children succeeded, and there seems to have been no limit to the succession in the descending line. It will assist the student to be informed, that ἀνεψιός signifies a first cousin. Ἀνεψιαδοῦς is a first cousin's son; formed in the same manner as ἀδελφιδοῦς from ἀδελφός, and θυγατριδοῦς from θυγατήρ. Κλῆρος is the subject-matter of inheritance, or (in one sense of the word) the inheritance; κληρονόμος the heir. Ἀγχιστεία, proximity of blood in reference to succession, and sometimes right of succession. Συγγένεια, natural consanguinity. Συγγενεῖς, collateral relations, are opposed to ἔκγονοι, lineal descendants.—(2) ROMAN. A person might become an heres by being named as such (institutus, scriptus, factus) in a will executed by a competent person, according to the forms required by law [TESTAMENTUM]. The testator might either name one person as heres, or he might name several heredes (coheredes), and he might divide the hereditas among them as he pleased. The shares of the heredes were generally expressed by reference to the divisions of the As: thus, "heres ex asse" is heres to the whole property; "heres ex dodrante," heres to three-fourths; "heres ex semuncia," heir to one twenty-fourth. If there were several heredes named, without any definite shares being given to them, the property belonged to them in equal shares. As a general rule, only Roman citizens could be named as heredes in the will of a Roman citizen; but a slave could also be named heres, though he had no power to make a will, and a filius-familias could also be named heres, though he was under the same incapacity. Persons, not Roman citizens, who had received the commercium, could take hereditates, legata and fideicommissa by testament.—Heredes were either Necessarii, Sui et Necessarii, or Extranei. The heres necessarius was a slave of the testator, who was made an heres and liber at the same time; and he was called necessarius, because of the necessity that he was under of accepting the hereditas. The heredes sui et necessarii were sons and daughters, and the sons and daughters of a son, who were in the power of a testator. These heredes sui were called necessarii, because of the necessity that they were under, according to the civil law, of taking the hereditas with its incumbrances. But the praetor permitted such persons to refuse the hereditas (abstinere se ab hereditate), and to allow the property to be sold to pay the testator's debts; and he gave the same privilege to a mancipated son (qui in causa mancipii est). All other heredes are called extranei, and comprehend all persons who are not in the power of a testator, such as emancipated children. A certain time was allowed to extranei for the cretio hereditatis, that is, for them to determine whether they would take the hereditas or not: hence the phrase, "cernere hereditatem."—If a man died intestate, the hereditas came to the heredes sui, and was then called legitima hereditas. If an intestate had no sui heredes, the Twelve Tables gave the hereditas to the agnati [COGNATI], and if there were no agnati, to the gentiles. If a man had a son in his power, he was bound either to make him heres, or to exheredate (exheredare) him expressly (nominatim). If he passed him over in silence (silentio praeterierit), the will was altogether void (inutile, non jure factum). Other liberi could be passed over, and the will would still be a valid will; but the liberi so passed over took a certain portion of the hereditas *adcrescendo*, as it was termed, or *jure adcrescendi*. It was necessary either to institute as heredes, or to exheredate posthumous children *nominatim*, otherwise the will, which was originally valid, became invalid (*ruptum*); and the will became invalid by the birth either of a posthumous son or daughter, or, as the phrase was, *adgnascendo rumpitur testamentum*. The heres represented the testator and intestate, and had not only a claim to all his property and all that was due to him, but was bound by all his obligations. He succeeded to the sacra privata, and was bound to maintain them, but only in respect of the property, for the obligation of the sacra privata was attached to property and to the heres only as the owner of it. Hence the expression "sine sacris hereditas" meant an hereditas unencumbered with sacra.

HERMAE (ἑρμαῖ), and the diminutive Hermuli (ἑρμίδια), statues composed of a head, usually that of the god Hermes, placed on a quadrangular pillar, the height of which corresponds to the stature of the human body. Such statues were very numerous at Athens. So great was the demand for these works that the words ἑρμογλύφος, ἑρμογλυφικὴ τέχνη, and ἑρμογλυφεῖον, were used as the generic terms for a sculptor, his art, and his studio. Houses in Athens had one of these statues placed at the door, called ἑρμῆς στροφαῖος or στροφεύς; and sometimes also in the peristyle. The great reverence attached to them is shown by the alarm and indignation which were felt at Athens in consequence of the mutilation of the whole number in a single night, just before the sailing of the Sicilian expedition. They were likewise placed in front of temples, near to tombs, in the gymnasia, palaestrae, libraries, porticoes, and public places, at the corners of streets, on high roads as sign-posts, with distances inscribed upon them, and on the boundaries of lands and states, and at the gates of cities. Small Hermae were also used as pilasters, and as supports for furniture and utensils. Many statues existed of other deities, of the same form as the Hermae; which no doubt originated in the same manner; and which were still called by the generic name of *Hermae*; even though the bust upon them was that of another deity. Some statues of this kind are described by a name compounded of that of Hermes and another divinity: thus we have *Hermanubis, Hermares, Hermathena, Hermeracles, Hermeros, Hermopan*. There is another class of these works, in which the bust represented no deity at all, but was simply the portrait of a man. Even these statues, however, retained the names of *Hermae* and *Termini*. The Hermae were used by the wealthy Romans for the decoration of their houses. The following engraving exhibits a Hermes decorated with garlands and surrounded with the implements of his worship.

Hermes. (From a Bas-relief.)

HERMAEA (ἑρμαῖα), festivals of Hermes, celebrated in various parts of Greece. As Hermes was the tutelary deity of the gymnasia and palaestrae, the boys at Athens celebrated the Hermaea in the gymnasia.

HESTIĀSIS (ἑστίασις), was a species of liturgy, and consisted in giving a feast to one of the tribes at Athens (τὴν φυλὴν ἑστιᾶν). It was provided for each tribe at the expense of a person belonging to that tribe, who was called ἑστιάτωρ.

HIĔRODŬLI (ἱερόδουλοι), persons of both sexes, who were devoted like slaves to the worship of the gods. They were of Eastern origin, and are most frequently met with in connection with the worship of the deities of Syria, Phoenicia, and Asia Minor. They consisted of two classes; one composed of slaves, properly so called, who attended to all the lower duties connected with the worship of the gods, cultivated the sacred lands, &c., and whose descendants continued in the same servile condition; and the other comprising persons who were personally free, but had dedicated themselves as slaves to the gods, and who were either attached to the temples, or were dispersed throughout the country and brought to the gods the money they had gained. To the latter class belonged the women, who prostituted their persons, and presented to the gods the money they had obtained by this means. This class was only found in Greece, in connection with the worship of those divinities who were of Eastern origin, or whose religious rites were borrowed from the East. This was the case with Aphrodite (Venus), who was originally an Oriental goddess.

HIEROMNEMONES (ἱερομνήμονες), the more honourable of the two classes of representatives who composed the Amphictyonic council. An account of them is given under AMPHICTYONES.—We also read of hieromnemones in Grecian states, distinct from the Amphictyonic representatives of this name. Thus the priests of Poseidon, at Megara, were called hieromnemones, and at Byzantium, which was a colony of Megara, the chief magistrate in the state appears to have been called by this name.

HIERONICAE. [ATHLETAE.]

HIEROPOII (ἱεροποιοί), sacrificers at Athens, of whom ten were appointed every year, and conducted all the usual sacrifices, as well as those belonging to the quinquennial festivals, with the exception of those of the Panathenaea.

HILARIA (ἱλάρια), a Roman festival, celebrated on the 25th of March, in honour of Cybele, the mother of the gods.

HIPPOBOTAE (ἱπποβόται), the feeders of horses, the name of the nobility of Chalcis in Euboea, corresponding to the ἱππεῖς in other Greek states.

HIPPODROMUS (ἱππόδρομος), the name by which the Greeks designated the place appropriated to the horse-races, both of chariots and of single horses, which formed a part of their games. The word was also applied to the races themselves. In Homer's vivid description (*Il.* xxiii., 262—650) the nature of the contest and the arrangements for it are very clearly indicated. There is no artificially constructed hippodrome; but an existing land-mark or monument (σῆμα) is chosen as the goal (τέρμα), round which the chariots had to pass, leaving it on the left hand, and so returning to the Greek ships on the sea-shore, from which they had started. The chariots were five in number, each with two horses and a single driver, who stood upright in his chariot. The critical point of the race was to turn the goal as sharp as possible, with the nave of the near wheel almost grazing it, and to do this safely: very often the driver was here thrown out, and the chariot broken in pieces. The account in Homer will give us an equally good idea of a chariot-race at Olympia, or in any other of the Greek games of later times. The general form of the hippodrome was an oblong, with a semicircular end. For an account of the chariot races at Rome see CIRCUS.

HISTRIO (ὑποκριτής), an actor.—(1) GREEK. It is shown in the articles CHORUS and DIONYSIA that the Greek drama originated in the chorus which at the festivals of Dionysus danced around his altar, and that at first one person detached himself from the chorus, and, with mimic gesticulation, related his story either to the chorus or in conversation with it. If the story thus acted required more than one person, they were all represented in succession by the same actor, and there was never more than one person on the stage at a time. This custom was retained by Thespis and Phrynichus. Aeschylus introduced a second and a third actor; and the number of three actors was but seldom exceeded in any Greek drama. The three regular actors were distinguished by the technical names of πρωταγωνιστής, δευτεραγωνιστής, and τριταγωνιστής, which indicated the more or less prominent part which an actor had to perform in the drama. The female characters of a play were always performed by young men. A distinct class of persons, who made acting on the stage their profession, was unknown to the Greeks during the period of their great dramatists. The earliest and greatest dramatic poets, Thespis, Sophocles, and probably Aeschylus also, acted in their own plays, and in all probability as protagonistae. It was not thought degrading in Greece to perform on the stage. At a later period persons began to devote themselves exclusively to the profession of actors, and distinguished individuals received even as early as the time of Demosthenes exorbitant sums for their performances.—(2) ROMAN. The word *histrio*, by which the Roman actor was called, is said to have been formed from the Etruscan *hister*, which signified a ludio or dancer. In the year 364 B.C. Rome was visited by a plague, and as no human means could stop it, the Romans are said to have tried to avert the anger of the gods by scenic plays (*ludi scenici*), which, until then, had been unknown to them; and as there were no persons at Rome prepared for such performances, the Romans sent to Etruria for them. The first histriones, who were thus introduced from Etruria, were dancers, and performed their movements to the accompaniment of a flute. Roman youths afterwards not only imitated these dancers, but also recited rude and jocose verses, adapted to the movements of the dance and the melody of the flute. This kind of amusement, which was the basis of the Roman drama, remained unaltered until the time of Livius Andronicus, who introduced a slave upon the stage for the purpose of singing or reciting the recitative, while he himself performed the appropriate dance and gesticulation. A further step in the development of the drama, which is likewise ascribed to Livius, was, that the dancer and reciter carried on a dialogue, and acted a story with the accompaniment of the flute. The name histrio, which originally signified a dancer, was now applied to the actors in the drama. The atellanae were played by freeborn Romans, while the regular drama was left to the histriones, who formed a distinct class of persons. The histriones were not citizens; they were not contained in the tribes, nor allowed to be enlisted as soldiers in the Roman legions; and if any citizen entered the profession of an histrio, he, on this account, was excluded from his tribe. The histriones were therefore always either freedmen, strangers, or slaves, and many passages of Roman writers show that they were generally held in great contempt. Towards the close of the republic it was only such men as Cicero, who, by their Greek education, raised themselves above the prejudices of their countrymen, and valued the person no less than the talents of an Aesopus and a Roscius. But notwithstanding this low estimation in which actors were generally held, distinguished individuals among them attracted immense crowds to the theatres, and were exorbitantly paid. Roscius alone received every day that he performed one thousand denarii, and Aesopus left his son a fortune of 200,000 sesterces, which he had acquired solely by his profession. The pay of the actors was called *lucar*, which word was perhaps confined originally to the payment made to those who took part in the religious services celebrated in groves.

HŌMOEI (ὅμοιοι), the Equals, were those Spartans who possessed the full rights of citizenship, and are opposed to the ὑπομείονες, or those who had undergone some kind of civil degradation. This distinction between the citizens was no part of the ancient Spartan constitution. In the institution ascribed to Lycurgus, every citizen had a certain portion of land; but as in course of time many citizens lost their lands through various causes, they were unable to contribute to the expenses of the syssitia, and therefore ceased to possess the full rights of Spartan citizens. Hence the distinction appears to have arisen between the ὅμοιοι and ὑπομείονες, the former being those who were in the possession of their land, and consequently able to contribute to the syssitia, the latter those who through having no land were unable to do so. The Homoei were the ruling class in the state. They filled all the public offices with the exception of the Ephoralty, and they probably met together to determine upon public affairs under the name of ἔκκλητοι in an assembly of their own, which is called ἡ μικρὰ ἐκκλησία, to distinguish it from the assembly of the whole body of Spartan citizens.

HŎNŌRES, the high offices of the state to which qualified individuals were called by the votes of the Roman citizens. The words "magistratus" and "honores" are sometimes coupled together. The capacity of enjoying the honores was one of the distinguishing marks of citizenship. [CIVITAS.] *Honor* was distinguished from *munus*. The latter was an office connected with the administration of the state, and was attended with cost (*sumptus*) but not with rank (*dignitas*). Honor was properly said *deferri*, *dari*; munus was said *imponi*. A person who held a magistratus might be said to discharge *munera*, but only as incident to the office, for the office itself was the *honor*. Such munera as these were public games and other things of the kind.

HOPLĪTAE. [EXERCITUS.]

HŌRA. [DIES.]

HŌROLŎGIUM (ὡρολόγιον), the name of the various instruments by means of which the ancients measured the time of the day and night. The earliest and simplest horologia of which mention is made, were called *polos* (πόλος) and *gnomon* (γνώμων). Both divided the day into twelve equal parts, and were a kind of sun-dial. The *gnomon*, which was also called *stoicheion* (στοιχεῖον), was the more simple of the two, and probably the more ancient. It consisted of a staff or pillar standing perpendicular, in a place exposed to the sun (σκιάθηρον), so that the length of its shadow might be easily ascertained. The shadow of the gnomon was measured by feet, which were probably marked on the place where the shadow fell. In later times the name gnomon was applied to any kind of sun-dial, especially to its finger which threw the shadow, and thus pointed to the hour. The *polos* or *heliotropion* (ἡλιοτρόπιον), on the other hand, seems to have been a more perfect kind of sun-dial; but it appears, nevertheless, not to have been much used. It consisted of a basin (λεκανίς), in the middle of which the perpendicular staff or finger (γνώμων) was erected, and in it the twelve parts of the day were marked by lines.— Another kind of horologium was the *clepsydra* (κλεψύδρα). It derived its name from κλέπτειν and ὕδωρ, as in its original and simple form it consisted of a vessel with several little openings (τρυπήματα) at the bottom, through which the water contained in it escaped, as it were by stealth. This instrument seems at first to have been used only for the purpose of measuring the time during which persons were allowed to speak in the courts of justice at Athens. It was a hollow globe, probably somewhat flat at the top-part, where it had a short neck (αὐλός), like that of a bottle, through which the water was poured into it. This opening might be closed by a lid or stopper (πῶμα), to prevent the water running out at the bottom. As the time for speaking in the Athenian courts was thus measured by water, the orators frequently use the term ὕδωρ instead of the time allowed to them. An especial officer (ὁ ἐφ' ὕδωρ) was appointed in the courts for the purpose of watching the clepsydra, and stopping it when any documents were read, whereby the speaker was interrupted. The time, and consequently the quantity of water allowed to a speaker, depended upon the importance of the case. The clepsydra used in the courts of justice was, properly speaking, no horologium; but smaller ones, made of glass, and of the same simple structure, were undoubtedly used very early in families for the purposes of ordinary life, and for dividing the day into twelve equal parts. In these glass-clepsydrae the division into twelve parts must have been visible, either on the glass globe itself, or in the basin into which the water flowed.—The first horologium with which the Romans became acquainted was a sun-dial (*solarium* or *horologium sciothericum*), and was said to have been brought to Rome by Papirius Cursor twelve years before the war with Pyrrhus. But as sun-dials were useless when the sky was cloudy, P. Scipio Nasica, in his censorship, 159 B.C., established a public clepsydra, which indicated the hours both of day and night. This clepsydra was in aftertimes generally called solarium. After the time of Scipio Nasica several horologia, chiefly solaria, seem to have been erected in various public places at Rome. Clepsydrae were used by the Romans in their camps, chiefly for the purpose of measuring accurately the four vigiliae into which the night was divided. The custom of using clepsydrae as a check upon the speakers in the courts of justice at Rome, was introduced by a law of Cn. Pompeius, in his third consulship. Before that time the speakers had been under no restrictions, but spoke as long as they deemed proper. At Rome, as at Athens, the time allowed to the speakers depended upon the importance of the case.

HORRĔUM (ὡρεῖον, σιτοφυλακεῖον, ἀποθήκη) was, according to its etymological signification, a place in which ripe fruits, and especially corn, were kept, and thus answered to our granary. During the empire the name horreum was given to any place destined for the safe preservation of things of any kind. Thus we find it applied to a place in which beautiful works of art were kept, to cellars (*horrea subterranea, horrea cinaria*), to depôts for merchandise, and all sorts of provisions (*horreum penarium*). Seneca even calls his library a horreum. But the more general application of the word horreum was to places for keeping fruit and corn ; and as some kinds of fruit required to be kept more dry than others, the ancients had besides the horrea subterranea, or cellars, two other kinds, one of which was built like every other house upon the ground; but others (*horrea pensilia* or *sublimia*) were erected above the ground, and rested upon posts or stone pillars, that the fruits kept in them might remain dry.—From about the year 140 after Christ, Rome possessed two kinds of public horrea. The one class consisted of buildings in which the Romans might deposit their goods, and even their money, securities, and other valuables. The second and more important class of horrea, which may be termed public granaries, were buildings in which a plentiful supply of corn was constantly kept at the expense of the state, and from which, in seasons of scarcity, the corn was distributed among the poor, or sold at a moderate price.

HORTUS (κῆπος), garden. Our knowledge of the horticulture of the Greeks is very limited. In fact the Greeks seem to have had no great taste for landscape beauties, and the small number of flowers with which they were acquainted afforded but little inducement to ornamental horticulture. At Athens the flowers most cultivated were probably those used for making garlands, such as violets and roses. In the time of the Ptolemies the art of gardening seems to have advanced in the favourable climate of Egypt so far, that a succession of flowers was obtained all the year round. The Romans, like the Greeks, laboured under the disadvantage of a very limited flora. This disadvantage they endeavoured to overcome, by arranging the materials they did possess in such a way as to produce a striking effect. We have a very full description of a Roman garden in a letter of the younger Pliny, in which he describes his Tuscan villa. In front of the *porticus* there was generally a *xystus*, or flat piece of ground, divided into flower-beds of different shapes by borders of box. There were also such flower-beds in other parts of the garden. Sometimes they were raised so as to form terraces, and their sloping sides planted with evergreens or creepers. The most striking features of a Roman garden were lines of large trees, among which the plane appears to have been a great favourite, planted in regular order; alleys or walks (*ambulationes*) formed by closely clipped hedges of box, yew, cypress, and other evergreens; beds of acanthus, rows of fruit-trees, especially of vines, with statues, pyramids, fountains, and summer-houses (*diaetae*). The trunks of the trees and the parts of the house or any other buildings which were visible from the garden, were often covered with ivy. In one respect the Roman taste differed most materially from that of the present day, namely, in their fondness for the *ars topiaria*, which consisted in tying, twisting, or cutting trees and shrubs (especially the box) into the figures of animals, ships, letters, &c. Their principal garden-flowers seem to have been violets and roses, and they also had the crocus, narcissus, lily, gladiolus, iris, poppy, amaranth, and others. Conservatories and hot-houses are frequently mentioned by Martial. Flowers and plants were also kept in the central place of the peristyle [DOMUS], on the roofs and in the windows of houses. An ornamental garden was also called *virida-*

Hortus, Garden. (From a Painting at Herculaneum.)

rium, and the gardener *topiarius* or *viridarius*. The common name for a gardener is *villicus* or *cultor hortorum*.

HOSPITIUM (ξενία, προξενία), hospitality, was in Greece, as well as at Rome, of a twofold nature, either private or public, in so far as it was either established between individuals, or between two states. (*Hospitium privatum* and *hospitium publicum*, ξενία and προξενία.) In ancient Greece the stranger, as such (ξένος and *hostis*), was looked upon as an enemy; but whenever he appeared among another tribe or nation without any sign of hostile intentions, he was considered not only as one who required aid, but as a suppliant, and Zeus was the protecting deity of strangers and suppliants (Ζεὺς ξένιος). On his arrival, therefore, the stranger was kindly received, and provided with every thing necessary to make him comfortable. It seems to have been customary for the host, on the departure of the stranger, to break a die (ἀστράγαλος) in two, one half of which he himself retained, while the other half was given to the stranger; and when at any future time they or their descendants met, they had a means of recognising each other, and the hospitable connection was renewed. Hospitality thus not only existed between the persons who had originally formed it, but was transferred as an inheritance from father to son. What has been said hitherto, only refers to *hospitium privatum*; but of far greater importance was the *hospitium publicum* (προξενία, sometimes simply ξενία) or public hospitality, which existed between two states, or between an individual or a family on the one hand, and a whole state on the other. Of the latter kind of public hospitality many instances are recorded, such as that between the Peisistratids and Sparta, in which the people of Athens had no share. The hospitium publicum among the Greeks arose undoubtedly from the hospitium privatum, and it may have originated in two ways. When the Greek tribes were governed by chieftains or kings, the private hospitality existing between the ruling families of two tribes may have produced similar relations between their subjects, which, after the abolition of the kingly power, continued to exist between the new republics as a kind of political inheritance of former times. Or a person belonging to one state might have either extensive connections with the citizens of another state, or entertain great partiality for the other state itself, and thus offer to receive all those who came from that state either on private or public business, and to act as their patron in his own city. This he at first did merely as a private individual, but the state to which he offered this kind of service would naturally soon recognise and reward him for it. When two states established public hospitality, and no individuals came forward to act as the representatives of their state, it was necessary that in each state persons should be appointed to show hospitality to, and watch over the interests of, all persons who came from the state connected by hospitality. The persons who were appointed to this office as the recognised agents of the state for which they acted were called *proxeni* (πρόξενοι), but those who undertook it voluntarily *etheloproxeni* (ἐθελοπρόξενοι). The office of *proxenus*, which bears great resemblance to that of a modern consul or minister-resident, was in some cases hereditary in a particular family. When a state appointed a proxenus, it either sent out one of its own citizens to reside in the other state, or it selected one of the citizens of this state, and conferred upon him the honour of proxenus. The former was, in early times, the custom of Sparta, where the kings had the right of selecting from among the Spartan citizens those whom they wished to send out as proxeni to other states. But in subsequent times this custom seems to have been given up, for we find that at Athens the family of Callias were the proxeni of Sparta, and at Argos, the Argive Alciphron. The principal duties of a proxenus were to receive those persons, especially ambassadors, who came from the state which he represented ; to procure for them admission to the assembly, and seats in the theatre ; to act as the patron of the strangers, and to mediate between the two states if any disputes arose. If a stranger died in the state, the proxenus of his country had to take care of the property of the deceased.—The hospitality of the Romans was, as in Greece, either hospitium privatum or publicum. Private hospitality with the Romans, however, seems to have been more accurately and legally defined than in Greece. The character of a *hospes*, i. e. a person connected with a Roman by ties of hospitality, was deemed even more sacred, and to have greater claims upon the host, than that of a person connected by blood or affinity. The relation of a hospes to his Roman friend was next in importance to that of a cliens. The obligations which the connection of hospitality with a foreigner imposed upon a Roman, were to receive in his house his hospes when travelling ; and to protect, and, in case of need, to represent him as his patron in the courts of justice. Private hospitality thus gave to the hospes the claims upon his host which the client had on his patron, but without any degree of the dependence implied in the clientela. Private hospitality was established between individuals by mutual presents, or by the mediation of a third person, and hallowed by religion ; for Jupiter hospitalis was thought to watch over the jus hospitii, as Zeus xenios did with the Greeks, and the violation of it was as great a crime and impiety at Rome as in Greece. When hospitality was formed, the two friends used to divide between themselves a *tessera hospitalis*, by which, afterwards, they themselves or their descendants— for the connection was hereditary as in Greece—might recognise one another. Hospitality, when thus once established, could not be dissolved except by a formal declaration (*renuntiatio*), and in this case the tessera hospitalis was broken to pieces. Public hospitality seems likewise to have existed at a very early period among the nations of Italy ; but the first direct mention of public hospitality being established between Rome and another city, is after the Gauls had departed from Rome, when it was decreed that Caere should be rewarded for its good services by the establishment of public hospitality between the two cities. The public hospitality after the war with the Gauls gave to the Caerites the right of isopolity with Rome, that is, the civitas without the suffragium and the honores. [COLONIA.] In the later times of the republic we no longer find public hospitality established between Rome and a foreign state ; but a relation which amounted to the same thing was introduced in its stead, that is, towns were raised to the rank of municipia, and thus obtained the civitas without the suffragium and the honores ; and when a town was desirous of forming a similar relation with Rome, it entered into clientela to some distinguished Roman, who then acted as patron of the client-town. But the custom of granting the honour of hospes publicus to a distinguished foreigner by a decree of the senate, seems to have existed down to the end of the republic. His privileges were the same as those of a municeps, that is, he had the civitas, but not the suffragium or the honores. Public hospitality was, like the hospitium privatum, hereditary in the family of the person to whom it had been granted.

HYACINTHIA (Ὑακίνθια), a great national

festival, celebrated every year at Amyclae by the Amyclaeans and Spartans, probably in honour of the Amyclaean Apollo and Hyacinthus together. This Amyclaean Apollo, however, with whom Hyacinthus was assimilated in later times, must not be confounded with Apollo, the national divinity of the Dorians. The festival was called after the youthful hero Hyacinthus, who evidently derived his name from the flower hyacinth (the emblem of death among the ancient Greeks), and whom Apollo accidentally struck dead with a quoit. The Hyacinthia lasted for three days, and began on the longest day of the Spartan month Hecatombeus, at the time when the tender flowers, oppressed by the heat of the sun, drooped their languid heads. On the first and last day of the Hyacinthia sacrifices were offered to the dead, and the death of Hyacinthus was lamented. During these two days, nobody wore any garlands at the repasts, nor took bread, but only cakes and similar things, and when the solemn repasts were over, everybody went home in the greatest quiet and order. The second day, however, was wholly spent in public rejoicings and amusements, such as horse-races, dances, processions, &c. The great importance attached to this festival by the Amyclaeans and Lacedaemonians is seen from the fact, that the Amyclaeans, even when they had taken the field against an enemy, always returned home on the approach of the season of the Hyacinthia, that they might not be obliged to neglect its celebration; and that in a treaty with Sparta, B.C. 421, the Athenians, in order to show their good-will towards Sparta, promised every year to attend the celebration of this festival.

HYBREOS GRAPHE (ὕβρεως γραφή), an action prescribed by the Attic law for wanton and contumelious injury to the person, whether in the nature of indecent (δι' αἰσχρουργίας) or other assaults (διὰ πληγῶν). The severity of the sentence extended to confiscation or death.

HYDRAULIS (ὕδραυλις), an hydraulic organ, invented by Ctesibius of Alexandria, who lived about B.C. 200. Its pipes were partly of bronze, and partly of reed. The number of its stops, and consequently of its rows of pipes, varied from one to eight. It continued in use so late as the ninth century of our era. The organ was well adapted to gratify the Roman people in the splendid entertainments provided for them by the emperors and other opulent persons. Nero was very curious about organs, both in regard to their musical effect and their mechanism. A contorniate coin of this emperor, in the British Museum, shows an organ with a sprig of laurel on one side, and a man standing on the other.

Hydraulis, water-organ. (Coin of Nero in British Museum.)

HYDRIAPHORIA (ὑδριαφορία), was the carrying of a vessel with water (ὑδρία), which service the married alien (μέτοικοι) women had to perform to the married part of the female citizens of Athens, when they walked to the temple of Athena in the great procession at the Panathenaea.

HYPORCHEMA (ὑπόρχημα), a lively kind of mimic dance which accompanied the songs used in the worship of Apollo, especially among the Dorians. A chorus of singers at the festivals of Apollo usually danced around the altar, while several other persons were appointed to accompany the action of the song with an appropriate mimic performance (ὑπορχεῖσθαι). The hyporchema was thus a lyric dance, and often passed into the playful and comic.

IDUS. [CALENDARIUM.]
IGNOMINIA. [CENSOR; INFAMIA.]
IGNOBILES. [NOBILES.]
IMAGO, a representation or likeness, an image or figure of a person. Among the Romans those persons, who had filled any of the higher or curule magistracies of the state, had the right of having images of themselves. Respecting this *jus imaginum* see NOBILES.

IMMUNITAS (from *in* and *munus*), signifies, (1) A freedom from taxes. (2) A freedom from services which other citizens had to discharge. With respect to the first kind of immunitas we find that the emperors frequently granted it to separate persons, or to certain classes of persons, or to whole states. The second kind of immunitas was granted to all persons who had a valid excuse (*excusatio*) to be released from such services, and also to other persons as a special favour. The immunitas might be either general, from all services which a citizen owed to the state, or special, such as from military service, from taking the office of tutor or guardian, and the like.

IMPĔRĀTOR. [IMPERIUM.]

IMPĔRĬUM, was under the republic a power, without which no military operation could be carried on as in the name and on the behalf of the state. It was not incident to any office, and was always specially conferred by a lex curiata, that is, a lex passed in the comitia curiata. Consequently, not even a consul could act as commander of an army, unless he were empowered by a lex curiata. It could not be held or exercised within the city in the republican period; but it was sometimes conferred specially upon an individual for the day of his triumph within the city, and at least, in some cases, by a plebiscitum. As opposed to *potestas*, *imperium* is the power which was conferred by the state upon an individual who was appointed to command an army. The phrases *consularis potestas* and *consulare imperium* might both be properly used; but the expression *tribunitia potestas* only could be used, as the tribuni never received the imperium. In respect of his imperium, he who received it was styled *imperator*. After a victory it was usual for the soldiers to salute their commander as imperator, but this salutation neither gave nor confirmed the title, since the title as a matter of course was given with the imperium. Under the republic the title came properly after the name; thus Cicero, when he was proconsul in Cilicia, could properly style himself M. Tullius Cicero Imperator, for the term merely expressed that he had the imperium. The emperors Tiberius and Claudius refused to assume the praenomen of imperator, but the use of it as a praenomen became established among their successors. The term imperium was applied in the republican period to express the sovereignty of the Roman state. Thus Gaul is said by Cicero to have come under the imperium and ditio of the populus Romanus.

IMPLŬVĬUM. [DOMUS.]

IMPŪBES. An infans was incapable of doing any legal act. An impubes, who had passed the limits of infantia, could do any legal act with the auctoritas of his tutor. With the attainment of pubertas, a person obtained the full power over his property, and the tutela ceased: he could also dispose of his property by will; and he could contract marriage. Pubertas, in the case of a male, was attained with the completion of the fourteenth, and, in a female, with the completion of the twelfth year. Upon attaining the age of puberty a Roman youth assumed the toga virilis, but until that time he wore the toga praetexta, the broad purple hem of which (*praetexta*) at once distinguished him from other persons. The toga virilis was assumed at the Liberalia in the month of March, and though no age appears to have been positively fixed for the ceremony, it probably took place as a general rule on the feast which next followed the completion of the fourteenth year; though it is certain that the completion of the fourteenth year was not always the time observed. Still, so long as a male wore the praetexta, he was impubes, and when he assumed the toga virilis, he was pubes.

INAUGŬRĀTĬO, was in general the ceremony by which the augurs obtained, or endeavoured to obtain, the sanction of the gods to something which had been decreed by man; in particular, however, it was the ceremony by which things or persons were consecrated to the gods, whence the terms *dedicatio* and *consecratio* were sometimes used as synonymous with inauguratio. Not only were priests inaugurated, but also the higher magistrates, who for this purpose were summoned by the augurs to appear on the capitol, on the third day after their election. This inauguratio conferred no priestly dignity upon the magistrates, but was merely a method of obtaining the sanction of the gods to their election, and gave them the right to take auspicia; and on important emergencies it was their duty to make use of this privilege.

INAURIS, an ear-ring; called in Greek ἐνώτιον, because it was worn in the ear (οὖς), and ἐλλόβιον, because it was inserted into the lobe of the ear (λοβός), which was bored for the purpose. Ear-rings were worn by both sexes in oriental countries. Among the Greeks and Romans they were worn only by females. This ornament consisted of the ring (κρίκος), and of the drops (*stalagmia*). The ring was generally of gold, although the common people also wore ear-rings of bronze. Instead of a ring a hook was often used. The drops were sometimes of gold, very finely wrought, and sometimes of pearls.

INCENDĬUM, the crime of setting any object on fire, by which the property of a man is endangered. A law of the Twelve Tables inflicted a severe punishment on the person who set fire to property maliciously (*sciens, prudens*); but if it was done by accident (*casu, id est, negligentia*), the law obliged the offender to repair the injury he

P 2

had committed. Sulla, in his *Lex Cornelia de Sicariis*, punished malicious (*dolo malo*) incendium, but only in the city, or within a thousand paces of it, with aquae et ignis interdictio. Cn. Pompeius, in u. c. 52, made incendium a crime of *Vis* by his *Lex Pompeia de Vi*, in consequence of the burning of the Curia and the Porcia Basilica on the burial of Clodius; and Julius Caesar also included it in his *Lex Julia de Vi*. Besides the two criminal prosecutions given by the Lex Cornelia and Lex Julia, a person could also bring actions to recover compensation for the injury done to his property.

INCESTUM or INCESTUS. Incestum is non castum, and signifies generally all immoral and irreligious acts. In a narrower sense it denotes the unchastity of a Vestal, and sexual intercourse of persons within certain degrees of consanguinity. Incest with a Vestal was punished with the death of both parties. [VESTALES.]

INCŪNĀBŪLA or CŪNĀBŪLA (σπάργανον), swaddling-clothes, in which a new-born child was wrapped. It was one of the peculiarities of the Lacedaemonian education to dispense with the use of incunabula, and to allow children to enjoy the free use of their limbs.

Incunabula, swaddling-clothes. (From a Bas-relief at Rome.)

INDUTUS. [AMICTUS.]

INFĀMĬA, was a consequence of condemnation for certain crimes, and also a direct consequence of certain acts, such as adultery, prostitution, appearing on the public stage as an actor, &c. A person who became *infamis* lost the suffragium and honores, and was degraded to the condition of an aerarian. Infamia should be distinguished from the *Nota Censoria*, the consequence of which was only *ignominia*. [CENSOR.]

INFANS, INFANTIA. In the Roman law there were several distinctions of age which were made with reference to the capacity for doing legal acts:—1. The first period was from birth to the end of the seventh year, during which time persons were called *Infantes*, or *Qui fari non possunt*. 2. The second period was from the end of seven years to the end of fourteen or twelve years, according as the person was a male or a female, during which persons were defined as those *Qui fari possunt*. The persons included in these first two classes were *Impuberes*. 3. The third period was from the end of the twelfth or fourteenth to the end of the twenty-fifth year, during which period persons were *Adolescentes, Adulti*. The persons included in these three classes were minores xxv annis or annorum, and were often, for brevity's sake, called minores only [CURATOR]; and the persons included in the third and fourth class were *Puberes*. 4. The fourth period was from the age of twenty-five, during which persons were *Majores*.

INFĔRIAE. [FUNUS.]

INFULA, a flock of white and red wool, which was slightly twisted, drawn into the form of a wreath or fillet, and used by the Romans for ornament on festive and solemn occasions. In sacrificing it was tied with a white band [VITTA] to the head of the victim and also of the priest.

INGĔNUI, were those free men who were born free. Consequently, freedmen (*libertini*) were not ingenui, though the sons of libertini were ingenui; nor could a libertinus by adoption become ingenuus. The words *ingenuus* and *libertinus* are often opposed to one another; and the title of freeman (*liber*), which would comprehend *libertinus*, is sometimes limited by the addition of *ingenuus* (*liber et ingenuus*.) Under the empire a person, not ingenuus by birth, could be made ingenuus by the emperor.

INJŪRIA. *Injuria*, in the general sense, is opposed to *Jus*. In a special sense *injuria* was done by striking or beating a man either with the hand or with anything; by abusive words (*convicium*); by the proscriptio bonorum, when the claimant knew that the alleged debtor was not really indebted to him; by libellous writings or verses; by soliciting a mater familias, &c. The Twelve Tables had various provisions on the subject of Injuria. Libellous songs or verses were followed by capital punishment. In the case of a limb being mutilated the punishment was Talio. In the case of a broken bone, the penalty was 300 asses if the injury was done to a freeman, and 150 if it was done to a slave. In other cases the Tables fixed the penalty at 25 asses. These penalties were afterwards considered to be insufficient; and the injured person was allowed by the praetor to claim such damages as he thought that he was entitled to, and the judex might give the full amount or less. Infamia was a consequence of condemnation in an actio Injuriarum.

INOA (ἰνῶα), festivals celebrated in several parts of Greece, in honour of Ino.

INQUILINUS. [EXSILIUM.]

INSTITA (περιπόδιον), a flounce; a fillet. The Roman matrons sometimes wore a broad fillet with ample folds, sewed to the bottom of the tunic and reaching to the instep. The use of it indicated a superior regard to decency and propriety of manners.

INSULA was, properly, a **house not joined to the neighbouring houses by a common wall.** An insula, however, generally contained several separate houses, or at least separate apartments or shops, which were let to different families; and hence the word *domus* under the emperors seems to be applied to the house where a family lived, whether it were an **insula** or not, and insula to any hired lodgings.

INTERCESSIO was the interference of a magistratus to whom an appeal [APPELLATIO] was made. The object of the intercessio was to put a **stop to** proceedings, on the ground of informality or other sufficient cause. Any magistratus might *intercedere*, who was of equal rank with or **of rank superior to the** magistratus from or against whom the appellatio was. Cases occur in which one of the praetors interposed (*intercessit*) against the proceedings of his colleague. The **intercessio** is most frequently spoken of with **reference** to the tribunes, who originally had not jurisdictio, but used the intercessio for **the** purpose of preventing wrong which was offered to a person in their presence. The intercessio of **the** tribunes of the plebs was auxilium, and it might be exercised either *in jure* or *in judicio*. The tribune *qui intercessit* could prevent a judicium **from** being instituted. The tribunes could also use the intercessio **to** prevent execution of a judicial **sentence.** A single tribune could effect this, **and against** the opinion of his **colleagues.**

INTERCISI DIES. [DIES.]

INTERDICTUM. "In certain cases (*certis ex causis*) the praetor or proconsul, in the first instance (*principaliter*), exercises his authority for **the termination of disputes.** This he chiefly **does when the** dispute is about possession or quasi-possession; and the exercise of his authority consists in ordering something to be done, or forbidding something to be done. The formulae and the terms, which he uses on such occasions, are called either *interdicta* or *decreta*. They are called *decreta* when he orders something to be done, as when he orders something to be produced (*exhiberi*) or to be restored; they are called *interdicta* when he forbids something to be done, as when he orders that force shall not be used against a person who is in possession rightfully (*sine vitio*), or that nothing shall be done on a piece of sacred ground. Accordingly all interdicta are either restitutoria, or exhibitoria, or prohibitoria." This passage, which is taken from Gaius, the Roman jurist, contains the essential distinction between an *actio* and an *interdictum*. In the case of an *actio*, the praetor pronounces no order or decree, but he gives a judex, whose business it is to investigate the matter in dispute, and to pronounce a sentence consistently with the formula, which is his authority for acting. In the case of an actio, therefore, the praetor neither orders nor forbids a thing to be done, but he says, *Judicium dabo*. In the case of an interdict, the praetor makes an order that something shall be done or shall not be done, and his words are accordingly words of command, *Restituas, Exhibeas, Vim fieri veto*. This *immediate* interposition of the praetor is appropriately expressed by the word *principaliter*.

INTERPRES, an interpreter. This class of persons became very numerous and necessary to the Romans as their empire extended. In large mercantile towns the interpreters, who formed a kind of agents through whom business was done, were sometimes very numerous. All Roman praetors, proconsuls, and quaestors, who were entrusted with the administration of a province, had to carry on all their official proceedings **in the Latin language,** and as they could not **be expected to** be acquainted with the language of the **provincials,** they had always among their **servants** [APPARITORES] one or more interpreters, who were generally Romans, but in most cases undoubtedly freedmen. These interpreters had not only to officiate at the conventus [CONVENTUS], but also explained **to** the Roman governor everything which **the provincials** might wish to be laid before **him.**

INTERREGNUM. [INTERREX.]

INTERREX. This office is said to have been instituted on the death of Romulus, when the senate wished to share the sovereign power among themselves, instead of electing a king. For this purpose, according to Livy, the senate, which then consisted of one hundred members, was divided into ten decuries; **and from each of** these decuries one senator **was** nominated. These together formed a board of ten, with the title of *Interreges*, each of whom enjoyed in succession the regal power and its badges for five days; and if no king was appointed at the expiration of fifty days, the rotation began anew. The period during which they exercised their power was called an *Interregnum*. These ten interreges were the *Decem Primi*, or ten leading senators, of whom the first was chief of the whole senate. The interreges agreed among themselves who should be proposed as king, and if the senate approved of their choice, they summoned the assembly of the curiae, and proposed the person whom they had previously agreed upon; the power of the curiae was confined to accepting or rejecting him. Interreges were appointed under the republic for holding the comitia for the election of the consuls, when the consuls, through civil commotions or other causes, had been unable to do so in their year of office. Each held the office for only five days, as under the kings. The comitia were hardly ever held by the first interrex; more usually by the second or third; but in one instance we read of an eleventh, and in another of a fourteenth interrex. The interreges under the republic, at least from B. C. 482, were elected by the senate from the whole body, and were not confined to the decem primi or ten chief senators, as under the kings. Plebeians, however, were not admissible to this office; and consequently, when plebeians were admitted into the senate, the patrician senators met without the plebeian members to elect an interrex. For this reason, as well as on account of the influence which the interrex exerted in the election of the magistrates, we find that the tribunes of the plebs were strongly opposed to the appointment of an interrex. The interrex had jurisdictio. Interreges continued to be appointed occasionally till the time of the second Punic war, but after that time we read of no interrex, till the senate, by command of Sulla, created an interrex to hold the comitia for his election as dictator, B. C. 82. In B. C. 55 another interrex was appointed, to hold the comitia in which Pompey and Crassus were elected consuls; and we also read of interreges in B. C. 53 and 52, in the latter of which years an interrex held the comitia in which Pompey was appointed sole consul.

ISTHMIA (ἴσθμια), the Isthmian games, one of the four great national festivals of the Greeks. This festival derived its name from the Corinthian isthmus, where it was held. Subsequent to the age of Theseus the Isthmia were celebrated in honour of Poseidon; and this innovation is ascribed to Theseus himself. The celebration of the Isthmia was conducted by the Corinthians, but Theseus had reserved for his Athenians some honourable distinctions: those Athenians who attended the Isthmia sailed across the Saronic gulf in a sacred vessel (θεωρίς), and an honorary place (προεδρία), as large as the sail of their vessel, was assigned to them during the celebration of the games. In times of war between the two states a sacred truce was concluded, and the Athenians were invited to attend at the solemnities. These games were celebrated regularly every other year, in the first and third years of each Olympiad. After the fall of Corinth, in 146 B. C., the Sicyonians were honoured with the privilege of conducting the Isthmian games; but when the town of Corinth was rebuilt by Julius Caesar, the right of conducting the solemnities was restored to the Corinthians. The season of the Isthmian solemnities was, like that of all the great national festivals, distinguished by general rejoicings and feasting. The contests and games of the Isthmia were the same as those at Olympia, and embraced all the varieties of athletic performances, such as wrestling, the pancratium, together with horse and chariot racing. Musical and poetical contests were likewise carried on, and in the latter women were also allowed to take part. The prize of a victor in the Isthmian games consisted at first of a garland of pine-leaves, and afterwards of a wreath of ivy. Simple as such a reward was, a victor in these games gained the greatest distinction and honour among his countrymen; and a victory not only rendered the individual who obtained it a subject of admiration, but shed lustre over his family, and the whole town or community to which he belonged. Hence Solon established by a law, that every Athenian who gained the victory at the Isthmian games should receive from the public treasury a reward of one hundred drachmae. His victory was generally celebrated in lofty odes, called Epinikia, or triumphal odes, of which we still possess some beautiful specimens among the poems of Pindar.

JACULUM. [HASTA.]

JANUA (θύρα), a door. Besides being applicable to the doors of apartments in the interior of a house, which were properly called *ostia*, this term more especially denoted the first entrance into the house, i. e. the front or street door, which was also called *anticum*, and in Greek θύρα αὔλειος, αὐλεία, αὔλιος, or αὐλία. The houses of the Romans commonly had a back door, called *posticum*, *postica*, or *posticula*, and in Greek παράθυρα, dium, παραθύριον. The door-way, when complete, consisted of four indispensable parts; the threshold, or sill (*limen, βηλός, οὐδας*); the lintel (*jugumentum, limen superum*); and the two jambs (*postes, σταθμοί*). The door itself was called *foris* or *valca*, and in Greek σανίς, κλισιάς, or θύρετρον. These words are commonly found in the plural, because the door-way of every building of the least importance contained two doors folding together. When *foris* is used in the singular, it denotes one of the folding doors only. The fastenings of the door (*claustra, obices*) commonly consisted of a bolt (*pessulus*; μάνδαλος, κατοχεύς, κλεῖθρον) placed at the base of each *foris*, so as to admit of being pushed into a socket made in the sill to receive it. By night, the front-door of the house was further secured by means of a wooden and sometimes an iron bar (*sera, repagula*, μοχλός) placed across it, and inserted into sockets on each side of the doorway. Hence it was necessary to remove the bar (τὸν μοχλὸν παραφέρειν) in order to open the door (*reserare*). It was considered improper to enter a house without giving notice to its inmates. This notice the Spartans gave by shouting; the Athenians and all other nations by using the knocker, or more commonly by rapping with the knuckles or with a stick (κρούειν, κόπτειν). In the houses of the rich a porter (*janitor, custos*, θυρωρός) was always in attendance to open the door. He was commonly an eunuch or a slave, and was chained to his post. To assist him in guarding the entrance, a dog was universally kept near it, being also attached by a chain to the wall; and in reference to this practice, the warning *cave canem*, εὐλαβοῦ τὴν κύνα, was sometimes written near the door. The appropriate name for the portion of the house immediately behind the door (θυρών) denotes that it was a kind of apartment; it corresponded to the hall or lobby of our houses. Immediately adjoining it, and close to the front door, there was in many houses a small room for the porter.

JENTACULUM. [COENA.]

JUDEX, JUDICIUM. A Roman magistratus generally did not investigate the facts in dispute in such matters as were brought before him: he appointed a judex for that purpose, and gave him instructions. [ACTIO.] Accordingly, the whole of civil procedure was expressed by the two phrases *Jus* and *Judicium*, of which the former comprehended all that took place before the magistratus (*in jure*), and the latter all that took place before the judex (*in judicio*). In many cases a single judex was appointed: in others, several were appointed, and they seem to have been sometimes called recuperatores, as opposed to the single judex. Under certain circumstances the judex was called arbiter: thus judex and arbiter are named together in the Twelve Tables. A judex when appointed was bound to discharge the functions of the office, unless he had some valid excuse (*excusatio*). There were certain seasons of the year when legal business was done at Rome, and at these times the services of the judices were required. These legal terms were regulated according to the seasons, so that there were periods of vacation. When the judex was appointed, the proceedings *in jure* or before the praetor were terminated. The parties appeared before the judex on the third day (*comperendinatio*), unless the praetor had deferred the judicium for some sufficient reason. The judex was generally aided by advisers (*jurisconsulti*) learned in the law, who were said *in consilio adesse*; but the judex alone was empowered to give judgment. The matter was first briefly stated to the judex (*causae conjectio, collectio*), and the advocates of each party supported his cause in a speech. Witnesses were produced on both sides, and examined orally; the witnesses on one side were also cross-examined by the other. After all the evidence was given and the advocates had finished, the judex gave sentence: if there were several judices, a majority decided. If the matter was one of difficulty, the hearing might be adjourned as often as was necessary (*ampliatio*); and if the judex could not come to a satisfactory conclusion, he might declare this upon oath, and so release himself from the difficulty. This was done by the form of words *non liquere* (N. L.). The sentence was pronounced orally, and was sometimes first written on a tablet. If the defendant did not make his appearance after being duly summoned, judgment might be given against him.—According to Cicero, all judicia had for their object, either the settlement of disputes between individuals (*controversiae*), or the punishment of crimes (*maleficia*). This refers to a division of judicia, which appears in the jurists, into *judicia publica* and *judicia privata*. The former, the *judicia publica*, succeeded to the *judicia populi* of the early republican period: the latter were so called because in them the populus acted as judices. Originally the kings presided in all criminal cases, and the consuls succeeded to their authority. But after the passing of the Lex Valeria (B. C. 507), which gave an appeal to the populus (that is, the comitia curiata) from the magistratus, the consul could not sit in judgment on the caput of a Roman citizen, but such cases were tried in the comitia, or persons were appointed to preside at such inquiries, who were accordingly called *Quaesitores* or *Quaestores parricidii* or *rerum capitalium*. In course of time, as such cases became of more frequent occurrence, such quaestiones were made perpetual, that is, particular magistrates were appointed for the purpose. It was eventually determined, that while the *praetor urbanus* and *peregrinus* should continue to exercise their usual jurisdictions, the other praetors should preside at public trials. In such trials any person might be an accuser (*accusator*). The praetor generally presided as quaesitor, assisted by a judex quaestionis, and a body of judices called his consilium. The judices were generally chosen by lot out of those who were qualified to act; but in some cases the accuser and the accused (*reus*) had the privilege of choosing (*edere*) a certain number of judices out of a large number, who were thence called *Edititii*. Both the accusator and the reus had the privilege of rejecting or challenging (*rejicere*) such judices as they did not like. In many cases a lex was passed for the purpose of regulating the mode of procedure.—The judices voted by ballot, at least generally, and a majority determined the acquittal or condemnation of the accused. Each judex was provided with three tablets (*tabulae*), on one of which was marked A, *Absolvo*; on a second C, *Condemno*; and on a third N. L., *Non liquet*. The judices voted by placing one of these tablets in the urns, which were then examined for the purpose of ascertaining the votes. It was the duty of the magistratus to pronounce the sentence of the judices; in the case of condemnation, to adjudge the legal penalty; of acquittal, to declare the accused acquitted; and of doubt, to declare that the matter must be further investigated (*amplius cognoscendum*).—A *judicium populi*, properly so called, was one in which the case was tried in the comitia curiata, but afterwards in the comitia centuriata and tributa. The accuser, who must be a magistratus, commenced by declaring in a contio that he would on a certain day accuse a certain person, whom he named, of some offence, which he also specified. This was expressed by the phrase *diem dicere*. If the offender held any high office, it was necessary to wait till his time of service had expired, before proceedings could be thus commenced against him. The accused was required to give security for his appearance on the day of trial; the security was called *vades* in a causa capitalis, and *praedes* when the penalty for the alleged offence was pecuniary. If such security was not given, the accused was kept in confinement. If nothing prevented the inquiry from taking place at the time fixed for it, the trial proceeded, and the accuser had to prove his case by evidence. The investigation of the facts was called *anquisitio* with reference to the proposed penalty: accordingly, the phrases *pecunia, capite* or *capitis anquirere*, are used. When the investigation was concluded, the magistratus promulgated a rogatio, which comprehended the charge and the punishment or fine. It was a rule of law that a fine should not be imposed together with another punishment in the same rogatio. The rogatio was made public during three nundinae, like any other lex, and proposed at the comitia for adoption or rejection. The accused sometimes withdrew into exile before the votes were taken; or he might make his defence. The offences which were the chief subject of judicia populi and publica were majestas, adulteria and stupra, parricidium, falsum, vis publica and privata, peculatus, repetundae, ambitus.—With the passing of special enactments for the punishment of particular offences, was introduced the practice of forming a body of judices for the trial of such offences as the enactments were directed against. The *Album Judicum* was the body out of which judices were to be chosen. It is not known what was the number of the body so constituted, but it has been conjectured that the number was 350, and that ten were chosen from each tribe, and thus the origin of the phrase *Decuriae Judicum* is explained. It is easy to conceive that the judicia populi, properly so called, would be less frequent, as special leges were framed for particular offences, the circumstances of which could be better investigated by a smaller body of judices than by the assembled people. The Lex Servilia (B. C. 104) enacted that the judices should not be under thirty nor above sixty years of age, that the accuser and accused should severally propose one hundred judices, and that each might reject fifty from the list of the other, so that one hundred would remain for the trial. Up to B. C. 122 the judices were always senators, but in this year the Sempronia Lex of C. Gracchus took the judicia from the senators and gave them to the equites. This state of things lasted nearly fifty years, till Sulla (B. C. 80) restored the judicia to the senate, and excluded the equites from the album judicum. A Lex Aurelia (B. C. 70) enacted that the judices should be chosen from the three classes—of senators, equites, and tribuni aerarii; and accordingly the judicia were then said to be divided between the senate and the equites. The tribuni aerarii were taken from the rest of the citizens, and were, or ought to have been, persons of some property. Thus the three decuriae of judices were formed; and it was either in consequence of the Lex Aurelia or the Lex Fufia that, instead of one urn for all the tablets, the decuriae had severally their balloting urn, so that the votes of the three classes were known. It is not known if the Lex Aurelia determined the number of judices in any given case. The Lex Pompeia de Vi and De Ambitu (B. C. 52) determined that eighty judices were to be selected by lot, out of whom the accuser and the accused might reject thirty. In the case of Clodius, in the matter of the Bona Dea, there were fifty-six judices. It is conjectured that the number fixed for a given case, by the Lex Aurelia, was seventy judices. Augustus added to the existing three decuriae judicum a fourth decuria, called that of the *Ducenarii*, who had a lower pecuniary qualification, and only decided in smaller matters. Caligula added a fifth decuria, in order to diminish the labours of the judices.

JŪGĒRUM, a Roman measure of surface, 240 feet in length and 120 in breadth, containing therefore 28,800 square feet. It was the double of the *Actus Quadratus*, and from this circumstance, according to some writers, it derived its name. [ACTUS.] The uncial division [As] was applied to the *jugerum*, its smallest part being the *scrupulum* of 10 feet square, = 100 square feet. Thus the *jugerum* contained 288 scrupula. The jugerum was the common measure of land among the Romans. Two *jugera* formed an *heredium*, a hundred *heredia* a *centuria*, and four *centuriae* a *saltus*. These divisions were derived from the original assignment of landed property, in which two *jugera* were given to each citizen as heritable property.

JŪGUM (ζυγός, ζυγόν), signified in general that which joined two things together, such as the transverse beam which united the upright posts of a loom, the cross-bar of a lyre, a scale-beam, &c., but it denoted more especially the yoke by which ploughs and carriages were drawn. The following woodcut shows two examples of the yoke: the upper one is provided with two collars, the lower one with excavations cut in the yoke, in order to give more ease and freedom to the animals. The latter figure shows the method of tying the yoke to the pole (*temo*, ῥυμός) by means of a leathern strap. The word *jugum* is often used to signify *slavery*, or the condition in which men are compelled, against their will, like oxen or horses, to labour for others. Hence, to express symbolically the subjugation of conquered nations, the Romans made their captives pass under a yoke (*sub jugum mittere*), which, however, was not made like the yoke used in drawing carriages or ploughs, but consisted of a spear supported transversely by two others placed upright.

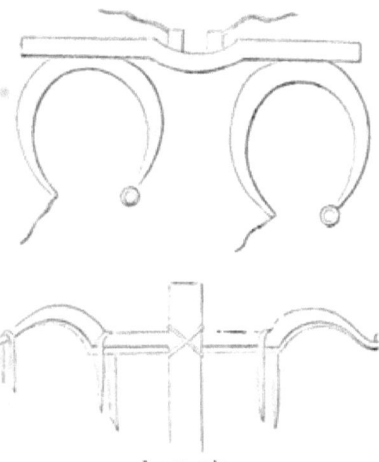

Jugum, yoke.

JŪRISCONSULTI or JŪRĒCONSULTI arose among the Romans after the separation of the Jus Civile from the Jus Pontificium. Such a body certainly existed before the time of Cicero, and the persons who professed to expound the law were called by the various names of *jurisperiti, jurisconsulti*, or *consulti* simply. They were also designated by other names, as *jurisprudentes, prudentiores, peritiores*, and *juris auctores*. The business of the early jurisconsulti consisted both in advising and acting on behalf of their clients (*consultores*) gratuitously. They gave their advice or answers (*responsa*) either in public places which they attended at certain times, or at their own houses; and not only on matters of law, but on any thing else that might be referred to them. The words *scribere* and *cavere* referred to their employment in drawing up formal instruments, such[1] as contracts or wills, &c. At a later period, many of these functions were performed by persons who were paid by a fee, and thus there arose a body of practitioners distinct from those who gave responsa and who were writers and teachers. Tiberius Coruncanius, a plebeian, who was consul B. C. 281, and also the first plebeian Pontifex Maximus, is mentioned as the first who publicly professed (*publice professus est*), and he was distinguished both for his knowledge of the law and his eloquence.

JURISDICTIO, signifies generally the authority of the magistrate " qui jus dicit," and is mostly applied to the authority of the praetor in civil cases, such as the giving of the formula in an actio and the appointment of a judex. [ACTIO.]

JUS. The law peculiar to the Roman state is sometimes called *Jus Civile Romanorum*, but more frequently *Jus Civile* only. The *Jus Quiritium* is equivalent to the *Jus Civile Romanorum*. The *jus civile* of the Romans is divisible into two parts, *jus civile* in the narrower sense, and *jus pontificium*, or the law of religion. This opposition is sometimes expressed by the words *Jus* and *Fas*. The law of religion, or the *Jus Pontificium*, was under the control of the pontifices, who in fact originally had the control of the whole mass of the law; and it was only after the separation of the jus civile in its wider sense into the two parts of the jus civile, in its narrower sense, and the jus pontificium, that each part had its proper and peculiar limits. Still, even after the separation, there was a mutual relation between these two branches of law; for instance, an adrogatio was not valid by the jus civile unless it was valid by the jus pontificium. Again, jus pontificium, in its wider sense, as the law of religion, had its subdivisions, as into jus augurum, pontificium, &c.

JUS CIVILE. [JUS.]
JUS LATII. [CIVITAS; LATINITAS.]
JUS PONTIFICIUM. [JUS.]
JUS QUIRITIUM. [JUS.]

JUSJURANDUM (ὅρκος), an oath. (1) GREEK. An oath is an appeal to some superior being, calling on him to bear witness that the swearer speaks the truth, or intends to perform the promise which he makes. We find early mention in the Greek writers of oaths being taken on solemn and important occasions, as treaties, alliances, vows, compacts, and agreements, both between nations and individuals. The Greeks paid high regard to the sanctity of oaths. The poets frequently allude to the punishment of perjury after death, which they assign to the infernal gods or furies, and we find many proofs of a persuasion that perjurers would not prosper in this world. Anciently the person who took an oath stood up, and lifted his hands to heaven, as he would in prayer; for an oath was a species of prayer, and required the same sort of ceremony. Oaths were frequently accompanied with sacrifice or libation. The parties used also to lay their hands upon the victims, or on the altar or some other sacred thing, as if by so doing they brought before them the deity by whom the oath was sworn, and made him witness of the ceremony. Hence the expressions πρὸς τὸν βωμὸν ἐξορκίζειν, ὁμνύναι καθ' ἱερῶν. The hand especially was regarded as a pledge of fidelity, and the allusions to the junction of hands in making contracts and agreements abound in the ancient writers. The different nations of Greece swore by their own peculiar gods and heroes; as the Thebans by Hercules, Iolaus, &c., the Lacedaemonians by Castor and Pollux, the Corinthians by Poseidon; the Athenians swore principally by Zeus, Athena, Apollo (their πατρῷος θεός), Demeter, and Dionysus. The office or character of the party, or the place, or the occasion often suggested the oath to be taken. As swearing became a common practice with men upon trivial occasions, and in ordinary conversation, they used to take oaths by any god, person, or thing, as their peculiar habits or predilections, or the fancy of the moment, dictated. Women also had their favourite oaths. As the men preferred swearing by Hercules, Apollo, &c., so the other sex used to swear by Aphrodite, Demeter, and Persephone, Hera, Hecate, Artemis; and Athenian women by Aglauros, Pandrosus, &c.—(2) ROMAN. I. *Oaths taken by magistrates and other persons who entered the service of the republic.*—After the establishment of the republic the consuls, and subsequently all the other magistrates, were obliged, within five days after their appointment, to promise on oath that they would protect and observe the laws of the republic (*in leges jurare*). Vestal virgins and the flamen dialis were not allowed to swear on any occasion. During the later period of the republic we also find that magistrates, when the time of their office had expired, addressed the people and swore that during their office they had undertaken nothing against the republic, but had done their utmost to promote its welfare. All Roman soldiers after they were enlisted for a campaign, had to take the military oath (*sacramentum*). It may here be remarked that any oath might be taken in two ways: the person who took it, either framed it himself, or it was put to him in a set form, and in this case he was said *in verba jurare*, or *jurare verbis conceptis*.—II. *Oaths taken in transactions with foreign nations in the name of the republic.* According to the most ancient form the pater patratus pronounced the oath in the name of his country, and struck the victim with a flint-stone, calling on Jupiter to destroy the Roman nation in like manner, as he (the pater patratus) destroyed the animal, if the people should violate the oath. The chiefs or priests of the other nation then swore in a similar manner by their own gods. In swearing to a treaty with a foreign nation, a **victim** (a pig or a lamb) was in the early times always sacrificed by the fetials (whence the expressions *foedus icere*, ὅρκια τέμνειν), and the priest while pronouncing the oath probably touched the victim or the altar. The jus fetiale, however, fell into disuse as the Romans extended their **conquests**; and as in most cases of treaties with foreign nations, the Romans were not the **party** that chose to promise anything on **oath**, we hear no more of oaths on their part. At first the Romans were very scrupulous in observing their oaths in contracts or treaties with foreigners, and even **with enemies**; but from the third Punic war to the end of the republic, perjury was **common** among the Romans in their dealings with foreigners as well as among themselves.—III. *Oaths or various modes of swearing in common life.* The practice of swearing in ordinary conversations, was as common among the **Romans** as among the Greeks. The forms used were sometimes simple invocations of one or more gods, as *Hercle* or *Mehercle*, that is, ita me Hercules juvet, amet, or **servet**; *Pol, Perpol* or *Aedepol*, that is, per Pollucem; *per Jovem Lapidem* or simply *per Jovem; per superos; per deos immortales; medius fidius*, that is, ita me Dius (Διός) filius juvet; *ita me deus amet*, or *dii ament*. **Women** as well as men swore by most of **the gods; but some oaths** were peculiar to one of the sexes. Thus women never swore by Hercules, **and men never** by Castor. Sometimes oaths were accompanied with an execration, in **case the swearer** was stating a falsehood : as *Dii me perdant ; dii me interficiant ; dispeream ; ne vivam ; ne salvus sim*, &c.—IV. *Oaths taken before the praetor or in courts of justice.* There might be a *jusjurandum* either *in jure* or *in judicio*. The *jusjurandum in jure* is the oath which one party proposed to his adversary (*detulit*) that he should make about the matter in dispute ; and the effect of the oath being taken or refused was equivalent to a judicium. The *jusjurandum in judicio* (*jusjurandum judiciale*) was required by the judex, and not by either of the parties, though either of the parties might suggest it.

JUSTITIUM, a cessation of public business of every kind. Thus the courts of law and the treasury were shut up, no ambassadors were received in the senate, and no auctions took place. The *Justitium* was proclaimed (*edicere, indicere*) by the senate and the magistrates in times of public alarm and danger; and **after confidence** and tranquillity had been restored, the **Justitium** was removed (*remittere, exuere*) **by** the same authorities. As such times of alarm **are** usually accompanied with general sorrow, **a** *Justitium* came in course of time to be ordained as a mark of public mourning, and under the empire was only employed for this reason.

JŬVĒNĀLĬA, or **JŬVĒNĀLES LŪDI**, scenic games instituted by Nero, in A. D. 59, in commemoration of his shaving his beard for the first time, thus intimating that he had passed from youth to manhood. He was then in the twenty-second year of his age. These games were not celebrated in the **circus**, but in a private theatre erected in a pleasure-ground (*nemus*), and consisted of every kind of theatrical performance, Greek and Roman plays, mimetic pieces, and the like. The Juvenalia continued to be celebrated by subsequent emperors, but not on the same occasion. The name was given to those games which were exhibited by the emperors on the 1st of January in each year. They no longer consisted of scenic representations, but **of** chariot races and combats of wild beasts.

LĀBĀRUM. [SIGNA MILITARIA.]
LĀBRUM. [BALNEUM.]
LĂBYRINTHUS (λαβύρινθος), a labyrinth, a large and complicated subterraneous cavern with **numerous and intricate passages, similar** to those of a mine. The earliest and most renowned labyrinth was that of Egypt, which lay beyond lake Moeris. It had 3000 apartments, 1500 under **ground, and the** same number above it, **and the whole** was surrounded by a wall. **It was divided** into courts, each of which was surrounded **by** colonnades of white marble. The second labyrinth mentioned **by** the ancients was that of Crete, in the neighbourhood of Cnossus, where the Minotaur is said to have dwelt. Although the Cretan labyrinth is very frequently mentioned by ancient authors, yet none of **them** speaks of it as an eyewitness. It was probably some natural cavern in the neighbourhood of Cnossus. A third labyrinth, the construction of which belongs to a more historical age, **was that in** the island of Lemnos. A fabulous **edifice in Etruria is also mentioned,** to which Pliny applies the name of labyrinth. It is described as being in the neighbourhood of Clusium, and as the tomb of Lar Porsena ; but no writer says that he ever saw it, or remains of it.

LĀCERNA (μανδύας, μανδύη), a **cloak** worn by the Romans over the toga. It differed from the paenula in being **an open** garment like the Greek pallium, **and** fastened on **the right** shoulder by means of a buckle (*fibula*), whereas the paenula was what is called a *vestimentum clausum* with an opening for the head. The Lacerna appears to have been commonly used in the army. In the time of Cicero it was not usually worn in the city, but it soon afterwards became quite common at Rome. The lacerna was sometimes thrown over the head for the purpose of concealment; but a *cucullus* or cowl was generally used for that purpose, which appears to have been frequently attached to the lacerna, and to have formed a part of the dress.

LACINIAE, the angular extremities of the toga, one of which was brought round over the left shoulder. It was generally tucked into the girdle, but sometimes was allowed to hang down loose.

LACONICUM. [BALNEUM.]
LACUNAR. [DOMUS.]
LACUS. [FONS.]

LAENA (χλαῖνα), a woollen cloak, the cloth of which was twice the ordinary thickness, shaggy upon both sides, and worn over the pallium or the toga for the sake of warmth. In later times the laena seems, to a certain extent, to have been worn as a substitute for the toga.

LAMPADEPHORIA (λαμπαδηφορία), *torch-bearing*, LAMPADEDROMIA (λαμπαδηδρομία), *torch-race*, and often simply LAMPAS (λαμπάς), was a game common throughout Greece. At Athens we know of five celebrations of this game: one to Prometheus at the Prometheia, a second to Athena at the Panathenaea, a third to Hephaestos at the Hephaesteia, a fourth to Pan, and a fifth to the Thracian Artemis or Bendis. The first three are of unknown antiquity; the fourth was introduced soon after the battle of Marathon; the last in the time of Socrates. The race was usually run on foot, horses being first used in the time of Socrates; sometimes also at night. The preparation for it was a principal branch of the *Gymnasiarchia*, so much so indeed in later times, that the *Lampadarchia* (λαμπαδαρχία) seems to have been pretty much equivalent to the *Gymnasiarchia*. The gymnasiarch had to provide the lampas, which was a candlestick with a kind of shield set at the bottom of the socket, so as to shelter the flame of the candle; as is seen in the following woodcut, taken from a coin. He had

Lampas. (From a Coin.)

also to provide for the training of the runners, which was of no slight consequence, for the race was evidently a severe one, with other expenses, which on the whole were very heavy, so that Isaeus classes this office with the *choregia* and *trierarchia*, and reckons that it had cost him 12 minae.

LAMPAS. [LAMPADEPHORIA.]
LANCEA. [HASTA.]
LANISTA. [GLADIATORES.]

LANX, a large dish, made of silver or some other metal, and sometimes embossed, used at splendid entertainments to hold meat or fruit; and consequently at sacrifices and funeral banquets.

LAPHRIA (Λάφρια), an annual festival, celebrated at Patrae in Achaia, in honour of Artemis, surnamed Laphria.

LAPICIDINAE. [LAUTUMIAE.]
LAQUEAR. [DOMUS, p. 144, *b*.]
LAQUEATORES. [GLADIATORES.]

LAQUEUS, a rope, was used to signify the punishment of death by strangling. This mode of execution was never performed in public, but only in prison and generally in the Tullianum. Hence we find the words *carcer* and *laqueus* frequently joined together. Persons convicted of treason were most frequently put to death by strangling, as for instance the Catilinarian conspirators (*laqueo gulam fregere*).

LARARIUM, a place in the inner part of a Roman house, which was dedicated to the Lares, and in which their images were kept and worshipped. It seems to have been customary for religious Romans in the morning, immediately after they rose, to perform their prayers in the lararium.

LARENTALIA, sometimes written LARENTINALIA and LAURENTALIA, a Roman festival in honour of Acca Larentia, the wife of Faustulus and the nurse of Romulus and Remus. It was celebrated in December, on the 10th before the calends of January.

LARGITIO. [AMBITUS.]

LATER (πλίνθος), a brick. The Romans distinguished between those bricks which were merely dried by the sun and air (*lateres crudi*), and those which were burnt in the kiln (*cocti* or *coctiles*). They preferred for brick making clay which was either whitish or decidedly red. Pliny calls the brickfield *lateraria*, and to make bricks *lateres ducere*, corresponding to the Greek πλίνθους ἕλκειν or ἐρύειν.

LATICLAVII. [CLAVUS.]
LATINAE FERIAE. [FERIAE.]

LATINITAS, LATIUM, JUS LATII. All these expressions are used to signify a certain status intermediate between that of *cives* and *peregrini*. Before the passing of the Lex

Julia de Civitate (b. c. 90) the above expressions denoted a certain nationality, and as part of it a certain legal status with reference to Rome; but after the passing of that lex, these expressions denoted only a certain status, and had no reference to any national distinction. About the year b. c. 89, a Lex Pompeia gave the jus Latii to all the Transpadani, and consequently the privilege of obtaining the Roman civitas by having filled a magistratus in their own cities. To denote the status of these Transpadani, the word Latinitas was used, which since the passing of the Lex Julia had lost its proper signification; and this was the origin of that Latinitas which thenceforth existed to the time of Justinian. This new Latinitas or jus Latii was given to whole towns and countries; as, for instance, by Vespasian to the whole of Spain. It is not certain wherein this new Latinitas differed from that Latinitas which was the characteristic of the Latini before the passing of the Lex Julia. It is, however, clear that all the old Latini had not the same right with respect to Rome; and that they could acquire the civitas on easier terms than those by which the new Latinitas was acquired.

LATRUNCŬLI (πεσσοί, ψῆφοι), draughts. The invention of a game resembling draughts was attributed by the Greeks to Palamedes; and it is mentioned by Homer. There were two sets of men, one set being black, the other white or red. Being intended to represent a miniature combat between two armies, they were called soldiers (milites), foes (hostes), and marauders (latrones, dim. latrunculi); also calculi, because stones were often employed for the purpose. The Romans often had twelve lines on the draughtboard, whence the game so played was called duodecim scripta.

LAUDĀTIO. [FUNUS.]
LAURENTĀLIA. [LARENTALIA.]
LAUTŬMIAE, LAUTŎMIAE, LĀTOMIAE, or LĀTUMIAE (λιθοτομίαι, λατομίαι, Lat. Lapicidinae), literally places where stones are cut, or quarries, and more particularly the public prison of Syracuse. It lay in the steep and almost inaccessible part of the town which was called Epipolae, and had been built by Dionysius the tyrant. It was cut to an immense depth into the solid rock, so that nothing could be imagined to be a safer or stronger prison, though it had no roof, and thus left the prisoners exposed to the heat of the sun, the rain, and the coldness of the nights. The Tullianum at Rome was also sometimes called lautumiae. [CARCER.]

LECTĬCA (κλίνη, κλινίδιον, or φορεῖον), was a kind of couch or litter, in which persons, in a lying position, were carried from one place to another. Lecticae were used for carrying the dead [FUNUS] as well as the living. The Greek lectica consisted of a bed or mattress, and a pillow to support the head, placed upon a kind of bedstead or couch. It had a roof, consisting of the skin of an ox, extending over the couch and resting on four posts. The sides of this lectica were covered with curtains. In the republican period it appears to have been chiefly used by women, and by men only when they were in ill health. When this kind of lectica was introduced among the Romans, it was chiefly used in travelling, and very seldom in Rome itself. But towards the end of the republic, and under the empire, it was commonly used in the city, and was fitted up in the most splendid manner. Instead of curtains, it was frequently closed on the sides with windows made of transparent stone (lapis specularis), and was provided with a pillow and bed. When standing, it rested on four feet, generally made of wood. Persons were carried in a lectica by slaves (lecticarii), by means of poles (asseres) attached to it, but not fixed, so that they might easily be taken off when necessary. The number of lecticarii employed in carrying one lectica varied according to its size, and the display of wealth which a person might wish to make. The ordinary number was probably two; but it varied from two to eight, and the lectica is called hexaphoron or octophoron, accordingly as it was carried by six or eight persons.

LECTISTERNIUM. Sacrifices being of the nature of feasts, the Greeks and Romans, on occasion of extraordinary solemnities, placed images of the gods reclining on couches, with tables and viands before them, as if they were really partaking of the things offered in sacrifice. This ceremony was called a lectisternium. The woodcut here introduced ex-

Pulvinar used at Lectisternium. (From the Glyptothek at Munich.)

hibits one of these couches, which is represented with a cushion covered by a cloth hanging in ample folds down each side. This beautiful *pulvinar* is wrought altogether in white marble, and is somewhat more than two feet in height.

LECTUS (λέχος, κλίνη, εὐνή), a bed. The complete bed (εὐνή) of a wealthy Greek in later times generally consisted of the following parts :—κλίνη, ἐπίτονοι, τυλεῖον or κνέφαλον, προσκεφάλειον, and στρώματα. The κλίνη is, properly speaking, merely the bedstead, and seems to have consisted only of posts fitted into one another and resting upon four feet. At the head part alone there was a board (ἀνάκλιντρον or ἐπίκλιντρον) to support the pillow and prevent its falling out. Sometimes, however, the bottom part of a bedstead was likewise protected by a board, so that in this case a Greek bedstead resembled what we call a French bedstead. The bedstead was provided with girths (τόνοι, ἐπίτονοι, κειρία) on which the bed or mattress (κνέφαλον, τυλεῖον, or τύλη) rested. The cover or ticking of a mattress was made of linen or woollen cloth, or of leather, and the usual material with which it was filled was either wool or dried weeds. At the head part of the bed, and supported by the ἐπίκλιντρον, lay a round pillow (προσκεφάλειον) to support the head. The bed-covers (στρώματα) were generally made of cloth, which was very thick and woolly, either on one or on both sides. The beds of the Romans (*lecti cubiculares*) in the earlier periods of the republic were probably of the same description as those used in Greece; but towards the end of the republic and during the empire, the richness and magnificence of the beds of the wealthy Romans far surpassed every thing we find described in Greece. The bedstead was generally rather high, so that persons entered the bed (*scandere*, *ascendere*) by means of steps placed beside it (*scamnum*). It was sometimes made of metal, and sometimes of costly kinds of wood, or veneered with tortoiseshell or ivory; its feet (*fulcra*) were frequently of silver or gold. The bed or mattress (*culcita* and *torus*) rested upon girths or strings (*restes*, *fasciae*, *institae*, or *funes*), which connected the two horizontal side-posts of the bed. In beds destined for two persons the two sides are distinguished by different names; the side at which persons entered was open, and bore the name *sponda*; the other side, which was protected by a board, was called *pluteus*. The two sides of such a bed are also distinguished by the names *torus exterior* and *torus interior*, or *sponda exterior* and *sponda interior*; and from these expressions it is not improbable that such lecti had two beds or mattresses, one for each person. Mattresses were in the earlier times filled with dry herbs or straw, and such beds continued to be used by the poor. But in subsequent times wool, and, at a still later period, feathers, were used by the wealthy for the beds as well as the pillows. The cloth or ticking (*operimentum* or *involucrum*) with which the beds or mattresses were covered, was called *toral*, *torale*, *linteum*, or *segestre*. The blankets or counterpanes (*vestes stragulae*, *stragula*, *peristromata*, *peripetasmata*) were in the houses of wealthy Romans of the most costly description, and generally of a purple colour, and embroidered with beautiful figures in gold. Covers of this sort were called *peripetasmata Attalica*, because they were said to have been first used at the court of Attalus. The pillows were likewise covered with magnificent casings. The *lectus genialis* or *adversus* was the bridal bed, which stood in the atrium, opposite the janua, whence it derived the epithet *adversus*. It was generally high, with steps by its side, and in later times beautifully adorned. Respecting the lectus funebris see FUNUS. An account of the disposition of the couches used at entertainments is given under TRICLINIUM.

LEGATIO LIBERA. [LEGATUS.]

LEGATUM, a part of the hereditas which a testator gives out of it, from the heres (*ab herede*); that is, it is a gift to a person out of that whole (*universum*) which is diminished to the heres by such gift. There were several laws limiting the amount of property which a person might give in legacies; and it was at last fixed by the Lex Falcidia (B.C. 40), that he should not bequeath more than three-fourths of his property in legacies, and thus a fourth was left to the heres. By the Law of the Twelve Tables a man could dispose of his property as he pleased, and he might exhaust (*erogare*) the whole hereditas by legacies and bequests of freedom to slaves, so as to leave the heres nothing. The consequence was that in such cases the scripti heredes refused to take the hereditas, and there was of course an intestacy. Legata were inutilia or void, if they were given before a heres was instituted by the will, for the will derived all its legal efficacy from such institution; there was the same rule as to a gift of freedom.

LEGATUS, from *lego*, a person commissioned or deputed to do certain things. They may be divided into three classes:—1. Legati or ambassadors sent to Rome by foreign nations; 2. Legati or ambassadors sent from Rome to foreign nations and into the provinces; 3. Legati who accompanied the Roman generals into the field, or the proconsuls and praetors into the provinces. 1. Foreign legati at Rome, from whatever country they came, had to go to the temple of Saturn, and deposit their names with the quaestors. Previous to their admission into the city, foreign ambassadors seem to have been obliged to give notice from what nation they came and for what purpose; for several instances are mentioned, in which ambassadors were prohibited from entering the city, especially in case of a war between Rome and the state from which they came. In such cases the ambassadors were either not heard at all, and obliged to quit Italy, or an audience was given to them by the senate (*senatus legatis datur*) outside the city, in the temple of Bellona. This was evidently a sign of mistrust, but the ambassadors were nevertheless treated as public guests, and some public villa outside the city was sometimes assigned for their reception. In other cases, however, as soon as the report of the landing of foreign ambassadors on the coast of Italy was brought to Rome, especially if they were persons of great distinction, or if they came from an ally of the Roman people, some one of the inferior magistrates, or a legatus of a consul, was despatched by the senate to receive, and conduct them to the city at the expense of the republic. When they were introduced into the senate by the praetor or consul, they first explained what they had to communicate, and then the praetor invited the senators to put their questions to the ambassadors. The whole transaction was carried on by interpreters, and in the Latin language. [INTERPRES.] After the ambassadors had thus been examined, they were requested to leave the assembly of the senate, who now began to discuss the subject brought before them. The result was communicated to the ambassadors by the praetor. In some cases ambassadors not only received rich presents on their departure, but were at the command of the senate conducted by a magistrate, and at the public expense, to the frontier of Italy, and even farther. By the Lex Gabinia it was decreed, that from the 1st of February to the 1st of March, the senate should every day give audience to foreign ambassadors. There was a place on the right-hand side of the senate-house, called Graecostasis, in which foreign ambassadors waited. All ambassadors, whencesoever they came, were considered by the Romans throughout the whole period of their existence as sacred and inviolable. 2. Legati to foreign nations in the name of the Roman republic were always sent by the senate; and to be appointed to such a mission was considered a great honour,

which was conferred only on men of high rank or eminence: for a Roman ambassador had the powers of a magistrate and the venerable character of a priest. If a Roman during the performance of his mission as ambassador died or was killed, his memory was honoured by the republic with a public sepulchre and a statue in the Rostra. The expenses during the journey of an ambassador were, of course, paid by the republic; and when he travelled through a province, the provincials had to supply him with every thing he wanted. 3. The third class of legati, to whom the name of ambassadors cannot be applied, were persons who accompanied the Roman generals on their expeditions, and in later times the governors of provinces also. They are mentioned at a very early period as serving along with the tribunes, under the consuls. They were nominated (*legabantur*) by the consul or the dictator under whom they served, but the sanction of the senate was an essential point, without which no one could be legally considered a legatus. The persons appointed to this office were usually men of great military talents, and it was their duty to advise and assist their superior in all his undertakings, and to act in his stead both in civil and military affairs. The legati were thus always men in whom the consul placed great confidence, and were frequently his friends or relations: but they had no power independent of the command of their general. Their number varied according to the greatness or importance of the war, or the extent of the province: three is the smallest number that we know of, but Pompey, when in Asia, had fifteen legati. Whenever the consuls were absent from the army, or when a proconsul left his province, the legati or one of them took his place, and then had the insignia as well as the power of his superior. He was in this case called legatus pro practore, and hence we sometimes read that a man governed a province as legatus without any mention being made of the proconsul whose vicegerent he was. During the latter period of the republic, it sometimes happened that a consul carried on a war, or a proconsul governed his province, through his legati, while he himself remained at Rome, or conducted some other more urgent affairs. When the provinces were divided at the time of the empire [PROVINCIA], those of the Roman people were governed by men who had been either consuls or practors, and the former were always accompanied by three legati, the latter by one. The provinces of the emperor, who was himself the proconsul, were governed by persons whom the emperor himself appointed, and who had been consuls or praetors, or were at least senators. These vicegerents of the emperor were called *legati augusti pro praetore*, *legati praetorii*, *legati consulares*, or simply *legati*, and they, like the governors of the provinces of the Roman people, had one or three legati as their assistants. During the latter period of the republic it had become customary for senators to obtain from the senate the permission to travel through or stay in any province at the expense of the provincials, merely for the purpose of managing and conducting their own personal affairs. There was no restraint as to the length of time the senators were allowed to avail themselves of this privilege, which was a heavy burden upon the provincials. This mode of sojourning in a province was called *legatio libera*, because those who availed themselves of it enjoyed all the privileges of a public legatus or ambassador, without having any of his duties to perform. At the time of Cicero the privilege of legatio libera was abused to a very great extent. Cicero, therefore, in his consulship (B. C. 63) endeavoured to put an end to it, but, owing to the opposition of a tribune, he only succeeded in limiting the time of its duration to one year. Julius Caesar afterwards extended the time during which a senator might avail himself of the legatio libera to five years.

LEGIO. [EXERCITUS.]

LEITURGIA (λειτουργία, from λεῖτον, Ion. λήϊτον, *i. e.* δημόσιον, or, according to others, πρυτανεῖον), a liturgy, is the name of certain personal services which, at Athens, every citizen who possessed a certain amount of property had to perform towards the state. These personal services, which in all cases were connected with considerable expenses, were at first a natural consequence of the greater political privileges enjoyed by the wealthy, who, in return, had also to perform heavier duties towards the republic; but when the Athenian democracy was at its height the original character of these liturgies became changed, for, as every citizen now enjoyed the same rights and privileges as the wealthiest, they were simply a tax upon property connected with personal labour and exertion. All liturgies may be divided into two classes: 1, ordinary or encyclic liturgies (ἐγκύκλιοι λειτουργίαι); and 2, extraordinary liturgies. The former were called encyclic, because they recurred every year at certain festive seasons, and comprised the *Choregia*, *Gymnasiarchia*, *Lampadarchia*, *Architheoria*, and *Hestiasis*. Every Athenian who possessed three talents and above was subject to them, and they were undertaken in turns by the members of every tribe who possessed the property qualification just mentioned, unless some one volunteered to undertake a liturgy for another person. But the law did not allow any one to be compelled to undertake more than one liturgy at a time, and he who had in one year performed a liturgy was free for the next, so that legally a person had to perform a liturgy only every other year. Those whose turn it was to undertake any of the ordinary liturgies were always appointed by their own tribe. The persons who were exempt from all kinds of liturgies were the nine archons, heiresses, and orphans until after the commencement of the second year of their coming of age. Sometimes the exemption from liturgies (ἀτέλεια) was granted to persons for especial merits towards the republic. The only kind of extraordinary liturgy to which the name is properly applied is the *trierarchia* (τριηραρχία); in the earlier times, however, the service in the armies was in reality no more than an extraordinary liturgy. [See EISPHORA and TRIERARCHIA.] In later times, during and after the Peloponnesian war, when the expenses of a liturgy were found too heavy for one person, we find that in many instances two persons combined to defray its expenses. Such was the case with the choragia and the trierarchy.

LEMBUS, a skiff or small boat, used for carrying a person from a ship to the shore. The name was also given to the light boats which were sent ahead of a fleet to obtain information of the enemy's movements.

LEMNISCUS (λημνίσκος), a kind of coloured ribbon which hung down from crowns or diadems at the back part of the head. Coronae adorned with lemnisci were a greater distinction than those without them. This serves to explain an expression of Cicero (*palma lemniscata*, *pro Rosc. Am.* 35), where palma means a victory, and the epithet lemniscata indicates the contrary of *infamis*, and at the same time implies an honourable as well as lucrative victory. Lemnisci were also worn alone and without being connected with crowns, especially by ladies, as an ornament for the head.

LEMURIA, a festival for the souls of the departed, which was celebrated at Rome every year in the month of May. It was said to have been instituted by Romulus to appease the spirit of Remus, whom he had slain, and to have been called originally Remuria. It was celebrated at night and in silence, and during three alternate days, that is, on the ninth, eleventh, and thirteenth of May. During this season the temples of the gods were closed, and it was thought unlucky for women to marry at this time and during the whole month of May, and those who ventured to marry were believed to die soon after, whence the proverb, *mense Maio malae nubent*. Those who celebrated the **Lemuria** walked barefooted, **washed their hands three times, and threw black beans nine times behind their backs, believing by this ceremony to secure themselves against the Lemures.** As regards the solemnities on each of the three days, we only know that on the second there were games in the circus in honour of Mars, and that on the third **day** the images of the thirty Argei, **made** of rushes, were thrown from the Pons Sublicius into the Tiber by the Vestal virgins [ARGEI] On the same day there was a festival of the merchants, probably because on this day the temple of Mercury had been dedicated in the year 495 B.C.

LĒNAEA. [DIONYSIA.]

LESCHĒ (λέσχη), an Ionic word, signifying *council* or *conversation*, and *a place for council or conversation*. There is frequent mention of places of public resort, in the Greek cities, by the name of *Leschae*, some **set apart for the purpose, and others so** called **because they were so used by loungers; to the latter class belong the agora and its porticoes, the gymnasia, and the shops of** various **tradesmen. The former class were small** buildings **or porticoes, furnished with seats,** and exposed **to the sun, to which the idle** resorted to enjoy **conversation, and the poor** to obtain warmth **and shelter: at Athens** alone there were 360 such. In the **Dorian** states the word retained the meaning **of a** place of meeting for deliberation and intercourse, a council-chamber or club-room. There were generally chambers for **council** and conversation, called by this name, attached to the temples of Apollo. The *Lesche* at Delphi was celebrated through Greece for the paintings with which it was adorned by Polygnotus.

LEX. **Of Roman** leges, viewed with reference to the mode of enactment, there were properly two kinds, *Leges Curiatae* and *Leges Centuriatae*. Plebiscita are improperly called leges, though **they were** laws, and in the course of time had the **same** effect as leges. [PLEBISCITUM.] Originally the leges curiatae were **the only** leges, and they **were passed by** the **populus in** the **comitia curiata.** After the establishment **of the comitia centuriata,** the comitia curiata fell almost **into disuse ;** but so **long as the republic** lasted, **and even** under Augustus, **a shadow** of the old constitution was preserved **in** the formal conferring of the imperium by a lex curiata only, and in the ceremony of adrogation being effected only in these comitia. [ADOPTIO.] Those leges, properly so called, with which we are acquainted, **were passed in** the comitia centuriata, and **were proposed** (*rogabantur*) by a magistratus of **senatorial rank,** after the senate had approved of them by a decretum. Such a lex was also designated by the name *Populi Scitum*.—The word **rogatio** (from the verb *rogo*) **properly means any measure proposed to the legislative body, and therefore is equally applicable to a proposed lex and a** proposed **plebiscitum**. It corresponds to our word *bill*, as opposed to *act*. When the **measure was** passed, it became **a lex or plebiscitum; though rogationes, after they had become laws, were sometimes, but improperly, called rogationes. A rogatio began with the words *velitis, jubeatis*, &c., and ended with the words *ita vos Quirites rogo*. The corresponding expression of assent to the rogatio on the part of the sovereign assembly was *uti rogas*. The phrases for proposing a law are *rogare legem, legem ferre,* and *rogationem promulgare ;* the phrase *rogationem accipere* applies to the enacting body. The **terms relating** to legislation are thus explained by Ulpian **the jurist :—" A lex is** said **either *rogari* or *ferri*; it is said *abrogari*, when it is repealed ; it is said *derogari*, when a part is repealed ; it is said *subrogari*, when some addition is made to it ; and it is said *obrogari*, when some part of it is changed."—A *privilegium* is an enactment** that had for its object a single person, **which** is indicated by the form of the **word** (*privilegium*), *privae res* being the same as *singulae res*. The word privilegium did not convey any notion of the character of the legislative measures; it might be beneficial to the party to whom it referred, or it might not. Under the empire, the word is used in the sense of a special grant proceeding from the imperial favour.—The title of a **lex** was generally derived from the gentile name of **the magistratus who proposed it, as the *Lex Hortensia* from** the dictator Hortensius. **Sometimes the lex took its name** from **the two consuls** or other magistrates, as the *Aelia Calpurnia, Aelia* or *Aelia Sentia, Papia* or *Papia Poppaea*, **and others.** It seems to have been the fashion **to omit the word *et*** between the two names, though instances occur in which it was used. A lex was also designated, with reference **to its object, as the** *Lex Cincia de Donis et Muneribus, Lex Furia Testamentaria, Lex Julia Municipalis*, and many others. Leges which related to a common object, were often designated by a collective name, as *Leges* **Agrariae,** *Judiciariae*, and others. A lex sometimes took its name from the chief contents **of** its first chapter, as *Lex Julia de Maritandis Ordinibus*. Sometimes a lex comprised very various provisions, relating to matters essentially different, and in that case it was called *Lex Satura*.—The number of leges was greatly increased in the later part of the republican period, and Julius Caesar is said to have contemplated a revision of the whole body. Under him and Augustus numerous enactments were passed, which are known under the general name of Juliae Leges. It is often stated that no leges, properly so called, or plebiscita, were passed after the time of Augustus; but this is a mistake. Though the voting might be a mere form, still the form was kept. Besides, various leges are mentioned as having been passed under the Empire, such as the Lex Junia under Tiberius, the Lex Visellia, the Lex Mamilia under Caligula, and a Lex Claudia on the tutela of women. It does not appear when the ancient forms of legislation were laid aside. A particular enactment is always referred to by its name. The following is a list of the principal leges, properly so called; but the list includes also various plebiscita and privilegia:—

ACĪLIA, De Coloniis Deducendis. (Liv. xxxii. 29.)
ACĪLIA. [REPETUNDAE.]
ACĪLIA CALPURNĪA or CALPURNIA. [AMBITUS.]
AEBUTĪA, of uncertain date, which with two Juliae Leges put an end to the Legis Actiones, except in certain cases. This or another lex of the same name prohibited the proposer of a lex, which created any office or power (*curatio ac potestas*), from having such office or power, and even excluded his collegae, cognati, and affines.
AELIA. This lex and a Fufia Lex, passed about the end of the sixth century of the city, gave to all the magistrates the obnunciatio, or power of preventing or dissolving the comitia, by observing the omens and declaring them to be unfavourable.
AELIA, De Coloniis Deducendis. (Liv. xxxiv. 53.)
AELIA SENTĪA, passed in the time of Augustus (about A. D. 3). This lex contained various provisions as to the manumission of slaves.
AEMĪLIA. A lex passed in the dictatorship of Mamercus Aemilius (B. C. 433), by which the censors were elected for a year and a half, instead of a whole lustrum. After this lex they had accordingly only a year and a half allowed them for holding the census and letting out the public works to farm.
AEMĪLIA BAEBĪA. [CORNELIA BAEBIA.]
AEMĪLIA. [LEGES SUMPTUARIAE.]
AGRĀRĪAE, the name of laws which had

relation to the ager publicus. [AGER PUBLICUS.] The most important of these are mentioned under the names of their proposers. [APPULEIA; CASSIA; CORNELIA; FLAMINIA; FLAVIA; JULIA; LICINIA; SEMPRONIA; SERVILIA; THORIA.]
AMBĪTUS. [AMBITUS.]
AMPĪA, to allow Cn. Pompeius to wear a crown of bay at the Ludi Circenses, &c. Proposed by T. Ampius and T. Labienus, tr. pl. B. C. 64.
ANNĀLIS or VILLĪA, proposed by L. Villius Tapulus in B. C. 179, fixed the age at which a Roman citizen might become a candidate for the higher magistracies. It appears that until this law was passed, any office might be enjoyed by a citizen after completing his twenty-seventh year. The Lex Annalis fixed 31 as the age for the quaestorship, 37 for the aedileship, 40 for the praetorship, and 43 for the consulship.
ANTĪA. [SUMPTUARIAE LEGES.]
ANTŌNIA DE THERMENSIBUS, about B. C. 72, by which Thermessus in Pisidia was recognised as Libera.
ANTŌNIAE, the name of various enactments proposed or passed by the influence of M. Antonius, after the death of the dictator J. Caesar.
APPŪLĒIA, respecting sureties.
APPŪLĒIA AGRĀRĪA, proposed by the tribune L. Appuleius Saturninus, B. C. 101.
APPŪLĒIA FRŪMENTĀRĪA, proposed about the same time by the same tribune.
APPŪLĒIA, DE COLONIIS DEDUCENDIS. (Cic. *pro Balbo*, 21.)
APPŪLĒIA MAJESTĀTIS. [MAJESTAS.]
ATERNIA TARPĒIA, B. C. 455. This lex empowered all magistrates to fine persons who resisted their authority; but it fixed the highest fine at two sheep and thirty cows, or two cows and thirty sheep, for the authorities vary in this.
ĀTĪA DE SĀCERDŌTIIS (B. C. 63), proposed by the tribune T. Atius Labienus, repealed the Lex Cornelia de Sacerdotiis.
ĀTĪLIA MARCĪA, B. C. 312, empowered the populus to elect 16 tribuni militum for each of four legions.
ĀTĪLIA, respecting tutores.
ĀTĪNIA, respecting thefts.
ĀTĪNIA, of uncertain date, was a plebiscitum which gave the rank of senator to a tribune. This measure probably originated with C. Atinius, who was tribune B. C. 130.
AUFĪDĪA. [AMBITUS.]
AURĒLIA (B. C. 70), enacted that the judices should be chosen from the senators, equites, and tribuni aerarii. [JUDEX.]
AURĒLIA TRĪBŪNĪCIA, respecting the tribunes.

BAEBĬA (B. c. 192 or 180), enacted that four praetors and six praetors should be chosen alternately; but the law was not observed.

BAEBĬA CORNĒLĬA. [AMBITUS.]

CAECĬLĬA DE CENSŌRĬBUS or CENSŌRIA (B. c. 54), proposed by Metellus Scipio, repealed a Clodia Lex (B. c. 58), which had prescribed certain regular forms of proceeding for the censors in exercising their functions as inspectors of mores, and had required the concurrence of both censors to inflict the nota censoria. When a senator had been already convicted before an ordinary court, the lex permitted the censors to remove him from the senate in a summary way.

CAECĬLĬA DE VECTĪGĀLĬBUS (B. c. 62), released lands and harbours in Italy from the payment of taxes and dues (portoria). The only vectigal remaining after the passing of this lex was the Vicesima.

CAECĬLĬA DĪDĬA (B. c. 98) forbade the proposing of a Lex Satura, on the ground that the people might be compelled either to vote for something which they did not approve, or to reject something which they did approve, if it was proposed to them in this manner. This lex was not always operative.

CAELIA. [LEGES TABELLARIAE.]

CĀLĬGŬLAE LEX AGRĀRĬA. [MAMILIA.]

CALPURNĬA DE AMBĬTU. [AMBITUS.]

CALPURNĬA DE RĔPĔTUNDIS. [REPETUNDAE.]

CĂNŬLĒIA (B. c. 445) established connubium between the patres and plebs, which had been taken away by the law of the Twelve Tables.

CASSĬA (B. c. 104), proposed by the tribune L. Cassius Longinus, did not allow a person to remain a senator who had been convicted in a judicium populi, or whose imperium had been abrogated by the populus.

CASSĬA empowered the dictator Caesar to add to the number of the patricii, to prevent their extinction.

CASSĬA AGRĀRĬA, proposed by the consul Sp. Cassius, B. c. 486. This is said to have been the first agrarian law. It enacted that of the land taken from the Hernicans, half should be given to the Latins, and half to the plebs, and likewise that part of the public land possessed by the patricians should be distributed among the plebeians. This law met with the most violent opposition, and appears not to have been carried. Cassius was accused of aiming at the sovereignty, and was put to death. [AGER PUBLICUS.]

CASSĬA TĂBELLĀRĬA. [LEGES TABELLARIAE.]

CASSĬA TĔRENTĬA FRŪMENTĀRĬA (B. c. 73) for the distribution of corn among the poor citizens and the purchasing of it.

CINCĬA DE DŌNIS ET MŪNĔRĬBUS, a plebiscitum passed in the time of the tribune M. Cincius Alimentus (B. c. 204). It forbade a person to take any thing for his pains in pleading a cause. In the time of Augustus, the Lex Cincia was confirmed by a senatusconsultum, and a penalty of four times the sum received was imposed on the advocate. The law was so far modified in the time of Claudius, that an advocate was allowed to receive ten sestertia; if he took any sum beyond that, he was liable to be prosecuted for repetundae. It appears that this permission was so far restricted in Trajan's time, that the fee could not be paid till the work was done.

CLAUDĬA, passed under the emperor Claudius, took away the agnatorum tutela in case of women.

CLAUDĬA DE SENATORIBUS, B.c. 218 (Liv. xxi. 63), the provisions of which are alluded to by Cicero as antiquated and dead in his time.

CLŌDIAE, the name of various plebiscita, proposed by Clodius, when tribune, B. c. 58.

CLODIA DE AUSPICIIS prevented the magistratus from dissolving the comitia tributa, by declaring that the auspices were unfavourable. This lex therefore repealed the Aelia and Fufia. It also enacted that a lex might be passed on the dies fasti. [AELIA LEX.]

CLODIA DE CENSORIBUS. [CAECILIA.]

CLODIA DE CIVIBUS ROMANIS INTEREMPTIS, to the effect that "qui civem Romanum indemnatum interemisset, ei aqua et igni interdiceretur." It was in consequence of this lex that the interdict was pronounced against Cicero, who considers the whole proceeding as a privilegium.

CLODIA FRUMENTARIA, by which the corn, which had formerly been sold to the poor citizens at a low rate, was given.

CLODIA DE SODALITATIBUS or DE COLLEGIIS restored the Sodalitia, which had been abolished by a senatus-consultum of the year B. c. 80, and permitted the formation of new Sodalitia.

CLODIA DE LIBERTINORUM SUFFRAGIIS. (Cic. pro Mil. 12, 33.)

CLODIA DE REGE PTOLEMAEO ET DE EXSULIBUS BYZANTINIS. (Vell. Pat. ii. 45.)

There were other so-called Leges Clodiae, which were however privilegia.

COMMISSŌRĬA LEX, respecting sales.

CORNĒLĬAE. Various leges passed in the dictatorship of Sulla, and by his influence, are so called.

Q 2

AGRARIA, by which many of the inhabitants of Etruria and Latium were deprived of the complete civitas, and retained only the commercium, and a large part of their lands were made public, and given to military colonists.
DE CIVITATE. (Liv., Epit. 86.)
DE FALSIS, against those who forged testaments or other deeds, and against those who adulterated or counterfeited the public coin, whence Cicero calls it *testamentaria* and *nummaria*.
DE INJURIIS. [INJURIA.]
JUDICIARIA. [JUDEX.]
DE MAGISTRATIBUS, partly a renewal of old plebiscita. (Appian, B. C. i. 100, 101.)
MAJESTATIS. [MAJESTAS.]
DE PARRICIDIO. [See below: DE SICARIIS.]
DE PROSCRIPTIONE ET PROSCRIPTIS. [PROSCRIPTIO.]
DE PROVINCIIS ORDINANDIS. (Cic. *ad Fam.* i. 9; iii. 6, 8, 10.)
DE REPETUNDIS. [REPETUNDAE.]
DE SACERDOTIIS. [SACERDOS.]
DE SICARIIS ET VENEFICIS, contained provisions as to death or fire caused by *dolus malus*, and against persons going about armed with the intention of killing or thieving. The law not only provided for cases of poisoning, but contained provisions against those who made, sold, bought, possessed, or gave poison for the purpose of poisoning; also against a magistratus or senator who conspired in order that a person might be condemned in a *judicium publicum*, &c.
SUMPTUARIAE. [LEGES SUMPTUARIAE.]
TRIBUNICIA, which diminished the power of the Tribuni Plebis.
UNCIARIA appears to have been a lex which lowered the rate of interest, and to have been passed about the same time with the Leges Sumptuariae of Sulla.
CORNELIAE, which were proposed by the tribune C. Cornelius about B. C. 67. One limited the edictal power by compelling the praetors *Jus dicere ex edictis suis perpetuis*.—Another lex of the same tribune enacted that no one *legibus solveretur*, unless such a measure was agreed on in a meeting of the senate at which two hundred members were present, and afterwards approved by the people; and it enacted that no tribune should put his veto on such a senatus-consultum.—There was also a Lex Cornelia concerning the wills of those Roman citizens who died in captivity (*apud hostes*).
CORNELIA DE NOVIS TABELLIS, proposed by P. Corn. Dolabella, B.C. 47.
CORNELIA ET CAECILIA, B. C. 57, gave Cn. Pompeius the superintendence of the Res Frumentaria for five years.
CORNELIA BAEBIA DE AMBITU, proposed by the consuls P. Cornelius Cethegus and M. Baebius Tamphilus, B.C. 181. This law is sometimes, but erroneously, attributed to the consuls of the preceding year, L. Aemilius and Cn. Baebius. [AMBITUS.]
CURIATA LEX DE IMPERIO. [IMPERIUM.]
CURIATA LEX DE ADOPTIONE. [ADOPTIO.]
DECEMVIRALIS. [LEX DUODECIM TABULARUM.]
DECIA DE DUUMVIRIS NAVALIBUS. (Liv. ix. 30.)
DIDIA. [LEGES SUMPTUARIAE.]
DOMITIA DE SACERDOTIIS. [SACERDOS.]
DUILIA (B.C. 449), a plebiscitum proposed by the tribune Duilius, which enacted that whoever left the people without tribunes, or created a magistrate from whom there was no appeal (*provocatio*), should be scourged and beheaded.
DUILIA MAENIA, proposed by the tribunes Duilius and Maenius (B. C. 357), restored the old uncial rate of interest (*unciarium fenus*), which had been fixed by the Twelve Tables. [FENUS.] The same tribunes carried a measure which was intended, in future, to prevent such unconstitutional proceedings as the enactment of a lex by the soldiers out of Rome, on the proposal of the consul.
DUODECIM TABULARUM. In the year B.C. 454 the Senate assented to a Plebiscitum, pursuant to which commissioners were to be sent to Athens and the Greek cities generally, in order to make themselves acquainted with their laws. Three commissioners were appointed for the purpose. On the return of the commissioners, B.C. 452, it was agreed that persons should be appointed to draw up the code of laws (decemviri Legibus scribundis), but they were to be chosen only from the Patricians, with a provision that the rights of the Plebeians should be respected by the decemviri in drawing up the laws. In the following year (B. C. 451) the Decemviri were appointed in the Comitia Centuriata, and during the time of their office no other magistratus were chosen. The body consisted of ten Patricians, including the three commissioners who had been sent abroad: Appius Claudius, Consul designatus, was at the head of the body. Ten Tables of Laws were prepared during the year, and after being approved by the Senate were confirmed by the Comitia Centuriata. As it was considered that some further Laws were wanted, Decemviri were again elected B.C. 450, consisting of Appius Claudius and his friends. Two more Tables were added by these Decemviri, which Cicero calls "Duae tabulae iniquarum legum." The provision

which allowed **no connubium between the** Patres and the **Plebs** is referred **to the** Eleventh Table. The whole Twelve **Tables were first** published in the consulship **of L. Valerius** and M. Horatius after the downfall **of the** Decemviri, B.C. 449. **This the first attempt to** make a code **remained also the only** attempt for near **one thousand years, until** the legislation of **Justinian. The Twelve** Tables are mentioned **by the Roman** writers under a great variety **of names :** *Leges Decemvirales, Lex* ***Decemviralis****, Leges XII., Lex XII.* *tabularum* or *Duodecim*, and sometimes they **are referred to under the** names of *Leges* **and** *Lex* simply, as being pre-eminently The **Law. The Laws were** cut on bronze tablets **and put up in a public** place. They contained matters **relating both** to the Jus Publicum and **the Jus Privatum** (*fons publici privatique juris*). The **Jus** Publicum underwent great changes in the course of years, but the Jus Privatum of the Twelve Tables continued to be the fundamental law of the Roman State. The Roman writers speak in high terms **of the precision** of the enactments contained **in the Twelve** Tables, and of the propriety **of the language** in which they were expressed.

FĂBIA DE PLĂGIO. [**PLAGIUM**.]
FĂBIA DE NUMERO **SECTATORUM.** (Cic. *pro Murena*, 34.)
FALCIDIA. [**LEX VOCONIA.**]
FANNIA. [**LEGES SUMPTUARIAE.**]
FANNIA. [**JUNIA DE PEREGRINIS.**]
FLĂMĬNIA was an Agraria Lex **for the** distribution of lands in Picenum, proposed by the tribune C. Flaminius, in B.C. 228 according to Cicero, or in B.C. 232 according to Polybius. The latter date is the more probable.
FLĀVIA AGRĀRIA, B.C. 60, for the distribution of lands among Pompey's soldiers, proposed by the tribune L. Flavius, who committed the consul Caecilius Metellus to prison for opposing it.
FRUMENTĀRIAE. Various leges were so called which had for their object the distribution of grain among the people, either **at** a low price or gratuitously. [**FRUMENTARIAE LEGES**, p. 182.]
FŬFIA DE RĔLĬGIŌNE, B.C. 61, **was a** privilegium which related to the trial **of** Clodius.
FŬFIA JŬDĬCIĀRIA. [**JUDEX**, p. 217.]
FŬRIA or FŬSIA CĂNĪNIA limited the number of slaves to be manumitted by testament.
FŬRIA or FŬSIA TESTĀMENTĀRIA, enacted that a testator should not give more than three-fourths of his property in legacies, thus securing one-fourth to the heres.

GĂBĪNIA TĂBELLĀRIA. [**LEGES TABELLARIAE.**] There were various Gabiniae Leges, some of which **were** privilegia, as that for conferring extraordinary **power on** Cn. Pompeius for conducting the **war** against the pirates. A Gabinia Lex, B. c. 58, forbade all loans **of** money at Rome **to** legationes from foreign parts. The object of the **lex** was to prevent money being borrowed **for the purpose** of bribing the senators at Rome.
GALLĬAE CISALPĪNAE. [**RUBRIA**.]
GELLIA CORNĒLIA, B. c. 72, **which gave to** Cn. Pompeius the extraordinary power **of** conferring the Roman civitas on Spaniards in Spain, with the advice of his consilium.
GENŬCIA, B. c. 341, forbade altogether the taking of interest for the use of money.
HIĔRŎNĬCA was not a lex properly so called. Before the Roman conquest of Sicily, the payment of the tenths of wine, oil, and other produce had been fixed by Hiero; and the Roman quaestors, in letting these tenths to farm, followed the practice which they found established.
HŎRĀTĬAE ET VALĔRIAE. [**LEGES VALERIAE.**]
HORTENSIA DE PLĒBISCĪTIS. [**LEGES PUBLILIAE**; **PLEBISCITUM**.] Another Lex Hortensia enacted that the nundinae, which had hitherto been feriae, should be dies fasti. This was done for the purpose of accommodating the inhabitants of the country.
ICILIA, B. c. 456, by which the Aventinus was assigned to the plebs. This was the first instance of the ager publicus being assigned to the plebs. Another **Lex Icilia**, proposed by the tribune Sp. Icilius, B. c. 470, had for its object to prevent all interruption to the tribunes while acting in the discharge of their duties. In some cases the penalty was death.
JŬLIAE. Most of the Juliae Leges were passed in the time of C. Julius Caesar and Augustus.
DE ADULTERIIS. [**ADULTERIUM.**]
AGRARIA, B. c. 59, in the consulship of Caesar, **for** distributing the ager publicus in Campania among 20,000 poor citizens, who had each three children or more.
DE AMBITU. [**AMBITUS.**]
DE BONIS CEDENDIS. This **lex** provided that a debtor might escape all personal molestation from his creditors **by** giving up his property to them **for** the purpose of sale and distribution. It **is** doubtful if this lex was passed in **the** time **of Julius** Caesar or of Augustus, though probably of the former.
DE CAEDE ET VENEFICIO (Suet. *Ver.* 35), perhaps the same as the Lex De Vi Publica.
DE CIVITATE was passed in the consulship of L. Julius Caesar and P. Rutilius

Lupus, B. C. 90. [CIVITAS; FOEDERATAE CIVITATES.]

DE FENORE, or rather De Pecuniis Mutuis or Creditis (B. c. 47), passed in the time of Julius Caesar. The object of it was to make an arrangement between debtors and creditors, for the satisfaction of the latter. The possessiones and res were to be estimated at the value which they had before the civil war, and to be surrendered to the creditors at that value; whatever had been paid for interest was to be deducted from the principal. The result was, that the creditor lost about one-fourth of his debt; but he escaped the loss usually consequent on civil disturbance, which would have been caused by novae tabulae.

JUDICIARIAE. [JUDEX.]
DE LIBERIS LEGATIONIBUS. [LEGATUS.]
DE MAJESTATE. [MAJESTAS.]
DE MARITANDIS ORDINIBUS. [See below: JULIA ET PAPIA POPPAEA.]

MUNICIPALIS, commonly called the Table of Heraclea. In the year 1732 there were found near the Gulf of Tarentum and in the neighbourhood of the city of ancient Heraclea, large fragments of a bronze table, which contained on one side a Roman lex, and on the other a Greek inscription. The whole is now in the Musco Borbonico at Naples. The lex contains various provisions as to the police of the city of Rome, and as to the constitution of communities of Roman citizens (*municipia, coloniae, praefecturae, fora, conciliabula civium Romanorum*). It was accordingly a lex of that kind which is called Satura. It was probably passed in B. C. 45.

JULIA ET PAPIA POPPAEA. Augustus appears to have caused a lex to be enacted about B. C. 18, which is cited as the *Lex Julia de Maritandis Ordinibus*, and is referred to in the Carmen Seculare of Horace, which was written in the year B. C. 17. The object of this lex was to regulate marriages, as to which it contained numerous provisions; but it appears not to have come into operation till the year B. C. 13. In the year A. D. 9, and in the consulship of M. Papius Mutilus and Q. Poppaeus Secundus (*consules suffecti*), another lex was passed as a kind of amendment and supplement to the former lex, and hence arose the title of Lex Julia et Papia Poppaea, by which this lex is often quoted. The lex is often variously quoted, according as reference is made to its various provisions; sometimes it is called *Lex Julia*, sometimes *Papia Poppaea*, sometimes *Lex Julia et Papia*, sometimes *Lex de Maritandis Ordinibus*, from the chapter which treated of the marriages of the senators, sometimes *Lex Cadu-caria, Decimaria*, &c. from the various chapters. The Lex Julia forbade the marriage of a senator or senator's children with a libertina, with a woman whose father or mother had followed an ars ludicra, and with a prostitute; and also the marriage of a libertinus with a senator's daughter. In order to promote marriage, various penalties were imposed on those who lived in a state of celibacy (*caelibatus*) after a certain age, and various privileges were given to those who had three or more children. A candidate for the public offices who had several children was preferred to one who had fewer. After the passing of this lex, it became usual for the senate, and afterwards the emperor (*princeps*), to give occasionally, as a privilege to certain persons who had not children, the same advantage that the lex secured to those who had children. This was called the *Jus Liberorum*, and sometimes the *Jus trium Liberorum*.

PECULATUS, cited in the Digest, related to sacrilege as well as peculatus.

JULIA ET PLAUTIA, respecting stolen things.
JULIA PAPIRIA. [PAPIRIA.]
DE PROVINCIIS. [PROVINCIAE.]
REPETUNDARUM. [REPETUNDAE.]
SACRILEGIS. [See above: JULIA PECULATUS.]
SUMPTUARIAE. [LEGES SUMPTUARIAE.]

THEATRALIS, which permitted Roman equites, in case they or their parents had ever had a census equestris, to sit in the fourteen rows (*quatuordecim ordines*) fixed by the Lex Roscia Theatralis, B. c. 69.

JULIA ET TITIA, respecting Tutors.
DE VI PUBLICA AND PRIVATA. [VIS.]
VICESIMARIA. [VICESIMA.]

JŪNIA DE PĒRĒGRĪNIS, proposed B. C. 126, by M. Junius Pennus, a tribune, banished peregrini from the city. A lex of C. Fannius, consul B. c. 122, contained the same provisions respecting the Latini and Italici; and a lex of C. Papius, perhaps B. c. 65, contained the same respecting all persons who were not domiciled in Italy.

JŪNIA LICĪNIA. [LICINIA JUNIA.]

JŪNIA NORBĀNA, of uncertain date, but probably about A. D. 17, enacted that when a Roman citizen had manumitted a slave without the requisite formalities, the manumission should not in all cases be ineffectual, but the manumitted person should have the status of a Latinus.

JŪNIA RĒPĒTUNDĀRUM. [REPETUNDAE.]

LAETŌRIA, the false name of the Lex Plactoria. [CURATOR.] Sometimes the lex proposed by Volero for electing plebeian magistrates at the comitia tributa is cited as a Lex Laetoria.

LĪCĪNIA DE SŎDĀLĪTIIS. [Ambitus.]
LĪCĪNIA. [Aebutia.]
LĪCĪNIA DE LŪDIS ĀPOLLĪNĀRĪBUS. (Liv. xxvii. 23.)

LĪCĪNIA JŪNIA, or, as it is sometimes called, Junia et Licinia, passed in the consulship of L. Licinius Murena and Junius Silanus, b. c. 62, enforced the Caecilia Didia, in connection with which it is sometimes mentioned.

LĪCĪNIA MŪCIA DE CĪVĪBUS RĒGUNDIS, passed in the consulship of L. Licinius Crassus and Q. Mucius Scaevola, b. c. 95, enacted a strict examination as to the title to citizenship, and deprived of the exercise of civic rights all those who could not make out a good title to them. This measure partly led to the Marsic war.

LĪCĪNIA SUMPTUĀRIA. [Leges Sumptuariae.]

LĪCĪNIAE, proposed by C. Licinius, who was tribune of the people from b. c. 376 to 367, and who brought the contest between the patricians and plebeians to a happy termination. He was supported in his exertions by his colleague L. Sextius. The laws which he proposed were: 1. That in future no more consular tribunes should be appointed, but that consuls should be elected as in former times, one of whom should always be a plebeian. 2. That no one should possess more than 500 jugera of the public land, nor keep upon it more than 100 head of large, or 500 of small cattle. It is related that Licinius was accused and condemned for violating his own law. Livy states that Licinius, together with his son, held 1000 jugera of the public land, and by emancipating his son had acted in fraud of the law. The son thus possessed 500 jugera in his own name, while his father had the actual enjoyment. 3. A law regulating the affairs between debtor and creditor, which ordained that the interest already paid for borrowed money should be deducted from the capital, and that the remainder of the latter should be paid back in three yearly instalments. 4. That the Sibylline books should be entrusted to a college of ten men (decemviri), half of whom should be plebeians, in order that no falsifications might be introduced in favour of the patricians. These rogations were passed after a most vehement opposition on the part of the patricians, and L. Sextius was the first plebeian who, in accordance with the first of them, obtained the consulship for the year b. c. 366.

LĪCĪNIA, also called MANLĪA, b. c. 196, created the triumviri epulones.

LĪVIAE, various enactments proposed by the tribune M. Livius Drusus, b. c. 91, for establishing colonies in Italy and Sicily, distributing corn among the poor citizens at a low rate, and admitting the foederatae civitates to the Roman civitas. He is also said to have been the mover of a law for adulterating silver by mixing with it an eighth part of brass. Drusus was assassinated, and the senate declared that all his laws were passed contra auspicia, and were therefore not leges.

LUTĀTIA DE VI, proposed by the consul Q. Lutatius Catulus, with the assistance of Plautius the tribune; usually called Lex Plautia or Plotia. [Vis.]

MAENĪA LEX, is only mentioned by Cicero, who says that M. Curius compelled the patres ante auctores fieri in the case of the election of a plebeian consul, "which," adds Cicero, "was a great thing to accomplish, as the Lex Maenia was not yet passed." The lex therefore required the patres to give their consent at least to the election of a magistratus, or, in other words, to confer or agree to confer the imperium on the person whom the comitia should elect. It was probably proposed by the tribune Maenius b. c. 287.

MAJESTĀTIS. [Majestas.]

MAMILIA DE JŪGURTHAE FAUTŌRIBUS. (Sall. Jug. 40.)

MAMILIA FINIUM REGUNDŌRUM, b. c. 239 or 165, respecting boundaries.

MĀNĪLIA, proposed by the tribune C. Manilius, b. c. 66, was a privilegium by which was conferred on Pompey the command in the war against Mithridates. The lex was supported by Cicero when praetor.

MANLĪA. [Licinia.]

MANLIA DE VĪCĒSĪMA, b. c. 357, imposed the tax of five per cent. (vicesima) on the value of manumitted slaves.

MARCĪA, probably about the year b. c. 352, adversus feneratores.

MARCIA, an agrarian law proposed by the tribune L. Marcius Philippus, b. c. 104.

MĀRIA, proposed by Marius when tribune, b. c. 119, for narrowing the pontes at elections.

MEMMIA or REMMIA. [Calumnia.]

MENSIA, respecting the marriage of a Roman woman with a peregrinus, declared the offspring of such marriages peregrini.

MĪNŪCIA, b. c. 216, created the triumviri mensarii.

NERVAE AGRĀRIA, the latest known instance of a lex.

OCTĀVIA, b. c. 91, one of the numerous leges frumentariae which repealed a Sempronia Frumentaria. It is mentioned by Cicero as a more reasonable measure than the Sempronia, which was too profuse.

OGULNIA, proposed by the tribunes, B. c. 300, increased the number of pontifices to eight, and that of the augurs to nine; it also enacted that four of the pontifices and five of the augurs should be taken from the plebes.

OPPIA. [LEGES SUMPTUARIAE.]
ORCHIA. [LEGES SUMPTUARIAE.]

OVINIA, of uncertain date, was a plebiscitum which gave the censors certain powers in regulating the lists of the senators (*ordo senatorius*) : the main object seems to have been to exclude all improper persons from the senate, and to prevent their admission, if in other respects qualified.

PAPIA DE PEREGRINIS. [LEX JUNIA DE PEREGRINIS.]

PAPIA POPPAEA. [LEX JULIA ET PAPIA POPPAEA.]

PAPIRIA or JULIA PAPIRIA DE MULCTARUM AESTIMATIONE (B. c. 430), fixed a money value according to which fines were paid, which formerly were paid in sheep and cattle. Some writers make this valuation part of the Aternian law [ATERNIA TARPEIA], but in this they appear to have been mistaken.

PAPIRIA, by which the as was made semuncialis, one of the various enactments which tampered with the coinage.

PAPIRIA, B. c. 332, proposed by the praetor Papirius, gave the Acerrani the civitas without the suffragium. It was properly a privilegium, but is useful as illustrating the history of the extension of the civitas Romana.

PAPIRIA, of uncertain date, enacted that no *aedes* should be declared *consecratae* without a plebiscitum.

PAPIRIA PLAUTIA, a plebiscitum of the year B. c. 89, proposed by the tribunes C. Papirius Carbo and M. Plautius Silvanus, in the consulship of Cn. Pompeius Strabo and L. Porcius Cato, is called by Cicero a lex of Silvanus and Carbo. [See CIVITAS; FOEDERATAE CIVITATES.]

PAPIRIA POETELIA. [LEX POETELIA.]
PAPIRIA TABELLARIA. [LEGES TABELLARIAE.]

PEDIA, relating to the murderers of Caesar.

PEDUCAEA, B. c. 113, a plebiscitum, seems to have been merely a privilegium, and not a general law against incestum.

PESULANIA, provided that if an animal did any damage, the owner should make it good, or give up the animal.

PETILLIA, DE PECUNIA REGIS ANTIOCHI. (Liv. xxxviii. 54.)

PETREIA, *de decimatione militum*, in case of mutiny.

PETRONIA, probably passed in the time of Augustus, and subsequently amended by various senatusconsulta, forbade a master to deliver up his slave to fight with wild beasts.

PINARIA, related to the giving of a judex within a limited time.

PLAETORIA. [CURATOR.]
PLAUTIA or PLOTIA DE VI. [VIS.]
PLAUTIA or PLOTIA JUDICIARIA, enacted that fifteen persons should be annually taken from each tribe to be placed in the Album Judicum.

PLAUTIA ET PLOTIA DE REDITU LEPIDANORUM. (Suet. *Caes*. 5.)

POETELIA, B. c. 358, a plebiscitum, was the first lex against ambitus.

POETELIA PAPIRIA, B. c. 326, made an important change in the liabilities of the Nexi.

POMPEIAE. There were various leges so called.

DE CIVITATE, proposed by Cn. Pompeius Strabo, the father of Cn. Pompeius Magnus, probably in his consulship B. c. 89, gave the jus Latii or Latinitas to all the towns of the Transpadani, and probably the civitas to the Cispadani.

DE AMBITU. [AMBITUS.]
DE IMPERIO CAESARI PROROGANDO. (Vell. Pat. ii. 46; Appian, *B. C*. ii. 18.)
JUDICIARIA. [JUDEX, p. 217, *a*.]
DE JURE MAGISTRATUUM, forbade a person to be a candidate for public offices (*petitio honorum*) who was not at Rome; but J. Caesar was excepted. This was doubtless the old law, but it had apparently become obsolete.

DE PARRICIDIIS. [PARRICIDIUM.]
TRIBUNITIA (B. c. 70), restored the old tribunitia potestas, which Sulla had nearly destroyed. [TRIBUNI.]

DE VI, was a privilegium, and only referred to the case of Milo.

PORCIAE DE CAPITE CIVIUM, or DE PROVOCATIONE, enacted that no Roman citizen should be scourged or put to death.

PORCIA DE PROVINCIIS, about B. c. 198, the enactments of which are doubtful.

PUBLICIA, permitted betting at certain games which required strength.

PUBLILIA. In the consulship of L. Pinarius and P. Furius, B. c. 471, the tribune Publilius Volero proposed, in the assembly of the tribes, that the tribunes should in future be appointed in the comitia of the tribes (*ut plebeii magistratus tributis comitiis fierent*), instead of by the centuries, as had formerly been the case; since the clients of the patricians were so numerous in the centuries, that the plebeians could not elect whom they wished. This measure was violently opposed by the patricians, who prevented the tribes from coming to any resolution respecting it throughout this year; but in the following year, B. c. 471, Publilius was re-elected tribune, and together with him C. Laetorius, a man of still greater resolution than Publilius. Fresh measures were added to the former proposition: the aediles were to be chosen by the tribes, as well as the tribunes, and the tribes were to be competent to deliberate and determine on all matters affecting the whole nation, and not such only as might concern the plebes. This proposition, though still more violently resisted by the patricians than the one of the previous year, was carried. Some said that the number of the tribunes was now for the first time raised to five, having been only two previously.

PUBLILIAE, proposed by the dictator Q. Publilius Philo, B. c. 339. According to Livy, there were three Publiliae Leges. 1. The first is said to have enacted, that plebiscita should bind all Quirites, which is to the same purport as the Lex Hortensia of B. c. 286. It is probable, however, that the object of this law was to render the approval of the senate a sufficient confirmation of a plebiscitum, and to make the confirmation of the curiae unnecessary. 2. The second law enacted, *ut legum quae comitiis centuriatis ferrerentur ante initum suffragium patres auctores fierent.* By patres Livy here means the curiae; and accordingly this law made the confirmation of the curiae a mere formality in reference to all laws submitted to the comitia centuriata, since every law proposed by the senate to the centuries was to be considered to have the sanction of the curiae also. 3. The third law enacted that one of the two censors should necessarily be a plebeian. It is probable that there was also a fourth law, which applied the Licinian law to the praetorship as well as to the censorship, and which provided that in each alternate year the praetor should be a plebeian.

PUPIA, mentioned by Cicero, seems to have enacted that the senate could not meet on comitiales dies.

QUINTIA, was a lex proposed by T. Quintius Crispinus, consul B. c. 9, for the preservation of the aquaeductus.

REGIA. A *Lex Regia* during the kingly period of Roman history might have a twofold meaning. In the first place it was a law which had been passed by the comitia under the presidency of the king, and was thus distinguished from a *Lex Tribunicia*, which was passed by the comitia under the presidency of the tribunus celerum. In later times all laws, the origin of which was attributed to the time of the kings, were called *Leges Regiae,* though it by no means follows that they were all passed under the presidency of the kings, and much less, that they were enacted by the kings without the sanction of the curies. Some of these laws were preserved and followed at a very late period of Roman history. A collection of them was made, though at what time is uncertain, by Papisius or Papirius, and this compilation was called the *Jus Civile Papirianum* or *Papisianum.* The second meaning of *Lex Regia* during the kingly period was undoubtedly the same as that of the *Lex Curiata de Imperio.* [IMPERIUM.] This indeed is not mentioned by any ancient writer, but must be inferred from the *Lex Regia* which we meet with under the empire, for the name could scarcely have been invented then; it must have come down from early times, when its meaning was similar, though not nearly so extensive. During the empire the curies continued to hold their meetings, though they were only a shadow of those of former times; and after the election of a new emperor, they conferred upon him the imperium in the ancient form by a *Lex Curiata de Imperio,* which was now usually called *Lex Regia.* The imperium, however, which this *Regia Lex* conferred upon an emperor, was of a very different nature from that which in former times it had conferred upon the kings. It now embraced all the rights and powers which the populus Romanus had formerly possessed, so that the emperor became what formerly the populus had been, that is, the sovereign power in the state. A fragment of such a lex regia, conferring the imperium upon Vespasian, engraved upon a brazen table, is still extant in the Lateran at Rome.

REMNIA. [CALUMNIA.]

REPETUNDARUM. [REPETUNDAE.]

RHODIA. The Rhodians had a maritime code which was highly esteemed. Some of its provisions were adopted by the Romans, and have thus been incorporated into the maritime law of European states. It was not, however, a lex in the proper sense of the term.

ROSCIA THEATRALIS, proposed by the tribune L. Roscius Otho, B.C. 67, which gave the equites a special place at the public spectacles in fourteen rows or seats (*in quatuordecim gradibus sive ordinibus*) next to the place of the senators, which was in the orchestra. This lex also assigned a certain place to spendthrifts. The phrase *sedere in quatuordecim ordinibus* is equivalent to having the proper census equestris which was required by the lex. There are numerous allusions to this lex, which is sometimes simply called the Lex of Otho, or referred to by his name. It is erroneously supposed by some writers to have been enacted in the consulship of Cicero, B.C. 63.

RUBRIA. The province of Gallia Cisalpina ceased to be a provincia, and became a part of Italia, about the year B.C. 43. When this change took place, it was necessary to provide for the administration of justice, as the usual modes of provincial administration would cease with the determination of the provincial form of government. This was effected by a lex, a large part of which, on a bronze tablet, is preserved in the Museum at Parma. The name of this lex is not known, but it is supposed by some to be the Lex Rubria.

RŬPĬLĬAE LEGES (B.C. 131), were the regulations established by P. Rupilius, and ten legati, for the administration of the province of Sicily, after the close of the first servile war. They were made in pursuance of a consultum of the senate. Cicero speaks of these regulations as a decretum of Rupilius, which he says they call Lex Rupilia; but it was not a lex proper. The powers given to the commissioners by the Lex Julia Municipalis were of a similar kind.

SĂCRĀTAE. Leges were properly so called which had for their object to make a thing or person *sacer*. A lex sacrata militaris is also mentioned by Livy.

SAENIA DE PATRICIORUM NUMERO AUGENDO, enacted in the 5th consulship of Augustus.

SĂTŬRA. [LEX, p. 226, *a.*]

SCANTĬNĬA, proposed by a tribune; the date and contents are not known, but its object was to suppress unnatural crimes. It existed in the time of Cicero.

SCRĪBŌNĬA. The date and whole import of this lex are not known; but it enacted that a right to servitutes should not be acquired by usucapion.

SCRĪBŌNIA VĬĀRIA or DE VIIS MUNIENDIS, B.C. 51.

SEMPRŌNĬAE, the name of various laws proposed by Tiberius and Caius Sempronius Gracchus.

AGRARIA. In B.C. 133 the tribune Tib. Gracchus revived the Agrarian law of Licinius [LEGES LICINIAE]: he proposed that no one should possess more than 500 jugera of the public land, and that the surplus land should be divided among the poor citizens, who were not to have the power of alienating it: he also proposed, as a compensation to the possessors deprived of the land on which they had frequently made improvements, that the former possessors should have the full ownership of 500 jugera, and each of their sons, if they had any, half that quantity: finally, that three commissioners (*triumviri*) should be appointed every year to carry the law into effect. This law naturally met with the greatest opposition, but it was eventually passed in the year in which it was proposed, and Tib. Gracchus, C. Gracchus, and Appius Claudius were the three commissioners appointed under it. It was, however, never carried fully into effect, in consequence of the murder of Tib. Gracchus. Owing to the difficulties which were experienced in carrying his brother's agrarian law into effect, it was again brought forward by C. Gracchus, B.C. 123.

DE CAPITE CIVIUM ROMANORUM, proposed by C. Gracchus B.C. 123, enacted that the people only should decide respecting the caput or civil condition of a citizen. This law continued in force till the latest times of the republic.

FRUMENTARIA, proposed by C. Gracchus B.C. 123, enacted that corn should be sold by the state to the people once a month at the price of 6½ asses for each modius, which was equal to 1 gallon and nearly 8 pints English. This was only a trifle more than half the market price.

JUDICIARIA. [JUDEX, p. 216.]

MILITARIS, proposed by C. Gracchus B.C. 123, enacted that the soldiers should receive their clothing gratis, and that no one should be enrolled as a soldier under the age of seventeen. Previously a fixed sum was deducted from the pay for all clothes and arms issued to the soldiers.

NE QUIS JUDICIO CIRCUMVENIRETUR, proposed by C. Gracchus, B.C. 123, punished all who conspired to obtain the condemnation of a person in a judicium publicum. One of the provisions of the Lex Cornelia de Sicariis was to the same effect.

DE PROVINCIIS CONSULARIBUS, proposed by C. Gracchus B.C. 123, enacted that the senate should fix each year, before the comitia for electing the consuls were held, the two provinces which were to be allotted to the two new consuls. There was also a Sempronian law concerning the province of Asia, which probably did not form part of the Lex de Provinciis Consularibus: it enacted that the taxes of this province should be let out to farm by the censors at Rome. This law was afterwards repealed by J. Caesar.

SEMPRŌNIA DE FĒNŎRE, B.C. 193, was a plebiscitum proposed by a tribune, M. Sempronius, which enacted that the law (*jus*) about money lent (*pecunia credita*) should be the same for the Socii and Latini (*Socii ac nomen Latinum*) as for Roman citizens. The object of the lex was to prevent Romans from lending money in the name of the Socii, who were not bound by the fenebres leges. The lex could obviously only apply within the jurisdiction of Rome.

SERVĪLIA AGRĀRIA, proposed by the tribune P. S. Rullus in the consulship of Cicero, B.C. 63, was a very extensive agrarian rogatio. It was successfully opposed by Cicero; but it was in substance carried by J. Caesar, B.C. 59 [LEX JULIA AGRARIA], and is the lex called by Cicero *Lex Campana*, from the public land called ager campanus being assigned under this lex.

SERVĪLIA GLAUCIA DE CĪVĪTĀTE. [REPETUNDAE.]

SERVĪLIA GLAUCIA DE RĒPĒTUNDIS. [REPETUNDAE.]

SERVĪLIA JŪDĪCIĀRIA, B.C. 106. [JUDEX, p. 216.] It is assumed by some writers that a lex of the tribune Servius Glaucia repealed the Servilia Judiciaria two years after its enactment.

SĪLIA, relating to Publica Pondera.

SILVĀNI ET CARBŌNIS. [LEX PAPIRIA PLAUTIA.]

SULPĪCIAE, proposed by the tribune P. Sulpicius Rufus, a supporter of Marius, B.C. 88, enacted the recall of the exiles, the distribution of the new citizens and the libertini among the thirty-five tribes, that the command in the Mithridatic war should be taken from Sulla and given to Marius, and that a senator should not contract debt to the amount of more than 2000 denarii. The last enactment may have been intended to expel persons from the senate who should get in debt. All these leges were repealed by Sulla.

SULPĪCIA SEMPRŌNĪA, B. c. 304. No name is given to this lex by Livy, but it was probably proposed by the consuls. It prevented the dedicatio of a templum or altar without the consent of the senate or a majority of the tribunes.

SUMPTUĀRIAE, the name of various laws passed to prevent inordinate expense (*sumptus*) in banquets, dress, &c. In the states of antiquity it was considered the duty of government to put a check upon extravagance in the private expenses of persons, and among the Romans in particular we find traces of this in the laws attributed to the kings, and in the Twelve Tables. The censors, to whom was entrusted the *disciplina* or *cura morum*, punished by the *nota censoria* all persons guilty of what was then regarded as a luxurious mode of living; a great many instances of this kind are recorded. But as the love of luxury greatly increased with the foreign conquests of the republic and the growing wealth of the nation, various leges sumptuariae were passed at different times with the object of restraining it. These, however, as may be supposed, rarely accomplished their object, and in the latter times of the republic they were virtually repealed. The following list of them is arranged in chronological order:—

OPPIA, proposed by the tribune C. Oppius in B. c. 215, enacted that no woman should have above half an ounce of gold, nor wear a dress of different colours, nor ride in a carriage in the city or in any town, or within a mile of it, unless on account of public sacrifices. This law was repealed twenty years afterwards, whence we frequently find the Lex Orchia mentioned as the first lex sumptuaria.

ORCHIA, proposed by the tribune C. Orchius in B. c. 181, limited the number of guests to be present at entertainments.

FANNIA, proposed by the consul C. Fannius, B. c. 61, limited the sums which were to be spent on entertainments, and enacted that not more than 100 asses should be spent on certain festivals named in the lex, whence it is called *centussis* by Lucilius; that on ten other days in each month not more than 30 asses, and that on all other days not more than 10 asses, should be expended; also that no other fowl but one hen should be served up, and that not fattened for the purpose.

DIDIA, passed B. c. 143, extended the Lex Fannia to the whole of Italy, and enacted that not only those who gave entertainments which exceeded in expense what the law had prescribed, but also all who were present at such entertainments, should be liable to the penalties of the law. We are not, however, told in what these consisted.

LICINIA, agreed in its chief provisions with the Lex Fannia, and was brought forward, we are told, that there might be the authority of a new law upon the subject, inasmuch as the Lex Fannia was beginning to be neglected. It allowed 200 asses to be spent on entertainments upon marriage days, and on other days the same as the Lex Fannia; also, that on ordinary days there should not be served up more than three pounds of fresh, and one pound of salt meat. It was probably passed in B. c. 103.

CORNELIA, a law of the dictator Sulla, B.C. 81, was enacted on account of the neglect of the Fannian and Licinian Laws. Like these, it regulated the expenses of entertainments. Extravagance in funerals, which had been forbidden even in the Twelve Tables, was also restrained by a law of Sulla.

AEMILIA, proposed by the consul Aemilius Lepidus, B. c. 78, did not limit the expenses of entertainments, but the kind and quantity of food that was to be used.

ANTIA, of uncertain date, proposed by Antius Resto, besides limiting the expenses of entertainments, enacted that no actual magistrate, or magistrate elect, should dine abroad anywhere except at the houses of certain persons. This law however was little observed; and we are told that Antius never dined out afterwards, that he might not see his own law violated.

JULIA, proposed by the dictator C. Julius Caesar, enforced the former sumptuary laws respecting entertainments which had fallen into disuse. He stationed officers in the provision market to seize upon all eatables forbidden by the law, and sometimes sent lictors and soldiers to banquets to take everything which was not allowed by the law.

JULIA, a lex of Augustus, allowed 200 sesterces to be expended upon festivals on dies profesti, 300 on those of the calends, ides, nones, and some other festive days, and 1000 upon marriage feasts. There was also an edict of Augustus or Tiberius, by which as much as from 300 to 2000 sesterces were allowed to be expended upon entertainments, the increase being made with the hope of securing thereby the observance of the law. Tiberius attempted to check extravagance in banquets; and a senatusconsultum was passed in his reign for the purpose of restraining luxury, which forbade gold vases to be employed, except for sacred purposes, and also prohibited the use of silk garments to men. This sumptuary law, however, was but little observed. Some regulations on the subject were also made by Nero and by succeeding emperors, but they appear to have been of little or no avail in checking the increasing love of luxury in dress and food.

TABELLARIAE, the laws by which the ballot was introduced in voting in the comitia. As to the ancient mode of voting at Rome, see COMITIA, p. 107.

GABINIA, proposed by the tribune Gabinius B. c. 139, introduced the ballot in the election of magistrates; whence Cicero calls the tabella *vindex tacitae libertatis*.

CASSIA, proposed by the tribune L. Cassius Longinus B. c. 137, introduced the ballot in the *judicium populi*, or cases tried in the comitia by the whole body of the people, with the exception of cases of perduellio.

PAPIRIA, proposed by the tribune C. Papirius Carbo, B. c. 131, introduced the ballot in the enactment and repeal of laws.

CAELIA, proposed by C. Caelius Caldus, B. c. 107, introduced the ballot in cases of perduellio, which had been excepted in the Cassian law. There was also a law brought

forward by Marius, B. c. 119, which was intended to secure freedom and order in voting.

TARPEIA ATERNIA. [ATERNIA TARPEIA.]

TERENTILIA, proposed by the tribune C. Terentilius, B. c. 462, but not carried, was a rogatio which had for its object an amendment of the constitution, though in form it only attempted a limitation of the imperium consulare. This rogatio probably led to the subsequent legislation of the decemviri.

TESTAMENTARIAE. Various leges, such as the Cornelia, Falcidia, Furia, and Voconia, regulated testamentary dispositions.

THORIA, passed B. c. 121, concerned the public land in Italy as far as the rivers Rubico and Macra, or all Italy except Cisalpine Gaul, the public land in the province of Africa, the public land in the territory of Corinth, and probably other public land besides. It relieved a great part of the public land of the land-tax (*vectigal*). Some considerable fragments of this lex have come down to us, engraved on the back part of the same bronze tablet which contained the Servilia Lex Judiciaria, and on Repetundae.

TITIA, similar in its provisions to the Lex Publicia.

TITIA, DE TUTORIBUS. [JULIA ET TITIA.]

TREBONIA, a plebiscitum proposed by L. Trebonius, B. c. 448, which enacted that if the ten tribunes were not chosen before the comitia were dissolved, those who were elected should not fill up the number (*co-optare*), but that the comitia should be continued till the ten were elected.

TREBONIA DE PROVINCIIS CONSULARIBUS. (Plut. *Cat. Min.* 43; Liv. *Epit.* 105.)

TRIBUNITIA. (1) A law passed in the times of the kings under the presidency of the tribunus celerum, and was so called by distinguish it from one passed under the presidency of the king. [LEX REGIA.]—(2) Any law proposed by a tribune of the plebs. —(3) The law proposed by Pompey in B. c. 70, restoring to the tribunes of the plebs the power of which they had been deprived by Sulla.

TULLIA DE AMBITU. [AMBITUS.]

TULLIA DE LEGATIONE LIBERA. [LEGATUS, p. 224.]

VALERIAE, proposed by the consul P. Valerius Publicola, B. c. 508, enacted, 1. That whoever attempted to obtain possession of royal power should be devoted to the gods, together with his substance. 2. That whoever was condemned by the sentence of a magistrate to be put to death, to be scourged, or to be fined, should possess the right of appeal (*provocatio*) to the people. The patricians possessed previously the right of appeal from the sentence of a magistrate to their own council the curiae, and therefore this law of Valerius probably related only to the plebeians, to whom it gave the right of appeal to the plebeian tribes, and not to the centuries. Hence the laws proposed by the Valerian family respecting the right of appeal are always spoken of as one of the chief safeguards of the liberty of the plebs. The right of appeal did not extend beyond a mile from the city, where unlimited imperium began, to which the patricians were just as much subject as the plebeians.

VALERIAE ET HORATIAE, three laws proposed by the consuls L. Valerius and M. Horatius, B.C. 449, in the year after the decemvirate, enacted, 1. That a plebiscitum should be binding on the whole people, respecting the meaning of which expression, see PLEBISCITUM. 2. That whoever should procure the election of a magistrate without appeal should be outlawed, and might be killed by any one with impunity. 3. Renewed the penalty threatened against any one who should harm the tribunes and the aediles, to whom were now added the judices and decemviri. There is considerable doubt as to who are meant by the *judices* and *decemviri*.

VALERIA, proposed by the consul M. Valerius, B.C. 300, re-enacted for the third time the celebrated law of his family respecting appeal (*provocatio*) from the decision of a magistrate. The law specified no fixed penalty for its violation, leaving the judges to determine what the punishment should be.

VARIA. [MAJESTAS.]

VATINIA DE PROVINCIIS, was the enactment by which Julius Caesar obtained the province of Gallia Cisalpina with Illyricum for five years, to which the senate added Gallia Transalpina. This plebiscitum was proposed by the tribune Vatinius. A Trebonia Lex subsequently prolonged Caesar's imperium for five years.

VATINIA DE COLONIS, under which the Latina Colonia [LATINITAS] of Novum-Comum in Gallia Cisalpina was planted, B.C. 59.

VATINIA DE REJECTIONE JUDICUM. (Cic. in *Vatin.* 11.)

DE VI. [VIS.]

VIARIA. A viaria lex which Cicero says the tribune C. Curio talked of; but nothing more seems to be known of it. Some modern writers speak of leges viariae, but there do not appear to be any leges properly so called. The provisions as to roads in many of the Agrarian laws were parts of such leges, and had no special reference to roads.

VISELLIA, made a Latinus who assumed the rights of an ingenuus liable to prosecution.

VILLIA ANNALIS. [LEX ANNALIS.]

VOCONIA, enacted on the proposal of Q. Voconius Saxa, a tribunus plebis, B.C. 169. One provision of the lex was, that no person who should be rated in the census at 100,000 sesterces (*centum millia aeris*) after the census of that year, should make any female (*virginem neve mulierem*) his heres. The lex allowed no exceptions, even in favour of an only daughter. It applied simply to testaments, and therefore a daughter or other female could inherit ab intestato to any amount. The vestal virgins could make women their heredes in all cases, which was the only exception to the provisions of the lex. Another provision of the lex forbade a person who was included in the census to give more in amount, in the form of a legacy to any person, than the heres or heredes should take. This provision secured something to the heres or heredes, but still the provision was ineffectual, and the object of the lex was only accomplished by the Lex Falcidia, B.C. 44, which enacted that a testator should not give more than three-fourths in legacies, thus securing a fourth to the heres.

LIBELLA, a small Roman silver coin, which existed in the early age of the city. The name was retained later as a proverbial expression for a very small value. The *libella* was equal in value to the old full-weight *as*; and it seems most probable that the coin ceased being struck at the time of the reduction of the *as*, on account of the inconveniently small size which it would have assumed. The *libella* was subdivided into the *sembella*, its half, and the *teruncius*, its quarter. Cicero uses these words to express fractions of an estate, with reference to the *denarius* as the unit, the *libella* signifying 1-10th, and the *teruncius* 1-40th of the whole.

LIBELLUS, the diminutive form of liber, signifies properly a little book. It was distinguished from other kinds of writings, by being written like our books by pages, whereas other writings were written *transversa charta*. It was used by the Romans as a technical term in the following cases:—
1. *Libelli accusatorum* or *accusatorii*, the written accusations which in some cases a plaintiff, after having received the permission to bring an action against a person, drew up, signed, and sent to the judicial authorities.
2. *Libelli famosi*, libels or pasquinades, intended to injure the character of persons. A law of the Twelve Tables inflicted very severe punishments on those who composed defamatory writings. 3. *Libellus memorialis*,

a pocket or memorandum book. 4. *Libellus* is used by the Roman jurists as equivalent to *Oratio Principis*. 5. The word libellus was also applied to a variety of writings, which in most cases probably consisted of one page only; such as short letters, advertisements, &c.

LĪBER (βιβλίον), a book. The most common material on which books were written by the Greeks and Romans, was the thin coats or rind (*liber*, whence the Latin name for a book) of the Egyptian papyrus. This plant was called by the Egyptians Byblos (βύβλος), whence the Greeks derived their name for a book (βιβλίον). The papyrus-tree grows in swamps to the height of ten feet and more, and paper (*charta*) was prepared from the thin coats or pellicles which surround the plant. Next to the papyrus, parchment (*membrana*) was the most common material for writing upon. It is said to have been invented by Eumenes II. king of Pergamus, in consequence of the prohibition of the export of papyrus from Egypt by Ptolemy Epiphanes. It is probable, however, that Eumenes introduced only some improvement in the manufacture of parchment, as Herodotus mentions writing on skins as common in his time, and says that

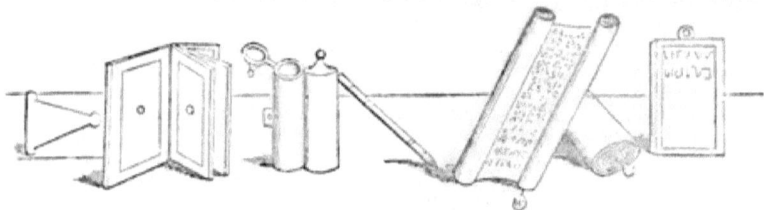

Ancient Writing Materials. (From a Painting at Herculaneum.)

the Ionians had been accustomed to give the name of skins (διφθέραι) to books. The ancients wrote usually on only one side of the paper or parchment. The back of the paper, instead of being written upon, was usually stained with saffron colour or the cedrus, which produced a yellow colour. As paper and parchment were dear, it was frequently the custom to erase or wash out writing of little importance, and to write upon the paper or parchment again, which was then called *Palimpsestus* (παλιμψήστος). The paper or parchment was joined together so as to form one sheet, and when the work was finished, it was rolled on a staff, whence it was called a *volumen*; and hence we have the expression *evolvere librum*. When an author divided a work into several books, it was usual to include only one book in a volume or roll, so that there was generally the same number of volumes as of books. In the papyri rolls found at Herculaneum, the stick on which the papyrus is rolled does not project from the papyrus, but is concealed by it. Usually, however, there were balls or bosses, ornamented or painted, called *umbilici* or *cornua*, which were fastened at each end of the stick and projected from the papyrus. The ends of the roll were carefully cut, polished with pumice-stone and coloured black; they were called the *geminae frontes*. The way in which a book was held while reading is shown in the following cut, taken from a painting at Herculaneum. To protect the roll from injury it was frequently put into a parchment case, which was stained with a purple colour or with the yellow of the Lutum. The title of the book (*titulus, index*) was written on a small strip of papyrus or parchment with a light red colour (*coccum* or *minium*).

Book held by a crowned Poet. (From a Painting at Herculaneum.)

LĪBERĀLIA. [DIONYSIA.]
LĪBERI. [INGENUI; LIBERTUS.]
LIBERTUS, LIBERTĪNUS. Freemen (*liberi*) were either *Ingenui* [INGENUI] or

Libertini. Libertini were those persons who had been released from legal servitude. A manumitted slave was *Libertus* (that is, *liberatus*) with reference to his master; with reference to the class to which he belonged after manumission, he was *Libertinus.* Respecting the mode in which a slave was manumitted, and his status after manumission, see MANUMISSIO.—At Athens, a liberated slave was called ἀπελεύθερος. When manumitted he did not obtain the citizenship, but was regarded as a *metoicus* [METOICUS], and, as such, he had to pay not only the *metoicion* (μετοίκιον), but a triobolon in addition to it. His former master became his patron (προστάτης), to whom he owed certain duties.

LIBITINARII. [FUNUS.]

LIBRA, *dim.* LIBELLA (σταθμός), a balance, a pair of scales. The principal parts of this instrument were, 1. The beam (*jugum*). 2. The two scales, called in Greek τάλαντα, and in Latin *lances.* The beam was made without a tongue, being held by a ring or other appendage (*ligula,* ῥῦμα) fixed in the centre.

LIBRA or AS, a pound, the unit of weight among the Romans and Italians. The uncial division, which has been noticed in speaking of the coin As, was also applied to the weight. —(See Tables at the end.) The divisions of the ounce are given under UNCIA. Where the word *pondo,* or its abbreviations P. or POND., occur with a simple number, the weight understood is the *libra.* The name *libra* was also given to a measure of horn, divided into twelve equal parts (*unciae*) by lines marked on it, and used for measuring oil.

LIBRARII, the name of slaves, who were employed by their masters in writing or copying, sometimes called *antiquarii.* They must be distinguished from the Scribae publici, who were freemen [SCRIBAE], and also from the booksellers [BIBLIOPOLA], to both of whom this name was also applied.

LIBRATOR, in general a person who examines things by a LIBRA; but specially applied to two kinds of persons.—(1) *Libratores aquae,* persons whose knowledge of hydrostatics was indispensable in the construction of aquaeducts, sewers, and other structures for the purpose of conveying a fluid from one place to another.—(2) *Libratores* in the armies were probably soldiers who attacked the enemy by hurling with their own hands (*librando*) lances or spears against them.

LIBRIPENS. [MANCIPIUM.]

LIBURNA, LIBURNICA, a light vessel, which derived its name from the Liburni. The ships of this people were of great assistance to Augustus at the battle of Actium; and experience having shown their efficiency, vessels of a similar kind were built and called by the name of the people.

LICTOR, a public officer, who attended on the chief Roman magistrates. The number which waited on the different magistrates is stated in the article FASCES. The office of lictor is said to have been derived by Romulus from the Etruscans. The lictors went before the magistrates one by one in a line; he who went last or next to the magistrate was called *proximus lictor,* to whom the magistrate gave his commands; and as this lictor was always the principal one, we also find him called *primus lictor.* The lictors had to inflict punishment on those who were condemned, especially in the case of Roman citizens; for foreigners and slaves were punished by the Carnifex; and they also probably had to assist in some cases in the execution of a decree or judgment in a civil suit. The lictors likewise commanded persons to pay proper respect to a magistrate passing by, which consisted in dismounting from horseback, uncovering the head, standing out of the way, &c. The lictors were originally chosen from the plebs, but afterwards appear to have been generally freedmen, probably of the magistrate on whom they attended. Lictors were properly only granted to those magistrates who had the Imperium. Consequently, the tribunes of the plebs never had lictors, nor several of the other magistrates. Sometimes, however, lictors were granted to persons as a mark of respect or for the sake of protection. Thus by a law of the Triumvirs every vestal virgin was accompanied by a lictor, whenever she went out, and the honour of one or two lictors was usually granted to the wives and other female members of the Imperial family. There were also thirty lictors called *Lictores Curiati,* whose duty it was to summon the curiae to the comitia curiata; and when these meetings became little more than a form, their suffrages were represented by the thirty lictors.

LIGULA, a Roman measure of fluid capacity, containing one-fourth of the CYATHUS. It signifies *a spoonful,* like *cochlear;* only the *ligula* was larger than the *cochlear.* The spoon which was called *ligula,* or *lingula* (dim. of *lingua*) from its shape, was used for various purposes, especially to clean out small and narrow vessels, and to eat jellies and such things. The word is also used for the leather tongue of a shoe.

LIMEN. [JANUA.]

LINTER, a light boat, frequently formed of the trunk of a tree, and drawing little water.

LĬTHOSTRŎTA. [DOMUS, p. 144.]
LITRA (λίτρα), a Sicilian silver coin, equal in value to the Aeginetan obol.
LĬTUUS, probably an Etruscan word signifying *crooked*.—(1) The crooked staff borne by the augurs, with which they divided the expanse of heaven, when viewed with reference to divination (*templum*), into regions

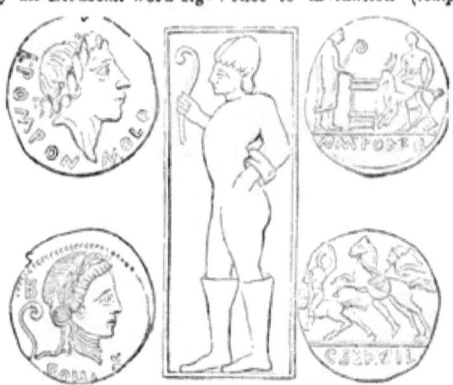

Lituus, Augur's Staff. (Centre figure from an Etruscan sculpture; the two others are Roman coins.)

(*regiones*).—(2) A sort of trumpet slightly curved at the extremity. It differed both from the *tuba* and the *cornu*, the former

Lituus, Trumpet. (From Fabretti.)

being straight, while the latter was bent round into a spiral shape. Its tones are usually characterised as harsh and shrill.

The Liticines, or blowers on the Lituus, formed a Collegium along with the Cornicines. [CORNU.]
LIXAE. [CALONES.]
LŎCŬPLĒTES or ASSĬDŬI, the name of the Roman citizens included in the five classes of the Servian constitution, and opposed to the *Proletarii.*
LŌDIX, a small shaggy blanket. It was also used as a carpet.
LOGISTAE. [EUTHYNE.]
LŌRĪCA (θώραξ), a cuirass. The cuirass was worn by the heavy-armed infantry both

Lorica, as worn by a Greek Warrior. (From a Vase.)

Lorica, as worn by a Roman Emperor. (Statue of Caligula in Louvre.)

among the Greeks and Romans. The soldiers commonly wore cuirasses made of flex-

Lorica, λεπιδωτός. Lorica, φολιδωτός.
(Bartoli, 'Arcus Triumph.')

ible bands of steel, or cuirasses of chain mail; but those of generals and officers usually consisted of two γύαλα, the breastpiece and back-piece, made of bronze, iron, &c., which were joined by means of buckles (περόναι). The epithets λεπιδωτός and φολιδωτός are applied to a cuirass; the former on account of its resemblance to the scales of fish (λεπίσιν), the latter to the scales of serpents (φολίσιν). Among the Asiatic nations the cuirass was frequently made of cotton, and among the Sarmatians and other northern nations of horn.

LŪCAR. [HISTRIO.]
LŪCĒRES. [TRIBUS.]

LŪCERNA (λύχνος), an oil lamp. The Greeks and Romans originally used candles; but in later times candles were chiefly confined to the houses of the lower classes. [CANDELA.] A great number of ancient lamps has come down to us; the greater part of which are made of terra cotta, but also a considerable number of bronze. Most of the lamps are of an oval form, and flat upon the top, on which there are frequently figures in relief. In the lamps there are one or more round holes, according to the number of wicks (*ellychnia*) burnt in them; and as these holes were called from an obvious analogy, μυκτῆρες or μύξαι, literally nostrils or nozzles, the lamp was also called *Monomyxos*, *Dimyxos*, *Trimyxos*, or *Polymyxos*, according as it contained one, two, three, or a greater number of nozzles or holes for the wicks. The following is an example of a *dimyxos lucerna*, upon which there is a winged boy

Lucerna, lamp. (Museo Borbon'co, vol. iv. pl. 10.)

with a goose. The next woodcut represents one of the most beautiful bronze lamps which has yet been found. Upon it is the figure of a standing Silenus. The lamps sometimes

Lucerna, lamp. (Museo Borbonico, vol. 1. pl. 10.)

hung in chains from the ceiling of the room, but they generally stood upon a stand. [CANDELABRUM.]

LUCTA, LUCTATIO (πάλη, πάλαισμα, παλαισμοσύνη, or καταβλητική), wrestling. The Greeks ascribed the invention of wrestling to mythical personages, and Hermes, the god of all gymnastic exercises, also presided over wrestling. In the Homeric age wrestling was much practised: during this period wrestlers contended naked, and only the loins were covered with the perizoma (περίζωμα), and this custom probably remained throughout Greece until Ol. 15, from which time the perizoma was no longer used, and wrestlers contended entirely naked. In the Homeric age the custom of anointing the body for the purpose of wrestling does not appear to have been known, but in the time of Solon it was quite general, and was said to have been adopted by the Cretans and Lacedaemonians at a very early period. After the body was anointed, it was strewed over with sand or dust, in order to enable the wrestlers to take a firm hold of each other. If one combatant threw the other down three times, the victory was decided. Wrestling was practised in all the great games of the Greeks. The most renowned wrestler was Milon, of Croton. [PANCRATIUM.]

LUDI, the common name for the whole variety of games and contests which were held at Rome on various occasions, but chiefly at the festivals of the gods; and as the ludi at certain festivals formed the principal part of the solemnities, these festivals themselves are called ludi. Sometimes ludi were also held in honour of a magistrate or a deceased person, in which case they may be considered as ludi privati. All ludi were divided by the Romans into two classes, *ludi circenses* and *ludi scenici*, accordingly as they were held in the circus or in the theatre; in the latter case they were mostly theatrical representations with their various modifications; in the former they consisted of all or of a part of the games enumerated in the articles CIRCUS and GLADIATORES. Another division of the ludi into *stati*, *imperativi*, and *votivi*, is analogous to the division of the feriae. [FERIAE.] The superintendence of the games, and the solemnities connected with them, was in most cases intrusted to the aediles. [AEDILES.] If the lawful rites were not observed in the celebration of the ludi, it depended upon the decision of the pontiffs whether they were to be held again (*instaurari*) or not. An alphabetical list of the principal ludi is subjoined.

LUDI APOLLINARES were instituted at Rome during the second Punic war, after the battle of Cannae (212 B. c.), at the command of an oracle contained in the books of the ancient seer Marcius, in order to obtain the aid of Apollo. They were held every year under the superintendence of the praetor urbanus, and ten men sacrificed to Apollo, according to Greek rites, a bull with gilt horns and two white goats also with gilt horns, and to Latona a heifer with gilt horns. The games themselves were held in the Circus Maximus, the spectators were adorned with chaplets, and each citizen gave a contribution towards defraying the expenses. In B. c. 208, it was ordained that they should always be celebrated on the 6th of July.

LUDI AUGUSTALES. [AUGUSTALES.]

LUDI CAPITOLINI were instituted B. c. 387, after the departure of the Gauls from Rome, as a token of gratitude towards Jupiter Capitolinus, who had saved the Capitol in the hour of danger. The superintendence of the games was entrusted to a college of priests called *Capitolini*.

LUDI CIRCENSES, ROMANI or MAGNI, were celebrated every year during several days, from the fourth to the twelfth of September, in honour of the three great divinities, Jupiter, Juno, and Minerva, or, according to others, in honour of Jupiter, Consus, and Neptunus Equestris. They were superintended by the curule aediles. For further particulars see CIRCUS.

LUDI COMPITALICII. [COMPITALIA.]

LUDI FLORALES. [FLORALIA.]

LUDI FUNEBRES were games celebrated at the funeral pyre of illustrious persons. Such games are mentioned in the very early legends of the history of Greece and Rome, and they continued with various modifications until the introduction of Christianity. It was at such a ludus funebris, in B. c. 264, that gladiatorial fights were exhibited at Rome for the first time, which henceforwards were the most essential part in all funeral games. [GLADIATORES.]

LUDI LIBERALES. [DIONYSIA.]

LUDI MEGALENSES. [MEGALESIA.]

LUDI PLEBEII were instituted probably in commemoration of the reconciliation between the patricians and plebeians after the first secession to the Mons Sacer, or, according to others, to the Aventine. They were held on the 16th, 17th, and 18th of November, and were conducted by the plebeian aediles.

LUDI SAECULARES. During the time of the republic these games were called *ludi Tarentini*, *Terentini*, or *Taurii*, and it was not till the time of Augustus that they bore the name of *ludi saeculares*. The names *Tarenti* or *Taurii* are perhaps nothing but different forms of the same word, and of the same root is Tarquinius. There were various accounts respecting the origin of the games, yet all agree in stating that they were celebrated for the purpose of averting from the state some great calamity by which it had been afflicted, and that they were held in honour of Dis and Proserpina. From the time of the consul Valerius Publicola down to that of Augustus, the Tarentine games were held only three times, and again only on certain emergencies, and not at any fixed period, so that we must conclude that their celebration was in no way connected with certain cycles of time (*saecula*). Not long after Augustus had assumed the supreme power in the republic, the quindecimviri announced that according to their books *ludi saeculares* ought to be held, and at the same time tried to prove from history that in former times they had not only been celebrated repeatedly, but almost regularly once in every century. The festival, however, which was now held, was in reality very different from the ancient Tarentine games; for Dis and Proserpina, to whom formerly the festival belonged exclusively, were now the last in the list of the divinities in honour of whom the ludi saeculares were celebrated. The festival took place in summer, and lasted for three days and three nights. On the first day the games commenced in that part of the Campus Martius, which had belonged to the last Tarquin, from whom it derived its name Tarentum, and sacrifices were offered to Jupiter, Juno, Neptune, Minerva, Venus, Apollo, Mercury, Ceres, Vulcan, Mars, Diana, Vesta, Hercules, Latona, the Parcae, and to Dis and Proserpina. The solemnities began at the second hour of the night, and the emperor opened them by the river side with the sacrifice of three lambs to the Parcae upon three altars erected for the purpose, and which were sprinkled with the blood of the victims. The lambs themselves were burnt. A temporary scene like that of a theatre was erected in the Tarentum, and illuminated with lights and fires. In this scene festive hymns were sung by a chorus, and various other ceremonies, together with theatrical performances, took place. During the morning of the first day the people went to the Capitol to offer solemn sacrifices to Jupiter; thence they returned to the Tarentum, to sing choruses in honour of Apollo and Diana. On the second day the noblest matrons, at an hour fixed by an oracle, assembled in the Capitol, offered supplications, sang hymns to the gods, and also visited the altar of Juno. The emperor and the quindecimviri offered sacrifices which had been vowed before, to all the great divinities. On the third day Greek and Latin choruses were sung in the sanctuary of Apollo by three times nine boys and maidens of great beauty, whose parents were still alive. The object of these hymns was to implore the protection of the gods for all cities, towns, and officers of the empire. One of these hymns was the *carmen saeculare* by Horace, which was especially composed for the occasion and adapted to the circumstances of the time. During the whole of the three days and nights, games of every description were carried on in all the circuses and theatres, and sacrifices were offered in all the temples. The first celebration of the ludi saeculares in the reign of Augustus took place in the summer of B. C. 17.

LUDI TARENTINI or TAURII. [LUDI SAECULARES.]

LŬDUS. [GLADIATORES.]

LŬDUS TRŌJAE. [CIRCUS.]

LUPERCĂLĬA, one of the most ancient Roman festivals, which was celebrated every year in honour of Lupercus, the god of fertility. It was originally a shepherd-festival, and hence its introduction at Rome was connected with the names of Romulus and Remus, the kings of shepherds. It was held every year, on the 15th of February, in the Lupercal, where Romulus and Remus were said to have been nurtured by the she-wolf; the place contained an altar and a grove sacred to the god Lupercus. Here the Luperci assembled on the day of the Lupercalia, and sacrificed to the god goats and young dogs. Two youths of noble birth were then led to the Luperci, and one of the latter touched their foreheads with a sword dipped in the blood of the victims; other Luperci immediately after wiped off the bloody spots with wool dipped in milk. Hereupon the two youths were obliged to break out into a shout of laughter. This ceremony was probably a symbolical purification of the shepherds. After the sacrifice was over, the Luperci partook of a meal, at which they were plentifully supplied with wine. They then cut the skins of the goats which they had sacrificed, into pieces: with some of which they covered parts of their body in imitation of the god Lupercus, who was represented half naked and half covered with goatskin. The other pieces of the skins they cut in the shape of thongs, and holding them in their hands they ran with them through the streets of the city, touching or striking with them all persons whom they met in their way, and especially women, who even used to come forward voluntarily for the purpose, since they believed that this ceremony rendered them fruitful, and procured them an easy delivery in childbearing. This act of running about with thongs of goatskin was a symbolic purification of the land, and that of touching persons a purification of men, for the words by which this act is designated are februare and lustrare. The goatskin itself was called februum, the festive day dies februata, the month in which it occurred Februarius, and the god himself Februus. The festival of the Lupercalia, though it necessarily lost its original import at the time when the Romans were no longer a nation of shepherds, was yet always observed in commemoration of the founders of the city. M. Antonius, in his consulship, was one of the Luperci, and not only ran with them half naked and covered with pieces of goatskin through the city, but even addressed the people in the forum in this rude attire.

LŬPERCI, the priests of the god Lupercus. They formed a college, the members of which were originally youths of patrician families, and which was said to have been instituted by Romulus and Remus. The college was divided into two classes, the one called *Fabii* or *Fabiani*, and the other *Quinctilii* or *Quinctiliani*. The office was not for life, but how long it lasted is not known. Julius Caesar added to the two classes of the college a third with the name of *Julii* or *Juliani*, and made Antonius their high-priest. He also assigned to them certain revenues (*vectigalia*) which were afterwards withdrawn from them.

LŬPUS FERREUS, the iron wolf used by the besieged in repelling the attacks of the besiegers, and especially in seizing the battering-ram and diverting its blows.

LUSTRATIO (κάθαρσις) was originally a purification by ablution in water. But the lustrations of which we possess direct knowledge are always connected with sacrifices and other religious rites, and consisted in the sprinkling of water by means of a branch of laurel or olive, and at Rome sometimes by means of the aspergillum, and in the burning of certain materials, the smoke of which was thought to have a purifying effect. Whenever sacrifices were offered, it seems to have been customary to carry them around the person or thing to be purified. Lustrations were made in ancient Greece, and probably at Rome also, by private individuals when they had polluted themselves by any criminal action. Whole cities and states also sometimes underwent purifications to expiate the crime or crimes committed by a member of the community. The most celebrated purification of this kind was that of Athens, performed by Epimenides of Crete, after the Cylonian massacre. Purification also took place when a sacred spot had been unhallowed by profane use, as by burying dead bodies in it, as was the case with the island of Delos. The Romans performed lustrations on many occasions, on which the Greeks did not think of them; and the object of most Roman lustrations was not to atone for the commission of crime, but to obtain the blessing of the gods upon the persons or things which were lustrated. Thus fields were purified after the business of sowing was over, and before the sickle was put to the corn. [ARVALES FRATRES.] Sheep were purified every year at the festival of the Palilia. All Roman armies before they took the field were lustrated; and as the solemnity was probably always connected with a review of the troops, the word lustratio is also used in the sense of the modern review. The establishment of a new colony was always preceded by a lustratio with solemn sacrifices. The city of Rome itself, as well as other towns within its dominion, always underwent a lustratio after they had been visited by some great calamity, such as civil bloodshed, awful prodigies, and the like. A regular and general lustratio of the whole Roman people took place after the completion of every lustrum, when the censor had finished his census and before he laid down his office. This lustratio (also called lustrum) was conducted by one of the censors, and held with sacrifices called *Suovetaurilia*, because the sacrifices consisted of a pig (or ram), a sheep, and an ox. It took place in the Campus Martius, where the people assembled for the purpose. The sacrifices were carried three times around the assembled multitude.

LUSTRUM (from *luo*, Gr. λούω) is properly speaking a lustration or purification, and in particular the purification of the whole Roman people performed by one of the censors in the Campus Martius, after the business of the census was over. [CENSUS; LUSTRATIO.] As this purification took place only once in five years, the word lustrum was also used to designate the time between two lustra. The first lustrum was performed in B.C. 566, by king Servius, after he had completed his census, and it is said to have taken place subsequently every five years, after the census was over. The census might be held without the lustrum, and indeed two cases of this kind are recorded which happened in B.C. 459 and 214. In these cases the lustrum was not performed on account of some great calamities which had befallen the republic. The time when the lustrum took place has been very ingeniously defined by Niebuhr. Six ancient Romulian years of 304 days each were, with the difference of one day, equal to five solar years of 365 days each, or the six ancient years made 1824 days, while the five solar years contained 1825 days. The lustrum, or the great year of the ancient Romans, was thus a cycle, at the end of which the beginning of the ancient year nearly coincided with that of the solar year. As the coincidence, however, was not perfect, a month of 24 days was intercalated in every eleventh lustrum. Now it is highly probable that the recurrence of such a cycle or great year was, from the earliest times, solemnised with sacrifices and purifications, and that Servius Tullius did not introduce them, but merely connected them with his census, and thus set the example for subsequent ages. Many writers of the latter period of the republic and during the empire, use the word lustrum for any space of five years, and without any regard to the census, while others even apply it in the sense of the Greek pentacteris or an Olympiad, which contained only four years.

LYCAEA (Λύκαια), a festival with contests, celebrated by the Arcadians in honour of Zeus surnamed Λυκαίος. It was said to have been instituted by the ancient hero Lycaon, the son of Pelasgus, who is also said, instead of the cakes which had formerly been offered to the god, to have sacrificed a child to Zeus, and to have sprinkled the altar with its blood.

LYRA (λύρα, Lat. *fides*), a lyre, one of the most ancient musical instruments of the stringed kind. The Greeks attributed the invention of the lyre to Hermes, who is said to have formed the instrument of a tortoise-shell, over which he placed gut-strings. The name λύρα, however, does not occur in the Homeric poems, and the ancient lyre, called in Homer *phorminx* (φόρμιγξ) and *citharis* (κίθαρις), seems rather to have resembled the *cithara* of later times, which was in some respects like a modern guitar. In the cithara the strings were drawn across the bottom, whereas in the lyra of ancient times they

were free on both sides. The lyre is also called χέλυς or χελώνη, and in Latin *testudo*, because it was made of a tortoise-shell. The lyre had originally three or four strings, but after the time of Terpander of Antissa (about B.C. 650), who is said to have added three more, it was generally made with seven. The ancients, however, made use of a variety of lyres; and about the time of Sappho and Anacreon several stringed instruments, such as *magadis, barbiton*, and others, were used in Greece, and especially in Lesbos. They had been introduced from Asia Minor, and their number of strings far exceeded that of the lyre, for we know that some had even twenty strings, so that they must have more resembled a modern harp than a lyre. But

Lyre with seven strings, from a coin of Chalcis. (British Museum.)

the lyra and cithara had in most cases no more than seven strings. The lyre had a great and full-sounding bottom, which continued as before to be made generally of tortoise-shell, from which the horns rose as from the head of a stag. A transverse piece of wood connecting the two horns at or near their top-ends served to fasten the strings, and was called ζύγον, and in Latin *transtillum*. The horns were called πήχεις or *cornua*. These instruments were often adorned in the most costly manner with gold and ivory. The lyre was considered as a more manly instrument than the cithara, which, on account of its smaller-sounding bottom, excluded full-sounding and deep tones, and was more calculated for the middle tones. The lyre when played stood in an upright position between the knees, while the cithara stood upon the knees of the player. Both instruments were held with the left hand, and played with the right. It has generally been supposed that the strings of these instruments were always

Lyre with four strings, from a Lycian coin. (Cabinet of Sir Charles Fellows.)

touched with a little staff called *plectrum* (πλῆκτρον), but among the paintings discovered at Herculaneum we find several instances where the persons play the lyre with their fingers. The lyre was at all times only played as an accompaniment to songs. The

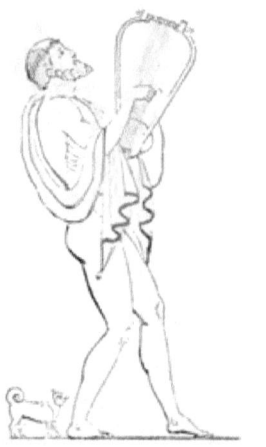

Anacreon playing the Lyre. (Vase-painting in the British Museum.)

Latin name *fides*, which was used for a lyre as well as a cithara, is probably the same as the Greek σφίδες, which signifies gut-string. The lyre (*cithara* or *phorminx*) was at first used in the recitations of epic poetry, though it was probably not played during the recitation itself, but only as a prelude before the minstrel commenced his story, and in the intervals or pauses between the several parts. The lyre has given its name to a species of poetry called lyric; this kind of poetry was originally never recited or sung without the accompaniment of the lyre, and sometimes also of an appropriate dance.

MAENIANUM, signified, originally, a projecting balcony, which was erected round the Roman forum, by the censor, C. Maenius, B.C. 318, in order to give more accommodation to the spectators of the gladiatorial combats. Hence balconies in general came to be called *maeniana*.

MAGADIS. [LYRA.]

MAGISTER, which contains the same root as *mag-is* and *mag-nus*, was applied at Rome to persons possessing various kinds of offices, and especially to the leading person in a collegium or corporation [COLLEGIUM]; thus the *magister societatis* was the president of the corporation of equites, who farmed the taxes at Rome.

MAGISTER EQUITUM. [DICTATOR.]

MAGISTRATUS was a person *qui juri dicundo praeerat*. The King was originally the sole Magistratus; he had all the Potestas. On the expulsion of the Kings, two Consuls were annually appointed, and they were Magistratus. In course of time other Magistratus were appointed; namely, dictators, censors, praetors, aediles, tribunes of the plebs, and the decemviri litibus judicandis. The governors of provinces with the title of propraetor or proconsul were also Magistratus. The word Magistratus contains the same element as *mag'ister*) and *mag(nus*); and it signifies both the person and the office, as we see in the phrase *se magistratu abdicare*. The auspicia maxima belonged to the consuls, praetors, and censors, and the minora auspicia to the other magistratus; accordingly the consuls, praetors, and censors were called *Majores*, and they were elected at the comitia centuriata; the other magistratus were called *Minores*. The former had the imperium, the latter had not. The magistratus were also divided into curules and those who were not curules: the magistratus curules were the dictator, consuls, praetors, censors, and the curule aediles, who were so called, because they had the jus sellae curulis. The magistrates were chosen only from the patricians in the early republic, but in course of time the plebeians shared these honours, with the exception of that of the Interrex: the plebeian magistratus, properly so called, were the plebeian aediles and the tribuni plebis.

MAJESTAS pretty nearly corresponds to treason in English law; but all the offences included under majestas comprehend more than the English treason. One of the offences included in majestas was the effecting, aiding in, or planning the death of a magistratus populi Romani, or of one who had imperium or potestas. Though the phrase *crimen majestatis* was used, the complete expression was *crimen laesae, imminutae, diminutae,* or *minutae majestatis*. The word majestas, consistently with its relation to *mag(nus)*, signifies the magnitude or greatness of a thing. Accordingly, the phrases *majestas populi Romani, imperii majestas*, signify the whole of that which constituted the Roman state; in other words, the sovereign power of the Roman state. The expression *minuere majestatem* consequently signifies any act by whence this majestas is impaired. In the republican period the term *majestas laesa* or *minuta* was most commonly applied to cases of a general betraying or surrendering his army to the enemy, exciting sedition, and generally by his bad conduct in administration impairing the majestas of the state. The old punishment of majestas was perpetual interdiction from fire and water. In the later imperial period, persons of low condition were thrown to wild beasts, or burnt alive; persons of better condition were simply put to death. In the early times of the republic, every act of a citizen which was injurious to the state or its peace was called *perduellio*, and the offender (*perduellis*) was tried before the populus (*populi judicio*), and, if convicted, put to death. *Perduellis* originally signified *hostis*; and thus the old offence of perduellio was equivalent to making war on the Roman state. The trial for perduellio (*perduellionis judicium*) existed to the later times of the republic; but the name seems to have almost fallen into disuse, and various leges were passed for the purpose of determining more accurately what should be majestas. These were a lex Apuleia, probably passed in the fifth consulship of Marius, the exact contents of which are unknown, a lex Varia b. c. 91, a lex Cornelia passed by L. Cornelius Sulla, and the lex Julia, which continued under the empire to be the fundamental enactment on this subject. This lex Julia is by some attributed to C. Julius Caesar, and assigned to the year b. c. 48. Under the empire the term majestas was applied to the person of the reigning Caesar, and we find the phrases majestas Augusta, imperatoria, and regia. It was, however, nothing new to apply the term to the emperor, considered in some of his various capacities, for it was applied to the magistratus under the republic, as to the consul and praetor. Horace even addresses Augustus in the terms *majestas tua*, but this can hardly be viewed otherwise than as a personal compliment, and not as said with reference to any of the offices which he held.

MALLĔŎLUS, a hammer, the transverse head of which was formed for holding pitch and tow, which, having been set on fire, was projected slowly, so that it might not be extinguished during its flight, upon houses and other buildings in order to set them on fire: it was therefore commonly used in sieges together with torches and falaricae.

MĀLUS. [NAVIS.]

MANCEPS has the same relation to Mancipium that Auspex has to Auspicium. It is properly *qui manu capit*. But the word has several special significations. Mancipes were they who bid at the public lettings of the censors for the purpose of farming any part of the public property. Sometimes the chief of the publicani generally are meant by this term, as they were no doubt the bidders and gave the security, and then they shared the undertaking with others or underlet it. The mancipes would accordingly have distinctive names according to the kind of revenue which they took on lease, as *Decumani*, *Portitores*, *Pecuarii*.

MANCĪPĀTĬO. [MANCIPIUM.]
MANCĪPĬUM, MANCĪPĀTĬO. These words are used to indicate the formal transfer of the ownership of a thing, and are derived from the fact that the person who received the thing took hold of it (*mancipatio dicitur quia manu res capitur*). It was not a simple corporeal apprehension, but one which was accompanied with certain forms described by Gaius the jurist:—"Mancipatio is effected in the presence of not less than five witnesses, who must be Roman citizens and of the age of puberty (*puberes*), and also in the presence of another person of the same status, who holds a pair of brazen scales, and hence is called *Libripens*. The purchaser (*qui mancipio accipit*), taking hold of the thing, says: I affirm that this slave (*homo*) is mine Ex Jure Quiritium, and he is purchased by me with this piece of money (*aes*) and brazen scales. He then strikes the scales with the piece of money, and gives it to the seller as a symbol of the price (*quasi pretii loco*)." This mode of transfer applied to all free persons or slaves, animals or lands, all of which persons and things were called *Res Mancipi*; other things were called *Nec Mancipi*. Lands (*praedia*) might be thus transferred, though the parties to the mancipatio were not on the lands; but all other things, which were objects of mancipatio, were only transferable in the presence of the parties, because corporeal apprehension was a necessary part of the ceremony. The party who transferred the ownership of a thing pursuant to these forms was said *mancipio dare*; he who thus acquired the ownership was said *mancipio accipere*. The verb *mancipare* is sometimes used as equivalent to *mancipio dare*. Mancipium may be used as equivalent to complete ownership, and may thus be opposed to *usus* and to *fructus*. Sometimes the word mancipium signifies a slave, as being one of the res mancipi.

MANDĀTUM, often signifies a command from a superior to an inferior. Under the empire the mandata principum were the commands and instructions given to governors of provinces and others.

MĂNĬPŬLUS. [EXERCITUS.]

MANSĬO (σταθμός), a post-station at the end of a day's journey. The word is derived from *manere*, signifying to pass the night at a place in travelling. On the great Roman roads the mansiones were at the same distance from one another as on those of the Persian empire, where such resting-places (khans or caravanseras) were first provided, viz. at intervals of about 20 English miles. They were originally called *castra*, being probably mere places of encampment formed by making earthen entrenchments. In process of time they included, not only barracks and magazines of provisions (*horrea*) for the troops, but commodious buildings adapted for the reception of travellers of all ranks, and even of the emperor himself, if he should have occasion to visit them. At those stations the cisiarii kept gigs for hire and for conveying government despatches. [CISIUM; ESSEDUM.] The *mansio* was under the superintendence of an officer called *mansionarius*.

MANUBIAE. [SPOLIA.]

MANUMISSIO was the form by which slaves were released from slavery. There were three modes by which this was effected, namely, Vindicta, Census, and Testamentum. Of these the manumissio by vindicta is probably the oldest, and perhaps was once the only mode of manumission. It is mentioned by Livy as in use at an early period; and, indeed, he states that some persons refer the origin of the vindicta to the event which he relates, and derive its name from Vindicius; the latter part, at least, of the supposition is of no value. The ceremony of the manumissio by the vindicta was as follows:—The master brought his slave before the magistratus, and stated the grounds (*causa*) of the intended manumission. The lictor of the magistratus laid a rod (*festuca*) on the head of the slave, accompanied with certain formal words, in which he declared that he was a free man ex jure quiritium, that is, *vindicavit in libertatem*. The master in the meantime held the slave, and after he had pronounced the words *hunc hominem liberum volo*, he turned him round and let him go (*emisit e manu*), whence the general name of the act of manumission. The word vindicta itself, which is properly the res *vindicata*, is used for festuca by Horace. In the case of the census the slave was registered by the censors as a citizen with his master's consent. The third mode of manumission was, when a master gave liberty to a slave by his will (*testamentum*). The act of manumission established the relation of patronus and libertus between the manumissor and the manumitted. When manumitted by a citizen, the libertus took the praenomen and the gentile name of the manumissor, and became in a sense a member of the gens of his patron. To these two names he added some other name as a cognomen, either some name by which he was previously known, or some

name assumed on the occasion: thus we find the names M. Tullius Tiro, P. Terentius Afer, and other like names. The relation between a patronus and libertus is stated under PATRONUS. Before the year B.C. 311, the libertini had not the suffragium, but in that year the censor Appius Claudius gave the libertini a place in the tribes, and from this time the libertini had the suffragium after they were duly admitted on the censors' roll. In the year B.C. 304, they were placed in the tribus urbanae, and not allowed to perform military service. In the censorship of Tiberius Gracchus, B.C. 169, they were placed in one of the tribus urbanae, determined by lot. Subsequently, by a law of Aemilius Scaurus, about B.C. 116, they were restored to the four city tribes, and this remained their condition to the end of the republic, though various attempts were made to give them a better suffrage. A tax was levied on manumission by a lex Manlia, B.C. 357: it consisted of the twentieth part of the value of the slave, hence called *Vicesima*.

MANUS FERREA. [HARPAGO.]

MARSUPIUM (μαρσύπιον, βαλάντιον), a purse. The purse used by the ancients was commonly a small leathern bag, and was often closed by being drawn together at the mouth (σύσπαστα βαλάντια). Mercury is commonly represented holding one in his hand. (See cut, p. 63.)

MARTYRIA (μαρτυρία), signifies strictly the deposition of a witness in a court of justice, though the word is applied metaphorically to all kinds of testimony. At Athens none but freemen could be witnesses. The incapacity of women may be inferred from the general policy of the Athenian law, and the absence of any example in the orators where a woman's evidence is produced. The same observation applies to minors. Slaves were not allowed to give evidence, unless upon examination by torture (βάσανος). Citizens who had been disfranchised (ἠτιμωμένοι) could not appear as witnesses (any more than as jurors or plaintiffs) in a court of justice; for they had lost all honourable rights and privileges. But there was no objection to alien freemen. The party who desired the evidence of a witness, summoned him to attend for that purpose. The summons was called πρόσκλησις. If the witness promised to attend and failed to do so, he was liable to an action called δίκη λειπομαρτυρίου. Whether he promised or not, he was bound to attend, and if his absence caused injury to the party, he was liable to an action (δίκη βλάβης). The attendance of the witness was first required at the ἀνάκρισις, where he was to make his deposition before the superintending magistrate (ἡγεμὼν δικαστηρίον). The party in whose favour he appeared, generally wrote the deposition at home upon a whitened board or tablet (λελευκωμένον γραμματεῖον), which he brought with him to the magistrate's office, and, when the witness had deposed thereto, put into the box (ἐχῖνος) in which all the documents in the cause were deposited. An oath was usually taken by the witness at the ἀνάκρισις, where he was sworn by the opposite party at an altar. The witness, whether he had attended before the magistrate or not, was obliged to be present at the trial, in order to confirm his testimony. The only exception was, when he was ill or out of the country, in which case a commission might be sent to examine him. [ΕϹΜΑΡΤΥΡΙΑ.] All evidence was produced by the party during his own speech, the κλεψύδρα being stopped for that purpose. The witness was called by an officer of the court, and mounted on the raised platform (βῆμα) of the speaker, while his deposition was read over to him by the clerk; he then signified his assent, either by express words, or bowing his head in silence.—We conclude by noticing a few expressions. Μαρτυρεῖν τινι is to testify in favour of a man, καταμαρτυρεῖν τινος to testify against. Μαρτύρεσθαι to call to witness (a word used poetically), διαμαρτύρεσθαι and sometimes ἐπιμαρτύρεσθαι τοὺς παρόντας, to call upon those who are present to take notice of what passes, with a view to give evidence. Ψευδομαρτυρεῖν and ἐπιορκεῖν are never used indifferently, which affords some proof that testimony was not necessarily on oath. The μάρτυς (witness in the cause) is to be distinguished from the κλητήρ or κλήτωρ, who merely gave evidence of the summons to appear.

MASTIGOPHORI or MASTIGONOMI (μαστιγοφόροι or μαστιγονόμοι), the name of the lower police officers in the Greek states, who carried into execution the corporal punishments inflicted by the higher magistrates. In the theatre the mastigophori preserved order, and were stationed for this purpose in the orchestra, near the thymele. In the Olympic games the ῥαβδοῦχοι performed the same duties. At Athens they were discharged by the public slaves, called bowmen (τοξόται), or Scythians (Σκύθαι). [DEMOSII.]

MATERFAMILIAS. [MATRIMONIUM.]

MATRALIA, a festival celebrated at Rome every year on the 11th of June, in honour of the goddess Mater Matuta, whose temple stood in the Forum Boarium. It was celebrated only by Roman matrons, and the sacrifices offered to the goddess consisted of cakes baked in pots of earthenware. Slaves were not allowed to take part in the solemnities, or to enter the temple of the goddess. One slave, however, was admitted by the matrons, but only to be exposed to a humiliating treatment, for one of the matrons gave her a blow on the cheek, and then sent her away from the temple. The matrons on this occasion took with them the children of their sisters, but not their own, held them in their arms, and prayed for their welfare.

MATRONALIA, a festival celebrated on the Kalends of March in honour of Juno Lucina. Hence Horace says, "Martiis caelebs quid agam Kalendis."

MATRIMONIUM NUPTIAE (γάμος), marriage. (1) GREEK. The ancient Greek legislators considered the relation of marriage as a matter not merely of private, but also of public or general interest. This was particularly the case at Sparta, where proceedings might be taken against those who married too late or unsuitably, as well as against those who did not marry at all. But independent of public considerations, there were also private or personal reasons, peculiar to the ancients, which made marriage an obligation. One of these was the duty incumbent upon every individual to provide for a continuance of representatives to succeed himself as ministers of the Divinity; and another was the desire felt by almost every one, not merely to perpetuate his own name, but to leave some one who might make the customary offerings at his grave. We are told that with this view childless persons sometimes adopted children. The choice of a wife among the ancients was but rarely grounded upon affection, and scarcely ever could have been the result of previous acquaintance or familiarity. In many cases a father chose for his son a bride whom the latter had never seen, or compelled him to marry for the sake of checking his extravagances. By the Athenian laws a citizen was not allowed to marry with a foreign woman, nor conversely, under very severe penalties, but proximity by blood (ἀγχιστεία), or consanguinity (συγγένεια), was not, with some few exceptions, a bar to marriage in any part of Greece; direct lineal descent was. At Athens the most important preliminary to marriage was the betrothal (ἐγγύησις), which was in fact indispensable to the complete validity of a marriage contract. It was made by the natural or legal guardian (ὁ κύριος) of the bride elect, and attended by the relatives of both parties as witnesses. The wife's dowry was settled at the betrothal. On the day before the gamos, or marriage, or sometimes on the day itself, certain sacrifices or offerings (προτέλεια γάμων or προγάμεια) were made to the gods who presided over marriage. Another ceremony of almost general observance on the wedding day, was the bathing of both the bride and bridegroom in water fetched from some particular fountain, whence, as some think, the custom of placing the figure of a λουτροφόρος or "water carrier" over the tombs of those who died unmarried. After these preliminaries, the bride was generally conducted from her father's to the house of the bridegroom at nightfall, in a chariot (ἐφ' ἁμάξης) drawn by a pair of mules or oxen, and furnished with a kind of couch (κλινίς) as a seat. On either side of her sat the bridegroom and one of his most intimate friends or relations, who from his office was called the *paranymph* (παράνυμφος or νυμφευτής); but as he rode in the carriage (ὄχημα) with the bride and bridegroom, he was sometimes called the πάροχος. The nuptial procession was probably accompanied, according to circumstances, by a number of persons, some of whom carried the nuptial torches. Both bride and bridegroom (the former veiled) were decked out in their best attire, with chaplets on their heads, and the doors of their houses were hung with festoons of ivy and bay. As the bridal procession moved along, the hymenaean song was sung to the accompaniment of Lydian flutes, even in olden times, as beautifully described by Homer, and the married pair received the greetings and congratulations of those who met them. After entering the bridegroom's house, into which the bride was probably conducted by his mother, bearing a lighted torch, it was customary to shower sweetmeats upon them (καταχύσματα), as emblems of plenty and prosperity. After this came the nuptial feast, to which the name *gamos* was particularly applied; it was generally given in the house of the bridegroom or his parents; and besides being a festive meeting, served other and more important purposes. There was no public rite, whether civil or religious, connected with the celebration of marriage amongst the ancient Greeks, and therefore no public record of its solemnisation. This deficiency then was supplied by the marriage feast, for the guests were of course competent to prove the fact of a marriage having taken place. To this feast, contrary to the usual practice amongst the Greeks, women were invited as well as men; but they seem to have sat at a separate table, with the bride still veiled amongst them. At the conclusion of this feast she was conducted by her husband into the bridal chamber; and a law of Solon required that on entering it they should eat a quince together, as if to indicate that their conversation ought to be sweet and agreeable. The song called the *Epithalamium* was then sung before the doors of the bridal chamber. The day after the marriage, the first of the bride's residence in her new abode, was called the *epaulia* (ἐπαύλια); on which their friends sent the customary presents to the newly married couple. On another day, the *apaulia* (ἀπαύλια), perhaps the second after marriage, the bridegroom left his house, to lodge apart from his wife at his father's-in-law. Some of the presents made to the bride by her husband and friends were called *anacalypteria* (ἀνακαλυπτήρια), as being given on the occasion of the bride first appearing unveiled: they were probably given on the *epaulia*, or day after the marriage. Another ceremony observed after marriage was the sacrifice which the husband offered up on the occasion of his bride being registered amongst his own phratores. The above account refers to Athenian customs.—At Sparta the betrothal of the bride by her father or guardian (κύριος) was requisite as a preliminary of marriage, as well as at Athens. Another custom peculiar to the Spartans, and a relic of ancient times, was the seizure of the bride by her intended husband, but of course with the sanction of her parents or guardians. She was not, however, immediately domiciled in her husband's house, but cohabited with him for some time clandestinely, till he brought her, and frequently her mother also, to his home.—The Greeks, generally speaking, entertained little regard for the female character. They considered women, in fact, as decidedly inferior to men, qualified to discharge only the subordinate functions in life, and rather necessary as helpmates than agreeable as companions. To these notions female education for the most part corresponded, and in fact confirmed them; it did not supply the elegant accomplishments and refinement of manners which permanently engage the affections, when other attractions have passed away. Aristotle states, that the relation of man to woman is that of the governor to the subject; and Plato, that a woman's virtue may be summed up in a few words, for she has only to manage the house well, keeping what there is in it, and obeying her husband. Among the Dorians, however, and especially at Sparta, women enjoyed much more estimation than in the rest of Greece.—(2) Roman. A legal Roman marriage was called *justae nuptiae, justum matrimonium*, as being conformable to *jus* (*civile*) or to law. A legal marriage was either *Cum conventione uxoris in manum viri* or it was without this conventio. But both forms of marriage agreed in this: there must be connubium between the parties, and consent. The legal consequences as to the power of the father over his children were the same in both. *Connubium* is merely a term which comprehends all the conditions of a legal marriage. Generally it may be stated, that there was only connubium between Roman citizens; the cases in which it at any time existed between parties, not both Roman citizens, were exceptions to the general rule. Originally, or at least at one period of the republic, there was no connubium between the patricians and the plebeians; but this was altered by the Lex Canuleia (B.C. 445.), which allowed connubium between persons of those two classes. There were various degrees of consanguinity and affinity, within which there was no connubium. An illegal union of a male and female, though affecting to be, was not a marriage: the man had no legal wife, and the children had no legal father: consequently they were not in the power of their reputed father. The marriage *Cum conventione* differed from that *Sine conventione*, in the relationship which it effected between the husband and the wife; the marriage *cum conventione* was a necessary condition to make a woman a *materfamilias*. By the marriage cum conventione, the wife passed into the familia of her husband, and was to him in the relation of a daughter, or, as it was expressed, *in manum convenit*. In the marriage sine conventione, the wife's relation to her own familia remained as before, and she was merely *uxor*. "*Uxor*," says Cicero, "is a genus of which there are two species; one is *materfamilias, quae in manum convenit*; the other is *uxor* only." Accordingly, a materfamilias is a wife who is in manu, and in the familia of her husband. A wife not in manu was not a member of her husband's familia, and therefore the term could not apply to her. *Matrona* was properly a wife not in manu, and equivalent to uxor; and she was called matrona before she had any children. But these words are not always used in these their original and proper meanings. It does not appear that any forms were requisite in the marriage sine conventione; and apparently the evidence of such marriage was cohabitation matrimonii causa. The matrimonii causa might be proved by various kinds of evidence. In the case of a marriage cum conventione, there were three forms, 1. *Usus*, 2. *Farreum*, and 3. *Coemptio*.—1. Marriage was effected by *usus*, if a woman lived with a man for a whole year as his wife; and this was by analogy to usucaption of movables

generally, in which usus for one year gave ownership. The Law of the Twelve Tables provided, that if a woman did not wish to come into the manus of her husband in this manner, she should absent herself from him annually for three nights (*trinoctium*) and so break the usus of the year. 2. *Farreum* was a form of marriage, in which certain words were used in the presence of ten witnesses, and were accompanied by a certain religious ceremony, in which panis farreus was employed; and hence this form of marriage was also called *confarreatio*. It appears that certain priestly offices, such as that of Flamen Dialis, could only be held by those who were born of parents who had been married by this ceremony (*confarreati parentes*). 3. *Coemptio* was effected by mancipatio, and consequently the wife was in mancipio. [MANCIPIUM.] A woman who was cohabiting with a man as uxor, might come into his manus by this ceremony, in which case the coemptio was said to be matrimonii causa, and she who was formerly uxor became *apud maritum filiae loco*. *Sponsalia* were not an unusual preliminary of marriage, but they were not necessary.—The sponsalia were an agreement to marry, made in such form as to give each party a right of action in case of non-performance, and the offending party was condemned in such damages as to the judex seemed just. The woman who was promised in marriage was accordingly called *sponsa*, which is equivalent to promissa; the man who was engaged to marry was called *sponsus*.—The sponsalia were of course not binding, if the parties consented to waive the contract. Sometimes a present was made by the future husband to the future wife by way of earnest (*arrha, arrha sponsalitia*), or, as it was called, *propter nuptias donatio*.—The consequences of marriage were—1. The power of the father over the children of the marriage, which was a completely new relation, an effect indeed of marriage, but one which had no influence over the relation of the husband and wife. [PATRIA POTESTAS.] 2. The liabilities of either of the parties to the punishments affixed to the violation of the marriage union. [ADULTERIUM; DIVORTIUM.] 3. The relation of husband and wife with respect to property. [DOS.] When marriage was dissolved, the parties to it might marry again; but opinion considered it more decent for a woman not to marry again. A woman was required by usage (*mos*) to wait a year before she contracted a second marriage, on the pain of infamia.—It remains to describe the customs and rites which were observed by the Romans at marriages. After the parties had agreed to marry and the persons in whose potestas they were had consented, a meeting of friends was sometimes held at the house of the maiden for the purpose of settling the marriage-contract, which was written on tablets, and signed by both parties. The woman after she had promised to become the wife of a man was called *sponsa*, *pacta*, *dicta*, or *sperata*. It appears that, at least during the imperial period, the man put a ring on the finger of his betrothed, as a pledge of his fidelity. This ring was probably, like all rings at this time, worn on the left hand, and on the finger nearest to the smallest. The last point to be fixed was the day on which the marriage was to take place. The Romans believed that certain days were unfortunate for the performance of the marriage rites, either on account of the religious character of those days themselves, or on account of the days by which they were followed, as the woman had to perform certain religious rites on the day after her wedding, which could not take place on a dies ater. Days not suitable for entering upon matrimony were the calends, nones, and ides of every month, all dies atri, the whole months of May and February, and a great number of festivals. On the wedding-day, which in the early times was never fixed upon without consulting the auspices, the bride was dressed in a long white robe with a purple fringe, or adorned with ribands. This dress was called *tunica recta*, and was bound round the waist with a girdle (*corona*, *cingulum*, or *zona*), which the husband had to untie in the evening. The bridal veil, called *flammeum*, was of a bright yellow colour, and her shoes likewise. Her hair was divided on this occasion with the point of a spear. The bride was conducted to the house of her husband in the evening. She was taken with apparent violence from the arms of her mother, or of the person who had to give her away. On her way she was accompanied by three boys dressed in the praetexta, and whose fathers and mothers were still alive (*patrimi et matrimi*). One of them carried before her a torch of white thorn (*spina*), or, according to others, of pine wood; the two others walked by her side, supporting her by the arm. The bride herself carried a distaff and a spindle, with wool. A boy called *camillus* carried in a covered vase (*cumera*, *cumerum*, or *camillum*), the so-called utensils of the bride and playthings for children (*crepundia*). Besides these persons who officiated on the occasion, the procession was attended by a numerous train of friends, both of the bride and the bridegroom. When the procession arrived at the house of the bridegroom, the door of which was adorned with garlands and flowers, the bride was carried across the threshold by *pronubi*, *i. e.* men who had been married to only one woman, that she might not knock against it with her foot, which would have been an evil omen. Before she entered the house, she wound wool around the door-posts of her new residence, and anointed them with lard (*adeps suillus*) or wolf's fat (*adeps lupinus*). The husband received her with fire and water, which the woman had to touch. This was either a symbolic purification, or a symbolic expression of welcome, as the interdicere aqua et igni was the formula for banishment. The bride saluted her husband with the words: *ubi tu Caius, ego Caia*. After she had entered the house with distaff and spindle, she was placed upon a sheep-skin, and here the keys of the house were delivered into her hands. A repast (*coena nuptialis*) given by the husband to the whole train of relatives and friends who accompanied the bride, generally concluded the solemnity of the day. Many ancient writers mention a very popular song, *Talasius* or *Talassio*, which was sung at weddings; but whether it was sung during the repast or during the procession is not quite clear, though we may infer from the story respecting the origin of the song, that it was sung while the procession was advancing towards the house of the husband. It may easily be imagined that a solemnity like that of marriage did not take place among the merry and humorous Italians without a variety of jests and railleries, and the ancient writers mention songs which were sung before the door of the bridal apartment by girls, after the company had left. These songs were probably the old Fescennina [FESCENNINA], and are frequently called *Epithalamia*. At the end of the repast the bride was conducted by matrons who had not had more than one husband (*pronubae*), to the lectus genialis in the atrium, which was on this occasion magnificently adorned and strewed with flowers. On the following day the husband sometimes gave another entertainment to his friends, which was called *repotia*, and the woman, who on this day undertook the management of the house of her husband, had to perform certain religious rites; on which account, as was observed above, it was necessary to select a day for the marriage which was not followed by a dies ater. These rites probably consisted of sacrifices to the Dii Penates. The position of a Roman woman after marriage was very different from that of a Greek woman. The Roman presided over the whole household; she educated her children, watched over and preserved the honour of the house, and as the materfamilias she shared the honours and respect shown to her husband. Far from being confined like the Greek women to a distinct apartment, the Roman matron, at least during the better centuries of the republic, occupied the most important part of the house, the atrium.

MAUSŌLĒUM (Μαυσωλεῖον), signified originally *the sepulchre of Mausolus*, which was a magnificent monument erected at Halicarnassus B. c. 353, by Artemisia, the widow of Mausolus. (See *Classical Dict.*, art. *Artemisia*.) It was adorned with beautiful works of art, and was regarded as one of the seven wonders of the world. The word *Mausoleum* was used by the Romans as a generic name for any magnificent sepulchral edifice. Mausolus, the dynast of Caria, having died in B. C. 353, his queen Artemisia evinced her sorrow by observing his funeral rites with the most expensive splendour, and by commencing the erection of a sepulchral monument to him at Halicarnassus, which should surpass any thing the world had yet seen. The building extended 63 feet from north to south, being shorter on the fronts, and its whole circuit was 411 feet (or, according to the Bamberg MS., 440); it rose to the height of 25 cubits (37½ feet); and was surrounded by 36 columns. This part of the building was called *Pteron*. It was adorned with sculptures in relief, on its eastern face by Scopas, on the northern by Bryaxis, on the southern by Timotheus, on the western by Leochares. Above this *pteron* was a pyramid equal to it in height, diminishing by 24 steps to its summit, which was surmounted by the marble quadriga made by Pythis. The total height, including this ornament, was 140 feet. In the Roman *Mausolea* the form chiefly employed was that of a succession of terraces in imitation of the *rogus*. Of these the most celebrated were those of Augustus and of Hadrian; the latter of which, stripped of its ornaments, still forms the fortress of modern Rome (the castle of S. Angelo); but of the other, which was on a still larger scale, and which was considered as one of the most magnificent buildings of Augustus, there are only some insignificant ruins.

MĒDIASTĪNI, the name given to slaves, used for any common purpose. The name is chiefly given to certain slaves belonging to the familia rustica, but it is also applied sometimes to slaves in the city.

MĒDIMNUS (μέδιμνος), the principal dry measure of the Greeks. It was used especially for measuring corn. The Attic medimnus was equal to six Roman modii. For its subdivisions see Tables at the end. [METRETES; CHOENIX; XESTES; COTYLA.]

MĒDIX TŪTICUS, the name of the supreme magistrate among the Oscan people. *Medix* appears to have signified a magistrate of any kind, and *tuticus* to have been equivalent to *magnus* or *summus*. Livy, therefore, in calling the medix tuticus the *summus magistratus*, gives a literal translation of the word.

MĒGĂLĒSĬA, MĔGĂLENSĬA, or MEGALENSES LŪDI, a festival with games, celebrated at Rome in the month of April and in honour of the great mother of the gods (Cybele, μεγάλη θεός, whence the festival derived its name). The statue of the goddess was brought to Rome from Pessinus in B. C. 203, and the day of its arrival was solemnised with a magnificent procession, lectisternia, and games, and great numbers of people carried presents to the goddess on the Capitol. The regular celebration of the Megalesia, however, did not begin till twelve years later (B. C. 191), when the temple, which had been vowed and ordered to be built in B. C. 203, was completed and dedicated by M. Junius Brutus. The festival lasted for six days, beginning on the 4th of April. The season of this festival, like that of the whole month in which it took place, was full of general rejoicings and feasting. It was customary for the wealthy Romans on this occasion to invite one another mutually to their repasts. The games which were held at the Megalesia were purely scenic, and not circenses. They were at first held on the Palatine, in front of the temple of the goddess, but afterwards also in the theatres. The day which was especially set apart for the performance of scenic plays was the third of the festival. Slaves were not permitted to be present at the games, and the magistrates appeared dressed in a purple toga and practexta, whence the proverb, *purpura Megalensis*. The games were under the superintendence of the curule aediles, and we know that four of the extant plays of Terence were performed at the Megalesia.

MEMBRĀNA. [LIBER.]

MENSA (τράπεζα), a table. The simplest kind of table was a round one with three legs, called in Greek τρίπους. Tables, however, must usually have had four legs, as the etymology of τράπεζα, the common word for table, indicates. For the houses of the opulent, tables were made of the most valuable and beautiful kinds of wood, especially of maple, or of the citrus of Africa, which was a species of cypress or juniper. As the table was not large, it was usual to place the dishes and the various kinds of meat upon it, and then to bring it thus furnished to the place where the guests were reclining. On many occasions, indeed, each guest either had a small table to himself, or the company was divided into parties of two or three, with a separate table for each party, as is distinctly represented in the cut under SYMPOSIUM. Hence we have such phrases as *mensam apponere* or *opponere*, and *mensam auferre* or *removere*. The two principal courses of a *deipnon* and *coena*, or a Greek and Roman dinner, were called respectively πρώτη τράπεζα, δευτέρα τράπεζα, and *mensa prima*, *mensa secunda*. [COENA; DEIPNON.]

MENSARII, MENSULARII, or NUMULARII, a kind of public bankers at Rome who were appointed by the state; they were distinct from the argentarii, who were common bankers, and did business on their own account. [ARGENTARII.] The mensarii had their tables or banks (*mensae*) like ordinary bankers, in the forum, and in the name of the aerarium they offered ready money to debtors who could give security to the state for it. Such an expediency was devised by the state only in times of great distress. The first time that mensarii (*quinqueviri mensarii*) were appointed was in B. C. 352, at the time when the plebeians were so deeply involved in debt, that they were obliged to borrow money from new creditors in order to pay the old ones, and thus ruined themselves completely. On this occasion they were also authorised to ordain that cattle or land should be received as payment at a fair valuation. With the exception of this first time, they appear during the time of the republic to have always been *triumviri mensarii*. One class of mensarii, however (perhaps an inferior order), the *mensularii* or *numularii*, seem to have been permanently employed by the state, and these must be meant when we read, that not only the aerarium, but also private individuals, deposited in their hands sums of money which they had to dispose of.

MENSIS. [CALENDARIUM.]
MERENDA. [COENA.]
METAE. [CIRCUS.]
METALLUM (μέταλλον), a mine and metal. The metals which have been known from the earliest period of which we have any information are those which were long distinguished as the seven principal metals, namely, gold, silver, copper, tin, iron, lead, and mercury. If to this list we add the compound of gold and silver called *electrum*, the compound of copper and tin called χαλκός and *aes* (bronze), and steel, we have, in all probability, a complete list of the metals known to the Greeks and Romans, with the exception of zinc, which they do not seem to have known as a metal, but only in its ores, and of brass, which they regarded as a sort of bronze. The early Greeks were no doubt chiefly indebted for a supply of the various metals to the commerce of the Phoenicians, who procured them principally from Arabia and Spain, and tin from our own island and the East. They were perfectly acquainted with the processes of smelting the metal from the ore, and of forging heated masses into the required shapes, by the aid of the hammer and tongs. The smith's instruments were the anvil (ἄκμων) with the block on which it rested (ἀκμόθετον), the tongs (πυράγρη), and the hammer (ῥαιστήρ, σφῦρα). The advances made in the art of metallurgy in subsequent times are chiefly connected with the improvements in the art of statuary. The method of working, as described in Homer, seems to have long prevailed, namely by heating out lumps of the material into the form proposed, and afterwards fitting the pieces together by means of pins or keys. It was called σφυρήλατον, from σφῦρα, a hammer. The next mode, among the Greeks, of executing metal works seems to have been by plating upon a nucleus, or general form, of wood—a practice which was employed also by the Egyptians. It is extremely difficult to determine at what date the casting of metal was introduced. According to the statements of Pausanias and Pliny, the art of casting in bronze and in iron was invented by Rhoecus and Theodorus of Samos, who probably lived in the sixth and fifth centuries before our era.

METOICI (μέτοικοι), the name by which, at Athens and in other Greek states, the *resident aliens* were designated. They must be distinguished from such strangers as made only a transitory stay in a place, for it was a characteristic of a *metoicus*, that he resided permanently in the city. No city of Greece perhaps had such a number of resident aliens as Athens, since none afforded to strangers so many facilities for carrying on mercantile business, or a more agreeable mode of living. In the census instituted by Demetrius Phalereus (B. C. 309), the number of resident aliens at Athens was 10,000, in which number women and children were probably not included. The jealousy with which the citizens of the ancient Greek republics kept their body clear of intruders, is also manifest in their regulations concerning aliens. However long they might have resided in Athens, they were always regarded as strangers, whence they are sometimes called ξένοι, and to remind them of their position, they had on some occasions to perform certain degrading services for the Athenian citizens [HYDRIAphoria]. These services were, however, in all probability not intended to hurt the feelings of the aliens, but were simply acts symbolical of their relation to the citizens. Aliens were not allowed to acquire landed property in the state they had chosen for their residence, and were consequently obliged to live in hired houses or apartments. As they did not constitute a part of the state, and were yet in constant intercourse and commerce with its members, every alien was obliged to select a citizen for his patron (προστάτης), who was not only the mediator between them and the state, through whom alone they could transact any legal business, whether private or public, but was at the same time answerable (ἐγγυητής) to the state for the conduct of his client. On the other hand, however, the state allowed the aliens to carry on all kinds of industry and commerce under the protection of the law; in fact, at Athens nearly all business was in the hands of aliens, who on this account lived for the most part in the Peiraceus. Each family of aliens, whether they availed themselves of the privilege of carrying on any mercantile business or not, had to pay an annual tax (μετοίκιον or ξενικά) of twelve drachmae, or if the head of the family was a widow, of only six drachmae. If aliens did not pay this tax, or if they assumed the right of citizens, and probably also in case they refused to select a patron, they not only forfeited the protection of the state, but were sold as slaves. Extraordinary taxes and liturgies (εἰσφοραί and λειτουργίαι) devolved upon aliens no less than upon citizens. The aliens were also obliged, like citizens, to serve in the regular armies and in the fleet, both abroad and at home, for the defence of the city. Those aliens who were exempt from the burthens peculiar to their class were called isoteles (ἰσοτελεῖς). They had not to pay the μετοίκιον (ἀτέλεια μετοικίου), were not obliged to choose a προστάτης, and in fact enjoyed all the rights of citizens, except those of a political nature. Their condition was termed ἰσοτέλεια, and ἰσοπολιτεία.

METOPA or METOPE (μετόπη), the name applied to each of the spaces between the triglyphs in the frieze of the Doric order, and by metonymy to the sculptured ornament with which those spaces were filled up. In the original significance of the parts the triglyphs represent the ends of the cross-beams or joists which rested on the architrave; the beds of these beams were called ὀπαί, and hence the spaces between them μετόπαι. Originally they were left open; next they were filled up with plain slabs, as in the propylaea at Eleusis, and many other buildings, and lastly, but still at an early period,

they were adorned with sculptures either in low or high relief. The metopes from the Parthenon in the British Museum are adorned with sculptures in high relief.

METRĒTES (μετρητής), the principal Greek liquid measure. The Attic metretes was equal in capacity to the amphora, containing 8 galls. 7·365 pints, English. See the Tables. [Chous: Choenix; Xestes; Cotyla.]

METROPOLIS. [Colonia.]

MILIĀRE, MILLIĀRIUM, or MILLE PASSUUM (μίλιον), the Roman mile, consisted of 1000 paces (passus) of 5 feet each, and was therefore = 5000 feet. Taking the Roman foot at 11·6496 English inches [Pes], the Roman mile would be 1618 English yards, or 142 yards less than the English statute mile. The most common term for the mile is mille passuum, or only the initials M. P.; sometimes the word passuum is omitted. The Roman mile contained 8 Greek stadia. The mile-stones along the Roman roads were called milliaria. They were also called lapides; thus we have ad tertium lapidem (or without the word lapidem) for 3 miles from Rome. Augustus erected a gilt pillar in the Forum, where the principal roads terminated, which was called milliarium aureum; but the miles were not reckoned from it, but from the gates of the city. Such central marks appear to have been common in the principal cities of the Roman empire. The "London-stone" in Cannon-street is supposed to have marked the centre of the Roman roads in Britain.

MIMUS (μῖμος), the name by which, in Greece and at Rome, a species of the drama was designated, though the Roman mimus differed essentially from the Greek. The Greek mimus seems to have originated among the Greeks of Sicily and southern Italy, and to have consisted originally of extemporary representations or imitations of ridiculous occurrences of common life at certain festivals. At a later period these rude representations acquired a more artistic form, which was brought to a high degree of perfection by Sophron of Syracuse (about B.C. 420). He wrote his pieces in the popular dialect of the Dorians and a kind of rhythmical prose. Among the Romans the word mimus was applied to a species of dramatic plays as well as to the persons who acted in them. It is certain that the Romans did not derive their mimus from the Greeks of southern Italy, but that it was of native growth. The Greek mimes were written in prose, and the name μῖμος was never applied to an actor, but if used of a person it signified one who made grimaces. The Roman mimes were imitations of foolish and mostly indecent occurrences, and scarcely differed from comedy except in consisting more of gestures and mimicry than of spoken dialogue. At Rome such mimes seem originally to have been exhibited at funerals, where one or more persons (*mimi*) represented in a burlesque manner the life of the deceased. If there were several mimi, one of them, or their leader, was called *archimimus*. These coarse and indecent performances had greater charms for the Romans than the regular drama. They were performed on the stage as farces after tragedies, and during the empire they gradually supplanted the place of the Atellanae. It was peculiar to the actors in these mimes, to wear neither masks, the cothurnus, nor the soccus, whence they are sometimes called planipedes.

MĪNA. [TALENTUM.]
MIRMILLŌNES. [GLADIATORES.]
MISSĬO. [EXERCITUS.]
MISSĬO. [GLADIATORES.]

MITRA ($\mu i \tau \rho a$), in general a band of any kind, and specifically, (1) A belt or girdle worn by warriors round the waist. [ZONA.]— (2) A broad band of cloth worn round the head, to which the name of *anadema* was sometimes given. [COMA.]

MŎDĬUS, the principal dry measure of the Romans, was equal to one-third of the amphora, and therefore contained nearly two gallons English. (See the Tables.) The modius was one-sixth of the medimnus.

MŌLA ($\mu \acute{v} \lambda o s$), a mill. All mills were anciently made of stone, the kind used being a volcanic trachyte or porous lava (*pyrites, silices, pumiceas*). Every mill consisted of two essential parts, the upper mill-stone, which was moveable (*catillus, ὄνος, τὸ ἐπιμύλιον*), and the lower, which was fixed and by much the larger of the two. Hence a mill is sometimes called *molae* in the plural. The principal mills mentioned by ancient authors are the following:—I. The hand-mill, or quern, called *mola manuaria, versatilis*, or *trusatilis*. The hand-mills were worked among the Greeks and Romans by slaves. Their pistrinum was consequently proverbial as a place of painful and degrading labour; and this toil was imposed principally on women. II. The cattle-mill, *mola asinaria*, in which human labour was supplied by the use of an ass or some other animal. III. The water-mill (*mola aquaria, ὑδραλέτης*). A cogged wheel, attached to the axis of the water wheel, turned another which was attached to the axis of the upper mill-stone: the corn to be ground fell between the stones out of a hopper (*infundibulum*), which was fixed above them. IV. The floating-mill. V. The saw-mill. VI. The pepper-mill.

MŎNARCHĬA ($\mu o v a \rho \chi \acute{\iota} a$), a general name for any form of government in which the supreme functions of political administration are in the hands of a single person. The term $\mu o v a \rho \chi \acute{\iota} a$ is applied to such governments, whether they are hereditary or elective, legal or usurped. In its commonest application, it is equivalent to $\beta a \sigma \iota \lambda \epsilon \acute{\iota} a$, whether absolute or limited. But the rule of an *aesymnetes* or a *tyrant* would equally be called a $\mu o v a \rho \chi \acute{\iota} a$. Hence Plutarch uses it to express the Latin *dictatura*. It is by a somewhat rhetorical use of the word that it is applied now and then to the δῆμος.

MŎNĒTA, the mint, or the place where money was coined. The mint of Rome was a building on the Capitoline, and attached to the temple of Juno Moneta, as the aerarium was to the temple of Saturn. The officers who had the superintendence of the mint were the *Triumviri Monetales*, who were perhaps first appointed about B. C. 269. Under the republic, the coining of money was not a privilege which belonged exclusively to the state. The coins struck in the time of the republic mostly bear the names of private individuals; and it would seem that every Roman citizen had the right of having his own gold and silver coined in the public mint, and under the superintendence of its officers. Still no one till the time of the empire had the right of putting his own image upon a coin; Julius Caesar was the first to whom this privilege was granted.

MŎNILE (ὅρμος), a necklace. Necklaces were worn by both sexes among the most polished of those nations which the Greeks called barbarous, especially the Indians, the Egyptians, and the Persians. Greek and Roman females adopted them more particularly as a bridal ornament. They were of various forms, as may be seen by the following specimens:—

Monilia, necklaces. (British Museum.)

MŌNŬMENTUM. [FUNUS.]
MŎRA. [EXERCITUS.]
MORTĀRIUM, also called **PĪLA** and **PĪ-LUM** (ὅλμος, ἰγδη, ἰγδις), a mortar. Before the invention of mills [MOLA] **corn was pounded and rubbed in mortars** (*pistum*), and hence the place for making bread, or the bake-house, was called *pistrinum*. Also **long after the introduction of mills this was an indispensable article of domestic furniture.** Those used in pharmacy **were sometimes made of Egyptian alabaster. The mortar was also employed in pounding charcoal, rubbing it with glue, in order to make black paint** (*atramentum*), **in making plaster for the walls of apartments, in mixing spices and fragrant herbs and flowers for the use of the kitchen, and in metallurgy, as in triturating cinnabar to obtain mercury from it by sublimation.**

MULSUM. [VINUM.]
MŪNĔRĀTOR. [GLADIATORES.]
MŪNĬCEPS, MŪNĬCĬPĬUM. [COLONIA; FOEDERATAE CIVITATES.]
MŬNUS. [HONORES.]
MŬNUS. [GLADIATORES.]
MŪRĀLIS CŎRŌNA. [CORONA.]
MURRHĪNA VĀSA, or MURRĒA VĀSA, were first introduced into Rome by Pompey, who **dedicated** cups of this kind to Jupiter Capitolinus. Their value was **very great.** Nero gave 300 talents for a capis **or drinking cup.** These murrhine vessels came **from the** East, principally from places within **the Parthian empire, and chiefly from Caramania.** They were made of **a substance formed by a moisture thickened in the earth by heat, and** were chiefly valued on account of the variety of their colours. Modern writers differ much respecting the material of which they **were composed, and some think they may have been true Chinese porcelain.**

MŪRUS, MOENIA (τεῖχος), the wall of a city, in contradistinction to PARIES (τοῖχος), the wall of a house, and *Maceria*, a boundary wall. We find cities surrounded by massive walls at **the** earliest periods of Greek and Roman history. Homer speaks of the chief cities of the Argive kingdom as "the walled Tiryns," and "Mycenae the well-built city," attesting the great antiquity of those identical gigantic walls which still stand at Tiryns and Mycenae, and which have been frequently attributed to the Cyclopes and Pelasgians. Three principal **species** can be clearly distinguished:—1. That in which the masses of **stone are of irregular shape and are put together without any attempt to fit them into one another, the interstices being** loosely filled in with smaller stones. An example is given in the annexed engraving. 2. In other cases we find the blocks still of irregular polygonal shapes, but their sides are suffici-

Ancient Wall at Tiryns.

ently smoothed to make each fit accurately into the angles between the others, and their faces are cut so as to give the whole wall a tolerably smooth surface. An example is given in the annexed engraving. 3. In the third spe-

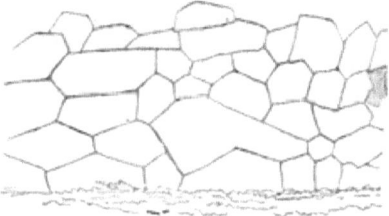

Ancient Wall of Larissa, the Acropolis of Argos.

cies, the blocks are laid in horizontal courses, more or less regular (sometimes indeed so irregular, that none of the horizontal joints are continuous), and with vertical joints either perpendicular or oblique, but with all the joints more or less accurately **fitted.** The walls of Mycenae present one of the ruder examples of this sort of structure; and the following engraving of the "Lion Gate" of that fortress (so called from the rudely sculptured figures of lions) shows also the manner **in which the gates of these three** species of **walls were built, by supporting an** immense **block of stone, for the lintel, upon** two others, **for jambs, the latter inclining** inwards, so as to give more space than if they were upright.—The materials employed in walls about the time of Pericles were various sorts of stone, and, in some of the most magnificent temples, marble. The practice of putting a facing of marble over a wall of a commoner material was introduced in the next period of architectural history. For buildings of a common sort, the materials employed were smaller stones, rough or squared, or flints, as well as bricks. These were bound together with various kinds of mortar or cement, composed of lime mixed with different sands and volcanic earths. The history of Roman masonry is not very different from that of the Greek.—The most ancient works at Rome, such as the *Carcer Mamertinus*, the *Cloaca Maxima*, and the Servian Walls, were constructed of massive quadrangular hewn stones, placed together without cement. [CLOACA.] Five species of Roman masonry may be distinguished; namely, 1. when the blocks of stone are laid in alternate courses, lengthwise in one course, and crosswise in the next; this is the most common; 2. when the stones in each course are laid alternately along and across; this construction was usual when the walls were to be faced with slabs of marble; 3. when they are laid entirely lengthwise; 4. entirely crosswise; and 5. when the courses are alternately higher and lower than each other. As by the Greeks, so by the Romans, walls of a commoner sort were built of smaller quarried stones (*caementa*) or of bricks. The excellence of the cement which the Romans used enabled them to construct walls of very small rough stones, not laid in courses, but held together by the mortar; this structure was called *opus incertum*. Another structure of which the Romans made great use, and which was one of the most durable of all, was that composed of courses of flat tiles. Such courses were also introduced in the other kinds of stone and brick walls, in which they both served as bond-courses, and, in the lower part of the wall, kept the damp from rising from the ground. Brick walls covered with stucco were exceedingly common with the Romans: even columns were made of brick covered with stucco.

Ancient Wall at Mycenae.

MUSCULUS was a kind of vinea, one of the smaller military machines, by which the besiegers of a town were protected.

MUSĒUM (μουσεῖον), the name of an institution founded by Ptolemy Philadelphus, about B. C. 280, for the promotion of learning and the support of learned men. The museum formed part of the palace, and contained cloisters or porticoes (περίπατος), a public theatre or lecture-room (ἐξέδρα), and a large hall (οἶκος μέγας), where the learned men dined together. The museum was supported by a common fund, supplied apparently from the public treasury; and the whole institution was under the superintendence of a priest, who was appointed by the king, and after Egypt became a province of the Roman empire, by the Caesar. Botanical and zoological gardens appear to have been attached to the museum.

MÝRII (μύριοι), the name given to the popular assembly of the Arcadians, which was established after the overthrow of the Spartan supremacy by the battle of Leuctra, and which used to meet at Megalopolis in order to determine upon matters affecting the whole people.

MYSIA (μύσια), a festival celebrated by the inhabitants of Pellene in Achaia in honour of Demeter Mysia, which lasted for 7 days.

MYSTĒRIA. The names by which mysteries or mystic festivals were designated in Greece, are μυστήρια, τελεταί, and ὄργια. The name ὄργια (from ἑοργα) originally signified only sacrifices accompanied by certain ceremonies, but it was afterwards applied especially to the ceremonies observed in the worship of Dionysus, and at a still later period to mysteries in general. Τελετή signifies, in general, a religious festival, but more particularly a lustration or ceremony performed in order to avert some calamity, either public or private. Μυστήριον signifies, properly speaking, the secret part of the worship, but was also used in the same sense as τελετή, and for mystic worship in general. Mysteries in general may be defined as sacrifices and ceremonies which took place at night or in secret within some sanctuary, which the uninitiated were not allowed to enter. What was essential to them, were objects of worship, sacred utensils, and traditions with their interpretation, which were withheld from all persons not initiated. The most celebrated mysteries in Greece were those of Samothrace and Eleusis, which are described in separate articles. [CABEIRIA; ELEUSINIA.]

NAENIA. [FUNUS.]
NATATIO, NATATORIUM. [BALNEUM.]
NAVALIA, docks at Rome where ships were built, laid up, and refitted. They were attached to the emporium outside of the Porta Trigemina, and were connected with the Tiber. The emporium and navalia were first included within the walls of the city by Aurelian.—The docks (νεώσοικοι or νεώρια) in the Peiraeeus at Athens cost 1000 talents, and having been destroyed in the anarchy were again restored and finally completed by Lycurgus, the contemporary of Demosthenes. They were under the superintendence of regular officers, called ἐπιμεληταὶ τῶν νεωρίων.

NAVALIS CORONA. [CORONA.]
NAVARCHUS (ναύαρχος), the name by which the Greeks designated both the captain of a single ship, and the admiral of a fleet. The office itself was called ναυαρχία. The admiral of the Athenian fleet was always one of the ten generals (στρατηγοί) elected every year, and he had either the whole or the chief command of the fleet. The chief officers who served under him were the trierarchs and the pentecontarchs, each of whom commanded one vessel; the inferior officers in the vessels were the κυβερνῆται or helmsmen, the κελευσταί or commanders of the rowers, and the πρωρᾶται, who must have been employed at the prow of the vessels. Other Greek states who kept a navy had likewise their navarchs. The chief admiral of the Spartan fleet was called navarchus, and the second in command epistoleus (ἐπιστολεύς). The same person was not allowed to hold the office of navarchus two successive years at Sparta. [EPISTOLEUS.]

NAUCRARIA (ναυκραρία), the name of a division of the inhabitants of Attica. The four ancient phylae were each divided into three phratries, and each of these twelve phratries into four naucraries, of which there were thus forty-eight. What the naucraries were previous to the legislation of Solon is not stated anywhere, but it is not improbable that they were political divisions similar to the demes in the constitution of Cleisthenes, and were made perhaps at the time of the institution of the nine archons, for the purpose of regulating the liturgies, taxes, or financial and military affairs in general. At any rate, however, the naucraries before the time of Solon can have had no connection with the navy, for the Athenians then had no navy; the word ναύκραρος therefore cannot be derived from ναῦς, ship, but must come from ναίω, and ναύκραρος is thus only another form for ναύκληρος in the sense of a householder, as ναῦλον was used for the rent of a house. Solon in his legislation retained the old institution of the naucraries, and charged each of them with the equipment of one trireme and with the mounting of two horsemen. All military affairs, as far as regards the defraying of expenses, probably continued as before to be regulated according to naucraries. Cleisthenes, in his change of the Solonian constitution, retained the division into naucraries for military and financial purposes; but he increased their number to fifty, making five for each of his ten tribes; so that now the number of their ships was increased from forty-eight to fifty, and that of horsemen from ninety-six to one hundred. The statement of Herodotus, that the Athenians in their war against Aegina had only fifty ships of their own, is thus perfectly in accordance with the fifty naucraries of Cleisthenes. The functions of the former ναύκραροι, or the heads of their respective naucraries, were now transferred to the demarchs. [DEMARCHI.] The obligation of each naucrary to equip a ship of war for the service of the republic may be regarded as the first form of trierarchy. As the system of trierarchy became developed and established, this obligation of the naucraries appears to have gradually ceased, and to have fallen into disuse. [TRIERARCHIA.]

NAUCRARUS. [NAUCRARIA.]
NAVIS, NAVIGIUM (ναῦς, πλοῖον), a ship. The numerous fleet, with which the Greeks are said to have sailed to the coast of Asia Minor, must on the whole be regarded as sufficient evidence of the extent to which navigation was carried on in those times, however much of the detail in the Homeric description may have arisen from the poet's own imagination. In the Homeric catalogue it is stated that each of the fifty Boeotian ships carried 120 warriors, and a ship which carried so many cannot have been of very small dimensions. What Homer states of the Boeotian vessels applies more or less to the ships of other Greeks. These boats were provided with a mast (ἱστός) which was fastened by two ropes (πρότονοι) to the two ends of the ship, so that when the rope connecting it with the prow broke, the mast would fall towards the stern, where it might kill the helmsman. The mast could be erected or taken down as necessity required. They also had sails (ἱστία), but no deck; each vessel however appears to have had only one sail, which was used in favourable winds; and the principal means of

s 2

propelling the vessel lay in the rowers, who sat upon benches (κληῖδες). The oars were fastened to the side of the ship with leathern thongs (τροποὶ δερμάτινοι), in which they were turned as a key in its hole. The ships in Homer are mostly called black (μέλαιναι), probably because they were painted or covered with a black substance, such as pitch, to protect the wood against the influence of the water and the air; sometimes other colours, such as μίλτος, minium (a red colour), were used to adorn the sides of the ships near the prow, whence Homer occasionally calls ships μιλτοπάρῃοι, i. e. red-cheeked; they were also painted occasionally with a purple colour (φοινικοπάρῃοι). When the Greeks had landed on the coast of Troy, the ships were drawn on land, and fastened at the poop to large stones with a rope which served as anchors. The Greeks then surrounded the fleet with a fortification to secure it against the attacks of the enemy. This custom of drawing the ships upon the shore, when they were not used, was followed in later times also, as every one will remember from the accounts in Caesar's Commentaries. In the Odyssey (v. 243, &c.) the building of a boat (σχεδία) is described, though not with the minuteness which an actual ship-builder might wish for. Ulysses first cuts down with his axe twenty trees, and prepares the wood for his purpose by cutting it smooth and giving it the proper shape. He then bores the holes for nails and hooks, and fits the planks together and fastens them with nails. He rounds the bottom of the ship like that of a broad transport vessel, and raises the bulwark (ἴκρια), fitting it upon the numerous ribs of the ship. He afterwards covers the whole of the outside with planks, which are laid across the ribs from the keel upwards to the bulwark: next the mast is made, and the sail-yard attached to it, and lastly the rudder. When the ship is thus far completed, he raises the bulwark still higher by a wicker-work which goes all around the vessel, as a protection against the waves. This raised bulwark of wickerwork and the like was used in later times also. For ballast Ulysses throws into the ship ὕλη, which according to the Scholiast consisted of wood, stones, and sand. Calypso then brings him materials to make a sail of, and he fastens the ὑπέραι or ropes which run from the top of the mast to the two ends of the yard, and also the κάλοι with which the sail is drawn up or let down. The πόδες mentioned in this passage were undoubtedly, as in the later times, the ropes attached to the two lower corners of the square sail. The ship of which the building is thus described was a small boat, a σχεδία, as Homer calls it; but it had like all the Homeric ships a round or flat bottom. Greater ships must have been of a more complicated structure, as ship-builders are praised as artists. Below (p. 266), a representation of two boats is given which appear to bear great resemblance to the one of which the building is described in the Odyssey.—The Corinthians were the first who brought the art of ship-building nearest to the point at which we find it in the time of Thucydides, and they were the first who introduced ships with three ranks of rowers (τριήρεις, Triremes). About B. C. 700, Ameinocles the Corinthian, to whom this invention is ascribed, made the Samians acquainted with it; but it must have been preceded by that of the Biremes, that is, ships with two ranks of rowers, which Pliny attributes to the Erythraeans.* These innovations however do not seem to have been generally adopted for a long time; for we read that about the time of Cyrus the Phocaeans introduced long sharp-keeled ships called πεντηκόντοροι. These belonged to the class of long war-ships (νῆες μακραί), and had fifty rowers, twenty-five on each side of the ship, who sat in one row. It is further stated that before this time

* Biremes are sometimes called by the Greeks δίκροτα. The name biremis is also applied to a little boat managed by only two oars.

vessels called στρογγύλαι, with large round or rather flat bottoms, had been used exclusively by all the Ionians in Asia. At this period most Greeks seem to have adopted the long ships with only one rank of rowers on each side (Moneris). Their name varied accordingly as they had fifty (πεντηκόντοροι), or thirty (τριακόντοροι), or even a smaller number of rowers. A ship of war of this class is represented in the preceding woodcut. The following cut contains a beautiful fragment of a Biremis with a complete deck. Another specimen of a small Biremis is given further on.—The first Greek people whom we know to have acquired a navy of importance were the Corinthians, Samians, and Phocaeans. About the time of Cyrus and Cambyses the Corinthian Triremes were generally adopted by the Sicilian tyrants and by the Corcyraeans, who soon acquired the most powerful navies among the Greeks. In other parts of Greece and even at Athens and in Aegina the most common vessels about this time were long ships with only one rank of rowers on each side. Athens, although the foundation of its maritime power had been laid by Solon [NAUCRARIA], did not obtain a fleet of any importance until the time of Themistocles, who persuaded the Athenians to build 200 Triremes for the purpose of carrying on the war against Aegina. But even then ships were not provided with complete decks (καταστρώματα) covering the whole of the vessel. Ships with only a partial deck or with no deck at all, were called ἄφρακτοι νῆες, and in Latin naves apertae. Even at the time of the Persian war, the Athenian ships were without a complete

Biremis. (Winckelmann, pl. 207.)

Navis Aperta. (Coin of Corcyra.)

deck. Ships which had a complete deck were called κατάφρακτοι, and the deck itself κατάστρωμα. At the time when Themistocles induced the Athenians to build a fleet of 200 sail he also carried a decree, that every year twenty new Triremes should be built from the produce of the mines of Laurium. After the time of Themistocles as many as twenty Triremes must have been built every year both in times of war and of peace, as the average number of Triremes which was always ready amounted to between three and four hundred. Such an annual addition was the more necessary, as the vessels were of a light structure and did not last long. The whole superintendence of the building of new Triremes was in the hands of the senate of the Five Hundred, but the actual business was entrusted to a committee called the τριηροποιοί, one of whom acted as their treasurer, and had in his keeping the money set apart for the purpose. Under the Macedonian supremacy the Rhodians became the greatest maritime power in Greece. The navy of Sparta was never of great importance. Navigation remained for the most part what it had been before; the Greeks seldom ventured out into the open sea, and it was generally considered necessary to remain in sight of the coast or of some island, which also served as guides in daytime: in the night the position, rising and setting of the different stars answered the same purpose. In winter navigation generally ceased altogether. In cases where it would have been necessary to coast around a considerable extent of country, which was connected with the main land by a narrow neck, the ships were sometimes drawn across the neck of land from one sea to the other, by machines called ὁλκοί. This was done most frequently across the isthmus of Corinth.—The various kinds of ships used by the Greeks might be divided, according to the number of ranks of rowers employed in them, into Moneres, Biremes, Triremes, Quadriremes, Quinqueremes, &c., up to the enormous ship with forty ranks of rowers, built by Ptolemaeus Philopator. But all these appear to have been constructed on the same principle, and it is more convenient to divide them into *ships of war* and *ships of burden* (φορτικὰ, φορτηγοὶ, ὁλκάδες, πλοῖα, στρογγύλαι, *naves onerariae*, *naves actuariae*). Ships of the latter kind were not calculated for quick movement or rapid sailing, but to carry the greatest possible quantity of goods. Hence their structure was bulky, their bottom round, and although they were not without rowers, yet the chief means by which they were propelled were their sails. The most common ships of war in the earlier times were the pentecontori (πεντηκόντοροι), but afterwards they were chiefly Triremes, and the latter are frequently designated only by the name νῆες, while all the others are called by the name indicating their peculiar character. Triremes however were again divided into two classes: the one consisting of real men-of-war, which were quick-sailing vessels (ταχεῖαι), and the other of transports either for soldiers (στρατιώτιδες or ὁπλιταγωγοί) or for horses (ἱππηγοί, ἱππαγωγοί). Ships of this class were more heavy and awkward, and were therefore not used in battle except in cases of necessity. The ordinary size of a war galley may be inferred from the fact that the average number of men engaged in it, including the crew and marines, was two hundred, to whom on some occasions as many as thirty epibatae were added. [EPIBATAE.]—Vessels with more than three ranks of rowers on each side were not constructed in Greece till about the year 400 B.C., when Dionysius I., tyrant of Syracuse, who bestowed great care upon his navy, built the first Quadriremes (τετρήρεις), and Quinqueremes (πεντήρεις). In the reign of Dionysius II., Hexeres (ἑξήρεις) are also mentioned. After the time of Alexander the Great the use of vessels with four, five, and more ranks of rowers became very general, and it is well known that the first Punic war was chiefly carried on with Quinqueremes. Ships with twelve, thirty, or even forty ranks of rowers, such as they were built by Alexander and the Ptolemies, appear to have been mere curiosities, and did not come into common use. The Athenians at first did not adopt vessels larger than Triremes, probably because they thought that with rapidity and skill they could do more than with large and unwieldy ships. In the year B.C. 356 they continued to use nothing but Triremes; but in B.C. 330 the republic had already a number of Quadriremes, which was afterwards increased. The first Quinqueremes at Athens are mentioned in a document belonging to the year B.C. 325.—Among the smaller vessels we may mention the ἄκατος or ἀκάτιον, which seems to have been sometimes used as a ship of burden. The name Scapha (σκάφη) denotes a small skiff or life-boat, which was commonly attached to merchantmen for the purpose of saving the crew in danger.—*Liburna*, or *Liburnica*, in Greek λιβυρνίς or λιβυρνόν, is a name given apparently to every war-ship, from a bireme up to those with six lines of rowers on each side, but in the time of Augustus, liburnae even with six lines of rowers were considered small and swift in comparison with the unwieldy ships of Antony at Actium. They were usually provided with a beak, whence a *navis rostrata* is generally the same as a Liburna. They were first constructed by the Liburnians (whence they derived their name), and formed the main part of the fleet of Augustus in the battle of Actium.—Every vessel at Athens, as in modern times, had a name given to it, which was generally of the feminine gender. The Romans sometimes gave to their ships masculine names. The Greek names were either taken from ancient heroines such as Nausicaa, or they were abstract words such as *Forethought*, *Safety*, *Guidance*, &c. In many cases the name of the builder also was added.—The Romans appear to have first become aware of the importance of a fleet during the second Samnite war, in the year B.C. 311: when *duumviri navales* were for the first time appointed by the people. The ships which the Romans now built were undoubtedly Triremes. This fleet, however insignificant it may have been, continued to be kept up until the time when Rome became a real maritime power. In the year B.C. 260, when the Romans saw that without a navy they could not carry on the war against Carthage with any advantage, the senate ordained that a fleet should be built. Triremes would now have been of no avail against the high-bulwarked vessels (Quinqueremes) of the Carthaginians. But the Romans would have been unable to build others had not fortunately a Carthaginian Quinquereme been wrecked on the coast of Bruttium, and fallen into their hands. This wreck the Romans took as their model, and after it built 120, or according to others 130 ships. From this time forward the Romans continued to keep up a powerful navy. Towards the end of the Republic they also increased the size of their ships, and built war vessels of from six to ten ranks of rowers. The construction of their ships, however, scarcely differed from that of Greek vessels: the only great difference was that the Roman galleys were provided with a greater variety of destructive engines of war than those of the Greeks. They even erected turres and tabulata upon the decks of their great men-of-war (*naves turritae*), and fought upon them as if they were standing upon the walls of a fortress (see cut, p. 260).

We now proceed to describe the parts of ancient vessels.—1. *The prow* (πρώρα or μέτωπον, *prora*) was generally ornamented on both sides with figures, which were either painted upon the sides or laid in. It seems to have been very common to represent an eye on each side of the prow. Upon the prow or fore-deck there was always some emblem (παράσημον, *insigne, figura*) by which the ship was distinguished from others. At the head of the prow there projected the στόλος, and its extremity was termed ἀκροστόλιον, which was frequently made in the shape of an animal or a helmet. It appears to have been sometimes covered with brass and to have served as an embole (ἐμβολή) against the enemy's vessels. The ἀκροστόλιον is sometimes designated by the name of χηνίσκος (from χήν, a goose), because it was formed in the shape of the head or neck of a goose or

BIREMIS.

A. Prora, πρώρα.
B. Oculus, ὀφθαλμός.
C. Rostrum, ἔμβολος.
D. Carinium, χηνίσκος.
E. Puppis, πρύμνη.
F. Aplustre, ἄφλαστον, with the pole containing the fascia or taenia.

G. τράφηξ.
H. Remi, κῶπαι.
I. Gubernaculum, πηδάλιον.
K. Malus, ἱστός.
L. Velum, ἱστός.
M. Antenna, κεραία, κέρας.
N. Cornua, ἀκροκέραιαι.

O. Ceruchi, κεροῦχοι.
P. Carchesium, καρχήσιον.
Q. κάλοι, καλώδια.
R. πρότονος.
S. Pedes, πόδες.
   Opifera, ὑπέραι.

swan, as in the accompanying woodcut. The cheniscus was often gilt and made of bronze.

Cheniscus. (From a Painting at Herculaneum.)

Just below the prow and projecting a little above the keel was the *Rostrum* (ἔμβολος, ἔμβολον) or beak, which consisted of a beam, to which were attached sharp and pointed irons, or the head of a ram and the like. This ἔμβολος was used for the purpose of attacking another vessel and of breaking its sides. These beaks were at first always above the water and visible; afterwards they were attached lower, so that they were invisible, and thus became still more dangerous to other ships. The annexed woodcuts represent three different beaks of ships. The command in the prow of a vessel was exercised by an officer called πρωρεύς, who seems to have been next in rank to the steersman, and to have had the care of the gear, and the command over the rowers.—2. *The stern* (πρύμνη, *puppis*) was generally above the other parts of the deck, and in it the helmsman had his elevated seat. It is seen in the representations of ancient vessels to be rounder than the prow, though its extremity is likewise sharp. The stern was, like the prow, adorned in various ways, but especially with the image of the tutelary deity of the vessel (*tutela*). In some representations a kind of roof is formed over the head of the steersman, and the upper part of the stern frequently has an elegant ornament called *aplustre*, and in Greek ἄφλαστον, which constituted the highest part of the poop. It formed a corresponding ornament to the ἀκροστόλιον at the prow. At the junction of the aplustre with the stern on

Rostra, Beaks of Ships. (Montfaucon, pl. 133.)

which it was based, we commonly observe an ornament resembling a circular shield: this was called ἀσπιδεῖον or ἀσπιδίσκη. It is seen on the two aplustria here represented. The aplustre rose immediately behind the gubernator, and served in some degree to protect him from wind and rain. Sometimes there appears, beside the aplustre, a pole, to which a fillet or pennon (ταινία) was attached, which served both to distinguish and adorn the vessel, and also to show the direction of the wind.—3. The τράφηξ is the bulwark of the vessel, or rather the uppermost edge of it. In small boats the pegs (σκαλμοί, *scalmi*) between which the oars move, and to which they are fastened by a thong (τροπωτήρ),

Aphlaston, Aplustre.

were upon the τράφηξ. In all other vessels the oars passed through holes in the side of the vessel (ὀφθαλμοί, τρήματα, or τρυπήματα). —4. The middle part of the deck in most ships of war appears to have been raised above the bulwark, or at least to a level with its upper edge, and thus enabled the soldiers to occupy a position from which they could see far around and hurl their darts against the enemy. Such an elevated deck appears in the annexed woodcut representing a *Moneris*. In this instance the flag is standing upon the hind-deck.—5. One of the most interesting, as well as important parts in the

Moneris. (From a Painting at Pompeii.)

arrangements of the Biremes, Triremes, &c., is the position of the ranks of rowers, from which the ships themselves derive their names. Various opinions have been entertained by those who have written upon this subject. Thus much is certain, that the different ranks of rowers, who sat along the sides of a vessel, were placed one above the other. In ordinary vessels, from the Moneris up to the Quinqueremis, each oar was managed by one man. The rowers sat upon little benches attached to the ribs of the vessel, and called ἑδώλια, and in Latin *fori* and *transtra*. The lowest row of rowers was called θαλάμος, the rowers themselves, θαλαμῖται or θαλάμιοι. The uppermost ordo of rowers was called θράνος, and the rowers themselves θρανῖται. The middle ordo or ordines of rowers were called ζυγὰ, ζύγιοι or ζυγῖται. Each of this last class of rowers had likewise his own seat, and did not, as some have supposed, sit upon benches running across the vessel. The gear of a vessel was divided into *wooden* and *hanging gear* (σκευὴ ξύλινα, and σκευὴ κρεμαστά).

I. WOODEN GEAR.—1. *Oars* (κώπαι, *remi*). The collective term for oars is ταρρός, which properly signified only the blade or flat part of the oar, but was afterwards used as a collective expression for all the oars, with the exception of the rudder. The oars varied in size accordingly as they were used by a lower or higher ordo of rowers, and from the name of the ordo by which they were used, they also received their special names, viz., κώπαι θαλάμιαι, ζύγιαι, and θρανίτιδες. Each Trireme had on an average 170 rowers. In a Roman Quinquereme during the first Punic war, the average number of rowers was 300; in later times we even find as many as 400. The lower part of the holes through which the oars passed appears to have been covered with leather (ἄσκωμα), which also extended a little way outside the hole.—2. *The rudder* (πηδάλιον, *gubernaculum*). Before the invention of the rudder, vessels must have been propelled and guided by the oars alone. This circumstance may account for the form of the ancient rudder, as well as for the mode of using it. It was like an oar with a very broad blade, and was commonly placed on each side of the stern, not at its extremity. The annexed woodcut presents examples of its appearance as it is frequently exhibited on gems, coins, and other works of art. The figure in the centre shows a Triton blowing the buccina, and holding a rudder over his shoulder. The left-hand figure represents a rudder with its helm or tiller crossed by the cornucopia. In the third figure Venus leans with her left arm upon a rudder to indicate her origin from the sea. The rudder was managed by the gubernator (κυβερνήτης), who is also called the *rector navis* as distinguished from the *magister*. A ship had sometimes one, but more commonly two rudders; but they were managed by the same steersman to prevent confusion. In larger ships the two rudders were joined

Gubernacula, rudders. (From an ancient Lamp and Gems.)

by a pole, which was moved by the gubernator, and kept the rudders parallel. The contrivances for attaching the two rudders to one another and to the sides of the ship, are called ζεῦγλαι or ζευκτηρίαι.—3. *Ladders* (κλιμακίδες, *scalae*). Each Trireme had two wooden ladders, and the same seems to have been the case in τριακόντοροι.—4. *Poles* or punt poles (κοντοί, *conti*). Three of these, of different lengths, belonged to every Trireme.—5. Παραστάται or supports for the masts. They seem to have been a kind of props placed at the foot of the masts.—6. The *mast* (ἱστός, *malus*). The ancients had vessels with one, two, or three masts. The foremast was called ἀκάτειος, the mainmast, ἱστός μέγας. A triaconter, or a vessel with 30 rowers, had likewise two masts, and the smaller mast here, as well as in a trireme, was near the prow. In three-masted vessels the largest mast was nearest the stern. The masts as well as the yards were usually of fir. The part of the mast immediately above the yard (*antenna*), formed a structure similar to a drinking-cup, and bore the name of *carchesium* (καρχήσιον). Into it the mariners ascended in order to manage the sail, to obtain a distant view, or to discharge mis-

Cerucbi. (From an ancient Lamp.)

siles. Breastworks (θωράκια) were fixed to these structures, so as to supply the place of defensive armour; and pulleys (τροχηλίαι, *trochleae*) for hoisting up stones and weapons from below. The continuation of the mast above the carchesium was called the "distaff" (ἡλακάτη), corresponding to our topmast or top-gallant mast.—7. The *yards* (κέρα, κεραῖαι, *antennae*). The mainyard was fastened to the top of the mast by ropes termed *ceruchi*, as seen in the preceding woodcut. To the mainyard was attached the mainsail, which was hoisted or let down as the occasion might require. In the two extremities of the yard (*cornua*, ἀκροκέραιαι), ropes (*ceruchi*, κηροῦχοι) were attached, which passed to the top of the mast; and by means of these ropes and the pulleys connected with them, the yard and sail, guided by the hoop, were hoisted to the height required. There are numerous representations of ancient ships in which the antenna is seen, as in the two woodcuts here appended. In the second of them there are ropes hanging down from the antenna, the object of which was to enable the sailors to turn the antenna and the sail according to the wind.

Antennae. (From ancient Gems.)

II. Hanging Gear.—1. *Hypozomata* (Ὑποζώματα), thick and broad ropes running in a horizontal direction around the ship from the stern to the prow, and intended to keep the whole fabric together. They ran round the vessel in several circles, and at certain distances from one another. The Latin name for ὑπόζωμα is *tormentum*. Sometimes they were taken on board when a vessel sailed, and not put on till it was thought necessary. The act of putting them on was called ὑποζων-νύναι, or διαζωννύναι, or ζῶσαι. A Trireme required four ὑποζώματα.—2. *The sail* ('ἱστίον, *velum*). Most ancient ships had only one sail, which was attached with the yard to the great mast. In a Trireme also one sail might be sufficient, but the trierarch might nevertheless add a second. As each of the two masts of a Trireme had two sail-yards, it further follows that each mast might have two sails, one of which was placed lower than the other. The two belonging to the main-mast were called ἱστία μεγάλα, and those of the fore-mast ἱστία ἀκάτεια. The former were used on ordinary occasions, but the latter probably only in cases when it was necessary to sail with extraordinary speed. The sails of the Attic war-galleys, and of most ancient ships in general, were of a square form. Whether triangular sails were ever used by the Greeks, as has been frequently supposed, is very doubtful. The Romans, however, used triangular sails, which they called *Suppara*, and which had the shape of an inverted Greek Δ (τ), the upper side of which was attached to the yard.—3. *Cordage* (τοπεῖα) differed from the σχοινία or κάλοι. The σχοινία (*funes*) are the strong ropes to which the anchors were attached, and by which a ship was fastened to the land; while the τοπεῖα were a lighter kind of ropes and made with greater care, which were attached to the masts, yards, and sails. Each rope of this kind was made for a distinct purpose and place (τόπος, whence the name τοπεῖα). The following kinds are most worthy of notice:—*a*. καλώδια or κάλοι, were probably the ropes by which the mast was fastened to both sides of the ship, so that the πρότονοι in the Homeric ships were only an especial kind of καλώδια, or the καλώδια themselves differently placed. In later times the πρότονος was the rope which went from the top of the mainmast (καρχήσιον) to the prow of the ship, and thus was what is now called the main-stay. *b. Ceruchi* (κεροῦχοι, ἱμάντες), ropes which ran from the two ends of the sail-yard to the top of the mast. In more ancient vessels the ἱμὰς consisted of only one rope; in later times it consisted of two, and sometimes four, which uniting at the top of the mast, and there passing through a ring, descended on the other side, where it formed the ἐπίτονος, by means of which the sail was drawn up or let down. *c*. ἄγκοινα, Latin *anquina*, was the rope which went from the middle of a yard to the top of the mast, and was intended to facilitate the drawing up and letting down of the sail. *d*. Πόδες (*pedes*) were in later times, as in the poems of Homer, the ropes attached to the two lower corners of a square sail. These πόδες ran from the ends of the sail to the sides of the vessel towards the stern, where they were fastened with rings attached to the outer side of the bulwark. *e*. Ὑπέραι were the two ropes attached to the two ends of the sail-yard, and thence came down to a part of the ship near the stern. Their object was to move the yard according to the wind. In Latin they are called *opifera*, which is, perhaps, only a corruption of *hypera*.—4. Παραρρύματα. The ancients as early as the time of Homer had various preparations raised above the edge of a vessel, which were made of skins and wicker-work, and which were intended as a protection against high waves, and also to serve as a kind of breast-work behind which the men might be safe against the darts of the enemy. These elevations of the bulwark are called παραρρύματα. They were probably fixed upon the edge on both sides of the vessel, and were taken off when not wanted. Each galley appears to have had several παραρρύματα, two made of hair and two white ones, these four being regularly mentioned as belonging to one ship.—5. Σχοινία are the stronger and heavier kinds of ropes. There were two kinds of these, viz. the σχοινία ἀγκύρεια, to which the anchor was attached, and σχοινία ἐπίγυα or ἐπίγεια (retinacula), by which the ship was fastened to the shore or drawn upon the shore.—6. The anchor (ἀγκύρα, ancora). We have already remarked that in the Homeric age anchors were not known, and large stones (εὐναί, sleepers) used in their stead. When anchors came to be used, they were generally made of iron, and their form resembled that of a modern anchor. Such an anchor was often termed bidens, διπλῆ, ἀμφίβολος or ἀμφίστομος, because it had two teeth or flukes; but sometimes it had only one, and was then called ἑτεροστόμος. The technical expressions in the use of the anchor are: ancoram solvere, ἀγκύραν χαλᾶν, to loose the anchor; ancoram jacere, ἀγκύραν βάλλειν or ῥίπτειν, to cast anchor; and ancoram tollere, ἀγκύραν αἴρειν or ἀναίρεσθαι, to weigh anchor, whence αἴρειν by itself means "to set sail," ἀγκύραν being understood. The following figure shows the cable (funis), passing through a hole in the prow (oculus). Each ship of course had several anchors. The last or most powerful anchor, "the last hope," was called ἱερά, sacra, and persons trying their last hope were said sacram solvere.—The preceding account of the different parts of the ship will be rendered still clearer by the drawing on p. 263.

Biremis. (From a Marble at Rome.)

NAUMACHIA, the name given to the representation of a sea-fight among the Romans, and also to the place where such engagements were exhibited. These fights sometimes took place in the circus or amphitheatre, sufficient water being introduced to float ships, but more generally in buildings especially devoted to this purpose. The combatants in these sea-fights, called Naumachiarii, were usually captives, or criminals condemned to death, who fought as in gladiatorial combats, until one party was killed, unless preserved by the clemency of the emperor. The ships engaged in the sea fights were divided into two parties, called respectively by the names of different maritime nations, as Tyrians and Egyptians, Rhodians and Sicilians, Persians and Athenians, Corcyraeans and Corinthians, Athenians and Syracusans, &c. These sea-fights were exhibited with the same magnificence and lavish expenditure of human life as characterised the gladiatorial combats and other public games of the Romans. In Nero's naumachia there were sea-monsters swimming about in the artificial lake. In the sea-fight exhibited by Titus there were 3000 men engaged, and in that exhibited by Domitian the ships were almost equal in number to two real fleets.

NAUTODICAE (ναυτοδίκαι), magistrates at Athens, who had jurisdiction in matters belonging to navigation and commerce, and in matters concerning such persons as had entered their names as members of a phratria without both their parents being citizens of Athens, or in other words, in the δίκαι ἐμπόρων and δίκαι ξενίας. The time when nautodicae were first instituted is not mentioned, but it must have been previous to Pericles, and perhaps as early as the time of Cleisthenes. The nautodicae were appointed every year by lot in the month of Gamelion, and probably attended to the δίκαι ἐμπόρων only during the winter, when navigation ceased, whereas the δίκαι ξενίας might be brought before them all the year round.

NEFASTI DIES. [Dies.]

NEGOTIĀTŌRES, signified specially during the later times of the republic Roman citizens settled in the provinces, who lent money upon interest or bought up corn on speculation, which they sent to Rome as well as to other places. Their chief business however was lending money upon interest, and hence we find the words *negotia, negotiatio,* and *negotiari* used in this sense. The *negotiatores* are distinguished from the *publicani,* and from the *mercatores.* The *negotiatores* in the provinces corresponded to the *argentarii* and *feneratores* at Rome.

NEMEA (νέμεα, νέμεια, or νεμαῖα), the Nemean games, one of the four great national festivals of the Greeks. It was held at Nemea, a place near Cleonae in Argolis, and is said to have been originally instituted by the Seven against Thebes in commemoration of the death of Opheltes, afterwards called Archemorus. The games were revived by Hercules, after he had slain the Nemean lion; and were from this time celebrated in honour of Zeus. They were at first of a warlike character, and only warriors and their sons were allowed to take part in them; subsequently, however, they were thrown open to all the Greeks. The various games were horse-racing, running in armour in the stadium, wrestling, chariot-racing and the discus, boxing, throwing the spear and shooting with the bow, to which we may add musical contests. The prize given to the victors was at first a chaplet of olive-branches, but afterwards a chaplet of green parsley. The presidency of these games, and the management of them, belonged at different times to Cleonae, Corinth, and Argos. They were celebrated twice in every Olympiad, viz. at the commencement of every second Olympic year, in the winter, and soon after the commencement of every fourth Olympic year, in the summer.

NENIA. [Funus, p. 188, a.]

NEŌCORI (νεωκόροι), signified originally temple-sweepers, but was applied even in early times to priestly officers of high rank, who had the supreme superintendence of temples and their treasures. Under the Roman emperors the word was especially applied to those cities in Asia, which erected temples to the Roman emperors, since the whole city in every such case was regarded as the guardian of the worship of the emperor. Accordingly we frequently find on the coins of Ephesus, Smyrna, and other cities, the epithet Νεωκόρος, which also occurs on the inscriptions of these cities.

NEPTŪNĀLIA, a festival of Neptune, celebrated at Rome, of which very little is known. The day on which it was held was probably the 23rd of July. In the ancient calendaria this day is marked as *Nept. ludi et feriae,* or *Nept. ludi,* from which we see that the festival was celebrated with games.

NEXUM, was either the transfer of the ownership of a thing, or the transfer of a thing to a creditor as a security; accordingly in one sense Nexum included Mancipium [Mancipium]; in another sense, Mancipium and Nexum are opposed in the same way in which Sale and Mortgage or Pledge are opposed. The formal part of both transactions consisted in a transfer *per aes et libram.* The person who became *nexus* by the effect of a *nexum* or *nexus* (for this form of the word also is used) was said *nexum inire.* The phrases *nexi datio, nexi liberatio,* respectively express the contracting and the release from the obligation. The Roman law as to the payment of borrowed money was very strict. By a law of the Twelve Tables, if the debtor admitted the debt, or had been condemned in the amount of the debt by a judex, he had thirty days allowed him for payment. At the expiration of this time, he was liable to be assigned over to the creditor (*addictus*) by the sentence of the praetor. The creditor was required to keep him for sixty days in chains, during which time he publicly exposed the debtor on three nundinae, and proclaimed the amount of his debt. If no person released the prisoner by paying the debt, the creditor might sell him as a slave or put him to death. If there were several creditors, the letter of the law allowed them to cut the debtor in pieces, and to take their share of his body in proportion to their debt. There is no instance of a creditor ever having adopted this extreme mode of satisfying his debt. But the creditor might treat the debtor, who was *addictus,* as a slave, and compel him to work out his debt; and the treatment was often very severe. The Lex Poetilia (B. c. 326) alleviated the condition of the nexi. So far as we can understand its provisions, it set all the nexi free, or made them *soluti,* and it enacted that for the future there should be no nexum, and that no debtor should for the future be put in chains.

NŌBILES, NŌBĪLĪTAS. In the early periods of the Roman state the Patricians were the Nobles as opposed to the Plebs. In B. c. 366, the plebeians obtained the right of being eligible to the consulship, and finally they obtained access to all the curule magistracies. Thus the two classes were put on the same footing as to political capacity; but now a new order of nobility arose. The descendants of plebeians who had filled curule magistracies, formed a class called Nobiles or men "known," who were so called by way of distinction from "Ignobiles" or people who were not known. The Nobiles had no legal privileges as such; but they were bound together by a common distinction derived from a legal title and by a common interest; and their common interest was to endeavour to confine the election to all the high magistracies to the members of their body, to the Nobilitas. Thus the descendants of those Plebeians who had won their way to distinction combined to exclude other Plebeians from the distinction which their own ancestors had transmitted to them. The external distinction of the Nobiles was the Jus Imaginum, a right or privilege which was apparently established on usage only, and not on any positive enactments. These Imagines were figures with painted masks of wax, made to resemble the person whom they represented; and they were placed in the Atrium of the house, apparently in small wooden receptacles or cases somewhat in the form of temples. The Imagines were accompanied with the tituli or names of distinction which the deceased had acquired; and the tituli were connected in some way by lines or branches so as to exhibit the pedigree (stemma) of the family. These Imagines were generally enclosed in their cases, but they were opened on festival days and other great ceremonials, and crowned with bay (laureatae): they also formed part of a solemn funeral procession. It seems probable that the Roman Nobilitas, in the strict sense of that term, and the Jus Imaginum, originated with the admission of the Plebeians to the consulship B. c. 366. A plebeian who first attained a Curule office was the founder of his family's Nobilitas (princeps nobilitatis; auctor generis). Such a person could have no imagines of his ancestors; and he could have none of his own, for such imagines of a man were not made till after he was dead. Such a person then was not nobilis in the full sense of the term, nor yet was he ignobilis. He was called by the Romans a "novus homo" or a new man; and his status or condition was called Novitas. The term novus homo was never applied to a Patrician. The two most distinguished "novi homines" were C. Marius and M. Tullius Cicero, both natives of an Italian municipium. The Patricians would of course be jealous of the new nobility; but this new nobility once formed would easily unite with the old aristocracy of Rome to keep the political power in their hands, and to prevent more novi homines from polluting this exclusive class. As early as the second Punic war this new class, compounded of Patricians or original aristocrats, and Nobiles or newly-engrafted aristocrats, was able to exclude novi homines from the consulship. They maintained this power to the end of the republican period, and the consulship continued almost in the exclusive possession of the Nobilitas. The *Optimates* were the Nobilitas and the chief part of the Equites, a rich middle class, and also all others whose support the Nobilitas and Equites could command, in fact all who were opposed to change that might affect the power of the Nobilitas and the interests of those whom the Nobilitas allied with themselves. Optimates in this sense are opposed to Plebs, to the mass of the people; and Optimates is a wider term than Nobilitas, inasmuch as it would comprehend the Nobilitas and all who adhered to them.

NŌMEN (ὄνομα), a name. The Greeks bore only one name, and it was one of the especial rights of a father to choose the names for his children, and to alter them if he pleased. It was customary to give to the eldest son the name of the grandfather on his father's side; and children usually received their names on the tenth day after their birth.—Originally every Roman citizen belonged to a gens, and derived his name (*nomen* or *nomen gentilicium*) from his gens, which *nomen gentilicium* generally terminated in *ius*. Besides this, every Roman had a name, called *praenomen*, which preceded the nomen gentilicium, and which was peculiar to him as an individual, *e. g.* Caius, Lucius, Marcus, Cneius, Sextus, &c. This praenomen was at a later time given to boys on the ninth day after their birth, and to girls on the eighth day. This day was called *dies lustricus, dies nominum,* or *nominalia*. The praenomen given to a boy was in most cases that of the father, but sometimes that of the grandfather or great-grandfather. These two names, a *praenomen* and a *nomen gentilicium*, or simply *nomen*, were indispensable to a Roman, and they were at the same time sufficient to designate him; hence the numerous instances of Romans being designated only by these two names, even in cases where a third or fourth name was possessed by the person. Every Roman citizen, besides belonging to a gens, was also frequently a member of a familia, contained in a gens, and accordingly might have a third name or *cognomen*. Such cognomina were derived by the Romans from a variety of mental or bodily peculiarities, or from some remarkable event in the life of the person who was the founder of the familia. Such cognomina are, Asper, Imperiosus, Magnus, Maximus, Publicola, Brutus, Capito, Cato, Naso, Labeo, Caecus, Cicero, Scipio, Sulla, Torquatus, &c. These names were in most cases hereditary, and descended to the latest members of a familia; in some cases they ceased with the death of the person to whom they were given for special reasons. Many Romans had a second cognomen (*cognomen secundum* or *agnomen*), which was given to them as an honorary distinction, and in commemoration of some memorable deed or event of their life, *e. g.* Africanus, Asiaticus, Hispallus, Cretensis, Macedonicus, Allobrogicus, &c. Such agnomina were sometimes given by one general to another, sometimes by the army and confirmed by the chief-general, sometimes by the people in the comitia, and sometimes they were assumed by the person himself, as in the case of L. Cornelius Scipio Asiaticus. The regular order in which these names followed one another was:—1. praenomen; 2. nomen gentilicium; 3. cognomen primum; 4. cognomen secundum or agnomen. Sometimes the name of the tribe to which a person belonged, was added to his name, in the ablative case, as Q. Verres Romilia, C. Claudius Palatina. If a person by adoption passed from one gens into another, he assumed the praenomen, nomen, and cognomen of his adoptive father, and added to these the name of his former gens, with the termination *anus*. Thus C. Octavius, after being adopted by his uncle C. Julius Caesar, was called C. Julius Caesar Octavianus, and the son of L. Aemilius Paullus, when adopted by P. Cornelius Scipio, was called P. Cornelius Scipio Aemilianus. [ADOPTIO.] Slaves had only one name, and usually retained that which they had borne before they came into slavery. If a slave was restored to freedom, he received the praenomen and nomen gentilicium of his former master, and to these was added the name which he had had as a slave. Instances of such freedmen are, T. Ampius Menander, a freedman of T. Ampius Balbus, L. Cornelius Chrysogonus, a freedman of L. Cornelius Sulla, and M. Tullius Tiro, freedman of M. Tullius Cicero.

NOMOPHYLACES (νομοφύλακες), certain magistrates or official persons of high authority, who exercised a control over other magistrates, and indeed over the whole body of the people, it being their duty to see that the laws were duly administered and obeyed. Mention is made of such officers at Sparta and elsewhere, but no such body existed at Athens, for they must have had a power too great for the existence of a democracy. The Senate of 500, or the Areopagitic council, performed in some measure the office of law-guardians; but the only persons designated by this name appear to have been inferior functionaries (a sort of police), whose business it was to prevent irregularities and disturbances in the public assemblies.

NOMOS (νόμος). This word comprehends the notion not only of established or statute law, but likewise of all customs and opinions to which long prescription or natural feeling gives the force of law. Before any written codes appeared, law was promulgated by the poets or wise men, who sang the great deeds of their ancestors, and delivered their moral and political lessons in verse. As civilisation advanced, laws were reduced to writing, in the shape either of regular codes or distinct ordinances, and afterwards publicly exhibited, engraved on tablets, or hewn on columns. The first written laws we hear of are those of Zaleucus. The first at Athens were those of Draco, called θεσμοί, and by that name distinguished from the νόμοι of Solon. The laws of Lycurgus were not written. He enjoined that they should never be inscribed on any other tablet than the hearts of his countrymen. Those of Solon were inscribed on wooden tablets, arranged in pyramidal blocks, turning on an axis, called ἄξονες and κύρβεις. They were first hung in the Acropolis, but afterwards brought down to the Prytaneum.

NOMOTHETAE (νομοθέται), movers or proposers of laws, the name of a legislative committee at Athens, which, by an institution of Solon, was appointed to amend and revise the laws. At the first κυρία ἐκκλησία in every year, any person was at liberty to point out defects in the existing code or propose alterations. If his motion was deemed worthy of attention, the third assembly might refer the matter to the Nomothetae. They were selected by lot from the Heliastic body; it being the intention of Solon to limit the power of the popular assembly by means of a superior board emanating from itself, composed of citizens of mature age, bound by a stricter oath, and accustomed to weigh legal principles by the exercise of their judicial functions. The number of the committee so appointed varied according to the exigency of the occasion. The people appointed five advocates (σύνδικοι) to attend before the board and maintain the policy of the existing institution. If the proposed measure met the approval of the committee, it passed into law forthwith. Besides this, the Thesmothetae were officially authorised to review the whole code, and to refer to the *Nomothetae* all statutes which they considered unworthy of being retained. Hence appears the difference between *Psephisma* (ψήφισμα) and *Nomos* (νόμος). The mere resolution of the people in assembly was a *psephisma*, and only remained in force a year, like a decree of the senate. Nothing was a *law* that did not pass the ordeal of the Nomothetae.

NŎNAE. [CALENDARIUM.]

NŎTA, which signified a mark or sign of any kind, was also employed for an abbreviation. Hence *notae* signified the marks or signs used in taking down the words of a speaker, and was equivalent to our short-hand writing, or stenography; and *notarii* signified short-hand writers. It must be borne in mind, however, that *notae* also signified writing in cipher; and many passages in the ancient reciters which are supposed to refer to short-hand, refer in reality to writing in cipher. Among the Greeks it is said to have been invented by Xenophon, and their short-hand writers were called ταχυγράφοι, ὀξυγράφοι and σημειογράφοι. The first introduction of the art among the Romans is ascribed to Cicero. He is said to have caused the debate in the senate on the punishment of the Catilinarian conspirators to be taken down in short-hand. Eusebius ascribes it to Tiro, the freedman of Cicero, and hence the system of abbreviated writing, in which some manuscripts are written, has received the name of *Notae Tironianae;* but there is no evidence to show whether this species of short-hand was really the invention of Tiro. The system of short-hand employed in the time of the Roman empire must have been of a much simpler and more expeditious kind than the *Notae Tironianae*, which were merely abbreviations of the words. Many of the wealthy Romans kept slaves, who were trained in the art. It was also learnt even by the Roman nobles, and the emperor Titus was a great proficient in it. At a later time, it seems to have been generally taught in the schools. There were, moreover, short-hand writers (*notarii*) by profession, who were chiefly employed in taking down (*notare, excipere*) the proceedings in the courts of justice. At a later period, they were called *exceptores*. These short-hand writers were also employed on some occasions to take down a person's will.

NOTĀRĪI, short-hand writers, spoken of under NOTA. They were likewise called Actuarii. They were also employed by the emperors, and in course of time the title of *Notarii* was exclusively applied to the private secretaries of the emperors, who, of course, were no longer slaves, but persons of high rank. The short-hand writers were now called *exceptores*, as is remarked under NOTA.

NŎTA CENSŌRĬA. [CENSOR.]

NŎVENDĬĀLE (sc. *sacrum*).—(1) A festival lasting nine days, which was celebrated as often as stones rained from heaven. It was originally instituted by Tullus Hostilius, when there was a shower of stones upon the Mons Albanus, and was frequently celebrated in later times.—(2) This name was also given to the sacrifice performed nine days after a funeral. [FUNUS.]

NŎVI HŎMĬNES. [NOBILES.]

NŪDUS (γυμνός). These words, besides denoting absolute nakedness, were applied to any one who, being without an AMICTUS, wore only his tunic or indutus. In this state of nudity the ancients performed the operations of ploughing, sowing, and reaping. This term applied to the warrior expressed the absence of some part of his armour. Hence the light-armed were called γυμνῆτες. [ARMA.]

NUMMŪLĀRĬI or NŬMŬLĀRII. [MENSARII.]

NUMMUS or NŪMUS. [SESTERTIUS.]

NUNDĬNAE is derived by all the ancient writers from *novem* and *dies*, so that it literally signifies the ninth day. Every eighth day, according to our mode of speaking, was a nundinae, and there were thus always seven ordinary days between two nundinae. The Romans in their peculiar mode of reckoning added these two nundinae to the seven ordinary days, and consequently said that the nundinae recurred every ninth day, and called them *nundinae*, as it were *novemdinae*. The number of nundinae in the ancient year of ten months was 38. They were originally market-days for the country folk, on which they came to Rome to sell the produce of their labour, and on which the king settled the legal disputes among them. When, therefore, we read that the nundinae were ferine, or dies *nefasti*, and that no comitia were allowed to be held, we have to understand this of the populus or patricians, and not of the plebes; and while for the populus the nundinae were feriae, they were real days of business (*dies fasti* or *comitiales*) for the plebeians, who on these occasions pleaded their causes with members of their own order, and held their public meetings (the ancient comitia of the plebeians). Afterwards the nundinae became fasti for both orders, and this innovation facilitated the attendance of the plebeians at the comitia centuriata. The subjects to be laid before the comitia, whether they were proposals for new laws, or the appointment of officers, were announced to the people three nundinae beforehand (*trinundino die proponere*). Instead of *nundinae* the form *nundinum* is sometimes used, but only when it is preceded by a numeral, as in *trinundinum*, or *trinum nundinum*.

NUPTIAE. [MATRIMONIUM.]

OBOLUS. [DRACHMA.]
OCREA (κνημίς), a greave, a leggin. A pair of greaves (κνημῖδες) was one of the six articles of armour which formed the complete equipment of a Greek warrior [ARMA], and likewise of a Roman soldier as fixed by Servius Tullius. They were made of various metals, with a lining probably of leather, felt, or cloth. Their form is shown in the accompanying cut. The figure is that of a fallen warrior, and in consequence of the bending of the knees, the greaves are seen to project a little above them. This statue also shows the ankle-rings (ἐπισφύρια), which were used to fasten the greaves immediately above the feet.

Ocreae, Greaves. (From the Aeginetan Marbles.)

ODEUM (ᾠδεῖον), a species of public building for contests in vocal and instrumental music. In its general form and arrangements it was very similar to the theatre; and it is sometimes called θέατρον. There were, however, some characteristic differences: the Odeum was much smaller than the theatre; and it was roofed over, in order to retain the sound. The earliest building of this kind was that erected by Pericles at Athens, for the purpose of celebrating the musical contests at the Panathenaea. Its proximity to the theatre suggested some of the uses made of it, namely, as a refuge for the audience when driven out of the theatre by rain, and also as a place in which the chorus could be prepared. Another Odeum was built at Athens by Herodes Atticus, and was the most magnificent edifice of the sort in the whole empire. The length of its largest diameter was 248 feet, and it is calculated to have furnished accommodation for about 8000 persons. There were also Odea in other Greek towns. The first Odeum, properly so called, at Rome, was built by Domitian, and the second by Trajan. There are ruins of such buildings in the villa of Hadrian at Tivoli, at Pompeii, and at Catana.

OLEA, OLIVA (ἐλαία); OLEUM, OLIVUM (ἔλαιον). The importance of the olive was recognised from the most remote period of antiquity in all civilised countries where the temperature admitted of its cultivation: and it was widely adopted as an emblem of industry and peace. Hence the honour paid to it at Athens, and hence the title of "prima omnium arborum," bestowed upon it by Columella. The fruit (*bacca*) of the olive was for the most part employed for one of two purposes. 1. It was eaten as a fruit, either fresh, pickled, or preserved in various ways. 2. It was pressed so as to yield the oil and other juices which it contained. And again, the oil was employed for a variety of purposes, but chiefly 1. As an article of food. 2. For anointing the body, and in this case was frequently made a vehicle for perfumes (*unguenta*). 3. For burning in lamps.

OLIGARCHIA (ὀλιγαρχία), the government of a few: a term applied to that perversion (παρέκβασις) of an *Aristocratia* into which the latter passed, when, owing to the rise of the *demus* [DEMOCRATIA], and the vanishing of those substantial grounds of pre-eminence which rendered an Aristocratia not unjust, the rule of the dominant portion of the community became the ascendancy of a faction, whose efforts were directed chiefly towards their own aggrandisement. The preservation of power under such circumstances of course depended chiefly upon the possession of superior wealth and the other appliances of wealth which were its concomitants. Thus it came to be regarded as essentially characteristic of an oligarchy, that the main distinction between the dominant faction and the subject portion of the community was the possession of greater wealth on the part of the former. Hence the term *Oligarchia* would not have been applied, if a small section of the community, consisting of poor persons, by any means got the reins of government into their hands.

OLLA (λέβης, χύτρος), a vessel of any material, round and plain, and having a wide mouth; a pot; a jar.

OLYMPIA (Ὀλύμπια), the Olympic games, the greatest of the national festivals of the Greeks. It was celebrated at Olympia in Elis, the name given to a small plain to the west of Pisa, which was bounded on the north and north-east by the mountains Cronius and Olympus, on the south by the river Alpheus, and on the west by the Cladeus, which flows into the Alpheus. Olympia does not appear to have been a town, but rather a collection of temples and public buildings. The origin of the Olympic games is buried in obscurity, but the festival was of very great antiquity. The first historical fact connected with this festival is its revival by Iphitus, king of Elis, who is said to have accomplished it with the assistance of Lycurgus, the Spartan lawgiver, and Cleosthenes of Pisa. The date of this event is given by some writers as B. C. 884, and by others as B.C. 828. The interval of four years between each celebration of the festival was called an Olympiad; but the Olympiads were not employed as a chronological aera till the victory of Coroebus in the foot-race, B. C. 776. [OLYMPIAS.] The most important point in the renewal of the festival by Iphitus was the establishment of the *Ececheiria* (ἐκεχειρία), or sacred armistice. The proclamation was made by peace-heralds (σπονδοφόροι), first in Elis and afterwards in the other parts of Greece; it put a stop to all warfare for the month in which the games were celebrated, and which was called the *sacred month* (ἱερομηνία). The territory of Elis itself was considered especially sacred during the games, and no armed force could enter it without incurring the guilt of sacrilege. The Olympic festival was probably confined at first to the Peloponnesians; but as its celebrity extended, the other Greeks took part in it, till at length it became a festival for the whole nation. No one was allowed to contend in the games but persons of pure Hellenic blood: barbarians might be spectators, but slaves were entirely excluded. After the conquest of Greece by the Romans, the latter were permitted to take part in the games. No women were allowed to be present or even to cross the Alpheus during the celebration of the games, under penalty of being hurled down from the Typaean rock, but women could send chariots to the races. The number of spectators at the festival was very great; and these were drawn together not merely by the desire of seeing the games, but partly through the opportunity it afforded them of carrying on commercial transactions with persons from distant places, as is the case with the Mohammedan festivals at Mecca and Medina. Many of the persons present were also deputies (θεωροί) sent to represent the various states of Greece; and we find that these embassies vied with one another in the number of their offerings, and the splendour of their general appearance, in order to support the honour of their native cities. The Olympic festival was a Pentaëteris (πενταετηρίς), that is, according to the ancient mode of reckoning, a space of four years elapsed between each festival, in the same way as there was only a space of two years between a *Trieteris*. It was celebrated on the first full moon after the summer solstice. It lasted, after all the contests had been introduced, five days, from the 11th to the 15th days of the month inclusive. The fourth day of the festival was the 14th of the month, which was the day of the full moon, and which divided the month into two equal parts. The festival was under the immediate superintendence of the Olympian Zeus, whose temple at Olympia, adorned with the statue of the god made by Phidias, was one of the most splendid works of art in Greece. There were also temples and altars to most of the other gods. The festival itself may be divided into two parts, the games or contests (ἀγὼν Ὀλυμπιακός), and the festive rites (ἑορτή) connected with the sacrifices, with the processions, and with the public banquets in honour of the conquerors.—The contests consisted of various trials of strength and skill, which were increased in number from time to time. There were in all twenty-four contests, eighteen in which men took part, and six in which boys engaged, though they were never all exhibited at one festival, since some were abolished almost immediately after their institution, and others after they had been in use only a short time. We subjoin a list of these from Pausanias, with the date of the introduction of each, commencing from the Olympiad of Coroebus:—1. The foot-race (δρόμος), which was the only contest during the first 13 Olympiads. 2. The δίαυλος, or foot-race, in which the stadium was traversed twice, first introduced in Ol. 14. 3. The δόλιχος, a still longer foot-race than the δίαυλος, introduced in Ol. 15. For a more particular account of the δίαυλος and δόλιχος, see STADIUM. 4. Wrestling (πάλη), and, 5. The Pentathlum (πένταθλον), which consisted of five exercises [PENTATHLUM], both introduced in Ol. 18. 6. Boxing (πυγμή) introduced in Ol. 23. [PUGILATUS.] 7. The chariot-race, with four full-grown horses (ἵππων τελείων δρόμος, ἅρμα), introduced in Ol. 25. 8. The Pancratium (παγκράτιον) [PANCRATIUM], and

9. The horse-race (ἵππος κέλης), both introduced in Ol. 33. 10 and 11. The foot-race and wrestling for boys, both introduced in Ol. 37. 12. The Pentathlum for boys,[1] introduced in Ol. 38., but immediately afterwards abolished. 13. Boxing for boys, introduced in Ol. 41. 14. The foot-race, in which men ran with the equipments of heavy-armed soldiers (τῶν ὁπλιτῶν δρόμος), introduced in Ol. 65., on account of its training men for actual service in war. 15. The chariot-race with mules (ἀπήνη), introduced in Ol. 70.; and 16. The horse-race with mares (κάλπη), introduced in Ol. 71., both of which were abolished in Ol. 84. 17. The chariot-race with two full-grown horses (ἵππων τελείων συνωρίς), introduced in Ol. 93. 18, 19. The contest of heralds (κήρυκες) and trumpeters (σαλπιγκταί), introduced in Ol. 96. 20. The chariot-race with four foals (πώλων ἅρμασιν), introduced in Ol. 99. 21. The chariot-race with two foals (πώλων συνωρίς), introduced in Ol. 128. 22. The horse-race with foals (πῶλος κέλης), introduced in Ol. 131. 23. The Pancratium for boys, introduced in Ol. 145. 24. There was also a horse-race (ἵππος κέλης) in which boys rode, but we do not know the time of its introduction.—The judges in the Olympic Games, called Hellanodicae (Ἑλλανοδίκαι), were appointed by the Eleans, who had the regulation of the whole festival. It appears to have been originally under the superintendence of Pisa, in the neighbourhood of which Olympia was situated, but after the conquest of Peloponnesus by the Dorians on the return of the Heraclidae, the Aetolians, who had been of great assistance to the Heraclidae, settled in Elis, and from this time the Aetolian Eleans obtained the regulation of the festival, and appointed the presiding officers. The Hellanodicae were chosen by lot from the whole body of the Eleans. Their number varied at different periods, but at a later time there were eight Hellanodicae. Their office probably lasted for only one festival. They had to see that all the laws relating to the games were observed by the competitors and others, to determine the prizes, and to give them to the conquerors. An appeal lay from their decision to the Elean senate. Under the direction of the Hellanodicae was a certain number of Alytae (ἀλύται) with an Alytarches (ἀλυτάρχης) at their head, who formed a kind of police, and carried into execution the commands of the Hellanodicae. There were also various other minor officers under the control of the Hellanodicae.—All free Greeks were allowed to contend in the games, who had complied with the rules prescribed to candidates. The equestrian contests were necessarily confined to the wealthy; but the poorest citizens could contend in the athletic games. This, however, was far from degrading the games in public opinion; and some of the noblest as well as meanest citizens of the state took part in these contests. The owners of the chariots and horses were not obliged to contend in person; and the wealthy vied with one another in the number and magnificence of the chariots and horses which they sent to the games. All persons, who were about to contend, had to prove to the Hellanodicae that they were freemen, and of pure Hellenic blood, that they had not been branded with atimia, nor guilty of any sacrilegious act. They further had to prove that they had undergone the preparatory training (προγυμνάσματα) for ten months previous. All competitors were obliged, thirty days before the festival, to undergo certain exercises in the Gymnasium at Elis, under the superintendence of the Hellanodicae. The competitors took their places by lot. The herald then proclaimed the name and country of each competitor. When they were all ready to begin the contest, the judges exhorted them to acquit themselves nobly, and then gave the signal to commence.—The only prize given to the conqueror was a garland of wild olive (κότινος), cut from a sacred olive tree, which grew in the sacred grove of Altis in Olympia. The victor was originally crowned upon a tripod covered over with bronze, but afterwards upon a table made of ivory and gold. Palm branches, the common tokens of victory on other occasions, were placed in his hands. The name of the victor, and that of his father and of his country, were then proclaimed by a herald before the representatives of assembled Greece. The festival ended with processions and sacrifices, and with a public banquet given by the Eleans to the conquerors in the Prytaneium. The most powerful states considered an Olympic victory, gained by one of their citizens, to confer honour upon the state to which he belonged; and a conqueror usually had immunities and privileges conferred upon him by the gratitude of his fellow-citizens. On his return home the victor entered the city in a triumphal procession, in which his praises were celebrated, frequently in the loftiest strains of poetry. [ATHLETAE.] As persons from all parts of the Hellenic world were assembled together at the Olympic Games, it was the best opportunity which the artist and the writer possessed of making their works known. It answered, to some extent, the same purpose as the press does in modern times. Before the invention of printing, the reading of an author's works to as large an assembly

as could be obtained, was one of the easiest and surest modes of publishing them; and this was a favourite practice of the Greeks and Romans. Accordingly we find many instances of literary works thus published at the Olympic festival. Herodotus is said to have read his history at this festival; but though there are some reasons for doubting the correctness of this statement, there are numerous other writers who thus published their works, as the sophist Hippias, Prodicus of Ceos, Anaximenes, the orator Lysias, Dion Chrysostom, &c. It must be borne in mind that these recitations were not contests, and that they formed properly no part of the festival. In the same way painters and other artists exhibited their works at Olympia.

OLYMPĬAS (ὀλυμπιάς), an Olympiad, the most celebrated chronological aera among the Greeks, was the period of four years which elapsed between each celebration of the Olympic Games. The Olympiads began to be reckoned from the victory of Coroebus in the foot-race, which happened in the year B.C. 776. Timaeus of Sicily, however, who flourished B.C. 264, was the first writer who regularly arranged events according to the conquerors in each Olympiad. His practice of recording events by Olympiads was followed by Polybius, Diodorus Siculus, Dionysius of Halicarnassus, &c. The writers who make use of the aera of the Olympiads, usually give the number of the Olympiad (the first corresponding to B.C. 776), and then the name of the conqueror in the foot-race. Some writers also speak of events as happening in the first, second, third, or fourth year, as the case may be, of a certain Olympiad; but others do not give the separate years of each Olympiad. The rules for converting Olympiads into the year B.C., and *vice versa*, are given under CHRONOLOGIA; but as this is troublesome, the student will find at the end of the book a list of the Olympiads, with the years of the Christian aera corresponding to them from the beginning of the Olympiads to A.D. 301. To save space, the separate years of each Olympiad, with the corresponding years B.C., are only given from the 47th to the 126th Olympiad, as this is the most important period of Grecian history; in the other Olympiads the first year only is given. In consulting the table it must be borne in mind that the Olympic Games were celebrated about midsummer, and that the Attic year commenced at about the same time. If, therefore, an event happened in the second half of the Attic year, the year B.C. must be reduced by 1. Thus Socrates was put to death in the 1st year of the 95th Olympiad, which corresponds in the table to B.C. 400; but as his death happened in Thargelion, the 11th month of the Attic year, the year B.C. must be reduced by 1, which gives us B.C. 399, the true date of his death.

OPĀLĬA, a Roman festival in honour of Opis, celebrated on the 19th of December, being the third day of the Saturnalia. It was believed that Opis was the wife of Saturnus, and for this reason the festivals were celebrated at the same time.

OPSŌNĬUM, or OBSŌNĬUM (ὄψον, dim. ὀψάριον; ὄψημα), denoted everything which was eaten with bread, the principal substance of every meal. Those numerous articles of diet called *opsonia* or *pulmentaria* were designed to give nutriment, but still more to add a relish to food. Some of these articles were taken from the vegetable kingdom, but were much more pungent and savoury than bread, such as olives, either fresh or pickled, radishes, and sesamum. Of animal food by much the most common kind was fish, whence the terms under explanation were in the course of time used in a confined and special sense to denote fish only, but fish variously prepared, and more especially salt fish, which was most extensively employed to give a relish to the vegetable diet. The Athenians were in the habit of going to markets (εἰς τοὔψον) themselves in order to purchase their opsonia (ὀψωνεῖν, *opsonare*). But the opulent Romans had a slave, called *opsonator* (ὀψώνης), whose office it was to purchase for his master.

OPTĬO. [CENTURIO.]

OPTĬMĀTES. [NOBILES.]

ŌRĀCŬLUM (μαντεῖον, χρηστήριον) was used by the ancients to designate both the revelations made by the deity to man, as well as the place in which such revelations were made. The deity was in none of these places believed to appear in person to man, and to communicate to him his will or knowledge of the future, but all oracular revelations were made through some kind of medium, which was different in the different places where oracles existed. It may, at first sight, seem strange that there were, comparatively speaking, so few oracles of Zeus, the father and ruler of gods and men. But although, according to the belief of the ancients, Zeus himself was the first source of all oracular revelations, yet he was too far above men to enter with them into any close relation; other gods therefore, especially Apollo, and even heroes, acted as mediators between Zeus and men, and were, as it were, the organs through which he communicated his will. The ancients consulted the will of the gods on all important occasions of public and private life, since they were unwilling to undertake anything of importance without their sanction.—The most celebrated oracle was that of Apollo at Delphi. Its ancient name was Pytho. In the centre of the temple there was a small opening (χάσμα) in the ground, from which, from time to time, an intoxicating smoke arose, which was believed to come from the well of Cassotis, which vanished into the ground close by the sanctuary. Over this chasm there stood a high tripod, on which the Pythia, led into the temple by the prophetes (προφήτης), took her seat whenever the oracle was to be consulted. The smoke rising from under the tripod affected her brain in such a manner that she fell into a state of delirious intoxication, and the sounds which she uttered in this state were believed to contain the revelations of Apollo. These sounds were carefully written down by the prophetes, and afterwards communicated to the persons who had come to consult the oracle. The Pythia (the προφῆτις) was always a native of Delphi, and when she had once entered the service of the god she never left it, and was never allowed to marry. In early times she was always a young girl, but subsequently no one was elected as prophetess who had not attained the age of fifty years. The Delphians, or, more properly speaking, the noble families of Delphi, had the superintendence of the oracle. Among the Delphian aristocracy, however, there were five families which traced their origin to Deucalion, and from each of these one of the five priests, called *Hosioi* (ὅσιοι), was taken. The *Hosioi*, together with the highpriest or prophetes, held their offices for life, and had the control of all the affairs of the sanctuary and of the sacrifices. That these noble families had an immense influence upon the oracle is manifest from numerous instances, and it is not improbable that they were its very soul, and that it was they who dictated the pretended revelations of the god. Most of the oracular answers which are extant are in hexameters, and in the Ionic dialect. Sometimes, however, Doric forms also were used.—No religious institution in all antiquity obtained such a paramount influence in Greece as the oracle of Delphi. When consulted on a subject of a religious nature, the answer was invariably of a kind calculated not only to protect and preserve religious institutions, but to command new ones to be established, so that it was the preserver and promoter of religion throughout the ancient world. Colonies were seldom or never founded without having obtained the advice and the directions of the Delphic god. The Delphic oracle had at all times a leaning in favour of the Greeks of the Doric race,

but the time when it began to lose its influence must be dated from the period when Athens and Sparta entered upon their struggle for the supremacy in Greece; for at this time the partiality for Sparta became so manifest that the Athenians and their party began to lose all reverence and esteem for it, and the oracle became a mere instrument in the hands of a political party. Of the other oracles, the most celebrated were that of Apollo at Didyma, usually called the oracle of the Branchidae, in the territory of Miletus; that of Zeus, at Dodona, where the oracle was given from sounds produced by the wind; that of Zeus Ammon, in an oasis in Libya, not far from the boundaries of Egypt; that of Amphiaraus, between Potniae and Thebes, where the hero was said to have been swallowed up by the earth; and that of Trophonius, at Lebadeia in Boeotia.

ORARIUM was a small handkerchief used for wiping the face, and appears to have been employed for much the same purposes as our pocket-handkerchief. It was made of silk or linen. Aurelian introduced the practice of giving *Oraria* to the Roman people to use *ad favorem*, which appears to mean for the purpose of waving in the public games in token of applause.

ORATOR. The profession of the Roman orator, who with reference to his undertaking a client's case is also called patronus, was quite distinct from that of the Jurisconsultus [JURISCONSULTI], and also from that of the Advocatus, at least in the time of Cicero, and even later. An orator who possessed a competent knowledge of the Jus Civile would, however, have an advantage. Some requisites of oratory, such as voice and gesture, could only be acquired by discipline, whereas a competent knowledge of the law of a case (*juris utilitas*) could be got at any time from the jurisconsulti (*periti*) or from books. Oratory was a serious study among the Romans. Cicero tells us by what painful labour he attained to excellence. Roman oratory reached its perfection in the century which preceded the Christian aera. Its decline dates from the establishment of the Imperial power. The old orators learned their art by constant attendance on some eminent orator and by actual experience of business: the orators of Messala's time were formed in the schools of Rhetoric, and their powers were developed in exercises on fictitious matters. But the immediate causes of the former flourishing condition of eloquence were the political power which oratory conferred on the orator under the Republic, and the party struggles and even the violence that are incident to such a state of society.

ORCHESTRA. [THEATRUM.]
ORCĪNUS SĒNĀTOR. [SENATUS.]
ORDO is applied to any body of men who form a distinct class in the community, either by possessing distinct privileges, pursuing certain trades or professions, or in any other way. Thus the whole body of sacerdotes at Rome is spoken of as an ordo, and separate ecclesiastical corporations are called by the same title. The libertini and scribae also formed separate ordines. The senate and the equites are also spoken of respectively as the ordo senatorius and ordo equestris, but this name is never applied to the plebes. Accordingly we find the expression, *uterque ordo*, used without any further explanation to designate the senatorial and equestrian ordines. The senatorial ordo, as the highest, is sometimes distinguished as *amplissimus ordo*.—The senate in colonies and municipia was called *ordo decurionum* [COLONIA], and sometimes simply *ordo*.—The term ordo is also applied to a company or troop of soldiers, and is used as equivalent to centuria : thus centurions are sometimes called *qui ordines duxerunt*, and the first centuries in a legion *primi ordines*. Even the centurions of the first centuries are occasionally called *primi ordines*.

ORGIA. [MYSTERIA.]

ORGYIA (ὀργυιά), a Greek measure of length, derived from the human body, was the distance from extremity to extremity of the outstretched arms, whence the name, from ὀρέγω. It was equal to 6 feet or to 4 cubits, and was 1-100th of the stadium.

ŎRĪCHALCUM, a metallic compound, akin to copper and bronze, which was highly prized by the ancients. It probably denotes *brass*, with which the ancients became acquainted by fusing zinc ore (*cadmium*, calamine) with copper, although they appear to have had scarcely any knowledge of zinc as a metal. The word is derived from ὄρος and χαλκός, that is, *mountain-bronze*.

OSCHŎPHŎRIA (ὠσχοφόρια, ὀσχοφόρια), an Attic festival, which, according to some writers, was celebrated in honour of Athena and Dionysus, and according to others in honour of Dionysus and Ariadne. It is said to have been instituted by Theseus. It was a vintage festival, and its name is derived from ὦσχος, ὄσχος, or ὄσχη, a branch of vines with grapes.

OSCILLUM, a diminutive through *osculum* from *os*, meaning "a little face," was the term applied to faces or heads of Bacchus, which were suspended in the vineyards to be turned in every direction by the wind. Whichsoever way they looked, they were supposed to make the vines in that quarter fruitful. The first cut represents the countenance of Bacchus with a beautiful, mild, and propitious expression. The other cut repre-

Oscillum. (From a Marble in the British Museum.)

sents a tree with four oscilla hung upon its branches. A syrinx and a pedum are placed at the root of the tree.

Oscillum. (From an ancient Gem.)

OSTĬĀRĬUM, a tax upon the doors of houses, which appears to have been sometimes levied in the provinces. There was a similar tax, called *columnarium*, imposed upon every pillar that supported a house.

OSTĬUM. [JANUA.]

ŎVĀTĬO, a lesser triumph. The circumstances by which it was distinguished from the more imposing solemnity [TRIUMPHUS] were the following :—The general did not enter the city in a chariot drawn by four horses, but on foot ; he was not arrayed in the gorgeous gold embroidered robe, but in the simple toga praetexta of a magistrate ; his brows were encircled with a wreath, not of laurel but of myrtle ; he bore no sceptre in his hand ; the procession was not heralded by trumpets, headed by the senate, and thronged with victorious troops, but was enlivened by a crowd of flute players, attended chiefly by knights and plebeians, frequently without soldiers : the ceremonies were concluded by the sacrifice, not of a bull but of a sheep. The word *ovatio* seems clearly to be derived from the kind of victim offered. An ovation was granted when the advantage gained, although considerable, was not sufficient to constitute a legitimate claim to the higher distinction of a triumph, or when the victory had been achieved with little bloodshed; or when hostilities had not been regularly proclaimed; or when the war had not been completely terminated; or when the contest had been carried on against base and unworthy foes; and hence when the servile bands of Athenion and Spartacus were destroyed by Perperna and Crassus, these leaders celebrated ovations only.

OVILE. [COMITIA.]

PAEAN (παιήων, παιάν, παιών), a hymn or song, which was originally sung in honour of Apollo. It was always of a joyous nature, and its tune and sounds expressed hope and confidence. It was a song of thanksgiving, when danger was passed, and also a hymn to propitiate the god. It was sung at the solemn festivals of Apollo, and especially at the Hyacinthia. The paean was also sung as a battle-song, both before an attack on the enemy and after the battle was finished. It is certain that the paean was in later times sung to the honour of other gods besides Apollo. Thus Xenophon relates that the Greek army in Asia sung a paean to Zeus.

PAEDAGOGUS (παιδαγωγός), a tutor. The office of tutor in a Grecian family of rank and opulence was assigned to one of the most trustworthy of the slaves. The sons of his master were committed to his care on attaining their sixth or seventh year, their previous education having been conducted by females. They remained with the tutor until they attained the age of puberty. His duty was rather to guard them from evil, both physical and moral, than to communicate instruction. He went with them to and from the school or the GYMNASIUM; he accompanied them out of doors on all occasions; he was responsible for their personal safety, and for their avoidance of bad company. In the Roman empire the name *paedagogi* or *paedagogia* was given to beautiful young slaves, who discharged in the imperial palace the duties of the modern *page*, which is in fact a corruption of the ancient name.

PAEDONOMUS (παιδονόμος), a magistrate at Sparta, who had the general superintendence of the education of the boys.

PAENULA, a thick cloak, chiefly used by the Romans in travelling, instead of the toga, as a protection against the cold and rain. It appears to have had no sleeves, and only an opening for the head, as shown in the following figure.

Paenula, travelling cloak. (From Bartholini.)

PAGANALIA. [PAGI.]
PAGANI. [PAGI.]
PAGI were fortified places in the neighbourhood of Rome, to which the country-people might retreat in case of a hostile inroad. Each of the country tribes is said to have been divided by Numa into a certain number of pagi; which name was given to the country adjoining the fortified village, as well as to the village itself. There was a magistrate at the head of each pagus, who kept a register of the names and of the property of all persons in the pagus, raised the taxes, and summoned the people, when necessary, to war. Each pagus had its own sacred rites, and an annual festival called *Paganalia*. The *pagani*, or inhabitants of the pagi, had their regular meetings, at which they passed resolutions. The division of the country-people into pagi continued to the latest times of the Roman empire. The term Pagani is often used in opposition to milites, and is applied to all who were not soldiers, even though they did not live in the country. The Christian writers gave the name of pagani to those persons who adhered to the old Roman religion, because the latter continued to be generally believed by the country-people, after Christianity became the prevailing religion of the inhabitants of the towns.

PALAESTRA (παλαίστρα), properly means

a place for wrestling (παλαίειν, πάλη), and appears to have originally formed a part of the gymnasium. At Athens, however, there was a considerable number of palaestrae, quite distinct from the gymnasia. It appears most probable that the palaestrae were chiefly appropriated to the exercises of wrestling and of the pancratium, and were principally intended for the athletae, who, it must be recollected, were persons that contended in the public games, and therefore needed special training. The Romans had originally no places corresponding to the Greek gymnasia and palaestrae; and when towards the close of the republic wealthy Romans, in imitation of the Greeks, began to build places for exercise in their villas, they called them indifferently gymnasia and palaestrae.

PĀLĪLIA, a festival celebrated at Rome every year on the 21st of April, in honour of Pales, the tutelary divinity of shepherds. The 21st of April was the day on which, according to the early traditions of Rome, Romulus had commenced the building of the city, so that the festival was at the same time solemnised as the dies natalitius of Rome. It was originally a shepherd-festival, and continued to be so among country people till the latest times, but in the city it lost its original character, and was only regarded as the dies natalitius of Rome. The first part of the solemnities was a public purification by fire and smoke. The things burnt in order to produce this purifying smoke were the blood of the *October-horse*, the ashes of the calves sacrificed at the festival of Ceres, and the shells of beans. The people were also sprinkled with water, they washed their hands in spring-water, and drank milk mixed with must. As regards the *October-horse* (*equus October*) it must be observed that in early times no bloody sacrifice was allowed to be offered at the palilia, and the blood of the October-horse mentioned above, was the blood which had dropped from the tail of the horse sacrificed in the month of October to Mars in the Campus Martius. This blood was preserved by the vestal virgins in the temple of Vesta for the purpose of being used at the palilia. The sacrifices consisted of cakes, millet, milk, and other kinds of eatables. The shepherds then offered a prayer to Pales. After these solemn rites were over, the cheerful part of the festival began: bonfires were made of heaps of hay and straw, and the festival was concluded by a feast in the open air, at which the people sat or lay upon benches of turf, and drank plentifully.

PALLIUM, dim. PALLIŎLUM, poet. PALLA (ἱμάτιον, dim. ἱματίδιον; Ion. and poet. φᾶρος), an outer garment. The English *cloak*, though commonly adopted as the translation of these terms, conveys no accurate conception of the form, material, or use of that which they denoted. The article designated by them was always a rectangular piece of cloth, exactly, or at least nearly square. It was indeed used in the very form in which it was taken from the loom, being made entirely by the weaver, without any aid from the tailor, except to repair the injuries which it sustained by time. Whatever additional richness and beauty it received from the art of the dyer, was bestowed upon it before its materials were woven into cloth or even spun into thread. Most commonly it was used without having undergone any process of this kind. The raw material, such as wool, flax, or cotton, was manufactured in its natural state, and hence pallia were commonly white, although from the same cause brown, drab, and grey were also prevailing colours. As the pallium was the most common outer garment, we find it continually mentioned in conjunction with the tunica, which constituted the indutus. Such phrases as "coat and waistcoat," or "shoes and stockings," are not more common with us than the following expressions, which constantly occur in ancient authors: *tunica palliumque*, ἱμάτιον καὶ χιτών, τὸ ἱμάτιον καὶ ὁ χιτωνίσκος, φᾶρος ἠδὲ χιτών, &c. To wear the pallium without

Pallium. (Museo Pio-Clement., vol. i. tav. 48.)

the underclothing indicated poverty or severity of manners, as in the case of Socrates. One of the most common modes of wearing the pallium was to fasten it with a brooch over the right shoulder, leaving the right arm at liberty, and to pass the middle of it either under the left arm so as to leave that arm at liberty also, or over the left shoulder so as to cover the left arm. The figure in the preceding cut is attired in the last-mentioned fashion.

PALMA. [PES.]

PALMIPES, a Roman measure of length, equal to a foot and a palm.

PALMUS, properly the width of the open hand, or, more exactly, of the four fingers, was used by the Romans for two different measures of length, namely, as the translation of the Greek παλαιστή, or δῶρον in old Greek, and σπιθαμή respectively. In the former sense it is equal to 4 digits, or 3 inches, or 1-4th of a foot, or 1-6th of the cubit. The larger palm of 9 inches only occurs in later Roman writers. From this large *palmus* the modern Roman *palmo* is derived.

PALUDAMENTUM, the cloak worn by a Roman general commanding an army, his principal officers and personal attendants, in contradistinction to the *sagum* of the common soldiers, and the *toga* or garb of peace. It was the practice for a Roman magistrate, after he had received the *imperium* from the comitia curiata and offered up his vows in the Capitol, to march out of the city arrayed in the paludamentum (*exire paludatus*, attended by his lictors in similar attire (*paludatis lictoribus*), nor could he again enter the gates until he had formally divested himself of this emblem of military power. The paludamentum was open in front, reached down to the knees or a little lower, and hung loosely over the shoulders, being fastened across the chest by a clasp. The colour of the paludamentum was commonly white or purple, and hence it was marked and remembered that Crassus on the morning of the fatal battle of Carrhae went forth in a dark-coloured mantle. In the cut below, representing the head of a warrior, we see the paludamentum flying back in the charge, and the clasp nearly in front.

Paludamentum, Military Cloak. (From a Mosaic at Pompeii.)

Paludamentum, Military Cloak. (Statue of a Roman Emperor.)

PAMBOEOTIA (παμβοιώτια), a festive panegyris of all the Boeotians, like the Panathenaea of the Atticans, and the Panionia of the Ionians. The principal object of the meeting was the common worship of Athena Itonia, who had a temple in the neighbourhood of Coronea, near which the panegyris was held.

PANATHENAEA (παναθήναια), the greatest and most splendid of the festivals celebrated in Attica in honour of Athena, in the character of Athena Polias, or the protectress of the city. It was said to have been instituted by Erichthonius, and its original name, down to the time of Theseus, was believed to have been Athenaea; but when Theseus united all the Atticans into one body, this festival, which then became the common festival of all the Attic tribes, was called Panathenaea. There were two kinds of Panathenaea, the greater and the lesser; the former were held every fourth year (πενταετηρίς), the latter every year. The lesser Panathenaea were probably celebrated on the 17th of the month

Hecatombaeon; the great Panathenaea in the third year of every Olympiad, and probably commenced on the same day as the lesser Panathenaea. The principal difference between the two festivals was, that the greater one was more solemn, and that on this occasion the peplus of Athena was carried to her temple in a most magnificent procession, which was not held at the lesser Panathenaea. The solemnities, games, and amusements of the Panathenaea were, rich sacrifices of bulls, foot, horse, and chariot races, gymnastic and musical contests, and the lampadephoria; rhapsodists recited the poems of Homer and other epic poets, philosophers disputed, cock-fights were exhibited, and the people indulged in a variety of other amusements and entertainments. The prize in these contests was a vase filled with oil from the ancient and sacred olive tree of Athena on the Acropolis. A great many of such vases, called Panathenaic vases, have in late years been found in Etruria, southern Italy, Sicily, and Greece. They represent on one side the figure of Athena, and on the other the various contests and games in which these vases were given as prizes to the victors. Of the discussions of philosophers and orators at the Panathenaea we still possess two specimens, the λόγος Παναθηναικός of Isocrates, and that of Aristeides. Herodotus is said to have recited his history to the Athenians at the Panathenaea. The management of the games and contests was entrusted to persons called *Athlothetae* (ἀθλοθέται), whose number was ten, one being taken from every tribe. Their office lasted from one great Panathenaic festival to the other. The chief solemnity of the great Panathenaea was the magnificent procession to the temple of Athena Polias, which probably took place on the last day of the festive season. The whole of the procession is represented in the frieze of the Parthenon, the work of Phidias and his disciples, now deposited in the British Museum. The chief object of the procession was to carry the peplus of the goddess to her temple. This peplus was a crocus-coloured garment for the goddess, and made by maidens, called ἐργαστῖναι. In it were woven Enceladus and the giants, as they were conquered by the goddess. The peplus was not carried to the temple by men, but suspended from the mast of a ship. The procession proceeded from the Ceramicus, near a monument called Leocorium, to the temple of Demeter at Eleusis, and thence along the Pelasgic wall and the temple of Apollo Pythius to the Pnyx, and thence to the Acropolis, where the statue of Minerva Polias was adorned with the peplus. In this procession nearly the whole population of Attica appears to have taken part, either on foot, on horseback, or in chariots, as may be seen in the frieze of the Parthenon. Aged men carried olive branches, and were called *Thallophori* (θαλλοφόροι); young men attended, at least in earlier times, in armour, and maidens who belonged to the noblest families of Athens carried baskets, containing offerings for the goddess, whence they were called *Canephori* (κανηφόροι). Respecting the part which aliens took in this procession, and the duties they had to perform, see HYDRIAPHORIA. Men who had deserved well of the republic were rewarded with a gold crown at the great Panathenaea, and the herald had to announce the event during the gymnastic contests.

PANCRATIUM (παγκράτιον), is derived from πᾶν and κράτος, and accordingly signifies an athletic game, in which all the powers of the fighter were called into action. The pancratium was one of the games or gymnastic contests which were exhibited at all the great festivals of Greece; it consisted of boxing and wrestling (πυγμή and πάλη), and was reckoned to be one of the heavy or hard exercises (ἀγωνίσματα βαρέα or βαρύτερα), on account of the violent exertions it required, and for this reason it was not much practised in the gymnasia. In Homer we find neither the game nor the name of the pancratium mentioned, and as it was not introduced at the Olympic games until Ol. 33, we may presume that the game, though it may have existed long before in a rude state, was not brought to any degree of perfection until a short time before that event. The name of the combatants was *Pancratiastae* (παγκρατιασταί) or *Pammachi* (πάμμαχοι). They fought naked, and had their bodies anointed and covered with sand, by which they were enabled to take hold of one another. When the contest began, each of the fighters might

Pancratiastae. (Krause, Gymnastik und Agonistik der Hellen., tav. 21.)

commence by boxing or by wrestling, accordingly as he thought he should be more successful in the one than in the other. The victory was not decided until one of the parties was killed, or lifted up a finger, thereby declaring that he was unable to continue the contest either from pain or fatigue.

PĀNĒGȲRIS (πανήγυρις), signifies a meeting or assembly of a whole people for the purpose of worshipping at a common sanctuary. The word is used in three significations:—1. For a meeting of the inhabitants of one particular town and its vicinity; 2. For a meeting of the inhabitants of a whole district, a province, or of the whole body of people belonging to a particular tribe [DELIA; PANIONIA]; and 3. For great national meetings, as the Olympic, Pythian, Isthmian, and Nemean games. Although in all panegyreis which we know, the religious character forms the most prominent feature, other subjects, political discussions and resolutions, as well as a variety of amusements, were not excluded, though they were perhaps more a consequence of the presence of many persons than objects of the meeting. Every panegyris, moreover, was made by tradespeople a source of gain, and it may be presumed that such a meeting was never held without a fair, at which all sorts of things were exhibited for sale.

PĀNIŌNĪA (πανιώνια), the great national panegyris of the Ionians on mount Mycalé, where the national god Poseidon Helicouius had his sanctuary called the Panionium. One of the principal objects of this national meeting was the common worship of Poseidon, to whom splendid sacrifices were offered on the occasion. But religious worship was not the only object for which they assembled at the Panionium; on certain emergencies, especially in case of any danger threatening their country, the Ionians discussed at their meetings political questions, and passed resolutions which were binding upon all.

PĀNOPLĪA (πανοπλία), a panoply or suit of armour. The articles of which it consisted both in the Greek and in the Roman army, are enumerated under ARMA.

PANTŌMĪMUS, the name of a kind of actors peculiar to the Romans, who very nearly resembled in their mode of acting the modern dancers in the ballet. They did not speak on the stage, but merely acted by gestures, movements, and attitudes. All movements, however, were rhythmical like those in the ballet, whence the general term for them is saltatio, saltare; the whole art was called musica muta; and to represent Niobe or Leda was expressed by saltare Nioben and saltare Ledam. During the time of the republic the name pantomimus does not occur, though the art itself was known to the Romans at an early period; for the first histriones said to have been introduced from Etruria were in fact nothing but pantomimic dancers [HISTRIO], whence we find that under the empire the names histrio and pantomimus were used as synonymous. The pantomimic art, however, was not carried to any degree of perfection until the time of Augustus. The greatest pantomimes of this time were Bathyllus, a freedman and favourite of Maecenas, and Pylades and Hylas. Mythological love-stories were from the first the favourite subjects of the pantomimes, which were disgraced by the most licentious scenes. In Sicily pantomimic dances were called ballismi (βαλλισμοί), whence perhaps the modern words ball and ballet.

PAPȲRUS. [LIBER.]

PĀRĀDĪSUS (παράδεισος), the name given by the Greeks to the parks or pleasure-grounds, which surrounded the country residences of the Persian kings and satraps. They were generally stocked with animals for the chase, were full of all kinds of trees, watered by numerous streams, and enclosed with walls.

PĀRĀGRĂPHĒ (παραγραφή). This word does not exactly correspond with any term in our language, but may without much impropriety be called a plea. It is an objection raised by the defendant to the admissibility of the plaintiff's action. The paragraphé, like every other answer (ἀντιγραφή) made by the defendant to the plaintiff's charge, was given in writing; as the word itself implies. If the defendant merely denied the plaintiff's allegations, a court was at once held for the trial of the cause. If, however, he put in a paragraphé, a court was to be held to try the preliminary question, whether the cause could be brought into court or not. Upon this previous trial the defendant was considered the actor. If he succeeded, the whole cause was at an end; unless the objection was only to the form of action, or some other such technicality, in which case it might be recommenced in the proper manner. If, however, the plaintiff succeeded, the original action, which in the mean time had been suspended, was proceeded with.

PĀRĂLUS (πάραλος), and SĂLĂMĪNĪA (σαλαμινία). The Athenians from very early times kept for public purposes two sacred or state vessels, the one of which was called Paralus and the other Salaminia : the crew of the one bore the name of πάραλιται or πάραλοι, and that of the other σαλαμίνιοι. The Salaminia was also called Δηλία or Θεωρίς, because it was used to convey the θεωροί to Delos, or which occasion the ship was adorned with garlands by the priest of Apollo. Both these vessels were quick-sailing triremes, and were used for a variety of state purposes: they conveyed theories, despatches, &c. from Athens, carried treasures from subject countries to Athens, fetched state criminals from foreign parts to Athens, and the like. In battles they were frequently used as the ships in which the admirals sailed. These vessels and their crews were always kept in readiness to act, in case of any necessity arising; and the crew, although they could not for the greater part of the year be in actual service, received their regular pay of four oboli per day all the year round. The names of the two ships seem to point to a very early period of the history of Attica, when there was no navigation except between Attica and Salamis, for which the Salaminia was used, and around the coast of Attica, for which purpose the Paralus was destined. In later times the names were retained, although the destination of the ships was principally to serve the purposes of religion, whence they are frequently called the sacred ships.

PĂRĂNOIAS GRĂPHĒ (παρανοίας γραφή). This proceeding may be compared to our commission of lunacy, or writ *de lunatico inquirendo*. It was a suit at Athens that might be instituted by a son or other relation against one who, by reason of madness or mental imbecility, had become incapable of managing his own affairs. If the complaint was well grounded, the court decreed that the next heir should take possession of the lunatic's property, and probably also made some provision for his being put in confinement, or under proper care and guardianship. The celebrated tale of Iophon, the son of Sophocles, accusing his father of lunacy, is related in the life of Sophocles in the *Classical Dictionary*.

PĂRĂNŎMŎN GRĂPHĒ (παρανόμων γραφή), an indictment at Athens for propounding an illegal, or rather unconstitutional measure or law. In order to check rash and hasty legislation, the mover of any law or decree, though he succeeded in causing it to be passed, was still amenable to criminal justice, if his enactment was found to be inconsistent with other laws that remained in force, or with the public interest. Any person might institute against him the γραφὴ παρανόμων within a year from the passing of the law. If he was convicted, not only did the law become void, but any punishment might be inflicted on him, at the discretion of the judges before whom he was tried. A person thrice so convicted lost the right of proposing laws in future. The cognizance of the cause belonged to the Thesmothetae.

PĂRĂPRESBEIA (παραπρεσβεία), signifies any corrupt conduct, misfeasance, or neglect of duty on the part of an ambassador; for which he was liable to be called to account and prosecuted on his return home. Demosthenes accused Aeschines of *Parapresbeia* on account of his conduct in the embassy to Philip.

PĂRĂPHERNA. [Dos.]

PĂRĂSANGA (ὁ παρασάγγης), a Persian measure of length, frequently mentioned by the Greek writers. It is still used by the Persians, who call it *ferseng*. According to Herodotus the parasang was equal to 30 Greek stadia. Xenophon must also have calculated it at the same, as he says that 16,050 stadia are equal to 535 parasangs. (16,050 ÷ 535 = 30.) Other ancient writers give a different length for the parasang. Modern English travellers estimate it variously at from 3½ to 4 English miles, which nearly agrees with the calculation of Herodotus.

PĂRĂSĪTI (παράσιτοι) properly denotes persons who dine with others. In the early history of Greece the name had a very different meaning, being given to distinguished persons, who were appointed as assistants to certain priests and to the highest magistrates. Their services appear to have been rewarded with a third of the victims sacrificed to their respective gods. Such officers existed down to a late period of Greek history. Solon in his legislation called the act of giving public meals to certain magistrates and foreign ambassadors in the prytaneum παρασιτεῖν, and it may be that the parasites were connected with this institution. The class of persons whom we call parasites was very numerous in ancient Greece, and appears to have existed from early times. The characteristic features common to all parasites are importunity, love of sensual pleasures, and above all the desire of getting a good dinner without paying for it. During the time of the Roman emperors a parasite seems to have been a constant guest at the tables of the wealthy.

PĂRĔDRI (πάρεδροι). Each of the three superior archons was at liberty to have two assessors (πάρεδροι) chosen by himself, to assist him by advice and otherwise in the performance of his various duties. The assessor, like the magistrate himself, had to undergo a *docimasia* (δοκιμασία) in the Senate of Five Hundred and before a judicial tribunal, before he could be permitted to enter upon his labours. He was also to render an account (εὔθυνη) at the end of the year. The duties of the archons, magisterial and judicial, were so numerous, that one of the principal objects of having assessors must have been to enable them to get through their business. From the *paredri* of the archons we must distinguish those who assisted the *euthyni* in examining and auditing magistrates' accounts.

PARENTĀLĬA. [FUNUS.]
PARIES. [DOMUS.]
PARMA, *dim.* PARMŬLA, a round shield, three feet in diameter, carried by the *velites* in the Roman army. Though small, com-

Parma. (From the Columna Trajana.)

pared with the CLIPEUS, it was so strongly made as to be a very effectual protection. This was probably owing to the use of iron in its frame-work. The parma was also worn by the cavalry. We find the term *parma* often applied to the target [CETRA], which was also a small round shield, and therefore very similar to the parma.

PAROCHI, certain people paid by the state to supply the Roman magistrates, ambassadors, and other official persons, when travelling, with those necessaries which they could not conveniently carry with them. They existed on all the principal stations on the Roman roads in Italy and the provinces, where persons were accustomed to pass the night. Of the things which the parochi were bound to supply, hay, fire-wood, salt, and a certain number of beds appear to have been the most important.

PAROPSIS (παροψίς), any food eaten with the ὄψον, as the μᾶζα, a kind of frumenty or soft cake, broth, or any kind of condiment or sauce. It was, likewise, the name of the dish or plate, on which such food was served up, and it is in this latter signification that the Roman writers use the word.

PARRĬCĪDA, PARRĬCĪDĬUM. A parricida signified originally a murderer generally, and is hence defined to be a person who kills another *dolo malo*. It afterwards signified the murderer of a parent, and by an ancient law such a parricide was sewed up in a sack (*culleus*), and thrown into a river. A law of the dictator Sulla contained some provisions against parricide, and probably fixed the same punishment for the parricide, as the Lex Pompeia de Parricidiis, passed in the time of Cn. Pompeius. This law extended the crime of parricide to the killing of a brother, sister, uncle, aunt, and many other relations, and enacted that he who killed a father or mother, grandfather or grandmother, should be punished (*more majorum*) by being whipped till he bled, sewed up in a sack with a dog, cock, viper, and ape, and thrown into the sea. Other parricides were simply put to death.

PASSUS, a measure of length, which consisted of five Roman feet. [PES.] The passus was not the step, or distance from heel to heel, when the feet were at their utmost ordinary extension, but the distance from the point which the heel leaves to that in which it is set down. The *mille passuum*, or thousand paces, was the common name of the Roman mile. [MILLIARE.]

PATER FAMILIAE. [FAMILIA; MATRIMONIUM.]

PATER PATRĀTUS. [FETIALES.]

PATĒRA, *dim.* PATELLA (φιάλη), a round plate or dish. The paterae of the most common kind were small plates of the

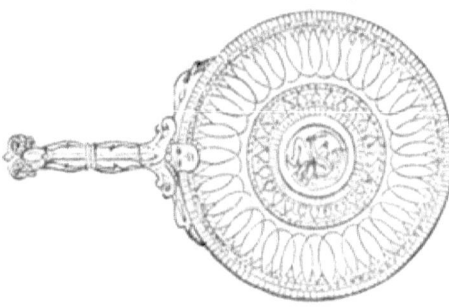

Patera. (From Pompeii.)

common red earthenware, on which an ornamental pattern was drawn, and which were sometimes entirely black. The more valuable paterae were metallic, being chiefly of bronze; but every family, raised above poverty, possessed one of silver, together with a silver salt-cellar. The accompanying cut exhibits a highly ornamented patera, made of bronze. The view of the upper surface is accompanied by a side-view, showing the form and depth of the vessel.

PĂTĬBŬLUM. [FURCA.]

PĂTĬNA (λεκάνη), a basin or bowl of earthenware, rarely of bronze or silver. The patina was of a form intermediate between the *patera* and the *olla*, not so flat as the former, nor so deep as the latter. The most frequent use of the *patina* was in cookery.

PATRES. [PATRICII.]

PĂTRĬA POTESTAS. Potestas signifies generally a power or faculty of any kind by which we do anything. "Potestas," says Paulus, a Roman jurist, "has several significations: when applied to magistrates, it is Imperium; in the case of children, it is the patria potestas; in the case of slaves, it is Dominium." According to Paulus then, potestas, as applied to magistrates, is equivalent to imperium. Thus we find potestas associated with the adjectives praetoria, consularis. But potestas is applied to magistrates who had not the imperium, as for instance to quaestors and tribuni plebis; and potestas and imperium are often opposed in Cicero. [IMPERIUM.] Thus it seems that this word potestas, like many other Roman terms, had both a wider signification and a narrower one. In its wider signification it might mean all the power that was delegated to any person by the state, whatever might be the extent of that power. In its narrower significations, it was on the one hand equivalent to imperium; and on the other, it expressed the power of those functionaries who had not the imperium. Sometimes it was used to express a magistratus, as a person; and hence in the Italian language the word podestà signifies a magistrate. Potestas is also one of the words by which is expressed the power that one private person has over another, the other two being manus and mancipium. The potestas is either dominica, that is, ownership as exhibited in the relation of master and slave [SERVUS]; or patria as exhibited in the relation of father and child. The mancipium was framed after the analogy of the potestas dominica. [MANCIPIUM.] Patria potestas then signifies the power which a Roman father had over the persons of his children, grandchildren, and other descendants (*filiisfamilias*, *filiae-*

familias), and generally all the rights which he had by virtue of his paternity. The foundation of the patria potestas was a legal marriage, and the birth of a child gave it full effect. [MATRIMONIUM.] It does not seem that the patria potestas was ever viewed among the Romans as absolutely equivalent to the dominica potestas, or as involving ownership of the child; and yet the original notion of the patria came very near to that of the dominica potestas. Originally the father had the power of life and death over his son as a member of his familia; and he could sell him, and so bring him into the mancipii causa. He could also give his daughter in marriage, or give a wife to his son, divorce his child, give him in adoption, and emancipate him at his pleasure.

PATRICII. This word is evidently a derivative from *pater*, which frequently occurs in the Roman writers as equivalent to senator. *Patricii* therefore signifies those who belonged to the *patres*, but it is a mistake to suppose that the patricii were only the offspring of the patres in the sense of senators. On the contrary, the patricians were, in the early history of Rome, the whole body of Roman citizens, the *populus Romanus*, and there were no real citizens besides them. The other parts of the Roman population, namely clients and slaves, did not belong to the populus Romanus, and were not burghers or patricians. The senators or patres (in the narrower sense of the word) were a select body of the populus or patricians, which acted as their representatives. The burghers or patricians consisted originally of three distinct tribes, which afterwards became united into the sovereign populus. These tribes had founded settlements upon several of the hills which were subsequently included within the precincts of the city of Rome. Their names were Ramnes, Tities, and Luceres, or Ramnenses, Titienses, and Lucerenses. Each of these tribes consisted of ten curiae, and each curia of ten gentes, and of the same number of decuries, which were established for representative and military purposes. [SENATUS.] The first tribe, or the Ramnes, were a Latin colony on the Palatine hill, said to have been founded by Romulus. As long as it stood alone, it contained only one hundred gentes, and had a senate of one hundred members. When the Tities, or Sabine settlers on the Quirinal and Viminal hills, under king Tatius, became united with the Ramnes, the number of gentes, as well as that of senators, was increased to 200. These two tribes after their union continued probably for a considerable time to be the patricians of Rome, until the third tribe, the Luceres, which chiefly consisted of Etruscans, who had settled on the Caelian hill, also became united with the other two as a third tribe. The amalgamation of these three tribes did not take place at once : the union between Latins and Sabines is ascribed to the reign of Romulus, though it does not appear to have been quite perfect, since the Latins on some occasions claimed a superiority over the Sabines. The Luceres existed for a long time as a separate tribe without enjoying the same rights as the two other tribes, until Tarquinius Priscus, himself an Etruscan, caused them to be placed on a footing of equality with the others. For this reason he is said to have increased the number of senators to 300. The Luceres, however, are, notwithstanding this equalisation, sometimes distinguished from the other tribes by the name *patres* or *patricii minorum gentium*. During the time of the republic, distinguished strangers and wealthy plebeians were occasionally made Roman patricians ; for instance, Appius Claudius and his gens, and Domitius Ahenobarbus. When the plebeians became a distinct class of citizens [PLEBES], the patricians, of course, ceased to be the only class of citizens, but they still retained the exclusive possession of all the power in the state. All civil and religious offices were in their possession, and they continued as before to be the populus, the nation now consisting of the populus and the plebes. In their relation to the plebeians or the commonalty, the patricians were a real aristocracy of birth. A person born of a patrician family was and remained a patrician, whether he was rich or poor, whether he was a member of the senate, or an eques, or held any of the great offices of the state, or not : there was no power that could make a patrician a plebeian. As regards the census, he might indeed not belong to the wealthy classes, but his rank remained the same. The only way in which a patrician might become a plebeian was when of his own accord he left his gens and curia, gave up the sacra, &c. A plebeian, on the other hand, or even a stranger, might be made a patrician by a lex curiata. But this appears to have been done very seldom ; and the consequence was, that in the course of a few centuries the number of patrician families became so rapidly diminished, that towards the close of the republic there were not more than fifty such families. Although the patricians throughout this whole period had the character of an aristocracy of birth, yet their political rights were not the same at all times. During the first centuries of the republic there was an almost uninterrupted struggle between patricians and plebeians, in which the former exerted every means to retain their exclusive rights, but which ended in the establishment of the political equality of the two orders. [PLEBES.] Only a few insignificant priestly offices, and the performance of certain ancient religious rites and ceremonies, remained the exclusive privilege of the patricians ; of which they were the prouder, as in former days their religious power and significance were the basis of their political superiority. At the time when the struggle between patricians and plebeians ceased, a new kind of aristocracy began to arise at Rome, which was partly based upon wealth, and partly upon the great offices of the republic, and the term nobiles was given to all persons whose ancestors had held any of the curule offices. (Compare NOBILES.) This aristocracy of nobiles threw the old patricians as a body still more into the shade, though both classes of aristocrats united as far as was possible to monopolise all the great offices of the state. In their dress and appearance the patricians were scarcely distinguished from the rest of the citizens, unless they were senators, curule magistrates, or equites, in which case they wore like others the ensigns peculiar to these classes. The only thing by which they seem to have been distinguished in their appearance from other citizens was a peculiar kind of shoe, which covered the whole foot and part of the leg, though it was not as high as the shoes of senators and curule magistrates. These shoes were fastened with four strings (*corrigiae* or *lora patricia*) and adorned with a lunula on the top.

PĀTRĪMI ET MĀTRĪMI were children born of parents, who had been married by the religious ceremony called confarreatio: they are almost always mentioned in connection with religious rites and ceremonies.

PĀTRŎNŎMI (πατρονόμοι), magistrates at Sparta, who exercised, as it were, a paternal power over the whole state. They did not exist till a late period, and they succeeded to the powers which the ephori formerly possessed.

PĀTRŌNUS. The act of manumission created a new relation between the manumissor and the slave, which was analogous to that between father and son. The manumissor became with respect to the manumitted person his patronus, and the manumitted person became the libertus of the manumissor. The word patronus (from pater) indicates the nature of the relation. If the manumissor was a woman, she became patrona. The libertus adopted the gentile name of the manumissor. Cicero's freedman Tiro was called M. Tullius Tiro. The libertus owed respect and gratitude to his patron, and in ancient times the patron might punish him in a summary way for neglecting those duties. This obligation extended to the children of the libertus, and the duty was due to the children of the patron. It was the duty of the patron to support his freedman in case of necessity, and if he did not, he lost his patronal rights; the consequence was the same if he brought a capital charge against him. The most important of the patronal rights related to the property of liberti, as in certain cases the patronus had a right to the whole or a part of the property of a libertus.

PAUPĔRIES, the legal term for mischief done by an animal (*quadrupes*) contrary to the nature of the animal, as if a man's ox gored another man. In such cases the law of the Twelve Tables gave the injured person an action against the owner of the animal for the amount of the damage sustained. The owner was bound either to pay the full amount of damages or to give up the animal to the injured person (*noxae dare*).

PĂVĪMENTUM. [DOMUS, p. 144, *b*.]

PECTEN (κτείς), a comb. The Greeks and Romans used combs made of box-wood. The Egyptians had ivory combs, which also came into use by degrees among the Romans. The wooden combs, found in Egyptian tombs, are toothed on one side only; but the Greeks used them with teeth on both sides. The principal use of the comb was for dressing the hair, in doing which the Greeks of both sexes were remarkably careful and diligent. To go with uncombed hair was a sign of affliction.

PECŬLĀTUS, is properly the misappropriation or theft of public property. The person guilty of this offence was *peculator*. The origin of the word appears to be *pecus*, a term which originally denoted that kind of moveable property which was the chief sign of wealth. Originally trials for *peculatus* were before the populus or the senate. In the time of Cicero matters of *peculatus* had become one of the quaestiones perpetuae.

PĔCŪLIUM. [SERVUS.]
PĔCŪNIA. [AES; ARGENTUM; AURUM.]
PĒDĀRII. [SENATUS.]
PĒDĬSĔQUI, a class of slaves, whose duty was to follow their master when he went out of his house. There was a similar class of female slaves, called *Pedisequae*.

PĒDUM (κορώνη), a shepherd's crook. On account of its connection with pastoral life, the crook is often seen in works of ancient art, in the hands of Pan, Satyrs, Fauns, and shepherds. It was also the usual attribute of Thalia, as the muse of pastoral poetry.

Pedum, Shepherd's Crook. (From a Painting found at Civita Vecchia.)

PEGMA (πῆγμα), a pageant, *i. e.* an edifice of wood, consisting of two or more stages (*tabulata*), which were raised or depressed at pleasure by means of balance weights. These great machines were used in the Roman amphitheatres, the gladiators who fought upon them being called *pegmares*. They were supported upon wheels so as to be drawn into the circus, glittering with silver and a profusion of wealth. When Vespasian and Titus celebrated their triumph over the Jews, the procession included pageants of extraordinary magnitude and splendour, consisting of three or four stages above one another, hung with rich tapestry, and inlaid with ivory and gold. By the aid of various contrivances they represented battles and their numerous incidents, and the attack and defence of the cities of Judaea. The pegma was also used in sacrifices. A bull having been slain in one of the stages, the high priest placed himself below in a cavern, so as to receive the blood upon his person and his garments, and in this state he was produced by the flamines before the worshippers.

PĒLĀTAE (πελάται), were free labourers working for hire, like the *thetes*, in contradistinction to the helots and penestae, who were bondsmen or serfs. In the later Greek writers, such as Dionysius of Halicarnassus, and Plutarch, the word is used for the Latin cliens, though the relations expressed by the two terms are by no means similar.

PELTA (πέλτη), a small shield. Iphicrates, observing that the ancient CLIPEUS was cumbrous and inconvenient, introduced among the Greeks a much smaller and lighter shield, from which those who bore it took the name of *peltastae*. It consisted principally of a frame of wood or wicker-work, covered with skin or leather.

PĔNESTAE (πενέσται), a class of serfs in Thessaly, who stood in nearly the same relation to their Thessalian lords as the helots of Laconia did to the Dorian Spartans, although their condition seems to have been on the whole superior. They were the descendants of the old Pelasgic or Aeolian inhabitants of Thessaly Proper. They occupied an intermediate position between freemen and purchased slaves, and they cultivated the land for their masters, paying by way of rent a portion of the produce of it. The Penestae sometimes accompanied their masters to battle, and fought on horseback as their vassals: a circumstance which need not excite surprise, as Thessaly was so famous for cavalry. There were Penestae among the Macedonians also.

PĔNĔTRĀLE. [TEMPLUM.]
PĔNĪCILLUS. [PICTURA, p. 295 a.]
PENTĀCOSIŎMĔDIMNI. [CENSUS.]
PENTATHLON (πένταθλον, *quinquertium*), was next to the pancratium the most beautiful of all athletic performances. The persons engaged in it were called *Pentathli* (πένταθλοι). The pentathlon consisted of five distinct kinds of games, viz. leaping (ἅλμα), the foot-race (δρόμος), the throwing of the discus (δίσκος), the throwing of the spear (σίγυννος or ἀκόντιον), and wrestling (πάλη), which were all performed in one day and in a certain order, one after the other, by the same athletae. The pentathlon was introduced in the Olympic games in Ol. 18.

PENTĒCOSTĒ (πεντηκοστή), a duty of two per cent. levied upon all exports and imports at Athens. The money was collected by persons called πεντηκοστολόγοι. The merchant who paid the duty was said πεντηκοντεύεσθαι. All the customs appear to have been let to farm, and probably from year to year. They were let to the highest bidders by the ten *Poletae*, acting under the authority of the senate. The farmers were called τελῶναι, and were said ὠνεῖσθαι τὴν πεντηκοστήν.

PEPLUM or PEPLUS (πέπλος), an outer garment or shawl, strictly worn by females, and thus corresponding to the himation or pallium, the outer garment worn by men. Like all other pieces of cloth used for the AMICTUS, it was often fastened by means of a brooch. It was, however, frequently worn without a brooch. The shawl was also often worn so as to cover the head while it enveloped the body, and more especially on occasion of a funeral or of a marriage, when a very splendid shawl (παστός) was worn by the bride. The following woodcut may be supposed to represent the moment when the bride, so veiled, is delivered to her husband at the door of the nuptial chamber. He wears the PALLIUM only; she has a long shift beneath her shawl, and is supported by the pronuba. Of all the productions of the loom, pepli were those on which the greatest skill and labour were bestowed. So various and tasteful were the subjects which they represented, that poets delighted to describe them. The art of weaving them was entirely oriental; and those of the most splendid dyes and curious workmanship were imported from Tyre and Sidon. They often constituted a very important part of the treasures of a temple, having been presented to the divinity by suppliants and devotees.

Peplum. (Bartoli, 'Admir. Rom. Ant.,' pl. 57.)

PERA (πήρα), a wallet, made of leather, worn suspended at the side by rustics and by travellers to carry their provisions, and adopted in imitation of them by the Cynic philosophers.

PERDUELLIO was in the ancient times of the republic nearly the same as the *Majestas* of the later times. [MAJESTAS.] *Perduellis* originally signified *hostis*, and thus the offence was equivalent to making war on the Roman state. Offenders were tried by two judges called *Perduellionis Duumviri*. In the time of the kings the duumviri perduellionis and the quaestores parricidii appear to have been the same persons; but after the establishment of the republic, the offices were distinct, for the quaestores were appointed regularly every year, whereas the duumviri were appointed very rarely, as had been the case during the kingly period. Livy represents the duumviri perduellionis as being appointed by the kings, but they were really proposed by the king and appointed by the populus. During the early part of the republic they were appointed by the comitia curiata, and afterwards by the comitia centuriata, on the proposal of the consuls. In the case of Rabirius (B.C. 63), however, this custom was violated, as the duumviri were appointed by the praetor instead of by the comitia centuriata. The punishment for those who were found guilty of perduellio was death; they were either hanged on the *arbor infelix*, or thrown from the Tarpeian rock. But when the duumviri found a person guilty, he might appeal to the people (in early times the populus, afterwards the comitia centuriata, as was done in the first case which is on record, that of Horatius, and in the last, which is that of Rabirius, whom Cicero defended before the people in the oration still extant.

PEREGRINUS, a stranger or foreigner. In ancient times the word *peregrinus* was used as synonymous with *hostis;* but in the times of which we have historical records, a peregrinus was any person who was not a Roman citizen. In B.C. 247, a second praetor (*praetor peregrinus*) was appointed for the purpose of administering justice in matters between Romans and peregrini, and in matters between such peregrini as had taken up their abode at Rome. [PRAETOR.] The number of peregrini who lived in the city of Rome appears to have had an injurious influence upon the poorer classes of Roman citizens, whence on some occasions they were driven out of the city. The first example of this kind was set in B.C. 127, by the tribune M. Junius Pennus. They were expelled a second time by the tribune C. Papius, in B.C.

66. During the last period of the republic and the first centuries of the empire, all the free inhabitants of the Roman world were, in regard to their political rights, either Roman citizens, or Latins, or peregrini, and the latter had, as before, neither commercium nor connubium with the Romans. They were either free provincials, or citizens who had forfeited their civitas, and were degraded to the rank of peregrini, or a certain class of freedmen, called peregrini dediticii.

PERIOECI (περίοικοι). This word properly denotes the inhabitants of a district lying around some particular locality, but is generally used to describe a dependent population, living without the walls or in the country provinces of a dominant city, and although personally free, deprived of the enjoyment of citizenship, and the political rights conferred by it. A political condition such as that of the *perioeci* of Greece, and like the vassalage of the Germanic nations, could hardly have originated in anything else than foreign conquest, and the *perioeci* of Laconia furnish a striking illustration of this. Their origin dates from the Dorian conquest of the Peloponnesus, when the old inhabitants of the country, the Achaeans, submitted to their conquerors on certain conditions, by which they were left in possession of their private rights of citizenship. They suffered indeed a partial deprivation of their lands, and were obliged to submit to a king of foreign race, but still they remained equal in law to their conquerors, and were eligible to all offices of state except the sovereignty. But this state of things did not last long: in the next generation after the conquest the relation between the two parties was changed. The Achaeans were reduced from citizens to vassals; they were made tributary to Sparta; their lands were subjected to a tax; and they lost their rights of citizenship, the right of voting in the general assembly, and their eligibility to important offices in the state, such as that of a senator, &c. It does not, however, appear that the *perioeci* were generally an oppressed people, though kept in a state of political inferiority to their conquerors. On the contrary, the most distinguished among them were admitted to offices of trust, and they sometimes served as heavy-armed soldiers; as, for instance, at the battle of Plataea. The Norman conquest of England presents a striking parallel to the Dorian conquest of Laconia, both in its achievement and consequences. The Saxons, like the old Achaeans, were deprived of their lands, excluded from all offices of trust and dignity, and reduced, though personally free, to a state of political slavery.

The Normans, on the contrary, of whatever rank in their own country, were all nobles and warriors, compared with the conquered Saxons, and for a long time enjoyed exclusively the civil and ecclesiastical administration of the land.

PÉRISCÉLIS (περισκελίς), an anklet or bangle, worn by the Orientals, the Greeks, and the Roman ladies also. It decorated the leg in the same manner as the bracelet adorns the wrist and the necklace the throat. The word, however, is sometimes used in the same sense as the Latin *feminalia*, that is, drawers reaching from the navel to the knees.

Periscelis, Anklet, worn by a Nereid. (Museo Borbonico, vol. vi. tav. 34.)

PERISTROMA, a coverlet large enough to hang round the sides of the bed or couch.

PERISTYLIUM. [DOMUS.]

PERO (ἀρβύλη), a low boot of untanned hide worn by ploughmen (*peronatus arator*), shepherds, and others employed in rural occupations. The term ἀρβύλη is applied to an appendage to the Greek chariot. It seems to have been a shoe fastened to the bottom of the chariot, into which the driver inserted his foot, to assist him in driving, and to prevent him from being thrown out.

PERSONA (*larva*, πρόσωπον or προσωπεῖον), a mask. Masks were worn by Greek and Roman actors in nearly all dramatic representations. This custom arose undoubtedly from the practice of smearing the face with certain juices and colours, and of appearing in disguise, at the festivals of Dionysus. [DIONYSIA.] Now, as the Greek drama arose out of these festivals, it is highly probable that some mode of disguising the face was as old as the drama itself. Choerilus of Samos, however, (about B.C. 500) is said to have been the first who introduced regular masks. Other writers attribute the invention of masks to Thespis or Aeschylus, though the latter had probably only the merit of perfecting and completing the whole theatrical apparatus and costume. Some masks covered,

Comic Mask. (Statue of Davus in British Museum.)

Masks. (From a Tomb at Sidyma in Lycia.)

like the masks of modern times, only the face, but they appear more generally to have covered the whole head down to the shoulders, for we always find the hair belonging to a mask described as being a part of it; and this must have been the case in tragedy more especially, as it was necessary to make the head correspond to the stature of an actor, which was heightened by the cothurnus.

PES (πούς), a foot, the standard measure of length among the Greeks and Romans, as well as among nearly all other nations, both ancient and modern. The Romans applied the uncial division [As] to the foot, which thus contained 12 *unciae*, whence our *inches*; and many of the words used to express certain numbers of unciae are applied to the parts of the foot. It was also divided into 16 *digiti* (finger-breadths): this mode of division was used especially by architects and land-surveyors, and is found on all the foot-measures that have come down to us. From the analogy of the as, we have also *dupondium* for 2 feet, and *pes sestertius* for 2½ feet. The probable value of the Roman foot is 11.6496 inches English. (See Tables at the end.)

PESSI. [LATRUNCULI.]
PESSULUS. [JANUA.]
PETALISMUS. [EXSILIUM.]
PETASUS. [PILEUS.]
PETITOR. [ACTOR.]
PETAURISTAE. [PETAURUM.]
PETAURUM (πέταυρον, πέτευρον), used in the Roman games, seems to have been a board moving up and down, with a person at each end, and supported in the middle, something like our see-saw; only it appears to have been much longer, and consequently went to a greater height than is common amongst us. The persons who took part in this game, were called *Petauristae* or *Petauristarii*.

PETORRITUM, a four-wheeled carriage, which, like the ESSEDUM, was adopted by the Romans in imitation of the Gauls. It differed from the HARMAMAXA in being uncovered. Its name is compounded of *petor*, four, and *rit*, a wheel.

PHALANX. [EXERCITUS.]
PHALARICA. [HASTA.]
PHALERAE (φάλαρον), a boss, disc, or crescent of metal, in many cases of gold, and beautifully wrought so as to be highly prized. They were usually worn in pairs; and we most commonly read of them as ornaments attached to the harness of horses, especially about the head, and often worn as pendants (*pensilia*), so as to produce a terrific effect when shaken by the rapid motions of the horse. These ornaments were often bestowed upon horsemen by the Roman generals, in

the same manner as the ARMILLA, the TORQUES, the hasta pura [HASTA], and the crown of gold [CORONA], in order to make a public and permanent acknowledgment of bravery and merit.

PHARETRA (φαρέτρα), a quiver, was principally made of hide or leather, and was adorned with gold, painting, and braiding. It had a lid (πῶμα), and was suspended from the right shoulder by a belt passing over the breast and behind the back. Its most common position was on the left hip, and is so seen in the annexed figures, the right-hand one representing an Amazon, and the left-hand an Asiatic archer.

Pharetrae, Quivers. (Left-hand figure from the Aeginetan Marbles; right-hand figure from a Greek Vase.)

PHARMACON GRAPHE (φαρμάκων or φαρμακείας γραφή), an indictment at Athens against one who caused the death of another by poison, whether given with intent to kill or to obtain undue influence. It was tried by the court of Areiopagus.

PHAROS or PHARUS (φάρος), a light-house. The most celebrated light-house of antiquity was that situated at the entrance to the port of Alexandria, on an island which bore the name of Pharos. It contained many stories, and the upper stories had windows looking seawards, and torches or fires were kept burning in them by night in order to guide vessels into the harbour. The name of Pharos was given to other light-houses, in allusion to that at Alexandria, which was the model for their construction.

PHASELUS (φάσηλος), a vessel rather long and narrow, apparently so called from its resemblance to the shape of a phaselus or kidney-bean. It was chiefly used by the Egyptians, and was of various sizes, from a mere boat to a vessel adapted for long voyages. The phaselus was built for speed, to which more attention seems to have been paid than to its strength: whence the epithet *fragilis* is given to it by Horace. These vessels were sometimes made of clay, to which the epithet of Horace may perhaps also refer.

PHASIS (φάσις, from φαίνω), one of the various methods by which public offenders at Athens might be prosecuted; but the word is often used to denote any kind of information; and we do not know in what respects the *Phasis* was distinguished from other methods of prosecution. The word *sycophantes* (συκοφάντης) is derived from the practice of laying information against those who exported figs. [SYCOPHANTES.]

PHORMINX. [LYRA.]
PHRATRIA. [TRIBUS.]

PHYLARCHI (φύλαρχοι) were at Athens after the age of Cleisthenes ten officers, one for each of the tribes, and were specially charged with the command and superintendence of the cavalry. There can be but little doubt that each of the phylarchs commanded the cavalry of his own tribe, and they were themselves collectively and individually under the control of the two hipparchs, just as the taxiarchs were subject to the two strategi. Herodotus informs us that when Cleisthenes increased the number of the tribes from four to ten, he also made ten phylarchs instead of four. It has been thought, however, that the historian should have said ten phylarchs in the place of the old phylobasileis, who were four in number, one for each of the old tribes.

PHYLOBASILEIS (φυλοβασιλεῖς) were four in number, representing each one of the four ancient Athenian tribes, and probably elected (but not for life) from and by them. They were nominated from the Eupatridae, and during the continuance of royalty at Athens these "kings of the tribes" were the constant assessors of the sovereign, and rather as his colleagues than counsellors. Though they were originally connected with the four ancient tribes, still they were not abolished by Cleisthenes when he increased the number of tribes, probably because their duties were mainly of a religious character. They appear to have existed even after his time, and acted as judges, but in unimportant or merely formal matters.

PICTURA (γραφή, γραφική, ζωγραφία), painting. I. *History of the Art*. It is singular that the poems of Homer do not contain any mention of painting as an imitative art. This is the more remarkable, since Homer speaks of rich and elaborate embroidery as a thing not uncommon. This embroidery is actual painting in principle, and is a species of painting in practice, and it was considered such by the Romans, who termed it "pictura textilis." The various allusions also to other arts, similar in nature to painting, are sufficient to prove that painting must have existed in some degree in Homer's time, although the only kind of painting he notices is the "red-cheeked" and "purple-cheeked ships," and an ivory ornament for the faces of horses, which a Maeonian or Carian woman colours with purple. Painting seems to have made considerable progress in Asia Minor while it was still in its infancy in Greece, for Candaules, king of Lydia (B.C. 716), is said to have purchased at a high price a painting of Bularchus, which represented a battle of the Magnetes. The old Ionic painting probably flourished at the same time with the Ionian architecture, and continued as an independent school until the sixth century B.C., when the Ionians lost their liberty, and with their liberty their art. Herodotus (i. 164) mentions that when Harpagus besieged the town of Phocaea (B.C. 544), the inhabitants collected all their valuables, their statues and votive offerings from the temples, leaving only their *paintings*, and such works in metal or of stone as could not easily be removed, and fled with them to the island of Chios; from which we may conclude that paintings were not only valued by the Phocaeans, but also common among them. Herodotus (iv. 88) also informs us that Mandrocles of Samos, who constructed for Darius Hystaspis the bridge of boats across the Bosporus (B.C. 508), had a picture painted, representing the passage of Darius's army, and the king seated on a throne reviewing the troops as they passed, which he dedicated in the temple of Hera at Samos. After the conquest of Ionia, Samos became the seat of the arts. The Heraeum at Samos, in which the picture of Mandrocles was placed, was a general depository for works of art, and in the time of Strabo appears to have been particularly rich in paintings, for he terms it a "picture-gallery" (πινακοθήκη). The first painter in Greece itself, whose name is recorded, is Cimon of Cleonae. His exact period is uncertain, but he was probably a contemporary of Solon, and lived at least a century before Polygnotus. It was with Polygnotus of Thasos that painting reached its full development (about B.C. 463). Previous to this time the only cities that had paid any considerable attention to painting were Aegina, Sicyon, Corinth, and Athens. Sicyon and Corinth had long been famous for their paintings upon vases and upon articles of furniture; the school of Athens had attained no celebrity whatever until the arrival of Polygnotus from Thasos raised it to that pre-eminence which it continued to maintain for more than two centuries, although very few of the great painters of Greece were natives of Athens. The principal contemporaries of Polygnotus were Dionysius of Colophon, Plistaenetus and Panaenus of Athens, brothers (or the latter perhaps a nephew) of Phidias, and Micon, also of Athens. The works of Polygnotus and his contemporaries were conspicuous for expression, character, and design; the more minute discriminations of tone and local colour, united with dramatic composition and effect, were accomplished in the succeeding generation, about 420 B.C., through the efforts of Apollodorus of Athens and Zeuxis of Heraclea. The contemporaries of Apollodorus and Zeuxis, and those who carried out their principles, were Parrhasius of Ephesus, Eupompus of Sicyon, and Timanthes of Cythnus, all painters of the greatest fame. Athens and Sicyon were the principal seats of the art at this period. Eupompus of Sicyon was the founder of the celebrated Sicyonian school of painting which was afterwards established by Pamphilus. The Alexandrian period was the last of progression or acquisition; but it only added variety of effect to the tones it could not improve, and was principally characterised by the diversity of the styles of so many contemporary artists. The most eminent painters of this period were Protogenes, Pamphilus, Melanthius, Antiphilus, Theon of Samos, Apelles, Euphranor, Pausias, Nicias, Nicomachus, and his brother Aristides. Of all these Apelles was the greatest. The quality in which he surpassed all other painters will scarcely bear a definition; it has been termed grace, elegance, beauty, χάρις, venustas. His greatest work was perhaps his Venus Anadyomene, Venus rising out of the waters. He excelled in portrait, and indeed all his works appear to have been portraits in an extended sense; for his pictures, both historical and allegorical, consisted nearly all of single figures. He enjoyed the exclusive privilege of painting the portraits of Alexander.—The works of Greek art brought from Sicily by Marcellus were the first to inspire the Romans with the desire of adorning their public edifices with statues and paintings, which taste was converted into a passion when they became acquainted with the great treasures and almost inexhaustible resources of Greece, and their rapacity knew no bounds. Mummius, after the destruction of Corinth, B.C. 146, carried off or destroyed more works of art than all his predecessors put together. Scaurus, in his aedileship, B.C. 58, had all the public pictures still remaining in Sicyon transported to Rome, on account of the debts of the former city, and he adorned the great temporary theatre which he erected upon that occasion with 3000 bronze statues. Verres ransacked Asia and Achaia, and plundered almost every temple and public edifice in Sicily of whatever was valuable in it. Amongst the numerous robberies of Verres, Cicero mentions particularly twenty-seven beautiful pictures taken from the temple of Minerva at Syracuse, consisting of portraits of the kings and tyrants of Sicily. Yet Rome was, about the end of the republic, full of painters, who appear, however, to have been chiefly occupied in portrait, or decorative and arabesque painting. Among the Romans the earliest painter mentioned is a member of the noble house of the Fabii, who received the surname of Pictor through some paintings which he executed in the temple of Salus at Rome, B.C. 304, which lasted till the time of the emperor Claudius, when they were destroyed by the fire that consumed that temple. Pacuvius also, the tragic poet, and nephew of Ennius, distinguished himself by some paintings in the temple of Hercules in the Forum Boarium, about 180 B.C. But generally speaking the artists at Rome were Greeks. Julius Caesar, Agrippa, and Augustus were among the earliest great patrons of artists. Caesar expended great sums in the purchase of pictures by the old masters. He gave as much as 80 talents for two pictures by his contemporary Timomachus of Byzantium, one an Ajax, and the other a Medea meditating the murder of her children. These pictures, which were painted in encaustic, were very celebrated works; they are alluded to by Ovid (*Trist.* ii. 525), and are mentioned by many other ancient writers.—There are three distinct periods observable in the history of painting in Rome. The first or great period of Graeco-Roman art may be dated from the conquest of Greece until the time of Augustus, when the artists were chiefly Greeks. The second, from the time of Augustus to the so-called Thirty Tyrants and Diocletian, or from the beginning of the Christian era until about the latter end of the third century, during which time the great majority of Roman works of art were produced. The third comprehends the state of the arts during the exarchate, when Rome,

in consequence of the foundation of Constantinople, and the changes it involved, suffered similar spoliations to those which it had previously inflicted upon Greece. This was the period of the total decay of the imitative arts amongst the ancients. About the beginning of the second period is the earliest age in which we have any notice of portrait painters (*imaginum pictores*) as a distinct class. Portraits must have been exceedingly numerous amongst the Romans; Varro made a collection of the portraits of 700 eminent men. The portraits or statues of men who had performed any public service were placed in the temples and other public places; and several edicts were passed by the emperors of Rome respecting the placing of them. The portraits of authors also were placed in the public libraries; they were apparently fixed above the cases which contained their writings, below which chairs were placed for the convenience of readers. They were painted also at the beginning of manuscripts. Several of the most celebrated ancient artists were both sculptors and painters; Phidias and Euphranor were both; Zeuxis and Protogenes were both modellers; Polygnotus devoted some attention to statuary; and Lysippus consulted Eupompus upon style in sculpture. Moreover scene-painting shows that the Greeks were acquainted with perspective at a very early period; for when Aeschylus was exhibiting tragedies at Athens, Agatharchus made a scene, and left a treatise upon it.—
II. *Methods of Painting.* There were two distinct classes of painting practised by the ancients—in water colours, and in wax, both of which were practised in various ways. Of the former the principal were fresco, al fresco; and the various kinds of distemper (a tempera), with glue, with the white of egg, or with gums (a guazzo); and with wax or resins when these were rendered by any means vehicles that could be worked with water. Of the latter the principal was through fire (διὰ πυρός), termed encaustic (ἐγκαυστική, *encaustica*). The painting in wax (κηρογραφία), or ship painting (*inceramenta navium*), was distinct from encaustic. It does not appear that the Greeks or Romans ever painted in oil; the only mention of oil in ancient writers in connection with painting is the small quantity which entered into the composition of encaustic varnish to temper it. They painted upon wood, clay, plaster, stone, parchment, and canvas. The use of canvas must have been of late introduction, as there is no mention of it having been employed by the Greek painters of the best periods. They generally painted upon panels or tablets (πίνακες, πινάκια, *tabulae, tabellae*), which when finished were fixed into frames of various descriptions and materials, and encased in walls. The style or cestrum used in drawing, and for spreading the wax colours, pointed at one end and broad and flat at the other, was termed γραφίς by the Greeks and cestrum by the Romans; it was generally made of metal. The hair pencil (*penicillus, penicillum*) was termed ὑπογραφίς, and apparently also ῥαβδίον. The ancients used also a palette very similar to that used by the moderns. Encaustic was a method very frequently practised by the Roman and later Greek painters; but it was in very little use by the earlier painters, and was not generally adopted until after the time of Alexander. Pliny defines the term thus : "ceris pingere ac picturam inurere," to paint with wax or wax colours, and to *burn in* the picture afterwards with the cauterium; it appears therefore to have been the simple addition of the process of *burning in* to the ordinary method of painting with wax colours. Cerae (waxes) was the ordinary term for painters' colours amongst the Romans, but more especially encaustic colours, and they kept them in partitioned boxes, as painters do at present.
—III. *Polychromy.* Ancient statues were often painted, and what is now termed polychrome sculpture was very common in Greece. The practice of colouring statues is undoubtedly as ancient as the art of statuary itself; although they were perhaps originally coloured more from a love of colour than from any design of improving the resemblance of the representation. The Jupiter of the Capitol, placed by Tarquinius Priscus, was coloured with minium. In later times the custom seems to have been reduced to a system, and was practised with more reserve. The practice also of colouring architecture seems to have been universal amongst the Greeks, and very general amongst the Romans.—IV. *Vase Painting.* The fictile-vase painting of the Greeks was an art of itself, and was practised by a distinct class of artists. The designs upon these vases (which the Greeks termed λήκυθοι) have been variously interpreted, but they have been generally considered to be in some way connected with the initiation into the Eleusinian and other mysteries. They were given as prizes to the victors at the Panathenaea and other games, and seem to have been always buried with their owners at their death, for they have been discovered only in tombs. Even in the time of the Roman empire painted vases were termed "operis antiqui," and were then sought for in the ancient tombs of Campania and other parts of Magna Graecia. We may form some idea of their immense value from

the statement of Pliny, that they were more valuable than the Murrhine vases. [MURRHINA VASA.] The paintings on the vases, considered as works of art, vary exceedingly in the detail of the execution, although in style of design they may be arranged in two principal classes, the black and the yellow; for those which do not come strictly under either of these heads are either too few or vary too slightly to require a distinct classification. The black are the most ancient, the yellow the most common.—V. *Mosaic*, or *pictura de musivo, opus musivum*, was very general in Rome in the time of the early emperors. It was also common in Greece and Asia Minor at an earlier period, but at the time of the Roman empire it began to a great extent even to supersede painting. It was used chiefly for floors, but walls and also ceilings were sometimes ornamented in the same way. There are still many great mosaics of the ancients extant. The most valuable is the one discovered in Pompeii a few years ago, which is supposed to represent the battle of Issus. The composition is simple, forcible, and beautiful, and the design exhibits in many respects merits of the highest order.

PILA (σφαῖρα), a ball. The game at ball (σφαιριστική) was one of the most favourite gymnastic exercises of the Greeks and Romans, from the earliest times to the fall of the Roman empire. It is mentioned in the Odyssey, where it is played by the Phaeacian damsels to the sound of music, and also by two celebrated performers at the court of Alcinous in a most artistic manner accompanied with dancing. The various movements of the body required in the game of ball gave elasticity and grace to the figure; whence it was highly esteemed by the Greeks. The Athenians set so high a value on it, that they conferred upon Aristonicus of Carystus the right of citizenship on account of his skill in this game. It was equally esteemed by the other states of Greece; the young Spartans, when they were leaving the condition of ephebi, were called σφαιρεῖς, probably because their chief exercise was the game at ball. Every complete gymnasium had a room (σφαιριστήριον, σφαίριστρα) devoted to this exercise [GYMNASIUM], where a special teacher (σφαιριστικός) gave instruction in the art. Among the Romans the game at ball was generally played at by persons before taking the bath, in a room (*sphaeristerium*) attached to the baths for the purpose. *Pila* was used in a general sense for any kind of ball: but the balls among the Romans seem to have been of three kinds; the *pila* in its narrower sense, a small ball; the *follis*, a great ball filled with air; and the *paganica*, of which we know scarcely anything, but which appears to have been smaller than the follis and

Pila, Game at Ball. (From the Baths of Titus.)

an the pila. The *Harpastum* (from seems to have been the name of a ich was thrown among the players, whom endeavoured to catch it.
(I. [EXERCITUS, p. 168 b.]
STUM, a splendid four-wheeled car-.rnished with soft cushions, which the Roman matrons in sacred pro- and in going to the Circensian and mes. The pilentum was probably the HARMAMAXA and CARPENTUM, at the sides, so that those who sat ht both see and be seen.

S or PĪLĔUM (πίλος, πίλημα, πι- any piece of felt; more especially a of felt, a hat. There seems no doubt that felting is a more ancient than weaving [TELA], nor that these arts came into Europe from from the Greeks, who were ac- with this article as early as the age er, the use of felt passed together name to the Romans. Its principal to make coverings of the head for sex, and the most common one was skull-cap.—Among the Romans the t was the emblem of liberty. When obtained his freedom he had his head and wore instead of his hair an un- leus. This change of attire took the temple of Feronia, who was

Cap, worn by a Greek Soldier. (From a Greek Vase.)

the goddess of freedmen. Hence the phrase *servos ad pileum vocare* is a summons to liberty, by which slaves were frequently called upon to take up arms with a promise of liberty. The figure of Liberty on some of the coins of Antoninus Pius, struck A. D. 145, holds this cap in the right hand. The *Petasus* (πέτασος) differed from the pileus or simple skull-cap in having a wide brim: the etymology of the word, from πετάννυμι, ex- presses the distinctive shape of these hats. It was preferred to the skull-cap as a protec- tion from the sun.

PĪLUM. [HASTA.]
PISCĪNA. [BALNEUM.]
PISTOR (ἀρτοποιός), a baker, from *pinsere*, to pound, since corn was pounded in mortars before the invention of mills. At Rome bread was originally made at home by the women of the house; and there were no persons at Rome who made baking a trade, or any slaves specially kept for this purpose in private houses, till B. C. 173. The name was also given to pastry-cooks and confec- tioners, in which case they were usually called *pistores dulciarii* or *candidarii*. Bread was often baked in moulds called *artoptae*, and the loaves thus baked were termed *ar- topticii*. Bread was not generally made at home at Athens, but was sold in the market- place, chiefly by women, called ἀρτοπώλιδες. These women seem to have been what the fish-women of London are at present; they excelled in abuse.

PLĂGIĀRĬUS. [PLAGIUM.]
PLĂGIUM, the offence of kidnapping, concealing, and selling freemen and other persons' slaves was the subject of a Fabia Lex (B. c. 183). The penalty of the lex was pecuniary; but this fell into disuse, and persons who offended against the lex were punished according to the nature of their offence; under the empire they were gene- rally condemned to the mines. The word *Plagium* is said to come from the Greek πλά- γιος, oblique, indirect, dolosus. He who com- mitted *plagium* was *plagiarius*, a word which Martial applies to a person who falsely gave himself out as the author of a book; and in this sense the word has come into common use in our language.

PLAUSTRUM or PLOSTRUM (ἅμαξα), a cart or waggon. It had commonly two wheels, but sometimes four, and it was then called the *plaustrum majus*. Besides the wheels and axle the plaustrum consisted of a strong pole (*temo*), to the hinder part of which was fastened a table of wooden planks. The blocks of stone, or other things to be car- ried, were either laid upon this table without any other support, or an additional security was obtained by the use either of boards at the sides, or of a large wicker basket tied upon the cart. The annexed cut exhibits a cart, the body of which is supplied by a basket. The commonest kind of cart-wheel was that called *tympanum*, "the drum," from its resemblance to the musical instrument of the same name. It was nearly a foot in thickness, and was made either by sawing the trunk of a tree across in a horizontal direction, or by nailing together boards of the requisite shape and size. (See the cut.) These wheels advanced slowly, and made a loud creaking, which was heard to a great distance.

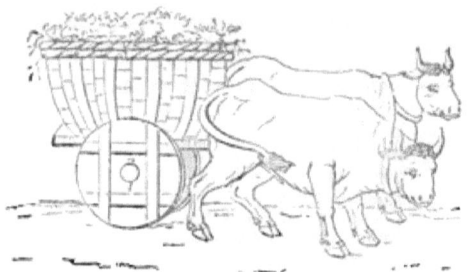

Plaustrum, Waggon. (From a Bas-Relief at Rome.)

PLĒBES or PLEBS. PLĒBĒII. This word contains the same root as *im-pleo*, *com-pleo*, &c., and is therefore etymologically connected with πλῆθος, a term which was applied to the plebeians by the more correct Greek writers on Roman history, while others wrongly called them δῆμος or οἱ δημοτικοί. The plebeians were the body of commons or the commonalty of Rome, and thus constituted one of the two great elements of which the Roman nation consisted, and which has given to the earlier periods of Roman history its peculiar character and interest. The time when the plebeians first appear as a distinct class of Roman citizens in contradistinction to the patricians, is in the reign of Tullus Hostilius. Alba, the head of the Latin confederacy, was in his reign taken by the Romans and razed to the ground. The most distinguished of its inhabitants were transplanted to Rome and received among the patricians; but the great bulk of Alban citizens, who were likewise transferred to Rome, received settlements on the Caelian hill, and were kept in a state of submission to the populus Romanus or the patricians. This new population of Rome, which in number is said to have been equal to the old inhabitants of the city or the patricians, were the plebeians. They were Latins, and consequently of the same blood as the Ramnes, the noblest of the three patrician tribes. After the conquest of Alba, Rome, in the reign of Ancus Martius, acquired possession of a considerable extent of country, containing a number of dependent Latin towns, as Medullia, Fidenae, Politorium, Tellenae, and Ficana. Great numbers of the inhabitants of these towns were again transplanted to Rome, and incorporated with the plebeians already settled there, and the Aventine was assigned to them as their habitation. Some portions of the land which these new citizens had possessed were given back to them by the Romans, so that they remained free land-owners as much as the conquerors themselves, and thus were distinct from the clients.—The plebeians were citizens, but not *optimo jure*; they were perfectly distinct from the patricians, and were neither contained in the three tribes, nor in the curiae, nor in the patrician gentes. The only point of contact between the two estates was the army. The plebeians were obliged to fight and shed their blood in the defence of their new fellow-citizens, without being allowed to share any of their rights or privileges, and without even the right of intermarriage (*connubium*.) In all judicial matters they were entirely at the mercy of the patricians, and had no right of appeal against any unjust sentence, though they were not, like the clients, bound to have a patronus. They continued to have their own sacra, which they had had before the conquest, but these were regulated by the patrician pontiffs. Lastly, they were free land-owners, and had their own gentes.—The population of the Roman state thus consisted of two opposite elements; a ruling class or an aristocracy, and the commonalty, which, though of the same stock as the noblest among the rulers, and exceeding them in numbers, yet enjoyed none of the rights which might enable them to take a part in the management of public affairs, religious or civil. Their citizenship resembled the relation of aliens to a state, in which they are merely tolerated on condition of performing certain services, and they are, in fact, sometimes called peregrini. That such a state of things could not last, is a truth which must have been felt by every one who was not blinded by his own selfishness and love of dominion. Tarquinius Priscus was the first who conceived the idea of placing the plebeians on a footing of equality with the old burghers, by dividing them into three tribes, which he intended to call after his own name and those of his friends. But this noble plan was frustrated by the opposition of the augur Attus Navius, who probably acted the part of a representative of the patricians. All that Tarquinius could do was to effect the admission of the noblest plebeian families into the three old tribes, who were distinguished from the old patrician families by the names of Ramnes, Tities, and Luceres secundi, and their gentes are sometimes distinguished by the epithet minores, as they entered into the same relation in which the Luceres had been to the first two tribes, before the time of Tarquinius. It was reserved to his successor, Servius Tullius, to give to the commonalty a regular internal organisation, and to determine their relations to the patricians. He first divided the city into four, and then the subject country around, which was inhabited by plebeians, into twenty-six regions or local tribes, and in these regions he assigned lots of land to those plebeians who were yet without landed property. [TRIBUS.] Each tribe had its praefect, called tribunus. The tribes had also their own sacra, festivals, and meetings (comitia tributa), which were convoked by their tribunes. This division into tribes with tribunes at their heads was no more than an internal organisation of the plebeians, analogous to the division of the patricians into thirty curiae, without conferring upon them the right to interfere in any way in the management of public affairs, or in the elections, which were left entirely to the senate and the curiae. These rights, however, they obtained by another regulation of Servius Tullius, which was made wholly independent of the thirty tribes. For this purpose he instituted a census, and divided the whole body of Roman citizens, plebeians as well as patricians, into five classes, according to the amount of their property. Taxation and the military duties were arranged according to these classes in such a manner, that the heavier burdens fell upon the wealthier classes. The whole body of citizens thus divided was formed into a great national assembly called comitiatus maximus, or comitia centuriata. [COMITIA.] In this assembly the plebeians now met the patricians apparently on a footing of equality, but the votes were distributed in such a way that it was always in the power of the wealthiest classes, to which the patricians naturally belonged, to decide a question before it was put to the vote of the poorer classes. A great number of such noble plebeian families, as after the subjugation of the Latin towns had not been admitted into the curies by Tarquinius Priscus, were now constituted by Servius into a number of equites, with twelve suffragia in the comitia centuriata. [EQUITES.] In this constitution, the plebeians, as such, did not obtain admission to the senate, nor to the highest magistracy, nor to any of the priestly offices. To all these offices the patricians alone thought themselves entitled by divine right. The plebeians also continued to be excluded from occupying any portion of the public land, which as yet was possessed only by the patricians, and they were only allowed to keep their cattle upon the common pasture. —In the early times of the republic there was a constant struggle between the two orders, the history of which belongs to a history of Rome, and cannot be given here. Eventually the plebeians gained access to all the civil and religious offices, until at last the two hostile elements became united into one great body of Roman citizens with equal rights, and a state of things arose, totally different from what had existed before. After the first secession, in B. C. 494, the plebeians gained several great advantages. First, a law was passed to prevent the patricians from taking usurious interest of money, which they frequently lent to impoverished plebeians; secondly, tribunes were appointed for the protection of the plebeians [TRIBUNI]; and lastly, plebeian aediles were appointed. [AEDILES.] Shortly after, they gained the right to summon before their own comitia tributa any one who had violated the rights of their order, and to make decrees (plebiscita), which, however, did not become binding upon the whole nation, free from the control of the curies, until the year B. C. 286. In (B. C. 445), the tribune Canuleius established, by his rogations, the connubium between patricians and plebeians. He also attempted to divide the consulship between the two orders, but the patricians frustrated the realisation of this plan by the appointment of six military tribunes, who were to be elected from both orders. [TRIBUNI.] But that the plebeians might have no share in the censorial power, with which the consuls had been invested, the military tribunes did not obtain that power, and a new curule dignity, the censorship, was established, with which patricians alone were to be invested. [CENSOR.] In

B.C. 421 the plebeians were admitted to the quaestorship, which opened to them the way into the senate, where henceforth their number continued to increase. [QUAESTOR; SENATUS.] In B.C. 367 the tribunes L. Licinius Stolo and L. Sextius placed themselves at the head of the commonalty, and resumed the contest against the patricians. After a fierce struggle, which lasted for several years, they at length carried a rogation, according to which decemvirs were to be appointed for keeping the Sibylline books instead of duumvirs, of whom half were to be plebeians. The next great step was the restoration of the consulship, on condition that one consul should always be a plebeian. A third rogation of Licinius, which was only intended to afford momentary relief to the poor plebeians, regulated the rate of interest. From this time forward the plebeians also appear in the possession of the right to occupy parts of the ager publicus. In B.C. 366, L. Sextius Lateranus was the first plebeian consul. The patricians, however, who always contrived to yield no more than what it was absolutely impossible for them to retain, stripped the consulship of a considerable part of its power, and transferred it to two new curule offices, viz. that of praetor and of curule aedile [AEDILES; PRAETOR.] But after such great advantages had been once gained by the plebeians, it was impossible to stop them in their progress towards a perfect equality of political rights with the patricians. In B.C. 356, C. Marcius Rutilus was the first plebeian dictator; in B.C. 351 the censorship was thrown open to the plebeians, and in B.C. 336 the praetorship. The Ogulnian law, in B.C. 300, also opened to them the offices of pontifex and augur. These advantages were, as might be supposed, not gained without the fiercest opposition of the patricians, and even after they were gained and sanctioned by law, the patricians exerted every means to obstruct the operation of the law. Such fraudulent attempts led, in B.C. 286, to the last secession of the plebeians, after which, however, the dictator Q. Hortensius successfully and permanently reconciled the two orders, secured to the plebeians all the rights they had acquired until then, and procured for their plebiscita the full power of leges binding upon the whole nation. After the passing of the Hortensian law, the political distinction between patricians and plebeians ceased, and, with a few unimportant exceptions, both orders were placed on a footing of perfect equality. Henceforth the name populus is sometimes applied to the plebeians alone, and sometimes to the whole body of Roman citizens, as assembled in the comitia centuriata or tributa. The term plebs or plebecula, on the other hand, was applied, in a loose manner of speaking, to the multitude or populace, in opposition to the nobiles or the senatorial party.—A person who was born a plebeian could only be raised to the rank of a patrician by a lex curiata, as was sometimes done during the kingly period, and in the early times of the republic. It frequently occurs in the history of Rome that one and the same gens contains plebeian as well as patrician families. In the gens Cornelia, for instance, we find the plebeian families of the Balbi, Mammulae, Merulae, &c., along with the patrician Scipiones, Sullae, Lentuli, &c. The occurrence of this phenomenon may be accounted for in different ways. It may have been, that one branch of a plebeian family was made patrician while the others remained plebeians. It may also have happened that two families had the same nomen gentilicium without being actual members of the same gens. Again, a patrician family might go over to the plebeians, and as such a family continued to bear the name of its patrician gens, this gens apparently contained a plebeian family. When a peregrinus obtained the civitas through the influence of a patrician, or when a slave was emancipated by his patrician master, they generally adopted the nomen gentilicium of their benefactor, and thus appear to belong to the same gens with him.

PLEBISCITUM, a name properly applied to a law passed at the comitia tributa on the rogation of a tribune. Originally, a plebiscitum required confirmation by the comitia curiata and the senate; but a Lex Hortensia was passed B.C. 286, to the effect that plebiscita should bind all the populus (*universus populus*), and this lex rendered confirmation unnecessary. The Lex Hortensia is always referred to as the lex which put plebiscita as to their binding force exactly on the same footing as leges. The principal plebiscita are mentioned under the article LEX.

PLECTRUM. [LYRA.]

PLETHRON (πλέθρον), the fundamental land measure in the Greek system, being the square of 100 feet, that is, 10,000 square feet. The later Greek writers use it as the translation of the Roman *jugerum*, probably because the latter was the standard land measure in the Roman system; but, in size, the *plethron* answered more nearly to the Roman *actus*, or half-jugerum, which was the older unit of land measures. As frequently happened with the ancient land measures, the side of the *plethron* was taken as a measure of length, with the same name.

This *plethron* was equal to 100 feet (or about 101 English feet) = 66⅔ πήχεις = 10 ἄκαιναι or κάλαμοι. It was also introduced into the system of itinerary measures, being 1-6th of the *stadium*.

PLŪTEUS, was applied in military affairs to two different objects. (1) A kind of shed made of hurdles, and covered with raw hides, which could be moved forward by small wheels attached to it, and under which the besiegers of a town made their approaches. (2) Boards or planks placed on the vallum of a camp, on moveable towers or other military engines, as a kind of roof or covering for the protection of the soldiers.

PLYNTĒRIA (πλυντήρια, from πλύνειν, to wash), a festival celebrated at Athens every year, on the 25th of Thargelion, in honour of Athena, surnamed Aglauros, whose temple stood on the Acropolis. The day of this festival was at Athens among the ἀποφράδες or *dies nefasti*; for the temple of the goddess was surrounded by a rope to preclude all communication with it; her statue was stripped of its garments and ornaments for the purpose of cleaning them, and was in the meanwhile covered over, to conceal it from the sight of man. The city was therefore, so to speak, on this day without its protecting divinity, and any undertaking commenced on it was believed to be necessarily unsuccessful.

PNYX. [ECCLESIA.]

POCULUM, any kind of drinking-cup, to be distinguished from the *Crater* or vessel in which the wine was mixed [CRATER], and from the *Cyathus*, a kind of ladle or small cup, used to convey the wine from the Crater to the Poculum or drinking-cup.

PŎDĪUM. [AMPHITHEATRUM.]

POENA (ποινή), a general name for any punishment of any offence. Multa is the penalty of a particular offence. A Poena was only inflicted when it was imposed by some lex or some other legal authority (*quo alio jure*). When no poena was imposed, then a multa or penalty might be inflicted.

POLEMARCHUS (πολέμαρχος). Respecting the polemarchus at Athens, see ARCHON. We read also of polemarchs at Sparta, and in various cities of Boeotia. As their name denotes, they were originally and properly connected with military affairs, being entrusted either with the command of armies abroad, or the superintendence of the war department at home; sometimes with both. The polemarchs of Sparta appear to have ranked next to the king, when on actual service abroad, and were generally of the royal kindred or house (γένος). They commanded single morae, so that they would appear to have been six in number, and sometimes whole armies. They also formed part of the king's council in war, and of the royal escort called *damosia*. At Thebes there appear to have been two polemarchs, perhaps elected annually; and in times of peace they seem to have been invested with the chief executive power of the state, and the command of the city, having its military force under their orders. They are not, however, to be confounded with the Boeotarchs.

PŌLĒTAE (πωληταί), a board of ten officers, or magistrates, whose duty it was to grant leases of the public lands and mines, and also to let the revenues arising from the customs, taxes, confiscations, and forfeitures. Of such letting the word πωλεῖν (not μισθοῦν) was generally used, and also the correlative words ὠνεῖσθαι and πρίασθαι. One was chosen from each tribe. In the letting of the revenue they were assisted by the managers of the theoric fund (τὸ θεωρικόν), and they acted under the authority of the senate of Five Hundred, who exercised a general control over the financial department of the administration. Resident aliens, who did not pay their residence tax (μετοίκιον), were summoned before them, and, if found to have committed default, were sold.

POLLINCTŌRES. [FUNUS.]

PŌMOERIUM. This word is compounded of *post* and *moerium* (*murus*), in the same manner as *pomeridiem* of *post* and *meridiem*, and thus signifies a line running by the walls of a town (*pone* or *post muros*). But the walls of a town here spoken of are not its actual walls or fortifications, but symbolical walls, and the course of the pomoerium itself was marked by stone pillars, erected at certain intervals. The sacred line of the Roman pomoerium did not prevent the inhabitants from building upon or taking into use any place beyond it, but it was necessary to leave a certain space on each side of it unoccupied, so as not to unhallow it by profane use. Thus we find that the Aventine, although inhabited from early times, was for many centuries not included within the pomoerium. The pomoerium was not the same at all times; as the city increased the pomoerium also was extended; but this extension could, according to ancient usage, only be made by such men as had by their victories over foreign nations increased the boundaries of the empire, and neither could a pomoerium be formed nor altered without the augurs previously consulting the will of the gods by augury: hence the *jus pomoerii* of the augurs.

POMPA (πομπή), a solemn procession, as on the occasion of a funeral, triumph, &c. It is, however, more particularly applied to the grand procession with which the games of the circus commenced (*Pompa Circensis*). [Circus.]

PONS (γέφυρα), a bridge. As the rivers of Greece were small, and the use of the arch known to them only to a limited extent, it is probable that the Greek bridges were built entirely of wood, or, at best, were nothing more than a wooden platform supported upon stone piers at each extremity. Pliny mentions a bridge over the Acheron 1000 feet in length; we also know that the island Euboea was joined to Bœotia by a bridge; but the only existing specimen of a Greek bridge is the one over a tributary of the Eurotas. The Romans regularly applied the arch to the construction of bridges, by which they were enabled to erect structures of great beauty and solidity, as well as utility. The width of the passage-way in a Roman bridge was commonly narrow, as compared with modern structures of the same kind, and corresponded with the road (*via*) leading to and from it. It was divided into three parts. The centre one, for horses and carriages, was denominated *agger* or *iter*; and the raised footpaths on each side *decursoria*, which were enclosed by parapet walls similar in use and appearance to the *pluteus* in the basilica. There were eight bridges across the Tiber. I. Of these the most celebrated, as well as the most ancient, was the PONS SUBLICIUS, so called because it was built of wood; *sublices*, in the language of the Formiani, meaning wooden beams. It was built by Ancus Martius, when he united the Janiculum to the city, and was situated at the foot of the Aventine.—II. PONS PALATINUS formed the communication between the Palatine and its vicinities and the Janiculum.—III. IV. PONS FABRICIUS and

Pons Cestius, and Pons Fabricius, at Rome, with the buildings between restored.

PONS CESTIUS were the two which connected the Insula Tiberina with the opposite sides of the river; the first with the city, and the latter with the Janiculum. Both are still remaining. They are represented in the preceding woodcut: that on the right hand is the pons Fabricius, and that on the left the pons Cestius.—V. PONS JANICULENSIS, which led direct to the Janiculum.—VI. PONS VATICANUS, so called because it formed the communication between the Campus Martius and Campus Vaticanus.—VII. PONS AELIUS, built by Hadrian, which led from the city to the mausoleum of that emperor, now the bridge and castle of St. Angelo.—VIII. PONS MILVIUS, on the Via Flaminia, now Ponte Molle,

Pons Aelius at Rome.

was built by Aemilius Scaurus the censor. —The Roman bridges without the city were too many to be enumerated here. They formed one of the chief embellishments in all the public roads; and their frequent and stupendous remains, still existing in Italy, Portugal, and Spain, attest, even to the present day, the scale of grandeur with which the Roman works of national utility were always carried on.—When the comitia were held, the voters, in order to reach the enclosure called *septum* and *ovile*, passed over a

Bridge at Ariminum.

wooden platform, elevated above the ground, which was called *pons suffragiorum*, in order that they might be able to give their votes without confusion or collusion. [COMITIA.] *Pons* is also used to signify the platform (ἐπιβάθρα, ἀποβάθρα), used for embarking in, or disembarking from, a ship.

PONTIFEX (ἱεροδιδάσκαλος, ἱερονόμος, ἱεροφύλαξ, ἱεροφάντης). The origin of this word is explained in various ways; but it is probably formed from *pons* and *facere* (in the signification of the Greek ῥέζειν, to perform a sacrifice), and consequently signifies the priests who offered sacrifices upon the bridge. The ancient sacrifice to which the name thus alludes, is that of the Argei on the sacred or sublician bridge. [ARGEI.] The Roman pontiffs formed the most illustrious among the great colleges of priests. Their institution, like that of all important matters of religion, was ascribed to Numa. The number of pontiffs appointed by this king was four, and at their head was the pontifex maximus, who is generally not included when the number of pontiffs is mentioned. It is probable that the original number of four pontiffs (not including the pontifex maximus) had reference to the two earliest tribes of the Romans, the Ramnes and Tities, so that each tribe was represented by two pontiffs. In the year B. C. 300 the Ogulnian law raised the number of pontiffs to eight, or, including the pontifex maximus, to nine, and four of them were to be plebeians. The pontifex maximus, however, continued to be a patrician down to the year B. C. 254, when Tib. Coruncanius was the first plebeian who was invested with this dignity. This number of pontiffs remained for a long time unaltered, until in B. C. 81 the dictator Sulla increased it to fifteen, and J. Caesar to sixteen. In both these changes the pontifex maximus is included in the number. During the empire the number varied, though on the whole fifteen appears to have been the regular number. The mode of appointing the pontiffs was also different at different times. It appears that after their institution by Numa, the college had the right of co-optation, that is, if a member of the college died (for all the pontiffs held their office for life), the members met and elected a successor, who, after his election, was inaugurated by the augurs. This election was sometimes called *captio*. In B. C. 104 a Lex Domitia was passed, which transferred the right of electing the members of the great colleges of priests to the people (probably in the comitia tributa); that is, the people elected a candidate, who was then made a member of the college by the co-optatio of the priests themselves, so that the co-optatio, although still necessary, became a mere matter of form. The Lex Domitia was repealed by Sulla in a Lex Cornelia de Sacerdotiis (B. c. 81), which restored to the great priestly colleges their full right of co-optatio. In B. c. 63 the law of Sulla was abolished, and the Domitian law was restored, but not in its full extent; for it was now determined, that in case of a vacancy the college itself should nominate two candidates, and the people elect one of them. M. Antonius again restored the right of co-optatio to the college. The college of pontiffs had the supreme superintendence of all matters of religion, and of things and persons connected with public as well as private worship. They had the judicial decision in all matters of religion, whether private persons, magistrates, or priests were concerned, and in cases where the existing laws or customs were found defective or insufficient, they made new laws and regulations (*decreta pontificum*), in which they always followed their own judgment as to what was consistent with the existing customs and usages. The details of these duties and functions were contained in books called *libri pontificii* or *pontificales, commentarii sacrorum* or *sacrorum pontificalium*, which they were said to have received from Numa, and which were sanctioned by Ancus Martius. As to the rights and duties of the pontiffs, it must first of all be borne in mind, that the pontiffs were not priests of any particular divinity, but a college which stood above all other priests, and superintended the whole external worship of the gods. One of their principal duties was the regulation of the sacra, both publica and privata, and to watch that they were observed in the proper times (for which purpose the pontiffs had the whole regulation of the calendar, see CALENDARIUM), and in their proper form. In the management of the sacra publica they were in later times assisted in certain duties by the Triumviri Epulones. [EPULONES.] The pontiffs convoked the assembly of the curies (*comitia calata* or *curiata*) in cases where priests were to be appointed, and flamines or a rex sacrorum were to be inaugurated; also when wills were to be received, and when a detestatio sacrorum and adoption by adrogatio took place. [ADOPTIO.] In most cases the sentence of the pontiffs only inflicted a fine upon the offenders; but the person fined had the right of appealing to the people, who might release him from the fine. In regard to the vestal virgins, and the persons who committed incest with them, the pontiffs had criminal jurisdiction, and might pronounce sentence of death. A man who had violated a vestal virgin was, according to an ancient law, scourged to death by the pontifex maximus in the comitium, and it appears that originally neither the vestal virgins nor the male offenders in such a case had any right of appeal. In later times we find that, even when the pontiffs had passed sentence upon vestal virgins, a tribune interfered, and induced the people to appoint a quaestor for the purpose of making a fresh inquiry into the case; and it sometimes happened that after this new trial the sentence of the pontiffs was modified or annulled. Such cases, however, seem to have been mere irregularities, founded upon an abuse of the tribunitian power. In the early times the pontiffs were in the exclusive possession of the civil as well as religious law, until the former was made public by Cn. Flavius. The regulations which served as a guide to the pontiffs in their judicial proceedings, formed a large collection of laws, which was called the *jus pontificium*, and formed part of the Libri Pontificii. The meetings of the college of pontiffs, to which in some instances the flamines and the rex sacrorum were summoned, were held in the curia regia on the Via Sacra, to which was attached the residence of the pontifex maximus and of the rex sacrorum. As the chief pontiff was obliged to live in a domus publica, Augustus, when he assumed this dignity, changed part of his own house into a domus publica. All the pontiffs were in their appearance distinguished by the conic cap, called tutulus or galerus, with an apex upon it, and the toga praetexta. The pontifex maximus was the president of the college, and acted in its name, whence he alone is frequently mentioned in cases in which he must be considered only as the organ of the college. He was generally chosen from among the most distinguished persons, and such as had held a curule magistracy, or were already members of the college. Two of his especial duties were to appoint (*capere*) the vestal virgins and the flamines [VESTALES; FLAMEN], and to be present at every marriage by confarreatio. When festive games were vowed, or a dedication made, the chief pontiff had to repeat over, before the persons who made the vow or the dedication, the formula in which it was to be performed (*praeire verba*). During the period of the republic, when the people exercised sovereign power in every respect, we find that if the pontiff, on constitutional or religious grounds, refused to perform this solemnity, he might be compelled by the people. The pontifex maximus wrote down what occurred in his year on tablets, which were hung up in his dwelling for the information of the people, and called *Annales Maximi*. A pontifex might, like all the members of the great priestly colleges, hold any other military, civil, or priestly office, provided the different offices did not interfere with one another. Thus we find one and the same person being pontiff, augur, and decemvir sacrorum; instances of a pontifex maximus being at the same time consul are very numerous. But whatever might be the civil or military office which a pontifex maximus held beside his pontificate, he was not allowed originally to leave Italy. The college of pontiffs continued to exist until the overthrow of paganism. The emperors themselves were always chief pontiffs, and as such the presidents of the college; hence the title of pontifex maximus (P. M. or PON. M.) appears on several coins of the emperors. If there were several emperors at a time, only one bore the title of pontifex maximus; but in the year A. D. 238 we find that each of the two emperors Maximus and Balbinus assumed this dignity.

From the time of Theodosius the emperors no longer appear with the dignity of **pontiff**; but at last the title was assumed **by the** Christian bishop of Rome.—There **were** other pontiffs at Rome, who were distinguished by the epithet *Minores*. They appear to have been originally only the secretaries of the pontiffs; and when the real pontiffs **began to** neglect their duties, and to leave **the principal** business to be done by their **secretaries**, it became customary to designate these scribes by the name of Pontifices **Minores**. The number of these secretaries is **uncertain**.

POPA. [SACRIFICIUM.]
POPINA. [CAUPONA.]
POPULARIA. [AMPHITHEATRUM.]
POPULUS. [PATRICII.]
POPULIFUGIA or POPLIFUGIA, the day of the people's flight, was celebrated on the nones of July, according to an ancient tradition, in commemoration of the flight of the people, when the inhabitants of Ficulae, Fidenae, and other places round about, appeared in arms against Rome shortly after the departure of the Gauls, and produced such a **panic** that the Romans suddenly fled before them. Other writers say that **the** Populifugia was celebrated in commemoration of the flight of the people before the Tuscans; while others again refer its origin to the flight **of the people on the death of** Romulus.

PORISTAE ($\pi o \rho \iota \sigma \tau a i$), magistrates at Athens, who **probably** levied the extraordinary supplies.

PORTA ($\pi \acute{\upsilon} \lambda \eta$, dim. $\pi \upsilon \lambda \acute{\iota} \varsigma$), **the gate of a** city, citadel, **or** other open space **inclosed by** a wall, in contradistinction to JANUA, which was the door of a house or any covered edifice. The terms *porta* and $\pi \acute{\upsilon} \lambda \eta$ are **often** found in the plural, even when applied to a single gate, because it consisted of two leaves. The gates of a city were of course various in **their** number and position. Thus Megara had **5** gates; Thebes, in Boeotia, had 7; Athens **had** 8; and Rome 20, or perhaps even more. The jambs of the gate were surmounted, **1.** by a lintel, which was large and strong **in proportion** to the width of the gate. 2. By **an** arch, as we see exemplified at Pompeii, **Paestum**, Sepianum, Volterra, Suza, Autun, Besançon, and Treves. **3. At** Arpinum, one of **the gates now remaining is** arched, whilst another **is constructed with** the stones projecting **one beyond** another. Gates sometimes had two passages close together, the one designed for carriages entering, and the other for carriages leaving the city. **In** other instances we find only one gate **for** carriages, but a smaller one on each side of it ($\pi \alpha \rho \alpha \pi \upsilon \lambda \acute{\iota} \varsigma$) for foot-passengers.

When there were no sideways, one of the **valves of the large** gate sometimes contained **a wicket** (*portula*, $\pi \upsilon \lambda \acute{\iota} \varsigma$: $\rho \iota \nu o \pi \acute{\upsilon} \lambda \eta$), large **enough to admit a single person.** The gateway had commonly a **chamber (called** $\pi \upsilon \lambda \acute{\omega} \nu$) **either** on one side or on both, **which served** as the residence of the porter **or guard.** Statues of the gods were often placed near **the** gate, or even within it in the barbican, **so as** to be ready to receive the adoration of **those** who entered the city.

PORTICUS ($\sigma \tau o \acute{a}$), a walk covered **with a roof,** and supported by columns, at least on one side. Such shaded walks and places **of** resort are almost indispensable in the **southern** countries of Europe, where people live **much in the open** air, as a protection from **the heat of the sun and** from rain. The **porticoes** attached **to the** temples were either constructed only **in front** of them, or went round the whole building, as is **the** case in **the** so-called Temple of Theseus **at** Athens. They were originally intended **as places for** those persons **to assemble and converse in who** visited the **temple for various purposes. As such** temple-porticoes, however, were **found too small, or not suited for the various purposes of private and public life, most** Grecian towns had **independent porticoes,** some of which were very **extensive; and in** most of these *stone*, seats (*exedrae*) were **placed, that those who were tired might sit down. They** were frequented not only **by idle loungers,** but also by philosophers, **rhetoricians, and other** persons fond **of intellectual conversation.** The Stoic school **of philosophy derived its** name from **the circumstance, that the** founder **of it** used **to converse with his** disciples in **a stoa. The Romans** derived their great **fondness for such** covered walks from the Greeks; **and as** luxuries among them were carried in every**thing to** a greater extent than in **Greece,** wealthy Romans had their private **porticoes,** sometimes in the city itself, and sometimes **in** their country-seats. In the public por**ticoes of** Rome, **which were exceedingly numerous and very extensive (as those around the Forum** and the Campus Martius), **a variety of** business was occasionally transacted: **we find that** law-suits **were** conducted here, meetings **of the senate held, goods** exhibited for sale, &c.

PORTISCULUS ($\kappa \epsilon \lambda \epsilon \upsilon \sigma \tau \acute{\eta} \varsigma$), an officer in **a ship, who gave the** signal **to** the rowers, **that they might keep** time in rowing. This officer **is sometimes called** *Hortator* or *Pausarius*.

PORTITORES. [PUBLICANI.]

PORTORIUM, a branch of the regular revenues of the Roman state, consisting of the duties paid on imported and exported goods. A portorium, or duty upon imported goods, appears to have been paid at a very early period, for it is said that Valerius Publicola exempted the plebes from the portoria at the time when the republic was threatened with an invasion by Porsena. The time of its introduction is uncertain; but the abolition of it, ascribed to Publicola, can only have been a temporary measure; and as the expenditure of the republic increased, new portoria must have been introduced. In conquered places, and in the provinces, the import and export duties, which had been paid there before, were generally not only retained, but increased, and appropriated to the aerarium. Sicily, and above all, Asia, furnished to the Roman treasury large sums, which were raised as portoria. In B.C. 60 all the portoria in the ports of Italy were done away with by a Lex Caecilia, but were restored by Julius Caesar and the subsequent emperors. Respecting the amount of the import or export duties we have but little information. In the time of Cicero the portorium in the ports of Sicily was one twentieth (*vicesima*) of the value of taxable articles; and it is probable that this was the average sum raised in all the other provinces. In the times of the emperors the ordinary rate of the portorium appears to have been the fortieth part (*quadragesima*) of the value of imported goods; and at a later period the exorbitant sum of one-eighth (*octava*) is mentioned. The portorium was, like all other vectigalia, farmed out by the censors to the publicani, who collected it through the *portitores*. [VECTIGALIA; PUBLICANI.]

POSSESSIO. [AGER PUBLICUS.]

POSTICUM. [JANUA.]

POSTLIMINIUM, POSTLIMINII JUS. If a Roman citizen during war came into the possession of an enemy, he sustained a *diminutio capitis maxima* [CAPUT], and all his civil rights were in abeyance. Being captured by the enemy, he became a slave; but his rights over his children, if he had any, were not destroyed, but were said to be in abeyance (*pendere*) by virtue of the *Jus Postliminii*: when he returned, his children were again in his power; and if he died in captivity, they became sui juris. Sometimes by an act of the state a man was given up bound to an enemy, and if the enemy would not receive him, it was a question whether he had the Jus Postliminii. This was the case with Sp. Postumius, who was given up to the Samnites, and with C. Hostilius Mancinus, who was given up to the Numantines; but the better opinion was, that they had no *Jus Postliminii*, and Mancinus was restored to his civic rights by a lex. It appears that the Jus Postliminii was founded on the fiction of the captive having never been absent from home; a fiction which was of easy application, for, as the captive during his absence could not do any legal act, the interval of captivity was a period of legal non-activity, which was terminated by his showing himself again.

POTESTAS. [PATRIA POTESTAS.]

PRACTORES (πράκτορες), subordinate officers at Athens, who collected the fines and penalties (ἐπιβολάς and τιμήματα) imposed by magistrates and courts of justice, and payable to the state.

PRAECINCTIO. [AMPHITHEATRUM.]

PRAECONES, criers, were employed for various purposes: 1. In sales by auction, they frequently advertised the time, place, and conditions of sale: they seem also to have acted the part of the modern auctioneer, so far as calling out the biddings and amusing the company, though the property was knocked down by the *magister auctionis*. [AUCTIO.] 2. In all public assemblies they ordered silence. 3. In the comitia they called the centuries one by one to give their votes, pronounced the vote of each century, and called out the names of those who were elected. They also recited the laws that were to be passed. 4. In trials, they summoned the accuser and the accused, the plaintiff and defendant. 5. In the public games, they invited the people to attend, and proclaimed the victors. 6. In solemn funerals they also invited people to attend by a certain form; hence these funerals were called *funera indictiva*. 7. When things were lost, they cried them and searched for them. 8. In the infliction of capital punishment, they sometimes conveyed the commands of the magistrates to the lictors. Their office, called *Praeconium*, appears to have been regarded as rather disreputable: in the time of Cicero a law was passed preventing all persons who had been praecones from becoming decuriones in the municipia. Under the early emperors, however, it became very profitable, which was no doubt partly owing to fees, to which they were entitled in the courts of justice, and partly to the bribes which they received from the suitors, &c.

PRAEDA signifies moveable things taken by an enemy in war. Such things were either distributed by the Imperator among the soldiers or sold by the quaestors, and the produce was brought into the Aerarium. The difference between Praeda and Manubiae is this:—Praeda is the things themselves that are taken in war, and Manubiae is the money realized by their sale. It was the practice to set up a spear at such sales, which was afterwards used at all sales of things by a magistratus in the name of the people. [SECTIO.]

PRAEFECTURA. [COLONIA.]

PRAEFECTUS AERARII. [AERARIUM.]

PRAEFECTUS ANNONAE, the praefect of the provisions, especially of the cornmarket, was not a regular magistrate under the republic, but was only appointed in cases of extraordinary scarcity, when he seems to have regulated the prices at which corn was to be sold. Augustus created an officer under the title of *Praefectus Annonae*, who had jurisdiction over all matters appertaining to the corn-market, and, like the *Praefectus Vigilum*, was chosen from the equites, and was not reckoned among the ordinary magistrates.

PRAEFECTUS AQUARUM. [AQUAE DUCTUS.]

PRAEFECTUS CASTRORUM, praefect of the camp, is first mentioned in the reign of Augustus. There was one to each legion.

PRAEFECTUS CLASSIS, the commander of a fleet. This title was frequently given in the times of the republic to the commander of a fleet; but Augustus appointed two permanent officers with this title, one of whom was stationed at Ravenna on the Adriatic, and the other at Misenum on the Tuscan sea, each having the command of a fleet.

PRAEFECTUS FABRUM. [FABRI.]

PRAEFECTUS JURI DICUNDO. [COLONIA.]

PRAEFECTUS LEGIONIS. [EXERCITUS.]

PRAEFECTUS PRAETORIO, was the commander of the troops who guarded the emperor's person. [PRAETORIANI.] This office was instituted by Augustus, and was at first only military, and had comparatively small power attached to it; but under Tiberius, who made Sejanus commander of the praetorian troops, it became of much greater importance, till at length the power of these praefects became only second to that of the emperors. From the reign of Severus to that of Diocletian, the praefects, like the vizirs of the east, had the superintendence of all departments of the state, the palace, the army, the finances, and the law; they also had a court in which they decided cases. The office of praefect of the praetorium was not confined to military officers; it was filled by Ulpian and Papinian, and other distinguished jurists. Originally there were two praefects; afterwards sometimes one and sometimes two; from the time of Commodus sometimes three, and even four. They were, as a regular rule, chosen only from the equites; but from the time of Alexander Severus the dignity of senator was always joined with their office.

PRAEFECTUS VIGILUM. [EXERCITUS, p. 171, a.]

PRAEFECTUS URBI, praefect or warden of the city, was originally called *Custos Urbis*. The name *praefectus urbi* does not seem to have been used till after the time of the decemvirs. The dignity of *custos urbis*, being combined with that of *princeps senatus*, was conferred by the king, as he had to appoint one of the decem primi as princeps senatus. The functions of the *custos urbis*, however, were not exercised except in the absence of the king from Rome; and then he acted as the representative of the king: he convoked the senate, held the comitia, if necessary, and on any emergency, might take such measures as he thought proper; in short, he had the imperium in the city. During the kingly period, the office of *custos urbis* was probably for life. Under the republic, the office, and its name of *custos urbis*, remained unaltered; but in B.C. 487 it was elevated into a magistracy, to be bestowed by election. The *custos urbis* was, in all probability, elected by the curiae. Persons of consular rank were alone eligible. In the early period of the republic the *custos urbis* exercised within the city all the powers of the consuls, if they were absent: he convoked the senate, held the comitia, and, in times of war, even levied civic legions, which were commanded by him. When the office of praetor urbanus was instituted, the wardenship of the city was swallowed up in it; but as the Romans were at all times averse to dropping altogether any of their old institutions, a praefectus urbi, though a mere shadow of the former office, was henceforth appointed every year, only for the time that the consuls were absent from Rome for the purpose of celebrating the Feriae Latinae. This praefectus had neither the power of convoking the senate nor the right of speaking in it; in most cases he was a person below the senatorial age, and was not appointed by the people, but by the consuls. An office very different from this, though bearing the same name, was instituted by Augustus on the suggestion of Maecenas. This new praefectus urbi was a regular and permanent magistrate, whom Augustus invested with all the powers necessary to maintain peace and order in the city. He had the superintendence of butchers, bankers, guardians, theatres, &c.; and to enable

x 2

him to exercise his power, he had distributed throughout the city a number of *milites stationarii*, whom we may compare to a modern police. His jurisdiction, however, became gradually extended; and as the powers of the ancient republican praefectus urbi had been swallowed up by the office of the praetor urbanus, so now the power of the praetor urbanus was gradually absorbed by that of the praefectus urbi; and at last there was no appeal from his sentence, except to the person of the princeps himself, while any body might appeal from the sentence of any other city magistrate, and, at a later period, even from that of a governor of a province, to the tribunal of the praefectus urbi.

PRAEFICAE. [FUNUS.]

PRAEJUDICIUM is used both in the sense of a precedent, in which case it is rather *exemplum* than *praejudicium* (*res ex paribus causis judicatae*); and also in the sense of a preliminary inquiry and determination about something which belongs to the matter in dispute (*judiciis ad ipsam causam pertinentibus*), from whence also comes the name Praejudicium.

PRAELUSIO. [GLADIATORES.]

PRAENOMEN. [NOMEN.]

PRAEROGATIVA TRIBUS. [COMITIA, p. 109.]

PRAES, is a surety for one who buys of the state. The goods of a Praes were called *Praedia*. The *Praediator* was a person who bought a *praedium*, that is, a thing given to the state as a security by a praes.

PRAESCRIPTIO, or rather TEMPORIS PRAESCRIPTIO, signifies the Exceptio or answer which a defendant has to the demand of a plaintiff, founded on the circumstance of the lapse of time. The word has properly no reference to the plaintiff's loss of right, but to the defendant's acquisition of a right by which he excludes the plaintiff from prosecuting his suit. This right of a defendant did not exist in the old Roman law.

PRAESES. [PROVINCIA.]

PRAESUL. [SALII.]

PRAETEXTA. [TOGA.]

PRAETOR (στρατηγός), was originally a title which designated the consuls as the leaders of the armies of the state. The period and office of the command of the consuls might appropriately be called *Praetorium*. Praetor was also a title of office among the Latins. The first praetor specially so called was appointed in B.C. 366, and he was chosen only from the patricians, who had this new office created as a kind of indemnification to themselves for being compelled to share the consulship with the plebeians. No plebeian praetor was appointed till the year B.C. 337. The praetor was called *collega consulibus*, and was elected with the same auspices at the comitia centuriata. The praetorship was originally a kind of third consulship, and the chief functions of the praetor (*jus in urbe dicere, jura reddere*) were a portion of the functions of the consuls. The praetor sometimes commanded the armies of the state; and while the consuls were absent with the armies, he exercised their functions within the city. He was a magistratus curulis, and he had the imperium, and consequently was one of the magistratus majores: but he owed respect and obedience to the consuls. His insignia of office were six lictors; but at a later period he had only two lictors in Rome. The praetorship was at first given to a consul of the preceding year.—In B.C. 246 another praetor was appointed, whose business was to administer justice in matters in dispute between peregrini, or peregrini and Roman citizens; and accordingly he was called *praetor peregrinus*. The other praetor was then called *praetor urbanus, qui jus inter cives dicit*, and sometimes simply *praetor urbanus* and *praetor urbis*. The two praetors determined by lot which functions they should respectively exercise. If either of them was at the head of the army, the other performed all the duties of both within the city. Sometimes the military imperium of a praetor was prolonged for a second year. When the territories of the state were extended beyond the limits of Italy, new praetors were made. Thus, two praetors were created B.C. 227, for the administration of Sicily and Sardinia, and two more were added when the two Spanish provinces were formed, B.C. 197. When there were six praetors, two stayed in the city, and the other four went abroad. The senate determined their provinces, which were distributed among them by lot. After the discharge of his judicial functions in the city, a praetor often had the administration of a province, with the title of *propraetor*. Sulla increased the number of praetors to eight, which Julius Caesar raised successively to ten, twelve, fourteen, and sixteen. Augustus, after several changes, fixed the number at twelve. Under Tiberius there were sixteen. Two praetors were appointed by Claudius for matters relating to fideicommissa, when the business in this department of the law had become considerable, but Titus reduced the number to one; and Nerva added a praetor for the decision of matters between the fiscus and individuals. Thus there were eventually eighteen praetors, who administered justice in the state.—The praetor urbanus was specially named praetor, and he was the first in rank. His duties confined him to Rome, as is implied by the name, and he could only leave the city for ten days at a time. It was part of his duty to superintend the Ludi Apollinares. He was also the chief magistrate for the administration of justice; and to the edicta of the successive praetors the Roman law owes in a great degree its development and improvement. Both the praetor urbanus and the praetor peregrinus had the jus edicendi, and their functions in this respect do not appear to have been limited on the establishment of the imperial power, though it must have been gradually restricted, as the practice of imperial constitutions and rescripts became common. [EDICTUM.] The chief judicial functions of the praetor in civil matters consisted in giving a judex. [JUDEX.] It was only in the case of interdicts that he decided in a summary way. [INTERDICTUM.] Proceedings before the praetor were technically said to be *in jure*. The praetors also presided at trials of criminal matters. These were the quaestiones perpetuae, or the trials for repetundae, ambitus, majestas, and peculatus, which, when there were six praetors, were assigned to four out of the number. Sulla added to these quaestiones those of falsum, de sicariis et veneficis, and de parricidis, and for this purpose he added two, or, according to some accounts, four praetors. On these occasions the praetor presided, but a body of judices determined by a majority of votes the condemnation or acquittal of the accused. [JUDEX.] The praetor, when he administered justice, sat on a sella curulis in a tribunal, which was that part of the court which was appropriated to the praetor and his assessors and friends, and is opposed to the subsellia, or part occupied by the judices, and others who were present.

PRAETORIA COHORS. [PRAETORIANI.]
PRAETORIANI, sc. *milites*, or *praetoriae cohortes*, a body of troops instituted by Augustus to protect his person and his power, and called by that name in imitation of the *praetoria cohors*, or select troops which attended the person of the praetor or general of the Roman army. They originally consisted of nine or ten cohorts, each comprising a thousand men, horse and foot. Augustus, in accordance with his general policy of avoiding the appearance of despotism, stationed only three of these cohorts in the capital, and dispersed the remainder in the adjacent towns of Italy. Tiberius, however, under pretence of introducing a stricter discipline among them, assembled them all at Rome in a permanent camp, which was strongly fortified. Their number was increased by Vitellius to sixteen cohorts, or 16,000 men. The praetorians were distinguished by double pay and especial privileges. Their term of service was originally fixed by Augustus at twelve years, but was afterwards increased to sixteen years; and when they had served their time, each soldier received 20,000 sesterces. They soon became the most powerful body in the state, and, like the janissaries at Constantinople, frequently deposed and elevated emperors according to their pleasure. Even the most powerful of the emperors were obliged to court their favour; and they always obtained a liberal donation upon the accession of each sovereign. After the death of Pertinax (A. D. 193) they even offered the empire for sale, which was purchased by Didius Julianus; but upon the accession of Severus in the same year they were disbanded, on account of the part they had taken in the death of Pertinax, and banished from the city. The emperors, however, could not dispense with guards, and accordingly the praetorians were restored on a new model by Severus, and increased to four times their ancient number. Diocletian reduced their numbers and abolished their privileges; they were still allowed to remain at Rome, but had no longer the guard of the emperor's person, as he never resided in the capital. Their numbers were again increased by Maxentius; but after his defeat by Constantine, A. D. 312, they were entirely suppressed by the latter, their fortified camp destroyed, and those who had not perished in the battle between Constantine and Maxentius were dispersed among the legions. The commander of the praetorians was called PRAEFECTUS PRAETORIO.

PRAETORIUM, the name of the general's tent in the camp, and so called because the name of the chief Roman magistrate was originally praetor, and not consul. [CASTRA.] The officers who attended on the general in the *praetorium*, and formed his council of war, were called by the same name. The word was also used in several other significations, which were derived from the original one. Thus the residence of a governor of a province was called the *praetorium*; and the same name was also given to any large house or palace. The camp of the praetorian troops at Rome, and frequently the praetorian troops themselves, were called by this name. [PRAETORIANI.]

PRANDIUM. [COENA, p. 96, b.]
PRELUM. [VINUM.]
PRIMIPILUS. [CENTURIO.]
PRINCEPS JUVENTUTIS. [EQUITES.]
PRINCEPS SENATUS. [SENATUS.]
PRINCIPES. [EXERCITUS, p. 168, b.]
PRINCIPIA, PRINCIPALIS VIA. [CASTRA.]

PRĪVĪLĒGĬUM. [Lex.]

PRŌBŎLĒ (προβολή), an accusation of a criminal nature, preferred before the people of Athens in assembly, with a view to obtain their sanction for bringing the charge before a judicial tribunal. The *probolé* was reserved for those cases where the public had sustained an injury, or where, from the station, power, or influence of the delinquent, the prosecutor might deem it hazardous to proceed in the ordinary way without being authorised by a vote of the sovereign assembly. In this point it differed from the *eisangelia*, that in the latter the people were called upon either to pronounce final judgment, or to direct some peculiar method of trial ; whereas, in the *probolé* after the judgment of the assembly, the parties proceeded to trial in the usual manner. The cases to which the *probolé* was applied were, complaints against magistrates for official misconduct or oppression ; against those public informers and mischief-makers who were called *sycophantae* (συκοφάνται); against those who outraged public decency at the religious festivals ; and against all such as by evil practices exhibited disaffection to the state.

PRŌBOULEUMA. [Boule.]

PRŌBOULI (πρόβουλοι), a name applicable to any persons who are appointed to consult or take measures for the benefit of the people. Ten *probouli* were appointed at Athens, after the end of the Sicilian war, to act as a committee of public safety. Their authority did not last much longer than a year ; for a year and a half afterwards Pisander and his colleagues established the council of Four Hundred, by which the democracy was overthrown.

PRŌCONSUL (ἀνθύπατος), an officer who acted in the place of a consul, without holding the office of consul itself. The proconsul, however, was generally one who had held the office of consul, so that the proconsulship was a continuation, though a modified one, of the consulship. The first time when the imperium of a consul was prolonged, was in B. C. 327, in the case of Q. Publilius Philo, whose return to Rome would have been followed by the loss of most of the advantages that had been gained in his campaign. The power of proconsul was conferred by a senatusconsultum and plebiscitum, and was nearly equal to that of a regular consul, for he had the imperium and jurisdictio, but it differed inasmuch as it did not extend over the city and its immediate vicinity, and was conferred, without the auspicia, by a mere decree of the senate and people, and not in the comitia for elections. When the number of Roman provinces had become great, it was customary for the consuls, who during the latter period of the republic spent the year of their consulship at Rome, to undertake at its close the conduct of a war in a province, or its peaceful administration, with the title of proconsuls. There are some extraordinary cases on record in which a man obtained a province with the title of proconsul without having held the consulship before. The first case of this kind occurred in B. C. 211, when young P. Cornelius Scipio was created proconsul of Spain in the comitia centuriata.

PRŌCŪRĀTOR, a person who has the management of any business committed to him by another. Thus it is applied to a person who maintains or defends an action on behalf of another, or, as we should say, an attorney [Actio] : to a steward in a family [Calculator] : to an officer in the provinces belonging to the Caesar, who attended to the duties discharged by the quaestor in the other provinces [Provincia] : to an officer engaged in the administration of the fiscus [Fiscus] : and to various other officers under the empire.

PRŌDIGĬUM, in its widest acceptation, denotes any sign by which the gods indicated to men a future event, whether good or evil, and thus includes omens and auguries of every description. It is, however, generally employed in a more restricted sense, to signify some strange incident or wonderful appearance which was supposed to herald the approach or misfortune, and happened under such circumstances as to announce that the calamity was impending over a whole community or nation rather than over private individuals. The word may be considered synonymous with *ostentum*, *monstrum*, *portentum*. Since prodigies were viewed as direct manifestations of the wrath of heaven, it was believed that this wrath might be appeased by prayers and sacrifices duly offered to the offended powers. This being a matter which deeply concerned the public welfare, the necessary rites were in ancient times regularly performed, under the direction of the pontifices, by the consuls before they left the city, the solemnities being called *procuratio prodigiorum*.

PRŌDŎSĬA (προδοσία) included not only every species of treason, but also every such crime as (in the opinion of the Greeks) would amount to a betraying or desertion of the interest of a man's country. The highest sort of treason was the attempt to establish a despotism (τυραννίς), or to subvert the constitution (καταλύειν τὴν πολιτείαν), and in democracies καταλύειν τὸν δῆμον or τὸ πλῆθος. Other kinds of treason were a secret correspondence with a foreign enemy ; a betraying of an important trust, such as a fleet, army, or fortress, a desertion of post, a disobedience of orders, or any other act of treachery, or breach of duty in the public service. But not only would overt acts of disobedience or treachery amount to the crime of προδοσία, but also the neglect to perform those active duties which the Greeks in general expected of every good citizen. Cowardice in battle (δειλία) would be an instance of this kind; so would any breach of the oath taken by the ἔφηβοι at Athens; or any line of conduct for which a charge of disaffection to the people (μισο-δημία) might be successfully maintained. The regular punishment appointed by the law for most kinds of treason appears to have been death, which, no doubt, might be mitigated by decree of the people, as in the case of Miltiades and many others. The goods of traitors, who suffered death, were confiscated, and their houses razed to the ground; nor were they permitted to be buried in the country, but had their bodies cast out in some place on the confines of Attica and Megara. Therefore it was that the bones of Themistocles, who had been condemned for treason, were brought over and buried secretly by his friends. The posterity of a traitor became ἄτιμοι, and those of a tyrant were liable to share the fate of their ancestor.

PROÉDRI. [BOULE.]
PROFESTI DIES. [DIES.]
PROLETARII. [CAPUT.]
PROMETHEIA (προμήθεια), a festival celebrated at Athens in honour of Prometheus. It was one of the five Attic festivals, which were held with a torch-race in the Cerameicus [comp. LAMPADEPHORIA], for which the gymnasiarchs had to supply the youths from the gymnasia. Prometheus himself was believed to have instituted this torch-race, whence he was called the torch-bearer.
PROMULSIS. [COENA, p. 96, b.]
PRONUBAE, PRONUBI. [MATRIMONIUM.]
PROPRAETOR. [PRAETOR.]
PROPYLAEA (προπύλαια), the entrance to a temple, or sacred enclosure, consisted of a gateway flanked by buildings, whence the plural form of the word. The Egyptian temples generally had magnificent propylaea, consisting of a pair of oblong truncated pyramids of solid masonry, the faces of which were sculptured with hieroglyphics. In Greek, except when the Egyptian temples are spoken of, the word is generally used to signify the entrance to the Acropolis of Athens, which was executed under the administration of Pericles.
PROQUAESTOR. [QUAESTOR.]

PRORA. [NAVIS, p. 263.]
PROSCENIUM. [THEATRUM.]
PROSCRIPTIO. The verb proscribere properly signifies to exhibit a thing for sale by means of a bill or advertisement. But in the time of Sulla it assumed a very different meaning, for he applied it to a measure of his own invention (B.C. 82), namely, the sale of the property of those who were put to death at his command, and who were themselves called proscripti. After this example of a proscription had once been set, it was readily adopted by those in power during the civil commotions of subsequent years. In the proscription of Antonius, Caesar, and Lepidus (B.C. 43), Cicero and some of the most distinguished Romans were put to death.
PROSTATES (προστάτης). [LIBERTUS.]
PROSTATES TOU DEMOU (προστάτης τοῦ δήμου), a leader of the people, denoted at Athens and in other democratical states, a person who by his character and eloquence placed himself at the head of the people, and whose opinion had the greatest sway amongst them: such was Pericles. It appears, however, that προστάτης τοῦ δήμου was also the title of a public officer in those Dorian states in which the government was democratical.
PROTHESMIA (προθεσμία), the term limited for bringing actions and prosecutions at Athens. The Athenian expression προθεσμίας νόμος corresponds to our statute of limitations. The time for commencing actions to recover debts, or compensation for injuries, appears to have been limited to five years at Athens.
PROVINCIA. This word is merely a shortened form of providentia, and was frequently used in the sense of "a duty" or "matter entrusted to a person." But it is ordinarily employed to denote a part of the Roman dominion beyond Italy, which had a regular organisation, and was under Roman administration. Livy likewise uses the word to denote a district or enemy's country, which was assigned to a general as the field of his operations, before the establishment of any provincial governments.—The Roman state in its complete development consisted of two parts with a distinct organisation, Italia and the Provinciae. There were no Provinciae in this sense of the word till the Romans had extended their conquests beyond Italy; and Sicily was the first country that was made a Roman province: Sardinia was made a province B.C. 235. The Roman province of Gallia Ulterior in the time of Caesar was sometimes designated simply by the term Provincia, a name which has been perpetuated in the modern Provence. A conquered country received its provincial organisation either

from the Roman commander, whose acts required the approval of the senate; or the government was organised by the commander and a body of commissioners appointed by the senate out of their own number. The mode of dealing with a conquered country was not uniform. When constituted a provincia, it did not become to all purposes an integral part of the Roman state; it retained its national existence, though it lost its sovereignty. The organisation of Sicily was completed by P. Rupilius with the aid of ten legates. The island was formed into two districts, with Syracuse for the chief town of the eastern and Lilybaeum of the western district: the whole island was administered by a governor annually sent from Rome. He was assisted by two quaestors, and was accompanied by a train of praecones, scribae, haruspices, and other persons, who formed his cohors. The quaestors received from the Roman aerarium the necessary sums for the administration of the island, and they also collected the taxes, except those which were farmed by the censors at Rome. One quaestor resided at Lilybaeum, and the other with the governor or praetor at Syracuse. For the administration of justice the island was divided into *Fora* or *Conventus*, which were territorial divisions. [CONVENTUS.] The island was bound to furnish and maintain soldiers and sailors for the service of Rome, and to pay tributum for the carrying on of wars. The governor could take provisions for the use of himself and his cohors on condition of paying for them. The Roman state had also the portoria which were let to farm to Romans at Rome. The governor had complete jurisdictio in the island, with the imperium and potestas. He could delegate these powers to his quaestors, but there was always an appeal to him, and for this and other purposes he made circuits through the different conventus.—Such was the organisation of Sicilia as a province, which may be taken as a sample of the general character of Roman provincial government. The governor, upon entering on his duties, published an edict, which was often framed upon the Edictum Urbanum. Cicero, when proconsul of Cilicia, says that on some matters he framed an edict of his own, and that as to others he referred to the Edicta Urbana. There was one great distinction between Italy and the provinces as to the nature of property in land. Provincial land could not be an object of Quiritarian ownership, and it was accordingly appropriately called Possessio. Provincial land could be transferred without the forms required in the case of Italian land, but it was subject to the payment of a land-tax (*vectigal*).—The Roman provinces up to the battle of Actium are: Sicilia, Sardinia et Corsica; Hispania Citerior et Ulterior; Gallia Citerior; Gallia Narbonensis et Comata; Illyricum; Macedonia; Achaia; Asia; Cilicia; Syria; Bithynia et Pontus; Cyprus; Africa; Cyrenaica et Creta; Numidia; Mauritania. Those of a subsequent date, which were either new or arose from division, are: Rhaetia; Noricum; Pannonia; Moesia; Dacia; Britannia; Mauritania Caesariensis and Tingitana; Aegyptus; Cappadocia; Galatia; Rhodus; Lycia; Commagene; Judaea; Arabia; Mesopotamia; Armenia; Assyria.—At first praetors were appointed as governors of provinces, but afterwards they were appointed to the government of provinces, upon the expiration of their year of office at Rome, and with the title of propraetores. In the later times of the republic, the consuls also, after the expiration of their year of office, received the government of a province, with the title of proconsules: such provinces were called consulares. The provinces were generally distributed by lot, but the distribution was sometimes arranged by agreement among the persons entitled to them. By a Sempronian Lex the proconsular provinces were annually determined before the election of the consuls, the object of which was to prevent all disputes. A senatusconsultum of the year 55 B.C. provided that no consul or practor should have a province till after the expiration of five years from the time of his consulship or praetorship. A province was generally held for a year, but the time was often prolonged. When a new governor arrived in his province, his predecessor was required to leave it within thirty days. The governor of a province had originally to account at Rome (*ad urbem*) for his administration, from his own books and those of his quaestors; but after the passing of a Lex Julia, B.C. 61, he was bound to deposit two copies of his accounts (*rationes*) in the two chief cities of his province, and to forward one (*totidem verbis*) to the aerarium. If the governor misconducted himself in the administration of the province, the provincials applied to the Roman senate, and to the powerful Romans who were their patroni. The offences of repetundae and peculatus were the usual grounds of complaint by the provincials; and if a governor had betrayed the interests of the state, he was also liable to the penalties attached to majestas. Quaestiones were established for inquiries into these offences; yet it was not always an easy matter to bring a guilty governor to the punishment that he deserved.—With the establishment of the imperial power under Augustus, a considerable change was made in the administration of the provinces. Augustus took the charge of those provinces where a large military force was required; the rest were left to the care of the senate and the Roman people. Accordingly we find in the older jurists the division of provinciae into those which were *propriae populi Romani*, and those which were *propriae Caesaris*; and this division, with some modifications, continued to the third century. The senatorian provinces were distributed among consulares and those who had filled the office of praetor, two provinces being given to the consulares and the rest to the praetorii: these governors were called *proconsules*, or *praesides*, which latter is the usual term employed by the old jurists for a provincial governor. The praesides had the jurisdictio of the praetor urbanus and the praetor peregrinus: and their quaestors had the same jurisdiction that the curule aediles had at Rome. The imperial provinces were governed by *legati Caesaris*, with praetorian power, the proconsular power being in the Caesar himself, and the legati being his deputies and representatives. The legati were selected from those who had been consuls or praetors, or from the senators. They held their office and their power at the pleasure of the emperor; and he delegated to them both military command and jurisdictio, just as a proconsul in the republican period delegated these powers to his legati. These legati had also legati under them. No quaestors were sent to the provinces of the Caesar. In place of the quaestors, there were *procuratores Caesaris*, who were either equites or freedmen of the Caesar. Egypt was governed by an eques with the title of praefectus. The procuratores looked after the taxes, paid the troops, and generally were intrusted with the interests of the fiscus. Judaea, which was a part of the province of Syria, was governed by a procurator, who had the powers of a legatus. It appears that there were also procuratores Caesaris in the senatorian provinces, who collected certain dues of the fiscus, which were independent of what was due to the aerarium. The regular taxes, as in the republican period, were the poll-tax and land-tax. The taxation was founded on a census of persons and property, which was established by Augustus. The portoria and other dues were farmed by the publicani, as in the republican period.

PROVOCATIO. [APPELLATIO.]
PROVOCATORES. [GLADIATORES.]
PROXENUS (πρόξενος). [HOSPITIUM.]
PRYTANEIUM (πρυτανεῖον), the public hall or town-hall in a Greek state. The *prytaneia* of the ancient Greek states and cities were to the communities living around them, what private houses were to the families which occupied them. Just as the house of each family was its home, so was the *prytaneium* of every state or city the common home of its members or inhabitants. This correspondence between the *prytaneium* or home of the city, and the private home of a man's family, was at Athens very remarkable. A perpetual fire was kept burning on the public altar of the city in the prytaneium, just as in private houses a fire was kept up on the domestic altar in the inner court of the house. Moreover, the city of Athens exercised in its prytaneium the duties of hospitality, both to its own citizens and to strangers. Thus foreign ambassadors were entertained here, as well as Athenian envoys, on their return home from a successful or well-conducted mission. Here, too, were entertained from day to day the successive prytanes or presidents of the senate, together with those citizens who, whether from personal or ancestral services to the state, were honoured with what was called the σίτησις ἐν πρυτανείῳ, or the privilege of taking their meals there at the public cost. This was granted sometimes for a limited period, sometimes for life, in which latter case the parties enjoying it were called ἀείσιτοι. Moreover, from the ever-burning fire of the prytaneium, or home of a mother state, was carried the sacred fire which was to be kept burning in the prytaneia of her colonies; and if it happened that this was ever extinguished, the flame was rekindled from the prytaneium of the parent city. Lastly, a prytaneium was also a distinguishing mark of an independent state. The prytaneium of Athens lay under the Acropolis on its northern side (near the ἀγορά), and was, as its name denotes, originally the place of assembly of the *prytanes*; in the earliest times it probably stood on the Acropolis. Officers called *prytanes* (πρυτανεῖς) were entrusted with the chief magistracy in several states of Greece, as Corcyra, Corinth, Miletus. At Athens they were in early times probably a magistracy of the second rank in the state (next to the archon), acting as judges in various cases (perhaps in conjunction with him), and sitting in the prytaneium. That this was the case is rendered probable by the fact, that even in aftertimes the fees paid into court by plaintiff and defendant, before they could proceed to trial, and received by the dicasts, were called *prytaneia*.

PRYTANES. [PRYTANEIUM; BOULE.]
PSEPHISMA. [BOULE; NOMOTHETES.]
PSEPHUS (ψῆφος), a ball of stone, used by

the Athenian dicasts in giving their verdict. [CADISCUS.] Hence ψηφίζεσθαι and its various derivatives are used so often to signify *voting*, *determining*, &c.

PSEUDENGRAPHĒS GRAPHĒ (ψευδεγγραφῆς γραφή). The name of every state debtor at Athens was entered in a register by the practores, whose duty it was to collect the debts, and erase the name of the party when he had paid it. If they made a false entry, either wilfully, or upon the suggestion of another person, the aggrieved party might institute a prosecution against them, or against the person upon whose suggestion it was made. Such prosecution was called γραφή ψευδεγγραφῆς. It would lie also, where a man was registered as debtor for more than was really due from him.

PSEUDOCLĒTEIAS GRAPHĒ (ψευδοκλητείας γραφή), a prosecution against one, who had appeared as a witness (κλητήρ or κλήτωρ) to prove that a defendant had been duly summoned, and thereby enabled the plaintiff to get a judgment by default. The false witness (κλητήρ) was liable to be criminally prosecuted, and punished at the discretion of the court. The γραφή ψευδοκλητείας came before the Thesmothetae, and the question at the trial simply was, whether the defendant in the former cause had been summoned or not.

PSILI (ψιλοί). [ARMA.]

PSYCTER (ψυκτήρ, *dim.* ψυκτηρίδιον), a wine-cooler, was sometimes made of bronze or silver. One of earthenware is preserved in the Museum of Antiquities at Copenhagen. It consists of one deep vessel for holding ice, which is fixed within another for holding wine. The wine was poured in at the top. It thus surrounded the vessel of ice and was cooled by the contact. It was drawn off so as to fill the drinking-cups by means of a cock at the bottom.

PŪBES, PŪBERTAS. [IMPUBES; INFANS.]

PUBLICANI, farmers of the public revenues of the Roman state (*vectigalia*). Their name is formed from *publicum*, which signifies all that belongs to the state, and is sometimes used by Roman writers as synonymous with *vectigal*. The revenues which Rome derived from conquered countries, consisting chiefly of tolls, tithes, harbour duties, the scriptura, or the tax which was paid for the use of the public pasture lands, and the duties paid for the use of mines and salt-works (*salinae*), were let out, or, as the Romans expressed it, were sold by the censors in Rome itself to the highest bidder. This sale generally took place in the month of Quinctilis, and was made for a lustrum. The terms on which the revenues were let, were fixed by the censors in the so-called *leges censoriae*. The people or the senate, however, sometimes modified the terms fixed by the censors, in order to raise the credit of the publicani; and in some cases even the tribunes of the people interfered in this branch of the administration. The tithes raised in the province of Sicily alone, with the exception of those of wine, oil, and garden produce, were not sold at Rome, but in the districts of Sicily itself, according to a practice established by Hiero. The persons who undertook the farming of the public revenue of course belonged to the wealthiest Romans, and during the latter period of the republic they belonged almost exclusively to the equestrian order. Their wealth and consequent influence may be seen from the fact, that as early as the second Punic war, after the battle of Cannae, when the aerarium was entirely exhausted, the publicani advanced large sums of money to the state, on condition of repayment after the end of the war. The words equites and publicani are sometimes used as synonymous. The publicani had to give security to the state for the sum at which they bought one or more branches of the revenue in a province; but as for this reason the property of even the wealthiest individual must have been inadequate, a number of equites generally united together, and formed a company (*socii, societas*, or *corpus*), which was recognised by the state, and by which they were enabled to carry on their undertakings upon a large scale. Such companies appear as early as the second Punic war. The shares which each partner of such a company took in the business were called *partes*, and if they were small, *particulae*. The responsible person in each company, and the one who contracted with the state, was called *manceps* [MANCEPS]; but there was also a *magister* to manage the business of each society, who resided at Rome, and kept an extensive correspondence with the agents in the provinces. He seems to have held his office only for one year; his representative in the provinces was called *sub magistro*, who had to travel about, and superintend the actual business of collecting the revenues. Nobody but a Roman citizen was allowed to become a member of a company of publicani; freedmen and slaves were excluded. No Roman magistrate, however, or governor of a province, was allowed to take any share whatever in a company of publicani, a regulation which was chiefly intended as a protection against the oppression of the provincials. The collection of the taxes in the provinces was performed by an inferior class of men, who were said *operas publicanis dare*, or *esse in operis societatis*. They were engaged by the publicani, and consisted of freemen as well as slaves, Romans as well as provincials. The separate branches of the public revenue in the provinces (*decumae*, *portoria*, *scriptura*, and the revenues from the mines and salt-works) were mostly leased to separate companies of publicani; whence they were distinguished by names derived from that particular branch which they had taken in farm; *e. g.* *decumani*, *pecuarii* or *scripturarii*, *salinarii* or *mancipes salinarum*, &c. [DECUMAE; PORTORIUM; SALINAE; SCRIPTURA.] The *portitores* were not publicani properly so called, but only their servants engaged in examining the goods imported or exported, and levying the custom-duties upon them. They belonged to the same class as the publicans of the New Testament.

PUBLĬCUM. [PUBLICANI.]

PŪGĬLĀTUS (πύξ, πυγμή, πυγμαχία, πυγμοσύνη), boxing, was one of the earliest athletic games among the Greeks, and is frequently mentioned in Homer. In the earliest times boxers (*pugiles*, πύκται) fought naked, with the exception of a girdle (ζῶμα) round their loins; but this was not used when boxing was introduced at Olympia, as the contests in wrestling and racing had been carried on there by persons entirely naked ever since Ol. 15. Respecting the leathern thongs with which pugilists surrounded their fists, see CESTUS, where its various forms are illustrated by woodcuts. The Ionians, especially those of Samos, were at all times more distinguished pugilists than the Dorians, and at Sparta boxing is said to have been forbidden by the laws of Lycurgus. But the ancients generally considered boxing as a useful training for military purposes, and a part of education no less important than any other gymnastic exercise.

PŬGILLĀRES. [TABULAE.]

PŪGĬO (μάχαιρα), a dagger; a two-edged knife, commonly of bronze, with the hand in many cases variously ornamented or enriched.

PULLĀRĬUS. [AUSPICIUM.]

PULPĬTUM. [THEATRUM.]

PULVĪNAR, a couch provided with cushions or pillows (*pulvini*), on which the Romans placed the statues of the gods at the *Lectisternia*. [EPULONES; LECTISTERNIUM.] There was also a *pulvinar*, on which the images of the gods were laid, in the Circus.

PŬPILLA, PŬPILLUS, the name given to every *impubes* not in the power of their father, but subject to a guardian. [IMPUBES; TUTELA.]

PUPPIS. [NAVIS.]

PŪTEAL, properly means the enclosure surrounding the opening of a well, to protect persons from falling into it. It was either round or square, and seems usually to have been of the height of three or four feet from the ground. It was the practice in some cases to surround a sacred place with an enclosure open at the top, and such enclosures, from the great similarity they bore to *putealia*, were called by this name. There were two such places in the Roman forum; one of these was called *Puteal Libonis* or *Scribonianum*, because a chapel (*sacellum*) in that place had been struck by lightning, and Scribonius Libo expiated it by proper ceremonies, and erected a puteal around it, open at the top, to preserve the memory of the place. The form of this puteal is preserved on several coins of the Scribonian gens. This puteal seems to have been near the atrium of Vesta, and was a common place of meeting for usurers. The other puteal was in the comitium, on the left side of the senate-house, and in it were deposited the whetstone and razor of Attus Navius.

Puteal on a Coin of the Scribonia Gens. (British Museum.)

PŬTĬCŬLI. [FUNUS.]

PYANEPSIA (πυανέψια), a festival celebrated at Athens every year on the seventh of Pyanepsion, in honour of Apollo, said to have been instituted by Theseus after his return from Crete. The festival, as well as the month in which it took place, are said to have derived their names from πύαμος, another form for κύαμος, *i. e.* pulse or beans, which were cooked at this season and carried about.

PYLĂGŎRAE. [AMPHICTYONES.]

PYRA. [FUNUS.]

PYRRHĬCA. [SALTATIO.]

PYTHIA (πύθια), one of the four great national festivals of the Greeks. It was celebrated in the neighbourhood of Delphi, anciently called Pytho, in honour of Apollo, Artemis, and Leto. The place of this solemnity was the Crissaean plain, which for this purpose contained a hippodromus or race-course, a stadium of 1000 feet in length, and a theatre, in which the musical contests took place. The Pythian games were, according to most legends, instituted by Apollo himself. They were originally perhaps nothing more than a religious panegyris, occasioned by the oracle of Delphi, and the sacred games are said to have been at first only a musical contest, which consisted in singing a hymn to the honour of the Pythian god, with the accompaniment of the cithara. They must, on account of the celebrity of the Delphic oracle, have become a national festival for all the Greeks at a very early period, and gradually all the various contests were introduced which occur in the Olympic games. [OLYMPIA.] Down to Ol. 48. the Delphians had been the agonothetae at the Pythian games; but in the third year of this Olympiad, after the Crissaean war, the Amphictyons took the management under their care, and appointed certain persons, called *Epimeletae* (ἐπιμεληταί), to conduct them. Some of the ancients date the institution of the Pythian games from this time. Previous to Ol. 48. the Pythian games had been an ἐνναετηρίς, that is, they had been celebrated at the end of every eighth year; but in Ol. 48. 3. they became, like the Olympia, a πενταετηρίς, i. e. they were held at the end of every fourth year; and a Pythiad, therefore, from the time that it was used as an aera, comprehended a space of four years, commencing with the third year of every Olympiad. They were in all probability held in the spring, and took place in the month of Bucatius, which corresponded to the Attic Munychion.

PYTHII (πύθιοι), four persons appointed by the Spartan kings, two by each, as messengers to the temple of Delphi. Their office was highly honourable and important; they were always the messmates of the Spartan kings.

PYXIS, *dim.* PYXIDULA (πύξις, *dim.* πυξίδιον), a casket; a jewel-box. The caskets in which the ladies of ancient times kept their jewels and other ornaments, were made of gold, silver, ivory, mother-of-pearl, tortoise-shell, &c. They were also much enriched with sculpture. The annexed woodcut represents a very plain jewel-box, out of which a dove is extracting a riband or fillet.

QUADRAGESIMA, the fortieth part of the imported goods, was the ordinary rate of the Portorium under the empire. [PORTORIUM.]

QUADRANS. [As.]

QUADRANTAL, or AMPHORA QUADRANTAL, or AMPHORA only, was the principal Roman measure of capacity for fluids. A standard model of the *Amphora* was kept with great care in the temple of Jupiter in the Capitol, and was called *amphora Capitolina*. It contained 5·77 imperial gallons, or a little more than 5¾ gallons, or than 5 gallons and 6 pints.

QUADRIGA. [CURRUS.]

QUADRIGATUS. [DENARIUS.]

QUADRUPLATORES: public informers or accusers were so called, either because they received a fourth part of the criminal's property, or because those who were convicted were condemned to pay fourfold (*quadrupli damnari*), as in cases of violation of the laws respecting gambling, usury, &c.

QUAESTIONES, QUAESTIONES PERPETUAE. [JUDEX: PRAETOR.]

QUAESTOR (ταμίας), a name given to two distinct classes of Roman officers. It is derived from *quaero*, and Varro gives a definition which embraces the principal functions of both classes of officers: *Quaestores a quaerendo, qui conquirerent publicas pecunias et maleficia*. The one class, therefore, had to do with the collecting and keeping of the public revenues, and the others were a kind of public accusers. The former bore the name of *Quaestores Classici*, the latter of *Quaestores Parricidii*.—The *Quaestores Parricidii* were public accusers, two in number, who conducted the accusation of persons guilty of murder or any other capital offence, and carried the sentence into execution. In the early period of the republic the quaestores parricidii appear to have become a standing office, which, like others, was held only for one year. They were appointed by the populus or the curies on the presentation of the consuls. When these quaestores discovered that a capital offence had been committed, they had to bring the charge before the comitia for trial. When the sentence had been pronounced by the people, the quaestores parricidii executed it; thus they threw Spurius Cassius from the Tarpeian rock. They were mentioned in the laws of the Twelve Tables, and after the time of the decemvirate they still continued to be ap-

Pyxis, jewel-box. (From a Painting at Herculaneum.)

QUAESTOR.

pointed, though probably no longer by the curies, but either in the comitia centuriata or tribute, which they therefore must have had the right of assembling in cases of emergency. From the year B.C. 366 they are no longer mentioned in Roman history, as their functions were gradually transferred to the triumviri capitales. [TRIUMVIRI CAPITALES.] —The *Quaestores Classici*, usually called *Quaestores* simply, were officers entrusted with the care of the public money. They were elected by the centuries, and the office is said to have been first instituted by Valerius Publicola. They were at first only two in number, and of course taken only from the patricians. As the senate had the supreme administration of the finances, the quaestors were in some measure only its agents or paymasters, for they could not dispose of any part of the public money without being directed by the senate. Their duties consequently consisted in making the necessary payments from the aerarium, and receiving the public revenues. Of both they had to keep correct accounts in their *tabulae publicae*. Demands which any one might have on the aerarium, and outstanding debts, were likewise registered by them. Fines to be paid to the public treasury were registered and exacted by them. Another branch of their duties, which, however, was likewise connected with the treasury, was to provide the proper accommodation for foreign ambassadors, and such persons as were connected with the republic by ties of public hospitality. —In B.C. 421 the number of quaestors was doubled, and the tribunes tried to effect, by an amendment of the law, that a part (probably two) of the quaestores should be plebeians. This attempt was indeed frustrated, but the interrex L. Papirius effected a compromise, that the election should not be restricted to either order. After this law was carried, eleven years passed without any plebeian being elected to the office: at last, in B.C. 409, three of the four quaestors were plebeians. A person who had held the office of quaestor had undoubtedly, as in later times, the right to take his seat in the senate, unless he was excluded as unworthy by the next censors. And this was probably the reason why the patricians so resolutely opposed the admission of plebeians to this office. Henceforth the consuls, whenever they took the field against an enemy, were accompanied by one quaestor each, who at first had only to superintend the sale of the booty, the produce of which was either divided among the legion, or was transferred to the aerarium. Subsequently, however, we find that these quaestors also kept the funds of the army, which they had received from the treasury at

317

QUAESTOR.

Rome, and gave the soldiers their pay; they were in fact the pay-masters of the army. The two other quaestors, who remained at Rome, continued to discharge the same duties as before, and were distinguished from those who accompanied the consuls by the epithet *urbani*. In B.C. 265, after the Romans had made themselves masters of Italy, and when, in consequence, the administration of the treasury and the raising of the revenues became more laborious and important, the number of quaestors was again doubled to eight; and it is probable that henceforth their number continued to be increased in proportion as the empire became extended. One of the eight quaestors was appointed by lot to the *Quaestura Ostiensis*, a most laborious and important post, as he had to provide Rome with corn. Besides the quaestor Ostiensis, who resided at Ostia, three other quaestors were distributed in Italy, to raise those parts of the revenue which were not farmed by the publicani, and to control the latter. One of them resided at Cales, and the two others probably in towns on the Upper Sea. The two remaining quaestors were sent to Sicily.—Sulla, in his dictatorship, raised the number of quaestors to twenty, that he might have a large number of candidates for the senate, and J. Caesar even to forty. In the year B.C. 49 no quaestors were elected, and Caesar transferred the keeping of the aerarium to the aediles. From this time forward the treasury was sometimes entrusted to the praetors, sometimes to the praetorii, and sometimes again to quaestors. [AERARIUM.] Quaestors, however, both in the city and in the provinces, occur down to the latest period of the empire. The proconsul or praetor, who had the administration of a province, was attended by a quaestor. This quaestor had undoubtedly to perform the same functions as those who accompanied the armies into the field; they were in fact the same officers, with the exception that the former were stationary in their province during the time of their office, and had consequently rights and duties which those who accompanied the armies could not have. In the provinces the quaestors had the same jurisdiction as the curule aediles at Rome. The relation existing between a praetor or proconsul of a province and his quaestor was, according to ancient custom, regarded as resembling that between a father and his son. When a quaestor died in his province, the praetors had the right of appointing a *proquaestor* in his stead; and when the praetor was absent, the quaestor supplied his place, and was then attended by lictors. In what manner the provinces were assigned to the quaestors after their election at Rome, is not mentioned, though it was probably by lot, as in the case of the quaestor Ostiensis.

QUAESTŌRĬUM. [Castra.]
QUĀLUS. [Calathus.]
QUARTĀRĬUS. [Sextarius.]
QUĀSILLĀRĬAE. [Calathus.]
QUĀSILLUM. [Calathus.]
QUĂTŬORVĬRI JŪRI DĪCUNDO. [Colonia.]
QUĂTŬORVĬRI VĬĀRUM CŪRANDĀRUM, four officers who had the superintendence of the roads (*viae*), were first appointed after the war with Pyrrhus, when so many public roads were made by the Romans.
QUĪNĀRĬUS. [Denarius.]
QUINCUNX. [As.]
QUINDĔCIMVĬRI. [Decimviri.]
QUINQUATRUS or **QUINQUATRĬA**, a festival sacred to Minerva, which was celebrated on the 19th of March. Ovid says that it was celebrated for five days, that on the first day no blood was shed, but that on the last four there were contests of gladiators. It would appear, however, that only the first day was the festival properly so called, and that the last four were merely an addition made perhaps in the time of Caesar, to gratify the people, who became so passionately fond of gladiatorial combats. On the fifth day of the festival, according to Ovid, the trumpets used in sacred rites were purified; but this seems to have been originally a separate festival called *Tubilustrium*, which was celebrated, as we know from the ancient calendars, on the 23rd of March, and would of course, when the Quinquatrus was extended to five days, fall on the last day of that festival. There was also another festival of this name, called *Quinquatrus Minusculae* or *Quinquatrus Minores*, celebrated on the Ides of June, on which the tibicines went through the city in procession to the temple of Minerva.

QUINQUENNĀLĬA, were games instituted by Nero, A.D. 60, in imitation of the Greek festivals, and celebrated like the Greek πενταετηρίδες, at the end of every four years: they consisted of musical, gymnastic, and equestrian contests.

QUINQUENNĀLIS. [Colonia, p. 101, *a*.]
QUINQUĔRĒMIS. [Navis.]
QUINQUERTĬUM. [Pentathlon.]
QUINQUĔVĬRI, or five commissioners, were frequently appointed under the republic as extraordinary magistrates to carry any measure into effect.
QUINTĀNA. [Castra.]
QUĪRĪNĀLĬA, a festival sacred to Quirinus, which was celebrated on the 17th of February, on which day Romulus (Quirinus) was said to have been carried up to heaven. This festival was also called *Stultorum feriae*, respecting the meaning of which see Fornacalia.

QUĪRĪTĬUM JUS. [Jus.]

RAMNES. [Patricii.]
RĂPĪNA. [Furtum.]
RĔCŬPĔRĀTŌRES. [Judex.]
RĔDEMPTOR, the general name for a contractor, who undertook the building and repairing of public works, private houses, &c., and in fact of any kind of work. The farmers of the public taxes were also called *Redemptores*.

RĔDĬMĪCULUM (καθετήρ), a fillet attached to the *calautica, diadema, mitra,* or other head-dress at the occiput, and passed over the shoulders, so as to hang on each side over the breast. *Redimicula* were properly female ornaments.

RĔGĬFŬGĬUM or **FŬGĀLĬA**, the king's flight, a festival which was held by the Romans every year on the 24th of February, and, according to some ancient writers, in commemoration of the flight of king Tarquinius Superbus from Rome. The day is marked in the Fasti as *nefastus*. In some ancient calendars the 24th of May is likewise called Regifugium. It is doubtful whether either of these days had anything to do with the flight of king Tarquinius: they may have derived their name from the symbolical flight of the Rex Sacrorum from the *comitium*; for this king-priest was generally not allowed to appear in the comitium, which was destined for the transaction of political matters in which he could not take part. But on certain days in the year, and certainly on the two days mentioned above, he had to go to the comitium for the purpose of offering certain sacrifices, and immediately after he had performed his functions there, he hastily fled from it; and this symbolical flight was called Regifugium.

RĔLĒGĀTĬO. [Exsilium.]
RĔMANCĬPĀTĬO. [Emancipatio.]
RĔMULCUM (ῥυμουλκεῖν τὰς ναῦς), a rope for towing a ship, and likewise a tow-barge.
RĔMŪRĬA. [Lemuria.]
RĒMUS. [Navis.]
RĔPĔTUNDAE, or **PĔCŪNĬAE RĔPĔTUNDAE**, was the term used to designate such sums of money as the socii of the Roman state or individuals claimed to recover from magistratus, judices, or publici curatores, which they had improperly taken or received in the Provinciae, or in the Urbs

Roma, either in the discharge of their jurisdictio, or in their capacity of judices, or in respect of any other public function. Sometimes the word Repetundae was used to express the illegal act for which compensation was sought, as in the phrase *repetundarum insimulari, damnari;* and Pecuniae meant not only money, but anything that had value. The first lex on the subject was the Calpurnia, which was proposed and carried by the tribunus plebis L. Calpurnius Piso (B.C. 149). By this lex a praetor was appointed for trying persons charged with this crime. It seems that the penalties of the Lex Calpurnia were merely pecuniary, and at least did not comprise exsilium. Various leges de repetundis were passed after the Lex Calpurnia, and the penalties were continually made heavier. The Lex Junia was passed probably about B.C. 126, on the proposal of M. Junius Pennus, tribunus plebis. The Lex Servilia Glaucia was proposed and carried by C. Servilius Glaucia, praetor, in the sixth consulship of Marius, B.C. 100. This lex applied to any magistratus who had improperly taken or received money from any private person; but a magistratus could not be accused during the term of office. The lex enacted that the praetor peregrinus should annually appoint 450 judices for the trial of this offence: the judices were not to be senators. The penalties of the lex were pecuniary and exsilium; the law allowed a comperendinatio. [JUDEX.] Before the Lex Servilia, the pecuniary penalty was simply restitution of what had been wrongfully taken; this lex seems to have raised the penalty to double the amount of what had been wrongfully taken; and subsequently it was made quadruple. Exsilium was only the punishment in case a man did not abide his trial, but withdrew from Rome. The lex gave the civitas to any person on whose complaint a person was convicted of repetundae. The Lex Acilia, which seems to be of uncertain date, was proposed and carried by M'. Acilius Glabrio, a tribune of the plebs, and enacted that there should be neither ampliatio nor comperendinatio. The Lex Cornelia was passed in the dictatorship of Sulla, and continued in force to the time of C. Julius Caesar. It extended the penalties of repetundae to other illegal acts committed in the provinces, and to judices who received bribes, to those to whose hands the money came, and to those who did not give into the aerarium their proconsular accounts (*proconsulares rationes*). The praetor who presided over this quaestio chose the judges by lot from the senators, whence it appears that the Servilia Lex was repealed by this lex, at least so far as related to the constitution of the court. This lex also allowed ampliatio and comperendinatio. The penalties were pecuniary (*litis aestimatio*) and the *aquae et ignis interdictio*. Under this lex were tried L. Dolabella, Cn. Piso, C. Verres, C. Macer, M. Fonteius, and L. Flaccus, the two last of whom were defended by Cicero. In the Verrine Orations Cicero complains of the comperendinatio or double hearing of the cause, which the Lex Cornelia allowed, and refers to the practice under the Lex Acilia, according to which the case for the prosecution, the defence, and the evidence were only heard once, and so the matter was decided. The last lex of repetundis was the Lex Julia, passed in the first consulship of C. Julius Caesar, B.C. 59. This lex repealed the penalty of exsilium, but in addition to the litis aestimatio, it enacted that persons convicted under this lex should lose their rank, and be disqualified from being witnesses, judices, or senators. The lex had been passed when Cicero made his oration against Piso, B.C. 55. A. Gabinius was convicted under this lex. Under the empire the offence was punishable with exile.

REPŌTIA. [MATRIMONIUM.]
REPŬDĬUM. [DIVORTIUM.]
RETIĀRĬI. [GLADIATORES.]
RĒTĬCŬLUM. [COMA.]
RĒTIS and RĒTE; *dim.* RĒTĬCŬLUM (δίκτυον), a net. Nets were made most commonly of flax or hemp, whence they are sometimes called *lina* (λίνα). The meshes (*maculae*, βρόχοι, *dim.* βροχίδες) were great or small according to the purposes intended. By far the most important application of network was to the three kindred arts of fowling, hunting, and fishing. In fowling the use of nets was comparatively limited. In hunting it was usual to extend nets in a curved line of considerable length, so as in part to surround a space into which the beasts of chace, such as the hare, the boar, the deer, the lion, and the bear, were driven through the opening left on one side. This range of nets was flanked by cords, to which feathers dyed scarlet and of other bright colours were tied, so as to flare and flutter in the wind. The hunters then sallied forth with their dogs, dislodged the animals from their coverts, and by shouts and barking drove them first within the *formido*, as the apparatus of string and feathers was called, and then, as they were scared with this appearance, within the circuit of the nets. In the drawing below three servants with staves carry on their shoulders a large net, which is intended to be set up as already described. In the lower figure the net is set up. At each end of it stands a watchman holding a staff. Being

intended to take such large quadrupeds as boars and deer (which are seen within it), the meshes are very wide (*retia rara*). The net is supported by three stakes (στάλικες, *ancones, vari*). To dispose the nets in this manner was called *retia ponere*, or *retia ten-*

Retia, Nets (From a Bas-Relief at Ince-Blundell.)

dere. Comparing it with the stature of the attendants, we perceive the net to be between five and six feet high. The upper border of the net consists of a strong rope, which was called σαρδών. Fishing-nets (ἁλιευτικὰ δίκ-*rυa*) were of different kinds. Of these the most common were the ἀμφίβληστρον, or casting-net (*funda, jaculum, retinaculum*) and the σαγήνη, *i. e.* the drag-net, or sean (*tragum, tragula, verriculum*).

Retia, Nets. (From the same.)

RĒUS. [ACTOR.]
REX (βασιλεύς, ἄναξ), king.—(1) GREEK. In the heroic age, as depicted in the poems of Homer, the kingly form of government was universal. The authority of these kings and its limitations were derived not from any definite scheme, or written code, but from the force of traditional usage, and the natural influence of the circumstances in which the kings were placed, surrounded as they were by a body of chiefs or nobles, whose power was but little inferior to that of the kings themselves. Even the title βασιλῆες is applied to them as well as to the king. The maintenance of regal authority doubtless depended greatly on the possession of personal superiority in bravery, military prowess, wisdom in council and eloquence in debate. When old age had blunted his powers and activity, a king ran a great chance of losing his influence. There was, however, an undefined notion of a sort of divine right connected with the kingly office, whence the epithet διοτρεφής, so commonly applied to kings in Homer. The characteristic emblem of the kingly office was the σκῆπτρον. [SCEPTRUM.] Our information respecting the Grecian kings in the more historical age is not ample or minute enough to enable us to draw out a detailed scheme of their functions. Respecting the kings of Sparta the reader is referred to the article EPHORI. As an illustration of the gradual limitation of the prerogatives of the king or chief magistrate, the reader may consult the article ARCHON. The title *Basileus* was sometimes applied to an officer who discharged the priestly functions of the more ancient kings, as in Athens. [ARCHON.]—(2) ROMAN. Rome was originally governed by kings. All the ancient writers agree in representing the king as elected by the people for life, and as voluntarily entrusted by them with the supreme power in the state. No reference is made to the hereditary principle in the election of the first four kings; and it is not until the fifth king Tarquinius Priscus obtained the sovereignty, that anything is said about the children of the deceased king. Since the people had conferred the regal power, it returned to them upon the death of the king. But as a new king could not be immediately appointed, an Interrex forthwith stepped into his place. The necessity for an immediate successor to the king arose from the circumstance that he alone had had the power of taking the auspicia on behalf of the state; and as the auspicia devolved upon the people at his death, it was imperative upon them to create a magistrate, to whom they could delegate the auspicia, and who would thus possess the power of mediating between the gods and the state. Originally the people consisted only of the patres or patricii; and accordingly on the death of the king, we read *res ad patres redit*, or, what is nearly the same thing, *auspicia ad patres redeunt*. [AUGUR.] The interrex was elected by the whole body of the patricians, and he appointed (*prodebat*) his successor, as it was a rule that the

first interrex could not hold the comitia for the election; but it frequently happened that the second interrex appointed a third, the third a fourth, and so on, till the election took place. The Interrex presided over the comitia curiata, which were assembled for the election of the king. The person whom the senate had selected was proposed by the interrex to the people in a regular *rogatio*, which the people could only accept or reject, for they had not the initiative and could not themselves propose any name. If the people voted in favour of the rogation, they were said *creare regem*, and their acceptance of him was called *jussus populi*. But the king did not immediately enter upon his office. Two other acts had still to take place before he was invested with the full regal authority and power. First, his *inauguratio* had to be performed, as it was necessary to obtain the divine will respecting his appointment by means of the auspices, since he was the high priest of the people. This ceremony was performed by an augur, who conducted the newly-elected king to the *arx*, or citadel, and there placed him on a stone seat with his face turned to the south, while the people waited below in anxious suspense until the augur announced that the gods had sent the favourable tokens confirming the king in his priestly character. The inauguratio did not confer upon him the auspicia; for these he obtained by his election to the royalty, as the comitia were held *auspicato*. The second act which had to be performed was the conferring of the imperium upon the king. The curiae had only determined by their previous votes who was to be king, and had not by that act bestowed the necessary power upon him; they had, therefore, to grant him the imperium by a distinct vote. Accordingly the king himself proposed to the curiae a *lex curiata de imperio*, and the curiae by voting in favour of it gave him the imperium. Livy in his first book makes no mention of the *lex curiata de imperio*, but he uses the expressions *patres auctores fierent, patres auctores facti*; but these expressions are equivalent to the *lex curiata de imperio* in the kingly period.—The king possessed the supreme power in the earliest times, and the senate and the comitia of the curiae were very slight checks upon its exercise. In the first place, the king alone possessed the right of taking the auspices on behalf of the state; and as no public business of any kind could be performed without the approbation of the gods expressed by the auspices, the king stood as mediator between the gods and the people, and in an early stage of society must necessarily have been regarded with religious awe. [AUGUR.] Secondly, the people surrendered to the king the supreme military and judicial authority by conferring the *imperium* upon him. The king was not only the commander in war, but the supreme judge in peace. Seated on his throne in the comitium, he administered justice to all comers, and decided in all cases which were brought before him, civil as well as criminal. Again, all the magistrates in the kingly period appear to have been appointed by the king and not elected by the curiae. Further, the king was not dependent upon the people for his support; but a large portion of the *ager publicus* belonged to him, which was cultivated at the expense of the state on his behalf. He had also the absolute disposal of the booty taken in war and of the conquered lands. It must not, however, be supposed that the authority of the king was absolute. The senate and the assembly of the people must have formed some check upon his power. But these were not independent bodies possessing the right of meeting at certain times and discussing questions of state. They could only be called together when the king chose, and further could only determine upon matters which the king submitted to them. The only public matter in which the king could not dispense with the co-operation of the senate and the curiae was in declarations of war. There is no trace of the people having had anything to do with the conclusion of treaties of peace.—The insignia of the king were the fasces with the axes (*secures*), which twelve lictors carried before him as often as he appeared in public, the *trabea*, the *sella curulis*, and the *toga praetexta* and *picta*. The *trabea* appears to have been the most ancient official dress, and is assigned especially to Romulus: it was of Latin origin, and is therefore represented by Virgil as worn by the Latin kings. The *toga praetexta* and *picta* were borrowed, together with the *sella curulis*, from the Etruscans, and their introduction is variously ascribed to Tullus Hostilius or Tarquinius Priscus.

REX SACRIFICŬLUS, REX SACRIFĬ-CUS, or REX SACRORUM. When the civil and military powers of the king were transferred to two praetors or consuls, upon the establishment of the republican government at Rome, these magistrates were not invested with that part of the royal dignity by virtue of which the king had been the high priest of his nation and had conducted several of the *sacra publica*, but this priestly part of his office was transferred to a priest called Rex Sacrificulus or Rex Sacrorum. The first rex sacrorum was designated, at the command of the consuls, by the college of pontiffs, and inaugurated by the augurs. He

Y

was always elected and inaugurated in the comitia curiata under the presidency of the pontiffs, and as long as a rex sacrificulus was appointed at Rome, he was always a patrician, for as he had no influence upon the management of political affairs, the plebeians never coveted this dignity. Considering that this priest was the religious representative of the kings, he ranked indeed higher than all other priests, and even higher than the pontifex maximus, but in power and influence he was far inferior to him. He held his office for life, was not allowed to hold any civil or military dignity, and was at the same time exempted from all military and civil duties. His principal functions were : 1. To perform those sacra publica which had before been performed by the kings; and his wife, who bore the title of *regina sacrorum*, had also, like the queens of former days, to perform certain priestly functions. These sacra publica he or his wife had to perform on all the Calends, Ides, and the Nundines; he to Jupiter, and she to Juno in the regia. 2. On the days called regifugium he had to offer a sacrifice in the comitium. [REGIFUGIUM.] 3. When extraordinary portenta seemed to announce some general calamity, it was his duty to try to propitiate the anger of the gods. 4. On the nundines, when the people assembled in the city, the rex sacrorum announced (*edicebat*) to them the succession of the festivals for the month. This part of his functions, however, must have ceased after the time of Cn. Flavius. He lived in a domus publica on the via sacra, near the regia and the house of the vestal virgins.

RHEDA or REDA, a travelling carriage with four wheels. Like the COVINUS and the ESSEDUM it was of Gallic origin, and may perhaps contain the same root as the German *reiten* and our *ride*. It was the common carriage used by the Romans for travelling, and was frequently made large enough not only to contain many persons, but also baggage and utensils of various kinds. The word *Epirhedium*, which was formed by the Romans from the Greek preposition ἐπί and the Gallic *rheda*, is explained by the Scholiast on Juvenal as " Ornamentum rhedarum aut plaustrum."

RHETRAE (ῥῆτραι), specially the name of the ordinances of Lycurgus. The word *Rhetra* means a solemn compact, either originally emanating from, or subsequently sanctioned by the gods, who are always parties to such agreements. The Rhetra of Lycurgus emanated from the Delphian god: but the kings, senators, and people all bound themselves, both to each other and to the gods, to obey it.

RHYTON (ῥυτόν), a drinking-horn (κέρας). Its original form was probably the horn of the ox, but one end of it was afterwards ornamented with the heads of various animals and birds. The *rhyton* had a small opening at the bottom, which the person who drank put into his mouth, and allowed the wine to run in : hence it derived its name.

Rhyton, drinking-horn. (Museo borbonico.)

RICA. [FLAMEN.]

RICINIUM, an article of female dress, appears to have been a kind of mantle, with a sort of cowl attached to it, in order to cover the head. The *mavortium*, *mavorte*, or *mavors* of later times was thought to be only another name for what had formerly been called ricinium.

ROBIGALIA, a public festival in honour of the god Robigus, to preserve the fields from mildew, is said to have been instituted by Numa, and was celebrated April 25th. The sacrifices offered on this occasion consisted of the entrails of a dog and a sheep, accompanied with frankincense and wine : a prayer was presented by a flamen in the grove of the ancient deity, whom Ovid and Columella make a goddess. A god Robigus or a goddess Robigo is a mere invention from the name of this festival, for the Romans paid no divine honours to evil deities.

ROGATIO. [LEX, p. 225.]
ROGATORES. [COMITIA, p. 107.]
ROGUS. [FUNUS, p. 188, b.]
ROMPHEA. [HASTA.]
RORARII. [EXERCITUS, p. 165.]

ROSTRA, or The Beaks, was the name applied to the stage (*suggestus*) in the Forum, from which the orators addressed the people. This stage was originally called *templum*, because it was consecrated by the augurs, but obtained its name of *Rostra* at the conclusion of the great Latin war, when it was adorned with the beaks (*rostra*) of the ships of the Antiates. The Greeks also mutilated galleys in the same way for the purpose of trophies; this was called by them ἀκρωτηριάζειν. [ACROTERIUM.] The rostra lay between the Comitium or place of meeting for the curies, and the Forum or place of meeting for the tribes, so that the speaker might turn either to the one or the other; but down to the time of C. Gracchus, even the tribunes in speaking used to front the Comitium; he first turned his back to it and spoke with his face towards the forum. The rostra was a circular building, raised on arches, with a stand or platform on the top, bordered by a parapet, the access to it being by two flights of steps, one on each side. It fronted towards the comitium, and the rostra were affixed to the front of it, just under the arches. Its form has been in all the main points preserved in the ambones or circular pulpits of the most ancient churches, which also had two flights of steps leading up to them, one on the east side, by which the preacher ascended, and another on the west side, for his descent. The speaker was thus enabled to walk to and fro, while addressing his audience. The suggestus or rostra was transferred by Julius Caesar to a corner of the Forum, but the spot where the ancient rostra had stood still continued to be called *Rostra Vetera*, while the other was called *Rostra Nova* or *Rostra Julia*. Both the rostra contained statues of illustrious men.

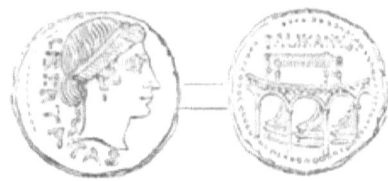

Rostra on Coin of M. Lollius Palicanus. (British Museum.)

ROSTRUM. [NAVIS.]
ROTA. [CURRUS.]
RUDIARII. [GLADIATORES.]
RUDIS. [GLADIATORES.]

SACCUS (σάκκος) signified in general any kind of sack or bag made of hair, cloth, or other materials. We have only to notice here its meaning as—(1) A head-dress. [COMA.]—(2) A sieve for straining wine. [COLUM.]—(3) A purse for holding money. Hence the phrase in Plautus *ire ad saccum*, "to go a begging."

SACELLUM is a diminutive of *sacer*, and signifies a small place consecrated to a god, containing an altar, and sometimes also a statue of the god to whom it was dedicated, but it was without a roof. It was therefore a sacred inclosure surrounded by a fence or wall, and thus answered to the Greek περίβολος.

SACERDOS, SACERDOTIUM. As all the different kinds of priests are treated of separately in this work, it is only necessary here to make some general remarks. In comparison with the civil magistrates, all priests at Rome were regarded as *homines privati*; though all of them, as priests, were *sacerdotes publici*, in as far as their office (*sacerdotium*) was connected with any worship recognised by the state. The appellation of *sacerdos publicus* was, however, given principally to the chief pontiff and the flamen dialis, who were at the same time the only priests who were members of the senate by virtue of their office. All priestly offices or sacerdotia were held for life, without responsibility to any civil magistrate. A priest was generally allowed to hold any other civil or military office besides his priestly dignity; some priests, however, formed an exception, for the duumviri, the rex sacrorum, and the flamen dialis were not allowed to hold any state office, and were also exempt from service in the armies. Their priestly character was, generally speaking, inseparable from their person as long as they lived: hence the augurs and fratres arvales retained their character even when sent into exile, or when they were taken prisoners. It also occurs that one and the same person held two or three priestly offices at a time. Thus we find the three dignities of pontifex maximus, augur, and decemvir sacrorum united in one individual. Bodily defects incapacitated a person at Rome, as among all ancient nations, from holding any priestly office. All priests were originally patricians, but from the year B.C. 367 the plebeians also began to take part in the sacerdotia [PLEBES]; and those priestly offices which down to the latest times remained in the hands of the patricians alone, such as that of the rex sacrorum, the flamines, salii, and others, had no influence upon the affairs of the state. As regards the appointment of priests, the ancients unanimously state, that at first they were appointed by the kings, but after the sacerdotia were once instituted, each college of priests—for nearly all priests constituted certain corporations called collegia—had the right of filling up, by cooptatio, the vacancies which occurred. [PONTIFEX.] Other priests, on the contrary, such as the vestal virgins and the flamines, were appointed (*capiebantur*) by the pontifex maximus, a rule which appears to have been observed down to the latest times; others again, such as the duumviri sacrorum, were elected by the people, or by the curiae, as the curiones. But in whatever manner they were appointed, all priests after their appointment required to be in. ugurated by the pontiffs and the augurs, or by the latter alone. Those priests who formed colleges had originally, as we have already observed, the right of cooptatio; but in the course of time they were deprived of this right, or at least the cooptatio was reduced to a mere form, by several leges, called leges de sacerdotiis, such as the Lex Domitia, Cornelia, and Julia; their nature is described in the article PONTIFEX, and what is there said in regard to the appointment of pontiffs applies equally to all the other colleges. All priests had some external distinction, as the apex, tutulus, or galerus, the toga praetexta, as well as honorary seats in the theatres, circuses, and amphitheatres. Most of the priestly colleges possessed landed property, and some priests had also a regular annual salary (stipendium), which was paid to them from the public treasury. This is expressly stated in regard to the vestal virgins, the augurs, and the curiones, and may therefore be supposed to have been the case with other priests also. The pontifex maximus, the rex sacrorum, and the vestal virgins had moreover a domus publica as their place of residence.

SACRA. This word, in its widest sense, expresses what we call divine worship. In ancient times, the state, as well as all its subdivisions, had their own peculiar forms of worship, whence at Rome we find sacra of the whole Roman people, of the curies, gentes, families, and even of private individuals. All these sacra, however, were divided into two great classes, the public and private sacra (sacra publica et privata), that is, they were performed either on behalf of the whole nation, and at the expense of the state, or on behalf of individuals, families, or gentes, which had also to defray their expenses. This division is ascribed to Numa. All sacra, publica as well as privata, were superintended and regulated by the pontiffs.

SACRAMENTUM, the military oath, which was administered in the following manner:— Each tribunus militum assembled his legion, and picked out one of the men, to whom he put the oath, that he would obey the commands of his generals, and execute them punctually. The other men then came forward, one after another, and repeated the same oath, saying that they would do like the first.

SACRARIUM was any place in which sacred things were deposited and kept, whether this place was a part of a temple or of a private house.

SACRIFICIUM (ἱερεῖον), a sacrifice. Sacrifices or offerings formed the chief part of the worship of the ancients. They were partly signs of gratitude, partly a means of propitiating the gods, and partly also intended to induce the deity to bestow some favour upon the sacrificer, or upon those on whose behalf the sacrifice was offered. Sacrifices in a wider sense would also embrace the DONARIA; in a narrower sense sacrificia were things offered to the gods, which merely afforded momentary gratification, and which were burnt upon their altars, or were believed to be consumed by the gods. All sacrifices may be divided into bloody sacrifices and unbloody sacrifices.—*Bloody sacrifices.* In the early times of Greece we find mention of human sacrifices, but with a few exceptions these had ceased in the historical ages. Owing to the influence of civilisation, in many cases animals were substituted for human beings; in others, a few drops of human blood were thought sufficient to propitiate the gods. The custom of sacrificing human life to the gods arose from the belief that the nobler the sacrifice and the dearer to its possessor, the more pleasing it would be to the gods. Hence the frequent instances in Grecian story of persons sacrificing their own children, or of persons devoting themselves to the gods of the lower world. That the Romans also believed human sacrifices to be pleasing to the gods, might be inferred from the story of Curtius and from the self-sacrifice of the Decii. The symbolic sacrifice of human figures made of rushes at the Lemuralia [LEMURALIA] also shows that in the early history of Italy human sacrifices were not uncommon. For another proof of this practice, see VER SACRUM. A second kind of bloody sacrifices were those of animals of various kinds, according to the nature and character of the divinity. The sacrifices of animals were the most common among the Greeks and Romans. The victim was called ἱερεῖον, and in Latin *hostia* or *victima*. In the early times it appears to have been the general custom to burn the whole victim (ὁλοκαυτεῖν) upon the altars of the gods, and the same was in some cases also observed in later times. But as early as the time of Homer it was the almost general practice to burn only the legs (μηροί, μηρία, μῆρα) enclosed in fat, and certain parts of the intestines, while the remaining parts of the victim were consumed by men at a festive meal. The gods delighted chiefly in the smoke arising from the burning victims, and the greater the number of victims, the more pleasing was the sacrifice. Hence it was not uncommon to offer a sacrifice of one hundred bulls (ἑκατόμβη) at once, though it must not be supposed that a hecatomb always signifies a sacrifice of a hundred bulls, for the name was used in a general way to designate any great sacrifice. Such great sacrifices were not less pleasing to men than to the gods, for in regard to the former they were in reality a donation of meat. Hence at Athens the partiality for such sacrifices rose to the highest degree. The animals which were sacrificed were mostly of the domestic kind, as bulls, cows, sheep, rams, lambs, goats, pigs, dogs, and horses; and each god had his favourite animals which he liked best as sacrifices. The head of the victim, before it was killed, was in most cases strewed with roasted barley meal (οὐλόχυτα or οὐλοχύται) mixed with salt (*mola salsa*). The persons who offered the sacrifice wore generally garlands round their heads, and sometimes also carried them in their hands, and before they touched anything belonging to the sacrifice they washed their hands in water. The victim itself was likewise adorned with garlands, and its horns were sometimes gilt. Before the animal was killed, a bunch of hair was cut from its forehead, and thrown into the fire as primitiae (κατάρχεσθαι). In the heroic ages the princes, as the high priests of their people, killed the victim; in later times this was done by the priests themselves. When the sacrifice was to be offered to the Olympic gods, the head of the animal was drawn heavenward; when to the gods of the lower world, to heroes, or to the dead, it was drawn downwards. While the flesh was burning upon the altar, wine and incense were thrown upon it, and prayers and music accompanied the solemnity. The most common animal sacrifices at Rome were the *suovetaurilia* or *solitaurilia*, consisting of a pig, a sheep, and an ox. They were performed in all cases of a lustration, and the victims were carried around the thing to be lustrated, whether it was a city, a people, or a piece of land. [Lustratio.] The Greek *trittya* (τριττύα), which likewise consisted of an ox, a sheep, and a pig, was the same sacrifice as the Roman suovetaurilia. The customs observed before and during the sacrifice of an animal were on the whole the same as those observed in Greece. But the victim was in most cases not killed by the priests who conducted the sacrifice, but by a person called *popa*, who struck the animal with a hammer before the knife was used. The better parts of the intestines (*exta*) were strewed with barley meal, wine, and incense, and were burnt upon the altar. Those parts of the animal which were burnt were called *proseeta*, *prosiciae*, or *ablegmina*. When a sacrifice was offered to gods of rivers, or of the sea, these parts were not burnt, but thrown into the water. Respecting the use which the ancients made of sacrifices to learn the will of the gods, see Haruspex and Divinatio.—*Unbloody sacrifices*. Among these we may first mention the libations (*libationes*, λοιβαί or σπονδαί). Bloody sacrifices were usually accompanied by libations, as wine was poured upon them. The wine was usually poured out in three separate streams. Libations always accompanied a sacrifice which was offered in concluding a treaty with a foreign nation, and that here they formed a prominent part of the solemnity, is clear from the fact that the treaty itself was called σπονδαί. But libations were also made independent of any other sacrifice, as in solemn prayers, and on many other occasions of public and private life, as before drinking at meals, and the like. Libations usually consisted of unmixed wine (ἄσπονδος, *merum*), but sometimes also of milk, honey, and other fluids, either pure or diluted with water. The libations offered to the Furies were always without wine. Incense was likewise an offering which usually accompanied bloody sacrifices, but it was also burned as an offering for itself. A third class of unbloody sacrifices consisted of fruit and cakes. The former were mostly offered to the gods as primitiae or tithes of the harvest, and as a sign of gratitude. They were sometimes offered in their natural state, sometimes also adorned or prepared in various ways. Cakes were peculiar to the worship of certain deities, as to that of Apollo. They were either simple cakes of flour, sometimes also of wax, or they were made in the shape of some animal, and were then offered as symbolical sacrifices in the place of real animals, either because they could not easily be procured, or were too expensive for the sacrificer.

SACRILEGIUM, the crime of stealing things consecrated to the gods, or things deposited in a consecrated place. A Lex Julia appears to have placed the crime of sacrilegium on an equality with peculatus. [Peculatus.]

SAECULUM was, according to the calculation of the Etruscans, which was adopted by the Romans, a space of time containing 110 lunar years. The return of each saeculum at Rome was announced by the pontiffs, who also made the necessary intercalations in such a manner, that at the commencement of a new saeculum the beginning of the ten months' year, of the twelve months' year, and of the solar year coincided. But in these arrangements the greatest caprice and irregularity appear to have prevailed at Rome, as may be seen from the unequal intervals at which the ludi saeculares were celebrated. [Ludi Saeculares.] This also accounts for the various ways in which a saeculum was defined by the ancients; some believed that it contained thirty, and others that it contained a hundred years: the latter opinion appears to have been the most common in later times, so that sacculum answered to our century.

SAGITTARII. [Arcus.]

SAGMINA, were the same as the *verbenae*, namely, herbs torn up by their roots from within the inclosure of the Capitoline, which were always carried by the Fetiales or ambassadors, when they went to a foreign people to demand restitution for wrongs committed against the Romans, or to make a treaty. [Fetiales.] They served to mark the sacred character of the ambassadors, and answered the same purpose as the Greek κηρύκεια.

SAGUM, the cloak worn by the Roman soldiers and inferior officers, in contradistinction to the paludamentum of the general and superior officers. [Paludamentum.] It is used in opposition to the toga or garb of peace, and we accordingly find, that when there was a war in Italy, all citizens put on the sagum even in the city, with the exception of those of consular rank (*saga sumere, ad saga ire, in sagis esse*). The sagum was open in the front, and usually fastened across the shoulders by a clasp: it resembled in form the paludamentum (see cut, p. 281). The cloak worn by the general and superior officers is sometimes called *sagum*, but the diminutive *sagulum* is more commonly used in such cases. The cloak worn by the northern nations of Europe is also called sagum. The German sagum is mentioned by Tacitus: that worn by the Gauls seems to have been a species of plaid (*versicolor sagum*).

SALAMINIA. [Paralus.]

SALII, priests of Mars Gradivus, said to have been instituted by Numa. They were twelve in number, chosen from the patricians even in the latest times, and formed an ecclesiastical corporation. They had the care of the twelve Ancilia, which were kept in the temple of Mars on the Palatine hill, whence these priests were sometimes called Salii Palatini, to distinguish them from the other Salii mentioned below. The distinguishing dress of the Salii was an embroidered tunic bound with a brazen belt, the trabea, and the apex, also worn by the Flamines. [Apex.] Each had a sword by his side, and in his right hand a spear or staff. The festival of Mars was celebrated by the Salii on the 1st of March and for several successive days; on which occasion they were accustomed to go through the city in their official dress, carrying the ancilia in their left hands or suspended from their shoulders, and at the same time singing and dancing, whence comes their name. The songs or hymns which they sang on this occasion were called *Asa-*

menta, Assamenta, or *Azamenta*, and were chiefly in praise of Mamurius Veturius, generally said to be the armourer, who made eleven ancilia like the one that was sent from heaven (ancile), though some modern writers suppose it to be merely another name of Mars. The praises of the gods were also celebrated in the songs of the Salii. In later times these songs were scarcely understood even by the priests themselves. At the conclusion of the festival the Salii were accustomed to partake of a splendid entertainment in the temple of Mars, which was proverbial for its excellence. The members of the collegium were elected by co-optation. We read of the dignities of praesul, vates, and magister in the collegium. The shape of the ancile is exhibited in the annexed cut, which illustrates the accounts of the ancient writers that its form was oval, but with the two sides receding inwards with an even curvature, and so as to make it broader at the ends than in the middle. The persons engaged in carrying these ancilia on their shoulders, suspended from a pole, are probably servants of the Salii. At the top of the cut is represented one of the rods with which the Salii were accustomed to beat the shield in their dance, as already described.

Salii carrying the Ancilia. (From an ancient Gem.)

Tullus Hostilius established another collegium of Salii, in fulfilment of a vow which he made in a war with the Sabines. These Salii were also twelve in number, chosen from the patricians, and appear to have been dedicated to the service of Quirinus. They were called the Salii Collini, Agonales or Agonenses. It is supposed that the oldest and most illustrious college, the Palatine Salii, were chosen originally from the oldest tribe, the Ramnes, and the one instituted by

Tullus Hostilius, or the Quirinalian, from the Tities alone: a third college for the Luceres was never established.

SALĪNAE (ἅλαι, ἁλοπήγιον), a salt-work. Throughout the Roman empire the salt-works were commonly public property, and were let by the government to the highest bidder. The first salt-works are said to have been established by Ancus Marcius at Ostia. The publicani who farmed these works appear to have sold this most necessary of all commodities at a very high price, whence the censors M. Livius and C. Claudius (B.C. 204) fixed the price at which those who took the lease of them were obliged to sell the salt to the people. At Rome the medius was, according to this regulation, sold for a sextans, while in other parts of Italy the price was higher and varied. The salt-works in Italy and in the provinces were very numerous.

SALĪNUM, a salt-cellar. All Romans who were raised above poverty had one of silver, which descended from father to son, and was accompanied by a silver plate, which was used together with the salt-cellar in the domestic sacrifices. [PATERA.] These two articles of silver were alone compatible with the simplicity of Roman manners in the early times of the republic.

SALTĀTIO (ὄρχησις, ὀρχηστύς), dancing. The dancing of the Greeks as well as of the Romans had very little in common with the exercise which goes by that name in modern times. It may be divided into two kinds, gymnastic and mimetic; that is, it was intended either to represent bodily activity, or to express by gestures, movements, and attitudes certain ideas or feelings, and also single events, or a series of events, as in the modern ballet. All these movements, however, were accompanied by music; but the terms ὄρχησις and saltatio were used in so much wider a sense than our word dancing, that they were applied to designate gestures, even when the body did not move at all. We find dancing prevalent among the Greeks from the earliest

A Dance. (Lamberti, Villa Borghese.)

times. It was originally closely connected with religion. In all the public festivals, which were so numerous among the Greeks, dancing formed a very prominent part. We find from the earliest times that the worship of Apollo was connected with a religious dance, called *Hyporchema* (ὑπόρχημα). All the religious dances, with the exception of the Bacchic and the Corybantian, were very simple, and consisted of gentle movements of the body, with various turnings and windings around the altar: such a dance was the *Geranus* (γέρανος), which Theseus is said to have performed at Delos on his return from Crete. The Dionysiac or Bacchic, and the Corybantian, were of a very different nature. In the former the life and adventures of the god were represented by mimetic dancing. [DIONYSIA.] The Corybantian was of a very wild character: it was chiefly danced in Phrygia and in Crete; the dancers were armed, struck their swords against their shields, and displayed the most extravagant fury; it was accompanied chiefly by the flute. Respecting the dances in the theatre, see CHORUS. Dancing was applied to gymnastic purposes and to training for war, especially in the Doric states, and was believed to have contributed very much to the success of the Dorians in war, as it enabled them to perform their evolutions simultaneously and in order. There were various dances in early times, which served as a preparation for war: hence Homer calls the Hoplites πρύλεες, a war-dance having been called πρύλις by the Cretans. Of such dances the most celebrated was the Pyrrhic (ἡ πυρρίχη), of which the πρύλις was probably only another name. It was danced to the sound of the flute, and its time was very quick and light, as is shown by the name of the Pyrrhic foot (``), which must be connected with this dance. In the non-Doric states it was probably not prac- tised as a training for war, but only as a mimetic dance: thus we read of its being danced by women to entertain a company.

Corybantian Dance. (Visconti, Mus. Pio Clem., vol. iv. tav. 9.)

It was also performed at Athens at the greater and lesser Panathenaea by ephebi, who were called Pyrrhichists (πυῤῥιχισταί), and were trained at the expense of the choragus. In the mountainous parts of Thessaly and Macedon dances are performed at the present day by men armed with muskets and swords. The Pyrrhic dance was introduced in the public games at Rome by Julius Caesar, when it was danced by the children of the leading men in Asia and Bithynia. There were other dances, besides the Pyrrhic, in which the performers had arms; but these seem to have been entirely mimetic, and not practised with any view to training for war. Such was the *Carpaea* (καρπαία), peculiar to the Aenianians and Magnetes, and described by Xenophon in the Anabasis. Such dances were frequently performed at banquets for the entertainment of the guests, where also the tumblers (κυβιστῆρες) were often intro-

Tumbler. (Museo Borbonico, vol. vii. tav. 58.)

duced, who in the course of their dance flung themselves on their head and alighted again upon their feet. These tumblers were also accustomed to make their somersets over knives and swords, which was called κυβιστᾶν εἰς μαχαίρας. We learn from Tacitus that the German youths also used to dance among swords and spears pointed at them. Other kinds of dances were frequently performed at entertainments, in Rome as well as in Greece, by courtezans, many of which were of a very indecent and lascivious nature. Among the dances performed without arms one of the most important was the *Hormos* (ὅρμος), which was danced at Sparta by youths and maidens together: the youth danced first some movements suited to his age, and of a military nature; the maiden followed in measured steps and with feminine gestures. Another common dance at Sparta was the *bibasis* (βίβασις), in which the dancer sprang rapidly from the ground and struck the feet behind.—Dancing was common among the Romans in ancient times, in connection with religious festivals and rites, because the ancients thought that no part of the body should be free from the influence of religion. The dances of the Salii, which were performed by men of patrician families, are described elsewhere. [ANCILE.] Dancing, however, was not performed by any Roman citizens except in connection with religion, and it was considered disgraceful for any freeman to dance. The mimetic dances of the Romans, which were carried to such perfection under the empire, are described under PANTOMIMUS. The dancers on the tight-rope (*funambuli*) under the empire were as skilful as they are in the present day.

SALUTATORES, the name given in the later

times of the republic, and under the empire, to a class of men who obtained their living by visiting the houses of the wealthy early in the morning, to pay their respects to them (*salutare*), and to accompany them when they went abroad. This arose from the visits which the clients were accustomed to pay to their patrons, and degenerated in later times into the above-mentioned practice: such persons seem to have obtained a good living among the great number of wealthy and vain persons at Rome, who were gratified by this attention. [SPORTULA.]

SAMBŪCA (σαμβύκη), a harp, was of oriental origin. The performances of *sambucistriae* (σαμβυκίστριαι) were only known to the early Romans as luxuries brought over from Asia. *Sambuca* was also the name of a military engine, used to scale the walls and towers of besieged cities. It was called by this name on account of its general resemblance to the form of a harp.

SAMNĪTES. [GLADIATORES.]

SANDĀLIUM (σανδάλιον or σάνδαλον), a kind of shoe worn only by women. The sandalium must be distinguished from the *hypodema* (ὑπόδημα), which was a simple sole bound under the foot, whereas the sandalium was a sole with a piece of leather covering the toes, so that it formed the transition from the *hypodema* to real shoes. The piece of leather over the toes was called ζυγός or ζυγόν.

SANDĀPĪLA. [FUNUS.]
SARCŌPHĀGUS. [FUNUS.]
SARISSA. [HASTA.]

SARRĀCUM, a kind of common cart or waggon, which was used by the country-people of Italy for conveying the produce of their fields, trees, and the like, from one place to another.

SATŪRA, the root of which is *sat*, literally means a mixture of all sorts of things. The name was accordingly applied by the Romans in many ways, but always to things consisting of various parts or ingredients, *e. g. lanx satura*, an offering consisting of various fruits, such as were offered at harvest festivals and to Ceres; *lex per saturam lata*, a law which contained several distinct regulations at once, and to a species of poetry, afterwards called *Satira*.

SATURNĀLIA, the festival of Saturnus, to whom the inhabitants of Latium attributed the introduction of agriculture and the arts of civilized life. Falling towards the end of December, at the season when the agricultural labours of the year were fully completed, it was celebrated in ancient times by the rustic population as a sort of joyous harvest-home, and in every age was viewed by all classes of the community as a period of absolute relaxation and unrestrained merriment. During its continuance no public business could be transacted, the law courts were closed, the schools kept holiday, to commence a war was impious, to punish a malefactor involved pollution. Special indulgences were granted to the slaves of each domestic establishment; they were relieved from all ordinary toils, were permitted to wear the *pileus*, the badge of freedom, were granted full freedom of speech, and partook of a banquet attired in the clothes of their masters, and were waited upon by them at table. All ranks devoted themselves to feasting and mirth, presents were interchanged among friends, *cerei* or wax tapers being the common offering of the more humble to their superiors, and crowds thronged the streets, shouting, *Io Saturnalia* (this was termed *clamare Saturnalia*), while sacrifices were offered with uncovered head, from a conviction that no ill-omened sight would interrupt the rites of such a happy day. Many of the peculiar customs of this festival exhibit a remarkable resemblance to the sports of our own Christmas and of the Italian Carnival. Thus on the Saturnalia public gambling was allowed by the aediles, just as in the days of our ancestors the most rigid were wont to countenance card-playing on Christmas-eve; the whole population threw off the toga, wore a loose gown, called *synthesis*, and walked about with the pileus on their heads, which reminds us of the dominos, the peaked caps, and other disguises worn by masques and mummers; the *cerei* were probably employed as the *moccoli* now are on the last night of the Carnival; and lastly, one of the amusements in private society was the election of a mock king, which at once calls to recollection the characteristic ceremony of Twelfth-night. During the republic, although the whole month of December was considered as dedicated to Saturn, only one day, the xiv. Kal. Jan., was set apart for the sacred rites of the divinity. When the month was lengthened by the addition of two days upon the adoption of the Julian Calendar, the Saturnalia fell on the xvi. Kal. Jan., which gave rise to confusion and mistakes among the more ignorant portion of the people. To obviate this inconvenience, and allay all religious scruples, Augustus enacted that three whole days, the 17th, 18th, and 19th of December, should in all time coming be hallowed, thus embracing both the old and new style. Under the empire the merry-making lasted for seven days, and three different festivals were celebrated during this period. First came the *Satur-*

nalia proper, commencing on xvi. Kal. Dec., followed by the *Opalia*, anciently coincident with the Saturnalia, on xiv. Kal. Jan.; these two together lasted for five days, and the sixth and seventh were occupied with the *Sigillaria*, so called from little earthenware figures (*sigilla, oscilla*) exposed for sale at this season, and given as toys to children.

SCALPTURA or SCULPTURA, originally signified cutting figures out of a solid material, but was more particularly applied to the art of cutting figures into the material (intaglios), which was chiefly applied to producing seals and matrices for the mints; and 2. the art of producing raised figures (cameos), which served for the most part as ornaments. *Sculpture* in our sense of the word was usually designated by the term STATUARIA. The first artist who is mentioned as an engraver of stones is Theodorus, the son of Telecles, the Samian, who engraved the stone in the ring of Polycrates. The most celebrated among them was Pyrgoteles, who engraved the seal-rings for Alexander the Great. Several of the successors of Alexander and other wealthy persons adopted the custom of adorning their gold and silver vessels, craters, candelabras, and the like, with precious stones on which raised figures (cameos) were worked. The art was in a particularly flourishing state at Rome under Augustus and his successors, in the hands of Dioscurides and other artists, many of whose works are still preserved. Numerous specimens of intaglios and cameos are still preserved in the various museums of Europe.

SCAMNUM, *dim.* SCABELLUM, a step which was placed before the beds of the ancients in order to assist persons in getting into them, as some were very high: others which were lower required also lower steps, which were called *scabella*. A scamnum was also used as a footstool. A scamnum extended in length becomes a bench, and in this sense the word is frequently used. The benches in ships were sometimes called scamna.

SCENA. [THEATRUM.]

SCEPTRUM (σκῆπτρον), which originally denoted a simple staff or walking-stick, was emblematic of station and authority. In ancient authors the sceptre is represented as belonging more especially to kings, princes, and leaders of tribes: but it is also borne by judges, by heralds, and by priests and seers. The sceptre descended from father to son, and might be committed to any one in order to express the transfer of authority. Those who bore the sceptre swore by it, solemnly taking it in the right hand and raising it towards heaven. The ivory sceptre of the kings of Rome, which descended to the consuls, was surmounted by an eagle.

SCHOENUS (ὁ, ἡ, σχοῖνος), an Egyptian and Persian measure, the length of which is stated by Herodotus at 60 stadia, or 2 parasangs. It was used especially for measuring land.

SCORPIO. [TORMENTUM.]

SCRIBAE, public notaries or clerks, in the pay of the Roman state. They were chiefly employed in making up the public accounts, copying out laws, and recording the proceedings of the different functionaries of the state. The phrase *scriptum facere* was used to denote their occupation. Being very numerous, they were divided into companies or classes (*decuriae*), and were assigned by lot to different magistrates, whence they were named Quaestorii, Aedilicii, or Praetorii, from the officers of state to whom they were attached. The appointment to the office of a "scriba" seems to have been either made on the nomination of a magistrate, or purchased. Horace, for instance, bought for himself a "patent place as clerk in the treasury" (*scriptum quaestorium comparavit*). In Cicero's time, indeed, it seems that any one might become a scriba or public clerk by purchase, and consequently, as freedmen and their sons were eligible, and constituted a great portion of the public clerks at Rome, the office was not highly esteemed, though frequently held by ingenui or free-born citizens. Very few instances are recorded of the scribae being raised to the higher dignities of the state. Cn. Flavius, the scribe of Appius Claudius, was raised to the office of curule aedile in gratitude for his making public the various forms of actions, which had previously been the exclusive property of the patricians [ACTIO]; but the returning officer refused to acquiesce in his election till he had given up his books and left his profession.

SCRINIUM. [CAPSA.]

SCRIPTA DUODECIM. [LATRUNCULI.]

SCRIPTURA, that part of the revenue of the Roman Republic which was derived from letting out, as pasture land, those portions of the ager publicus which were not taken into cultivation. The names for such parts of the ager publicus were, *pascua publica, saltus*, or *silvae*. They were let by the censors to the publicani, like all other vectigalia; and the persons who sent their cattle to graze on such public pastures had to pay a certain tax or duty to the publicani, which of course varied according to the number and quality of the cattle which they kept upon them. The publicani had to keep the lists of persons who sent their cattle upon the public pastures, together with the number and quality of the cattle. From this registering (*scribere*) the duty itself was called *scriptura*, the public pasture land *ager scripturarius*, and the publicani, or their agents who raised the tax, *scripturarii*. The Lex Thoria (B.C. 111) did away with the scriptura in Italy, where the public pastures were very numerous and extensive, especially in Apulia, and the lands themselves were now sold or distributed. In the provinces, where the public pastures were also let out in the same manner, the practice continued until the time of the empire; but afterwards the scriptura is no longer mentioned.

SCRŪPŬLUM, or more properly SCRIPŬLUM or SCRIPLUM (γραμμα), the smallest denomination of weight among the Romans. It was the 24th part of the UNCIA, or the 288th of the LIBRA, and therefore = 18·06 grains English, which is about the average weight of the scrupular aurei still in existence. [AURUM.] As a square measure, it was the smallest division of the jugerum, which contained 288 scrupula. [JUGERUM.]

SCŪTUM (θυρεος), the Roman shield worn by the heavy-armed infantry, instead of being round, like the Greek CLIPEUS, was adapted to the form of the human body, by being made either oval or of the shape of a door, (θύρα), which it also resembled in being

Scuta, shields. (Bartoli, Arcus Triumph.)

made of wood or wicker-work, and from which consequently its Greek name was derived. Polybius says that the dimensions of the scutum were 4 feet by 2½.

SCŸTĂLĒ (σκυτάλη) is the name applied to a secret mode of writing, by which the Spartan ephors communicated with their kings and generals when abroad. When a king or general left Sparta, the ephors gave to him a staff of a definite length and thickness, and retained for themselves another of precisely the same size. When they had any communications to make to him, they cut the material upon which they intended to write into the shape of a narrow riband, wound it round their staff, and then wrote upon it the message which they had to send to him. When the strip of writing material was taken from the staff, nothing but single letters appeared, and in this state the strip was sent to the general, who, after having wound it round his staff, was able to read the communication.

SCŸTHAE (Σκύθαι). [DEMOSII.]

SĔCESPĪTA, an instrument used by the Roman priests in killing the victims at sacrifices, probably an axe. In the annexed coin, the reverse represents a culter, a simpuvium, and a secespita.

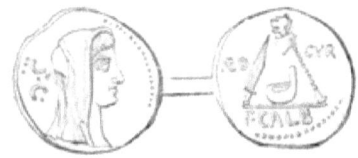

Secespita, Culter, and Simpuvium. (Coin of Sulpicia Gens.)

SECTĬO, the sale of a man's property by the state (*publice*). This was done in consequence of a condemnatio, and for the purpose of repayment to the state of such sums of money as the condemned person had improperly appropriated; or in consequence of a proscriptio. Sometimes the things sold were called *sectio*. Those who bought the property were called *sectores*. The property was sold *sub hasta*.

SECTOR. [SECTIO.]

SĔCŪRIS (ἀξίνη, πέλεκυς), an axe or hatchet. The axe was either made with a single edge, or with a blade or head on each side of the haft, the latter kind being denominated *bipennis*. The axe was used as a weapon of war chiefly by the Asiatic nations. It was a part of the Roman fasces. [FASCES.]

SECŪTŌRES. [GLADIATORES.]

SELLA, the general term for a seat or chair of any description.—(1) SELLA CURŪLIS, the chair of state. *Curulis* is derived by the ancient writers from *currus*, but it more probably contains the same root as *curia*. The sella curulis is said to have been used at Rome from a very remote period as an emblem of kingly power, having been imported, along with various other insignia of royalty, from Etruria. Under the republic the right of sitting upon this chair belonged to the consuls, praetors, curule aediles, and censors; to the flamen dialis; to the dictator, and to those whom he deputed to act under himself, as the *magister equitum*, since he might be said to comprehend all magistracies within himself. After the downfal of the constitution, it was assigned to the emperors also, or to their statues in their absence; to the augustales, and perhaps, to the praefectus urbi. It was displayed upon all great public occasions, especially in the circus and theatre; and it was the seat of the praetor when he administered justice. In the provinces it was assumed by inferior magistrates, when they exercised proconsular or propraetorian authority. We find it occasionally exhibited on the medals of foreign monarchs likewise, as on those of Ariobarzanes II. of Cappadocia, for it was the practice of the Romans to present a curule chair, an ivory sceptre, a toga praetexta, and such-like ornaments, as tokens of respect and confidence to those rulers whose friendship they desired to cultivate. The sella curulis appears from the first to have been ornamented with ivory; and at a later period it was overlaid with gold. In shape it was extremely plain, closely resembling a common folding camp-stool with crooked legs. The sella curulis is frequently represented upon the denarii of Roman families. In the following cut are represented

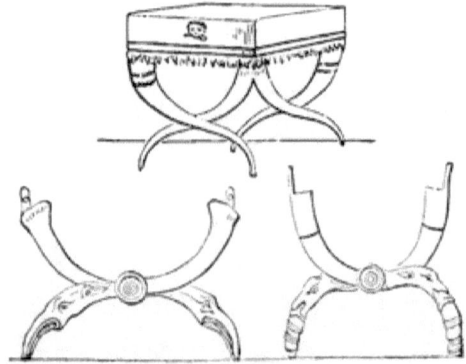

Sellae Curules. (The top figure from the Vatican collection; the two bottom figures from the Museum at Naples.)

two pair of bronze legs, belonging to a sella curulis, and likewise a sella curulis itself. —(2) SELLA GESTATORIA, or FERTORIA, a sedan used both in town and country, and by men as well as by women. It is expressly distinguished from the LECTICA, a portable bed or sofa, in which the person carried lay in a recumbent position, while the *sella* was a portable chair, in which the occupant sat upright. It differed from the *cathedra* also, but in what the difference consisted, it is not easy to determine. [CATHEDRA.] It appears not to have been introduced until long after the lectica was common, since we scarcely, if ever, find any allusion to it until the period of the empire. The sella was sometimes entirely open, but more frequently shut in. It was made sometimes of plain leather, and sometimes ornamented with bone, ivory, silver, or gold, according to the fortune of the proprietor. It was furnished with a pillow to support the head and neck (*cervical*); the motion was so easy that one might study without inconvenience, while at the same time it afforded a healthful exercise.—(3) Chairs for ordinary domestic purposes have been discovered in excavations, or are seen represented in ancient frescoes, many displaying great taste.

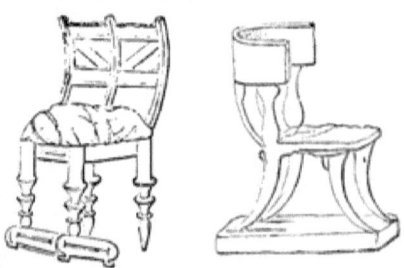

Sellae, Chairs. (The right-hand figure from the Vatican collection; the left-hand figure from a Painting at Pompeii.)

SĒMIS, SĒMISSIS. [AS.]
SĒMUNCIA. [UNCIA.]
SĒMUNCIĀRIUM FĒNUS. [FENUS.]
SĒNĀTUS. In all the republics of antiquity the government was divided between a senate and a popular assembly; and in cases where a king stood at the head of

affairs, as at Sparta and in early Rome, the king had little more than the executive. A senate in the early times was always regarded as an assembly of elders, which is in fact the meaning of the Roman senatus, as of the Spartan (γερουσία), and its members were elected from among the nobles of the nation. The number of senators in the ancient republics always bore a distinct relation to the number of tribes of which the nation was composed. [BOULE; GEROUSIA.] Hence in the earliest times, when Rome consisted of only one tribe, its senate consisted of one hundred members (*senatores* or *patres*; compare PATRICII), and when the Sabine tribe or the Tities became united with the Latin tribe or the Ramnes, the number of senators was increased to two hundred. This number was again augmented to three hundred by Tarquinius Priscus, when the third tribe or the Luceres became incorporated with the Roman state. The new senators added by Tarquinius Priscus were distinguished from those belonging to the two older tribes by the appellation *patres minorum gentium*, as previously those who represented the Tities had been distinguished, by the same name, from those who represented the Ramnes. Under Tarquinius Superbus the number of senators is said to have become very much diminished, as he is reported to have put many to death and sent others into exile. This account however appears to be greatly exaggerated, and it is probable that several vacancies in the senate arose from many of the senators accompanying the tyrant into his exile. The vacancies which had thus arisen were filled up immediately after the establishment of the republic, when several noble plebeians of equestrian rank were made senators. These new senators were distinguished from the old ones by the name of *Conscripti*; and hence the customary mode of addressing the whole senate henceforth always was: *Patres Conscripti*, that is, *Patres et Conscripti*.—The number of 300 senators appears to have remained unaltered for several centuries. The first permanent increase to their number was made by Sulla, and the senate seems henceforth to have consisted of between five and six hundred. Julius Caesar augmented the number to 900, and raised to this dignity even common soldiers, freedmen, and peregrini. Augustus cleared the senate of the unworthy members, who were contemptuously called by the people *Orcini senatores*, and reduced its number to 600.—In the time of the kings the senate was probably elected by the gentes, each gens appointing one member as its representative; and as there were 300 gentes,

there were consequently 300 senators. The whole senate was divided into decuries, each of which corresponded to a curia. When the senate consisted of only one hundred members, there were accordingly only ten decuries of senators; and ten senators, one being taken from each decury, formed the *Decem Primi*, who represented the ten curies. When subsequently the representatives of the two other tribes were admitted into the senate, the Ramnes with their decem primi retained for a time their superiority over the two other tribes, and gave their votes first. The first among the decem primi was the *princeps senatus*, who was appointed by the king, and was at the same time custos urbis. [PRAEFECTUS URBI.] Respecting the age at which a person might be elected into the senate during the kingly period, we know no more than what is indicated by the name senator itself, that is, that they were persons of advanced age.—Soon after the establishment of the republic, though at what time is uncertain, the right of appointing senators passed from the gentes into the hands of the consuls, consular tribunes, and subsequently of the censors. At the same time, the right which the magistrates possessed of electing senators was by no means an arbitrary power, for the senators were usually taken from among those whom the people had previously invested with a magistracy, so that in reality the people themselves always nominated the candidates for the senate, which on this account remained, as before, a representative assembly. After the institution of the censorship, the censors alone had the right of introducing new members into the senate from among the ex-magistrates, and of excluding such as they deemed unworthy. [CENSOR.] The exclusion was effected by simply passing over the names, and not entering them on the lists of senators, whence such men were called *Praeteriti Senatores*. On one extraordinary occasion the eldest among the ex-censors was invested with dictatorial power for the purpose of filling up vacancies in the senate.—As all curule magistrates, and also the quaestors, had by virtue of their office a seat in the senate, even if they had not been elected senators, we must distinguish between two classes of senators, viz., real senators, or such as had been regularly raised to their dignity by the magistrates or the censors, and such as had, by virtue of the office which they held or had held, a right to take their seats in the senate and to speak (*sententiam dicere, jus sententiae*), but not to vote. To this ordo senatorius also belonged the pontifex maximus and the flamen dialis. Though these senators had no right to vote, they might, when the real senators had voted, step over or join the one or the other party, whence they were called *Senatores Pedarii*, an appellation which had in former times been applied to those juniores who were not consulars. When at length all the state offices had become equally accessible to the plebeians and the patricians, and when the majority of offices were held by the former, their number in the senate naturally increased in proportion. The senate had gradually become an assembly representing the people, as formerly it had represented the populus, and down to the last century of the republic the senatorial dignity was only regarded as one conferred by the people. But notwithstanding this apparently popular character of the senate, it was never a popular or democratic assembly, for now its members belonged to the nobiles, who were as aristocratic as the patricians. [NOBILES.] The office of princeps senatus, which had become independent of that of praetor urbanus, was now given by the censors, and at first always to the eldest among the ex-censors, but afterwards to any other senator whom they thought most worthy; and unless there was any charge to be made against him, he was re-elected at the next lustrum. This distinction, however, great as it was, afforded neither power nor advantages, and did not even confer the privilege of presiding at the meetings of the senate, which only belonged to those magistrates who had the right of convoking the senate.—During the republican period no senatorial census existed, although senators naturally always belonged to the wealthiest classes. The institution of a census for senators belongs to the time of the empire. Augustus first fixed it at 400,000 sesterces, afterwards increased it to double this sum, and at last even to 1,200,000 sesterces. Those senators whose property did not amount to this sum received grants from the emperor to make it up. As regards the age at which a person might become a senator, we have no express statement for the time of the republic, although it appears to have been fixed by some custom or law, as the aetas senatoria is frequently mentioned, especially during the latter period of the republic. But we may by induction discover the probable age. We know that, according to the lex annalis of the tribune Villius, the age fixed for the quaestorship was 31. Now as it might happen that a quaestor was made a senator immediately after the expiration of his office, we may presume that the earliest age at which a man could become a senator was 32. Augustus at last fixed the senatorial age at 25, which appears to have remained unaltered throughout the time of the empire.—No senator was allowed to carry on any mercantile business. About the commencement of the second Punic war, some senators appear to have violated this law or custom, and in order to prevent its recurrence a law was passed, with the vehement opposition of the senate, that none of its members should be permitted to possess a ship of more than 300 amphorae in tonnage, as this was thought sufficiently large to convey to Rome the produce of their estates abroad. It is clear, however, that this law was frequently violated.—Regular meetings of the senate (*senatus legitimus*) took place during the republic, and probably during the kingly period also, on the calends, nones, and ides of every month extraordinary meetings (*senatus indictus*) might be convoked on any other day, with the exception of those which were atri, and those on which comitia were held. The right of convoking the senate during the kingly period belonged to the king, or to his vicegerent, the custos urbis. This right was during the republic transferred to the curule magistrates, and at last to the tribunes also. If a senator did not appear on a day of meeting, he was liable to a fine, for which a pledge was taken (*pignoris captio*) until it was paid. Towards the end of the republic it was decreed, that during the whole month of February the senate should give audience to foreign ambassadors on all days on which the senate could lawfully meet, and that no other matters should be discussed until these affairs were settled.—The places where the meetings of the senate were held (*curiae, senacula*) were always inaugurated by the augurs. [TEMPLUM.] The most ancient place was the Curia Hostilia, in which alone originally a senatus-consultum could be made. Afterwards, however, several temples were used for this purpose, such as the temple of Concordia, a place near the temple of Bellona [LEGATUS], and one near the porta Capena. Under the emperors the senate also met in other places: under Caesar, the Curia Julia, a building of extraordinary splendour, was commenced; but subsequently meetings of the senate were frequently held in the house of a consul.—The subjects laid before the senate belonged partly to the internal affairs of the state, partly to legislation, and partly to finance; and no measure could be brought before the populus without having previously been discussed and prepared by the senate. The senate was thus the medium through which all affairs of the whole government had to pass: it considered and discussed whatever measures the king thought proper to introduce, and had, on the other hand, a perfect control over the assembly of the populus, which could only accept or reject what the senate brought before it. When a king died, the royal dignity, until a successor was elected, was transferred to the Decem Primi, each of whom in rotation held this dignity for five days. Under the republic, the senate had at first the right of proposing to the comitia the candidates for magistracies, but this right was subsequently lost: the comitia centuriata became quite free in regard to elections, and were no longer dependent upon the proposal of the senate. The curies only still possessed the right of sanctioning the election; but in the year u. c. 299 they were compelled to sanction any election of magistrates which the comitia might make, before it took place, and this soon after became law by the Lex Maenia. When at last the curies no longer assembled for this empty show of power, the senate stepped into their place, and henceforth in elections, and soon after also in matters of legislation, the senate had previously to sanction whatever the comitia might decide. After the Lex Hortensia a decree of the comitia tributa became law, even without the sanction of the senate. The original state of things had thus gradually become reversed, and the senate had lost very important branches of its power, which had all been gained by the comitia tributa. In its relation to the comitia centuriata, however, the ancient rules were still in force, as laws, declarations of war, conclusions of peace, treaties, &c., were brought before them, and decided by them on the proposal of the senate.—The powers of the senate, after both orders were placed upon a perfect equality, may be thus briefly summed up. The senate continued to have the supreme superintendence in all matters of religion; it determined upon the manner in which a war was to be conducted, what legions were to be placed at the disposal of a commander, and whether new ones were to be levied; it decreed into what provinces the consuls and praetors were to be sent [PROVINCIA], and whose imperium was to be prolonged. The commissioners who were generally sent out to settle the administration of a newly-conquered country, were always appointed by the senate. All embassies for the conclusion of peace or treaties with foreign states were sent out by the senate, and such ambassadors were generally senators themselves, and ten in number. The senate alone carried on the negotiations with foreign ambassadors, and received the complaints of subject or allied nations, who always regarded the senate as their common protector. By virtue of this office of protector it also settled all disputes which might arise among the municipia and colonies of Italy, and punished all heavy crimes committed in Italy, which might endanger the public peace and security. Even in Rome itself, the judices to whom the praetor referred important cases, both public and private, were taken from among the senators, and in extraordinary cases the senate appointed especial commissions to investigate them; but such a commission, if the case in question was a capital offence committed by a citizen, required the sanction of the people. When the republic was in danger, the senate might confer unlimited power upon the magistrates by the formula, *Videant consules, ne quid respublica detrimenti capiat*, which was equivalent to a declaration of martial law within the city. This general care for the internal and external welfare of the republic included, as before, the right of disposing of the finances requisite for these purposes. Hence all the revenue and expenditure of the republic were under the direct administration of the senate, and the censors and quaestors were only its ministers or agents. [CENSOR; QUAESTOR.] All the expenses necessary for the maintenance of the armies required the sanction of the senate, before anything could be done, and it might even prevent the triumph of a returning general, by refusing to assign the money necessary for it. There are, however, instances of a general triumphing without the consent of the senate.—How many members were required to be present in order to constitute a legal assembly, is uncertain, though it appears that there existed some regulations on this point, and there is one instance on record, in which at least one hundred senators were required to be present. The presiding magistrate opened the business with the words *Quod bonum, faustum, felix fortunatumque sit populo Romano Quiritibus*, and then laid before the assembly (*referre, relatio*) what he had to propose. Towards the end of the republic the order in which the question was put to the senators appears to have depended upon the discretion of the presiding consul, who called upon each member by pronouncing his name; but he usually began with the princeps senatus, or if consules designati were present, with them. The consul generally observed all the year round the same order in which he had commenced on the first of January. A senator when called upon to speak might do so at full length, and even introduce subjects not directly connected with the point at issue. It depended upon the president which of the opinions expressed he would put to the vote, and which he would pass over. The majority of votes always decided a question. The majority was ascertained either by *numeratio* or *discessio*; that is, the president either counted the votes, or the members who voted on the same side separated from those who voted otherwise. The latter mode seems to have been the usual one. What the senate determined was called *senatus consultum*, because the consul, who introduced the business, was said *senatum consulere*. In the enacting part of a lex the populus were said *jubere*, and in a plebiscitum *scire*; in a senatusconsultum the senate was said *censere*. Certain forms were observed in drawing up a senatusconsultum, of which there is an example in Cicero: "S. C. Auctoritates Pridie Kal. Octob. in Aede Apollinis, scribendo adfuerunt L. Domitius Cn. Filius Ahenobarbus, &c. Quod M. Marcellus Consul V. F. (*verba fecit*) de prov. Cons. D. E. R. I. C. (*de ea re ita censuerunt Uti, &c.*)" The names of the persons who were witnesses to the drawing up of the senatusconsultum were called the *auctoritates*, and these auctoritates were cited as evidence of the fact of the persons named in them having been present at the drawing up of the S. C. There can be no doubt that certain persons were required to be present *scribendo*, but others might assist if they chose, and a person in this way might testify his regard for another on behalf of whom or with reference to whom the S. C. was made. Besides the phrase *scribendo adesse*, there are *esse ad scribendum* and *poni ad scribendum*. When a S. C. was made on the motion of a person, it was said to be made *in sententiam ejus*. If the S. C. was carried, it was written on tablets, and placed in the Aerarium. Senatusconsulta were, properly speaking, laws, for it is clear that the senate had legislative power even in the republican period; but it is difficult to determine how far their legislative power extended. A *decretum* of the senate was a rule made by the senate as to some matter which was strictly within its competence, and thus differed from a *senatusconsultum*, which was a law; but these words are often used indiscriminately and with little precision. Many of the senatusconsulta of the republican period were only determinations of the senate, which became leges by being carried in the comitia. One instance of this kind occurred on the occasion of the trial of Clodius for violating the mysteries of the Bona Dea. A rogatio on the subject of the trial was proposed to the comitia ex senatusconsulto, which is also spoken of as the *auctoritas* of the senate. A senate was

not allowed to be held before sunrise or to be prolonged after sunset: on extraordinary emergencies, however, this regulation was set aside.—During the latter part of the republic the senate was degraded in various ways by Sulla, Caesar, and others, and on many occasions it was only an instrument in the hands of the men in power. In this way it became prepared for the despotic government of the emperors, when it was altogether the creature and obedient instrument of the princeps. The emperor himself was generally also princeps senatus, and had the power of convoking both ordinary and extraordinary meetings, although the consuls, praetors and tribunes continued to have the same right. The ordinary meetings, according to a regulation of Augustus, were held twice in every month. In the reign of Tiberius the election of magistrates was transferred from the people to the senate, which, however, was enjoined to take especial notice of those candidates who were recommended to it by the emperor. At the demise of an emperor the senate had the right of appointing his successor, in case no one had been nominated by the emperor himself; but the senate very rarely had an opportunity of exercising this right, as it was usurped by the soldiers. The aerarium at first still continued nominally to be under the control of the senate, but the emperors gradually took it under their own exclusive management, and the senate retained nothing but the administration of the funds of the city (*arca publica*), which were distinct both from the aerarium and from the fiscus. Augustus ordained that no accusations should any longer be brought before the comitia, and instead of them he raised the senate to a high court of justice, upon which he conferred the right of taking cognisance of capital offences committed by senators, of crimes against the state and the person of the emperors, and of crimes committed by the provincial magistrates in the administration of their provinces. Respecting the provinces of the senate, see PROVINCIA. Under the empire, senatusconsulta began to take the place of leges, properly so called, and as the senate was, with the exception of the emperor, the only legislating body, such senatusconsulta are frequently designated by the name of the consuls in whose year of office they were passed.—The distinctions and privileges enjoyed by senators were: 1. The tunica with a broad purple stripe (*latus clavus*) in front, which was woven in it, and not, as is commonly believed, sewed upon it. 2. A kind of short boot, with the letter C. on the front of the foot. This C. is generally supposed to mean *centum*, and to refer to the original number of 100 (*centum*) senators. 3. The right of sitting in the orchestra in the theatres and amphitheatres. This distinction was first procured for the senators by Scipio Africanus Major, 194 B. C. 4. On a certain day in the year a sacrifice was offered to Iupiter in the Capitol, and on this occasion the senators alone had a feast in the Capitol; the right was called the *jus publice epulandi*. 5. The *jus liberae legationis*. [LEGATUS, p. 224.]

SENIORES. [COMITIA.]
SEPTEMVIRI EPULONES. [EPULONES.]
SEPTIMONTIUM, a Roman festival which was held in the month of December. It was celebrated by the montani, or the inhabitants of the seven ancient hills or rather districts of Rome, who offered on this day sacrifices to the gods in their respective districts. These sacra were, like the Paganalia, not sacra publica, but privata. They were believed to have been instituted to commemorate the enclosure of the seven hills of Rome within the walls of the city, and must certainly be referred to a time when the Capitoline, Quirinal, and Viminal were not yet incorporated with Rome.

SEPTUM. [COMITIA, p. 107.]
SEPTUNX. [AS.]
SEPULCRUM. [FUNUS.]
SERA. [JANUA.]
SERICUM (σηρικόν), silk, also called *bombycinum*. Raw silk was brought from the interior of Asia, and manufactured in Cos, as early as the fourth century B. C. From this island it appears that the Roman ladies obtained their most splendid garments [COA VESTIS], which were remarkably thin, sometimes of a fine purple dye, and variegated with transverse stripes of gold. Silk was supposed to come from the country of the Seres in Asia, whence a silk garment is usually called *Serica vestis*. Under the empire the rage for such garments was constantly on the increase. Even men aspired to be adorned with silk, and hence the senate, early in the reign of Tiberius, enacted *ne vestis Serica viros foedaret*. The eggs of the silkworm were first brought into Europe in the age of Justinian, A. D. 530, in the hollow stem of a plant from "Serinda," which was probably Khotan in Little Bucharia, by some monks who had learnt the method of hatching and rearing them.

SERTA. [CORONA.]
SERVUS (δοῦλος), a slave. (1) GREEK. Slavery existed almost throughout the whole of Greece; and Aristotle says that a complete household is that which consists of slaves and freemen, and he defines a slave to be a living working-tool and possession. None of the Greek philosophers ever seem to have objected to slavery as a thing morally wrong; Plato in his perfect state only desires that no Greeks should be made slaves by Greeks, and Aristotle defends the justice of the institution on the ground of a diversity of race, and divides mankind into the free and those who are slaves by nature; under the latter description he appears to have regarded all barbarians in the Greek sense of the word, and therefore considers their slavery justifiable. In the most ancient times there are said to have been no slaves in Greece, but we find them in the Homeric poems, though by no means so generally as in later times. They are usually prisoners taken in war, who serve their conquerors: but we also read as well of the purchase and sale of slaves. They were, however, at that time mostly confined to the houses of the wealthy. There were two kinds of slavery among the Greeks. One species arose when the inhabitants of a country were subdued by an invading tribe, and reduced to the condition of serfs or bondsmen. They lived upon and cultivated the land which their masters had appropriated to themselves, and paid them a certain rent. They also attended their masters in war. They could not be sold out of the country or separated from their families, and could acquire property. Such were the Helots of Sparta [HELOTES], and the Penestae of Thessaly [PENESTAE]. The other species of slavery consisted of domestic slaves acquired by purchase, who were entirely the property of their masters, and could be disposed of like any other goods and chattels: these were the δοῦλοι properly so called, and were the kind of slaves that existed at Athens and Corinth. In commercial cities slaves were very numerous, as they performed the work of the artisans and manufacturers of modern towns. In poorer republics, which had little or no capital, and which subsisted wholly by agriculture, they would be few: thus in Phocis and Locris there are said to have been originally no domestic slaves. The majority of slaves was purchased; few comparatively were born in the family of the master, partly because the number of female slaves was very small in comparison with the male, and partly because the cohabitation of slaves was discouraged, as it was considered cheaper to purchase than to rear slaves. It was a recognised rule of Greek national law that the persons of those who were taken prisoners in war became the property of the conqueror, but it was the practice for Greeks to give liberty to those of their own nation on payment of a ransom. Consequently almost all slaves in Greece, with the exception of the serfs above-mentioned, were bar-

barians. The chief supply seems to have come from the Greek colonies in Asia Minor, which had abundant opportunities of obtaining them from their own neighbourhood and the interior of Asia. A considerable number of slaves also came from Thrace, where the parents frequently sold their children.— At Athens, as well as in other states, there was a regular slave-market, called the κύκλος, because the slaves stood round in a circle. They were also sometimes sold by auction, and were then placed on a stone, as is now done when slaves are sold in the United States of North America: the same was also the practice in Rome, whence the phrase *homo de lapide emtus*. [AUCTIO.] At Athens the number of slaves was far greater than the free population. Even the poorest citizen had a slave for the care of his household, and in every moderate establishment many were employed for all possible occupations, as bakers, cooks, tailors, &c.—Slaves either worked on their masters' account or their own (in the latter case they paid their masters a certain sum a day); or they were let out by their master on hire, either for the mines or any other kind of labour, or as hired servants for wages. The rowers on board the ships were usually slaves, who either belonged to the state or to private persons, who let them out to the state on payment of a certain sum. It appears that a considerable number of persons kept large gangs of slaves merely for the purpose of letting out, and found this a profitable mode of investing their capital. Great numbers were required for the mines, and in most cases the minelessees would be obliged to hire some, as they would not have sufficient capital to purchase as many as they wanted. The rights of possession with regard to slaves differed in no respect from any other property; they could be given or taken as pledges. The condition, however, of Greek slaves was upon the whole better than that of Roman ones, with the exception perhaps of Sparta, where, according to Plutarch, it is the best place in the world to be a freeman, and the worst to be a slave. At Athens especially the slaves seem to have been allowed a degree of liberty and indulgence which was never granted to them at Rome. The life and person of a slave at Athens were also protected by the law: a person who struck or maltreated a slave was liable to an action; a slave too could not be put to death without legal sentence. He could even take shelter from the cruelty of his master in the temple of Theseus, and there claim the privilege of being sold by him. The person of a slave was, of course, not considered so sacred as that of a free-

man: his offences were punished with corporal chastisement, which was the last mode of punishment inflicted on a freeman; he was not believed upon his oath, but his evidence in courts of justice was always taken with torture. Notwithstanding the generally mild treatment of slaves in Greece, their insurrection was not unfrequent: but these insurrections in Attica were usually confined to the mining slaves, who were treated with more severity than the others. Slaves were sometimes manumitted at Athens, though not so frequently as at Rome. Those who were manumitted (ἀπελεύθεροι) did not become citizens, as they might at Rome, but passed into the condition of *metoici*. They were obliged to honour their former master as their patron (προστάτης), and to fulfil certain duties towards him, the neglect of which rendered them liable to the δίκη ἀποστασίου, by which they might again be sold into slavery. Respecting the public slaves at Athens, see DEMOSII. It appears that there was a tax upon slaves at Athens, which was probably three oboli a year for each slave.— (2) ROMAN. The Romans viewed liberty as the natural state, and slavery as a condition which was contrary to the natural state. The mutual relation of slave and master among the Romans was expressed by the terms *Servus* and *Dominus*; and the power and interest which the dominus had over and in the slave was expressed by *Dominium*. Slaves existed at Rome in the earliest times of which we have any record; but they do not appear to have been numerous under the kings and in the earliest ages of the republic. The different trades and the mechanical arts were chiefly carried on by the clients of the patricians, and the small farms in the country were cultivated for the most part by the labours of the proprietor and of his own family. But as the territories of the Roman state were extended, the patricians obtained possession of large estates out of the *ager publicus*, since it was the practice of the Romans to deprive a conquered people of part of their land. These estates probably required a larger number of hands for their cultivation than could readily be obtained among the free population, and since the freemen were constantly liable to be called away from their work to serve in the armies, the lands began to be cultivated almost entirely by slave labour. Through war and commerce slaves could easily be obtained, and at a cheap rate, and their number soon became so great, that the poorer class of freemen was thrown almost entirely out of employment. This state of things was one of the chief arguments used by Licinius and the Gracchi for

ity of public land which a
... In Sicily, which sup-
... great a quantity of corn,
gricultural slaves was im-
...sions to which they were
... twice to open rebellion,
...s enabled them to defy for
... power. The first of these
... n in B. C. 134 and ended in
second commenced in B. C.
...lmost four years. Long,
had become the custom to
...gs of slaves in the cultiva-
... the number of those who
... attendants still continued
...ons in good circumstances
...ave had one only to wait
was generally called by the
...er with the word *por* (that
to it, as *Caipor*, *Lucipor*,
...or, *Quintipor*, &c. But
times of the republic and
... the number of domestic
... eased, and in every family
... re were separate slaves to
...ecessities of domestic life.
a reproach to a man not to
...de number of slaves. The
...ked respecting a person's
pascit servos, "How many
...ep ?" Ten slaves seem to
...est number which a person
... age of Augustus, with a
... respectability in society.
...nber of prisoners taken in
...s of the republic, and the
...h and luxury, augmented
...ives to a prodigious extent.
...r Augustus, who had lost
... the civil wars, left at his
... 4,116. Two hundred was
...ber for one person to keep.
...arts, which were formerly
...e clients, were now entirely
...es ; a natural growth of
...e slaves perform certain
certain arts, such duties or
... degrading to a freeman.
...orgotten, that the games of
...required an immense num-
...ed for the purpose. [GLA-
...the slaves in Sicily, the
...ly rose in B. C. 73 against
...and under the able general-
...s, defeated a Roman con-
... were not subdued till B. C.
... of them are said to have
—A slave could not contract
cohabitation with a woman
... ; and no legal relation
his children was recognized.

A slave could have no property. He was
not incapable of acquiring property, but his
acquisitions belonged to his master. Slaves
were not only employed in the usual domestic offices and in the labours of the field,
but also as factors or agents for their masters
in the management of business, and as mechanics, artisans, and in every branch of
industry. It may easily be conceived that,
under these circumstances, especially as they
were often entrusted with property to a large
amount, there must have arisen a practice of
allowing the slave to consider part of his
gains as his own; this was his *Peculium*, a
term also applicable to such acquisitions of a
filiusfamilias as his father allowed him to
consider as his own. [PATRIA POTESTAS.]
According to strict law, the *peculium* was
the property of the master, but according to
usage, it was considered to be the property
of the slave. Sometimes it was agreed between master and slave, that the slave
should purchase his freedom with his *peculium* when it amounted to a certain sum. A
runaway slave (*fugitivus*) could not lawfully
be received or harboured. The master was
entitled to pursue him wherever he pleased;
and it was the duty of all authorities to give
him aid in recovering the slave. It was the
object of various laws to check the running
away of slaves in every way, and accordingly a runaway slave could not legally be
an object of sale. A class of persons called
Fugitivarii made it their business to recover
runaway slaves. A person was a slave either
jure gentium or jure civili. Under the republic, the chief supply of slaves arose from
prisoners taken in war, who were sold by
the quaestors with a crown on their heads
(*sub corona venire, vendere*), and usually on
the spot where they were taken, as the care
of a large number of captives was inconvenient. Consequently slave-dealers usually
accompanied an army, and frequently after a
great battle had been gained many thousands
were sold at once, when the slave-dealers
obtained them for a mere nothing. The
slave trade was also carried on to a great
extent, and after the fall of Corinth and
Carthage, Delos was the chief mart for this
traffic. When the Cilician pirates had possession of the Mediterranean, as many as
10,000 slaves are said to have been imported
and sold there in one day. A large number
came from Thrace and the countries in the
north of Europe, but the chief supply was
from Africa, and more especially Asia,
whence we frequently read of Phrygians,
Lycians, Cappadocians, &c. as slaves. The
trade of slave-dealers (*mangones*) was considered disreputable; but it was very lucra-

tive, and great fortunes were frequently realised from it. Slaves were usually sold by auction at Rome. They were placed either on a raised stone (hence *de lapide emtus*), or a raised platform (*catasta*), so that every one might see and handle them, even if they did not wish to purchase them. Purchasers usually took care to have them stripped naked, for slave-dealers had recourse to as many tricks to conceal personal defects as the horse-jockeys of modern times: sometimes purchasers called in the advice of medical men. Newly imported slaves had their feet whitened with chalk, and those that came from the East had their ears bored, which we know was a sign of slavery among many eastern nations. The slave-market, like all other markets, was under the jurisdiction of the aediles, who made many regulations by edicts respecting the sale of slaves. The character of the slave was set forth in a scroll (*titulus*) hanging around his neck, which was a warranty to the purchaser: the vendor was bound to announce fairly all his defects, and if he gave a false account had to take him back within six months from the time of his sale, or make up to the purchaser what the latter had lost through obtaining an inferior kind of slave to what had been warranted. The chief points which the vendor had to warrant, were the health of the slave, especially freedom from epilepsy, and that he had not a tendency to thievery, running away, or committing suicide. Slaves sold without any warranty wore at the time of sale a cap (*pileus*) upon their head. Slaves newly imported were generally preferred for common work: those who had served long were considered artful (*veteratores*); and the pertness and impudence of those born in their master's house, called *vernae*, were proverbial. The value of slaves depended of course upon their qualifications; but under the empire the increase of luxury and the corruption of morals led purchasers to pay immense sums for beautiful slaves, or such as ministered to the caprice or whim of the purchaser. Eunuchs always fetched a very high price, and Martial speaks of beautiful boys who sold for as much as 100,000 or 200,000 sesterces each (885*l.* 8*s.* 4*d.* and 1770*l.* 16*s.* 8*d.*). Slaves who possessed a knowledge of any art which might bring profit to their owners, also sold for a large sum. Thus literary men and doctors frequently fetched a high price, and also slaves fitted for the stage.—Slaves were divided into many various classes: the first division was into public or private. The former belonged to the state and public bodies, and their condition was preferable to that of the common slaves. They were less liable to be sold, and under less control, than ordinary slaves: they also possessed the privilege of the testamenti factio to the amount of one half of their property, which shows that they were regarded in a different light from other slaves. Public slaves were employed to take care of the public buildings, and to attend upon magistrates and priests. A body of slaves belonging to one person was called *familia*, but two were not considered sufficient to constitute a *familia*. Private slaves were divided into urban (*familia urbana*) and rustic (*familia rustica*); but the name of urban was given to those slaves who served in the villa or country residence as well as in the town house; so that the words urban and rustic rather characterised the nature of their occupations than the place where they served. Slaves were also arranged in certain classes, which held a higher or a lower rank according to the nature of their occupation. These classes are *ordinarii*, *vulgares*, and *mediastini*. —*Ordinarii* seem to have been those slaves who had the superintendence of certain parts of the housekeeping. They were always chosen from those who had the confidence of their master, and they generally had certain slaves under them. To this class the *actores*, *procuratores*, and *dispensatores* belong, who occur in the familia rustica as well as the familia urbana, but in the former are almost the same as the *villici*. They were stewards or bailiffs. To the same class also belong the slaves who had the charge of the different stores, and who correspond to our housekeepers and butlers: they are called *cellarii*, *promi*, *condi*, *procuratores peni*, &c.—*Vulgares* included the great body of slaves in a house who had to attend to any particular duty in the house, and to minister to the domestic wants of their master. As there were distinct slaves or a distinct slave for almost every department of household economy, as bakers (*pistores*), cooks (*coqui*), confectioners (*dulciarii*), picklers (*salmentarii*), &c., it is unnecessary to mention these more particularly. This class also included the porters (*ostiarii*), the bed-chamber slaves (*cubicularii*), the litter-bearers (*lecticarii*), and all personal attendants of any kind.—*Mediastini*, the name given to slaves used for any common purpose, was chiefly applied to certain slaves belonging to the familia rustica. —The treatment of slaves of course varied greatly, according to the disposition of their masters, but they were upon the whole, as has been already remarked, treated with greater severity and cruelty than among the Athenians. Originally the master could use the slave as he pleased; under the republic the law does not seem to have protected the person or life of the slave at all; but the cruelty of masters was to some extent restrained under the empire by various enactments. In early times, when the number of slaves was small, they were treated with more indulgence, and more like members of the family: they joined their masters in offering up prayers and thanksgivings to the gods, and partook of their meals in common with their masters, though not at the same table with them, but upon benches (*subsellia*) placed at the foot of the lectus. But with the increase of numbers and of luxury among masters, the ancient simplicity of manners was changed: a certain quantity of food was allowed them (*dimensum* or *demensum*), which was granted to them either monthly (*menstruum*) or daily (*diarium*). Their chief food was the corn called *far*, of which either four or five modii were granted them a month, or one Roman pound (*libra*) a day. They also obtained an allowance of salt and oil: Cato allowed his slaves a sextarius of oil a month and a modius of salt a year. They also got a small quantity of wine, with an additional allowance on the Saturnalia and Compitalia, and sometimes fruit, but seldom vegetables. Butcher's meat seems to have been hardly ever given them. Under the republic they were not allowed to serve in the army, though after the battle of Cannae, when the state was in imminent danger, 8000 slaves were purchased by the state for the army, and subsequently manumitted on account of their bravery. The offences of slaves were punished with severity, and frequently with the utmost barbarity. One of the mildest punishments was the removal from the familia urbana to the rustica, where they were obliged to work in chains or fetters. They were frequently beaten with sticks or scourged with the whip. Runaway slaves (*fugitivi*) and thieves (*fures*) were branded on the forehead with a mark (*stigma*), whence they are said to be *notati* or *inscripti*. Slaves were also punished by being hung up by their hands with weights suspended to their feet, or by being sent to work in the Ergastulum or Pistrinum. [ERGASTULUM.] The carrying of the furca was a very common mode of punishment. [FURCA.] The toilet of the Roman ladies was a dreadful ordeal to the female slaves, who were often barbarously punished by their mistresses for the slightest mistake in the arrangement of the hair or a part of the dress. Masters might work their slaves as many hours in the day as they pleased, but they usually allowed them holidays on the public festivals. At the festival of Saturnus, in particular, special indulgences were granted to all slaves, of which an account is given under SATURNALIA. There was no distinctive dress for slaves. It was once proposed in the senate to give slaves a distinctive costume, but it was rejected, since it was considered dangerous to show them their number. Male slaves were not allowed to wear the toga or bulla, nor females the stola, but otherwise they were dressed nearly in the same way as poor people, in clothes of a dark colour (*pullati*) and slippers (*crepidae*). The rights of burial, however, were not denied to slaves, for, as the Romans regarded slavery as an institution of society, death was considered to put an end to the distinction between slaves and freemen. Slaves were sometimes even buried with their masters, and we find funeral inscriptions addressed to the Dii Manes of slaves (*Dis Manibus*).

SESCUNX. [As.]

SESTERTIUS, a Roman coin, which properly belonged to the silver coinage, in which it was one-fourth of the denarius, and therefore equal to $2\frac{1}{2}$ asses. Hence the name, which is an abbreviation of *semis tertius* (sc. *nummus*), the Roman mode of expressing $2\frac{1}{2}$. The word *nummus* is often expressed with *sestertius*, and often it stands alone, meaning *sestertius*. Hence the symbol II S or I I S, which is used to designate the sestertius. It stands either for L L S (*Libra Libra et Semis*), or for I I S, the two I's merely forming the numeral two (sc. *asses* or *librae*), and the whole being in either case equivalent to *dupondius et semis*. When the as was reduced to half an ounce, and the number of asses in the denarius was made sixteen instead of ten [As, DENARIUS], the sestertius was still $\frac{1}{4}$ of the denarius, and therefore contained no longer $2\frac{1}{2}$, but 4 asses. The old reckoning of 10 asses to the denarius was kept, however, in paying the troops. After this change the sestertius was coined in brass as well as in silver; the metal used for it was that called *aurichalcum*, which was much finer than the common *aes*, of which the asses were made. The sum of 1000 *sestertii* was called *sestertium*. This was also denoted by the symbol II S, the obvious explanation of which is "I I S ($2\frac{1}{2}$ millia)." The *sestertium* was always a sum of money, never a *coin*; the *coin* used in the payment of large sums was the denarius. According to the value we have assigned to the DENARIUS, up to the time of Augustus, we have—

	£.	s.	d.	*farth.*
the sestertius =	0	0	2	·5
the sestertium =	8	17	1	

After the reign of Augustus—

	£.	s.	d.	*farth.*
the sestertius =	0	0	1	3·5
the sestertium =	7	16	3	

The sestertius was the denomination of money almost always used in reckoning considerable amounts. There are a very few examples of the use of the denarius for this purpose. The mode of reckoning was as follows:— *Sestertius* = *sestertius nummus* = *nummus*. Sums below 1000 *sestertii* were expressed by the numeral adjectives joined with either of these forms. The sum of 1000 sestertii = *mille sestertii* = M *sestertium* (for *sestertiorum*) = M *nummi* = M *nummum* (for *nummorum*) = M *sestertii nummi* = M *sestertium nummum* = *sestertium*. These forms are used with the numeral adjectives below 1000: sometimes *millia* is used instead of *sestertia*: sometimes both words are omitted: sometimes *nummum* or *sestertium* is added. For example, 600,000 sestertii = *sescenta sestertia* = *sescenta millia* = *sescenta* = *sescenta sestertia nummum*. For sums of a thousand *sestertia* (i.e. a million *sestertii*) and upwards, the numeral adverbs in *ies* (*decies*, *undecies*, *vicies*, &c.) are used, with which the words *centena millia* (a hundred thousand) must be understood. With these adverbs the neuter singular *sestertium* is joined in the case required by the construction. Thus, *decies sestertium* = *decies centena millia sestertium* = *ten times a hundred thousand sestertii* = 1,000,000 sestertii = 1000 *sestertia*: *millies* II S = *millies centena millia sestertium* = a thousand times one hundred thousand sestertii = 100,000,000 *sestertii* = 100,000 *sestertia*. When the numbers are written in cypher, it is often difficult to know whether *sestertii* or *sestertia* are meant. A distinction is sometimes made by a line placed over the numeral when *sestertia* are intended, or in other words, when the numeral is an adverb in *ies*. Thus

HS. M.C. = 1100 sestertii, but

HS. M̄.C̄. = HS millies centies
= 110,000 sestertia =
110,000,000 sestertii.

Sesterce is sometimes used as an English word. If so, it ought to be used only as the translation of *sestertius*, never of *sestertium*.

SĒVIR. [EQUITES.]

SEX SUFFRAGIA. [EQUITES.]

SEXTANS. [As.]

SEXTARIUS, a Roman dry and liquid measure. It was one-sixth of the congius, and hence its name. It was divided, in the same manner as the As, into parts named *uncia*, *sextans*, *quadrans*, *triens*, *quincunx*, *semissis*, &c. The uncia, or twelfth part of the sextarius, was the CYATHUS; its *sextans* was therefore two cyathi, its *quadrans* three, its *triens* four, its *quincunx* five, &c. (See Tables.)

SIBYLLĪNI LIBRI. These books are said to have been obtained in the reign of Tarquinius Priscus, or according to other accounts in that of Tarquinius Superbus, when a Sibyl (Σίβυλλα), or prophetic woman, presented herself before the king, and offered nine books for sale. Upon the king refusing to purchase them, she went and burnt three, and then returned and demanded the same price for the remaining six as she had done for the nine. The king again refused to purchase them, whereupon she burnt three more, and demanded the same sum for the remaining three as she had done at first for the nine; the king's curiosity now became excited, so that he purchased the books, and then the Sibyl vanished. These books were probably written in Greek, as the later ones undoubtedly were. They were kept in a stone chest under ground in the temple of Jupiter Capitolinus, under the custody of certain officers, at first only two in number, but afterwards increased successively to ten and fifteen, of whom an account is given under DECEMVIRI. The public were not allowed to inspect the books, and they were only consulted by the officers, who had the charge of them, at the special command of the senate. They were not consulted, as the Greek oracles were, for the purpose of getting light concerning future events; but to learn what worship was required by the gods, when they had manifested their wrath by national calamities or prodigies. Accordingly we find that the instruction they give is in the same spirit; prescribing what honour was to be paid to the deities already recognised, or what new ones were to be imported from abroad. When the temple of Jupiter Capitolinus was burnt in B. C. 82, the Sibylline books perished in the fire; and in order to restore them, ambassadors were sent to various towns in Italy, Greece, and Asia Minor, to make fresh collections, which on the rebuilding of the temple were deposited in the same place that the former had occupied. The Sibylline books were also called *Fata Sibyllina* and *Libri Fatales*. Along with the Sibylline books were preserved, under the guard of the same officers, the books of the two prophetic brothers, the Marcii, the Etruscan prophecies of the nymph Bygoe, and those of Albuna or Albunea of Tibur. Those of the Marcii, which had not been placed there at the time of the battle of Cannae, were written in Latin.

SĪCA, *dim.* SĪCĪLA, whence the English *sickle*, a curved dagger, adapted by its form to be concealed under the clothes, and therefore carried by robbers and murderers. *Sica* may be translated *a scimitar*, to distinguish it from *pugio*, which denoted a dagger of the common kind. *Sicarius*, though properly meaning one who murdered with the sica, was applied to murderers in general. Hence the forms *de sicariis* and *inter sicarios* were used in the criminal courts in reference to murder. Thus *judicium inter sicarios*, "a trial for murder;" *defendere inter sicarios*, "to defend against a charge of murder."

SIGILLĀRIA. [SATURNALIA.]

SIGNA MILITĀRIA (σημεῖα, σημαῖαι), military ensigns or standards. The most ancient standard employed by the Romans is said to have been a handful of straw fixed to the top of a spear or pole. Hence the company of soldiers belonging to it was called *Manipulus*. The bundle of hay or fern was soon succeeded by the figures of animals, viz. the eagle, the wolf, the minotaur, the horse, and the boar. These appear to have corresponded to the five divisions of the Roman army as shown on p. 165. The eagle (*aquila*) was carried by the *aquilifer* in the midst of the *hastati*, and we may suppose the wolf to have been carried among the *principes*, and so on. In the second consulship of Marius, B. C. 104, the four quadrupeds were entirely laid aside as standards, the eagle being alone retained. It was made of silver, or bronze, and with expanded wings, but was probably of a small size, since a standard-bearer (*sig-nifer*) under Julius Caesar is said in circumstances of danger to have wrenched the eagle from its staff, and concealed it in the folds of his girdle. Under the later emperors the eagle was carried, as it had been for many centuries, with the legion, a legion being on that account sometimes called *aquila*, and at the same time each cohort had for its own ensign the serpent or dragon (*draco*, δράκων), which was woven on a square piece of cloth, elevated on a gilt staff, to which a cross-bar was adapted for the purpose, and carried by the *draconarius*. Another figure used in the standards was a ball (*pila*), supposed to have been emblematic of the dominion of Rome over the world; and for the same reason a bronze figure of Victory was sometimes fixed at the top of the staff. Under the eagle or other emblem was often placed a head of the reigning emperor, which was to the army the object of idolatrous adoration. The minor divisions of a cohort, called *centuries*, had also each an ensign, inscribed with the number both of the cohort and of the century. By this provision every soldier was enabled with the greatest ease to take his place. The standard of the cavalry, properly called *vexillum*, was a square piece of cloth expanded upon a cross in the manner already indicated, and perhaps surmounted by some figure. The following cut, contain-

Military Standards. (Bellori, Vet. Arc. Aug.)

ing several standards, represents the performance of the sacrifice called *suovetaurilia*. The imperial standard from the time of Constantine was called *labarum*; on it a figure or emblem of Christ was woven in gold upon purple cloth, and this was substituted for the head of the emperor. Since the movements of a body of troops and of every portion of it were regulated by the standards, all the evolutions, acts, and incidents of the Roman army were expressed by phrases derived from this circumstance. Thus *signa inferre* meant to advance, *referre* to retreat, and *convertere* to face about; *efferre*, or *castris vellere*, to march out of the camp; *ad signa convenire*, to re-assemble. Notwithstanding some obscurity in the use of terms, it appears that, whilst the standard of the legion was properly called *aquila*, those of the cohorts were in a special sense of the term called *signa*, their bearers being *signiferi*, and that those of the manipuli or smaller divisions of the cohort were denominated *vexilla*, their bearers being *vexillarii*. In time of peace the standards were kept in the AERARIUM, under the care of the QUAESTOR.

SILICERNIUM. [FUNUS.]

SIMPULUM or SIMPUVIUM, the name of a small cup used in sacrifices, by which libations of wine were offered to the gods. It is represented on the coin figured under SECESPITA. There was a proverbial expression *excitare fluctus in simpulo*, "to make much ado about nothing."

SIPARIUM, a piece of tapestry stretched on a frame, which rose before the stage of the theatre, and consequently answered the purpose of the drop-scene with us, although, contrary to our practice, it was depressed when the play began, so as to go below the level of the stage (*aulaea premuntur*), and was raised again when the performance was concluded (*tolluntur*). It appears that human figures were represented upon it, whose feet seemed to rest upon the stage when this screen was drawn up. These figures were sometimes those of Britons woven in the canvass, and raising their arms in the attitude of lifting up a purple curtain, so as to be introduced in the same manner as Atlantes, Persae, and Caryatides. [CARYATIDES.] In a more general sense, *siparium* denoted any piece of cloth or canvass stretched upon a frame.

SISTRUM (σεῖστρον), a mystical instrument of music, used by the ancient Egyptians in their ceremonies, and especially in the worship of Isis. It was held in the right hand (see cut), and shaken, from which circumstance it derived its name. The introduction of the worship of Isis into Italy shortly before the commencement of the Christian aera made the Romans familiar with this instrument.

Sistra. (The two figures on the left hand from paintings found at Portici; the right-hand figure represents a Sistrum formerly belonging to the library of St. Genovefa at Paris.)

SITELLA. [SITULA.]

SITOPHYLACES (σιτοφύλακες), a board of officers, chosen by lot, at Athens. They were at first three, afterwards increased to fifteen, of whom ten were for the city, five for the Peiraeus. Their business was partly to watch the arrival of the corn ships, take account of the quantity imported, and see that the import laws were duly observed; partly to watch the sales of corn in the market, and take care that the prices were fair and reasonable, and none but legal weights and measures used by the factors; in which respect their duties were much the same as those of the Agoranomi and Metronomi with regard to other saleable articles.

SITOS (σῖτος), corn. The soil of Attica, though favourable to the production of figs, olives, and grapes, was not so favourable for corn; and accordingly a large quantity of corn was annually imported. Exportation was entirely prohibited, nor was any Athenian or resident alien allowed to carry corn to any other place than Athens. Whoever did so, was punishable with death. Of the corn brought into the Athenian port two-thirds was to be brought into the city and sold there. No one might lend money on a ship that did not sail with an express condition to bring a return cargo, part of it corn, to Athens. Strict regulations were made with

rn in the market. corn-dealers (σιτο-n (συνωνεῖσθαι), or ας τὰς τιμάς), were ιε sale of **corn was** vision of a **special** *tophylaces* (σιτοφύ- other marketable ended by the agora-**ess to see** that meal proper quality, and .d price. Notwith- ovisions, scarcities **curred at** Athens. it efforts to supply **by** importing large **elling** it at **a low were** kept in the Porch, and naval *Sitonae* (σιτῶναι) n the supply and is called *apodectae* rn, measured **it out**, in quantities. κη). If anything riage contract, the ative was bound **to** n (προὶξ); **or, if he** ble to **pay interest** .iteen per cent. per rtune **was usually the husband's pro- was so or not, her action against the .ld it**; δίκη προικὸς, δίκη σίτου, **for the** is called σῖτος (ali- recause it was **the** woman had **to be** σῖτος is often **used** just as we use the

A (ὑδρία), was pro- for drawing and more usually applied i lots were drawn. owever, was more gnification. It ap- illed with water (as re the word ὑδρία), vere made of wood; z **in size below**, it one lot could come at the same time, he **vessel** used for led *urna* or *orca* as **t is important to un-** meaning, between use in the comitia ce they nave been The *Sitella* was the

urn, from which the names of the tribes **or centuries were drawn out** by lot, so that each **might have its proper place** in voting, and the *Cista* was the ballot-box into which the tabellae were cast in voting. The *Cista* seems to have been made of wicker or similar **work.**

Cista. Sitella.

SOCCUS, *dim.* SOCCULUS, was **nearly if** not altogether equivalent in meaning to CRE- PIDA, and denoted a slipper or low shoe, which did not fit closely, and was not fas- tened by any tie. The Soccus was worn by comic actors, and was in this respect opposed **to the COTHURNUS.**

Socci, slippers, worn by a Mimus or Buffoon. **(From an** ancient Painting.)

SŎCĬI (σύμμαχοι). In the early times, **when** Rome formed equal alliances with any of the surrounding nations, these nations were called *Socii*. After the dissolution of **the** Latin league, when the name *Latini*, or *Nomen Latinum*, was **artificially** applied to a great **number** of Italians, only a few of **whom** were **real inhabitants** of the old **Latin towns,** and **the majority of whom** had been made Latins **by the will and the law of Rome,** there necessarily arose a **difference between** these Latins and the **Socii**, and the expres- sion *Socii Nomen Latinum* is one of the old asyndeta, instead of *Socii et Nomen Latinum*. The Italian allies again must be distinguished from foreign allies. The Italian allies con- sisted, for the most part, of such nations as had either been conquered by the Romans, or had come under their dominion through other circumstances. When such nations formed an alliance with Rome, they generally retained their own laws; or if they were not allowed this privilege at first, they usually obtained it subsequently. The condition of the Italian allies varied, and mainly depended upon the manner in which they had come under the Roman dominion; but in reality they were always dependent upon Rome. The following are the principal duties which the Italian Socii had to perform towards Rome: they had to send subsidies in troops, money, corn, ships, and other things, whenever Rome demanded them. The number of troops requisite for completing or increasing the Roman armies was decreed every year by the senate, and the consuls fixed the amount which each allied nation had to send, in proportion to its population capable of bearing arms, of which each nation was obliged to draw up accurate lists, called *formulae*. The consul also appointed the place and time at which the troops of the socii, each part under its own leader, had to meet him and his legions. The infantry of the allies in a consular army was usually equal in numbers to that of the Romans; the cavalry was generally three times the number of the Romans: but these numerical proportions were not always observed. The consuls appointed twelve praefects as commanders of the socii, and their power answered to that of the twelve military tribunes in the consular legions. These praefects, who were probably taken from the allies themselves, and not from the Romans, selected a third of the cavalry, and a fifth of the infantry of the socii, who formed a select detachment for extraordinary cases, and who were called the *extraordinarii*. The remaining body of the socii was then divided into two parts, called the right and the left wing. The infantry of the wings was, as usual, divided into cohorts, and the cavalry into turmae. In some cases also legions were formed of the socii. Pay and clothing were given to the allied troops by the states or towns to which they belonged, and which appointed quaestors or paymasters for this purpose: but Rome furnished them with provisions at the expense of the republic: the infantry received the same pay as the Roman infantry, but the cavalry only received two-thirds of what was given to the Roman cavalry. In the distribution of the spoil and of conquered lands they frequently received the same share as the Romans. They were never allowed to take up arms of their own accord, and disputes among them were settled by the senate. Notwithstanding all this, the socii fell gradually under the arbitrary rule of the senate and the magistrates of Rome; and after the year B. C. 173, it even became customary for magistrates, when they travelled through Italy, to demand of the authorities of allied towns to pay homage to them, to provide them with a residence, and to furnish them with beasts of burden when they continued their journey. The only way for the allies to obtain any protection against such arbitrary proceedings, was to enter into a kind of clientela with some influential and powerful Roman. Socii who revolted against Rome were frequently punished with the loss of their freedom, or of the honour of serving in the Roman armies. Such punishments however varied according to circumstances. After the civitas had been granted to all the Italians by the Lex Julia de Civitate (B. c. 90), the relation of the Italian socii to Rome ceased. But Rome had long before this event applied the name Socii to foreign nations also which were allied with Rome, though the meaning of the word in this case differed from that of the Socii Italici. There were two principal kinds of alliances with foreign nations: 1. *foedus aequum*, such as might be concluded either after a war in which neither party had gained a decisive victory, or with a nation with which Rome had never been at war; 2. a *foedus iniquum*, when a foreign nation conquered by the Romans was obliged to form the alliance on any terms proposed by the conquerors. In the latter case the foreign nation was to some extent subject to Rome, and obliged to comply with anything that Rome might demand. But all foreign socii, whether they had an equal or unequal alliance, were obliged to send subsidies in troops when Rome demanded them; these troops, however, did not, like those of the Italian socii, serve in the line, but were employed as light-armed soldiers, and were called *milites auxiliares, auxiliarii, auxilia*, or sometimes *auxilia externa*. Towards the end of the republic all the Roman allies, whether they were nations or kings, sank down to the condition of mere subjects or vassals of Rome, whose freedom and independence consisted in nothing but a name. [Compare FOEDERATAE CIVITATES.]

SŎDĀLĪTĬUM. [AMBITUS.]

SŎLĀRĬUM. [HOROLOGIUM.]

SŎLĔA was the simplest kind of sandal [SANDALIUM], consisting of a sole with little more to fasten it to the foot than a strap across the instep.

SŎLĬDUS. [AURUM.]

SOLITAURILIA. [SACRIFICIUM; LUSTRATIO; and woodcut on p. 313.]

SOPHRONISTAE. [GYMNASIUM.]

SORTES, lots. It was a frequent practice among the Italian nations to endeavour to ascertain a knowledge of future events by drawing lots (*sortes*): in many of the ancient Italian temples the will of the gods was consulted in this way, as at Praeneste, Caere, &c. These sortes or lots were usually little tablets or counters, made of wood or other materials, and were commonly thrown into a sitella or urn, filled with water, as is explained under SITULA. The lots were sometimes thrown like dice. The name of sortes was in fact given to anything used to determine chances, and was also applied to any verbal response of an oracle. Various things were written upon the lots according to circumstances, as for instance the names of the persons using them, &c.: it seems to have been a favourite practice in later times to write the verses of illustrious poets upon little tablets, and to draw them out of the urn like other lots, the verses which a person thus obtained being supposed to be applicable to him.

SPECULARIA. [DOMUS.]

SPECULATORES, or EXPLORATORES, were scouts or spies sent before an army, to reconnoitre the ground and observe the movements of the enemy. Under the emperors there was a body of troops called Speculatores, who formed part of the praetorian cohorts, and had the especial care of the emperor's person.

SPECULUM (κάτοπτρον, ἔσοπτρον, ἔνοπτρον), a mirror, a looking-glass. The looking-glasses of the ancients were usually made of metal, at first of a composition of tin and copper, but afterwards more frequently of silver. The ancients seem to have had glass mirrors also like ours, consisting of a glass plate covered at the back with a thin leaf of metal. They were manufactured as early as the time of Pliny at the celebrated glasshouses of Sidon, but they must have been inferior to those of metal, since they never came into general use, and are never mentioned by ancient writers among costly pieces of furniture, whereas metal mirrors frequently are. Looking-glasses were generally small, and such as could be carried in the hand. Instead of their being fixed so as to be hung against the wall or to stand upon the table or floor, they were generally held by female slaves before their mistresses when dressing.

SPECUS. [AQUAEDUCTUS.]

SPHAERISTERIUM. [GYMNASIUM.]

SPICULUM. [HASTA.]

SPIRA (σπεῖρα), *dim.* SPIRULA, the base of a column. This member did not exist in the Doric order of Greek architecture, but was always present in the Ionic and Corinthian, and, besides the bases properly belonging to those orders, there was one called the Attic, which may be regarded as a variety of the Ionic [ATTICURGES]. In the Ionic and Attic the base commonly consisted of two tori (*torus superior* and *torus inferior*) divided by a scotia (τρόχιλος), and in the Corinthian of two tori divided by two scotiae. The upper torus was often fluted (ῥαβδωτός), and surmounted by an astragal [ASTRAGALUS], as in the left-hand figure of the annexed woodcut, which shows the form of the base

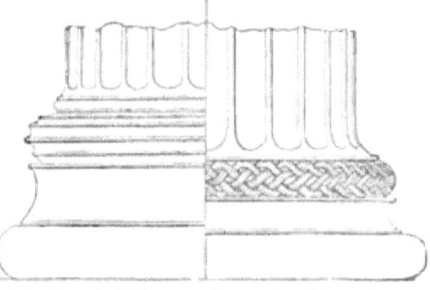

Spirae (bases) of Columns. (From ancient Columns.)

in the Ionic temple of Panops on the Ilissus. The right-hand figure in the same woodcut shows the corresponding part in the temple of Minerva Polias at Athens. In this the upper torus is wrought with a plaited ornament, perhaps designed to represent a rope or cable. In these two temples the spira rests not upon a plinth (*plinthus*, πλίνθος), but on a podium.

SPOLIA. Four words are commonly employed to denote booty taken in war, *Praeda*,

Looking-glass held by a Nymph. (From a Painting at Herculaneum.)

Manubiae, Exuviae, Spolia. Of these *Praeda* bears the most comprehensive meaning, being used for plunder of every description. *Manubiae* would seem strictly to signify that portion of the spoil which fell to the share of the commander-in-chief, the proceeds of which were frequently applied to the erection of some public building. *Exuviae* indicates anything stripped from the person of a foe, while *Spolia*, properly speaking, ought to be confined to armour and weapons, although both words are applied loosely to trophies, such as chariots, standards, beaks of ships and the like, which might be preserved and displayed. Spoils collected on the battlefield after an engagement, or found in a captured town, were employed to decorate the temples of the gods, triumphal arches, porticoes, and other places of public resort, and sometimes in the hour of extreme need served to arm the people; but those which were gained by individual prowess were considered the undoubted property of the successful combatant, and were exhibited in the most conspicuous part of his dwelling, being hung up in the atrium, suspended from the door-posts, or arranged in the vestibulum, with appropriate inscriptions. They were regarded as peculiarly sacred, so that even if the house was sold the new possessor was not permitted to remove them. But while on the one hand it was unlawful to remove spoils, so it was forbidden to *replace* or *repair* them when they had fallen down or become decayed through age; the object of this regulation being doubtless to guard against the frauds of false pretenders. Of all spoils the most important were the *spolia opima*, a term applied to those only which the commander-in-chief of a Roman army stripped in a field of battle from the leader of the foe. Plutarch expressly asserts that Roman history up to his own time afforded but three examples of the *spolia opima*. The first were said to have been won by Romulus from Acro, king of the Caeninenses, the second by Aulus Cornelius Cossus from Lar Tolumnius, king of the Veientes, the third by M. Claudius Marcellus from Viridomarus, king of the Gaesatae. In all these cases, in accordance with the original institution, the spoils were dedicated to Jupiter Feretrius.

SPONSA, SPONSUS, SPONSALIA. [MATRIMONIUM.]

SPORTŬLA. In the days of Roman freedom, clients were in the habit of testifying respect for their patron by thronging his atrium at an early hour, and escorting him to places of public resort when he went abroad. As an acknowledgment of these courtesies, some of the number were usually invited to partake of the evening meal. After the extinction of liberty, the presence of such guests, who had now lost all political importance, was soon regarded as an irksome restraint, while at the same time many of the noble and wealthy were unwilling to sacrifice the pompous display of a numerous body of retainers. Hence the practice was introduced under the empire of bestowing on each client, when he presented himself for his morning visit, a certain portion of food as a substitute and compensation for the occasional invitation to a regular supper (*coena recta*), and this dole, being carried off in a little basket provided for the purpose, received the name of *sportula*. For the sake of convenience it soon became common to give an equivalent in money, the sum established by general usage being a hundred quadrantes. The donation in money, however, did not entirely supersede the sportula given in kind, for we find in Juvenal a lively description of a great man's vestibule crowded with dependents, each attended by a slave bearing a portable kitchen to receive the viands and keep them hot while they were carried home. Under the empire great numbers of the lower orders derived their whole sustenance, and the funds for ordinary expenditure, exclusively from this source, while even the highborn did not scruple to increase their incomes by taking advantage of the ostentatious profusion of the rich and vain.

STADIUM (ὁ στάδιος and τὸ στάδιον), a Greek measure of length, and the chief one used for itinerary distances. It was equal to 600 Greek or 625 Roman feet, or to 125 Roman paces; and the Roman mile contained 8 stadia. Hence the stadium contained 606 feet 9 inches English. This standard prevailed throughout Greece, under the name of the Olympic stadium, so called because it was the exact length of the stadium or foot-race course at Olympia, measured between the pillars at the two extremities of the course. The first use of the measure seems to be contemporaneous with the formation of the stadium at Olympia when the Olympic games were revived by Iphitus (B. C. 884 or 828). This distance doubled formed the δίαυλος, the ἱππικόν was 4 stadia, and the δόλιχος is differently stated at 6, 7, 8, 12, 20, and 24 stadia. A day's journey by land was reckoned at 200 or 180 stadia, or for an army 150 stadia. The stadium at Olympia was used not only for the foot-race, but also for the other contests which were added to the games from time to time [OLYMPIA], except the horse-races, for which a place was set apart, of a similar form with the stadium, but larger; this was called the Hippodrome (ἱππόδρόμος). The name stadium was also given to all other places throughout Greece wherever games were celebrated. The stadium was an oblong area terminated at one end by a straight line, at the other by a semicircle having the breadth of the stadium for its base. Round this area were ranges of seats rising above one another in steps.

STATER (στατήρ), which means simply a standard (in this case both of weight and more particularly of money), was the name of the principal gold coin of Greece, which was also called Chrysus (χρυσοῦς). The stater is said to have been first coined in Lydia by Croesus, and probably did not differ materially from the stater which was afterwards current in Greece, and which was equal in weight to two drachmae, and in value to twenty. The Macedonian stater, which was the one most in use after the time of Philip and his son Alexander the Great, was of the value of about 1l. 3s. 6d. In calculating the value of the stater in our money the ratio of gold to silver must not be overlooked. Thus the stater of Alexander, which we have valued, according to the present worth of gold, at 1l. 3s. 6d., passed for twenty drachmae, which, according to the present value of silver, were worth only 16s. 3d. But the former is the true worth of the stater, the difference arising from the greater value of silver in ancient times than now.

STATIONES. [CASTRA.]

STATOR, a public servant, who attended on the Roman magistrates in the provinces. The Statores seem to have derived their name from standing by the side of the magistrate, and thus being at hand to execute all his commands; they appear to have been chiefly employed in carrying letters and messages.

STATUARIA ARS is in its proper sense the art of making statues or busts, whether they consist of stone or metal or other materials, and includes the art of making the various kinds of reliefs (alto, basso, and mezzo relievo). These arts in their infant state existed among the Greeks from time immemorial. There is no material applicable to statuary which was not used by the Greeks. As soft clay is capable of being shaped without difficulty into any form, and is easily dried, either by being exposed to the sun or by being baked, we may consider this substance to have been the earliest material of which figures were made. The name plastic art (ἡ πλαστική), by which the ancients sometimes designate the art of statuary, properly signifies to form or shape a thing of clay. The second material was wood, and figures made of wood were called ξόανα, from ξέω, "polish" or "carve." It was chiefly used for making images of the gods, and probably more on account of the facility of working in it, than for any other reason. Stone was little used in statuary during the early ages of Greece, though it was not altogether unknown, as we may infer from the relief on the Lion-gate of Mycenae. In Italy, where the soft peperino afforded an easy material for working, stone appears to have been used at an earlier period and more commonly than in Greece. But in the historical times the Greeks used all the principal varieties of marble for their statues. Different kinds of marble and of different colours were sometimes used in one and the same statue, in which case the work is called Polylithic statuary. Bronze (χάλκος, aes), silver, and gold were used profusely in the state of society described in the Homeric poems. At that period, however, and long after, the works executed in metal were made by means of the hammer, and the different pieces were joined together by pins, rivets, cramps, or other mechanical fastenings, and, as the art advanced, by a kind of glue, cement, or solder. Iron came into use much later, and the art of casting both bronze and iron is ascribed to Rhoecus and to Theodorus of Samos. Ivory was employed at a later period than any of the before-mentioned materials, and then was highly valued both for its beauty and rarity. In its application to statuary, ivory was generally combined with gold, and was used for the parts representing the flesh. The history of ancient art, and of statuary in particular, may be divided into five periods.

I. *First Period, from the earliest times till about 580 B. C.*—Three kinds of artists may be distinguished in the mythical period. The first consists of gods and daemons; such as Athena, Hephaestus, the Phrygian or Dardanian Dactyli, and the Cabiri. The second contains whole tribes of men distinguished from others by the mysterious possession of superior skill in the practice of the arts, such as the Telchines and the Cyclopes. The third consists of individuals who are indeed described as human beings, but yet are nothing more than personifications of particular branches of art, or the representatives of families of artists. Of the latter the most celebrated is *Daedalus*, whose name indicates nothing but a smith, or an artist in general, and who is himself the mythical ancestor of a numerous family of artists (*Daedalids*), which can be traced from the time of Homer to that of Plato, for even Socrates is said to have been a descendant of this family. *Smilis* (from σμίλη, a carving-knife) exercised his art in Samos, Aegina, and other places, and some remarkable works were attributed to him. *Endoeus* of Athens is called a disciple of Daedalus. According to the popular traditions of Greece, there was no period in which the gods were not represented in some form or other, and there is no doubt that for a long time there existed no other statues in Greece than those of the gods. The earliest representations of the gods, however, were only symbolic. The presence of a god was indicated by the simplest and most shapeless symbols, such as unhewn blocks of stone (λίθοι ἀργοί), and by simple pillars or pieces of wood. The general name for a representation of a god not consisting of such a rude symbol was ἄγαλμα. In the Homeric poems there are sufficient traces of the existence of statues of the gods; but they probably did not display any artistic beauty. The only work of art which has come down to us from the heroic age is the relief above the ancient gate of Mycenae, representing two lions standing on their hind legs, with a sort of pillar between them (woodcut under MURUS). The time which elapsed between the composition of the Homeric poems and the beginning of the fifth century before our aera may be termed the age of discovery; for nearly all the inventions, upon the application of which the developement of the arts is dependent, are assigned to this period. Glaucus of Chios or Samos is said to have invented the art of soldering metal (σιδήρου κόλλησις). The two artists most celebrated for their discoveries were the two brothers Telecles and Theodorus of Samos, about the time of Polycrates. They invented the art of casting figures of metal. During the whole of this period, though marble and bronze began to be extensively applied, yet wood was more generally used for representations of the gods. These statues were painted [PICTURA], and in most cases dressed in the most gorgeous attire. The style in which they are executed is called the *archaic* or the *hieratic* style. The figures are stiff and clumsy, the countenances have little or no individuality, the eyes long and small, and the outer angles turned a little upwards; the mouth, which is likewise drawn upwards at the two corners, has a smiling appearance. The hair is carefully worked, but looks stiff and wiry, and hangs generally down in straight lines, which are curled at the ends. The arms hang down the sides of the body, unless the figure carries something in its hands. The drapery is likewise stiff, and the folds are very symmetrical and worked with little regard to nature.

II. *Second Period, from 580 to 480 B. C.*—The number of artists who flourished during this period is truly astonishing. The Ionians of Asia Minor and the islanders of the Aegean, who had previously been in advance of the other Greeks in the exercise of the fine arts, had their last flourishing period from 560 to 528 B. C. Works in metal were produced in high perfection in Samos, in Aegina and Argos, while Chios gained the greatest reputation from its possessing the earliest great school of sculptors in marble, in which Bupalus and Anthermus were the most distinguished about 540 B. C. Their works were scattered over various parts of Greece, and their value may be inferred from the fact that Augustus adorned with them the pediment of the temple of Apollo on the Palatine. Sicyon also possessed a celebrated school of sculptors in marble, and about 580 B. C. Dipoenus and Scyllis, who had come from Crete, were at the head of it, and executed several marble statues of gods. Respecting Magna Graecia and Sicily we know few particulars, though it appears that the arts here went on improving and continued to be in advance of the mother-country. The most celebrated artists in southern Italy were Dameas of Croton, and Pythagoras of Rhegium. In Athens the arts made great progress under the patronage of the Pisistratids. The most celebrated among the Athenian sculptors of this period were Critias and Hegias, or Hegesias, both distinguished for their works in bronze. The former of them made in 477 B. C. the statues of Harmodius and Aristogiton. Argos also distinguished itself, and it is a curious circumstance, that the greatest Attic artists with whom the third period opens, and who brought the Attic art to its culminating point, are disciples of the Argive Ageladas (about 516 B. C.) In the statues of the gods (ἀγάλματα), which were made for temples as objects of worship, the hieratic style was more or less conscientiously retained, and it is therefore not in these statues that we have to seek for proofs of the progress of art. But even in temple-statues wood began to give way to other and better materials. Besides bronze, marble also, and ivory and gold were now applied to statues of the gods, and it was not uncommon to form the body of a statue of wood, and to make its head, arms, and feet of stone (ἀκρόλιθοι), or to cover the whole of such a wooden figure with ivory and gold. From the statues of the gods erected for worship we must distinguish those statues which were dedicated in temples as ἀναθήματα, and which now became customary instead of craters, tripods, &c. In these the artists were not only not bound to any traditional or conventional forms, but were, like the poets, allowed to make free use of mythological subjects, to add, and to omit, or to modify the stories, so as to render them more adapted for their artistic purposes. A third class of statues, which were erected during this period in great numbers, were those of the victors in the national games, and, though more rarely, of other distinguished persons (ἀνδριάντες). Those of the latter kind appear generally to have been portraits (εἰκόνες, statuae iconicae). The first iconic statues of Harmodius and Aristogiton were made by Antenor in 509 B. C., and in 477 B. C. new statues of the same persons were made by Critias. It was also at the period we are now describing that it became customary to adorn the pediments, friezes, and other parts of temples with reliefs or groups of statues of marble. We still possess two great works of this kind which are sufficient to show their general character during this period. 1. The *Selinuntine Marbles*, or the metopes of two temples on the acropolis of Selinus in Sicily, which were discovered in 1823, and are at present in the Museum of Palermo. 2. The *Aeginetan Marbles*, which were discovered in 1812 in the island of Aegina, and are now at Munich. They consist of eleven statues, which adorned two pediments of a temple of Athena, and represent the goddess leading the Aeacids against Troy, and contain manifest allusions to the war of the Greeks with the Persians.

III. *Third Period, from 480 to 336 B. C.*— During this period Athens was the centre of the fine arts in Greece. Statuary went hand in hand with the other arts and with literature: it became emancipated from its ancient fetters, from the stiffness and conventional forms of former times, and reached its culminating point in the sublime and mighty works of Phidias. His career begins about 452 B. C. The genius of this artist was so great and so generally recognised, that all the great works which were executed in the age of Pericles were placed under his direction, and thus the whole host of artists who were at that time assembled at Athens were engaged in working out his designs and ideas. Of these we have still some remains:—1. Parts of the eighteen sculptured metopes, together with the frieze of the small sides of the cella of the temple of Theseus. Ten of the metopes represent the exploits of Hercules, and the eight others those of Theseus. The figures in the frieze are manifestly gods, but their meaning is uncertain. Casts of these figures are in the British Museum. 2. A considerable number of the metopes of the Parthenon, which are all adorned with reliefs in marble, a great part of the frieze of the cella, some colossal figures, and a number of fragments of the two pediments of this temple. The greater part of these works is now in the British Museum, where they are collected under the name of the Elgin Marbles. Besides the sculptures of these temples, there are also similar ornaments of other temples extant, which show the influence which the school of Phidias exercised in various parts of Greece. Of these the most important are, the Phigalian marbles, which belonged to the temple of Apollo Epicurius, built about 436 B. C., by Ictinus. They were discovered in 1812, and consist of twenty-three plates of marble belonging to the inner frieze of the cella. They are now in the British Museum. The subjects represented in them are fights with Centaurs and Amazons, and one plate shows Apollo and Artemis drawn in a chariot by stags. About the same time that the Attic school rose to its highest perfection under Phidias, the school of Argos was likewise raised to its summit by Polycletus. The art of making bronze statues of athletes was carried by him to the greatest perfection: ideal youthful and manly beauty was the sphere in which he excelled. One of his statues, a youthful Doryphorus, was made with such accurate observation of the proportions of the parts of the body, that it was looked upon by the ancient artists as a canon of rules on this point. Myron of Eleutherae, about 432 B. C., adhered to a closer imitation of nature than Polycletus, and as far as the impression upon the senses was concerned, his works were most pleasing. The cow of Myron in bronze was celebrated in all antiquity. The change which took place after the Peloponnesian war in the public mind at Athens could not fail to show its influence upon the arts also. It was especially Scopas of Paros and Praxiteles of Athens, about one generation after Myron and Polycletus, who gave the reflex of their time in their productions. Their works expressed the softer feelings and an excited state of mind, such as would make a strong impression upon and captivate the senses of the beholders. Both were distinguished as sculptors in marble, and both worked in the same style; the legendary circles to which most of their ideal productions belong are those of Dionysus and Aphrodite, a fact which also shows the character of the age. Cephissodorus and Timarchus were sons of Praxiteles. There were several works of the former at Rome in the time of Pliny; he made his art subservient to passions and sensual desires. Most of the above-mentioned artists, however widely their works differed from those of the school of Phidias, may yet be regarded as having only continued and developed its principles of art in a certain direction; but towards the end of this period Euphranor and

Lysippus of Sicyon carried out the principles of the Argive school of Polycletus. Their principal object was to represent the highest possible degree of physical beauty and of athletic and heroic power. The chief characteristic of Lysippus and his school is a close imitation of nature, which even contrived to represent bodily defects in some interesting manner, as in his statues of Alexander.

IV. *Fourth Period, from 336 to 146 B.C.*— During the first fifty years of this period the schools of Praxiteles and Lysippus continued to flourish, especially in works of bronze; but after this time bronze statues were seldom made, until the art was carried on with new vigour at Athens about the end of the period. The school of Lysippus gave rise to that of Rhodes, where his disciple Chares formed the most celebrated among the hundred colossal statues of the sun. It was seventy cubits high, and partly of metal. It stood near the harbour, and was thrown down by an earthquake about 225 B.C. Antiquarians assign to this part of the fourth period several very beautiful works still extant, as the magnificent group of Laocoon and his sons, which was discovered in 1506 near the baths of Titus, and is at present at Rome. This is, next to the Niobe, the most beautiful group among the extant works of ancient art; it was according to Pliny the work of three Rhodian artists: Agesander, Polydorus, and Athenodorus. The celebrated Farnesian bull is likewise the work of two Rhodian artists, Apollonius and Tauriscus. In the various kingdoms which arose out of the conquests of Alexander the arts were more or less cultivated. Not only were the great master-works of former times copied to adorn the new capitals, but new schools of artists sprang up in several of them. At Pergamus the celebrated groups were composed which represented the victories of Attalus and Eumenes over the Gauls. It is believed by some that the so-called dying gladiator at Rome is a statue of a Gaul, which originally belonged to one of these groups. The Borghese gladiator in the Louvre is supposed to be the work of an Ephesian Agasias, and to have originally formed a part of such a battle-scene. About the close of this period, and for more than a century afterwards, the Romans, in the conquest of the countries where the arts had flourished, made it a regular practice to carry away the works of art. The triumphs over Philip, Antiochus, the Aetolians, the Gauls in Asia, Perseus, Pseudo-Philip, and above all the taking of Corinth, and subsequently the victories over Mithridates and Cleopatra, filled the Roman temples and porticoes with the greatest variety of works of art. The sacrilegious plunder of temples and the carrying away of the sacred statues from the public sanctuaries became afterwards a common practice. The manner in which Verres acted in Sicily is but one of many instances of the extent to which these robberies were carried on. The emperors, especially Augustus, Caligula, and Nero, followed these examples, and the immense number of statues which, notwithstanding all this, remained at Rhodes, Delphi, Athens, and Olympia, is truly astonishing.— We can only briefly advert to the history of statuary among the Etruscans and Romans down to the year 146 B.C. The Etruscans were on the whole an industrious and enterprising people. With the works of Grecian art they must have become acquainted at an early time through their intercourse with the Greeks of southern Italy, whose influence upon the art of the Etruscans is evident in numerous cases. The whole range of the fine arts was cultivated by the Etruscans at an early period. Statuary in clay (which here supplied the place of wood, ξόανα, used in Greece) and in bronze appears to have acquired a high degree of perfection. In 267 B.C. no fewer than 2000 bronze statues are said to have existed at Volsinii, and numerous works of Etruscan art are still extant, which show great vigour and life, though they do not possess a very high degree of beauty. Some of their statues are worked in a Greek style; others are of a character peculiar to themselves, and entirely different from works of Grecian art, being stiff and ugly: others again are exaggerated and forced in their movements and attitudes, and resemble the figures which we meet with in the representations of Asiatic nations. The Romans previously to the time of the first Tarquin are said to have had no images of the gods; and for a long time afterwards their statues of gods in clay or wood were made by Etruscan artists. During the early part of the republic the works executed at Rome were altogether of a useful and practical, and not of an ornamental character; and statuary was in consequence little cultivated. But in the course of time the senate and the people, as well as foreign states which desired to show their gratitude to some Roman, began to erect bronze statues to distinguished persons in the Forum and other places.

V. *Fifth Period, from B.C. 146 to the fall of the Western Empire.*—During this period Rome was the capital of nearly the whole of the ancient world, not through its intellectual superiority, but by its military and political power. But it nevertheless became the centre of art and literature, as the artists resorted thither from all parts of the empire for the purpose of seeking employment in the houses of the great. The mass of the people, however, had as little taste for and were as little concerned about the arts as ever. In the time of Nero, who did much for the arts, we meet with Zenodorus, a founder of metal statues, who was commissioned by the emperor to execute a colossal statue of 110 feet high, representing Nero as the Sun. In the reign of Hadrian the arts seem to begin a new aera. He himself was undoubtedly a real lover of art, and encouraged it not only at Rome, but in Greece and Asia Minor. The great Villa of Hadrian below Tivoli, the ruins of which cover an extent of ten Roman miles in circumference, was richer in works of art than any other place in Italy. Here more works of art have been dug out of the ground than anywhere else within the same compass. Some statues executed at this time are worthy of the highest admiration. Foremost among these stand the statues and busts of Antinous, for whom the emperor entertained a passionate partiality, and who was represented in innumerable works of art. The colossal bust of Antinous in the Louvre is reckoned one of the finest works of ancient art, and is placed by some critics on an equality with the best works that Greece has produced. There are also some very good works in red marble which are referred to this period, as that material is not known to have been used before the age of Hadrian. As the arts had received such encouragement and brought forth such fruits in the reign of Hadrian, the effects remained visible for some time during the reigns of the Antonines. The frieze of a temple, which the senate caused to be erected to Antoninus Pius and Faustina, is adorned with griffins and vessels of very exquisite workmanship. The best among the extant works of this time are the equestrian statue of M. Aurelius of gilt bronze, which stands on the Capitol, and the column of M. Aurelius with reliefs representing scenes of his war against the Marcomanni. After the time of the Antonines the symptoms of decline in the arts became more and more visible. The most numerous works continued to be busts and statues of the emperors, but the best among them are not free from affectation and mannerism. In the time of Caracalla many statues were made, especially of Alexander the Great. Alexander Severus was a great admirer of statues, not from a genuine love of art, but because he delighted in the representations of great and good men. The reliefs on the triumphal arch of Septimius Severus, representing his victories over the Parthians, Arabs, and Adia-

benians, have scarcely any artistic merits. Art now declined with great rapidity: busts and statues were more seldom made than before, and are awkward and poor; the hair is frequently indicated by nothing else but holes bored in the stone. The reliefs on the sarcophagi gradually become monotonous and lifeless. The reliefs on the arch of Constantine, which are not taken from that of Trajan, are perfectly rude and worthless, and those on the column of Theodosius were not better. Before concluding, it remains to say a few words on the destruction of ancient works of art. During the latter part of the reign of Constantine many statues of the gods were destroyed, and not long after his time a systematic destruction began, which under Theodosius spread to all parts of the empire. The spirit of destruction, however, was not directed against works of art in general and as such, but only against the pagan idols. The opinion, therefore, which is entertained by some, that the losses we have sustained in works of ancient art, are mainly attributable to the introduction of Christianity, is too sweeping and general. Of the same character is another opinion, according to which the final decay of ancient art was a consequence of the spiritual nature of the new religion. The coincidence of the general introduction of Christianity with the decay of the arts is merely accidental. That the early Christians did not despise the arts as such, is clear from several facts. We know that they erected statues to their martyrs, of which we have a specimen in that of St. Hippolytus in the Vatican library. The numerous works, lastly, which have been found in the Christian catacombs at Rome, might alone be a sufficient proof that the early Christians were not hostile towards the representation of the heroes of their religion in works of art. In fact, Christianity during the middle ages became as much the mother of the arts of modern times, as the religion of Greece was the mother of ancient art. Another very general and yet incorrect notion is, that the northern barbarians after the conquest of Rome intentionally destroyed works of art. This opinion is not supported by any of the contemporary historians, nor is it at all probable. The barbarians were only anxious to carry with them the most precious treasures in order to enrich themselves; a statue must have been an object of indifference to them. What perished, perished naturally by the circumstances and calamities of the times. In times of need bronze statues were melted down and the material used for other purposes; marble statues were frequently broken to pieces and used for building materials. If we consider the history of Rome during the first centuries after the conquest of Italy by the Germans, we have every reason to wonder that so many specimens of ancient art have come down to our times. The greatest destruction, at one time, of ancient works of art is supposed to have occurred at the taking of Constantinople, in the beginning of the thirteenth century. Among the few works saved from this devastation are the celebrated bronze horses which now decorate the exterior of St. Mark's church at Venice. They have been ascribed, but without sufficient authority, to Lysippus.

STILUS or STYLUS is in all probability the same word with the Greek στύλος, and conveys the general idea of an object tapering like an architectural column. It signifies, (1) An iron instrument, resembling a pencil in size and shape, used for writing upon waxed tablets. At one end it was sharpened to a point for scratching the characters upon the wax, while the other end, being flat and circular, served to render the surface of the tablets smooth again, and so to obliterate what had been written.

Stilus. (Museo Borbonico, vol. vi. tav. 35.)

Thus, *vertere stilum* means *to erase*, and hence *to correct*. The stylus was also termed *graphium*, and the case in which it was kept *graphiarium*.—(2) A sharp stake or spike placed in pitfalls before an entrenchment, to embarrass the progress of an attacking enemy.

STIPENDIARII. The stipendiariae urbes of the Roman provinces were so denominated, as being subject to the payment of a fixed money-tribute, *stipendium*, in contradistinction to the vectigales, who paid a certain portion as a tenth or twentieth of the produce of their lands, their cattle, or customs. The word *stipendium* was used to signify the tribute paid, as it was originally imposed for and afterwards appropriated to the purpose of furnishing the Roman soldiers with pay. The condition of the urbes stipendiariae is generally thought to have been more honourable than that of the vectigales, but the distinction between the two terms was not always observed. The word stipendiarius is also applied to a person who receives a fixed salary or pay, as a *stipendiarius miles*.

STIPENDIUM, a pension or pay, from *stipem* and *pendo*, because before silver was coined at Rome the copper money in use was paid by weight and not by tale. According to Livy, the practice of giving pay to the Roman soldiers was not introduced till B.C. 405, on the occasion of the taking of Tarracina or Anxur. It is probable, however, that they received pay before this time, but, since it was not paid regularly, its first institution was referred to this year. In B.C. 403 a certain amount of pay was assigned to the knights also, or EQUITES, p. 136, b. This, however, had reference to the citizens who possessed an equestrian fortune, but had no horse (*equus publicus*) assigned to them by the state, for it had always been customary for the knights of the 18 centuries to receive pay out of the common treasury, in the shape of an allowance for the purchase of a horse, and a yearly pension of 2000 asses for its keep. [AES EQUESTRE; AES HORDEARIUM.] In the time of the republic the pay of a legionary soldier amounted to two oboli, or $3\frac{1}{3}$ asses; a centurion received double, and an eques or horseman triple. Polybius states that foot soldiers also received in corn every month an allowance (*demensum*) of $\frac{2}{3}$ of an Attic medimnus, or about 2 bushels of wheat: the horsemen 7 medimni of barley and 2 of wheat. The infantry of the allies received the same allowance as the Roman: the horsemen $1\frac{1}{3}$ medimni of wheat and 5 of barley. But there was this difference, that the allied forces received their allowances as a gratuity; the Roman soldiers, on the contrary, had deducted from their pay the money value of whatever they received in corn, armour, or clothes. There was indeed a law passed by C. Gracchus, which provided that besides their pay the soldiers should receive from the treasury an allowance for clothes; but this law seems either to have been repealed or to have fallen into disuse. The pay was doubled for the legionaries by Julius Caesar before the civil war. He also gave them corn whenever he had the means, without any restrictions. Under Augustus it appears to have been raised to 10 asses a day (three times the original sum). It was still further increased by Domitian. The praetorian cohorts received twice as much as the legionaries.

STOLA, a female dress worn over the tunic; it came as low as the ankles or feet, and was fastened round the body by a girdle, leaving above the breast broad folds. The tunic did not reach much below the knee, but the essential distinction between the tunic and stola seems to have been that the latter always had an *instita* or flounce sewed to the bottom and reaching to the instep. Over the stola the palla or pallium was worn [PALLIUM], as we see in the cut annexed. The stola was the characteristic dress of the Roman matrons, as the toga was of the Roman men. Hence the meretrices were not allowed to wear it, but only a dark-coloured toga; and accordingly Horace speaks of the *matrona* in contradistinction to the *togata*. For the same reason, women who had been divorced from their husbands on account of adultery, were not allowed to wear the stola, but only the toga.

Stola, female dress. (Museo Borbonico, vol. iii. tav. 37.)

STRATĒGUS (στρατηγός), general. This office and title seems to have been more especially peculiar to the democratic states of ancient Greece: we read of them, for instance, at Athens, Tarentum, Syracuse, Argos, and Thurii; and when the tyrants of the Ionian cities in Asia Minor were deposed by Aristagoras, he established strategi in their room, to act as chief magistrates. The strategi at Athens were instituted after the remodelling of the constitution by Clisthenes, to discharge the duties which had in former times been performed either by the king or the archon polemarchus. They were ten in number, one for each of the ten tribes, and chosen by the suffrages (χειροτονία) of the people. Before entering on their duties they were required to submit to a *docimasia*, or examination of their character; and no one was eligible to the office unless he had legitimate children, and was possessed of landed property in Attica. They were, as their name denotes, entrusted with the command on military expeditions, with the superintendence of all warlike preparations, and with the regulation of all matters in any way connected with the war department of the state. They levied and enlisted the soldiers, either personally or with the assistance of the taxiarchs. They were entrusted with the collection and management of the property taxes (εἰσφοραί) raised for the purposes of war; and also presided over the courts of justice in which any disputes connected with this subject or the trierarchy were decided. They nominated from year to year persons to serve as trierarchs. They had the power of convening extraordinary assemblies of the people in cases of emergency. But their most important trust was the command in war, and it depended upon circumstances to how many of the number it was given. At Marathon all the ten were present, and the chief command came to each of them in turn. The archon polemarchus also was there associated with them, and, according to the ancient custom, his vote in a council of war was equal to that of any of the generals. Usually, however, three only were sent out; one of these (τρίτος αὐτός) was considered as the commander-in-chief, but his colleagues had an equal voice in a council of war. The military chiefs of the Aetolian and Achaean leagues were also called *strategi*. The Achaean *strategi* had the power of convening a general assembly of the league on extraordinary occasions. Greek writers on Roman affairs give the name of *strategi* to the praetors.

STRĒNA, a present given on a festive day, and for the sake of good omen. It was chiefly applied to a new year's gift, to a present made on the calends of January. In accordance with a senatusconsultum, new year's gifts had to be presented to Augustus in the Capitol, even when he was absent.

STRĬGIL. [BALNEUM.]

STROPHĬUM (ταινία, ταινίδιον, ἀπόδεσμος), a girdle or belt worn by women round the breast and over the inner tunic or chemise. It appears to have been usually made of leather.

STUPRUM. [ADULTERIUM.]

SUBSIGNĀNI, privileged soldiers in the time of the empire, who fought under a standard by themselves, and did not form part of the legion. They seem to have been the same as the *vexillarii*.

SUFFRĀGIA SEX. [EQUITES.]

SUFFRĀGĬUM, a vote. At Athens the voting in the popular assemblies and the courts of justice was either by show of hands (χειροτονία) or by ballot (ψῆφος). Respecting the mode of voting at Rome, see COMITIA, p. 107, and LEGES TABELLARIAE.

SUGGESTUS, means in general any elevated place made of materials heaped up (*sub* and *gero*), and is specially applied: (1) To the stage or pulpit from which the orators addressed the people in the comitia. [ROSTRA.]—(2) To the elevation from which a general addressed the soldiers.—(3) To the elevated seat from which the emperor beheld the public games, also called *cubiculum*. [CUBICULUM.]

SUOVETAURILIA. [SACRIFICIUM, p. 325; LUSTRATIO; and woodcut on p. 343.]

SUPPARUM. [NAVIS, p. 267, *b*.]

SUPPLICATIO, a solemn thanksgiving or supplication to the gods, decreed by the senate, when all the temples were opened, and the statues of the gods frequently placed in public upon couches (*pulvinaria*), to which the people offered up their thanksgivings and prayers. [LECTISTERNIUM.] A *supplicatio* was decreed for two different reasons. 1. As a thanksgiving, when a great victory had been gained: it was usually decreed as soon as official intelligence of the victory had been received by a letter from the general in command. The number of days during which it was to last was proportioned to the importance of the victory. Sometimes it was decreed for only one day, but more commonly for three or five days. A supplication of ten days was first decreed in honour of Pompey at the conclusion of the war with Mithridates, and one of fifteen days after the victory over the Belgae by Caesar, an honour which had never been granted to any one before. Subsequently a supplicatio of twenty days was decreed after his conquest of Vercingetorix. A supplicatio was usually regarded as a prelude to a triumph, but it was not always followed by one. This honour was conferred upon Cicero on account of his suppression of the conspiracy of Catiline, which had never been decreed to any one before in a civil capacity (*togatus*).— 2. A *supplicatio*, a solemn supplication and humiliation, was also decreed in times of public danger and distress, and on account of prodigies, to avert the anger of the gods.

SYCOPHANTES (συκοφάντης). At an early period in Attic history a law was made prohibiting the exportation of figs. Whether it was made in a time of dearth, or through the foolish policy of preserving to the natives the most valuable of their productions, we cannot say. It appears, however, that the law continued in force long after the cause of its enactment, or the general belief of its utility, had ceased to exist; and Attic fig-growers exported their fruit in spite of prohibitions and penalties. To inform against a man for so doing was considered harsh and vexatious; as all people are apt to think that obsolete statutes may be infringed with impunity. Hence the term συκοφαντεῖν, which originally signified *to lay an information against another for exporting figs*, came to be applied to all ill-natured, malicious, groundless, and vexatious accusations. *Sycophantes* in the time of Aristophanes and Demosthenes designated a person of a peculiar class, not capable of being described by any single word in our language, but well understood and appreciated by an Athenian. He had not much in common with our *sycophant*, but was a happy compound of the *common barrator, informer, pettifogger, busybody, roguliar, and slanderer*. The Athenian law permitted any citizen (τὸν βουλόμενον) to give information against public offenders, and prosecute them in courts of justice. It was the policy of the legislator to encourage the detection of crime, and a reward (such as half the penalty) was frequently given to the successful accuser. Such a power, with such a temptation, was likely to be abused, unless checked by the force of public opinion, or the vigilance of the judicial tribunals. Unfortunately, the character of the Athenian democracy and the temper of the judges furnished additional incentives to the informer. Eminent statesmen, orators, generals, magistrates, and all persons of wealth and influence were regarded with jealousy by the people. The more causes came into court, the more fees accrued to the judges, and fines and confiscations enriched the public treasury. The prosecutor therefore in public causes, as well as the plaintiff in civil, was looked on with a more favourable eye than the defendant, and the chances of success made the employment a lucrative one. It was not always necessary to go to trial, or even to commence legal proceedings. The timid defendant was glad to compromise the cause, and the conscious delinquent to avert the threat of a prosecution, by paying a sum of money to his opponent. Thriving informers found it not very difficult to procure witnesses, and the profits were divided between them.

SYLAE (σῦλαι). When a Greek state, or any of its members, had received an injury or insult from some other state or some of its members, and the former was unwilling, or not in a condition, to declare open war, it was not unusual to give a commission, or grant public authority to individuals to make reprisals. This was called συλας, or σῦλα, διδόναι. This ancient practice may be compared with the modern one of granting letters of marque and reprisal.

SYLLOGEIS (συλλογεῖς), usually called Συλλογεῖς τοῦ δήμου, or the Collectors of the People, were special commissioners at Athens, who made out a list of the property of the oligarchs previously to its confiscation.

SYMBOLAEON, SYNALLAGMA, SYNTHĒCĒ (συμβόλαιον, συνάλλαγμα, συνθήκη), are all words used to signify a contract, but are distinguishable from one another. Συμβόλαιον is used of contracts and bargains between private persons, and peculiarly of loans of money. Thus, συμβαλεῖν εἰς ἀνδράποδον is, to lend upon the security of a slave. Συνάλλαγμα signifies any matter negotiated or transacted between two or more persons, whether a contract or anything else. Συνθήκη is used of more solemn and important contracts, not only of those made between private individuals, but also of treaties and conventions between kings and states.

SYMPOSIUM (συμπόσιον, comissatio, conticinium), a drinking-party. The symposium must be distinguished from the deipnon (δεῖπνον), for though drinking almost always followed a dinner-party, yet the former was regarded as entirely distinct from the latter, was regulated by different customs, and frequently received the addition of many guests, who were not present at the dinner. For the Greeks did not usually drink at their dinner, and it was not till the conclusion of the meal that wine was introduced. Symposia were very frequent at Athens. Their enjoyment was heightened by agreeable conversation, by the introduction of music and dancing, and by games and amusements of various kinds; sometimes, too, philosophical subjects were discussed at them. The symposia of Plato and Xenophon give us a lively idea of such entertainments at Athens. The name itself shows, that the enjoyment of drinking was the main object of the symposia: wine from the juice of the grape (οἶνος ἀμπέλινος) was the only drink partaken of by the Greeks, with the exception of water. The wine was almost invariably mixed with water, and to drink it unmixed (ἄκρατον) was considered a characteristic of barbarians. The mixture was made in a large vessel called the CRATER, from which it was conveyed into the drinking-cups. The guests at a symposium reclined on couches, and were crowned with garlands of flowers. A master of the revels (ἄρχων τῆς πόσεως, συμποσίαρχος, or βασιλεύς) was usually chosen to conduct the symposium, whose commands the whole company had to obey, and who regulated the whole order of the entertainment, proposed the amusements, &c. The same practice prevailed among the Romans, and their symposiarch was called Magister, or Rex Convivii, or the Arbiter Bibendi. The choice was generally determined by the throwing of astragali or tali. The proportion in which the wine and water were mixed was fixed by him, and also how much each of the company was to drink, for it was not usually left to the option of each of the company to drink as much or as little as he pleased. The cups were always carried round from right to left (ἐπὶ δεξιά), and the same order was observed in the conversation, and in everything that took place in the entertainment. The company frequently drank to the health of one another, and each did it especially to the one to whom he handed the same cup. Respecting the games and amusements by which the symposia were enlivened, it is unnecessary to say much here, as most of them are described in separate articles in this work. Enigmas or riddles (αἰνίγματα or γρῖφοι) were among the most usual and favourite modes of diversion. Each of the company proposed one in turn to his right-

Symposium. (From a Painting on a Vase.)

hand neighbour; if he solved it, he was rewarded with a crown, a garland, a cake, or something of a similar kind, and sometimes with a kiss; if he failed, he had to drink a cup of unmixed wine, or of wine mixed with salt water, at one draught. The cottabos was also another favourite game at symposia, and was played at in various ways. [COTTABUS.] Representations of symposia are very common on ancient vases. Two guests usually reclined on each couch (κλίνη), as is explained on p. 95, but sometimes there were five persons on one couch. A drinking-party among the Romans was sometimes called *concivium*, but the word *comissatio* more nearly corresponds to the Greek symposium. [COMISSATIO.] The Romans, however, usually drank during their dinner (*coena*), which they frequently prolonged during many hours, in the later times of the republic and under the empire. Their customs connected with drinking differed little from those of the Greeks, and have been incidentally noticed above.

SYNDICUS (σύνδικος), *an advocate*, is frequently used as synonymous with the word *synegorus* (συνήγορος), to denote any one who pleads the cause of another, whether in a court of justice or elsewhere, but was peculiarly applied to those orators who were sent by the state to plead the cause of their countrymen before a foreign tribunal. Aeschines, for example, was appointed to plead before the Amphictyonic council on the subject of the Delian temple; but a certain discovery having been made, not very creditable to his patriotism, the court of Areiopagus took upon themselves to remove him, and appoint Hyperides in his stead. There were other *syndici*, who acted rather as magistrates or judges than as advocates, though they probably derived their name from the circumstance of their being appointed to protect the interests of the state. These were extraordinary functionaries, created from time to time to exercise a jurisdiction in disputes concerning confiscated property.

SYNEDRI (σύνεδροι), a name given to the members of any council, or any body of men who sat together to consult or deliberate. The congress of Greeks at Salamis is called συνέδριον. Frequent reference is made to the general assembly of the Greeks, τὸ κοινὸν τῶν Ἑλλήνων συνέδριον, at Corinth, Thermopylae, or elsewhere. The congress of the states belonging to the new Athenian alliance, formed after B. C. 377, was called συνέδριον, and the deputies σύνεδροι, and the sums furnished by the allies συντάξεις, in order to avoid the old and hateful name of φόρος or tribute. The name of συνέδριον was given at Athens to any magisterial or official body, as to the court of Areiopagus, or to the place where they transacted business, their board or council-room.

SYNEGORUS (συνήγορος). In causes of importance, wherein the state was materially interested, more especially in those which were brought before the court upon an εἰσαγγελία, it was usual to appoint public advocates (called συνήγοροι, σύνδικοι, or κατήγοροι) to manage the prosecution. In ordinary cases however the accuser or prosecutor (κατήγορος) was a distinct person from the συνήγορος, who acted only as auxiliary to him. It might be, indeed, that the συνήγορος performed the most important part at the trial, or it might be that he performed a subordinate part, making only a short speech in support of the prosecution, which was called ἐπίλογος. But however this might be, he was in point of law an auxiliary only, and was neither entitled to a share of the reward (if any) given by the law to a successful accuser, nor liable, on the other hand, to a penalty of a thousand drachms, or the ἀτιμία consequent upon a failure to get a fifth part of the votes. The fee of a drachm (τὸ συνηγορικόν) mentioned by Aristophanes was probably the sum paid to the public advocate whenever he was employed on behalf of the state. There appears to have been (at least at one period) a regular appointment of συνήγοροι, ten in number. For what purpose they were appointed, is a matter about which we have no certain information: but it is not unreasonable to suppose that these ten συνήγοροι were no other than the public advocates who were employed to conduct state prosecutions.

SYNGRAPHE (συγγραφή), signifies a written contract: whereas συνθήκη and συμβόλαιον do not necessarily import that the contract is in writing; and ὁμολογία is, strictly speaking, a verbal agreement. At Athens important contracts were usually reduced to writing; such as leases (μισθώσεις), loans of money, and all executory agreements, where certain conditions were to be performed. The whole was contained in a little tablet of wax or wood (βιβλίον or γραμματεῖον, sometimes double, δίπτυχον), which was sealed, and deposited with some third person, mutually agreed on between the parties.

SYNOIKIA (συνοίκια).—(1) A festival celebrated every year at Athens on the 16th of Hecatombaeon in honour of Athena. It was believed to have been instituted by Theseus to commemorate the concentration of the government of the various towns of Attica at Athens.—(2) A house adapted to hold several families, a lodging-house, *insula*, as the Romans would say. The lodging-houses were let mostly to foreigners who came to Athens on business, and especially to the μέτοικοι, whom the law did not allow to acquire real property, and who therefore could not purchase houses of their own. The rent was commonly paid by the month. Lodging-houses were frequently taken on speculation by persons called ναύκληροι or σταθμοῦχοι, who made a profit by underletting them.

SYNTHĔSIS, a garment frequently worn at dinner, and sometimes also on other occasions. As it was inconvenient to wear the toga at table, on account of its many folds, it was customary to have dresses especially appropriated to this purpose, called *vestes coenatoriae*, or *coenatoria*, *accubitoria*, or *syntheses*. The synthesis appears to have been a kind of tunic, an *indumentum* rather than an *amictus*. [AMICTUS.] That it was, however, an easy and comfortable kind of dress, as we should say, seems to be evident from its use at table above mentioned, and also from its being worn by all classes at the SATURNALIA, a season of universal relaxation and enjoyment. More than this respecting its form we cannot say; it was usually dyed with some colour, and was not white, like the toga.

SYRINX (σύριγξ), the Pan's pipe, or Pandean pipe, was the appropriate musical instrument of the Arcadian and other Grecian shepherds, and was regarded by them as the invention of Pan, their tutelary god. When the Roman poets had occasion to mention it, they called it *fistula*. It was formed in general of seven hollow stems of cane or reed, fitted together by means of wax, having been previously cut to the proper lengths, and adjusted so as to form an octave; but sometimes nine were admitted, giving an equal number of notes. A syrinx of eight reeds is represented on p. 278.

SYRMA (σύρμα), which properly means that which is drawn or dragged (from σύρω), is applied to a dress with a train. It was more especially the name of the dress worn by the tragic actors, which had a train to it trailing upon the ground. Hence we find *syrma* used metaphorically for tragedy itself.

SYSSĬTĬA (συσσίτια). The custom of taking the principal meal of the day in public prevailed extensively amongst the Greeks from very early ages, but more particularly in Crete and at Sparta. The Cretan name for the syssitia was *Andreia* (ἀνδρεία), the singular of which is used to denote the building or public hall where they were given. This title affords of itself a sufficient indication that they were confined to men and youths only. All the adult citizens partook of the public meals amongst the Cretans, and were divided into companies or "messes," called *hetaeriae* (ἑταιρίαι), or sometimes *andreia*. The syssitia of the Cretans were distinguished by simplicity and temperance. They always *sat* at their tables, even in later times, when the custom of reclining had been introduced at Sparta. In most of the Cretan cities, the expenses of the syssitia were defrayed out of the revenues of the public lands, and the tribute paid by the perioeci, the money arising from which was applied partly to the service of the gods, and partly to the maintenance of all the citizens, both male and female; so that in this respect there might be no difference between the rich and the poor. The Spartan syssitia were in the main so similar to those of Crete, that one was said to be borrowed from the other. They differed from the Cretan in the following respects. The expenses of the tables at Sparta were not defrayed out of the public revenues, but every head of a family was obliged to contribute a certain portion at his own cost and charge; those who were not able to do so were excluded from the public tables. The guests were divided into companies, generally of fifteen persons each, and all vacancies were filled up by ballot, in which unanimous consent was indispensable for election. No persons, not even the kings, were excused from attendance at the public tables, except for some satisfactory reason, as when engaged in a sacrifice, or a chase, in which latter case the individual was required to send a present to his table. Each person was supplied with a cup of mixed wine, which was filled again when required: but drinking to excess was prohibited at Sparta as well as in Crete. The repast was of a plain and simple cha-

Pan with a Syrinx. (Mus. Worsleyanum, pl. 9.)

racter, and the contribution of each member of a mess (φειδίτης) was settled by law. The principal dish was the black broth (μέλας ζωμός), with pork. Moreover, the entertainment was enlivened by cheerful conversation, though on public matters. Singing also was frequently introduced. The arrangements were under the superintendence of the polemarchs.

TABELLA, *dim.* of TABULA, a billet or tablet, with which each citizen and judex voted in the comitia and courts of justice. For details see pp. 107, 236.

TABELLARIUS, a letter-carrier. As the Romans had no public post, they were obliged to employ special messengers, who were called *tabellarii*, to convey their letters (*tabellae*, *literae*), when they had not an opportunity of sending them otherwise.

TABERNACULUM. [TEMPLUM.]
TABLINUM. [DOMUS.]
TABULAE. This word properly means planks or boards, whence it is applied to several objects, as gaming-tables, pictures, but more especially to tablets used for writing. Generally, *tabulae* and *tabellae* signify waxen tablets (*tabulae ceratae*), which were thin pieces of wood, usually of an oblong shape, covered over with wax (*cera*). The wax was written on by means of the stilus. These tabulae were sometimes made of ivory and citron-wood, but generally of the wood of a more common tree, as the beech, fir, &c. The outer sides of the tablets consisted merely of the wood; it was only the inner sides that were covered over with wax. They were fastened together at the back by means of wires, which answered the purpose of hinges, so that they opened and shut like our books; and to prevent the wax of one tablet rubbing against the wax of the other, there was a raised margin around each, as is clearly seen in the woodcut on p. 354. There were sometimes two, three, four, five, or even more, tablets fastened together in the above-mentioned manner. Two such tablets were called *diptycha* (δίπτυχα), which merely means "twice-folded" (from πτύσσω, "to fold"), whence we have πτυκτίον, or with the τ omitted, πυκτίον. The Latin word *pugillares*, which is the name frequently given to tablets covered with wax, may perhaps be connected with the same root, though it is usually derived from *pugillus*, because they were small enough to be held in the hand. Three tablets fastened together were called *triptycha*; in the same way we also read of *pentaptycha*, and of *polyptycha* or *multiplices*

(*cerae*). The pages of these tablets were frequently called by the name of *cerae* alone: thus we read of *prima cera*, *altera cera*, "first page," "second page." In tablets containing important legal documents, especially wills, the outer edges were pierced through with holes (*foramina*), through which a triple thread (*linum*) was passed, and upon which a seal was then placed. This was intended to guard against forgery, and if it was not done such documents were null and void. Waxen tablets were used among the Romans for almost every species of writing, where great length was not required. Thus letters were frequently written upon them, which were secured by being fastened together with packthread and sealed with wax. Legal documents, and especially wills, were almost always written on waxen tablets. Such tablets were also used for accounts, in which a person entered what he received and expended (*tabulae* or *codex accepti et expensi*), whence *novae tabulae* mean an abolition of debts either wholly or in part. The tablets used in voting in the comitia and the courts of justice were also called tabulae, as well as tabellae. [TABELLA.]

TABULARII were notaries or accountants, who are first mentioned under this name in the time of the empire. Public notaries, who had the charge of public documents, were also called tabularii. They were first established by M. Antoninus in the provinces, who ordained that the births of all children were to be announced to the tabularii within thirty days from the birth.

TABULARIUM, a place where the public records (*tabulae publicae*) were kept. These records were of various kinds, as for instance senatusconsulta, tabulae censoriae, registers of births, deaths, of the names of those who assumed the toga virilis, &c. There were various tabularia at Rome, all of which were in temples; we find mention made of tabularia in the temples of the Nymphs, of Lucina, of Juventus, of Libitina, of Ceres, and more especially in that of Saturn, which was also the public treasury.

TAGUS (ταγός), a leader or general, was more especially the name of the military leader of the Thessalians. He is sometimes called *king* (βασιλεύς). His command was of a military rather than of a civil nature, and he seems only to have been appointed when there was a war or one was apprehended. We do not know the extent of the power which the Tagus possessed constitutionally, nor the time for which he held the office; probably neither was precisely fixed, and depended on the circumstances of the times and the character of the individual.

TALARIA, small wings, fixed to the ancles of Hermes and reckoned among his attributes (πέδιλα, πτηνοπέδιλος). In many works of ancient art they are represented growing from his ancles (see cut, p. 63); but more frequently he is represented with sandals, which have wings fastened to them on each side over the ancles.

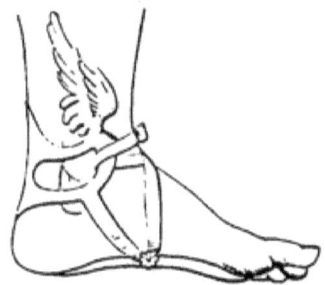

Talaria. (From a Statue of Hermes at Naples.)

TALASSIO. [MATRIMONIUM.]

TALENTUM (τάλαντον) meant originally a *balance* [LIBRA], then the substance weighed, and lastly and commonly a certain weight, *the talent*. The Greek system of money, as well as the Roman [AS], was founded on a reference to weight. A certain weight of silver among the Greeks, as of copper among the Romans, was used as a representative of a value, which was originally and generally that of the metal itself. The talent therefore and its divisions are denominations of money as well as of weight. The Greek system of weights contained four principal denominations, which, though different in different times and places, and even at the same place for different substances, always bore the same relation *to each other*. These were the talent (τάλαντον), which was the largest, then the mina (μνᾶ), the drachma (δραχμή), and the obolus (ὀβολός). [See Tables.] The Attic and Aeginetan were the two standards of money most in use in Greece. The Attic mina was 4*l*. 1*s*. 3*d*., and the talent 243*l*. 15*s*. The Aeginetan mina was 5*l*. 14*s*. 7*d*., and the talent 343*l*. 15*s*. The Euboic talent was of nearly the same weight as the Attic. A much smaller talent was in use for gold. It was equal to six Attic drachmae, or about $\frac{3}{4}$ oz. and 71 grs. It was called the *gold talent*, or the *Sicilian talent*, from its being much used by the Greeks of Italy and Sicily. This is the talent always meant when the word occurs in Homer. This small talent explains the use of the term *great talent* (*magnum talentum*), which we find in Latin authors, for the silver Attic talent was *great* in comparison with this. But the use of the word by the Romans is altogether very inexact. Where talents are mentioned in the classical writers without any specification of the standard, we must generally understand the Attic.

TALIO, from Talis, signifies an equivalent, but it is used only in the sense of a punishment or penalty the same in kind and degree as the mischief which the guilty person has done to the body of another. Talio, as a punishment, was a part of the Mosaic law.

TALUS (ἀστράγαλος), a huckle-bone. The huckle-bones of sheep and goats were used to play with from the earliest times, principally by women and children, occasionally by old men. To play at this game was some-

Game of Tali. (From an ancient Painting.)

times called πενταλιθίζειν, because five bones or other objects of a similar kind were employed; and this number is retained among ourselves. When the sides of the bone were marked with different values, the game became one of chance. [ALEA; TESSERA.] The two ends were left blank, because the bone could not rest upon either of them on account of its curvature. The four remaining sides were marked with the numbers 1, 3, 4, 6; 1 and 6 being on two opposite sides, and 3 and 4 on the other two opposite sides. The Greek and Latin names of the numbers were as follows:—1. Μονάς, εἷς, κύων, Χῖος; Ion. Οἴνη: Unio, Vulturius, canis: 3. Τρίας, Ternio; 4. Τετράς, Quaternio; 6. Ἑξάς, ἑξίτης, Κῷος; Senio. Two persons played together at this game, using four bones, which they threw up into the air, or emptied out of a dice-box, and observing the numbers on the uppermost sides. The numbers on the four sides of the four bones admitted of thirty-five different combinations. The lowest throw of all was four aces (jacere vulturios quatuor). But the value of a throw was not in all cases the sum of the four numbers turned up. The highest in value was that called Venus, or jactus Venereus, in which the numbers cast up were all different, the sum of them being only fourteen. It was by obtaining this throw that the king of the feast was appointed among the Romans [SYMPOSIUM], and hence it was also called Basilicus. Certain other throws were called by particular names, taken from gods, illustrious men and women, and heroes. Thus the throw, consisting of two aces and two trays, making eight, which number, like the jactus Venereus, could be obtained only once, was denominated Stesichorus.

TAMIAE (ταμίαι), the treasurers of the temples and the revenue at Athens. The wealthiest of all the temples at Athens was that of Athena on the Acropolis, the treasures of which were under the guardianship of ten tamiae, who were chosen annually by lot from the class of pentacosiomedimni, and afterwards, when the distinction of classes had ceased to exist, from among the wealthiest of Athenian citizens. The treasurers of the other gods were chosen in like manner; but they, about the 90th Olympiad, were all united into one board, while those of Athena remained distinct. Their treasury, however, was transferred to the same place as that of Athena, viz., to the opisthodomus of the Parthenon, where were kept not only all the treasures belonging to the temples, but also the state treasure (ὅσια χρήματα, as contradistinguished from ἱερά), under the care of the treasurers of Athena. All the funds of the state were considered as being in a manner consecrated to Athena; while on the other hand the people reserved to themselves the right of making use of the sacred monies, as well as the other property of the temples, if the safety of the state should require it. Payments made to the temples were received by the treasurers in the presence of some members of the senate, just as public monies were by the Apodectae; and then the treasurers became responsible for their safe custody. — The treasurer of the revenue (ταμίας or ἐπιμελητὴς τῆς κοινῆς προσόδου) was a more important personage than those last mentioned. He was not a mere keeper of monies, like them, nor a mere receiver, like the apodectae; but a general paymaster, who received through the apodectae all money which was to be disbursed for the purposes of the administration (except the property-taxes, which were paid into the war-office, and the tribute from the allies, which was paid to the hellenotamiae [HELLENOTAMIAE]), and then distributed it in such manner as he was required to do by the law; the surplus (if any) he paid into the war-office or the theoric fund. As this person knew all the channels in which the public money had to flow, and exercised a general superintendence over the expenditure, he was competent to give advice to the people upon financial measures, with a view to improve the revenue, introduce economy, and prevent abuses; he is sometimes called ταμίας τῆς διοικήσεως, or ὁ ἐπὶ τῆς διοικήσεως, and may be regarded as a sort of minister of finance. He was elected by vote (χειροτονία), and held his office for four years, but was capable of being re-elected. A law, however, was passed during the administration of Lycurgus, the orator, prohibiting re-election; so that Lycurgus, who is reported to have continued in office for twelve years, must have held it for the last eight years under fictitious names. The power of this officer was by no means free from control; inasmuch as any individual was at liberty to propose financial measures, or institute criminal proceedings for malversation or waste of the public funds; and there was an ἀντιγραφεὺς τῆς διοικήσεως appointed to check the accounts of his superior. Anciently there were persons called Poristae (πορίσται), who appear to have assisted the tamiae in some part of their duties. The money disbursed by the treasurer of the revenue was sometimes paid directly to the various persons in the employ of the government, sometimes through subordinate pay offices. Many public functionaries had their own paymasters, who were dependent on the treasurer of the evenue, receiving their funds from him, and then distributing them in their respective departments. Such were the τριηροποιοί, τειχοποιοί, ὁδοποιοί, ταφροποιοί, ἐπιμεληταὶ νεωρίων, who received through their own tamiae such sums as they required from time to time for the prosecution of their works. The payment of the judicial fees was made by the *Colacretae* (κωλακρέται), which, and the providing for the meals in the Prytaneium, were the only duties that remained to them after the establishment of the apodectae by Cleisthenes. The tamiae of the sacred vessels (τῆς Παράλου and τῆς Σαλαμινίας) acted not only as treasurers, but as trierarchs, the expenses (amounting for the two ships together to about sixteen talents) being provided by the state. They were elected by vote. Other trierarchs had their own private tamiae.—The war fund at Athens (independently of the tribute) was provided from two sources: first, the property-tax (εἰσφορά), and secondly, the surplus of the yearly revenue, which remained .fter defraying the expenses of the civil .dministration. Of the ten strategi, who were annually elected to preside over the war department, one was called στρατηγὸς ὁ ἐπὶ τῆς διοικήσεως, to whom the management of the war fund was entrusted. He had under him a treasurer, called the ταμίας τῶν στρατιωτικῶν, who gave out the pay of the troops, and defrayed all other expenses incident to the service. So much of the surplus revenue as was not required for the purposes of war, was to be paid by the treasurer of the revenue into the theoric fund; of which, after the archonship of Euclides, special managers were created. [THEORICA.] —Lastly, we have to notice the treasurers of the demi (δήμων ταμίαι), and those of the tribes (φυλῶν ταμίαι), who had the care of the funds belonging to their respective communities, and performed duties analogous to those of the state treasurers. The demi, as well as the tribes, had their common lands, which were usually let to farm. The rents of those formed the principal part of their revenue.

TAXIARCHI (ταξίαρχοι), military officers at Athens, next in rank to the strategi. They were ten in number, like the strategi, one for each tribe, and were elected by vote χειροτονία). In war each commanded the nfantry of his own tribe, and they were frequently called to assist the strategi with their dvice at the war-council. In peace they assisted the strategi in levying and enlisting oldiers, and seem to have also assisted the trategi in the discharge of many of their ther duties. The taxiarchs were so called rom their commanding *taxeis* (τάξεις), which were the principal divisions of the hoplites in the Athenian army. Each tribe (φυλή) formed a *taxis*. As there were ten tribes, there were consequently in a complete Athenian army ten *taxeis*, but the number of men contained in each would of course vary according to the importance of the war. Among the other Greeks, the *taxis* was the name of a much smaller division of troops. The *lochus* (λόχος) among the Athenians was a subdivision of the *taxis*, and the *lochagi* (λοχαγοί) were probably appointed by the taxiarchs.

TEGULA (κέραμος, dim. κεραμίς), a roofing-tile. Roofing-tiles were originally made, like bricks, of baked clay (γῆς ὀπτῆς). Byzes of Naxos first introduced tiles of marble about the year 620 B.C. A still more expensive and magnificent method of roofing consisted in the use of tiles made of bronze and gilt. At Rome the houses were originally roofed with shingles, and continued to be so down to the time of the war with Pyrrhus, when tiles began to supersede the old roofing material.

TEICHOPOII (τειχοποιοί), magistrates at Athens, whose business it was to build and keep in repair the public walls. They appear to have been elected by vote (χειροτονία), one from each tribe, and probably for a year. Funds were put at their disposal, for which they had their treasurer (ταμίας) dependent on the treasurer of the revenue. They were liable to render an account (εὔθυνη) of their management of these funds, and also of their general conduct, like other magistrates. This office has been invested with peculiar interest in modern times, on account of its having been held by Demosthenes, and its having given occasion to the famous prosecution of Ctesiphon, who proposed that Demosthenes should receive the honour of a crown before he had rendered his account according to law.

TELA (ἱστός), a loom. Although weaving was among the Greeks and Romans a distinct trade, carried on by a separate class of persons (ὑφάνται, *textores* and *textrices*, *linteones*), yet every considerable domestic establishment, especially in the country, contained a loom, together with the whole apparatus necessary for the working of wool (*lanificium*, ταλασία, ταλασιουργία). [CALATHUS.] These occupations were all supposed to be carried on under the protection of Athena or Minerva, specially denominated *Ergane* (Ἐργάνη). When the farm or the palace was sufficiently large to admit of it, a portion of it called the *histon* (ἱστών) or *textrinum* was devoted to this purpose. The work was there principally carried on by female slaves (*quasillariae*), under the superintendence of the mistress of the house. Every thing woven consists of two essential parts, the warp and the woof, called in Latin *stamen* and *subtegmen*, *subtemen*, or *trama*; in Greek στήμων and κρόκη. The warp was called *stamen* in Latin (from *stare*) on account of its erect posture in the loom. The corresponding Greek term στήμων, and likewise ἱστός, have evidently the same derivation. For the same reason, the very first operation in weaving was to set up the loom (ἱστὸν στήσασθαι); and the web or cloth, before it was cut down or "descended" from the loom, was called *vestis pendens* or *pendula tela*, because it hung from the transverse beam, or *jugum*. These particulars are all clearly exhibited in the picture of Circe's loom given in the annexed cut. We

Tela, Loom. (From the Vatican MS. of Virgil.)

observe in the preceding woodcut, about the middle of the apparatus, a transverse rod passing through the warp. A straight cane was well adapted to be so used, and its application is clearly expressed by Ovid in the words *stamen secernit arundo*. In plain weaving it was inserted between the threads of the warp so as to divide them into two portions, the threads on one side of the rod alternating with those on the other side throughout the whole breadth of the warp. In a very ancient form of the loom there was a roller underneath the *jugum*, turned by a handle, and on which the web was wound as the work advanced. The threads of the warp, besides being separated by a transverse rod or plank, were divided into thirty or forty parcels, to each of which a stone was suspended for the purpose of keeping the warp in a perpendicular position, and allowing the necessary play to the strokes of the *spatha*. Whilst the comparatively coarse, strong, and much-twisted thread designed for the warp was thus arranged in parallel lines, the woof remained upon the spindle [FUSUS], forming a *spool*, *bobbin*, or *pen* (πήνη). This was either conveyed through the warp without any additional contrivance, or it was made to revolve in a shuttle (*radius*). This was made of box brought from the shores of the Euxine, and was pointed at its extremities, that it might easily force its way through the warp. All that is effected by the shuttle is the conveyance of the woof across the warp. To keep every thread of the woof in its proper place, it is necessary that the threads of the warp should be decussated. This was done by the leashes, called in Latin *licia*, in Greek μίτοι. By a leash we are to understand a thread having at one end a loop, through which a thread of the warp was passed, the other end being fastened to a straight rod called *liciatorium*, and in Greek κανών. The warp, having been divided by the arundo, as already mentioned, into two sets of threads, all those of the same set were passed through the loops of the corresponding set of leashes, and all these leashes were fastened at their other end to the same wooden rod. At least one set of leashes was necessary to decussate the warp, even in the plainest and simplest weaving. The number of sets was increased according to the complexity of the pattern, which was called *bilix* or *trilix*, δίμιτος, τρίμιτος, or πολύμιτος, according as the number was two, three, or more. The process of annexing the leashes to the warp was called *ordiri telam*, also *licia telae addere*, or *adnectere*. It occupied two women at the same time, one of whom took in regular succession each separate thread of the warp, and handed it over to the other (παραφέρειν, παραδιδόναι, or προσφωρεῖσθαι); the other, as she received each thread, passed it through the loop in proper order; an act which we call "entering," in Greek διάζεσθαι. Supposing the warp to have been thus adjusted, and the pen or the shuttle to have been carried through it, it was then decussated by drawing forwards the proper rod, so as to carry one set of the threads of the warp across the rest, after which the woof was shot back again, and by the continual repetition of this process the warp and woof were interlaced. Two staves were occasionally used to fix the rods in such a position as was most convenient to assist the weaver in drawing her woof across her warp. After the woof had been conveyed by the shuttle through the warp, it was driven sometimes downwards, as is represented in the woodcut, but more commonly upwards. Two different instruments were used in this part of the process. The simplest, and probably the most ancient, was in the form of a large wooden sword (*spatha*, σπάθη). The spatha was, however, in a great degree superseded by the comb (*pecten*, κερκίς), the teeth of which were inserted between the threads of the warp, and thus made by a forcible impulse to drive the threads of the woof close together.—The lyre, the favourite musical instrument of the Greeks, was only known to the Romans as a foreign invention. Hence they appear to have described its parts by a comparison with the loom, with which they were familiar. The terms *jugum* and *stamina* were transferred by an obvious resemblance from the latter to the former object; and, although they adopted into their own language the Greek word *plectrum*, they used the Latin *pecten* to denote the same thing, not because the instrument used in striking the lyre was at all like a comb in shape and appearance, but because it was held in the right hand, and inserted between the stamina of the lyre, as the comb was between the stamina of the loom.

TELAMŌNES. [ATLANTES.]

TELŌNES (τελώνης), a farmer of the public taxes at Athens. The taxes were let by auction to the highest bidder. Companies often took them in the name of one person, who was called ἀρχώνης or τελωνάρχης, and was their representative to the state. Sureties were required of the farmer for the payment of his dues. The office was frequently undertaken by resident aliens, citizens not liking it, on account of the vexations proceedings to which it often led. The farmer was armed with considerable powers: he carried with him his books, searched for contraband or uncustomed goods, watched the harbour, markets, and other places, to prevent smuggling, or unlawful and clandestine sales; brought a phasis (φάσις) or other legal process against those whom he suspected of defrauding the revenue; or even seized their persons on some occasions, and took them before the magistrate. To enable him to perform these duties, he was exempted from military service. Collectors (ἐκλογεῖς) were sometimes employed by the farmers; but frequently the farmer and the collector were the same person. The taxes were let by the commissioners (πωληταί), acting under the authority of the senate. The payments were made by the farmer on stated prytaneias in the senate-house. There was usually one payment made in advance, προκαταβολή, and one or more afterwards, called προσκαταβλήματα. Upon any default of payment, the farmer became *atimus*, if a citizen, and he was liable to be imprisoned at the discretion of the court, upon an information laid against him. If the debt was not paid by the expiration of the ninth prytaneia, it was doubled; and if not then paid, his property became forfeited to the state, and proceedings to confiscation might be taken forthwith. Upon this subject, see the speech of Demosthenes against Timocrates.

TELOS (τέλος), a tax. The taxes imposed by the Athenians, and collected at home, were either ordinary or extraordinary. The former constituted a regular or permanent source of income; the latter were only raised in time of war or other emergency. The ordinary taxes were laid mostly upon *property*, and upon citizens *indirectly*, in the shape of toll or customs; though the resident aliens paid a poll-tax (called μετοίκιον), for the liberty of residing at Athens under protection of the state. There was a duty of two per cent. (πεντηκοστή), levied upon all exports and imports. An excise was paid on all sales in the market (called ἐπωνία), though we know not what the amount was. Slave-owners paid a duty of three obols for every slave they kept; and slaves who had been emancipated paid the same. This was a very productive tax before the fortification of Deceleia by the Lacedaemonians. The justice fees (πρυτανεῖα, παράστασις, &c.) were a lucrative tax in time of peace. The extraordinary taxes were the property-tax, and the compulsory services called *liturgies* (λειτουργίαι). Some of these last were regular, and recurred annually; the most important, the *trierarchia*, was a war-service, and performed as occasion required. As these services were all performed, wholly or partly, at the expense of the individual, they may be regarded as a species of tax. [EISPHORA; LEITOURGIA; TRIERARCHIA.] The tribute (φόρος) paid by the allied states to the Athenians formed, in the flourishing period of the republic, a regular and most important source of revenue. In Olymp. 91 2, the Athenians substituted for the tribute a duty of five per cent. (εἰκοστή) on all commodities exported or imported by the subject states, thinking to raise by this means a larger income than by direct taxation. This was terminated by the issue of the Peloponnesian war, though the tribute was afterwards revived, on more equitable principles, under the name of σύνταξις. Other sources of revenue were derived by the Athenians from their mines and public lands, fines, and confiscations. The public demesne lands, whether pasture or arable, houses or other buildings, were usually let by auction to private persons. The conditions of the lease were engraven on stone. The rent was payable by prytaneias. These various sources of revenue produced, according to Aristophanes, an annual income of two thousand talents in the most flourishing period of Athenian empire. Τελέω signifies " to settle, complete, or perfect," and hence " to settle an account," and generally " to pay." Thus Τέλος comes to mean any payment in the nature of a tax or duty. The words are connected with *zahlen* in German, and the old sense of *tale* in English, and the modern word *toll*. Though τέλος may signify any payment in the nature of a tax or duty, it is more commonly used of the ordinary taxes, as customs, &c. Ἰσοτέλεια signifies the right of being taxed on the same footing, and having other privileges, the same as the citizens; a right sometimes granted to resident aliens. Ἀτέλεια signifies an exemption from taxes, or other duties and services; an honour very rarely granted by the Athenians. As to the farming of the taxes, see TELONES.

TEMPLUM is the same word as the Greek *Temenos* (τέμενος, from τέμνω, to cut off); for *templum* was any place which was circumscribed and separated by the augurs from the rest of the land by a certain solemn formula. The technical terms for this act of the augurs are *liberare* and *effari*, and hence a templum itself is a *locus liberatus et effatus*. A place thus set apart and hallowed by the augurs was always intended to serve religious purposes, but chiefly for taking the auguries. The place in the heavens within which the observations were to be made was likewise called templum, as it was marked out and separated from the rest by the staff of the augur. When the augur had defined the templum within which he intended to make his observations, he fixed his tent in it (*tabernaculum capere*), and this tent was likewise called *templum*, or, more accurately, *templum minus*. The place chosen for a templum was generally an eminence, and in the city it was the *arx*, where the fixing of a tent does not appear to have been necessary, because here a place called *auguraculum* was once for all consecrated for this purpose. Besides this meaning of the word templum in the language of the augurs, it also had that of a temple in the common acceptation. In this case, however, the sacred precinct within which a temple was built, was always a *locus liberatus et effatus* by the augurs, that is, a *templum* or a *fanum*; the consecration was completed by the pontiffs, and not until inauguration and consecration had taken place, could sacra be performed or meetings of the senate be held in it. It was necessary then for a temple to be sanctioned by the gods, whose will was ascertained by the augurs, and to be consecrated or dedicated by the will of man (pontiffs.) Where the sanction of the gods had not been obtained, and where the mere act of man had consecrated a place to the gods, such a place was only a *sacrum*, *sacrarium*, or *sacellum*. The ceremony performed by the augurs was essential to a temple, as the consecration by the pontiffs took place also in

other sanctuaries which were not templa, but mere *sacra* or *aedes sacrae*. Thus the sanctuary of Vesta was not a templum, but an aedes sacra, and the various curiae (Hostilia, Pompeia, Julia) required to be made templa by the augurs before senatusconsulta could be made in them. It is impossible to determine with certainty in what respects a templum differed from a *delubrum*.—Temples appear to have existed in Greece from the earliest times. They were separated from the profane land around them (τόπος βέβηλος or τὰ βέβηλα), because every one was allowed to walk in the latter. This separation was in early times indicated by very simple means, such as a string or a rope. Subsequently, however, they were surrounded by more efficient fences, or even by a wall (ἕρκος, περίβολος). The whole space enclosed in such a περίβολος was called τέμενος, or sometimes ἱερόν; and contained, besides the temple itself, other sacred buildings, and sacred ground planted with groves, &c. Within the precincts of the sacred enclosure no dead were generally allowed to be buried, though there were some exceptions to this rule, and we have instances of persons being buried in or at least near certain temples. The religious laws of the island of Delos did not allow any corpses to be buried within the whole extent of the island, and when this law had been violated, a part of the island was first purified by Pisistratus, and subsequently the whole island by the Athenian people. The temple itself was called ναός or νεώς, and at its entrance fonts (περιῤῥαντήρια) were generally placed, that those who entered the sanctuary to pray or to offer sacrifices might first purify themselves. The act of consecration, by which a temple was dedicated to a god, was called ἵδρυσις. The character of the early Greek temples was dark and mysterious, for they had no windows, and they received light only through the door, which was very large, or from lamps burning in them. Architecture in the construction of magnificent temples, however, made great progress even at an earlier time than either painting or statuary, and long before the Persian wars we hear of temples of extraordinary grandeur and beauty. All temples were built either in an oblong or round form, and were mostly adorned with columns. Those of an oblong form had columns either in the front alone, in the fore and back fronts, or on all the four sides. Respecting the original use of these porticoes see PORTICUS. The friezes and metopes were adorned with various sculptures, and no expense was spared in embellishing the abodes of the gods. The light, which was formerly let in at the door, was now frequently let in from above through an opening in the middle. Most of the great temples consisted of three parts : 1. the πρόναος or πρόδομος, the vestibule ; 2. the cella (ναός, σηκός); and 3. the ὀπισθόδομος. The cella was the most important part, as it was, properly speaking, the temple or the habitation of the deity whose statue it contained. In one and the same cella there were sometimes the statues of two or more divinities, as in the Erechtheum at Athens, the statues of Poseidon, Hephaestus, and Butas. The statues always faced the entrance, which was in the centre of the prostylus. The place where the statue stood was called ἕδος, and was surrounded by a balustrade or railings. Some temples also had more than one cella, in which case the one was generally behind the other, as in the temple of Athena Polias at Athens. In temples where oracles were given, or where the worship was connected with mysteries, the cella was called ἄδυτον, μέγαρον, or ἀνάκτορον, and to it only the priests and the initiated had access. The ὀπισθόδομος was a building which was sometimes attached to the back front of a temple, and served as a place in which the treasures of the temple were kept, and thus supplied the place of θησαυροί, which were attached to some temples.—*Quadrangular Temples* were described by the following terms, according to the number and arrangement of the columns on the fronts and sides. 1. Ἄστυλος, *astyle*, without any columns. 2. Ἐν παραστάσι, *in antis*, with two columns in front between the antae. 3. Πρόστυλος, *prostyle*, with four columns in front. 4. Ἀμφιπρόστυλος, *amphiprostyle*, with four columns at each end. 5. Περίπτερος or ἀμφικίων, *peripteral*, with columns at each end and along each side. 6. Δίπτερος, *dipteral*, with two ranges of columns (πτερά) all round, the one within the other. 7. Ψευδοδίπτερος, *pseudodipteral*, with one range only, but at the same distance from the walls of the *cella* as the outer range of a δίπτερος. To these must be added a sort of sham invented by the Roman architects, namely : 8. Ψευδοπερίπτερος, *pseudoperipteral*, where the sides had only half-columns (at the angles threequarter columns), attached to the walls of the *cella*, the object being to have the *cella* large without enlarging the whole building, and yet to keep up something of the splendour of a peripteral temple. Names were also applied to the temples, as well as to the porticoes themselves, according to the number of columns in the portico at either end of the temple : namely, τετράστυλος, *tetrastyle*, when there were *four* columns in front, ἑξάστυλος, *hexastyle*, when there were *six*, ὀκτάστυλος,

octastyle, when there were *eight*, δεκάστυλος, *decastyle*, when there were *ten*. There were never more than ten columns in the end portico of a temple ; and when there were only two, they were always arranged in that peculiar form called *in antis* (ἐν παραστάσι). The number of columns in the end porticoes was never uneven, but the number along the sides of a temple was generally uneven. The number of the side columns varied : where the end portico was tetrastyle, there were never any columns at the sides, except false ones, attached to the walls : where it was hexastyle or octastyle, there were generally 13 or 17 columns at the sides, counting in the corner columns : sometimes a hexastyle temple had only eleven columns on the sides. The last arrangement resulted from the rule adopted by the Roman architects, who counted by intercolumniations (the spaces between the columns), and whose rule was to have *twice as many intercolumniations along the sides of the building as in front*. The Greek architects on the contrary, counted by columns, and their rule was to have *twice as many columns along the sides as in front, and one more*, counting the corner columns in each case. Another set of terms, applied to temples and other buildings having porticoes, as well as to the porticoes themselves, was derived from the distances between the columns as compared with the lower diameters of the columns. They were the following :—1. Πυκνόστυλος, *pycnostyle*, the distance between the columns a diameter of a column and half a diameter. 2. Σύστυλος, *systyle*, the distance between the columns two diameters of a column. 3. Εὔστυλος, *eustyle*, the distance between the columns two diameters and a quarter, except in the centre of the front and back of the building, where each intercolumniation (*intercolumnium*) was three diameters ; called eustyle, because it was best adapted both for beauty and convenience. 4. Διάστυλος, *diastyle*, the intercolumniation, or distance between the columns, three diameters. 5. Ἀραιόστυλος, *araeostyle*, the distances excessive, so that it was necessary to make the epistyle (ἐπιστύλιον), or architrave, not of stone, but of timber. These five kinds of intercolumniation are illustrated by the following diagram. Independently of the

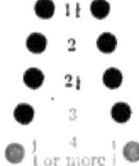

immense treasures contained in many of the Greek temples, which were either utensils or ornaments, and of the tithes of spoils, &c., the property of temples, from which they derived a regular income, consisted of lands (τεμένη), either fields, pastures, or forests. These lands were generally let out to farm, unless they were, by some curse which lay on them, prevented from being taken into cultivation. Respecting the persons entrusted with the superintendence, keeping, cleaning, &c., see AEDITUI. In the earliest times there appear to have been very few temples at Rome, and on many spots the worship of a certain divinity had been established from time immemorial, while we hear of the building of a temple for the same divinity at a comparatively late period. Thus the foundation of a temple to the old Italian divinity Saturnus, on the Capitoline, did not take place till B. C. 498. In the same manner, Quirinus and Mars had temples built to them at a late period. Jupiter also had no temple till the time of Ancus Martius, and the one then built was certainly very insignificant. We may therefore suppose that the places of worship among the earliest Romans were in most cases simple altars or sacella. The Roman temples of later times were constructed in the Greek style. As regards the property of temples, it is stated that in early times lands were assigned to each temple, but these lands were probably intended for the maintenance of the priests alone. [SACERDOS.] The supreme superintendence of the temples of Rome, and of all things connected with them, belonged to the college of pontiffs. Those persons who had the immediate care of the temples were the AEDITUI.

TEPIDARIUM. [BALNEUM, p. 56.]

TERMINALIA, a festival in honour of the god Terminus, who presided over boundaries. His statue was merely a stone or post stuck in the ground to distinguish between properties. On the festival the two owners of adjacent property crowned the statue with garlands, and raised a rude altar, on which they offered up some corn, honeycombs, and wine, and sacrificed a lamb or a sucking-pig. They concluded with singing the praises of the god. The public festival in honour of this god was celebrated at the sixth milestone on the road towards Laurentum, doubtless because this was originally the extent of the Roman territory in that direction. The festival of the Terminalia was celebrated on the 23rd of February, on the day before the Regifugium. The Terminalia was celebrated on the last day of the old Roman year, whence some derive its name. We know that February was the last month of the Roman year, and that when the intercalary month Mercedonius was added, the last five days of February were added to the intercalary month, making the 23rd of February the last day of the year.

TERUNCIUS. [As.]

TESSERA (κύβος), a square or cube; a die; a token. The dice used in games of chance were tesserae, small squares or cubes, and were commonly made of ivory, bone, or wood. They were numbered on all the six sides, like the dice still in use; and in this respect as well as in their form they differed from the tali. [TALUS.] Whilst four tali were used in playing, only three tesserae were anciently employed. Objects of the same materials with dice, and either formed like them, or of an oblong shape, were used as tokens for different purposes. The *tessera hospitalis* was the token of mutual hospitality, and is spoken of under HOSPITIUM. This token was probably in many cases of earthenware, having the head of Jupiter Hospitalis stamped upon it. *Tesserae frumentariae* and *nummariae* were tokens given at certain times by the Roman magistrates to the poor, in exchange for which they received a fixed amount of corn or money. From the application of this term to tokens of various kinds, it was transferred to the *word* used as a token among soldiers. This was the *tessera militaris*, the σύνθημα of the Greeks. Before joining battle it was given out and passed through the ranks, as a method by which the soldiers might be able to distinguish friends from foes.

TESTAMENTUM, a will. In order to be able to make a valid Roman will, the Testator must have the Testamentifactio, which term expresses the legal capacity to make a valid will. The testamentifactio was the privilege only of Roman citizens who were patresfamilias. The following persons consequently had not the testamentifactio: those who were in the Potestas or Manus of another, or in Mancipii causa, as sons and daughters, wives In manu and slaves: Latini Juniani, Dediticii : Peregrini could not dispose of their property according to the form of a Roman will: an Impubes could not dispose of his property by will even with the consent of his Tutor; when a male was fourteen years of age, he obtained the testamentifactio, and a female obtained the power, subject to certain restraints, on the completion of her twelfth year : muti, surdi, furiosi, and prodigi " quibus lege bonis interdictum est " had not the testamentifactio. In order to constitute a valid will, it was necessary that a heres should be instituted, which might be done in such terms as follow :—

Titius heres esto, Titium heredem esse jubeo. [HERES (ROMAN.)] Originally there were two modes of making wills; either at Calata Comitia, which were appointed twice a year for that purpose; or *in procinctu*, that is, when a man was going to battle. A third mode of making wills was introduced, which was effected *per aes et libram*, whence the name of Testamentum per aes et libram. If a man had neither made his will at Calata Comitia nor In procinctu, and was in imminent danger of death, he would mancipate (*mancipio dabat*) his Familia, that is, his Patrimonium to a friend and would tell him what he wished to be given to each after his death. There seems to have been no rule of law that a testament must be written. The heres might either be made by oral declaration (*nuncupatio*) or by writing. Written wills however were the common form among the Romans at least in the later republican and in the imperial periods. They were written on tablets of wood or wax, whence the word "cera" is often used as equivalent to "tabella;" and the expressions prima, secunda cera are equivalent to prima, secunda pagina. The will must have been in some way so marked as to be recognized, and the practice of the witnesses (*testes*) sealing and signing the will at last became common. It was necessary for the witnesses both to seal (*signare*), that is, to make a mark with a ring (*annulus*) or something else on the wax and to add their names (*adscribere*). Wills were to be tied with a triple thread (*linum*) on the upper part of the margin which was to be perforated at the middle part, and the wax was to be put over the thread and sealed. Tabulae which were produced in any other way had no validity. A man might make several copies of his will, which was often done for the sake of caution. When sealed, it was deposited with some friend, or in a temple, or with the Vestal Virgins; and after the testator's death it was opened (*resignare*) in due form. The witnesses or the major part were present, and after they had acknowledged their seals, the thread (*linum*) was broken and the will was opened and read, and a copy was made; the original was then sealed with the public seal and placed in the archium, whence a fresh copy might be got, if the first copy should ever be lost.

TESTIS, a witness.—(1) GREEK, [MARTYRIA.]—(2) ROMAN. [JUSJURANDUM.]

TESTUDO (χελώνη), a tortoise, was the name given to several other objects.—(1) To the Lyra, because it was sometimes made of a tortoise-shell.—(2) To an arched or vaulted roof.—(3) To a military machine moving upon wheels and roofed over, used in besieging cities, under which the soldiers worked in undermining the walls or otherwise destroying them. It was usually covered with raw hides, or other materials which could not easily be set on fire. The battering-ram [ARIES] was frequently placed under a testudo of this kind, which was then called *Testudo Arietaria*.—(4) The name of testudo was also applied to the covering made by a close body of soldiers who placed their shields over their heads to secure themselves against the darts of the enemy. The shields fitted so

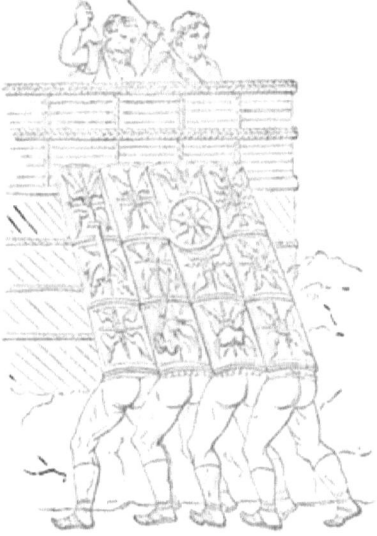

Testudo. (From the Antonine Column.)

closely together as to present one unbroken surface without any interstices between them, and were also so firm that men could walk upon them, and even horses and chariots be driven over them. A testudo was formed (*testudinem facere*) either in battle to ward off the arrows and other missiles of the enemy, or, which was more frequently the case, to form a protection to the soldiers when they advanced to the walls or gates of a town for the purpose of attacking them. Sometimes the shields were disposed in such a way as to make the testudo slope. The soldiers in the first line stood upright, those in the second stooped a little, and each line successively was a little lower than the preceding down to the last, where the soldiers rested on one knee. Such a disposition of the shields was called *fastigata testudo*, on account of their sloping like the roof of a

2 B

building. The advantages of this plan were obvious: the stones and missiles thrown upon the shields rolled off them like water from a roof; besides which, other soldiers frequently advanced upon them to attack the enemy upon the walls. The Romans were accustomed to form this kind of testudo, as an exercise, in the games of the circus.

TETRARCHES or TETRARCHA (τετράρχης). This word was originally used, according to its etymological meaning, to signify the governor of the fourth part of a country (τετραρχία or τετραδαρχία). We have an example in the ancient division of Thessaly into four tetrarchies, which was revived by Philip. Each of the three Gallic tribes which settled in Galatia was divided into four tetrarchies, each ruled by a tetrarch. Some of the tribes of Syria were ruled by tetrarchs, and several of the princes of the house of Herod ruled in Palestine with this title. In the later period of the republic and under the empire, the Romans seem to have used the title (as also those of *ethnarch* and *phylarch*) to designate those tributary princes who were not of sufficient importance to be called kings.

TETTARAKONTA, HOI (οἱ τετταράκοντα), *the Forty*, were certain officers chosen by lot, who made regular circuits through the demi of Attica, whence they are called δικασταὶ κατὰ δήμους, to decide all cases of αἰκία and τὰ περὶ τῶν βιαίων, and also all other private causes, where the matter in dispute was not above the value of ten drachmae. Their number was originally thirty, but was increased to forty after the expulsion of the thirty tyrants, and the restoration of the democracy by Thrasybulus, in consequence, it is said, of the hatred of the Athenians to the number of thirty.

THARGELIA (θαργήλια), a festival celebrated at Athens on the 6th and 7th of Thargelion, in honour of Apollo and Artemis. The real festival, or the Thargelia in a narrower sense of the word, appears to have taken place on the 7th; and on the preceding day, the city of Athens or rather its inhabitants were purified. The manner in which this purification was effected is very extraordinary, and is certainly a remnant of very ancient rites, for two persons were put to death on that day, and the one died on behalf of the men and the other on behalf of the women of Athens. The name by which these victims were designated was *pharmaci* (φαρμακοί). It appears probable, however, that this sacrifice did not take place annually, but only in case of a heavy calamity having befallen the city, such as the plague, a famine, &c. The victims appear to have been criminals sentenced to death. The second day of the thargelia was solemnized with a procession and an agon, which consisted of a cyclic chorus, performed by men at the expense of a choragus. The prize of the victor in this agon was a tripod, which he had to dedicate in the temple of Apollo which had been built by Pisistratus. On this day it was customary for persons who were adopted into a family to be solemnly registered, and received into the genos and the phratria of the adoptive parents. This solemnity was the same as that of registering one's own children at the Apaturia.

THEATRUM (θέατρον), a theatre. The Athenians before the time of Aeschylus had only a wooden scaffolding on which their dramas were performed. Such a wooden theatre was only erected for the time of the Dionysiac festivals, and was afterwards pulled down. The first drama that Aeschylus brought upon the stage was performed upon such a wooden scaffold, and it is recorded as a singular and ominous coincidence that on that occasion (500 B. C.) the scaffolding broke down. To prevent the recurrence of such an accident, the building of a stone theatre was forthwith commenced on the south-eastern descent of the Acropolis, in the Lenaea; for it should be observed, that throughout Greece theatres were always built upon eminences, or on the sloping side of a hill. The new Athenian theatre was built on a very large scale, and appears to have been constructed with great skill in regard to its acoustic and perspective arrangements. Subsequently theatres were erected in all parts of Greece and Asia Minor, although Athens was the centre of the Greek drama, and the only place which produced great masterworks in this department of literature. All the theatres, however, which were constructed in Greece were probably built after the model of that of Athens, and, with slight deviations and modifications, they all resembled one another in the main points, as is seen in the numerous ruins of theatres in various parts of Greece, Asia Minor, and Sicily. The Attic theatre was, like all the Greek theatres, placed in such a manner that the place for the spectators formed the upper or north-western, and the stage with all that belonged to it the south-eastern part, and between these two parts lay the orchestra. The annexed plan has been made from the remains of Greek theatres still extant, and from a careful examination of the passages in ancient writers which describe the whole or parts of a theatre.—1. The place for the spectators was in a narrower sense of the word called *theatrum*. The seats for the spectators, which were in most cases cut out of the rock, consisted of rows of benches rising one above another; the rows themselves (*a*) formed parts (nearly three-fourths) of concentric circles, and were at intervals divided into compartments by one or more broad passages (*b*) running between them, and parallel with the benches. These pas-

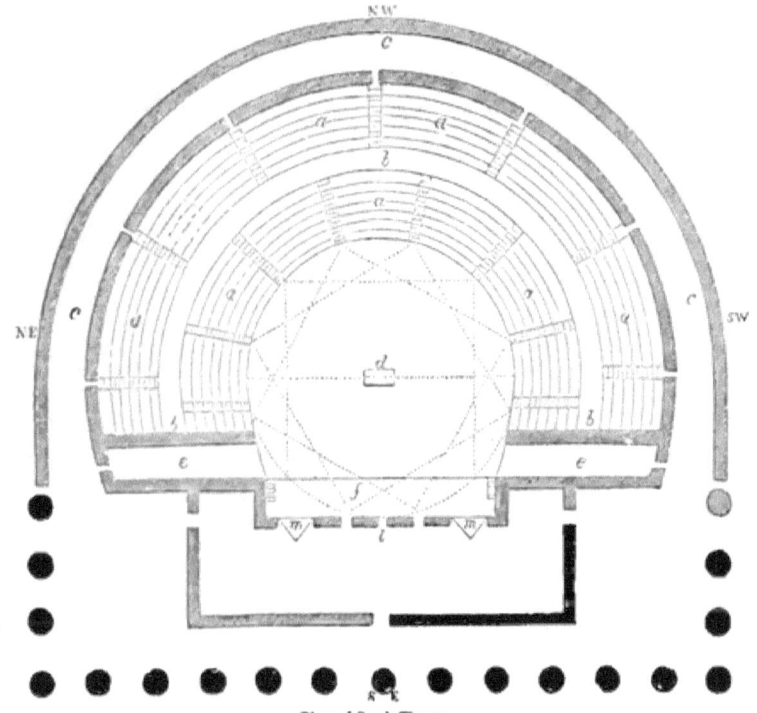

Plan of Greek Theatre.

sages were called διαζώματα, or κατατομαί, Lat. *praecinctiones*, and when the concourse of people was very great in a theatre, many persons might stand in them. Across the rows of benches ran stairs, by which persons might ascend from the lowest to the highest. But these stairs ran in straight lines only from one praecinctio to another; and the stairs in the next series of rows were just between the two stairs of the lower series of benches. By this course of the stairs the seats were divided into a number of compartments, resembling cones from which the tops are cut off; hence they were termed κεοκίδες, and in Latin *cunei*. The whole of the place for the spectators (θέατρον) was sometimes designated by the name κοῖλον, Latin *cavea*, it being in most cases a real excavation of the rock. Above the highest row of benches there rose a covered portico (*c*), which of course far exceeded in height the opposite buildings by which the stage was surrounded, and appears to have also contributed to increase the acoustic effect. The entrances to the seats of the spectators were partly underground, and led to the lowest rows of benches, while the upper rows must have been accessible from above. —2. The orchestra (ὀρχήστρα) was a circular level space extending in front of the spectators, and somewhat below the lowest row of benches. But it was not a complete circle, one segment of it being appropriated to the stage. The orchestra was the place for the chorus, where it performed its evolutions and dances, for which purpose it was covered with boards. As the chorus was the element out of which the drama arose, so the orchestra was originally the most important part of a theatre: it formed the centre around which all the other parts of the building were grouped. In the centre of the circle of the orchestra was the *thymele* (θυμέλη), that is, the altar of Dionysus (*d*),

2 B 2

which was of course nearer to the stage than to the seats of the spectators, the distance from which was precisely the length of a radius of the circle. In a wider sense the orchestra also comprised the broad passages (πάροδοι, e) on each side, between the projecting wings of the stage and the seats of the spectators, through which the chorus entered the orchestra. The chorus generally arranged itself in the space between the thymele and the stage. The thymele itself was of a square form, and was used for various purposes, according to the nature of the different plays, such as a funeral monument, an altar, &c. It was made of boards, and surrounded on all sides with steps. It thus stood upon a raised platform, which was sometimes occupied by the leader of the chorus, the flute-player, and the rhabdophori. The orchestra as well as the *theatrum* lay under the open sky; a roof is nowhere mentioned.—3. The stage. Steps led from each side of the orchestra to the stage, and by them the chorus probably ascended the stage whenever it took a real part in the action itself. The back side of the stage was closed by a wall called the *scena* (σκηνή), from which on each side a wing projected which was called the *parascenium* (παρασκήνιον). The whole depth of the stage was not very great, as it only comprised a segment of the circle of the orchestra. The whole space from the scena to the orchestra was termed the *proscenium* (προσκήνιον), and was what we should call the real stage. That part of it which was nearest to the orchestra, and where the actors stood when they spoke, was the *logeium* (λογείον), also called *ocribas* (ὀκρίβας), in Latin *pulpitum*, which was of course raised above the orchestra, and probably on a level with the thymele. The *scena* was, as we have already stated, the wall which closed the stage (*proscenium* and *logeium*) from behind. It represented a suitable back-ground, or the locality in which the action was going on. Before the play began it was covered with a curtain (παραπέτασμα, προσκήνιον, αὐλαίαι), Latin *aulaea* or *siparium*. When the play began this curtain was let down, and was rolled up on a roller underneath the stage. The proscenium and logeium were never concealed from the spectators. As regards the scenery represented on the *scena*, it was different for tragedy, comedy, and the satyric drama, and for each of these kinds of poetry the scenery must have been capable of various modifications, according to the character of each individual play; at least that this was the case with the various tragedies, is evident from the scenes described in the tragedies still extant. In the latter however the back-ground (*scena*) in most cases represented the front of a palace with a door in the centre (*i*) which was called the *royal door*. This palace generally consisted of two stories, and upon its flat roof there appears to have been some elevated place from which persons might observe what was going on at a distance. The palace presented on each side a projecting wing, each of which had its separate entrance. These wings generally represented the habitations of guests and visitors. All the three doors must have been visible to the spectators. The protagonistes always entered the stage through the middle or royal door, the deuteragonistes and tritagonistes through those on the right and left wings. In tragedies like the Prometheus, the Persians, Philoctetes, Oedipus in Colonus, and others, the back-ground did not represent a palace. There are other pieces again in which the scena must have been changed in the course of the performance, as in the Eumenides of Aeschylus and the Ajax of Sophocles. The dramas of Euripides required a great variety of scenery; and if in addition to this we recollect that several pieces were played in one day, it is manifest that the mechanical parts of stage performance, at least in the days of Euripides, must have been brought to great perfection. The scena in the satyric drama appears to have always represented a woody district with hills and grottos; in comedy the scena represented, at least in later times, the fronts of private dwellings or the habitations of slaves. The art of scene-painting must have been applied long before the time of Sophocles, although Aristotle ascribes its introduction to him. The whole of the cavea in the Attic theatre must have contained about 50,000 spectators. The places for generals, the archons, priests, foreign ambassadors, and other distinguished persons, were in the lowest rows of benches, and nearest to the orchestra, and they appear to have been sometimes covered with a sort of canopy. The rows of benches above these were occupied by the senate of 500, those next in succession by the ephebi, and the rest by the people of Athens. But it would seem that they did not sit indiscriminately, but that the better places were let at a higher price than the others, and that no one had a right to take a place for which he had not paid. The usual fee for a place was two obols, which was subsequently given to the poorer classes by a law of Pericles. [THEORICA.] Women were allowed to be present during the performance of tragedies, but not of comedies.—The Romans must have become acquainted with the theatres of the Italian Greeks at an early period, whence they erected their own theatres in similar positions upon the sides of hills. This is still clear from the ruins of very ancient theatres at Tusculum and Faesulae. The Romans themselves, however, did not possess a regular stone theatre until a very late period, and although dramatic representations were very popular in earlier times, it appears that a wooden stage was erected when necessary, and was afterwards pulled down again, and the plays of Plautus and Terence were performed on such temporary scaffoldings. In the mean while, many of the neighbouring towns of Rome had their stone theatres, as the introduction of Greek customs and manners was less strongly opposed in them than in the city of Rome itself. Wooden theatres, adorned with the most profuse magnificence, were erected at Rome even during the last period of the republic. In B. C. 55 Cn. Pompey built the first stone theatre at Rome, near the Campus Martius. It was of great beauty, and is said to have been built after the model of that of Mytilene; it contained 40,000 spectators. The construction of a Roman theatre resembled, on the whole, that of a Greek one. The principal differences are, that the seats of the spectators, which rose in the form of an amphitheatre around the

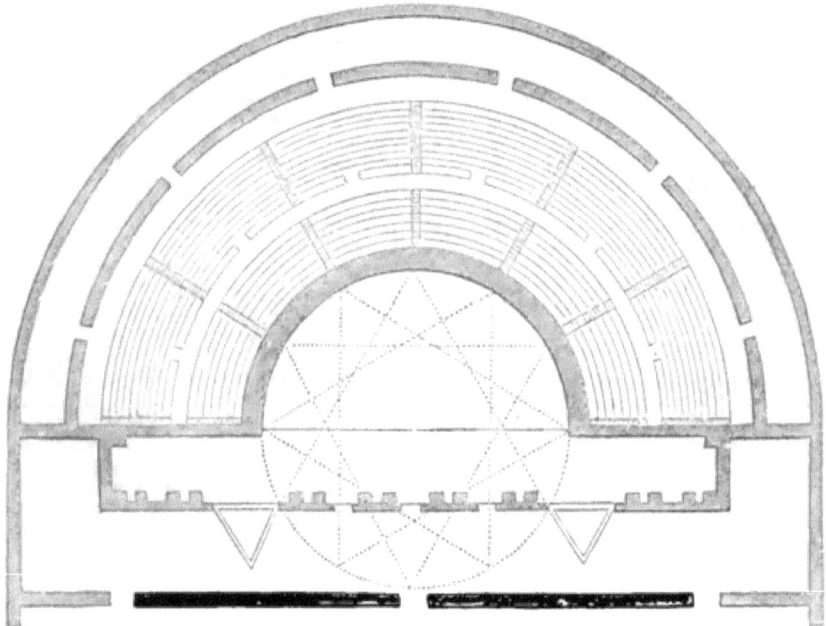

Plan of Roman Theatre.

orchestra, did not form more than a semicircle; and that the whole of the orchestra likewise formed only a semicircle, the diameter of which formed the front line of the stage. The Roman orchestra contained no thymele, and was not destined for a chorus, but contained the seats for senators and other distinguished persons, such as foreign ambassadors, which are called *primus subselliorum ordo*. In B. C. 68 the tribune L. Roscius Otho carried a law which regulated the places in the theatre to be occupied by the different classes of Roman citizens: it enacted that fourteen ordines of benches were to be assigned as seats to the equites. Hence these quatuordecim ordines are sometimes mentioned without any further addition, as the honorary seats of the equites. They were undoubtedly close behind the seats of the senators and magistrates, and thus consisted of the rows of benches immediately behind the orchestra.

THENSAE or TENSAE, highly ornamented sacred vehicles, which, in the solemn pomp of the Circensian games, conveyed the statues of certain deities with all their decorations to the pulvinaria, and after the sports were over bore them back to their shrines. We are ignorant of their precise form. We know that they were drawn by horses, and escorted (*deducere*) by the chief senators in robes of state, who, along with pueri patrimi [PATRIMI], laid hold of the bridles and traces, or perhaps assisted to drag the carriage by means of thongs attached for the purpose (and hence the proposed derivation from *tendo*). So sacred was this duty considered, that Augustus, when labouring under sickness, deemed it necessary to accompany the tensae in a litter. If one of the horses knocked up, or the driver took the reins in his left hand, it was necessary to recommence the procession, and for one of the attendant boys to let go the thong, or to stumble, was profanation. The only gods distinctly named as carried in tensae are Jupiter and Minerva, though others appear to have had the same honour paid them.

THEŌPHĂNĬA (θεοφάνια), a festival celebrated at Delphi, on the occasion of which the Delphians filled the huge silver crater which had been presented to the Delphic god by Croesus.

THĔŌRĬA. [THEORI.]

THĔŌRĬCA (θεωρικά). Under this name at Athens were comprised the monies expended on festivals, sacrifices, and public entertainments of various kinds; and also monies distributed among the people in the shape of largesses from the state. There were, according to Xenophon, more festivals at Athens than in all the rest of Greece. At the most important of the public festivals, such as the Dionysia, Panathenaea, Eleusinia, Thargelia, and some others, there were not only sacrifices, but processions, theatrical exhibitions, gymnastic contests, and games, celebrated with great splendour and at a great expense. A portion of the expense was defrayed by the individuals upon whom the burden of the liturgies devolved; but a considerable, and perhaps the larger, part was defrayed by the public treasury. Demosthenes complains, that more money was spent on a single Panathenaic or Dionysiac festival than on any military expedition. The religious embassies to Delos and other places, and especially those to the Olympian, Nemean, Isthmian, and Pythian games, drew largely upon the public exchequer, though a part of the cost fell upon the wealthier citizens who conducted them. The largesses distributed among the people had their origin at an early period, and in a measure apparently harmless, though from a small beginning they afterwards rose to a height most injurious to the commonwealth. The Attic drama used to be performed in a wooden theatre, and the entrance was free to all citizens who chose to go. It was found, however, that the crushing to get in led to much confusion and even danger. On one occasion, about B. C. 500, the wooden scaffolding of the theatre fell down, and caused great alarm. It was then determined that the entrance should no longer be gratuitous. The fee for a place was fixed at two obols, which was paid to the lessee of the theatre, (called θεατρώνης, θεατροπώλης, or ἀρχιτέκτων,) who undertook to keep it in repair, and constantly ready for use, on condition of being allowed to receive the profits. This payment continued to be exacted after the stone theatre was built. Pericles, to relieve the poorer classes, passed a law which enabled them to receive the price of admission from the state; after which all those citizens who were too poor to pay for their places applied for the money in the public assembly, which was then frequently held in the theatre. In process of time this donation was extended to other entertainments besides theatrical ones; the sum of two oboli being given to each citizen who attended; if the festival lasted two days, four oboli; and if three, six oboli; but not beyond. Hence all theoric largesses received the name of *diobelia* (διωβελία). It is calculated that from 25 to 30 talents were spent upon them annually. So large an expenditure of the public funds upon shows and amusements absorbed the resources, which were demanded for services of a more important nature. By the ancient law, the whole surplus of the annual revenue which remained after the expense of the civil administration (τὰ περίοντα χρήματα τῆς διοικήσεως) was to be carried to the military fund, and applied to the defence of the commonwealth. Since the time of Pericles various demagogues had sprung up, who induced the people to divert all that could be spared from the other branches of civil expenditure into the theoric fund, which at length swallowed up the whole surplus, and the supplies needed for the purpose of war or defence were left to depend upon the extraordinary contributions, or property-tax (εἰσφοραί). An attempt was made by the demagogue Eubulus to perpetuate this system. He passed a law, which made it a capital offence to propose that the theoric fund should be applied to military service. The law of Eubulus was a source of great embarrassment to Demosthenes, in the prosecution of his schemes for the national defence; and he seems at last, but not before

B. C. 339, to have succeeded in repealing it. In the earlier times there was no person, or board of persons, expressly appointed to manage the theoric fund. The money thus appropriated was disbursed by the Hellenotamiae. After the anarchy, the largess system having been restored by Agyrrhius, a board of managers was appointed. They were elected by show of hands at the period of the great Dionysia, one from each tribe.

THEORI (θεωροί), persons sent on special missions (θεωρίαι) to perform some religious duty, as to consult an oracle, or to offer a sacrifice, on behalf of the state. There were among some of the Dorian states, as the Aeginetans, Troezenians, Messenians, and Mantineans, official priests called *Theori*, whose duty it was to consult oracles, interpret the responses, &c., as among the Spartans there were men called *Pythii*, chosen by the kings to consult the oracle at Delphi. At Athens there were no official persons called *Theori*, but the name was given to those citizens who were appointed from time to time to conduct religious embassies to various places; of which the most important were those that were sent to the Olympian, Pythian, Nemean, and Isthmian games, those that went to consult the God at Delphi, and those that led the solemn procession to Delos, where the Athenians established a quadriennial festival, in revival of the ancient Ionian one, of which Homer speaks. The expense of these embassies was defrayed partly by the state, and partly by wealthy citizens, to whom the management of them was entrusted, called *Architheori* (ἀρχιθέωροι), chiefs of the embassy. This was a sort of liturgy, and frequently a very costly one; as the chief conductor represented the state, and was expected to appear with a suitable degree of splendour; for instance, to wear a golden crown, to drive into the city with a handsome chariot, retinue, &c. The Salaminian, or Delian, ship was also called θεωρὶς ναῦς, and was principally used for conveying embassies to Delos, though, like the Paralus, it was employed on other expeditions besides.

THERMAE. [BALNEUM.]

THESAURUS (θησαυρός), a treasure-house. Tradition points to subterranean buildings in Greece, of unknown antiquity and of peculiar formation, as having been erected during the heroic period, for the purpose of preserving precious metals, arms, and other property (κειμήλια). Such are the treasury of Minyas, at Orchomenus, of which some remains still exist, and those of Atreus and his sons at Mycenae, the chief one of which, the so-called Treasury of Atreus, still exists almost in a perfect state. It is, however, very questionable whether these edifices were treasuries at all: some of the best archaeologists maintain that they were tombs. In the historical times, the public treasury was either in a building attached to the *agora*, or in the *opisthodomus* of some temple. Respecting the public treasury at Rome, see AERARIUM.

THESEIA (θησεῖα), a festival celebrated by the Athenians in honour of their national hero Theseus, whom they believed to have been the author of their democratical form of government. In consequence of this belief donations of bread and meat were given to the poor people at the Theseia, which was thus for them a feast at which they felt no want, and might fancy themselves equal to the wealthiest citizens. The day on which this festival was held was the eighth of every month (ὀγδόαι), but more especially the eighth of Pyanepsion, whence the festival was sometimes called ὀγδώδιον. It is probable that the festival of the Theseia was not instituted till B. C. 469, when Cimon brought the remains of Theseus from Scyrus to Athens.

THESMOPHORIA (θεσμοφόρια), a great festival and mysteries, celebrated in honour of Demeter in various parts of Greece, and only by women, though some ceremonies were also performed by maidens. It was intended to commemorate the introduction of the laws and regulations of civilised life, which was universally ascribed to Demeter. The Attic thesmophoria probably lasted only three days, and began on the 11th of Pyanepsion, which day was called ἄνοδος or κάθοδος, because the solemnities were opened by the women with a procession from Athens to Eleusis. In this procession they carried on their heads sacred laws (νόμιμοι βίβλοι or θεσμοί), the introduction of which was ascribed to Demeter (Θεσμοφόρος), and other symbols of civilised life. The women spent the night at Eleusis in celebrating the mysteries of the goddess. The second day, called νηστεία, was a day of mourning, during which the women sat on the ground around the statue of Demeter, and took no other food than cakes made of sesame and honey. On this day no meetings either of the senate or the people were held. It was probably in the afternoon of this day that the women held a procession at Athens, in which they walked barefooted behind a waggon, upon which baskets with mystical symbols were conveyed to the thesmophorion. The third day, called καλλιγένεια, from the circumstance that Demeter was invoked under this name, was a day of merriment and raillery among the women themselves, in commemoration of Iambe, who was said to have made the goddess smile during her grief.

THESMŎTHĔTAE. [ARCHON.]
THĒTES. [CENSUS.]
THOLOS (θόλος, also called σκιάς), a name given to any round building which terminated at the top in a point, whatever might be the purpose for which it was used. At Athens the name was in particular applied to the new round prytaneium near the senate-house, which should not be confounded with the old prytaneium at the foot of the acropolis. It was therefore the place in which the prytanes took their common meals and offered their sacrifices. It was adorned with some small silver statues, and near it stood the ten statues of the Attic Eponymi.

THŌRAX. [LORICA.]
THRĀCES. [GLADIATORES.]
THRANĪTAE. [NAVIS.]
THRŎNUS (θρόνος), a throne, is a Greek word, for which the proper Latin term is *Solium*. This did not differ from a chair (καθέδρα) [CATHEDRA; SELLA] except in being higher, larger, and in all respects more magnificent. On account of its elevation it was always necessarily accompanied by a footstool (*subsellium*, ὑποπόδιον, θράνιον). The accompanying cut shows two gilded thrones with cushions and drapery, intended to be the thrones of Mars and Venus, which is expressed by the helmet on the one and the dove on the other.

Throni. (From an ancient Painting.)

THỸMĔLĒ. [THEATRUM.]
THYRSUS (θύρσος), a pole carried by Bacchus, and by Satyrs, Maenades, and others who engaged in Bacchic festivities and rites. [DIONYSIA.] It was sometimes terminated by the apple of the pine, or fir-cone, that tree (πεύκη) being dedicated to Bacchus in consequence of the use of the turpentine which flowed from it, and also of its cones, in making wine. The monuments of ancient art, however, most commonly exhibit, instead of the pine-apple, a bunch of vine or ivy-leaves, with grapes or berries, arranged into the form of a cone. The fabulous history of Bacchus relates that he converted the thyrsi carried by himself and his followers into dangerous weapons, by concealing an iron point in the head of the leaves. Hence his thyrsus is called "a spear enveloped in vine-leaves," and its point was thought to incite to madness.

TIĀRA or TIĀRAS (τιάρα or τιάρας: *Att.* κυρβασία), a hat with a large high crown.

Tiara. (From a Coin in the British Museum.)

This was the head-dress which characterised the north-western Asiatics, and more especially the Armenians, Parthians, and Persians, as distinguished from the Greeks and Romans, whose hats fitted the head, or had only a low crown. The king of Persia wore an erect tiara, whilst those of his subjects were soft and flexible, falling on one side. The Persian name for this regal head-dress was *cidaris*.

Tiara. (From a Coin in the British Museum.)

TĪBĬA (αὐλός), a pipe, the commonest musical instrument of the Greeks and Romans. It was very frequently a hollow cane, perforated with holes in the proper places. In other instances it was made of some kind of wood, especially box, and was bored with a gimblet. When a single pipe was used by itself, the performer upon it, as well as the instrument, was called *monaulos*. Among the varieties of the single pipe the most remarkable were the bagpipe, the performer on which was called *utricularius* or ἀσκαύλης; and the αὐλὸς πλάγιος or πλαγίαυλος, which, as its name implies, had a mouth-piece inserted into it at right angles. Pan was the reputed inventor of this kind of tibia as well as of the *fistula* or *syrinx* [SYRINX]. But among the Greeks and Romans it was much more usual to play on two pipes at the same time. Hence a performance on this instrument (*tibicinium*), even when executed by a single person, was called *canere* or *cantare tibiis*. This act is exhibited in very numerous works of ancient art, and often in such a way as to make it manifest that the two pipes were perfectly distinct, and not connected, as some have supposed, by a common mouth-piece. The mouth-pieces of the two pipes often passed through a capistrum. Three different

Woman Playing on two Pipes, Tibiæ. (From a Vase in the British Museum.)

kinds of pipes were originally used to produce music in the Dorian, Phrygian, and Lydian modes. It appears, also, that to produce the Phrygian mode the pipe had only two holes above, and that it terminated in a horn bending upwards. It thus approached to the nature of a trumpet, and produced slow, grave, and solemn tunes. The Lydian mode was much quicker, and more varied and animating. Horace mentions "Lydian pipes" as a proper accompaniment, when he is celebrating the praise of ancient heroes. The Lydians themselves used this instrument in leading their troops to battle; and the pipes employed for the purpose are distinguished by Herodotus as "male and female," i. e. probably bass and treble, corresponding to the ordinary sexual difference in the human voice. The corresponding Latin terms are *tibia dextra* and *sinistra*: the respective instruments are supposed to have been so called, because the former was more properly

held in the right hand and the latter in the left. The "tibia *dextra*" was used to lead or commence a piece of music, and the "sinistra" followed it as an accompaniment. The comedies of Terence having been accompanied by the pipe, the following notices are prefixed to explain the kind of music appropriate to each: *tibiis paribus*, i. e. with pipes in the same mode; *tib. imparibus*, pipes in different modes; *tib. duabus dextris*, two pipes of low pitch; *tib. par. dextris et sinistris*, pipes in the same mode, and of both low and high pitch. The use of the pipe among the Greeks and Romans was threefold, viz. at sacrifices (*tibiae sacrificae*), entertainments (*ludicrae*), and funerals. The pipe was not confined anciently, as it is with us, to the male sex, but αὐλητρίδες, or female tibicines were very common.

TIMEMA (τίμημα). The penalty imposed in a court of criminal justice at Athens, and also the damages awarded in a civil action, received the name of Τίμημα, because they were estimated or assessed according to the injury which the public or the individual might respectively have sustained. The penalty was either fixed by the judge, or merely declared by him according to some estimate made before the cause came into court. In the first case the trial was called ἀγὼν τιμητός, in the second case ἀγὼν ἀτίμητος, a distinction which applies to civil as well as to criminal trials. Where a man sought to recover an estate in land, or a house, or any specific thing, as a ring, a horse, a slave, nothing further was required, than to determine to whom the estate, the house, or the thing demanded, of right belonged. The same would be the case in an action of debt, χρέους δίκη, where a sum certain was demanded. In these and many other similar cases the trial was ἀτίμητος. On the other hand, wherever the damages were in their nature *unliquidated*, and no provision had been made concerning them either by the law or by the agreement of the parties, they were to be assessed by the dicasts. The following was the course of proceeding in the τιμητοὶ ἀγῶνες. The bill of indictment (ἔγκλημα) was always superscribed with some penalty by the person who preferred it. He was said ἐπιγράφεσθαι τίμημα, and the penalty proposed is called ἐπίγραμμα. If the defendant was found guilty, the prosecutor was called upon to support the allegation in the indictment, and for that purpose to mount the platform and address the dicasts (ἀναβαίνειν εἰς τίμημα). If the accused submitted to the punishment proposed on the other side, there was no further dispute; if he thought it too severe, he made a counter proposition. He was then said ἀντιτιμᾶσθαι, or ἑαυτῷ τιμᾶσθαι. He was allowed to address the court in mitigation of punishment. After both parties had been heard, the dicasts were called upon to give their verdict. Sometimes the law expressly empowered the jury to impose an additional penalty (προστίμημα) besides the ordinary one. Here the proposition emanated from the jury themselves, any one of whom might move that the punishment allowed by the law should be awarded. He was said προστιμᾶσθαι, and the whole dicasts, if (upon a division) they adopted his proposal, were said προστιμᾶν.

TINTINNABULUM (κώδων), a bell. Bells were of various forms among the Greeks and Romans, as among us.

TIRO, the name given by the Romans to a newly enlisted soldier, as opposed to *veteranus*, one who had had experience in war. The mode of levying troops is described under EXERCITUS. The age at which the liability to military service commenced was 17. From their first enrolment the Roman soldiers, when not actually serving against an enemy, were perpetually occupied in military exercises. They were exercised every day, the tirones twice, in the morning and afternoon, and the veterani once. The state of a tiro was called *tirocinium*; and a soldier who had attained skill in his profession was then said *tirocinium ponere*, or *deponere*. In civil life the terms *tiro* and *tirocinium* were applied to the assumption of the toga virilis, which was called *tirocinium fori* [TOGA], and to the first appearance of an orator at the rostrum, *tirocinium eloquentiae*.

TIROCINIUM. [TIRO.]

TITII SODALES, a sodalitas or college of priests at Rome, who represented the second tribe of the Romans, or the Tities, that is, the Sabines, who, after their union with the Ramnes or Latins, continued to perform their own ancient Sabine sacra. To superintend and preserve these, T. Tatius is said to have instituted the Titii sodales. During the time of the republic the Titii sodales are no longer mentioned, as the sacra of the three tribes became gradually united into one common religion. Under the empire we again meet with a college of priests bearing the name of Sodales Titii or Titienses, or Sacerdotes Titiales Flaviales; but they had nothing to do with the sacra of the ancient tribe of the Tities, but were priests instituted to conduct the worship of an emperor, like the Augustales.

TITIES or TITIENSES. [PATRICII.]

TOGA (τήβεννος), a gown, the name of the principal outer garment worn by the Romans, seems to have been received by them from the Etruscans. The toga was the peculiar distinction of the Romans, who were thence called *togati* or *gens togata*. It was originally worn only in Rome itself, and the use of it was forbidden alike to exiles and to foreigners. Gradually, however, it went out of common use, and was supplanted by the pallium and lacerna, or else it was worn in public under the lacerna. [LACERNA.] But it was still used by the upper classes, who regarded it as an honourable distinction, in the courts of justice, by clients when they received the SPORTULA, and in the theatre or at the games, at least when the emperor was present. The exact form of the toga,

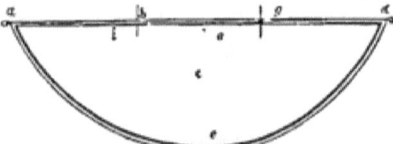

Fig. 1.—Form of the Toga spread out.

and the manner of wearing it, have occasioned much dispute; but the following account, for which the writer is indebted to his friend Mr. George Scharf, jun., will set these matters in a clearer light than has hitherto been the case. The complete arrangement of this dress may be seen in many antique statues, but especially in that of Didius Julianus,

Fig. 2.—Statue of Didius Julianus. (From the Louvre.)

in the Louvre, and a bronze figure of the elder Drusus discovered at Herculaneum. (See figs. 2, 3.) The letters upon particular parts

Fig. 3.—Bronze of the elder Drusus. (From Herculaneum.)

of the illustrations correspond with each other, and refer to the same places upon the general form of the toga given above. The method of adjusting the toga is simply this: the straight edge (a b g d) being kept towards the neck, and the rounded towards the hand, the first part of the toga hangs in front over the left shoulder to the ground (a, fig. 4), so as to cover that entire half of the figure viewed in front. The remainder falling behind is wrapped round the body, being carried under the right arm, and brought upwards, like a belt, across the chest, covering the left arm and shoulder for a second time. It again falls behind, and terminates in the point d (fig. 5), somewhat higher than the front portion (a). So far any mantle of sufficient length might be folded, but two distinctive features of Roman dress, the umbo (f) and the sinus (e e), have yet to be considered. The sinus (e e) is that upper hanging portion with the curved edge downwards which shows conspicuously upon the right thigh. When the toga has been brought round to the front of the right leg, it has attained its greatest width (c c e), although on the figure less space is required for it. It is therefore folded over at the top, the upper

part falling forward, down almost to the knee. It may be easily raised (see fig. 5) and used as a lap—hence the name sinus—

Fig. 4.   Fig. 5.
Mode of putting on the Toga.

to carry fruits and flowers, so often represented in ancient art. The fold at c thus becomes the upper edge, and forms the balteus, which may be made still more effective by being rolled round and slightly twisted, as in figs. 2 and 5. A variety again was sometimes produced by lifting the hanging edge (e) of this sinus up on to the shoulder, so as to cover the right arm with that alone, and Quintilian hints that it is not ungraceful to throw back the extreme edge of that again, an effect still to be admired in some of the ancient sculptures. Fig. 5 is in the act of raising the edge. The umbo (f), a projecting mass of folds in front of the body, like the boss of a shield, was formed *after* the rest of the dress had been put on in a very simple manner: a part of the front upright line (a b), almost covered up by the adjustment of the upper shoulder portion (g), was pulled out and made to hang down over the balteus or belt-like part (fig. 6). It is clearly traceable in both statues here given (figs. 2 and 3), and fig. 4 is intended to show the formation of the umbo more clearly by the right hand holding the edge, which falls over the fingers instead of the balteus. In proportion as the umbo (f) projects, so of course the end (a) is raised from the ground. The smaller figures (4 and 5) are both drawn without under-garments in order to avoid confusion. During sacrifice, when necessary to cover the head, the edge (b) nearest the neck was pulled up and made to cover the head, as in fig. 3, where the entire length of the edge, passing from the umbo into the sinus, is very clearly visible. The dress here is very ample, and can spare an extra length, but in the statue of a priest in the Louvre the head is covered at the expense of the umbo, which has entirely disappeared. Fig. 6 is intended to show the interlacing and arrangement of the toga by following the course of the straight edge alone from *a* to *d*. In many ancient sta-

Fig. 6.

tues the sleeves and folds of the tunic, being very full, are apt to be confounded with the rest, but in the best style of art this is not the case. Quintilian cautions his orators against these incumbrances. A difference in size and fulness of the toga, modified according to the rank of the wearer, may be detected in coins and sculpture, but in all cases the mode of adjustment appears to be the same.—One mode of wearing the toga was the Cinctus Gabinus. It consisted in forming a part of the toga itself into a girdle, by drawing its outer edge round the body and tying it in a knot in front, and at the same time covering the head with another portion of the garment. It was worn by persons offering sacrifices, by the consul when he declared war, and by devoted persons, as in the case of Decius. Its origin was Etruscan, as its name implies. Persons wearing this dress were said to be *procincti* (or *incincti*) *cinctu* (or *ritu*) *Gabino*.—The colour of the toga worn by men (*toga virilis*) was generally white, that is, the natural colour of white wool. Hence it was called *pura* or *vestimentum purum*, in opposition to the *praetexta* mentioned below. A brighter white was given to the toga of candidates for offices (*candidati* from their *toga candida*) by rubbing it with chalk. There is an allusion to this custom in the phrase *cretata ambitio*. White togas are often mentioned as worn at festivals, which does not imply that they were not worn commonly, but that new or fresh-cleaned togas were first put on at festivals. The toga was kept white and clean by the fuller. When this was neglected, the toga was called *sordida*, and those who wore such garments *sordidati*. This dress (with disarranged hair and other marks of disorder about the person) was worn by accused persons, as in the case of Cicero. The *toga pulla*, which was of the natural colour of black wool, was worn in private mourning, and sometimes also by artificers and others of the lower orders.— The *toga picta*, which was ornamented with Phrygian embroidery, was worn by generals in triumphs [TRIUMPHUS], and under the emperors by the consuls, and by the praetors when they celebrated the games. It was also called *Capitolina*. The *toga palmata* was a kind of toga picta.—The *toga praetexta* had a broad purple border. It was worn with the BULLA, by children of both sexes. It was also worn by magistrates, both those of Rome, and those of the colonies and municipia; by the sacerdotes, and by persons engaged in sacred rites or paying vows. Among those who possessed the *jus togae praetextae habendae*, the following may be more particularly mentioned: the dictator, the consuls, the praetors (who laid aside the praetexta when about to condemn a Roman citizen to death), the augurs (who, however, are supposed by some to have worn the trabea), the decemviri sacris faciundis, the aediles, the triumviri epulones, the senators on festival days, the magistri collegii, and the magistri vicorum when celebrating games. In the case of the tribuni plebis, censors, and quaestors, there is some doubt upon the subject. The toga praetexta is said to have been derived from the Etruscans, and to have been first adopted, with the latus clavus [CLAVUS LATUS], by Tullus Hostilius as the royal robe, whence its use by the magistrates in the republic. The toga praetexta and the bulla aurea were first given to boys in the case of the son of Tarquinius Priscus, who, at the age of fourteen, in the Sabine war, slew an enemy with his own hand. Respecting the leaving off of the toga praetexta, and the assumption of the toga virilis, see IMPUBES and CLAVUS LATUS. The occasion was celebrated with great rejoicings by the friends of the youth, who attended him in a solemn procession to the Forum and Capitol. This assumption of the toga virilis was called *tirocinium fori*, as being the young man's introduction to public life. Girls wore the praetexta till their marriage.—The *trabea* was a toga ornamented with purple horizontal stripes. There were three kinds of trabeae; one wholly of purple, which was sacred to the gods, another of purple and white, and another of purple and saffron, which belonged to augurs. The purple and white trabea was a royal robe, and is assigned to the Latin and early Roman kings, especially to Romulus. It was worn by the consuls in ublic solemnities, such as opening the temple of Janus. The equites wore it at the *transvectio*, and in other public solemnities. Hence the *trabea* is mentioned as the badge of the equestrian order. Lastly, the toga worn by the Roman emperors was wholly of purple. It appears to have been first assumed by Julius Caesar.—The material of which the toga was commonly made was wool. It was sometimes thick and sometimes thin. The former was the *toga densa, pinguis*, or *hirta*. A new toga, with the nap neither worn off nor cut close, was called *ucra*, to which is opposed the *trita* or *rasa*, which was used as a summer dress. The toga was originally worn by both sexes; but when the stola came to be worn by matrons, the toga was only worn by the meretrices, and by women who had been divorced on account of adultery. [STOLA.] In war the toga was laid aside, and replaced by the PALUDAMENTUM and SAGUM. Hence *togatus* is opposed to *miles*.

TONSOR. [BARBA.]

TORCŬLAR, TORCŬLUM. [VINUM.]

TORMENTUM (ἀφετήρια ὄργανα), a military engine, so called from the twisting (*torquendo*) of hairs, thongs, and vegetable fibres. The principal military engines were the *balista* and *catapulta*. The *balista* (πετροβόλος) was used to shoot stones; the *catapulta* (καταπέλτης, καταπελτική) to project darts, especially the falarica [HASTA], and a kind of missile, 4½ feet long, called *trifax*. Whilst in besieging a city the ram [ARIES] was employed in destroying the lower part of the wall, the balista was used to overthrow the battlements (*propugnacula*, ἐπάλξεις), and the catapult to shoot any of the besieged who appeared between them: the forms of these machines being adapted to the objects which they were intended to throw; the catapult was long, the balista nearly square. Instances are recorded in which the balista threw stones to the distance of a quarter of a mile. Some balistae threw stones weighing three hundredweight. Of the *scorpio* or *onager*, which was also a species of tormentum, we know next to nothing.

TORMENTUM (βάσανος), torture. (1) GREEK.—By a decree of Scamandrius it was ordained that no free Athenian could be put to the torture, and this appears to have been the general practice. The evidence of slaves was, however, always taken with torture, and their testimony was not otherwise received. From this circumstance their testimony appears to have been considered of more value than that of freemen. Any person might offer his own slave to be examined by torture, or demand that of his adversary, and he offer or demand was equally called πρόκλησις εἰς βάσανον. The parties interested either superintended the torture themselves, or chose certain persons for this purpose, hence called βασανισταί, who took the evidence of the slaves. (2) ROMAN.—During the time of the republic freemen were never put to the torture, and slaves only were exposed to this punishment. Slaves, moreover, could not be tortured to prove the guilt of their own master, except in the case of incestus, which was a crime against the gods, or unless the senate made an exception in some special instance. At a later time slaves might be tortured to bear witness against their masters in cases of majestas and adultery. Under the emperors even free persons were put to the torture to extract evidence from them in cases of majestas; and although this indignity was confined for the most part to persons in humble circumstances, we read of cases in which even Roman senators and equites were exposed to it.

TORQUES or TORQUIS (στρεπτός), an ornament of gold, twisted spirally and bent into a circular form, which was worn round the neck by men of distinction among the Persians, the Gauls, and other Asiatic and northern nations. It was by taking a collar from a Gallic warrior that T. Manlius obtained the cognomen of *Torquatus*. Such collars were among the rewards of valour bestowed after an engagement upon those who had most distinguished themselves.

TŎRUS, a bed covered with sheets or blankets, called *Toralia*.

TRĂBEA. [TOGA.]

TRAGOEDIA (τραγῳδία), tragedy. (1) GREEK. The tragedy of the ancient Greeks as well as their comedy confessedly originated in the worship of the god Dionysus. The peculiarity which most strikingly distinguishes the Greek tragedy from that of modern times, is the lyrical or choral part. This was the offspring of the dithyrambic and choral odes from which, as applied to the worship of Dionysus, Greek tragedy took its rise. The name of Tragedy (τραγῳδία) is probably derived from the goatlike appearance of the Satyrs who sang or acted with mimetic gesticulations (ὄρχησις) the old Bacchic songs, with Silenus, the constant companion of Dionysus, for their leader. The Dionysian dithyrambs were sometimes of a gay and at other times of a mournful character: it was from the latter that the stately and solemn tragedy of the Greeks arose. Great improvements were introduced in the dithyramb by Arion, a contemporary of Periander. Before his time the dithyramb was sung in a wild and irregular manner; but he is said to have invented the Cyclic chorus, by which we are to understand that the

Dithyramb was danced by a chorus of fifty men round an altar. The choral Dithyrambic songs prevailed to some extent, as all choral poetry did, amongst the Dorians of the Peloponnesus; whence the choral element of the Attic tragedy was always written in the Dorian dialect, thus showing its origin. The lyrical poetry was, however, especially popular at Sicyon and Corinth. In the latter city Arion made his improvements; in the former "tragic choruses," i. e. dithyrambs of a sad and plaintive character, were very ancient. From the more solemn Dithyrambs then, as improved by Arion, ultimately sprang the dramatic tragedy of Athens, somewhat in the following manner. The choruses were under the direction of a leader or exarchus, who, it may be supposed, came forward separately, and whose part was sometimes taken by the poet himself. We may also conjecture that the exarchus in each case led off by singing or reciting his part in a solo, and that the chorus dancing round the altar then expressed their feelings of joy or sorrow at his story, representing the perils and sufferings of Dionysus, or some hero, as it might be. The subjects of this Dithyrambic tragedy were not, however, always confined to Dionysus. Even Arion wrote Dithyrambs, relating to different heroes, a practice in which he was followed by succeeding poets. It is easy to conceive how the introduction of an actor or speaker independent of the chorus might have been suggested by the exarchs coming forward separately and making short off-hand speeches, whether learnt by heart beforehand, or made on the spur of the moment. [CHORUS.] But it is also possible, if not probable, that it was suggested by the rhapsodical recitations of the epic and gnomic poets formerly prevalent in Greece : the gnomic poetry being generally written in Iambic verse, the metre of the Attic dialogue. This however is certain, that the union of the Iambic dialogue with the lyrical chorus took place at Athens under Pisistratus, and that it was attributed to Thespis, a native of Icaria, one of the country demes or parishes of Attica where the worship of Dionysus had long prevailed. The alteration made by him, and which gave to the old tragedy a new and dramatic character, was very simple but very important. He introduced an actor, as it is recorded, for the sake of giving rest to the chorus, and independent of it, in which capacity he probably appeared himself, taking various parts in the same piece, under various disguises, which he was enabled to assume by means of linen masks, the invention of which is attributed to him. Now as a chorus, by means of its leader, could maintain a dialogue with the actor, it is easy to see how with one actor only a dramatic action might be introduced, continued, and concluded, by the speeches between the choral songs expressive of the joy or sorrow of the chorus at the various events of the drama. With respect to the character of the drama of Thespis there has been much doubt: some writers, and especially Bentley, have maintained that his plays were all satyrical and ludicrous, i. e. the plot of them was some story of Bacchus, the chorus consisted principally of satyrs, and the argument was merry. But perhaps the truth is that in the early part of his career Thespis retained the satyrical character of the older tragedy, but afterwards inclined to more serious compositions, which would almost oblige him to discard the Satyrs from his choruses. That he did write serious dramas is intimated by the titles of the plays ascribed to him, as well as by the character of the fragments of Iambic verse quoted by ancient writers as his. It is evident that the introduction of the dialogue must also have caused an alteration in the arrangement of the chorus, which could not remain cyclic or circular, but must have been drawn up in a rectangular form about the thymele or altar of Bacchus in front of the actor, who was elevated on a platform or table (ἐλεός), the forerunner of the stage. The lines of Horace (*Ar. Poet.* 276) :—

" Dicitur et plaustris vexisse poemata Thespis,
Quae canerent agerentque peruncti faecibus ora "—

are founded on a misconception of the origin of the Attic tragedy, and the tale about the waggons of Thespis probably arose out of a confusion of the waggon of the comedian Susarion with the *platform* of the Thespian actor. The first representation of Thespis was in B. c. 535. His immediate successors were the Athenian Choerilus and Phrynichus, the former of whom represented plays as early as B. c. 524. Phrynichus was a pupil of Thespis, and gained his first victory in the dramatic contests B.C. 511. In his works, the lyric or choral element still predominated over the dramatic, and he was distinguished for the sweetness of his melodies, which in the time of the Peloponnesian war were very popular with the admirers of the old style of music. The first use of female masks is also attributed to him, and he so far deviated from the general practice of the Attic tragedians as to write a drama on a subject of contemporary history, the capture of Miletus by the Persians, B. c. 494.—We now come to the first writer of Satyrical dramas, Pratinas of Phlius, a town not far from Sicyon, and which laid claim to the invention of tragedy as well as comedy.

For some time previously to this poet, and probably as early as Thespis, tragedy had been gradually departing more and more from its old characteristics, and inclining to heroic fables, to which the chorus of Satyrs was not a fit accompaniment. But the fun and merriment caused by them were too good to be lost. Accordingly the Satyrical drama, distinct from the recent and dramatic tragedy, but suggested by the sportive element of the old Dithyramb, was founded by Pratinas, who however appears to have been surpassed in his own invention by Choerilus. It was always written by tragedians, and generally three tragedies and one Satyrical piece were represented together, which in some instances at least formed a connected whole, called a tetralogy (τετραλογία). The Satyrical piece was acted last, so that the minds of the spectators were agreeably relieved by a merry after-piece at the close of an earnest and engrossing tragedy. The distinguishing feature of this drama was the chorus of Satyrs, in appropriate dresses and masks, and its subjects seem to have been taken from the same class of the adventures of Bacchus and of the heroes as those of tragedy; but of course they were so treated and selected, that the presence of rustic satyrs would seem appropriate. In their jokes and drollery consisted the merriment of the piece; for the kings and heroes who were introduced into their company were not of necessity thereby divested of their epic and legendary character, though they were obliged to conform to their situation and suffer some diminution of dignity, from their position. Hence Horace (*Ar. Poet.* 231) says:—

"Effutire leves indigna Tragoedia versus
Intererit Satyris paulum pudibunda protervis."—

alluding in the first line to the mythic or epic element of the Satyric drama, which he calls Tragoedia, and in the second representing it as being rather ashamed of its company. The "Cyclops" of Euripides is the only Satyric drama now extant.—The great improvements in tragedy were introduced by Aeschylus. This poet added a second actor, diminished the parts of the chorus, and made the dialogue the principal part of the action. He also availed himself of the aid of Agatharchus, the scene-painter, and improved the costume of his actors by giving them thick-soled boots (ἐμβάται), as well as the masks, which he made more expressive and characteristic. Horace (*Ar. Poet.* 278) thus alludes to his improvements:—

"personae pallaeque repertor honestae
Aeschylus, et modicis instravit pulpita tignis
Et docuit magnumque loqui, nitique cothurno."—

The custom of contending with trilogies (τριλογίαι), or with three plays at a time, is said to have been also introduced by him. In fact he did so much for tragedy, and so completely built it up to its "towering height," that he was considered the father of it. The subjects of his dramas were not connected with the worship of Dionysus; but rather with the great cycle of Hellenic legends and some of the myths of the Homeric Epos. Accordingly, he said of himself that his dramas were but scraps and fragments from the great feasts of Homer. In the latter part of his life Aeschylus made use of one of the improvements of Sophocles, namely the τριταγωνιστής, or third actor. This was the finishing stroke to the dramatic element of Attic tragedy, which Sophocles is said to have matured by further improvements in costume and scene-painting. Under him tragedy appears with less of sublimity and sternness than in the hands of Aeschylus, but with more of calm grandeur and quiet dignity and touching incident. The plays of Sophocles are the perfection of the Grecian tragic drama, as a work of art and poetic composition in a thoroughly chastened and classic style. In the hands of Euripides tragedy deteriorated not only in dignity, but also in its moral and religious significance. He introduces his heroes in rags and tatters, and busies them with petty affairs, and makes them speak the language of every-day life. As Sophocles said of him, he represented men not as they ought to be, but as they are, without any ideal greatness or poetic character. His dialogues too were little else than the rhetorical and forensic language of his day cleverly put into verse: full of sophistry and quibbling distinctions. One of the peculiarities of his tragedies was the πρόλογος, an introductory monologue, with which some hero or god opens the play, telling who he is, what is the state of affairs, and what has happened up to the time of his address, so as to put the audience in possession of every fact which it might be necessary for them to know: a very business-like proceeding no doubt, but a poor make-shift for artistical skill. The "Deus ex machina," also, though not always, in a "nodus, tali vindice dignus," was frequently employed by Euripides to effect the dénoûment of his pieces. The chorus too no longer discharged its proper and high functions either as a representative of the feelings of unprejudiced observers, or, as one of the actors, and a part of the whole, joining in the development of the piece. Many of his choral odes in fact are but remotely connected in subject with the action of the play. Another novelty of Euripides was the use of the monodies or lyrical songs, in which not the chorus, but the principal persons of the drama, declare their emotions and sufferings. Euripides was also the inventor of tragi-comedy. A specimen of the Euripidean tragi-comedy is still extant in the Alcestis, acted B. c. 438, as the last of four pieces, and therefore as a substitute for a Satyrical drama. Though tragic in its form and some of its scenes, it has a mixture of comic and satyric characters (e. g. Hercules) and concludes happily.—The parts which constitute a Greek tragedy, *as to its form*, are, the prologue, episode, exode, and choral songs; the last divided into the parode and stasimon. The πρόλογος is all that part of a tragedy which precedes the parodos of the chorus, *i. e.* the first act. The ἐπεισόδιον is all the part between whole choral odes. The ἔξοδος that part which has no choral ode after it. Of the choral part the πάροδος is the first speech of the whole chorus (not broken up into parts): the stasimon is without anapaests and trochees. These two divisions were sung by all the choreutae, but the "songs on the stage" and the κόμμοι by a part only. The commus, which properly means a wailing for the dead, was generally used to express strong excitement, or lively sympathy with grief and suffering, especially by Aeschylus. It was common to the actors and a portion only of the chorus. Again the πάροδος was so named as being the passage-song of the chorus sung while it was advancing to its proper place in the orchestra, and therefore in anapaestic or marching verse: the στάσιμον, as being chaunted by the chorus when standing still in its proper position.—The materials of Greek tragedy were the national mythology,

"Presenting Thebes, or Pelop's line,
Or the tale of Troy divine."

The exceptions to this were the two historical tragedies, the "Capture of Miletus," by Phrynichus, and the "Persians" of Aeschylus; but they belong to an early period of the art. Hence the plot and story of the Grecian tragedy were of necessity known to the spectators, a circumstance which strongly distinguishes the ancient tragedy from the modern.—The functions of the Chorus in Greek Tragedy were very important, as described by Horace (Ar. Poet. 193),

"Actoris partes chorus officiumque virile
Defendat: neu quid medios intercinat actus,
Quod non proposito conducat, et haereat apte," &c.

It often expresses the reflections of a dispassionate and right-minded spectator, and inculcates the lessons of morality and resignation to the will of heaven, taught by the occurrence of the piece in which it is engaged. With respect to the number of the chorus see CHORUS.—(2) ROMAN. The tragedy of the Romans was borrowed from the Greek; but the construction of the Roman theatre afforded no appropriate place for the chorus, which was therefore obliged to appear on the stage, instead of in the orchestra. The first tragic poet and actor at Rome was Livius Andronicus, a Greek by birth, who began to exhibit in B. c. 240. In his monodies (or the lyrical parts sung, not by a chorus, but by one person), it was customary to separate the singing from the mimetic dancing, leaving the latter only to the actor, while the singing was performed by a boy placed near the flute-player (*ante tibicinem*); so that the dialogue only (*diverbia*) was left to be spoken by the actors. Livius Andronicus was followed by Naevius, Ennius, Pacuvius, and Attius. These five poets belong to the earlier epoch of Roman tragedy, in which little was written but translations and imitations of the Greek, with occasional insertions of original matter. How they imitated the structure of the choral odes is doubtful—perhaps they never attempted it. In the age of Augustus the writing of tragedies, whether original or imitations, seems to have been quite a fashionable occupation. The emperor himself attempted an Ajax, but did not succeed. One of the principal tragedians of this epoch was Asinius Pollio, to whom the line (Virg. *Eclog.* viii. 10) applies—

"Sola Sophocleo tua carmina digna cothurno."

Ovid wrote a tragedy on the subject of Medea. Quintilian says of Varius, who was distinguished in epic as well as tragic poetry, that his Thyestes might be compared with any of the Greek tragedies. Some fragments of this Thyestes are extant, but we have no other remains of the tragedy of the Augustan age. The loss perhaps is not great. The only complete Roman tragedies that have come down to us are the ten attributed to the philosopher Seneca; but whether he wrote any of them or not is a disputed point. To whatever age they belong, they are beyond description bombastic and frigid, utterly unnatural in character and action, full of the most revolting violations of propriety, and barren of all theatrical effect. Still they have had admirers: Heinsius calls the Hippolytus "divine," and prefers the Troades to the Hecuba of Euripides: even Racine has borrowed from the Hippolytus in Phèdre. Roman tragedians sometimes wrote tragedies on subjects taken from their national history Pacuvius, *e. g.* wrote a *Paulus*, L. Accius a *Brutus* and a *Decius*. Curiatius Maternus, also a distinguished orator in the reign of Domitian, wrote a Domitius and a Cato, the latter of which gave offence to the rulers of the state.

TRĀGŬLA. [HASTA.]
TRANSTRA. [NAVIS.]
TRANSVECTIO EQUITUM. [EQUITES, p. 157.]
TRIARII. [EXERCITUS.]
TRIBŬLA or **TRIBŬLUM** (τρίβολος), a corn-drag, consisting of a thick and ponderous wooden board, which was armed underneath with pieces of iron or sharp flints, and drawn over the corn by a yoke of oxen, either the driver or a heavy weight being placed upon it, for the purpose of separating the grain and cutting the straw.

TRIBŬLUS (τρίβολος), a caltrop, also called *murex*. When a place was beset with troops, the one party endeavoured to impede the cavalry of the other party, either by throwing before them caltrops, which necessarily lay with one of their four sharp points turned upwards, or by burying the caltrops with one point at the surface of the ground.

TRIBŪNAL, a raised platform, on which the praetor and judices sat in the Basilica. [BASILICA.] There was a tribunal in the camp, which was generally formed of turf, but sometimes, in a stationary camp, of stone, from which the general addressed the soldiers, and where the consul and tribunes of the soldiers administered justice. When the general addressed the army from the tribunal the standards were planted in front of it, and the army placed round it in order. The address itself was called *Allocutio*.

TRIBŪNUS, a tribune. This word seems originally to have indicated an officer connected with a tribe (*tribus*), or who represented a tribe for certain purposes; and this is indeed the character of the officers who were designated by it in the earliest times of Rome, and may be traced also in the later officers of this name.—(1) TRIBUNES OF THE THREE ANCIENT TRIBES.—At the time when all the Roman citizens were contained in the three tribes of the Ramnes, Tities, and Luceres, each of them was headed by a tribune, and these three tribunes represented their respective tribes in all civil, religious, and military affairs; that is to say, they were in the city the magistrates of the tribes, and performed the *sacra* on their behalf, and in times of war they were their military commanders. The *tribunus celerum* was the commander of the *celeres*, the king's bodyguard, and not the tribune of the tribe of the Ramnes, as is supposed by some modern writers. In what manner the tribunus celerum was appointed is uncertain, but it is probable that he was elected by the tribes; for we find that when the imperium was to be conferred upon the king, the comitia were held under the presidency of the tribunus celerum; and in the absence of the king, to whom this officer was next in rank, he convoked the comitia: it was in an assembly of this kind that Brutus proposed to deprive Tarquinius of the imperium. A law passed under the presidency of the tribunus celerum was called a *lex tribunicia*, to distinguish it from one passed under the presidency of the king. The tribunes of the three ancient tribes ceased to be appointed when these tribes themselves ceased to exist as political bodies, and when the patricians became incorporated in the local tribes of Servius Tullius. [TRIBUS.]—(2) TRIBUNES OF THE SERVIAN TRIBES (φύλαρχοι, τριττυάρχοι).—When Servius Tullius divided the commonalty into thirty local tribes, we again find a tribune at the head of these tribes. The duties of these tribunes, who were without doubt the most distinguished persons in their respective districts, appear to have consisted at first in keeping a register of the inhabitants in each district, and of their property, for purposes of taxation, and for levying the troops for the armies. When subsequently the Roman people became exempted from taxes, the main part of their business was taken from them, but they still continued to exist. The *tribuni aerarii*, who occur down to the end of the republic, were perhaps only the successors of the tribunes of the tribes. When (B.C. 406) the custom of giving pay (*stipendium*) to the soldiers was introduced, each of the tribuni aerarii had to collect the tributum in his own tribe, and with it to pay the soldiers; and in case they did not fulfil this duty, the soldiers had the right of pignoris capio against them. In later times their duties appear to have been confined to collecting the tributum, which they made over to the military quaestors who paid the soldiers. [QUAESTOR.] The Lex Aurelia, B.C. 70, called the tribuni aerarii to the exercise of judicial functions, along with the senators and equites, as these tribunes represented the body of the most respectable citizens. But of this distinction they were subsequently deprived by Julius Caesar.—(3) TRIBUNI PLEBIS (δήμαρχοι, the office δημαρχία).—The ancient tribunes of the plebeian tribes had undoubtedly the right of convoking the meetings of their tribes, and of maintaining the privileges granted to them by king Servius, and subsequently by the Valerian laws. But this protection was very inadequate against the insatiable ambition and usurpations of the patricians. When the plebeians, impoverished by long wars, and cruelly oppressed by the patricians, at last seceded in B.C. 494 to the Mons Sacer, the patricians were obliged to grant to the plebeians the right of appointing tribunes (*tribuni plebis*) with more efficient powers to protect their own order than those which were possessed by the heads of the tribes. The purpose for which they were appointed was only to afford protection against any abuse on the part of the patrician magistrates; and that they might be able to afford such protection their persons were declared sacred and inviolable, and it was agreed that whoever invaded this inviolability should be an outlaw, and that his property should be forfeited to the temple of Ceres. A subsequent law enacted that no one should oppose or interrupt a tribune while addressing the people, and that whoever should act contrary to this ordinance should give bail to the tribunes for the payment of whatever fine they should affix to his offence in arraigning him before the commonalty; if he refused to give bail, his life and property were forfeited. The tribunes were thus enabled to afford protection to any one who appealed to the assembly of the commonalty or required any other assistance. They were essentially the representatives and the organs of the plebeian order, and their sphere of action was the comitia tributa. With the patricians and their comitia they had nothing to do. The tribunes themselves, however, were not judges, and could inflict no punishments, but could only propose the imposition of a fine to the commonalty (*multam irrogare*). The tribunes were thus in their origin only a protecting magistracy of the plebs, but in the course of time their power increased to such a degree that it surpassed that of all other magistrates, and the tribunes then became a magistracy for the whole Roman people, in opposition to the senate and the oligarchical party in general, although they had nothing to do with the administration or the government. During the latter period of the republic they became true tyrants, and may be compared to the national convention of France during the first revolution. At first the number of the tribunes was only two, but soon afterwards they were increased to five, one being taken from each of the five classes, and subsequently to ten, two being taken from each of the five classes. This last number appears to have remained unaltered down to the end of the empire. The tribunes entered upon their office on the 10th of December, but were elected, at least in the time of Cicero, on the 17th of July. It is almost superfluous to state that none but plebeians were eligible to the office of tribune; hence when, towards the end of the republic, patricians wished to obtain the office, they were obliged first to renounce their own order and to become plebeians; hence also under the empire it was thought that the princeps should not be tribune because he was a patrician. But the influence which belonged to this office was too great for the emperors not to covet it. Hence Augustus was made tribune for life. During the republic, however, the old regulation remained in force, even after the tribunes had ceased to be the protectors of the plebs alone. There is only one instance recorded in which patricians were elected to the tribuneship, and this was probably the consequence of an attempt to divide the tribuneship between the two orders. Although nothing appears to be more natural than that the tribunes should originally have been elected by that body of Roman citizens which they represented, yet the subject is involved in considerable obscurity. Some writers state that they were elected by the comitia of the curies; others suppose that they were elected in the comitia of the centuries; but whether they were elected in the latter or in the comitia of the tribes, it is certain that at first the sanction of the curies to the election was at all events necessary. But after the time of the Lex Publilia (B.C. 472) the sanction of the curies is not heard of, and the election of the tribunes was left entirely to the comitia tributa, which were convoked and held for this purpose by the old tribunes previous to the expiration of their office. One of the old tribunes was appointed by lot to preside at the election. As the meeting could not be prolonged after sunset, and the business was to be completed in one day, it sometimes happened that it was obliged to break up before the election was completed, and then those who were elected filled up the legitimate number of the college by cooptatio. But in order to prevent this irregularity, the tribune L. Trebonius, in 448 B.C., got an ordinance passed, according to which the college of the tribunes should never be completed by cooptatio, but the elections should be continued on the second day, if they were not completed on the first, till the number ten was made up. The place where the election of the tribunes was held was originally and lawfully the Forum, afterwards also the Campus Martius, and sometimes the area of the Capitol.—We now proceed to trace the gradual growth of the tribunitian power. Although its original character was merely protection (*auxilium* or βοήθεια) against patrician magistrates, the plebeians appear early to have regarded their tribunes also as mediators or arbitrators in matters among themselves. The whole power possessed by the college of tribunes was designated by the name *tribunicia potestas*, and extended at no time farther than one mile beyond the gates of the city; at a greater distance than this they came under the imperium of the magistrates, like every other citizen. As they were the public guardians, it was necessary that every one should have access to them and at any time; hence the doors of their houses were open day and night for all who were in need of help and protection, which they were empowered to afford against any one, even against the highest magistrates. For the same reason a tribune was not allowed to be absent from the city for a whole day, except during the Feriae Latinae, when the whole people were assembled on the Alban Mount. In B. c. 456 the tribunes, in opposition to the consuls, assumed the right of convoking the senate, in order to lay before it a rogation, and discuss the same; for until that time the consuls alone had had the right of laying plebiscita before the senate for approbation. Some years after, B. c. 452, the tribunes demanded of the consuls to request the senate to make a senatusconsultum for the appointment of persons to frame a new legislation; and during the discussions on this subject the tribunes themselves were present in the senate. The written legislation which the tribunes then wished can only have related to their own order; but as such a legislation would only have widened the breach between the two orders, they afterwards gave way to the remonstrances of the patricians, and the new legislation was to embrace both orders. From the second decemvirate the tribuneship was suspended, but was restored after the legislation was completed, and now assumed a different character from the change that had taken place in the tribes. [TRIBUS.] The tribunes now had the right to be present at the deliberations of the senate; but they did not sit among the senators themselves, but upon benches before the opened doors of the senate house. The inviolability of the tribunes, which had before only rested upon a contract between the two estates, was now sanctioned and confirmed by a law of M. Horatius. As the tribes now also included the patricians and their clients, the tribunes might naturally be asked to interpose on behalf of any citizen, whether patrician or plebeian. Hence the patrician ex-decemvir, Appius Claudius, implored the protection of the tribunes. About this time the tribunes also acquired the right of taking the auspices in the assemblies of the tribes. They also assumed again the right, which they had exercised before the time of the decemvirate, of bringing patricians who had violated the rights of the plebeians before the comitia of the tribes. By the Lex Valeria passed in the Comitia Centuriata (B. c. 449), it was enacted that a plebiscitum, which had been voted by the tribes, should bind the patricians as well. While the college thus gained outwardly new strength every day, a change took place in its internal organisation, which to some extent paralysed its powers. Before B.C. 394, every thing had been decided in the college by a majority; but about this time, we do not know how, a change was introduced, which made the opposition (*intercessio*) of one tribune sufficient to render a resolution of his colleagues void. This new regulation does not appear in operation till 394 and 393 B. c.; the old one was still applied in B. c. 421 and 415. From their right of appearing in the senate, and of taking part in its discussions, and from their being the representatives of the whole people, they gradually obtained the right of intercession against any action which a magistrate might undertake during the time of his office, and this even without giving any reason for it. Thus we find a tribune preventing a consul from convoking the senate, and preventing the proposal of new laws or elections in the comitia; they interceded against the official functions of the censors; and even against a command issued by the praetor. In the same manner a tribune might place his veto upon an ordinance of the senate; and he could thus either compel the senate to submit the subject to a fresh consideration, or could raise the session. In order to propose a measure to the senate they might themselves convene a meeting, or when it had been convened by a consul they might make their proposal even in opposition to the consul, a right which no other magistrates had in the presence of the consuls. The senate, on the other hand, had itself, in certain cases, recourse to the tribunes. Thus, in B. c. 431 it requested the tribunes to compel the consuls to appoint a dictator, in compliance with a decree of the senate, and the tribunes compelled the consuls, by threatening them with imprisonment, to appoint A. Postumius Tubertus dictator. From this time forward we meet with several instances in which the tribunes compelled the consuls to comply with the decrees of the senate, *si non essent in auctoritate senatus*, and to execute its commands. In their relation to the senate a change was introduced by the *Plebiscitum Atinium*, which ordained that a tribune, by virtue of his office, should be a senator. When this plebiscitum was made is uncertain; but we know that in B. c. 170 it was not yet in operation. It probably originated with C. Atinius, who was tribune in B. c. 132.

But as the quaestorship, at least in later times, was the office which persons held previously to the tribuneship, and as the quaestorship itself conferred upon a person the right of a senator, the law of Atinius was in most cases superfluous.—In their relation to other magistrates we may observe, that the right of intercessio was not confined to stopping a magistrate in his proceedings, but they might even command their viatores to seize a consul or a censor, to imprison him, or to throw him from the Tarpeian rock. When the tribunes brought an accusation against any one before the people, they had the right of *prehensio*, but not the right of *vocatio*, that is, they might command a person to be dragged by their viatores before the comitia, but they could not summon him. They might, as in earlier times, propose a fine to be inflicted upon the person accused before the comitia, but in some cases they dropped this proposal and treated the case as a capital one. The college of tribunes had also the power of making edicts. In cases in which one member of the college opposed a resolution of his colleagues nothing could be done, and the measure was dropped; but this useful check was removed by the example of Tiberius Gracchus, in which a precedent was given for proposing to the people that a tribune obstinately persisting in his veto should be deprived of his office. From the time of the Hortensian law the power of the tribunes had been gradually rising to such a height that at length it was superior to every other in the state. They had acquired the right of proposing to the comitia tributa or the senate measures on nearly all the important affairs of the state, and it would be endless to enumerate the cases in which their power was manifested. Their proposals were indeed usually made ex auctoritate senatus, or had been communicated to and approved by it; but cases in which the people itself had a direct interest, such as a general legal regulation, granting of the franchise, a change in the duties and powers of a magistrate, and others, might be brought before the people, without their having been previously communicated to the senate, though there are also instances of the contrary. Subjects belonging to the administration could not be brought before the tribes without the tribunes having previously received through the consuls the auctoritas of the senate. This, however, was done very frequently, and hence we have mention of a number of plebiscita on matters of administration. It sometimes even occurs that the tribunes brought the question concerning the conclusion of peace before the tribes, and then compelled the senate to ratify the resolution, as expressing the wish of the whole people. Sulla, in his reform of the constitution on the early aristocratic principles, left to the tribunes only the jus auxiliandi, and deprived them of the right of making legislative or other proposals, either to the senate or the comitia, without having previously obtained the sanction of the senate. But this arrangement did not last, for Pompey restored to them their former rights. During the latter period of the republic, when the office of quaestor was in most cases held immediately before that of tribune, the tribunes were generally elected from among the senators, and this continued to be the case under the empire. Sometimes, however, equites also obtained the office, and thereby became members of the senate, where they were considered of equal rank with the quaestors. Tribunes of the people continued to exist down to the fifth century of our era, though their powers became naturally much limited, especially in the reign of Nero. They continued however to have the right of intercession against decrees of the senate, and on behalf of injured individuals.—(4) TRIBUNI MILITUM CUM CONSULARI POTESTATE. When in B. C. 445 the tribune C. Canuleius brought forward the rogation that the consulship should not be confined to either order, the patricians evaded the attempt by a change in the constitution; the powers which had hitherto been united in the consulship were now divided between two new magistrates, viz. the *Tribuni militum cum consulari potestate* and the censors. Consequently, in B. C. 444, three military tribunes, with consular power, were appointed, and to this office the plebeians were to be equally eligible with the patricians. For the years following, however, the people were to be at liberty, on the proposal of the senate, to decide whether consuls were to be elected according to the old custom, or consular tribunes. Henceforth, for many years, sometimes consuls and sometimes consular tribunes were appointed, and the number of the latter varied from three to four, until in B. C. 405 it was increased to six, and as the censors were regarded as their colleagues, we have sometimes mention of eight tribunes. At last, however, in B. C. 367, the office of these tribunes was abolished by the Licinian law, and the consulship was restored. These consular tribunes were elected in the comitia of the centuries, and undoubtedly with less solemn auspices than the consuls.—(5) TRIBUNI MILITARES [EXERCITUS, p. 169.]

TRIBUS (φῦλον, φυλή), a tribe. (1) GREEK. In the earliest times of Greek history mention is made of people being divided into tribes and clans. Homer speaks of such divisions in terms which seem to imply that they were elements that entered into the composition of every community. A person not included in any clan (ἀφρήτωρ), was regarded as a vagrant or outlaw. These divisions were rather natural than political, depending on family connection, and arising out of those times, when each head of a family exercised a patriarchal sway over its members. The bond was cemented by religious communion, sacrifices and festivals, which all the family or clansmen attended, and at which the chief usually presided. —Of the Dorian race there were originally three tribes, traces of which are found in all the countries which they colonised. Hence they are called by Homer Δωριέες τριχάικες. These tribes were the *Hylleis* (Ὑλλεῖς), *Pamphyli* (Πάμφυλοι), and *Dymanatae* or *Dymanes* (Δυμανάται or Δυμᾶνες). The first derived their name from Hyllus, son of Hercules, the two last from Pamphylus and Dymas, who are said to have fallen in the last expedition when the Dorians took possession of the Peloponnesus. The Hyllean tribe was perhaps the one of highest dignity; but at Sparta there does not appear to have been much distinction, for all the freemen there were by the constitution of Lycurgus on a footing of equality. To these three tribes others were added in different places, either when the Dorians were joined by other foreign allies, or when some of the old inhabitants were admitted to the rank of citizenship or equal privileges. Thus the Cadmean Aegeids are said by Herodotus to have been a great tribe at Sparta, descended (as he says) from Aegeus, grandson of Theras, though others have thought they were incorporated with the three Doric tribes. The subdivision of tribes into *phratriae* (φρατρίαι) or *patrae* (πάτραι), *gene* (γένη), *trittyes* (τρίττυες), &c. appears to have prevailed in various places. At Sparta each tribe contained ten *obae* (ὠβαί), a word denoting a local division or district; each *obe* contained ten *triacades* (τριακάδες), communities containing thirty families. But very little appears to be known of these divisions, how far they were local, or how far genealogical. After the time of Cleomenes the old system of tribes was changed; new ones were created corresponding to the different quarters of the town, and they seem to have been five in number. —The first Attic tribes that we read of are said to have existed in the reign, or soon after the reign, of Cecrops, and were called *Cecropis* (Κεκροπίς), *Autochthon* (Αὐτόχθων), *Actaea* (Ἀκταία), and *Paralia* (Παραλία). In the reign of a subsequent king, Cranaus,

these names were changed to *Cranais* (Κραναίς), *Atthis* (Ἀτθίς), *Mesogaea* (Μεσόγαια), and *Diacris* (Διακρίς). Afterwards we find a new set of names; *Dias* (Διάς), *Athenais* (Ἀθηναίς), *Posridonias* (Ποσειδωνιάς), and *Hephaestias* (Ἡφαιστιάς); evidently derived from the deities who were worshipped in the country. Some of those secondly mentioned, if not all of them, seem to have been geographical divisions; and it is not improbable that, if not independent communities, they were at least connected by a very weak bond of union. But all these tribes were superseded by four others, which were probably founded soon after the Ionic settlement in Attica, and seem to have been adopted by other Ionic colonies out of Greece. The names *Geleontes* (Γελέοντες), *Hopletes* (Ὁπλῆτες), *Argades* (Ἀργάδεις), *Aegicores* (Αἰγικορεῖς), are said by Herodotus to have been derived from the sons of Ion, son of Xuthus. Upon this, however, many doubts have been thrown by modern writers. The etymology of the last three names would seem to suggest, that the tribes were so called from the occupations which their respective members followed; the *Hopletes* being the armed men, or warriors; the *Argades*, labourers or husbandmen; the *Aegicores*, goatherds or shepherds. But whatever be the truth with respect to the origin of these tribes, one thing is certain, that before the time of Theseus, whom historians agree in representing as the great founder of the Attic commonwealth, the various people who inhabited the country continued to be disunited and split into factions.—Theseus in some measure changed the relations of the tribes to each other, by introducing a gradation of ranks in each; dividing the people into *Eupatridae* (Εὐπατρίδαι), *Geomori* (Γεωμόροι), and *Demiurgi* (Δημιουργοί), of whom the first were nobles, the second agriculturists or yeomen, the third labourers and mechanics. At the same time, in order to consolidate the national unity, he enlarged the city of Athens, with which he incorporated several smaller towns, made it the seat of government, encouraged the nobles to reside there, and surrendered a part of the royal prerogative in their favour. The tribes or *phylae* were divided, either in the age of Theseus or soon after, each into three *phratriae* (φρατρίαι, a term equivalent to fraternities, and analogous in its political relation to the Roman *curiae*), and each *phratria* into thirty *gene* (γένη, equivalent to the Roman *Gentes*, the members of a *genos* (γένος) being called *gennetae* (γεννῆται) or *homogalactes* (ὁμογαλάκτες). Each *genos* was distinguished by a particular name of a patronymic form, which was derived from some hero or mythic ancestor. These divisions, though the names seem to import family connection, were in fact artificial; which shows that some advance had now been made towards the establishment of a closer political union. The members of the *phratriae* and *gene* had their respective religious rites and festivals, which were preserved long after these communities had lost their political importance, and perhaps prevented them from being altogether dissolved.—After the age of Theseus, the monarchy having been first limited and afterwards abolished, the whole power of the state fell into the hands of the *Eupatridae* or nobles, who held all civil offices, and had besides the management of religious affairs, and the interpretation of the laws. Attica became agitated by feuds, and we find the people, shortly before the legislation of Solon, divided into three parties, *Pediaci* (Πεδιαῖοι) or lowlanders, *Diacrii* (Διάκριοι) or highlanders, and *Parali* (Πάραλοι) or people of the seacoast. The first two remind us of the ancient division of tribes, *Mesogaea* and *Diacris;* and the three parties appear in some measure to represent the classes established by Theseus, the first being the nobles, whose property lay in the champaign and most fertile part of the country; the second, the smaller landowners and shepherds; the third, the trading and mining class, who had by this time risen in wealth and importance. To appease their discords, Solon was applied to; and thereupon framed his celebrated constitution and code of laws. Here we have only to notice that he retained the four tribes as he found them, but abolished the existing distinctions of *rank,* or at all events greatly diminished their importance, by introducing his property qualification, or division of the people into *Pentacosiomedimni* (Πεντακοσιομέδιμνοι), *Hippeis* (Ἱππεῖς), *Zeugitae* (Ζευγῖται), and *Thetes* (Θῆτες). [CENSUS, GREEK.] The enactments of Solon continued to be the *law* at Athens, though in great measure suspended by the tyranny, until the democratic reform effected by Clisthenes. He abolished the old tribes, and created ten new ones, according to a geographical division of Attica, and named after ten of the ancient heroes: *Erechtheis, Aegeis, Pandionis, Leontis, Acamantis, Oeneis, Cecropis, Hippothoontis, Acantis, Antiochis.* These tribes were divided each into ten *demi* (δῆμοι), the number of which was afterwards increased by subdivision; but the arrangement was so made that several *demi* not contiguous or near to one another were joined to make up a tribe. [DEMUS.] The object of this arrangement was, that by the breaking of old associations a perfect and lasting revolution might be effected, in the habits and feelings, as well as the political organisation of the people. Solon allowed the ancient *phratriae* to exist, but they were deprived of all political importance. All foreigners admitted to the citizenship were registered in a phyle and demus, but not in a phratria or genos. The functions which had been discharged by the old tribes were now mostly transferred to the *demi.* Among others, we may notice that of the forty-eight *naucrariae* into which the old tribes had been divided for the purpose of taxation, but which now became useless, the taxes being collected on a different system. The reforms of Clisthenes were destined to be permanent. They continued to be in force (with some few interruptions) until the downfall of Athenian independence. The ten tribes were blended with the whole machinery of the constitution. Of the senate of five hundred, fifty were chosen from each tribe. The allotment of dicasts was according to tribes; and the same system of election may be observed in most of the principal offices of state, judicial and magisterial, civil and military, &c. In B. C. 307, Demetrius Poliorcetes increased the number of tribes to twelve by creating two new ones, namely, *Antigonias* and *Demetrias,* which afterwards received the names of *Ptolemais* and *Attalis;* and a thirteenth was subsequently added by Hadrian, bearing his own name.—(2) ROMAN. The three ancient Romulian tribes, the Ramnes, Tities, and Luceres, or the Ramnenses, Titienses, and Lucerenses, to which the patricians alone belonged, must be distinguished from the thirty plebeian tribes of Servius Tullius, which were entirely local, four for the city, and twenty-six for the country around Rome. The history and organisation of the three ancient tribes are spoken of under PATRICII. They continued of political importance almost down to the period of the decemviral legislation; but after this time they no longer occur in the history of Rome, except as an obsolete institution. The institution and organisation of the thirty plebeian tribes, and their subsequent reduction to twenty by the conquests of Porsena, are spoken of under PLEBES. The four city tribes were called by the same names as the regions which they occupied, viz. *Suburana, Esquilina, Collina,* and *Palatina.* The names of the sixteen country tribes which continued to belong to Rome after the conquest of Porsena, are in their alphabetical order as follows: *Aemilia, Camilia, Cornelia, Fabia, Galeria, Horatia, Lemonia, Menenia, Papiria, Pollia, Papillia,*

Pupinia, Romilia, Sergia, Teturia, and Voltinia. As Rome gradually acquired possession of more of the surrounding territory, the number of tribes also was gradually increased. When Appius Claudius, with his numerous train of clients, emigrated to Rome, lands were assigned to them in the district where the Anio flows into the Tiber, and a new tribe, the *tribus Claudia*, was formed. This tribe was subsequently enlarged, and was then designated by the name *Crustumina* or *Clustumina*. This name is the first instance of a country tribe being named after a place, for the sixteen older ones all derived their name from persons or heroes. In B. C. 387, the number of tribes was increased to twenty-five by the addition of four new ones, viz. the *Stellatina, Tromentina, Sabatina*, and *Arniensis*. In B. C. 358 two more, the *Pomptina* and *Publilia*, were formed of Volscians. In B. C. 332, the censors Q. Publilius Philo and Sp. Postumius increased the number of tribes to twenty-nine, by the addition of the *Maecia* and *Scaptia*. In B. C. 318 the *Ufentina* and *Falerina* were added. In B. C. 299 two others, the *Aniensis* and *Terentina*, were added by the censors, and at last in B. C. 241, the number of tribes was augmented to thirty-five, by the addition of the *Quirina* and *Velina*. Eight new tribes were added upon the termination of the Social War, to include the Socii, who then obtained the Roman franchise; but they were afterwards incorporated among the old 35 tribes, which continued to be the number of the tribes to the end of the republic. When the tribes, in their assemblies, transacted any business, a certain order (*ordo tribuum*) was observed, in which they were called upon to give their votes. The first in the order of succession was the Suburana, and the last the Arniensis. Any person belonging to a tribe had in important documents to add to his own name that of his tribe, in the ablative case. Whether the local tribes, as they were established by the constitution of Servius Tullius, contained only the plebeians, or included the patricians also, is a point on which the opinions of modern scholars are divided: but it appears most probable that down to the decemviral legislation the tribes and their assemblies were entirely plebeian. From the time of the decemviral legislation, the patricians and their clients were undoubtedly incorporated in the tribes. Respecting the assemblies of the tribes, see COMITIA TRIBUTA.

TRIBŪTUM, a tax which was partly applied to cover the expenses of war, and partly those of the fortifications of the city.

The usual amount of the tax was one for every thousand of a man's fortune, though in the time of Cato it was raised to three in a thousand. The tributum was not a property-tax in the strict sense of the word, for the accounts respecting the plebeian debtors clearly imply, that the debts were not deducted in the valuation of a person's property, so that he had to pay the tributum upon property which was not his own, but which he owed, and for which he had consequently to pay the interest as well. It was a direct tax upon objects without any regard to their produce, like a land or house-tax, which indeed formed the main part of it. That which seems to have made it most oppressive, was its constant fluctuation. It was raised according to the regions or tribes instituted by Servius Tullius, and by the tribunes of these tribes, subsequently called tribuni aerarii. It was not, like the other branches of the public revenue, let out to farm, but being fixed in money it was raised by the tribunes, unless (as was the case after the custom of giving pay to the soldiers was introduced) the soldiers, like the knights, demanded it from the persons themselves who were bound to pay it. [AES EQUESTRE and HORDEARIUM.] When this tax was to be paid, what sum was to be raised, and what portion of every thousand asses of the census, were matters upon which the senate alone had to decide. But when it was decreed, the people might refuse to pay it when they thought it too heavy, or unfairly distributed, or hoped to gain some other advantage by the refusal. In later times the senate sometimes left its regulation to the censors, who often fixed it very arbitrarily. No citizen was exempt from it, but we find that the priests, augurs, and pontiffs made attempts to get rid of it: but this was only an abuse, which did not last. After the war with Macedonia (B. C. 147), when the Roman treasury was filled with the revenues accruing from conquests and from the provinces, the Roman citizens became exempted from paying the tributum, and this state of things lasted down to the consulship of Hirtius and Pansa (43 B. C.), when the tributum was again levied, on account of the exhausted state of the aerarium. After this time it was imposed according to the discretion of the emperors. Respecting the tributum paid by conquered countries and cities, see VECTIGALIA.

TRICLĪNĬUM, the dining-room of a Roman house, the position of which, relatively to the other parts of the house, is seen in the "house of the Tragic poet" (see p. 144). It was of an oblong shape, and was twice as long as it was broad. The superintendence of the dining-room in a great house was intrusted to a slave called *tricliniarcha*, who, through other slaves, took care that everything was kept and proceeded in proper order. A *triclinium* generally contained three couches, and as the usual number of persons occupying each couch was three, the triclinium afforded accommodation for a party of nine. Sometimes, however, as many as four lay on each of the couches. Each man in order to feed himself lay flat upon his breast or nearly so, and stretched out his hand towards the table; but afterwards, when his hunger was satisfied, he turned upon his left side, leaning on his elbow. To this Horace alludes in describing a person sated with a particular dish, and turning in order to repose upon his elbow. (*Sat.* ii. 4, 39.) We find the relative positions of two persons who lay next to one another, commonly expressed by the prepositions *super* or *supra*, and *infra*. A passage of Livy (xxxix. 43), in which he relates the cruel conduct of the consul L. Quintius Flamininus, shows that *infra aliquem cubare* was the same as *in sinu alicujus cubare*, and consequently that each person was considered as *below* him to whose breast his own head approached. On this principle we are enabled to explain the denominations both of the three couches, and of the three places on each couch. Supposing the annexed arrangement to represent

of their accubation—an order exhibited in the annexed diagram.

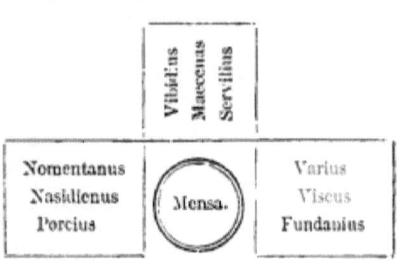

TRĪDENS. [FUSCINA.]
TRIENS. [AS.]
TRIĒRARCHĪA (τριηραρχία), one of the extraordinary war services or liturgies at Athens, the object of which was to provide for the equipment and maintenance of the ships of war belonging to the state. The persons who were charged with it were called trierarchs (τριήραρχοι), as being the captains of triremes, though the name was also applied to persons who bore the same charge in other vessels. It existed from very early times in connection with the forty-eight naucraries of Solon, and the fifty of Clisthenes: each of which corporations appears to have been obliged to equip and man a vessel. [NAUCRARIA.] Under the constitution of Clisthenes the ten tribes were at first severally charged with five vessels. This charge was of course superseded by the later forms of the trierarchy. The state furnished the ship, and either the whole or part of the ship's rigging and furniture, and also pay and provisions for the sailors. The trierarchs were bound to keep in repair the ship and its furniture, and were frequently put to great expense in paying the sailors and supplying them with provisions, when the state did not supply sufficient money for the purpose. Moreover, some trierarchs, whether from ambitious or patriotic motives, put themselves to unnecessary expense in fitting

the plan of a triclinium, it is evident that, as each guest reclined on his left side, the countenances of all when in this position were directed, first, from No. 1 towards No. 3, then from No. 4 towards No. 6, and lastly, from No. 7 towards No. 9; that the guest No. 1 lay, in the sense explained, *above* No. 2, No. 3 *below* No. 2, and so of the rest; and that, going in the same direction, the couch to the right hand was *above* the others, and the couch to the left hand *below* the others. It will be found, that in a passage in the eighth satire of the second book of Horace, the guests are enumerated in the order

out and rigging their ships, from which the state derived an advantage. The average expense of the trierarchy was 50 minae. In ancient times one person bore the whole charge of the trierarchy, afterwards it was customary for two persons to share it, who were then called *syntrierarchs* (συντριήραρχοι). When this practice was first introduced is not known, but it was perhaps about the year 412 B. C., after the defeat of the Athenians in Sicily, when the union of two persons for the choregia was first permitted. The syntrierarchy, however, did not entirely supersede the older and single form, being only meant as a relief in case of emergency, when there was not a sufficient number of wealthy citizens to bear the expense singly. In the case of a syntrierarchy the two trierarchs commanded their vessel in turn, six months each, according as they agreed between themselves.—The third form of the trierarchy was connected with, or suggested by, the syntrierarchy. In B. C. 358, the Athenians were unable to procure a sufficient number of legally appointed trierarchs, and accordingly they summoned volunteers. This, however, was but a temporary expedient; and as the actual system was not adequate to the public wants, they determined to manage the trierarchy somewhat in the same way as the property-tax (eisphora), namely, by classes or symmoriae, according to the law of Periander passed in B. C. 358, and which was the primary and original enactment on the subject. With this view 1200 *synteleis* (συντελεῖς) or partners were appointed, who were probably the wealthiest individuals of the state, according to the census or valuation. These were divided into 20 *symmoriae* (συμμορίαι) or classes; out of which a number of persons (σώματα) joined for the equipment or rather the maintenance and management of a ship, under the title of a *synteleia* (συντέλεια) or union. To every ship there was generally assigned a *synteleia* of fifteen persons of different degrees of wealth, as we may suppose, so that four ships only were provided for by each symmoria of sixty persons. It appears, however, that before Demosthenes carried a new law on this subject (B. C. 340), it had been customary for *sixteen* persons to unite in a synteleia or company for a ship, who bore the burden in equal shares. This being the case, it follows either that the members of the symmoriae had been by that time raised from 1200 to 1280, or that some alterations had taken place in their internal arrangements, of which no account has come down to us. The superintendence of the whole system was in the hands of the 300 wealthiest members, who were therefore called the "leaders of the symmoriae" (ἡγεμόνες τῶν συμμοριῶν), on whom the burdens of the trierarchy chiefly fell, or rather ought to have fallen. The services performed by individuals under this system appear to have been the same as before the state still provided the ship's tackle, and the only duty then of the trierarchs under this system was to keep their vessels in the same repair and order as they received them. But even from this they managed to escape: for the wealthiest members, who had to serve for their synteleia, let out their trierarchies for a talent, and received that amount from their partners (συντελεῖς), so that in reality they paid next to nothing, or, at any rate, not what they ought to have done, considering that the trierarchy was a ground of exemption from other liturgies.—To remedy these abuses Demosthenes carried a law when he was the ἐπιστάτης τοῦ ναυτικοῦ, or the superintendent of the Athenian navy, thereby introducing the *Fourth form* of the trierarchy. The provisions of the law were as follows: The naval services required from every citizen were to depend upon and be proportional to his property, or rather to his taxable capital, as registered for the symmoriae of the property-tax, the rate being one trireme for every ten talents of taxable capital, up to three triremes and one auxiliary vessel (ὑπηρέσιον) for the largest properties; *i. e.* no person, however rich, could be required to furnish more. Those who had not ten talents in taxable capital were to club together in synteleiae till they had made up that amount. By this law great changes were effected. All persons paying taxes were rated in proportion to their property, so that the poor were benefited by it, and the state likewise: for, as Demosthenes says, those who had formerly contributed one-sixteenth to the trierarchy of one ship were now trierarchs of two, in which case they must either have served by proxy, or done duty in successive years. He adds, that the consequences were highly beneficial. We do not know the amount of property which rendered a man liable to serve a trierarchy or syntrierarchy, but we read of no instance of liability arising from a property of less value than 500 minae. The appointment to serve under the first and second forms of the trierarchy was made by the strategi, and in case any person was appointed to serve a trierarchy, and thought that any one else (not called upon) was better able to bear it than himself, he offered the latter an exchange of his property [ANTIDOSIS] subject to the burden of the trierarchy. In cases of extreme hardship, persons became suppliants to the people, or fled to the altar of Artemis at Munychia. If not ready in time, they were sometimes liable to imprisonment. On the contrary, whoever got his ship ready first was to be rewarded with the "crown of the trierarchy;" so that in this way considerable emulation and competition were produced. Moreover, the trierarchs were ὑπεύθυνοι, or liable to be called to account for their expenditure; though they applied their own property to the service of the state. It has been already stated that the trierarchy was a ground of exemption from the other liturgies, any of which, indeed, gave an exemption from all the rest during the following year.

TRINUNDINUM. [NUNDINAE.]

TRIOBOLON (τριώβολον), the fee of three obols, which the Athenian dicasts received. [DICASTAE.]

TRIPOS (τρίπους), a tripod, i.e. any utensil or article of furniture supported upon three feet. More especially (1) A three-legged table.—(2) A pot or caldron, used for boiling meat, and either raised upon a three-legged stand of bronze, or made with its three feet in the same piece.—(3) A bronze altar, not differing probably in its original form from the tall tripod caldron already described. It was from a tripod that the Pythian priestess at Delphi gave responses. [CORTINA.] The celebrity of this tripod produced innumerable imitations of it, which were made to be used in sacrifice, and still more frequently to be presented to the treasury both in that place and in many other Greek temples.

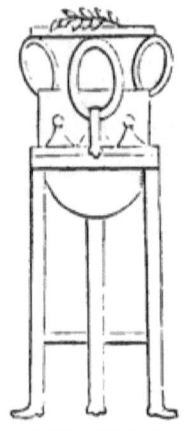

Tripod of Apollo at Delphi. (Böttiger's Amalthea, vol. 1. p. 119.)

TRIPUDIUM. [AUSPICIUM.]
TRIREMIS. [NAVIS.]

TRIUMPHUS (θρίαμβος), a solemn procession, in which a victorious general entered the city in a chariot drawn by four horses. He was preceded by the captives and spoils taken in war, was followed by his troops, and after passing in state along the Via Sacra, ascended the Capitol to offer sacrifice in the temple of Jupiter. From the beginning of the republic down to the extinction of liberty a regular triumph (*justus triumphus*) was recognised as the summit of military glory, and was the cherished object of ambition to every Roman general. A triumph might be granted for successful achievements either by land or sea, but the latter were comparatively so rare that we shall for the present defer the consideration of the naval triumph. After any decisive battle had been won, or a province subdued by a series of successful operations, the imperator forwarded to the senate a laurel-wreathed dispatch (*literae laureatae*), containing an account of his exploits. If the intelligence proved satisfactory, the senate decreed a public thanksgiving. [SUPPLICATIO.] After the war was concluded, the general with his army repaired to Rome, or ordered his army to meet him there on a given day, but did not enter the city. A meeting of the senate was held without the walls, usually in the temple either of Bellona or Apollo, that he might have an opportunity of urging his pretensions in person, and these were then scrutinised and discussed with the most jealous care. The following rules were for the most part rigidly enforced, although the senate assumed the discretionary power of relaxing them in special cases. 1. That no one could be permitted to triumph unless he had held the office of dictator, of consul, or of praetor. The honours granted to Pompey, who triumphed in his 24th year (B.C. 81) before he had held any of the great offices of state, and again ten years afterwards, while still a simple eques, were altogether unprecedented. 2. That the magistrate should have been actually in office both when the victory was gained and when the triumph was to be celebrated. This regulation was insisted upon only during the earlier ages of the commonwealth. Its violation commenced with Q. Publilius Philo, the first person to whom the senate ever granted a *prorogatio imperii* after the termination of a magistracy, and thenceforward proconsuls and propraetors were permitted to triumph without question. 3. That the war should have been prosecuted or the battle fought under the auspices and in the province and with the troops of the general seeking the triumph. Thus if a victory was gained by the legatus of a general who was absent from the army, the honour of it did not belong to the former, but to the latter, inasmuch as he had the auspices. 4. That at least 5000 of the enemy should have been slain in a single battle, that the advantage should have been positive, and not merely a compensation for some previous disaster, and that the loss on the part of the Romans should have been small compared with that of their adversaries. But still we find many instances of triumphs granted for general results, without reference to the numbers slain in any one engagement. 5.

e been a legitimate
:s, and not a civil
celebrated no tri-
Antonius over Cati-
s over their antago-
, nor Caesar after
did subsequently
over the sons of
ersal disgust. 6.
state should have
merely something
The absolute ac-
not appear to have
he war should have
on and the province
, so as to permit of
n, the presence of
ig considered indis-
The senate claimed
liberating upon all
or withholding the
for the most part
without question,
olitical excitement.
eople, however, in
t a very early date,
have been voted by
Horatius, the con-
t opposition to the
, and in a similar
itilus the first ple-
ostumius Megellus,
rated a triumph,
nate and seven out
, more, we read of
s, consul B. C. 143,
celebrating a tri-
h the senate and
by his daughter (or
irgin, and by her
eing dragged from
. A disappointed
ventured to resort
but satisfied him-
the forms on the
first introduced by
senate gave their
time voted a sum
ing the necessary
ribunes *ex auctori-*
plebiscitum to per-
in his imperium on
the city. This last
d with either in an
ause the imperium
curiata did not in-
hen a general had
, his military power
-entered the gates,
ad been previously
enactment; and in

this manner the resolution of the senate was,
as it were, ratified by the plebs. For this
reason no one desiring a triumph ever entered
the city until the question was decided, since
by so doing he would ipso facto have forfeited
all claim. We have a remarkable example of
this in the case of Cicero, who after his return
from Cilicia lingered in the vicinity of Rome
day after day, and dragged about his lictors
from one place to another, without entering
the city, in the vain hope of a triumph.—In
later times these pageants were marshalled
with extraordinary pomp and splendour, and
presented a most gorgeous spectacle. Minute
details would necessarily be different according to circumstances, but the general arrangements were as follows. The temples were all
thrown open, garlands of flowers decorated
every shrine and image, and incense smoked
on every altar. Meanwhile the imperator
called an assembly of his soldiers, delivered
an oration commending their valour, and
concluded by distributing rewards to the most
distinguished, and a sum of money to each
individual, the amount depending on the
value of the spoils. He then ascended his
triumphal car and advanced to the Porta Triumphalis, where he was met by the whole body
of the senate headed by the magistrates. The
procession then defiled in the following order.
1. The senate headed by the magistrates.
2. A body of trumpeters. 3. A train of
carriages and frames laden with spoils, those
articles which were especially remarkable
either on account of their beauty or rarity
being disposed in such a manner as to be
seen distinctly by the crowd. Boards were
borne aloft on ferculа, on which were
painted in large letters the names of vanquished nations and countries. Here, too,
models were exhibited in ivory or wood of
the cities and forts captured, and pictures
of the mountains, rivers, and other great
natural features of the subjugated region,
with appropriate inscriptions. Gold and
silver in coin or bullion, arms, weapons,
and horse furniture of every description,
statues, pictures, vases, and other works of
art, precious stones, elaborately wrought
and richly embroidered stuffs, and every
object which could be regarded as valuable
or curious. 4. A body of flute players.
5. The white bulls or oxen destined for
sacrifice, with gilded horns, decorated with
infulae and serta, attended by the slaughter-
ing priests with their implements, and followed by the Camilli bearing in their hands
paterae and other holy vessels and instruments. 6. Elephants or any other strange
animals, natives of the conquered districts.
7. The arms and insignia of the leaders of

the foe. 8. The leaders themselves, and such of their kindred as had been taken prisoners, followed by the whole band of inferior captives in fetters. 9. The coronae and other tributes of respect and gratitude bestowed on the imperator by allied kings and states. 10. The lictors of the imperator in single file, their fasces wreathed with laurel. 11. The imperator himself in a circular chariot of a peculiar form, drawn by four horses, which were sometimes, though rarely, white. He was attired in a gold-embroi-

Triumphal Procession. (Zoega, Bassa-rilievi, tav. 9, 76.)

dered robe (*toga picta*) and flowered tunic (*tunica palmata*): he bore in his right hand a laurel bough, and in his left a sceptre; his brows were encircled with a wreath of Delphic laurel, in addition to which in ancient times, his body was painted bright red. He was accompanied in his chariot by his children of tender years, and sometimes by very dear or highly honoured friends, while behind him stood a public slave, holding over his head a golden Etruscan crown ornamented with jewels. The presence of a slave in such a place at such a time seems to have been intended to avert *invidia* and the influence of the evil eye, and for the same purpose a fascinum, a little bell, and a scourge were attached to the vehicle. Tertullian tells us, that the slave ever and anon whispered in the ear of the imperator the warning words *Respice post te, hominem memento te*, but this statement is not confirmed by any earlier writer. 12. Behind the chariot or on the horses which drew it rode the grown-up sons of the imperator, together with the legati, the tribuni, and the equites, all on horseback. 13. The rear was brought up by the whole body of the infantry in marching order, their spears adorned with laurel, some shouting Io Triumphe, and singing hymns to the gods, while others proclaimed the praises of their leader or indulged in keen sarcasms and coarse ribaldry at his expense, for the most perfect freedom of speech was granted and exercised. Just as the pomp was ascending the Capitoline hill, some of the hostile chiefs were led aside into the adjoining prison and put to death, a custom so barbarous that we could scarcely believe that it existed in a civilised age, were it not attested by the most unquestionable evidence. Pompey, indeed, refrained from perpetrating this atrocity in his third triumph, and Aurelian on like occasion spared Zenobia, but these are quoted as exceptions to the general rule. When it was announced that these murders had been completed, the victims were then sacrificed, an offering from the spoils was presented to Jupiter, the laurel wreath was deposited in the lap of the god, the imperator was entertained at a public feast along with his friends in the temple, and returned home in the evening preceded by torches and pipes, and escorted by a crowd of citizens. The whole of the proceedings, generally speaking, were brought to a close in one day; but when the quantity of plunder was very great, and the troops very numerous, a longer period was required for the exhibition, and thus the triumph of Flaminius continued for three days in succession. But the glories of the imperator did not end with the show, nor even with his life. It was customary (we know not if the practice was invariable) to provide him at the public expense with a site for a house, such mansions being styled *triumphales domus*. After death his kindred were permitted to deposit his ashes within the walls, and laurel-wreathed statues standing erect in triumphal cars, displayed in the vestibulum of the family mansion, transmitted his fame to posterity.— A TRIUMPHUS NAVALIS appears to have differed in no respect from an ordinary triumph, except that it must have been upon a smaller scale, and would be characterised by the exhibition of beaks of ships and other nautical trophies The earliest upon record was granted to C. Duillius, who laid the foundation of the supremacy of Rome by sea in the first Punic war; and so elated was he by his success, that during the rest of his life, whenever he returned home at night from supper, he caused flutes to sound and torches to be borne before him. A second naval triumph was celebrated by Lutatius Catulus for his victory off the Insulae Aegates, B. c. 241; a third by Q. Fabius Labeo, B. c. 189, over the Cretans; and a fourth by C. Octavins over King Perseus, without captives and without spoils.—TRIUMPHUS CASTRENSIS was a procession of the soldiers through the camp in honour of a tribunus or some officer inferior to the general, who had performed a brilliant exploit. After the extinction of freedom, the emperor being considered as the commander-in-chief of all the armies of the state, every military achievement was understood to be performed under his auspices, and hence, according to the forms of even the ancient constitution, he alone had a legitimate claim to a triumph. This principle was soon fully recognised and acted upon; for although Antonius had granted triumphs to his legati, and his example had been freely followed by Augustus in the early part of his career, yet after the year B. c. 14, he entirely discontinued the practice, and from that time forward triumphs were rarely, if ever, conceded to any except members of the imperial family. But to compensate in some degree for what was then taken away, the custom was introduced of bestowing what were termed Triumphalia Ornamenta, that is, permission to receive the titles bestowed upon and to appear in public with the robes worn by the imperatores of the commonwealth when they triumphed, and to bequeath to descendants triumphal statues. These triumphalia ornamenta are said to have been first bestowed upon Agrippa or upon Tiberius, and ever after were a common mark of the favour of the prince.

TRIUMVIRI, or TRESVIRI, were either ordinary magistrates or officers, or else extraordinary commissioners, who were frequently appointed at Rome to execute any public office.* The following is a list of the most important of both classes.

1. TRIUMVIRI AGRO DIVIDUNDO. [TRIUM-VIRI COLONIAE DEDUCENDAE.]

2. TRIUMVIRI CAPITALES were regular magistrates, first appointed about B. c. 292. They were elected by the people, the comitia being held by the praetor. They succeeded to many of the functions of the Quaestores Parricidii. [QUAESTOR.] It was their duty to inquire into all capital crimes, and to receive informations respecting such, and consequently they apprehended and committed to prison all criminals whom they detected. In conjunction with the aediles, they had to preserve the public peace, to prevent all unlawful assemblies, &c. They enforced the payment of fines due to the state. They had the care of public prisons, and carried into effect the sentence of the law upon criminals. In these points they resembled the magistracy of the Eleven at Athens.

4. TRIUMVIRI COLONIAE DEDUCENDAE were persons appointed to superintend the formation of a colony. They are spoken of under COLONIA, p. 99, b. Since they had besides to superintend the distribution of the land to the colonists, we find them also called Triumviri Coloniae Deducendae Agroque Dividundo, and sometimes simply Triumviri Agro Dando.

5. TRIUMVIRI EPULONES. [EPULONES.]

6. TRIUMVIRI EQUITUM TURMAS RECOGNOSCENDI, or LEGENDIS EQUITUM DECURIIS, were magistrates first appointed by Augustus to revise the lists of the equites, and to admit persons into the order. This was formerly part of the duties of the censors.

7. TRIUMVIRI MENSARII. [MENSARII.]

8. TRIUMVIRI MONETALES. [MONETA.]

9. TRIUMVIRI NOCTURNI were magistrates elected annually, whose chief duty it was to prevent fires by night, and for this purpose they had to go round the city during the night (vigilias circumire). If they neglected their duty they appear to have been accused before the people by the tribunes of the plebs. The time at which this office was instituted is unknown, but it must have been previously to the year B. c. 304. Augustus transferred their duties to the Praefectus Vigilum. [PRAEFECTUS VIGILUM.]

10. TRIUMVIRI REFICIENDIS AEDIBUS, extraordinary officers elected in the Comitia Tributa in the time of the second Punic war, were appointed for the purpose of repairing and rebuilding certain temples.

11. TRIUMVIRI REIPUBLICAE CONSTITUENDAE. When the supreme power was shared between Caesar (Octavianus), Antony, and Lepidus, they administered the affairs of the state under the title of Triumviri Reipublicae Constituendae. This office was conferred upon them in B. c. 43, for five years; and on the expiration of the term, in B. c. 38, was

conferred upon them again, in B.C. 37, for five years more. The coalition between Julius Caesar, Pompey, and Crassus, in B.C. 60, is usually called the first triumvirate, and that between Octavianus, Antony, and Lepidus, the second; but it must be borne in mind that the former never bore the title of triumviri, nor were invested with any office under that name, whereas the latter were recognised as regular magistrates under the above-mentioned title.

12. TRIUMVIRI SACRIS CONQUIRENDIS DONISQUE PERSIGNANDIS, extraordinary officers elected in the Comitia Tributa in the time of the second Punic war, seem to have had to take care that all property given or consecrated to the gods was applied to that purpose.

13. TRIUMVIRI SENATUS LEGENDI were magistrates appointed by Augustus to admit persons into the senate. This was previously the duty of the censors.

TROCHUS (τροχός), a hoop. The Greek hoop was a bronze ring, and had sometimes bells attached to it. It was impelled by means of a hook with a wooden handle, called *clavis*, and ἐλατήρ. From the Greeks this custom passed to the Romans, who consequently adopted the Greek term. The following woodcuts from gems exhibit naked youths trundling the hoop by means of the hook or key. They are accompanied by the jar of oil and the laurel branch, the signs of effort and of victory.

Trochi, Hoops. (From ancient Gems.)

TROJAE LŪDUS. [CIRCUS.]

TRŎPAEUM (τρόπαιον, Att. τροπαῖον), a trophy, a sign and memorial of victory, which was erected on the field of battle where the enemy had turned (τρέπω, τροπή) to flight; and in case of a victory gained at sea, on the nearest land. The expression for raising or erecting a trophy is τροπαῖον στῆσαι or στήσασθαι, to which may be added ἀπὸ or κατὰ τῶν πολεμίων. When the battle was not decisive, or each party considered it had some claims to the victory, both erected trophies. Trophies usually consisted of the arms, shields, helmets, &c. of the enemy that were defeated; and these were placed on the trunk of a tree, which was fixed on some elevation. The trophy was consecrated to some divinity, with an inscription (ἐπίγραμμα), recording the names of the victors and of the defeated party; whence trophies were regarded as inviolable, which even the enemy were not permitted to remove. Sometimes, however, a people destroyed a trophy, if they considered that the enemy had erected it without sufficient cause. That rankling and hostile feelings might not be perpetuated by the continuance of a trophy, it seems to have been originally part of Greek international law that trophies should be made only of wood, and not of stone or metal, and that they should not be repaired when decayed. It was not, however, uncommon to erect trophies of metal. Pausanias speaks of several which he saw in Greece. The trophies erected to commemorate naval victories were usually ornamented with the beaks or acroteria of ships [ACROTERIUM; ROSTRA]; and were generally consecrated to Poseidon or Neptune. Sometimes a whole ship was placed as a trophy. The Romans, in early times, never erected any trophies on the field of battle, but carried home the spoils taken in battle, with which they decorated the public buildings, and also the private houses

Trophy of Augustus. (Museo Capitolino, vol. I. tav. 5.)

of individuals. [SPOLIA.] Subsequently, however, the Romans adopted the Greek practice of raising trophies on the field of battle. The first trophies of this kind were erected by Domitius Ahenobarbus and Fabius Maximus in B. c. 121, after their conquest of the Allobroges, when they built at the junction of the Rhone and the Isara towers of white stone, upon which trophies were placed adorned with the spoils of the enemy. Pompey also raised trophies on the Pyrenees after his victories in Spain; Julius Caesar did the same near Ziela, after his victory over Pharnaces; and Drusus, near the Elbe, to commemorate his victory over the Germans. Still, however, it was more common to erect some memorial of the victory at Rome than on the field of battle. The trophies raised by Marius to commemorate his victories over Jugurtha and the Cimbri and Teutoni, which were cast down by Sulla, and restored by Julius Caesar, must have been in the city. In the later times of the republic, and under the empire, the erection of triumphal arches was the most common way of commemorating a victory, many of which remain to the present day. [ARCUS.]

TROSSULI. [EQUITES, p. 157, a.]
TRUA, dim. TRULLA (τορύνη), derived from τρύω, τόρω, &c., to perforate; a large and flat spoon or ladle, pierced with holes; a trowel. The annexed woodcut represents such a ladle. The trulla vinaria seems to

Trua. (From the House of Pansa at Pompeii.)

have been a species of colander [COLUM], used as a wine-strainer.

TRUTĪNA (τρυτάνη), a general term, including both libra, a balance, and statera, a steelyard. Payments were originally made by weighing, not by counting. Hence a balance (trutina) was preserved in the temple of Saturn at Rome.

TŪBA (σάλπιγξ), a bronze trumpet, distinguished from the cornu by being straight while the latter was curved. [CORNU.] The tuba was employed in war for signals of every description, at the games and public festivals, and also at the last rites to the dead: those who sounded the trumpet at funerals were termed siticines, and used an instrument of a peculiar form. The tones of the tuba are represented as of a harsh and fear-inspiring character. The invention of the tuba is usually ascribed by ancient writers to the Etruscans. It has been remarked that

Homer never introduces the σάλπιγξ in his narrative except in comparisons, which leads us to infer that, although known in his time, it had been but recently introduced into Greece; and it is certain that, notwithstanding its eminently martial character, it was not until a late period used in the armies of the leading states. By the Greek tragedians its Tuscan origin is fully recognised. According to one account it was first fabricated for the Tyrrhenians by Athena, who in consequence was worshipped by the Argives under the title of Σάλπιγξ, while at Rome the tubilustrium, or purification of sacred trumpets, was performed on the last day of the Quinquatrus. [QUINQUATRUS.] There appears to have been no essential difference in form between the Greek and Roman or Tyrrhenian trumpets. Both were long, straight, bronze tubes, gradually increasing in diameter, and terminating in a bell-shaped aperture.

Soldiers blowing Tubae and Cornua. (From Column of Trajan.)

TŪBILUSTRIUM. [QUINQUATRUS.]
TULLIĀNUM. [CARCER.]
TUMULTUĀRII. [TUMULTUS.]
TUMULTUS, the name given to a sudden or dangerous war in Italy or Cisalpine Gaul, and the word was supposed by the ancients to be a contraction of timor multus. It was, however, sometimes applied to a sudden or dangerous war elsewhere; but this does not appear to have been a correct use of the word. Cicero says that there might be a war without a tumultus, but not a tumultus without a war; but it must be recollected that the word was also applied to any sudden alarm respecting a war; whence we find a tumultus often spoken of as of less importance than a war, because the results were of

less consequence, though the fear might have been much greater than in a regular war. In the case of a tumultus there was a cessation from all business (*justitium*), and all citizens were obliged to enlist without regard being had to the exemptions (*vacationes*) from military service, which were enjoyed at other times. As there was not time to enlist the soldiers in the regular manner, the magistrate who was appointed to command the army displayed two banners (*vexilla*) from the Capitol, one red, to summon the infantry, and the other green, to summon the cavalry, and said, *Qui rempublicam salvam vult, me sequatur.* Those that assembled took the military oath together, instead of one by one, as was the usual practice, whence they were called *conjurati*, and their service *conjuratio.* Soldiers enlisted in this way were termed *Tumultuarii* or *Subitarii.*

TŬNĬCA (χιτών, dim. χιτωνίσκος, χιτώνιον), an under-garment. (1) GREEK. The chiton was the only kind of ἔνδυμα, or under-garment worn by the Greeks. Of this there were two kinds, the Dorian and Ionian. The Dorian chiton, as worn by males, was a short woollen shirt, without sleeves; the Ionian was a long linen garment, with sleeves. The former seems to have been originally worn throughout the whole of Greece; the latter was brought over to Greece by the Ionians of Asia. The Ionic chiton was commonly worn at Athens by men during the Persian wars, but it appears to have entirely gone out of fashion for the male sex about the time of Pericles, from which time the Dorian chiton was the under-garment universally adopted by men through the whole of Greece. The distinction between the Doric and Ionic chiton still continued in the dress of women. The Spartan virgins only wore this one garment, and had no upper kind of clothing, whence it is sometimes called *Himation* [PALLIUM] as well as *Chiton*. They appeared in the company of men without any further covering; but the married women never did so without wearing an upper garment. This Doric chiton was made, as stated above, of woollen stuff; it was without sleeves, and was fastened over both shoulders by clasps or buckles (πόρπαι, περόναι), which were often of considerable size. It was frequently so short as not to reach the knee. It was only joined together on one side, and on the other was left partly open or slit up (σχιστὸς χιτών), to allow a free motion of the limbs. The following cut represents an Amazon with a chiton of this kind: some parts of the figure appear incomplete, as the original is mutilated. The Ionic chiton, on the contrary, was a long and loose garment, reaching to the feet (ποδήρης), with wide sleeves (κόραι), and was usually made of

Doric Chiton. (From a Bas-relief in the British Museum.)

linen. The sleeves, however, appear generally to have covered only the upper part of the arm; for in ancient works of art we seldom find the sleeve extending farther than the elbow, and sometimes not so far. The sleeves were sometimes slit up, and fastened together with an elegant row of brooches. The Ionic chiton, according to Herodotus, was originally a Carian dress, and passed over to Athens from Ionia, as has been already remarked. The women at Athens originally wore the Doric chiton, but were compelled to change it for the Ionic, after they had killed with the buckles or clasps of their dresses the single Athenian who had returned alive from the expedition

Ionic Chiton. (From a Statue in the British Museum.)

against Aegina, because there were no buckles or clasps required in the Ionic dress. The preceding cut represents the Muse Thalia wearing an Ionic chiton. The peplum has fallen off her shoulders, and is held up by the left hand. Both kinds of dress were fastened round the middle with a girdle, and as the Ionic chiton was usually longer than the body, part of it was drawn up so that the dress might not reach farther than the feet, and the part which was so drawn up overhung or overlapped the girdle, and was called κόλπος.—There was a peculiar kind of dress, which seems to have been a species of double chiton, called *Diplois* (διπλοΐς), *Diploidion* (διπλοΐδιον), and *Hemidiploidion* (ἡμιδιπλοΐδιον). It appears not to have been a separate article of dress, but merely the upper part of the cloth forming the chiton, which was larger than was required for the ordinary chiton, and was therefore thrown over the front and back. The following cuts will give a clearer idea of the form of this garment than any description. Since the

Diploidia, double Chitons. (Museo Borbonico, vol. ii. tav. 4, 6.)

Diploidion was fastened over the shoulders by means of buckles or clasps, it was called *Epomis* (ἐπωμίς), which is supposed by some writers to have been only the end of the garment fastened on the shoulder. The chiton was worn by men next their skin; but females were accustomed to wear a chemise (χιτώνιον) under their chiton. It was the practice among most of the Greeks to wear an himation, or outer garment, over the chiton, but frequently the chiton was worn alone. A person who wore only a chiton was called μονοχίτων (οἰοχίτων in Homer), an epithet given to the Spartan virgins. In the same way, a person who wore only an hima-

tion, or outer garment, was called ἀχίτων. The Athenian youths, in the earlier times, wore only the chiton, and when it became the fashion, in the Peloponnesian war, to wear an outer garment over it, it was regarded as a mark of effeminacy.—(2) ROMAN. The *Tunica* of the Romans, like the Greek chiton, was a woollen under garment, over which the toga was worn. It was the *Indumentum* or *Indutus*, as opposed to the *Amictus*, the general term for the toga, pallium, or any other outer garment. [AMICTUS.] The Romans are said to have had no other clothing originally but the toga; and when the tunic was first introduced, it was merely a short garment without sleeves, and was called *Colobium*. It was considered a mark of effeminacy for men to wear tunics with long sleeves (*manicatae*) and reaching to the feet (*talares*). The tunic was girded (*cincta*) with a belt or girdle around the waist, but it was usually worn loose, without being girded, when a person was at home, or wished to be at his ease. Hence we find the terms *cinctus*, *praecinctus*, and *succinctus*, applied, like the Greek εὔζωνος, to an active and diligent person, and *discinctus* to one who was idle or dissolute. The form of the tunic, as worn by men, is represented in many woodcuts in this work. In works of art it usually terminates a little above the knee; it has short sleeves, covering only the upper part of the arm, and is girded at the waist: the sleeves sometimes, though less frequently, extend to the hands.—Both sexes at Rome usually wore two tunics, an outer and an under, the latter of which was worn next the skin, and corresponds to our shirt and chemise. The under tunics were called *Subucula* and *Indusium*, the former of which is supposed to be the name of the under tunic of the men, and the latter of that of the women: but this is not certain. The word *Interula* was of later origin, and seems to have been applied equally to the under tunic of both sexes. It is doubtful whether the *Supparus* or *Supparum* was an outer or an under garment. Persons sometimes wore several tunics, as a protection against cold: Augustus wore four in the winter, besides a subucula. As the dress of a man usually consisted of an under tunic, an outer tunic, and the toga, so that of a woman, in like manner, consisted of an under tunic, an outer tunic, and the palla. The outer tunic of the Roman matron was properly called stola [STOLA], and is represented in the woodcut on p. 355; but the annexed woodcut, which represents a Roman empress in the character of Concordia, or Abundantia, gives a better idea of its form. Over the tunic or stola the palla is thrown in many folds, but the shape of the former is still distinctly shown. The tunics of women

Roman Tunic. (Visconti, Monumenti Gabini, n. 34.)

were larger and longer than those of men, and always had sleeves; but in ancient paintings and statues we seldom find the sleeves covering more than the upper part of the arm. Sometimes the tunics were adorned with golden ornaments called *Leria*. Poor people, who could not afford to purchase a toga, wore the tunic alone, whence we find the common people called *Tunicati*. A person who wore only his tunic was frequently called NUDUS. Respecting the clavus latus and the clavus angustus, worn on the tunics of the senators and equites respectively, see CLAVUS LATUS, CLAVUS ANGUSTUS. When a triumph was celebrated, the conqueror wore, together with an embroidered toga (*Toga picta*), a flowered tunic (*Tunica palmata*), also called *Tunica Jovis*, because it was taken from the temple of Jupiter Capitolinus. Tunics of this kind were sent as presents to foreign kings by the senate.

TŪRĪBŬLUM (θυμιατήριον), a censer. The Greeks and Romans, when they sacrificed, commonly took a little frankincense out of the ACERRA and let it fall upon the flaming altar. [ARA.] More rarely they used a censer, by means of which they burnt the incense in greater profusion, and which was in fact a small moveable grate or FOCULUS. The annexed cut shows the performance of both of these acts at the same time. Winckelmann supposes it to represent Livia, the wife, and Octavia, the sister of Augustus, sacrificing to Mars in gratitude for his safe return from Spain. The censer here represented has two handles for the purpose of carrying it from place to place, and it stands upon feet so that the air might be admitted underneath, and pass upwards through the fuel.

TURMA. [EXERCITUS, p. 166, b.]

Livia and Octavia Sacrificing. (From an ancient Painting.)

TURRIS (πύργος), a tower. Moveable towers were among the most important engines used in storming a fortified place. They were generally made of beams and planks, and covered, at least on the three sides which were exposed to the besieged, with iron, not only for protection, but also to increase their weight, and thus make them steadier. They were also covered with raw hides and quilts, moistened, and sometimes with alum, to protect them from fire. Their height was such as to overtop the walls, towers, and all other fortifications of the besieged place. They were divided into stories (*tabulata* or *tecta*), and hence they are called *turres contabulatae*. The sides of the towers were pierced with windows, of which there were several to each story. The use of the stories was to receive the engines of war (*tormenta*). They contained balistae and catapults, and slingers and archers were stationed in them and on the tops of the towers. In the lowest story was a battering-ram [ARIES]; and in the middle one or more bridges (*pontes*) made of beams and planks, and protected at the sides by hurdles. Scaling-ladders (*scalae*) were also carried in the towers, and when the missiles had cleared the walls, these bridges and ladders enabled the besiegers to rush upon them. These towers were placed upon wheels (generally 6 or 8), that they might be brought up to the walls. These wheels were placed for security inside of the tower.

TUTOR. [CURATOR.]

TYMPĀNUM (τύμπανον), a small drum carried in the hand. Of these, some resembled in all respects a modern tambourine with bells. Others presented a flat circular disk on the upper surface and swelled out beneath like a kettle-drum. Both forms are represented in the cuts below. Tympana

Tympana. (From ancient Paintings.)

were covered with the hides of oxen, or of asses; were beaten with a stick, or with the hand, and were much employed in all wild enthusiastic religious rites, especially the orgies of Bacchus and Cybelé.—(2) A solid wheel without spokes, for heavy waggons, such as is shown in the cut on p. 298.

TYRANNUS (τύραννος). In the heroic age all the governments in Greece were monarchical, the king uniting in himself the functions of the priest, the judge, and military chief. In the first two or three centuries following the Trojan war various causes were at work, which led to the abolition, or at least to the limitation, of the kingly power. Emigrations, extinctions of families, disasters in war, civil dissensions, may be reckoned among these causes. Hereditary monarchies became elective; the different functions of the king were distributed; he was called *Archon* (ἄρχων), *Cosmus* (κόσ-

μος), or *Prytanis* (πρύτανις), instead of *Basileus* (βασιλεύς), and his character was changed no less than his name. Noble and wealthy families began to be considered on a footing of equality with royalty; and thus in process of time sprang up oligarchies or aristocracies, which most of the governments that succeeded the ancient monarchies were in point of fact, though not as yet called by such names. These oligarchies did not possess the elements of social happiness or stability. The principal families contended with each other for the greatest share of power, and were only unanimous in disregarding the rights of those whose station was beneath their own. The people, oppressed by the privileged classes, began to regret the loss of their old paternal form of government; and were ready to assist any one who would attempt to restore it. Thus were opportunities offered to ambitious and designing men to raise themselves, by starting up as the champions of popular right. Discontented nobles were soon found to prosecute schemes of this sort, and they had a greater chance of success, if descended from the ancient royal family. Pisistratus is an example; he was the more acceptable to the people of Athens, as being a descendant of the family of Codrus. Thus in many cities arose that species of monarchy which the Greeks called *tyrannis* (τυραννίς), which meant only *a despotism*, or irresponsible dominion of one man; and which frequently was nothing more than a revival of the ancient government, and, though unaccompanied with any recognised hereditary title, or the reverence attached to old name and long prescription, was hailed by the lower orders of people as a good exchange, after suffering under the domination of the oligarchy. All *tyrannies*, however, were not so acceptable to the majority; and sometimes we find the nobles concurring in the elevation of a despot, to further their own interests. Thus the Syracusan *Gamori*, who had been expelled by the populace, on receiving the protection of Gelon, sovereign of Gela and Camarina, enabled him to take possession of Syracuse, and establish his kingdom there. Sometimes the conflicting parties in the state, by mutual consent, chose some eminent man, in whom they had confidence, to reconcile their dissensions; investing him with a sort of dictatorial power for that purpose, either for a limited period or otherwise. Such a person they called *Aesymnetes* (αἰσυμνήτης). The *tyrannus* must be distinguished, on the one hand, from the *aesymnetes*, inasmuch as he was not elected by general consent, but commonly owed his elevation to some violent movement or stratagem, such as the creation of a body-guard for him by the people, or the seizure of the citadel ; and on the other hand, from the ancient king, whose right depended, not on usurpation, but on inheritance and traditionary acknowledgment. The power of a king might be more absolute than that of a *tyrant;* as Phidon of Argos is said to have made the royal prerogative greater than it was under his predecessors ; yet he was still regarded as a king; for the difference between the two names depended on title and origin, and not on the manner in which the power was exercised. The name of *tyrant* was originally so far from denoting a person who abused his power, or treated his subjects with cruelty, that Pisistratus is praised for the moderation of his government. Afterwards, when *tyrants* themselves had become odious, the name also grew to be a word of reproach, just as *rex* did among the Romans. Among the early *tyrants* of Greece those most worthy of mention are : Clisthenes of Sicyon, grandfather of the Athenian Clisthenes, in whose family the government continued for a century since its establishment by Orthagoras, about B. c. 672 ; Cypselus of Corinth, who expelled the Bacchiadae, B. c. 656, and his son Periander, both remarkable for their cruelty; their dynasty lasted between seventy and eighty years ; Procles of Epidaurus ; Pantaleon of Pisa, who celebrated the thirty-fourth Olympiad, depriving the Eleans of the presidency ; Theagenes of Megara, father-in-law to Cylon the Athenian ; Pisistratus, whose sons were the last of the early *tyrants* on the Grecian continent. In Sicily, where *tyranny* most flourished, the principal were Phalaris of Agrigentum, who established his power in B. c. 568 ; Theron of Agrigentum ; Gelon, already mentioned, who, in conjunction with Theron, defeated Hamilcar the Carthaginian, on the same day on which the battle of Salamis was fought ; and Hieron, his brother : the last three celebrated by Pindar. The following also are worthy of notice : Polycrates of Samos ; Lygdamis of Naxos ; Histiaeus and Aristagoras of Miletus. Perhaps the last mentioned can hardly be classed among the *Greek tyrants,* as they were connected with the Persian monarchy. The general characteristics of a *tyranny* were, that it was bound by no laws, and had no recognised limitation to its authority, however it might be restrained *in practice* by the good disposition of the *tyrant* himself, or by fear, or by the spirit of the age. It was commonly most odious to the wealthy and noble, whom the *tyrant* looked upon with jealousy as a check upon his power, and whom he often sought to get rid of by sending them into exile or putting them to death. The *tyrant* usually kept a body-guard of foreign mercenaries, by aid of whom he controlled the people at home ; but he seldom ventured to make war, for fear of giving an opportunity to his subjects to revolt. The causes which led to the decline of *tyranny* among the Greeks were partly the degeneracy of the *tyrants* themselves, corrupted by power, indolence, flattery, and bad education ; for even where the father set a good example, it was seldom followed by the son ; partly the cruelties and excesses of particular men, which brought them all into disrepute ; and partly the growing spirit of inquiry among the Greek people, who began to speculate upon political theories, and soon became discontented with a form of government, which had nothing in theory, and little in practice, to recommend it. Few dynasties lasted beyond the third generation. Most of the tyrannies, which flourished before the Persian war, are said to have been overthrown by the exertions of Sparta, jealous, probably, of any innovation upon the old Doric constitution, especially of any tendency to ameliorate the condition of the Perioeci, and anxious to extend her own influence over the states of Greece by means of the benefits which she conferred. Upon the fall of *tyranny*, the various republican forms of government were established, the Dorian states generally favouring oligarchy, the Ionian democracy. Of the tyrants of a later period, the most celebrated are the two Dionysii. The corruption of the Syracusans, their intestine discords, and the fear of the Carthaginian invaders, led to the appointment of Dionysius to the chief military command, with unlimited powers ; by means of which he raised himself to the throne, B. c. 406, and reigned for 38 years, leaving his son to succeed him. The younger Dionysius, far inferior in every respect to his father, was expelled by Dion, afterwards regained the throne, and was again expelled by Timoleon, who restored liberty to the various states of Sicily.

UDO, a sock of goat's-hair or felt, worn by countrymen with the low boots called *perones*. [PERO.]
ULNA. [PES.]
UMBILICUS. [LIBER.]
UMBO. [CLIPEUS.]
UMBRACULUM, UMBELLA (σκιάδειον, σκιάδιον, σκιαδίσκη), a parasol, was used by Greek and Roman ladies as a protection

against the sun. They seem not to have been carried generally by the ladies themselves, but by female slaves, who held them over their mistresses. The daughters of the aliens (μέτοικοι) at Athens had to carry parasols after the Athenian maidens at the Panathenaea, as is mentioned under HYDRIAPHORIA. The parasols of the ancients seem to have been exactly like our own parasols or umbrellas in form, and could be shut up and opened like ours. It was considered a mark of effeminacy for men to make use of parasols. The Roman ladies used them in the amphitheatre to defend themselves from the sun or some passing shower, when the wind or other circumstances did not allow the velarium to be extended. [AMPHITHEATRUM.] To hold a parasol over a lady was one of the common attentions of lovers, and it seems to have been very common to give parasols as presents. Instead of parasols, the

Umbraculum, Parasol. (From an ancient Vase.)

Greek women in later times wore a kind of straw hat or bonnet, called *tholia* (θολία). The Romans also wore a hat with a broad brim (*petasus*) as a protection against the sun.

UNCIA (ὀγκία, οὐγκία, οὐγγία), the twelfth part of the As or LIBRA, is derived by Varro from *unus*, as being the unit of the divisions of the as. Its value as a weight was 433·666 grains, or ¾ of an ounce and 105·36 grains avoirdupois. [LIBRA.] In connecting the

Roman system of weights and money with the Greek another division of the uncia was used. When the drachma was introduced into the Roman system as equivalent to the denarius of 96 to the pound [DENARIUS; DRACHMA], the uncia contained 8 drachmae, the drachma 3 scrupula, the scrupulum 2 oboli (since 6 oboli made up the drachma), and the obolos 3 siliquae (κεράτια). In this division we have the origin of the modern Italian system, in which the pound is divided into 12 ounces, the ounce into 3 drams, the dram into 3 scruples, and the scruple into 6 carats. In each of these systems 1728 κεράτια, siliquae, or carats, make up the pound. The Romans applied the uncial division to all kinds of magnitude. [As.] In length the uncia was the twelfth of a foot, whence the word *inch* [PES], in area the twelfth of a jugerum [JUGERUM], in content the twelfth of a sextarius [SEXTARIUS; CYATHUS], in time the twelfth of an hour.

UNCLARIUM FENUS. [FENUS.]
UNCTORES. [BALNEUM.]
UNGUENTA, ointments, oils, or salves. The application of unguenta in connection with the bathing and athletic contests of the ancients is stated under BALNEUM and ATHLETAE. But although their original object was simply to preserve the health and elasticity of the human frame, they were in later times used as articles of luxury. They were then not only employed to impart to the body or hair a particular colour, but also to give to them the most beautiful fragrance possible; they were, moreover, not merely applied after a bath, but at any time, to render one's appearance or presence more pleasant than usual. In short, they were used then as oils and pomatums are at present. At Rome these luxuries did not become very general till towards the end of the republic, while the Greeks appear to have been familiar with them from early times. The wealthy Greeks and Romans carried their ointments and perfumes with them, especially when they bathed, in small boxes of costly materials and beautiful workmanship, which were called *Narthecia*. The traffic which was carried on in these ointments and perfumes in several towns of Greece and southern Italy was very considerable. The persons engaged in manufacturing them were called by the Romans *Unguentarii*, or, as they frequently were women, *Unguentariae*, and the art of manufacturing them *Unguentaria*. In the wealthy and effeminate city of Capua there was one great street, called the Seplasia, which consisted entirely of shops in which ointments and perfumes were sold.

URAGUS. [CENTURIO.]

URCEUS, a pitcher or water-pot, generally made of earthenware, was used by the priests at Rome in the sacrifices, and thus appears with other sacrificial emblems on Roman coins.

Urceus and Lituus on obverse of Coin of Pompey.

URNA, an urn, a Roman measure of capacity for fluids, equal to half an AMPHORA. This use of the term was probably founded upon its more general application to denote a vessel for holding water, or any other substance, either fluid or solid. An urn was used to receive the names of the judges (*judices*) in order that the praetor might draw out of it a sufficient number to determine causes: also to receive the ashes of the dead.

USTRĪNA, USTRĪNUM. [BUSTUM.]

USŪCĂPĬO, the possession of property for a certain time without interruption. The Twelve Tables declared that the ownership of land, a house, or other immoveable property, could be acquired by usucapio in two years; and of moveable property by usucapio in one year.

USŪRAE. [FENUS.]

USUS. [MATRIMONIUM.]

USUSFRUCTUS was the right to the enjoyment of a thing by one person, while the ownership belonged to another. He who had the ususfructus was *Ususfructuarius* or *Fructuarius*, and the object of the ususfructus was *Res Fructuaria*.

UTRĬCŬLĀRĬUS. [TIBIA.]

UXOR. [MATRIMONIUM.]

UXŌRĬUM. [AES UXORIUM.]

VĂCĀTĬO. [EXERCITUS, EMERITI.]

VĂDĬMŌNĬUM, VAS. [ACTIO; PRAES.]

VĂGĪNA. [GLADIUS.]

VALLUM, a term applied either to the whole or a portion of the fortifications of a Roman camp. It is derived from *vallus* (a stake), and properly means the palisade which ran along the outer edge of the agger, but it very frequently includes the agger also. The *vallum*, in the latter sense, together with the *fossa* or ditch which surrounded the camp outside of the *vallum*, formed a complete fortification. The *valli* (χάρακες), of which the *vallum*, in the former and more limited sense, was composed, are described by Polybius and Livy, who make a comparison between the *vallum* of the Greeks and that of the Romans, very much to the advantage of the latter. Both used for *valli* young trees or arms of larger trees, with the side branches on them; but the *valli* of the Greeks were much larger and had more branches than those of the Romans, which had either two or three, or at the most four branches, and these generally on the same side. The Greeks placed their valli in the agger at considerable intervals, the spaces between them being filled up by the branches; the Romans fixed theirs close together, and made the branches interlace, and sharpened their points carefully. Hence the Greek vallus could easily be taken hold of by its large branches and pulled from its place, and when it was removed a large opening was left in the vallum. The Roman vallus, on the contrary, presented no convenient handle, required very great force to pull it down, and even if removed left a very small opening. The Greek valli were cut on the spot; the Romans prepared theirs beforehand, and each soldier carried three or four of them when on a march. They were made of any strong wood, but oak was preferred. The word *vallus* is sometimes used as equivalent to *vallum*. In the operations of a siege, when the place could not be taken by storm, and it became necessary to establish a blockade, this was done by drawing defences similar to those of a camp round the town, which was then said to be *circumvallatum*. Such a circumvallation, besides cutting off all communication between the town and the surrounding country, formed a defence against the sallies of the besieged. There was often a double line of fortifications, the inner against the town, and the outer against a force that might attempt to raise the siege. In this case the army was encamped between the two lines of works. This kind of circumvallation, which the Greeks called ἀποτειχισμός and περιτειχισμός, was employed by the Peloponnesians in the siege of Plataeae. Their lines consisted of two walls (apparently of turf) at the distance of 16 feet, which surrounded the city in the form of a circle. Between the walls were the huts of the besiegers. The wall had battlements (ἐπάλξεις), and at every tenth battlement was a tower, filling up by its depth the whole space between the walls. There was a passage for the besiegers through the middle of each tower. On the outside of each wall was a ditch (τάφρος). This description would almost exactly answer to the Roman mode of

| VALVAE. | 407 | VECTIGALIA. |

circumvallation, of which some of the best examples are that of Carthage by Scipio, that of Numantia by Scipio, and that of Alesia by Caesar. The towers in such lines were similar to those used in attacking fortified places, but not so high, and of course not moveable. [TURRIS.]

VALVAE. [JANUA.]

VANNUS (λικμός, λίκνον), a winnowing-van, *i. e.* a broad basket, into which the corn mixed with chaff was received after thrashing, and was then thrown in the direction of the wind. Virgil dignifies this simple implement by calling it *mystica vannus Iacchi*. The rites of Bacchus, as well as those of Ceres, having a continual reference to the occupations of rural life, the vannus was borne in the processions celebrated in honour of both these divinities. In the cut annexed the infant Bacchus is carried in a vannus by two dancing bacchantes clothed in skins.

Bacchus carried in a Vannus. (From an Antefixa in the British Museum.)

VAS (pl. *vasa*), a general term for any kind of vessel. Thus we read of *vas vinarium*, *vas argenteum*, *vasa Corinthia et Deliaca*, *vasa Samia*, that is, made of Samian earthenware, *vasa Murrhina*. [MURRHINA VASA.] The word *vas* was used in a still wider signification, and was applied to any kind of utensil used in the kitchen, agriculture, &c. The utensils of the soldiers were called *vasa*, and hence *vasa colligere* and *vasa conclamare* signify to pack up the baggage, to give the signal for departure.

VECTIGALIA, the general term for all the regular revenues of the Roman state. It means anything which is brought (*vehitur*) into the public treasury, like the Greek φόρος. The earliest regular income of the state was in all probability the rent paid for the use of the public land and pastures. This revenue was called *pascua*, a name which was used as late as the time of Pliny, in the tables or registers of the censors for all the revenues of the state in general. The senate was the supreme authority in all matters of finance, but as the state did not occupy itself with collecting the taxes, duties, and tributes, the censors were entrusted with the actual business. These officers, who in this respect may not unjustly be compared to modern ministers of finance, used to let the various branches of the revenue to the publicani for a fixed sum, and for a certain number of years. [CENSOR; PUBLICANI.] As most of the branches of the public revenues of Rome are treated of in separate articles, it is only necessary to give a list of them here, and to explain those which have not been treated of separately. 1. The tithes paid to the state by those who occupied the ager publicus. [DECUMAE; AGER PUBLICUS.] 2. The sums paid by those who kept their cattle on the public pastures. [SCRIPTURA.] 3. The harbour duties raised upon imported and exported commodities. [PORTORIUM.] 4. The revenue derived from the salt-works. [SALINAE.] 5. The revenues derived from the mines (*metalla*). This branch of the public revenue cannot have been very productive until the Romans had become masters of foreign countries. Until that time the mines of Italy appear to have been worked, but this was forbidden by the senate after the conquest of foreign lands. The mines of conquered countries were treated like the salinae. 6. The hundredth part of the value of all things which were sold (*centesima rerum venalium*). This tax was not instituted at Rome until the time of the civil wars ; the persons who collected it were called *coactores*. Tiberius reduced this tax to a two-hundredth (*ducentesima*), and Caligula abolished it for Italy altogether, whence upon several coins of this emperor we read B. C. C., that is, *Remissa Ducentesima*. Respecting the tax raised upon the sale of slaves, see QUINQUAGESIMA. 7. The vicesima hereditatum et manumissionum. [VICESIMA.] 8. The tribute imposed upon foreign countries was by far the most important branch of the public revenue during the time of Rome's greatness. It was sometimes raised at once, sometimes paid by instalments, and sometimes changed into a poll-tax, which was in many cases regulated according to the census. In regard to Cilicia and Syria we know that this tax amounted to one per cent. of a person's census, to which a tax upon houses and slaves was added. In some cases the tribute was not paid according to the census, but consisted in a land-tax. 9. A tax upon bachelors. [AES UXORIUM.] 10. A door-tax. [OSTIARIUM.] 11. The *octavae*. In the time of Caesar all liberti living in Italy, and possessing property of 200 sestertia, and above it, had to pay a tax consisting of the eighth part of their property.—It would be interesting to ascertain the amount of income which Rome at various periods derived from these and other sources; but our want of information renders it impossible. We have only the general statement, that previously to the time of Pompey the annual revenue amounted to fifty millions of drachmas, and that it was increased by him to eighty-five millions.

VELARIUM. [AMPHITHEATRUM, p. 23.]

VELITES, the light-armed troops in a Roman army. [EXERCITUS, p. 169.]

VELUM (αὐλαία).—(1) A curtain. Curtains were used in private houses as coverings over doors, or they served in the interior of the house as substitutes for doors.—(2) *Velum*, and more commonly its derivative *velamen*, denoted the veil worn by women. That worn by a bride was specifically called *flammeum*. [MATRIMONIUM.]—(3) ('Ιστίον.) A sail. [NAVIS, p. 267.]

VENABULUM, a hunting-spear. This may have been distinguished from the spears used in warfare by being barbed; at least it is often so formed in ancient works of art. It was seldom, if ever, thrown, but held so as to slant downwards and to receive the attacks of the wild boars and other beasts of chace.

VENATIO, hunting, was the name given among the Romans to an exhibition of wild beasts, which fought with one another and with men. These exhibitions originally formed part of the games of the circus. Julius Caesar first built a wooden amphitheatre for the exhibition of wild beasts, and others were subsequently erected; but we frequently read of venationes in the circus in subsequent times. The persons who fought with the beasts were either condemned criminals or captives, or individuals who did so for the sake of pay, and were trained for the purpose. [BESTIARII.] The Romans were as passionately fond of this entertainment as of the exhibitions of gladiators, and during the latter days of the republic, and under the empire, an immense variety of animals was collected from all parts of the Roman world for the gratification of the people, and many thousands were frequently slain at one time. We do not know on what occasion a venatio was first exhibited at Rome; but the first mention we find of any thing of the kind is in the year B. C. 251, when L. Metellus exhibited in the circus 142 elephants, which he had brought from Sicily after his victory over the Carthaginians. But this can scarcely be regarded as an instance of a venatio, as it was understood in later times, since the elephants are said to have been only killed because the Romans did not know what to do with them, and not for the amusement of the people. There was, however, a venatio in the later sense of the word in B. C. 186, in the games celebrated by M. Fulvius in fulfilment of the vow which he had made in the Aetolian war; in these games lions and panthers were exhibited. It is mentioned as a proof of the growing magnificence of the age that in the ludi circenses, exhibited by the curule aediles P. Cornelius Scipio Nasica and P. Lentulus B. C. 168, there were 63 African panthers and 40 bears and elephants. From about this time combats with wild beasts probably formed a regular part of the ludi circenses, and many of the curule aediles made great efforts to obtain rare and curious animals, and put in requisition the services of their friends. Elephants are said to have first fought in the circus in the curule aedileship of Claudius Pulcher, B. C. 99, and twenty years afterwards, in the curule aedileship of the two Lucullii, they fought against bulls. A hundred lions were exhibited by Sulla in his praetorship, which were destroyed by javelin-men sent by king Bocchus for the purpose. This was the first time that lions were allowed to be loose in the circus; they were previously always tied up. The games, however, in the curule aedileship of Scaurus, B. C. 58, surpassed anything the Romans had ever seen; among other novelties, he first exhibited an hippopotamos and five crocodiles in a temporary canal or trench (*euripus*). At the venatio given by Pompey in his second consulship, B. C. 55, upon the dedication of the temple of Venus Victrix, there was an immense number of animals slaughtered, among which we find mention of 600 lions, and 18 or 20 elephants; the latter fought with Gaetulians, who hurled darts against them, and they attempted to break through the railings (*clathri*) by which they were separated from the spectators. To guard against this danger Julius Caesar surrounded the arena of the amphitheatre with trenches (*euripi*). In the games exhibited by J. Caesar in his third consulship, B. C. 45, the venatio lasted for five days, and was conducted with extraordinary splendour. Cameleopards or giraffes were then for the first time seen in Italy. The venationes seem to have been first confined to the ludi circenses, but during the later times of the republic, and under the empire, they were frequently exhibited on the celebration of triumphs, and on many other occasions, with the view of pleasing the people. The passion for these shows continued to increase under the empire, and the number of beasts sometimes slaughtered seems almost incredible. Under the emperors we read of a particular kind of venatio, in which the beasts were not killed by bestiarii, but were given up to the people, who were allowed to rush into the area of the circus and carry away what they pleased. On such occasions a number of large trees, which had been torn up by the roots, was planted in the circus, which thus resembled a forest, and none of the more savage animals were admitted into it. One of the most extraordinary venationes of this kind was that given by Probus, in which there were 1000 ostriches, 1000 stags, 1000 boars, 1000 deer, and numbers of wild goats, wild sheep, and other animals of the same kind. The more savage animals were slain by the bestiarii in the amphitheatre, and not in the circus. Thus, in the day succeeding the venatio of Probus just mentioned, there were slain in the amphitheatre 100 lions and 100 lionesses, 100 Libyan and 100 Syrian leopards, and 300 bears.

Venationes. (From Bas-reliefs on the Tomb of Scaurus at Pompeii.)

VENEFICIUM, the crime of poisoning, is frequently mentioned in Roman history. Women were most addicted to it: but it seems not improbable that this charge was frequently brought against females without sufficient evidence of their guilt, like that of witchcraft in Europe in the middle ages. We find females condemned to death for this crime in seasons of pestilence, when the people are always in an excited state of mind, and ready to attribute the calamities under which they suffer to the arts of evil-disposed persons. Thus the Athenians, when the pestilence raged in their city during the Peloponnesian war, supposed the wells to have been poisoned by the Peloponnesians, and similar instances occur in the history of almost all states. Still, however, the crime of poisoning seems to have been much more frequent in ancient than in modern times;

and this circumstance would lead persons to suspect it in cases when there was no real ground for the suspicion. At Athens the PHARMACON GRAPHE was brought against poisoners. At Rome the first legislative enactment especially directed against poisoning was a law of the dictator Sulla—Lex Cornelia de Sicariis et Veneficis—passed in B. C. 82, which continued in force, with some alterations, to the latest times. It contained provisions against all who made, bought, sold, possessed, or gave poison for the purpose of poisoning. The punishment fixed by this law was the interdictio aquae et ignis.

VER SACRUM (ἔτος ἱερόν). It was a custom among the early Italian nations, especially among the Sabines, in times of great danger and distress, to vow to the deity the sacrifice of everything born in the next spring, that is, between the first of March and the last day of April, if the calamity under which they were labouring should be removed. This sacrifice in the early times comprehended both men and domestic animals, and there is little doubt that in many cases the vow was really carried into effect. But in later times it was thought cruel to sacrifice so many infants, and accordingly the following expedient was adopted. The children were allowed to grow up, and in the spring of their twentieth or twenty-first year they were with covered faces driven across the frontier of their native country, whereupon they went whithersoever fortune or the deity might lead them. Many a colony had been founded by persons driven out in this manner; and the Mamertines in Sicily were the descendants of such devoted persons. In the two historical instances in which the Romans vowed a ver sacrum, that is, after the battle of lake Trasimenus and at the close of the second Punic war, the vow was confined to domestic animals.

VERBENA. [SAGMINA.]
VERBENARIUS. [FETIALIS.]
VERNA. [SERVUS.]
VERSURA. [FENUS.]
VERU, VERUTUM. [HASTA.]
VESPAE, VESPILLONES. [FUNUS, p. 188.]

VESTALES, the virgin priestesses of Vesta, who ministered in her temple and watched the eternal fire. Their existence at Alba Longa is connected with the earliest Roman traditions, for Silvia the mother of Romulus was a member of the sisterhood; their establishment in the city, in common with almost all other matters connected with state religion, is generally ascribed to Numa, who selected four, two from the Titienses and two from the Ramnes; and two more were subsequently added from the Luceres, by Tarquinius Priscus according to one authority, by Servius Tullius according to another. This number of six remained unchanged to the latest times. They were originally chosen (*capere* is the technical word) by the king, and during the republic and empire by the pontifex maximus. It was necessary that the maiden should not be under six nor above ten years of age, perfect in all her limbs, in the full enjoyment of all her senses, patrima et matrima [PATRIMI], the daughter of free and freeborn parents who had never been in slavery, who followed no dishonourable occupation, and whose home was in Italy. The Lex Papia ordained that when a vacancy occurred the pontifex maximus should name at his discretion twenty qualified damsels, one of whom was publicly (*in concione*) fixed upon by lot, an exemption being granted in favour of such as had a sister already a vestal, and of the daughters of certain priests of a high class. The above law appears to have been enacted in consequence of the unwillingness of fathers to resign all control over a child, and this reluctance was manifested so strongly in later times, that in the age of Augustus *libertinae* were declared eligible. The casting of lots moreover does not seem to have been practised if any respectable person came forward voluntarily, and offered a daughter who fulfilled the necessary conditions. As soon as the election was concluded, the pontifex maximus took the girl by the hand and addressed her in a solemn form. After this was pronounced she was led away to the atrium of Vesta, and lived thenceforward within the sacred precincts, under the special superintendence and control of the pontifical college. The period of service lasted for thirty years. During the first ten the priestess was engaged in learning her mysterious duties, being termed *discipula*, during the next ten in performing them, during the last ten in giving instructions to the novices, and so long as she was thus employed she was bound by a solemn vow of chastity. But after the time specified was completed, she might, if she thought fit, throw off the emblems of her office, unconsecrate herself (*exaugurare*), return to the world, and even enter into the marriage state. Few however availed themselves of these privileges; those who did were said to have lived in sorrow and remorse (as might indeed have been expected from the habits they had formed); hence such a proceeding was considered ominous, and the priestesses for the most part died, as they had lived, in the service of the goddess. The senior sister was entitled *Vestalis Maxi-*

ma, or *Virgo Maxima*, and we find also the expressions *Vestalium vetustissima* and *tres maximae*. Their chief office was to watch by turns, night and day, the everlasting fire which blazed upon the altar of Vesta, its extinction being considered as the most fearful of all prodigies, and emblematic of the extinction of the state. If such misfortune befell, and was caused by the carelessness of the priestess on duty, she was stripped and scourged by the pontifex maximus, in the dark and with a screen interposed, and he rekindled the flame by the friction of two pieces of wood from a *felix arbor*. Their other ordinary duties consisted in presenting offerings to the goddess at stated times, and in sprinkling and purifying the shrine each morning with water, which according to the institution of Numa was to be drawn from the Egerian fount, although in later times it was considered lawful to employ any water from a living spring or running stream, but not such as had passed through pipes. When used for sacrificial purposes it was mixed with *muries*, that is, salt which had been pounded in a mortar, thrown into an earthen jar, and baked in an oven. They assisted moreover at all great public holy rites, such as the festivals of the Bona Dea, and the consecration of temples; they were invited to priestly banquets, and we are told that they were present at the solemn appeal to the gods made by Cicero during the conspiracy of Catiline. They also guarded the sacred relics which formed the *fatale pignus imperii*, the pledge granted by fate for the permanency of the Roman sway, deposited in the inmost adytum, which no one was permitted to enter save the virgins and the chief pontifex. What this object was no one knew; some supposed that it was the palladium, others the Samothracian gods carried by Dardanus to Troy, and transported from thence to Italy by Aeneas, but all agreed in believing that something of awful sanctity was here preserved, contained, it was said, in a small earthen jar closely sealed, while another exactly similar in form, but empty, stood by its side. We have seen above that supreme importance was attached to the purity of the vestals, and a terrible punishment awaited her who violated the vow of chastity. According to the law of Numa, she was simply to be stoned to death, but a more cruel torture was devised by Tarquinius Priscus, and inflicted from that time forward. When condemned by the college of pontifices, she was stripped of her vittae and other badges of office, was scourged, was attired like a corpse, placed in a close litter and borne through the forum attended by her weeping kindred, with all the ceremonies of a real funeral, to a rising ground called the *Campus Sceleratus*, just within the city walls, close to the Colline gate. There a small vault underground had been previously prepared, containing a couch, a lamp, and a table with a little food. The pontifex maximus, having lifted up his hands to heaven and uttered a secret prayer, opened the litter, led forth the culprit, and placing her on the steps of the ladder which gave access to the subterranean cell, delivered her over to the common executioner and his assistants, who conducted her down, drew up the ladder, and having filled the pit with earth until the surface was level with the surrounding ground, left her to perish deprived of all the tributes of respect usually paid to the spirits of the departed. In every case the paramour was publicly scourged to death in the forum. The honours which the vestals enjoyed were such as in a great measure to compensate for their privations. They were maintained at the public cost, and from sums of money and land bequeathed from time to time to the corporation. From the moment of their consecration they became as it were the property of the goddess alone, and were completely released from all parental sway, without going through the form of *emancipatio* or suffering any *capitis deminutio*. They had a right to make a will, and to give evidence in a court of justice without taking an oath. From the time of the triumviri each was preceded by a lictor when she went abroad; consuls and praetors made way for them, and lowered their fasces; even the tribunes of the plebs respected their holy character, and if any one passed under their litter he was put to death. Augustus granted to them all the rights of matrons who had borne three children, and assigned them a conspicuous place in the theatre, a privilege which they had enjoyed before at the gladiatorial shows. Great weight was attached to their intercession on behalf of those in danger and difficulty, of which we have a remarkable example in the entreaties which they addressed to Sulla on behalf of Julius Caesar, and if they chanced to meet a criminal as he was led to punishment, they had a right to demand his release, provided it could be proved that the encounter was accidental. Wills, even those of the emperors, were committed to their charge, for when in such keeping they were considered inviolable; and in like manner very solemn treaties, such as that of the triumvirs with Sextus Pompeius, were placed in their hands. That they might be honoured in death as in life, their ashes were interred within the pomoerium. They were attired in a stola over which was an upper vestment made of linen, and in addition to the infula and white woollen vitta, they wore when sacrificing a peculiar head-dress called *suffibulum*, consisting of a piece of white cloth bordered with purple, oblong in shape, and secured by a clasp. In dress and general deportment they were required to observe the utmost simplicity and decorum, any fanciful ornaments in the one or levity in the other being always regarded with disgust and suspicion. Their hair was cut off, probably at the period of their consecration: whether this was repeated from time to time does not appear, but they are never represented with flowing locks. The following cut represents the vestal Tuccia who, when wrongfully accused,

Vestal Virgin. (From a Gem.)

appealed to the goddess to vindicate her honour, and had power given to her to carry a sieve full of water from the Tiber to the temple. The form of the upper garment is well shown.

VESTĬBŬLUM. [Domus, p. 142, a.]
VĚTĔRĀNUS. [Tiro.]
VEXILLĀRĬI. [Exercitus, p. 170, b.]
VEXILLUM. [Signa Militaria.]

VIA, a public road. It was not until the period of the long protracted Samnite wars that the necessity was felt of securing a safe communication between the city and the legions, and then for the first time we hear of those famous paved roads, which, in after ages, connected Rome with her most distant provinces, constituting the most lasting of all her works. The excellence of the principles upon which they were constructed is sufficiently attested by their extraordinary durability, many specimens being found in the country around Rome which have been used without being repaired for more than a thousand years. The Romans are said to have adopted their first ideas upon this subject from the Carthaginians, and it is extremely probable that the latter people may, from their commercial activity and the sandy nature of their soil, have been compelled to turn their attention to the best means of facilitating the conveyance of merchandise to different parts of their territory. The first great public road made by the Romans was the Via Appia, which extended in the first instance from Rome to Capua, and was made in the censorship of Appius Claudius Caecus (B. C. 312.) The general construction of a Roman road was as follows:— In the first place, two shallow trenches (*sulci*) were dug parallel to each other, marking the breadth of the proposed road; this in the great lines is found to have been from 13 to 15 feet. The loose earth between the *sulci* was then removed, and the excavation continued until a solid foundation (*gremium*) was reached, upon which the materials of the road might firmly rest; if this could not be attained, in consequence of the swampy nature of the ground or from any peculiarity in the soil, a basis was formed artificially by driving piles (*fistucationibus*). Above the *gremium* were four distinct strata. The lowest course was the *statumen*, consisting of stones not smaller than the hand could just grasp; above the statumen was the *rudus*, a mass of broken stones cemented with lime, (what masons call *rubble-work*,) rammed down hard, and nine inches thick; above the rudus came the *nucleus*, composed of fragments of bricks and pottery, the pieces being smaller than in the rudus, cemented with lime, and six inches thick. Uppermost was the *pavimentum*, large polygonal blocks of the hardest stone (*silex*), usually, at least in the vicinity of Rome, basaltic lava, irregular in form, but fitted and jointed with the greatest nicety, so as to present a perfectly even surface, as free from gaps or irregularities as if the whole had been one solid mass. The general aspect will be understood from the cut given below. The centre of the way was a little elevated, so as to permit the water to run off easily. Occasionally, at least in cities, rectangular slabs of softer stone were employed instead of the irregular polygons of silex, and hence the distinction between the phrases *silice sternere* and *saxo quadrato sternere*. Nor was this all. Regular foot-paths (*margines, crepidines, umbones*) were raised upon each side and strewed with gravel, the different parts were strengthened and bound together with *gomphi* or stone wedges, and stone blocks were set up at moderate intervals on the side of the foot-paths, in order that travellers on horseback might be able to mount

Street at the entrance of Pompeii.

without assistance. Finally, Caius Gracchus erected mile-stones along the whole extent of the great highways, marking the distances from Rome, which appear to have been counted from the gate at which each road issued forth, and Augustus, when appointed inspector of the viae around the city, erected in the forum a gilded column (*milliarium aureum*), on which were inscribed the distances of the principal points to which the viae conducted. During the earlier ages of the republic the construction and general superintendence of the roads without, and the streets within the city, were committed like all other important works to the censors. These duties, when no censors were in office, devolved upon the consuls, and in their absence on the praetor urbanus, the aediles, or such persons as the senate thought fit to appoint. There were also under the republic four officers, called *quatuorviri viarum*, for superintending the streets within the city, and two called *curatores riarum*, for superintending the roads without. Under the empire the *curatores riarum* were officers of high rank. The chief roads which issued from Rome are:—1. The Via Appia, the Great South Road. It issued from the Porta Capena, and passing through *Aricia, Tres Tabernae, Appii Forum, Tarracina, Fundi, Formiae, Minturnae, Sinuessa,* and *Casili-num,* terminated at *Capua*, but was eventually extended through *Calatia* and *Caudium* to *Beneventum*, and finally from thence through *Venusia, Tarentum,* and *Uria,* to *Brundusium*.—2. The Via Latina, from the Porta Capena, another great line leading to Beneventum, but keeping a course farther inland than the Via Appia. Soon after leaving the city it sent off a short branch (Via Tusculana) to *Tusculum*, and passing through *Compitum Anaginum, Ferentinum, Frusino, Fregellae, Fabrateria, Aquinum, Casinum, Venafrum, Teanum, Allifae,* and *Telesia,* joined the Via Appia at *Beneventum*. A cross-road called the Via Hadriana, running from *Minturnae* through *Suessa Aurunca* to *Teanum*, connected the Via Appia with the Via Latina.—3. From the Porta Esquilina issued the Via Labicana, which passing Labicum fell into the Via Latina at the station *ad Bicium*, 30 miles from Rome. —4. The Via Praenestina, originally the Via Gabina, issued from the same gate with the former. Passing through *Gabii* and *Praeneste*, it joined the Via Latina just below *Anagnia*.—5. The Via Tiburtina, which issued from the Porta Tiburtina, and proceeding N. E. to *Tibur*, a distance of about 20 miles, was continued from thence, in the same direction, under the name of the Via Valeria, and traversing the country of the

Sabines passed through *Carseoli* and *Corfinium* to *Aternum* on the Adriatic, thence to *Adria*, and so along the coast to *Castrum Truentinum*, where it fell into the *Via Salaria*.—6. The VIA NOMENTANA, anciently FICULNENSIS, ran from the *Porta Collina*, crossed the *Anio* to *Nomentum*, and a little beyond fell into the *Via Salaria* at *Eretum*.—7. The VIA SALARIA, also from the *Porta Collina* (passing *Fidenae* and *Crustumerium*) ran north and east through Sabinum and Picenum to *Reate* and *Asculum Picenum*. At *Castrum Truentinum* it reached the coast, which it followed until it joined the *Via Flaminia* at *Ancona*.—8. The VIA FLAMINIA, the *Great North Road*, carried ultimately to *Ariminum*. It issued from the *Porta Flaminia*, and proceeded nearly north to *Ocriculum* and *Narnia* in Umbria. Here a branch struck off, making a sweep to the east through *Interamna* and *Spoletium*, and fell again into the main trunk (which passed through *Mevania*) at *Fulginia*. It continued through *Fanum Flaminii* and *Nuceria*, where it again divided, one line running nearly straight to *Fanum Fortunae* on the Adriatic, while the other diverging to *Ancona* continued from thence along the coast to *Fanum Fortunae*, where the two branches uniting passed on to *Ariminum* through *Pisaurum*. From thence the *Via Flaminia* was extended under the name of the VIA AEMILIA, and traversed the heart of Cisalpine Gaul through *Bononia*, *Mutina*, *Parma*, *Placentia* (where it crossed the Po), to *Mediolanum*.—9. The VIA AURELIA, the *Great Coast Road*, issued originally from the *Porta Janiculensis*, and subsequently from the *Porta Aurelia*. It reached the coast at *Alsium*, and followed the shore of the lower sea along Etruria and Liguria by *Genoa* as far as *Forum Julii* in Gaul. In the first instance it extended no farther than *Pisa*.—10. The VIA PORTUENSIS kept the right bank of the Tiber to *Portus Augusti*.—11. The VIA OSTIENSIS originally passed through the *Porta Trigemina*, afterwards through the *Porta Ostiensis*, and kept the left bank of the Tiber to *Ostia*. From thence it was continued under the name of VIA SEVERIANA along the coast southward through *Laurentum*, *Antium*, and *Circaei*, till it joined the *Via Appia* at *Taracina*. The VIA LAURENTINA, leading direct to *Laurentum*, seems to have branched off from the *Via Ostiensis* at a short distance from Rome.—12. The VIA ARDEATINA from Rome to *Ardea*. According to some this branched off from the *Via Appia*, and thus the circuit of the city is completed.

VIATICUM is, properly speaking, everything necessary for a person setting out on a journey, and thus comprehends money, provisions, dresses, vessels, &c. When a Roman magistrate, praetor, proconsul, or quaestor went to his province, the state provided him with all that was necessary for his journey. But as the state in this, as in most other cases of expenditure, preferred paying a sum at once to having any part in the actual business, it engaged contractors (*redemptores*), who for a stipulated sum had to provide the magistrates with the viaticum, the principal parts of which appear to have been beasts of burden and tents (*muli et tabernacula*). Augustus introduced some modification of this system, as he once for all fixed a certain sum to be given to the proconsuls (probably to other provincial magistrates also) on setting out for their provinces, so that the redemptores had no more to do with it.

VIATOR, a servant who attended upon and executed the commands of certain Roman magistrates, to whom he bore the same relation as the lictor did to other magistrates. The name *viatores* was derived from the circumstance of their being chiefly employed on messages either to call upon senators to attend the meeting of the senate, or to summon people to the comitia, &c. In the earlier times of the republic we find viatores as ministers of such magistrates also as had their lictors: viatores of a dictator and of the consuls are mentioned by Livy. In later times, however, viatores are only mentioned with such magistrates as had only potestas and not imperium, such as the tribunes of the people, the censors, and the aediles.

VICTIMA. [SACRIFICIUM.]

VICESIMA, a tax of five per cent. Every Roman, when he manumitted a slave, had to pay to the state a tax of one-twentieth of his value, whence the tax was called *vicesima manumissionis*. This tax was first imposed by the Lex Manlia (B. c. 357), and was not abolished when all other imposts were done away with in Rome and Italy. A tax called *vicesima hereditatum et legatorum* was introduced by Augustus (*Lex Julia Vicesimaria*): it consisted of five per cent., which every Roman citizen had to pay to the aerarium militare, upon any inheritance or legacy left to him, with the exception of such as were left to a citizen by his nearest relatives, and such as did not amount to above a certain sum. It was levied in Italy and the provinces by procuratores appointed for the purpose.

VICOMAGISTRI. [VICUS.]

VICUS, the name of the subdivisions into which the four regions occupied by the four city tribes of Servius Tullius were divided, while the country regions, according to an institution ascribed to Numa, were subdivided into pagi. This division, together with that of the four regions of the four city tribes, remained down to the time of Augustus, who made the vici subdivisions of the fourteen regions into which he divided the city. In this division each vicus consisted of one main street, including several smaller by-streets; their number was 424, and each was superintended by four officers, called *vico-magistri*, who had a sort of local police, and who, according to the regulation of Augustus, were every year chosen by lot from among the people who lived in the vicus. On certain days, probably at the celebration of the compitalia, they wore the praetexta, and each of them was accompanied by two lictors. These officers, however, were not a new institution of Augustus, for they had existed during the time of the republic, and had had the same functions as a police for the vici of the Servian division of the city.

VICTŌRIĀTUS. [DENARIUS.]
VĬGĬLES. [EXERCITUS, p. 171.]
VĬGĬLIAE. [CASTRA.]
VĪGINTĪSEXVĪRI, twenty-six magistratus minores, among whom were included the Triumviri Capitales, the Triumviri Monetales, the Quatuorviri Viarum Curandarum for the city, the two Curatores Viarum for the roads outside the city, the Decemviri Litibus (*stlitibus*) Judicandis, and the four praefects who were sent into Campania for the purpose of administering justice there. Augustus reduced the number of officers of this college to twenty (*vigintiviri*), as the two curatores viarum for the roads outside the city and the four Campanian praefects were abolished. Down to the time of Augustus the sons of senators had generally sought and obtained a place in the college of the vigintisexviri, it being the first step towards the higher offices of the republic; but in A. D. 13 a senatusconsultum was passed, ordaining that only equites should be eligible to the college of the vigintiviri. The consequence of this was that the vigintiviri had no seats in the senate, unless they had held some other magistracy which conferred this right upon them. The age at which a person might become a vigintivir appears to have been twenty.

VĬGINTĪVĬRI. [VIGINTISEXVIRI.]

VILLA, a farm or country-house. The Roman writers mention two kinds of villa, the *villa rustica* or farm-house, and the *villa urbana* or *pseudo-urbana*, a residence in the country or in the suburbs of a town. When both of these were attached to an estate they were generally united in the same range of buildings, but sometimes they were placed at different parts of the estate. The interior arrangements of the *villa urbana* corresponded for the most part to those of a town-house. [DOMUS.]

VILLĬCUS, a slave who had the superintendence of the *villa rustica*, and of all the business of the farm, except the cattle, which were under the care of the *magister pecoris*. The word was also used to describe a person to whom the management of any business was entrusted.

VĪNĀLIA. There were two festivals of this name celebrated by the Romans: the *Vinalia urbana* or *priora*, and the *Vinalia rustica* or *altera*. The vinalia urbana were celebrated on the 23rd of April, when the wine-casks which had been filled the preceding autumn were opened for the first time, and the wine tasted. The rustic vinalia, which fell on the 19th of August, and was celebrated by the inhabitants of all Latium, was the day on which the vintage was opened. On this occasion the flamen dialis offered lambs to Jupiter, and while the flesh of the victims lay on the altar, he broke with his own hands a bunch of grapes from a vine, and by this act he, as it were, opened the vintage, and no must was allowed to be conveyed into the city until this solemnity was performed. This day was sacred to Jupiter, and Venus too appears to have had a share in it.

VINDĒMĬĀLIS FĒRĬA. [FERIAE.]
VINDEX. [ACTIO.]
VINDICTA. [MANUMISSIO.]

VĪNEA, in its literal signification, is a bower formed of the branches of vines, and, from the protection which such a leafy roof affords, the name was applied by the Romans to a roof under which the besiegers of a town protected themselves against darts, stones, fire, and the like, which were thrown by the besieged upon the assailants. The whole machine formed a roof, resting upon posts eight feet in height. The roof itself was generally sixteen feet long and seven broad. The wooden frame was in most cases light, so that it could be carried by the soldiers; sometimes, however, when the purpose which it was to serve required great strength, it was heavy, and then the whole fabric probably was moved by wheels attached to the posts. The roof was formed of planks and wicker-work, and the uppermost layer or layers consisted of raw hides or wet cloth, as a protection against fire, by which the besieged frequently destroyed the vineae. The sides of a vinea were likewise protected by wicker-work. Such machines were constructed in a safe place at some distance from the besieged town, and then carried or wheeled (*agere*) close to its walls. Here several of them were frequently joined together, so that a great number of soldiers might be employed under them. When vineae had taken their place close to the walls, the soldiers began their operations, either by undermining the walls, and thus opening a breach, or by employing the battering-ram (*aries*).

VINUM (οἶνος). The general term for the fermented juice of the grape. In the Homeric poems the cultivation of the grape is represented as familiar to the Greeks. It is worth remarking that the only wine upon whose excellence Homer dilates in a tone approaching to hyperbole is represented as having been produced on the coast of Thrace, the region from which poetry and civilisation spread into Hellas, and the scene of several of the more remarkable exploits of Bacchus. Hence we might infer that the Pelasgians introduced the culture of the vine when they wandered westward across the Hellespont, and that in like manner it was conveyed to the valley of the Po, when at a subsequent period they made their way round the head of the Adriatic. It seems certain that wine was both rare and costly in the earlier ages of Roman history. As late as the time of the Samnite wars, Papirius the dictator, when about to join in battle with the Samnites, vowed to Jupiter only a small cupful (*vini poeillum*) if he should gain the victory. In the times of Marius and Sulla foreign wines were considered far superior to native growths; but the rapidity with which luxury spread in this matter is well illustrated by the saying of M. Varro, that Lucullus when a boy never saw an entertainment in his father's house, however splendid, at which Greek wine was handed round more than once, but when in manhood he returned from his Asiatic conquests he bestowed on the people a largess of more than a hundred thousand cadi. Four different kinds of wine are said to have been presented for the first time at the feast given by Julius Caesar in his third consulship (B. C. 46), these being Falernian, Chian, Lesbian, and Mamertine, and not until after this date were the merits of the numerous varieties, foreign and domestic, accurately known and fully appreciated. But during the reign of Augustus and his immediate successors the study of wines became a passion, and the most scrupulous care was bestowed upon every process connected with their production and preservation. Pliny calculates that the number of wines in the whole world deserving to be accounted of high quality (*nobilia*) amounted to eighty, of which his own country could claim two-thirds; and that 195 distinct kinds might be reckoned up, and that if all the varieties of these were to be included in the computation, the sum would be almost doubled.—The process followed in wine-making was essentially the same among both the Greeks and the Romans. After the grapes had been gathered they were first trodden with the feet in a vat (ληνός, *torcular*); but as this process did not press out all the juice of the grapes, they were subjected to the more powerful pressure of a thick and heavy beam (*prelum*) for the purpose of obtaining all the juice yet remaining in them. From the press the sweet unfermented juice flowed into another large vat, which was sunk below the level of the press, and therefore called the *under wine-vat*, in Greek ὑπολήνιον, in Latin *lacus*. A portion of the must was used at once, being drunk fresh after it had been clarified with vinegar. When it was desired to preserve a quantity in the sweet state, an amphora was taken and coated with pitch within and without, and corked so as to be perfectly air-tight. It was then immersed in a tank of cold fresh water or buried in wet sand, and allowed to remain for six weeks or two months. The contents after this process were found to remain unchanged for a year, and hence the name ἀεὶ γλεῦκος, *i. e. semper mustum*. A considerable quantity of must from the best and oldest vines was inspissated by boiling, being then distinguished by the Greeks under the general names of ἕψημα or γλύξις, while the Latin writers have various terms according to the extent to which the evaporation was carried. Thus, when the must was reduced to two-thirds of its original volume it became *carenum*, when one-half had evaporated *defrutum*, when two-thirds *sapa* (known also by the Greek names *siraeum* and *hepsema*), but these words are frequently interchanged. Similar preparations are at the present time called in Italy *musto cotto* and *sapa*, and in France *sabe*. The process was carried on in large caldrons of lead (*vasa defrutaria*), over a slow fire of chips, on a night when there was no moon, the scum being carefully removed with leaves, and the liquid constantly stirred to prevent it from burning. These grape-jellies, for they were nothing else, were used extensively for giving body to poor wines and making them keep, and entered as ingredients into many drinks, such as the *burranica potio*, so called from its red colour, which was formed by mixing *sapa* with milk. The whole of the mustum not employed for some of the above purposes was conveyed from the *lacus* to the *cella vi-*

naria, an apartment on the ground-floor or a little below the surface. Here were the *dolia* (πίθοι), otherwise called *seriae* or *cupae*, long bell-mouthed vessels of earthenware, very carefully formed of the best clay, and lined with a coating of pitch. They were usually sunk (*depressa, defossa, demersa*) one-half or two-thirds in the ground; to the former depth, if the wine to be contained was likely to prove strong, to the latter if weak. In these *dolia* the process of fermentation took place, which usually lasted for about nine days, and as soon as it had subsided, and the *mustum* had become *vinum*, the dolia were closely covered. The lids (*opercula doliorum*), were taken off about once every thirty-six days, and oftener in hot weather, in order to cool and give air to the contents, to add any preparation required to preserve them sound, and to remove any impurities that might be thrown up. The commoner sorts of wine were drunk direct from the dolium, and hence draught wine was called *vinum doliare* or *vinum de cupa*, but the finer kinds were drawn off (*diffundere*, μεταγγίζειν), into *amphorae*. On the outside the title of the wine was painted, the date of the vintage being marked by the names of the consuls then in office. [AMPHORA.] The amphorae were then stored up in repositories (*apothecae, horrea, tabulata*), completely distinct from the *cella vinaria*, and usually placed in the upper story of the house (whence *descende, testa*, and *deripere horreo* in Horace), for a reason explained afterwards. It is manifest that wine prepared and bottled in the manner described above must have contained a great quantity of dregs and sediment, and it became absolutely necessary to separate these before it was drunk. This was sometimes effected by fining with yolks of eggs, those of pigeons being considered most appropriate by the fastidious, but more commonly by simply straining through small cup-like utensils of silver or bronze perforated with numerous small holes. Occasionally a piece of linen cloth (σάκκος, *saccus*) was placed over the *colum*, and the wine filtered through. [COLUM.] In all the best wines hitherto described the grapes are supposed to have been gathered as soon as they were fully ripe, and fermentation to have run its full course. But a great variety of sweet wines were manufactured by checking the fermentation, or by partially drying the grapes, or by converting them completely into raisins. *Passum* or *raisin-wine* was made from grapes dried in the sun until they had lost half their weight, or they were plunged into boiling oil, which produced a similar effect, or the bunches after they were ripe were allowed to hang for some weeks upon the vine, the stalks being twisted or an incision made into the pith of the bearing shoot so as to put a stop to vegetation. The stalks and stones were removed, the raisins were steeped in must or good wine, and then trodden or subjected to the gentle action of the press. The quantity of juice which flowed forth was measured, and an equal quantity of water added to the pulpy residuum, which was again pressed, and the product employed for an inferior *passum* called *secundarium*. The passum of Crete was most prized, and next in rank were those of Cilicia, Africa, Italy, and the neighbouring provinces. The kinds known as *Psythium* and *Melampsythium* possessed the peculiar flavour of the grape and not that of wine. The grapes most suitable for passum were those which ripened early, especially the varieties *Apiana, Scirpula*, and *Psithia*. The Greeks recognised three colours in wines: red (μέλας), *white*, i. e. pale straw-colour (λευκός), and brown or amber-coloured (κιρρός). The Romans distinguish four: *albus*, answering to λευκός, *fulvus* to κιρρός, while μέλας is subdivided into *sanguineus* and *niger*, the former being doubtless applied to bright glowing wines like Tent and Burgundy, while the *niger* or *ater* would resemble Port. We have seen that wine intended for keeping was racked

Silenus astride upon a Wine-skin. (Museo Borbonico, vol. iii. tav. 23.)

off from the dolia into amphorae. When it was necessary in the first instance to transport it from one place to another, or when carried by travellers on a journey, it was contained in bags made of goat-skin (ἀσκοί, *utres*) well pitched over so as to make the seams perfectly tight. As the process of wine-making among the ancients was for the most part conducted in an unscientific manner, it was found necessary, except in the case of the finest varieties, to have recourse to various devices for preventing or correcting acidity, heightening the flavour, and increasing the durability of the second growths. The object in view was accomplished sometimes by merely mixing different kinds of wine together, but more frequently by throwing into the dolia or amphorae various condiments or seasonings (ἀρτύσεις, *medicamina, conditurae*). The principal substances employed as *conditurae* were, 1. sea-water; 2. turpentine, either pure, or in the form of pitch (*pix*), tar (*pix liquida*), or resin (*resina*). 3. Lime, in the form of gypsum, burnt marble, or calcined shells. 4. Inspissated must. 5. Aromatic herbs, spices, and gums; and these were used either singly, or cooked up into a great variety of complicated confections. But not only were spices and gums steeped in wine or incorporated during fermentation, but even the precious perfumed essential oils (*unguenta*) were mixed with it before it was drunk (μυρρίνη, *murrhina*.) Of these compound beverages the most popular was the *oenomeli* (οἰνόμελι) of the Greeks, the *mulsum* of the Romans. This was of two kinds; in the one honey was mixed with wine, in the other with must. The former was said to have been invented by the legendary hero Aristaeus, the first cultivator of bees, and was considered most perfect and palatable when made of some old rough (*austerum*) wine, such as Massic or Falernian (although Horace objects to the latter for this purpose), and new Attic honey. The proportions were four, by measure, of wine to one of honey, and various spices and perfumes, such as myrrh, cassia, costum, malobathrum, nard, and pepper, might be added. The second kind was made of must evaporated to one half of its original bulk, Attic honey being added in the proportion of one to ten. This, therefore, was merely a very rich fruit syrup, in no way allied to wine. *Mulsum* was considered the most appropriate draught upon an empty stomach, and was therefore swallowed immediately before the regular business of a repast began and hence the whet (*gustatio*) coming before the cup of mulsum was called the *promulsis*. *Mulsum* was given

at a triumph by the imperator to his soldiers. *Mulsum* (sc. *vinum*) or *oenomeli* (οἰνόμελι) is perfectly distinct from *mulsa* (sc. *aqua*). The latter, or *mead*, being made of honey and water mixed and fermented, is the *melicraton* (μελίκρατον) or *hydromeli* (ὑδρόμελι) of the Greeks. The ancients considered old wine not only more grateful to the palate, but also more wholesome and invigorating. Generally speaking the Greek wines do not seem to have required a long time to ripen. Nestor in the Odyssey, indeed, drinks wine ten years old; but the connoisseurs under the empire pronounced that all transmarine wines arrived at a moderate degree of maturity in six or seven. Many of the Italian varieties, however, required to be kept for twenty or twenty-five years before they were drinkable (which is now considered ample for our strongest ports), and even the humble growths of Sabinum were stored up for from four to fifteen. Hence it became a matter of importance to hasten, if possible, the natural process. This was attempted in various ways, sometimes by elaborate condiments, sometimes by sinking vessels containing the must in the sea, by which an artificial mellowness was induced (*praecox vetustas*) and the wine in consequence termed *thalassites*; but more usually by the application of heat. Thus it was customary to expose the amphorae for some years to the full fervour of the sun's rays, or to construct the *apothecae* in such a manner as to be exposed to the hot air and smoke of the bath-furnaces, and hence the name *fumaria* applied to such apartments, and the phrases *fumosos, fumum bibere, fuligine testae*, in reference to the wines. If the operation was not conducted with care, and the amphorae not stoppered down perfectly tight, a disagreeable effect would be produced on the contents. In Italy, in the first century of the Christian aera, the lowest market price of the most ordinary quality of wine was 300 sesterces for 40 urnae, that is, 15 sesterces for the amphora, or 6d. a gallon nearly. At a much earlier date, the triumph of L. Metellus during the first Punic war (b. c. 250), wine was sold at the rate of 8 asses the amphora. The price of native wine at Athens was four drachmas for the metretes, that is, about 4½d. the gallon, when necessaries were dear, and we may perhaps assume one half of this sum as the average of cheaper times. On the other hand, high prices were given freely for the varieties held in esteem, since as early as the time of Socrates a metretes of Chian sold for a mina.—With respect to the way in which wine was drunk, and the customs observed by the Greeks and

Romans at their drinking entertainments, the reader is referred to the article SYMPOSIUM.—The **wine** of most early celebrity was **that** which **the** minister of Apollo, Maron, **who** dwelt upon the skirts of Thracian Ismarus, gave to Ulysses. It was red (ἐρυθρόν), and honey-sweet (μελιηδέα), **so precious, that it** was unknown to all in **the mansion save** the wife of the priest and one **trusty housekeeper**; so strong, that a single **cup was mingled** with twenty of water; **so fragrant, that** even when thus diluted **it diffused a divine** and most tempting perfume. **Homer** mentions also more than once *Pramnian wine* (**οἶνος** Πραμνεῖος), an epithet which **is variously interpreted** by different **writers**. In after times a wine bearing **the same name was produced** in the island **of Icaria,** around the **hill village** of Latorea **in the** vicinity of Ephesus, in the neighbourhood **of** Smyrna, **near the** shrine **of Cybele,** and **in** Lesbos. But **the** wines **of greatest** renown at a later period were grown in the islands of Thasos, Lesbos, Chios, and Cos, and in a few favoured spots on the opposite coast of Asia, such as the slopes of Mount Tmolus, **the ridge** which separates the valley of the **Hermus** from that of **the Caÿster,** Mount **Messogis, which divides the tributaries of the Caÿster from** those **of the** Meander, **the volcanic region of** the **Catacecaumene, which** still retains its fame, the environs **of Ephesus, of Cnidus, of** Miletus, and **of** Clazomenae. **Among these** the first place seems to have **been by general** consent conceded to the **Chian, of which** the most delicious varieties were **brought** from the heights of Ariusium **in the central** parts, and from the promontory **of Phanae** at the southern extremity **of the island.** The *Thasian* and *Lesbian* occupied the second place, and the *Coan* disputed the palm with them. In Lesbos the most highly **prized** vineyards were around Mytilene and **Methymna.** There is no foundation whatever **for the** remark that the finest Greek wines, especially the products of the islands in the Aegean and Ionian seas, belonged for the most part to the luscious sweet class. **The** very reverse is proved by the epithets αὐστηρός, σκληρός, λεπτός, and the like, applied to a great number, while γλυκύς and γλυκάζων are designations comparatively rare, except in the vague language of poetry.—The most noble Italian wines, with a very few exceptions, were derived from Latium and Campania, and for the most part grew within a short distance of the sea. In **the** first rank we must place the *Setinum*, which fairly deserves the title of *Imperial*, since it was the chosen beverage of Augustus and most of his courtiers. It grew upon the hills of Setia, above Forum Appii, looking down upon the Pomptine marshes. Before the age of Augustus the *Caecubum* was the most prized of all. It grew in the poplar swamps bordering on the gulf of Amyclae, close to Fundi. In the time of Pliny its reputation was entirely gone, partly in consequence of the carelessness of the cultivators, and partly from its proper soil, originally a very limited space, having been **cut up** by **the canal** of Nero extending from **Baiae to Ostia.** It was full-bodied and heady, not arriving at maturity until it had been kept for many years. The second rank was occupied by **the *Falernum*,** of which the *Faustianum* was **the most** choice variety, having gained its character from the care and skill exercised in the cultivation of the vines. **The *Falernus ager* commenced at the Pons Campanus, on the left hand of those journeying towards the Urbana Colonia of Sulla, the *Faustianus ager*** at a village about six miles from Sinuessa, so that the **whole district in question may be** regarded **as stretching from the Massic hills** to the **river Vulturnus.** Falernian became fit for drinking in ten years, and might be used until twenty years old, but when kept longer gave headachs, and proved injurious to **the nervous system.** Pliny distinguishes three kinds, the rough (*austerum*), the sweet (*dulce*), **and** the thin (*tenue*). Others arranged the varieties differently; that which grew upon the hill tops they called *Caucinum,* that on the middle slopes *Faustianum,* and that on the plain *Falernum.* In the third rank was the *Albanum,* from the Mons Albanus, **of various** kinds, very sweet (*praedulce*), sweetish, rough, and sharp; it was invigorating (*nervis utile*), and in perfection after being kept for fifteen years. Here too we place the *Surrentinum,* from the promontory forming the southern horn of the bay **of** Naples, which was not drinkable until it had been kept for five-and-twenty **years,** for, being destitute of richness, and **very** dry, it required a long time to ripen, **but** was strongly recommended to convalescents, on account of its thinness and wholesomeness. Of equal reputation were the *Massicum,* from the hills which formed the boundary between Latium and Campania, although somewhat harsh, and the *Gauranum,* from the ridge above Baiae and Puteoli, produced in small quantity, but of very high quality, full-bodied, and thick. In the same class are to be included the *Calenum* from Cales, and the *Fundanum* from Fundi. The *Calenum* was light and better for the stomach than Falernian; the *Fundanum* was full-bodied and nourishing, but apt to attack both stomach and head; therefore little sought after at banquets. This list is closed by the *Veliturninum, Privernatinum,* and *Signinum,* from Velitrae, Privernum, and Signia, towns on the Volscian hills; the first was a sound wine, but had this peculiarity, that it always tasted as if mixed with some foreign substance; the second was thin and pleasant; the last was looked upon only in the light of a medicine valuable for its astringent qualities. We may safely bring in one more, the *Formianum,* from the Gulf of Caieta, associated by Horace with the Caecuban, Falernian, and Calenian. The fourth rank contained the *Mamertinum,* from the neighbourhood of Messana, first brought into fashion by Julius Caesar. The finest was sound, light, and at the same time not without body.

VIRGINES VESTALES. [VESTALES VIRGINES.]

VIS. Leges were passed at Rome for the purpose of preventing acts of violence. The Lex Plotia or Plautia was enacted against those who occupied public places and carried arms. The lex proposed by the consul Q. Catulus on the subject, with the assistance of Plautius the tribunus, appears to be the Lex Plotia. There was a Lex Julia of the dictator Caesar on this subject, which imposed the penalty of exile. Two Juliae Leges were passed as to this matter in the time of Augustus, which were respectively entitled De Vi Publica and De Vi Privata.

VISCERATIO. [FUNUS, p. 190, b.]

VITIS. [CENTURIO.]

VITRUM (ὕαλος), glass. A story has been preserved by Pliny, that glass was first discovered accidentally by some merchants who, having landed on the Syrian coast at the mouth of the river Belus, and being unable to find stones to support their cooking-pots, fetched for this purpose from their ships some of the lumps of nitre which composed the cargo. This being fused by the heat of the fire, united with the sand upon which it rested, and formed a stream of vitrified matter. No conclusion can be drawn from this tale, even if true, in consequence of its vagueness; but it probably originated in the fact, that the sand of the district in question was esteemed peculiarly suitable for glass-making, and was exported in great quantities to the workshops of Sidon and Alexandria, long the most famous in the ancient world. Alexandria sustained its reputation for many centuries: Rome derived a great portion of its supplies from this source, and as late as the reign of Aurelian we find the manufacture still flourishing. There is some difficulty in deciding by what Greek author glass is first mentioned, because the term ὕαλος unquestionably denotes not only artificial glass but rock-crystal, or indeed any transparent stone or stone-like substance. Thus the ὕελος of Herodotus, in which the Ethiopians encased the bodies of their dead, cannot be glass, for we are expressly told that it was dug in abundance out of the earth; and hence commentators have conjectured that rock-crystal or rock-salt, or amber, or oriental alabaster, or some bituminous or gummy product, might be indicated. But when the same historian, in his account of sacred crocodiles, states that they were decorated with ear-rings made of melted stone, we may safely conclude that he intends to describe some vitreous ornament for which he knew no appropriate name. Glass is, however, first mentioned with certainty by Theophrastus, who notices the circumstance alluded to above, of the fitness of the sand at the mouth of the river Belus for the fabrication of glass. Among the Latin writers Lucretius appears to be the first in which the word *vitrum* occurs; but it must have been well known to his countrymen long before, for Cicero names it along with paper and linen, as a common article of merchandise brought from Egypt. Scaurus, in his aedileship (B. C. 58), made a display of it such as was never witnessed even in after-times; for the *scena* of his gorgeous theatre was divided into three tiers, of which the under portion was of marble, the upper of gilded wood, and the middle compartment of glass. In the poets of the Augustan age it is constantly introduced, both directly and in similes, and in such terms as to prove that it was an object with which every one must be familiar. Strabo declares that in his day a small drinking-cup of glass might be purchased at Rome for half an as, and so common was it in the time of Juvenal and Martial, that old men and women made a livelihood by trucking sulphur matches for broken fragments. When Pliny wrote, manufactories had been established not only in Italy, but in Spain and Gaul also, and glass drinking-cups had entirely superseded those of gold and silver; and in the reign of Alexander Severus we find *vitrearii* ranked along with curriers, coachmakers, goldsmiths, silversmiths, and other ordinary artificers whom the emperor taxed to raise money for his thermae. The numerous specimens transmitted to us prove that the ancients were well acquainted with the art of imparting a great variety of colours to their glass; they were probably less successful in their attempts to render it perfectly pure and free from all colour, since we are told that it was considered most valuable in this state. It was wrought according to the different methods now practised, being fashioned into the required shape by the blowpipe, *cut*, as we term it, although *ground* (*teritur*) is a more accurate phrase, upon a wheel, and engraved with a sharp tool like silver. The art of etching upon glass, now so common, was entirely unknown, since it depends upon the properties of fluoric acid, a chemical discovery of the last century. The following were the chief uses to which glass was applied:—1. Bottles, vases, cups, and cinerary urns. 2. Glass pastes, presenting fac-similes either in relief or intaglio of engraved precious stones. 3. Imitations of coloured precious stones, such as the carbuncle, the sapphire, the amethyst, and, above all, the emerald. 4. Thick sheets of glass of various colours appear to have been laid down for paving floors, and to have been attached as a lining to the walls and ceilings of apartments in dwelling houses, just as scagliuola is frequently employed in Italy, and occasionally in our own country also. Rooms fitted up in this way were called *vitreae camerae*, and the panels *vitreae quadraturae*. Such was the kind of decoration introduced by Scaurus for the scene of his theatre, not columns nor pillars of glass as some, nor bas-reliefs as others have imagined. 5. Glass was also used for windows. [DOMUS, p. 144.]

VITTA, or plural VITTAE, a ribbon or fillet, is to be considered, 1. As an ordinary portion of female dress. 2. As a decoration of sacred persons and sacred things. 1. When considered as an ordinary portion of female dress, it was simply a band encircling the head, and serving to confine the tresses (*crinales vittae*), the ends when long (*longae taenia vittae*) hanging down behind. It was worn by maidens, and by married women also, the vitta assumed on the nuptial day being of a different form from that used by virgins. The Vitta was *not* worn by libertinae even of fair character, much less by meretrices; hence it was looked upon as an *insigne pudoris*, and, together with the *stola* and *instita*, served to point out at first sight the freeborn matron. The colour was probably a matter of choice: white and purple are both mentioned. When employed for sacred purposes, it was usually twisted round the infula [INFULA], and held together the loose flocks of wool. Under this form it was employed as an ornament for 1. Priests, and those who offered sacrifice. 2. Priestesses, especially those of Vesta, and hence *vittata sacerdos* for a vestal, κατ' ἐξόχην. 3. Prophets and poets, who may be regarded as priests, and in this case the vittae were frequently intertwined with chaplets of olive or laurel. 4. Statues of deities. 5. Victims decked for sacrifice. 6. Altars. 7. Temples. 8. The ἱκετήρια of suppliants. The sacred vittae, as well as the infulae, were made of wool, and hence the epithets *lanea* and *mollis*. They were white (*niveae*), or purple (*puniceae*), or azure (*caeruleae*), when wreathed round an altar to the manes.

VOLONES is synonymous with *Voluntarii* (from *volo*), and might hence be applied to all those who volunteered to serve in the Roman armies without there being any obligation to do so. But it was applied more especially to slaves, when in times of need they offered or were allowed to fight in the Roman armies. Thus when during the second Punic war, after the battle of Cannae, there was not a sufficient number of freemen to complete the army, about 8000 young and able-bodied slaves offered to serve. Their proposal was accepted; they received armour at the public expense, and as they distinguished themselves they were honoured with the franchise. In after times the name volones was retained whenever slaves chose or were allowed to take up arms in defence of their masters, which they were the more willing to do, as they were generally rewarded with the franchise.

VOLUMEN. [LIBER.]
VOLUNTARII. [VOLONES.]
VOMITORIA. . [AMPHITHEATRUM.]
VULCANALIA, a festival celebrated at Rome in honour of Vulcan, on the 23rd of August, with games in the circus Flaminius, where the god had a temple. The sacrifice on this occasion consisted of fishes, which the people threw into the fire. It was also customary on this day to commence working by candle-light, which was probably considered as an auspicious beginning of the use of fire, as the day was sacred to the god of this element.

VULGARES. [SERVUS.]

XENAGI (ξεναγοί). The Spartans, as being the head of that Peloponnesian and Dorian league, which was formed to secure the

Vittae. (Statue from Herculaneum.)

independence of the Greek states, had the sole command of the confederate troops in time of war, ordered the quotas which each state was to furnish, and appointed officers of their own to command them. Such officers were called *Xenagi*. The generals whom the allies sent with their troops were subordinate to these Spartan *xenagi*, though they attended the council of war, as representatives of their respective countries. After the peace of Antalcidas, the league was still more firmly established, though Argos refused to join it; and the Spartans were rigorous in exacting the required military service, demanding levies by the *scytale*, and sending out *xenagi* to collect them. The word *Xenagus* may be applied to any leader of a band of foreigners or mercenaries.

XENELASIA (ξενηλασία). The Lacedaemonians appear in very early times, before the legislation of Lycurgus, to have been averse to intercourse with foreigners. This disposition was encouraged by the lawgiver, who made an ordinance forbidding strangers to reside at Sparta without special permission, and empowering the magistrate to expel from the city any stranger who misconducted himself, or set an example injurious to public morals.

XENIAS GRAPHE (ξενίας γραφή). As no man could be an Athenian citizen except by birth or creation (γένει or ποιήσει), if one, having neither of those titles, assumed to act as a citizen, either by taking part in the popular assembly, or by serving any office, judicial or magisterial, or by attending certain festivals, or doing any other act which none but a citizen was privileged to do, he was liable to a γραφὴ ξενίας, which any citizen might institute against him; or he might be proceeded against by εἰσαγγελία.

XENUS (ξένος). [HOSPITIUM.]

XESTES (ξέστης), a Greek measure of capacity, both fluid and solid, which contained 12 cyathi or 2 cotylae, and was equal to $\frac{1}{6}$ of the chous, $\frac{1}{73}$ of the Roman amphora or quadrantal, and $\frac{1}{72}$ of the Greek amphora or metretes; or, viewing it as a dry measure, it was half the choenix and $\frac{1}{96}$ of the medimnus. It contained ·9911 of a pint English. At this point the Roman and Attic systems of measures coincide; for there is no doubt that the Attic xestes was identical with the Roman sextarius.

ZACORI. [AEDITUI.]

ZETETAE (ζητηταί), *Inquisitors*, were extraordinary officers, appointed by the Athenians to discover the authors of some crime against the state, and bring them to justice. They were more frequently appointed to search for confiscated property, the goods of condemned criminals and state debtors; to receive and give information against any persons who concealed, or assisted in concealing them, and to deliver an inventory of all such goods (ἀπογράφειν) to the proper authorities.

ZONA, also called CINGULUM (ζώνη, ζῶμα, ζωστήρ, μίτρα), a girdle or zone, worn about the loins by both sexes. The chief use of this article of dress was to hold up the tunic (ζώννυσθαι), which was more especially requisite to be done when persons were at work, on a journey, or engaged in hunting. The zona is also represented in many statues and pictures of men in armour as worn round the cuirass. The girdle, mentioned by Homer, seems to have been a constituent part of the cuirass, serving to fasten it by means of a buckle, and also affording an additional protection to the body, and having a short kind of petticoat attached to it, as is shown in the figure of the Greek warrior in p. 240. The cut at p. 4 shows that the ancient cuirass did not descend low enough to secure that part of the body which was covered by the ornamental kilt or petticoat. To supply this defect was the design of the *mitra* (μίτρα), a brazen belt lined probably on the inside with leather and stuffed with wool, which was worn next to the body. Men used their girdles to hold money instead of a purse. As the girdle was worn to hold up the garments for the sake of business or of work requiring despatch, so it was loosened and the tunic was allowed to fall down to the feet to indicate the opposite condition, and more especially in preparing to perform a sacrifice (*veste recincta*), or funeral rites (*discincti*, *incinctae*). A girdle was worn by young women, even when their tunic was not girt up, and removed on the day of marriage, and therefore called ζώνη παρθενική.

ZOPHORUS (ζωφόρος or διάζωμα), the frieze of an entablature.

TABLES

OF

GREEK AND ROMAN MEASURES, WEIGHTS, AND MONEY.

Table	Page	Table	Page
I. Greek Measures of Length.		IX. Greek Measures of Capacity.	
(1) Smaller Measures	424	(2) Dry Measures	430
II. Roman Measures of Length.		X. Roman Measures of Capacity.	
(1) Smaller Measures	424	(2) Dry Measures	430
III. Greek Measures of Length.		XI. Greek Weights	431
(2) Land and Itinerary	425	XII. Greek Money	432
IV. Roman Measures of Length.		XIII. Roman Weights.	
(2) Land and Itinerary	426	(1) The As and its Uncial Divisions	433
V. Greek Measures of Surface	426		
VI. Roman Measures of Surface	427	XIV. Roman Weights.	
		(2) Subdivisions of the Uncia	432
VII. Greek Measures of Capacity.		XV. Roman Money.	
(1) Liquid Measures	428	(1) Before Augustus	434
III. Roman Measures of Capacity.		XVI. Roman Money.	
(1) Liquid Measures	429	(2) After Augustus	434

TABLE I.

GRECIAN MEASURES OF LENGTH.

									I. Smaller Measures.					Feet.	Inches.
Δάκτυλος														,,	·7584375
2	Κόνδυλος													,,	1·516875
4	2	Παλαιστή, Δῶρον, Δοχμή, or Δακτυλοδοχμή												,,	3·03375
8	4	2	Διχάς, or Ἡμιπόδιον											,,	6·0675
10	5	2½	1¼	Λιχάς										,,	7·584375
11	5½	2¾	1⅜	1 1/10	Ὀρθόδωρον									,,	8·3428125
12	6	3	1½	1⅕	1 1/11	Σπιθαμή								,,	9·10125
16	8	4	2	1⅗	1 5/11	1⅓	ΠΟΥΣ							1	0·135
18	9	4½	2¼	1⅘	1 7/11	1½	1⅛	Πυγμή						1	1·651875
20	10	5	2½	2	1 9/11	1⅔	1¼	1⅑	Πυγών					1	3·16875
24	12	6	3	2⅖	2 2/11	2	1½	1⅓	1⅕	ΠΗΧΥΣ				1	6·2025
72	36	18	9	7⅕	6 6/11	6	4½	4	3⅗	3	Ξύλον			4	6·6075
96	48	24	12	9⅗	8 8/11	8	6	5⅓	4⅘	4	1⅓	ΟΡΓΥΙΑ		6	0·81

N.B.—*Approximate Values.* From the above Table, it will be seen that the Greek *Foot, Cubit,* and *Orguia*, only exceed the English *Foot, Foot and a half,* and *Fathom,* by about 1-10th, 2-10ths, and 8-10ths of an inch respectively.

TABLE II.

ROMAN MEASURES OF LENGTH.

					I. Smaller Measures.		Feet.	Inches.
Digitus							,,	·7281
1⅓	Uncia or Pollex						,,	·9708
4	3	Palmus					,,	2·9124
12	9	3	Palmus Major (of late times)				,,	8·7372
16	12	4	1⅓	Pes			,,	11·6496
20	15	5	1⅔	1¼	Palmipes		1	2·562
24	18	6	2	1½	1⅕	Cubitus	1	5·4744

N.B.—*Approximate Values.* The Roman *Uncia, Pes,* and *Cubitus* only fall short of our *Inch, Foot,* and *Foot and a half,* by less than 1-10th, 4-10ths, and 6-10ths of an inch respectively.

TABLE III.

GRECIAN MEASURES OF LENGTH.

II. LARGER MEASURES, LAND AND ITINERARY.*

ΠΟΥΣ	ΒΗΜΑ	Βῆμα	ΟΡΓΥΙΑ	Κάλαμος, Ἀκαινα, or Δεκάπους	Ἅμμα	Πλέθρον	ΣΤΑΔΙΟΝ or ΣΤΑΔΙΟΣ	Δίαυλος	Ἱππικόν	ROMAN MILE (μίλιον)	Παρασάγγης	Σχοῖνος	Degree	Miles	Feet	Inches
1½														‥	—	0·15
2½	1⅔													‥	—	6·25
6	4	2⅖												‥	2	6·375
10	6⅔	4	1⅔											‥	6	0·8
60	40	24	10	6										‥	30	1·35
100	66⅔	40	16⅔	10	1⅔									‥	60	8·1
600	400	240	100	60	10	6								‥	101	1·5
1200	800	480	200	120	20	12	2							‥	6·6	9
2400	1600	960	400	240	40	24	4	2						‥	1213	6
4800	3200	1920	800	480	80	48	8	4	2					‥	2427	‥
16,000	12,000	7200	3000	1800	300	180	30	15	7½	3½				‥	4854	‥
36,000	24,000	14,400	6000	3600	600	360	60	30	15	7½	2			3	2152	6
242,000																
362,000	242,000	144,000	60,000	36,000	6000	3600	600	300	150	75	30	10	Degree	69½	5110	‥

* In order to show the relations more clearly, the foreign measures most familiar to the Greeks are included in this Table.

† This is, of course, not the true number of English statute miles contained in a degree of a great circle of the earth, but the number computed from the data exhibited in the Table, some of which are only approximate; namely, 1 Degree = 75 Roman miles = 600 Greek Stadia, and 1 Greek foot = 12·135 inches. The true value of a degree in English miles is $(69)_{81}^{1}$ = $69·0165$, and the difference is only about 7-100ths of a mile.

TABLE IV.

ROMAN MEASURES OF LENGTH.

II. Larger Measures.—Land and Itinerary.								Miles	Feet	Inches
Pes	.	.	.	.	.	.	.	,,	,,	11·6496
1½	Cubitus	.	.	.	.	.	.	,,	1	5·4744
2½	1⅔	Gradus, or Pes Sestertius	.	.	.	.	.	,,	2	5·124
5	3⅓	2	Passus	.	.	.	.	,,	4	10·248
10	6⅔	4	2	Decempeda, or Pertica	.	.	.	,,	9	8·496
120	80	48	24	12	Actus (in length)	.	.	,,	116	5·952
5000	3333⅓	2000	1000	500	41⅔	Mille Passuum	.	,,	4854	,,
7500	5000	3000	1500	750	62½	1½	Gallic Leuga	1	2003	,,
375,000	250,000	150,000	75,000	37,500	3125	75	50 Degree*	68	5110	,,

* See Note to Table III.

N.B.—The Roman mile only differs from the English by less than 1-10th.

TABLE V.

GRECIAN MEASURES OF SURFACE.

Ordinary Land Measures.							Perches.	Square Feet.
ΠΟΥΣ (Square Foot)	.	.	.	.	.	.	,,	1·0226
36	Ἑξαπόδης	.	.	.	.	.	,,	36·81456
100	2⅞	Ακαινα (Square of the κάλαμος)	.	.	.	.	,,	102·26266
833⅓	23 4/27	8⅓	Ἡμίεκτος	.	.	.	3	35·439
1666⅔	46 8/27	16⅔	2	Ἕκτος	.	.	6	70·877
2500	69 4/9	25	3	1½	Ἄρουρα	.	9	106·318
10,000	277 7/9	100	12	6	4	ΠΛΕΘΡΟΝ	37	153·02*

* This differs from a rood, or a quarter of an acre, by little more than 2 perches; for the rood contains 40 perches.

ROMAN MEASURES OF SURFACE.

Pes Quadratus	Ordinary Land Measures								Acres	Roods	Perches	Square Feet
100	.	.	.	.	.	.	.	.	..	..	..	·9415
10	Scrupulum, or Decempeda Quadrata	.	.	.	.	.	.	.	..	..	..	94·245
480	4⅘	Actus Simplex	.	.	.	.	.	.	..	..	1	160·127
2,400	24	5	Uncia*	.	.	.	.	.	..	..	8	85·885
3600	36	7½	1½	Clima	.	.	.	.	..	..	12	155·85
14,400	144	30	6	4	Actus Quadratus	.	.	.	..	1	9	231·07
28,800	288	60	12	8	2	Jugerum	.	.	..	2	19	189·89†
57,600	576	120	24	16	4	2	Heredium	.	1	0	39	107·53‡
5,760,000	57,600	12,000	2400	1600	400	200	100	Centuria	124	2	19	155·25
23,040,000	230,400	48,000	9600	6400	1600	800	400	4	Saltus	498	1	37	268·75§

* The As to which this *Uncia* and the above *Scrupulum* belong is the *Jugerum*. The other uncial divisions of the *Jugerum* may easily be calculated from the *Uncia*. The *Semissis* is, of course, the *Actus Quadratus*.

† i.e. almost 5-8ths of an acre.   ‡ i.e. almost an acre and a quarter.   § i.e. almost 500 acres.

TABLE VII.

GRECIAN MEASURES OF CAPACITY.

I. Attic Liquid Measures.

Κοχλιάριον	Χήμη	Μύστρον	Κόγχη	ΚΥΑΘΟΣ	Ὀξύβαφον	Τέταρτον	Κοτύλη, Τρυβλίον, or Ἡμίνα	ΞΕΣΤΗΣ (Sextarius)	ΧΟΥΣ	Roman Amphora (κεράμιον)	ΑΜΦΟΡΕΥΣ ΜΕΤΡΗΤΗΣ	Gallons	Pints	Approximate.* Gallons	Approximate.* Pints
1															
2	1											..	·008	..	1/120
2½	1¼	1										..	·016	..	1/60
5	2½	2	1									..	·02	..	1/48
10	5	4	2	1								..	·04	..	1/24
15	7½	6	3	1½	1							..	·08	..	1/12
30	15	12	6	3	2	1						..	·12	..	1/8
60	30	24	12	6	4	2	1					..	·24	..	1/4
120	60	48	24	12	8	4	2	1				..	·48	..	1/2
720	360	288	144	72	48	24	12	6	1			..	·96	..	1
5760	2880	2304	1152	576	384	192	96	48	8	1		..	5·76	..	6
8640	4320	3456	1728	864	576	288	144	72	12	1½	1	5	6·08	6	..
												8	5·12	9	..

* As the *Sextarius* differs from the English pint by only 1-25th part of the latter, it will be found useful, in ordinary rough calculations, to take it at exactly a pint, and so with the other measures in this table. The results thus obtained may be corrected by subtracting from each of them its 1-25th part.

N.B.—The *Aeginetan* measures of capacity may be easily calculated from these, according to the ratio given under QUADRANTAL.

ROMAN MEASURES OF CAPACITY.

I. LIQUID MEASURES.

Ligula										Gallons.	Pints.	Approximate.* Gallons.	Approximate.* Pints.
4	Cyathus									..	·02	..	$\frac{1}{48}$
6	1½	Acetabulum								..	·08	..	$\frac{1}{12}$
12	3	2	Quartarius, i.e. 1-4th of the Sextarius							..	·12	..	$\frac{1}{8}$
24	6	4	2	Hemina or Cotyla						..	·24	..	$\frac{1}{4}$
48	12	8	4	2	Sextarius, i.e. 1-6th of the Congius					..	·48	..	$\frac{1}{2}$
288	72	48	24	12	6	Congius				..	2·88	..	3
1152	288	192	96	48	24	4	Urna			2	7·04	..	..
2304	576	384	192	96	48	8	2	Amphora Quadrantal		5	6·08	..	..
46,080	11,520	7680	3840	1920	960	160	40	20	Culeus	115	1·6	120	..

* See the Note to Table VII.   † According to the uncial division, the *Sextarius* was the *As*, and the *Cyathus* the *Uncia*.

TABLE IX.

GRECIAN MEASURES OF CAPACITY.

II. Attic Dry Measures.							Gallons	Pints	Approxima Gallons	Pi
Κοχλιάριον						.	,,	·008	,,	
10	ΚΥΑΘΟΣ						,,	·08	,,	
15	1½	Ὀξύβαφον					,,	·12	,,	
60	6	4	ΚΟΤΥΛΗ or Ἡμίνα				,,	·48	,,	
120	12	8	2	ΞΕΣΤΗΣ (*Sextarius*)			,,	·96	,,	
240	24	16	4	2	ΧΟΙΝΙΞ		,,	1·92	,,	
960	96	64	16	8	4	Ἡμίεκτον	,,	7·68	1	
1920	192	128	32	16	8	2	Ἕκτος (equal to the Roman *Modius*.)	1	7·36	2
11,520	1152	768	192	96	48	12	6	ΜΕΔΙΜΝΟΣ	11	4·16	12‡

* See the Note to Table VII.   † Or one quart.   ‡ Or one bushel and a half.
N.B.—Respecting the *Aeginetan* Measures, see the Note to Table VII.

TABLE X.

ROMAN MEASURES OF CAPACITY.

II. Dry Measures.							Gallons	Pints	Approxima Gallons	Pi
Ligula						.	,,	·02	,,	
4	Cyathus†						,,	·08	,,	
6	1½	Acetabulum					,,	·12	,,	
12	3	2	Quartarius, *i.e.* 1-4th of the *Sextarius*				,,	·24	,,	
24	6	4	2	Hemina, or Cotyla			,,	·48	,,	
48	12	8	4	2	Sextarius, *i.e.* 1-6th of the *Congius*.		,,	·96	,,	
384	96	64	32	16	8	Semimodius	,,	7·68	1	
768	192	128	64	32	16	2	Modius	1	7·36	2‡

* See the Note to Table VII   † See the Note to Table VIII
‡ Or a quarter of a bushel.

TABLE XI.
GRECIAN WEIGHTS.

1. Ratios of the three chief Systems.

Aeginetan : Euboic or old Attic	::	6 : 5
Aeginetan : Solonian or later Attic	::	5 : 3
Euboic : Solonian	::	$136\frac{8}{9}$: 100
	or ::	100 : 72
	or ::	25 : 18

The Aeginetan Talent = 6000 Aeginetan Drachmae = 7200 Euboic = 10,000 Solonian
Euboic ,, = 5000 ,, = 6000 ,, = $8,333^1$,,
Solonian * ,, = 3600 ,, = 4320 ,, = 6,000 ,,

* Also called the **Attic Silver Talent**. When Attic **weights are** spoken of without any further distinction, these are generally intended.

2. Aeginetan Weights.

				Exact.*			Approximate.		
				lb.	oz.	grs.	lb.	oz.	grs.
Obol (Ὀβολός)				,,	,,	$16.472\frac{2}{9}$	,,	,,	20
6	Drachma (Δραχμή)			,,	,,	$110.63\frac{1}{3}$	,,	$\frac{1}{4}$	,,
600	100	Mina (Μνᾶ)		1	9	$143.83\frac{1}{3}$†	$1\frac{2}{3}$	,,	,,
36,000	6000	60	Talent (Τάλαντον)	95	,,	,,	100	,,	,,

* In this and **the other** tables the English weights used **are those of the avoirdupois** scale as fixed by statute; namely, the grain = the Troy grain, the ounce = $437\frac{1}{2}$ grains, the pound = 16 ounces = 7000 grains. † Or $\frac{1}{8}$ of an oz.

3. Euboic or Attic Commercial Weights.

				Exact.			Approximate.		
				lb.	oz.	grs.	lb.	oz.	grs.
Obol				,,	,,	$15.39\frac{14}{27}$	,,	,,	$15\frac{1}{2}$
6	Drachma			,,	,,	$92.36\frac{11}{9}$	,,	,,	$93\frac{1}{2}$
600	100	Mina		1	5	$48.611\frac{1}{9}$	1	,,	,,
36,000	6000	60	Talent	79	2	$291.63\frac{1}{3}$	80	,,	,,

4. Attic Commercial Weights increased.

	Exact.			Approximate.		
	lb.	oz.	grs.	lb.	oz.	grs.
1 Mina = 150 Drachmae (silver)	1	6	$350\frac{2}{9}$	$1\frac{1}{2}$	,,	,,
5 Minae = 6 Minae (commercial)	7	14	$291.6\frac{2}{3}$	$7\frac{1}{2}$	,,	,,
1 Talent = 65 Minae (commercial)	86	,,	$143.8\frac{1}{3}$	86	,,	,,

5. Attic Silver Weights.

				Exact.			Approximate.		
				lb.	oz.	grs.	lb.	oz.	grs.
Obol				,,	,,	$11.0833\frac{1}{3}$	,,	,,	11
6	Drachma			,,	,,	66.5	,,	,,	70
600	100	Mina		,,	15	87.5*	1	,,	,,
36,000	6000	60	Talent	57	,,	,,	60	,,	,,

* Or $\frac{1}{8}$ of an oz.

TABLE XII.

GRECIAN MONEY.

I. Attic Copper and Silver.

												£	s.	d.	Farthings.
Lepton (Λεπτόν)	.	.	.	.	.	.	.	.	.	.	.	,,	,,	,,	·116
7	Chalchus (Χαλκοῦς)	.	.	.	.	.	.	.	.	.	.	,,	,,	,,	·8125
14	2	Dichalcon, or Quarter Obol (Δίχαλκον)	.	.	.	.	.	.	.	.	.	,,	,,	,,	1·625
28	4	2	Half Obol (Ἡμιωβόλιον)	.	.	.	.	.	.	.	.	,,	,,	,,	3·25
56	8	4	2	Obol (Ὀβολός)	.	.	.	.	.	.	.	,,	,,	,,	2·5
112	16	8	4	2	Diobolus (Διόβολον)	.	.	.	.	.	.	,,	,,	1	1
168	24	12	6	3	1½	Triobolus (Τριόβολον)	.	.	.	.	.	,,	,,	3	1·5
224	32	16	8	4	2	1⅓	Tetrobolus (Τετρώβολον)	.	.	.	.	,,	,,	4	2
336	48	24	12	6	3	2	1½	Drachma * (Δραχμή)	.	.	.	,,	,,	6	1
672	96	48	24	12	6	4	3	2	Didrachm (Δίδραχμον)	.	.	,,	,,	9	2
1344	192	96	48	24	12	8	6	4	2	Tetradrachm (Τετράδραχμον)	.	,,	1	7	,,
33,600	4800	2400	1,200	600	300	200	150	100	50	25	Mina (Μνᾶ)	,,	3	2	,,
2,016,000	288,000	144,000	72,000	36,000	18,000	12,000	9000	6000	3000	1500	60	Talent (Τάλαντον)	243	15¾	,,

* The Drachma was very nearly equal to the French Franc. † Or, approximately, 250d., the difference being only 1·50d.

II. *Æginetan and Euboic Silver*.—The coins of these systems can be easily calculated from the Attic, according to the ratios given in Table XI., No. 1. As thus calculated, the Æginetan Talent was equal to 406l. 5s., and the Euboic was equal to 338l. 10s. 10d., and the Drachmae were equal respectively to 1s. 4½d. for the Æginetan, and 1s. 1¾d. + ⅔ of a farthing for the Euboic.

III. *Grecian Gold*.—The values of the Grecian gold money cannot be conveniently reduced to the tabular form; they will be found in the articles Stater and Darkius.

TABLE XIII.

ROMAN WEIGHTS.

I. THE UNCIAL DIVISIONS OF THE POUND.													Avoirdupois Weight. Oz.	Grs.
UNCIA													..	$430·83\frac{1}{3}$*
$1\frac{1}{2}$	Sescuncia, or Sescunx												1	203·75
2	$1\frac{1}{3}$	Sextans											1	$404·16\frac{2}{3}$
3	2	$1\frac{1}{2}$	Quadrans, or Teruncius										2	168·7500
4	$2\frac{1}{3}$	2	$1\frac{1}{3}$	Triens									3	$270·83\frac{1}{3}$
5	$3\frac{1}{3}$	$2\frac{1}{2}$	$1\frac{2}{3}$	$1\frac{1}{4}$	Quincunx								4	$354·16\frac{2}{3}$
6	4	3	2	$1\frac{1}{2}$	$1\frac{1}{5}$	SEMIS, or Semissis							5	337·5
7	$4\frac{2}{3}$	$3\frac{1}{2}$	$2\frac{1}{3}$	$1\frac{3}{4}$	$1\frac{2}{5}$	$1\frac{1}{6}$	Septunx						6	$320·33\frac{1}{3}$
8	$5\frac{1}{3}$	4	$2\frac{2}{3}$	2	$1\frac{3}{5}$	$1\frac{1}{3}$	$1\frac{1}{7}$	Bes, or Bessis					7	$104·16\frac{2}{3}$
9	6	$4\frac{1}{2}$	3	$2\frac{1}{4}$	$1\frac{4}{5}$	$1\frac{1}{2}$	$1\frac{2}{7}$	$1\frac{1}{8}$	Dodrans				8	277·5
10	$6\frac{1}{3}$	5	$3\frac{1}{3}$	$2\frac{1}{2}$	2	$1\frac{2}{3}$	$1\frac{3}{7}$	$1\frac{1}{4}$	$1\frac{1}{9}$	Dextans			9	$270·83\frac{1}{3}$
11	$7\frac{1}{3}$	$5\frac{1}{2}$	$3\frac{2}{3}$	$2\frac{3}{4}$	$2\frac{1}{5}$	$1\frac{5}{6}$	$1\frac{4}{7}$	$1\frac{3}{8}$	$1\frac{2}{9}$	$1\frac{1}{10}$	Deunx		10	$260·83\frac{1}{3}$
12	8	6	4	3	$2\frac{2}{5}$	2	$1\frac{5}{7}$	$1\frac{1}{2}$	$1\frac{1}{3}$	$1\frac{1}{5}$	$1\frac{1}{11}$	As, or LIBRA	11	237·5

* This only differs from the ounce avoirdupois by less than 7 grains.

TABLE XIV.

ROMAN WEIGHTS.

II. SUBDIVISIONS OF THE UNCIA.										Grains.
Siliqua										2·9224
3	Obolus									8·767361
6	2	SCRUPULUM								17·53472
12	4	2	Semisextula							35·0694
24	8	4	2	SEXTULA						70·138
36	12	6	3	$1\frac{1}{2}$	Sicilicus					105·2083
48	16	8	4	2	$1\frac{1}{3}$	Duella				140·277
72	24	12	6	3	2	$1\frac{1}{2}$	Semuncia			120·416
144	48	24	12	6	4	3	2	UNCIA		420·833
1728	576	288	144	72	48	36	24	12	As or LIBRA	5050

TABLE XV.

ROMAN MONEY.

I. Before the Reign of Augustus: when the Denarius was 1-7th of an Ounce, or about 60 Grains.

1. Copper Coins.						2. Silver Coins.					£.	s.	d.	Farthings.
Sextula											,,	,,	,,	·35416
1½	Quadrans							Teruncius			,,	,,	,,	·53125
2	1⅓	Triens									,,	,,	,,	·7083
3	2	1½	Semissis			2	Sembella				,,	,,	,,	1·0625
6	4	3	2	As .		4	2	Libella			,,	,,	,,	2·125
12	8	6	4	2	Dupondius	.	.	.	.		,,	,,	1	·25
24	16	12	8	4	2	Sestertius	16	8	4	Sestertius	,,	,,	2	·5
48	32	24	16	8	4	2	.	32	16	8	2	Quinarius	4	1
96	64	48	32	16	8	4	.	24	32	16	4	2	Denarius	8	2

| 3. Gold Coins. Aureus* (value in proportion to Roman Silver) | ,, | 17 | 8 | 2 |
| (value in English current Coin) | 1 | 1 | 1 | 2 |

| 4. Money of Account (not a Coin). Sestertium, or Mille Nummi | 8 | 17 | 1 | ,, |

* For the subdivisions of the gold money, see Aurum.

TABLE XVI.

ROMAN MONEY.

II. After the Reign of Augustus: when the Denarius was 1-8th of an Ounce, or 52·5 Grains.

							£.	s.	d.	Farthings.
Sextula							,,	,,	,,	·3125
1½	Quadrans						,,	,,	,,	·46875
2	1⅓	Triens					,,	,,	,,	·625
3	2	1½	Semissis				,,	,,	,,	·9375
6	4	3	2	As .			,,	,,	,,	1·875
12	8	6	4	2	Dupondius		,,	,,	,,	3·75
24	16	12	8	4	2	Sestertius	,,	,,	1	3·5
48	32	24	16	8	4	2 Quinarius, or Victoriatus	,,	,,	3	3
96	64	48	32	16	8	4 2 Denarius	,,	,,	7	2

Aureus, reckoned at 25 Denarii	,,	15	7	2
,, reckoned in English Current Coin	,,	18	5	3·25
Sestertium, or Mille Nummi	7	16	3	,,

PARALLEL YEARS.

(*See page 276.*)

B.C.	Ol.	B.C.	Ol.	B.C.	Ol.	B.C.	Ol.	B.C.	Ol.	B.C.	Ol.
776.	1. 1.	616.	41. 1.	558.	55. 3.	518.	65. 3.	478.	75. 3.	438.	85. 3.
772.	2. 1.	612.	42. 1.	557.	4.	517.	4.	477.	4.	437.	4.
768.	3. 1.	608.	43. 1.	556.	56. 1.	516.	66. 1.	476.	76. 1.	436.	86. 1.
764.	4. 1.	604.	44. 1.	555.	2.	515.	2.	475.	2.	435.	2.
760.	5. 1.	600.	45. 1.	554.	3.	514.	3.	474.	3.	434.	3.
756.	6. 1.	596.	46. 1.	553.	4.	513.	4.	473.	4.	433.	4.
752.	7. 1.	592.	47. 1.	552.	57. 1.	512.	67. 1.	472.	77. 1.	432.	87. 1.
748.	8. 1.	591.	2.	551.	2.	511.	2.	471.	2.	431.	2.
744.	9. 1.	590.	3.	550.	3.	510.	3.	470.	3.	430.	3.
740.	10. 1.	589.	4.	549.	4.	509.	4.	469.	4.	429.	4.
736.	11. 1.	588.	48. 1.	548.	58. 1.	508.	68. 1.	468.	78. 1.	428.	88. 1.
732.	12. 1.	587.	2.	547.	2.	507.	2.	467.	2.	427.	2.
728.	13. 1.	586.	3.	546.	3.	506.	3.	466.	3.	426.	1.
724.	14. 1.	585.	4.	545.	4.	505.	4.	465.	4.	425.	4.
720.	15. 1.	584.	49. 1.	544.	59. 1.	504.	69. 1.	464.	79. 1.	424.	89. 1.
716.	16. 1.	583.	2.	543.	2.	503.	2.	463.	2.	423.	2.
712.	17. 1.	582.	3.	542.	3.	502.	3.	462.	3.	422.	3.
708.	18. 1.	581.	4.	541.	4.	501.	4.	461.	4.	421.	4.
704.	19. 1.	580.	50. 1.	540.	60. 1.	500.	70. 1.	460.	80. 1.	420.	90. 1.
700.	20. 1.	579.	2.	539.	2.	499.	2.	459.	2.	419.	2.
696.	21. 1.	578.	3.	538.	3.	498.	3.	458.	3.	418.	3.
692.	22. 1.	577.	4.	537.	4.	497.	4.	457.	4.	417.	4.
688.	23. 1.	576.	51. 1.	536.	61. 1.	496.	71. 1.	456.	81. 1.	416.	91. 1.
684.	24. 1.	575.	2.	535.	2.	495.	2.	455.	2.	415.	2.
680.	25. 1.	574.	3.	534.	3.	494.	3.	454.	3.	414.	3.
676.	26. 1.	573.	4.	533.	4.	493.	4.	453.	4.	413.	4.
672.	27. 1.	572.	52. 1.	532.	62. 1.	492.	72. 1.	452.	82. 1.	412.	92. 1.
668.	28. 1.	571.	2.	531.	2.	491.	2.	451.	2.	411.	2.
664.	29. 1.	570.	3.	530.	3.	490.	3.	450.	3.	410.	3.
660.	30. 1.	569.	4.	529.	4.	489.	4.	449.	4.	409.	4.
656.	31. 1.	568.	53. 1.	528.	63. 1.	488.	73. 1.	448.	83. 1.	408.	93. 1.
652.	32. 1.	567.	2.	527.	2.	487.	2.	447.	2.	407.	2.
648.	33. 1.	566.	3.	526.	3.	486.	3.	446.	3.	406.	3.
644.	34. 1.	565.	4.	525.	4.	485.	4.	445.	4.	405.	4.
640.	35. 1.	564.	54. 1.	524.	64. 1.	484.	74. 1.	444.	84. 1.	404.	94. 1.
636.	36. 1.	563.	2.	523.	2.	483.	2.	443.	2.	403.	2.
632.	37. 1.	562.	3.	522.	3.	482.	3.	442.	3.	402.	3.
628.	38. 1.	561.	4.	521.	4.	481.	4.	441.	4.	401.	4.
624.	39. 1.	560.	55. 1.	520.	65. 1.	480.	75. 1.	440.	85. 1.	400.	95. 1.
620.	40. 1.	559.	2.	519.	2.	479.	2.	439.	2.	399.	2.

APPENDIX

B.C.	Ol.	B.C.	Ol.	B.C.	Ol.	B.C.	Ol.	B.C.	Ol.	A.D.	Ol.
398.	95. 3.	352.	107. 1.	306.	118. 3.	224.	139. 1.	40.	183. 1.	121.	225. 1.
397.	4.	351.	2.	305.	4.	220.	140. 1.	36.	186. 1.	125.	226. 1.
396.	96. 1.	350.	3.	304.	119. 1.	216.	141. 1.	32.	187. 1.	129.	227. 1.
395.	2.	349.	4.	303.	2.	212.	142. 1.	28.	188. 1.	133.	228. 1.
394.	3.	348.	108. 1.	302.	3.	208.	143. 1.	24.	189. 1.	137.	229. 1.
393.	4.	347.	2.	301.	4.	204.	144. 1.	20.	190. 1.	141.	230. 1.
392.	97. 1.	346.	3.	300.	120. 1.	200.	145. 1.	16.	191. 1.	145.	231. 1.
391.	2.	345.	4.	299.	2.	196.	146. 1.	12.	192. 1.	149.	232. 1.
390.	3.	344.	109. 1.	298.	3.	192.	147. 1.	8.	193. 1.	153.	233. 1.
389.	4.	343.	2.	297.	4.	188.	148. 1.	4.	194. 1.	157.	234. 1.
388.	98. 1.	342.	3.	296.	121. 1.	184.	149. 1.			161.	235. 1.
387.	2.	341.	4.	295.	2.	180.	150. 1.			165.	236. 1.
386.	3.	340.	110. 1.	294.	3.	176.	151. 1.			169.	237. 1.
385.	4.	339.	2.	293.	4.	172.	152. 1.			173.	238. 1.
384.	99. 1.	338.	3.	292.	122. 1.	168.	153. 1.			177.	239. 1.
383.	2.	337.	4.	291.	2.	164.	154. 1.	A.D.	Ol.	181.	240. 1.
382.	3.	336.	111. 1.	290.	3.	160.	155. 1.	1.	195. 1.	185.	241. 1.
381.	4.	335.	2.	289.	4.	156.	156. 1.	5.	196. 1.	189.	242. 1.
380.	100. 1.	334.	3.	288.	123. 1.	152.	157. 1.	9.	197. 1.	193.	243. 1.
379.	2.	333.	4.	287.	2.	148.	158. 1.	13.	198. 1.	197.	244. 1.
378.	3.	332.	112. 1.	286.	3.	144.	159. 1.	17.	199. 1.	201.	245. 1.
377.	4.	331.	2.	285.	4.	140.	160. 1.	21.	200. 1.	205.	246. 1.
376.	101. 1.	330.	3.	284.	124. 1.	136.	161. 1.	25.	201. 1.	209.	247. 1.
375.	2.	329.	4.	283.	2.	132.	162. 1.	29.	202. 1.	213.	248. 1.
374.	3.	328.	113. 1.	282.	3.	128.	163. 1.	33.	203. 1.	217.	249. 1.
373.	4.	327.	2.	281.	4.	124.	164. 1.	37.	204. 1.	221.	250. 1.
372.	102. 1.	326.	3.	280.	125. 1.	120.	165. 1.	41.	205. 1.	225.	251. 1.
371.	2.	325.	4.	279.	2.	116.	166. 1.	45.	206. 1.	229.	252. 1.
370.	3.	324.	114. 1.	278.	3.	112.	167. 1.	49.	207. 1.	233.	253. 1.
369.	4.	323.	2.	277.	4.	108.	168. 1.	53.	208. 1.	237.	254. 1.
368.	103. 1.	322.	3.	276.	126. 1.	104.	169. 1.	57.	209. 1.	241.	255. 1.
367.	2.	321.	4.	275.	2.	100.	170. 1.	61.	210. 1.	245.	256. 1.
366.	3.	320.	115. 1.	274.	3	96.	171. 1.	65.	211. 1.	249.	257. 1.
365.	4.	319.	2.	273.	4.	92.	172. 1.	69.	212. 1.	253.	258. 1.
364.	104. 1.	318.	3.	272.	127. 1.	88.	173. 1.	73.	213. 1.	257.	259. 1.
363.	2.	317.	4.	268.	128. 1.	84.	174. 1.	77.	214. 1.	261.	260. 1.
362.	3.	316.	116. 1.	264.	129. 1.	80.	175. 1.	81.	215. 1.	265.	261. 1.
361.	4.	315.	2.	260.	130. 1.	76.	176. 1.	85.	216. 1.	269.	262. 1.
360.	105. 1.	314.	3.	256.	131. 1.	72.	177. 1.	89.	217. 1.	273.	263. 1.
359.	2.	313.	4.	252.	132. 1.	68.	178. 1.	93.	218. 1.	277.	264. 1.
358.	3.	312.	117. 1.	248.	133. 1.	64.	179. 1.	97.	219. 1.	281.	265. 1.
357.	4.	311.	2.	244.	134. 1.	60.	180. 1.	101.	220. 1.	285.	266. 1.
356.	106. 1.	310.	3.	240.	135. 1.	56.	181. 1.	105.	221. 1.	289.	267. 1.
355.	2.	309.	4.	236.	136. 1.	52.	182. 1.	109.	222. 1.	293.	268. 1.
354.	3.	308.	118. 1.	232.	137. 1.	48.	183. 1.	113.	223. 1.	297.	269. 1.
353.	4.	307.	2.	228.	138. 1.	44.	184. 1.	117.	224. 1.	301.	270. 1.

CALENDARIUM.

Our days of the Month.	March, May, July, October, have 31 days.	January, August, December, have 31 days.	April, June, September, November, have 30 days.	February has 28 days, and in Leap Year 29.
1.	KALENDIS.	KALENDIS.	KALENDIS.	KALENDIS.
2.	VI. ⎫	IV. ⎫ ante	IV. ⎫ ante	IV. ⎫ ante
3.	V. ⎬ ante	III. ⎭ Nonas.	III. ⎭ Nonas.	III. ⎭ Nonas.
4.	IV. ⎭ Nonas.	Pridie Nonas.	Pridie Nonas.	Pridie Nonas.
5.	III. ⎭	NONIS.	NONIS.	NONIS.
6.	Pridie Nonas.	VIII. ⎫	VIII. ⎫	VIII.
7.	NONIS.	VII.	VII.	VII.
8.	VIII. ⎫	VI. ⎬ ante	VI. ⎬ ante	VI.
9.	VII.	V. ⎭ Idus.	V. ⎭ Idus.	V.
10.	VI. ⎬ ante	IV.	IV.	IV.
11.	V. ⎭ Idus.	III.	III.	III.
12.	IV. ⎭	Pridie Idus.	Pridie Idus.	Pridie Idus.
13.	III. ⎭	IDIBUS.	IDIBUS.	IDIBUS.
14.	Pridie Idus.	XIX. ⎫	XVIII. ⎫	XVI. ⎫
15.	IDIBUS.	XVIII.	XVII.	XV.
16.	XVII	XVII.	XVI.	XIV.
17.	XVI.	XVI.	XV.	XIII.
18.	XV.	XV.	XIV.	XII.
19.	XIV.	XIV.	XIII.	XI.
20.	XIII.	XIII.	XII.	X.
21.	XII. ⎬ Ante Kalendas (of the month following).	XII. ⎬ Ante Kalendas (of the month following).	XI. ⎬ Ante Kalendas (of the month following).	IX. ⎬ Ante Kalendas Martias.
22.	XI.	XI.	X.	VIII.
23.	X.	X.	IX.	VII.
24.	IX.	IX.	VIII.	VI.
25.	VIII.	VIII.	VII.	V.
26.	VII.	VII.	VI.	IV.
27.	VI.	VI.	V.	III.
28.	V.	V.	IV.	Pridie Kalendas Martias.
29.	IV.	IV.	III.	
30.	III.	III.	Pridie Kalendas (of the month following).	
31.	Pridie Kalendas (of the month following).	Pridie Kalendas (of the month following).		

GREEK INDEX.

The numerals indicate the pages, and the letters a *and* b *the first and second columns respectively.*

A.

Ἄβαξ, 1, a.
Ἄγαλμα, 13, b; 350, a.
Ἀγαθοεργοί, 13, b.
Ἀγγαρεία, 25, a.
Ἀγέλη, 13, b.
Ἄγημα, 13, b.
Ἀγητής, 72, b.
Ἀγητόρειον, 72, b.
Ἀγητόρια, 72, b.
Ἄγκιστρον, 191, b.
Ἄγκοινα, 267, b.
Ἀγκύλη, 200, a.
Ἄγκυρα, 268, a.
Ἀγορά, 15, b.
Ἀγορανόμος, 8, b; 15, b.
Ἀγρονόμοι, 16, a.
Ἀγροτέρας θυσία, 16, a.
Ἀγύρται, 16, a.
Ἀγχεμάχοι, 41, b.
Ἀγχιστεία, 203, a.
Ἀγωνάρχαι, 15, a.
Ἀγῶνες, 15, a; 131, b.
  ἀτίμητοι, 132, b; 377, b.
  τίμητοι, 132, b; 377, b.
Ἀγωνισταί, 47, a.
Ἀγωνοδίκαι, 15, a.
Ἀγωνοθέται, 15, a.
Ἀδελφιδοῦς, 203, a.
Ἀδελφός, 203, a.
Ἀδέσποτοι, 202, a.
Ἀδύνατοι, 8, b.
Ἀδώνια, 7, a.
Ἄδυτον, 367, a.
Ἀείσιτοι, 313, b.
Ἀέτωμα, 176, a.
Ἀθληταί, 47, a.
Ἀθλητῆρες, 47, a.
Ἀθλοθέται, 15, a; 282, a.
Αἰγικορεῖς, 189, b.
Αἰγίοχος, 10, b.
Αἰγίς, 10, b.
Αἰθουσα, 16, b.
Αἰκίας δίκη, 16, a.
Αἴνιγμα, 11, a; 357, b.
Αἰσυμνήτης, 12, b; 15, a.
Αἰχμή, 199, b.

Αἰχμοφόροι, 587, b.
Αἰώρα, 11, a.
Ἄκαινα, Ἀκαίνη, 1, b.
Ἀκάτειος, 266, b.
Ἀκάτιον, 1, b; 262, b.
Ἄκατος, 1, b; 262, a.
Ἀκινάκης, 3, b.
Ἀκμόθετον, 254, b.
Ἄκμων, 254, b.
Ἀκόντιον, 200, b.
Ἀκράτισμα, 95, a.
Ἀκροκέραια, 267, a.
Ἀκρόλιθοι, 4, a; 350, b.
Ἀκρόπολις, 4, a.
Ἀκροστόλιον, 4, a; 263, b.
Ἀκρωτηριάζειν, 4, b; 322, b.
Ἀκρωτήριον, 4, a.
Ἄκτια, 5, a.
Ἀκωκή, 199, b.
Ἄκων, 200, b.
Ἀλαβάρχης, 16, b.
Ἁλαί, 327, a.
Ἀλείπται, 17, b.
Ἀλία, 15, b.
Ἀλλῆξ, or Ἄλλιξ, 17, a.
Ἄλμα, 289, a.
Ἀλοπήγιον, 327, a.
Ἀλυσίδιον, 76, b.
Ἄλυσιον, 76, b.
Ἄλυσις, 76, b.
Ἁλύται, 18, a; 275, a.
Ἀλυτάρχης, 18, a; 275, a.
Ἁλώα, 18, a; 37, a.
Ἁλῶα, 18, a.
Ἅλως, 37, a.
Ἅμαξα, 297, b.
Ἀμαρύνθια, 18, a.
Ἀμαρύσια, 18, a.
Ἀμβροσία, 19, a.
Ἀμπεχόνη, 19, b.
Ἀμπίτταρες, 202, a.
Ἀμπυκτήρ, 24, a.
Ἄμπυξ, 24, a.
Ἀμφίβληστρον, 320, b.
Ἀμφίβολος, 268, b.
Ἀμφιδέαι, 42, b.
Ἀμφιδρόμια, 21, a.
Ἀμφιθάλαμος, 141, b.
Ἀμφικίων, 367, a.

Ἀμφικτύονες, 19, b.
Ἀμφιπρόστυλος, 367, a.
Ἀμφίστομος, 268, b.
Ἀμφορεύς, 23, a.
Ἀναβαθμοί, 140, a.
Ἀνάγλυπτα, 24, b.
Ἀνάγλυφα, 24, b.
Ἀναγώγια, 25, a.
Ἀναδικία, 29, a.
Ἀναθήματα, 145, a; 350, b.
Ἀνακαλυπτήρια, 230, b.
Ἀνακειμένα, 145, a.
Ἀνάκειον, 24, b.
Ἀνάκλιντρον, 222, a.
Ἀνάκρισις, 24, b; 34, b.
Ἀνάκτορον, 367, a.
Ἄναξ, 320, a.
Ἀναξυρίδες, 62, a.
Ἀνδρεία, 359, b.
Ἀνδριάς, 351, a.
Ἀνδρογεώνια, 25, a.
Ἀνδροληψία, 25, a.
Ἀνδρολήψιον, 25, a.
Ἀνδρῶνες, 140, b.
Ἀνδρωνῖτις, 140, a.
Ἀνεύθυνος, 160, a.
Ἀνεψιαδοῦς, 203, a.
Ἀνεψιός, 203, a.
Ἀνθεστήρια, 135, b.
Ἀνθεστηριών, 65, b.
Ἀνθεσφόρια, 26. b.
Ἀνθράκια, 141, b.
Ἀνθύπατος, 310, a.
Ἀνθυπωμοσία, 132, a.
Ἄνοδος, 375, b.
Ἄνοπλοι, 41, b.
Ἀντιγόνεια, 390, b.
Ἀντιγραφή, 27, a; 132, a.
Ἀντίδοσις, 26, b.
Ἀντιτίμησις, 81, b.
Ἀντιχειροτονεῖν, 83, b.
Ἀντλία, 27, a.
Ἄντυξ, 27, a; 94, a.
Ἀντωμοσία, 132, a.
Ἀξίνη, 331, b.
Ἄξονες, 54, b; 271. b.
Ἄξων, 124, a.
Ἄορ, 196, a.
Ἀπαγωγή, 27, b.

GREEK INDEX.

Ἀπατούρια.

Ἀπατούρια, 27, b.
Ἀπαυλια, 250, b.
Ἀπελεύθερος, 239, a; 338, b.
Ἀποβάθρα, 303, a.
Ἀπογραφή, 28, b.
Ἀποδέκται, 28, a; 345, a.
Ἀπόδεσμος, 355, b.
Ἀποθέωσις, 28, b.
Ἀποθήκη, 28, b; 207, b.
Ἀποικία, 98, b.
Ἀποικοι, 93, a.
Ἀπόκλητοι, 13, a.
Ἀπολείψεως δίκη, 139. a.
Ἀπολλώνια, 28, b.
Ἀποπέμψεως δίκη, 139, a.
Ἀπόρρητα, 28, b.
Ἀποστασίου δίκη, 338, b.
Ἀποστολεύς, 28, b.
Ἀποτειχισμός, 406, b.
Ἀποτελεσματικός, 45, b.
Ἀποτίμημα, 145, b.
Ἀπόφασις, 38, a.
Ἀποφορά, 28, b.
Ἀποφράδες ἡμέραι, 301, a.
Ἀποχειροτονεῖν, 35. a.
Ἀποχειροτονία, 85, b.
Ἀπωμοσία, 171, b.
Ἀραιόστυλος, 367, b.
Ἀρβύλη, 291, a.
Ἀργάδεις, 389, b.
Ἀργυράσπιδες, 40, a.
Ἀργυροκοπεῖον, 40, a.
Ἄργυρος, 40, a.
Ἀρδάλιον, 185, a.
Ἀρδάνιον, 185, a.
Ἄρειος πάγος, 37, a.
Ἀριστοκρατία, 40, b.
Ἄριστον, 95, a.
Ἅρμα, 123, b; 274, b.
Ἁρμάμαξα, 199, b.
Ἄροτρον, 31, b.
Ἄρουρα, 43, a.
Ἁρπαγή, 199, a.
Ἀρπαστόν, 297, a.
Ἄρπη, 175, b.
Ἀρρηφόρια, 42, b.
Ἀρρηφόροι, 42, b.
Ἀρτάβη, 43, a.
Ἀρτεμίσια, 43, a.
Ἀρτοποιος, 297, b.
Ἀρτοπώλαι, 96, a.
Ἀρτοπωλίδες, 96, a; 297, b.
Ἀρτύσεις, 418, a.
Ἀρχεῖον, 33, a.
Ἀρχή, 35, b.
Ἀρχίατρος, 33, a.
Ἀρχιθέωρος, 129, a; 375, a.
Ἀρχιτεκτονία, 33, a.
Ἀρχιτεκτονική, 33, a.
Ἀρχιτέκτων, 374, b.
Ἄρχων, 34, b.
  βασιλεύς, 35, a.
  ἐπώνυμος, 35, a; 66, a; 86, a.
Ἀρχώνης, 363, a.
Ἀσάμινθος, 54, b.
Ἄσβολος, 183, b.
Ἀσεβείας γραφή, 44, a.
Ἀσκαύλης, 376, b.
Ἀσκληπίεια, 44, b.

Βοιωτάρχης.

Ἀσκοί, 418, a.
Ἀσκωλιασμός, 44, b.
Ἄσκωμα, 265, b.
Ἀσπιδεῖον, 264, a.
Ἀσπιδίσκη, 264, a.
Ἀσπίς, 41, b; 94, a.
Ἀσπισταί, 41, b.
Ἀσσάριον, 44, a.
Ἀστράβη, 154, a.
Ἀστράγαλος, 45, a; 361, b.
Ἀστρατείας γραφή, 45, b.
Ἄστυλος, 367, a.
Ἀστυνόμοι, 46, a.
Ἀσυλία, 46, a.
Ἄσυλον, 46, a.
Ἀτέλεια, 46, b; 366, a.
Ἀτιμία, 8, a; 47, b.
Ἄτιμος, 36, a; 47, b.
Ἀτλαντες, 47, b.
Ἄτρακτος, 191, b.
Αὐθέψης, 54, a.
Αὐλαία, 372, a; 408, a.
Αὐλακες, 32, b.
Αὔλειος θύρα, 140, b.
Αὐλή, 16, b; 48, a; 140, b.
Αὐλητρίδες, 377, b.
Αὐλός, 207, a; 376, b.
Αὐτόνομοι, 54, a.
Αὐτοψία, 150, b.
Ἀφέται, 202, a.
Ἀφετήριον ὄργανον, 381, a.
Ἀφλαστον, 264, b.
Ἄφοδος, 85, b.
Ἄφρακτος ναῦς, 261, b.
Ἀφρήτορ, 389, a.
Ἀφροδίσια, 28, a.
Ἀχίτων, 401, b.
Ἅψις, 29, b.

Β.

Βαλανεῖον, 54, b.
Βαλαντιον, 248, b.
Βαλλισμοί, 283, b.
Βάραθρον, 57, a.
Βάρβιτον, -ος, 57, b; 245, b.
Βασανισταί, 381, b.
Βάσανος, 248, b; 381, a.
Βασίλεια, 156, b.
Βασίλειος, 320, a; 360, b.
Βασίλισσα, 35, a.
Βασκανία, 175, a.
Βελόνη, 6, b.
Βελονίς, 6, b.
Βέμβηξ, 148, a.
Βενέδεια, 58, a.
Βηλός, 215, a.
Βῆμα, 146, b; 249, a.
Βίβωσις, 328, b.
Βιβλιοθήκη, 58, b.
Βιβλίον, 236, a.
Βιδιαίοι, 59, a.
Βίκος, 51, a.
Βίος, 37, b.
Βοηδρομια, 59, b.
Βοηδρομιών, 65, b.
Βοιωτάρχης, -ος, 59, b.

Γυμνῆτες.

Βολίς, 76, a.
Βομβύλιος, 23, b.
Βορεασμοί, 61, a.
Βορεασμός, 61, a.
Βουλευτήριον, 62, a.
Βουλή, 3, b; 15, b; 61, a.
Βοῶναι, 60, b.
Βραβεῖς, 15, b.
Βραβευταί, 15, b.
Βραυρωνια, 62, a.
Βρόχοι, 319, b.
Βύβλος, 238, a.
Βυκάνη, 62, b.
Βυσσός, 63, a.
Βωμός, 31, a.

Γ.

Γαισός, 192, b.
Γάλως, 13, b.
Γαμηλία, 193, a.
Γάμοροι, 91, a.
Γάμος, 249, b.
Γελέοντες, 389, b.
Γενεθλιαλογία, 45, b.
Γενέσιον, 57, a.
Γενέσια, 187, b.
Γένεσις, 46, a.
Γένη, 389, a.
Γεννῆται, 389, b.
Γένος, 301, a.
Γέρανος, 327, a.
Γερουσία, 191, b.
Γέρρα, 194, a.
Γέφυρα, 302, a.
Γεφυρίζειν, 151, a.
Γεφυρισμός, 151, a.
Γεωμόροι, 389, b.
Γλεῦκος, 416, b.
Γλύξις, 416, b.
Γναφεύς, 184, a.
Γνήσιος, 7, a.
Γνώμων, 206, a.
Γοργύρα, 72, a.
Γράμμα, 331, a.
Γραμματεύς, 3, b; 196, a.
Γραφή, 131, b; 293, b.
Γραφή δωροδοκίας, 127, a.
  δώρων, 127, a.
  ξενίας, 422, a.
  παρανοίας, 284, a.
  παρανόμων, 147, b; 284, a.
  ὕβρεως, 210, a.
  φαρμάκων, 292, b.
  ψευδεγγραφῆς, 314, a.
Γραφικη, 293, b.
Γραφίς, 295, b.
Γρίφος, 357, b.
Γρόσφος, 200, b.
Γύης, 31, b.
Γυμνασιάρχης, 197, b.
Γυμνασίαρχος, 197, b.
Γυμνάσιον, 197, a.
Γυμνασταί, 197, b.
Γυμνασιον, 198, a.
Γυμνῆται, 41, b.
Γυμνῆτες, 41, b; 193, b.

Γυμνοί.

Γυμνοί, 41, b; 272, b.
Γυμνοπαιδία, 198, b.
Γυναικοκόσμοι, 198, b.
Γυναικονόμοι, 198, b.
Γυναικωνῖτις, 140, a.
Γωρυτός, 37, b.

Δ.

Δᾳδοῦχος, 150, b.
Δαίδαλα, 126, b.
Δαιδάλεια, 126, b.
Δακτύλιος, 25, b.
Δάκτυλος, 126, b.
Δαμαρέτειον χρύσιον, 126, b.
Δαμοσία, 161, b; 301, b.
Δανάκη, 126, b; 185, a.
Δαρεικος, 126, b.
Δᾳφνηφόρια, 126, b.
Δεῖγμα, 128, b.
Δείλη, 134, b.
Δεῖπνον, 95, a.
Δεκαδαρχία, 127, a.
Δεκαδοῦχοι, 127, a.
Δεκαρχία, 127, a.
Δεκασμός, 127, a.
Δεκάστυλος, 367, b.
Δεκατευταί, 128, b.
Δεκάτη, 128, b.
Δεκατηλόγοι, 128, a.
Δεκατῶναι, 128, a.
Δελφίνια, 129, a.
Δελφίς, 129, a.
Δεσμωτήριον, 72, a.
Δεσποσιοναῦται, 202, a.
Δευτεραγωνιστής, 205, b.
Δήγμα, 182, b.
Δήλια, 128, b; 283, b.
Δήμαρχοι, 129, a; 385, b.
Δημιούργοι, 3, b; 129, a; 389, b.
Δήμιος, 202, a.
Δημοκρατία, 129, b.
Δῆμος, 129, b; 130, a.
Δημόσιοι, 129, b.
Δημόσιοι, 11, b; 33, a.
Δημόται, 130, a.
Διαγραφεῖς, 149, a.
Διάζωμα, 422, b.
Διαζώματα, 371, a.
Διαιτηταί, 130, b.
Διάκριοι, 390, a.
Διαμαρτυρία, 24, b.
Διαμαστίγωσις, 130, b.
Διάσια, 131, a.
Διάστυλος, 367, b.
Δίαυλος, 274, b; 348, b.
Διαχειροτονία, 83, b.
Διαψήφισις, 130, b.
Διελκυστίνδα παίζειν, 198, a.
Διῆρες, 141, b.
Δίκαι ἔμμηνοι, 152, a.
Διπόλεια, 135, b.
Διπόλια, 135, b.
Δικαστής, 131, a.
Δικαστικόν, 131, a.
Δίκη, 131, b.
  ἀποστασίου, 338, b.

Εἰσαγγελία.

Δίκη αὐτοτελής, 132, b.
  βλάβης, 248, b.
  ἐξούλης, 152, a.
  λειπομαρτυρίου, 248, b.
  προικός, 345, a.
  σίτου, 345, a.
  χρέους, 377, b.
Δίκροτα, 260, b.
Δικτύννια, 134, b.
Δίκτυον, 319, b.
Διμάχαι, 135, b; 164, a.
Δίμιτος, 364, b.
Διοικήσεως, ὁ ἐπὶ, 362, b.
Διόλειa, 135, b.
Διονύσια, 135, b.
  ἐν ἄστει, or μεγάλα, 135, b.
  κατ' ἀγρούς, or μικρά, 135, b.
Διοσημεία, 138, b.
Διοσκούρια, 137, a.
Διπλοίδιον, 401, a.
Διπλοῖς, 401, a.
Διπόλεια, 135, b.
Δίπτερος, 367, a.
Δίπτυχα, 137, b; 358, b; 360, a.
Δίσκος, 137, b.
Διφθέρα, 137, a; 238, a.
Δίφρος, 124, b.
Διωβελία, 374, b.
Δόκανα, 139, b.
Δοκιμασία, 139, b; 153, b.
Δόλιχος, 274, b; 348, b.
Δόλων, 140, a.
Δοράτιον, 159, b.
Δόρπον, 95, a.
Δόρυ, 41, b; 199, b.
Δοῦλος, 337, a.
Δράκων, 343, b.
Δραχμή, 145, b.
Δρεπάνη, Δρέπανον, 173, b.
Δροῖται, 185, b.
Δρόμος, 274, b.
Δυμανάται, 389, a.
Δυμάνες, 389, a.
Δωμάτια, 140, b.
Δῶρα, 145, a.
Δωροδοκίας γραφή, 127, a.
Δῶρον, 281, a.
Δώρων γραφή, 127, a.

Ε.

Ἐγγύησις, 249, b.
Ἔγκλημα, 131, b.
Ἔγκτημα, 152, b.
Ἔγκτησις, 91, a; 152, b.
Ἔγχος, 41, b; 199, b.
Ἔδνα, 145, a.
Ἕδος, 367, a.
Ἐδώλια, 265, b.
Ἑεδνα, 145, a.
Ἐθελοπρόξενος, 209, a.
Εἰκόνες, 151, a.
Εἰκοστή, 148, b.
Εἰκοστολόγος, 148, b.
Εἴλωτες, 201, b.
Εἴρην, 148, b.
Εἰσαγγελία, 148, b.

Ἐξηγηταί.

Εἰσιτήρια, 148, b
Εἰσποιεῖσθαι, 7, a.
Εἰσποίησις, 7, a.
Εἰσποιητός, 7, a.
Εἰσφέρειν, 149, a.
Εἰσφορά, 148, b.
Ἑκατόμβαια, 203, a.
Ἑκαταμβαιών, 65, b.
Ἑκατομβή, 203, a; 324, b
Ἔκγονοι, 203, a.
Ἔκδικος, 148, a.
Ἔκδοσις, 176, b.
Ἐκεχειρία, 274, a.
Ἐκκλησία, 146, b.
  κυρία, 146, b.
  νόμιμος, 146, b.
  σύγκλητος, 146, b.
Ἔκκλητοι, 206, b.
Ἐκκομιδή, 185, b.
Ἐκλογεῖς, 149, a.
Ἐκμαρτυρία, 24, b; 148, a.
Ἐκποιεῖν, 7, a.
Ἐκποιεῖσθαι, 7, a.
Ἐκτεύς, Ἕκτη, 201, a.
Ἐκφορά, 185, a.
Ἐκφυλλοφορία, 172, b.
Ἐλαία, Ἔλαιον, 273, b.
Ἐλατήρ, 198, a.
Ἐλαφηβολιών, 65, b.
Ἐλέος, 382, b.
Ἐλευθέρια, 151, b.
Ἐλευσίνια, 149, b.
Ἐλκυστίνδα παίζειν, 198, a.
Ἑλλανοδίκαι, 18, a; 201, b; 275, a.
Ἑλληνοταμίαι, 201, b.
Ἐλλόβιον, 211, b.
Ἐλλώτια, or Ἑλλώτια, 151, b.
Ἔλυμα, 31, b.
Ἐμβάς, 151, b.
Ἐμβατεία, 151, b.
Ἔμβλημα, 152, a.
Ἐμβολή, 40, b.
Ἔμβολον, 264, a.
Ἔμβολος, 124, a; 264, a.
Ἐμμέλεια, 85, b.
Ἔμμηνοι δίκαι, 152, a.
Ἐμπαισμα, 152, a.
Ἐμπόριον, 152, b.
Ἔμπορος, 152, b.
Ἔμφρουρος, 161, a.
Ἐναγίσματα, 187, b.
Ἔνατα, 187, a.
Ἔνδειξις, 152, b.
Ἔνδεκα οἱ, 202, b.
Ἐνδοῦναι, 152, b.
Ἐνδρομίς, 152, b.
Ἔνδυμα, 19, b.
Ἔννατα, 187, a.
Ἐννεάκρουνος, 29, b.
Ἐννεατηρίς, 316, a.
Ἔνοπτρον, 347, a.
Ἔντεα, 41, a.
Ἐνωμο:ίαι, 161, a.
Ἐνώτιον, 211, b.
Ἐξάστυλος. 367, a.
Ἐξέδρα, 140, b; 160, b; 258, b.
Ἐξέτασται, 160, b.
Ἐξηγηταί, 160, a; 160, b.

GREEK INDEX. 441

Ἡμέρα.

Ἑστιάτωρ, 204, b.
Ἐσχάρα, 31, a; 141, b; 180, b.
Ἐσχαρίς, 31, a; 141, b; 160, b.
Ἑταιρία, 98, a; 159, a; 359, b.
Ἕταιροι, 163, b.
Ἑτεροστόμος, 268, b.
Εὔδειπνος, 11, a.
Εὔζωνος, 401, b.
Εὐθυδικία, 132, a.
Εὐθύνη, 154, b; **160**, a.
Εὔθυνοι, 160, b.
Εὐμολπίδαι, 159, b.
Εὐνή, 222, a.
Εὐπατρίδαι, 91, a; **160**, a.
Εὔστυλος, 167, b.
Εὐφημεῖτε, 138, b.
Εὐφημία, 138, b.
Ἐφελκύσασθαι, 140, b.
Ἔφεσις, 29, a.
Ἐφέται, 153, b.
Ἐφηβεία, 153, a.
Ἔφηβος, 153, a.
Ἐξήγησις, 133, b.
Ἐφίππειον, 154, a.
Ἐφίππιον, 154, a.
Ἔφοροι, 154, a.
Ἔφυροι, 150, b.
Ἐχῖνος, 24, b; 132, a; 249, a.
Εὔχημα, 416, b.
Ἑώρα, 11, a.

Z.

Ζάκοροι, 10, a.
Ζευγῖται, 81, b; 162, a; 190, a.
Ζευγλαι, 266, a.
Ζευκτηρίαι, 266, a.
Ζητηταί, 422, b.
Ζυγά, 265, b.
Ζύγιοι, 124, b; **265**, b.
Ζυγῖται, 124, b; 265, b.
Ζυγόν, 161, a; **217**, a; 245, b; 329, a.
Ζυγός, 217, a; 329, a.
Ζύθος, 82, b.
Ζωγραφία, 293, b.
Ζῶμα, 422, b.
Ζωμὸς μέλας, **160**, a.
Ζώνη, 41, a; **422**, b.
Ζωστήρ, 41, b; **422**, b.
Ζωφόρος, **102**, a; **422**, b.

H.

Ἡγεμόνες συμμοριῶν, 393, a.
Ἡγεμονία δικαστηρίου, 247, a.
Ἠθμος, 191, a.
Ἠλακάτη, 141, b; 267, a.
Ἤλεκτρον -ος, 149, b.
Ἡλιοτρόπιον, 207, a.
Ἦμαρ δείελον, 134, b.
μέσον, 134, b.
Ἡμέρα εὐσία τοῦ νομοῦ, 94, a.
μέση, 134, b.

Θυρωρός.

Ἡμεροδρόμοι, 202, a.
Ἡμιδιπλοΐδιον, 401, a.
Ἡμιεκτέον, 201, a.
Ἡμίεκτον, 201, a.
Ἡμικύκλιον, 202, a.
Ἡμίμνα, or Ἡμιμνα, **120**, b; 202, b.
Ἡνίοχος, **124**, b.
Ἡραῖα, 202, b.
Ἡρῷον, 186, a.
Ἡώς, 134, b.

Θ.

Θαλάμιοι, 265, b.
Θαλαμῖται, 265, b.
Θάλαμος, 141, b; 265, b.
Θαλλοφόροι, 282, b.
Θάπτειν, 185, b.
Θαργήλια, 370, a.
Θαργηλιών, 65, b.
Θέατρον, 273, a; 370, b.
Θεατροπώλης, 374, b.
Θεατρώνης, 374, b.
Θέμα, 46, a.
Θεοφάνια, 374, a.
Θεράπων, 161, b; **202**, a.
Θερμά, **55**, a.
Θέσις, 7, a.
Θεσμοθέται, 35, a.
Θεσμός, 35, b; 271, b.
Θεσμοφόριος, 375, b.
Θετοί, **7**, a.
Θεωρία, 373, a.
Θεωρικά, 374, a.
Θεωρίς, 128, b; **283**, b.
Θεωροί, 128, b; **375**, a.
Θῆκαι, 186, a.
Θηριομάχοι, 58, b.
Θησαυρός, 367, a; **375**, a.
Θησεία, 375, b.
Θῆτες, 81, b; 190, a.
Θίασος, 135, b.
Θολία, 405, a.
Θόλος, 376, a.
Θόωκος, 15, b.
Θρανίον, 376, a.
Θρανῖται, 265, b.
Θρᾶνος, 265, b.
Θρηνῳδοί, 185, h.
Θρίαμβος, 194, a.
Θρόνος, 376, a.
Θυμέλη, 371, b.
Θυμιατήριον, **2**, a; **422**, b.
Θύρα, 214, b.
αὔλειος, **140**, b.
βαλανωτός, 141, a.
κηπαία, 141, b.
μέσαυλος, 141, a.
μέταυλος, 141, a.
Θυρεός, 331, a.
Θυρετρον, 215, a.
Θυρίδες, 141, b.
Θύρσος, 376, a.
Θυρών, 140, b.
Θυρωρεῖον, 140, b.
Θυρωρος, 140, b; **215**, a.

GREEK INDEX.

Θύσανοι.

Θύσανοι, 10, b.
Θυτήριον, 31, a.
Θώραξ, 41, a; 240, b.

Ι.

Ἴακχος, 150, b.
Ἰγδη, Ἰγδις, 257, a.
Ἵδρυσις, 366, b.
Ἱερεῖον, 324, a.
Ἱεροδιδάσκαλος, 303, a.
Ἱερόδουλοι, 204, b.
Ἱερομαντεία, 138, a.
Ἱερομηνία, 274, a.
Ἱερομνήμονες, 20, a; 205, a.
Ἱερόν, 362, a; 366, b
Ἱερονῖκαι, 47, a.
Ἱερανόμος, 303, a.
Ἱεροποιοί, 205, a.
Ἱεροσκοπία, 138, a.
Ἱεροφάντης, 150, a; 159, b; 303, a.
Ἱεροφύλαξ, 303, a.
Ἱκετηρία, 421, b.
Ἴκρια, 260, a.
Ἱλάρια, 205, a.
Ἴλη, 163, b.
Ἱμάντες, 82, b; 267, b.
Ἱμάντες πυκτικοί, 82, b.
Ἱματίδιον, 280, a.
Ἱμάτιον, 19, a; 280, a.
Ἰνῶα, 213, a.
Ἱππαρμοστής, 161, a.
Ἵππαρχος, 3, b; 162, b.
Ἱππεῖς, 13, b; 81, b; 390, a.
Ἱππικόν, 348, b.
Ἱπποβόται, 205, a.
Ἱππόδρομος, 348, b.
Ἱπποκόμος, 162, b.
Ἴρην, 148, b.
Ἴσθμια, 214, a.
Ἰσοπολιτεία, 91, a; 255, a.
Ἰσυτέλεια, 91, a; 255, a; 366, a.
Ἰσοτελεῖς, 91, a; 255, a.
Ἰστίον, 259, b; 267, a.
Ἱστοβοεύς, 31, b.
Ἱστός, 259, b; 266, a; 363, b.
Ἱστών, 141, b; 363, b.
Ἴτυς, 124, a.
Ἰφικρατίδες, 163, a.

Κ.

Καβείρια, 63, a.
Κάδος, Κάδδος, 23, b; 63, b.
Καθάπαξ, 47, b.
Κάθαρσις, 244, a.
Καθετήρ, 318, b.
Κάθοδος, 375, b.
Καίειν, 185, b.
Κάλαθος, 64, a.
  κάθοδος, 150, b.
Κάλαμος, 301, a.
Καλλιγένεια 375, b

Κληῖδες.

Καλλιερεῖν, 138, b.
Καλλιστεῖα, 68, b.
Καλοβάτης, 184, b.
Κάλοι, 260, b; 267, b.
Καλῳδία, 267, b.
Καμάρα, 69, a.
Κάναβος, or Κίναβος, 69, a.
Κάναθρον, 69, a.
Κάνδυς, 70, a.
Κάνεον, 70, a.
Κανηφόρος, 70, a; 282, b.
Κανών, 364, b.
Καπηλεῖον, 77, a.
Κάπηλος, 77, a; 152, b.
Καπνοδόκη, 141, b.
Καρνεᾶται, 72, b.
Καρνεῖα, 72, b.
Καρπαία, 328, a.
Καρχήσιον, 72, a.
Κάρυα, 73, a.
Καρυατίς, 73, a.
Καταβλητική, 242, a.
Καταγώγιον, 77, a.
Κατάλογος, 76, a.
Κατάλυσις, 77, a.
Καταπειρατήρια, 76, a.
Καταπέλτης, 381, a.
Καταπελτική, 381, a.
Καταρράκτης, 76, a.
Κατάστασις, 162, b.
Καταστρώματα, 261, a.
Κατατομαί, 371, a.
Κατάφρακτοι, 261, a.
Καταχειροτονία, 83, b.
Καταχύσματα, 250, a.
Κατήγορος, 358, b.
Κάτοπτρον, 347, a.
Καταρύττειν, 185, b.
Κατοχεύς, 215, a.
Καυσία, 77, b.
Κεάδας, 72, a; 78, a.
Κειρία, 222, a.
Κεκρύφαλος, 103, b.
Κελευστής, 259, a; 305, b.
Κεραία, 267, a.
Κεραμεύς, 178, b.
Κεράμιον, 178, b.
Κέραμος, 178, b; 363, b.
Κέρας, 163, b; 322, b.
Κερατίον, 405, b.
Κερκίδες, 364, b; 371, a.
Κεροῦχοι, 267, b.
Κεφαλή, 40, b.
Κηπαία θύρα, 141, b.
Κῆπος, 207, b.
Κηρογραφία, 295, a.
Κηρός, 82, b.
Κηρύκειον, 63, a.
Κηρύκιον, 63, a.
Κιβωτός, 32, a.
Κίθαρις, 243, a.
Κίονες, 186, a.
Κίστη, 90, a.
Κιστοφόρος, 90, b.
Κίων, 101, b.
Κλεῖθρον, 215, a.
Κλεῖς, 178, b.
Κλεψύδρα, 249, a.
Κληῖδες, 260, a.

Κῦμα.

Κληρονόμος, 203, a.
Κλῆρος, 203, a.
Κληρουχία, 91, a; 98, b.
Κληροῦχοι, 91, a.
Κλητῆρες, 91, a.
Κλήτορες, 93, a.
Κλιμακίδες, 266, a.
Κλίνη, 221, a; 222, a.
Κλινίδιον, 221, a.
Κλισίας, 215, a.
Κναφεύς, 184, a.
Κνέφαλον, 222, a.
Κνῆμαι, 124, a.
Κνημίς, 41, a; 273, a.
Κόγξ, 150, b.
Κόθορνος, 120, a.
Κοῖλοι, 65, b.
Κοῖλον, 371, a.
Κοινὸν τῶν Αἰτώλων, 13, a.
Κοιτῶνες, 140, b.
Κολεός, 196, a.
Κολοσσός, 101, a.
Κόλπος, 401, a.
Κολῶναι, 186, a.
Κόμη, 103, a.
Κομμός, 384, a.
Κοντός, 266, a.
Κοπίς, 123, a.
Κόρδαξ, 85, b; 111, a.
Κόρη, 400, b.
Κορυβαντικά, 119, b.
Κόρυμβος, 103, a.
Κόρυς, 41, b; 192, b.
Κορώνη, 288, a.
Κορωνίς, 102, b; 119, b.
Κοσμοί, 120, a.
Κότινος, 275, b
Κόττaβoς, 120, b.
Κοτύλη, 120, b.
Κοτύττια, 120, b.
Κουρά, 103, a.
Κόφινος, 117, a.
Κοχλιάριον, 94, b.
Κοχλίας, 94, b.
Κράνος, 192, b.
Κρατήρ, 121, a.
Κρεάγρα, 199, b.
Κρήνη, 29, b; 181, a.
Κρηπίς, 121, a.
Κρίκος, 211, b.
Κριός, 40, a.
Κριταί, 121, a.
Κροκή, 364, a.
Κροκωτόν -ός, 121, a.
Κρόταλον, 126, a.
Κρούειν, 215, a.
Κρυπτεία, 121, b.
Κρωβύλος, 103, a.
Κτείς, 288, a.
Κύαθος, 125, a.
Κύαμος, 96, a.
Κυβερνῆται, 259, a.
Κυβιστῆρες, 328, a.
Κύβος, 368, b.
Κύκλα, 124, a.
Κυκλάς, 125, b.
Κύκλος, 338, a.
Κύλιξ, 68, a.
Κῦμα, 125, b.

GREEK INDEX. 443

Κύμβαλον.
Κύμβαλον, 125, b.
Κύμβη, 125, b.
Κυνέη, 41, b; 192, b.
Κυρβασία, 376, b.
Κύρβεις, 54, b; 271, b.
Κύριος, 123, b; 230, b.
Κύων, 362, a.
Κώδων, 378, a.
Κωλακρέται, 98, a; 363, a.
Κῶμος, 110, b.
Κωμῳδία, 110, b.
Κωνοπεῖον, 113, a.
Κώπη, 265, b.

Λ.

Λαμπαδαρχία, 220, a.
Λαμπαδηδρομία, 220, a.
Λαμπαδηφορία, 220, a.
Λαμπάς, 220, a.
Λάρνακες, 185, b.
Λάφαια, 220, b.
Λέβης, 273, b.
Λειτουργία, 224, a.
Λεκάνη, 286, a.
Λεκανίς, 207, a.
Λέσχη, 223, a.
Λέχος, 222, a.
Λήκυθος, 23, b; 185, a; 295, b.
Λήναια, 135, b.
Ληνοί, 185, b.
Ληνός, 416, b.
Ληξιαρχικὸν γραμματεῖον, 130, a.
Λῆξις, 131, b.
Λιβανωτρίς, 2, b.
Λιβυρνίς, 239, a; 262, b.
Λιβυρνόν, 239, a; 262, b.
Λιθοτομίαι, 221, a.
Λικμός, 407, a.
Λίκνον, 407, a.
Λίνα, 319, b.
Λίτρα, 240, a.
Λογεῖον, 372, a.
Λογισταί, 160, b.
Λογιστής, 65, a.
Λόγχη, 199, b.
Λοετρόν, 54, b.
Λοιβαί, 325, b.
Λουτήρ, 55, a.
Λουτήριον, 55, a.
Λουτρόν, 54, b.
Λουτροφόρος, 250, a.
Λόφος, 192, b.
Λοχαγοί, 161, a; 163, b.
Λόχος, 161, a; 162, b; 363, b.
Λύκαια, 245, a.
Λύκος, 199, a.
Λύρα, 245, a.
Λύχνος, 241, b.
Λυχνοῦχος, 70, a.

Μυστίλη.

M.

Μάζα, 96, a; 285, a.
Μαιμακτηριών, 65, b.
Μαίανδρος, 215, a.
Μανδύας, 219, b.
Μανδύη, 219, b.
Μαντεῖον, 276, b.
Μάντεις, 137, b.
Μαντική, 137, b.
Μαρσύπιον, 248, b.
Μαρτυρία, 24, b; 248, b.
Μαστιγονόμοι, 249, a.
Μαστιγοφόροι, 249, a.
Μάστιξ, 179, b.
Μάχαιρα, 122, a; 315, a.
Μέγαρον, 367, a.
Μέδιμνος, 253, a.
Μεθίστασθαι, 172, a.
Μελία, 199, b.
Μελίκρατον, 418, b.
Μελιττοῦτα, 185, a.
Μελλείρην, 148, b.
Μεσαύλιος θύρα, 141, a.
Μέσαυλος θύρα, 141, a.
Μεσημβρία, 134, b.
Μεταγειτνιών, 65, b.
Μέταλλον, 254, a.
Μετάστασις, 85, b.
Μέταυλος θύρα, 141, a.
Μετεωρολογία, 45, b.
Μετοίκιον, 233, a; 365, b.
Μέτοικοι, 234, b.
Μετόπη, 255, a.
Μετρητής, 255, b.
Μέτωπον, 263, a.
Μὴν ἐμβόλιμος, 65, b.
Μητροπολις, 98, b.
Μήτρωον, 33, a.
Μῖμος, 255, b.
Μισθὸς ἐκκλησιαστικός, 147, a.
Μίτοι, 364, b.
Μίτρα, 103, a; 256, a; 422, b.
Μίτρη, 41, a.
Μνᾶ, 361, b.
Μνήματα, 186, a.
Μνημεῖα, 186, a.
Μόθακες, 202, a.
Μόθωνες, 202, a.
Μοιχείας γραφή, 8, a.
Μολυβδίδες, 184, b.
Μοναρχία, 256, b.
Μονομάχοι, 194, b.
Μονοχίτων, 401, a.
Μόρα, 161, a.
Μουνυχιών, 65, b.
Μουσεῖον, 258, b.
Μοχλός, 215, a.
Μυκτῆρες, 241, b.
Μύλοι, 256, a.
Μύξαι, 241, b.
Μύριοι, 258, b.
Μυρρίναι, 418, a.
Μυσία, 258, b.
Μυσταγωγός, 150, a; 159, b.
Μύσται, 150, a.
Μυστήρια, 258, b.
Μυστίλη, 95, b.

Οἶκος.

Μύστρον, 95, b.
Μύστρος, 95, b.

Ν.

Ναΐδιοι, 186, a.
Ναός, 366, b.
Ναυαρχία, 259, a.
Ναύαρχος, 259, a.
Ναύκληροι, 259, b; 359, a.
Ναυκραρία, 259, a.
Ναύκραρος, 259, a.
Ναῦς, 259, b.
Ναυτικόν, 176, b.
Ναυτοδίκαι, 268, b.
Νεάζεσθαι, 32, b.
Νεκρόδειπνον, 187, a.
Νεκύσια, 187, b.
Νεμαῖα, 269, a.
Νέμεα, 269, a.
Νεμεία, 269, a.
Νεοδαμώδεις, 202, a.
Νέος, 32, b.
Νεοῦσθαι, 32, b.
Νεωκόροι, 10, a; 269, a.
Νεώς, 366, b.
Νῆες, 262, a.
Νῆμα, 191, b.
Νηστεία, 375, b.
Νομοθέτης, 35, b; 271, b.
Νόμος, 271, b.
Νομοφύλακες, 271, a.
Νουμηνία, 65, a.
Νυμφευτής, 250, a.
Νυχθήμερον, 134, b.

Ξ.

Ξεναγία, 163, a.
Ξεναγοί, 421, b.
Ξεηλασία, 422, a.
Ξενία, 208, a.
Ξενίας γραφή, 427, a.
Ξενικά, 235, a.
Ξένος, 208, a; 254, b.
Ξεώνες, 141, b.
Ξέστης, 422, a.
Ξίφος, 41, b; 196, a.
Ξόανον, 349, a.
Ξυήλη, 161, b.
Ξυλοκοπία, 191, b.
Ξυστήρ, 17, b.
Ξύστρα, 56, b.

O.

Ὀβολός, 145, a; 361, b.
Ὀγδόδιον, 375, b.
Ὀγκία, or Οὐγκία, 405, a.
Ὀδοποιοί, 363, a.
Οἰκήματα, 140, b.
Οἰκίστης, 98, b.
Οἶκος, 140, a.

GREEK INDEX.

Οἰνιστήρια.

Οἰνιστήρια, 103, a.
Οἰνόμελι, 418, a.
Οἶνος, 416, a.
Οἰωνιστική, 138, b.
Οἰωνοπόλος, 49, b.
Οἰωνοσκόποι, 49, b.
Ὀκρίβας, 372, a.
Ὀκτάστυλος, 367, a.
Ὀλιγαρχία, 41, a; 273, b.
Ὁλκάδες, 262, a.
Ὁλκοί, 261, b.
Ὁλμος, 257, a.
Ὁλοκαυτεῖν, 324, b.
Ὀλύμπια, 274, a.
Ὀλυμπιάς, 276, a.
Ὁμογάλακτες, 389, b.
Ὁμοιοι, 91, b; 161, b; 206, a.
Ὁμολογία, 358, b.
Ὀμφάλος, 94, a; 163, b.
Ὀνειροπολία, 138, b.
Ὄνομα, 270, b.
Ὄνος, 256, a.
Ὀξίς, 2, b.
Ὀξυβάφιον, 2, b.
Ὀξύβαφον, 2, b; 120, b.
Ὀξυγράφοι, 272, a.
Ὀπή, 255, a.
Ὀπισθόδομος, 367, a.
Ὅπλα, 41, a.
Ὁπλῆτες, 389, b.
Ὁπλῖται, 41, b.
Ὄργια, 258, b.
Ὀργυιά, 278, a.
Ὀρείχαλκος, 278, a.
Ὅρκος, 218, a.
Ὅρμος, 256, b; 328, b.
Ὄρυγμα, 57, a.
Ὄρχησις, 327, b.
Ὀρχήστρα, 371, b.
Ὀρχηστύς, 327, b.
Ὅσιοι, 277, a.
Ὀστράκιον, 178, b.
Ὀστρακισμός, 172, a.
Ὄστρακον, 172, b; 178, b; 185, a.
Ὀσχοφόρια, 278, a.
Οὐγγία, 405, a.
Οὐγκία, 405, a.
Οὖδας, 215, a.
Οὐλαμοί, 161, b.
Οὐλόχυτα, 325, a.
Οὐλοχύται, 325, a.
Οὐραγός, 161, b; 166, b.
Οὐρίαχος, 200, a.
Ὄφεις, 42, b.
Ὀχάνη, 94, a.
Ὄχανον, 94, a.
Ὀχλοκρατία, 129, b.
Ὄψημα, 276, b.
Ὄψον, 276, b.
Ὀψώνης, 276, b.

Π.

Παγκρατιασταί, 282, b.
Παγκράτιον, 282, b.
Παιάν, 279, a.

Πεντάπτυχα.

Παιδαγωγός, 279, a.
Παιδονόμος, 279, a.
Παιδοτριβαί, 197, b.
Παιήων, 279, a.
Παίων, 279, a.
Πάλαισμα, 242, a.
Παλαισμοσύνη, 242, a.
Παλαιστή, 281, a.
Παλαίστρα, 279, b.
Πάλη, 242, a.
Παμβοιώτια, 281, b.
Πάμμαχοι, 282, b.
Πάμφυλοι, 389, a.
Παναθήναια, 281, b.
Πανδοκεῖον, 77, a.
Πανήγυρις, 283, a.
Πανιώνια, 283, a.
Πανοπλία, 283, a.
Παράβασις, 111, a.
Παραγναθίδες, 192, b.
Παραγραφή, 283, b.
Παράδεισος, 283, b.
Παραθύρα, 215, a.
Παραιβάτης, 124, b.
Παραλῖαι, 283, b.
Πάραλοι, 283, b; 390, a.
Πάραλος, 283, b.
Παράμεσος δάκτυλος, 25, b.
Παρανοίας γραφή, 284, a.
Παρανόμων γραφή, 147, b; 284, a.
Παρανύμφος, 250, a.
Παραπέτασμα, 140, b; 372, a.
Παραπρεσβεία, 284, b.
Παραστάδες, 26, a.
Παραπυλίς, 305, a.
Παραρρύματα, 267, b.
Παρασάγγης, 284, b.
Παράσημον, 263, b.
Παράσιτος, 284, b.
Παρασκήνιον, 372, a.
Παραστάς, 141, a.
Παράστασις, ἐν, 367, a.
Παραστάται, 266, a.
Πάρεδροι, 284, b.
Παρήορος, 124, b.
Πάροδοι, 172, a.
Πάροδος, 85, b.
Πάροχος, 250, a.
Παστός, 289, b.
Πάτραι, 389, a.
Πεδιαῖοι, 390, a.
Πέδιλον, 64, b.
Πεζέταιροι, 163, b.
Πελάται, 288, b.
Πέλεκυς, 331, b.
Πελτασταί, 42, a; 163, a; 289, a.
Πέλτη, 42, a; 288, b.
Πενέσται, 289, a.
Πενταετηρίς, 274, b.
Πένταθλοι, 289, a.
Πένταθλον, 289, a.
Πεντακοσιαρχία, 163, b.
Πεντακοσιομέδιμνοι, 81, b; 390, a.
Πενταλιθίζειν, 362, a.
Πεντάλιθος, 198, a.
Πεντάπτυχα, 360, a.

Πομπή.

Πεντηκόντορος, 260, b; 262, a.
Πεντηκοστή, 289, a.
Πεντηκοστήρ, 161, a.
Πεντηκοστολόγοι, 289, b.
Πεντηκοστύς, 161, a.
Πεντήρεις, 262, a.
Πέπλος, 289, b.
Περίαμμα, 24, a.
Περίαπτον, 24, a.
Περίβλημα, 19, b.
Περιβόλαιον, 19, b.
Περίβολος, 323, a.
Περίδειπνον, 187, a.
Περίοικοι, 290, b.
Περίπατος, 258, b.
Περιπόδιον, 213, a.
Περίπολοι, 153, b; 162, a.
Περίπτερος, 367, a.
Περιρῥαντήρια, 366, b.
Περισκελλίς, 291, a.
Περιστύλιον, 102, a; 140, b.
Περιτειχισμός, 406, b.
Περόνη, 178, b.
Πεσσοί, 221, a.
Πεταλισμός, 172, b.
Πέτασος, 297, b.
Πέταυρον, 292, a.
Πέτευρον, 292, a.
Πετροβόλος, 381, a.
Πηδάλιον, 265, b.
Πῆληξ, 192, b.
Πήνη, 364, a.
Πηνίκη, 104, a.
Πηνίον, 192, a.
Πήρα, 290, a.
Πῆχυς, 122, a; 245, b.
Πίθος, 417, a.
Πιθοιγία, 136, a.
Πίλημα, 297, a.
Πῖλος, 297, a.
Πιλωτόν, 297, a.
Πινακική, 45, b.
Πινακοθήκη, 293, b.
Πλαγίαυλος, 376, b.
Πλαστική, 349, a.
Πλέθρον, 300, b.
Πλῆκτρον, 246, a.
Πλήμνη, 124, a.
Πλημοχόαι, 151, a.
Πλημοχόη, 151, a.
Πληρεῖς, 65, b.
Πλίνθος, 220, b.
Πλοῖον, 259, b; 262, a.
Πλυντήρια, 301, a.
Πόδες, 260, b; 267, b.
Ποιεῖν, 7, a.
Ποιεῖσθαι, 7, a.
Ποίησις, 7, a.
Ποιητός, 7, a.
Ποιηή, 301, a.
Πολέμαρχος, 35, a; 162, 301, a.
Πόλις, 91, b.
Πολιτεία, 90, b; 203, a.
Πολίτης, 90, b.
Πόλος, 206, a.
Πολύμιτος, 364, b.
Πολύπτυχα, 360, a.
Πομπή, 301, b.

GREEK INDEX. 445

Πορισταί.
όρισταί, 305, a; 362, b.
όρπαξ, 161, b.
όρπη, 178, b.
οσειδεών, 65, b.
ούς, 292, a.
ράκτορες, 306, b.
ροάγνευσις, 150, a.
ροβολή, 310, a.
ροβούλευμα, 61, b.
ρόβουλοι, 310, a.
ρογάμεια, 250, a.
ρόδομος, 367, a.
ροδοσία, 310, b.
ρόδρομος, 141, a.
ροεδρία, 214, b.
ρόεδροι, 61, b.
ρόθεσις, 185, a.
ροθεσμία, 311, b.
ροθεσμίας νόμος, 311, b.
ρόθυρα, 140, a.
ρόθυρον, 16, b.
ροικὸς δίκη, 345, a.
ροίξ, 145, a.
ροκάθαρσις, 150, a.
ροκαταβολή, 365, a.
ρόκλησις, 132, a.
ρόλογος, 383, b.
ρόμαχοι, 41, b.
ρομήθεια, 311, a.
ρόναος, 367, a.
ροξενία, 208, a.
ρόξενος, 209, a.
ροπύλαια, 311, a.
ροσκατοβλημα, 367, a.
ροσκεφάλειον, 222, a.
ροσκήνιον, 372, a.
ρόσκλησις, 131, b; 248, b.
ροσκύνησις, 7, b.
ροστάς, 141, a.
ροστάτης, 91, a.
τοῦ δήμου, 311, b.
ροστιμᾶν, 378, a.
ροστιμᾶσθαι, 378, a.
ροστίμημα, 132, b; 378, a.
ροστόον, 140, b.
ρόστυλος, 367, a.
ροσωπείον, 291, a.
ρόσωπον, 291, a.
ροτέλεια γάμων, 249, b.
ροτομή, 40, b.
ρότονοι, 259, b; 267, b.
ροθήτης, 150, a.
ροθῆτις, 277, a.
ροχειροτονία, 62, a.
ροωμοσία, 132, a.
ρυλέες, 327, b.
ρύλις, 327, b.
ρύμνη, 264, b.
ρυτανεία, 61, b.
ρυτανεία, 131, b; 313, b.
ρυτανεῖον, 313, a.
ρυτανεῖς, 61, b; 313, b.
ρωί, 131, b.
ρῶρα, 263, a.
ρωρᾶται, 259, a.
ρωρεύς, 264, b.
ρωταγωνιστής, 205, b.
ρωτοστάτης, 161, b.
ψανέψια, 315, b.

Σημαίαι.
Πυανεψιών, 65, b.
Πυγμαχία, 315, a.
Πυγμή, 115, a.
Πυγμοσύνη, 315, a.
Πυέλοι, 54, b; 185, b.
Πύθια, 315, b.
Πύθιοι, 316, a.
Πυκνόστυλος, 367, b.
Πύκται, 115, a.
Πυλαγόραι, 20, a.
Πυλαια, 20, a.
Πύλη, 105, a.
Πυλίς, 105, a.
Πυλών, 140, b; 305, b.
Πύξ, 315, a.
Πυξίδιον, 316, a.
Πύξις, 316, a.
Πυράγρα, 254, b.
Πυραί, 185, b.
Πύργος, 402, a.
Πυρία, 55, b.
Πυριατήριον, 55, b.
Πυρρ.χη, 327, b.
Πυρρίχισται, 328, a.
Πώγων, 57, a.
Πωλῆται, 301, b.
Πῶμα, 207, a.

P.
Ῥαβδίον, 295, b.
Ῥαβδονόμοι, 15, a.
Ῥαβδοῦχοι, 15, a; 249, a.
Ῥαιστήρ, 254, b.
Ῥαφίς, 6, b.
Ῥήτρα, 322, a.
Ῥινοπύλη, 305, b.
Ῥιπίς, 179, b.
Ῥόμβος, 198, a.
Ῥυμός, 31, b; 124, a.
Ῥυτόν, 322, b.

Σ.
Σαγήνη, 320, b.
Σάκκος, 101, b; 103, a; 323, a.
Σάκος, 41, b.
Σαλαμίνια, 285, b.
Σαλαμίνιοι, 285, b.
Σάλπιγξ, 399, a.
Σαμβύκη, 329, a.
Σαμβυκιστριαί, 129, a.
Σανδάλιον, 329, a.
Σάνδαλον, 329, a.
Σανίς, 215, a.
Σαρδών, 320, a.
Σάρισα, or Σάρισσα, 163, a.
Σαυρωτήρ, 200, a.
Σεβαστός, 53, a.
Σειραφόρος, 124, b.
Σείστρον, 341, a.
Σηκός, 367, a.
Σημαίαι, 343, a.

Συλλογεῖς.
Σήματα, 186, a.
Σημειογράφοι, 272, a
Σημεῖον, 343, a.
Σίγυννος, 289, a.
Σίκιννις, 85, b.
Σιτηρέσιον, 162, b.
Σιτοδείαι, 345, a.
Σιτοπῶλαι, 345, a.
Σῖτος, 344, b.
Σίτου δίκη, 345, a.
Σιτοφυλακεῖον, 207, b.
Σιτοφύλακες, 15, b; 344, b
Σιτώναι, 345, a.
Σκαλμοί, 264, b.
Σκαπέδρα, 198, a.
Σκάφη, 262, b.
Σκέπαρνον, 44, a.
Σκεύη κρεμαστά, 265, b.
ξύλινα, 265, b.
Σκηνή, 372, a.
Σκῆπτρον, 330, a.
Σκιάδειον, 404, b.
Σκιάδιον, 404, b.
Σκιαδίσκη, 404, b.
Σκίαθηρον, 206, a.
Σκιάς, 376, a.
Σκιροφοριών, 65, b.
Σκόλοψ, 121, a.
Σκύθαι, 129, b; 147, a.
Σκυτάλη, 331, a.
Σμίλη, 139, b.
Σοροί, 185, b.
Σπάθη, 364, b.
Σπάργανον, 212, a.
Σπεῖρα, 347, b.
Σπονδαί, 323, b.
Σπονδοφόροι, 274, a.
Στάδιον, 348, b.
Στάδιος, 348, b.
Σταθμός, 215, a; 239, a; 247, b.
Σταθμοῦχοι, 359, a.
Στάσιμον, 111, a; 384, a.
Στατήρ, 349, a.
Σταυρός, 121, a.
Στέφανος, 118, a.
Στῆλαι, 186, a.
Στήμων, 364, a.
Στλεγγίς, 17, b; 56, b.
Στοά, 140, b; 305, b.
Στόλος, 261, b.
Στόμιον, 182, b.
Στοιχεῖον, 206, a.
Στρατηγός, 3, b; 13, a; 308, a;
  355, a.
ὁ ἐπὶ διοικήσεως, 363, a.
Στρατός, 160, b.
Στρεπτός, 381, b.
Στρόβιλος, 198, a.
Στρογγύλαι, 261, a; 262, a.
Στρῶμα, 154, a; 222, a.
Στῦλος, 101, b; 354, a.
Στύραξ, 200, a.
Συγγένεια, 201, a.
Συγγενεῖς, 201, a.
Συγγραφή, 358, b.
Σύγκλητος ἐκκλησία, 146, b.
Συκοφάντης, 356, a.
Σύλαι, 356, b.
Συλλογεῖς, 357, a

Συμβόλαιον.

Συμβόλαιον, 357, a.
Συμβολή, 95, b.
Σύμμαχοι, 145, b.
Συμμορία, 149, a; 393, a.
Συμπόσιον, 357, a.
Συνάλλαγμα, 357, a.
Σύνδικος, 271, b; 358, a.
Συνέδριον, 358, a.
Σύνεδροι, 358, a.
Συνηγορικόν, 158, b.
Συνήγορος, 160, b; 358, a.
Συνθήκη, 357, a.
Σύνθημα, 168, b.
Σύνοδος, 117, a.
Συνοικία, 358, b.
Σύνταγμα, 163, a.
Συντάξεις, 358, a.
Σύνταξις, 365, b.
Συντέλεια, 393, a.
Συντελείς, 393, a.
Συντριήραρχοι, 392, b.
Συνωρίς, 124, b.
Σύριγξ, 359, a.
Σύρμα, 354, b.
Σύσκηνοι, 116, b.
Συσσίτια, 349, b.
Σύστασις, 163, b.
Σύστυλος, 367, b.
Σφαγίς, 122, a.
Σφαίρα, 296, a.
Σφαιρείς, 296, b.
Σφαιριστήριον, 198, a; 296, b.
Σφαιριστική, 198, a; 296, a.
Σφαιριστικός, 296, b.
Σφαιρίστρα, 296, b.
Σφενδόνη, 103, b; 184, b.
Σφενδονήται, 184, b.
Σφίδες, 246, a.
Σφραγίς, 25, b.
Σφύρα, 254, b.
Σφυρήλατον, 254, b.
Σχεδίαι, 260, a.
Σχοινία, 267, b; 268, a.
Σχοινοβάτης, 184, b.
Σχοίνος, 330, b.
Σωφρονίσται, 197, b.
Σωφροσύνη, 197, b.

Τ.

Ταγός, 360, b.
Ταινία, 264, b; 355, b.
Ταινίδιον, 355, b.
Τάλαντα, 239, a.
Τάλαντον, 361, a.
Τάλαρος, 64, a.
Ταλασία, 363, b.
Ταλασιουργία, 363, b.
Ταμίας, 316, b; 362. a.
Ταξίαρχοι, 163, b; 363, a.
Τάξις, 162, b; 163, a.
Ταρρός, 265, b.
Τάφοι, 186, a.
Ταφροποιοί, 363, a.
Τάφρος, 406, b.
Ταχυγράφοι, 272, a.
Τεύμιππος, 124, a.

Τρυγωδία.

Τειχοποιός, 363, b.
Τείχος, 257, a.
Τελαμών, 47, b; 57, a.
Τελεταί, 258, b.
Τέλος, 163, b; 365, b.
Τελωνάρχης, 165, a.
Τελώνης, 289, b; 365, a.
Τέμενος, 166, b.
Τέρμα, 205, b.
Τετράδραχμον, 145, b.
Τετραλογία, 383, a.
Τετραορία, 124, a.
Τετράρχης, 370, a.
Τεταρχία, 163, a; 370, a.
Τετράστυλος, 367, a.
Τετήρεις, 262, a.
Τετταράκοντα, οἱ, 16, a; 370, a.
Τεύχεα, 41, a.
Τήβεννος, 378, a.
Τιάρα, 376, b.
Τιάρας, 376, b.
Τίμημα, 81, b; 377, b.
Τιμητεία, 78, b.
Τιμητής, 78, b.
Τόκοι ἔγγειοι, 176, b.
ἔγγυοι, 176, b.
ναυτικοί, 176, b.
Τόκος, 176, b.
Τολύπη, 191, b.
Τόνοι, 222, a.
Τόξαρχοι, 129, b.
Τοξοθήκη, 37, b.
Τόξον, 37, b.
Τοξόται, 129, b; 147, a.
Τοπεία, 267, b.
Τορευτική, 63, b.
Τορύνη, 399, a.
Τραγωδία, 381, b.
Τράπεζα, 253, b.
Τράπεζαι, 186, b.
δεύτεραι, 96, a.
πρῶται, 95, a.
Τραπεζῖται, 39, a.
Τράφηξ, 264, b.
Τρίαινα, 191, b.
Τριακάδες, 183, a.
Τριακοσιομέδιμνοι, 81, b.
Τριβόλος, 385, a.
Τριετηρίς, 65, b.
Τριηραρχία, 224, b; 392, b.
Τριήραρχοι, 392, b.
Τριήρεις, 260, b.
Τριηροποιοί, 261, a; 363, a.
Τρίμιτος, 364, b.
Τρίπολος, 32, b.
Τρίπους, 253, b; 394, a.
Τρίπτυχα, 360, a.
Τρίτα, 187, a.
Τριταγωνιστής, 205, b.
Τρίτυια, 325, a.
Τρίττύς, 389, a.
Τριώβολον, 394, a.
Τροπαίον, 398, a.
Τροπωτήρ, 265, a.
Τρόχιλος, 347, b.
Τροχός, 124, a; 178, b; 398, a.
Τρυβλίον, 120, b.
Τρύγοιπος, 101, b.
Τρυγωδία, 110, b.

Φαρμάκων.

Τρυτάνη, 399, a.
Τρυφάλεια, 193, a.
Τυλείον, 222, a.
Τύλη, 222, a.
Τύμβος, 186, a.
Τύμπανον, 403, a.
Τύπος, 178, b.
Τυραννίς, 401, b.
Τύραννος, 403, a.

Υ.

Ὑακίνθια, 209, b.
Ὕαλος, 420, a.
Ὕβρεως γραφή, 16, b; 210, a.
Ὑδραγωγία, 29, b.
Ὑδραλέτης, 256, a.
Ὑδρανός, 150, a.
Ὑδραύλις, 210, a.
Ὑδρία, 345, a.
Ὑδριαφορία, 210, b.
Ὑδρόμελι, 418, b.
Ὕδωρ, 207, a.
Ὕλη, 260, b.
Ὑλλεῖς, 389, a.
Ὕπαιθρον, 147, b.
Ὕπαιθρος, 102, a.
Ὑπασπισταί, 161, b; 163, b.
Ὕπατος, 111, b.
Ὑπέραι, 260, b; 267, b.
Ὑπερῷον, 140, a; 141, b.
Ὑπεύθυνος, 34, a; 160, a; 391, b.
Ὑπήνη, 57, a.
Ὑπηρεσία, 393, b.
Ὑπηρέτης, 162, b.
Ὑπόγαιον, 186, a.
Ὑπόγειον, 186, a.
Ὑπογραφίς, 295, b.
Ὑπόδημα, 64, b; 329, a.
Ὑποζάκοροι, 10, a.
Ὑποζώματα, 267, a.
Ὑποκριτής, 205, b.
Ὑπολήνιον, 416, b.
Ὑπομείονες, 91, b; 206, a.
Ὑπόνομος, 122, b; 132, a.
Ὑποπόδιον, 376, a.
Ὑπόρχημα, 210, b; 327, a.
Ὑποστρατηγός, 3, b.
Ὑπωμοσία, 132, a.
Ὑσσός, 200, a.
Ὑφάνται, 363, b.

Φ.

Φάλαγγες, 163, b.
Φαλαγγαρχία, 163, b.
Φάλαγξ, 160, b; 163, b.
Φάλαρον, 292, a.
Φάλος, 192, b.
Ψανός, 176, a.
Φαρέτρα, 292, b.
Φαρμακείας γραφή, 292, b.
Φαρμακοί, 370, a.
Φαρμάκων γραφή, 292, b.

GREEK INDEX.

Φᾶρυς.

ἶρος, 280, b.
ἶρος, 292, b.
ἴσγανον, 196, a.
ἴσηλος, 293, a.
ἴσις, 293, a.
ἰδίτης, 360, a.
ἰνάκη, 104, a.
ῥνῆ, 145, a.
ὕγειν, 172, a.
ἰορά, 8, a.
ἀλη, 285, b.
μος, 162, b.
ιρβειά, 70, b.
ιρεῖον, 221, a.
ιρμιγξ, 245, a.
ιρος, 348, a.
ιρτηγοί, 262, a.
ιρτικά, 262, a.
ιατρία, 389, a.
ιατρικὸν **γραμματεῖον,** 7, a.
ιγή, **172, a.**
ικος, **185, b.**
ιλακες, 155, b.
ιλακτήριον, 24, a.
ιλαρχοι, 162, b; **293, a.**
ιλή, 162, a; 388, a.
ιλοβασιλεῖς, 293, a.
ιλον, 388, a.
ωταγωγία, 150, b.

X.

αλδαίων **μέθοδοι, 45, b.**
αλδαίων **ψηφίδες, 45, b.**

Χρυσός.

Χαλινός, 182, a.
Χαλκιοικια, 83, a.
Χαλκός, 12, a.
Χαλκοῦς, 12, a; **83, a.**
Χάρακες, 406, b.
Χειρόγραφον, 83, b.
Χειροτονεῖν, 83, b.
Χειροτονητοί, 83, b.
Χειροτονια, 34, a; **83, b.**
Χέλυς, 245, b.
Χελώνη, 245, b; **369, a.**
Χηνίσκος, 263, b.
Χιλιαρχία, 163, b.
Χιτών, 400, a.
  σχιστός, 400, a.
Χιτώνιον, 400, a; **401, a.**
Χιτωνίσκος, **400, a.**
Χλαῖνα, 220, a.
Χλαμύς, 84, a.
Χλαμύδιον, 84, a.
Χλιδών, 42, b.
Χοαί, 185, b.
Χόες, 136, a.
Χοεύς, 85, b.
Χοίνιξ, 84, b.
Χορηγία, 84, b.
Χορηγός, 84, b.
Χοροδιδάσκαλος, 84, b.
Χορός, 85, a; 198, b.
  κυκλικος, 85, a.
Χοῦς, 85, b.
Χρέους δίκη, 377, b.
Χρησμόλογοι, 138, a.
Χρηστήριον, 276, b.
Χρονολογια, 85, b.
Χρυσός, 53, b.

Ὠσχοφόρια.

Χρυσοῦς, 349, a.
Χύτρα, 271, b.
Χύτροι, 136, a.
Χώμα, 14, b; **186, a.**

Ψ.

Ψάλιον, 42, b.
Ψέλιον, or Ψέλλιον, 42, b.
Ψευδεγγραφῆς γραφή, 314, a.
Ψευδοδίπτερος, 367, a.
Ψευδοπερίπτερος, 367, a.
Ψήφισμα, **62, a;** 147, b; **272, a.**
Ψῆφος, 221, a; 313, b.
Ψιλοί, 41, b.
Ψυκτήρ, 314, a.

Ω.

Ὠβαί, 191, b; **389, a.**
Ὠδεῖον, 273, a.
Ὠρεῖον, 207, b.
Προλόγιον, 206, b.
Προσκόπος, 46, a.
Ὠσχοφόρια, 276, a.

LATIN INDEX.

A.

Abacus, 1, a.
Ablegmina, 325, a.
Abolla, 1, a.
Abrogare legem, 225, b.
Absolutio, 216, a.
Accensi, 165, b; 168, b.
Accensus, 1, b.
Acclamatio, 2, a.
Accubatio, 2, a.
Accubitoria vestis, 359, a.
Accusatio, 121, a.
Accusator, 6, a; 216, a.
Accusatorum libelli, 237, b.
Acerra, 2, b.
Acetabulum, 2, b.
Achaicum fœdus, 3, a.
Acies, 199, b.
Acilia lex, 226, a.
Acilia Calpurnia lex, 18, b.
Acinaces, 3, b.
Acisculus, 44, b.
Aclis, 4, a; 201, a.
Acroama, 4, a.
Acropolis, 4, a.
Acroterium, 4, a.
Acta, 4, b.
  diurna, 4, b.
  forensia, 4 b.
  jurare in, 4, b.
  militaria, 4 b.
  patrum, 4, b.
  senatus, 4, b.
Actio, 5, a; 213, b.
  exercitoria, 160, b.
  fiduciaria, 179, a.
  injuriarum, 213, a.
  in jure, 6, a.
  Legis or Legitima, 5, a.
  de pauperie, 288, a.
  de peculio, 339, b.
  rei uxoriæ, or dotis, 145, b.
  restitutoria, 213, b.
  Sepulchri violati, 190, b.
Actionem dare, 5, b.
  edere, 5, b.
Actor, 6, a.
  publicus, 6, a.
Actuariæ naves, 6, a; 262, a.
Actuarii, 6, a; 272, b.
Actus, 6, b; 300, b.
  minimus, 6, b.
  quadratus, 6, b.

Actus simplex, 6, b.
Acus, 6, b.
Adcrescendi jure, 204, a.
Addico, 48, b; 50, a.
Addicti, 269, b.
Ademptio equi, 80, b.
Adfines, 13, a.
Adfinitas, 13, a.
Adgnati, 98, a.
Adgnatio, 98, a.
Adlecti, 6, b.
Admissionales, 6, b.
Admissionum proximus, 6, b.
Adolescentes, 212, b.
Adoptio, 7, a.
Adoratio, 7, b.
Adrogatio, 7, a.
Adsertor, 45, a.
Adsessor, 45, a.
Adversaria, 8, a.
Adversarius, 6, a.
Adulterium (Greek), 7, b.
Adulterium (Roman), 8, a.
Adulti, 6, b; 212, b.
Advocatus, 8, b.
Aebutia lex, 226, a.
Aedes, 366, b.
  sacra, 366, b.
Aediles, 8, b.
  cereales, 9, b.
Aeditimi, 10, a.
Aeditui, 10, a.
Aedituml, 10, a.
Aegis, 10, b.
Aelia lex, 226, a.
  Sentia lex, 226, a.
Aemilia lex, 226, a.
  Baebia lex, 228, a.
  Lepidi lex, 235, b.
  Scauri lex, 248, b.
Aenatores, 11, a
Aenei nummi, 12, a; 341, b
Aenum, 11, a.
Aeora, 11, a.
Aera, 12, a.
Aerarii, 11, a.
  Tribuni, 12, b; 385, b.
Aerarium, 11, b.
  militare, 11, b.
  Praetores ad, 11, b.
  sanctum, 11, b.
Aerii nummi, 341, b.
Aes, 12, a.
Aes (money), 12, a.
  alienum, 12, a.
  circumforaneum, 12, a.
  equestre, 12, a; 156, b.

Aes grave, 12, a; 43, b.
  hordearium, or hordiarium 12, a; 156, b.
  militare, 12, a.
  uxorium, 12, b.
Aestivae feriae, 177. b.
Aetolicum fœdus, 13, a.
Affines, 13, a.
Affinitas, 13, a.
Agaso, 13, b.
Agema, 13, b.
Ager, 13, b.
  iteratus, 32, b.
  publicus, 13, b.
  scripturarius, 331, a.
Agger, 14, b; 75, a; 302, b.
Agitator, 89, a.
Agmen, 167, a.
  pilatum, 167, a.
  quadratum, 167, a.
Agnati, 98, a.
Agnatio, 98, a.
Agnomen, 271, b.
Agonales, 316, b.
Agonalia, 15, a.
Agonensis, 316, b.
Agonia, 15, a.
Agonium Martiale, 15, a.
Agonus, 15, a.
Agoranomi, 15, b.
Agrariae leges, 14, b.
Agraulia, 15, b.
Agrimensores, 16, a.
Agronomi, 16, a.
Ahenum, 11, a.
Ala, 16, b.
Alae, 142, b; 171, b.
Alabaster, 16, b.
Alabastrum, 16, b.
Alares, 16, b.
Alarii, 16, b.
Alauda, 17, a.
  legio, 17, a.
Albogalerus, 28, a.
Album, 17, a.
  judicum, 17, a.
  Senatorium, 17, a
Alea, 17, a.
Aleator, 17, a.
Ales, 50, a.
Alicula, 17, a.
Alimentarii pueri et puellæ, 17, b.
Alipilus, 17, b.
Aliptae, 17, b.
Alites, 50, a.
Allocutio, 17, b; 385, a.

ALTARE.

Altare, 31, a.
Aluta, 65, b.
Amanuensis, 18, a.
Ambarvalia, 43, a.
Ambitus, 18, a.
Ambrosia, 19, a.
Ambubaiae, 19, a.
Ambulationes, 207, a.
Amburbiale, 19, a.
Amburbium, 19, a.
Amentum, 200, a.
Amicire, 19, a.
Amictorium, 19, a; 335, b.
Amictus, 19, a.
Amphictyones, 19, b.
Amphitheatrum, 21, a.
Amphora, 23, a; 316, b; 417, a.
Ampliatio, 23, b; 215, b.
Ampulla, 17, b; 23, b; 36, b.
Ampullarius, 24, a.
Amuletum, 24, a.
Amussis, or Amussium, 24, b.
Anagnostae, 24, b.
Anatocismus, 177, a.
Ancilla, 326, b.
Ancora, 268, a.
Ancones, 320, b.
Andabatae, 195, a.
Angaria, 25, a.
Angariarum exhibitio, or praestatio, 25, a.
Angiportus, or Angiportum, 25, a.
Angustus clavus, 92, b.
Animadversio censoria, 80, a.
Anio novus, 30, a.
    vetus, 30, a.
Annales maximi, 175, b; 104, b.
Annalis lex, 226, b; 344, a.
Annona, 25, a.
    civica, 183, b.
Annuli aurei jus, 25, b.
Annulorum jus, 25, b.
Annulus, 24, b.
Annus magnus, 66, a.
Anquina, 267, b.
Anquisitio, 26, a; 216 b.
Antae, 26, a.
Anteambulones, 26, b.
Antecessores, 16, b.
Antecoena, 96, b.
Antecursores, 26, b.
Antefixa, 26, b.
Antemeridianum tempus, 134, b.
Antenna, 267, a.
Antepilani, 165, b; 168, b.
Antesignani, 168, b.
Antia lex, 236, a.
Anticum, 214, b.
Antiquarii, 239, a.
Antlia, 27, a.
Antoniae leges, 226, b.
Apaturia, 27, b.
Aperta navis. 261, b.
Apex, 28, a.
Aplustre, 264, b.
Apodectae, 28, a.

ARBA.

Apodyterium, 56, a.
Apollinares ludi, 24*, b.
Apophoreta, 28, b.
Apotheca, 28, b; 58, b.
Apotheosis, 28, b.
Apparitio, 29, a.
Apparitores, 29, a.
Appellatio (Greek), 29, a.
    (Roman), 29, a.
Aprilis, 66, a.
Apuleia lex, 226, b.
    agraria lex, 226, b.
    frumentaria lex, 226, b.
    majestatis lex, 226, b.
Aqua, 29, b.
    Alexandrina, 30, b.
    Algentia, 30, b.
    Alsietina, or Augusta, 30, a.
    Appia, 30, a.
    Claudia, 30, a.
    Crabra, 30, b.
    Julia, 30, a.
    Marcia, 30, a.
    Septimiana, 30, b.
    Tepula, 30, a.
    Trajana, 30, b.
    Virgo, 30, a.
Aquae ductus, 29, b.
    et ignis interdictio, 173, a.
Aquarii, 31, a.
Aquila, 343, a.
Aquilifer, 169, b.
Ara, 31, a.
Aratrum, 31, b.
Arbiter, 215, b.
Arbiter bibendi, 357, b.
Arbitrium, 188, a.
Arca, 32, a; 188, b.
Arca, ex, 39, b.
Arca publica, 336, b.
Arcera, 33, a.
Archiater, 33, a.
Archimagirus, 97, a.
Archimimus, 188, a; 256, a.
Architectura, 33, a.
Archon, 34, b.
Arcus, 36, a; 37, b.
    triumphalis, 36, b.
    Constantini, 37, b.
    Drusi, 37, a.
    Gallieni, 37, b.
    Septimii Severi, 37, a.
    Titi, 37, a.
Area, 37, a.
Areiopagus, 17, a.
Arena, 21, a.
Aretalogi, 39, a.
Argei, 39, a.
Argentarii, 39, a.
Argentum, 40, a.
Argyraspides, 40, a.
Aries, 40, a.
Arma, Armatura, 41, a.
Armarium, 42, a.
Armatura levis, 170, a.
Armilla, 42, b.
Armilustrium, 42, a.
Arra, Arrabo, or Arrha, Arrhabo, 42, a.

AUSPICIUM.

Arrogatio, 7, a.
Ars Chaldaeorum, 45, b.
Artaba, 43, a.
Artopta, 197, a.
Artopticii, 197, a.
Arvales Fratres, 43, a.
Arundo, 364, a.
Arura, 43, a.
Aruspices, 159, b.
Arx, 44, b.
As, 43, b.
As libralis, 43, b.
Asamenta, 326, b.
Ascia, 44, a.
Asiarchae, 45, a.
Assamenta, 326, b.
Assarius, 44, a.
Asseres lecticarii, 221, b.
Assertor, 45, a.
Assertus, 45, a.
Asses Usurae, 176, b.
Assessor, 45, a.
Assidui, 240, b.
Assiduitas, 18, b.
Astragalus, 45, a.
Astrologi, 45, b.
Astrologia, 45, b.
Astronomi, 45, b.
Asyli jus, 46, a.
Asylum, 46, a.
Atellanae Fabulae, 46, b.
Aternia Tarpeia lex, 226, b.
Athenaeum, 46, b.
Athletae, 47, a.
Atia lex, 226, b.
Atilia lex, 226, b.
Atinia lex, 226, b.
Atlantes, 47, b.
Atramentum, 48, a.
Atrium, 48, a; 141, b.
Auctio, 48, b.
Auctor, 48, b.
Auctores fieri, 49, b.
Auctoramentum, 58, b; 194, b.
Auctorati, 194, b.
Auctoritas, 49, b.
    senatus, 336, a.
Auditorium, 49, b.
Aufidia lex, 18, b.
Augur, 49, b.
Auguraculum, 41, b; 50, b; 366, a.
Augurale, 50, b; 74, b.
Augurium, 49, b; 118, b.
Augustales, 42, b.
Augustalia, 52, b.
Augustus, 53, a; 68.
Avia, 13, a.
Aulaeum, 272, a.
Aurelia lex, 226, b.
Aures, 32, a.
Aureus nummus, 51, b; 341, b.
Aurichalcum, 341, b.
Auriga, 89, a.
Aurum, 51, b.
    coronarium, 54, a.
    vicesimarium, 11, b.
Auspex, 49, b.
Auspicium, 49, b; 118, b.

2 G

450 LATIN INDEX.

AUTHEPSA.

Authepsa, 54, a.
Autonomi, 54, a.
Auxilia, 346, b.
Auxiliares, 170, b.
Auxiliarii, 170, b.
Axamenta, 326, b.
Axis, 124, a.

B.

Babylonii, 45, b.
  numeri, 45, b.
Bacchanalia, 116, b.
Baebia lex, 227, a.
  Aemilia lex, 228, a.
Balineae, 54, b.
Balineum, 54, b.
Balista, Ballista, 381, a.
Balneae, 54, b.
Balneator, 55, b.
Balneum, 54, b.
Balteus, or Baltea, 379, b.
Balteus, 57, a.
Baptisterium, 56, a.
Barathrum, 57, a.
Barba, 57, a.
Barbati bene, 57, b.
Barbatuli, 57, b.
Bascauda, 57, b.
Basilica, 57, b.
Basis, 101, b.
Basterna, 58, a.
Baxa, or Baxea, 58, a.
Bellaria, 97, a.
Beneficiarius, 58, b.
Beneficium, 58, b.
Benignitas, 18, b.
Bes, 44, a.
Bessis, 176, b.
Bestiarii, 58, b.
Bibasis, 328, b.
Bibliopola, 58, b.
Bibliotheca, 58, b.
Bidens, 59, a; 268, b.
Bidental, 59, a.
Didiaei, 59, a.
Biga, or Bigae, 124, b.
Bigati, 136, b.
Billix, 364, b.
Bipennis, 331, b.
Biremis, 59, b; 260, a.
Bissextilis annus, 67, b.
Bissextum, 67, b.
Bissextus, 67, b.
Bombycinum, 337, a.
Bona, 59, b.
  caduca, 60, a.
  fides, 62, a.
Bonorum cessio, 60, a.
  collatio, 60, a.
  emtio, et emtor, 60, b.
  possessio, 5, b; 60, b.
Bracae, or Braccae, 62, a.
Bravium, 90, a.
Bruttiani, 62, b.
Buccina, 62, b.

CAPISTRUM.

Buccinator, 11, a.
Buccinae, 191, b.
Bulla, 62, b.
Bura, or Buris, 31, b.
Bustuarii, 63, a.
Bustum, 63, a; 189, a.
Buxum, 63, a.
Byssus, 63, a.

C.

Caduceator, 63, b.
Caduceus, 63, a.
Caducum, 60, a.
Cadus, 23, b; 63, b.
Caecilia lex de censoribus, 227, a.
  lex de vectigalibus, 227, a.
  Didia lex, 227, a.
Caelatura, 63, b.
Caelia lex, 236, a.
Caementa, 258, a.
Caesar, 64, a.
Caetra, 83, a.
Calamistrum, 64, a.
Calamus, 64, a.
Calantica, 103, a.
Calathus, 64, a.
Calatores, 104, a.
Calceamen, 64, b.
Calceamentum, 64, b.
Calceus, 64, b.
Calculator, 65, a.
Calculi, 65, a; 221, a.
Calda lavatio, 56, a.
Caldarium, 56, a.
Calendae, 67, b.
Calendarium, 65, a; 176, b.
Calida, 77, a.
Caliga, 68, a.
Calix, 68, a.
Callis, 68, a.
Calones, 68, b.
Calpurnia lex de ambitu, 18, b.
  lex de repetundis, 319, a.
Calvatica, 103, a.
Calumnia, 68, b.
Calx, 88, a.
Camara, 69, a.
Camera, 69, a.
Camillae, Camilli, 69, a; 252, a.
Caminus, 145, a.
Campestre, 69, a.
Canalis, 30, b.
Cancellarius, 69, b.
Cancelli, 69, a; 107, b.
Candela, 69, b.
Candelabrum, 69, b.
Candidarii, 197, b.
Candidatus, 18, b; 380, a.
Canephorus, 70, a.
Canistrum, 70, a.
Cantharus, 70, b.
Canthus, 124, a.
Canticum, 70, b.
Canuleia lex, 227, a.
Capistrum, 70, b.

CENSUS.

Capite censi, 71, a.
Capitis deminutio, 71, a.
Capitis minutio, 71, a.
Capitolini, 242, b.
  ludi, 242, b.
Capsa, 70, b.
Capsarii, 56, a; 71, a.
Captio, 103, b.
Capulum, 188, a.
Capulus, 32, a.
Caput, 71, a.
  extorum, 71, b.
Caracalla, 72, a.
Carcer, 72, a.
Carceres, 87, b; 107, b.
Carchesium, 72, a; 266, b.
Carenum, 416, b.
Carmen seculare, 241, b.
Carmentalia, 72, a.
Carnifex, 72, b.
Carpentum, 72, b.
Carptor, 97, a.
Carrago, 73, a.
Carruca, 73, a.
Carrus, or Carrum, 73, a.
Caryatides, 73, a.
Caryatis, 73, a.
Cassia lex, 227, a.
  agraria, 227, a.
  tabellaria, 216, a.
  Terentia frumentaria, 227, b.
Cassis, 41, b; 192, b.
Castellarii, 31, a.
Castellum aquae, 31, a.
Castra, 71, a.
  stativa, 71, b.
Castrensis corona, 118, b.
Cataphracti, 76, a.
Catapulta, 381, a.
Cataracta, 76, a.
Catasta, 340, a.
Cateia, 76, b; 201, a.
Catella, 76, b.
Catena, 76, b.
Catervarii, 195, a.
Cathedra, 76, b.
Catilium, or Cutillus, 77, a.
Catillus, 256, a.
Catinum, or Catinus, 77, a.
Cavaedium, 142, b.
Cavea, 87, a; 371, a.
Cavere, 217, b; 77, b.
Caupo, 77, a.
Caupona, 77, a.
Causia, 77, b.
Cauterium, 295, b.
Cautio, 77, b.
Cavum aedium, 142, b.
Celeres, 78, a.
Celerum tribunus, 385, a.
Cella, 78, a; 142, b; 367, a.
  caldaria, 56, a.
Cellarius, 78, a.
Celtes, 139, b.
Cenotaphium, 78, b.
Censere, 116, a.
Censor, 78, b; 101, a.
Censura, 78, b.
Census, 78, b; 81, b; 248, a.

LATIN INDEX. 451

CENSUS.

Census (Greek), 81, b.
Centesima, 82, a.
　rerum venalium, 82, a.
Centesimae usurae, 176, b.
Centumviri, 82, a.
Centuria, 105, b; 166, b; 168, a; 217, a.
Centuriata comitia, 105, a
Centurio, 165, a; 166, b; 169, a.
　primus, 169, b.
　primipili, 169, b.
Centussis, 44, a.
Cera, 82, b.
Cerae, 295, b; 360, b.
Ceratae tabulae, 360, a.
Cerealia, 82, b.
Cerevisia, 82, b.
Cernere hereditatem, 203, b.
Ceroma, 82, b.
Certamen, 52, b.
Ceruchi, 267, a.
Cessio bonorum, 60, a.
Cestius pons, 102, a.
Cestrum, 295, b.
Cestus, 82, b.
Cetra, 83, a.
Chaldaei, 45, b.
Charistia, 83, b.
Charta, 238, b.
Cheironomia, 83, b.
Cheniscus, 263, b.
Chirographum, 83, b.
Chlamys, 84, a.
Choregia, 84, b.
Choregus, 84, **b.**
Chorus, 85, a.
Chronologia, 85, **b.**
Chrysendeta, 86, b.
Cidaris, 376, b.
Cincia, or Muneralis, lex, 22- b.
Cinctus, 401, b.
　Gabinus, 380, a.
Cinerarius, 64, a.
Cingulum, 41, b; 422, b.
Ciniflo, 64, a.
Cippus, 86, b.
Circenses ludi, 89, a.
Circuitores, 31, a.
Circus, 87, a.
Cisium, 92, a.
Cista, 90, a; 141, b.
Cistophorus, 50, b.
Cithara, 245, a.
Civica corona, 118. a
Civile jus, 218, **a.**
Civis, 91, b
Civitas (Greek), 92, b
　(Roman), 91, b
Clarigatio, 178, b
Classica corona, 118 b
Classici, 171, a.
Classicum, 118, a.
Clathri, 144, b; 409, a.
Claudia lex, 237, b.
Clavis, 398, a.
Claustra, 88, a; 215, a.
Clavus angustus, 92, b.
　annalis, 92, b.
　latus, 92, b.

COMPITALIA.

Clepsydra, 207, a.
Clibanarii, 76, a.
Cliens, 93, b.
Clientela, 93, **b.**
Clipeus, 41, b; 94, a.
Clitellae, 94, a.
Cloaca, 94. **a.**
Cloacarium, 94. **a.**
Cloacarum curatores, 94, b.
Clodiae leges, 18 , a ; 237, b.
Coa vestis, 94, b.
Coactor, 82, a; 94, b; 477, b.
Cochlea, 27, a; 94, b.
Cochlear, 94, b.
Codex, 33, b; 95, a.
Codex Gregorianus et Hermogianus, 95, a.
　Justinianus, 95, a.
　Theodosianus, 95, a.
Coelia, or Caelia, lex, 136, a.
Coemptio, 251, a.
Coena, 95, a ; 96, b.
Coenaculum, 143, b.
Coenatio, 97, b.
Coenatoria, 97, b; 359, a.
Cognati, 98, a.
Cognatio, 98, a.
Cognitor, 6, a.
Cognomen, 271, b.
Cohors, 203, b.
Cohors, 167, **b.**
Cohortes **Alariae**, 16, b.
　equitatae, 171, a.
　peditatae, 171, a.
　vigilum, 171, a.
　urbanae, 171, a.
Collectio, 215, b.
Collegae, 98, a.
Collegium, 98, **a.**
Colobium, 401, **b.**
Colonia, 98, **b.**
Colonus, 98, **b.**
Colores, 235, a.
Colossus, 101, **a.**
Colum, 101, a.
Columbarium, 101, b; 190, a
Columna, 101, b.
　rostrata, 102, b.
Columnarium, 102, **b.**
Colus, 191, b.
Coma, 103, a.
Commentarii senatus, 4. b.
Commissatio, 104, a ; 357, a.
Comitia, 104, **a.**
　caiata, **105, a.**
　centuriata, **105, a.**
　curiata, **104, b.**
　tributa, **108, a.**
Commeatus, 110, b.
Commentarii sacrorum, 324, a
Commentarium, 110, **b.**
Commentarius, 110, **b.**
Commercium, 92, a.
Commissoria lex, 227, b.
Concordia, 110, b.
Comperendinatio, 215, b.
Comperendini dies, 135, b
Competitor, 18, b.
Compitalia, 112, b.

CORNELIA UNCIARIA.

Compitalicii ludi, 112, b.
Compluvium, 142, b.
Concamerata sudatio. 56, a.
Conceptivae feriae, 112, b.
Concilium, 112, b.
Conditivum, 190, a.
Conditorium, 190, a.
Conditurae, 418, a.
Conductor, 81, a.
Condus, 78, a.
Confarreatio, 251, b.
Congiarium, 112, b.
Congius, 113, a.
Conjurati, 400, a.
Conjuratio, 400, a.
Connubium, 251, a.
Conopeum, 113, a.
Conquisitores, 113, a.
Consanguinei, 98, a.
Conscripti, 331, a.
Consecratio, 19, a; **211, b.**
Consilium, 104, a.
Consualia, 113, a.
Consul, 113, b.
Consulares, 116, b.
Consularis, 1 6, b.
Consulti, 217, b.
Consultores, 217, b.
Contio, 116, b.
Controversia, 215, b.
Contubernales, 116, b.
Contubernium, 117, a; 168, b 339, a.
Contus, 266, b.
Conventio in manum, 251, a.
Conventus, 117, b; 117, a.
Convicium, 212, b.
Convivii magister, 357, b.
　rex, 357, b.
Convivium, 357, a.
Cooptari, 98, b.
Cophinus, 117, a.
Corbicula, 117, b.
Corbis, 117, b.
Corbitae, 117, b.
Corbula, 117, b.
Cornelia lex—
　agraria, 228, a.
　de alea, 17, a.
　de civitate, 228, a.
　de falsis, 173, b. a.
　frumentaria, 178, a.
　de injuriis, 212, b.
　judiciaria, 216, b
　majestatis, 247, a.
　de novis tabellis, 228, b
　sumaria, 228, a.
　de parricidio, 228, a.
　de proscriptione et proscriptis, 311, b.
　de repetundis, 319, a.
　de sacerdotiis, 324, a.
　de sicariis et veneficis, 217 a; 228, a.
　sumptuaria, 215, b.
　testamentaria, 173, b; 228. a.
　tribunicia, 228, a.
　unciaria, 228, a.

2 G 2

CORNELIA.

Cornelia Baebia lex, 18, b; 228, a.
  Caecilia lex, 18?, a.
  et Caecilia lex, 228, a.
Cornicines, 11, a.
Cornu, 117, a.
Cornua, 218, a; 242, b; 267, a.
Corona, 102, b; 1-8, a.
  castrensis, 118, b.
  civica, 118, a.
  classica, 118, b.
  convivialis, 119, b.
  funebris, 119, a.
  graminea, 118, a.
  muralis, 118, b.
  natalitia, 119, b.
  navalis, 118, b.
  nuptialis, 119, b.
  obsidionalis, 118, a.
  oleagina, 118, b.
  ovalis, 118, b.
  rostrata, 118, b.
  sacerdotalis, 119, a.
  sepulchralis, 119, a.
  triumphalis, 118, b.
  vallaris, 118, b.
Coronis, 102, b; 119, b.
Corporati, 98, a.
Corporatio, 98, a.
Corpus, 98, a.
Cortina, 119, b.
Corvus, 119, b.
Corytos, 37, b.
Cosmetae, 120, a.
Cosmi, 120, a.
Cothurnus, 120, a.
Cotyla, 120, b.
Covinarii, 121, a.
Covinus, 120, b.
Crater, Cratera, 121, a.
Creditum, 39, b.
Crepida, 121, a.
Crepidata tragoedia, 112, a.
Crepidines, 412, b.
Creta, 88, a.
Cretio hereditatis, 203, b.
Crimen, 121, a.
Crista, 192, b.
Crocota, 121, a.
Crotalistria, 126, a.
Crotalum, 126, a.
Crusta, 64, a; 152, a.
Crux, 121, a.
Crypta, 84, a; 121, b.
Cryptoporticus, 121, b.
Ctesibica machina, 27, a.
Cubicularii, 122, a.
Cubiculum, 22, b; 78, a; 122. a; 143, b.
Cubitoria, 97, b.
Cubitus, 122, a.
Cucullus, 122, a.
Cudo, or Cudon, 122, a.
Culcita, 122, a.
Culeus, 122, a.
Culina, 141, a.
Culleus, 122, a.
Culter, 12, a; 122, a.
Cultrarius, 12, b.

DEDUCTORES.

Cumatium, 125, b.
Cumera, 252, a.
Cumerum, 252, a.
Cunabula, 212, a.
Cuneus, 23, a; 122, b; 371, a.
Cuniculus, 122, b.
Cupa, 122, b; 417, a.
Curator, 101, a; 122, b.
Curatores, 123, a.
  annonae, 123, a.
  aquarum, 31, a.
  ludorum, 123, a.
  religionum, 123, a.
  viarum, 413, a.
Curia, 100, b; 123, a.
Curiae, 100, b; 334, b.
Curiales, 100, b.
Curiata comitia, 104, b.
Curio, 123, b.
  maximus, 123, b.
Curriculum, 123, b.
Currus, 123, b.
Cursores, 125, a.
Cursus, 89, a.
Curulis sella, 311, b.
Cuspis, 199, b.
Custodes, Custodiae, 75, b.
Custos urbis, 307, b.
Cyathus, 125, a.
Cyclas, 125, b.
Cyma, 125, b.
Cymatium, 125, b.
Cymba, 125, b.
Cymbalum, 125, b.

D.

Dare actionem, 5, b.
Daricus, 126, b.
Decanus, 117, a.
December, 66, a.
Decempeda, 212, a.
Decemviri, 127, a.
  legibus scribendis, 127, a; 228, b.
  litibus, or stlitibus, judicandis, 127, b.
  sacrorum, or sacris faciendis, 127, b.
Decennalia, or Decennia, 128, a.
Decimatio, 128, a.
Decretum, 128, a; 213, b; 336, a.
Decumae, 128, a.
Decumani, 128, a.
Decuncis, 128, b.
Decuriae, 310, b.
Decuriones, 120, b; 166, b.
Decursoria, 302, b.
Decussis, 44, a.
Dedicare, 145, a.
Dedicatio, 211, b.
Dediticii, 128, b.
Deditio, 128, a.
Deductores, 18, b.

DIVINATIO.

Defrutum, 416, b.
Delator, 128, b.
Delectus, 167, a.
Delia, 128, b.
Delphinae, 87, b.
Delphinia, 129, a.
Delubrum, 366, b.
Demarchi, 129, a.
Demens, 123, a.
Demensum, 129, a; 341, a.
Dementia, 123, a.
Deminutio capitis, 71, a.
Demiurgi, 129, a.
Demus, 130, a.
Denarius, 130, a
  aureus, 53, b.
Denicales feriae, 190, b.
Dens, or Dentale, 31, b; 191, b.
Deportatio, 173, b.
  in insulam, 173, b.
Deportatus, 173, b.
Depositum, 39, b.
Derogare legem, 225, b.
Designator, 188, a.
Desultor, 130, b.
Detestatio sacrorum, 105, a.
Deversorium, 77, a.
Deunx, 44, a.
Dextans, 44, a.
Diadema, 130, b.
Diaeta, 97, b; 141, b.
Diaetetae, 130, b.
Dialis flamen, 182, a.
Diarium, 341, a.
Dicere, 133, a.
Dictator, 132, b.
Didia lex, 235, b.
Diem dicere, 216, a.
Dies, 134, b.
  civilis, 134, b.
  comitiales, 135, b.
  comperendini, 135, b.
  fasti, 135, a; 175, a.
  feriati, 177, b.
  festi, 135, a.
  intercisi, 135, a.
  Naturalis, 134, b.
  nefasti, 135, a.
  proeliales, 135, b.
  profesti, 135, a.
  stati, 135, b.
Diffarreatio, 119, b.
Digitus, 292, a.
Dimachae, 135, b.
Dimensum, 341, a.
Diminutio capitis, 71, a.
Dionysia, 135, b.
Diota, 137, a.
Diploma, 137, a.
Diptycha, 137, b.
Diribitores, 107, b.
Discessio, 336, a.
Discinctus, 401, b.
Discipula, 410, b.
Discus, 137, b.
Dispensator, 65, a.
Diversorium, 77, a.
Divinatio, 137, b.
  (law term), 139, a.

DIVISORES.

Divisores, 18, b.
Divortium, 139, a.
Divus, 29, a.
Dodrans, 44, a.
Dolabella, 139, b.
Dolabra, 139, b.
Dolium, 140, b; 417, a.
Dolo, 140, a.
Dominium, 14, a; 140, a.
Dominus, 140, a; 194, b; 338, b.
  funeris, 188, a.
Domitia lex, 324, a.
Domo, de, 39, b.
Domus, 140, a.
Dona, 145, a.
Donaria, 145, a.
Donatio, 182, b.
Donativum, 113, a.
Dormitoria, 141, a.
Dos (Greek), 145, a.
  (Roman), 141, b.
Drachma, 145, b; **405, b.**
Draco, 343, b.
Draconarius, 343, b.
Ducenarii, 146, a; 217, a.
Ducentesima, 82, a; 408, a.
Duillia lex, 228, b.
  Maenia lex, 228, **b.**
Dulciarii, 297, b.
Duodecim scripta, 221, a.
Duplarii, 146, a.
Duplicarii, 146, a.
Duplicatio, 6, a.
Dupondium, 292, **a.**
Dupondius, 44, a.
Dussis, 44, **a.**
Duumviri, 101, a; **146, a.**
  juri dicundo, 100, **b.**
  navales, 146, a.
  perduellionis, 290, a.
  quinquennales, 146, **b.**
  sacri, 146, b.
  sacrorum, 146, b.

E.

Eculeus, 159, **a.**
Edere actionem, 5, **b.**
Edictum, 148, a.
  novum, 148, **a.**
  perpetuum, 148, **a.**
  repentinum, 148, **a.**
  tralatitium, 148, **b.**
  vetus, 148, a.
Edituii, 216, a.
Editor, 194, b.
Elaeothesium, 36, a.
Electrum, 149, b.
Eleusinia, 149, b.
Ellychnium, 241, b.
Emancipatio, 151, b.
Emblema, 152, a.
Emeriti, 152, a; 167, **b.**
Emissarium, 152, a.
Emporium, 152, b.
Encaustica, 195, a.

FABULA TABERNARIA.

Endromis, **152, b.**
Ensis, 41, b; **196, a.**
Entasis, 101, b; **152, b.**
Ephebia, **153, b.**
Ephippium, **154, a.**
Ephori, **154, a.**
Epibatae, **155, a.**
Epidemiurgi, **129, b.**
Epirhedium, **322, a.**
Epistylium, **155, b.**
Epitaphium, **189, a.**
Epithalamium, **250, b; 251, b.**
Epulones, **156, a.**
Epulum Jovis, **156, a.**
Equestris ordo, **157, b.**
Equiria, **156, a.**
Equites, **156, a; 314, a.**
Equitum transvectio, **157, a.**
Equuleus, 159, a.
Equus October, **280, a.**
  Publicus, **156, b.**
Ergastulum, **159, a.**
Ericius, **159, a.**
Esseda, **159, b.**
Essedarii, **159, b; 195, b.**
Essedum, 153, b.
Everriator, 190, **b.**
Evocati, 167, b.
Euripus, 22, a; **408, b.**
Exauctorati, 170, **b.**
Exauguratio, 160, **b.**
Exceptio, **5, b; 308, a.**
Exceptores, 272, a.
Excubiae, **75, b.**
Excubitores, 160, b.
Exedra, 141, a; 160, b.
Exercitor navis, 160, **b.**
Exercitoria actio, **160, b.**
Exercitus, **160, b.**
Exodia, **171, a.**
Exostra, **171, b.**
Expeditus, 170, a; **171, b.**
Exploratores, **147, a.**
Exsequiae, 188, a.
Exsilium, 171, a.
  liberum, 173, **b.**
Exsul, 173, a.
Exta, 325, a.
Extispices, 199, b.
Extispicium, 199, b.
Extranei heredes, 203, b.
Extraordinarii, 167, a; **146, a.**
Exverrae, 190, b.
Exverriator, 190, b.
Exuviae, 140, **a.**

F.

Fabia lex, 297, **b.**
Fabiani, 244, a.
Fabii, 244, a.
Fabri, 173, b.
Fabula palliata, 112, a.
  praetextata, 112, a.
  togata, 113, a.
  tabernaria, 112, a.

FIDUCIARIA ACTIO.

Fabula trabeata, 112, a.
Fabulae Atellanae, 46, b.
Factiones aurigarum, 89, a.
Falarica, **201, a.**
Falcidia **lex, 237, b.**
Falcula, 173, b.
Falsum, 173, b.
Falx, **171, b.**
Familia, 174, b; 194, b; 340, b
Familiae emptor, 174, a.
Famosi libelli, 237, b.
Famulus, **174, a.**
Fannia **lex, 235, b.**
Fanum, 366, a.
Farreum, 251, a.
Fartor, **174, a.**
Fas, 218, a.
Fasces, 114, b; 174, a.
Fascia, 175, a; 222, a.
Fascinum, 175, a.
Fasti, 175, a.
  annales, 175, b.
  calendares, 175, b.
  Capitolini, 175, b.
  dies, 175, a.
  historici, 175, b.
  sacri, 175, b.
Fastigium, 175, b.
Fata Sibyllina, 347, b.
Fauces, 88, a; **141, a.**
Favete linguis, **138, b.**
Fax, 176, a.
Februare, 244, a.
Februarius, 67, a; 244, a.
Februum, 244, a.
Februus, 244, a.
Feciales, 178, a.
Feminalia, 176, a.
Fenestra, 144, b.
Fenus, 176, a.
  nauticum, **176, b.**
Feralia, 191, a.
Ferculum, 97, a; 177, a.
Ferentarii, **168, b.**
Feretrum, **183, a.**
Feriae, 177, **b.**
  aestivae, **177, b.**
  conceptivae, or conceptae, 177, b.
  denicales, **190, b.**
  imperativae, **177, b.**
  Latinae, **177, b.**
  publicae, **177, b.**
  stativae, **177, b.**
  stultorum, 181, a.
  vindemiales, 177, b.
Ferre legem, 225, b.
Fescennina, 178, a.
Festi dies, 113, a.
Festuca, 242, a.
Feciales, 178, a.
Fibula, 178, b.
Fictile, 11, a; 178, b.
Fideicommissarii praetores, 108, b.
Fideicommissum, 179, a.
Fides, 245, a.
Fiducia, 179, a.
Fiduciaria actio, 179, a.

LATIN INDEX.

FIGULINA.

Figulina ars, 178, b.
Figulus, 178, b.
Filiafamilias, 286, a.
Filiusfamilias, 286, a.
Filum, 191, b.
Fiscus, 11, b; 179, a.
Fistuca, 144, b.
Fistucatio, 412, b.
Fistula, 359, a.
Flabelliferae, 179, b.
Flabellum, 179, b.
Flagellum, 179, b.
Flagrum, 179, b.
Flamen, 180, a.
   Dialis, 180, a.
   Martialis, 180, a.
   Quirinalis, 180, a.
   Pomonalis, 180, a.
Flaminia lex, 229, a.
Flaminica, 180, b.
Flammeum, 252, a.
Flavia agraria lex, 229, a.
Flexumines, 157, a.
Floralia, 180, b.
Focale, 180, b.
Foculus, 145, a; 180, b.
Focus, 180, b.
Foederatae civitates, 181, a.
Foederati, 181, a.
Foedus, 181, a; 346, b.
Foenus, 176, a.
   nauticum, 176, b.
Follis, 181, b; 296, b.
Fons, 181, a.
Fores, 88, a; 142, b.
Fori, 87, a; 265, b.
Foris, 215, a.
Forma, 178, b.
Formido, 319, b.
Formula, 5, b; 346, a.
Fornacalia, 182, a.
Fornax, 182, a.
Fornix, 16, a; 187, a.
Foro cedere, or abire, 39, b.
   mergi, 39, b.
Foruli, 87, a.
Forum, 74, b; 117, a; 190, a.
Fossa, 14, b; 75, a.
Framea, 201, a.
Fratres arvales, 43, a.
Frenum, 182, a.
Frigidarium, 56, a.
Fritillus, 182, b.
Frontale, 24, a.
Fructuaria res, 406, a.
Fructuarius, 406, a.
Frumentariae leges, 152, b.
Frumentarii, 183, b.
Fucus, 181, b.
Fuga lata, 173, b.
   libera, 173, b.
Fugalia, 318, b.
Fugitivarii, 339, b.
Fugitivus, 339, b.
Fulcra, 222, a.
Fullo, 184, a.
Fullonica, 184, a.
Fullonicum, 184, a.
Fullonium, 164, a.

HARMOSTAE.

Fumarium, 418, b.
Funalis equus, 114, b.
Funambulus, 184, b; 328, b.
Funda, 184, b; 310, b.
Funditores, 184, b.
Funes, 222, a; 267, b.
Funus, 184, b.
   indictivum, 188, a.
   plebeium, 188, a.
   publicum, 188, a.
   tacitum, 188, a.
   translatitium, 188, a.
Furca, 191, a.
Furcifer, 191, a.
Furia, or Fusia Caninia lex, 229, a.
Furiosus, 123, a.
Fuscina, 191, b.
Fustuarium, 191, b.
Fusus, 191, b.

G.

Gabinia lex, 229, b; 216, a.
Gabinus cinctus, 380, a.
Gaesum, 192, a.
Galea, 41, b; 192, b.
Galerus, -um, 104, a; 193, a.
Galli, 193, a; 195, b.
Ganea, 77, a.
Gausapa, 193, a.
Gausape, 193, a.
Gausapum, 193, a.
Geminae frontes, 238, a.
Gener, 13, a.
Genethliaci, 45, b.
Genitura, 46, a.
Gens, 193, a.
Gentilitia sacra, 193, b.
Germani, 98, a.
Gerrae, 194, a.
Gladiatores, 194, a.
Gladiatorium, 194, b.
Gladius, 41, b; 196, a.
Glandes, 184, b.
Glomus, 191, b.
Glos, 13, b.
Gomphi, 413, a.
Gradus, 21, b; 182, b.
Graecostasis, 196, a.
Graphiarium, 354, a.
Gregorianus codex, 95, a.
Gremium, 412, b.
Gubernaculum, 265, b.
Gubernator, 266, a.
Gustatio, 96, b.
Guttus, 17, b; 56, b.
Gymnasium, 197, a.

H.

Haeres, 203, a.
Halteres, 198, b.
Harmamaxa, 119, a.
Harmostae, 199, a.

JANUA.

Harpago, 199, a.
Harpastum, 297, a.
Haruspices, 199, b.
Haruspicina ars, 138, a; 199, b.
Haruspicium, 138, a.
Hasta, 41, b; 82, a; 199, b.
   celibaris, 201, a.
   pura, 201, a.
   vendere sub, 48, a.
Hastarium, 201, a.
Hastati, 165, a; 168, b.
Helepolis, 201, b.
Heliocaminus, 145, a.
Hellanodicae, 201, b.
Hellenotamiae, 201, b.
Helotes, 201, b.
Hemina, 120, b; 202, b.
Heraea, 202, b.
Hereditas, 203, b.
Heredium, 217, a.
Heres (Greek), 203, a.
   (Roman), 203, a.
Hermae, 204, a.
Hermaea, 204, a.
Hermanubis, 204, b.
Hermares, 204, b.
Hermathena, 204, b.
Hermeracles, 204, b.
Hermogenianus codex, 95, a.
Hermuli, 88, a; 204, a.
Hexaphoron, 221, b.
Hexeres, 262, a.
Hieronica lex, 229, b.
Hieronicae, 47, a.
Hilaria, 205, a.
Hippodromus, 205, a.
Hister, 205, b.
Histrio, 188, a; 205, b.
Honorarii, 116, b.
Honorarium, 8, b.
Honores, 206, b.
Hoplomachi, 195, b.
Hora, 115, a.
Hordearium aes, 12, b; 156, b.
Horologium, 206, b.
Horreum, 207, b; 417, a.
Hortator, 305, b.
Hortensia lex, 229, b; 330, b.
Hortus, 207, b.
Hospes, 209, a.
Hospitium, 208, a.
Hostia, 174, b.
Hostia ambarvalis, 43, b.
Hostis, 208, a.
Humare, 189, b.
Hyacinthia, 209, b.
Hydraulis, 210, a.
Hypaethrae, 107, a.
Hypocaustum, 56, a.
Hypogeum, 186, a.

I, J.

Jaculatores, 201, a.
Jaculum, 209, b; 320, b.
Janitor, 142, b; 215, a.
Janua, 142, b; 214, b.

LATIN INDEX. 455

JANUARIUS.

Januarius, 67, a.
Iconicae statuae, 351, a.
Idus, 67, a.
Jentaculum, 96, a.
Ignominia, 80, a; 212, a.
Licet, 189, a.
Imagines, 210, b; 270, a.
Immunitas, 210, b.
Imperativae feriae, 177, b.
Imperator, 211, a.
Imperium, 211, a.
Impluvium, 142, b.
Impubes, 211, a.
In Ionis, 59, b.
Inauguratio, 211, b.
regis, 321, a.
Inauris, 211, b.
Incendium, 211, b.
Incensus, 71, b; 79, b.
Incrementa navium, **295, a.**
Incestum, -us, 212, a.
Incunabula, 212, a.
Index, 238, b.
Induere, 19, a.
Indumentum, 359, a; **401**, b.
Indusium, 401, b.
Indutus, 19, a; 401, b.
Infamia, 212, a.
Infans, 212, b.
Infantia, 212, **b.**
Inferiae, 191, a.
Infula, 212, b.
Infundibulum, 256, a.
Ingenui, 212, b.
Injuria, 212, b.
Injuriarum actio, 213, a.
Inlicium, 106, b.
Inquilinus, 173, a.
Insigne, 161, b.
Instita, 213, a; 222, a.
Insula, 213, a.
Intentio, 5, b.
Interessio, 213, a.
Intercisi dies, 135, a.
Interdictio aquae et ignis, 171, a.
Interdictum, 213, a.
prohibitorium, 213, a.
restitutorium, 213, a.
Interpres, 18, b; 19, b; 213, b.
Interregnum, 214, a.
Interrex, **213**, b; **320, b.**
Intorula, 401, b.
Iselastici ludi, **47, a.**
Iter, 302, **b.**
Iterare, **32,** b.
Jubere, 336, a.
Judex, 215, a.
Judices editi, 216, **a.**
editii, 216, a.
Judicium, 215, a.
album, 216, b.
populi, 215, b; 216, **a.**
privatum, 215, b.
publicum, 215, b.
Jugerum, 217, a.
Jugum, 217, a; 239, a; **364, a.**
Jugumentum, 215, a.
Juliae leges, 229, b.

JUVENALIA.

Julia lex de civitate, 181, b; 219, b.
de foenore, 230, a.
judiciaria, 216, b. •
de liberis legationibus, **224**, a.
majestatis, 247, a.
municipalis, 219, a.
et Papia Poppaea, 237, a.
peculatus, 230, b.
et Plautia, 230, b.
de provinciis, 312, b.
repetundarum, 319, b.
de sacerdotiis, 324, a.
de sacrilegiis, 230, b.
sumptuaria, 238, a.
theatralis, 230, b.
et Titia, 230, b.
de vi publica et privata, 212, a.
vicesimaria, 414, b.
Julius, **67**, b.
Junea, **or Junia**, Norbana lex, 230, b.
Junia lex repetundarum, 319; a
Juniores, 195, b.
Junius, 66, a.
Jure, actio in, 5, b.
adcrescendi, 204, a.
agere, 9, a.
Jure cessio, in, **7**, b; 60, a.
Jureconsulti, 217, b.
Juris auctores, 217, b.
Jurisconsulti, 217, b.
Jurisdictio, 117, a; **218**, a.
Jurisperiti, 217, b.
Jurisprudentes, **217**, b.
Jus, 218, a.
annuli aurei, **25, b.**
annulorum, **25,** b.
applicationis, 173, a
augurium, or auguruc:, 52, b.
Censurae, **79, a.**
civile, **218, a.**
civile Papirianum, or Papi-sianum, **233**, b.
civitatis, 92, a.
commercii, 92, **a.**
connubii, 92, a.
edicendi, 9, a; 148, a.
exsulandi, 173, a.
feriae, 219, a.
honorum, 92, **a.**
Latii, **92**, a; **230**, b.
Iberorum, 230, b.
Pontificium, **218**, a; **304**, a.
postliminii, **306**, a.
privatum, 92, **a.**
publice epulandi, **317**, **a.**
publicum, 92, a.
Quiritium, **79**, b; **218**, a.
senatus, 333, b.
suffragiorum, 92, **a.**
vocatio, in, **5,** a.
Jusjurandum, 218, a.
judiciale, 219, a.
Justa funera, 188, a.
Justinianeus codex, 95, a.
Justitium, 191, a; 219, a.
Juvenalia, or juvenales ludi, 219, b.

LEMURALIA.

L.

Labarum, 344, **a.**
Labrum, 56, a.
Labyrinthus, **219**, **b.**
Lacerna, 219, b.
Laciniae, **220,** a.
Laconicum, **56**, **a.**
Lacunar, **144**, **b.**
Lacus, **182**, a; **416**, b.
Laena, **220**, a.
Laesa majestas, 246, b.
Lancea, **200**, **a.**
Lances, **219**, a.
Lanificium, 363, **b.**
Lanista, **194**, b.
Lanx, 220, **b.**
Lapicidinae, **221**, a.
Lapis, **255, b.**
specularis, 144, b.
Laquear, **144**, **b.**
Laqueatores, **195**, **b.**
Laqueus, **220**, **b.**
Lararium, **220**, **b.**
Larentalia, 220, b.
Larentinalia, **220**, b.
Largitio, **18**, **b.**
Larva, **191**, a.
Lata fuga, 173, b.
Later, **220**, **b.**
Lateraria, **220**, **b.**
Laticlavius, **92**, **b.**
Latii jus, **230**, **b.**
Latinae feriae, 177, **b.**
Latinitas, **220**, **b.**
Latinus, 92, a; 181, a.
Latium, **220**, **b.**
Latomiae, **221**, **a.**
Latrones, **221**, a.
Latrunculi, **221, a.**
Laudimiae, **221**, a.
Latus clavus, 92, b.
Lavatio calda, 56, a.
Laudatio funebris, 188, **b.**
Laurentalia, 220, b.
Lautomiae, **221**, **a.**
Lautumiae, **221**, a.
Lectica, 221, **a.**
Lecticarii, 221, **b.**
Lectisternium, 221, b.
Lectus, **222**, **a.**
funebris, **188**, **a.**
Legatio libera, 224, **a.**
Legatum, **222**, **b.**
Legatus, 222, b; 313, a.
Leges, 225, a.
censoriae, 81, a.
centuriatae, 79, a; 225, a.
curiatae, 225, a.
Juliae, 229, a.
Legio, 164, a; 170, b.
Legis actiones, 5, a.
Legitima hereditas, 207, b.
Legitimae actiones, 5, a.
Lembus, 224, b.
Lemnisens, 224, b.
Lemuralia, **224**, b.

LEMURIA.

Lemuria, 224, b.
Lenaea, 135, b.
Leria, 402, a.
Lessus, 188, a.
Levir, 13, b.
Lex, 225, a; 229, a.
  Acilia, 226, a.
  Acilia Calpurnia, 18, b.
  Aebutia, 226, a.
  Aelia, 226, a.
  Aelia Sentia, 226, a.
  Aemilia, 226, a.
  Aemilia, de censoribus, 226, a.
  Aemilia Baebia, 228, a.
  Aemilia Lepidi, 235, b.
  Aemilia Scauri, 248, b.
  agraria, 14, b; 226, a.
  ambitus, 18, b.
  Ampia, 226, b.
  annalis, or Villia, 226, b; 334, a.
  annua, 148, b.
  Antia, 236, a.
  Antonia, 226, b.
  Apuleia, 226, b.
  Apuleia agraria, 226, b.
  Apuleia frumentaria, 226, b.
  Apuleia majestatis, 247, a.
  Aternia Tarpeia, 226, b.
  Atia de sacerdotiis, 226, b.
  Atilia, 226, b.
  Atilia Marcia, 226, b.
  Atinia, 226, b.
  Aufidia, 18, b.
  Aurelia, 226, b.
  Aurelia Tribunicia, 226, b.
  Baebia, 227, a.
  Baebia Aemilia, 228, a.
  Caecilia de Censoribus, or Censoria, 227, a.
  Caecilia de Vectigalibus, 227, a.
  Caecilia Didia, 227, a.
  Calpurnia de ambitu, 18, b.
  Calpurnia de repetundis, 319, a.
  Campana, 215, a.
  Canuleia, 227, a.
  Cassia, 227, a.
  Cassia agraria, 227, a.
  Cassia tabellaria, 216, a.
  Cassia Terentia frumentaria, 227, b.
  Centuriata, 79, a.
  Cincia, 227, b.
  Claudia, 227, b.
  Claudia de Senatoribus, 227, b.
  Clodiae, 181, a; 227, b.
  Coelia or Caelia, 236, a.
  Lex Cornelia—
    agraria, 228, a.
    de civitate, 228, a.
    de falsis, 173, b.
    frumentaria, 181, a.
    de injuriis, 212, b.
    judiciaria, 216, b.
    de magistratibus, 228, a.
    majestatis, 247, a.

LEX MAJESTATIS.

Lex Cornelia—
  de novis tabellis, 228, a.
  nummaria, 228, a.
  de parricidio, 228, a.
  de proscriptione et proscriptis, 311, b.
  de repetundis, 319, a.
  de sacerdotiis, 324, a.
  de sicariis et veneficis, 212, a; 228, a.
  sumptuaria, 235, b.
  testamentaria, 173, b; 228, a.
  tribunicia, 228, a.
  unciaria, 228, a.
  Baebia, 18, b; 228, a.
  Caecilia, 183, a.
  et Caecilia, 228, a.
Lex Curiata de imperio, 49, a; 104, b; 233, b.
Curiata de adoptione, 7, b.
Decemviralis, 228, b.
Decia de duumviris navalibus, 228, b.
Didia, 235, b.
Domitia de sacerdotiis, 324, a.
Duilia, 228, b.
Duilia maenia, 228, b.
Duodecim Tabularum, 228, b.
Fabia de plagio, 297, b.
Fabia de numero sectatorum, 229, a.
Falcidia, 217, b.
Fannia, 235, b.
Flaminia, 229, a.
Flavia agraria, 229, a.
  frumentariae, 182, b; 229, a.
Fufia de religione, 229, a.
Fufia judiciaria, 217, a.
Furia or Fusia Caninia, 229, a.
Furia or Fusia testamentaria, 229, a.
Gabinia tabellaria, 229, b; 236, a.
Gellia Cornelia, 229, b.
Genucia, 229, b.
Hieronica, 229, b.
Hortensia de plebiscitis, 229, b; 300, b.
Icilia, 229, b.
Julia de adulteriis, 8, a.
Julia de ambitu, 18, b.
Juliae, 229, b.
Junia de peregrinis, 230, b.
Junia Licinia, 231, a.
Junia Norbana, 230, b.
Junia repetundarum, 319, a.
Laetoria, 230, b.
Licinia de sodalitiis, 19, a.
Licinia de ludis Apollinaribus, 231, a.
Licinia Junia, 211, a.
Licinia Mucia de civibus regundis, 211, a.
Licinia sumptuaria, 235, a.
Liciniae rogationes, 231, a.
Livine, 211, a.
Lutatia de vi, 231, b.
Maenia, 231, b.
majestatis, 246, b.

LEX ROSCIA.

Lex Mamilia de Jugurthae Fautoribus, 231, b.
Mamilia finium regundarum, 231, b.
mancipii, 247, b.
Manilia, 231, b.
Manlia de vicesima, 231, b.
Marcia, 211, b.
Maria, 231, b.
Memmia, or Remmia, 69, a.
Mensia, 231, b.
Minucia, 231, b.
Nervae Agraria, 211, b.
Octavia, 182, b; 231, b.
Ogulnia, 232, a.
Oppia, 235, b.
Orchia, 235, b.
Ovinia, 212, a.
Papia de peregrinis, 232, a.
Papia Poppaea, 230, a.
Papiria, or Julia Papiria de mulctarum aestimatione, 212, a.
Papiria, 232, a.
Papiria Plautia, 232, a.
Papiria Poetelia, 232, a.
Papiria tabellaria, 236, a.
Pedia, 232, a.
Peducaea, 232, a.
Pesulania, 232, a.
Petreia, 232, a.
Petronia, 232, b.
Pinaria, 232, b.
Plaetoria, 122, b.
Plautia, or Plotia de vi, 231, b.
Plautia, or Plotia judiciaria, 232, b.
Plautia Papiria, 232, a.
Poetelia, 232, b.
Poetelia Papiria, 232, b.
Pompeia, 212, b.
Pompeia de ambitu, 217, a.
Pompeia de civitate, 212, b.
Pompeia de imperio Caesari prorogando, 232, b.
Pompeia judiciaria, 217, b.
Pompeia de jure magistratuum, 232, b.
Pompeia de parricidiis, 285, b.
Pompeia tribunitia, 232, b.
Pompeia de vi, 212, a; 232, b.
Pompeiae, 232, b.
Popilia, 212, a.
Porciae de capite civium, 232, b.
Porcia de provinciis, 232, b.
Publicia, 232, b.
Publilia, 232, b.
Publiliae, 233, a.
Pupia, 233, a.
Quina vicemaria, 122, b.
Quintia, 233, a.
regia, 233, a.
regiae, 233, b.
Remmia, 69, a.
repetundarum, 319, a.
Rhodia, 233, b.
Roscia theatralis, 233, b.

LATIN INDEX.

LEX RUBRIA.

Lex Rubria, **214, a.**
Rupiliae, 214, a.
sacratae, 234, a.
Saenia de patriciorum numero augendo, 234, a.
Satura, 226, a.
Scantinia, 214, a.
Scribonia, 234, a.
Scribonia viaria, 234. a.
Sempronia de foenore, 234, b.
Semproniae, 234, a.
Servilia agraria, 215, a.
Servilia Glaucia de civitate, 319, a.
Servilia Glaucia de repetundis, 319, a.
Servilia judiciaria, 235, a.
Silia, 235, a.
Silvani et Carbonis, 92, a.
Sulpicia Sempronia, 235, a.
Sulpiciae, 235, a.
Sumptuariae, 235. a.
Tabellariae, 236, a.
Tarpeia Aternia, **236, b.**
Terentia Cassia, 183, a.
Terentilia, 236, b.
Testamentariae, **236, b.**
Thoria, 216, b.
Titia, 236, b.
Titia de alea, 17, a.
Titia de tutoribus, 230, b.
Trebonia, 236, b.
Trebonia de provinciis consularibus, 236, b.
Tribunicia, 231, a; **236, b.**
Tullia de ambitu, **18, b.**
Tullia de legatione libera, **224,** a.
Valeria, 237, a.
Valeriae, 236, b.
Valeria et Horatiae, **29, b;** 237, a.
Varia, 247, a.
Vatinia de provinciis, 237, a.
Vatinia de colonis, 237, a.
Vatinia de rejectione judicum, 237, a.
de vi, 420, a.
viaria, 237, a.
vicesimaria, 414, b.
Villia annalis, 226, b.
Visellia, 237, a.
Voconia, 237, b.
Abatio, 325, b.
Abella, 90, a; 237, **b.**
Abellus, 194, b; 237, **b.**
Aber, 238, a.
Abera fuga, 173, b.
Aberales ludi, 137, a.
Aberalia, 137, a.
Aberalis causa, 45, a.
manus, 45, a.
Aberalitas, 18, b.
Aberi, 238, b.
Abertus, 238, b.
Abertinus, 212, b; 238, b.
Abitinarii, 187, b.
Abra, 239, a.
or as, 239, a.

LYRA.

Librarium, 48, a.
Libraria taberna, 52, b.
Librarii, 58, b; **239,** a.
Librator, 239, a.
Libripens, 247, b.
Liburna, 239, a; **262, b.**
Liburnica, 239, a; **262, b.**
Liceri, 48, b.
Licia, 364, b.
Liciatorum, **164, b.**
Licinia lex de sodalitiis, 19, a.
Junia lex, 231, a.
Mucia lex, 231, a.
lex sumptuaria, 235, b.
Licinlae rogationes, 231, a.
Licitari, 48, b.
Lictor, 219, b.
Ligula, 239, b.
Limen, 215, a.
Linteones, 363, b.
Linter, 239, b.
Linteum, 17, b; 222, b.
Linum, 360, b.
Lirare, 32, b.
Literae, 360, a.
Lithostrotum, **144, b.**
Lituus, 240, a.
Lixae, 68, b.
Locatio, 80, b.
Loculus, 32, b; 188, b.
Locuples, 240, b.
Locus liberatus et effatus, **166,** a.
Lodix, 247, a.
Logistae, 160, b.
Lorica, 41, a; **240, b.**
Lucar, 206, a.
Lucerences, 286, b.
Luceres, **286, b.**
Lucerna, 241, b.
Lucta, 242, a.
Luctatio, **242,** a.
Ludi, 242, a.
Apollinares, 242, a.
Augustales, 52, b.
Capitolini, 242, b.
Circenses, 89, a; **242,** a.
compitalitii, 112, b.
Florales, 180, b.
funebres, 191, b; 242, b.
liberales, 137, a.
magni, 242, b.
Megalenses, **253, b.**
Osci, 46, b.
plebeii, **242, b.**
Romani, 242, b.
saeculares, 242, b.
scenici, 206, a; **242,** a.
Tarentini, **242, b.**
Tauri, 242, b.
Ludus, 194, b.
Trojae, 90, a.
Lupanar, 77, a.
Lupatum, 182, b.
Lupercalia, 243, b.
Luperci, 243, b; 244, b.
Lupus ferreus, 244, a.
Lustratio, 41, b; 244, a.
Lustrum, 66, a; 244, b.
Lyra, 245, a.

MEMMIA LEX.

M.

Maceria, 257, a.
Maculae, **319, b.**
Maenia lex, 231, b.
Maenianum, **22, b; 246, a.**
Magadis, 245, b.
Magister, 246, a.
admissionum, 6, b.
auctionis, 48, b.
equitum, **114,** b.
populi, 132, b.
societatis, 246, a.
Magistratus, 246, b.
Maius, 66, a.
Majestas, 246, b.
Majores, 212, b; 246, b.
Malleolus, 247, a.
Malus, 266, a.
Malus oculus, 175, a.
Mamilia lex, 231, b.
Manceps, 81, a; 247, a.
Mancipatio, **247, b.**
Mancipi res, **247,** b.
Mancipium, **247,** b.
Mandatum, **247,** b.
Mangones, **339, b.**
Manilia lex, **231, b.**
Manipulares, 168, a.
Manipularii, 168, a.
Manipulus, 165, a; 168, a**; 341, a.**
Manlia lex, 231, b.
Mansio, **247, b.**
Mansionarius, 248, a.
Mansiones, 248, a.
Manubiae, 106, b; 348, a.
Manum, conventio in, 251, a.
Manumissio, 248, a.
Manus **ferrea, 199, b.**
Mappa, 97, **b.**
Marcia lex, 231, b.
Margines, 412, b.
Maria lex, 231, b.
Marsupium, 248, b.
Martialis flamen, 180, a.
Martius, 66, a.
Materfamilias, **251,** a.
Mathematici, 45, b.
Mathesis, 45, b.
Matralia, 249, a.
Matrimonium, 249, b.
Matrona, 251, a.
Matronales **feriae, 249, b.**
Matronalia, **249, b.**
Matura, 201, a.
Mausoleum, 190, a; 257, a.
Mediastini, 253, a; 340, b.
Medicamina, 412, a.
Medimnus, 253, a.
Medix tuticus, 253, b.
Megalenses ludi, **253, b.**
Megalensia, 251, b.
Megalesia, 253, b.
Membrana, 238, b.
Memmia lex, 69, a

MENSA.

Mensa, 253, b.
  de, 39, b.
Mensae scripturam, per, 39, b.
Mensam per, 39, b.
Mensarii, 254, a.
Mensularii, 254, a.
Mensia lex, 231, b.
Mensis, 66, a.
Menstruum, 341, a.
Mercedonius, 66, b.
Meridiani, 195, b.
Meridies, 134, b.
Metae, 87, a.
Metallum, 254, a.
Metator, 73, b.
Metretes, 23, b; 255, b.
Mille passuum, 255, b.
Milliare, 255, b.
Milliarium, 255, b.
  aureum, 255, b.
Mimus, 255, b.
Minores, 123, a; 246, b.
Minucia lex, 231, b.
Minutio capitis, 71, a.
Mirmillones, 195, b.
Missio, 167, b; 195, a.
  causaria, 167, b.
  honesta, 167, b.
  ignominiosa, 167, b.
Missus, 90, a.
  aerarius, 90, a.
Mitra, 104, a; 256, a.
Modiolus, 124, a.
Modius, 256, a.
Moenia, 257, a.
Mola, 256, a.
  aquaria, 256, a.
  asinaria, 256, a.
  manuaria, 256, a.
  trusatilis, 256, a.
  versatilis, 256, a.
  salsa, 325, a.
Monarchia, 256, b.
Monaulos, 376, b.
Moneris, 261, a.
Moneta, 256, b.
Monetales triumviri, 256, b.
Monile, 256, b.
Monstrum, 310, b.
Monumentum, 190, a.
Murator, 89, b.
Morbus comitialis, 108, a.
Mortarium, 257, a.
Morum cura, or praefectura, 79, a.
Mos, 251, b.
Motio e senatu, 80, b.
  e tribu, 80, b.
Mulleus, 65, b.
Mulsa, 418, b.
Mulsum, 418, a.
Munerator, 194, b.
Municeps, 100, b.
Municipes, 100, b.
Municipium, 100, b.
Munus, 194, b; 206, b.
Muralis corona, 118, b.
Muries, 411, a.
Murrea vasa, 257, a.

NURUS.

Murrhina vasa, 257, a.
Murus, 257, a.
Musculus, 258, b.
Museum, 258, b.
Musica muta, 281, a.
Musivum opus, 144, b; 296, a.
Mustum, 416, b.
Mysteria, 258, b.

N.

Naeca, 184, a.
Naenia, 188, a.
Narthecia, 405, b.
Natatio, 56, a.
Natatorium, 56, a.
Nationes, 170, b.
Navales Socii, 171, a.
Navalis corona, 118, b.
Navarchus, 259, a.
Navis, 259, b.
  aperta, 261, b.
Naumachia, 268, a.
Naumachiarii, 268, a.
Necessarii heredes, 203, b.
Nefasti dies, 135, a.
Negotiatores, 269, a.
Nenia, 188, a.
Neptunalia, 269, b.
Nexum, 269, b.
Nexus, 269, b.
Nobiles, 270, a.
Nobilitas, 270, a.
Nomen, 270, b.
  expedire, or expungere, 39, b.
  Latinum, 345, b.
  (Greek), 270, b.
  (Roman), 270, b.
Nomenclator, 18, b.
Nonae, 66, a.
Nota, 272, a.
  censoria, 80, a.
Notarii, 272, a.
Notatio censoria, 80, a.
Novale, 32, b.
Novare, 32, b.
November, 66, a.
Novendiale, 190, b; 272, b.
Noverca, 13, b.
Novi homines, 270, a.
Novitas, 270, a.
Nucleus, 412, b.
Nudus, 272, b.
Numeratio, 336, a.
Numeri, 168, a.
Nummularii, 254, a.
Numularii, 254, a.
Nummus, or Numus, 341, a.
  aureus, 53, b.
Nuncupatio, 369, a.
Nundinae, 66, a; 272, b.
Nundinum, 273, a.
Nuntiatio, 51, a.
Nuptiae, 249, b.
Nurus, 13, a.

OSTIARIUS.

O.

Obices, 215, a.
Obnuntiatio, 51, a.
Obolus, 145, a; 405, b.
Obrogare legem, 225, b.
Obsidionalis corona, 118, a.
Obsonium, 276, b.
Occatio, 32, b.
Ocrea, 41, a; 273, a.
Octavae, 408, a.
Octavia lex, 182, b; 231, b.
October, 66, a.
  equus, 280, a.
Octophoron, 221, b.
Odeum, 273, a.
Oecus, 143, a.
Oenomelum, 418, a.
Officium admissionis, 6, b.
Offringere, 32, b.
Ogulnia lex, 232, a.
Olea, 273, b.
Oleagina corona, 118, b.
Oleum, 273, b.
Oliva, 273, b.
Olla, 190, b; 273, b.
Olympia, 274, a.
Onager, 381, a.
Onerariae naves, 117, b; 262, a.
Onyx, alabaster, 16, b.
Opalia, 276, b; 330, a.
Opifera, 267, b.
Opima spolia, 348, a.
Oppia lex, 235, b.
Oppidum, 87, b.
Opsonator, 276, b.
Opsonium, 276, b.
Optio, 166, b.
Optimates, 270, b.
Opus incertum, 258, a.
Oraculum, 276, b.
Orarium, 277, b.
Oratio, 7, b.
Orator, 277, b.
Orbis, 178, b.
Orca, 345, a.
Orchestra, 371, b.
Orchia lex, 235, b.
Orcinus senator, 333, a.
Ordinarii servi, 340, b.
Ordinum ductores, 166, b; 168, b; 169, a.
Ordo, 100, b; 165, b; 168, a; 278, a.
  decurionum, 100, b.
  equestris, 157, b.
  senatorius, 333, b.
Oreae, 182, b.
Orichalcum, 278, a.
Ornamenta triumphalia, 397, a.
Ornatrix, 103, b.
Oscines, 50, a.
Oscillum, 278, a.
Ostentum, 310, b.
Ostiarium, 278, b.
Ostiarius, 142, b.

LATIN INDEX.   459

OSTIUM.
Ostium, 88, a; 142, b; 214, b.
Ova, 87, b.
Ovalis corona, 118, b.
Ovatio, 278, b.
Ovile, 107, b.
Ovinia lex, 232, a.

P.
Paean, 279, a.
Paedagogia, 279, a.
Paedagogus, 279, a.
Paenula, 279, a.
Paganalia, 279, b.
Pagani, 279, b.
Paganica, 296, b.
Pagi, 279, b.
Pala, 26, a.
Palaestra, 198, a; 279, b.
Palangae, 160, b.
Palilia, 280, a.
Palimpsestus, 238, a.
Palla, 280, a.
Palliata fabula, 112, a.
Palliolum, 280, a.
Pallium, 280, a.
Palmipes, 281, a.
Palmus, 281, a.
Paludamentum, 281, a.
Paludatus, 195, a.
Panathenaea, 281, b.
Pancratiastae, 282, b.
Pancratium, 282, b.
Panegyris, 281, a.
Pantomimus, 283, a.
Papia lex de peregrinis, 232, a.
  Poppaea lex, 225, a.
Papiria lex, 232, a.
  Plautia lex, 212, a.
  Poetelia lex, 232, a.
  tabellaria lex, 216, a.
Papyrus, 233, a.
Paradisus, 283, b.
Parapherna, 144, b.
Parasiti, 284, b.
Parentalia, 291, a.
Paries, 143, a.
Parma, 284, a.
Parmula, 285, a.
Parochi, 285, a.
Paropsis, 285, a.
Parricida, 285, b.
Parricidium, 285, b.
Partes, 114, b.
Particulae, 314, b.
Pascua, 407, a.
  publica, 330, b.
Passum, 417, b.
Passus, 285, b.
Patella, 285, b.
Pater, 286, b.
  familias, 174, a.
  patratus, 178, a.
Patera, 285, b.
Patibulum, 191, a.
Patina, 286 a

PIGNORIS CAPTIO.
Patres, 286, b.
  conscripti, 131, a.
Patria potestas, 286, a.
Patricii, 286, b.
Patrimi et matrimi, or Patrimes et matrines, 287, b.
Patrimonium, 174, a.
Patronomi, 287, b.
Patronus, 93, b; 287, b.
Pavimentum, 144, b; 412, b.
Pauperie, actio de, 288, a.
Pauperies, 288, a.
Pausarii, 305, b.
Pecten, 268, a; 364, b.
Peculator, 288, a.
Peculatus, 288, a.
Peculio, actio de, 339, b.
Peculium, 339, b.
Pecunia, 12, a; 40, a; 53, b.
  vacua, 39, b.
Pecuniae repetundae, 318, b.
Pecus, 288, a.
Pedarii senatores, 334, a.
Pedisequi, 288, a.
Peducaea lex, 232, a.
Pedum, 288, a.
Pegma, 288, b.
Pegmares, 288, b.
Pelta, 288, b.
Penicillus -um, 295, b.
Pentacosiomedimni, 81, b; 290, a.
Pentathli, 289, a.
Pentathlon, 289, a.
Peplum, 289, b.
Pera, 290, a.
Perduellio, 247, a; 290, a.
Perduellionis duumviri, 2,0, a.
Peregrinus, 92, a; 290, a.
Perferre legem, 225, b.
Peripetasmata, 222, b.
Periscelis, 291, a.
Peristroma, 222, b; 291, a.
Peristylium, 102, a; 143, a.
Peritiores, 217, b.
Permutatio, 39, b.
Pero, 291, a.
Perscriptio, 19, b.
Persona, 291, a.
Pes, 267, b; 292, a.
  sestertius, 292, a.
Pessulus, 215, a.
Pesulania lex, 212, a.
Petasus, 297, a; 405, a.
Petauristae, 292, a.
Petaurum, 297, a.
Petitor, 6, a; 18, b.
Petorritum, 262, a.
Petreia lex, 212, a.
Petronia lex, 232, b.
Phalangae, 160, b.
Phalanx, 160, b; 163, b.
Phalerica, 201, a.
Phalera, 292, a.
Pharetra, 222, b.
Pharos, or Pharus, 292, b.
Phaselus, 293, a.
Pictura, 293, b.
Pignoris captio, 334, b.

PORTA POMPAE.
Pila, 257, a; 296, a; 343, b.
Pilani, 168, b.
Pileati, 188, a.
Pilentum, 297, a.
Pileum, 297, a.
Pileus, 297, a.
Pilum, 200, a; 257, a.
Pinacotheca, 141, a.
Pinaria lex, 232, b.
Piscina, 30, a; 31, a; 56, a.
Pistor, 297, b.
Pistrinum, 257, a.
Plaetoria lex, 122, b.
Plagiarius, 297, b.
Plagium, 297, b.
Planetarii, 45, b.
Planipedes, 256, a.
Plaustrum, or Plostrum, 297, b.
Plautia, or Plotia lex de vi, 231, b.
  judiciaria, 232, b.
Plebeii, 298, a.
  ludi, 242, b.
Plebes, 298, a.
Plebiscitum, 225, b; 300, b.
Plebs, 298, a.
Plectrum, 246, a.
Pluteus, 58, a; 222, a; 301, a.
Pnyx, 146, b.
Poculum, 301, a.
Podium, 21, b; 101, b.
Poena, 301, a.
Poetelia Papiria lex, 232, b.
Pollinctores, 187, b.
Polus, 206, a.
Polychromy, 295, b.
Pomerianum tempus, 134, b.
Pomerium, 301, b.
Pompa, 301, b.
  Circensis, 89, b.
Pompeiae leges, 232, b.
Pons, 107, b; 302, a.
  Aelius, 302, b.
  Cestius, 302, a.
  Fabricius, 302, b.
  Janiculensis, 302, a.
  Milvius, 302, a.
  Palatinus, 302, b.
  Sublicius, 302, b.
  suffragiorum, 301, a.
  Vaticanus, 302, b.
Pontifex, 303, a.
Pontificales libri, 304, a.
Pontifices minores, 303, a.
Pontificii libri, 304, a.
Pontificium jus, 218, a; 304, a.
Popa, 77, a; 122, b; 305, a.
Popilia lex, 232, b.
Popina, 77, a.
Popularia, 23, a.
Populi scitum, 225, b.
Popullfugia, or Poplifugia, 305, a.
Populus, 100, a; 286, a.
Porcae, 32, b.
Porciae leges, 232, b.
Porta, 305, a.
  decumana, 75, a.
  pompae, 88, a.

PORTA PRAETORIA.

Porta praetoria, or extraordinaria, 75, a.
principalis, 75, a.
Portentum, 138, b; 199, b.
Porticus, 305, b.
Portisculus, 305, b.
Portitores, 306, a.
Portorium, 305, b.
Portula, 305, b.
Possessio, 14, a.
Possessor, 14, a.
Postes, 215, a.
Posticum, 214, b.
Postliminium, 306, a.
Postmeridianum tempus, 135, a.
Postsignani, 168, b.
Potestas, 286, a.
Praecinctio, 21, a; 171, a.
Praecinctus, 401, b.
Praecones, 306, b.
Praeconium, 306, b.
Praeda, 306, b; 347, b.
Praedes, 216, a.
Praedia, 308, a.
Praediator, 308, a.
Praefecti sociorum, 167, a
Praefectus, 307, a.
    aerarii, 11, b.
    annonae, 182, b; 307, a.
    aquarum, 31, a.
    castrorum, 307, a.
    classis, 307, a.
    fabrûm, 173, a.
    juri dicundo, 100, b.
    praetorio, 307, a.
    vigilum, 171, a.
    urbi, 10, a; 307, b.
Praefectura, 101, a.
    morum, 79, a.
Praeficae, 188, a.
Praejudicium, 308, a.
Praelusio, 194, b.
Praemium, 167, b.
Praenomen, 270, b.
Praerogativa tribus, 109, a.
Praerogativae, 109, a.
Praes, 308, a.
Praescriptio, 308, a.
Praeses, 311, a.
Praesidia, 75, b.
Praeteriti senatores, 80, b; 333, b.
Praetexta, 380, b.
Praetextata fabula, 46, b; 112, a.
Praetor, 308, a.
    peregrinus, 308, b.
    urbanus, 308, b.
Praetoria cohors, 309, a.
Praetoriani, 309, a.
Praetorium, 308, a; 309, b.
Prandium, 96, b.
Prehensio, 388, a.
Prelum, or Praelum, 416, b.
Prensatio, 18, b.
Primipilus, 169, b.
Primitiae, 125, b.
Princeps juventutis, 129, a.
Princeps senatus, 333, b.

PUPILLUS.

Principes, 165, b; 168, b.
Principia, 168, b.
    via, 75, a.
Principium, 109, a.
Privatum jus, 92, a.
Privilegium, 223, b.
Privigna, 13, b
Privignus, 13, b.
Probatio nummorum, 39, b.
Proconsul, 310, a.
Procubitores, 164, b.
Procuratio prodigiorum, 310, b.
Procurator, 6, a; 65, a; 179, b; 310, b; 313, a.
    peni, 78, a.
Prodigium, 310, b.
Prodigus, 123, a.
Proeliales dies, 135, b.
Profesti dies, 135, a.
Progener, 13, b.
Proletarii, 71, a.
Promulsis, 96, b; 418, a.
Promus, 78, a; 97, a.
Pronubae, 252, b.
Pronubi, 252, b.
Pronurus, 13, b.
Propraetor, 308, b.
Propugnaculum, 381, a.
Proquaestor, 317, b.
Prora, 263, a.
Proscenium, 372, a.
Proscindere, 32, b.
Proscribere, 311, b.
Proscripti, 311, b.
Proscriptio, 311, b.
Prosecta, 325, a.
Prosiciae, 325, a.
Prosocrus, 13, b.
Provincia, 311, b.
Provocatio, 29, b.
Provocatores, 195, b.
Proximus admissionum, 6, b.
Prudentiores, 217, b.
Pteron, 253, a.
Pubertas, 211, a.
Pubes, 212, b.
Publicae feriae, 177, b.
Publicani, 314, a.
Publicia lex, 232, b.
Publicum, 314, a.
    jus, 92, a.
Publicus ager, 13, b.
Publilia lex, 232, b.
Publiliae leges, 232, b.
Pugilatus, 315, a.
Pugiles, 315, a.
Pugillares, 360, a.
Pugio, 315, a.
Pugna equestris et pedestris, 50, a.
Pullarius, 50, b.
Pullati, 23, a.
Pulmentarium, 276, b.
Pulpitum, 372, a.
Pulvinar, 87, a; 315, a.
Pulvinus, 315, a.
Punctae, 107, a.
Pupia lex, 233, a.
Pupillus, 315, a.

RATIONES.

Puppis, 264, b.
Puteal, 315, a.
Puteus, 56, a.
Puticulae, 189, b.
Puticuli, 189, b.
Pyra, 188, b.
Pyrgus, 182, b.
Pythia, 277, a; 315, b.
Pyxidula, 316, a.
Pyxis, 316, a.

Q.

Quadragesima, 316, b.
Quadrans, 44, a.
Quadrantal, 316, b.
Quadriga, 124, b.
Quadrigati, 130, b.
Quadriremes, 261, b.
Quadrupes, 288, a.
Quadruplatores, 316, b.
Quadruplicatio, 6, a.
Quadrussis, 44, a.
Quaesitor, 216, a.
Quaestiones, 216, a; 316, b.
    perpetuae, 309, a.
Quaestor, 316, b.
Quaestores classici, 316, b.
    parricidii, 216, a; 316, b.
    rerum capitalium, 216, a.
    urbani, 317, b.
Quaestorium, 74, b.
Quaestura Ostiensis, 317, b.
Qualus, 64, b.
Quasillariae, 64, b.
Quasillus, 64, b.
Quatuorviri juri dicundo, 100, b.
    viarum curandarum, 318, a; 413, a.
Quinctiliani, 244, a
Quinctilii, 244, a.
Quinctilis, 66, a.
Quincunx, 44, a.
Quindecemviri, 128, a.
Quinquatria, 318, a.
Quinquatrus, 318, a.
    minores or minusculae, 318, a.
Quinquennalia, 318, a.
Quinquennalis, 101, a.
Quinqueremes, 261, b.
Quinquertium, 289, a.
Quinqueviri, 318, a.
    mensarii, 254, a.
Quintana, 74, b.
Quintia lex, 233, a.
Quirinalia, 318, a.
Quirinalis flamen, 180, a.
Quiritium jus, 79, b; 218, a.

R.

Radius, 124, a; 364, b.
Ramnenses, 286, b.
Ramnes, 286, b.
Rationes, 39, b.

LATIN INDEX. 461

RATIONES CHALDAICAE.

Rationes Chaldaicae, 45, b.
Recuperatores, 5, b; 215, b.
Reda, 322, a.
Redemptor, 81, a; 318, b.
Redimiculum, 318, b.
Regia, 15, a.
  lex, 233, a.
Regifugium, 318, b.
Regimen morum, 80, a.
Regina sacrorum, 322, a.
Rei uxoriae, or dotis actio, 145, b.
Relatio, 335, b.
Relegatio, 173, a.
Relegatus, 173, b.
religiosus, 190, b.
Remancipatio, 139, b.
Remmia lex, 69, a.
Romulcum, 318, b.
Remuria, 224, b.
Remus, 265, b.
Renuntiatio, 109, a.
Repagula, 88, a; 215, a.
Repetundae, 318, b.
Replicatio, 6, a.
Repositorium, 97, a.
Repotia, 252, b.
Repudium, 139, b.
Res mancipi, 247, b.
  nec mancipi, 247, b.
  privatae, 225, b.
  singulae, 225, b.
Responsa, 217, b.
Restitutoria actio, 213, b.
Rete, 319, b.
Retiarii, 195, b.
Reticulum, 101, a; 319, b.
Retinaculum, 268, a; 320, b.
Retis, 319, b.
Reus, 6, a; 216, a.
Rex, 320, a.
  sacrificulus, 321, b.
  sacrificus, 15, a; 321, b.
  sacrorum, 304, a; 321, b.
Rheda, 322, a.
Rhinthonica, 112, a.
Rhodia lex, 233, b.
Rica, 322, b.
Ricinium, 322, b.
Robigalia, 322, b.
Robur, 72, a.
Rogare legem, 225, b.
Rogatio, 107, a; 216, b; 225, b.
Rogationem accipere, 225, b.
  promulgare, 224, b.
Rogationes Liciniae, 231, a.
Rogator, 107, b.
Rogus, 188, b.
Romphea, 201, a.
Rorarii, 165, b; 168, b.
Roscia theatralis lex, 233, b.
Rostra, 322, b.
Rostrata columna, 102, b.
  corona, 118, b.
Rostrum, 264, a.
Rota, 124, a; 178, b.
Rubria lex, 234, a.
Rubrica, 179, a.
Ruderatio, 144, b.

SCRIBAE.

Rudiarii, 195, a.
Rudis, 194, b.
Rudus, 412, b.
Rupiliae leges, 234, a.

S.

Saccus, 101, b; 323, a; 417, a.
Sacellum, 193, b; 323, a; 366, a.
Sacer, 234, a.
Sacerdos, 323, b.
Sacerdotes Augustales, 53, a.
Sacerdotium, 323, b.
Sacra, 268, b; 324, a.
  gentilitia, 193, b.
  privata, 324, a.
  publica, 324, a.
Sacramentum, 218, b; 324, a.
Sacrarium, 324, a; 366, a.
Sacratae leges, 234, a.
Sacrificium, 324, a.
Sacrilegium, 324, b.
Sacrorum detestatio, 105, a.
Sacrum novemdiale, 272, b.
Saeculares ludi, 242, b.
Saeculum, 325, b.
Sagittarii, 37, b.
Sagmina, 326, a.
Sagulum, 326, a.
Sagum, 326, a.
Salaminia, 283, b.
Salii, 326, a.
Salinae, 327, a.
Salinum, 327, a.
Saltatio, 281, a; 327, b.
Saltus, 217, a; 310, b.
Salutatores, 328, b.
Sambuca, 329, a.
Samnites, 195, a.
Sandalium, 329, a.
Sandapila, 188, a.
Sapa, 416, b.
Sarcophagus, 188, b.
Sarissa, 201, a.
Sarracum, 329, a.
Satira, 329, a.
Satura, 329, a.
  lex, 226, a; 329, a.
Saturnalia, 329, a.
Scabellum, 330, a.
Scalae, 23, a; 266, a.
Scalmi, 264, b.
Sculptura, 330, a.
Scamnum, 222, a; 330, a.
Scantinia lex, 234, a.
Scapha, 1, b; 262, b.
Scapus, 101, b.
Scena, 372, a.
Scenici ludi, 206, a; 242, a.
Sceptrum, 330, a.
Schoenus, 330, b.
Sciothericum, 207, a.
Scire, 336, a.
Scissor, 97, a.
Scitum populi, 225, b.
Scorpio, 180, a; 381, a.
Scotia, 347, b.
Scribae, 330, b.

SABINA.

Scribere, 331, a.
Scribonia lex, 234, a.
Scrinium, 70, b.
Scriplum, 331, a.
Scripta, 221, a.
Scriptura, 330, b.
Scripturarii, 331, a.
Scripulum, 331, a.
Scrupulum, 53, b; 331, a; 405, b.
Sculptura, 330, a.
Scutica, 180, a.
Scutum, 41, b; 331, a.
Scytale, 331, a.
Secespita, 331, b.
Sectatores, 18, b.
Sectio, 331, b.
Sector, 331, b.
Secundarium, 417, b.
Securis, 331, b.
Secutores, 195, b.
Seges, 32, b.
Segestre, 222, b.
Sella, 154, a; 331, b.
Sembella, 237, b.
Semis, Semissis, 44, a, 54, a.
Semproniae leges, 234, a.
Sempronia lex de foenore, 234, b.
Semunciarium fenus, 177, a.
Senator, 333, a.
Senatores Orcini, 333, a.
  pedarii, 331, a.
Senatus, 332, a.
  auctoritas, 336, a.
  consultum, 336, a.
  jus, 333, b.
Seniores, 105, b.
Sepelire, 189, b.
September, 66, a.
Septemviri Epulones, 156, b.
Septimontium, 337, a.
Septum, 107, b.
Septunx, 44, a.
Sepulchri violati actio, 190, b.
Sepulchrum, 189, b.
Sequestres, 18, b.
Sera, 215, a.
Seriae, 417, a.
Sericum, 337, a.
Serrati, sc. nummi, 130, b.
Serta, 337, a.
Servare de coelo, 51, a.
Servilia agraria lex, 235, a.
  Glaucia lex, 319, a.
  judiciaria lex, 235, a.
Servus (Greek), 337, a.
  (Roman), 338, b.
  ad manum, 12, a.
  publicus, 340, a.
Sescuncia, 44, a.
Sescunx, 44, a.
Sestertium, 341, b.
Sestertius, 341, b.
Sevir turmae equitum, 172, a.
Seviri, 53, a.
Sex suffragia, 156, a.
Sextans, 44, a.
Sextarius, 342, a; 405, b.
Sextilis, 66, a.
Sabina, 201, a.

462   LATIN INDEX.

SIBYLLINI LIBRI.

Sibyllini libri, 342, b.
Sica, 342, b.
Sicarius, 343, a.
Sicila, 342, b.
Sidus natalitium, 46, a.
Sigillaria, 330, a.
Signa militaria, 341, a.
Signifer, 166, b; 343, b.
Signum, 138, b; 168, a.
Silentium, 51, a.
Silia lex, 235, a.
Silicarii, 31, a.
Silicernium, 140, b.
Siliqua, 405, b.
Silvae, 330, b.
Silvani et Carbonis lex, 92, a.
Simpulum, or Simpuvium, 311, b; 344, a.
Siparium, 344, a; 372, a.
Sistrum, 344, a.
Sitella, 345, a.
Siticines, 188, a.
Situla, 345, a.
Socculus, 345, b
Soccus, 345, b.
Socer, 13, a.
  magnus, 13, b.
Societas, 39, b.
Socii, 170, b; 181, a; 345, b.
Socrus, 13, a.
  magna, 13, b.
Sodales, 98, a.
  Augustales, 53, a.
  Titii, 43, a.
Sodalitium, 19, a.
Solarium, 135, a; 143, b; 227, a.
Solea, 346, b.
Solidorum venditio, 79, b.
Solidus, 54, a.
Solitaurilia, 325, a; 244, b.
Solium, 56, a; 376, a.
Solum, 144, b.
Sophronistae, 179, b
Sordidati, 380, a.
Sortes, 345, a; 347, a.
Sparus, 200, b.
Spectacula, 87, a.
Spectio, 51, a.
Specularia, 144, b
Specularis lapis, 144, b.
Speculatores, 347, a.
Speculum, 347, a.
Specus, 30, b.
Sperata, 252, b.
Sphaeristerium, 296, b.
Spiculum, 199, b; 200, b.
Spina, 87, a.
Spira, 101, b; 347, b.
Spirula, 347, b.
Spolia, 347, b.
Sponda, 222, a.
Sponsa, 251, b.
Sponsalia, 251, b.
Sponsus, 251, b.
Sportula, 348, a.
Stadium, 348, b.
Stalagmia, 211, b.
Stamen, 191, b; 364, a.
Stater, 349, a.

TABELLARIAE LEGES.

Statera, 399, a.
Stati dies, 135, b.
Stationes, 75, b.
Stativae feriae, 177, b.
Stator, 349, a.
Statuaria ars, 349, a.
Statumen, 412, b.
Stesichorus, 362, a.
Stilus, 354, a.
Stipendiarii, 354, a.
Stipendium, 354, b.
Stiva, 32, a.
Stola, 354, b.
Stragulum, 222, b.
Stratum, 154, a.
Strena, 355, b.
Strigil, 56, b.
Strophium, 355, b.
Structor, 97, a.
Stultorum feriae, 182, a.
Stuprum, 8, a.
Stylus, 354, a.
Subitarius exercitus, 167, a.
Subitarii, 400, a.
Subrogare legem, 225, b.
Subscriptores, 133, a.
Subscriptio censoria, 80, a.
Subsellium, 376, a.
Subsignanus, 168, b; 355, b.
Subtegmen, 364, a.
Subtemen, 364, a.
Subucula, 401, b.
Suburana, 197, b.
Succinctus, 401, b.
Sudatio concamerata, 56, a.
Sudatorium, 56, a.
Suffibulum, 412, a.
Suffitio, 190, b.
Suffragia sex, 156, a.
Suffraginm, 355, b.
Suggestus, 22, b; 322, b; 356, a
Suggrundarium, 188, b.
Sui heredes, 203, b.
Sulci, 412, b.
Sulcus, 32, b.
Sulpiciae leges, 235, a.
Sulpicia Sempronia lex, 233, a.
Sumptuariae leges, 215, a.
Suovetaurilia, 244, b; 325, a.
Supparum, 267, b; 401, b.
Supparus, 401, b.
Supplicatio, 356, a.
Supposititii, 193, b.
Susceptores, 81, a.
Suspensura, 56, a.
Sutorium, 48, a.
Symposium, 357, a.
Syndicus, 358, a.
Syngrapha, 358, b.
Synthesis, 329, b; 359, a.
Syrinx, 359, a.
Syssitia, 359, b.

T.

Tabella, 360, a.
Tabellariae leges, 236, a.

TIARAS.

Tabellarius, 360, a.
Taberna, 39, b; 77, a.
  diversoria, 77, a.
Tabernaria fabula, 112, a.
Tablinum, 142, b.
Tabulae, 39, b; 360, a.
  censoriae, 79, b.
  novae, 360, b.
  publicae, 317, a.
Tabulam, adesse ad, 48, b.
Tabularii, 360, b.
Tabularium, 360, b.
Tabulatum, 417, a.
Talaria, 361, a.
Talasius, 252, b.
Talassio, 252, b.
Talentum, 361, a.
Talio, 361, b.
Talus, 361, b.
Tarentini ludi, 242, b.
Tarpeia Aternia lex, 226, b.
Taurii ludi, 242, b.
Tectores, 31, a.
Tectorium, 48, a.
Tegula, 363, b.
Tela, 363, b.
Telamones, 47, b.
Temo, 31, b; 124, a; 297, b.
Templum, 322, b.
Temporis praescriptio, 308, a.
Tensae, 373, b.
Tepidarium, 56, a.
Terentilia lex, 236, b.
Terentini ludi, 242, b
Terminalia, 368, a.
Termini, 204, b.
Tertiare, 32, b.
Teruncius, 44, a; 237, b.
Tessera, 368, b.
  hospitalis, 209, b.
  nummaria, or frumentaria, 183, a.
Testamentariae leges, 236, b.
Testamentifactio, 368, b.
Testamentum, 248, a; 368, b.
Testator, 368, b.
Testis, 248, a; 218, b.
Testudo, 40, b; 245, b; 367, a.
Tetrarcha, 370, a.
Tetrarches, 370, a.
Textores, 363, b.
Textrices, 363, b.
Textrinum, 363, b.
Thalassites, 418, b.
Thargelia, 370, a.
Theatrum, 370, b.
Thensae, 373, b.
Theodosianus codex, 95, a.
Thermae, 54, b.
Thermopolium, 77, a.
Thesmophoria, 375, b.
Thorax, 240, b.
Thoria lex, 236, b.
Thraces, 195, b.
Threces, 195, b.
Thronus, 376, a.
Thyrsus, 176, a.
Tiara, 376, b.
Tiaras, 376, b.

TIBIA.

Tibia, 376, b.
Tibicinium, 377, a.
Tintinnabulum, 378, a.
Tirocinium, 378, a.
Tiro, 378, a.
Titia lex, 236, b.
Titienses, 286, b.
Tities, 286, b.
Titii Sodales, 378, a.
Titulus, 189, a; 238, b.
Toga, 378, a.
  candida, 380, a.
  palmata, 380, b.
  jacta, 380, b.
  praetexta, 380, b.
  pulla, 380, b.
  pura, 380, a.
  sordida, 380, a.
  virilis, 380, a.
Togata fabula, 112, a.
Togatus, 378, b.
Tonsor, 381, a.
Topiaria ars, 208, b.
Topiarius, 208, a.
Toralia, 222, b.
Torcular, 416, b.
Torculum, 416, b.
Tormentum, 267, a; 381, a.
Torques, 381, b.
Torquis, 381, b.
Torus, 222, a; 347, b; 381, b.
Trabea, 380, b.
Trabeata fabula, 112, a.
Tragoedia, 381, b.
Tragula, 201, a; 320, b.
Tragum, 320, b.
Trama, 364, a.
Transactio in via, 5, a.
Transtillum, 245, b.
Transtra, 265, b.
Transvectio equitum, 152, b.
Trebonia lex, 236, b.
Tremissis, 54, a.
Tressis, 44, a.
Tresviri, 397, a.
Triarii, 165, b; 168, b.
Tribula, 385, a.
Tribulum, 385, a.
Tribulus, 385, a.
Tribunal, 385, a.
Tri**buni** Laticlavii, 169, a.
  militum, 166, a; 169, a.
Tribunicia lex, 233, a; 236, b.
  potestas, 387, a.
Tribunus, 385, a.
  celerum, 78, a.
Tribus (Greek), 188, a.
  (Roman), 390, b.
Tributa comitia, 108, a.
Tributum, 391, a.
Triclinlarchia, 392, a.
Triclinium, **391**, b.
Tridens, 191, **b.**
Triens, 44, a.
Trifax, 381, a.
Triga, 124, a.
Trilix, 164, b.
Trinum nundinum, 273, a.
Trinundinum, 273, a.

VALERIAE LEGES.

Triplicatio, 6, a.
Tripos, 394, a.
Tripudium, 50, b.
Triremes, 260, b.
Triticum, 182, b.
Triumphalia ornamenta, 397, a.
Triumphalis corona, 118, b.
Triumphus, 394, a.
  castrensis, 397, a.
  navalis, 397, a.
Triumviri, 397, a.
  agro dividundo, 397, b.
  capitalis, 397, b.
  coloniae deducendae, 99, b; 397, b.
  epulones, 156, a.
  equitum turmas recognoscendi, or legendis equitum decuriis, 397, b.
  mensarii, 254, a.
  monetales, 256, b.
  nocturni, 397, b.
  reficiendis aedibus, 397, b.
  reipublicae constituendae, 397, b.
  sacris conquirendis donisque persignandis, 398, a.
  senatus legendi, 192, a.
Trochleae, 267, a.
Trochus, 398, a.
Trojae ludus, 90, a.
Tropaeum, 398, a.
Trossuli, 157, a.
Trua, 399, a.
Trulla, 399, a.
Trutina, 399, a.
Tuba, 400, a.
Tubicen, 11, a.
Tubilustrium, 318, a.
Tullia lex de ambitu, 18, b.
  de legatione libera, 224, a.
Tullianum, 72, a.
Tumultuarii, 400, c.
Tumultuarius Exercitus, 167, a.
Tumultus, 399, b.
Tunica, 400, a.
Tunica recta, 252, a.
Tunicati, 402, b.
Turibulum, **402**, **b**.
Turma, 166, b.
Turricula, 182, b.
Turris, 402, a.
Tutela, 264, b.
Tutor, 122, b.
Tympanum, 27, a; 298, a; 403, a.

U, V.

Vacatio, 142, a; 167, b.
Vadari reum, 5, b.
Vades, 216, a.
Vades dare, 5, b.
Vadimonium, Vas, 5, b.
Vagina, 196, a.
Valeriae leges, 236, **b.**

VINDEMIALIS FERIA.

Valeriae et Horatiae leges, 29, b; 237, a.
Valeria lex, 237, a.
Vallaris corona, 118, b.
Vallum, 14, b; 75, a; 406, a.
Vallus, 75, a; 406, b.
Valva, 213, a.
Vannus, 407, a.
Vari, 120, b.
Varia lex, 247, a.
Vas, 407, a.
Vatinia lex, 237, a.
Udo, 404, b.
Vectigal rerum venalium, 82, a.
Vectigalia, 407, a.
Velarium, 23, a.
Velites, 166, b; 168, b; 408, a.
Velum, 267, a; 408, a.
Venabulum, 408, a.
Venatio, 21, a; 408, a.
Venditio, 80, b.
Veneficium, 409, a.
Venereus jactus, 362, a.
Venus, 362, a.
Ver sacrum, 410, a.
Verbena, 11, b; 326, a.
Verbenarius, 178, a.
Verna, 147, a.
Verriculum, 320, b.
Versura, 177, a.
Veru, 200, b.
Vervactum, 32, b.
Verutum, 200, b.
Vespae, 188, a.
Vespillones, 188, a.
Vestalis, 410, a.
  maxima, 410, b.
Vestibulum, 142, a.
Veteranus, 167, b; 378, a.
Veteratores, 340, a.
Vexillarii, 165, b; 170, b.
Vexillum, 165, b; 141, b.
Via Principalis, 75, a.
Viae, 412, a.
Viaria lex, 237, a.
Viaticum, 414, a.
Viator, 414, b.
Victima, 324, b.
Vicesima, 11, b; 414, b.
  hereditatum et legatorum, 414, b.
  manumissionis, 248, b; 414, b.
Vicesimaria lex, 414, b.
Vicesimarii, 414, b.
Vico magistri, 415, a.
Vicus, 414, b.
Victoriatus, 330, a.
Vigiles, 171, a.
Vigiliae, 75, b.
Vigintisexviri, 414, a.
Vigintiviri, 415, a.
Villa, 415, a.
  publica, 79, a.
  rustica, 415, a.
Villia annalis lex, 226, b.
Villicus, 31, a; 208, a; 347, b; 415, b.
Vinalia, 415, b.
Vindemialis feria, 177, b.

VINDEX.

Vindex, 5, a.
Vindicta, 248, a.
Vinea, 415, b.
Vinum, 416, a.
Virgines Vestales, 410, a.
Virgo maxima, 411, a.
Viridarium, 208, b.
Viridarius, 208, a.
Virilis toga, 380, a.
Vis, 420, a.
Visceratio, 190, b.
Viscellia lex, 237, a.
Vitis, 169, a.
Vitium, 51, a.
Vitrearii, 420, b.
Vitricus, 13, b.
Vitrum, 420, a.
Vitta, Vittae, 421, a.
Vittata sacerdos, 421, b.
Ulna, 404, b.
Umbella, 404, b.
Umbilicus, 238, a.
Umbo, 94, a; 379, b; 412, b.
Umbraculum, 404, b.

USUS.

Uncia, 44, a; 176, b; 405, a.
Unciarum fenus, 177, a.
Unctores, 17, b.
Uncturium, 56, a.
Unguenta, 405, b.
Unguentaria, 405, b.
Unguentariae, 405, b.
Unguentarii, 405, b.
Universitas, 98, a.
Vocatio, 188, a.
Voconia lex, 237, b.
Volones, 421, b.
Volumen, 218, a.
Voluntarii, 421, b.
Vomer, 32, a.
Vomitoria, 23, a.
Vorticellum, 191, b.
Urceus, 406, a.
Urna, 189, a; 345, a; 406, a.
Ustrina, 63, a; 189, a.
Ustrinum, 189, a.
Usucapio, 406, a.
Usurae, 176, b.
Usus, 251, a.

ZOPHORUS.

Usus fructuarius, 406, a.
Ususfructus, 406, a.
Uterini, 98, a.
Utres, 418, a.
Utricularius, 376, b.
Vulcanalia, 421, b.
Vulgares, 340, b.
Uxor, 251, a.
Uxorium, 12, b.

X.

Xystus, 208, a.

Z.

Zona, 422, b.
Zophorus, 102, a; 422, b.

ENGLISH INDEX.

ACTORS.

A.

Actors (Greek), 205, b.
— (Roman), 205, b.
Adoption (Greek), 7, a.
— (Roman), 7, a.
Advocate, 358, a.
Adze, 44, a.
Altar, 31, a.
Ambassadors, 223, a.
Anchor, 268, a.
Anvil, 254, b.
Aqueduct, 29, b.
Arch, 36, a.
Archers, 37, b.
Armour, 41, a.
Arms, 41, a.
Army (Greek), 162, b.
— (Roman), 164, a.
Astronomy, 45, b.
Auction (sale), 43, b.
Axe, 311, b.
Axle, 124, a.

B.

Bail (Greek), 152, b.
— (Roman), 5, b.
Bakers, 297, b.
Balance, the, 239, a.
Ball, game at, 181, b; 296, a.
Bankers, 39, a.
Banishment (Greek), 172, a.
— (Roman), 173, a.
Barber, 57, a.
Basket, 57, b.
Baths (Greek), 54, a.
— (Roman), 55, b.
Beard, 57, a.
Beds, 222, a.
Beer, 82, b.
Bell, 378, a.
Bellows, 181, b.
Belt, 57, a.
Bit (of horses), 182, b.
Boeotian constitution, 59, b.
Books, 238, a.
Bookseller, 239, a.
Boots, 64, b; 120, a.

COMEDY.

Bottomry, 176, b.
Bow, 37, b.
Boxing, 315, a.
Bracelet, 42, b.
Brass, 12, a; 278, a.
Brazier, 180, b.
Breakfast, 95, a.
Bribery (Greek), 127, a.
— (Roman), 18, b.
Bricks, 220, b.
Bridge, 302, a.
Bridle, 182, a.
Bronze, 12, a.
Brooch, 178, b.
Burial (Greek), 184, a.
— (Roman), 187, b.

C.

Calendar (Greek), 65, a.
— (Roman), 66, a.
Cameos, 330, a.
Camp, 73, a.
— breaking up of, 76, a.
— choice of ground for, 73, b.
— construction of, 74, a.
Candle, 69, b.
Candlestick, 69, b.
Canvassing, 18, a.
Capital (of columns), 101, b.
Cart, 72, b.
Casque, 192, b.
Ceilings, 144, b.
Celt, 139, b.
Censer, 402, b.
Chain, 76, b.
Chariot, 123, b.
Chimneys, 145, a.
Chisel, 139, b.
Circumvallation, 406, b.
Citizenship (Greek), 90, b.
— (Roman), 91, b.
Clerks (Athenian), 196, a.
— (Roman), 6, a.
Clocks, 206, b.
Coffins, 185, b; 188, b.
Colony (Greek), 98, b.
— (Roman), 99, b.
Column, 101, b.
Combs, 288, a.
Comedy (Greek), 110, b.

EXECUTIONER.

Comedy (Roman), 111, b.
Cooks, 97, a.
Cordage, 267, b.
Corn crops, 344, b.
— preservation of, 345, a.
Couches, 221, a.
Cowl, 122, a.
Cretan constitution, 120, a.
Criers, 306, b.
Crook, 288, a.
Crops, 344, b.
Cross, 121, a.
Crown, 118, a.
Crucifixion, 121, a.
Cubit, 122, a.
Cup, 68, a.
Cymbal, 125, b.

D.

Daggers, 315, a; 342, b.
Dance, the Pyrrhic, 328, a.
Dancing, 327, b.
Day, 134, a.
Dice, 368, b.
Dice-box, 182, b.
Dinner, 95, a.
Dish, 77, a; 285, a.
Distaff, 191, b.
Dithyramb, 381, b.
Divorce (Greek), 139, a.
— (Roman), 139, a.
Door, 214, b.
Dowry (Greek), 145, a.
— (Roman), 145, b.
Drains, 94, a.
Draughts, game of, 221, a.
Drum, 403, a.
Dynasty, 34, b.

E.

Ear-ring, 211, b.
Earthenware, 178, b.
Eleven, the, 202, b.
Ensigns, military, 343, a.
Era, 86, a.
Evil Eye, 175, a.
Executioner, 72, b.

2 H

F

Fan, 179, b.
Felting, 297, a.
Fire-place, 180, b.
Floors of houses, 144, b.
Fresco, 295, a.
Fuller, 184, a.
Funerals (Greek), 184, b.
   (Roman), 187, b.
Furnace, 56, a; 182, a.

G.

Gambler, Gaming, 17, a.
Garden, 207, b.
Gates of cities, 305, a
Girdle, 422, b.
Gladiators, 194, a.
Glass, 420, a.
Gold, 53, b.
Granary, 207, b.
Greaves, 273, a.
Guards, 75, b.

H.

Hair (Greek), 103, a.
   (Roman), 103, b.
Hammers, 247, a; 254, b.
Harp, 329, a.
Hatchet, 331, b.
Hearth, 180, b.
Heir (Greek), 203, a.
   (Roman), 203, a.
Helmet, 192, b.
Hemlock, 202, b.
Heraclean tablet, 230, a.
Holidays, 177, b.
Hoop, 398, a.
Hospitality, 208, a.
Hour, 207, a.
House (Greek), 140, a.
   (Roman), 142, a.
Hunting, 408, a.
Hunting-spear, 408, a.

I, J.

Informer, 128, b.
Inheritance (Greek), 203, a.
   (Roman), 203, a.
Ink, 48, a.
Inn, 77, a.
Intaglios, 330, a.
Intercalary month, 66, b.
Interest of money (Greek), 176, b.
   (Roman), 176, b.
Isthmian games, 214, a.

Italy, 100, b.
Judges (Greek), 121, a; 131, a.
   (Roman), 215, a.

K.

Kiln, 182, a.
King (Greek), 320, a.
   (Roman), 320, b.
Kitchen, 143, a.
Knife, 122, a.
Knights (Athenian), 81, o.
   Roman), 156, a.
Knockers, 215, a.

L.

Ladders, 266, a.
Lamps, 241, b.
Law, 218, a; 225, a.
Legacy, 222, b.
Legion, 164, a.
Letter-carrier, 360, a.
Levy, 167, a.
Library, 58, b.
Light-house, 293, a.
Litters, 221, a.
Liturgies, 224, a.
Looking-glass, 347, a.
Loom, 363, b.
Lots, 347, a.
Luncheon, 95, a.
Lyre, the, 245, a.

M.

Marriage (Greek), 249, b.
   (Roman), 250, b.
Masks, 291, a.
Masts, 266, a.
Meals (Greek), 95, a.
   (Roman), 96, a.
Mile, 255, b.
Mile-stones, 255, b; 413, a.
Mills, 256, a.
Mines, 407, b.
Mint, 256, b.
Mirror, 347, a.
Money, coined, 12, a.
   (Greek), gold, 53, b.
   (Roman), „ 53, b.
Month (Greek), 65, a.
   (Roman), 66, a
Mortars, 257, a; 258, a.
Mosaics, 141, b; 144, b.
Mourning for the dead, 190, b; 187, a.

N.

Names (Greek), 270, b.
   (Roman), 270, b.

Necklaces, 256, b.
Nemean games, 269, a.
Nets, 319, b.
Notary, 360, b.

O.

Oars, 265, b.
Oath (Greek), 218, a.
   (Roman), 218, b.
October-horse, 280, a.
Officers, duty of, 75, b.
   parade of, 75, b.
Olympiad, 276, a.
Olympic games, 274, a.
Oracles, 276, b.
Orders of architecture, 101, b; 102, a.
Organ, 210, a.
Ostracism, 172, a.
Oven, 182, a.
Ounce, 105, a.

P.

Painting, 293, b.
Paper, 238, b.
Parasol, 404, b.
Parchment, 238, b.
Pay of soldiers, 354, b.
Pediment, 176, a.
Pen, 64, a.
Perfumes, 405, b.
Pipe, 376, b.
Plough, 31, b.
Poisoning, 409, a.
Poles, 266, a.
Portcullis, 76, a.
Pottery, 178, b.
Priests, 323, b.
Prison, 72, a.
Prodigies, 310, b.
Property-tax (Greek), 148
   (Roman), 391, b.
Prow, 263, a.
Purification, 244, a.
Purses, 248, b.
Pyrrhic dance, 328, a.
Pythian games, 315, b.

Q.

Quiver, 292, b.

R.

Races, 87, a.
Rings, 25, b.
Road, 412, a.
Rope-dancers, 184, b.

ROPES.

Ropes, 267, b.
Rounds, 75, b.
Rudder, 265, b.

S.

Sacrifices, 324, a.
Saddles, 154, a.
Sails, 267, a.
Salt, 327, a.
Salt-cellar, 327, a.
Salt-works, 327, a.
Sandal, 58, a.
Scales, 239, a.
Screw, 94, b.
Scythe, 173, b.
Senate (Greek), 61, a; **193, b.**
  (Roman), 332, b.
Sentinels, 75, b.
Shawl, 289, b.
Shields, 94, a; **285, a; 331, a; 288,** b.
Ships, 259, b.
Shoe, 64, b; 151, **b.**
Shops, 39, b.
Sibyl, 342, b.
Sickle, 342, b.
Silk, 337, a.
Silver, 40, a.
Slaves (Greek), 337, a.
  (Roman), 338, b.
Sling, 184, b.
Slingers, 184, b.
Spartan constitution, **193, b.**
Spear, 199, b.
Speusinians, 129, b.

TROUSERS.

Spindle, 191, b.
Standards, military, **343, a.**
Statuary, 349, a.
Stern, 264, b.
Stoves, 145, a.
Sun-dial, 206, **b.**
Sword, 196, a.

T.

Tables, 253, **b.**
Talent, 361, a.
Tapestry, 344, a.
Taxes (Greek), 365, **b.**
  (Roman), 365, b; **391, a.**
Temple, 366, a.
Testament, 368, b.
Theatre, 370, b.
Thessalian constitution, **360, b.**
Threshold, 214, b.
Throne, 376, **a.**
Tiles, roofing, **363, b.**
Tombs, 186, a.
Torch, 176, a.
Torture, 381, a.
Tower, 402, a.
Tragedy (Greek), **381, b.**
  (Roman), 384, a.
Triangle, the, 181, **a.**
Tribes (Greek), **388, b.**
  (Roman), 390, b.
Tribunes, 385, a.
Trident, 191, b.
Tripod, 394, a.
Trophy, 398, a.
Trousers, 62, a.

YOKE.

Trumpet, 62, b; 399, a.
Tumblers, 328, a.

U, V.

Vase-painting, 295, **b.**
Veil, 408, a.
Voting (Greek), **355, b.**
  (Roman), 107, **a; 355, b.**
Usurers, 176, **b.**

W.

Waggon, 297, **b.**
Wall, 257, b; 301, b.
Weaving, 164, a.
Wheel, 124, a.
Whip, 179, b.
Wills, 368, **b.**
Window, 144, **b.**
Wine, 416, **a.**
Witnesses (Greek), **248, b**
  (Roman), 218, a.
Wrestling, **242, a.**

Y.

Yards of a sail, 267, a
Year (Greek), 65, a.
  (Roman), 66, b.
Yoke, 217, a.

CLASSIFIED INDEX.

Under each head the names of the articles in the Index are given in which the subject is explained.

AGRICULTURE.

Hortus.
Olea, Oliva.
Oscillum.
Scamnum.
Sitos.
Villa rustica.
Vinum.

AGRICULTURAL IMPLEMENTS.

Aratrum.
Jugum.
Pala.
Pecten.
Pedum.
Plaustrum.
Prelum.
Sarracum.
Stilus.
Tintinnabulum.
Torculum.
Tribula.
Tympanum.
Vannus.

AMUSEMENTS AND PLAYTHINGS.

Abacus.
Aenigma.
Alea.
Ascoliasmus.
Buxum.
Calculi.
Cottabos.
Follis.
Fritillus.
Latrunculi.
Talus.
Tessera.
Trochus.

ARCHITECTURE.

Abacus.
Acroterium.
Antae.
Antefixa.
Apsis.
Architectura.
Arcus.
Astragalus.
Atlantes.
Balteus.
Camara.
Canalis.
Columbaria.
Columna.
Coronis.
Cortina.
Crypta.
Cyma.
Entasis.
Epistylium.
Fascia.
Fastigium.
Janua.
Jugum.
Later.
Maenianum.
Metopa.
Peristylium.
Podium.
Porticus.
Spira.
Testudo.
Tholus.
Tympanum.
Zophorus.

ARITHMETIC.

Abacus.
Calculi.

ARMOUR AND WEAPONS.

Acinaces.
Aegis.

Armour and Weapons—continued.

Arcus.
Arma.
Armatura.
Capulus.
Cateia.
Cetra.
Clipeus.
Dolo.
Funda.
Galea.
Gerrha.
Gladius.
Hasta.
Lorica.
Ocrea.
Palma.
Pelta.
Pharetra.
Pugio.
Scutum.
Securis.
Sica.
Venabulum.

ASSEMBLIES AND COUNCILS.

Agora.
Amphictyones.
Areiopagus.
Boule.
Comitia calata.
    curiata.
    centuriata.
    tributa.
Concilium.
Concio.
Conventus.
Curia.
Ecclesia.
Eccleti.
Gerousia.
Myrii.
Panegyris.

Assemblies and Councils—continued.

Panionia.
Senatus.
Synedri.

ASTRONOMY.

Astrologia.

CAMPS AND FORTS.

Acropolis.
Agger.
Arx.
Carrago.
Castra.
    stativa.
Pagi.
Praetorium.
Turris.
Vallum.

CHARITIES AND DONATIONS.

Alimentarii.
Congiaria.
Dianomae.
Donaria.
Frumentariae Leges.
Strena.

CIVIL PUNISHMENTS.

Arca.
Barathron, or Orugma.
Carcer.
Ceadas.
Crux.
Equuleus.

CLASSIFIED INDEX.

Civil Punishments—
continued.
Ergastulum.
Flagrum.
Furca, patibulum.
Laqueus.
Latumiae.
Sestertium.

CLASSES OF CITIZENS AND OTHERS.
Adlecti.
Aerarii.
Agela.
Aretalogi.
Camilli.
Canephoros.
Dediticii.
Delator.
Demos.
Eiren.
Empbruri.
Ephebus.
Equites.
Eupatridae.
Geomori.
Hetaerae.
Hippobotae.
Homoei.
Libertus.
Locupletes
Metoeci.
Naucraria.
Nobiles.
Ordo.
Parasiti.
Patricii.
Patrimi et Matrimi.
Perioeci.
Plebes.
Quadruplatores.
Salutatores.

COLONIES & MOTHER COUNTRY.
Apoikia.
Cleruchiae.
Colonia.
Metropolis.

CRIMES.
Ambitus.
Calumnia.
Falsum.
Incendium.
Injuria.
Leges Corneliae et Juliae.
Majestas.
Parricidium.
Plagium.

Crimes—*continued.*
Sacrilegium.
Sodalitium.
Stuprum.
Talio.
Veneficium.
Vis.

DIVISION OF LAND.
Ager publicus.
Cippus.
Pyrgos.
Temenos.

DRAMA, DRAMATIC ENTERTAINMENTS.
Comoedia.
Exodia.
Exostra.
Mimus.
Pantomimus.
Periactos.
Persona.
Siparium.
Theatrum.
Tragoedia.
Velum.

DRESS, ORNAMENTS, THE TOILET.
Abolla.
Alicula.
Amictorium.
Amictus.
Ampyx.
Annulus.
Apex.
Armilla.
Barba.
Baxa.
Braccae.
Bulla.
Calamistrum.
Calceus.
Campestre.
Candys.
Caracalla.
Catena.
Causia.
Cestus.
Chlamys.
Clavus latus.
  angustus.
Coma.
Cothurnus.
Crepida.
Crocota.
Cucullus.
Cudo.
Cyclas.

Dress, &c.—*continued.*
Diadema.
Embas.
Emblema.
Endromis.
Exomis.
Fascia.
Feminalia.
Fibula.
Fimbriae.
Flabellum.
Focale.
Fucus.
Galerus.
Inauris.
Incunabula.
Infula.
Instita.
Lacerna.
Laciniae.
Laena.
Lemniscus.
Marsupium.
Mitra.
Monile.
Nudus.
Orarium.
Paenula.
Pallium.
Pecten.
Peplum.
Pera.
Periscelis.
Pero.
Phalera.
Pileus.
Redimiculum.
Reticulum.
Ricinium.
Saccus.
Sandalium.
Serta.
Soccus.
Solea.
Stola.
Strophium.
Synthesis.
Tiara.
Toga.
Torques.
Tunica.
Udo.
Velum.
Vitta.
Umbraculum.
Unguenta.
Zona.

ENGINEERING.
Aquaeductus.
Cloaca.
Crypta.
Emissarium.
Fistula.
Fons.
Librator aquae.
Murus, moenia.

Engineering — *continued.*
Navalia.
Pharos.
Piscina.
Pons.
Porta.
Syrinx.

ENGRAVING AND CHASING.
Caelatura.

ENTERTAINMENTS, FOOD
Apophoreta.
Calida.
Cerevisia.
Coena.
Commissatio.
Erani.
Opsonium.
Paropsis.
Posca.
Sportula.
Symposium.
Syssitia.
Vinum.

EPOCHS AND DIVISIONS OF TIME.
Calendarium, 1. Greek.
  2. Roman.
Chronologia.
Clavus annalis.
Dies.
  fasti et nefasti.
Fasti.
  sacri, or kalendares.
  annales, or historici.
Feriae.
Hora.
Horologium.
Lustrum.
Nundinae.
Olympias.
Saeculum.

EXERCISES.
Ceroma.
Cestus.
Cheironomia.
Desultor.
Discus.
Gymnasium.
Halteres.
Harpastum.
Hippodromus.

CLASSIFIED INDEX.

Exercises—*continued.*
Lucta, luctatio.
Palaestra.
Pancratium.
Pentathlon.
Petaurum.
Pila.
Pugilatus.
Saltatio.

FESTIVALS, GAMES, AND SHOWS.

Actia.
Adonia.
Aeora.
Agonalia.
Agones.
Agraulia.
Agroteras thusia.
Aloa or haloa.
Amarynthia.
Ambrosia.
Amphidromia.
Anagogia.
Androgeonia.
Anthesphoria.
Apaturia.
Aphrodisia.
Apollonia.
Ariadneia.
Armilustrium.
Arrhephoria.
Artemisia.
Asclepieia.
Augustales.
Bendideia.
Boedromia.
Boreasmus.
Brauronia.
Cabeiria.
Callisteia.
Carmentalia.
Carneia.
Carya.
Cerealia.
Chalciolkia.
Charistia.
Compitalia.
Consualia.
Cotyttia.
Daedala.
Decennalia.
Delia.
Delphinia.
Diipoleia.
Diocleia.
Dionysia.
Eleusinia.
Eleutheria.
Eliotia.
Equiria.
Floralia.
Fornacalia.
Gymnopaedia.
Heraea.
Hermaea.
Hestiasis.

Festivals, &c.—*continued.*
Hilaria.
Hyacinthia.
Inoa.
Isthmia.
Juvenalia.
Lampadephoria.
Laphria.
Larentalia.
Lectisternium.
Lemuralia.
Ludi.
[*In the text an alphabetical list of the principal ludi is given.*]
Lupercalia.
Lycaea.
Matralia.
Matronalia.
Megalensia.
Mysia.
Mysteria.
Neptunalia.
Novendiale.
Olympia.
Opalia.
Oschophoria.
Palilia.
Pamboeotia.
Panathenaea.
Plynteria.
Poplifugia.
Prometheia.
Pyanepsia.
Pythia.
Quinquatrus.
Quinquennalia.
Quirinalia.
Regifugium.
Robigalia.
Saturnalia.
Septimontium.
Sthenia.
Synoikia.
Terminalia.
Theophania.
Theseia.
Thesmophoria.
Vinalia.
Vulcanalia.

FORMS OF GOVERNMENT.

Aristocratia.
Democratia.
Monarchia.
Ochlocratia.
Oligarchia.

FUNERALS.

Arca.
Cenotaphium.

Funerals—*continued.*
Cippus.
Columbarium.
Crypta.
Funus, 1. Greek.
      2. Roman.
Mausoleum.
Urna.

FURNITURE.

Abacus.
Armarium.
Balnea.
Cathedra.
Conopeum.
Cortina.
Incitega.
Lectus.
Mensa.
Pluteus.
Pulvinar.
Scamnum.
Sella.
Speculum.
Thronus.
Torus.
Triclinium.
Tripos.

GREEK LAW.

Adoptio.
Aikias dike.
Anakrisis.
Androlepsia.
Antidosis.
Antigraphe.
Apographe.
Apophasis.
Aporrheta.
Apostasiou dike.
Appellatio.
Asebeias graphe.
Astrateias graphe.
Ateleia.
Atimia.
Axones.
Civitas, politeia.
Cleteres.
Decasmus.
Diaetetae.
Diapsephisis.
Dicastes.
Dike.
Divortium.
Dokimasia.
Dos.
Ecmartyria.
Eisangelia.
Embateia.
Emmeni dikae.
Endeixis, ephegesis.
Epangelia.
Epibole.
Epiclerus.

Greek Law—*continued.*
Epitropus.
Epobelia.
Euthyne.
Exomosia.
Exsilium.
Fenus.
Gamelia.
Graphe.
Heres.
Hieromenia.
Hybreos graphe.
Jusjurandum.
Prodosia.
Proeisphoras dike.
Prostates tou demou.
Prothesmia.
Psephus.
Pseudengraphes graphe.
Pseudocleteias graphe
Rhetrae.
Sitou dike.
Sycophantes.
Sylae.
Syndicus.
Synegorus.
Syngraphe.
Timema.
Tormentum.
Xenias graphe.

HORSE FURNITURE.

Ephippium.
Frenum.
Habenae.
Hippoperae.

INCOME, PUBLIC AND PRIVATE.

Aes uxorium.
Apophora.
Arca.
Census.
Centesima.
Columnarium.
Decumae.
Eicoste.
Eisphora.
Epidoseis.
Fiscus.
Ostiarium.
Pentecoste.
Phoros.
Portorium.
Quadragesima.
Salinae.
Scriptura.
Stipendiarii.
Telones.
Telos.
Theorica.
Tributum.
Vectigalia.
Vicesima.

CLASSIFIED INDEX. 471

INSIGNIA AND ATTRIBUTES.

Caduceus.
Fasces.
Insignia.
Sceptrum.
Talaria.
Thyrsus.

LEAGUES.

Achaicum Foedus.
Aetolicum Foedus.
Socii.

LITERATURE.

Commentarius.
Fescennina.
Logographi.
Paean.
Satura.

MACHINES AND CONTRIVANCES.

Antlia.
Catena.
Clitellae.
Cochlea.
Columbarium.
Ephippium.
Exostra.
Ferculum.
Fistula.
Follis.
Forma.
Fornax.
Jugum.
Libra, Libella.
Mortarium, pila.
Pegma.
Phalangae.
Retis, Rete.
Scalae.
Tela.
Tintinnabulum.
Torculum.
Trutina.

MAGISTRATES AND RULERS.

Acta.
Adlecti.
Aesymnetes.

Magistrates, &c.—continued.

Alabarches.
Amphictyones.
Archon.
Areiopagus.
Bidiaei.
Boetarches.
Boule.
Censor.
Centumviri.
Consul.
Consularis.
Cosmi.
Decaduchi.
Decarchia.
Decemviri.
  legibus scribendis.
  litibus judicandis.
  sacris faciundis.
  agris dividundis.
Demarchi.
Demiurgi.
Dictator.
Duumviri.
Ephetae.
Ephori.
Epimeletae.
Eponymus.
Gerousia.
Gynaeconomi.
Harmostae.
Hendeka, hoi.
Hieromnemones.
Interrex.
Magistratus.
Medix tuticus.
Nomophylaces.
Paedonomus.
Patronomi.
Perduellionis duumviri.
Phylarchi.
Phylobasileis.
Polemarchus.
Poletae.
Poristae.
Praetor.
Probouli.
Proconsul.
Rex.
Senatus.
Tetrarches.
Tribunus.
Triumviri.
Tyrannus.
Vigintisex viri.

MANUFACTURES AND MATERIALS.

Byssus.
Coa vestis.
Fictile.
Gausapa.
Lodix, lodicula.
Salinae.

Manufactures, &c.—continued.

Sericum.
Serta.
Vitrum.

MANNERS AND CUSTOMS.

Acclamatio.
Acta.
Angaria.
Cheirotonia.
Chelidonia.
Chirographum.
Corona convivialis.
  nuptialis.
  natalitia.
Crypteia.
Diploma.
Hospitium.
Hydriaphoria.
Immunitas.
Jusjurandum,
  1. Greek.
  2. Roman.
Leiturgia.
Matrimonium,
  1. Greek.
  2. Roman.
Nomen.
Nudus.
Proscriptio.
Prytaneium.
Suffragium.
Synoikia.
Syssitia.
Tabella.
Tribus, 1. Greek.
  2. Roman
Trierarchia.
Venatio.
Viaticum.
Xenelasia.

MARITIME AFFAIRS.

Camara.
Carchesium.
Cataphracti.
Corbitae.
Cymba.
Delphis.
Dolo.
Epibatae.
Epistoleus.
Harpago.
Insignia.
Jugum.
Lembus.
Navarchus.
Navis.
Naumachia.
Paralus.

Maritime Affairs—continued.

Phaselus.
Portisculus.
Praefectus classis.
Remulcum.
Rudens.

MARKETS.

Agora.
Deigma.
Emporium.
Forum.
Macellum.

MEASURES AND WEIGHTS.

Acaena.
Acetabulum.
Actus.
Amphora.
Artaba.
Arura.
As.
Choenix.
Chous.
Congius.
Cotyla.
Cubitus.
Culeus.
Cyathus.
Dactylus.
Decempeda.
Gradus.
Hecte.
Hemina.
Hippicon.
Jugerum.
Libra, as.
Ligula.
Litra.
Medimnus.
Metretes.
Milliare.
Modius.
Obolus.
Orgyia.
Palmipes.
Palmus.
Parasanga.
Passus.
Pes.
Plethron.
Quadrantal.
Schoenus.
Scrupulum.
Sextarius.
Stadium.
Ulna.
Uncia.
Urna.
Xestes.

CLASSIFIED INDEX.

METALS.
Aes.
Argentum.
Aurum.
Electrum.
Metallum.
Orichalcum.

MILITARY COSTUME.
Abolla.
Alicula.
Balteus.
Bulla.
Caliga.
Paludamentum.
Sagum.

MILITARY ENGINES.
Aries.
Catapulta.
Cataracta.
Corvus.
Cuniculus.
Ericius.
Helepolis.
Lupus ferreus.
Pluteus.
Scalae.
Stylus.
Testudo.
Tormentum.
Tribulus.
Turris.
Vinea.

MILITARY ENSIGNS.
Signa Militaria.

MILITARY LEVIES.
Catalogus.
Conquisitores.
Emphruri.
Epariti.
Tumultus.

MILITARY MANŒUVRES.
Cuneus.
Forfex.
Testudo.

MILITARY PAY AND ALLOWANCES.
Acta.
Aes eqnestre.
  hordearium.
  militare.
Praeda.
Stipendium.

MILITARY PUNISHMENTS.
Decimatio.
Fustuarium.

MILITARY REWARDS.
Anrum coronarium.
Corona obsidionalis.
  civica.
  navalis.
  muralis.
  castrensis, vallaris.
  ovalis.
  oleagina.
Hasta pura.
Ovatio.
Praeda.
Spolia.
Triumphus.
Tropaeum.

MONEY.
Aes.
  circumforaneum.
Argentum.
As.
Assarius nummus.
Aurum.
Chalcus.
Cistophorus.
Damaretion.
Danace.
Daricus.
Denarius.
Drachma.
Hecte.
Libella.
Litra.
Nummus.
Obolus.
Sestertius.
Stater.
Uncia.

MUSIC AND MUSICAL INSTRUMENTS.
Aeroama.
Aeneatores.

Music, &c.—continued.
Buccina.
Canticum.
Capistrum.
Chorus.
Cornu.
Crotalum.
Cymbalum.
Hydraula.
Lituus.
Lyra.
Pecten.
Sambuca.
Sistrum.
Syrinx.
Testudo.
Tibia.
Tuba.
Tympanum.

OFFICERS AND SOLDIERS.
Accensi.
Aeneatores.
Agathoergi.
Ala.
Alauda.
Antecessores.
Argyraspides.
Catalogus.
Cataphracti.
Celeres.
Conquisitores.
Contubernales.
Damosia.
Dimachae.
Ducenarii.
Duplarii.
Epariti.
Evocati.
Excubitores.
Exercitus, 1. Greek.
  2. Roman.
Libratores.
Phylarchi.
Praefectus castrorum.
  praetorio.
Praetor.
Praetoriani.
Strategus.
Tagus.
Taxiarchi.
Tiro.
Volones.
Xenagi.

ORACLES AND DIVINATION.
Angurium, auspicium.
Caput extorum.
Oraculum.
Sibyllini Libri.
Sortes.

PRIESTS AND PRIESTLY OFFICES.
Aeditui.
Agyrtae.
Arvales fratres.
Asiarchae.
Augur, auspex.
Augustales.
Curio.
Epulones.
Eumolpidae.
Exegetae.
Fetiales.
Flamen.
Galli.
Haruspices.
Luperci.
Neocori.
Pausarii.
Pontifex.
Rex sacrificulus.
Sacerdos.
Salii.
Theori.
Titii sodales.
Vestales.

PRIVATE BUILDINGS.
Aithousa.
Apotheca.
Armarium.
Atrium.
Bibliotheca.
Caupona.
Cella.
Cubiculum.
Domus, 1. Greek.
  2. Roman.
  vestibulum.
  ostium.
  atrium.
  alae.
  tablinum.
  fauces.
  perystylum.
  cubicula.
  triclinia.
  oeci.
  exedrae.
  culina.
  coenacula.
  diaeta.
  solaria.
Exedrae.
Focus.
Fornax.
Fornix.
Hemicyclium.
Janua.
Lararium.
Later.
Paries cratitius.
  formaceus.
  lateritius.
  reticulata structura

CLASSIFIED INDEX. 473

Private Buildings—
continued.
Paries structura antiqua.
 emplecton.
 e lapide quadrato.
Pergula.
Pinacotheca.
Pluteus.
Puteal.
Scalae.
Synoikia.
Taberna.
Tegula.
Triclinium.
Villa.

PUBLIC BUILDINGS.
Aerarium.
Amphitheatrum.
Archeion.
Arcus triumphalis.
Argyrocopeion.
Athenaeum.
Auditorium.
Balneae.
Basilica, chalcidicum.
Bibliotheca.
Carcer.
 ircus.
 ochlea.
 uria.
Forum.
Graecostasis.
Hippodromus.
Horreum.
Labyrinthus.
Lautumiae.
Lesche.
Moneta.
Museum.
Paradisus.
Porticus.
Prytaneion.
Rostra.
Stadium.
Suggestus.
Tabularium.
Thesaurus.
Tribunal.

PUBLIC OFFICERS.
Accensi.
Actuarii.
Adlecti.
Admissionales.
Aediles.
Agathoergi.
Agonothetae.
Agoranomi.
Agrimensores.
Agronomi.
Apodectae.
Apostoleis.
Apparitores.
Asiarchae.
Astynomi.

Public Officers—*continued.*
Boonae.
Carnifex.
Choregus.
Coactor.
Critae.
Curatores.
 [*An alphabetical list of* curatores *is given.*]
Diaetetae.
Diribitores.
Ducenarii.
Ecdicus.
Episcopi.
Epistates.
Euthyni.
Exetastae.
Frumentarii.
Grammateus.
Hieropoii.
Hodopoei.
Legatus.
Leiturgia.
Lictor.
Magister
 [*An alphabetical list of* magistri *is given.*]
Manceps.
Mastigophori.
Mensarii.
Notarii.
Paredri.
Parochi.
Practores.
Praecones.
Praefectus **Annonae.**
 Urbi.
Probouli.
Procurator.
Publicani.
Pythii.
Quaestores classici.
 parricidii.
Quinqueviri.
Scribae.
Sitophylaces.
Stator.
Stratores.
Syllogeis.
Tabularii.
Tamias.
Teichopoeus.
Tettaraconta, **hoi.**
Theori.
Trierarchia.
Triumviri.
Viatores.
Zetetae.

ROADS AND STREETS.
Angiportus.
Callis.
Mansio.
Viae.
Vicus.

ROMAN LAW.
Actio.
Actor.
Adoptio.
Advocatus.
Aediles.
Affinitas.
Agrariae leges.
Album.
Ambitus.
Appellatio.
Arra, Arrha.
Arrabo, Arrhabo.
Assertor.
Assessor.
Auctio.
Auctor, **Auctoritas.**
Basilica.
Beneficium.
Bona.
 caduca.
 fides.
Bonorum cessio.
 collatio.
 emptio.
 possessio.
Calumnia.
Caput.
Caupo.
Cautio, cavere.
Centumviri.
Certi, incerti actio.
Chirographum.
Civitas.
Cliens.
Codex Gregorianus.
 Hermogenianus.
 Justinianeus.
 Theodosianus.
Cognati.
Collegium.
Colonia.
Commissoria lex.
Crimen, delictum.
Curator.
Decretum.
Dediticii.
Depositum.
Divortium.
Dominium.
Dominus.
Dos.
Edictum.
 Theodorici.
Emancipatio.
Exercitoria actio.
Exsilium.
Falsum.
Familia.
Fenus.
Fidei commissum.
Fiducia.
Fiscus.
Foederatae civitates.
Frumentariae leges.
Gens.
Heres.
Honores.
Imperium.

Roman Law—*continued.*
Impubes.
Incendium.
Incestum.
Infamia.
Infans.
Ingenui.
Injuria.
Intercessio.
Interdictum.
Judex.
Jure, **cessio in.**
Jurisconsulti.
Jurisdictio.
Jus.
 Civile Papirianum.
Jusjurandum.
Latinitas.
Legatum.
Lex.
 [*Under this head an alphabetical list of the principal laws is given.*]
Libelli accusatorum.
 famosi.
Libertus.
Magistratus.
Majestas.
Mancipium.
Mandatum.
Manumissio.
Negotiatores.
Nexum.
Orator.
Patria potestas.
Patronus.
Pauperies.
Peculatus.
Plagium.
Plebiscitum.
Poena.
Possessio.
Postliminium.
Praedium.
Praejudicium.
Praes.
Praescriptio.
Praetor.
Procurator.
Proscriptio.
Provincia.
Repetundae pecuniae
Sectio.
Senatus consultum
Societas.
Sumptuariae leges.
Tabellariae leges.
Talio.
Testamentum.
Tormentum.
Tutor.
Vindicta.
Vis.
Universitas.
Usufructus.

2 I

CLASSIFIED INDEX.

SACRIFICES AND RELIGIOUS RITES.

Acerra.
Amburbium.
Anakleteria.
Antigoneia.
Apotheosis.
Ara.
Canephoros.
Corona sacerdotalis.
Cortina.
Diamastigosis.
Eisiteria.
Eleusinia.
Exauguratio.
Inauguratio.
Lituus.
Lustratio.
Lustrum.
Sacra.
Sacrificium.
Sagmina.
Secespita.
Simpulum.
Supplicatio.
Thensae.
Tripos.
Turibulum.

SLAVES AND BONDSMEN.

Agaso.
Alipilus.
Aliptae.
Amanuensis.
Anagnostae.
Anteambulones.
Aquarii.
Bruttiani.
Calones.
Capsarii.
Coloni.
Cosmetae.
Cubicularii.
Cursores.
Demosii.
Fartor.
Gymnesii.
Helotes.
Ieroduli.
Librarii.
Mediastini.
Notarii.
Paedagogus.
Pedisequi.
Penestae.
Servus, 1. Greek.
  2. Roman.
Tabellarius.
Thetes.
Villicus.

STATUARY.

Acrolithi.
Caryatides.
Colossus.
Daedala.
Hermae.
Imago.
Sculptura.
Statuaria ars.
Typus.

SUPERSTITIONS.

Amuletum.
Apophrades hemerai.
Astrologia.
Fascinum.
Oscillum.
Prodigium.
Sortes.

TEMPLES AND HOLY PLACES.

Argei.
Asylum.
Bidental.
Docana.
Propylaea.
Sacellum.
Sacrarium.
Templum.
Velum.

TITLES.

Augustus.
Caesar.

TOOLS AND IMPLEMENTS.

Acus.
Amussis.
Apsis.
Ascia.
Colus.
Contus.
Culter.
Dolabra, Dolabella.
Falx.
Fistuca.
Follis.
Fuscina.
Fusus.
Harpago.
Jugum.
Malleolus.

Tools, &c.—continued.

Norma.
Securis.

TRADES AND OCCUPATIONS.

Ambubaiae.
Argentarii.
Athletae.
Bestiarii.
Bibliopola.
Calculator.
Caupo.
Fabri.
Fullo.
Funambulus.
Gladiatores.
Hemerodromi.
Histrio.
Interpres.
Notarii.
Pelatae.
Pistor.
Redemtor.

VEHICLES AND THEIR PARTS.

Antyx.
Arcera.
Basterna.
Canathron.
Capistrum.
Carpentum.
Carruca.
Chiramaxium.
Cisium.
Covinus.
Currus.
Esseda.
Harmamaxa.
Jugum.
Lectica.
Petorritum.
Pilentum.
Rheda.
Sella.

UTENSILS.

Acetabulum.
Aenum.
Alabastrum.
Amphora.
Ampulla.
Anaglypha.
Anthepsa.
Bascauda.
Bicos.

Utensils—continued.

Cadus.
Calathus.
Calix.
Candela.
Candelabrum.
Cantharus.
Capsa.
Carchesium.
Catinus.
Chrysendita.
Cista.
Cochlear.
Colum.
Cophinus.
Corbis, Corbula, Corbicula.
Cortina.
Crater.
Cupa.
Cyathus.
Fax.
Ferculum.
Guttus.
Lanx.
Lecythus.
Lucerna.
Modiolus.
Murrhina vasa.
Oenophorum.
Olla, aula.
Patera, Patella.
Patina.
Poculum.
Psycter.
Pyxis.
Rhyton.
Salinum.
Situla, Sitella.
Tripos.
Trua, Trulla.
Vas.
Urceus.

WRITING AND WRITING MATERIALS.

Adversaria.
Album.
Atramentum.
Buxum.
Calamus.
Codex.
Libellus.
  memorialis.
Liber.
Nota.
Regula.
Scytale.
Stylus.
Tabulae.

THE END.

LONDON: PRINTED BY WILLIAM CLOWES AND SONS, STAMFORD STREET, AND CHARING CROSS.

www.ingramcontent.com/pod-product-compliance
Lightning Source LLC
Chambersburg PA
CBHW051856300426
44117CB00006B/425